GURPS® Fourth Edition

DISCWORLD

ROLEPLAYING GAME

Adventures on the Back of the Turtle

The Discworld Created by TERRY PRATCHETT

***GURPS* Game Adaptation by PHIL MASTERS**

**Additional Material by
JOHN M. FORD and TERRY PRATCHETT**

Edited by SEAN PUNCH

Cover Art by PAUL KIDBY

**Interior Illustrations by
PAUL KIDBY and SEAN MURRAY**

Discworld Map by STEPHEN PLAYER

Ankh-Morpork Map by STEPHEN BRIGGS

Port Duck Map by ERIC HOTZ

The authors gratefully acknowledge the help of that invaluable guide, *The Discworld Companion,*
by Terry Pratchett and Stephen Briggs.

GURPS System Design ❚ STEVE JACKSON
GURPS Line Editor ❚ SEAN PUNCH
Asst. *GURPS* Line Editor ❚ JASON "PK" LEVINE
GURPS Project Manager ❚ STEVEN MARSH
GURPS FAQ Maintainer ❚
VICKY "MOLOKH" KOLENKO

Managing Editor ❚ MIRANDA HORNER
Asst. Art Director ❚ BRIDGET WESTERMAN
Cover Design ❚ ALEX FERNANDEZ
Production Artist and Indexer ❚ NIKOLA VRTIS
Page Design ❚ LILLIAN BUTLER, JACK ELMY,
PHIL REED, JUSTIN DE WITT,
MONICA STEPHENS, NIKOLA VRTIS

Chief Executive Officer ❚ PHILIP REED
Chief Operating Officer ❚ SAMUEL MITSCHKE
Director of Sales ❚ ROSS JEPSON
Licensing Manager ❚ ELISABETH ZAKES
Prepress Checker ❚ MONICA STEPHENS
Print Buyer ❚ PHILIP REED

Lead Playtester: Jeff Wilson   *Assistant Lead Playtester:* Roger Burton West

Playtesters: W. "Ian" Blanton, Frederick Brackin, Peter V. Dell'Orto, Scott Harris, MA Lloyd, Alden Loveshade, Garðar Steinn Ólafsson,
Andrew Rivett, Scott Rochat, Kristof Sardemann, William H. Stoddard, Antoni Ten Monrós, Hans-Christian Vortisch, and Bryan Weaver

ISBN 978-1-55634-806-8   1 2 3 4 5 6 7 8 9 10

STEVE JACKSON GAMES

CONTENTS

9. "SUICIDALLY GLOOMY WHEN SOBER, HOMICIDALLY INSANE WHEN DRUNK" 305

10. BEWARE THE AMBIGUOUS PUZUMA. 351

11. BAD FOOD, NO SLEEP, AND STRANGE PEOPLE. . . . 367

INTRODUCTION

Somewhere . . .

There is a flat, circular world which rests on the backs of four elephants, which in turn stand on the back of a giant turtle, which swims through space. Magic works here. Well, most of the time. Some of the time, anyway. There are gods and heroes.

It is a fantasy world, albeit with odd similarities to our own, and a setting for fantasy stories. Some of these stories have been told over the last quarter-century or so in a series of novels – and the occasional short story, novella, and so on – by Terry Pratchett. (For convenience, this body of stories is hereafter referred to as *the chronicles*.) The *Discworld Roleplaying Game* enables you to create Discworld stories of your own, in the form of games, with the collaboration of your friends.

The Discworld is a comedy setting, but with room for occasional bits of tragic relief. Hence, this book is about running comedy games, and getting the atmosphere right. But these stories are also about people, and stories told and games played in this setting can be as complex and character-driven as any you could set anywhere else.

So dive in. Don't eat the meat pies, don't frighten the swamp dragons, and be careful how you refer to the Librarian.

What Is a Roleplaying Game?

As some Discworld fans who buy this book may not know much about these "roleplaying game" things, a word of explanation is in order.

Non-computer roleplaying games (RPGs) – sometimes called "tabletop" or "pencil-and-paper" RPGs – go back to the 1970s, preceding the Discworld by just a few years. They've sometimes been described as "collaborative improvised radio drama"; a group of people get together, take the parts of characters, and create a story by describing what happens and what those characters do in response to events. But it's just as accurate (somewhat, but not very) to compare them to computer games, including "first-person shooters" and, yes, "roleplaying games"; the game provides an environment, in which each player operates one character, usually an adventurous sort, who can go through the game world, exploring or fighting or trading or talking to other characters. Apart from anything else, unlike radio dramas but like computer games, tabletop RPGs have rules and systems to determine whether the characters succeed or fail in their actions.

An important way in which RPGs differ from either of those other things, though, is in the presence of a Game Master (GM). Like the designer of a computer game, the GM defines settings, creates situations to which the player characters (PCs) must respond, and manages the use of the rules. Unlike a computer-game designer, however, the GM is present in person; among other things, he gets to play all the non-player characters (NPCs), giving them dialogue and personality. He's a bit like the director of that radio drama, except that he plays characters – often *many* characters – and he doesn't have the right to *tell* anyone else what to do, although he does make rules decisions and subtly steer events to keep the story interesting.

And that's why tabletop RPGs are so exciting. As there are humans on both sides of things, every character can have personality and individual mannerisms. Since the GM has the freedom to make decisions and improvise, the PCs can go off track or try unexpected tricks – but because there are rules and systems, things are fair, and the PCs' successes have the taste of real victories. You can fight monsters if you want, and those fights can be as exciting as in any computer game or radio play, but you can also talk, trade, or sneak around, and that's just as important as fighting, if you want it to be.

> *"How can you hope to win without sacrificing the occasional pawn?"*
> *"Oh, I never play to win."*
> *She smiled. "But I do play not to lose."*
> – *Fate and the Lady, in Interesting Times*

ROLEPLAYING ON THE DISC

The *Discworld Roleplaying Game* does what it says; it enables you to play an RPG with the Disc as its game world. Over the decades and dozens of novels, the Disc has developed into a huge and detailed setting – an ideal location for roleplaying. (Actually, it's a whole *collection* of settings, from the scholar-pirate nation of Krull to the jungle kingdoms of Howondaland, the snows of the Ramtops, the swamps of Genua, the ancient Agatean Empire, and the Fourecksian Outback.) At the same time, the legion of readers who've enjoyed the chronicles provide a ready-made supply of players who are familiar with the world, and who therefore won't need many explanations before they start – although it's perfectly possible to play here without having read any of the stories, and indeed to treat a game as your introduction to the Disc.

The only snag with this is that some people may feel intimidated by the idea of creating their own stories in a setting with so much depth, which people love so much. Please don't! The Disc is meant to be a place for readers to enjoy, where stories happen. The entire point of this book is to help you have fun making up your own.

THE *GURPS* RULES

This game uses a set of rules based on the current (fourth) edition of *GURPS*, the *Generic Universal RolePlaying System*, from Steve Jackson Games. See Chapters 2-5 for these. *GURPS* is versatile and allows you to define characters in enough detail to make them interesting individuals, with real advantages and problems, and unique abilities, skills, and flaws.

There are plenty of other **GURPS** books (starting with the two-volume **Basic Set,** which contains a more comprehensive set of rules), which will be of interest to those who want to get deeper into the system or who desire more detail in particular areas of play. See the Bibliography (pp. 402-403).

WHAT ELSE YOU WILL NEED

To use the rules, you'll need at least three ordinary six-sided dice, pencils, and scratch paper. You may want to run off a few photocopies of the blank character sheet on p. 24 (you have our permission to do so for your personal use) – at least one copy per player – or download a similar sheet from the Steve Jackson Games website and print copies of that. Other Discworld-related books are of course strongly recommended; again, see the Bibliography (pp. 402-403).

This Book

The first chapter of the **Discworld Roleplaying Game** is a basic introduction to the Discworld, for the benefit of gamers who don't know the setting well and anyone who wants a refresher. Chapters 2-5 are about the *game* part, providing most of the rules. The next five chapters explore the setting in greater detail, with reference to those game mechanics; they cover society, nonhuman races, geography, the supernatural side, major characters from the chronicles, and animals. Chapter 11 puts everything together, discussing how to run games set on the Disc, and illustrating this with a number of example settings and adventures. The book wraps up with a bibliography.

PUBLICATION HISTORY

The original **Discworld Roleplaying Game** was released in 1998, initially under the title **GURPS Discworld,** and was followed in 2001 by a companion volume, **GURPS Discworld Also.** The book in your hands is the second edition, which combines content from both of those earlier works, adds material from the latest novels, updates the rules to the most recent version of **GURPS,** and includes a new magic system. All of which should answer the question of *why* there's a new edition – the Discworld doesn't stand still, and neither do we.

This book refers to all of the "adult" Discworld novels published up to the time of writing, plus a few short stories and such. For practical and stylistic reasons, though, it doesn't encompass any of the "younger readers" books set on the Disc.

Some Warnings

Spoiler Alert: We don't set out to spoil anyone's pleasure in the chronicles, or to give away the plots gratuitously. We'd rather that you read and enjoyed everything. However, it's impossible to talk about the current state of the Disc without mentioning how things got that way and how important events turned out. In other words, reading this book from cover to cover means you're in for fewer surprises if you read the novels later.

What It's Not: This book isn't an attempt to retell the entire history of the Discworld, or even the entire history-so-far of the chronicles. It merely attempts to give a feel for most parts of the Disc, with some interesting specifics.

About the Authors

Phil Masters has been roleplaying and writing for RPGs for more than three-fifths of his life, which is a thought he finds . . . very strange. He is the author, co-author, or compiler of several books for **GURPS** and other RPGs (including **Champions, Ars Magica,** and **Eclipse Phase**), and is line editor for the **Transhuman Space** hard-SF, near-future **GURPS** sub-line. He lives in England with a wife who is smarter than him and a computer which he still suspects of ambition.

Terry Pratchett, it turns out, wrote his first RPG scenario when Phil Masters was still running around the playground. It had a toilet in it. It also had an intelligent box called The Luggage, which walked around on legs. Some ten years later, when he had the idea of writing a fantasy novel that'd be an antidote to too many bad fantasy books, he remembered it . . .

Since then, the Discworld series has sold about 85 million copies (but who's counting?) in 38 languages worldwide, the books have achieved bestseller status in the U.K. and U.S. mainstream lists. *Sir* Terry was knighted for services to literature by Queen Elizabeth II. His numerous awards include a Carnegie Medal, Locus Awards, and an Andre Norton Award, while his documentaries have garnered a Grierson Award, several BAFTAs, and an International Emmy.

On the BACK of FOUR ELEPHANTS...

GREAT A'TUIN

The bard walked into the throne room, and looked about himself with the confidence of a man who knows far too much about the history of his profession and the privileges traditionally granted to its members. He had never reflected much on the difference between "traditionally" and "actually."

His serious pose properly established, at least in his own eyes, he fixed what was definitely intended to be a piercing gaze on the figure seated atop the podium at the far end of the room. (Not far enough, as it seemed to him – didn't royal architects take their jobs seriously?) Then he drew breath.

"Know You, O Prince," he began grandly in his Llamedese accent, "that between the years when the oceans drank Leshp and its brass gongs for the fifth or possibly sixth time, and the years of the rise of the Middle Classes, there was an Age undreamed of . . ."

Atop his throne, King Verence II of Lancre stifled a deep sigh. His own training had been in a completely different branch of show business, but he could tell a string of clichés when he heard one. After a few more sparklings and gleamings and grandeurs, his impatience got the better of his good manners.

"Yes, yes," he interrupted the bard, "I believe that I have the idea. But really, you know, all I'm looking for just now is a summary of the current political situation on the Sto Plains – from your expert point of view, of course."

*The bard, thrown by the unusual experience of being interrupted, glowered slightly from beneath bushy eyebrows. "A **summary**,*

Majesty?" he enquired unhappily.

"Yes – a summary," said the king. He was a man who normally derived most of his ideas from books, but some of those books were quite insistent about the Ancient Wisdom of the Bardic Orders, and so he'd opted to investigate the oral tradition, just this once.

The bard took a few moments to chew this new idea over. "It's a little irregular," he said, "but I suppose that a précis might be possible . . ."

"Give it a try," said Verence encouragingly.

"Well," said the bard, "you are aware, O prince, of the recent wars between Borogravia and, well, practically everyone else?"

"Sadly," said Verence.

"And of the Undertaking in mighty Ankh-Morpork of the brazen beasts and the mighty smell . . . ah, in Ankh-Morpork?"

"Only the basics," said Verence, leaning forward. "Do you have details?"

The bard was the one who stifled a sigh now. Civil engineering wasn't really his forte – but such were the times . . .

The Discworld is quite strange, even by the standards of fantasy settings. Thus, it's prudent to begin with a few words on life and reality in this eccentric world.

Why a Disc? Why the Turtle?

The Discworld, which looks like an extraordinarily improbable object (at least until one examines some terrestrial concepts of cosmic structure), can exist because it occupies a region of Highly Stressed Reality. There can be wizards, trolls, and dragons because the physical constraints that prevent them in other parts of the multiverse are relaxed – in fact, downright limp. There are still rules of existence, but they're permissive, not exclusive.

Or, to put it another way, the Disc is the handiwork of a Creator working to a specification that was more poetic than usual.

Either way, it exists at the far end of the probability curve. It is consistent, in its way, but not *likely*. Furthermore, this improbability – and the laws of narrative causality which have real force here – are important to more than just its origins. They pervade life on the Disc.

The Power of Story

Part of what enables the Discworld to exist as it does is the power of narrative. Stories have *serious* clout in a universe like this. A flat world carried on top of four elephants may be unlikely, but it makes a good story. Part of the fundamental structure of the Disc's universe is a material – or particle, or something – called *narrativium*, which holds the whole thing together. The effects propagate down to the level where it's hard for a royal family to produce three sons without the lads being bound to go off on adventures at some point, the youngest achieving the most impressive results.

This is known to scholars and philosophers on the Disc, is a part of the local system of magic, and can be manipulated. Indeed, there are people on the Discworld who've built lengthy careers on the power of their personal story. But this isn't always a safe or easy thing to do. Stories can turn round and get nasty if you're not very careful – and you have to make sure that you're playing the right part in the right story.

METAPHOR AND BELIEF

Metaphors, too, tend not to sit like Patience on a monument smiling at grief, but to get off the monument, hunt Grief down, and demand to know why he done her wrong and how about the maintenance payments? Death is not an abstract concept represented by a robed skeleton with a scythe; he *is* a robed skeleton with a scythe.

Belief has powerful effects. Discworld gods are created – or at least empowered and maintained in their power – by their followers' collective belief. Wizards and witches draw power as much from other people believing in their abilities as from their command of magical energy. (After all, convince enough people that you can turn them into frogs with a hard stare, and you may never have to prove it.) Conversely, disbelief can prevent something from existing, or from being seen even if it does exist.

A side-effect of this tendency towards personification is the recurrent and sometimes tiresome literal-mindedness of the Disc's inhabitants. People take metaphors literally because metaphors all too often become literal. Talk about your true love as a rose, and people are likely to point out that she (a) isn't green and red, (b) doesn't have thorns, and (c) walks about a lot. Poets, like engineers, can have a tough time of it on the Disc – and indeed have been severely controlled by law on occasion. On the Disc, "poetic licence" isn't metaphor, either.

NARRATIVE CAUSALITY

Narrative causality is the fundamental power of stories. People want and need events to follow certain courses and come to proper resolutions. A war is supposed to end with the "right" side winning and the "wrong" side having learned its lesson forever. The fact that in the extremely long history of warfare this has hardly ever happened doesn't alter the fact that people want it to happen and resolutely believe, at the start of each new war, that it'll happen again. And on the Disc, there's a chance that it *will* happen – but the power of that story must battle human nature and the personal stories of the war-leaders.

Great A'Tuin

The Disc is borne through space on the back of a world-turtle, of the species *Chelys galactica*. This *is* a species, not a unique specimen; a cluster of eight baby turtles, each bearing four elephant-calves and a little Discworld in its geological youth, were once observed to hatch from moon-sized eggs that had been left in orbit around a full-sized star. They spent a little time orbiting Great A'Tuin, but have since departed on their own cosmic voyages. It's possible that they're the literal offspring of Great A'Tuin, but the turtle's gender remains unknown, despite heroic research programs.

Great A'Tuin is 10,000 miles long – slightly smaller than the Disc it carries. Its shell is encrusted with methane ice and pocked with meteor impacts; its eyes are like oceans. Wizards have tried for centuries to peek telepathically into its consciousness, and they discovered one thing: it's *slow*. Time is of little importance to a turtle; to a really big turtle, time is *really* unimportant. Its thoughts move like glaciers, although it *does* think, and it seems quite content.

Berilia, Tubul, Great T'Phon, and Jerakeen

Even less is known about the four elephants who stand on Great A'Tuin, and on whose backs the Disc rests. It's even harder to get a look at them – they're well under the rim. They are not completely static, however. The Disc's sun and moon trace complex orbits, ensuring phases for the moon and seasons for the Disc, and every now and again, an elephant has to cock a leg to let one of them go past safely.

Nor is it clear how the Disc rotates round its hub, or how the elephants avoid chafing. There is some evidence that the direction of rotation changes at geological intervals, which may be part of the arrangement to avoid such problems.

Incidentally, the Disc's moon seems to generate its own light. It *appears* like our world's moon, waxing and waning regularly, whereas a lunar cycle generated by the Disc's sun's motion coupled with the local physics of light would be too complex to contemplate.

The trick, for the insanely brave, is to ride the tiger of story until it gets you where you want to be. Then you have to work out how to get off.

On the Disc, narrative becomes a powerful force indeed. Fate and destiny are the stories of things that haven't happened yet – and they're written down, somewhere. But writing can be changed. There's a whole class of people (the History Monks, p. 13) whose job is to observe history, making sure that it happens as it is supposed to. Genuinely heroic efforts to get off-script have failed because of the innate power of plot[1] – but even more heroic efforts can change it.

It helps that more than one story might share the same beginning. The trick seems to be to provide a new plot that's *better* – to beat the power of stories with a different story. Because even Death will bend the rules in the service of a more satisfying resolution.

FURTHER COROLLARIES

Rules have logical consequences, not least rules about the power of story. Most of them are conditional and vague, but a couple are worth mentioning.

First, there's the *Rule of Universal Humour*. On the Discworld, when an event can happen in a variety of slightly different ways, it tends to unfold in the most satisfying manner from the point of view of narrative. Because even tragedies have jokes and comic interludes, this means that some things happen because they're funny. This is especially true when magic or heroes are involved.

For instance, if a wizard turns someone into a pumpkin, the spell of course encompasses any clothes the victim may be wearing – it's magic, and involves morphic fields and symbolism, not boring questions of molecular rearrangement. Nonetheless, the pumpkin will almost certainly be wearing the victim's hat. Similarly, in any Disc society advanced enough to have invented plate glass, the main function of large sheets of the stuff is to be carried by two men into the path of anyone engaged in a chase, while arrows deflected off some hard object usually hit innocent passing birds. In game terms, the GM shouldn't be afraid to throw a cliché detail into a scene if it will raise a laugh. Don't get addicted to this, though; "funny" can too easily turn into "boring."

Second, there's the *Million-to-One Rule*. As everyone knows, in stories, million-to-one chances come up nine times in 10. This is certainly true on the Disc. For more on this, see *1,000,000-1* (p. 369).

THE ART OF NARRATIVE MANIPULATION

Players should be extremely careful when attempting to *use* narrative causality, just as they ought to think twice about trying to exploit million-to-one chances. For one thing, it's unreliable. Stories *can* be subtle and can take many forms, and they even seem to *resent* being exploited. A character who tries to cast himself as the Brave Peasant Lad Who Outwits The Troll may find that he's actually one of the Twenty Poor Peasants Eaten By The Troll Before The Knight Comes Along. He might even end up as the Devious Little Human Squashed By The Troll Hero. (Troll fairy-stories aren't especially subtle.)

Second, it's ethically tricky. A lot of what happens in stories involves unpleasant things happening to minor characters.

---

1. *This is a definition of Tragedy, of course.*

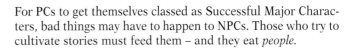

Other Worlds

As previously mentioned (*Great A'Tuin*, p. 8), there are at least eight other world-turtles in the Disc's universe. There are also other discs with other arrangements; one is ringed by a great dragon, its tail in its mouth. However, this fact is likely to remain purely of academic interest. Interstellar flight is *not* a feasible concept for this setting without a *lot* of plot tweaking: Discworld technology is nowhere near up to the idea, magic depends on the availability of a strong thaumic field, and gods depend even more on the proximity and fervent belief of a large group of worshippers. Still, the GM who wants to develop his own disc from scratch is free to do so.

For PCs to get themselves classed as Successful Major Characters, bad things may have to happen to NPCs. Those who try to cultivate stories must feed them – and they eat *people*.

Morphic Fields

In our world, there are some highly disputed theories about "morphic resonance" or "morphic fields." On the Discworld, these theories are all true. Even the contradictory ones.

Everything – every stone, every insect, every person – has a natural form, which is entrenched in its morphic field. This field is *much* harder to change, by magic or brute force, than the thing's physical shape. If someone has an arm or a leg chopped off, he sometimes talks about feeling as if a "ghost limb" is still there, which shows that he's dimly sensing his morphic field. (Indeed, actual ghosts retain the image of their former human form by holding on to some of their morphic field.) If a change is magical, the true morphic field struggles to reassert itself, eventually overcoming the magic; this is why transformation spells usually wear off. To make the change permanent, the caster must make a permanent adjustment to the field, which is *difficult*.

Furthermore, morphic fields exhibit resonance effects. Once one exists, other objects can imitate it. Thus, if something has been made once – a type of tool, say, or a style of art – then it's fairly easy to repeat the trick. Genuine creativity is hard because it means shaping new morphic fields.

But once a change has been made, it can be just as hard to undo or control, because a morphic field may become distorted. For example, Greebo the cat (pp. 343-344) was once the subject of a short-term transformation spell, and ever since, he has had an embarrassing tendency to switch to human form in times of stress. Werewolves exhibit some lupine attributes in human form (extra hair, superior senses), and human intelligence – or at least cunning and sometimes too-sophisticated malice – in wolf form, because while they can adjust their morphic field between two states, each tends to carry "echoes" of the other. Sometimes these echoes grow faint, causing the special abilities to fade with time; sometimes they don't.

Thus, in Discworld biology inheritance does not operate as it does in our world. To get technical, it's at least as much Lamarckian as Mendelian. Morphic fields change (if slowly) and resonate, so that acquired characteristics can be passed on to offspring. In fact, characteristics can even pass to *adopted* offspring.

For example: Susan, the child of Death's adopted daughter, exhibits Death's powers of invisibility and memory (functions of his office, which she sometimes performs); moreover, when she blushes or is angry, marks on her face become visible which match marks left on her father's face when Death slapped him. Part of this sort of thing can be put down to magical action, which can not only change animals deliberately but can affect them accidentally (as with all the intelligent animals found around the highly magical Unseen University); part is a much more general function of the universe.

Discworld genes can also react intelligently, or at least take hints. The appearance of a supersonic, jet-propelled swamp dragon

shows what a truly focussed mutation can accomplish, although those genes may have borrowed something from the dragon's cousins or ancestors.

Finally, there are even more subtle resonances, which play a major part in the humour of the chronicles. As Ankh-Morpork's City Watch becomes more organised, it becomes more familiar – it's as though it's being shaped by the field generated by every cop show you've ever seen. This can be so overt that in times of stress a watchman might attempt to shoot the lock off a door – difficult with a crossbow.

But Really . . .

Let's be honest for a moment: The Discworld doesn't exist.[1]

More precisely, the Discworld is a place where *stories happen*. It was created as a setting for the chronicles. Things have appeared or happened there because they fitted the stories, more than out of deep logic.

That's what makes the Discworld work so well as a setting for fiction. But when it comes to RPGs, it means that a little common sense is required.

To begin with, there may be a few inconsistencies in the chronicles. Fortunately, the Disc is first and foremost a place where magic works. Thus, many of these can be explained away as the product of supernatural influences.

Perhaps more confusingly, the Disc has changed through the evolution of the novels, from a parody of a

rambunctious sword-and-sorcery world to something rather more modern. This is explicable as the result of the setting being dragged through a peculiar and accelerated sort of Renaissance (something the novels do actually support). Remember, however, that while the words "Victorian times" conjure up images of steamships, railways, and the telegraph, what that actually *meant* for the majority of people – even those living within 100 miles of the most developed cities of the Western world – was "living pretty much as your ancestors did, but with a few changes of fashion."

This even raises some gaming possibilities. Apart from the fact that periods of change are always interesting, games can be set before, during, or after such changes, depending on what people want to play *with*.

Most of all, though, there's a moral of sorts – because roleplaying games are stories, too. If you, as a GM, need to tinker with the setting to get your game to work, then go ahead. Try to be consistent – it's fairer to your players – but don't treat the place as sacred.

---

1. *This may be news to the millions of beings who live there, but there you go. Or, in their case, there they don't go.*

Practical Basics

To return to material facts, for those who worry about such things: The Disc has a diameter of about 10,000 miles. It is around 30 miles thick at the Rim and is thought to be considerably thicker in the centre; certainly, it seems to have a substantial internal pocket of molten lava, necessary for interesting volcanoes. (There's some evidence of continental drift, too, suggesting either a molten interior or a really strange arrangement of wheels.) There are fossils in the rocks, and also lots of signs of sedimentary layering, which are widely blamed on the Creator trying to confuse people.

Where the Disc's internal heat comes from is unknown. One theory says that it's the result of high pressure acting on deep-lying deposits of octiron (p. 275). This might also explain its strong magical field, which is so intense that it can slow light to a crawl in places. But there are plenty of mysteries about the Disc; for example, no one can explain why the oceans remain at the same level when water is forever pouring over 30,000 miles of circumference. Arrangements are presumably made. Anyway, we've

been taking oil out of our spinning Earth for years now, so why aren't we kept awake at night by the axles squeaking?

Directions

Obviously, the Disc has no north or south. Rather, directions are given as *hubwards* (toward the Disc's centre), *rimwards* (away from the centre), *turnwise* or *spinwards* (the direction of rotation – clockwise as seen from above), or *widdershins* or occasionally *trailing* (opposite to the direction of rotation).

Weather and Temperature

The Disc is orbited by a small, hot sun and a moon, which whirl under and over it as the whole assembly moves through space. The hottest place on the Disc, at any particular time, must be where the sun is closest at the start or end of the day. In other words, points on the Rim currently adjacent to the sun's orbit experience the equivalent of a tropical summer. Other points on the Rim receive less heat, and hence should be downright cold at times – but in fact they're usually no worse than "mild."

Heat is somehow transferred around the Rim; most theories say that this is through the dense magical flux there. (There's also ocean round almost the entire Rim, and water is a great conductor and store of heat.)

The Hublands, on the other hand, never get more than distant sunlight and are surrounded by a lot of land, so this is a cold and wintry region. Ankh-Morpork – the location of many novels in the chronicles – is just over halfway from the Hub to the Rim, and is a temperate city with some hot summers.

One other point: The moon's orbit is fairly close to the Disc. During summer, points on the Rim can see it from fairly close up. On the Disc, the tropical moon looks bigger because it really does occupy a larger portion of the sky.

Time

Discworld time is a mess.

This isn't just a matter of the calendars being unreliable and the clocks being erratic, although there's plenty of that, too. The secret truth, known to a few paranormal beings and the History Monks (p. 13), is that time and history themselves have been *broken* at least once. It's possible, using sufficiently mad science, to construct a device (an excessively accurate clock) which causes the flow of time to waver – at which point the whole system proves to be far more fragile than it ought to be, and falls apart. The first time this happened, by honest accident, the History Monks got time moving again and then had to put a great deal of work into patching over the shattered mess that was left. Still, they bodged the job. Some years ended up repeated, some incidents had very different results depending on how you looked at them, and causality went entirely to pieces in spots throughout history.

Still, the Monks got things working again – and more important, humans and other supposedly intelligent races proved obligingly willing to accept things as they found them, without wondering too much about inconsistencies. Subsequently, the only attempt to repeat that effect was due to meddling by the Auditors (pp. 296-297); fortunately, that merely stopped time for a while. The History Monks can be assumed to be on the lookout for other repetitions, and meanwhile they continue to patch over any remaining inconsistencies. But there are some, and anyone who looks hard enough at Discworld history tends to end up scratching his head and muttering about poor-quality sources.

In addition, the past has, on rare occasions, been changed at the whim of powerful supernatural beings (although this usually seems to require the consent of the gods on Cori Celesti; see pp. 300-301). It turns out that time can not only divide into two separate historical paths, but also later remerge, leaving people with a hazy sense that various things happened in the past, but no strong sense of causality. To add to the confusion, time can be stopped by mere mortal magic, over limited areas. For example, the entire kingdom of Lancre was once put into stasis for well over a decade by a heroine-ic piece of witchcraft.

(And to be honest, the chronicles weren't written to a tight, pre-planned chronology. Trying to fit a consistent historical timeline to recent events described there isn't just inherently difficult but actively misguided. This book contains what is merely a best guess.)

Still, the Discworld does have working calendars of a sort. They're slightly messy and confused, but they hold together despite all that damage to history.

The Disc Year

There are two sorts of year on the Disc. In one sense, a year is 800 days, the time it takes for the Disc to revolve once relative to the Turtle. This is known as a "spin year," among those with sufficiently advanced astronomical knowledge and time on their hands. There are eight seasons in the spin year – two of each. It is summer when a point on the Rim is directly under the sun's orbit, winter when it's 90° away.

In the days when Ankh-Morpork was an empire, the eight-season year was known as the Great Year, with differently named seasons: Winter Prime, Spring Prime, Summer Prime, Autumn Prime, Winter Secundus, Spring Secundus, and so on.

Discworld Light

The Disc's magical field can actually slow the speed of light – down to about the speed of sound (750 mph), in fact. Thunder and lightning are often seen and heard simultaneously. Viewed from vantage points available to the gods, a Disc sunrise involves the light of dawn spreading across the landscape like incandescent honey.

There are problems with the assumption that this is true everywhere on the Disc, though. As Didactylos the Ephebian pointed out, it would mean that sunlight would take longer to cross the Disc's 10,000-mile diameter than the sun takes to go from rising to setting, and the sun would have to travel faster than its own light. Working out illumination levels at any point on the Disc at a given time would be astoundingly headache-inducing. Thus, it seems possible that light is severely slowed only in places where the magical field is dense.

Some light definitely behaves like a thick fluid, pooling in low-lying areas and piling up behind mountain ranges so that valleys get no dawn until it spills over the ridge. (Tribes in the Great Nef capture it behind light dams for their own purposes.) But there is also a thin, fast sort, which allows people to see what happens to the thick sort.

Light passing through strong magical fields also gets split into the traditional seven-colour spectrum plus an eighth colour: *octarine*, the colour of magic. This is visible only to the magically adept and said to resemble a sort of fluorescent greenish-yellow-purple.

The Nonexistent Horizon

Given that the Discworld is flat, it should logically be possible to see across it for unlimited distances. As the inhabitants happily point out, however, this isn't true because things get in the way.

On open sea on the Disc, on a clear, calm day, one can in fact see a heck of a distance. However, Discworld light is typically distorted and diffused by minor local variations in the magical field, along with the usual water vapour in the atmosphere. In practise, this makes recognising anything smaller than a mountain at distances greater than a few miles simply impossible. But if players insist on asking – no, their characters *don't* see a proper horizon, just haze, and if they're in the right place, the edge of the Disc.

However, this was of interest only to wizards and astrologers. For most people, the year was and is four seasons – more specifically, a year is ploughing, planting, growing, and harvest – except that in half of them the sun comes up on the left of the Hub, and in half it comes up on the right.

Discworld Holidays

Due the double nature of the Disc year, its festival days come in pairs, one instance in each half of the Great Year. For example, there are two major, widely observed festival pairs, in a cycle that starts with *Small Gods' Eve* and *Crueltide* in the first half of the Great Year, then follows with *Midsummer Eve* (also known as *All's Fallow*) and *Hogswatchnight* in the second half of the Great Year. Many people, especially in rural areas, use only two names: Midsummer Eve and Hogswatchnight.

Hogswatchnight (or Crueltide) is the last day of the year – a traditional day for slaughtering pigs, hence the name. Witches are expected to stay at home on this one night, although no one likes to insist. The same has been claimed of All's Fallow (with as much effect). On the following *Hogswatchday*, first day of the year, shops do not open. This is also the night when the Hogfather (pp. 302-303) brings gifts to children.

The other noted dates on Sto Plains and Ramtops calendars are Soul Cake Days – the first Tuesday, Wednesday, and Thursday after the first half-moon in Sektober. This is a Halloween/Bonfire Night sort of festival. Human traditions include trickle-treating, all-comers morris dancing, and rolling boiled eggs down the Tump in Ankh-Morpork (see p. 251), while dwarfs engage in bobbing for trout and enjoy toffee rats on a stick. Don't ask why; it's an excuse for a party. The festival has its own aviomorphic personification, the Soul Cake Tuesday Duck, which doesn't seem to do very much – perhaps wisely, as the festival also marks the start of duck-hunting season.

Genua (pp. 241-242) has its own favourite festival, Mardi Gras (also known as Fat Tuesday), which culminates in Samedi Nuit Mort, the night halfway between the Living and the Dead, which is marked by processions and a ball at the palace. It suffices to say that Genua *really* knows how to party.

This gives a "year" of 400 days – close enough to one of our terrestrial years for all practical purposes, and treated as such in this book. All references to a "year" in Disc-related sources should be taken to mean such a 400-day unit unless clearly stated otherwise.

A year is divided into 13 months: *Offle, February, March, April, May, June, Grune, August, Spune, Sektober, Ember, December,* and *Ick.* There are eight days in a week: our usual seven, plus *Octeday.* There are 50 weeks in a year.

Years and (especially) centuries are also named, usually by astrologers using obscure logic. Events in the early chronicles mostly took place during the last years of the Century of the Fruitbat; the previous era was the Century of the Three Lice. In recent novels, the Disc has plunged – kicking and screaming, of course – into the Century of the Anchovy.

Ankh-Morpork uses a numeric calendar – less poetic but theoretically easier to work with. This was originally dated from the city's founding (or at least the official foundation of its old empire), but is now dated from the formal foundation of Unseen University (pp. 279-289) in a year then given as AM 1282: 1,282 years after the foundation of the Ankh-Morporkian Empire, which ended shortly after the University was founded (probably by coincidence). There are at least two explanations given for this change.

One is that the city has so often been destroyed – or all but destroyed, or sufficiently damaged – that people wanted to forget the whole thing and start over, and so many kings have decided that the beginning of their reign ought rightly to be the Year One, that no one is sure any more what the old city calendar relates to. The University, on the other hand, began counting years from its own starting point, with no reference to what the city outside was doing, since they didn't care. Citizens eventually began following the University calendar because it didn't gain or lose time like a pendulum clock on a ship in a hurricane. Because wizards, for all their faults, can be precise about things that can be useful to them, its calendar seemed guaranteed.

The other explanation says that the old city calendar was technically far superior to the UU version (and it's certainly true that the year 1456 happened twice by the University count, for reasons still not clear), but it gets a bit complicated sometimes, whereas the University calendar happens to fit the farming seasons fairly well, which is all that most people on the Disc want a calendar for.

Calendar experts, like most experts, love to argue, but the UU-based calendar has now spread across much of the Disc, so it's too late to worry. By its reckoning, the Century of the Fruitbat is in fact the 20th century, while the Century of the Anchovy is the 21st.

History (Slightly Frayed)

The history of intelligent life on the Disc is a slightly under-researched topic, partly because of the way it gets a little hazy when examined closely. But it has certainly been long, confused, and sometimes depressing. What follows is a brief outline of the business; more details appear later in this book.

Prehistory

The universe was evidently created, though how and by whom isn't clear. (Discworld astronomers have a Big Bang Theory, but it relates to what may happen when two world-turtles of opposite genders chance to meet.) Certainly, the Disc was constructed by a being known as the Creator (perceived as a sharp-faced, put-upon little man by humans who meet him), who seems to have been working to a tight budget and eccentric specifications. Who employed him remains unclear, although they were apparently creating the universe in general at the time. The Creator himself may not have had much imagination; any entity who could leave his working manual, the Octavo, lying around when he had finished must have had some mental limitations.

It's even possible that the universe came into being through the operation of natural forces, the Creator and his ilk are simply personifications of these in a situation where everything is personified, and human imagination can echo back through time.

It would be tactless to say so, however. While these forces aren't worshipped, lesser gods would likely become dangerously irate if people went round saying that they were subordinate to blind chance.

How long ago this was is also uncertain, but there's evidence of continental drift, evolution from less to more complex forms of life, and devastating meteor (and stray world-elephant) impacts. Even given the accelerated way these things happen here, a timescale in the hundreds of millions of years seems indicated. On the other hand, it's entirely possible that some of that evidence was faked. Somewhere along the way, the Tower of Art appeared on the site of what is now Ankh-Morpork; this structure is believed to pre-date humanity.

THE MAGE WARS

Humans, dwarfs, trolls, and other races seem to have evolved at around the same time, and they promptly started believing in gods. This is the time that most Disc religions and histories mean when they refer to "the creation."[1] However, once the humans had looked around and found out a little more, they quite naturally lost their temper. As there was a great deal of magic around in those days, the wars between men and gods were balanced and extremely violent; many of the Disc's more unstable high-magic zones and bizarre species date to this period. Eventually, the Old High Ones (p. 291) intervened, exiling the gods to the mountaintops (in theory – the more powerful ones who were around at the time, anyway), shrinking mortals considerably in size, and reducing the Disc's magic level.

Still, a great deal of raw magic remained. Human history continued to be dominated by sourcerers (p. 274) for some time, until eventually, things were brought under control by human agreement or other powers. Magic was focussed in relatively controlled bodies such as Unseen University (pp. 279-289).

Human Civilisations

The great city of Ankh-Morpork goes back somewhat over 3,000 years in something like its current form. Other urban Disc cultures – such as the Agatean Empire and Klatch – date back about as far, give or take a millennium. However, there has been civilisation of a sort for much longer, especially around the Circle Sea (the Disc's counterpart to our Mediterranean). But paranormal distortions aside, even the history that's written down is largely lies or half-truths, and things get cloudy at a distance.

The earliest human civilisation – in the sense of a hierarchical urban culture, rather than a bunch of people who happened to know each other – was apparently the City of Um, which probably emerged in the wake of the fading away of sourcery, when it finally became possible for large groups of humans to live together without someone rearranging the scenery in a fit of pique. Not much is remembered about Um (this *was* about 60,000 years ago) except that it was destroyed in a continent-wide flood. However, its society seems to have been based almost entirely on the use of golems (pp. 104-106), of which it had many, rendering any other sort of technology or practical magic somewhat superfluous. Even the wheel was just a child's toy in Um.

---

1. *Anything earlier was just mechanical and unobserved, and so doesn't really count.*

The History Monks

Somewhere in the High Ramtops dwells an order of monks whose first task is to observe history as it happens. (We don't know who *gave* them the task, even though their records discuss their founding in some detail – they're mythic that way.) They guard great books wherein the history of the Discworld – past and future – is written, and often go forth to make sure that it happens properly, not (officially) by intervening, but by observing. As large-scale quantum mechanics, in their way, they know that this is essential for what occurs to be *history* and not just events.

The Monks are quintessential enlightened, meditating little bald men, with a taste for saffron robes and incredible skill in martial arts (which they use strictly defensively, of course). Advanced training at their timeless monastery makes most of them effectively unageing, although the abbot – their greatest theoretician – never quite got the hang of that, and has to keep reincarnating instead (so the monastery sometimes finds itself administered by a bald, saffron-clad infant with a brilliant mind and teething trouble). This calm enlightenment, and their nominal role as *observers,* should in theory make them rather passive. However, as watchers of time and history, they inevitably become aware that there are some problems which only they can resolve.

Their expertise with their subject gives them formidable powers. They can even travel back and forth through history, while the ability to stop or accelerate time locally helps explain their formidable reputation as martial artists. They have shrines and temples in a number of places around the Disc, including Ankh-Morpork, from where they act to preserve history against accidents or meddling. Powerful though they are, however, they're always up against quantum uncertainty. Like a swan, their stately progress may be because of frantic paddling down below. A man need only drop the wrong glass or miss with the wrong arrow to send a History Monk scurrying to put everything right. In addition, novice monks are doubtless sent out to observe small historical events and, like apprentices everywhere, may get things wrong – with, as they say, hilarious results.

Other civilisations have risen since, but they've also fallen. Djelibeybi (p. 235) is probably the Disc's oldest extant culture, claiming 7,000 years of history, although much of it was recycled. It ruled vast areas for a while, but ultimately declined. At the end of that long, slow fall, the region around the Circle Sea shattered into several nations, leading to the patchwork of competing states we see today. For much of fairly recent history, the two mightiest have been Ankh-Morpork, with its wizards and commercial strength, and Klatch, with its sophisticated deviousness. Recently, both have been challenged to some extent by the resurgent ancient nation of Tsort, although the Tsortean army has never been quite strong enough to conquer other major powers.

Omnia, another coastal nation, may be acquiring more long-term influence thanks to its successful exportation of its increasingly popular religion.

Closer to the Hub, the region now known as Uberwald was at one point the centre of what was identified simply as the Dark Empire – and no, that name wasn't misleading (see p. 241). The Empire fell apart over the decades and centuries, though, leaving Uberwald less a nation than a patchwork of towns, races, and factions (including vampire lords, werewolf packs, mad doctors, and dwarf clans). Its neighbours are still sorting out their relationships, often with swords and crossbows. Elsewhere, less organised regions were occasionally colonised by stronger powers and then gained independence, leading to the appearance of oddities such as Genua. Far across the Disc, the insanely wealthy Agatean Empire long ago found a stable equilibrium, based on bureaucracy, careful control of thought, and paddy fields, and no sane ruler sought to challenge or invade it. The Agateans weren't interested in expanding (too destabilising), but were very good at revenge.

RECENT DECADES

During the chronicles, the Discworld has gone through some accelerated progress. A key turning point was the appointment[1] of Lord Havelock Vetinari as Patrician of squabbling, lawless Ankh-Morpork. He has entirely transformed the city, finding ways to canalise the relentless self-interest of its warring factions. Ankh-Morpork remains squabbling but is not exactly lawless, and it is something of a boomtown. Vetinari governs it anyway (see Chapter 7). Today, rather than brutal thugs and scarred assassins round every corner, there are polite thugs and gentlemanly assassins, the latter waiting round only the best corners.

Indirectly or by example, this has triggered a period of further changes round the Disc. Djelibeybi has woken from its cyclic history, forcing Tsort and Ephebe to revise their ancient enmity. Omnia has completed its transformation from a land of psychotic religious fanatics to a land of polite missionary religious fanatics. Even the Agatean Empire has been changed, admittedly by the traditional means of a barbarian conquest (but only a *very* small one). Threats that might have brought the whole Disc down in flames – such as the brief rise of Coin the Sorcerer, or the even briefer rule of a full-size dragon in Ankh-Morpork – have been contained, by luck or judgement or inadvertent bravery. Theatre is going through a golden age; opera is at a peak (but never mind). All this is combined with a small-scale industrial revolution based in part on low-key magic.

Not that anyone would ever admit that things are improving, or credit the people responsible – and not that there are no longer any adventures or threats to civilisation. In fact, more civilisation means more threats, many from inside the walls.

Basic Geography

The map shows the Disc's basic geography, and Chapter 6 goes into more detail. However, a quick run-down may be useful.

The Circle Sea

The Circle Sea lies about halfway between the Hub and the Rim, and it empties into the Rim Ocean on its turnwise side. Its name is accurate, if unimaginative. The temperate Sto Plains lie to hubward, "Arabian" Klatch and "African" Howondaland are to rimward, and nations such as Omnia, Djelibeybi, and Tsort are ranged along its coasts. These civilisations have fought, traded, and exchanged ideas over many centuries, and the great city of Ankh-Morpork on the Sto Plains is currently seen as the beating heart of progress on the Disc.

Hubward Lands

The lands of the Disc rise toward the Hub, which is surrounded by mountain ranges which sprawl almost to the edge of the great central continent. Where the Sto Plains meet the great Ramtops lies the little kingdom of Lancre, which features in the chronicles as a place to go for great witchcraft and the occasional interdimensional incursion.

---

1. *Or assumption, or usurpation . . .*

Widdershins of there is the vast "gothic" land of Uberwald. Beyond that are warmer regions, including the swamp-city of Genua – while if one turns hubwards and climbs a lot of mountains, one ends up amidst the saffron-robed monks and hairy-chested barbarians of the Hublands.

Hub and Rimfall

The design of the Disc includes a number of spectacular features. At its dead centre is the towering spire of Cori Celesti (p. 242), less a mountain than a damn great spike, sticking out of the middle of the whole assembly and often surrounded by the *Aurora Corialis* – silent streamers of blue, green, and octarine (p. 401). Cori Celesti, or at least the aurora, can be glimpsed from almost anywhere on the Disc.

Far from that, all around the edge, the Rim Ocean tumbles endlessly into mist and empty space. It refracts light into the *Rimbow*, a double rainbow of eight colours – the terrestrial seven, spread out close to the Disc, plus a broad band of octarine some distance farther out. The Rimbow is visible at dawn and sunset, when the Disc's little sun is at just the right angle.

You really *don't* need to worry about how the water gets back on the Disc.

The Far Rim

The Discworld has reasonably good communications by fantasy-world standards, but there's still no radio or regular air travel. From the perspective of most of the chronicles' protagonists, the region beyond the Hub is distant, mysterious, and *weird*. Trade with such parts is mostly conducted through a lot of intermediaries. However, direct contact with a couple of powers there is increasing, and some brave folk travel the full distance. Still, that's mostly a new phenomenon.

The Counterweight Continent – about a third of the way round the Disc from Ankh-Morpork – is extremely rich. Thus, those bold travellers are very interested in it. This continent is dominated by the ancient, formalistic Agatean Empire, and it has considerable resources of gold and of magical materials such as sapient pearwood (p. 158) and octiron (p. 275).

Another third of the way round the Disc from *there* is an island continent, EcksEcksEcksEcks (or Fourecks), which for most of human history was effectively isolated by freak climatic conditions. However, it had some inhabitants from early on, and the population has grown substantially in recent centuries thanks to a small-but-steady flow of shipwrecked mariners. It was actually a separate creation from most of the Disc, explaining its peculiar fauna, while some accidents during its creation explained its peculiar weather conditions. Recent events have brought it back into contact with the rest of the Disc.

Living and Adventuring

Disc society is made up of many species, dozens of cultures, and a sprinkling of magic. It's kept together by a certain amount of compromise and by the recognition – at least some of the time – that intelligent beings can't spend *all* their time hitting each other.

It is also changing, as the place is currently being dragged through a kind of warped and confused Renaissance with Victorian trimmings. Not everyone even wants to admit this, but it's the kind of thing that leads to lots of adventures. That is, a few people have an uncomfortable, confusing, sometimes miserable, and occasionally fatal time so that a lot more people can live in a bit more comfort – if they're lucky.

For convenience, this book assumes that gamers will wish to play in the world as it's seen in the more recent novels. That isn't a firm rule, though. For example, anyone who wants to have fun with the conventions of heroic high fantasy is welcome to set their game in and around the more medieval Ankh-Morpork of *The Colour of Magic*. At least one novel, *Small Gods*, can best be interpreted as lying a good century in the past of the main sequence, so the GM wishing to use the tyrannical, pre-Brutha version of Omnia is going to have to go back that far, or tinker with history. Feel free! It's the stories that count, not the numbers.

Languages

The language of modern Ankh-Morpork is known as *Morporkian*. This is also the language of the Sto Plains and up into the Ramtops at least as far as Lancre, and it is spoken (sometimes with odd accents and dialect variations) in colonies and "cultural outliers" such as Genua, Krull, and distant Fourecks. The more widespread it has become, the more other peoples have adopted it for trade, and in some cases ended up using it in place

of their original tongue. For game purposes, players can use English. Even English puns and wordplay work in Morporkian.

However, some regions do still have their own languages, and the Disc has enough of them that a gift for learning them could earn Rincewind the failed wizard a living of sorts on the lower rungs of Ankh-Morpork society. For example, the language of the Sto Plains state of Quirm fills some of the same roles as French in our world (being, among other things, the language of fancy restaurant menus[1]). Likewise, the distinctive accent of Llamedos (p. 234) hints at the existence of an old (Welsh-like) language, which doubtless survives for ceremonial purposes at least. Brindisi, some way Widdershins of the Circle Sea, has a language resembling Italian; *Brindisian* is often heard in operas on the Disc.

Ephebian, *Tsortean*, *Omnian*, and *Djelibeybian* are spoken in coastal nations around the Circle Sea, and may in fact be related, while *Klatchian* is spoken not only in the nation of Klatch itself, but also by many desert tribes and city-states. It's said that the D'Regs (p. 236) have a language in which the same word means "traveller," "stranger," and "target," but that's probably a dialect of Klatchian.

Deeper in that continent, numerous tribes and peoples – often cut off from their neighbours by excesses of geography or warfare – have their own very local languages. Back toward the Hub, the vast region of Uberwald (p. 240) also has its own language, which resembles some kind of Germanic or Slavic tongue to an English-speaker's ears. Beyond that are more tribes, all proudly linguistically independent. Known minor tribal languages include *Cumhoolie* and *K'turni*.

---

1. *With good reason. Even the ordinary citizens of Ankh-Morpork have to admit that Quirmian cooking is actually better than their own if they try it and after they've stopped going on about the garlic.*

The other major human language of the Disc is that of the Agatean Empire (pp. 243-244), which is tonal and subtle, and written in an intricate script of thousands of ideograms. Besides this, the only modern language which ordinary Agateans were (very occasionally) known to learn before recent times was *Trob*, as used by sailors who visit their ports from the nearest island chain.

DEAD LANGUAGES

There are also plenty of dead languages. Most are of interest only to academics and priests of religions with very old holy books, but one, *Latatian,* is used in Ankh-Morpork as a language of law, heraldry, and fancy jargon. For practical purposes, it can be treated as Latin. (However, this might not be *good* Latin; "dog Latin" tags can pass as Latatian.) Anyone from the Sto Plains who has the Heraldry or Law skill can attempt to puzzle out a few words with an IQ roll (see pp. 165-166).

Ancient magical tomes may be written in all sorts of dead (and *un*dead) languages. The one certainty is that wizards can read books that they shouldn't, yet have immense difficulties with books of what turn out to be basic horticultural spells.

NONHUMAN LANGUAGES

Nonhuman races sometimes have their own languages, perhaps better suited for nonhuman vocal apparatus. Trolls and dwarfs have *Trollish* and *Dwarfish* respectively, which are relatively standard across their widespread populations – they're both culturally conservative races, not prone to divergence merely because they're scattered over thousands of miles. Still, even these long-lived beings aren't immune to linguistic shifts. Anyone studying *really* ancient texts will need to know other, archaic dwarf or troll languages.

Humans can learn to speak both Trollish and Dwarfish, albeit with some difficulty, although a human learning either tongue to the Native fluency level might require some explanation – they may need a Cultural Familiarity (pp. 32-33) for the race's own culture to understand some of the concepts, which in turn might require an Unusual Background (pp. 48-49).[1] Dwarfs and trolls themselves, on the other hand, learn Morporkian more than well enough. Pictsies (pp. 101-102) also speak their own language, although speakers of Morporkian can usually get the gist of what they're saying if they pay attention, and a few humans have learned Pictsie. Goblins (pp. 102-104) have what turns out to be an amazingly complex, highly contextual language, of which human scholars are completely ignorant; the *very* few humans who speak it have had to spend years in close contact with goblins.

By and large, though, humans don't bother learning nonhuman languages, as most nonhumans end up learning human languages out of necessity. This lets humans feel superior, as it means that they don't have to go to any trouble themselves. Few worry that it gives the nonhumans a private communication channel . . .

There are even more obscure languages around, too. For example, golems always learn the languages in which other races order them about, but they also seem to share a language of their own, which is 20,000 years old. Humans need an Unusual Background to learn it at better than the Broken level, as may be necessary for some work with golems (it's hell on the tongue); this costs 1 point, or more to be a true golem friend. Most golems also know the ritual language of whichever priests created them.

---

1. *An unusual throat would also help.*

Orang-utans have a sophisticated, complex, and expressive language, which unfortunately has only one word; humans can get the hang of *understanding* but not *speaking* it (see p. 53). Then there are the languages used by unusually intelligent but essentially "normal" dogs (p. 354). Other races may or may not once have had their own languages, but they've ended up using human languages for convenience.

Oggham

Oggham is an ancient runic alphabet, still used by some dwarfs in the Ramtops. Nanny Ogg (pp. 340-341) claims that it's somehow connected to her own (very long-established) family; it *is* intimately related to the old languages of the region. It isn't a magical language as such, but it *is* used in some old inscriptions of interest to those researching ceremonial magic or rituals. There are doubtless scholars at Unseen University with theoretical knowledge of it, and any witch, dwarf, or amateur historian from the Ramtops could have picked it up. See *Oggham Reader* (p. 52) for game rules.

Technology

At first glance, the Discworld appears to be a medieval-to-Renaissance society with some high-fantasy trimmings. Soldiers use swords, spears, and halberds at close quarters, and bows and crossbows at range; they wear mail or scale, with the odd piece of plate (often rusty or ill-fitting, as it's expensive stuff, much reused). A few foppish aristocrats carry rapiers, largely for show. Gunpowder is known but used mostly for fireworks. A crude form of printing, based on well-paid engravers, has long sustained a publishing industry in Ankh-Morpork; recently, the arrival of moveable type, developed elsewhere on the Disc, has revolutionised that. Architecture still mostly looks medieval, but there are some huge and elegant stone and brick buildings. See also *Travel* (p. 18).

But just calling Disc technology "late medieval" or even "Renaissance" misses the richness and perversity of the thing. To begin with, there's magic. It isn't so much the high-end spellcasters, who aren't always especially practical and don't disseminate their achievements efficiently. It's the odd ideas that come from alchemists, apprentices, and whoever got hold of the spell for summoning and binding small and (supposedly) efficient imps (see *Demon-Based Devices*, pp. 159-160) that really make things interesting for most people.

This is typical of the Disc. A great deal is possible here, even in the field of nonmagical technology, *given the idea and the determination*. It's a quasi-Renaissance society all right, but with huge masses of higher-tech potentiality lurking in the wings, plus magical augmentation. Mad inventors, of whom there are a few, can construct astonishing devices on a one-off basis – but like all such crazed geniuses, they can never seem to repeat their strokes of genius, let alone mass-produce things.

Nor is even widespread technology exploited effectively. The Agatean Empire has endured for centuries and has huge reserves of inventions. It knows more about explosives than most nations, and it has even applied gunpowder to warfare; handguns are a way off yet, but Agatean armies do employ cannon.

Travel

Transport on the Disc is still rather basic. Land travel is by foot, horse (or other beast of burden), or coach. Terrain varies enormously, but roads are usually poor, restricting even riders to a walking pace when they aren't falling into potholes.

Stagecoach travel is mostly limited to the Sto Plains, up to the foothills of the Ramtops. Proper stagecoaches, with their relatively advanced suspensions, are actually fairly sophisticated pieces of engineering (TL4, in game terms; see *Technology Level*, pp. 30-31), although the passengers might not think so as they bump along. This development was one of the first signs of the current era of technological progress. A stagecoach with fresh horses can carry nine normal-human-sized passengers in addition to the driver – albeit with a number of them hanging on the outside looking worried (guards sometimes replace some of those). It can manage 18 mph for a few miles or 12 mph for hours at a time, but only on good roads.

Criminals who prey on travellers add to the fun; see *Banditry and Piracy* (p. 222). The threat of banditry in wilder regions leads to caravans, usually organised by a major merchant, who may hire professional guards for exceptionally dangerous routes, and who will charge other travellers a small fee for the safety of joining. By tradition, wizards aren't charged but are *paid* to join caravans, as their powers can prove useful.

At sea, ships generally use the wind, exploiting it with some fairly advanced rigging, although inshore vessels on more placid bodies of water often employ rowers (usually well-paid professionals, not slaves). Sailing ships may manage 8-10 mph for quite long periods, but that of course depends on the wind. There's also the option of river travel. Large boats on some major rivers have treadmill-powered paddlewheels; the great floating palaces of the Vieux River (p. 241) traditionally employ trolls for this, but on other waterways, oxen are more usual. Smaller boats use sails, oars, or draft animals on towpaths. They invariably go significantly faster downstream than upstream.

Air travel, by broomstick or flying carpet, is available to some of the magically inclined, and to individuals who don't mind heights and are owed favours by the right people. Flying is generally safe, but not especially fast. Most forms are also tiring and poorly protected against bad weather.

However, the system that creates this stability also creates problems. Those cannon are designed by bureaucrats who are selected for their traditional grasp of the fine arts, not for their technical ability. The best place to be when an Agatean "Barking Dog" is fired is about two miles behind it.[1]

One extremely important recent invention is long-distance semaphore communication, using a system of signalling towers. The social and political consequences of this are vast, radical, and unexpected. See *The Semaphore Revolution* (pp. 222-225).

Medicine

Medicine on the Disc is one area where things are primitive by real-world standards, although not *quite* as bad as they may appear at first glance. Surgery, at least in Ankh-Morpork, involves carpentry tools and hot pitch, and is best avoided. Doctors are often seen as well-educated con artists who have not only worked out literally how to get away with murder, but how to charge the victim for it.

Magic isn't as useful here as people hope – not because it's weak, but because it's too insidiously powerful. Magic *could* remove injury or disease, but then the patient's body would become magical and thus prone to erratic behaviour; it would no longer be entirely under his control. The cure would almost certainly be, quite literally, worse than the disease.

On the other hand, magic can be used reasonably safely for diagnostic work, and also for anaesthesia by those who can afford it or who know a sympathetic witch. This alone improves survival rates significantly, while other medicines can help less severe cases. Witches, especially, have a repertoire of useful and subtle spells that assist healing without imposing on the patient – by, say, suppressing pain by moving it to an inanimate object, or delaying the effects of an injury until the witch is in a position to do something about it.

The Disc does have a huge and effective repertoire of herbal medicine, mostly in the hands of witches. Despite their concentration on the placebo effect, haphazard methods, and semiliterate recordkeeping, Disc witches can work near-miracles with a few scraggly leaves extracted from under old logs. They're helped in this by several factors. For one thing, intense magical fields in areas such as the Ramtops have evolved a huge and bizarre flora to use for raw material. For another, a little careful magic can help in preparing, purifying, and testing herbal preparations. Many witches have a comfortable commercial sideline in medicine-making; their folk wisdom extends into areas such as contraception, making them especially popular, at least among women. They also have other useful techniques; for example, they're often talented chiropractors.[2]

Another useful set of medical practitioners are the Igors (pp. 140-141), who originated in Uberwald and who are only now spreading across the Disc. Igors deal more with physical injuries than with disease, being repairmen and gadgeteers at heart (and their hearts are covered by this). However, they employ an interesting array of alchemical salves and ointments, and their anachronistic brilliance with transplant surgery means that limb amputations or malfunctioning organs need not have permanent deleterious effects.

Disease is also relatively rare on the Disc, at least at truly serious levels. This is true even in Ankh-Morpork, where sanitation and water supplies are, err, not to advanced standards. This can be credited to a combination of evolution (most Ankh-Morpork natives have well-hardened immune systems and are descended from people who survived even worse conditions), the long-term efforts of various specialists, and literary convention. (And maybe even the odd god of medicine, although such deities aren't always terribly helpful – too many of them double as gods of thieves or bureaucrats, having discovered that standard Disc-human levels of belief in medicine aren't sufficient to power a decent thunderbolt.)

---

1. And even then, only maybe.

2. They derive this art from a basic belief that what most people need is a hard shove in the right place.

Still, there *have* been occasional plagues, and Pestilence still rides with the other Horsemen of the Apocalypse. If an adventure plot calls for disease, then disease there can be.

For notes on the quality of Discworld medical skills in game terms, see p. 77.

The Position of Magic

Magic is an accepted part of life on the Disc, and isn't usually regarded as evil. However, like excess firepower, it does sometimes worry people – often for similar reasons.

Exponents of magic are not always above exploiting such worry. Witches work on the theory that much of their power comes from the respect (or fear) in which they're held. The wizards of Unseen University don't so much keep accounts with local tradesmen as have *arrangements*.[1] And the ability to work magic is closely linked to the ability to see things as they really are, rather than as people assume they must be, which in turn gives magic-workers a slightly unnerving, detached air. Where other characters take part in stories, witches and wizards *shape* stories, and sometimes it shows.

There's also a divide between truly powerful magic-workers – witches, wizards, and exotic variants on these types, such as voodoo-users – and the large class of less-versatile supernatural specialists. Mediums, wandering fortune-tellers, dwarf broomstick-mechanics, and some alchemists may all possess a scrap of true power, but most aren't in the same league as spell-hurling pointy-hat wearers and are somewhat easier to live with. One exception is demonologists, who are generally authentic (if not overly powerful) wizards, but who choose voluntarily to have dealings with beings whose job descriptions mention Infinite Evil and Corrupting the Souls of Mankind. This *does* tend to aggravate the neighbours, and demonologists quickly learn not to tell other folk what they do in their attics.

Magic-users have been persecuted on rare occasions, sometimes even systematically. Individuals may earn their profession a bad name (by indiscriminate frog-making, demonology, or whatever), and nearby communities might develop a prejudice that can take years to change. There's also a traditional rivalry between magic and religion. Magic-workers know enough that they don't take the gods as seriously as the gods would like, and they see priests as people who encourage stupidity. Priests, meanwhile, feel that spellcasters undermine the significance of divine miracles; they also have a pretty good idea about the very real dangers of demonology and the Dungeon Dimensions. This enmity mostly remains on the name-calling level, but some powerful and expansionist religions have been known to progress to bonfires and inquisitions.[2]

The social status of magic might give non-spellcaster PCs ideas about making false claims – dressing up in pointy hats, waving sticks around, and demanding better service. This might even work sometimes, but it's really, really not clever. Discworlders mostly know enough about magic to be aware that small effects are easy for true experts to accomplish, and the majority have seen smarter con games than this in their time. They're likely to

---

1. *The tradesmen deliver groceries, and the wizards don't have as many accidents as they might if they weren't so fat and contented.*

2. *Seldom against real magic-users, of course, precisely because they can use magic. But a good inquisitor can always find a helpless old woman if the need for a victim arises.*

demand demonstrations of any claimed power – politely or brusquely, according to their mood and the claim's apparent plausibility. Furthermore, real spellcasters get irritated by such fakery. Unseen University still has some quite medieval statutes on its books related to the subject and has jurisdiction in the matter, while a typical Ramtops village witch would probably do something milder but seriously humiliating.

Caroc Cards

Caroc cards are used for both divination (p. 202) and card games. The deck contains eight suits: Octagrams, Turtles, Elephants, Swords, Sceptres, Cups, Coins, and Crowns. Each suit has numbered cards from Ace to Eight, a Knave, a Knight, a Queen, and a King. There are also Major Arcana, which are dealt out of simpler games; these include the Ruler, the Star, the Importance of Washing the Hands, the Dome of the Sky, the Pool of Night (which may be the same as the Moon), and Death. As with our world's tarot, fortune-tellers insist that Death doesn't always mean death. It's symbolic. Really.

Caroc-readers also claim that the deck contains the distilled wisdom of the universe (or the ancients). Other people – even some wizards – mutter that this is rubbish. Shrewd witches regard the cards as a concentration aid that helps focus innate powers. Both fortune-tellers and gamblers need above-average dexterity to shuffle a 100-card deck.

These days, the cards are mostly used for games (for the skills involved, see *Game/Sport Skills*, pp. 73-74). These include a hideously complex game of bids, partnerships, ruffs, and grand slams, whose name has been identified as "Aqueduct," and the slightly less arcane and accordingly more popular Cripple Mr. Onion.

This latter is played by two sorts of Discworlders: "Winners" and "Losers." It uses the eight Minor Suits only (you don't want to play with people who deal in the Major Arcana). It's similar to poker, with an initial deal, followed by a series of betting rounds until all but one player has folded or the bets are equalised, in which case a showdown follows. One may also buy extra cards. Combinations include the Two-, Three-, and Five-Card Onions, Broken Flush, Double Bagel, Double and Triple Onions, Great Onion (the second-best hand), and Nine-Card Run (a nine-card straight flush – the best possible hand).

Warfare

Wars do happen on the Disc, and in the past, some of them have been quite large. Certainly, the Agatean Empire maintains a sizeable standing army (because it *can*), while expansionist powers such as Klatch (pp. 234-237) use healthy armed forces to enforce their foreign policies. Meanwhile, regional conflicts – such as those between Borogravia (p. 241) and anyone else – have involved as much manpower as the participants could muster. Mostly, though, the Disc is *fairly* peaceful just now. Most of the time.

The overall shape of local military technology is what our world would call "Early Renaissance." The core of each army is a large number of infantry wearing a bit of armour – as much as someone can afford. The majority carry spears or polearms, and provide a stable centre to the army in battle and cover for the smaller number who carry missile weapons – mostly crossbows. This approach depends on drill and discipline to maintain cohesion, which is why amateurish armies suffer so badly. Supporting the infantry is usually a smaller force of cavalry – either nobles and aristocrats (people who can afford horses and heavy armour), or mercenary nomads (people who *have* to own horses and ride well). A well-rounded army is filled out by a train of mechanical artillery, essential in sieges and useful in open battle because it can rain down modest but demoralising amounts of damage on enemies at extreme ranges. Some modern "engines" are quite ingenious and can produce terrifying volumes of missile fire for short periods, but their cost is equally frightening.

Naturally, there's a lot of local variation in army composition, and some rulers field flashy if questionably effective things such as war elephants merely because they can. Most leaders with dreams of military glory find their local resources tediously limited, however. Thus, there's always work for wandering mercenaries who can look tougher and more *credible* than locally raised soldiers.

Magic tends to be used in warfare only when someone is foolish enough to attack a witch or a wizard directly, and it is mostly seen as against the unwritten laws of war. Not that people are especially good at obeying laws, of course – especially when the laws are unwritten, and personal advantage or one's neck is at stake – but witches and wizards don't want to be dragged into dangerous and uncomfortable positions if they can avoid it, and magic isn't terribly good at making the user invulnerable. "No first use of magic" is the sort of slogan that Discworld politicians and strategists trundle out during wars when they want to claim the moral high ground.

Currencies

The Disc has a huge array of very confused currencies. Most are *theoretically* based on the value of precious metals but *actually* depend on what governments can get away with. There's no system of international money markets, just a lot of shrewd merchants who know how desperate different governments have been at different dates, and who keep alchemists on retainer to check the worth of any new coins that come along.

The Ankh-Morpork dollar has long been the most internationally useful currency. The dollar coin is (or maybe now *was*) the size of a sequin: half the width of a United States nickel, but fairly thick due to the state of coin-making technology. While theoretically gold, in practise it has been debased so often over the centuries that it contains no meaningful quantity of gold. However, as the Ankh-Morporkian economy is productive and relatively stable, its currency is seen as stable as well, and it is the *de facto* standard for all the nations around the Circle Sea. Other currencies tend to be defined by their value relative to this. Faked coins have always been possible, of course – especially given the poor quality of the coin's metal content – but as plenty of commercial factions regard this as Bad For Business, forgers faced serious dangers to life and limb.

This is little different from paper money on our world, really – the currency was based on confidence more than metal value, which had become a joke. With radical social change and commercial expansion in Ankh-Morpork, though, concepts of simple confidence were becoming shaky. (Not to mention that increasing trade with the gold-rich Agatean Empire must be pulling a lot more gold into the Sto Plains, which is likely to play havoc with the metal's supposed value.) But Discworlders find the feel of real metal coins reassuring and were sure to resist the idea of changing the system.

The Patrician (pp. 306-308) saw that the Ankh-Morpork financial system was a mess and that plans for the city's future demanded reform, so he put Moist von Lipwig (pp. 309-311) in charge of the Bank of Ankh-Morpork. Moist's solution was to introduce paper money, persuading people to accept it partly through his own brilliant salesmanship and partly by declaring that the currency was now backed by the value of an army of golems which had conveniently become available, and which was now buried outside the city. This didn't mean any more than saying that it was based on (nonexistent) gold, of course, but it proved convincing enough, and Ankh-Morpork and its neighbours are now getting used to banknotes.

The dollar is divided into 100 pence, or pennies. For convenience and by tradition, there are other coins and units: the *shilling* is 10 pence, while a 50-pence quantity is known as a *nob, ton, half a bar,* or *knocker,* and 25 pence is *half a ton.*

In Ephebe, the standard coinage is a *derechmi,* worth one Ankh-Morpork dollar and divided into 50 *cercs.* The Djelibeybi *talent* and the Omnian *obol* are each worth about one Ankh-Morpork penny. In small nations such as Lancre, silver pennies, weighing more than an ounce, are used on the rare occasions when coinage is needed. These *do* have some measurable silver content; country folk are old-fashioned about value.

The least-valuable coin on the Discworld is the lead *quarteriotum* of Zchloty, which is worth less than the lead from which it's made. It is run close by the Hershebian *half-dong,* which is worth one-eighth of a penny.

That leaves the Agatean Empire, where gold is barely a semi-precious metal. The Agatean *rhinu* is pure gold; its value relative to the traditional Ankh-Morpork dollar isn't calculable, because if rhinu had started appearing in Ankh-Morpork in quantity, the whole economy would have buckled. Today, the conversion rate is whatever merchants and tourists can haggle out. There's scope for profit from what economists call *arbitrage* in transactions between the two regions, with different products having widely divergent relative values, but travel times are long enough that there isn't much of this going on.

Nonhumans and Money

Discworld nonhumans can usually comprehend basic trade, but they don't necessarily think naturally in terms of fixed units of exchange. Trolls, for example, base their intra-species trade on lumps of rock. Dwarfs have a keen and precise idea of the values of precious metals, but only shape it into standardised lumps because humans expect it. They would prefer to measure nugget weights to the microgram and argue for hours over purity.

And some creatures are still firmly at the barter stage. Gargoyles, for example, define their needs and desires in terms of pigeons.

MAKING CHARACTERS

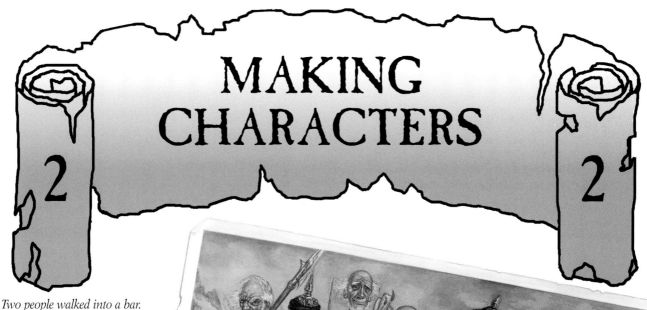

Two people walked into a bar.

In most bars, this is nothing unusual. In the case of Biers, though, quite a lot of the regular customers didn't qualify as "people" by conventional standards. Furthermore, while Biers wasn't as actively dangerous as many bars in Ankh-Morpork for visitors in uniform, they weren't entirely popular there either – but one of these two was wearing the uniform of a captain of the Watch. However, she was the only one of the two who actually belonged in there.

"You're certain that the human we're looking for will be here?" asked the other one, who didn't.

"I'm sure that she's here sometimes," said Captain Angua. "And I think that, at worst, all we'll have to do is wait a few minutes."

Her companion, a dwarf in plain, well-maintained mail, looked around himself nervously. "But why?" he asked. "I mean, she's human. Okay, she's a wizard . . ."

"No she isn't," said Angua. "You should know that. She's a she, and so she can't be a wizard."

Hunchbroad Modoscousin shrugged the shrug of a dwarf who was still getting used to this bizarre human obsession with gendered pronouns. "Witch?" he ventured.

"No. I think that the word for this case, if it matters, may be 'enchantress.' Although that's probably wrong too."

"Deeply," said a voice from a corner table. "And don't pretend that you didn't know I was here, Captain. I'm pretty sure that your senses are better than that."

Angua scowled at the speaker, who leaned forward over her drink to bring her jet-black face out of the shadows. "Jemzarkiza of Krull," Angua said, "this is Hunchbroad Modoscousin. Hunchbroad, this is Jemzarkiza. I'm told that you two have something in common."

"What's that?" asked Jemzarkiza.

"A wish for adventure."

"What do you . . ." the dwarf began.

"You were told wrong," Jemzarkiza stated flatly at the same moment.

"I'm sorry. I should have said, 'A wish for adventure, if the price is right.'"

There was a very short pause. "Right in very large amounts?" Jemzarkiza asked.

Angua shrugged. "I'm not here to haggle," she said, "and I don't play this mysteriousness game very well . . ."

"Don't you?" muttered Jemzarkiza.

". . . even if I have been sent here by the Patrician. But he'd have sent one of his clerks if that was how he wanted things done. I'm just here to make an introduction and pass on a message."

"So pass it," said Jemzarkiza. Then she took another swig of her drink. "Please?" she added.

Angua pulled out two stools, one for herself and one for Hunchbroad. "I can't, yet, I'm afraid," she said. "We need to get some more people first . . ."

The Discworld is a place to have adventures, among other things, and perhaps whether you want to or not. A roleplaying game uses rules to mediate what happens to characters in play, and the next few chapters are specifically about those rules. Once we've described them, we can use them when discussing those Discworld adventures.

GURPS

The rules that follow are a cut-down, dedicated version of **GURPS,** another roleplaying game from Steve Jackson Games. **GURPS** stands for "Generic Universal RolePlaying System." Why is it called that? Well . . .

"Generic." **GURPS** starts with simple rules and builds up to as much optional detail as you like.

"Universal." The basic rules are designed to emphasise realism, but they can adapt to any situation – fantasy or historical; past, present, or future.

"RolePlaying." This isn't just a "hack-and-slash" game. The rules are written to make true roleplaying possible – indeed, to encourage it. In **GURPS,** you pretend, for a little while, to be someone else.

"System." Over 200 different books have been published for **GURPS,** in eight different languages (so far). It's one of the recognised standards for roleplaying, worldwide.

Hence, **GURPS** is ideal for Discworld games. The version presented here cuts it back to the rules and components necessary for that purpose, but if you want more detail, you can pick up more books later – probably starting with the **GURPS Basic Set,** which details the full rules. The Bibliography (pp. 402-403) describes what's available.

The Example Characters

To illustrate the character-creation process, two examples run through the next three chapters: *Jemzarkiza of Krull* is a moderately powerful character with magical abilities, demonstrating a range of options and ideas. *Hunchbroad Modoscousin* is designed using the rules for nonhuman characters and the quick template-based option introduced in Chapter 3.

Glossary

Like any hobby, roleplaying games have their own language. Thus, we'll start with a few definitions:

adventure: The basic "unit of play" in a roleplaying game, representing a single mission or plot. It might require several sessions of play, or just one.

campaign: A continuing series of *adventures*. A campaign usually has a returning cast of *player characters,* and the same *GM*.

character: Any being – person, animal, robot, etc. – played by the *GM* or a player.

d: Abbreviation for "six-sided dice," usually preceded by a number (of dice); e.g., "3d" means "roll three dice and add them up." May be followed by a modifier for the result; for example, "2d-2" means "roll two dice, add them up, and subtract 2 from the result," while "1d+1" means "roll one die and add 1 to the result."

encounter: One "scene" of an *adventure,* usually a meeting between the *PCs* and one or more *NPCs*.

Game Master (GM): The referee, who chooses the *adventure,* talks the players through it, judges the results, and awards bonus points.

game world: A background for play; a setting. "World" might mean "planet," but it could also refer to a region and historical period . . . or an entire universe. In the **Discworld Roleplaying Game,** the game world is of course the Disc.

nonplayer character (NPC): Any *character* played by the *GM*.

party: A group of *PCs* taking part in the same *adventure*.

player character (PC): A *character* created and played by one of the players.

Quick Contest: One way of resolving conflicts between *characters'* traits or abilities; see p. 166.

Regular Contest: Another way of resolving trait or ability conflicts; see p. 166.

roll: As in "skill roll," "HT roll," etc.; a test of some ability or probability, usually involving rolling 3d and hoping to score less than or equal to a set number. Explained in detail in Chapter 5.

statistics: The numerical values that describe a *character,* piece of equipment, etc., taken collectively. Often called "stats."

Character Basics

As a player, the first thing you need for this game is a *character,* which you create for yourself. You imagine a person living on the Disc – say, a watchman or a witch, or just someone who's going to get involved in interesting events by accident – and then define him in game terms. At the end of this process, you'll have a useful representation of your character's abilities, failings, and peculiarities. Once you've got the hang of the basics, you can speed things up a bit by using *Occupational Templates* (pp. 119-145).

You should start with a vision of the sort of character you want, although you're free to refine and adjust this throughout the process. Talk to your GM and make sure that your idea fits with his general plans for the game. For example, "A veteran watchman, a bit like Colon but better in a fight" would often be a perfectly good idea, but it wouldn't really suit a game of exploration and treasure-hunting in darkest Klatch. Likewise,

"A powerful, megalomaniac wizard" would be fine in some games, but isn't going to work, or even be possible, in a situation comedy about peasants in a Ramtops village.

Next, the GM will give you a number of *character points* with which to "buy" your abilities. For instance, the more physical strength you want, the more points it will cost. You can also buy favourable social traits, such as wealth, and special abilities called *advantages* (pp. 28-49 and 85-93). If you want more capabilities than you can afford on this budget, you can get extra points by accepting below-average strength, appearance, wealth, social status, etc., or by taking *disadvantages* (pp. 28-49, 53-68, and 94-98) – specific handicaps such as bad vision or fear of heights. The point budget your GM hands out tells you how powerful starting PCs can expect to be, in combat, with magic, or socially; see *Starting Points* (pp. 23-25).

But the two most important things to know about your character are *who he is* and *what role you want him to play in his adventures*. You can even play a nonhuman being, such as a dwarf, troll, or zombie, although it adds a little complexity. See Chapter 3 for rules.

Once you've settled this much about your character, you can start filling in details. There are several ways to approach this.

You can choose the abilities you want, spend your character points, and work out a detailed background that fits the abilities. While a good character is much more than a collection of abilities, "shopping" for abilities can be a great inspiration.

You might instead decide on your character's focal qualities first, the handful of things that *define* him: personal history, appearance, behaviour, aptitudes, and skills. Think about how he acquired those qualities, and then spend your points on features that go with them.

It's also sometimes possible to play characters from the novels as PCs; see Chapter 9 for detailed character sheets for some of them. This can be quite entertaining in one-off games, and we certainly don't prohibit it. In general, though, we recommend that you create your own characters from scratch. For one thing, this avoids arguments with other players about whether Carrot or Rincewind would *actually* do what you've just said. For another, it permits the GM to make sure that the PCs fit well with his ideas about the game's style and specific location. But most of all, this game is about making your *own* Discworld stories – for which you really need your own protagonists.

THE COMEDY FACTOR

A key piece of wisdom is worth spelling out here: "Funny" isn't the same as "stupid."

Because Discworld games should (mostly) be comic, some players may come up with silly, inconsistent, or unbalanced characters. This indicates a misunderstanding. The Disc is a strange place, and much that happens in the chronicles is funny – but the inhabitants are more than straight-men and victims. They live their lives, try to avoid unpleasantness and Death, and deal with each other as best they can. Discworld games are about more than laughs.

Certainly, characters in the chronicles include some obviously comic concepts: a wizard who knows no magic, a geriatric swordsman, a New Age witch. Some of them even have silly names.[1] However, each of them has a real, rounded personality, and each is genuinely competent at some things, whether survival, languages, swordsmanship, or magic. More to the point, the novels in which they appear don't consist entirely of jokes at their expense. There are plots and adventures and ideas. Comedy on the Discworld arises from situation and personality.

Thus, if players can't come up with funny characters, they don't have to try. Let them design simple, straightforward PCs, and then turn those loose in some typical Discworld situations. Comedy enough should ensue.

On the other hand, Discworld games should be about much more than slaughtering monsters and taking their property. It's more important that the PCs be *interesting* than invulnerable. Players who seem to be trying to squeeze every ounce of lethality out of their points should be gently discouraged.

---

1. As opposed to un-silly names like . . . err . . . Finkelstein, Pressburger, and Oral Roberts.

Converting Existing Characters

This version of the **Discworld Roleplaying Game** is rooted in **GURPS** *Fourth Edition*, but its original incarnation was based on **GURPS** *Third Edition*. Some groups may want to update existing campaigns from the old edition to the new one, and some GMs might allow players to bring PCs over from earlier games (although they're advised to review such characters carefully first). It's perfectly possible to convert characters for these purposes – **GURPS** hasn't changed too radically – but certain things differ enough to demand a bit of thought. A general guide to such conversions, **GURPS Update,** is available on the Steve Jackson Games website as a free PDF: **gurps.sjgames.com/resources/4eupdate.pdf**. That should answer the majority of questions, although the GM may have to apply a little common sense to Discworld-specific issues.

The biggest change between editions of the **Discworld Roleplaying Game** is the magic system. The old version used the default **GURPS** system, which treats each spell as a distinct skill, whereas this book takes a different, more flexible and open-ended approach. If you've been playing with the earlier system, the simplest approach might be simply to carry on doing so; the spell-based system is still included in the **GURPS Basic Set,** and hasn't changed much (although the Fourth Edition version of **GURPS Magic** describes many additional spells). Alternatively, if you want to use the new system, the best bet is probably to take the points that the character spent on spells and reassign them to the Magic skill (p. 76) and Magical Forms (pp. 76-77) – and optionally to Standardised Spells (p. 203), if you're using that rule.

Character Points

Character points are the "currency" of character creation. Anything that improves your abilities has a cost: You must spend points equal to the listed price of an ability to add it to your character sheet and use it in play. Anything that reduces your capabilities has a negative cost – that is, it *gives you back* some points. For instance, if you start with 125 points, buy 75 points of advantages, and take -15 points of disadvantages, you have 125 - 75 + 15 = 65 points remaining.

STARTING POINTS

The GM decides how many character points the player characters (PCs) start with. This depends on how capable he wants them to be, and on the nature of the specific game. Many different styles of game are possible on the Disc. Starting points are one of the things that help determine how a game plays.

Once the GM and players have decided what sort of entertainment they're after, it's time to fix some numbers. Options range from less than 25 points (children, incompetent peasants, etc.) up to 250-300 points for major figures of an entire culture – or even higher for living legends. Below are some common examples. This beginning point level is sometimes referred to as the game's *power level*.

DISCWORLD
ROLEPLAYING GAME

Character Sheet

Name _____ Player _____ Point Total _____

Ht _____ Wt _____ Size Modifier _____ Age _____ Unspent Pts _____

Notes _____

_____

ST [___] [ ] **HP** [___ | CURRENT ___] [ ]   **MP** [___ | CURRENT ___]

Magery: _____ [ ]
Staff: _____ [ ]

DX [___] [ ] **WILL** [___] [ ]

Languages	Spoken	Written
_____		[ ]
_____		[ ]
_____		[ ]
_____		[ ]

IQ [___] [ ] **PER** [___] [ ]

HT [___] [ ] **FP** [___ | CURRENT ___] [ ]

DR	TL _____ [ ]
	Cultural Familiarities
	_____ [ ]
	_____ [ ]
PARRY	_____ [ ]

BASIC LIFT (ST × ST)/5 _____ **DAMAGE Thr** _____ **Sw** _____

BASIC SPEED _____ [ ] **BASIC MOVE** _____ [ ]

			Reaction Modifiers
BLOCK			**Appearance, Status, Reputation, etc.:** _____

ENCUMBRANCE	MOVE	DODGE
None (0) = BL _____	BM × 1 _____	Dodge _____
Light (1) = 2 × BL _____	BM × 0.8 _____	Dodge -1 _____
Medium (2) = 3 × BL _____	BM × 0.6 _____	Dodge -2 _____
Heavy (3) = 6 × BL _____	BM × 0.4 _____	Dodge -3 _____
X-Heavy (4) = 10 × BL _____	BM × 0.2 _____	Dodge -4 _____

Reaction Modifiers section continued:
_____
_____
_____

ADVANTAGES AND PERKS

_____ [ ]
_____ [ ]
_____ [ ]
_____ [ ]
_____ [ ]
_____ [ ]
_____ [ ]
_____ [ ]
_____ [ ]
_____ [ ]
_____ [ ]

Total Points in Advantages and Perks [ ]

DISADVANTAGES AND QUIRKS

_____ [ ]
_____ [ ]
_____ [ ]
_____ [ ]
_____ [ ]
_____ [ ]
_____ [ ]
_____ [ ]
_____ [ ]
_____ [ ]
_____ [ ]
_____ [ ]
_____ [ ]

Total Points in Disadvantages and Quirks [ ]

SKILLS

Name	Level	Relative Level
_____		[ ] [ ]
_____		[ ] [ ]
_____		[ ] [ ]
_____		[ ] [ ]
_____		[ ] [ ]
_____		[ ] [ ]
_____		[ ] [ ]
_____		[ ] [ ]
_____		[ ] [ ]
_____		[ ] [ ]
_____		[ ] [ ]
_____		[ ] [ ]
_____		[ ] [ ]
_____		[ ] [ ]
_____		[ ] [ ]
_____		[ ] [ ]
_____		[ ] [ ]
_____		[ ] [ ]
_____		[ ] [ ]
_____		[ ] [ ]
_____		[ ] [ ]
_____		[ ] [ ]

Total Points in Skills [ ]

Pawns of The Lady (25-75 points)

Many folktales and fairy-stories feature unremarkable people who are plunged into bizarre situations. Such things certainly happen on the Disc! If the players are willing to have their characters rely on wits rather than raw power, this can make for an interesting game.

Starting with 25 to 50 points creates PCs who can be moderately competent specialists, in a best-in-the-village sort of way. Few wizards or witches will be so low-powered, but students and trainees with just a touch of magic may be feasible. Going up to 75 points allows for characters who look like *fairly* credible heroes, although they wouldn't be advised to try storming the evil demonologist's tower without first checking that the demonologist is out.

One option is to start with low points, but to allow substantial disadvantages and to award generous bonus character points (p. 219). This can produce plots similar to that of *Mort*, wherein unimpressive, even incompetent characters are plunged into adventures, and they learn and grow through the experience. However, such a plot is necessarily limited in time; no one can carry on learning and growing that fast forever. The game can always mutate into a slower-changing series of adventures for the newly matured heroes, though.

Honest Working Adventurers (100-200 points)

Slightly higher starting values generate PCs who can take a hand in their own destiny, but who shouldn't hope to save the Disc or alter the fate of Ankh-Morpork every week. For many *GURPS* settings, 150 points is considered the default standard. The chief drawback to this starting level is that PCs may be too tough to feel comically stressed by problems, yet not powerful enough to emulate the achievements of the heroes of the chronicles. However, it does make for stable games, which may be preferable to trying to emulate the books' feel too slavishly. Roleplaying games aren't the same thing as novels, and it's a mistake to try to make them work in exactly the same way.

Small Gods, Large Heroes, and Inflated Wizards (250+ points)

Some Discworld stories revolve around seriously capable individuals – the sort who get to save the Disc, repel extradimensional invasions, and dent the special-effects budget. (Think of the young Carrot taking on the entire clientèle of the Mended Drum, or the Silver Horde's conquest of the Agatean Empire.) Certainly, well-qualified Discworld spellcasters often have *significant* abilities, even if they aren't always clever about how they use them. And comedy isn't the same thing as incompetence. Therefore, games may have high power levels.

The snag here is that the GM must come up with plots that employ and stretch the heroes, shaking the Disc without knocking it off its axis. Fortunately, there are always gods and other powers to help straighten matters out after especially weird days (although this plot device should be used with caution). There's also the example of Cohen and his Horde, who kept doing this stuff for years – and yet they couldn't retire, because they never got the hang of saving, and they didn't know any other way to live.

However, if a game is going to involve high-powered PCs, it's *especially* important to give serious prior consideration to the question of what sorts of stories will be involved. A barbarian hero, a Doctor of Morbid Spellbinding, and a Genuan court assassin

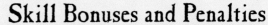

Skill Bonuses and Penalties

Many advantages, disadvantages, perks, and quirks in these rules give *modifiers* to skills – that is, *bonuses* (+1 or better) or *penalties* (-1 or less). These change effective skill levels (see *Success and Failure*, p. 165), but don't worry about those details for now. Just note that the modifiers exist and continue reading.

Example: Jemzarkiza of Krull – Concept

Anne is about to start playing in a new Discworld saga, which the GM has said will be a dramatic, free-wheeling game based in Ankh-Morpork, with PCs on a par with many of the city's more formidable denizens, such as tough watchmen and competent Unseen University faculty. The heroes could be experienced magic-workers, high-ranking nobles (with some good sense), and so on. To make this possible, the characters will start at 250 points. To ensure that they aren't hobbled by excess player enthusiasm, there's a disadvantage limit of -75 points.

Anne has played *GURPS* before and knows her way around the rules, so she decides to play a fairly complex character: a trained magic-wielder and scholar. Being especially fond of some scenes in *The Colour of Magic*, she opts for something out of the ordinary: a spellcaster from the exotic land of Krull (p. 238), who has left home for some reason and is trying to make her way in Ankh-Morpork. She invents the name "Jemzarkiza," and agrees with the GM that she'll be more capable than influential or well-connected – not a figure in high society yet, but if the game calls for serious action, able to mix in. Anne will work out more details later; the game's power level and disadvantage limit certainly give her plenty of options.

might all be 300-pointers, but it could be hard to bring them together for an adventure, let alone an extended "campaign."

DISADVANTAGE LIMITS

A *disadvantage* is anything with a negative point cost, including low attributes (pp. 26-28), reduced social status (p. 37), and all the specific disabilities under *Disadvantages* (pp. 53-66). In theory, you could keep adding disadvantages until you had enough points to buy whatever advantages and skills you wanted. In practise, most GMs will set a limit on the disadvantage points a PC may have. It's customary to hold disadvantages to 50% of starting points – for instance, -75 points in a 150-point game – but this is entirely up to the GM. If the campaign has very low starting points – say, 50 points – the limit will probably have to be significantly more than 50%, as someone with low Status, below-average Wealth, and a strong personality can reach -25 points without even trying.

"More disadvantages" can often mean "funnier," but don't overdo this. If characters are entirely dominated by psychological problems, handicaps, and misfortunes, they can end up looking less comic than pathetic or stupid. Even in a comedy game, people like to play characters with a chance of achieving something. As well as setting starting points to define the game's power level, then, the

GM may set disadvantage limits to determine its seriousness – the more disadvantages he allows, the more the PCs are prisoners of their impulses and misfortunes.

Disadvantage limits don't apply to NPCs. Your serious, capable heroes may well encounter physically crippled or insane individuals on their journeys. In fact, on the Disc, that's a certainty.

Basic Attributes

Four numbers called "attributes" define your basic abilities: Strength (ST), Dexterity (DX), Intelligence (IQ), and Health (HT).

A score of 10 in any attribute is *free*, and it represents the human average. Higher scores cost points: 10 points to raise ST or HT by one level, 20 points to raise DX or IQ by one level. Similarly, scores lower than 10 have a negative cost: -10 points per level for ST or HT, -20 points per level for DX or IQ. (Remember that negative point values mean you get those points back to spend elsewhere!)

Most characters have attributes in the 1-20 range, and most normal humans have scores in the 8-12 range. Scores above 20 are possible but typically reserved for superhuman beings – ask the GM before buying such a value. At the other end of the scale, 1 is the minimum score for a human.

Your decisions here will determine your most fundamental strengths and weaknesses throughout the game. Choose wisely:

6 or less: *Crippling.* An attribute this bad severely constrains your lifestyle.

7: *Poor.* Your limitations are immediately obvious to anyone who meets you. This is the lowest score you can have and still pass for "able-bodied."

8 or 9: *Below average.* Such scores are limiting but within the human norm. The GM may forbid attributes below 8 to adventurers in traditional high-action games.

10: *Average.* Most humans get by just fine with a score of 10!

11 or 12: *Above average.* These scores are superior but within the human norm.

13 or 14: *Exceptional.* The attribute is immediately apparent – as bulging muscles, feline grace, witty dialogue, or glowing health – to those who meet you.

15 or more: *Amazing.* An attribute this high draws constant comment and probably guides your career choices.

These guidelines suit humans and most other beings living in human society, though nonhumans may adjust them somewhat; e.g., trolls can easily possess truly superhuman Strength. See *Rolling the Dice* (pp. 165-167) for how attribute scores are used in play.

STRENGTH (ST)

±10 points/level

Strength measures physical power and bulk. It's crucial to old-fashioned warriors, as high ST lets you dish out *and absorb* more damage in hand-to-hand combat. Any professional adventurer will find ST useful for lifting and throwing things, moving quickly with a load, and so on.

Strength is more "open-ended" than other attributes. Scores greater than 20 are common among large or supernatural creatures, while tiny nonhumans often have low ST.

Larger creatures purchase ST at a discount; see *Character Size* (p. 27). Quadrupeds (p. 96) buy it at 40% off because, lacking hands, they can do less with it. Both situations might pertain, but no one can ever get ST at more than 80% off in total (that is, for less than 2 points/level). These discounts don't affect the amount you get *back* for ST less than 10. However, if your race's normal ST is less than 10 and you have Quadruped, you *do* get 40% off the cost of ST above your racial base, even if it's still less than 10.

DEXTERITY (DX)

±20 points/level

Dexterity measures agility, coordination, and fine motor ability. It controls your basic ability at athletics and combat, and at craft skills that call for a delicate touch. DX also helps determine Basic Speed (p. 28) and Basic Move (p. 28).

Quadrupeds (p. 96) buy DX at 40% off, or for 12 points/level, because they can do less with it.

INTELLIGENCE (IQ)

±20 points/level

Intelligence broadly measures brainpower, including creativity, intuition, memory, and reason. It rules your basic ability with "mental" skills: philosophy, negotiation, etc. Any wizard, strategist, or politician needs a high IQ. A creature with IQ less than 6 isn't "sapient" – it can't learn to talk or acquire technological skills (p. 69). The secondary characteristics of Will (below) and Perception (below) are based on IQ.

Intelligence comes in many forms, which may be reflected by advantages, disadvantages, and skills. The Patrician, Archchancellor Ridcully, and Leonard of Quirm all have high intelligence, but apply it *very* differently!

HEALTH (HT)

±10 points/level

Health represents energy, vitality, stamina, resistance (to poison, disease, etc.), and basic "grit." High HT is good for anyone and *vital* for barbarian warriors. HT determines Fatigue Points (below) and helps determine Basic Speed (p. 28) and Basic Move (p. 28).

Secondary Characteristics

"Secondary characteristics" are quantities calculated from your attributes. You can raise or lower these by adjusting your attributes – or independently, if the GM permits. The latter is *optional* because it complicates the game. Regardless, normal humans rarely have scores more than about three levels different from their base values, or maybe a bit more for special cases (a couple of extra HP for someone who's overweight, say – or almost anything for an Igor, to represent Igor engineering).

Size Modifier (see below) is often listed with secondary characteristics for convenience, but it isn't modified with points.

Hit Points (HP)

±2 points per ±1

Hit Points represent your body's ability to sustain injury. You start with HP equal to your ST; e.g., ST 10 gives 10 HP. As with ST, you get a discount on the point cost of HP if you're exceptionally large; see *Character Size*.

Will

±5 points per ±1

Will measures your ability to withstand psychological stress (brainwashing, fear, hypnotism, interrogation, seduction, torture, etc.) and your resistance to certain exotic attacks (e.g., elven mind-bending). It starts equal to IQ. Will doesn't represent *physical* resistance – buy HT for that!

Perception (Per)

±5 points per ±1

Perception rates your general alertness. The GM makes a "Sense roll" against your Per to determine whether you notice something. Per starts equal to IQ.

Character Size

Nonhuman or unusual characters may be larger or smaller than the human norm. This is represented by an abstract *Size Modifier* (SM). Any object can be assigned an SM to rate how hard it is to see from afar or hit in combat.

Normal humans – from about 5' to 6'6" in height – have an SM of 0. For other creatures and objects, consult this table:

Longest Dimension	SM	Longest Dimension	SM
2.5"	-9	3'	-2
3.5"	-8	4'6"	-1
5"	-7	6'6"	0
7"	-6	9'	+1
10"	-5	15'	+2
18"	-4	21'	+3
2'	-3	30'	+4

For intermediate heights, use the next-*higher* value; e.g., 2'6" is SM -2. All this assumes an approximately human shape – just one long dimension. For an "elongated box" shape (e.g., a cart), add +1 to SM; for something like a cube or a sphere, add +2.

A person with SM +1 or greater is easier to hit and may have problems fitting into rooms, vehicles, etc. meant for normal humans, but is often stronger and harder to kill than most humans. To reflect this, he gets 10% off the point cost of ST and HP per +1 SM (round all fractions up).

Smaller-than-human characters (SM -1 or less) *don't* modify these costs. The benefits and drawbacks of tiny size – such as being harder to hit but unable to use a lot of standard human gear – are considered to balance out. Such folk *might* have to take disadvantages that reflect their size, such as reduced Basic Move (p. 28) or Short Arms (p. 96), but that depends on the specific case.

Finally, being larger is *intimidating*. When using Intimidation (p. 74), add your SM to your skill and subtract the target's SM. However, you can't get better than +4 this way; a 100' giant isn't *that* much more worrying than a 50' giant. Also, many small beings on the Disc have better-than-human Will, Fearlessness, or the perk Unfazed by Size (p. 94).

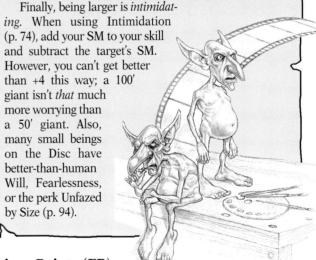

Fatigue Points (FP)

±3 points per ±1

Fatigue Points represent your body's "energy supply." You start with FP equal to your HT.

Basic Lift (BL)

Basic Lift is the maximum weight you can lift overhead with *one* hand in *one* second. It's equal to (ST×ST)/5 lbs. If BL is 10 lbs. or more, round to the nearest whole number; e.g., 16.2 becomes 16 lbs. Other rules – notably *Encumbrance and Move* (p. 168) – also use this statistic. BL for some possible ST values is as follows:

ST	BL	ST	BL	ST	BL
1	0.2	9	16	18	65
2	0.8	10	20	20	80
3	1.8	11	24	22	97
4	3.2	12	29	25	125
5	5	13	34	30	180
6	7.2	14	39	35	245
7	9.8	15	45	45	405
8	13	16	51	50	500

Damage

Your ST determines how much damage you inflict in unarmed combat or with a melee weapon. Two types of damage derive from ST:

- *Thrusting* damage (abbreviated "thrust" or "thr") is your basic damage with a punch, kick, or bite, or a thrusting weapon such as a spear.
- *Swinging* damage (abbreviated "swing" or "sw") is your basic damage with a swung weapon such as an axe – anything that acts as a lever to multiply your ST.

Consult the *Damage Table* for your basic damage (sometimes abbreviated "Dmg."). This is given in "dice+adds" format. On your character sheet, list thrust followed by swing, separated by a slash; e.g., with ST 13, a lookup shows that you have 1d thrust and 2d-1 swing, which you would write as "Damage 1d/2d-1."

Damage Table

ST	Thrust	Swing	ST	Thrust	Swing
1	1d-6	1d-5	11	1d-1	1d+1
2	1d-6	1d-5	12	1d-1	1d+2
3	1d-5	1d-4	13	1d	2d-1
4	1d-5	1d-4	14	1d	2d
5	1d-4	1d-3	15	1d+1	2d+1
6	1d-4	1d-3	16	1d+1	2d+2
7	1d-3	1d-2	17	1d+2	3d-1
8	1d-3	1d-2	18	1d+2	3d
9	1d-2	1d-1	19	2d-1	3d+1
10	1d-2	1d	20	2d-1	3d+2

Follow the sequence for higher ST values: Every +8 ST gives +1d to thrust, while every +4 ST gives +1d to swing. For example, ST 22 gives 2d/4d, ST 31 gives 3d+1/6d+1, and ST 54 gives 6d/12d.

Basic Speed

±5 points per ±0.25

Basic Speed gauges your reflexes and general physical quickness. It helps determine your running speed, your chance of dodging an attack, and the order in which you act in combat (a high Basic Speed lets you "out-react" your foes). To calculate starting Basic Speed, add your HT and DX together, and then divide the total by 4. *Do not round it off.* A 5.25 is better than a 5!

Dodge: Your Dodge defence (see *Dodging*, p. 180) equals Basic Speed + 3, dropping all fractions. For instance, if your Basic Speed is 5.25, your Dodge is 8.

Basic Move

±5 points per ±1 yard/second

Basic Move is how fast you can run. It's your usual ground speed in yards per second (you can go a little faster if you "sprint" in a straight line; see *Running*, p. 168). Basic Move starts equal to Basic Speed, less any fractions; e.g., Basic Speed 5.75 gives Basic Move 5. An average person has Basic Move 5; therefore, he can run about five yards per second if unencumbered.

Magic Points (MP)

Magic Points only matter to characters with Magery (pp. 44-45). To determine these, see *Magic Points* (p. 192).

Image, Looks, and Physique

Next, consider your character's intrinsic "social" traits – appearance, manner, and bearing – and anything exceptional about his build. Traits with positive point values (e.g., above-average Appearance, Voice) are considered advantages (p. 41) for all purposes. Those with negative point values (e.g., below-average Appearance, Odious Personal Habits) are deemed disadvantages (p. 53), and obey all the usual rules for such. Anything without a point value (e.g., height within the normal human range, handedness) merely adds "colour."

APPEARANCE

Variable

You may choose any physical appearance you like – it's mostly a "special effect." However, looks good or bad enough to influence how people respond to you have a point value, for which purpose appearance is rated in levels. Most people are "Average," for 0 points. Pleasing looks give a bonus to reaction rolls (pp. 171-172), and are an advantage that costs points. Unappealing looks give a reaction penalty, making them a disadvantage that gives back points.

Hideous: Any sort of disgusting looks: severe skin disease, wall-eye . . . preferably several things at once. This gives -4 on reaction rolls. *-16 points.*

Ugly: As above, but not so bad – maybe only stringy hair and snaggle teeth. Gives -2 on reaction rolls. *-8 points.*

Unattractive: You look vaguely unappealing, but it's nothing anyone can put a finger on. Gives -1 on reaction rolls. *-4 points.*

Average: The default level. *0 points.*

Attractive: You don't enter beauty contests, but are definitely good-looking. Gives +1 on reaction rolls. *4 points.*

Handsome (or Beautiful): You *could* enter beauty contests. Gives +4 on reaction rolls made by those attracted to members of your sex, +2 from everyone else. *12 points.*

Very Handsome (or Very Beautiful): You could regularly *win* beauty contests. Gives +6 on reaction rolls made by those attracted to members of your sex, +2 from others. *16 points.*

These reaction modifiers only influence people who can see you. For this purpose, "people" means your species and other species that happen to share the same aesthetics. For rules on how different species view each other, and what this means for characters, see *Racial and Personal Appearance* (p. 85).

BUILD

Variable

If your physique differs *significantly* from the norm, you suffer penalties to your Disguise skill, and to Shadowing skill if trying to follow someone in a crowd. There are usually other consequences, too.

Weight

Skinny: -2 to those skills, and -2 to ST when you resist knockback (p. 186). Your HT may not exceed 14. *-5 points.*

Overweight: -1 to those skills. However, you get +1 to Swimming rolls, and +1 to ST to resist knockback. *-1 point.*

Fat: -2 to those skills. However, you get +3 to Swimming rolls, and +2 to ST to resist knockback. Your HT may not exceed 15. *-3 points.*

Very Fat: -3 to those skills. However, you get +5 to Swimming rolls, and +3 to ST to resist knockback. Your HT may not exceed 13. *-5 points.*

Height

Dwarfism: -2 to those skills. You also have -1 Size Modifier relative to the norm for adults of your species (see *Character Size,* p. 27), and -1 to Basic Move (short legs). In combat, your reach (pp. 176-177) with any weapon is reduced by one yard (to a minimum of C), because you have shorter arms and related problems with your build. This is a personal physical abnormality, and it has nothing to do with the race of dwarfs; indeed, it would be possible to be a dwarf with dwarfism. Humans with dwarfism will always be less than 4'4" tall. *-15 points.*

Gigantism: -2 to those skills. You also have +1 Size Modifier relative to the norm for your species (see *Character Size,* p. 27), possibly giving you a discount on your ST and HP, and you get +1 to Basic Move (long legs). *0 points.*

In addition, Dwarfism and Gigantism affect some equipment costs; see *Unusual Sizes and Shapes* (p. 161).

CHARISMA

5 points/level

You have a natural ability to impress and lead others. Anyone can acquire a semblance through looks, manners, and intelligence, but *real* charisma is independent of

these things. Each level gives +1 on all reaction rolls made by sapient beings with whom you actively interact (converse, lecture, etc.); +1 to Influence rolls (pp. 172-173); and +1 to Fortune-Telling, Leadership, Panhandling, and Public Speaking skills.

Handedness

Decide whether you're right-handed or left-handed. Whenever you try to do anything significant with the other hand (apart from unarmed combat), you're at -4 to skill. This doesn't apply to things *normally* done with the "off" hand, like using a shield. *GURPS* doesn't distinguish between left- and right-handed characters; either is 0 points. However, Ambidexterity (p. 41) is an advantage worth 5 points.

ODIOUS PERSONAL HABITS

Variable

You usually or always behave in a repugnant fashion. An Odious Personal Habit (OPH) is worth -5 points for every -1 to reaction rolls made by people who notice it. Specify the behaviour when you create your character, and work out the point value with the GM.

Examples: Body odour, constant scratching, or tuneless humming give -1 to reactions and are worth -5 points apiece. Constant bad puns or spitting on the floor would give -2 to reactions, worth -10 points apiece. We leave -15-point habits (-3 to reactions) to the imagination!

Two such habits merit special mention:

Barbarian Heroism may be worth -5 or -10 points, depending on severity. It involves a lot of quaffing, shouting, brawling, moroseness when sober, petty thievery when short of cash, attacking anyone whom you take for an evil wizard, and interminable quotation of tribal epics, pedigree, and feuds. Other would-be heroes might not react negatively to this, but those who don't will probably join in, competitively.

Throat-Staring is only appropriate for *known* vampires, werewolves, and other "monsters." If you can't break the habit of noticeably contemplating human throats, humans either avoid you or prepare the stakes and silverware. This is worth -5 points if you just dart the odd glance, -10 points if you're blatant about it.

PITIABLE

5 points

Something about you makes people pity you and want to take care of you. You get +3 on reaction rolls from those who consider you to be in a position of weakness or need (which *never* includes those with the Callous disadvantage). Taken in conjunction with above-average looks, Pitiable means you're "cute" instead of "sexy"; in combination with below-average looks, it means you're "appealingly homely."

UNNATURAL FEATURES

-1 point/level

You are superficially "normal" but have one or more disturbing cosmetic features. To qualify for points, these must be unnatural *for your race*. Grey, stony skin would be unnatural for a human, but not for troll! Specify the origin of your Unnatural Features: magical curse, bungled surgery, rare disease, etc.

Unnatural Features need not be unattractive (if they are, you can also claim points for below-average Appearance), but they make it easy for others to identify you and hard for you to blend into a crowd. Each level, to a maximum of five levels, gives -1 to your Disguise and Shadowing skills, and +1 to others' attempts to identify or follow you (including *their* Observation and Shadowing rolls), unless almost everyone else in the crowd happens to share your features.

VOCAL FEATURES

Variable

You may have a notably good *or* bad voice. This modifies reaction rolls when you have to talk to people, and it affects the skills Diplomacy, Fast-Talk, Mimicry, Performance, Politics, Public Speaking, Sex Appeal, and Singing.

Disturbing Voice: Your voice is unpleasant or obviously artificial. It might be raspy, hollow, or squeaky, or monotonous and uninflected. The most common version of this among normal humans is stuttering. You have -2 to reaction rolls and the skills listed above. Certain occupations (interpreter, town crier, etc.) are closed to you. *-10 points.*

Voice: You have a clear and attractive voice, giving you +2 on reaction rolls and the skills listed above. *10 points.*

Social Background

Now it's time to round out your character by defining his background. Being technologically advanced or culturally cosmopolitan is an advantage. *Inadequacy* in either area can be a crippling disadvantage.

Technology Level (TL)

"Technology level" ("tech level") is a number that rates technological development. The more advanced a society, the higher its TL. The TL of the society where the game is going to be set (mostly, at least to start) is the "campaign TL" or "setting TL."

Characters *also* have a TL, equal to that of the technology with which they're most familiar. Unless you're especially primitive or advanced, your personal TL will be the same as the setting's TL. Some skills have an associated TL (p. 69), too, reflecting the equipment and knowledge involved – learning to sail a TL2 longship isn't the same as working aboard a TL4 galleon. Personal TL limits the TL of the skills you can learn.

THE MEANING OF TECH LEVELS

Tech levels on the Discworld range from 0 to 5, defined as follows:

TL0: *Stone Age.* This does *not* mean "no technology"; low-tech peoples can do some amazing things with stone, wood, and string. But they don't have metals, glass, or writing, and they don't live in cities. Only a few remote parts of the Disc are still at this level.

TL1: *Bronze Age.* Swords, literacy, and cities are possible, and many animals are domesticated – although long-distance transport tends to use chariots rather than horses. But it's all a bit *basic;* for instance, architecture uses stone blocks and low doorways rather than soaring arches or domes. Most of the Disc is more advanced than this, but Djelibeybi stuck obstinately there until recently, and there are a few scary jungle kingdoms still going for the step-pyramid look.

TL2: *Iron Age.* Think Greece and Rome – elegant columns, very clever thinking, and reasonable iron swords and armour to resolve the problems caused by certain kinds of cleverness. No stirrups on the horses, and no glass lenses, mind. Backward lands may be stuck at this level, and it still provides the design aesthetic for Tsort and Ephebe.

TL3: *"Medieval"* (on our world). Knights in armour, big castles, and large-but-sordid cities. Ankh-Morpork was at this level in the earliest novels in the series, the pattern had spread across the Sto Plains to places like Lancre, and much of the Disc is still there. Hence, games set in backwoods areas, or at the time of the start of Rincewind's wanderings, may have a setting TL of 3.

TL4: *"Renaissance"* (again, on our world). Sophisticated thinking and craftsmanship creates things like telescopes, printing presses, ever-so-elegant rapiers, stagecoaches with suspension good enough that travel doesn't *actually* qualify as torture, and oceangoing galleys or junks. This is the level to which Ankh-Morpork and its neighbours progress later in the chronicles (although gunpowder remains rare). The most sophisticated cities of the Agatean Empire have been there for a while, though that society is too static for such advances to spread much. Games set in "modern" Ankh-Morpork will have a setting TL of 4.

TL5: *"Steam Age."* This implies gadgets and ideas that would look "Victorian" on our world: steam power, iron ships, not just guns but maybe even reliable rifles, scarily powerful explosives, and so on. No *society* is at this level on the Disc, but some individual inventors have jumped that far ahead, at least in limited areas.

Magic doesn't count as a technology, but it has effects on society if it's sufficiently widespread. Hence, a TL3 society on the Disc can have the equivalent of cameras and pocket watches, and might sustain cities larger than anything seen in our world's medieval period. Also, as the advance from TL3 to TL4 is actually a theme of some recent Discworld novels, many games may end up featuring a mix of TLs.

PERSONAL TL

Your personal TL *may* differ from the game average. A Hubland warrior wandering into Ankh-Morpork might not understand some of the devices (or ideas) he encounters, while a brilliant philosopher-inventor may actually be ahead of his surroundings. Hence, *Low TL* and *High TL* count as a disadvantage and an advantage, respectively.

Low TL

-5 points/TL below campaign TL

Your personal TL is below the campaign standard. You start with *no* knowledge (or default skills) relating to equipment above your personal TL. Even if a skill doesn't have a /TL qualifier, the GM may rule that the necessary equipment wasn't available in your home society (e.g., crossbows don't exist before TL2, and fencing weapons don't appear until TL4). You can learn DX-based technological skills (pertaining to vehicles, weapons, etc.) in play, but fundamental differences in thinking prevent you from learning IQ-based technological skills until you buy off this disadvantage. To prevent physically oriented characters from treating a level or two of Low TL as free points, the GM should rule that they're confused by many details of higher-tech life, and hint that they're being mocked as yokels behind their backs.

High TL

5 points/TL above campaign TL

Your personal TL is above the campaign standard. You may enter play with skills relating to equipment up to your personal TL. This is most useful if you also have access to high-TL equipment, but some high-tech knowledge can be useful in a low-tech setting even without. You *may* enter play with equipment from your background TL, with the GM's permission, but its cost is

doubled for each TL by which it exceeds the campaign standard (e.g., if TL4 gear is available in a basically TL2 game, it costs 4× the listed price); this reflects special import costs and the like. The GM may set some prices even higher, or simply prohibit certain equipment. You don't start with more *money* than other characters merely because you have High TL, though – standard starting funds (p. 33) are determined purely by the *setting's* TL.

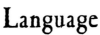

Character Age

You can choose any age you like for your character, within your race's normal lifespan. (See also *Longevity*, p. 52, and *Short Lifespan*, p. 99.) This is mostly a special effect – although very young or old characters might suffer from Social Stigmas (p. 36). You may also have to explain how a youngster could acquire many skills in his short life, or how a wizened individual could have exceptionally good looks, but such matters are between you and the GM.

Language

Most characters can read and write their native tongue. This costs no points, but you should note it under "Languages" on your character sheet; e.g., "Morporkian (Native) [0]." Additional competencies cost extra. For a discussion of languages on the Disc, see *Languages* (pp. 16-17). The PCs will typically need at least some grasp of Morporkian – but a lot depends on the game.

LANGUAGE COMPREHENSION LEVELS

The point cost to learn an additional language depends on your "comprehension level" – a measure of how well you function in that language overall. There are four such levels:

None: You don't know the language at all. *0 points.*

Broken: You know just enough to get by in daily life, but have -3 when using skills that depend on language. When reading, roll vs. IQ just to get the basic meaning. *1 point for spoken, 1 point for written.*

Accented: You can communicate clearly. You're only at -1 when using skills that depend on language. *2 points for spoken, 2 points for written.*

Native: You use the language as well as a native. *3 points for spoken, 3 points for written.*

Skill penalties are doubled (to -6 or -2) for artistic skills when beauty and subtlety are required; e.g., for composing poetry.

Native-level comprehension of your native language is free. Being less literate in that language is a *disadvantage:* -1 point for Accented (a passable writing style, but with some bizarre spelling and punctuation), -2 points for Broken (sometimes called "semi-literacy"), or -3 points for None (illiteracy). Poor or nonexistent literacy is widespread in barbarian societies and among trolls, and the GM may choose not to count it against the campaign disadvantage limit (if any).

When describing characters, assume by default that they write languages as well as they speak them; somebody described simply as having Klatchian (Accented) speaks *and* writes Klatchian at Accented level (and probably paid 4 points for this).

If they don't write as well as they speak, or vice versa, the description should give two levels; the first defines how well they *speak* the language, the second is how well they *write* it. For example, many trolls in Ankh-Morpork have Morporkian (Accented/None), for 2 points; they can chat quite well to locals, in distinctly trollish tones, but they're completely illiterate in the language. A more complicated example might be somebody with Uberwaldian (Broken/Native), for 4 points; this person has perhaps learned to write fluent and chatty letters to acquaintances in Uberwald, but if he ever tries *talking* to them, he mangles the pronunciation and trips over his tongue.

Example: Jemzarkiza of Krull – Social Background

Jemzarkiza's origins, while somewhat exotic, aren't *that* different from the Ankh-Morpork norm. Krull is quite technologically advanced, and Jemzarkiza soon learned her way around most of the odd gadgets that she encountered in Ankh-Morpork, so she starts play at the standard campaign tech level (TL4). Krull uses Morporkian as its language, so Jemzarkiza has that as her native tongue. (She's fully literate, of course.) Likewise, Krullian society shares broad cultural assumptions with Ankh-Morpork, so she gets "Sto Plains/Uberwald" as her native Cultural Familiarity.

To add a little interest, though, Ann says that Jemzarkiza picked up a few things on her travels before arriving in the city. Her first ship dropped her on the hubward side of Klatch, where she spent a little time before finding passage to the Circle Sea. Ann adds the Klatchian language at the Broken level (spoken and written) to her character sheet, costing 2 points, and Cultural Familiarity (Klatchian), for another 1 point. This puts Jemzarkiza at 154 points.

LANGUAGE-RELATED ADVANTAGES

Variable

You may have special abilities involving languages:

Language Talent: You're naturally good at learning languages. When you learn one at a comprehension level above None, you automatically function at one level higher; thus, 4 points rather than the usual 6 gets you Native-level fluency and literacy in a foreign tongue. You also receive +1 to Shouting at Foreigners skill (p. 74). *10 points.*

Multilingual: You have enormous experience with languages, from years of study or extensive travel. You focus on one application of this knowledge – see *Rincewind* (pp. 330-332) and *The Librarian* (pp. 333-335) for examples – and may have the equivalent of a foreign accent when you're out of practise with a specific tongue, although you shed this once you've had a chance to re-immerse yourself, and you can usually get by for any routine purposes. However, while your language ability is probably beyond anything possible in the dull reality of our own world, it isn't supernatural. The GM can always rule that you haven't had a chance to learn some language (especially if it's a secret, long-forgotten, or

from another universe), and can decide that you make occasional small mistakes whenever that would be funny. You may also have to spend a few seconds mentally switching gears when shifting between languages. *20 points.*

Universal Translator: You can talk – and read, and write – any language you encounter, with Native-level fluency. This may involve one second of concentration as you switch tracks mentally, and it only works with one language at a time, but it *is* a supernatural advantage, normally limited to nonhuman beings. However, it's the kind of thing which a powerful god *might* grant to a devout worshipper (the "gift of tongues") to facilitate missionary work. *30 points.*

Culture

A culture is a set of basic assumptions and ground rules for behaviour. In game terms, characters have no penalty to operate socially in cultures they understand – but in ones where they're strangers, they're in danger of making unfortunate or catastrophic errors, such as eating with the wrong hand or speaking to the wrong person. The *Cultural Familiarity* (CF) trait represents proper understanding of a culture. Each distinct culture has its own CF.

Characters are assumed to be comfortable with their "native" culture for free. Record this under "Cultural Familiarities"; e.g., "Klatchian [0]." Familiarity with other cultures costs 1 point per culture. If you *don't* have CF for the culture in which you're trying to operate, you're at -3 to the skills Carousing, Dancing, Detect Lies, Diplomacy, Directing, Fast-Talk, Gesture, Heraldry, Leadership, Politics, Public Speaking, Savoir-Faire (all forms), Streetwise, and Teaching. This penalty extends to Acting if the GM decides that the act requires cultural background knowledge; to Criminology when dealing with criminal *behaviour* rather than *methods;* to Performance, Poetry, and anything else artistic when trying to emulate a local style; and to Intimidation and Sex Appeal when used as Influence skills (pp. 74-75).

Cultures are defined broadly; minor local differences don't make a different culture. On the Disc, "contemporary" Cultural Familiarities include *Sto Plains/Uberwald* (covering everything from the Circle Sea through Ankh-Morpork to Lancre and beyond, and also such colonies and cultural outliers as Genua, Fourecks, and even Krull), *Agatean* (the formal, ancient culture of the Counterweight Continent), and *Klatchian* (actually the culture of the desert-dwelling peoples of the hubward edge of the great continent of Klatch, generally applicable in most neighbouring countries, too), along with surviving distinct local cultures in countless remote regions. Most adventurers should be able to get away with taking no more than two or three CFs, but those who want to spend long periods in remote communities may have to learn more – and games set in slightly earlier periods might feature distinct CFs for virtually every nation-state around the Circle Sea (Djelibeybi, Ephebe, Tsort, etc.).

NONHUMAN CULTURES

Trolls and dwarfs have distinct cultures and hence Cultural Familiarities of their own, but they adopt many human assumptions (that is, acquire human CFs) when moving to human communities. This might be news to their human neighbours, but the fact is that dwarfs who are even *speaking* to humans are making an adjustment from the conservative norms of traditional dwarf culture, while trolls simply find it impossible to carry on living in the old mountain-troll way among other peoples.

Both races can be proud and secretive. While this has always been clear with dwarfs, humans underestimate trolls in this regard. Dwarfs won't explain more than they have to – you must already be initiated in dwarf culture for a dwarf to talk to you about it – but it would be difficult for a human to physically survive the immersion in trollish society that would be needed to acquire CF (Trollish). Carrot Ironfoundersson (pp. 321-322) is one of the few living humans with CF (Dwarfish)[1], enabling him

to deal with dwarf society and avoid annoying dwarfs in dangerous situations.

Other, less-common nonhuman races *may* have their own cultures, but most either emulate nearby humans, or live in small, self-reliant groups with few complex assumptions.

---

1. As is required to, for example, understand "mine sign" – the symbols which dwarfs mark on their walls, reflecting the community's mood.

Rincewind switched to High Borogravian, to Vanglemesht, Sumtri and even Black Oroogu, the language with no nouns and only one adjective, which is obscene. Each was met with polite incomprehension. In desperation he tried heathen Trob . . .
— **The Colour of Magic**

Wealth and Influence

You need to determine your *position* in your society, too: How much money do you have, what privileges do you enjoy, and how do others react to you?

Wealth

Personal prosperity is rated in "wealth levels." A level of "Average" costs no points and lets you support an average lifestyle. If you're unusually poor or rich, the following rules apply.

WEALTH

Variable

Above-average Wealth is an advantage; below-average Wealth, a disadvantage. Each level of Wealth has a *Wealth Multiplier* attached to it; this applies to both your starting funds (below) and your income from regular jobs (p. 173), although not to any money that you pick up while adventuring. Each level also has a typical level of Status (pp. 37-38) associated with it, but this is *not* mandatory – plenty of people are poorer or richer than their position in society implies.

Dead Broke: You have *no* job, *no* source of income, *no* money, and *no* property other than the clothes you're wearing. Either you're unable to work or there are no jobs to be found. You're almost certainly Status -2. *-25 points.*

Poor: Wealth Multiplier 1/5. Some jobs aren't available to you, and no job you'll ever find pays very well. You're probably Status -2. *-15 points.*

Struggling: Wealth Multiplier 1/2. Almost any job is open to you (you *can* be a Struggling lawyer or opera soloist), but you don't earn much. You're most likely Status -1. *-10 points.*

Average: Wealth Multiplier 1. The default wealth level, which usually accompanies the default Status level: Status 0. *0 points.*

Comfortable: Wealth Multiplier 2. You likely work for a living, but your lifestyle is better than most. You probably make enough to support Status 1. *10 points.*

Wealthy: Wealth Multiplier 5. You live very well indeed. You're likely to be Status 2. *20 points.*

Very Wealthy: Wealth Multiplier 20, potentially taking you to Status 3+, although in many places that needs aristocratic birth or at least political power. *30 points.*

Filthy Rich: Wealth Multiplier 100! You can buy almost anything you want without considering the cost. You probably rate high Status whatever your birth; money always talks, and yours shouts. *50 points.*

Multimillionaire: This represents additional Wealth *beyond* Filthy Rich, and it must be purchased on top of that. For every 25 points you spend beyond the 50 points for Filthy Rich, increase Wealth Multiplier by another factor of 10: Multimillionaire 1 costs 75 points and gives Wealth Multiplier 1,000, Multimillionaire 2 costs 100 points and gives Wealth Multiplier 10,000, and so on. *50 points + 25 points/level of Multimillionaire.*

Starting Funds

Average starting money depends on campaign TL (pp. 30-31); more advanced societies are richer. Base personal funds – measured in Ankh-Morpork dollars (AM$, or $ for short) – are as follows:

Campaign TL	Base Value
0	AM$12.50
1	AM$25
2	AM$37.50
3	AM$50
4	AM$100

Multiply the base value for the campaign's TL by your Wealth Multiplier to find your starting funds. For example, a Struggling character in a TL2 campaign starts play with $37.50 × 0.5 = $18.75, some of which he can spend on personal equipment.

The GM may choose to set an upper limit on Wealth, especially if he wants the PCs to go on traditional sorts of adventures. Someone who has spent many points on Wealth can get a lot done by paying someone else to do it, but might not be very competent himself. Being Wealthy should be plenty in most games – and the player who wants more than Multimillionaire 3 will need to explain how his PC came to be richer than the richest man in Ankh-Morpork!

Reputation

It's possible to be so well-known that your reputation affects reaction rolls made by NPCs (pp. 171-172).

REPUTATION

Variable

Reputation can be an advantage or a disadvantage, depending on what people think of you. You can be known for bravery, ferocity, eating green snakes, or whatever you want. However, you *must* give specifics.

Specify the reaction-roll modifier that you get from people who recognise you. This determines your reputation's base cost. For every +1 bonus to reactions (up to +4), the cost is 5 points. For every -1 penalty (down to -4), the cost is -5 points. This cost may then be modified further.

People Affected

The size of the group of people who might have heard of you adjusts the base cost:

Almost everyone on the Disc: ×*1*.
Almost everyone on the Disc except one large class (everyone but barbarian warriors, everyone but dwarfs): ×*2/3*.
Large class of people (all people of a particular faith, all mercenaries, all tradesmen, etc.): ×*1/2*.
Small class of people (all priests of Offler, all well-travelled people in the Ramtops, all resident foreigners in the Agatean Empire): ×*1/3*.

If the class of people affected is so small that, in the GM's opinion, you wouldn't meet even one in the average adventure, your reputation isn't worth points.

Frequency of Recognition

Either your name or your face is enough to trigger a "reputation roll" to see if the people you meet have heard of you. Roll once for each person or small group you meet. For a large group, the GM may opt to roll more than once.

The frequency with which you're recognised modifies your reputation's cost:

All the time: ×*1*.
Sometimes (roll of 10 or less): ×*1/2*.
Occasionally (roll of 7 or less): ×*1/3*.

Apply multipliers for people affected and frequency of recognition, and then drop all fractions at the end. *Exception:* A reputation with an absolute value of less than 1 point is worth 1 point if good or -1 point if bad.

Your reputation extends only within a certain area. If you travel far enough away, the GM may require you to "buy off" the disadvantage points received for a bad reputation. There's no corresponding bonus for losing a good reputation.

Multiple Reputations

You may have more than one reputation, and your reputations can overlap. The GM should check each one before determining how an NPC reacts to you. Your total reaction modifier from reputations cannot be better than +4 or worse than -4 in a given situation.

Example: Brother Poll is well-respected (Reputation +2) among worshippers of Om (a large class), recognised occasionally (7 or less); that costs 1 point (10 × 1/2 × 1/3, dropping fractions). He's also *very* well-regarded (Reputation +3) among Ephebian philosophers (a small class in the context of the Disc as a whole, although in an Ephebe-based game, they might count as a large class) for giving good value during an invitational debate last year, and helping solve a crisis with the drinks supply at the after-match party, and is recognised all the time: 5 points (15 × 1/3). Lastly, he's deeply disliked (Reputation -3) by many pirates on the Circle Sea (another small class), having had a successful career as a naval officer before entering the church, and is recognised sometimes (10 or less): -2 points (-15 × 1/3 × 1/2, dropping fractions).

If Poll should meet an Ephebian philosopher who's also a worshipper of Om (it *could* happen, although most philosophers preserve a battered agnosticism), and should the philosopher recognise him as a churchman (rolling 7 or less) as well as that good talker, the philosopher will react to Poll at +4 – the total bonus would be +5, but +4 is the limit. On the other hand, should Poll meet a pirate who's somehow sustaining a belief in Omnianism, and should the pirate recognise him as both the church father (rolling 7 or less) and the old pirate-hunter (10 or less), the pirate will react at a net -1, respect for religious work not quite compensating for old feuds.

Importance

Your formally recognised *place* in society is distinct from your personal fame and fortune.

CLERICAL INVESTMENT

5 points

You're a priest of a recognised religion. This gives +1 to reactions from those who share your religion or otherwise respect your faith – that is, most *sensible* people, as gods and their temples can be touchy, although wizards and witches make a point of not being impressed. You may also buy Religious Rank (p. 35) *if* your church or temple uses it.

Technically, this is a purely social advantage, granting no particular spiritual insight or powers. However, your god will (probably!) recognise your status and feel obliged to listen to your prayers. He *may* actually respond, if anything seems important enough to *him* – although if interesting events are taking place elsewhere, or something amusing is happening on Cori Celesti, you're out of luck. You might even be permitted to take him as a Patron (p. 41), which is allowed to very few nonclerics. (You can only get *personal* aid if your deity *is* your Patron; otherwise, there's no point in bothering him about such matters.) Lastly, divine protocol means that you're generally immune to being zapped by other gods, unless you do something *really* stupid.

Clerics may also be required to take a Duty (pp. 59-60), although that will usually be Nonhazardous.

LEGAL ENFORCEMENT POWERS

5 to 15 points

You're an agent of the law. For 5 points, you have local jurisdiction, and you can arrest and search people (e.g., a constable in a well-run town). For 10 points, you have national jurisdiction, *or* may disregard some significant legal limits, *or* can even kill with relative impunity (e.g., many royal guardsmen). For 15 points, you enjoy broad privileges *and* discretion (e.g., some ruler's personal agent). You probably also possess a Duty (pp. 59-60) and Rank (below).

Powers broad enough to be worth 15 points are rare on the Disc, though not unknown. Special agents may be granted special powers – but rulers with the authority to set that up *also* tend to arrange matters so that the agent is left to dangle in the wind if the mission goes wrong. You need to be exceptionally well regarded by a powerful ruler to qualify.

LEGAL IMMUNITY

5 to 15 points

You're exempt from some or all laws. Should you break them, ordinary law enforcers don't have the power to charge you. Only one authority – e.g., your temple, a guild court, or the king – can judge or punish you. If the rules that govern your behaviour are merely different from ordinary law, but just as strict, this costs 5 points. If they're less strict, it's 10 points. And if you can do nearly anything you please provided that you don't injure your group's long-term interests, pay 15 points.

Legal Immunity is usually accompanied by high Status (pp. 37-38), Clerical Investment (p. 34), and/or a Duty (pp. 59-60). Wizards at Unseen University *don't* have this advantage, although they theoretically claim a degree of immunity to civil law, because civil law is patchily and informally enforced in Ankh-Morpork anyway, and a wizard who breaks the rules can expect much the same consequences as anyone else. Members of the Assassins' and Thieves' Guilds *do* have the 5-point version, however, because while the Watch will try to stop assassinations and a lot of non-contractual thievery, the chance of a Guild member being tracked down and brought to justice is pretty low. On the other hand, both are subject to their respective guilds' rules.

A special version of this is available to Igors (pp. 140-141):

Igor Immunity: This only works in Uberwald and some adjacent areas, where Igors are considered essentially *neutral*. It's understood by most people that an Igor can take no particular blame for his employer's actions. Furthermore, it isn't prudent to annoy the Igors, who provide low-cost medical services for the community. They're lickspittle toadies, sure, but there's no point in lynching them for it.

An Igor caught, say, robbing a graveyard may be told to push off, with a threat or two for the look of the thing – but no more than that. And when the mob arrives with the pitchforks and the torches, the Igor employed by the vampire or mad doctor is allowed to slip out a side door and vanish into the night. Likewise, an Igor's employer is unlikely to do anything fatal to him, although whippings, insults to the intelligence, and extended rants are part of the contract of employment. *5 points.*

RANK

5 points/level

Rank represents position in some structured organisation that gives higher-ranked members *significant* authority over lower-ranked ones. The lowest Rank in a structure is always 0, which is free and grants no particular benefits. The highest depends on the organisation's size and nature, but never exceeds 8.

The classic example is *Military Rank,* ranging from 0 (Private, Footman, etc.) to 8 (Supreme Commander of an empire's army or navy). The Ankh-Morpork City Watch has *Watch Rank* (p. 256), and other cities are doubtless imitating that structure as they imitate Ankh-Morpork generally. Formal, powerful religions have hierarchies with *Religious Rank* (p. 302). The governing bureaucracy of the Agatean Empire has *Administrative Rank;* other Discworld bureaucracies aren't sufficiently structured and disciplined to count as having a Rank structure – although in Ankh-Morpork, the Patrician's palace and the Post Office *may* both come close.

If you have high Rank, you can order those of lower Rank to assist you – but *only* for purposes related to the organisation. Individuals with higher Rank can likewise command *you,* so Rank often comes with a Duty (pp. 59-60).

SOCIAL REGARD

5 points per +1 reaction

You belong to a class, race, or group that your society respects. Every 5 points in Social Regard gives you +1 to reaction rolls (maximum +4). This isn't a Reputation, despite the similarities – you're treated well because of *what* you are, not because of *who* you are. Exactly how you're treated on a good reaction roll will depend on the *type* of Regard:

Feared: Others react as if you had successfully used Intimidation (p. 74). People stand aside or run away.

Respected: You receive polite deference. Noncombat interactions usually go smoothly for you – but sometimes, the kowtowing gets in the way.

Venerated: Total strangers react to you in a caring way, give up their seats, and receive your every word as pearls of wisdom. They also try to prevent you from putting yourself in danger.

Witches may be either Feared or Respected, depending on their personal style – how much they emphasise the dangerous, cackling old hag or the useful wise-woman thing – but trainee witches don't enjoy either until they've acquired a bit of credibility.

SOCIAL STIGMA

Variable

You belong to a group or a category that your society deems inferior, and this is obvious from your physical appearance, dress, manner, or speech; *or* easily learned by anyone who cares to check up on you; *or* the result of public denouncement (e.g., by a chieftain or a priest). This trait is the opposite of Social Regard (p. 36), and it gives you a reaction penalty and/or restricts your social mobility. It's unrelated to Status (pp. 37-38) – you can hold a high position in society and still be stigmatised. Some Stigmas can be combined; e.g., a member of an enslaved minority might have both Minority Group *and* Valuable Property.

Some examples and special cases:

Logical Impossibility: Even on the Disc, certain things are generally considered impossible, and some of them turning out to be real doesn't change people's minds. You are an example. This doesn't give you a

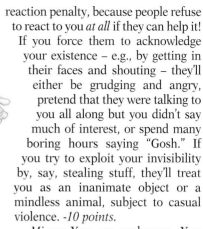

reaction penalty, because people refuse to react to you *at all* if they can help it! If you force them to acknowledge your existence – e.g., by getting in their faces and shouting – they'll either be grudging and angry, pretend that they were talking to you all along but you didn't say much of interest, or spend many boring hours saying "Gosh." If you try to exploit your invisibility by, say, stealing stuff, they'll treat you as an inanimate object or a mindless animal, subject to casual violence. *-10 points.*

Minor: You are under-age. You suffer -2 on reaction rolls whenever you try to deal with others as an adult; they might like you, but they don't respect you. You may be barred from drinking dens, war parties, guild membership, etc. You must buy this off when you reach "legal age." *-5 points.*

Minority Group: You belong to a minority that people around you regard as "barbarians" or "inferior." You get -2 on reaction rolls made by anyone except your own kind. In an area, profession, or situation where your minority is *especially* rare, you get +2 on reaction rolls made by your own kind. This disadvantage also fits undead and lycanthropes in many parts of the Disc; however well-behaved they are, people don't quite trust them. *-10 points.*

Monster: You're a monstrosity or other being that's hated or feared, regardless of *actual* appearance or disposition. This gives you -3 on all reaction rolls, and you're liable to be hunted on sight. However, you get +3 to Intimidation rolls in situations where you have the upper hand (GM's opinion). *-15 points.*

Overdressed Foreigner: Because of the way that you talk, act, or dress, people in most places regard you as "not one of us," and probably as flashy and annoyingly rich. This usually only nets you a -1 reaction penalty (though *not* from others who share your background, or from self-consciously cosmopolitan individuals), and many people will suppress their hostility – but only because they want your money. You're a magnet for con artists, pickpockets, overcharging merchants, would-be guides, and other rogues, some blatant and annoying, some subtle and skilled. Should you be taken for a *wizard*, you suffer -3 reactions from Unseen University graduates (who look upon you with suspicion) and would-be barbarian heroes (who consider you a possible target), although you may also attract a few interested followers. *-10 points.*

Second-Class Citizen: You belong to a sex, species, etc., that receives fewer rights and privileges than "full citizens." This gives -1 on all reaction rolls except from others of your own kind. *-5 points.*

Uneducated: You're thought to be wilfully ignorant and a bit stupid, probably because you lack much education. People with even a minimal "normal" education react to you at -1 and treat you as a bit of an idiot. *-5 points.*

Valuable Property: Society regards you as somebody's property rather than as a legal person. This takes the form of limited freedom or lack of intellectual respect, rather than a reaction modifier. Enslaving sapient beings is illegal on *most* of the Disc these days, but it was fairly widespread in the past, and not all sapient beings are recognised as such. *-10 points.*

Regarding Female Characters

Many leading characters in the Discworld stories are female, but parts of the Disc have undeniably sexist ideas about the role of women. For example, novels such as *Small Gods* and *Monstrous Regiment* depict societies with seriously narrow views, while true wizardry is universally restricted to men.

This is no excuse for preventing players from running characters of whatever sex they prefer. Numerous women in Discworld canon choose their own path; some fit within their societies' attitudes, others defy them. In the sword-and-sorcery world of the earlier stories, the very shortage of career opportunities makes the heroic tradition of swordswomen who take no nonsense from men quite appealing to some,[1] while in later tales, a kind of feminist movement appears to be emerging. As in some of the novels, this may lead to exploring the questions of social roles, if the GM and players would enjoy that.

Unless the gaming group would rather ignore the whole subject, though, there are *also* places and times where female characters should have Social Stigma (Second-Class Citizen) – not a crippling disability, but certainly an inconvenience. Alternatively, a woman can disguise herself as a man; *Monstrous Regiment* hints that this is practically commonplace. (It could conceivably have spread to the least likely seeming places; see p. 288.) Maintaining this requires reasonable Acting and Disguise skills, and gives a Secret (p. 65) worth -5 points if being revealed would merely wreck your marital prospects, draw unwelcome comments, etc., or -10 points if it would lose you your job, friends, and family.

---

1. *However, chainmail bikinis were never widespread; practical swordswomen favoured practical armour.*

STATUS

5 points/level

Status is the primary measure of social standing. Levels range from -2 to 8, with an ordinary citizen being Status 0. If you don't specifically buy Status, you have Status 0. Status costs 5 points per level; e.g., Status 5 costs 25 points, while Status -2 is -10 points. High Status costs money to support, so you'll probably need high Wealth (pp. 33-34) to go with it.

Status greater than 0 means you're a member of the dominant classes. Consequently, others *in your culture only* defer to you, giving you a bonus on all reaction rolls equal to the difference between your Status and theirs; e.g., a Status 2 merchant reacts to a Status 5 duke at +3. However, criminals and street rabble may *hate* the upper classes, and react to them at large penalties if they can get away with it (GM's option). Some figures, such as witches and Hubland monks, see themselves as standing outside normal hierarchies, so Status is unlikely to influence their reactions either way. A high-Status character will normally treat somebody of lower but non-negative Status with distant politeness (no reaction modifier), but gaffes can quickly turn differences into penalties for the lower-Status person; e.g., if that merchant did something actively annoying to the duke, the duke would remember the difference between them and react at -3.

However, Status less than 0 means you're definitely of the lower orders. Higher-Status characters will often react to you at a penalty equal to the difference in level, although they'll tolerate your existence so long as you seem to know your place. Alternatively, they may carefully *ignore* you.

All of which said, Discworlders are often a remarkably democratic lot, considering that most of them are traditionalist monarchists. Much of the time, they only really acknowledge four social categories: Proper Gentlefolk (to whom other people are polite out of tradition or fear), *Nouveau Riche* (about whom people are often quite rude in private, but who have the power to purchase at least a working facsimile of respect), the Supernatural Lot (wizards, witches, and priests, who are a bit weird but who might be able to turn you into a frog, so be careful), and Everyone Else (common folk). For dealings within a single category, the GM can safely ignore fine gradations of Status except when portraying nitpicking snobs or inverted snobs.

The *Status Table* shows what each Status level typically signifies. "Monthly Cost" is the cost of living at that Status level; it keeps you alive and looking the part. If you can't raise the money to match your Status each month, then you must live in a style that you *can* afford – and so you'll be *treated* as having lower Status than you've paid the points for. (If you can't make Status -2 expenses, you're literally starving to death on the street.) If you live below your nominal Status for more than a couple of months, you'll probably have to do something impressive to restore your credibility later (give a good party, say, or acquire a big house). If your Status comes partly or entirely from Rank (see *Special Cases for Status*, p. 38), then the salary attached to that Rank will generally be enough to support it – but

your lifestyle may be somewhat circumscribed by the job. See *Living Expenses* (pp. 148-149) and *Characters With Jobs* (p. 173) for more on all this.

Status Table

Level	Typical Jobs or People	Monthly Cost
8	Agatean Emperor, Pharaoh of Djelibeybi	*
7	King of a large nation, Seriph of Al Khali	*
6	Minor king or seriph, Patrician, Cenobiarch of the Church of Om	*
5	Independent duke, Archchancellor, high priest of a major god, grand vizier	*
4	Major guild master, high priest of a lesser god, major court functionary, lesser duke	$3,000
3	Lesser guild master, tenured academic, senior priest, earl, assertive baron, rising civil servant	$600
2	Master craftsman, small-town wizard, affluent merchant, minor baron, Ephebian philosopher, civil servant	$150
1	Recent graduate wizard, witch, independent craftsman, small landowner, ordinary priest, mercenary or watch captain	$60
0	Apprentice witch, salt-of-the-earth peasant, student wizard, common citizen, Ephebian slave	$30
-1	Common ruffian, grubby peasant, watchman in an unreformed watch	$15
-2	Beggar, *bungling* thug†, golem	$5

* On the Disc, the Status *is* the job at this level, and it incorporates its own means of support. The Discworld doesn't really have

the concept of a salaried head of state, but all jobs or positions associated with Status 5+ are assumed to carry with them enough rents, gifts, tithes, and socks of coins stuffed behind furniture to keep the incumbent and a few family members in appropriate style. That's "assumed," mind. Many a God-King or Supreme Patriarch has had to double as a cook and sometimes ask his butler to lend him a few dollars until next week. Precise details of such situations are up to the GM; NPCs should be played as best fits the game, and if any PC ever attains those heights, the question of their finances should be a topic for scenarios and a running joke, not an exercise in arithmetic.

† Merely being a known professional criminal is rarely a great social liability on the Disc – certainly not in Ankh-Morpork. However, crude and incompetent thugs are disdained.

Special Cases for Status

In Discworld societies, wealth and official power grant *effective* Status. Hence, anyone who's Wealthy or better receives +1 Status for free, increasing to +2 with Multimillionaire 1 and to +3 – the maximum Status bonus for Wealth – with Multimillionaire 2. Being rich makes you a bit posh. Likewise, characters get +1 Status for free at Rank 3-5, and +2 Status at Rank 6 or higher. Being important in any major organisation gives you an elevated place in society. Occasionally, this simply cancels out low Status; for example, in the old days, when the Ankh-Morpork Night Watch was regarded with contempt, its constables and corporals were Status -1, and its sergeants and captains could just about rate Status 0 thanks to the small, grudging respect granted to their titles and slightly better pay.

In a peculiar democratic nation like Ephebe, with a formally structured government, the tyrant might have only a few levels of Status in his own right (from family background, education, etc.), but he would add +1 for Wealth and another +2 for his Administrative Rank 7 in the government, giving him effective Status 5-6! In such places, it may be that no character can buy more than Status 1-4 (GM's decision) directly with points; any more *must* come from Rank and Wealth.

Alternatively, in theocracies like pre-Brutha Omnia, Religious Rank might *replace* Status. Characters from such societies *cannot* buy Status as such. Instead, the relevant variety of Rank costs double (10 points/level) and gives all its usual benefits *plus* the effect of an equivalent level of Status.

Friends and Foes

Some specific NPCs may be inclined to help you in various ways. You might be obliged to take care of others. And yet others may want to *harm* you.

Frequency of Appearance

These types of NPCs aren't constant fixtures in the game. At the beginning of each adventure, the GM rolls 3d for each individual or group. In most cases, the roll required for them to show up in the course of events multiplies their point value as an advantage or a disadvantage, as follows:

Roll	15 or less	12 or less	9 or less	6 or less
Multiplier	×3	×2	×1	×1/2 (round up)

CONGREGATION

10, 12, or 15 points

You have a group of faithful followers – perhaps even worshippers – who will do whatever you ask of them, within reason. They won't give you lots of money, but they *will* do odd jobs for you, and if you're a deity, they *believe* in you, which is important. However, if you abuse them or fail to help them when they make reasonable requests, they'll drift away from you. If they get killed, it's up to you to recruit replacements – and most candidates will have heard what happened to the first lot.

For 10 points, you get a Congregation of up to 20 people; for 12 points, you get up to 50; and for 15 points, you get up to 100. Bigger Congregations than this are out of PC territory. A Congregation always has a frequency of appearance (above) of 15 or less; this is already factored into the point cost. On a roll of 16 or higher, they all have taxes to pay, there's a secular festival, they're all stuck in traffic, or whatever.

No one in your Congregation can be worth more than 10% of your own point value, so they're quite fragile and thus best used as a source of noncombat aid and, if you need it, worship. Still, they'll defend themselves if attacked (unless you're the sort of priest or god who attracts fanatical pacifists). The GM should design Congregation members as characters, subject to this point limit (though you can offer *suggestions* regarding their abilities and histories); most will be broadly similar and interchangeable, although they may have a range of job skills. None can have Congregations of their own!

CONTACTS

Variable

A "Contact" is someone – from a beggar in the right gutter to a head of state – who's willing to lend you his ability with a noncombat skill, either by providing you with useful information or by doing you *small* favours (pick any two of "quick," "nonhazardous," and "inexpensive"). The Contact's point value is based on the skill he supplies, the frequency with which he helps you, and his reliability.

Effective Skill

First, choose the skill your Contact provides (see *Skills*, pp. 69-83). This should match his background; e.g., Accounting for a clerk or Alchemy for an alchemist.

Next, select an effective skill level. This reflects the Contact's connections, other skills, Status, etc. It need not be his actual skill level; for instance, the head of a merchant family might have Finance-12, but his *effective* skill might be Finance-18 because of his position. This determines the Contact's base cost:

Effective Skill	12	15	18	21
Base Cost	1 point	2 points	3 points	4 points

Add 1 point to these costs for ghosts, wizards, and other Contacts who can obtain information using supernatural talents (magical divination, etc.).

Frequency of Appearance

Select a frequency of appearance (above) and apply its multiplier to the Contact's base cost. When you wish to reach your Contact, the GM will roll against this. Failure means the Contact is busy or cannot be located that day – and a 17 or 18 means the Contact cannot be reached for the *entire adventure*. On a success, the GM will roll against the Contact's effective skill once per piece of information or favour you request.

No Contact may be reached more than once per day, even if several PCs share the same Contact. If you have several questions to ask, you should have them all in mind when you first reach your Contact. The Contact answers the first question at his full effective skill. Subsequent questions suffer a cumulative -2. Don't overuse Contacts!

A Contact can never supply information outside his area of knowledge. Use common sense. Likewise, the GM must not allow a Contact to give information that short-circuits an important part of an adventure.

Reliability

Contacts aren't guaranteed to be truthful. Reliability multiplies the Contact's point cost:

Completely Reliable: Even on a critical failure on his effective skill roll, the Contact's worst response will be "I can't help you." On an ordinary failure, he can find or accomplish something in 1d days. *×3.*

Usually Reliable: On a critical failure, the Contact lies. On any other failure, he can't help now, ". . . but check back in (1d) days." Roll again at that time; a failure then means he can't find out at all. *×2.*

Somewhat Reliable: On a failure, the Contact simply can't help. On a *critical* failure, he lies – and on a natural 18, he lets the opposition or authorities (as appropriate) know who's asking questions. *×1.*

Money Talks

Bribery – blatant with cash or polite with a favour – can motivate Contacts. This is rated in "levels" of improvement; a level can change "somewhat reliable" to "usually reliable," or grant +1 to effective skill, but bribery cannot make anyone "completely reliable." A cash bribe should be roughly equivalent to one day's income for one level of improvement, one week's income for two levels, one month's income for three, and one year's income for four. See *Characters With Jobs* (p. 173) for figures. Favours should be of equivalent worth.

The bribe must also be appropriate to the Contact. A noble diplomat would be insulted by a cash offer but might welcome an introduction into the right social circle; a criminal might ask for cash but settle for dubious favours.

Acquiring New Contacts

You may add new Contacts in play, provided that you can come up with a good in-game justification. The GM might even turn an existing NPC into a Contact for one or more PCs – possibly in lieu of character points for the adventure in which the PCs "cultivated" the NPC.

Example: Brother Dewlap, an Omnian missionary, has helped a clacks engineer set up a relay station in what turned out to be a haunted house. The GM tells his player that the engineer is now a Contact, providing Mechanic/TL4 (Low-Tech Machines) skill. (While the Clacks specialisation might be more logical, that wouldn't be much use to Dewlap, so the GM fudges this.) This NPC has access to his company's workshop, making his effective skill 18 (3 points); can *usually* be found in his rooming-house of an evening (12 or less, ×2); and is *fairly* grateful (Somewhat Reliable, ×1). A 6-point advantage is a good reward for the adventure!

Later, Dewlap discovers that the sewers beneath his shrine are occupied by an albino alligator – and the rules say that no blood should be spilled on the site! So he calls on the engineer. The GM rolls a 10 for availability, and Dewlap's player says that he'll chat before requesting help. This is a good move, because the engineer mentions that his sister is getting married to a wealthy merchant's son and would like to find a venue that will impress the groom's family. Normally, for Dewlap to bribe the engineer would cost a day's pay for an Average Wealth TL4 job – $1.35, too much for the impoverished priest – but Dewlap has some pull in the Temple of Om, so he offers use of a side-chapel there. This is well worth a week's pay, so the GM raises the engineer's reliability from "somewhat" to "usually" *and* adds +1 to his effective skill – he's willing to throw more resources at the problem.

Dewlap asks the engineer to rig an alligator-proof cage with a remote-release door over the entrance to the sewers. He also needs this the next day, despite a -5 skill penalty for haste. With an effective skill of 14, the engineer succeeds. Now Dewlap just has to entice the alligator into the cage, dispose of it somewhere, and arrange a wedding.

DEPENDENTS

Variable

A "Dependent" is an NPC for whom you are or feel responsible; e.g., your child, kid brother, spouse, or even "boyfriend/girlfriend of the week." You *must* take care of Dependents, and your foes can strike at *you* through them. If your Dependent is kidnapped or otherwise in danger, you *must* go to the rescue immediately, or the GM will deny you bonus character points (p. 219) for "acting out of character." Furthermore, you never earn bonus character points for a game session in which your Dependent is killed or badly hurt.

Three factors determine a Dependent's disadvantage value: *competence, importance* (to you!), and *frequency of appearance.* Regardless of these details, you cannot earn points for more than two Dependents.

Competence

Specify the number of points your Dependent is built on. The more points you use, the *fewer* points he's worth as a disadvantage. Below, "Point Total" is the Dependent's point total as a fraction of the PC's, except for the last line, which is absolute. "Cost" is the base disadvantage value.

Point Total	Cost
No more than 100%	-1 point
No more than 75%	-2 points
No more than 50%	-5 points
No more than 25%	-10 points
0 or fewer points	-15 points

Importance

The more important your Dependent is to you, the more you multiply his base cost to reflect his intrinsic "nuisance value":

Employer or Acquaintance: You feel a responsibility toward this person, but may weigh risks to him rationally. ×1/2.

Friend: You must always try to protect this person, only risking harm to him if something very important (such as the safety of many other people) is at stake. ×1.

Loved One: You may not put *anything* before this person's safety! ×2.

Frequency of Appearance

Choose a *frequency of appearance* (p. 38) and adjust cost for this, too. This reflects how often the Dependent gets caught up in your adventures, not how important he is in your life.

Dependents in Play

When you earn points, the GM will scale your Dependent's abilities proportionally to keep his point total a fixed percentage of your own. For example, if you start as a 150-point character, a "No more than 50%" Dependent may be worth 75 points; if you

gain 20 points in play, your Dependent can go up to 85 points. Thus, his value as a disadvantage doesn't change.

If your Dependent is killed or so seriously injured that he's effectively out of play, you *must* make up the points you got for him. You have three options: buy off the amount by spending earned character points, take a new disadvantage (a mental disability brought on by shock is good), or get a new Dependent.

ENEMIES

Variable

Some NPC, group, or organisation is actively working against *you*, personally. Three factors determine the disadvantage value of this "Enemy": *power, intent,* and *frequency of appearance.* Regardless of such things, you may not take more than two distinct Enemy disadvantages, or claim more than -60 points from Enemies. (Going right up to these limits is your choice, but might well mean being jailed or killed before long!)

Power

The GM sets this value. If the Enemy is an organisation, its base point value depends on the number of individuals who are after *you*, not on total group size. For example, the City Watch might assign a dozen watchmen to pursue an important suspect.

- One person, less powerful than the PC (built on about 50% of the PC's starting points). *-5 points.*
- One person, equal in power to the PC (with about 100% of the PC's starting points), or a small group (3 to 5 individuals) of less-powerful people. *-10 points.*
- One person, more powerful than the PC (with at least 150% of the PC's starting points), or a medium group (6 to 20 individuals) of less-powerful people. *-20 points.*
- A large group (21 to 1,000 individuals) of less-powerful people, or a medium group that includes some formidable individuals. *-30 points.*
- An utterly formidable group; e.g., an entire government. *-40 points.*

Intent

The more unpleasant the Enemy's intentions, the more you multiply its worth in points:

Watcher: Your Enemy stalks or spies on you – a journalist dogging a politician, say, or plainclothes watchmen shadowing a suspect. This makes it hard to keep secrets, but is rarely more than a minor inconvenience. ×1/4.

Rival: Your Enemy wishes to upstage or inconvenience you, or plays cruel practical jokes, but stops short of anything physically dangerous. ×1/2.

Hunter: The Enemy intends to arrest, bankrupt, injure, or otherwise harm you in some lasting way – or to kill you. ×1.

Frequency of Appearance

Finally, choose a *frequency of appearance* (p. 38).

Enemies in Play

If you kill or otherwise eliminate an Enemy, you have three choices: pay enough character points to buy off its original value, find some other disadvantage to cover the shortfall (e.g., an injury suffered in the final battle), or take a new Enemy of the same value (e.g., the old Enemy's vengeful brother).

PATRON

Variable

You have a more-powerful individual or organisation looking out for you *personally*; e.g., a wealthy relative, or a politician who sees you as his chosen successor. An ordinary employer isn't such a "Patron," but a commanding officer who will go out of his way to help you might be. If a leader is looking after you and can command the resources of a city, nation, or organisation, you may treat that whole body as your Patron, although the motivation happens to come from the individual at the top.

The Patron's base point cost depends on its power. Use the following categories as a guide, but be aware that some Patrons won't fit neatly into any of them:

- A powerful individual (usually built on at least 150% of the PC's starting points) or fairly powerful organisation (assets of at least 1,000 times average starting money). *10 points.*
- An extremely powerful individual (built on at least twice the PC's starting points) or powerful organisation (assets of at least 10,000 times average starting money). *15 points.*
- An ultra-powerful individual (e.g., a god, built on as many points as the GM wants!) or a very powerful organisation (assets of at least 100,000 times average starting money). *20 points.*
- A city-state or other small nation. *25 points.*
- A large nation or empire. *30 points.*

Modify this cost for *frequency of appearance* (p. 38).

Advantages

Advantage List

An "advantage" is a useful trait that gives you a mental, physical, or social "edge." Several examples have appeared already; e.g., superior Appearance and above-average Wealth. This section details many more.

Each advantage has a cost in points. This is fixed for some, while others are bought in "levels," at a cost per level (e.g., Acute Vision costs 2 points/level, so if you want Acute Vision 6, you pay 12 points). Advantages with "Variable" cost are more complicated; read the advantage description for details.

Some advantages have *prerequisites*: traits you must purchase separately before you can buy the advantage. Where skills are noted as prerequisites, you need only one point in the skill if no minimum level is specified – although such advantages are often more *useful* if you're really good at the skill.

The GM has the final say as to whether a particular advantage suits a given character concept.

Limited Advantages: Some advantages have variant, restricted forms. For examples, see *Magery* (pp. 44-45) and *Speak With Animals* (p. 46). These are explained where they appear, with reduced point costs to reflect lower utility.

ACUTE SENSES

2 points/level

You have superior senses. Each Acute Sense is a separate advantage that gives +1 per level to all Sense rolls (pp. 169-170) you make – or the GM makes for you – using that one sense. Available types:

- Acute Hearing
- Acute Taste and Smell
- Acute Touch
- Acute Vision

AMBIDEXTERITY

5 points

You can fight or otherwise work equally well with either hand and never suffer the -4 DX penalty for using the "off" hand (p. 29).

CHANNELLING

10 points

You can allow spirits to speak through you. To do so, you must enter a trance, taking one minute of concentration and a Will roll (at +2 if you have Autotrance, p. 50). You're unaware of the world around you while you're in this state. After that, any spirit in the immediate vicinity can enter your body and use it to speak. The GM controls what the spirit says. The spirit will answer questions put to it by others, but it isn't bound to tell the truth.

The spirit can use your body only to communicate. However, if it has the ability to possess and control living beings, it can attempt to possess you. It's effectively touching you, but you're considered "wary," which is worth +5 to resist.

COMBAT REFLEXES

15 points

You have fast reactions and are rarely surprised for long. You get +1 to all active defence rolls (p. 180), +1 to Fast-Draw skill, and +2 to Fright Checks (pp. 170-171). You never "freeze" in a surprise situation, and you have +6 on all IQ rolls to wake up.

This advantage is mostly found among experienced warriors, but it's also useful to devout cowards and criminals. Alchemists and wizards sometimes acquire it as a way to survive their own experiments: When the crucible starts to fizz, *duck*.

DANGER SENSE

15 points

You can't depend on it, but sometimes you get a *feeling* that something's wrong. The GM rolls once against your Perception, secretly, in any situation involving an ambush, impending disaster, etc. On a success, you get enough warning that you can take action. A roll of 3 or 4 means you get a little detail as to the nature of the danger.

EMPATHIC ABILITIES

5 to 15 points

You have a "feeling" for a certain class of beings, which is useful for spotting imposters, brainwashing, etc., and for determining the attitudes of NPCs. When you first meet a suitable subject, or are reunited after an absence, you may ask the GM to roll against your IQ. He'll tell you what you "feel" about that individual's emotional state – friendly, frightened, hostile, hungry, etc. – and whether he or it is under some kind of control. On a failure, you get an uncertain or misleading answer.

There are several advantages in this category:

Animal Empathy: Works on animals, usually defined as non-supernatural beings with IQ 5 or below. A few creatures with IQ 6+, such as the smartest sorts of Discworld dogs, also count as "animals." In addition to reading animals' moods, you can use Influence skills (pp. 74-75) on them just as you would on sapient beings. *5 points.*

Empathy: Works on "ordinary" creatures of IQ 6+: humans, dwarfs, trolls, etc. In addition to mood-reading, it gives you +3 to Detect Lies and Fortune-Telling skills, and to Psychology rolls to analyse a subject you can converse with. *15 points.*

Sensitive: As Empathy, but less reliable. The IQ roll for mood-reading is at -3, and the skill bonus is only +1. *5 points.*

Spirit Empathy (Full): Works on spirits (magical, usually immaterial beings), golems, and anything else the GM decides is extraordinary enough to belong in this category. Your Influence skills (pp. 74-75) affect these entities normally. This doesn't prevent evil spirits from seeking to harm you, but it makes it easier to detect their hostility. *10 points.*

Spirit Empathy (Specialised): As Spirit Empathy (Full), but all benefits are limited to one specific class of spirits; e.g., demons, djinn, ghosts, or golems. *5 points.*

ENHANCED DEFENCES

5 to 15 points

There are three advantages in this category:

Enhanced Block: You have +1 to your Block score (p. 180). *5 points.*

Enhanced Dodge: You have +1 to your Dodge score (p. 28). *15 points.*

Enhanced Parry: You have +1 to your Parry score (pp. 180-181). You may take this for bare hands (5 points), for any one melee weapon skill (5 points), or for all parries (10 points). *5 or 10 points.*

Combat Reflexes gives +1 to *all* defences for 15 points. Buy it *before* spending 15 or more points on Enhanced Defences!

There was a sudden blur and the nearest man collapsed in a small gurgling heap. Then Conina's elbows went back and into the stomachs of the men behind her. Her left hand rebounded past Rincewind's ear with a noise like tearing silk and felled the man behind him.

– Sourcery

EXTRA ATTACK

25 points/attack

You can attack more than once per turn, using different body parts. You can't have more attacks than you have limbs, plus one for a bite.

A normal human can buy just one Extra Attack, representing exceptional combat ability. This would allow him to stab with a sword in each hand (although his attack with the "off" hand would still be at -4), punch *and* kick, or whatever. An animal might have *several* Extra Attacks.

You *cannot* strike with some attacks while trading others for Aim, All-Out Defence, Change Posture, Concentrate, Move, or Ready manoeuvres. You *can* All-Out Attack (p. 175), in which case you have three options: make *all* of your attacks Strong, make *all* of them Determined, *or* use Double to add *one* more attack to your overall total.

Extra Life

25 points/life

You can come back from the dead! No matter how sure your foes were that they killed you, you didn't *really* die. This may represent a favour from Fate, amazing luck (perhaps courtesy of The Lady, p. 303), or an overdose of narrative importance. Every time you come back, you use up one Extra Life – remove it from your character sheet and reduce your point total by 25 points.

Fearlessness

2 points/level

You're difficult to frighten or intimidate! Add your level to your Will whenever you make a Fright Check (pp. 170-171) or must resist the Intimidation skill (p. 74). You also subtract your Fearlessness level from all Intimidation rolls made against you.

Flexibility

5 or 15 points

Your body is unusually flexible. This advantage comes in two levels:

Flexibility: You get +3 on Climbing rolls, and on Escape rolls to get free of ropes, handcuffs, etc. You may ignore up to -3 in penalties for working in close quarters (including many Explosives and Mechanic rolls). *5 points.*

Double-Jointed: As above, but more so. You cannot stretch or squeeze yourself abnormally, but any part of your body may bend any way. You get +5 to Climbing, Escape, and attempts to break free. You may ignore up to -5 in penalties for close quarters. *15 points.*

Gadgeteer

25 points

You're a natural inventor. You can modify existing equipment and – given time and money – invent entirely new gadgets. This lets you design gadgets quickly and makes it easy to realise higher-TL innovations. Gadgeteers on the Disc aren't comic-book super-inventors, though; your work takes days or months, and it requires money and equipment.

High Manual Dexterity

5 points/level

You have remarkably fine motor skills. Each level (to a maximum of four) gives +1 to DX for tasks that require a delicate touch. This includes all DX-based rolls against Artist, Jeweller, Knot-Tying, Lockpicking, Pickpocket, Sewing, Sleight of Hand, and Surgery, as well as DX-based rolls to do fine work with Mechanic (e.g., on clockwork). This bonus doesn't apply to IQ-based tasks, to large-scale DX-based tasks, or to combat-related dice rolls of any kind.

High Pain Threshold

10 points

You are as susceptible to injury as anyone else, but you don't *feel* it as much. You *never* suffer a shock penalty when you're injured. In addition, you get +3 on HT rolls to avoid knockdown and stunning, and +3 to resist physical torture. The GM may let you roll at Will+3 to ignore pain in other situations.

Indomitable

15 points

You're impossible to influence through ordinary words or actions. Those who wish to use Influence skills on you (see *Influence Rolls*, pp. 172-173) must possess a suitable Empathic Ability (p. 42): Empathy if you're a human, dwarf, troll, etc.; Animal Empathy if you're an animal; or Spirit Empathy if you're a demon, ghost, etc. Everyone else – however convincing – fails automatically.

Less Sleep

2 points/level

A normal human requires eight hours of sleep per night. Each level of this advantage – to a maximum of four – lets you get by with one hour less.

Lifting ST

3 points per +1 ST

You have exceptional lifting capacity. This can be a racial quality of species such as dwarfs (who have rugged frames) and trolls (who are made of rock), but anyone can buy up to three levels to represent practise in hauling loads. Add your Lifting ST to your ordinary ST when you determine Basic Lift (p. 28). Lifting ST also adds to ST in situations where you can apply slow, steady pressure (grappling, choking, drawing crossbows, etc.). Lifting ST *does not* boost ST (or Basic Lift) for the purposes of determining HP, throwing distance, damage inflicted by melee attacks or thrown weapons, or whether you can use a weapon without a penalty for being too weak.

If your SM is +1 or higher, you get a discount (-10% per +1 SM) on the cost of Lifting ST, just as for ordinary ST. You do *not* get a discount for the Quadruped disadvantage (p. 96), however.

Luck Advantages

Variable

You were born lucky! The three traits in this category can be combined:

Daredevil: The Lady smiles on you when you take risks. Any time you take an unnecessary risk (in the GM's opinion), you get +1 to all skill rolls. Furthermore, you may reroll any critical failure that occurs during such high-risk behaviour. For example, if a gang of bandits start firing arrows at you, and you crouch down behind a wall and return fire, you get no bonuses. If you vault the wall and charge, screaming, Daredevil provides all of its benefits. *15 points.*

Luck: At limited intervals in a game session, you may reroll a single dice roll twice and take the best of the three rolls. You must declare that you're using your Luck immediately after you roll the dice. Your Luck only applies to your own success, damage, or reaction rolls; *or* on outside events that affect you or your whole party; *or* when you're being attacked (in which case you may make the attacker roll three times and take the *worst* roll!). "Ordinary" *Luck* lets you reroll something once per hour of play, *Extraordinary Luck* is usable every 30 minutes, and *Ridiculous Luck* works every 10 minutes. *15 points for Luck, 30 points for Extraordinary Luck, 60 points for Ridiculous Luck.*

Serendipity: Each level of Serendipity entitles you to one fortuitous coincidence per game session, details being up to the GM. For instance, one of the guards you need to talk your way past happens to be your cousin, or there's a fast horse tied up in front of the bank just as you run outside in pursuit of fleeing robbers. If you have several levels, the GM may on occasion rule that a single implausible coincidence counts as some or all of your lucky breaks for a given session (e.g., the local blacksmith has multiple parts you need to complete your fancy rapid-fire siege engine, just lying around). You're free to *suggest* serendipitous occurrences to the GM, but he gets the final say. Should he reject all your suggestions but fail to work Serendipity into the game session, you'll get your lucky breaks next game session. *15 points/level.*

Working for The Lady?

Heroes with Extra Lives, Extraordinary Luck, and multiple levels of Serendipity are clearly under the eye of The Lady (p. 303). This could imply all manner of other complications, including strange Enemies up to and including Fate. A PC might theoretically take The Lady as an actual Patron, but that is *not* wise; She is whimsical, and She *never* helps when She is asked.

MAD MEDICINE

15 points

Prerequisites: Gadgeteer (p. 43) *and* the ability to operate at TL5 in the Physician and Surgery skills (requires the High TL advantage, p. 31, or a Cutting-Edge Training perk, p. 51).

You're a brilliant inventor (thanks to the prerequisite Gadgeteer advantage), able to work with and even create all sorts of new and innovative devices – but in the field of medicine, your brilliance hurtles into the realms of insanity and heads for the horizon. Just for a start, you can perform *ad hoc* transplant surgery, using an array of peculiar drugs and treatments to sidestep any boring questions of tissue rejection. You can also create exotic monsters from bits and pieces, or grow them from scratch if you have the patience. You probably apply your Gadgeteer ability in combination with other technical skills in support of your medical work.

MAGERY

Variable

You're magically adept. This advantage comes in levels. You *must* purchase Magery 0 (for 5 points) before buying higher levels (for another 10 points apiece).

Magery 0

5 points

This is basic "magical awareness": a prerequisite for learning "proper" magic. It's said that people with this ability have octagons as well as rods and cones in their eyes, enabling them to perceive octarine, the eighth colour of the spectrum, the "colour of magic" – but that may be a metaphor or something.

The GM makes a Sense roll (pp. 169-170) when you first see a magic item, and again when you first touch it. On a success, you intuitively know that the item is magical. A roll of 3 or 4 also tells you whether the magic is helpful or dangerous, and about how strong it is. With a similar roll, you sometimes get a "sense" about other supernatural things, though never any details; for instance, you might notice that a werewolf is "strange," but that's all. Individuals without Magery don't get these rolls.

In addition, you can operate certain magical items – relatively safely and reliably, even – because you can sense the operational energies, read the invisible control runes, or whatever. You can also sense that invisible spirits (such as ghosts) are around, although you can't locate them; you just get "a feeling." And you usually perceive beings using the Unnoticed advantage (p. 48), as you're used to seeing what's truly there and aren't so easily persuaded to ignore things.

Magery 1+

10 points/level

Further levels of Magery make it much easier to learn and use magic. Add your Magery to your IQ when you learn Magic, Magical Form, and Thaumatology skills (and also spells, if the GM uses the optional rule on p. 203). For instance, if you have IQ 14, Magery 3 lets you learn those skills as though you had IQ 17. As well, your Magery level adds to Perception when you roll to sense magic items and beings, and it may benefit some rolls required when operating magical devices. Finally, higher Magery levels grant you access to more powerful spells and let you channel more energy into certain "variable" magics; see pp. 195-196.

Limited Magery

Some people have restricted forms of Magery. They possess magical talent, but their practical options are limited. At worst, they can't be "proper" witches or wizards (and wizards tend to be condescending toward those with such serious restrictions), though they can still get good jobs if they play their cards right.

Magery (No Spellcasting): While you have a sensitivity to magic, you just can't get spells to work – possibly because of a mental block. You still receive the standard rolls to sense magic items and can operate them like any proper mage. However, this version of Magery does *not* grant any skill bonuses. *1 point for Magery 0, 2 points/level for Magery 1+.*

Magery (Engineering Only): You can learn all the magical skills like a full-powered mage, but you can't cast spells as such. You *can* work them into magical items, though. While obviously of limited use to adventurers, this can get you very well-paid employment. It's often found among dwarfs, who don't produce many witches or wizards, but who are famously good magical craftsmen. You can only roll to sense magic items when you first touch them – not on sight – but you can operate them just fine using your Magery level. This only grants bonuses to Magic or Magical Form skills when they're being used for engineering purposes and gives no bonus to Thaumatology. *4 points for Magery 0, 6 points/level for Magery 1+.*

Magery (Non-Improvisational): You can learn a full set of magical skills and cast effective spells, but you can't whip up spells on the fly. Either you've never learned to improvise with magic or you've lost the knack over years of routine magical work.

Before you cast any spell, you must sit down and work out what needs doing and how to do it, taking 2 minutes per Magic Point required to cast the spell in its simplest form (e.g., reminding yourself how to cast a fireball takes 2 minutes, because you could always throw a 1 MP fireball, although many are more powerful), with a minimum of 2 minutes. Once you've done this, you have to cast the spell within a number of minutes equal to *four times your IQ*, after which the magical forces will have shifted too much, or you'll have forgotten some of the fine details. For example, an IQ 13 wizard looking to cast a 3 MP spell must spend 6 minutes working out the details, then must use the spell within 52 minutes or lose it. The GM might opt to let someone with Magery (Non-Improvisational) buy a perk (p. 49) that lets him always know how to cast a single spell with a casting requirement of no more than 1 MP. Wizards – that is, casters with Magic (Wizardry) skill – who have this kind of Magery face one additional problem: -3 to *all* spellcasting skill rolls unless they have their staff (pp. 192-193) in hand, except for ritual casting (p. 200).

This limitation is common among both young wizards (Unseen University doesn't teach much about improvisation, being in the business of producing wizards who *won't* blow the world up too often, not ones who can do it on the fly) and old wizards (who get terribly out of practise). It also crops up among young witches who lack confidence in their magic. As most student wizards don't even receive a staff until they graduate (see *No Staff*, p. 68), this makes most of the undergraduate body at UU relatively useless as spellcasters, but don't assume that they're *all* that hopeless.

Magery (Non-Improvisational) *does* give full bonuses to Magic, Magical Form, and Thaumatology skills. *4 points for Magery 0, 7 points/level for Magery 1+.*

MEDIUM

10 points

You can perceive and communicate with spirits, particularly spirits of the dead. You don't see them visually, but you know when they're nearby. You can speak with any spirit in your presence, provided that you share a language. You can also call spirits to you; there's no guarantee that they'll respond, but they'll hear you if they're the sort who pick up such things. This does *not* give you a reaction bonus with spirits, or any power over them.

MENTAL GIFTS

Variable

Your brain has some capability which most people lack:

Absolute Direction: You always know which way is hubwards, and you can retrace any path you've followed within the past month. This gives you +3 to Navigation skill. This knack works even underground and underwater. *5 points.*

Eidetic Memory: Anyone may attempt an IQ roll to recall the general sense of past events, but you automatically succeed, and you can recall *specific* details by making an IQ roll. *5 points.*

Lightning Calculator: You can do arithmetic in your head, instantly. You, the *player*, can always keep a calculator handy. *2 points.*

Photographic Memory: Like Eidetic Memory, but better – you automatically succeed at even the roll for specific details. *10 points.*

MIND SHIELD

4 points/level

You have a "shield" that warns you of and defends against mental attacks. Add your level to IQ or Will whenever you resist a supernatural effect or magic spell that seeks to read or control your mind, "mental blasts," and so on. Your shield also resists attempts to *locate* your mind; such abilities must win a Quick Contest against your Will + Mind Shield level to find you.

You may voluntarily lower your Mind Shield – say, to let a friend read your mind. Lowering or raising your shield is a free action, but it must take place at the start of your turn. Mind Shield *does* protect you while you are asleep or unconscious, unless you fell asleep or were knocked out while your shield was voluntarily lowered.

NIGHT VISION

1 point/level

Your eyes adapt rapidly to darkness. Each level of this ability (maximum nine) allows you to ignore -1 in combat or vision penalties due to darkness, provided that there is *some* light.

PATCHWORK MAN

10 points

Prerequisites: High Pain Threshold (p. 43), Resistant to Disease at the +8 or Immunity level (p. 46), *and* either Very Rapid Healing (p. 46) or Repairable (pp. 90-91).

You have a body constructed of parts from other bodies, rendered functional by Mad Medicine (p. 44). You might be an Igor or the product of some mad doctor's researches. This permits you to purchase the occasional strange physical advantage, thanks to the ingenuity of your rebuilding. Acute Senses, High Manual Dexterity, and minor "racial" advantages (see Chapter 3) such as Claws or one or two levels of Damage Resistance (Tough Skin) would all be perfectly feasible, along with high ST or Lifting ST. The weirder your advantages, the more likely the GM is to insist that you should have, say, bad Appearance or Unnatural Features as well. In fact, Patchwork Man might also allow you to take odd physical *disadvantages*, such as Semi-Upright.

You're also immune to Fright Checks and other psychological problems caused by the discovery of what a surgeon has done to you. You'll never come round from the anaesthetic screaming "What have you done to me, you fiend?" – although if you're an Igor, you may critique the stitching.

The eyes were on different levels. One ear was larger than the other. The face was a network of scars.

– The Truth

PERFECT BALANCE

15 points

Under normal conditions, you can always keep your footing – no matter how narrow the walking surface (tightrope, ledge, tree limb, etc.) – without having to make a roll. If the surface is wet, slippery, or unstable, you get +6 on rolls to keep your feet. In combat, you get +4 to DX and DX-based skill rolls to keep your feet or avoid being knocked down. Finally, you get +1 to Acrobatics, Climbing, and Piloting skills.

RAPID HEALING

5 or 15 points

You heal wounds quickly. This comes in two levels:

Rapid Healing: Whenever you roll to recover lost HP (p. 187), you get +5 to your effective HT. You must have HT 10+ to take this. *5 points.*

Very Rapid Healing: As above, but on a successful HT+5 roll, you heal *two* HP, not one. You must have HT 12+ to take this. *15 points.*

Neither level helps recovery from short-term injury effects such as stunning.

RESISTANT

Variable

You're naturally resistant or immune to diseases, poisons, or some specific concern. *Resistant* gives you a bonus on all HT rolls to resist the item in question. Total *Immunity* to a broad range of effects is usually limited to supernatural beings.

Resistant to Disease: Protects against all diseases. You get a +3 bonus for 3 points, +8 for 5 points, or *Immunity* for 10 points.

Resistant to Poison: Protects against all toxins. You get a +3 bonus for 5 points, +8 for 7 points, or *Immunity* for 15 points.

Resistant to Specific Item: Protects against one particular drug, disease, or poison. You get a +3 bonus for 1 point, +8 for 2 points, or *Immunity* for 5 points. You can also buy Resistant to seasickness and general motion sickness as such a "specific item"; the 1-point version is treated as a perk (p. 49) called *Sea Legs*.

SEE INVISIBLE

15 points

You can see objects or individuals that are normally *truly* invisible. Two types of "proper" invisibility exist in Discworld games: *Magical*, granted by spells and the like, and *Spirit*, possessed by certain immaterial, possibly extradimensional beings. Buy this advantage separately for each – See Invisible (Magical) or See Invisible (Spirit). *Either* variety allows you to perceive people using Unnoticed (p. 48), because Unnoticed doesn't work very well on anyone who's used to seeing what's really there, and not just what they want to see.

SILENCE

5 points/level

You move and breathe noiselessly. You get +2 per level to Stealth skill when you're perfectly motionless, or +1 if moving – but only when your opponents must use *hearing* to detect you, such as in the dark.

SINGLE-MINDED

5 points

You get +3 to success rolls for any lengthy mental task on which you concentrate to the exclusion of everything else *if* the GM feels that total concentration would help. You ignore everything else (roll vs. Will to avoid this), and you have -5 to all rolls to notice interruptions.

The GM may rule that some tasks (e.g., inventing, magic, and social activities) *require* divided attention. This trait has no effect in such situations.

SPEAK WITH ANIMALS

Variable

You can converse with animals (as defined for Animal Empathy, p. 42). This requires a good explanation! It takes one minute to ask one question and get the answer – if the animal decides to talk at all. The GM may require a reaction roll (at +2 if you offer food). The quality of information you receive depends on the beast's IQ and the GM's decision on what it has to say. Insects might only convey "hunger" or "fear," while a chimp or a cat might engage in reasonably intelligent discussion.

Cost depends on scope: "All animals" costs 25 points; "All land animals" (including birds, insects, and land-dwelling mammals and reptiles) or "All aquatic animals" (including amphibians, fish, molluscs, crustaceans, and cetaceans), 15 points; one class (e.g., "Mammals" or "Birds"), 13 points; one family (e.g., "Felines" or "Parrots"), 10 points; and one species (e.g., "House Cats" or "Macaws"), 5 points.

Superior Staff

5 points/level

Prerequisites: Magery (pp. 44-45) *and* Magic (Wizardry) skill (p. 76).

You've somehow acquired an unusually good wizard's staff (see *The Wizard's Staff*, pp. 192-193). This serves as a Magic Point "battery," as usual, but each level of Superior Staff gives +1 to the number of Magic Points you can store in it. Moreover, you get +1 per level to Magic skill and all Magical Form skills (pp. 202-217), so long as you're *holding* the staff.

The drawback is that the staff can be snatched away from you by an opponent. First, he has to use a grab attack (pp. 183-184) to get hold of it. Then he must win a Regular Contest of ST to take it from you. Fortunately, he can't then turn it against you, even if he's a wizard (see below).

You can take up to three levels of this advantage. There are legends of more powerful staffs, but they're true one-offs, with built-in problems you wouldn't want to know about. The only one to appear in the chronicles was carried by Coin the Sourcerer, which says it all.

Normally, you can only purchase Superior Staff at character creation. Acquiring it once you've started a career in wizardry is a tricky and lengthy process at best. The traditional method for ruthless wizards is to take such a staff off another wizard (usually implying something homicidal). To benefit from this, you must then spend one month "detuning" your old staff and two months per level "attuning" to the new one, during which time you can't do much else. Other wizards who realise what you've done will despise you if they have any morals, and envy you bitterly if they don't.

Sapient Pearwood Staff: If you buy three levels of Superior Staff (for 15 points), you can further specify that the staff is made of *sapient pearwood* (p. 158), for +10 points, bringing total cost to 25 points. This makes the staff invulnerable to damage from magic and more resistant to mundane damage (see *Losing Your Staff*, pp. 192-193). If you lose it, it will always return to you in some way after a few minutes, hours, or days; perhaps someone drops it accidentally at your feet, or maybe you just wake up and find it in the corner of the room. Other wizards will recognise the material and respond with respect (+2 to reactions) or, if they're prone to jealousy, with that (-2 to reactions); the GM decides which.

Talent

Variable

You have an aptitude for a set of closely related skills. "Talents" come in levels and give a bonus of +1 per level with all affected skills, even for default use. This effectively raises your attribute scores for the purpose of *those skills only*. Talents also impress other people who understand the skills; anyone who notices and can appreciate your gift reacts to you at +1 per level.

You may never have more than four levels of a given Talent. However, overlapping Talents *can* give skill bonuses (only) in excess of +4.

Some examples:

Animal Friend: Animal Handling, Falconry, Packing, Riding, Teamster, and Veterinary. The reaction bonuses it gives are from animals! *5 points/level.*

Artificer: Engineer, repair skills (p. 80), and any other skill for making, building, or fixing practical stuff. Impresses customers. *10 points/level.*

Born to Hang: Larcenous skills (pp. 75-76), along with Disguise, Fast-Talk, Fortune-Telling, and Sleight of Hand. This is a gift for misdirection, deception, spotting loopholes, and working systems. It mostly garners reaction bonuses from any crooks who are "honest" enough to acknowledge an expert in their own field – who may be the only people who realise how good you are, at least until you get to court. *10 points/level.*

Born War-Leader: Officer skills (p. 79), plus Leadership and Savoir-Faire (Military). Impresses veteran soldiers and warriors. *5 points/level.*

Gifted Artist: Artistic and "craft" skills such as Artist, Jeweller, and Photography. Mostly impresses critics and connoisseurs. *5 points/level.*

Healer: Medical skills (p. 77) and Psychology. Impresses patients, not doctors! *10 points/level.*

Mathematical Ability: Accounting, Astronomy, Cryptography, Engineer, Finance, Mathematics, and so on. You may also add your level to skill rolls for forms of "philosophy" that lean heavily on mathematics, and for magical studies that you can convince the GM require mathematical analysis (although those can be fiercely theoretical), but it *doesn't* add to those skills in general, only to specific applications. Impresses mathematically inclined wizards and philosophers, and "creative" accountants. *10 points/level.*

Metalwork: Armoury, Engineer (for any metal-related specialisation, which is most but not all of them), Jeweller, Mechanic, Metallurgy, Prospecting, and Smith. This is virtually universal at some level among dwarfs, and occasionally appears in individuals of other races. Impresses other skilled metalworkers. *10 points/level.*

Musical Ability: Any skill related to the composition or performance of music. Impresses most listeners. *5 points/level.*

Outdoorsman: Camouflage, Fishing, Mimicry, Naturalist, Navigation, Survival, and Tracking. Impresses other outdoors types. *10 points/level.*

Sense of the City: Area Knowledge, Current Affairs, Hidden Lore, and History relating to one specific town or city, and Urban Survival when in that place. Impresses watchmen, tour guides, and amateur historians there. *5 points/level.*

Smooth Operator: Influence skills (pp. 74-75), plus Acting, Carousing, Detect Lies, Leadership, Panhandling, Politics, and Public Speaking. Impresses other social operators, so long as you aren't using it on them! *15 points/level.*

TENURE

5 points

You have a job from which you cannot normally be fired. You can only lose it (and this trait) as the result of *extraordinary* misbehaviour. Otherwise, your employment and salary are guaranteed for life. Senior wizards at Unseen University have this. In some places and times, this may tempt lower-ranking rivals to clear you off the ladder of seniority in a *permanent* fashion.

Example: Jemzarkiza of Krull – Advantages

Jemzarkiza needs a few advantages, especially if she's going to work magic. She starts with Magery 3 (35 points); consulting *Magic Points* (p. 192), Anne determines that she therefore has 6 MP. Anne has also decided that Jemzarkiza is particularly interested in working with animals, magically and academically, and might be fairly good at it – she might even seem better with animals than with people. A level of Animal Friend (a Talent) costs 5 points.

With her IQ, Jemzarkiza is going to end up as the brains of the party a lot of time, and she has been through the intensive Krullian academic system, so Anne throws in Lightning Calculator (2 points). Lastly, travelling at TL4 and living in Ankh-Morpork are tests for the immune system, so Anne takes Resistant to Disease (+8) (5 points).

With her advantages, Jemzarkiza is at 196 points.

TRUE FAITH

15 points

You have a profound religious faith that protects you from certain supernatural beings such as demons and vampires. To enjoy this protection, you must actively wield a physical holy symbol, chant, dance, or do whatever else is appropriate to your god. If you wish to use this ability in combat, you must choose the Concentrate manoeuvre each turn, and can do nothing else.

For as long as you assert your faith, no malign supernatural entity (GM's judgement as to what this covers) may approach within one yard of you. If one is forced into this radius, it must leave by the most direct route possible. If it cannot leave without coming closer, it must make a Will roll. Success means it may run past you to escape, pushing you aside if necessary (but using only minimum force). On a failure, the monster cowers, helplessly; it cannot move, defend itself, or take any other action.

To keep True Faith, you must behave in a manner consistent with your religion. You should take a disadvantage such as Disciplines of Faith (p. 59) or Vow (p. 66), and *stick to it*. You don't have to be kind or loving, though; there are plenty of stern and narrow-minded gods.

UNFAZEABLE

15 points

Nothing surprises or frightens you! Intimidation (p. 74) doesn't work on you, nor do magic spells that cause fear. The *only* thing on the Disc that can cause you to make a Fright Check (pp. 170-171) is becoming *knurd* (p. 187) – and even then, you get +8 to your roll.

The GM may wish to limit this to characters with very appropriate personal histories, or even ban it; PCs who refuse to be unnerved by *anything* don't always fit in comedy games. However, there *are* people like this on the Disc.

UNNOTICED

70 points

You have the ability to *not be noticed* by normal people. This isn't true invisibility – light doesn't pass through you, and a fair number of beings can see you just fine – but it serves. This is basically what Death himself uses as he goes about his job. However, it doesn't work – or at least not well – against anyone who's accustomed to seeing things that "aren't supposed to be there."

You can turn this ability on and off at will with a one-second Concentrate manoeuvre. It works not only for you but also for anything you're carrying up to Heavy encumbrance (p. 168). People get a chance to notice you, though, which requires a successful Will roll at -5. They try automatically when you first enter their view after at least five minutes out of their sight, or when you turn on your ability in their presence, and may be allowed to try again if you make loud noises, do something violent, etc., at the GM's discretion. If you physically attack someone, your victim gets a roll to notice in time to defend himself, and automatically notices you after being hit once. Optionally, the GM can give very small children a bonus of +1 to +5 to all of these Will rolls, as they haven't always learned to ignore inconvenient truths yet.

Unnoticed fails automatically against gods, spirits, and anyone with any version of See Invisible (p. 46). Individuals with Magery (pp. 44-45) or Medium (p. 45) aren't immune, but they roll at +2 to Will instead of at -5 (having both advantages *doesn't* give a double bonus), and enjoy an *additional* +2 per Magery level; e.g., someone with Magery 0 or Medium rolls at Will+2, Magery 1 gives Will+4, and Magery 3 gives Will+8. If someone like this succeeds three times against you, your ability will never again work on him!

This supernatural advantage is mostly associated with a job as some kind of anthropomorphic personification, such as Death or a Tooth Fairy. Indeed, it "comes with the job"; anyone accompanying Death on his rounds, or standing in for him, gains the full benefits of his ability (under his control, if he's present), while Tooth Fairies – who are perfectly ordinary young women in most respects – gain the ability while they are at work. At the GM's option, anyone else who wants this ability may require an Unusual Background (below).

UNUSUAL BACKGROUND

Variable

This is a "catchall" trait that the GM can use to adjust the point total of anyone with special abilities that aren't widely available on the Disc; e.g., being a creature that has somehow fallen there from another world. Not every unusual character concept merits it!

The GM should only charge points when the character enjoys a tangible benefit. For instance, it would be unusual for a human to be raised by wolves, but unless this gave him capabilities that opponents wouldn't expect or for which employers would pay a large premium, such as the ability to speak to wolves, it would merely be background colour, worth 0 points.

Versatile

5 points

You're extremely imaginative. You have +1 on success rolls for any task that requires creativity or invention. This includes most rolls against Artist skill, all Engineer rolls for new inventions, and all skill rolls made to use the Gadgeteer advantage (p. 43).

Versatile (Inspiration Magnet): This variant of Versatile costs 5 points, just like the ordinary version – it's more powerful but also highly erratic. Your capacity for original thought stems from the fact that your brain is a natural attractor for *inspirations.* Before making any skill rolls for a task that you or the GM think involves *any* significant creativity, roll 1d:

1 – The inspirations fail you. You get no bonus at all.
2, 3 – You get the usual +1.
4, 5 – You get *+2* to *any* relevant rolls, but the thing you produce is radical, unusual, or just *too* creative. Users or assistants require twice the usual time to get the hang of what you've created, and conventional observers and critics will react to it at -2.
6 – Your brain overloads! You automatically produce something brilliant but wildly unorthodox, and only semi-relevant to your task – perhaps vaguely akin to what you set out to create, perhaps at a complete tangent, such as a new system of urban traffic management when trying to build a war chariot, or a new genre of publishing when attempting to develop a cosmological theory.

You cannot turn off this effect; your brain permanently fizzes with sensitivity. Also, because this advantage involves insight, the ideas that it grants tend to be fundamentally *truthful.* Using it to create propaganda or theories built on flawed foundations will produce bizarre results.

Voice of Command

90 points + 5 points per +2 to IQ roll

When you tell someone to do something – in a particular tone of voice – they tend to obey. This affects everyone within eight yards, but only if they can hear you tolerably clearly (so noise, deafness, etc. can pose a problem) *and* understand your words

Inspirations

In the Discworld universe, new ideas are *literally* sparked off, like flickers in a physics experiment, and in a similar way: by collisions with fundamental particles. *Inspirations,* the particles responsible, possess the time-hopping unpredictability of tachyons or neutrinos, and there's no known way of screening against them. However, most sapient brains possess a receptor which can interact with them. Elves are missing this organ.

Anyone can get lucky and stop the odd inspiration, but some people are hypersensitive, even attractive, to them. This may be considered a huge blessing or a curse – Versatile (Inspiration Magnet) is often accompanied by disadvantages such as Absent-Mindedness, Confused, Impulsiveness, and Klutz.

(thus, complex instructions in a language which you or your subject speak at Broken levels might not work). Issuing the command requires a one-second Concentrate manoeuvre (p. 176) – or longer, if the GM thinks it's complicated enough. Then roll a Quick Contest between your IQ and each possible victim's Will. If you win, that person *must* obey; if he wins, he's immune to your ability for the next 24 hours.

The effect will last anywhere from one second for a nigh-suicidal instruction ("Attack that army!") to a minute or two for something which the victim might well do anyway ("Give the doggy a biscuit."). If the command is one which *requires* an extended duration, assume that it persists for up to a minute per point by which you won the Quick Contest.

To make your Voice of Command more effective, you can buy bonuses to your IQ roll. Every +2 to your roll costs 5 points. If the advantage affects only specific categories of victim, the GM might *reduce* its cost by 5 to 25 points, depending on how much this constrains the ability. For example, "Only affects humans" would be worth -5 points, "Only on trolls" or "Only on males" would be -10 points, and "Only affects redheads" would be -25 points.

This is a supernatural trait, but one or two *slightly* supernatural beings in the stories have acquired it. Gaspode the Wonder Dog (pp. 316-317) gains it because people assume that anything they hear from a talking dog must actually be their own idea. Still, it does require a justification, possibly involving an Unusual Background (pp. 48-49).

Perks

"Perks" are minor advantages that cost just 1 point apiece. They give *small* benefits in highly specific situations. Some let you pull off unusual tricks using particular skills, others represent special permissions, and still others simply let you look really *cool.*

A few perks bear symbols that indicate special properties:

* – *Requires specialisation.* You must link the perk to a particular skill, weapon, piece of equipment, etc. Read the description!
† – *Comes in levels.* You can buy the perk more than once for cumulative benefits. Each level counts as one perk, but write the perk just once on your character sheet, along with its level; e.g., Cutting-Edge Training 3 (Astronomy).

Some perks have *prerequisites,* which work as explained under *Advantages* (see p. 41).

The following perks are merely examples; many others are possible. When inventing new ones, remember that perks cost only 1 point. They shouldn't give *too* great a benefit. If something can be represented using ordinary advantages or skills, it's *not* a perk.

ALCOHOL TOLERANCE

You can handle your drink. You get +2 on any HT roll related to drinking. (Trolls can take Sulphur Tolerance instead, for similar benefit.)

ARCHAIC TRAINING*†

You've learned to use old-fashioned tools or methods with one of your technological skills (p. 69). Each level of this perk lets you treat that skill as one TL lower whenever that would be convenient. This is handy not only because parts of the Disc are behind the times technologically, but also because lower-tech equipment is often easier to improvise.

Example: Vog the Wanderer trained in Navigation skill aboard a state-of-the-art Agatean junk and has Navigation/TL4 (Sea)-13. However, he's also sailed on old-fashioned ships and learned to use their instruments. He has Archaic Training 2 (Navigation); if necessary, he can use TL3 or TL2 Navigation tools at full skill.

ASSASSIN IN GOOD STANDING

You're a graduate of the Assassins' Guild School (pp. 259-261) or have otherwise been granted Guild membership. (The GM may insist that you have skills and advantages enough to make this plausible.) If you kill someone for money in a place where the Guild operates, the Guild will make no objection so long as you can plausibly claim to have followed procedure. In addition, if you happen to kill somebody who's on the Guild's open target list, you can claim the fee.

AUTOTRANCE

You can enter a trance at will. This requires one minute of complete concentration and a successful Will roll, at -1 per additional attempt per hour. This trance gives +2 on rolls to contact spirits, etc. You must make another Will roll to break your trance; if you fail, you can try again every five minutes.

BLADE-PROOF BARE-CHESTEDNESS

Prerequisite: -15 points from Compulsive Barbarian Heroism (p. 58) and/or Odious Personal Habit (Barbarian Heroism) (p. 58).

When wearing an outfit that bares your legs, chest, or midriff, you get +1 to all active defences (pp. 180-181). In just a loincloth or otherwise skimpy wear, that becomes +2. Topless females get

an *extra* +1. Total nudity gives no further bonus to defence, but adds +1 to your ground Move and +2 to water Move.

This perk does *not* make you immune to cold weather or public decency laws. It fits well with *Benefits of the Barbarian Lifestyle* (p. 58) – and if the GM chooses not to use that optional rule, he might also prohibit this perk.

CHECK THE EXITS

Whenever you enter a room, you reflexively look to see where the exits are – and if you're going to be staying for long, you try to ensure that there's at least one plausible escape route. This doesn't mean that you respond instantly to threats (buy Combat Reflexes for that), or that your escape plan is perfect, but you need not specify that you *have* such a plan.

CLIMATIC EMPHASIS

On dark nights or during overcast and potentially stormy days, if you say something really significant and dramatic or portentous, or if you succeed with an Intimidation skill roll, you get a flash of lightning and a roll of thunder to emphasise the point. This has no specific game effects – although it may amplify the effects of Intimidation, at the GM's option – but it's *stylish*.

COBBLESTONE SENSE*

Prerequisite: Area Knowledge (p. 71) for the city in question.

You know the unique patterns and textures of a specific city's cobblestones by *touch*. If you have bare feet or are wearing thin-soled footwear (no DR on the bottom!), then when walking or running along that city's streets, you may roll against the associated Area Knowledge skill. Success tells you exactly where you are. You may attempt this as a free action once every 30 seconds.

This perk is known to work for Ankh-Morpork. Other cities may or may not have such recognisable cobbling. It wouldn't be valid for a city where the streets have only been laid or re-laid recently, or one so organised that they all feel identical.

COLD OR HEAT RESISTANCE*

These perks refer to the rules for ambient temperature under *Temperature Extremes* (p. 191) and are equivalent to the 1-point versions of the racial advantage Temperature Tolerance (p. 92):

Cold Resistance: You can go out in just a loincloth on Freezing days. If you wear lots of furs, you can treat Extreme Cold the way most people treat Freezing temperatures.

Heat Resistance: You can remain fully active without penalty in Hot conditions, and you treat Very Hot temperatures as most people treat Hot.

CONTROLLABLE DISADVANTAGE*

You can inflict a specific disadvantage on yourself by taking 3d seconds and rolling against Will for a mental disadvantage or HT for a physical one. It then lasts until you choose to drop it. If you make multiple attempts, this roll is at -1 per previous attempt in the last hour, successful or not.

Valid options for mental disadvantages include Callous (which benefits Intimidation), Easy to Read (helpful for convincing others you're not lying), and various forms of fake insanity. Berserk is *prohibited*. Physical disadvantages are mainly useful to weird people out or facilitate disguise: talking strangely to emulate Disturbing Voice, dislocating your shoulder to simulate One Arm, and so on.

CROSSBOW SAFETY

You somehow carry full-sized or pistol crossbows on your back or slung from your belt, string drawn and a bolt ready to shoot, without wear or stress on bow or string – and more important, without *serious* accidents. As soon as you have the weapon in your hand, you can get a shot off. This may involve ingenious clips, good weapons maintenance, or just a lot of *style*.

CUTTING-EDGE TRAINING*†

You've received instruction in a technological skill (p. 69) above your personal TL; e.g., a TL3 blacksmith might have Cutting-Edge Training (Armoury/TL4 (Melee Weapons)) to know how to make rapiers and smallswords. At the GM's option, this perk *might* give access to two or even three *closely related* higher-tech skills. For example, a TL4 inventor who dabbles with steam power might know Engineer/TL5 (Steam Engines) and Mechanic/TL5 (Steam Engines) – and even Driving/TL5 (Steam Wagon) – with just one perk, because it's all about one machine. Cutting-Edge Training (Physician and Surgery) is always permitted, as those two skills are closely linked.

This perk is cheaper than High TL (p. 31) for those with fewer than five specialisations. If someone gets Cutting-Edge Training in five areas, the GM may let him "trade in" those five perks for High TL 1.

This perk can have levels, one per TL. For example, Urn of Ephebe, in *Small Gods*, had three levels: while living in a TL2 society, he got a TL5 steam vehicle working.

DEEP SLEEPER

You can fall asleep in all but the worst conditions, and sleep through most disturbances. You never suffer any ill effects due to quality of sleep. You get an IQ roll to notice disturbances and awaken, just like anyone else; success is automatic if you have Combat Reflexes (p. 42).

DIVINE NEWS-FEED

Thanks to a gift from your god (well, *a* god), you can learn about the latest goings-on atop Cori Celesti (pp. 300-301) simply by concentrating for a second or two. This news usually takes the form of something that sounds like a plot summary from a bad soap opera, but it allows priests to track which other cults they should be friendly with and which they should disdain. Demonstrating this ability may be good for +1 or more to reactions from serious believers.

This gift is usually granted only to high-ranking priests. However, every now and again, a whimsical or careless deity inflicts it on some hermit or junior monk, to the consternation of the temple hierarchy.

DUAL READY*

You can use a *single* Ready manoeuvre to draw a weapon with either hand. Specialise by weapon combination in left-hand/right-hand order; e.g., Dual Ready (Axe/Pick) lets you ready an axe in your left hand and a pick in your right.

FORGETTABLE FACE

You blend in. Your face is hard to pick out or remember. You get +1 to Shadowing in crowds, while others have -1 to rolls made to recognise you in a line-up, or even to recall meeting you! Forgettable Face is mutually incompatible with Unnatural Features (p. 30), Distinctive Features (p. 68), and Appearance above Attractive or below Unattractive.

GOOD WITH (ANIMAL)*

You have the Animal Empathy advantage (p. 42) for one specific species – dogs, horses, whatever.

GOOD WITH (SOCIAL GROUP)*

You enjoy the Sensitive advantage (p. 42) – an IQ-3 roll to sense intent and +1 to Detect Lies and Psychology – when dealing with one *specific* group: children (anyone under 12 years of age), old people (adults over 65), wizards, witches, etc. "Men" and "women" are much too broad for this purpose, as are "dwarfs," "trolls," and "undead," although some less common nonhuman races might be allowed.

HIGH-HEELED HEROINE

You can run, climb, and fight while wearing high heels without suffering any special penalty for "bad footing." You can also kick with such footwear, dealing thrust-1 *large piercing* damage, plus unarmed skill bonuses.

HONEST FACE

You look honest, reliable, or generally harmless. People who don't know you tend to pick you as the one to confide in – or *not* pick you, if they're seeking a potential criminal or troublemaker. You won't be spot-checked by gate guards unless they have another reason to suspect you, or unless they're truly choosing at random. You have +1 to Acting skill for the sole purpose of "acting innocent." None of this has anything to do with the truth about you!

HYPER-SPECIALISATION*

You're an expert in an extremely *specific* area. You must specialise by one IQ-based "knowledge" skill, or magical or philosophical "theory" skill, and then *further* choose some obscure speciality that takes at least three words to describe. You get +5 to rolls regarding that specific topic. Examples include Hyper-Specialisation (Thaumatology: Left-Handed Narrativium Charm Inversions), (Philosophy (Agatean): Aesthetic Butterfly Related Dreaming), and (Theology (Omnian): Angelic Choreographic Geometries). These may seem useless, but smart players can be surprisingly clever with such things.

Improvised Weapons*

You're accustomed to fighting with the first object that comes to hand. This lets you avoid any penalties the GM assesses for using such improvised weapons in combat. You must select one weapon skill (pp. 77-78) to which this perk applies (buy it several times to use it with multiple weapon skills) – or choose Brawling (p. 82) or Karate (p. 83) to avoid penalties from improvised fist loads.

Longevity

You have a significantly longer lifespan than most humans – meaning anything from "you'll be hale and hearty at 80" to "you don't physically age." Details vary by race, and several nonhuman races have this as an innate quality. Longevity has little direct effect in play, but it does grant you immunity to weird magical ageing effects, and can help you explain remarkably broad experience or memories of historical events that most people only read about in books.

No Hangover

You get drunk just like anybody else (pp. 187-188), but you always wake up feeling fine the next day. This doesn't eliminate the immediate consequences of drinking – just the after-effects. Persistently acting cheerful and hearty while your friends are groping for the Klatchian coffee, or telling others not to fuss about their "imaginary" hangovers, can qualify as an Odious Personal Habit (p. 29).

Off-Hand Training*

You've practised a particular skill (usually but not necessarily a combat skill) with your "off" hand enough that you can ignore the -4 for using that hand; see *Handedness* (p. 29). This extends to defences based on that skill. You must specialise by skill; any skill qualifies, provided that it has applications that normally use only one hand.

This is cheaper than Ambidexterity (p. 41) for those with fewer than five specialisations. If someone is dedicated enough to buy the perk five times, the GM should let him "trade in" the points for full-fledged Ambidexterity.

Oggham Reader

Prerequisite: At least Accented-level literacy (p. 31) in one appropriate language.

You can read the Oggham runes (p. 17). Normally, literacy in a language that used to use Oggham implies command of a more modern script (dwarfs use human scripts a lot these days, even for their own languages), and you've got that, but you've also acquired knowledge of this ancient writing.

Penetrating Voice

You can really make yourself heard! In situations where you want to be heard over noise, others get +3 to their Hearing rolls. At the GM's option, you may get +1 to Intimidation rolls if you surprise someone by yelling or roaring.

Secret Name

Prerequisite: Magery (pp. 44-45).

A wizard who wants to transform another wizard by magic must know his subject's correct name; see *Arbitrary Limitations* (pp. 193-194). This perk means that you've succeeded in keeping your true, full name secret, to protect yourself from transformation magic. It's known only to you, and perhaps to a few trusted friends or relations (your choice). The only snag is that if you ever suffer some kind of magical affliction and can't fix it yourself, you might have to give your name away to another wizard anyway, so that he can help.

Self-Styling Hair

Your hair has the supernatural ability to adopt any style by itself, in response to your mood. This is helpful because it will automatically look right on social occasions (provided that you genuinely *want* to look right), and it will get out of the way within seconds if things get dangerous. You can't exert fine conscious control over it, though, and it can't exert any significant strength.

Statuesque

Whatever your appearance in general, you have an excellent figure. You count as one Appearance level higher than usual when dealing with someone who judges purely by shape and not at all by face, when you're glimpsed at a distance while dressed appropriately, or when you can get away with wearing a veil combined with close-fitting or revealing clothes.

This perk is mutually incompatible with all the traits under *Build* (p. 29). Its benefits work only on other members of your species – and dwarfs can pick it only if they're the modern, outrageous sort who admit what sex they are. Don't bother with Statuesque if you're Very Beautiful or Very Handsome; if you're *that* good-looking, you already have a perfect figure.

There on Call

Prerequisites: Savoir-Faire (Servant) (p. 75), Stealth (p. 81), *and* Traps (p. 82).

If your current paying employer calls out your name and you could reach his side within two seconds, or if you're in his home and an unexpected visitor knocks on the front door, you can appear behind your boss with a "Yes, master?" (or more likely a "Yeth, mathter?", this largely being the province of Igors) or open the door within seconds, as appropriate. You automatically avoid any traps or pitfalls that might get in your way, and no one can ever work out how you accomplished this.

You cannot use this perk for any sort of combat advantage. You just do your job right.

UNDERSTANDS THE LIBRARIAN

The Librarian (pp. 333-335) insists that orang-utans have a rich and complex language, but as it has only one word ("ook"), humans can't really master it. It also happens to be all he speaks, although he can *understand* Morporkian and numerous other languages. Hence, many wizards and servants at Unseen University (and a few other people) have learned to understand what he says, although they don't try to speak his language. The GM may rule that especially complex or technical concepts require gestures or visual illustration.

WORDLESS INFLUENCE*

This is a *category* of perks, each of which enables you to use one Influence skill (pp. 74-75) as such without saying a word, thanks to your posture and manner, even if you don't know the local language.

Fearsome Stare: You can use Intimidation by crossing your arms and glowering. This leaves no evidence of recorded threats or bruises, and scores lots for style.

Haughty Sneer: You can make bank tellers and waiters fawn over you just by peering down your nose and making a Savoir-Faire (High Society) roll. This saves time and makes you look like a proper aristocrat.

Street Swagger: Your casual walk and steely stare amount to use of Streetwise. If you're good enough at the skill, you can walk through the Shades (pp. 252-253) unmolested.

> ## Example: Jemzarkiza of Krull – Perks
>
> Anne gives Jemzarkiza a couple of perks to round her out. She's upper class by upbringing, so Haughty Sneer looks fun, and she's a showy dresser but has to survive on adventures, so High-Heeled Heroine fits. Jemzarkiza is up to 198 points now.

Disadvantages

A "disadvantage" is any problem or imperfection that renders you less capable. In addition to the traits in this section, this includes anything described earlier with a negative point cost: low Status, below-average Wealth, etc.

Because disadvantages have negative point costs, they *give you extra points.* You can spend these to improve your character in other ways. Just as important, an imperfection or two makes your character more interesting and realistic, adding to the fun of roleplaying!

Note: You *cannot* take a disadvantage that one of your advantages would counter or negate. For instance, if you have Acute Hearing, you cannot take Hard of Hearing.

VILLAIN DISADVANTAGES

Some disadvantages (e.g., Sadism) aren't very suitable for "heroes." The GM is free to forbid these to PCs. They're often found among villains, though, so they're included in the interest of good NPC creation.

SELF-CONTROL

Some mental disadvantages don't affect you constantly. An asterisk (*) appears next to the name of any disadvantage that gives you a chance to control your urges. In circumstances likely to trigger your problem, you may opt to roll 3d. If the total is less than or equal to a set *target number,* you succeed in restraining yourself. This is a *self-control roll.* You never *have* to attempt it – it's good roleplaying to give in willingly.

If you take the listed value for one of these disadvantages, the target number is 12: a roll of 12 or less means you control yourself, while a 13 or higher means you fail and suffer the disadvantage's effects. However, it's possible to have worse or better self-control, and to get different numbers of points for the disadvantage accordingly:

Target Number	6	9	12	15
Cost Multiplier	×2	×1.5	×1	×0.5

Drop all fractions. Record the self-control number with the disadvantage; e.g., "Overconfidence (9)."

Example: Dave is creating a wannabe barbarian warrior who's dangerously sure of his abilities, but who's actually one of the ones who's born every minute. He takes Overconfidence, which is worth a base -5 points – but as he doesn't want to get into *too* much trouble, he goes for Overconfidence (15), making the value just -2 points. On the other hand, he doesn't mind if his character is *really* gullible, so he takes Gullibility (9), adjusting that disadvantage's value from -10 to -15 points.

MITIGATED DISADVANTAGES

With the GM's permission, you may also have disadvantages that you can suppress most of the time, thanks to some substance or condition to which you have reasonably easy access; e.g., an herbal potion that you take daily to control a medical condition. However, this *mitigator* must be vulnerable to being lost, taken away, or denied – otherwise, the disadvantage is just a quirk (p. 66). The commonest mitigator is ordinary glasses for Bad Sight (p. 63), but many other possibilities exist if the GM doesn't mind a little extra complexity. Reduce the disadvantage's value by 60%, dropping fractions.

Example: Moist von Lipwig suffers from Compulsive Risk-Taking (9) (p. 58), which is normally worth -22 points. However, this problem disappears so long as he's able to socialise daily with Adora Belle Dearheart (that relationship is danger enough for any man). She acts as a mitigator, reducing the value to -8 points.

Disadvantage List

Remember when choosing from this list that your GM may cap the points you can gain from disadvantages; see *Disadvantage Limits* (pp. 25-26).

ABSENT-MINDEDNESS

-15 points

You have trouble focussing on anything not of immediate interest. You have -5 on IQ and IQ-based skill rolls except for the task on which you're currently concentrating. If no engaging topic presents itself, you'll ignore your immediate surroundings until something brings you back. Once adrift, you must roll against Perception at -5 to *notice* anything short of personal injury. You may attempt to rivet your attention on a boring topic (small talk, guard duty, driving a cart down a straight highway, etc.) by making a Will-5 roll once every five minutes.

Also, the GM may call for an IQ-2 roll for you to remember to do something small but significant, such as reloading your crossbow after firing it.

The watchmen realised that the man holding them up had paused to redesign his weapon and had given it to them to hold while he looked for a screwdriver. This was a thing that did not often happen.

– Jingo

ADDICTION

Variable

You're addicted to a drug. A habit which is legal, costs no more than a few pence a day, leaves you generally functional, and can be suppressed fairly easily – for instance, light smoking or caffeine addiction – is merely a quirk (p. 66). Some addictions are more severe, however. Disadvantage value depends on the particulars:

Cost: If your habit is *expensive*, costing you $0.20-$0.50 per day, that's worth -5 points. If it's *very expensive*, costing dollars per day, that's worth -15 points.

Legality: If the drug is *illegal*, that's worth -5 points.[1]

Addictiveness: If you can't get hold of your drug, you must make Will or HT rolls to avoid problems (see *Withdrawal*, below). If it's *highly addictive*, these are at -5, which is worth an extra -5 points. *Totally addictive* drugs give -10 and are worth an extra -10 points.

Extreme Effects: A drug that renders you unconscious or "blissed out" for a couple of hours a day, that makes you hallucinate blue elephants or talk to gods who aren't actually there, or that will make your head explode if you don't come off it within the year, is worth an extra -10 points.

Drugs that lack extreme effects still have some consequences, perhaps making the user feel energised for an hour or two (roleplay this!) . . . until they wear off. After drugs wear off, addicts are often depressed and irritable for a while (roleplay that, too).

---

1. *Most authorities on the Disc don't care much what people do to their own brains. However, if a drug causes serious harm, selling it is widely classed as assault or murder, and possession may be taken as evidence of intent to sell.*

Examples: Tobacco can be highly addictive; a chain smoker has a -5-point Addiction. The troll drug slab (a mixture of chloric ammonium and radium) is expensive, illegal, highly addictive, and incapacitating; a -25-point Addiction. (There's a reason why Sergeant Detritus nails slab dealers to walls by their ears.) A backwoods shaman living in Ankh-Morpork who *needs* obscure, specially imported mushrooms from the Forest of Skund has an Addiction that's very expensive and hallucinogenic, also worth -25 points.

Withdrawal

If you decide or are forced to do without your drug, you have a problem.

If your dependency is *psychological*, make daily rolls against Will. Failure means you must either start taking the drug again or acquire an extra quirk (pp. 66-68) of the GM's choosing – or start building already-acquired quirks up into full disadvantages, a point at a time.

If the dependency is *physiological*, make daily rolls against HT. Failure means you must either start taking the drug again or suffer 1 HP of injury, which you can't heal until you either lose the addiction or go back on the drug.

Treat Will or HT higher than 13 as only 13 for these rolls. Without your drug, you'll eventually get locked up or die – unless you buy off the Addiction with bonus character points (p. 219), in which case you lose the mental effects at the rate of one point per day, or can start healing HP lost to physical ones.

ALCOHOLISM

-15 points (-10 points if Withdrawn)

Alcoholism uses the Addiction rules (above). Being cheap, incapacitating, and usually legal, it would normally be a -10-point Addiction. However, it's also *insidious*, so it's worth -15 points.

Most of the time, you may confine your drinking to the evenings, and therefore function normally for many purposes. However, *any time* you're in the presence of alcohol, you must roll vs. Will to avoid partaking (treat Will 14+ as 13 for this purpose). Failure means you go on a binge lasting 2d hours, probably followed by a hangover; see *Drinking* (pp. 187-188). Binging Alcoholics will go very quickly to being fully drunk, and are prone to sudden, extreme mood swings between friendliness and hostility.

It might seem that alcoholics with high HT and Will won't suffer much. However, being able to handle more booze with less effect simply causes an alcoholic to drink *more*. High-HT alcoholics spend a *lot* on booze – and still frequently end up incapacitated or annoying in the evenings or when they binge.

Continued alcoholism destroys your abilities. Roll yearly against HT+2. Failure means you lose a level from one of your four basic attributes; roll randomly to determine which.

Withdrawn Alcoholics

Alcoholism is hard to get rid of. If you roleplay coming off the booze for some time, and spend 5 bonus character points, you can become a "withdrawn" alcoholic. You can also start play in this state, with a -10-point disadvantage. Either way, you no longer need to drink daily . . . but you must still make a Will+4 roll whenever you're in the presence of alcohol, or when you come under severe stress and the booze might help you forget. *Really* bad experiences might require an unmodified Will roll, or even a roll at a penalty. A failed roll sets off a binge.

Three binges in a week turns you back into a full alcoholic, but you don't get those points back for this!

There's no normal way to get rid of Alcoholism *completely*. For the sake of allowing playable characters who don't face the risk of sudden disasters, however, withdrawn alcoholics may buy the disadvantage down to a quirk, Former Alcoholic (p. 67). The GM should require a player whose character consistently avoids the worst problems to find the points to reduce the disadvantage to this level.

Troll Sulphurism

Trolls suffer from *Sulphurism* instead of Alcoholism. They consume drinks with a high molten sulphur content rather than alcohol, but the effects are exactly the same for game purposes, and so is the point value.

BAD BACK

-15 or -25 points

Your spine is in bad shape. This may be *Mild* (-15 points) or *Severe* (-25 points). Whenever you miss a roll against a movement skill (pp. 78-79), fail an attack or defence roll in melee by 3 or more, or critically fail such a roll, and *any time* you must attempt a ST roll, make a HT roll as well. This is at -2 if your problem is Severe. Any modifiers to the roll that triggered the problem apply here, too.

Failure means you throw your back. Until someone helps you by making a First Aid roll at -2, or you lie down and rest for an hour, you'll suffer problems. The consequences depend on the severity of your case:

Mild: You're at -3 DX – and at -3 IQ during the second after your back goes (on your next turn, in combat). Critical failure

means you're at -5 DX and must make a Will roll to perform *any* physical action.

Severe: Your DX and IQ are both at -4 for the duration. Critical failure means your muscles lock up completely, leaving you like a statue.

High Pain Threshold (p. 43) *halves* all DX and IQ penalties (drop fractions).

If you have enough bonus character points (p. 219) to buy off this problem, you may choose to do so immediately after someone succeeds at that First Aid-2 roll, for comic effect. Roleplay your gratitude!

BAD SMELL

-10 points

You exude an appalling odour that you cannot remove, such as the stench of decay. This causes a -2 reaction from most people and animals (although pests or carrion-eating scavengers might be *attracted*). You can mask the smell with perfume, but the amount needed results in the same reaction penalty.

BERSERK*

-10 points

You tend to run amok when you or a loved one is harmed, attacking whatever you see as the cause of the trouble. Make a self-control roll any time you suffer injury over 1/4 of your HP in the space of one second, and whenever you witness equivalent harm to a loved one. Failure means you go berserk. You go berserk automatically if you fail a self-control roll for Bad Temper (p. 64)!

While berserk, you make All-Out Attacks (p. 175) and never bother to Aim (p. 175). If you run out of ammunition for a ranged weapon, you either draw another weapon or charge into melee. You're immune to stunning and shock, and injuries cause no penalty to your Move score. You make HT rolls to remain conscious or alive at +4. If you don't fail any rolls, you remain alive and madly attacking until you reach -5×HP. Then you fall dead.

Whenever you down an opponent, you may (if you wish) attempt another self-control roll. If you fail (or don't roll), you continue to the next foe. Treat any friend who attempts to restrain you as a foe. You get one extra roll when no more enemies remain; if you're still berserk, you start to attack your friends. Once you snap out of the berserk state, all your wounds immediately affect you. Roll at normal HT to see whether you remain conscious and alive.

BLINDNESS

-50 points

You cannot see *at all*. In unfamiliar territory, you must travel slowly and carefully, or have a companion or a guide animal lead you. You're at -6 to all combat skills. You can make melee attacks, but you cannot target a particular hit location. With a ranged weapon, you can only attack randomly, or engage targets so close that you can hear them. Many other actions are *impossible* for you.

All this assumes that you're accustomed to blindness. Someone who *suddenly* loses his eyesight fights at -10, just as if he were in total darkness.

This isn't an easy disadvantage to buy off with bonus character points, but a very few blind witches *have* refocused their precognitive powers onto the present.

CALLOUS

-5 points

You are merciless. You can decipher others' emotions, but do so only to manipulate people. This gives you -3 to Teaching skill, on Psychology rolls made to help others (as opposed to deduce weaknesses), and on any skill roll made to interact with those who've previously suffered from your callousness. Past victims react to you at -1, as does anyone with Empathy. However, you *do* get an extra +1 to Interrogation and Intimidation rolls when you use threats or torture.

CANNOT SPEAK

-15 or -25 points

You have a limited capacity for speech. This comes in two levels:

Cannot Speak: You can make vocal sounds (maybe bark, growl, trill, etc.), but your speech organs are incapable of the subtleties of language. You may still have the Mimicry skill (though not the Speech specialisation), the Voice advantage, or the Disturbing Voice disadvantage. Most animals have this trait. *-15 points.*

Mute: You cannot vocalise *at all.* All communications with others must be non-verbal: writing, gestures, telepathy, etc. You cannot have any other voice-related traits. *-25 points.*

CHUMMY

-5 or -10 points

You *much* prefer company to being alone. This comes in two levels:

Chummy: When alone, you're unhappy and distracted: -1 to IQ-based skills. Chummy NPCs usually react to others at +2. *-5 points.*

Gregarious: You're miserable when alone: -2 to IQ-based skills – or -1 if in a group of four or less. Gregarious NPCs usually react to others at +4. *-10 points.*

CODE OF HONOUR

-5 to -15 points

You take pride in following a set of "honourable" principles. The specifics can vary. You'll do nearly anything, maybe even risk death, to avoid looking "dishonourable."

The point value of a Code of Honour depends on how much trouble it gets you into, and on how arbitrary and irrational its requirements are. An informal Code, or one that shouldn't ever get you killed, is worth -5 points. A formal Code, or one that often sends you into danger, is worth -10 points. A highly formal Code that regularly jeopardises your life is worth -15 points.

Many social classes and groups have an associated Code of Honour. This doesn't necessarily mean that all or even most such people actually possess the disadvantage – although high-minded and idealistic ones usually will, and many others may follow it at quirk level (p. 66), obeying it when convenient but not at serious risk to their lives. On the other hand, *openly* disregarding your group's Code is a good way to become a social outcast; a "gentleman" who fails to act the part may be expelled from his club and possibly sent far away by his family, while a watchman who doesn't watch his colleagues' backs may find his gear vandalised and can't expect much help when *he* gets into trouble. Failing to pay lip-service to a Code can be the basis for a negative Reputation (p. 34).

As the Disc is a realistic-comedy world, many people who espouse strict Codes come across as stiff-necked, pompous, and even stupid. However, the sincere ones get credit for trying – and there are those who believe that sometimes, when *Narrative Causality* (pp. 8-9) kicks in, living by one of the stricter Codes can save your life. The hero will win, but only if he *acts* like a hero; the dark lord will live to scheme another day, but only if he plays his part. Certainly, a Code may well mean allowing opponents a better chance provided that *they* played by the rules as well, whether this is a soldier treating prisoners better if they, too, recognise the Soldier's Code, or a dark lord putting a proper barbarian hero in a fallible death-trap when he'd outright massacre mere rebellious peasants. Thus, living by a Code *can* save your life.

Examples:

Academic: Pursue learning diligently, and never lie about it. Respect fellow academics and their work. Only conceal knowledge if lives are at stake. Acknowledge your sources. *-5 points.*

Assassins': As a member of the Assassins' Guild (pp. 259-261) – *not* a vulgar hired killer – you must behave with courtesy to other gentlemen, keep your word to fellow Guild members (and in general, when not performing your Guild duty), and never kill except for hire or in self-defence. If you take an advance payment, complete the mission or return it with an apology. Killing a target's guards, let alone mere servants, is questionable manners; it can be forgiven in exceptional circumstances, but it's a matter for stern self-criticism, as bypassing guards with stealth and agility is always preferable. Never employ gross or clumsy methods; you disdain explosives in any great quantity (a small charge, perfectly placed, might show *just* enough style), or heavy weapons. Offer a personal service; you might *possibly* deal with two or three problems at the same time, but you refuse bulk orders. Nor will you shoot down a victim in the street like a crude thug; you deliver at home or at the office, and always leave a receipt. Wear black or very dark colours, unless there's some clear off-duty reason not to; this inspires respect (and helps you hide in shadows, although solid black isn't perfect for that), but it can also attract the attention of lower-class persons who regard killing an Assassin as something to boast about. *-10 points.*

Chivalry: Never break your word. Never ignore an insult. Defend all ladies (women of Status 1+). *Always* fight fair, and accept any challenge to arms from anyone of equal or higher Status. Serve your lord faithfully in all things. *-15 points.*

Dark Lord's: Aim to win in a way that demonstrates your superiority, and only break your word in large matters. Never ignore an insult to yourself, your schemes, or the symbols of your rule – rant a lot at whoever is responsible, and then take a complicated revenge. (This Code only applies between dark lords and hero types, though; disrespect from peasants calls for a sneer and overwhelming force, not a rant.) Always take advantage of opponents in dramatic ways; if your enemies are defeated and helpless, engage in some token gloating and then ignore them while you get on with important matters. Use over-complicated death-traps and ornate, flared, barbed, and smoke-blackened blades. Talk to upper-class or good-looking prisoners and guests with florid courtesy, but treat people you find attractive as interesting decorations, never as your equals. Compliment them on their looks by leering at them; it shows that you care.

The Code of the Igors was very strict.

Never Contradict: it was no part of an Igor's job to say things like "No, thur, that'th an artery." The marthter was always right.

Never Complain: an Igor would never say "But that'th a thouthand mileth away!"

Never Make Personal Remarks: no Igor would dream of saying anything like "I thould have thomething done about that laugh, if I wath you."

And never, ever Ask Questions.

– Thief of Time

Provide visiting heroes who aren't yet scheduled for the death-trap with comfortable lodgings, submissive servants, and a change of clothes.[1] *-10 points.*

D'reg's: Seek revenge for insults. Protect your sworn friends. If you take in a guest or *are* a guest, treat the hospitality as sacred for exactly 72 hours. In battle, when someone says "Charge!" you charge. However, you don't have to fight fair, and you aren't *automatically* sworn to loyalty to anyone – not even family. *-5 points.*

Gentleman's: Never break your word. Never ignore an insult to yourself, a lady, or your flag (insults must be wiped out by an apology or a duel, *not* necessarily to the death!). Never take advantage of an opponent – weapons and circumstances must be equal (except in open war). All this applies only between gentlemen; discourtesy from anyone of Status 0 or less calls for a whipping, not a duel! *-10 points.*

Igor's: This is a form of Professional Code (below) that just about demands the skills, tolerance, and detachment of a true Igor (pp. 140-141). Obey instructions, never complain, and get the job done. Accept routine physical abuse from your employer with calm resignation, and don't cave in to screaming angry villagers – although you may whimper and cower a bit for the look of the thing. You aren't obliged to die for your master, though. If and when his career approaches a catastrophic climax, you may collect enough knick-knacks from his collection to cover wages owed and quietly depart by the back door. *-5 points.*

Klatchian: Never break your word. Never ignore an insult to yourself, a family member, or your tribe (insults must be wiped out by an apology or a duel, *not* necessarily to the death!). If you take in a guest or *are* a guest, treat the hospitality as sacred for exactly 72 hours. *-10 points.*

Pirate's: Always avenge an insult, regardless of the danger. Your buddy's foe is your own. Never attack a fellow crewman or buddy except in a fair, open duel. Anything else goes. Similar Codes often appear among bandits, Hublander tribesmen, etc. *-5 points.*

Professional: Many professions have formalised ethics, which some professionals treat as a matter of honour. This generally involves obeying rules of procedure, paying professional membership dues, not undermining a fellow professional who's playing by the rules himself, and only ripping off customers in the polite, time-honoured fashion. *-5 points.*

---

1. *Your guest wardrobe tends to have a lot of black leather or metallic swimwear; you know that guests will appreciate this.*

Soldier's: An officer should be tough but fair, lead from the front, and look out for his men; an ordinary soldier should look out for his pals and take care of his kit. Be willing to fight and die for the honour of your unit, service, and country. Follow orders. Obey the "rules of war." Treat an honourable enemy with respect (a dishonourable one deserves a knife). Wear the uniform with pride. *-10 points.*

Watchman's: Serve your community by upholding the law – and most importantly, by catching the bad guys. Wear the uniform with pride. Defend the honour of the watch. Protect and assist your fellow officers; when they call for assistance, *run* to help. Don't embarrass your buddies, and protect them if they make mistakes, but if *they're* knowingly damaging the watch, they forfeit your loyalty. While all this sometimes requires bending the written rules, don't lose track of the objective. *-5 points.*

Wise-Woman's: This Professional Code (above) is mostly found among witches of the more ethical sort. It's chiefly a set of principles for a medical practitioner, the main components of which are "Do your best for your patients," "Only charge what people can afford," and "What's said in the sickroom stays in the sickroom." The last applies double to the *delivery* room; any working midwife hears things yelled that the mother won't want repeated later. This rule is the one thing that limits some witches' gossiping. *-5 points.*

COMBAT PARALYSIS

-15 points

You "freeze up" in combat situations and receive -2 to all Fright Checks. This has nothing to do with Cowardice (p. 64); you might be brave, but your body betrays you. Conversely, a coward may respond very promptly to danger – by running away!

In any situation in which personal harm seems imminent, make a HT roll. Don't roll until the instant you need to fight, run, pull the trigger, or whatever. Any roll over 13 is a failure, even if you have HT 14+. Success lets you act normally. Failure means you're mentally stunned (see *Mental Stunning*, p. 171); make another HT roll every second, at a cumulative +1 per turn after the first, to break the freeze. A quick slap from a friend gives +1 to your cumulative roll.

Once you unfreeze, you won't freeze again until the immediate danger is over. Then, in the next dangerous situation, you may freeze once again.

This is the opposite of Combat Reflexes (p. 42). You cannot have both.

COMPULSIVE BEHAVIOUR*

-5 to -15 points

You have a habit or a vice that wastes a good deal of your time or money. You *must* indulge at least once per day, if possible, and do so *any* time you have the opportunity unless you can make a self-control roll. You must also make a self-control roll to enter a situation where you'll be unable to indulge for more than a day; if you succeed (or are forced into the situation), you suffer from Bad

Temper (p. 64) the whole time, with the same self-control roll as your Compulsive Behaviour. Some people may be amused by your habits, but anyone who disapproves will react to you at -1 or worse.

This disadvantage's point value depends on the trouble it causes. Examples include:

Compulsive Barbarian Heroism: You live the loincloth-and-broadsword life. Your preferred solution to any problem is to grab a weapon – although your tactics *may* be cunning. But it isn't the violence that appeals to you, it's the *attitude.* You suffer from intermittent wanderlust, which makes it difficult for you to own a home or hold any permanent job (such as, say, king) for long. This is obviously closely related to the similarly named Odious Personal Habit (p. 29), and you may have both, but that's externalised and annoying to others, whereas this is personal and dangerous to you. *-10 points.*

Compulsive Carousing: You never miss a party and *always* hit the bars when in town. You like strong booze, loud music, and messy romantic relationships. *-5 points, or -10 points in puritanical settings.*

Compulsive Gambling: You can't resist a bet – any bet! *-5 points.*

Compulsive Lying: Even your friends and allies can't know whether to trust *anything* you say. Business partners will very soon decide that you're a liability. *-15 points.*

Compulsive Neatness: You want everything to be *just so*, both physical objects (especially your possessions) and numbers and information. You drive friends and colleagues to distraction with all the polishing, tidying, aligning, and double-checking. *-5 points.*

Compulsive Risk-Taking: You're addicted to excitement. You climb mountains, sail through storms, take up extreme sports, drink in strange dark taverns, plunder tombs, or commit pointless showy crimes – all just for the rush. You *may* be able to limit yourself to stuff covered by your personal skills, but this compulsion is liable to get you killed eventually. *-15 points.*

Compulsive Spending: You like buying stuff! Make a self-control roll whenever you get a chance to purchase something interesting and you have the money. This raises your cost of living and gives you a penalty to your Merchant skill when you're bargaining for something cool, depending on your self-control number: +10%/-1 for a self-control number of 15, +20%/-2 for 12, +40%/-3 for 9, and +80%/-4 for 6. *-5 points.*

Compulsive Vowing: You never just *decide* to do things. You always *vow* to do them – and you take all your vows seriously, whether they're ludicrously trivial or insanely difficult. *-5 points.*

Kleptomania: You're compelled to steal – not necessarily things of value, but anything you can get away with. Make a self-control roll *whenever* you're presented with a chance to steal, at up to -3 if the item is especially interesting to you (not necessarily *valuable*, unless you're poor or have Greed). If you fail, you must try to steal it. You may keep or sell stolen items, but not return or discard them. *-15 points.*

Trickster: You crave the excitement of outwitting *dangerous* foes. Playing simple tricks on harmless folk is no fun at all – it has to be perilous! Make a self-control roll each day. If you fail, you must try to trick a dangerous subject: a skilled warrior, a terrible monster, a whole group of reasonably competent victims, etc. If you resist, you get a cumulative -1 per day to your self-control roll until you finally fail! *-15 points.*

Many of the above are very similar in effect. Characters cannot take two such disadvantages which lead to the same results most of the time.

Optional Rule: Benefits of the Barbarian Lifestyle

Traditional barbarian heroes refer to their lifestyle – as defined by their Odious Personal Habit (p. 29) and Compulsive Behaviour (above) – as "the Code," although it isn't a Code of Honour (pp. 56-57) for game purposes. (Many of them do have the Pirate's Code, however.) The Code is very important to them.

Many of them believe that the Code is one thing that enables them to survive in this high-risk career; so long as they live by it, they'll survive as a hero should (however painfully). In the narrative-dominated world of Disc adventuring, they may actually be *right*. This optional rule provides a way to reflect this, at the cost of a little complexity.

If a character has both disadvantages and gets at least -20 points from them together, he may buy any advantage that helps him operate as a "proper" hero at a 20% discount (rounding up). For example, High Pain Threshold costs just 8 points, while Extraordinary Luck costs 24. However, advantages bought with this discount only work while the hero obeys the Code *to the letter*. Forget the Code, behave other than as a barbarian hero really should, or let other motivations take precedence, and it'll turn round and have your blood! Those advantages *will* fail you – probably at the worst possible moment – and stay "off" until you do something *really* heroic.

Appropriate advantages here include Absolute Direction, Combat Reflexes, Danger Sense, High Pain Threshold, Indomitable, Luck Advantages, Mind Shield, and Rapid Healing.

The Dark Lord Code

If this works for barbarian heroes, something very similar might work for dark lords. If they take and live by their Code of Honour, they can buy advantages such as Born War-Leader, Enhanced Defences, Indomitable, and Luck Advantages at a 10% discount.

Two Sides of the Same Coin

Whether or not these rules apply, sensible barbarian heroes and dark lords recognise that, at some level, they *need* each other. That's why dark lords are forever putting captive heroes in ludicrous death-traps or flimsy cells, and why barbarian heroes never check for escape tunnels before storming an enemy lair.

DEAFNESS

-20 points

You cannot hear *anything*. You must receive information in writing (if you're literate) or sign language, and you won't hear that runaway cart careering down the street toward your back . . .

DELUSIONS

-5 to -15 points

You believe something that simply isn't true. Other people may consider you insane – and they may be right! You *must* roleplay your belief at all times. Point value depends on the Delusion's nature:

Minor Delusions affect your behaviour. They don't keep you from functioning more-or-less normally, but anyone around you will soon notice them and react to you at -1. *-5 points.*

Major Delusions have a *strong* effect on your behaviour. While they still don't keep you from living a fairly normal life, others react at -2. *-10 points.*

Severe Delusions influence your behaviour so severely that they may keep you from functioning in the everyday world. Others react at -3, but are more likely to fear or pity you than to attack. *-15 points.*

Two specific examples:

Megalomania: The Major Delusion that you're destined for greatness. Choose some grand goal, and let nothing stand between you and destiny! Young or naïve characters, and fanatics looking for a new cause, may actually react to you at +2; others react at the usual penalty.

Paranoia: The Major Delusion that everyone is plotting against you. You trust no one except old friends – and you keep an eye on *them*. Paranoid NPCs react at -4 to *any* stranger, and *double* any "legitimate" reaction penalty (e.g., for an unfriendly nationality).

Two other, tragically common Major Delusions are "My combat sports training is fully effective in a real fight" and "My superior social class automatically makes me a good warrior." The latter requires Status 1+, is usually associated with Status 3+, and isn't allowed to anyone who's genuinely competent in a fight. These are slightly unusual in that neither tends to earn reaction penalties – except from veteran warriors who know what sort of mess they cause – and neither is much of a disadvantage outside combat. They just get sufferers killed, a lot; the second unfortunately also gets people serving under the sufferer killed.

DISCIPLINES OF FAITH

-5 to -15 points

You express your metaphysical beliefs by following a strict set of rules. Few gods actually *care* whether their followers do this stuff, but some find it a useful way to test and reinforce faith, so such rules end up written into a lot of holy books. Also, some monkish orders based near the Hub – who perhaps serve powers beyond the gods – find that such practises help them achieve useful mystical results.

Some specific Disciplines:

Asceticism: You lead a life of self-denial and self-discipline, often involving isolation in bleak wilderness, and possibly bouts of self-punishment. You cannot have above-average Wealth, or Status beyond that granted by your Religious Rank (if any). Some temples find it safer to suggest this sort of thing to extremely devout followers than to keep them hanging around causing trouble. *-15 points.*

Monasticism: You live in a monastery, are completely devoted to religious pursuits, and must spend at least 75% of your time sequestered from the world. You cannot have above-average Wealth, or Status beyond that granted by your Religious Rank (if any). *-10 points.*

Mysticism: You spend most of your time in deep meditation and trance-like contemplation, complete with chanting, consumption of exotic mushrooms, or other trappings. Individuals other than devout coreligionists consider you a bit mad: -2 to reactions. *-10 points.*

Ritualism: You stick faithfully to elaborate rituals regarding every aspect of life, from waking to eating to bathing to sex. Each ritual has its proper place, time, words, trappings, and ceremony. *-5 points.*

DUTY

Variable

You have an official responsibility to a cause or an organisation, and can't easily avoid it. Most ordinary jobs don't qualify – a real Duty is likely to be hazardous and often inconvenient. Military service, however, *is* often both a job and a Duty.

The GM rolls at the beginning of each adventure to see whether your Duty comes into play. Being "called to duty" could delay your plans, or be the *reason* for the adventure – or your master might give you a secret agenda to pursue.

A Duty's basic point value depends on the frequency with which it arises in play:

Roll	15 or less*	12 or less	9 or less	6 or less
Base Cost	-15 points	-10 points	-5 points	-2 points

* At this level, the GM may rule that you're *always* on duty.

Modify base cost if the Duty is more or less dangerous than average:

Extremely Hazardous: You're *always* at risk of death or serious injury when your Duty comes up. *-5 points.*

Nonhazardous: Your Duty never *requires* you to risk your life. (This can raise the cost to 0 points or more; if so, the obligation is too trivial to qualify.) *+5 points.*

EASY TO READ

-10 points

Your body language betrays your intentions. This is *not* the same as Truthfulness (p. 66). You have no moral problem with lying, and may possess Fast-Talk at a high level, but your face or stance gives the game away.

Easy to Read gives *others* +4 on all Empathy, Body Language, and Psychology rolls to discern your intentions or the truth of your words, and +4 to their IQ, Detect Lies, and Gambling rolls in any Quick Contest with your Acting, Fast-Talk, or Gambling skill when you try to lie or bluff.

This is a mental disadvantage, despite its physical manifestations. With enough practise, you can "buy it off."

FEARFULNESS

-2 points/level

Fearfulness gives -1 per level to Will whenever you must make a Fright Check (pp. 170-171) or resist Intimidation (p. 74), and +1 per level to all Intimidation rolls made against you. You may not reduce your Will roll below 3; e.g., if you have Will 11, you're limited to Fearfulness 8.

GULLIBILITY*

-10 points

There's one born every minute, and you're it. You'll swallow even the most ridiculous story if it's told with conviction. Whenever you're confronted with a lie – or an improbable truth, for that matter – make a self-control roll, modified for the story's plausibility. Failure means you believe what you were told.

As well, you're at -3 (to IQ, skills, etc.) in any situation in which your credulity might be exploited. This includes all Merchant skill rolls. You can *never* learn the Detect Lies skill.

HAM-FISTED

-5 points

You have poor fine motor skills and suffer -3 on rolls for any kind of small-detail work. You also tend to be badly groomed and messy, giving -1 to reaction rolls when this matters.

INNUMERATE

-5 points

You have little or no grasp of mathematics. You cannot learn – and get no default with – Computer Programming or any of the skills that benefit from Mathematical Ability (p. 47). This has many frustrating side-effects: you must use your fingers to count or perform arithmetic, and you're easily cheated by dishonest merchants (-4 to rolls to notice you've been had).

This disadvantage is widespread in "barbarian" societies, and the GM may choose not to count it against the campaign disadvantage limit (if any) for characters from such backgrounds. It's also quite common among trolls, although they have a traditional numbering system that's a bit more sophisticated than many people realise, allowing multiple compounded applications of the concept of "many."

INTOLERANCE

Variable

You dislike and distrust some or all people who are different from you. You may be prejudiced on the basis of class, species, nationality, religion, or sex. Roleplay this! (An NPC with Intolerance reacts at -3 to the hated group.) Victims of your Intolerance will return the favour, reacting to you at -1 to -5 (GM's decision).

Point value depends on the *scope* of your Intolerance. Total Intolerance of *anyone* not of your own class, species, nationality, or religion (pick one) is a -10-point disadvantage. Intolerance directed at one *specific* class, species, nationality, religion, or sex is worth from -5 points for a commonly encountered victim to -1 point (a nasty quirk) for a rare victim.

Jealousy is Intolerance of anyone who seems smarter, more attractive, or better off than you! This is worth -10 points, because it often affects you very badly. You resist any plan proposed by such a "rival," and *hate* it if someone else is in the limelight.

KLUTZ

-5 points

You have a talent for physical blunders. You cannot have DX higher than 13, and you must make a DX roll to get through the day without at least one annoying or embarrassing accident. Avoid laboratories, explosives, and china shops!

LAZINESS

-10 points

You're violently averse to work, especially physical labour. Your chances of getting a raise or promotion in *any* job are halved. If you're self-employed, halve your monthly pay. Roleplay it!

LOW PAIN THRESHOLD

-10 points

You're very sensitive to pain. *Double* the shock from any injury; e.g., if wounded for 3 HP, you're at -6 to DX and IQ on your next turn. Also, you roll at -4 to resist knockdown, physical stunning, and physical torture. Whenever you suffer a wound that inflicts more than 1 HP of injury, you must make a Will roll to avoid crying out. Failure can give away your presence and earn -1 to reactions from "macho" individuals.

MENTAL LIMITATIONS

Variable

You have a limited approach to the world, which makes you seem stupid or dull (and often annoying). You may actually be fairly bright and even have high IQ. The problem is that you're often incapable of *applying* whatever brains you've got.

This category includes several disadvantages, many of which penalise skills. Except as noted, you can still *learn* those skills – you just aren't as good at them as other people.

Clueless: You totally miss the point of any wit aimed at you, and are oblivious to attempts at seduction (+4 to resist Sex Appeal). Sophisticated manners are beyond you (giving you -4 to Savoir-Faire), while colloquial expressions escape you. Most people react to you at -2. Unlike No Sense of Humour (p. 65), you may make jokes – lame ones – and you can appreciate slapstick and written humour. However, you rarely "get" verbal humour, and must roll vs. IQ-4 to realise you're the butt of a joke. And unlike Gullibility (p. 60), you normally realise when someone is trying to take advantage of you, except in social situations; you're no more susceptible to Fast-Talk than usual, save when someone is trying to convince you that an attractive member of the appropriate sex is interested in you. *-10 points.*

Confused*: The world seems strange and incomprehensible to you, and you're slow to pick up on new facts or situations. In particular, you respond poorly to excessive stimulation. Alone in peace and quiet, somewhere familiar, you function normally – but in a strange place, or when there's a commotion going on, you must make a self-control roll. Failure means you freeze up. The GM should adjust the roll in accordance with the stimuli in the area: resisting confusion from two friends chatting quietly in a familiar room would require an unmodified roll, but a raucous tavern might give -5, and a full-scale riot would give -10! If this disadvantage strikes in combat, you must take the Do Nothing manoeuvre each turn. You aren't stunned, you can defend yourself normally if you're directly and physically attacked, and you can even launch a counterattack against that one foe – but you don't *act*, only *react*. *-10 points.*

Hidebound: You find it difficult to come up with an original thought. You have -2 on any task that requires creativity or invention, including most rolls against Artist skill, all Engineer rolls for

new inventions, and all skill rolls made to use the Gadgeteer advantage. *-5 points.*

Incurious*: You hardly ever notice things unrelated to the business at hand. Make a self-control roll when confronted with something strange. Failure means you ignore it! Incurious NPCs react at -1 to novelty. *-5 points.*

Literal-Minded: This is mostly found among dwarfs – although they can buy it off with bonus character points, and many *other* Discworlders seem to have literal-minded tendencies. You use language literally, cannot grasp metaphors, and take rhetorical exaggerations at face value. While people can explain metaphors to you, you find them bizarre. Similes are easier, but they still worry you ("I am NOT attracted to gold like a moth to a flame; I cannot fly . . ."). Ordinary humans find conversations with you annoying, reacting at -1 when the problem becomes evident (-2 for would-be wits and poets), and you may suffer from -1 to -3 to Poetry and most social skills (especially Fast-Talk and Public Speaking) when dealing with a more metaphor-prone audience, at the GM's option. This is *not* the same as No Sense of Humour (you just favour rather blunt comedy, full of face-pulling and prat-falls) or Clueless (it doesn't exclude good manners); but as these things overlap, Literal-Minded is worth fewer points if you take either of these disadvantages. *-10 points, or -5 points if you also have Clueless and/or No Sense of Humour.*

Low Empathy: You cannot understand emotions *at all*. This doesn't prevent you from *having* emotions – just from analysing them. You may not take any Empathic Abilities (p. 42), and suffer -3 to Acting, Carousing, Criminology, Detect Lies, Diplomacy, Fast-Talk, Interrogation, Leadership, Merchant, Politics, Psychology, Savoir-Faire, Sex Appeal, and Streetwise. *-20 points.*

Oblivious: You understand emotions but not *motivations*, making you bad at social manipulation. You have -1 to all Influence skills (pp. 74-75) – and also to *resist* those skills! *-5 points.*

Totally Oblivious: This is a worse version of Oblivious, taken to the extreme. Play it for comedy! It has all the same effects and more: You cannot spend points on Acting, Fast-Talk, Fortune-Telling, Intimidation, Interrogation, or Politics, and if you try to use any of those skills at default, you're at -4 (rather than the -1 that applies to only some of them for normal-level Oblivious). *-10 points.*

MISERLINESS*

-10 points

You must always hunt for the best deal possible. Make a self-control roll any time you're called on to spend money; the GM may penalise your roll for large expenditures. Failure means you refuse to spend. If you absolutely *must* spend the money, you haggle and complain interminably.

OBSESSIVE IDEAS

Variable

You place *something* ahead of all other concerns. This can take various forms:

Fanaticism: You value a country, organisation, philosophy, or religion (specify this!) above yourself. This *doesn't* make you mindless or evil – a wild-eyed priest may be a fanatic, but so is a devoted patriot who dies for his country. Optionally, you may qualify this as *Extreme Fanaticism,* at no change in point value. Extreme Fanaticism works like regular Fanaticism but means you'll accept suicide missions unquestioningly, in return for which you get +3 on Will rolls to resist brainwashing, interrogation, and supernatural mind control in any situation where failure would lead you to betray your cause. *-15 points.*

Obsession:* Your entire life revolves around a single objective. Make a self-control roll whenever it would be wise to deviate from this path. Failure means you continue to pursue your Obsession, regardless of consequences. Point value depends on the time needed to realise your goal. *-5 points for a short-term goal (e.g., assassinating someone), or -10 points for a long-term goal (e.g., becoming Tyrant of Ephebe).*

You could become famous just for being, well, famous. It occurred to him that this was an extremely dangerous thing and he might probably have to have someone killed one day, although it would be with reluctance.
– Moving Pictures

OVERCONFIDENCE*

-5 points

You believe that you're far more powerful, intelligent, or competent than you really are. You might be proud and boastful, or just quietly determined, but you must roleplay this! The GM may request a self-control roll any time he feels you show an unreasonable degree of caution. Failure means you *must* go ahead as though you were able to handle the situation.

You receive +2 on reaction rolls from young or naïve individuals (who believe you *are* that good), but -2 on reactions from experienced NPCs.

PACIFISM

-5 to -15 points

You're opposed to violence. This can take several forms. The first is a fairly normal human lack of "killer instinct"; the others are moral standpoints.

Reluctant Killer: You have -4 to hit a person (*not* a monster, machine, etc.) with a deadly attack, and you can't Aim (p. 175). However, if you can't see his face, you suffer only -2 and you *can* Aim. If you kill someone, roll 3d – you're traumatised and useless (roleplay it!) for that many days. You won't stop your allies from killing; you might even encourage them. *-5 points.*

Cannot Harm Innocents: You may fight, and even start fights, but you may only use deadly force on a foe who's attempting to do you serious harm. (Capture is not "serious harm"!) You must avoid actions that might harm bystanders. *-10 points.*

Self-Defence Only: You may only fight to defend yourself or those in your care, using only as much force as necessary (no pre-emptive strikes!). You must do your best to discourage others from starting fights, too. *-15 points.*

PHOBIAS*

Variable

A "Phobia" is fear of an item, creature, or circumstance; the more common the object of your fear, the more points you get. You may attempt a self-control roll to master your Phobia temporarily. Failure means you cringe, flee, panic, or otherwise lose control. Pick something amusing; what's important is that you're *useless.* Even if you succeed, the fear persists – you suffer -2 to all IQ, DX, and skill rolls while the cause of your fear is present, and you must roll again every 10 minutes to see if the fear overcomes you.

Even the *threat* of the feared object requires a self-control roll at +4. If your enemies actually inflict the feared object on you, you must make an unmodified self-control roll.

Some common phobias:

Crowds (Demophobia): Any group of a dozen people or more. Your self-control roll may be penalised for much larger groups. *-15 points.*

Darkness (Scotophobia): Nothing to do with bagpipes. *-15 points.*

Enclosed Spaces (Claustrophobia): *-15 points.*

Fire (Pyrophobia): This comes in two varieties. *Minor Pyrophobia* is about uncontrolled flames – you're fine around enclosed lamps (so long as you don't have to think about what's inside them), cigarettes (still, *you* don't smoke), or even a fire in a hearth (though you have nightmares about the place burning down). But if someone waves a lit torch in your face, or you encounter a forest or a building on fire, or a wizard hurls a fireball at you, you flee or cower. *Major Pyrophobia* means that you cannot deal with any fire, not even a lit cigarette within five yards, which means that you won't be spending much time with sane humans after dark or in cold regions. *-5 points for Minor, -10 points for Major.*

Heights (Acrophobia): You'll only willingly go more than 15' above the ground in a large, solid building – and then you'll stay well back from the windows. If there's some chance of an actual fall, self-control rolls are at -5. *-10 points.*

Monsters
(Teratophobia):
Trolls, gargoyles, etc.,
don't count as "monsters"
on the Disc; they're widely
known to be talking, (slow-)thinking
beings. However, adventurers will meet
plenty of *actual* monsters – and from the
viewpoint of typical citizens of Ankh-Morpork, this
category might include huge "mundane" animals such
as rhinoceroses and large squid. *-15 points.*

The Number 8 (Octophobia): Your self-control roll is at -5 if
obvious supernatural powers are involved! *-5 points.*

Open Spaces (Agoraphobia): You're uncomfortable when
you're outdoors, and frightened if there are no walls within 50'.
This isn't actually common among old-fashioned dwarfs, but it
isn't unknown. *-10 points.*

Strange and Unknown Things (Xenophobia): You're upset by
strange circumstances, and especially by strange people. Make a
self-control roll when you're surrounded by people of a different
nationality, at -3 if they're a different species to you. If you fail,
you may well attack strangers in your panic. This isn't usually
suitable for adventurers, but some Agateans and deep-dwelling
dwarfs are sufferers. *-15 points.*

The Sun (Heliophobia): The sun is another problem more associated with old-school monsters than sane humans. If you think
that the terrible yellow eye is out to burn you, you're unlikely to
go out in daytime, even on deeply overcast days; who knows when
a gap in the clouds might allow It to get you? *-15 points.*

One variant problem uses the Phobias rules, but isn't so specific:

Squeamish*: You have a strong dislike of "yucky stuff": little
bugs and crawly things, blood and dead bodies, slime, etc. You
don't suffer from simple fears of insects, reptiles, dirt, or the dead,
because huge bugs or reptiles, ordinary dirt, and ghosts don't
especially bother you; it's nasty creepy things, filth, and bits of
grue that make you jump back. *-10 points.*

PHYSICAL PROBLEMS

Variable

You have a serious physical disability or permanent injury.
Unless noted otherwise, assume that where the problem is obvi-
ous, any effects on others' reactions are factored into your
Appearance rating.

Examples:

Bad Grip: Each level of this
trait (maximum three levels)
gives -2 to skill or DX rolls for
melee weapons, climbing,
catching things, and anything
else the GM decides is appropriate. *-5 points/level.*

Bad Sight: You have poor
vision, which comes in two
varieties. If *Nearsighted*, you
cannot read small writing more
than a foot away, or shop signs,
etc., at more than about 10
yards; have -6 to Vision rolls to
spot items more than a yard
away; are at -2 to skill when
making a melee attack; and
must *double* the actual distance
to your target when calculating
the range modifier for a ranged
attack. If *Farsighted*, you cannot
read text except with great difficulty and triple normal time;
are at -6 to Vision rolls to spot
items within one yard; and
have -3 to DX on any close manual task, including close com-
bat. Either can sometimes be corrected with eyeglasses, which act
as a mitigator (p. 53). *-25 points, or -10 points with mitigator.*

Hard of Hearing: You're at -4 on any Hearing roll, and on any
skill roll where it's important that you understand someone
else. *-10 points.*

Hunchback: You have a spinal deformity that forces you into a
twisted or hunched position, resulting in a noticeable hump or
lump on one or both shoulders. You're about 10% shorter than a
normal being of your ST. Normal clothing and armour will fit
badly, giving you -1 to DX; to avoid this, you must pay an extra
10% for specially made gear. Most people find you disturbing and
react at -1. This penalty is cumulative with regular Appearance
modifiers, and you may have no better than Average looks. Your
appearance is also distinctive, giving you -3 to Disguise and
Shadowing skills, and +3 to others' attempts to identify or follow
you. *-10 points.*

Lame: You're at -3 to use any skill that requires use of your
legs, including all melee weapon and unarmed combat skills (but
not *ranged* combat skills). You *must* reduce your Basic Move to
half your Basic Speed (round down) or less, but you get the
usual -5 points/level for this (see *Basic Move*, p. 28). *-10 points.*

Motion Sickness: You're miserable whenever you're in a moving vehicle such as a stagecoach or ship. You may never learn any
vehicle-operation skill. You must roll vs. HT as soon as you're
aboard a moving vehicle. Failure means you vomit and are at -5
on all DX, IQ, and skill rolls for the rest of the journey. On a success, you're merely miserably queasy and at -2 on DX, IQ, and
skill rolls. Roll daily on long journeys. *-10 points.*

No Legs: Either you've lost both legs or they're completely
paralysed. You're at -6 to use any skill that requires use of your
legs, and you cannot stand, kick, or walk at all. You *must* reduce
your Basic Move to 0, but you get full points for this. A wheelchair
will give you ground Move equal to 1/4 your ST (round down), but
has many problems with manoeuvring and doorways. *-30 points.*

One Arm: You've lost one arm. You get -4 on tasks that are *possible* with one arm but that are usually executed with two (e.g., most Climbing and Wrestling rolls). You have no penalty on tasks that require only one arm. In all cases, the GM's ruling is final. *-20 points.*

One Eye: You have only one eye. You suffer -1 to DX in melee combat (that is, -1 to melee weapon, Shield, and unarmed combat skills) and on any task involving hand-eye coordination. This worsens to -3 on ranged attacks, unless you Aim (p. 175) first, and on rolls to operate vehicles at high speeds in tricky situations. *-15 points.*

One Hand: You have only one hand. For the most part, use the rules for One Arm. The difference is that you may make unarmed parries with a handless arm, and possibly strap something to it (e.g., a shield). You can also have a hook or claw fitted, which counts as an undroppable large knife in combat and gives +1 to Intimidation skill if waved at your foes. *-15 points.*

One Leg: You've lost one leg, giving you -6 to any skill that requires use of your legs. Using crutches or a peg leg, you can stand up and walk slowly. You *must* reduce your Basic Move to 2 or less, but you get full points for this. You can still kick, but between the standard -2 for a kick and -6 for this disadvantage, you do so at -8! Without your crutches or peg leg, you cannot stand, walk, or kick at all. *-20 points.*

Poor Impulse Control*

Variable

You have incomplete control over some unfortunate psychological tendency. When exposed to an appropriate stimulus, you must make a self-control roll or do something *unwise*. The GM may penalise this roll for unusually strong temptations. Even if you don't give in, you should roleplay your struggle! Those who witness your behaviour will often react poorly: -1 to reaction rolls per full -5 points of disadvantage value.

Bad Temper: Roll in any stressful situation. Failure means you must insult, attack, or otherwise act against the cause of the stress. *-10 points.*

Bloodlust: An enemy is always an enemy, and should *die!* Roll whenever you must accept a surrender, evade a sentry, take a prisoner, etc. Failure means you attempt to kill your foe instead. (You don't get carried away in bar-room brawls though, unless knives or swords come out.) This isn't especially heroic, but it may pass as "excess enthusiasm" in, say, a wartime army. Among watchmen or Guild thieves, though – or even Guild Assassins – it'll soon get you thrown out, or dead. *-10 points.*

Bully: Roll whenever you have a chance to degrade another person – physically, mentally, or socially – to make yourself look "better." Failure means you do that . . . and usually make yourself look worse. *-10 points.*

Cowardice: Roll whenever you're called on to risk physical danger (at -5 if you face *death*). Failure means you refuse to endanger yourself (unless threatened with *greater* danger), and perhaps even flee! You also suffer a penalty to Fright Checks whenever physical danger is involved: -1 for a self-control number of 15, -2 for 12, -3 for 9, and -4 for 6. *-10 points.*

Curious: Roll whenever you're presented with an interesting item or situation. Failure means you try the interesting-looking mushrooms, pull the big creaky lever, ask impertinent questions, etc. *-5 points.*

Gluttony: Roll whenever food or drink is present, or any time you have the chance to acquire provisions. Failure means you partake when you shouldn't, burden yourself with extra rations, etc. *-5 points.*

Greed: Roll whenever wealth is offered (at -5 for large sums). Failure means you do whatever it takes to get the payoff – even if that means crime. *Dwarfish Greed* is a minor variant of Greed with the same value; it involves a peculiar obsession with *gold*, and to a lesser extent silver, so that an offer of coins or nuggets gets the same response as offers of much higher value in other forms. Sufferers from Dwarfish Greed are also quite unwilling to spend or let go of gold, although they may not be especially miserly in other ways (unless they also have Miserliness). Dwarfs don't react badly to Dwarfish Greed, considering it natural. *-15 points.*

Impulsiveness: Roll whenever debate and planning threaten to hold up action, and any time you should stop to think about what you're doing. Failure means you act immediately! *-10 points.*

Lecherousness: Roll whenever you have contact with an appealing member of the sex you find attractive (-5 if this person is Handsome/Beautiful, -10 if Very Handsome/Very Beautiful). Failure means you make a pass. *-15 points.*

Sadism: Roll whenever you have an opportunity to engage in physical or mental cruelty for its own sake. Failure means you behave in an *evil* way. The GM may wish to disallow this trait for PCs, who are normally *supposed* to be the heroes. *-15 points.*

Post-Combat Shakes*

-5 points

You're shaken and sickened by combat, but only after it's over. Make a self-control roll at the end of any fight. It's up to the GM to determine when combat has truly ended, and he may apply a penalty if it was particularly dangerous or gruesome. If you fail, roll 3d, add the amount by which you failed your self-control roll, and look up the result on the *Fright Check Table* (pp. 170-171). For instance, if your self-control number is 12 but you rolled a 14, roll 3d+2 on the table. This result affects you immediately!

Pyromania*

-5 points

You like fires! You like to set fires, too; make a self-control roll whenever you have the opportunity. For good roleplaying, you should never miss a chance to employ fire, or to appreciate one you encounter.

SECRET

Variable

You have a secret that you *really* don't want revealed. The GM sets the point value, which can range from -5 points (exposure would be terribly embarrassing) to -30 points (run for your life or you're *dead*). The GM also decides when your Secret is threatened; if in doubt, a roll of 6 or less on 3d at the start of a game session is reason enough. You should always bear this problem in mind, though – just in case. If for whatever reason your Secret *is* revealed, the GM will replace it with new, permanent disadvantages equal to *twice* its value.

Secret Identity: A "double life" is one interesting type of Secret. Such a Secret is worth an extra -10 points if you have Status 3+, because you are watched more closely – the problem comes up on a roll of 7 or less, not 6 or less – and have more to lose.

SENSE OF DUTY

-2 to -20 points

You feel a strong commitment toward a particular class of people. You'll never betray them, abandon them when they're in trouble, or let them suffer or go hungry if you can help it. This isn't the same as an externally imposed Duty (pp. 59-60); it comes from within. Point value depends on how large a group you look out for:

Individual (e.g., the king, your little brother): *-2 points.*
Small Group (e.g., your close friends, your watch squad): *-5 points.*
Large Group (e.g., a nation, a religion, everyone you know personally): *-10 points.*
Entire Race (e.g., all humanity): *-15 points.*
Every Living Being: -20 points.

SHORT ATTENTION SPAN*

-10 points

You find it difficult to concentrate on a single task for longer than a few minutes. Make a self-control roll whenever you must maintain interest in something for an extended period of time, or whenever a distraction is offered. If you fail, you automatically fail at the task at hand. The GM might give you a small bonus to the self-control roll in situations where, say, your survival is at stake.

SHYNESS

-5, -10, or -20 points

You're uncomfortable around strangers. Roleplay it! This disadvantage comes in three levels:

Mild: You have -1 on skills that require you to deal with people: Acting, Carousing, Diplomacy, Fast-Talk, Intimidation, Leadership, Merchant, Panhandling, Politics, Public Speaking, Savoir-Faire, Sex Appeal, Streetwise, and Teaching. *-5 points.*
Severe: You tend to be quiet even among friends, and you have -2 to the above skills. *-10 points.*
Crippling: You may not learn the listed skills *at all,* and you have -4 on default rolls for them. *-20 points.*

UNLUCKINESS

-10 points

Things go badly for you – persistently. Once per play session, the GM will arbitrarily and maliciously make something go wrong for you: you miss a vital dice roll, the enemy shows up at the worst possible time, etc. If the adventure's plot calls for something bad to happen to someone, it's *you.* The GM may *not* kill you outright with "bad luck," but anything less is fine.

UNSOCIABLE FLAWS

Variable

These problems make you hard to live with. Roleplay them!

No Sense of Humour: You never get jokes, think everyone is earnestly serious at all times, and never joke yourself. Others react to you at -2 when they notice. *-10 points.*
Selfish*: You're self-important and status-conscious, spending much of your time striving for social dominance. Make a self-control roll whenever you experience a social slight or snub. Failure means you lash out at the offending party as if you had Bad Temper (p. 64), giving -3 to the target's reactions toward you. Selfish *NPCs* react to perceived slights at -2 if their self-control number is 15, -3 if it's 12, -4 if it's 9, or -5 if it's 6. *-5 points.*
Stubbornness: You always want your own way. Your friends have to make a lot of Fast-Talk rolls to get you to go along with reasonable plans. Others react to you at -1 when they notice. *-5 points.*

VIRTUOUS FLAWS*

Variable

A few traits often regarded as virtues are considered *disadvantages* because they severely limit your options:

Charitable: You are acutely aware of others' emotions and feel compelled to help those around you – even legitimate enemies. Make a self-control roll in any situation where you could render aid or are specifically asked for help, but should resist the urge. If you fail, you must offer assistance, even if that means violating orders or walking into a potential trap. *-15 points.*

The sight of a waterfall or a soaring bird would send him spinning down some new path of practical speculation that invariably ended in a heap of wire and springs and a cry of "I think I know what I did wrong."

– Jingo

Honesty: You *must* obey the law and do your best to get others to do so, too. In areas with little or no law, you don't "go wild" – you act as though the laws of your own home were in force. You also assume that others are honest unless you *know* otherwise. Make a self-control roll when faced with unreasonable laws; if you fail, you *must* obey them, whatever the consequences. If you resist your urges and break the law, make a second self-control roll afterwards. Failure means you must turn yourself in to the authorities! *-10 points.*

Selfless: You're deeply altruistic and self-sacrificing. You must make a self-control roll to put your needs – even survival – before those of someone else. *-5 points.*

Truthfulness: You hate to tell a lie, or are just very bad at it. Make a self-control roll whenever you must keep silent about an uncomfortable truth (lying by omission); this is at -5 if you actually have to *tell* a falsehood! Failure means you blurt out the truth, or stumble so much that your lie is obvious. You have a permanent -5 to Fast-Talk skill, and your Acting skill is at -5 when your purpose is to deceive. *-5 points.*

Vow

-5 to -15 points

You've *seriously* sworn to do (or *not* do) something. Point value depends on the inconvenience this causes; the GM is the final judge. Examples:

Minor Vow: Silence during daylight hours; vegetarianism; chastity (yes, for game purposes, this is *minor*). *-5 points.*

Major Vow: Use no edged weapons; keep silence at all times; own no more than you can carry with you. *-10 points.*

Great Vow: Never refuse any request for aid; always fight with the wrong hand; hunt a certain dangerous foe until you destroy him. *-15 points.*

Quirks

A "quirk" is a minor personal trait. Neither an advantage nor necessarily a disadvantage, it's just something specific about you. For instance, Compulsive Carousing is a disadvantage; you're forever getting sidetracked by offers of a good time, and you annoy quiet companions by trying to involve them. But if you merely have a taste for Quirmian wine, have difficulty turning down the offer of a bottle, and can be a little boring about vintages, that's a quirk.

You may take up to five quirks at -1 point apiece . . . giving you five more points to spend. You can also "buy off" a quirk later by *paying* a point – although you shouldn't, as a rule. Quirks might have a small cost, but they're a big part of what makes a character seem "real"!

Mental Quirks

These are minor personality traits. You *must* roleplay them. If you choose "Dislikes heights," but blithely climb trees and cliffs whenever you need to, the GM will penalise you for bad roleplaying.

To qualify as a mental quirk, a personality trait must meet one of two criteria:

- It requires a specific action, behaviour, or choice on your part on occasion.
- It gives you a *small* penalty very occasionally, or to a narrow set of actions.

Be creative – the quirks below are merely examples!

Attentive

You stick to one task until it's done. You get +1 when working on lengthy tasks – but -3 to notice any important interruption!

Autocondimentor

Whenever you sit down to eat, you immediately add salt, pepper, and probably any available sauces to your food, without even tasting it first. This makes you easier to drug or poison if you aren't careful, and it causes serious chefs and cooks to react to you at -3 or worse, possibly with violence.

Broad-Minded

You get along well with other races and species, and strange looks rarely bother you.

CAREFUL

This is quirk-level Cowardice (p. 64) – you're naturally cautious, always on the lookout for danger. You spend extra time and money on preparations before venturing into danger.

CHAUVINISTIC

This extremely low-level Intolerance (p. 60) means you're always *aware* of differences in sex, skin colour, etc. even if you don't actually react poorly to others. Thin-skinned individuals might occasionally react to you at -1.

CODE OF HONOUR

You may take a minor Code of Honour (pp. 56-57) as a quirk. For instance, you might insist on exhibiting "gentlemanly" behaviour toward all women, or spurning "chauvinistic" behaviour.

CONGENIAL

This milder version of Chummy (p. 56) means you like company and work well with others. You always choose group action over individual action.

DELUSIONS

A completely trivial Delusion (p. 59) makes a good quirk. This doesn't affect your everyday behaviour, and casual acquaintances are unlikely to notice it – but you truly believe it! *Examples:* "The world is a sphere." "The Temple of Offler controls all the restaurants in Ankh-Morpork." "Socks cause diseases of the feet."

DISLIKES

You can have any Phobia (pp. 62-63) at the level of a mere "dislike." If you dislike something, you must avoid it whenever possible, but it doesn't actually harm you as a Phobia would. Dislikes don't *have* to be watered-down Phobias. There's a whole Disc full of things to dislike: carrots, cats, fancy travelling cloaks, violence, the clacks, taxes . . .

DISTRACTIBLE

This is quirk-level Short Attention Span (p. 65). You are easily distracted and don't do well on long-term projects. You're at -1 when rolling to accomplish long tasks.

DREAMER

You have -1 on any long task, because you tend to spend time thinking of better ways to do it, rather than working.

DULL

While not quite Hidebound (p. 61), you tend to stick with tried-and-true methods.

FORMER ALCOHOLIC

You used to have Alcoholism (pp. 54-55), but have shed the addiction so successfully that you *don't* have to roll to resist booze

if it's offered – you really have learned to handle things. However, being teetotal is sometimes socially inconvenient, and you may get slightly twitchy or terse in the presence of drink.

GIGGLES A LOT

This is a trifling Odious Personal Habit (p. 29) which is slightly annoying for other people, especially in high-stress moments, and may get -1 or worse reactions from very serious individuals.

HABITS OR EXPRESSIONS

Saying "By Mighty Zephyrus!" or "Bless my cloak-pin" constantly, say, or carrying a silver coin that you habitually flip into the air.

HUMBLE

A weak form of Selfless (p. 66) – you tend to put the concerns of others, or of the group, before your own.

IMAGINATIVE

You're a font of ideas and are more than willing to share them with others. They may or may not be *good* ideas.

LIKES

You like something, seeking it out whenever possible. Gadgets, kittens, shiny knives, fine art . . . whatever. This isn't a compulsion – just a preference.

NOSY

This lesser version of Curious (p. 64) means you're always poking your nose into corners and everyone else's business.

OBSESSIONS

An almost-rational, not especially unusual Obsession (p. 62) can be a quirk. For instance, you may hope to get just enough money to buy a farm (or a ship, or a castle) of your own.

PERSONALITY CHANGE

You suffer from a full-blown mental disadvantage, but only in circumstances that are normally under your control – Bully when you drink too much, say, or Pyromania when you work with fire magic.

Example: Jemzarkiza of Krull – Quirks

To add some colour (and save points), Anne opts to give Jemzarkiza a few quirks. First, there's that academic focus. Anne decides that Jemzarkiza learned a bit about turtles and other aquatic reptiles in her studies, but that she found the small versions *much* more interesting than Great A'Tuin – making her extremely un-cool by Krullian standards. So she gets a quirk-level Obsession: "Small aquatic reptiles fan." (One symptom of this will be that Jemzarkiza usually has a pet turtle in her luggage.)

Second, Anne thinks that Jemzarkiza will be *seriously* unhappy about her unwanted image as some kind of cool and mysterious foreign enchantress, which she'll take as a sign that non-Krullians are almost as stupid as the people of Krull assume. This will be something to roleplay; Jemzarkiza may have trouble getting on with others, at least until they get to know her. Anne notes this as "Annoyed by crass foreign assumptions," and tells the GM that Jemzarkiza will end up drinking in Biers (p. 266) a lot of the time, just to get some peace. The fact that she was able to find that place, and that the other patrons tolerate her, is ironic – *everyone* seems to see her as not quite *normal*.

Finally, Jemzarkiza *is* an academic at heart, and Anne reckons that she needs more reasons to interact with other PCs – she's in danger of being *too* surly and standoffish, which could be boring to play. Thus, Jemzarkiza's third quirk is "Loves intellectual argument – gets voluble."

That's another -3 points to Jemzarkiza's total; she's down to 180 points.

Proud

This is quirk-level Selfish (p. 65). Individual success, wealth, or social standing concerns you greatly. Proud NPCs react at -1 to orders, insults, or social slights.

Responsive

A mild case of Charitable (p. 65) – all other things being equal, you're inclined to help others.

Staid

With this very low level of Incurious (p. 61), you're likely to ignore matters that don't immediately affect you.

Terrifying Singer

Prerequisites: HT 12+ *and* no Singing skill.

You like singing, despite a complete lack of ability, and your singing voice is loud and penetrating enough to wake the neighbourhood and frighten animals.

Uncongenial

You prefer to be alone, and you always choose individual action over group action if you have a choice.

Vow

A trivial Vow (p. 66) – e.g., never drink alcohol, treat all elders with courtesy, or pay 10% of your income to your temple – is a quirk.

Physical/Social Quirks

These are physical or practical disadvantages that are only mildly or rarely limiting. They don't require roleplaying, but give specific, minor penalties in play. Again, these examples only begin to describe what's possible.

Alcohol Intolerance

Alcohol "goes right to your head." You become intoxicated much more quickly than normal. You get -2 on any HT roll related to drinking.

Bowlegged

You're bowlegged. This doesn't normally affect Move, but you have -1 to Jumping skill. This quirk may elicit a -1 reaction from those who think it looks funny.

Distinctive Features

You have a physical feature – e.g., "Brilliant blue hair" – that makes you stand out in a crowd. This gives -1 to your Disguise and Shadowing skills, and +1 to others' attempts to identify or follow you. Compare Unnatural Features (p. 30) and Supernatural Features (p. 97).

Horrible Hangovers

You suffer an additional -3 to any penalties the GM assesses for excessive drinking the previous evening, and you add three hours to hangover duration.

Minor Handicap

You may take most mundane physical disadvantages at quirk level. For instance, you could use a watered-down version of Lame for a "creaky knee." Difficulties rarely crop up, but are inconvenient when they do. The GM may give you -1 to attribute, skill, or reaction rolls, as appropriate, in situations where the handicap would logically interfere.

Nervous Stomach

You have -3 to HT rolls to avoid illness (typically in the form of attribute penalties or vomiting) brought on by rich or spicy food, strong drink, etc.

No Staff

Prerequisite: Magic (Wizardry) skill (p. 76).

You haven't yet acquired a wizard's staff, so you lack the extra power that grants. You must buy off this quirk if you receive a staff (upon graduation, from a mentor, etc.).

Skills

A "skill" is a particular kind of knowledge; for instance, boxing, philosophy, or blacksmithing. Every skill is separate, though some skills help you to learn others. Just as in real life, you start your career with some skills and can learn more later.

A number called "skill level" measures your ability with each of your skills: the higher the number, the better. For instance, "Shortsword-17" means a skill level of 17 with the shortsword. See *Rolling the Dice* (pp. 165-167) for how this is used.

CONTROLLING ATTRIBUTE

Each skill is based on one of DX, IQ, HT, Per, or Will:

- *DX-based* skills rely on coordination, reflexes, and steady hands.
- *IQ-based* skills require knowledge, creativity, and reasoning ability.
- *HT-based* skills are governed by physical fitness.
- *Per-based* skills involve spotting subtle differences.
- *Will-based* skills hinge on mental focus and clarity.

Your skill level is calculated directly from this "controlling attribute": the higher your attribute score, the more effective you are with *every* skill based on it! If your character concept calls for *many* skills based on a given attribute, consider starting with a high level in that attribute – it will prove cost-effective.

DIFFICULTY LEVEL

Some fields demand more study and practise than others. Four "difficulty levels" rate the effort required to learn and improve a skill. The more difficult the skill, the more points you must spend to buy it at a given level:

- *Easy* skills are things that anyone could do reasonably well after a short learning period.
- *Average* skills include most combat skills, mundane job skills, and the practical social and survival skills that ordinary people use daily.
- *Hard* skills require intensive study or training.
- *Very Hard* skills require intensive formal study of a huge body of knowledge, and they probably need to be got just right.

TECHNOLOGICAL SKILLS

Certain skills are different at each tech level (see *Technology Level*, pp. 30-31). These are designated by "/TL." When you learn such a skill, you must learn it at a specific tech level (TL). Always note the TL when you write down such a skill. Navigation/TL0 (look at the stars and consider your instincts about your surroundings) isn't much like Navigation/TL4 (employ a fancy astrolabe and lots of charts).

You learn most technological skills at your personal TL. You may also choose skills from a *lower* TL. You can only learn skills from a *higher* TL in play – and only if you have a teacher *and* the skill isn't based on IQ. To learn IQ-based technological skills from a higher TL, you must first raise your personal TL. See *Cutting-Edge Training* (p. 51) for one exception.

Buying Skills

To learn or improve a skill, you must spend character points. Points spent on a skill imply training in that field. Skills are easy to learn at first – a little training goes a long way! But added improvement costs more.

A skill's point cost depends on two things: its difficulty and the final skill level you wish to attain. Use the *Skill Cost Table* (p. 70) to calculate this cost.

The first column shows the skill level you're trying to attain, *relative to the skill's controlling attribute* – DX for DX-based skills, IQ for IQ-based skills, and so forth. For instance, if your DX were 12, a level of "Attribute-1" would be DX-1, or 11; "Attribute+0" would be DX, or 12; and "Attribute+1" would be DX+1, or 13.

The next four columns show the point costs to learn skills of different difficulties – *Easy*, *Average*, *Hard*, and *Very Hard* – at the desired skill level. Harder skills cost more to learn! A dash ("–") means you *can't* have the skill at such a low level; if you haven't spent at least a point, use your default (p. 70).

Using a Skill With a Different Attribute

If the GM doesn't mind complicating things, skills can sometimes be used based on a different attribute from usual: Take the skill level relative to the controlling attribute and apply it to the alternative attribute instead. Relevant Talents add to skills, whatever attribute is used!

Example 1: Artist is IQ-based – artistic work depends primarily on creativity and thoughtfulness. However, Triana the Artist needs to produce a simple sketch quickly, to show the watchmen what the stranger who just tried to assassinate the duke looks like. Never mind originality or flair; this is a matter of deftness. Triana has DX 11, IQ 14, and Artist-16 (IQ+2). Her roll to produce this sketch is against DX+2; that is, 13.

Example 2: Broadsword is DX-based but includes a little practical knowledge of weapons. Lionel the Guard has just met someone who looks like a street thug, but who's really a spy in disguise. The spy is carrying his expensive, high-quality sword, and the GM has decided that Lionel has a chance to notice this – a task that surely uses Per. Lionel has DX 13, Per 10, and Broadsword-13 (DX+0). The GM rolls Lionel's chance to spot the nice blade against Per+0; that is, 10.

SKILL COST TABLE

Your Final Skill Level	— Difficulty of Skill —			
	Easy	Average	Hard	Very Hard
Attribute-3	–	–	–	1
Attribute-2	–	–	1	2
Attribute-1	–	1	2	4
Attribute+0	1	2	4	8
Attribute+1	2	4	8	12
Attribute+2	4	8	12	16
Attribute+3	8	12	16	20
Extra +1	+4	+4	+4	+4

APPROPRIATE LEVELS

The final skill level you buy is up to you (and your budget). As a guideline, assume that anything below 10 indicates someone who's still learning, or a very casual hobby; most normal jobs require level 12+ in the relevant skill (you succeed more often than not at routine tasks); level 15+ indicates serious expertise, sometimes demanded in well-paid jobs where skill use is a matter of life and death (assuming that the *recruiter* knows what he's doing); and level 20+ may be unique on the Disc, or at least the mark of a true genius.

Defaults (Skills You Don't Know)

Most skills have a "default level": the level at which you use the skill if you have *no* training. A skill has a default level if it's something that everybody can do . . . a little bit. Anyone can *try* to climb a tree, make a speech, or even jiggle a lock open with a small tool. But some skills have *no* default. For instance, Karate is complex enough that you cannot use it *at all* without training.

THE RULE OF 20

Treat any attribute score that's greater than 20 as though it were 20 when figuring defaults involving it. Superhuman characters get *good* defaults, but not *super* ones.

WHO GETS A DEFAULT?

Only individuals from a society where a skill is known may attempt a default roll against that skill. For instance, the default for Boating skill assumes you've at least seen a boat before and have some idea – if only from stories – of how one is operated. Someone born and raised in the depths of the Klatchian jungle would be less than no use whatsoever if he suddenly found himself dropped onto a small sailing boat.

Skill List

This list is sorted alphabetically by skill name. Each entry gives the following information:

Name: The skill's name. Technological skills are noted as such; e.g., "Mechanic/TL."

Type: The skill's controlling attribute and difficulty level; e.g., "IQ/A." **E** stands for Easy, **A** for Average, **H** for Hard, and **VH** for Very Hard.

Default: Your level with the skill if you haven't studied it, given as an attribute with a penalty. "None" means *no* default – you *cannot* attempt to use the skill without training.

Description: An explanation of what the skill is for and how it works in play.

Many skills require the player to pick a particular *specialisation* when he buys them – a category of technology, a geographical area, etc. Characters may buy such skills more than once, for multiple specialisations. Record the chosen speciality in parentheses after the skill name; e.g., "Area Knowledge (Genua)" or "Artillery (Catapult)."

ACADEMIC SKILLS (IQ/H)

Default: IQ-6.

Philosophers, theoretical wizards, and scholars study a whole range of subjects. Some may seem rarefied, even useless – but role-players can be good at finding uses for things. Those available:

Astronomy/TL: The study of the heavens and of how the sun and moon move around the Disc – the foundation of much navigation, astrological wizardry, etc.

Astrozoology: The study of Great A'Tuin and the four elephants which support the Disc is largely highly theoretical, even philosophical, but does derive some data from magic, observations over the edge of the Disc, and studies of smaller turtles and elephants.

History: This needs a specialisation such as a period and a theme ("Ancient Military"), a period and a region ("Modern Klatchian"), or a small nation over its entire history ("Genuan").

Literature: The study of great (nonmagical) writings, poetry, stories, etc., can be useful for picking up hidden written clues or subtle allusions.

Mathematics/TL: This has two specialisations: *Applied* (used by especially sophisticated engineers and a few wizards) and *Pure* (the really abstract stuff, beloved of academics who want to avoid practical work). Most *practical* uses of mathematics require other skills, such as Engineer or Navigation.

Metallurgy/TL: The study of metals serves mainly as the primary skill for intellectual dwarfs, although it's also known to some alchemists.

At which point someone tried to slap Vetinari on the back.

It happened with remarkable speed and ended possibly even faster than it began, with Vetinari still seated in his chair with his beer mug in one hand and the man's wrist gripped tightly at head height.

– Unseen Academicals

Natural Philosophy/TL: "Science" as we know it hasn't really developed on the Disc, and it might never work well, thanks to the influence of narrativium and magic. There aren't separate studies of chemistry, biology, physics, and so on; instead, scholars may learn this skill, which covers all sorts of book-learned ideas about how the physical world works. On a *really* good skill roll, it may even provide useful information.

Philosophy: The study of ideas in general, and of non-religious principles to live by. This requires specialisation by tradition, which usually corresponds to a culture: Philosophy (Sto Plains Schools), Philosophy (Agatean), etc. It can provide insights into the behaviour of followers of an ideology, abstract ideas about how the world works, and (with a secret roll by the GM) hints about the least-worst solutions to moral dilemmas.

ACTING (IQ/A)

Default: IQ-5.

The skill of counterfeiting moods, emotions, and voices, and of lying convincingly over a period of time. Impersonating someone comprehensively requires this *and* Disguise (p. 72).

ADMINISTRATION (IQ/A)

Default: IQ-5.

The skill of running a large organisation, required by government officials, guild leaders, military staff officers, etc. A successful roll gives +2 to reactions when dealing with a bureaucrat and/or tells you how best to deal with a bureaucracy.

ALCHEMY/TL (IQ/VH)

Default: None.

The not-quite-magical skill of manipulating materials and substances. Discworld alchemists don't require Magery, although they sometimes tinker at the edges of magic; see *Alchemists* (p. 290). They possess a wide range of chemically related knowledge, but most spend their time trying unsuccessfully to turn lead into gold and blowing up their workshops.

ANIMAL HANDLING (IQ/A)

Default: IQ-5.

The ability to train and work with a category of animals – choose a specialisation. When working with a trained animal, roll against skill for each task you give it. Smarter animals and herbivores are easier to train; low-intelligence carnivores won't understand what you're trying to get them to do and may well end up taking your arm off, although this skill will tell you to keep your arm out of their way.

On the Disc, Animal Handling often includes odd little secrets bordering on herbalism, alchemy, or even magic, which offer shortcuts to controlling particular animals. In game terms, this means that on a good roll you can achieve results very quickly, although the GM may require cash expenditure, or a roll against Naturalist skill to find ingredients.

Falconry, the skill of hunting small game with a trained hawk, is a variant of Animal Handling.

AREA KNOWLEDGE (IQ/E)

Default: IQ-4.

This represents familiarity with the people, places, and politics of a specific region. Specialise in an area – anything from the whole Disc down to a neighbourhood, even a *large* building. The smaller the area, the more detailed the information you have. With a small neighbourhood or a hamlet, you know the names of every inhabitant, their personal rivalries, and something about every house; with a city or a nation, you're aware of major regions or districts, leaders, important organisations, festival days, etc. Area Knowledge (The Disc) covers significant nations, empires, and geographical features, important trade routes, and individuals who are famous across the whole world. You only have a default for the area you'd consider your "home base."

ARTISTIC SKILLS (VARIES)

Default: Varies.

All manner of skills exist to represent artistic accomplishments. These can earn the user a living, be satisfying hobbies, or impress other people. Only some have defaults. Examples include *Artist* (you must specialise in a medium; IQ/H, defaults to IQ-6), *Conducting* (getting a group of musicians to work together; IQ/A, defaults to IQ-5), *Dancing* (DX/A, defaults to DX-5), *Directing* (taking charge of a group of actors in a play; IQ/A, defaults to IQ-5), *Jeweller/TL* (fine decorative metalwork and work with gemstones; IQ/H, defaults to IQ-6), *Musical Composition* (IQ/H, no default), *Musical Instrument* (you must specialise by instrument; IQ/H, no default), *Performance* (*stage* acting; IQ/A, defaults to IQ-5), *Poetry* (IQ/A, defaults to IQ-5), and *Singing* (HT/E, defaults to HT-4). Roll to produce a competent artwork or performance.

BODY LANGUAGE (PER/A)

Default: None.

The ability to read people's body language to judge emotions or intentions. It works like the Empathy advantage (p. 42) or Detect Lies skill (p. 72), but only on people you can *see* – so baggy clothing gives -1 to the skill, a shield gives -2, and a mask gives -5. It can also help you coordinate with friends without speaking, including in battle, but it doesn't work fast enough to be any help against enemies in combat.

CAMOUFLAGE (IQ/E)

Default: IQ-4.

The ability to use natural materials, special fabrics and paints, etc., to hide yourself, your position, or your equipment.

CAROUSING (HT/E)

Default: HT-4.

The art of socialising, partying, etc. A successful roll, under the right circumstances, gives you +2 on a request for aid or information, or just on a general reaction. Failure means you made a fool of yourself in some way: -2 on any reaction roll made by those you caroused with.

Combat Sports

Some people on the Disc study "combat sports" like boxing under the Marquis of Fantailler rules, or the sort of fencing that involves a gymnasium, a mask, and a padded jacket. These recreations *do* teach skills that are useful in a real fight. Dangerously, however, they fail to cover a lot of dirty tricks.

In game terms, individuals who pursue such activities may learn combat skills to reasonable levels, but they *also* divert time and character points toward a Games skill (p. 73) that covers the sport's rules. In a sporting bout, they must roll at least once per match (more often, at the GM's whim) to remember what is or isn't a legal move. Failure means they risk disqualification, unless the referee misses a Perception roll.

Unfortunately, some such athletes also acquire Overconfidence (p. 62), or a Delusion (p. 59) that they're as good in a real fight as in a sporting bout – or perhaps just a quirk-level tendency to fair play. A character with combat sports training who loses to someone without (perhaps because his opponent put more points into combat skills, not having to invest any in the Games skill) may well have slipped into "sports fighting" style and suffered as a result. This happens to Captain Carrot against Wolf von Uberwald in *The Fifth Elephant*.

COMPUTER PROGRAMMING (IQ/H)

Default: None.

Two classes of "computers" exist on the Disc, neither of them much like computers on other worlds. This skill covers their use. Each category is its own specialisation:

Magical Computers used to be a category with just one member – Hex, at Unseen University (pp. 279-289) – but recently, other teams of wizards have been *trying* to emulate that invention. Anyone who wants to learn this skill needs access to such a device, and will probably only be granted that if he has Magery and several other skills, such as Engineer (Clockwork), Engineer (Magical), and Thaumatology. (The ability to subsist on pizzas is also traditional.) Roll to get the computer to solve tricky problems in magical analysis, work out how to control large flows of magical energy, or balance insanely complex magical operations.

Stone Circles – such as are found on the Vortex Plains and in Llamedos – can be programmed using chants and rituals. Successful use of this skill can get an accurate weather prediction covering the next few days or even weeks, assist astronomical calculations, and enhance the benefits (if any) of religious rituals and sacrifices.

In either case, the skill's precise results and applications are left to the GM. Both types of computers should be genuinely useful to experts, but mostly serve as plot devices.

CONNOISSEUR (IQ/A)

Default: IQ-5.

An *educated* appreciation of art, luxury items, or collectibles. Choose a specialisation; possibilities include Antiques, Music, Painting, Sculpture, Theatre, and Wine. Roll to judge the quality of an example of the form, tell fakes from the genuine article, put a date on things, or recognise the name or work of a famous master. This skill *doesn't* let you create anything, apart from convincing criticism.

CRIMINOLOGY/TL (IQ/A)

Default: IQ-5.

The study of crime and the criminal mind. Roll to find and interpret clues, guess how criminals might behave, etc. In some worlds, this can be an academic study; on the Disc, it's a practical skill for career watchmen, mostly learned by grinding experience.

CRYPTOGRAPHY/TL (IQ/H)

Default: None.

Making and breaking codes and ciphers. These days, whole government departments across the Sto Plains and beyond are engaged in contests of Cryptography.

CURRENT AFFAIRS/TL (IQ/E)

Default: IQ-4.

The skill of absorbing news quickly and efficiently, and hence of being up-to-date on events. Roll to know what's going on, and why! Choose a specialisation: *Business* (trade and exchange rates), *Headline News* (stuff that gets on the front of the papers), *Politics* (what's going on in the corridors of power), *Regional* (everything that's happening in one particular town or city), or *Sports* (which teams, horses, or athletes are winning or losing, and why).

DETECT LIES (PER/H)

Default: Per-6.

The ability to tell when someone is lying to you. This isn't the same as Interrogation (p. 75); Detect Lies works in a casual or social situation. When you ask to use it, the GM rolls a secret Quick Contest: your skill vs. your subject's IQ (or Fast-Talk or Acting skill, if they're better). Victory means the GM tells you whether the subject is lying. Otherwise, the GM may lie to you about whether you were lied to, or just say, "You can't tell."

DISGUISE/TL (IQ/A)

Default: IQ-5.

The art of altering your appearance using clothing, make-up, and prosthetics. A *good* disguise requires a Disguise roll and 30-60 minutes of preparation. Strictly speaking, you should specialise by species, but very few members of any Discworld race can pass as members of any other.

ENGINEER/TL (IQ/H)

Default: None.

The ability to design and build technological devices. You must specialise; common options are Artillery, Civil (roads, aqueducts, etc.), Clacks (designing and constructing signalling towers, including theoretical knowledge of the coding systems they employ), Clockwork, Combat (fortifications), Low-Tech Machines (big assemblies of beams and ropes or cables), Mining, and various types of vehicle. Roll to design a new system, diagnose a glitch, identify the purpose of a strange device, or improvise a solution to a problem.

A further special version is *Engineer (Magical)*, the skill required to combine magical forces or miniature demons with material objects, and get the combination to do something useful. At TL1, it's used to create and maintain flying broomsticks. It really comes into its own at TL4, though, when it's exploited to create imp-infested cameras and watches, magical computers, and so on. Anyone can learn this skill, but applying it to new purposes usually requires either magical ability or Alchemy skill.

ESCAPE (DX/H)

Default: DX-6.

The ability to slip out of ropes, handcuffs, etc. If you've been tied up, roll a Quick Contest vs. your captor's Knot-Tying skill. Against chains, manacles, etc., make an uncontested Escape roll, modified for restraint quality. Well-made hardware gives a penalty – but underfunded watch departments often skimp on the handcuff budget, and old-school dark lords use over-ornate restraints that cunning prisoners can slip with ease. The first escape attempt takes one minute; each subsequent attempt takes 10 minutes.

> *"Thunder Clay is terribly powerful stuff," said Ridcully. "But it needs a special detonator. You have to smash a jar of acid inside the mixture. The acid soaks into it, and then – kablooie, I believe the term is."*
> *– The Last Hero*

EXPLOSIVES/TL (IQ/A)

Default: IQ-5.

The skill of working with explosives and incendiaries – rare on the Disc, but not unknown. Alchemists using TL4 knowledge have concocted various substances akin to gunpowder (indeed, *stopping* alchemists from inventing explosives can be the real problem), and some worrying character in the Agatean Empire has created "Thunder Clay," a TL5 explosive. You must specialise in either *Demolition* (setting explosives for seriously destroying stuff) or *Fireworks* (manufacturing low-powered explosive devices that produce pretty colours, gratifying amounts of smoke, or loud bangs).

FAST-DRAW (DX/E)

Default: None.

Drawing a weapon from a sheath, belt, etc., normally requires a one-second Ready manoeuvre. A successful Fast-Draw roll at the start of your turn means the weapon is ready instantly, and you can do something else. An ordinary failure means you spend the whole turn drawing it after all; on a critical failure, you drop it. You must specialise by weapon type: *Arrow/Bolt* (to reduce reload times for bows or crossbows), *Knife, Knuckledusters, Pistol Crossbow, Sword, Throwing Star,* or *Two-Handed Sword.*

FISHING (PER/E)

Default: Per-4.

The ability to catch fish with a net, hook and line, or whatever you're used to.

FORTUNE-TELLING (IQ/A)

Default: IQ-5.

The non-supernatural art of subtly interviewing someone in order to learn more about him, and then making educated guesses that you can pass off as supernatural divination. It requires specialisation in one method of divination, for use as a prop – but as some of these *work* on the Disc, certain versions of Fortune-Telling can sometimes also be used for somewhat valid predictions, even by people without magical ability. Many witches and a few shrewd consultant wizards learn this skill; it's often safer than messing about with real magic, and frankly, people tend to be happier with a bit of well-judged waffle than with real knowledge of their future.

Specialisations include Astrology, Caroc Cards (similar to our world's tarot), Ching Aling (a Hublander method resembling our I Ching), Crystal Ball, Cuisinomancy (much like reading tea leaves, but using a good stew), Palmistry, and Tea-Leaf Reading.

GAME/SPORT SKILLS (VARIES)

Default: Varies.

These skills relate to various sorts of competition. Some such events use other skills (a wrestling bout calls for Wrestling, while traditional Ankh-Morpork football is mostly about Brawling and Intimidation), but otherwise, in a game where skill genuinely affects the outcome – if only in the sense of recognising that the odds are good or bad – roll a Quick Contest between opponents' skills. If the match is important and the game is moderately complex, the GM may call for *several* Quick Contests and narrate the back-and-forth of play.

Gambling (IQ/A): Skill at playing games of *chance*. A successful roll can (among other things) tell you if a game is rigged, identify a fellow gambler in a group of strangers, or "estimate the odds" in *any* tricky situation. You can't *change* the odds without cheating, though. Defaults to IQ-5.

Games (IQ/E): Knowledge of and ability to play games of *skill.* You must specialise by game: Aqueduct (p. 19), Chess, Craps (much as on our world, but played with *eight*-sided dice), Cripple Mr. Onion (p. 19), Shibo Yangcong-san (popular in the Agatean Empire), Thud (an ancient game among both dwarfs and trolls, sometimes called *Hnaflbaflsniflwhifltafl*), etc. Apart from other uses, a successful roll can tell you what the rules say about a given situation. You can also take Games specialisations that represent knowledge of the rules of some sport or physical contest; e.g., boxing, or football under the new Ankh-Morpork rules. Referees require this, while players *should* spend points to avoid accidental disqualification. Defaults to IQ-4 for games generally known in your culture.

Sports (DX/A): Any physical sport which can't be represented by other skills. Modern Ankh-Morpork Football is one specialisation; others include Darts and Aargrooha (a troll version of football, played with obsidian boots and a human head, and so *of course* never played by any troll you'll meet these days). Defaults to DX-5.

Magical Cheating

Characters with occult precognitive or fate-warping abilities can sometimes use them to improve their chances in games of luck or skill. Make whatever roll you need to operate the ability – use IQ for one that doesn't normally involve a roll – and add your margin of success to your Gambling, Games, or Sports skill. This never *guarantees* victory, though.

HEAVY WEAPON SKILLS (VARIES)

Default: Varies.

Operating big, essentially non-portable long-range weapons. These are skills for career soldiers, especially those who'd prefer not to get mixed up in messy personal combat too often. (Mind you, accidents with heavy weapons can get *very* messy, if amusing for people who are a safe distance away.) They can also be a comfort to heroes when some really *huge* monster shows up. There are two types:

Artillery/TL (IQ/A): "Indirect-fire" weapons – trebuchets, big guns, etc. which you don't simply point at a target, but which lob massive projectiles in high arcs. Defaults to IQ-5.

Gunner/TL (DX/E): Weapons fired at targets to which you have line of sight. Despite the name, this skill also applies to pre-gunpowder devices such as ballistas. Defaults to DX-4.

Each skill further requires specialisation by weapon type – either *Cannon* (for big gunpowder weapons, only widely known in the Agatean Empire) or *Catapult* (for older-style mechanical "engines").

HOBBY SKILLS (DX/E OR IQ/E)

Default: DX-4 or IQ-4, as appropriate.

You can study all sorts of "useless" interests – juggling, stamp collecting, kite flying, pin collecting, needlepoint, origami, and so on. Clever PCs may find uses for these, and they can certainly pass as "accomplishments" for high-Status characters with too much time on their hands. The GM decides whether a Hobby Skill is DX-based or IQ-based.

HOUSEKEEPING (IQ/E)

Default: IQ-4.

Managing a household. This covers both home economics and domestic chores: cleaning, plain home cooking, minor repairs, etc. As well as keeping a dwelling-place vaguely civilised, House-keeping can come in handy on adventures – for instance, to clean up evidence.

IMPROVISED COMMUNICATION SKILLS (IQ/E)

Default: Varies.

Use these skills to communicate with people with whom you don't share a language. Roll to convey about a sentence's worth of *simple* ideas, taking 20 seconds per attempt. Critical success transmits a clear idea of your *intentions.* Any failure may annoy or amuse the target – if he's an NPC, make an immediate reaction roll at -3 (-6 for a critical failure).

Gesture: Communicating through improvised hand signals or other movements. Roll against the skill of the person gesturing or his target, whichever is *higher.* Defaults to IQ-4.

Shouting at Foreigners: Communicating by speaking loudly, slowly, and clearly in your own language, maybe with some half-remembered foreign words. (Yes, on the Disc, this sometimes works.) Cannot be used to understand what others are trying to say! Language Talent gives +1 to this skill. Cultural Familiarity penalties do *not* apply. Defaults to IQ-4 or HT-5.

INFLUENCE SKILLS (VARIES)

Default: Varies.

Several distinct skills exist for influencing others in various ways. When you use such an Influence skill in an appropriate encounter, see *Influence Rolls* (pp. 172-173) for rules and treat all reaction modifiers that apply in the situation as skill modifiers, regardless of whether they're noted as modifying that skill. Influence skills have *other* uses, too – but for those, reaction modifiers add only where specifically noted. For example, Attractive appearance (+1 reactions) and Reputation -2 would give a net -1 to use Savoir-Faire (High Society) to mingle at a posh party, but *not* to a Savoir-Faire roll made to plan seating arrangements for a dinner.

Diplomacy (IQ/H): Negotiation and compromise. Also serves as a professional skill for all sorts of negotiators. Diplomacy at level 20+ gives you +2 on all reaction rolls! Defaults to IQ-6.

Fast-Talk (IQ/A): Lying and deceit – including befuddling people for just long enough to get away from or past them through sheer speed and confusion (this use often requires a Quick Contest versus IQ). The GM may assess a bonus or a penalty if you suggest an especially clever or feeble story. Fast-Talk at level 20+ gives you +2 on all reaction rolls when you're able to speak! Defaults to IQ-5.

Intimidation (Will/A): Threats and the implication of violence. This takes modifiers for whether you're in a superior or inferior position, armed or not, displaying strength, power, or bloodthirstiness, and so on. Defaults to Will-5.

Savoir-Faire (IQ/E): Manners and etiquette, and practise in using them. *Savoir-Faire (High Society)* is useful among the aristocracy, while other specialisations apply to the military, organised crime, etc. (although *Savoir-Faire (Organised Crime)* is a defunct skill in Ankh-Morpork, where thieves and assassins are out of the closet and don't need fancy rules about kissed cheeks and hidden tattoos). *Savoir-Faire (Servant)* is the skill of knowing how to lay tables right, serve trays of drinks smoothly while barely being noticed, and so on. In all cases, roll at +2 if you have higher standing in the social group than the people you're trying to impress, or -2 if you're of lower standing ("standing" is Status in high society, Rank in many other situations). You also get +2 if you seem to have important friends. All versions default to IQ-4.

Sex Appeal (HT/A): Vamping and seduction, usually of the opposite sex (but we don't judge). Often handy for stage performers and suchlike, too. In all applications – not just when used as an Influence skill – add the standard bonus for above-average Appearance (pp. 28-29) or *double* the penalty for below-average looks. Defaults to HT-3.

Streetwise (IQ/A): Making contacts and (usually) subtle intimidation. Only useful in "street" and criminal situations, but often a matter of life and death there. Also used to find where the action is, know how to slip a bribe to the right sort of person, and so on. Being an obvious stranger can earn serious penalties – the underworld is a suspicious place – while a "tough" Reputation, even if negative in itself, can get you a bonus (all at the GM's option). Defaults to IQ-5.

INTERROGATION (IQ/A)

Default: IQ-5.

The ability to get information out of someone by asking leading or forceful questions, whether in a prison cell or an interview. It need not involve brute force – smart interrogators know that torture is often counterproductive – but the concept of "human rights" isn't exactly advanced on the Discworld, so most interrogators know how to twist an arm or throw a bucket of cold water to make a point. Brutality *can* give skill bonuses, and can also earn deadly enemies and lose useful prisoners. Taking a lot of extra time is another way to get a bonus. Such measures are useful against fanatical subjects, who give skill penalties.

Roll a Quick Contest vs. the subject's Will for each question. This requires 5 minutes per question. Victory extracts a truthful answer. If you tie or lose, the victim remains silent or lies. Loss by more than five points means he tells you a *good, believable* lie!

KNOT-TYING (DX/E)

Default: DX-4.

The ability to tie a variety of knots quickly and efficiently. A successful skill roll lets you make a noose, tie someone up, etc.

High Manual Dexterity (p. 43) gives +1 per level; Ham-Fisted (p. 60) gives -3.

KNOWLEDGE SKILLS (IQ/A)

Default: Varies.

These skills represent large bodies of knowledge. They involve little theory or analysis, mostly just a lot of facts.

Heraldry: Knowledge of coats of arms, flags, etc. Roll to recognise a crest or badge, analyse the significance of a design, or create appropriate symbolism. Defaults to IQ-5.

Hidden Lore: Forgotten, lost, or deliberately hidden knowledge. Specialise in one set of secrets: Demon Lore (the politics of Hell), Secrets of the City (dark and hidden happenings in back alleys, sewers, and the rulers' private chambers; further specialise by city), Spirit Lore (weird stuff involving immaterial beings), etc. A few librarians across the multiverse possess Hidden Lore (L-Space), which enables them to enter L-Space (p. 285) in any sufficiently large library and then find their way around that multiply connected labyrinth. To start play with Hidden Lore, you need an explanation of how you learned these secrets – an aspect of your job, an Unusual Background (pp. 48-49), or possibly something involving Enemies, Secrets, or Vows. If you spend enough time in play talking to the right (or wrong) people or reading old books[1], the GM may assign you a point in some specialisation. No default.

Occultism: The study of the folklore of the mysterious and supernatural (the *science* of magical forces is Thaumatology, p. 82). Most undergraduate wizards take a few exams in this subject and then forget what they learned as soon as possible, regarding it as messy and superstitious. It's also studied by witches and a few philosophers. Occultists can derive ancient secrets (or horrible warnings) from their studies, and the skill helps when dealing with all sorts of spirits, undead, and related phenomena. Defaults to IQ-5.

Sacred Texts: Knowledge of the Disc's huge array of known sacred writings. Someone with Theology (p. 82) knows about *one* religion, but this skill can cover anything where a holy book survives. Unlike Theology, Sacred Texts says nothing about interpretation, morality, divine psychology, etc. – it just lets you quote the books. No default.

LARCENOUS SKILLS (VARIES)

Default: Varies.

These skills mostly see use in nonviolent crime or espionage, although some also have legitimate applications.

Counterfeiting/TL (IQ/H): Duplicating coins or banknotes. Defaults to IQ-6.

Filch (DX/A): Shoplifting, swiping documents or pens off a desk, etc. If someone is actively watching the item, roll a Quick Contest: Filch vs. his Observation skill or Vision. Dim light and distractions can earn you a bonus. Defaults to DX-5.

---

1. The approved term is "mouldy tomes."

Forced Entry (DX/E): Roll against skill to hit unresisting, inanimate objects with boots, sledgehammers, crowbars, etc. Add +1 per die to basic thrust or swing damage when smashing such stuff if you know this skill at DX+1, or +2 per die if you have it at DX+2 or better. Add the same bonus to ST rolls when trying to force your way in somewhere, lever open a door, etc. No default.

Forgery/TL (IQ/H): The ability to create falsified documents (wills, letters of credit, etc.). When using a forged document, roll against the forger's skill *each time* it's inspected – unless the first attempt was a critical success. Failure means someone spots the forgery. Defaults to IQ-6.

Holdout (IQ/A): Concealing items on your person or on other people (usually with their cooperation). An item's size and shape govern its concealability, from +4 for a small jewel or a postage stamp, to -6 or worse for a battleaxe. Likewise, voluminous or skimpy clothes give bonuses or penalties. Defaults to IQ-5.

Lockpicking/TL (IQ/A): Opening locks without the key or combination. Each attempt requires one minute. If you make the roll and open the lock, each point of success shaves five seconds off the required time. Cheaper or better locks give bonuses or penalties to the roll. Defaults to IQ-5.

Pickpocket (DX/H): The ability to steal a purse, knife, etc., from someone's person – or to "plant" something on him. Roll a Quick Contest against the victim's Per (or his Streetwise if he has it and knows he's a possible target). Distractions can give you a bonus. Defaults to DX-6.

Smuggling (IQ/A): Concealing items in baggage and vehicles, or hiding something in a room or a building. In an active search, the searchers must win a Quick Contest of Search vs. your Smuggling to find the item. Defaults to IQ-5.

LAW (IQ/H)

Default: IQ-6.

Knowledge of one specific set of legal codes and jurisprudence. Choose a specialisation, usually meaning a nation's approach to a particular subject (e.g., "Genuan Criminal" or "Ankh-Morpork Commercial") – or "International Agreements," for treaties *between* nations. Roll to remember or deduce the answer to a question about the law, or to present a case in court. The GM may opt to resolve a court case as a Quick Contest, although one side or the other might have significant bonuses or penalties depending on what they have to work with ("My client was indeed discovered with a bloody knife in one hand and the victim's wallet in the other . . .").

LEADERSHIP (IQ/A)

Default: IQ-5.

The ability to coordinate a group. Roll to lead NPCs into a dangerous or stressful situation (PCs can decide for themselves if they want to follow you!).

MAGIC (IQ/VH)

Default: None.
Prerequisite: Magery (pp. 44-45).

This is the basic skill for any kind of spellcasting, representing the methods and procedures taught to you from the beginning of your training in whatever sort of magic you use. It defines your general grasp of magical operations, and sets an upper limit on your Magical Form skills (below); e.g., if you know Magic at 13, none of your Magical Form skills can exceed 13.

You require at least Magery 0 to learn the Magic skill because you must be able to perceive magical forces to manipulate them safely. Higher levels of Magery add to your IQ when learning this skill.

You *must* specialise in a branch of magic. The two most common specialisations are Wizardry and Witchcraft. There are others – Voodoo, Demonology, Enchantressing, and so on – but these tend to give access to a narrower range of options and spells.

It's almost impossible to learn multiple Magic specialisations; the mindset needed to work one sort of magic locks you out of the others. Eskarina Smith (see *Equal Rites*) seems to be the only person to have learned both Magic (Wizardry) and Magic (Witchcraft). Matching her feat would require an Unusual Background (pp. 48-49), if the GM permitted it at all.

MAGICAL FORMS (IQ/VH)

Default: Magic skill-6.
Prerequisite: Magic skill (above).

The rules for magic (pp. 191-217) divide things up into eight "Forms": *Divination* (the magic of information), *Elementalism* (the magic of energy and inert matter), *Magianism* (direct manipulation of the basic forces of magic), *Necromancy* (death, the dead, and the undead), *Physiomancy* (living things' bodies), *Psychomancy* (mind-magic), *Sortilege* (chance and fate), and *Summonation* (summoning and warding against supernatural spirits). Each has an associated Magical Form skill. You must normally study a Form to use spells which fit within it, although skilled casters can sometimes get them to work without. As with the Magic skill, levels of Magery add to your IQ when learning Magical Form skills.

Each Magical Form skill defaults to basic Magic skill at -6; treat Magic skill levels higher than 20 as 20 for this purpose. If this special default is better than the skill level you could buy with 1 point, you can buy up the Form skill from default level by paying the difference. If you subsequently improve your Magic skill level, you may need to reassign some points to keep the numbers right – just don't let any of your skills go *down* as a result.

Example: Augustus Sump has IQ 12 and Magery 2, so he's effectively IQ 14 when purchasing magical skills. He buys Magic (Wizardry)-17 for 20 points, giving him every Magical Form skill at 11. Normally, buying one of those skills at that level would cost him 1 point. Augustus also decides that he wants Magical Form (Elementalism)-12. This would normally cost him 2 points, but he need only pay the difference between the new level and the default: 1 point.

Sump subsequently accumulates some bonus character points, and decides to raise his Magic (Wizardry) skill to 18. He could handle this in two ways: He might put 3 bonus points into Magic and move the 1 from Elementalism, leaving that at 12, or he might put 4 bonus points into Magic and also put 1 more into Elementalism, raising that to 13.

Some styles of magic *don't* permit specific Form skills to be bought up from default, though – and certain minor styles ignore some Forms altogether. Finally, remember that no Form skill level can ever exceed your Magic skill level.

MEDICAL SKILLS (IQ/VARIES)

Default: Varies.

This is a *set* of skills related to healing. Strictly, everything except Veterinary should specialise by species (Human, Troll, Dwarf, etc.) – although a generous GM might allow cross-species use at moderate penalties.

Diagnosis/TL (IQ/H): The ability to tell what's wrong with a sick or injured person, or what killed a corpse. It might not determine the exact problem, but it gives hints and rules out impossibilities. Defaults to IQ-6.

First Aid/TL (IQ/E): The ability to patch up injuries in the field (see *Recovery*, pp. 186-187). Make a skill roll to halt bleeding, restart breathing, etc. Defaults to IQ-4.

Herbalism (IQ/H): The skill of preparing medicines from natural ingredients. *Finding* the ingredients may require Naturalist (p. 79); exotic and nigh-magical drugs (which can be *very* risky) might call for Alchemy (p. 71). Defaults to IQ-6.

Midwifery (IQ/A): Theoretically, delivering babies is an aspect of Physician. Even on our world, though, some people are trained purely for this task – and on most of the Disc, witches and competent local midwives are far safer than the average doctor. This skill also includes a fair amount of practical psychology specific to dealing with worried mothers (and fathers). However, if serious complications arise during a birth, a sensible non-witch midwife will try to call in a witch – or a *competent* doctor, if she somehow knows of one. Defaults to IQ-5.

Physician/TL (IQ/H): The ability to aid the sick and the injured, prescribe drugs and care, etc. Make a skill roll to hasten natural recovery from injury (see *Recovery*, pp. 186-187), and whenever the GM requires a test of general medical competence or knowledge. Physician can also be used in place of First Aid. Defaults to IQ-7.

Surgery/TL (IQ/VH): Using invasive techniques to repair damage to the body, transplant organs, etc. On the Disc, only Igors have this at a skill level and TL high enough to make it much better than any alternative – but *they* can work wonders. No default.

Veterinary/TL (IQ/H): Caring for sick or wounded animals. This uses a lot of general principles, so it can sometimes be employed to help sick people, too – but usually at penalties, and with a lot of odd advice thrown in by reflex ("Make sure that he gets plenty of oats and keep his stable warm"). No default.

Sadly, on the Disc, many physicians operate at a TL *below* that of their society. On one hand, most people are fatalistic about the consequences of injury or disease, so the medical profession can get away with poor results and lack of progress (despite charging large fees); on the other, any better medical ideas that do come along tend to be counterintuitive, so Discworlders just ignore them, or refuse to be "experimented on." In Ankh-Morpork or elsewhere on the Sto Plains, First Aid and Veterinary[1] are limited to TL3, while other medical skills are limited to TL2. For a doctor (or vet) from that region to be trained at a higher TL requires a 5-point Unusual Background (pp. 48-49), probably indicating time spent in Klatch. One reason for the recent popularity of Uberwaldian Igors (pp. 140-141) as doctors, despite their little eccentricities, is that they're trained to at least TL4, and usually TL5. Witches can learn medical skills up to TL3, or even TL4 for the ones that read a lot and really try, but nobody sophisticated pays any attention to the medical skills of a bunch of rustic wise-women.

MELEE WEAPON SKILLS (DX/VARIES)

Default: Varies.

This is not one but a *collection* of skills – one per class of closely related melee weapons. Melee weapon skills are based on DX, and default to DX-4 if Easy, DX-5 if Average, or DX-6 if Hard.

Fencing Weapons

Fencing weapons are light, one-handed blades, optimised for parrying. Fencing relies on quick footwork; all fencing skill rolls *and* parries take a penalty equal to your encumbrance level (p. 168). The metalworking required to make fencing blades needed sophisticated knowledge; thus, characters with a personal TL lower than TL4 cannot usually learn these skills.

Skills: Rapier (DX/A), for long fencing blades used by serious swashbucklers; *Smallsword* (DX/A), for elegant blades mostly worn by people who are primarily concerned with the look of the thing, and one or two fancy-pants dwarfs.

Flails

Flails are weapons with a chain or linkage in the middle, allowing them to whirl around in a way that's even more dangerous to the enemy than to the user. Some are farming tools adapted to warfare; others are fancy Agatean martial-arts equipment (which started out as farming tools), and they are extremely popular among fans of Agatean ninjas. Attempts to block them are at -2; attempts to parry them are at -4, and fencing weapons and knives cannot parry them at all.

Skills: Flail (DX/H).

---

1. Yes, the vets are more sophisticated than the people-doctors. It makes sense. People aren't worth much, but a good racehorse can be worth a fortune.

Impact Weapons

An *impact* weapon is any rigid, unbalanced weapon with most of its mass concentrated in the head. Such a weapon cannot parry if you've already attacked with it on your turn.

Skills: Axe/Mace (DX/A); *Two-Handed Axe/Mace* (DX/A), which is also used for scythes.

Pole Weapons

Pole weapons have long shafts.

Skills: Polearm (DX/A), for halberds and the like; *Spear* (DX/A); *Staff* (DX/A), which has +2 to Parry.

Swords

A *sword* is a rigid, hilted blade, distinguished for game purposes from lighter, slimmer fencing weapons.

Skills: Broadsword (DX/A); *Knife* (DX/E), which has -1 to Parry; *Shortsword* (DX/A); *Two-Handed Sword* (DX/A). The weapons used with Broadsword and Shortsword are sufficiently similar that those from either category can be used with the other skill at -2.

MERCHANT (IQ/A)

Default: IQ-5.

The skill of buying, selling, and trading retail and wholesale goods. It involves bargaining, salesmanship, and an understanding of trade practises.

MIMICRY (IQ/H)

Default: IQ-6.

Convincingly imitating voices or sounds. Choose a specialisation:

Animal Sounds and *Bird Calls* are mostly used in the wilderness to attract game – or to deter predators, in a pinch. Roll a Quick Contest vs. Per-6 or Naturalist-3 to use either specialisation to fool an observer.

Speech is mostly learned by actors, criminals, and spies. It doesn't let you converse in any foreign language, but you can catch the *sound* of one. Imitating a specific individual is at -3. To trick someone with a specific human voice, roll a Quick Contest against IQ.

MISSILE WEAPON SKILLS (DX/VARIES)

Default: Varies.

Another *collection* of skills – one per class of closely related personal missile weapons. Some require specialisation by specific weapon. Defaults are usually DX-4 if the skill is Easy, DX-5 if Average, or DX-6 if Hard.

Blowpipe (DX/H): Shooting small (usually poisoned!) darts from a blowpipe.

Bow (DX/A): For all sorts of short bows and longbows.

Crossbow (DX/E): Covers all types of crossbows, including fancy little pistol things – and even one or two sneaky and widely banned dart-firing assassination devices.

Guns/TL (DX/E): While personal firearms are vanishingly rare on the Disc (and various people are labouring to keep things that way), they can work; this is the skill to use them. Specialise by type: *Pistol*, *Rifle*, or *Shotgun*.

Innate Attack (DX/E): This isn't for weapons as such; rather, it's the skill of attacking *at range* with effects generated from your person, such as dragon's breath, magical fireballs, or divine lightning. For instance, to strike effectively with a fireball, you must first use a magical skill to create it and then use Innate Attack to hit with it. Choose a specialisation: *Beam*, *Breath*, *Gaze* (attacks from the eyes), or *Projectile* (for fireballs and other solid or pseudo-solid missiles).

Sling (DX/H): The skill for a cheap, handy weapon often used by shepherds and other poor rustics.

Throwing (DX/A): The ability to throw any small, relatively smooth object that fits in the palm of your hand, such as the balls used in many sports, convenient pebbles, and some types of dwarfish battle bread. Defaults to DX-3.

Thrown Weapon (DX/E): The ability to hurl *one* type of purpose-made throwing weapon. Specialisations include Axe/Mace, Knife, Spear, and Throwing Star. *Thrown Weapon (Stick)* is used with dwarf-made boomerang croissants, among other things.

MOUNT (DX/A)

Default: DX-5.

The skill of *being ridden.* A riding animal with *any* points in Mount gives anyone whom it allows to ride it at least +1 to Riding skill; if its Mount is better than the rider's Riding, use the average of the two (rounded up) for the rider's Riding rolls. The animal can throw an unwelcome rider by winning a Quick Contest of Mount vs. Riding.

MOVEMENT SKILLS (VARIES)

Default: Varies.

These skills cover agility and efficient movement.

Acrobatics (DX/H): The ability to perform gymnastic stunts, roll, take falls, etc. Defaults to DX-6.

Aerobatics (DX/H): May be learned by anyone who acquires the ability to fly, using a magic broomstick or otherwise. Covers looping the loop, flying through narrow gaps, etc. Defaults to DX-6.

Climbing (DX/A): The ability to climb mountains, rock walls, trees, the sides of buildings, etc. See *Climbing* (p. 167). Defaults to DX-5.

Hiking (HT/A): Training for endurance walking, hiking, and marching. See *Hiking* (pp. 167-168). Defaults to HT-5.

Jumping (DX/E): When attempting a difficult jump, roll against the *higher* of Jumping or DX. Likewise, you may use half of your Jumping skill (round down) instead of Basic Move when calculating jumping distance, if that's better. See *Jumping* (p. 168). No default.

Running (HT/A): Covers both sprints and long-distance running. Roll against the *higher* of Running or HT to avoid fatigue due to running. When racing someone of equal Move on foot, a Quick Contest of Running skill determines the winner. Defaults to HT-5.

Swimming (HT/E): The skill of swimming and lifesaving. Roll against the *higher* of Swimming or HT to avoid fatigue or injury due to aquatic misfortunes. Defaults to HT-4.

NATURALIST (IQ/H)

Default: IQ-6.

Practical knowledge of nature – how to tell dangerous plants and animals from benign ones, locate a cave to shelter in, and "read" weather patterns to know when to take shelter.

NAVIGATION/TL (IQ/A)

Default: IQ-5.

Finding your position through careful observation and use of instruments. A successful roll tells you where you are or lets you plot a course. *Land* and *Sea* are separate specialisations; *Air* is another, occasionally used by witches on broomsticks, albeit mostly at default.

OBSERVATION (PER/A)

Default: Per-5.

Observing dangerous or interesting situations efficiently and discreetly. Roll to pick up concealed or tactically significant details concerning a location, a group of people, or your immediate surroundings without letting others know you're watching.

OFFICER SKILLS (IQ/H)

Default: IQ-6.

These skills are used mainly by military officers to plan successful operations and predict enemy actions – although some civilians pick them up, too.

Intelligence Analysis/TL: Analysing and interpreting intelligence data, evaluating sources, and deducing enemy plans and capabilities.

Strategy: Planning successful large-scale operations. There are two distinct specialisations: *Land* and *Naval*.

Tactics: Outmanoeuvring the enemy in small-scale combat. When commanding a small unit, roll against Tactics to place your troops correctly for an ambush, know where to post sentries, etc. In personal combat, you may make a Tactics roll before hostilities commence if you had *any* time to prepare. Success lets you start the fight in an advantageous position – e.g., behind cover or on higher ground – as determined by the GM.

PHOTOGRAPHY (IQ/A)

Default: IQ-5.

The ability to use an imp-infested iconograph (pp. 159-160) to take recognisable and attractive pictures. The skill includes knowing when to supply the imp with more paints, what it is or isn't likely to be able to achieve, and how to talk to it.

POISONS/TL (IQ/H)

Default: IQ-6.

Practical knowledge of poisons – what works, what can be obtained from natural sources, how to recognise characteristics or symptoms of effects, what antidotes might work, etc.

POLITICS (IQ/A)

Default: IQ-5.

The ability to get into office (in a place where that involves something other than being the late ruler's eldest son) and get along with other politicians. Roll to trade favours, pull strings, and generally work the system. A successful skill roll can also give +2 on reactions from fellow politicians. Actually *running* a polity requires Administration (p. 71).

PROFESSIONAL SKILLS (VARIES)

Default: Varies.

Many skills exist which enable people to perform ordinary jobs. These can sometimes come in handy on adventures, too. Some examples:

Accounting (IQ/H): Keeping (or cooking) the books for a business or government. Defaults to IQ-6.

Architecture/TL (IQ/A): Designing buildings – and analysing the design of existing structures. Defaults to IQ-5.

Carpentry (IQ/E): Building things from wood. Defaults to IQ-4.

Cartography (IQ/A): Making (or interpreting) maps or charts. Defaults to IQ-5.

Finance (IQ/H): Managing money and working as a banker. No default.

Fool's Lore (IQ/A): The body of knowledge taught by the Fools' Guild (pp. 262-263): formalised clowning practises, standard punch lines, and stock puns. Some of these are quite clever, but very few are actually funny. Guild teachers hammer the skill in hard; a graduate of the school may have to make a Will roll to *avoid* responding to a recognised feed line. Defaults to IQ-6.

Gardening (IQ/E): Growing plants on a *small* scale. Defaults to IQ-4.

Packing (IQ/A): Getting loads on and off pack animals efficiently, choosing the best animals and routes, and managing the beasts on the road. Defaults to IQ-5.

Panhandling (IQ/E): Begging on the streets, making yourself look pathetic or amusing enough to receive a few coins without too many beatings or legal problems. Defaults to IQ-4.

Printing/TL (IQ/A): Operating the printing technology available at your TL: woodblocks at TL3, metal-plate engraving and moveable type at TL4. Defaults to IQ-5.

Seamanship/TL (IQ/E): Working as *crew* on a seagoing ship – operating rigging, oars, and pumps, arguing about superstitions, etc. At least one person aboard will also need Shiphandling (p. 81). Defaults to IQ-4.

Smith/TL (IQ/A): Working non-precious metals. Although this is IQ-based, many smith's tools need a minimum ST for proper use. There are three specialisations: *Blacksmith* (working with iron), *Coppersmith* (copper, bronze, and brass), and *Tinsmith* (lead, tin, and other "soft" metals). Any serious Discworld village has its own blacksmith, usually a brawny fellow with knowledge of small rituals that get him treated as almost-but-not-quite magical. The other specialisations are less common, though any large town will have a range of competent metalworkers. Defaults to IQ-5.

Telegraphy/TL (IQ/E): Operating a "clacks" system. Covers knowledge of the coding system and practise at working the mechanisms. Make a roll to send a message faster than usual or in difficult conditions. No default.

Other Professional Skills include Bartender, Cooking (covering *haute cuisine,* not just the basics included in Housekeeping), Farming (very widespread on the Disc, but traditionally avoided by adventurers), Filing Clerk, Freight Handling/TL (*organising* the loading and unloading of ships), and a huge variety of "crafts." Should it matter in play, most such skills are IQ/A with an IQ-5 default – although as the examples show, the GM has latitude to make some easier or harder. Extremely physical skills might even be DX-based (typically DX/A, defaulting to DX-5).

PROPAGANDA/TL (IQ/A)

Default: IQ-5.

Persuading large groups of people by indirect means: popular ballads, concerted rumour campaigns, newspaper stories, advertising, etc. Details depend on your TL and what's available. A rare skill on the Disc, but not unknown.

PROSPECTING/TL (IQ/A)

Default: IQ-5.

Practical, applied geology. Prospecting includes assessing potential mines and mineral samples, and finding water in the wild.

PSYCHOLOGY (IQ/H)

Default: IQ-6.

Applied psychology regarding a particular species (choose a specialisation), learned through study or observation. Roll against skill to predict the *general* behaviour of an individual or a small group in a given situation, especially under stress. Psychological *therapy* (always informal on the Discworld, but often performed by witches and others) also requires social skills, to influence the subject's behaviour.

PUBLIC SPEAKING (IQ/A)

Default: IQ-5.

General talent with the spoken word. A successful roll lets you (for instance) give a good political speech, entertain a group around a campfire, incite or calm a riot, or put on a successful court jester act.

How many ways can you fight a war? Polly wondered. We have the clacks now. I know a man who writes things down.
– Monstrous Regiment

RELIGIOUS RITUAL (IQ/H)

Default: None.

The practical day-to-day skill of the professional priest. Choose a religion as a specialisation; you know the required words, gestures, and movements for its ceremonies and sacrifices. Roll to impress a congregation – or your god, if he's paying attention.

REPAIR SKILLS (IQ/A)

Default: IQ-5.

These abilities are used to maintain and repair technological artefacts, or to construct them from standard components. A successful roll lets you find a problem, if it isn't obvious, *or* fix something. Time and equipment required are up to the GM. There are two skills here, both specialised by type of item:

Armoury/TL: Repairing weapons or armour. Specialisations include Body Armour, Heavy Weapons (anything covered by Artillery or Gunner skills), Melee Weapons (including shields), and Missile Weapons (bows, crossbows, and slings). A blacksmith can handle some of the basics and may be required to make metal gear from scratch, but serious armoury work involves a body of specialised knowledge.

Mechanic/TL: Repairing mechanical devices. Specialisations include Animal-Drawn Vehicle (for chariots, carts, and coaches), Clacks (for everything that's used inside the signalling tower system), Clockwork (for various small mechanisms that are invented at late TL3 and come into their own at TL4), and Low-Tech Machines (for all sorts of large contraptions at TL4 or below).

RESEARCH/TL (IQ/A)

Default: IQ-5.

Doing library and file research. Roll to find a useful piece of data in an appropriate place . . . *if* the information is there to be found.

RIDING (DX/A)

Default: DX-5.

The ability to ride a particular kind of mount. Choose from among mostly obvious specialisations: Camels, Equines (for mules and horses), Elephants, etc. Roll when you first try to mount a riding animal, and again each time something happens to frighten or challenge the creature (e.g., a jump).

SCROUNGING (PER/E)

Default: Per-4.

The ability to find, salvage, or improvise useful items that others can't locate. Each attempt takes an hour. You don't necessarily steal your booty, just locate it somehow and then acquire it by any means necessary.

SEARCH (PER/A)

Default: Per-5.

The ability to search people, baggage, and vehicles for items that aren't in plain sight. The GM rolls once – *in secret* – per article of interest. For *deliberately* concealed things, this is a Quick Contest: Search vs. Holdout or Smuggling. If you fail, the GM simply says, "You found nothing."

SEWING/TL (DX/E)

Default: DX-4.

Working with needle and thread. A standard domestic skill, also invaluable to adventurers in games where the GM pays attention to what can happen to clothes and gear during long wilderness journeys.

SHADOWING (IQ/A)

Default: IQ-5.

The ability to follow another person through a town, city, or crowd without being noticed. Roll a Quick Contest every 10 minutes: Shadowing vs. the subject's Vision roll. If you lose, you lost the subject; if you lose by more than 5, you were *seen*.

SHIELD (DX/E)

Default: DX-4.

Using a shield to protect yourself in combat. Your Block score (p. 180) is (skill/2) + 3, rounded down. You also use this skill when bashing opponents with your shield.

SHIPHANDLING/TL (IQ/H)

Default: IQ-6.
Prerequisites: Leadership (p. 76), plus the Navigation (Sea) (p. 79) *and* Seamanship (p. 80) skills for the same TL.

Acting as the *master* of a seagoing ship – directing the crew, standing watch on the bridge, etc.

SLEIGHT OF HAND (DX/H)

Default: None.

The skill of "palming" small objects, performing card tricks, etc., used by criminals and professional entertainers. You may have to win a Quick Contest vs. Vision or Observation skill to get away with some things.

SOLDIER/TL (IQ/A)

Default: IQ-5.

Basic military training and experience, battlefield discipline, and routine equipment use and care. Roll to perform standard military tasks correctly, and to avoid minor inconveniences in battle or on the march.

STEALTH (DX/A)

Default: DX-5 or IQ-5.

The ability to hide and to move silently. A successful roll lets you conceal yourself practically anywhere, move so quietly that nobody will hear you, or follow someone without being noticed. If someone is *specifically* on the alert, the GM will roll a Quick Contest: your Stealth vs. his Perception.

SURVIVAL (PER/A)

Default: Per-5.

The ability to "live off the land," find food and water, trap small game, build shelter, etc. Living safely in the wilderness requires a successful Survival roll once per day. Failure inflicts 2d-4 injury on you and anyone in your care. You can also roll to find the best route in some direction.

You must specialise. Standard specialisations are *Arctic, Desert, Fourecks Outback, Island/Beach, Jungle, Mountain, Plains, Swampland,* and *Woodlands.* Roll at -3 to use Survival for one of these environments in any of the others.

Survival (L-Space) is a rare version that provides detailed knowledge of the peculiar hazards found in L-Space (p. 285). It isn't useful in other environments, even at a penalty.

Urban Survival is a separate skill used in cities, similar to Survival in purpose but very different in detail. It allows you to find clean rainwater, warm sleeping places, and safe spots to hole up, and also to locate particular types of buildings or businesses by the "feel" of the neighbourhood.

TEACHING (IQ/A)

Default: IQ-5.

The skill of instructing others can be used to get a job, as an excuse for characters to acquire useful skills from one another (using bonus character points, p. 219), to convert raw recruits into useful watchmen or militia, etc.

THAUMATOLOGY (IQ/VH)

Default: IQ-7.

Abstract, theoretical study of magic – as a science rather than as a practical art – is almost entirely the province of academic wizards (who disagree widely and sometimes violently about it), although anyone with enough intelligence could study it in principle. Thaumatology is much easier to learn if you can perceive magical energies, however; add your level of Magery (pp. 44-45) to IQ when learning it.

While this is a highly theoretical skill, it can be useful "in the field" if a wizard must whip up a complicated new spell from first principles, understand some bizarre magical effect, make sense of another wizard's research notes, or recognise why casting a particular spell might lead to disaster.

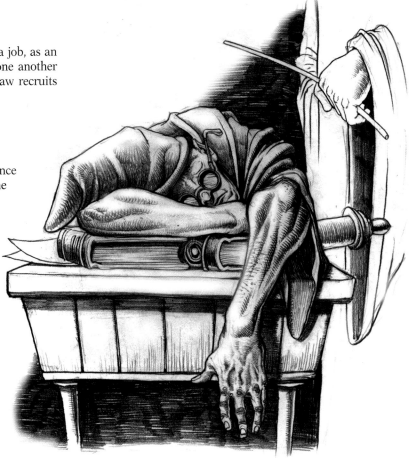

THEOLOGY (IQ/H)

Default: IQ-6.

Religious ideas and divine rules and behaviour are studied almost solely by priests; other people *could* learn this, but it's rare. (Wizards disdain the subject.) Theology takes specialisations, usually by religion – which may correspond to a single god, as with Theology (Church of Om), or to a pantheon whose members share responsibilities and broadly support each other's cults, as with Theology (Gods of Djelibeybi). Roll to determine what the religion believes (useful when dealing with other believers) or what a god expects of worshippers (essential when dealing with a god).

Theology (Small Gods), as studied in the Temple of Small Gods in Ankh-Morpork, covers what's known about the crowded and ever-changing roster of petty deities.

Theology (Research) is the cautious study of gods in general – how many there are, which are growing in power and which are fading, and which might actually be some other deity in a different costume or a wig.

TRACKING (PER/A)

Default: Per-5.

The ability to follow a man or an animal by its tracks. Roll to pick up the trail, then again every 15 minutes to avoid losing it, at a modifier ranging from 0 for soft terrain to -6 for city streets.

TRAPS/TL (IQ/A)

Default: IQ-5.

Building and nullifying traps and "security systems." This skill covers everything from covered pits to elaborate anti-burglary devices.

UNARMED COMBAT SKILLS (DX/VARIES)

Default: None.

Another *collection* of skills, ranging from the simple-but-effective to the refined. As with melee weapons, unarmed parries are at (skill/2) + 3, rounded down. Unarmed attacks and parries take no penalties if performed using the "off" hand.

While these skills offer no defaults, untrained fighters can use DX to punch, grapple, or barge, and can parry at (DX/2) + 3.

Boxing (DX/A): Trained stand-up punching (kicking isn't covered). Roll to hit with a punch. If you know Boxing at DX+1, add +1 damage *per die* to boxing punch damage; if you know it at DX+2 or better, that becomes +2 *per die*. You can also parry two *different* attacks per turn using empty hands, one with each hand – but you parry kicks at -2 and non-thrusting weapons at -3. You get an improved retreating bonus with these parries; see *Retreating* (pp. 181-182).

Brawling (DX/E): "Unscientific" unarmed combat, learned (usually the hard way) in playgrounds and bar-rooms. Roll to hit with a punch, or at -2 to hit with a kick. Brawling can also be used for biting, with horns or claws (if you have them), and with blackjacks and saps. If you know Brawling at DX+2 or better, add +1 damage *per die* to damage with any Brawling attack. You can also parry two *different* attacks per turn using empty hands, one with each hand – but at -3 vs. non-thrusting weapons.

Judo (DX/H): Advanced training at unarmed throws and grapples. Use Judo for the moves described in *Judo Throws* (p. 178), and in place of DX for grappling and throwing moves in close

combat. You can also parry two *different* attacks per turn using empty hands, one with each hand; this has *no* penalty against weapons. Any hand with which you wish to attack or defend using Judo must be empty. Moreover, Judo relies on quick footwork – all skill rolls *and* parries suffer a penalty equal to your encumbrance level (p. 168), though you get an improved retreating bonus when parrying.

Karate (DX/H): Advanced training at unarmed striking. Roll to hit with a punch, or at -2 to hit with a kick. If you know Karate at DX, add +1 damage *per die* to damage with Karate attacks; if you know it at DX+1 or better, that becomes +2 *per die*. You can also parry two *different* attacks per turn using empty hands, one with each hand; this has *no* penalty against weapons. Karate, too, relies on footwork – skill rolls and parries take a penalty equal to your encumbrance level, but you get an improved retreating bonus when parrying.

Wrestling (DX/A): The skill of grappling and pinning. You can roll against Wrestling instead of DX when grappling, or when resisting being taken down to the ground by an opponent. If you know Wrestling at DX+1, add +1 to your effective ST when making or resisting grapples, chokes, pins, takedowns, etc., or when breaking free of holds; if you know it at DX+2 or better, that becomes +2. You can also parry with empty hands once per turn, using *both* hands – but at -3 vs. *any* weapon.

VEHICLE SKILLS (VARIES)

Default: Varies.

Roll to get a vehicle underway without complications, to execute fancy or dangerous vehicular moves, to deal with hazards, and to avoid practical problems on long journeys (roll once per day). Failure indicates lost time, even an accident. This category includes many skills:

Boating/TL (DX/A): Handling one type of small watercraft. Choose a specialisation: *Sailboat* (for dinghies, etc.) or *Unpowered* (for canoes, kayaks, punts, etc.). Defaults to DX-5 or IQ-5.

Teamster (IQ/A): Driving a team of animals which draw a cart, chariot, etc., including choosing, harnessing, and caring for the beasts. Specialise by animal type; Equines (horses and mules) is most common by far. Defaults to IQ-5.

Powered and flying vehicles appear *very* occasionally in the chronicles. Possible skills include *Bicycling* (DX/E, defaults to DX-4), *Driving* (DX/A, defaults to DX-5 or IQ-5) for land vehicles, *Piloting* (DX/A, defaults to IQ-6) for aircraft and spacecraft, and *Submarine* (DX/A, defaults to IQ-6). Specialise by precise vehicle type: Driving (Steam Car), Driving (Giant Mechanical Statue), Piloting (Hang Glider), Piloting (Swamp Dragon-Powered Spacecraft), etc.

WEATHER SENSE/TL (IQ/A)

Default: IQ-5.

The study of the weather and how to predict it, using appropriate equipment or data. Working out what tomorrow is likely to be like in a region you know well is fairly easy; more than that tends to take severe penalties, except in places and seasons when the weather is very stable. The GM always rolls for you, secretly!

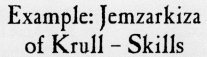

Example: Jemzarkiza of Krull – Skills

Anne starts with Jemzarkiza's magical training. With her IQ and Magery, Magic-20 costs her 16 points. A 20 is high, but she's supposed to be good and it sounds like a nice number; higher wouldn't improve her Magical Form defaults, so she'll stop there. She has to have a specialisation for this, which the GM dubs "Krullian Wizardry." They agree that Magic (Krullian Wizardry) mostly works like Magic (Wizardry), except when the GM decides that it doesn't. The most obvious difference will be that a Krullian wizard won't attach as much importance to a big, cumbersome staff as someone from the mainland would; Jemzarkiza will use a neat little wand to achieve similar, if lesser, effects.

With Magic-20, she has every Magical Form at 14, which is less than she'd get for 1 point, so she saves no points when buying Forms. Anyway, Anne wants Jemzarkiza to be especially good at stuff that's relevant when working with animals; she buys Magical Form (Physiomancy)-16 for 2 points and Magical Form (Psychomancy)-18 for 8 points. (She may deny that she's an enchantress, but she *is* good at working with minds – she says that they're much like turtles, only with a layer of extra confusion.) Talking of magic, Jemzarkiza knows a bit of theory, too; Thaumatology-16 costs 2 points. Oh, and she might get desperate enough to throw the occasional fireball; Innate Attack (Projectile)-14 costs 4 points.

Jemzarkiza's more mundane skills fall into three broad categories. First, she has had Krullian-style academic training: Alchemy/TL4-14 (4 points), Astrozoology-13 (1 point), Natural Philosophy/TL4-15 (4 points), Naturalist-15 (4 points), Philosophy (Krullian Scholasticism)-13 (1 point), and Research/TL4-16 (4 points). Also, Savoir-Faire (High Society)-16 (2 points) seems to fit.

Second, Jemzarkiza gets on well with animals. Anne adds Animal Handling (Reptiles)-15 (1 point) and Veterinary/TL3-16 (4 points). The rule on p. 69 limits her TL with Veterinary. Both skills benefit from her Animal Friend advantage.

Finally, Jemzarkiza has been travelling by sea a lot, and probably having to fend off trouble with whatever came to hand. Anne adds Fishing-15 (1 point), Knife-14 (4 points), Navigation/TL4 (Sea)-14 (1 point), Seamanship/TL4-15 (1 point), Shouting at Foreigners-16 (2 points), Staff-12 (2 points), and Weather Sense/TL4-15 (2 points).

That's 70 points in skills, making 250 points in total. Jemzarkiza is balanced – in game terms, anyway.

WRITING (IQ/A)

Default: IQ-5.

The ability to write in a clear or entertaining manner. A successful roll means the work is readable and accurate.

NONHUMANS and OCCUPATIONAL TEMPLATES

Crowds in Ankh-Morpork don't normally part in front of two striking and strikingly different-looking women walking side by side. Far too many people would hope that one or both of the women would bump into them, and in any case, Ankh-Morpork crowds don't part for much. However, there are things about a Watch uniform and a businesslike staff that command enough respect to overcome lechery. Much of the time, anyway.

*"Very well," said Jemzarkiza of Krull, after the pair had walked a little way, "I might as well try just asking. What **are** you, Captain?"*

Captain Angua scowled. "I'm a Watchman," she said.

"That's not what I meant."

"But it's what I am." Angua sighed. "I know that you think you can tell something else about me, Miss, ah, . . ."

"Just call me Jemzarkiza."

"As you wish. And you can call me Captain."

"As you wish."

"Aft'noon, big girl. 'Oos your friend?" said somebody else.

Jemzarkiza's brow furrowed, and she looked around. "Did you just hear something?" she asked.

"Nobody important," Angua said, throwing a hard look at a small, scruffy street-dog which was sitting in the entrance to a nearby alley, scratching itself vigorously.

"Charmin'," said nobody important.

Jemzarkiza shook her head and walked on. "I need to get out of this city," she muttered.

The rules so far let you create a wide range of *human* characters. However, there are other intelligent races and types of beings on the Disc who may be treated as characters – often as playable ones. And regardless of race, it can be helpful to have a quick way of defining characters. A single mechanism can handle both requirements: *templates*. Templates come in two types:

Racial templates are collections of attribute modifiers, advantages, disadvantages, etc. which are standard for normal members of a particular nonhuman race. A race's template defines the baseline for its members, in the same way that "10 in all basic attributes, no particular advantages or disadvantages" defines the human baseline. Individuals of that race will also have personal traits and may sometimes even be missing things from the template, but that makes them unusual.

Occupational templates are a quick way of creating characters. They outline attribute levels, abilities, problems, skills, etc. for typical people in particular jobs or social positions. There's nothing mandatory about them – they're optional game aids.

Traits for Nonhuman Characters

Before discussing racial templates, we need a number of additional traits which are mostly only used when creating nonhuman characters.

Attribute and Secondary Characteristic Modifiers

Racial templates often have basic attribute or secondary characteristic *modifiers*; e.g., "ST+2" or "HP-3." Apply attribute modifiers to the attributes you buy for your character. Next, recalculate your secondary characteristics to reflect your modified attributes. Finally, apply secondary characteristic modifiers. If an attribute or a secondary characteristic doesn't appear in the racial template, assume that it's unchanged from the human norm.

Racial and Personal Appearance

Some racial templates have appearance modifiers, positive or negative. These represent how typical members of the race appear *to human beings* – who are, after all, the Disc's dominant sapient species. Members of the race ignore this racial appearance in their interactions with each other; they regard average members of their own species as, well, average.

Other beings who share human-like tastes *may* respond to racial appearance in the same way as humans. Mostly, though, dwarfs aren't terribly interested in the personal appearance of non-dwarfs, trolls can't easily tell all these squishy things apart, and other races are even less like humans in all this.

Any nonhuman character can also take a *personal* appearance modifier, good or bad. This reflects *either* how he appears to other members of his race *or* how he looks to humans – choose when selecting the advantage or disadvantage. Alternatively, you can have appearance that affects both humans *and* your own species. In that case, mark it as "Universal" and add 25% to the feature's value, positive or negative.

Examples: Trolls have Ugly appearance as a racial feature: humans see them as big, lumpy, and frankly *scary* walking rocks, and therefore react to them at -2. However, an ordinary troll sees another ordinary troll as ordinary, and no appearance modifiers apply in their interactions. But Ruby, the wife of Sergeant Detritus (pp. 325-326), is notably good-looking by troll standards (she used to sing in a troll nightclub). She has Beautiful appearance *to trolls*, which costs 12 points. Male trolls react to her at +4; females, at +2. To humans, however, she looks like a bizarrely curvaceous lump of rock; they still react to her at -2, although they're polite about it if her husband is present.

Golems don't have a racial appearance modifier: to humans, most of them just look like big, bland clay statues. Crazk the Golem, though, was sculpted by a skilled artist and animated to guard the temple of a god of beauty. He's Attractive *to humans,* who react to him at +1. Other golems don't pay any attention to that stuff. Hence, the advantage costs him the usual 4 points.

Gnomes, too, don't have a racial appearance modifier: to humans, they just look like tiny people. However, Rifvrik the Unfortunate had a bad experience with a snake while hunting a few years ago, and he was left scarred. Other gnomes don't find him a pleasant sight, and neither do humans – they see him as a tiny, *ugly* person. Hence, he has Ugly (Universal), worth -10 points, and fellow gnomes and humans alike react to him at -2.

Example: Hunchbroad Modoscousin

Steve is new to roleplaying games but has been persuaded to join a Discworld game. To keep things simple for him, he'll use an occupational template – but to add a bit of interest, he has decided to play a dwarf character. Dwarfs aren't really that weird, after all, and Steve has read enough Discworld books to have a good idea of how to play one. This offers an example of using both racial *and* occupational templates.

The GM has set the power level for starting characters at 100 points, with a maximum of -50 points in disadvantages. Steve notes that playing a dwarf costs 27 points (p. 100), so if he adds that to a 75-point template, he could hit 100 points with a little adjustment. He decides to play a thaumaturgist (p. 137) – a wizard's errand-runner – which should be a good excuse to go adventuring.

One of the best-known dwarfs in wizardly employ in the chronicles is Modo, the gardener at Unseen University. Perhaps Steve's character is a distant relative who has landed a job at UU through some mild nepotism (though getting someone a job tracking down rare materials for wizards may not be doing them *that* great a favour). Steve chooses his name on that basis, anyway.

Racial Advantages

Some advantages are only available to nonhuman characters, or to individuals with extraordinarily superhuman or paranormal abilities – no "normal" human can have them, even on the Discworld (although the line between "normal" and "supernatural" gets a bit fuzzy there). Generally, these can be purchased only as part of a racial template, or by highly unusual characters when the GM agrees that they fit.

ALTERNATE FORM

Variable

Some supernatural creatures have the ability to change shape; e.g., werewolves can transform into wolves, while some vampires can turn into bats (either single bats or swarms of them). This is a hugely variable capability; thus, the advantage to represent it is moderately complicated. See *Vampires* (pp. 109-114) and *Werewolves and Wolfmen* (pp. 114-116), and the character sheets for Angua (pp. 322-324) and Greebo (pp. 343-344), for worked examples.

She had to stay human. She thought better when she was human. Unfortunately, here and now, as a human, the thought occupying her mind in no small measure was that she was naked.

*— **Feet of Clay***

The base version of Alternate Form allows you to assume a form different from your "native" one by concentrating for 10 seconds. Fatigue, injury, etc., carry over between forms; HP and FP losses scale in proportion to the form's HP and FP. For instance, if you suffer 9 HP of injury while in a form with 18 HP, and then switch to a form with 10 HP, you'll have 5 HP of injury. If you're knocked out or killed, you'll immediately revert to your native form – and it, too, will be unconscious or dead. It's also possible to force you to revert with magic-suppressing spells, by carrying you into an area where magic doesn't work, or perhaps by using "folk charms" from dusty books or half-forgotten rural lore. You can adjust some of these assumptions with modifiers (see below).

To calculate advantage cost, you'll need a racial template for the form you take. This template might include such traits as Flight (Winged), Quadruped, modified attributes, or special senses, as well as abilities like Regeneration (for werewolves who just won't stay dead). It doesn't *have* to include reduced IQ, even if you adopt the shape of an unintelligent animal; some shapeshifters retain their intellect. If a new racial template is needed, the GM designs it.

Alternate Form's base cost is 15 points. If your alternate racial template costs *more* than your native one, then there's an additional premium of 90% of the cost difference between the two, rounding all fractions up. If you add Once On, Stays On (below), that 90% becomes 100%. The base form of a normal human has a "null" template, worth 0 points – so if you're a human, simply add 90% (or 100%) of the cost of your alternate racial template, where that's positive.

Example 1: Ingvar the Were-Badger is a normal human who can transform into a huge badger with a 37-point racial template. The cost of his Alternate Form is 15 + (90% of 37) = 49 points.

Example 2: Clay the Troll is a were-*human* – he once accidentally drank a magic potion that gave him the power to transform into a human being with +3 ST (30 points), -1 DX (-20 points), and grey-tinged skin (Distinctive Features, -1 point). His alternate racial template is thus worth 9 points. As his normal troll racial template costs more than that (83 points), the base cost of his Alternate Form is a flat 15 points.

While Alternate Form is turned on, its racial template *replaces* your native one (that "null" template, if you start as a normal human). Apply its traits – attribute modifiers, racial advantages and disadvantages, etc. – *instead of* those of your native race. Personal traits (including attribute levels, advantages, disadvantages, and skills bought over and above racial norms) remain intact, although your skill levels are affected by changes to the controlling attribute scores. It's worth making up a second character sheet for your secondary form, so that you'll have all the attributes, abilities, modified skill levels, and so on instantly to hand whenever you change.

If the Alternate Form's racial template has traits that conflict with your personal traits, your Alternate Form's traits take precedence. For instance, if you become a wolf, with no hands, you temporarily lose personal advantages that affect your hands, such as High Manual Dexterity – and some skills (e.g., Lockpicking) will be relatively useless, although you'll still remember them.

Some shapeshifters have special advantages that apply in *both* forms. For example, Angua the werewolf has an uncanny sense of smell, even in her human shape, and she retains this advantage in wolf form. Thus, she buys Discriminatory Smell as a *personal* trait, rather than including it in the wolf template used to calculate Alternate Form cost. Conversely, remember to include all the things that are unique to the beast form on the beast template. For example, if you're a werewolf that behaves properly in human guise but turns bestially savage when changed, your template can include disadvantages such as Berserk, Bestial, or Bloodlust.

Multiple Forms: If you have more than one Alternate Form, buy the most expensive form normally and then pay a flat 15 points per form for the others.

Example: Shalnak the Shaman is a Howondaland werecat with the power to change into both a large cat (template cost 50 points) and an outsize meerkat (template cost 10 points). His player determines the full base cost for the first form (15 + 90% of 50 = 60 points) and adds a flat 15 points for the second – a total of 75 points.

Modifiers

Having determined the nature of your Alternate Form(s), you can apply modifiers to the advantage cost to reflect better or worse shape-changing abilities. These are given as *percentages* – add them together and modify the 15-point cost per form, and only that cost, accordingly, rounding all fractions up. Modifiers ***don't*** *affect the added cost for a form with an expensive template.* For example, if you have Trigger (Only during the full moon, -40%) and Reduced Change Time (5 seconds, +20%), reduce the 15 points per form by 20%, to 12 points/form.

Absorptive Change: You "absorb" worn and carried clothing and items into your Alternate Forms instead of leaving them in a heap on the ground. These reappear when you change back. The added cost depends on how much encumbrance (p. 168) you can be carrying when you change: +5% for None, +10% for Light, +15% for Medium, +20% for Heavy, or +25% for Extra-Heavy. If you're carrying more than you can absorb, the GM decides what's left behind. He can also rule that magical or unique and exotic items can't be absorbed.

Emergencies Only: You can only shift when frightened or excited, as a response to danger – never under "routine" conditions. The GM decides what counts as sufficient provocation. You *might* be able to whip yourself into enough of a fury to trigger the change, but at best, that'll take time and make everyone around you nervous or amused. -30%.

Once On, Stays On: If you remain in your changed form even when rendered unconscious, you pay 100% rather than 90% of the difference in template costs, *and* you add a +50% modifier to the base 15 points.

Reduced Change Time: A change that takes just 5 seconds costs +20%; 3 seconds, +40%; 2 seconds, +60%; and 1 second (the fastest possible), +80%.

Trigger: Something is *required* to set off your change. The percentage reduction depends on how common this trigger is – from -10% for something available almost anywhere (say, a glass of water) to -40% for something *seriously* expensive or inconvenient. Some Discworld werewolves can only change during the period of the full moon, broadly defined as one week in every month, but can shift by night or day during that period, which is worth -25%. If you can only change under the light of a *completely* full moon, just three *nights* in every month, that's -40%.

Unconscious Only: You can only take this in conjunction with Uncontrollable (below). You have *no* conscious control over your change – it only ever happens when the GM says so, as the result of stress or environmental effects. -20%.

Uncontrollable: You change at inconvenient times, when you really don't want to. This happens *either* at fixed times *or* when the GM rules that the situation is stressful for you (which always includes but isn't limited to any time you must make a Fright Check). In the latter case, you can make a Will roll to control the change, but a roll of 14 or higher always fails, and the GM can require another roll if the situation continues for more than a minute or gets significantly worse. Changing at fixed times is worth from -10% to -30%; examples include "three nights a month" for -10%, "eight nights a month" for -15%, "eight nights a month *and* if touched directly by moonlight" for -20%, and "continuously for eight days in each month" for -30%. Changing when under stress is worth -10%, or -15% if some specific and moderately common provocation (such as the sight or smell of blood) automatically counts as stressful for you even if it wouldn't for most people.

Example 1: Ingvar the Were-Badger was initially going to pay the full 49 points for his Alternate Form. However, his player decides that he can only change during the week of the full moon (-25%), he can change in 5 seconds (+20%), and he sometimes changes involuntarily when under stress (-10%). That adds up to -15%, reducing the cost of the advantage to (85% of 15) + (90% of 37) = 13 + 34 = 47 points.

Example 2: Shalnak the Shaman's player decides that Shalnak needs a special amulet, which would take him some time and effort to replace, to trigger his change (-20%); that he can "absorb" loads up to Medium encumbrance into his animal forms (+15%); and he can transform in one second flat (+80%). This adds up to +75%. The cost works out as (175% of 15) + (90% of 50) = 27 + 45 = 72 points for the first form and (175% of 15) = 27 points for the second – a total of 99 points.

BRACHIATOR

5 points

You can travel by swinging on vines, tree branches, ropes, chandeliers, etc. You get +2 to Climbing skill, and you move at half your Basic Move while brachiating.

BURNING ATTACK

Variable

You can inflict *burning* damage on opponents at range, though perhaps only short range. This may be dragon-like fiery breath, or the ability (frequently) demonstrated by gods to smite mortals with lightning. These attacks will also ignite flammable materials – paper, dry wood, etc. Cost per die of damage caused depends on the form:

Short-Range Flame: This is similar to a swamp dragon (pp. 359-360) breath attack. You can produce a blast of flame which is treated as a melee weapon with reach C, 1 (see p. 149), although it cannot parry. Each attack costs you 1 FP. *4 points/die.*

Flame Jet: You can throw or breathe a jet of fire. It can do full damage to targets up to five yards away, and half damage from there out to 10 yards. You *don't* take penalties for target range and speed, and you can't Aim for greater accuracy – it's more like a melee weapon in these respects. It *doesn't* cost FP to use. *5 points/die.*

Lightning Bolt: You can cause lightning bolts to smite opponents. Because these drop from above, you ignore cover behind which the target is hiding, along with any penalties to hit crouching, kneeling, sitting, or prone victims. Treat this as a ranged attack, with 1/2D and Max both 100, and Acc 4 (see p. 150 for what all this signifies). Someone who takes damage from a bolt must make a HT roll, at -1 per 2 points of damage that penetrated his DR, or be physically *stunned* (pp. 185-186). He can roll against HT once per second to recover, at the same penalty as for the initial roll. Lightning bolts don't cost FP to use. *10 points/die.*

To hit with your Burning Attack, roll against the appropriate specialisation of Innate Attack skill (p. 78), typically Beam or Breath.

Some enormous monsters (such as true dragons) and really powerful gods may be able to generate *huge* blasts that affect everyone in an area. However, this is beyond the capabilities of any reasonable PC.

CAST-IRON STOMACH

3 points

You can eat rotten vegetables and blue-green meat, and drink gutter water and sour milk. Your food bill is 5% of that of a normal person of your size, and you can survive in many situations where ordinary humans would starve – although you do need food and water of *some* kind. You also get +3 to resist food-borne poisons or diseases not specific to your species. However, humans and similar beings react at -3 if they must watch you consume things they wouldn't touch.

CATFALL

10 points

You subtract five yards from any fall. This counts as an automatic Acrobatics success (see *Falls*, pp. 189-190) – don't check again for it. Make a DX roll, however; success *halves* damage from the fall. To enjoy these benefits, your limbs must be unbound and your body free to twist as you fall.

CLAWS/HOOVES

Variable

You have something on your hands or feet that helps in a fight:

Blunt Claws: Add +1 *per die* to the damage you inflict with a punch or kick; e.g., 2d-3 becomes 2d-1. *3 points.*

Hooves: Add +1 *per die* to the damage you inflict with a kick, and give your feet (only) +1 DR. *3 points.*

Sharp Claws: Change the damage you inflict with a punch or kick from crushing to cutting. *5 points.*

Talons: Long claws (up to 12"). Change the damage you inflict with a punch or kick from crushing to your choice of cutting or impaling (choose before rolling to hit). *8 points.*

Long Talons: Claws like sword blades! Treat as Talons, but damage is +1 *per die. 11 points.*

DAMAGE RESISTANCE

5 points/level

Your body itself has a Damage Resistance (DR) score, as if it had built-in armour. Subtract this from the damage done by any physical or energy attack *after* the DR of artificial armour but *before* multiplying the injury for damage type. This DR *does not* protect your eyes, or help against purely mental attacks like magical mind-blasts or elven hypnotism.

Ordinary animals with natural armour can usually buy DR 1 to 5. Thick skin or a pelt would be DR 1; pig hide, armadillo shell, a heavy pelt, or scales like those of a lizard would be DR 2; rhinoceros hide would be DR 3; alligator scales or elephant hide would be DR 4; and a giant tortoise can have DR 5.

Trolls and other silicon-based life forms – and golems – can purchase up to DR 8, although most have less. Odd supernatural beings, such as gods who've learned how to manifest as walking metal statues, might have more (GM's decision).

Damage Resistance usually costs 5 points/level but sometimes has flaws that reduce this cost:

Can't Wear Armour: Your body is designed in such a way that you cannot practically wear personal armour. Reduce cost by 2 points/level.

Only vs. X: Damage Resistance that only works against specific forms of attack has a price reduction, depending on how common the threat is. Two possibilities are "Only vs. Heat and Fire" (which also protects against lightning) and "Only vs. Impaling Damage"; both reduce cost by 2 points/level.

Tough Skin: Your DR isn't rigid, leaving you vulnerable to being slowly squeezed or crushed. Furthermore, if a poisoned or drugged weapon, or some other exotic attack such as a stunning electrical blast, strikes your skin, the poison, drug, shock, etc., has full effect, even if your DR saves you from actual injury. Reduce cost by 2 points/level.

You can combine these qualifiers, but regardless of which ones you choose, minimum final cost is 1 point/level.

DIMENSION SHIFT

80 points

You can shift at will to and from another plane or realm of existence, such as Death's Domain or Hell, which you must specify when you buy this advantage. Oddly enough, the gods' realm *isn't* another plane – they divide their time between hanging around with mortals and lounging on top of Cori Celesti. The "astral plane" that gods sometime speak of visiting is more like an abstract state of being.

Each use requires 10 seconds of concentration and an IQ roll. A roll of 14 or more always fails. Succeed or fail, you must spend 1 FP per attempt. If you later return to your starting plane using this ability, you always come back to the place from which you left.

DISCRIMINATORY SMELL

15 or 23 points

Your sense of smell is far beyond human. You can recognise people, places, and things by scent. You may memorise a scent by sniffing it for at least one minute and making a successful IQ roll. On a failure, you must wait at least one full day before making a repeated attempt.

You get +4 (in addition to any Acute Taste and Smell bonuses) on any task that uses the sense of smell, and +4 to Tracking skill. Very strong or pungent smells can overload your senses, negating your Tracking bonus and causing you extreme discomfort.

The basic version of this advantage costs 15 points.

Discriminatory Smell (Emotion Sense): This augmented version also lets you "read" the *emotions* of humans or animals as if you had the Empathy advantage (p. 42) – but only if they're within two yards. *23 points.*

DOESN'T BREATHE

20 points

You don't need to breathe. Choking and strangulation cannot harm (or silence!) you, and you're immune to *inhaled* poisons.

DOESN'T EAT OR DRINK

10 points

You don't require food or water. Your body is powered in some other manner – probably magical or spiritual energy. (You may have the *option* to eat or drink. Many gods do so, for fun or for the look of the thing.)

DOESN'T SLEEP

20 points

You don't have to sleep, at all.

ENHANCED MOVE

20 points/level

Each level of Enhanced Move *doubles* your top speed in one environment: Air, Ground, or Water. You may also take a half-level of Enhanced Move, either alone or with any whole number of levels; this costs 10 points and multiplies Move by 1.5.

Example: A cheetah has Enhanced Move 2.5 (Ground), for 50 points. This multiplies its Move by $2 \times 2 \times 1.5 = 6$. If its Basic Move were 6, it could run at 36 yards/second (72 mph).

Your multiplied Move is your *top speed*. Record it in parentheses after your Enhanced Move trait. For instance, that cheetah, if detailed as a character, would have "Enhanced Move 2.5 (Ground Speed 36)."

Enhanced Move does *not* affect Basic Speed, Basic Move, or Dodge. Its benefits apply only when moving along a relatively straight, smooth course. It does have some defensive value, however: anyone attacking you with a ranged attack must take your speed into account when calculating speed/range modifiers (p. 179).

FLIGHT

Variable

You can fly! Flight comes in two basic forms:

Levitation: You fly without wings – probably thanks to supernatural levitation. You can hover, and you also "fly" at half-speed underwater. *40 points.*

Winged: You use large wings to fly. Your wingspan is at least twice your height. To take off, land, or manoeuvre, you require an open area with a radius equal to your wingspan in all directions. This may mean that you're unable to hover – and if you can't, you must continue flying forward with at least 1/4 your top airspeed (rounded up) at all times. *30 points if you can hover, 24 points if you have to keep moving.*

In either case, your basic flight Move is Basic Speed ×2 (drop all fractions). You can adjust this for ±2 points per ±1 yard/second. For very high speeds, take Enhanced Move (Air) (above).

They had touched down on the mountain peak, above the clouds. She felt warm and light, which was wrong. Even on a broomstick she'd never felt like this . . .

– Carpe Jugulum

FOOT MANIPULATORS

4 points

You can use your feet as extra hands. You can't walk on them at the same time, but this can still be quite, um, handy. However, because legs aren't articulated like arms, your feet can only work as hands at fairly close quarters. When wielding a melee weapon with your foot, the weapon's reach is reduced by one yard (see *Range, Reach, and Close Combat*, pp. 176-177) and you lack the leverage to deliver swing-based damage (see *Damage*, p. 28, and *Weapons*, pp. 149-150).

INJURY TOLERANCE

Variable

You lack certain physiological weaknesses. Cost depends on the frailties eliminated:

No Blood: You don't rely on a vital bodily fluid for survival. You don't bleed, are unaffected by blood-borne toxins, and are immune to attacks that rely on cutting off blood to part of your body. *5 points.*

No Vitals: You have no vital organs (such as a heart) and no tricky soft spots (knees to the groin don't worry you much). *5 points.*

Unliving: Your body isn't composed of living flesh or of its silicon-based counterpart. You take reduced injury from some attacks; see *Wounding Modifiers and Injury* (pp. 182-183). *20 points.*

INSUBSTANTIALITY

Variable

The basic version of this advantage allows you to become intangible, passing through solid objects as though they weren't there. In this state, gravity doesn't affect you – you can "fly" in *any* direction at full Move, and you make no noise when you move. You can perceive the tangible world and speak normally to those within it, but you *cannot* pick up material objects or affect them in any way. The GM may allow you to retain some minimal, non-protective clothing while insubstantial, but even that's a stretch.

While insubstantial, physical and energy attacks *cannot* harm you, but you're still vulnerable to mental and some "nonmaterial" magical attacks (fireballs won't hurt you, but "mind blasts" will). Likewise, *your* physical and energy attacks can't affect material opponents. If you're capable of casting magic spells, these can affect the physical world, but at -3 to all skill rolls – and you have to pay significantly more for this advantage (see *Variations*, below). However, you can always affect other beings who are using the same form of Insubstantiality, exactly as if both of you were substantial.

Unless you also possess Invisibility (p. 90), you're still visible while insubstantial, although you may be misty, hazy, or translucent. And while you can pass through solids, you must still breathe; treat moving through a solid object as though you were swimming underwater for purposes of suffocation. You cannot materialise *inside* a solid object.

There's always *some* way to block or contain you, which opponents may figure out. You must specify this when you buy the advantage. In addition, Insubstantiality may not work in some other dimensions, such as Death's home – it's all about shifting to "spirit form," which doesn't work if you're in a "spirit world."

The basic version of this advantage costs 80 points.

Variations

If your Insubstantiality is better or worse than the basic version, the cost changes:

Affect Substantial: If you have *any* abilities that can affect the substantial world while you're insubstantial – including magic – the advantage costs more. *+80 points.*

Always On: You are always insubstantial and cannot materialise. If you have this drawback, there's no -3 to use magic. *-40 points.*

Can Carry Objects: You can carry or wear objects, including clothing and armour, while insubstantial. These become physical if dropped. You cannot materialise them *inside* other objects or characters – you'll find that you simply can't release your grip. You may even be able to carry other living beings along with you if you're strong enough. *+8 points to carry up to No encumbrance, +16 points for Light encumbrance, +40 points for Medium, or +80 points for Heavy.*

Usually On: Similar to Always On (you cannot have both), except that you can materialise for short periods with an effort. Materialisation costs 1 FP *per second. -32 points.*

Example: Grrfoozzzar the Djinni is usually insubstantial, but can make himself solid by an effort of will (Usually On), and he can carry or wear things like a fancy turban, a bit of jewellery, and a scimitar (up to Light encumbrance). His Insubstantiality costs 64 points.

INVISIBILITY

Variable

You're truly invisible. Unlike most advantages, this one is "always on" in its basic form. You still make noise, leave footprints, and have a scent – and by default, anything you *carry* remains visible. (Yes, this may mean that you must wander around naked to avoid attention, although ghosts and spirits can treat the appearance of clothing as part of their bodies.) You don't cast a shadow or show up in mirrors, however. When carrying nothing, you get +9 to Stealth in any situation where being seen would matter.

Individuals using magical remote viewing (crystal balls, etc.) cannot see you if you would be invisible to their normal vision. *Devices* with these powers can still sense you, as can paranormal abilities that detect enemies, life, and so on non-visually. Similarly, iconographs (pp. 159-160) will capture your image and golems can see you; both have fundamentally magical perceptions. You're also visible to Sonar (p. 91), unless you're insubstantial as well.

The basic version of this advantage costs 40 points.

Variations

If your Invisibility is better or worse than the basic version, the cost changes:

Affects Devices: You're invisible even to supernatural mechanisms – including iconographs and golems. *+20 points.*

Can Carry Objects: Objects you carry – including clothing and armour – become invisible, regaining visibility when put down. *+4 points to carry up to No encumbrance, +8 points for Light encumbrance, +20 points for Medium, or +40 points for Heavy.*

Only While Insubstantial: You must also have Insubstantiality (p. 89). Your Invisibility only works when you make yourself insubstantial. *-4 points.*

Substantial Only: Your invisibility only hides you in the material world. Immaterial beings (ghosts, etc.) can see you normally. *-4 points.*

Switchable: You are normally visible, but can become invisible at will. *+4 points.*

Usually On: You are normally invisible, but can become visible for short periods, with effort. Turning visible costs 1 FP *per second. +2 points.*

Visible Reflection/Shadow: You can be seen in mirrors *or* you cast a shadow. *-4 points each.*

PRESSURE-PROOF

15 points

You suffer no ill effects from any level of pressure – say, from water or burial in earth – provided that it's applied reasonably evenly over your entire surface. Crushing attacks and squeezing can still harm you, though, and you still need to breathe.

PROTECTED EYES

1 point/level

You have well-shielded eyeballs. Each level of Protected Eyes gives your eyes (only) DR 1. This lets you see normally underwater, and it protects your eyes from sand, irritants, etc., giving +1/level to all HT rolls concerned with eye damage.

REGENERATION

Variable

Your wounds heal in mere hours, minutes, or seconds! To regenerate lost body parts, you'll also need Regrowth (below) – but Regeneration greatly accelerates that ability. Regeneration includes Rapid Healing (p. 46) at no extra cost. You cannot have Regeneration if you have Unhealing (p. 98), but see *Repairable* (below).

Cost depends on your regeneration speed:

Regeneration (Slow): You recover 1 HP every 12 hours, in addition to normal healing. *10 points.*

Regeneration (Regular): You recover 1 HP per hour. *25 points.*

Regeneration (Fast): You recover 1 HP per minute. *50 points.*

Regeneration (Very Fast): You recover 1 HP per second. *100 points.*

If your ability requires some special condition, such as close contact with a moderate quantity of blood (common with vampires), reduce cost by 40%. If it doesn't heal injury from certain types of damage, or doesn't work in some specific and reasonably plausible circumstances (e.g., if you have a stake through the heart), reduce cost by 20%. These reductions can be combined.

REGROWTH

40 points

You can regrow lost limbs and organs! A lost ear, finger, toe, claw, tentacle tip, etc. regrows in 1d weeks; a lost hand or foot, in 1d+1 months; and a lost eye, arm, or leg, in 2d+2 months. If you also have Regeneration (above), Regrowth works *much* faster: all lost body parts regrow in the time it takes you to heal to full HP.

REPAIRABLE

50 points

You don't recover HP through normal healing *at all*, but you can regain lost HP by being physically repaired, which is *fairly* easy. This requires one minute per lost HP, an appropriate skill roll from the person performing the repair, and some cheap materials.

The roll is at -1 per full 5 HP you've lost. If you try to repair yourself, there's an extra -3 due to tricky angles and a further -4 if you lack High Pain Threshold – but most beings with Repairable learn the relevant skill anyway, just in case. It's even possible to reattach severed body parts, though you must either find them or fashion a convincing substitute from appropriate materials (for which purpose the GM may apply *another* penalty to the roll).

Success restores the HP and reattaches the body parts, but except on a critical success, you'll show signs of the repair: stitches, surface patches, etc. Ordinary failure means you regain no HP but can try again, taking twice as long. Repeated failures can lead to multiple doublings of time – unskilled repairs can be a lengthy process! On a *critical* failure, however, you not only suffer the effects of a normal failure, but also lose 1 HP and any severed body parts *permanently*. Repairable characters who get into a lot of fights will go to pieces eventually. It's up to the GM whether they can buy replacement HP with bonus character points, but they should face the very real risk of permanent destruction.

The two most common examples of Repairable are found among those zombies who can be repaired with Sewing skill and a needle and strong thread, and golems, who can be repaired using Professional Skill (Potter) and good-quality clay.

Sonar

20 points

You can "see" your surroundings by making high-pitched sounds and "reading" the echoes. You can't perceive colours or read text with this, obviously, but it's good enough for you to avoid any penalties for darkness when in combat. You can scan up to 20 yards away in a 120° arc in front of you. Anyone with Ultrahearing (p. 92) will notice you using this from up to 40 yards away.

Super Climbing

6 points

You move three times as fast when climbing on any surface (see *Climbing*, p. 167).

Supernatural Durability

150 points

You can "shake off" most wounds. Injury comes off your HP as usual, and you suffer knockback (p. 186), but you're *completely immune* to shock, physical stunning, and being knocked out. You don't need High Pain Threshold (p. 43) – this advantage *includes* that one.

As long as you have 0 or more HP, you have your full Move. Below 0 HP, you're at half Move. Most important, though, you won't *die* unless you're wounded by an attack to which you're specifically vulnerable.

To die, you must first be wounded to -HP or worse. After that, one specific attack form can kill you. You must specify this when you buy Supernatural Durability, and it has to be something that you'll encounter at least occasionally, even if your opponents don't know about it; e.g., "magical energies" or "bronze blades." Once you're at -HP, if wounds from this attack form – or from anything toward which you have a Vulnerability disadvantage (p. 98) – ever reduce your HP to the point where a normal human would have to make HT rolls to survive, *you* must make those HT rolls. If such attacks wound you to -5×HP, you die automatically. And if you're *already* below -5×HP for whatever reason, *any* such wound will kill you.

The sole exception to all this is a *single attack* of any kind that inflicts an injury of 10× your HP or more. That much damage at once will blow you apart or smash you to a pulp, killing you!

Swarm Body

135 points

Your "body" consists of a number of small flying creatures; bats are traditional, but magpies aren't unknown. The flock must stay together in a loose swarm. (If you *change shape* into a Swarm Body, it will usually be +1 SM larger than your normal form.) You retain a single intelligence controlling the entire horde. If you take damage, this usually means that some of the component creatures were injured or killed.

While in this form, you can fly at your Basic Speed ×2 (just as for Flight, p. 89), and the swarm can in effect hover – although the creatures within it are doubtless moving all over the place. You have no ground movement, though; even if the component creatures have legs, coordinating them in that unfamiliar situation is just too confusing. You can also see in all directions at once, thanks to all those eyes. However, you don't have much in the way of hands; you might be able to do a *little* with mouths, beaks, or claws (GM's decision), but they aren't made for manipulation and you find it impossibly complex to exert fine control over them. You probably have low ST; if so, you get the points for that separately.

Most important, you're extremely hard to injure seriously, as most attacks pass right through the swarm with a bit of squawking and fluttering. Impaling and piercing attacks never do you more than 1 HP of injury, while other attacks inflict at most 2 HP.

The exception is area-effect attacks and explosions (usually the result of magic, alchemy, or *really big* rocks falling on you), which cause full damage.

This advantage is most often part of an Alternate Form (pp. 85-87) template for vampires who have mastered the shapeshifting trick but still find themselves bound by tiresome conservation-of-mass limitations. And yes, it would technically be more correct to call it "Flock Body" . . . but that sounds like it's something to do with the wallpaper in a Klatchian restaurant.

TEETH

1 or 2 points

Anyone with a mouth has *blunt* teeth (or a beak) that can bite for thrust-1 crushing damage; this costs 0 points. You have a more damaging bite:

Sharp Teeth: Inflict thrust-1 *cutting* damage. *1 point.*
Sharp Beak: Inflicts thrust-1 *large piercing* damage. *1 point.*
Fangs: Inflict thrust-1 *impaling* damage. *2 points.*

Supernaturally Powered Beings

If you have Doesn't Breathe, Doesn't Eat or Drink, Doesn't Sleep, and both Temperature Tolerance 3 (Cold) *and* Temperature Tolerance 3 (Heat) on your racial template, then you function entirely on magical or spiritual forces rather than mundane energy. In that case, you don't have a Fatigue Points (FP) score, and thus can't alter that characteristic for points.

This has the drawback that you can't spend FP to perform exceptional feats such as climbing faster than usual or carrying more than Extra-Heavy encumbrance (p. 168), and you can't have advantages that require FP to use. The benefit is that *you never get tired.* You can exert your full strength or run at top speed for days – or centuries – without penalty. You *may* sometimes pause or lie down, but that's for psychological reasons, not physical ones.

TEMPERATURE TOLERANCE

1, 3, or 6 points

Using the terms defined in *Temperature Extremes* (p. 191), normal humans are fine in Chilly through Warm temperatures, and they can put up with Hot weather. These advantages increase your tolerance range:

Temperature Tolerance 1 (Cold): You can operate in Freezing temperatures without special arrangements, and you can handle Extreme Cold the way normal humans do Freezing temperatures if you wrap up well. *1 point.*
Temperature Tolerance 2 (Cold): You have no problems at all in Freezing temperatures, can handle Extreme Cold the way normal

humans do Freezing temperatures, and can cope with any natural level of Intolerable Cold the way that humans deal with Extreme Cold (although magical refrigeration may be enough to get through to you eventually). *3 points.*
Temperature Tolerance 3 (Cold): You can put up with *any* naturally occurring cold temperatures without problems. Magical refrigeration may cause you *minor* inconvenience (such as icing over), at the GM's whim. *6 points.*
Temperature Tolerance 1 (Heat): You can remain fully active on Hot days without penalty, and treat Very Hot temperatures as normal humans treat Hot. *1 point.*
Temperature Tolerance 2 (Heat): You can remain fully active on Hot days without difficulty, treat Very Hot temperatures as Hot, Severe Heat as Very Hot, and Intolerable Heat as Severe Heat, up to the point where things start spontaneously combusting. *3 points.*
Temperature Tolerance 3 (Heat): You disregard *all* potential FP loss due to heat. Intolerable Heat can still inconvenience you by causing things you're carrying or using to melt or char. *6 points.*

Temperature Tolerance confers no special resistance to "blast" attacks which use rapid *changes* of temperature.

ULTRAHEARING

5 points

You can hear sounds in the frequencies above the normal range of human hearing – dog whistles, bat squeaks, etc.

UNKILLABLE

50 or 100 points

You cannot (easily) be killed! In the absence of other advantages, perks, etc., you're subject to *all* of the less-than-fatal effects of injury: pain, being slowed by your wounds, stunning, knockout, and even losing body parts. You have no special immunity to the countless ill effects of disease or poison, either; while these things might not kill you, they can surely make your life horrible. And you still age normally and will eventually expire of old age. However, you'll only die *before* that time if your body is physically destroyed – and sometimes not even then.

This advantage comes in two levels:

Unkillable 1: Injury affects you normally, but you need never make a HT roll to stay alive. You can survive (and even function, if you remain conscious) down to -10×HP, at which point your body is physically destroyed and you finally get the hint and die. As long as you're alive, you heal at your usual rate – typically 1 HP/day, modified for any Regeneration (p. 90) you may have. Crippled limbs do heal, but *severed* limbs are gone for good unless you have Regrowth (p. 90). *50 points.*
Unkillable 2: As Unkillable 1, but you don't die at -10×HP. When you reach that level, you're reduced to an effectively indestructible remnant and automatically fall unconscious. You sustain no further effective damage from *any* attack. After the damage stops, you heal normally – even if you've been hacked to pieces – and any severed body parts will grow back. You regain consciousness once you have *positive* HP. However, your enemies may imprison your remains while you're unconscious, or even expose them to a source of continuous damage (fire is popular) to prevent you from healing. *100 points.*

Variations

Many Unkillable characters have restrictions on their nigh-immortality, reducing the point cost. Below, the discount for Unkillable 1 is given before the slash, and the more sizeable one for Unkillable 2 appears after. These drawbacks cannot reduce the cost of Unkillable 1 below 10 points, or that for Unkillable 2 below 20 points.

Achilles' Heel: Damage from one particular source (possibly one to which you have a Vulnerability, p. 98) can kill you normally. You must make normal HT rolls to survive at -HP and below if you've taken any damage from this source, and you die automatically if you go below -5×HP after taking such damage. Cost savings depend on the attack's rarity: -5/-10 points if rare (e.g., octiron or some exotic alchemical preparation), -15/-30 points if it might come up occasionally (e.g., bronze weapons or lightning), or -25/-50 points if it's fairly common (e.g., wooden weapons or magical attacks).

Hindrance: A specific substance (e.g., silver or wood) prevents healing – whether of the normal type or Regeneration – for as long as it remains in your body. Once you pass out from your injuries, you remain dormant until this substance is removed. Cost savings depend on substance's rarity, as for Achilles' Heel: -2/-5 points if rare, -7/-15 points if occasional, or -12/-25 points if common.

Trigger: Only available for Unkillable 2. Once reduced to -10×HP, you require some substance (such as blood) or condition (such as a ritual) before you'll start to heal. Until then, you'll remain dormant. Cost reduction depends on the trigger's rarity: -25 points if it's something rare (e.g., your friends or minions have to go on a quest for a unique flower that grows at the foot of Cori Celesti), -15 points if it's occasional (e.g., the blood of another creature of your rare kind dribbled on your remains), or -5 points if it's reasonably common (e.g., just add water for instant demigod).

Example: Count von Vonkevve wants to be an old-school vampire who always comes back for the sequel. However, his sort of vampirism leaves him seriously vulnerable to fire, and he hasn't quite mastered the art of fitting the narrative, so he got hold of an ancient magical amulet that grants protection against normal fire and had an Igor implant it in his chest. He has Unkillable 2 (100 points), but he can still be killed permanently by magical or alchemical fire, which overloads the amulet – and it's just possible that various Igors know this (Achilles' Heel, Occasional, -30 points). As well, he'll remain "dead" if he's left with a stake through his heart in the time-honoured and well-known fashion (Hindrance, Common, -25 points). And to his annoyance, if he's reduced to dust, he can only be brought back by having blood dripped on his remains (though that does seem to happen remarkably easily: Trigger, Common, -5 points). His shaky immortality costs 40 points.

Racial Perks

Some advantageous racial features are minor enough to rate as perks.

BOREDOM IMMUNITY

You're absolutely and completely immune to boredom. If your basic requirements (if any) for food, drink, air, and exercise are met, you can sit in the same place for millennia without your mind going. You also get +3 on any rolls required to ignore distractions while working on some task.

FEATHERS, FUR, OR SCALES*

You have feathers, fur, or scales. This prevents sunburn and probably looks either cute or scary-animalistic. Any of the three can also justify a little Damage Resistance (p. 88), but you must buy that separately in all cases.

Feathers help shed water, eliminating up to -2 in penalties for being wet (notably for *Cold*, p. 191), and they may justify Damage Resistance 1 if they're good and thick. *Fur* might justify buying Damage Resistance 1-3 and Temperature Tolerance 1 (Cold), if thick enough. *Scales* can justify Damage Resistance 1-5.

FULLY DRESSED RESURRECTION

Prerequisite: Unkillable 2 (p. 92).

Whenever you're reduced to an indestructible remnant thanks to Unkillable, your current clothing disappears with your body. When you come back, the clothes reappear, too, keeping you decent and stylish. This works strictly for *ordinary clothing;* jewellery, anything that would rate as armour, magical items, and stuff in your pockets all ends up on the ground when you're killed.

The perk is available to (and standard for) male vampires, but not female ones.

Heartbeat Counter

Prerequisites: Base Hearing roll of 18+ (e.g., Per 18, or Per 14 plus Acute Hearing 4), and neither Hard of Hearing nor Deafness.

You can scan an area around you for heartbeats by taking a Concentrate manoeuvre (p. 176) and making a Hearing roll. This is at -1 per three yards of radius, with a further -1 for each intervening wall or door – or larger penalties, at the GM's whim, for especially thick barriers, other noises, etc. Success reveals exactly how many living things of cat size or larger there are in the chosen area, and it gives you a good idea of each creature's size and heart rate.

This perk is mostly associated with vampires, who find it tactful not to mention it too often; humans find it unnerving.

Limited Camouflage*

Your surface (fur, hide, etc.) blends in with a particular terrain or vegetation type, giving +2 to Camouflage and Stealth when posed *still* and *unclad* against a suitable backdrop. For instance, a gargoyle with Limited Camouflage (Stone) would get a bonus next to a rock face and could easily "impersonate" a statue around observers who don't know about living gargoyles, while a tiger with Limited Camouflage (Jungle) would be hard to see in his home territory.

Name Hearing

You must be a god or other spirit of some kind to take this perk. If anyone, anywhere on the Disc, speaks your name, you hear it (along with a few words of the associated speech) and can locate the speaker to within a few yards. This needn't distract you much; if a lot of people speak your name, it's just a soft continuous whisper in the back of your mind, from which you can extract useful information at the GM's whim.

Recognised Divinity

To take this perk, you usually have to be an actual god – a spirit which draws power from worship – although it's *just* conceivable that someone else with a remarkable backstory and an Unusual Background (pp. 48-49) could claim the status. Certainly, you must have at least one worshipper who honestly believes in your divinity.

Other deities acknowledge your standing, however grudgingly, and must address you as an equal. There are conventions and rules governing relations between deities, which are just sufficient to prevent all-out divine civil war, direct inter-god violence being frowned upon (that's what worshippers are for). So long as you respect these, other deities will usually respect them with regard to you. Also, any god may request a boon of any other; the snag is that the one who performs the favour may require any vaguely plausible price, and may decide what that should be, and when and where to take it, later. Naturally, such prices are rarely small.

Sordid Claws

Prerequisite: Sharp Claws, Talons, or Long Talons (p. 88).

You not only have claws, but they tend to be caked in filth – and thanks to your racial tolerance for the stuff, this is worse for others than for you. If you injure an opponent with your claws, he must roll for some kind of possible infection (see *Disease*, p. 189). Severity is up to the GM, and might depend on how dirty local conditions are, but this should always be at least potentially unpleasant, and something that's actually lethal without treatment is entirely possible.

Striking Surface

Prerequisite: Damage Resistance 3+ *without* the Tough Skin option (p. 88).

You have a hard body surface that increases barehanded damage. Your punch counts as using brass knuckles and your kick works as if wearing heavy boots. This gives +1 to damage, but you can't get more by wearing boots or knuckledusters.

Unfazed by Size

Prerequisite: SM -1 or less.

Your species is smaller than humanity, but this doesn't worry you. When somebody with a larger SM uses Intimidation skill on you, you may disregard up to three levels of SM difference (see *Character Size*, p. 27), while anyone bigger gets a flat +1 for size.

Example: An SM -3 creature trying to intimidate an SM -4 to -6 victim who has this perk gets no bonus. Even a troll with SM +1, which normally has +4 against SM -3 or smaller creatures, receives just +1 if its tiny target has Unfazed by Size.

Racial Disadvantages

As with racial advantages, racial disadvantages can only be taken as part of a racial template unless the GM agrees that one suits a particularly unusual character.

Aerial

0 points

Prerequisite: Flight (p. 89).

You fly rather than walk, and you don't have useful legs; your ground Move is 0. While this is recorded with disadvantages, it isn't worth any points – flying everywhere works just fine, and the lack of legs with which to kick is balanced by both the lack of legs to get injured and the fact that you can't be knocked over while resting on the ground.

Arcane Automaton

-55 points

You're a magical or supernatural construct or unmotivated spirit; you were created or summoned to serve, and you can't do much else unless you get rid of this disadvantage. You can be programmed or mystically assigned to obey a master, and it's hard, although not necessarily impossible, for unauthorised people to alter this "programming" (resolve the details with the GM if necessary). Consequently, you must obey slavishly, remaining strictly within the letter of your master's commands. As you lack real initiative, you may become confused and ineffectual – most likely just standing around – without someone to give you orders. You might have built-in "commandments" which override everything else; you'll *probably* explain this to your current master.

You must make an IQ roll at -8 before you can take any action that isn't either obeying a direct order or part of an established routine. You *automatically* fail any Will roll to assert yourself or resist social influence unless the GM decides that you might just have a reason to succeed, in which case you roll at -6. However, because your programming always takes priority, it's *very* difficult for anyone to manipulate you socially or psychologically.

You suffer all the effects of being Hidebound (p. 61) – which is included in this disadvantage – and you may also have other psychological limitations such as Incurious (p. 61), Low Empathy (p. 61), or No Sense of Humour (p. 65).

This trait doesn't necessarily imply low IQ or Will. You might be intelligent enough to obey the command, "Perform the Greater Rituals of Offler and Blind Io thrice per day on every ninth day," but if you needed to eat, were starving, and found a coin, you would have to roll vs. IQ-8 to decide to pick up the money and go buy food. Similarly, you might be strong-willed enough to succeed at Fright Checks in the presence of terrifying monsters, yet roll at Will-6 to resist the manipulations of an obvious con man.

This disadvantage should generally be limited to non-player entities such as non-free golems, as it doesn't make for a very playable character.

BESTIAL

-10 or -15 points

You think and act like a wild animal – not necessarily savage, but you have no conception of property, art, or formal manners (although you may understand *territory* or pack hierarchy). You mostly ignore those who leave you alone, and you respond to threats with fight or flight.

This is normally worth -10 points. You can't take an Odious Personal Habit to reflect "animalistic" behaviour – this disadvantage covers that – but if your "animal" behaviour is *really* unpleasant, Bestial can be worth -15 points. You *can* have Odious Personal Habits that aren't the norm with wild animals.

DREAD/FIXATION

Variable

Dread compels you to keep a certain, minimum distance from a particular item or substance; e.g., a holy symbol. If outside forces bring you and that thing any closer together, you must move away as fast as you can, by the most direct route possible. You may do nothing else until you're beyond the range of your Dread. If you cannot put that much distance between yourself and the object of your aversion, you collapse and whimper helplessly.

You can instantly sense the presence of the dreaded substance as soon as you enter the forbidden radius. You don't know exactly where it is, but you know what direction it lies in, and you are compelled to go the other way.

The base value of Dread is -10 points, which prohibits you from coming within one yard of the dreaded substance. A larger radius gives an additional -1 point per yard, to a maximum of -20 points at 11 yards. If the object of your Dread is rare (e.g., a particularly obscure holy symbol), *halve* the value. If it's notably common (e.g., any of an array of different holy symbols, or "anything magical"), *double* it. And if it's very common (e.g., sunlight, or *anything* that anyone would recognise as *possibly* a holy symbol), *triple* it.

Fixation means that, instead of being repelled by something, you must remain effectively motionless and pay attention to it in some way, usually taking a certain amount of time – minutes to hours – until you can act again. If you're attacked, you can defend yourself, but no more. If the object of your Fixation is removed, you'll try to follow it, but if it's moved out of the disadvantage's radius of effect, you can make a Will roll at -2 each turn to stop

pursuing it. You don't *automatically* sense the thing upon which you're fixated, but any hint of its presence obliges you to check for it. This costs the same as Dread of the same thing; see *Optional Vampire Traits* (pp. 110-112) for an example.

FAITH MAINTENANCE

-25, -30, or -35 points

You draw power from mortal worship and belief. The GM decides what, exactly, constitutes "belief." There are known examples of gods with nation-sized congregations, *none* of whom *really* believed – but if people are prepared to pray to you at least weekly, for no less than an hour at a time, and you or your priests give them *some* reason to believe, you should be okay. (The strategy developed by Om, p. 299, of not promising much while offering a *comfortable* faith, and making his inaction somehow proof of his reality, demands a really well-run church and won't work for most deities.) If you've paid points for a Congregation (p. 38), you can assume that they believe in you and continue to provide belief even when they aren't present in person. If you have Social Regard (p. 35) *and* Recognised Divinity (p. 94), you start play with adequate worship from about 25 people per week per level of Social Regard.

Major Discworld deities need the belief of thousands, but smaller gods can get by with smaller cults, and this disadvantage fits them. Pricing depends on how many worshippers you require:

Number of Believers	Point Value
11-20	-25
21-50	-30
51-100	-35

You don't need prayers from the same people every week – plenty of pantheons share a pool of believers – but you do have to have *enough* people showing up *each* week. A well-run campaign of persecution can put you in danger, although the GM may agree that's the sort of thing that drives believers underground and makes their faith stronger. You still have to worry about your followers getting wiped out, though.

If you don't get enough belief from enough people in a one-week period, your HT drops by 1 and you must roll against your new HT. Failure means one of your divine powers is weakened or lost. Details are up to the GM; perhaps your lightning bolts lose a couple of dice of damage or start to require a large FP expenditure, or you can no longer change into a different shape, or your flight speed is halved, or you have -3 to ST. On a critical failure, something *really* bad happens – maybe your main temple spontaneously collapses, or you lose a power permanently, or one of your priests proclaims that you're just a solar myth. If your HT ever falls to 3 or less, you become almost entirely powerless; at HT 0, you're effectively dead, reduced to a sad voice on the wind.

Regaining lost HT and abilities takes *work*. Your cult must start praying again, for a period of two weeks for every week by which you missed out. You have to work several convincing miracles for them per lost point of HT. And your priests should run a preaching campaign with plenty of successful Public Speaking rolls.

You can *never* buy off or reduce this disadvantage with bonus character points. Once you've hit the big time, there's no going back.

FRIGHTENS ANIMALS

-10 points

You upset animals just by being what you are. Dogs shy away or attack you, and you can forget about riding anywhere. Your mere scent is enough to panic most creatures. You get -4 on reaction rolls made by animals – and people who see how animals react to you, and those with Animal Empathy, react to you at -1. Watchmen, hunters, etc. with guard animals or "sniffer" dogs will probably decide how to deal with you based on their *animal's* reaction roll.

ODIOUS RACIAL HABITS

Variable

This disadvantage is almost identical to Odious Personal Habits (p. 29), and it uses the same rules and pricing. However, the behaviour is associated with your *whole species*, and other members of your species aren't annoyed by it. On the other hand, it does fuel stereotyping and prejudice, adding an extra twist of trouble.

QUADRUPED

-35 points

You're a four-legged creature with a horizontal posture. You take up more space horizontally than a humanoid of the same size, and you don't reach up as high. (You might stand on your hind legs for short periods, but you find this very uncomfortable.) If you lose use of one leg, you can continue to move at half Move (round down). Loss of a second leg causes you to fall down.

You have no "hands" more agile than paws or hooves. Consequently, you cannot use your limbs to make repairs, pick locks, wield weapons, etc., or even to grasp firmly. This gets you a 40% discount when improving ST (p. 26) and DX (p. 26), however.

Your build doesn't let you put your full weight behind a kick; your thrusting damage is at -1 *per die* when kicking. Ignore this if you have Claws (p. 88) – that trait includes the necessary adaptations to strike at full power. The penalty *does* apply if you have Hooves, however.

RESTRICTED DIET

-10 to -40 points

You require a specialised food or fuel that's hard to come by. You don't take damage if you go without – you just can't eat and will eventually starve. Point value depends on the rarity of the needed item. Something really rare, like precious stones, would be worth -40 points; something common but difficult, like human flesh, would get you -20 points (although *that* example would probably earn you all sorts of other disadvantages, too). Reasonably fresh blood of any sort, as required by most Discworld vampires, is worth just -10 points; while it's trickier than "ordinary" food, a vampire who wants to avoid trouble can generally make an arrangement with a local butcher.

SEMI-UPRIGHT

-5 points

You have a semi-upright posture, like many apes. You can stand up more-or-less comfortably, allowing you to use your forelimbs to bash, hold books, etc. You can manage a clumsy gait while upright (-40% to Move), but you must use all of your limbs to run at full Move. If you have DX 12+, you can carry a small object or two while walking.

SHORT ARMS

-10 points

You have fully functional arms, but they're *significantly* shorter than the human norm – most likely because you're much smaller than a human. As a result, when you wield a melee weapon, its reach is reduced by one yard (see *Range, Reach, and Close Combat*, pp. 176-177) and you lack the leverage to deliver swing-based damage (see *Damage*, p. 28, and *Weapons*, pp. 149-150). Moreover, you have -2 on attempts to grapple – you can't get your hands around an opponent. In practise, characters with SM -2 or less usually have this disadvantage and are limited to knife- and dagger-sized weapons for practical purposes, whatever their ST.

If you also have the One Arm disadvantage (p. 64), the value of Short Arms becomes just -5 points.

Discworld dwarfs and goblins *don't* take this disadvantage; they have little trouble wielding all sorts of human-sized weapons normally. Gnomes and pictsies (pp. 101-102) qualify, however. They may use certain weapons with a swinging motion, but as they can't get as much leverage as a human-sized fighter, it's easiest to treat all of their weapons as daggers doing thrust-based damage, regardless of blade shape (and pictsies use *many* different blades – with enthusiasm).

SHORT LEGS

-2 points

Prerequisite: Quadruped (above).

Your legs are significantly shorter than the human norm, probably simply because you're small. The game effect is that you can kick no further than reach C (see *Range, Reach, and Close Combat*, pp. 176-177). This disadvantage is only considered *significant*, and thus worth points, for quadrupeds; other beings don't have to worry about kicking reach that much.

SUPERNATURAL FEATURES

Variable

You have disturbing features that mark you as a supernatural being. You can pass for a normal mortal to casual observers, but closer inspection reveals that you are *not quite right.*

Supernatural Features differ from Unnatural Features (p. 30) in that they *aren't* usually obvious; they only become apparent under specific circumstances. When they *are* noticed, though, they give a reaction penalty: -1 for every -5 points from this trait. They also give a bonus to any skill roll made to identify your true nature: +1 for every -5 points.

If the features can only be detected on close contact and might pass as just slightly odd (e.g., No Body Heat), they're worth -5 points. However, most are blatantly unnatural and fairly easy to spot in appropriate circumstances or good light (e.g., No Reflection in Mirrors, No Shadow, and Deathly Pallor), and are worth -10 points. Many traditional vampires have *several* different Supernatural Features.

TROLL BRAIN

-10 points

You're a troll or similar, with a silicon brain which operates best in cold conditions. Your purchased IQ represents your intelligence in *Chilly* or *Moderate* temperatures (see *Temperature Extremes,* p. 191). This value falls as ambient temperatures rise.

In Warm conditions, you suffer -1 to IQ. This becomes -2 in a Hot environment, -3 in Very Hot temperatures, and -5 in Severe Heat. Intolerable Heat would cause you to turn even more thoroughly stupid! Your Will and Per – and all skills based on IQ, Will, or Per – are adjusted in line with your modified IQ.

If your effective IQ drops to 3 or 4, you can do little more than grunt and hit back if attacked; moreover, your DX and all DX-based skills are at -4. (Trolls in this condition generally lumber off into a corner and go to sleep.) At IQ 2, you run on pure instinct and can do nothing but shamble around at half Move until you find a place to fall over safely (most trolls consider falling on top of a human to be perfectly safe). In addition, at IQ 2 or less, you get *no* natural DR against heat-based damage, as your nervous system becomes highly vulnerable. At IQ 1 or below, you lock up and "turn to stone." Old trolls can spend years like this – although at the GM's option, they may respond to extreme provocation, running on the troll equivalent of adrenaline.

Heat-based attacks (magical flame, incendiary weapons, etc.) cause shorter-lived penalties. Divide the attack's damage roll by (2 + your SM), round down, and subtract the result from your IQ, even if no damage penetrates your DR; e.g., a troll with SM +2, hit by a fireball that rolls 15 points of damage, suffers -3 to IQ. You then recover a level of IQ per second. A salvo of small fireballs can thus heat you into temporary immobility, even if none of them really hurt. You may dislike very bright illumination, perhaps as a quirk (p. 66), because it's associated with heat, but most urban trolls put up with the human preference for daytime. A few old-fashioned trolls might have an actual Dread (p. 95) of daylight.

Balancing all this, you gain some benefits when the temperature is especially cool: Freezing conditions give a temporary +1 to IQ, Extreme Cold gives +2, and Intolerable Cold can grant even more, at the GM's whim. If you're locked in a magical freezer, you may gain genius-level insights into your situation – or the nature of the universe. This is left to roleplaying and GM discretion; the burst of advanced intelligence need not grant anything *useful,* and you might not know what to do with it. And be aware that even trolls suffer serious danger at these temperatures!

In a campaign which is set to take place mostly in cooler locations, Troll Brain is less of a disadvantage; the GM may reduce its point value. In a campaign set, say, in high mountains, trolls may be required to have higher "base" IQ scores than their usual racial template implies – that being their level in the usual local Freezing conditions – and get -5 points for Troll Brain, as they would remain vulnerable to fire attacks and unusually warm weather.

TROLL NOCTURNALISM

-20 points, or -8 points with mitigator
Prerequisite: Troll Brain (above).

This disadvantage is far more serious than the biologist's meaning of "nocturnal" in our world. It represents an extreme version of the effects noted for Troll Brain (above). It's mostly limited to backwoods trolls – if only because sufferers have such a hard time of it in more cosmopolitan communities. They're said to "turn to stone" in daylight. In fact they don't (they're *already* stone), but in warm conditions, they lose so much brain function that they stop moving. There may be a large psychosomatic component involved; these trolls aren't sensitive to small differences in temperature, but the moment the sun rises, they just *stop.*

If you have Troll Nocturnalism, you can only be active while the sun is below the horizon. As soon as dawn starts to break, you grow lethargic – and when the sun clears the horizon, you become paralysed and comatose until the sun goes down again. In theory, you should take several minutes to warm up; in practise, you cease functioning almost instantly. The GM may require a Will roll *each second* for you to keep going.

As a special effect, trolls look almost like odd-but-natural lumps of rock when they're in this condition. Human travellers can walk right by a stationary troll without giving it a second glance. The tendency of rural trolls to wear very few clothes but to let moss grow on their surfaces may contribute to this.

Most trolls found in human cities don't seem to suffer from this problem; they're doubtless overwhelmingly descended from migrants who didn't. A few, though, have Troll Nocturnalism with a mitigator (p. 53), in the form of an alchemical concoction referred to as "high-strength sunscreen." This reduces disadvantage value to -8 points. The GM should occasionally threaten trolls with this version of the trait with problems when they can't get to alchemists' shops, are out of cash to pay for the stuff, or get so thoroughly soaked that the sunscreen washes off.

UNCONTROLLABLE APPETITE*

-15 points

This sort of problem is associated with some less self-controlled vampires and a few demons and monstrosities from the Dungeon Dimensions. You consume something (blood, "life force," etc.) that you must obtain from other sapient beings through force or guile . . . and you have difficulty controlling your appetites.

Whenever you have an opportunity to indulge, you must make a self-control roll, at -2 if someone deliberately tempts you or if the item on which you feed is available in large quantities within range of your senses. If feeding would restore lost HP, this roll is at -1 per missing HP. Failure means you *must* feed. Make a second self-control roll to stop once you've had your fill. If you fail, you go into frenzy and overindulge.

A vampire with an Uncontrollable Appetite for human blood doesn't have to roll just because he's in the same room as a living being – *unless* he's seriously hungry (having gone for at least a day without any sort of blood, not necessarily that of a sapient), the blood is directly visible (there's a wounded human present, the blood is in a cup, etc.), or he's being deliberately tempted somehow (and a lot of vampires regard nubile young women in gauzy nightwear as inherently tempting). For every 12 hours past the one-day mark he has gone without feeding, the self-control roll is at -1. Many modern vampires have found ways to mitigate this urge, but in that case, losing the mitigator can make them very dangerous; see *The Mitigator* (p. 114).

UNHEALING

-20 or -30 points

You cannot heal *naturally*. You get no daily HT roll to recover lost HP (see *Natural Recovery*, p. 187). Bandaging, the First Aid skill, or the Physician skill cannot restore missing HP for you, and magic or drugs that accelerate natural healing are useless. This trait comes in two levels:

Partial: You can heal naturally if a rare condition is met (e.g., when immersed in blood or bathed in lava). *-20 points.*
Total: You can *never* heal naturally. *-30 points.*

Depending on your nature, you might be able to regain lost HP "unnaturally" through surgery, mechanical repairs, or exotic means (special spells, alchemy, etc.). However, this should be a lengthy, complicated, and expensive process, requiring help from people with specialised skills. If you can't heal by natural processes but *can* be repaired fairly easily, don't take Unhealing – buy Repairable (pp. 90-91) instead.

UNNATURALLY FRAGILE

-50 points

Your body lacks the vitality of a normal living thing, so it tends to go to pieces as soon as you take serious levels of damage – probably because you're a supernatural construct (e.g., a golem, some kind of undead, or a demon in a temporary body bodged together by summoning magic). You *automatically* fail the HT roll to stay alive if reduced to -HP or below (p. 185).

VULNERABILITY

Variable

You suffer extra harm from a particular attack form. Point value depends on how much extra and how common the attack mode; e.g., ×2 injury from silver weapons is worth -10 points, whereas ×4 injury from all metal is worth -80 points. Apply the multiplier to any damage that penetrates your DR; regular wounding modifiers (for cutting, impaling, etc.) then *further* increase the injury.

WEAK BITE

-2 points

You do -2 damage *per die* with biting attacks (pp. 92 and 178).

WEAKNESS

Variable

You suffer painful physical injury from something that's harmless to normal humans. It's worth -20 points to lose 1d HP a minute to something you encounter occasionally (e.g., intense cold, salt water). If you take more than 1d, multiply the point value by the number of dice. If the problem is rare (e.g., holy water, pure gold), *halve* the value; if it's common (e.g., *direct sunlight, smoke*), *double* it; and if it's very common (*any daylight, living plants*), *triple* it. You take the first batch of injury the moment you're exposed to the problem, and then more every minute thereafter.

Racial Quirks

Some races have problems worth only -1 point each. Many of these would make valid quirks (p. 66) for an individual human, but those below tend to be specifically racial.

BRAWLING SOCIETY

Your culture regards brawls as part of normal personal relations. You need very little excuse to throw a punch at another member of your species; conversely, you don't regard being punched, or even hit with crushing weapons, as a great problem. You've *probably* learned not to act this way with humans, though you may secretly regard them as feeble.

CANNOT FLOAT

You always sink in water, possibly because you're made of rock or ceramic.

CANNOT RUN LONG DISTANCES

When running (p. 168), halve the time intervals at which you check for FP loss; thus, you tire twice as quickly as a normal human.

DELUSION (SPELLING MY NAME BACKWARDS DISGUISES IT PERFECTLY)

This is tragically common among vampires – many a hunted Count von Vogelheim has cheerfully signed into hotels as "Miehlegov." This is only worth a point if you're genuinely likely to use a pseudonym on occasion, though.

DOGGY RESPONSES

You have numerous psychological foibles that humans associate with dogs, such as catching and fetching thrown sticks, and not liking baths. This is typical of werewolves, to their annoyed embarrassment. They like to think of themselves as free-willed beings, or at least *wild* animals, so reacting when told to "Sit!" seems like betrayal.

HUNTER'S HABITS

This quirk-level carnivore version of Bestial (p. 95) is another common foible of werewolves and other sapient predators. You like to go out and hunt your own food, and whine and complain if forced to stay at home. You can control *what* you hunt to a fair degree; werewolves who live in human communities raid a lot of henhouses, although they may worry about losing control and doing something worse. Vampires suffer from this trait occasionally, which can be more dangerous, as they favour larger prey; Black Ribboners (pp. 113-114) try to suppress such instincts.

SHORT LIFESPAN

A lifespan that's merely a bit less than the human average isn't terribly important in most Discworld games. It might be something for the character to suffer a bit of angst about, but it's unlikely to affect day-to-day activity. Hence, it's considered a quirk.

SILVER AVERSION

Prerequisite: Vulnerability (p. 98) to silver weapons.

Beyond being hurt more by silver, you have a kind of allergy to the stuff. It acts as a poison if you somehow ingest it (take 2d or more damage); biting down on silver objects or inhaling silver dust is at the very least unpleasant for you (spit, curse audibly, and roll HT-4 to avoid being physically stunned); and having it pressed against your skin is painful. A werewolf with this quirk can be trapped in wolf form by a silver collar; trying to change back involves hard contact, and the pain disrupts the change.

SUNBURNS EASILY

If you're exposed to direct sunlight, roll against HT once per hour to avoid suffering -1 to DX for a day thereafter.

WEAK SPOT

Prerequisite: Racial Damage Resistance (p. 88) of 2+.

You have a small but fairly well-known weak spot where your racial DR doesn't apply. The GM decides how hard this is to hit in combat, but the penalty is usually at least -4.

Racial Skills

These represent things that a human would have to study but which come naturally to most members of the race. To get a better level in such a skill, simply pay the difference between the racial level and your desired level; e.g., a dwarf would pay 2 points for Axe/Mace skill at DX+1, 6 points for DX+2, and so on.

Racial Templates

For game purposes, "race" means either "species" (in the biological sense, broadly) or "class of supernatural being" (e.g., "werewolf" or "vampire"). The Discworld has quite a few of both. "Races" in the mundane, real-world sense also exist on the Disc, but nobody worries about them much – differences in skin colour seem trivial when there are trolls and elves around!

Each nonhuman race has a template with a point cost, positive or negative. To play a member of that race, you must buy the associated template. For convenience, record this as an advantage if its value is positive or as a disadvantage if negative. Negative-value racial templates *don't* count against disadvantage limits, though.

Each racial template is made up of a bundle of attribute and secondary characteristic modifiers, advantages, disadvantages, required skills, etc. The point value of each trait appears in square brackets; e.g., "ST+2 [20]." Skills in racial templates are given with difficulty, level relative to the controlling attribute, point cost, and level assuming a racial average attribute level; e.g., "Tracking (A) Per+1 [4]-11." The template's point cost is the sum of the point values of all these parts. Disadvantages included in racial templates don't count against disadvantage limits, either.

Advantages, disadvantages, etc. included in racial templates are found in *at least* 50% of all members of the species, and usually many more – but they need not be 100% universal. Eliminating a racial advantage gives you back its point cost, and those points *do* count against disadvantage limits, because this *is* a disadvantage by that race's standards. You can usually pay points to buy off racial disadvantages and quirks, too, as most such traits are actually products of culture and upbringing, rather than hard-wired.

For example, you could play a dwarf with no Metalwork Talent (a -10-point "disadvantage") and Greed with the self-control number improved from 12 to 15 (paying 8 points to partly buy off the disadvantage). Many other dwarfs *will* think he's a bit odd, though. He might even have a negative Reputation as a non-dwarfish freak.

What follows are templates for an assortment of (more-or-less) intelligent races that might make reasonable PCs. Some may be more reasonable than others! Always seek the GM's permission first, especially for weirder races – they don't all fit every campaign.

Hunchbroad Modoscousin: The Dwarf

Steve begins by taking the dwarf racial template (below). This gives him ST 11, HT 11, 13 HP, and various other traits. He has to choose what sort of Greed Hunchbroad suffers from; Steve opts for Dwarfish Greed, as he wants to play a *dwarfish* dwarf.

Dwarfs

27 points

Dwarfs are discussed at length on pp. 226-228. They're typically around 4' tall, but very stocky and hence much heavier than a human of that height – around 130 lbs., even without all the armour they habitually wear.

This template represents a dwarf with a fairly complete set of cultural baggage, although a fully "traditional" individual would add Intolerance (Trolls) [-5] and Literal-Minded [-10]; don't count those against campaign disadvantage limits if you take them. Likewise, many add "Likes wearing metal to the point of obsession" to their quirks, which again need not count against campaign limits. Recently, though, some dwarfs have shown a willingness to discard their old prejudice against trolls, and dwarfs in the Ankh-Morpork City Watch are *required* to act as watchmen first and dwarfs second, and also not to start too many fights when somebody nearby uses the word "short." This shows that dwarfs can restrain their psychological disadvantages and quirks if they try. Dwarfs who've come to moderate their behaviour – usually as a result of living in human cities – may also raise the self-control number on their Greed or Dwarfish Greed to 15, or even change the disadvantage to a quirk (usually "Insists on being paid in gold"). A few real dwarf sophisticates have abandoned the old attitude to gender and come out of the closet as female (or for that matter male), although some other dwarfs may display Intolerance toward *them*.

Dwarfs may purchase extra levels of Metalwork. However, while that Talent gives bonuses to Engineer and Mechanic, those skills – aside from Engineer (Mining) – aren't *especially* common among dwarfs, who mostly like their metal in big, plain lumps.

Some other disadvantages are more common among dwarfs than among humans, although nothing like as common as humans assume. These include Berserk, Chummy, Clueless, Hidebound, Miserliness, and Stubbornness. A dwarf character could have any

of those at quirk level. Alcoholism is an occasional unfortunate consequence of dwarfish behaviour on getting away from home. Urban dwarfs often have high skill in a profitable craft, while their backwoods cousins may well have good levels of Prospecting or Engineer (Mining).

Dwarfs rarely if ever learn to cast spells, but their craft skills do extend into the realm of magical devices. In game terms, if they have Magery at all, it will probably be Magery (Engineering Only). They can certainly learn Engineer (Magical) and apply their racial Metalwork bonus to it.

Attribute Modifiers: ST+1 [10]; HT+1 [10].
Secondary Characteristic Modifiers: SM -1; HP+2 [4].
Advantages: Lifting ST 3 [9]; Metalwork 1 [10].
Perks: Longevity [1].
Disadvantages: Dwarfish Greed (12) [-15] *or* Greed (12) [-15].
Quirks: Cannot Run Long Distances; Considers dwarf gender a very private matter; Personality Change (gains Bad Temper when drinking); Touchy about height and beard. [-4]
Racial Skills: Axe/Mace (A) DX [2]-10.

Gargoyles

46 points

Gargoyles *appear* to be a race akin to trolls. However, while they're definitely creatures of living stone, they may not be one of the ancient Discworld races at all, but something altogether different. One possibility is that they're a product of high-speed Disc evolution: creatures who've developed a symbiosis with architecture, and a close relationship with guttering that ideally suits an unfussy filter-feeder. Another theory is that they're descended from the inanimate decorations on some wizards' towers – there's a type of spell-user who *insists* on having amusing carvings on his home, and a high level of ambient magic interacting with inanimate stone over decades *might* produce animation. Certainly, Unseen University has its own gargoyle population.

Gargoyles mostly just sit around on ledges and cornices, letting water flow off their surroundings and through their mouths, and extracting nutrition from what comes with it. However, they like variety in their diet (usually in the form of pigeons) enough to make them amenable to the occasional paying job. The big practical problem in negotiating with them is that a gargoyle's mouth cannot close properly, so they cannot pronounce many consonants. Roleplay this!

Many gargoyles have disadvantages such as Clueless, Low TL, No Sense of Humour, illiteracy, and low Status and Wealth; their normal lifestyle doesn't require much in the way of education or social interaction. However, they get on tolerably with other races, and sometimes take jobs other than "architectural feature." They certainly make excellent observers.

Gargoyles are around human size or a bit bulkier, but appear shorter owing to their habitual hunched posture. Due to their stony composition, they obviously weigh a lot more – about 400 lbs.

Attribute Modifiers: ST+5 [50]; DX-1 [-20]; IQ-3 [-60].
Secondary Characteristic Modifiers: Will+4 [20]; Per+4 [20]; Basic Move-1 [-5].
Advantages: Cast-Iron Stomach [3]; Claws (Blunt Claws) [3]; Damage Resistance 5 (Can't Wear Armour) [15]; High Pain Threshold [10]; Night Vision 4 [4]; Protected Eyes 4 [4]; Single-Minded [5]; Temperature Tolerance 3 (Cold) [6]; Temperature Tolerance 1 (Heat) [1]; Unfazeable [15].

Perks: Boredom Immunity; Limited Camouflage (Stone); Longevity. [3]
Disadvantages: Appearance (Ugly) [-8]; Disturbing Voice [-10]; Hidebound [-5]; Innumerate [-5]; Troll Brain [-10].
Quirks: Cannot Float; Prefers to be above ground level. [-2]
Racial Skills: Climbing (A) DX+3 [12]-12.

OTHER GARGOYLE TRAITS

Depending on its exact form, a gargoyle could have a Sharp Beak or other physical features. Any gargoyle can buy up to three additional levels of DR to reflect a more robustly stony structure. Despite often having wings, gargoyles can't fly – they *are* slow-moving and made of stone, after all. However, in a sufficiently strong ambient magical field, the odd gliding mutant cannot be ruled out entirely.

GARGOYLE NPCS

Gargoyles can be used simply as setting "furniture," lurking on roofs and watching the world go by, but they can also make useful Contacts for city-based adventurers who want to know about events on a given street. Owners of gothic castles might also employ them as part of the defences; while gargoyles are averse to actual combat, they make excellent lookouts and could be persuaded to drop the odd heavy object on attackers. Gargoyles may also develop sentimental feelings towards the inhabitants of "their" buildings, or even seek revenge for the destruction of their habitat by some besieger. Having troll-like bodies, they must also have troll-like brains, so one who has settled on some icicle-draped mountaintop tower near the Hub could prove quite bright.

Gnomes and Pictsies

18 points

Gnomes and pictsies (or pixies) are the Disc's smallest humanoids, ranging from 4" (SM -7) to 2' (SM -3) tall, tending toward the lower end of that scale. This implies weights of about 0.5 oz.-6 lbs. It isn't certain whether they're in fact the same species – there are many differences in behaviour and psychology, and the races may have completely different histories – but they're similar enough to use the same template for game purposes. They're often startlingly strong, and the smallest of them might even be among the strongest. Gnomes who live above ground are occasionally referred to as "goblins," but that name is better used for a different race (pp. 102-104).

Gnomes are solitary and reclusive, with little culture of their own beyond a traditional fondness for setting up home in large mushrooms, which they outfit with windows and chimneys. Like many small creatures, they tend to be quick on their feet and good at hiding. Until recently, many humans believed them to be extinct, but some have shown up in Ankh-Morpork in recent years. They're basically hunter-gatherers, a lifestyle which has adapted well to human cities (even if what they gather there may already have an owner). It also turns out that many jobs in human cities are ideally suited to beings with tiny fingers, and a modest payment in human terms can provide a gnome-sized worker with a very comfortable lifestyle. Gnomes mostly speak Morporkian and have shown no aptitude for magic.

Banshees

72 points

Banshees are a sapient species, but they wouldn't make very good PCs in most games. They're rare and largely solitary, with no taste for small talk; they're also aggressive, little-loved *predators*. However, they can serve as scary antagonists for the heroes.

These flying humanoids are believed to have originated in some jungle region, but are now found occasionally in the forests of Uberwald. They have wings that fold around them like leather capes, sinewy bodies with powerful muscles, and two hearts. While about the same height as a human being when standing on the ground, they're much lighter thanks to hollow bones and a light build. Though their claws aren't *very* long or sharp, they can deliver a vicious swipe with more reach than people expect (hence the Long Talons advantage). They instinctively snatch at small prey without even thinking.

When a banshee is closing on a victim, it will almost always scream. Handle this as use of Intimidation with the bonus from Penetrating Voice. However, it will close its eyes when it does so – treat it as suffering from Blindness (p. 55) on that turn.

A very few banshees find employment in human societies. Those often have Brawling and Stealth skills, and probably Merchant and Streetwise (to help them find work). Banshees that remain in the wilderness focus on Tracking and Survival.

(The chronicles also feature one *supernatural* banshee, Mr. Ixolite. See p. 366.)

Attribute Modifiers: ST-1 [-10]; DX+2 [40]; HT+1 [10].
Secondary Characteristic Modifiers: HP+4 [8]; Per+4 [20]; Basic Speed+0.25 [5].
Advantages: Acute Taste and Smell 2 [4]; Claws (Long Talons) [11]; Combat Reflexes [15]; Damage Resistance 2 (Can't Wear Armour; Tough Skin) [2]; Discriminatory Smell [15]; Fearlessness 2 [4]; Flight (Winged, Can't Hover) [24]; High Pain Threshold [10]; Night Vision 4 [4]; Teeth (Sharp Teeth) [1].
Perks: Penetrating Voice [1].
Disadvantages: Appearance (Hideous) [-16]; Bad Temper (15) [-5]; Bloodlust (12) [-10]; Callous [-5]; Odious Racial Habit (Habitual Killer) [-15]; Social Stigma (Minority Group) [-10]; Vulnerability (Crushing Attacks ×2) [-30].
Quirks: Blunt and tactless; Closes eyes and screams to intimidate victims; Dislikes cramped conditions; Reflexively grabs and consumes small flying creatures; Uncongenial. [-5]
Racial Skills: Intimidation (A) Will+1 [4]-11.

Humans have been known to enslave gnomes. Trying this on the wrong gnome is a quick route to a pair of broken kneecaps, though. Sentimental humans will side with the gnome, while unsentimental humans will just laugh at whoever comes off worst.

Elf-Kin

16 points

Elves (pp. 362-365) aren't suitable as PCs. However, during past incursions on the Disc, these extradimensional parasites sometimes mated with humans, and the results included pregnancies. The descendants of those relationships often group together, partly because they get on better with each other than with anybody else and partly for mutual defence – other beings who know a bit about real elves may seek to eradicate them. Hence, there are families and small communities of "elf-kin," who less-knowledgeable humans just call "elves." Real elves treat such half-breeds with casual disdain (but then, elves treat *everyone* with casual disdain).[1] They might make viable PCs in games that don't involve many dealings with trolls or dwarfs.

Elf-kin are slim (on a par with slender humans) and graceful, with pointed ears and large eyes. Although they can be stronger than they look, they never match the strongest humans, and quite a few are Skinny. They share the aesthetics of personal appearance with humans, so their Attractive appearance applies to both races. (Yes, this implies a streak of racial vanity.)

While elf-kin don't *have* to have serious mental problems, enough take after their ancestors that Bully, Callous, Compulsive Carousing, and Selfish show up all too often. They may also be Hidebound, lacking true creativity. They have a human side too, however, and the genetic mix may grace them with *style* in the form of perks or advantages such as Gifted Artist, Haughty Sneer, High-Heeled Heroine, Perfect Balance, and Voice. Finally, they might have enough sensitivity to metals or magnetic fields to give them traits like Absolute Direction, Dread (Iron), or Vulnerability (Iron Weapons ×2) (worth -20 points).

Attribute Modifiers: DX+1 [20].
Advantages: Appearance (Attractive) [4]; Reputation +1 (As wondrous magical folk, among naïve romantics) [2].
Disadvantages: Reputation -1 (As a poseur with nothing to boast about, among humans who know the full truth about elves) [-1]; Reputation -3 (As a sinister psycho case, among dwarfs, trolls, and humans who know a bit about elves) [-7].
Quirks: Giggles a Lot; Sunburns Easily. [-2]

---

1. *Elves might call elf-kin contemptible mongrels, or they may merely laugh coldly at their pretensions. As elves aren't widely encountered, and are nasty and callous to everyone, this isn't worth any points.*

Pictsies (also known as the *Nac mac Feegle*) are much more aggressive than gnomes, but find it amusing to hide from view when it suits them; they're still generally seen as an obscure oddity limited to rural upland regions. They have a well-developed tribal culture, largely built around brawling and drinking. Each tribe is governed from an underground lair by its only adult female member, the *kelda*, who is immensely fertile, very shrewd, and sometimes knowledgeable in herbalism and a kind of magic akin to witchcraft. Pictsies have their own language, or rather dialect (resembling our world's Scots, delivered with a lot of aggressive expression), but can understand Morporkian.

Attribute Modifiers: ST-6 [-60]; DX+2 [40]; HT+1 [10].
Secondary Characteristic Modifiers: SM -7 to -3; Per+1 [5]; Basic Move-2 [-10].
Advantages: Catfall [10]; Damage Resistance 2 (Can't Wear Armour; Tough Skin) [2]; Damage Resistance 15 (Only vs. Falling Damage) [15]; Silence 2 [10].
Disadvantages: Short Arms [-10].
Racial Skills: Camouflage (E) IQ+1 [2]-11; Stealth (A) DX+1 [4]-13.

VARIANT TRAITS

The ST this template gives is appropriate for a modest-sized gnome. Pictsie warriors can be *much* stronger! Groups of four pictsies have been known to carry off live cows, one to a leg, implying that each has an effective lifting ST of 13+. It's possible that specialist pictsie cattle-rustlers acquire a few levels of Lifting ST (p. 43).

Likewise, a gnome or a pictsie may have significantly better Basic Move than the template implies. Some are *amazingly* quick on their feet. However, those feet *are* on short legs, so they might also have the quirk Cannot Run Long Distances (p. 99).

Pictsies have the quirk Brawling Society (p. 99), while quirk-level Paranoia (p. 59) is practically a racial feature among gnomes, though *not* pictsies. None of the quirks mentioned so far count against campaign disadvantage limits. Disadvantages such as Bad Temper and Berserk are common among gnomes and *very* common with pictsies (who also tend to add a Pirate's Code of Honour and sometimes Alcoholism), but these *do* count against limits.

This template's built-in DR 2 represents an extraordinary robustness. Many gnomes and pictsies respond to being trodden on by much larger creatures with extreme violence at knee height, and they can roll with most blows. The additional resistance to falling damage represents the innate ability of any small creature to fall long distances safely, due to air resistance. Gnomes and pictsies can't buy additional DR, however.

Finally, neither race can take Dwarfism or Gigantism (see *Build*, p. 29). Extreme size variations are normal among them.

Goblins

-7 points

Goblins are an extremely *marginal* race – usually cave-dwellers – who've long been disregarded by other Disc inhabitants, even classified as barely sapient vermin. It hasn't helped that goblins themselves concur with this opinion, or that their difficult lives all too often force brutal choices on them, up to and including cannibalism. They're widely regarded not only as sordid and malodorous, but also as stupid, thieving, and vicious. Killing a goblin isn't always seen as murder, although picking a fight with one may be unwise; they're notorious berserkers, and a scratch from a goblin's claws all too often becomes infected.

Unfortunately for goblins, they're easily psychologically dominated. It only takes a small group of bullying humans to enslave a larger group of goblins. The race has only survived by hiding as much as possible. However, a very few have shown up in Ankh-Morpork, all of whom have ended up working in the waste-disposal business.

A handful of dwarfs and curious humans understand that there's a little more to goblins, realising that while goblins are rarely particularly intelligent, they aren't *totally* stupid. A *very* few, exceptionally broad-minded observers understand goblins even better, but even they face another problem: the goblin language is surprisingly complex, highly contextual, and subtle. In game terms, it's highly unlikely that any non-goblin could have more than one point in it, if that. Goblin names translate as things like "Sound of the Rain on Hard Ground" or "The Pleasant Contrast of the Orange and Yellow Petals in the Flower of the Gorse."

A typical goblin is about 3' tall and weighs around 30 lbs., with a spindly, wiry body and an outsize head. Goblins typically dress in rags, and they smell unpleasant to other races. If they're armed at all, it's usually with crude stone axes.

Attribute Modifiers: ST-3 [-30]; DX+1 [20]; IQ-1 [-20]; HT+1 [10].
Secondary Characteristic Modifiers: SM -2; Will-1 [-5]; Per+2 [10].
Advantages: Claws (Sharp Claws) [5]; Night Vision 6 [6]; Resistant to Disease (+3) [3]; Temperature Tolerance 1 (Cold) [1].
Perks: Sordid Claws [1].
Disadvantages: Appearance (Ugly) [-8]; Bad Smell [-10]; Berserk (15) [-5]; Illiterate in Native Language (Goblin) [-3]; Odious Racial Habit (General Sordidness) [-5].
Quirks: Collects own snot and earwax [-1].*
Racial Skills: Pot-Making (A) IQ+6 [24]-15.*

* Goblins have these traits for a reason; see *Unggue* (p. 104).

OTHER GOBLIN TRAITS

Goblins often display exceptional senses. Discriminatory Smell and some level of Acute Hearing are common, possibly universal. Goblins have on occasion demonstrated an uncanny gift for music, too. To represent this, give them Musical Ability, or just some Musical Instrument skill such as Harp at 15+.

In places where they're officially classed as vermin, goblins have Social Stigma (Minority Group), and possibly *also* Social Stigma (Uneducated). The legal situation has recently changed across most of the Sto Plains, but in practise, goblins will probably still suffer from one or both Social Stigmas in many areas for some years yet. Many goblins have Low TL, often down as low as TL0, but cases vary. Most have negative Status and are Poor; a goblin with positive Status would be truly extraordinary. Extra disadvantages such as Cowardice, Impulsiveness, Innumerate, Kleptomania, Laziness, and Shyness are quite likely – goblins rarely try to behave better than their reputation suggests – and the GM may decide that some such disadvantages need not count against campaign limits.

No goblin can be Skinny (if they were any thinner, they'd be dead) or Overweight or heavier (in the unlikely event of them getting too much food, they just burn it off).

Gnolls

-14 points

Gnolls are another minor race who wouldn't make great PCs in most games, being smelly scavengers with limited intellect and social gifts. They can be useful Contacts, though, and can live almost anywhere.

Sometimes described as a kind of low-grade troll, if only to annoy trolls, gnolls are in fact a midway point between trolls and humans. While the former are made of stone and the latter are made of meat, gnolls seem to be made of *soil*. (If any wizards know more, their work hasn't been widely published – but then, Gnoll Studies isn't a fashionable field.) They appear to be covered in a matted mixture of hair, rags, and rubbish; actually, that *is* the gnoll.

Like most scavengers, gnolls aren't above giving something that's already dying a thump. Sensible gnolls avoid killing other sapient beings – and certainly avoid being *caught* doing so, or eating corpses – but they don't convey the impression of an over-refined morality. In the country, they're furtive foragers. However, they've recently come to more attention in cities; there's a small community in Ankh-Morpork, keeping the streets a bit cleaner. They don't *need* civilisation, but they'll trade for interesting rubbish. Most gnolls know Survival or Urban Survival, and probably Scrounging.

Gnolls speak human languages in slurred tones, and they have a rough manner. Whether they're naturally surly or this is just their response to the way they're treated is a moot point. A typical human's poor reactions to a gnoll usually cause the former to avoid the latter, not to attack. Hitting a gnoll is unlikely to be *fun*, even for those who define "fun" as "hitting things."

Gnolls are about the same weight as humans, perhaps a bit bulkier thanks to the vegetation they often have growing on them. They would be about the same height if they didn't walk around bent double. Their DR is fixed – no gnoll will be significantly more or less robust.

Attribute Modifiers: ST+2 [20]; IQ-2 [-40]; HT+3 [30].
Secondary Characteristic Modifiers: HP+2 [4]; Per+2 [10]; Basic Move-1 [-5].
Advantages: Cast-Iron Stomach [3]; Fearlessness 3 [6]; Damage Resistance 2 (Can't Wear Armour; Tough Skin) [2]; Resistant to Disease (+8) [5]; Temperature Tolerance 1 (Cold) [1]; Temperature Tolerance 1 (Heat) [1].
Disadvantages: Appearance (Hideous) [-16]; Bad Smell [-10]; Callous [-5]; Disturbing Voice [-10]; Odious Racial Habit (Surly) [-5]; Social Stigma (Uneducated) [-5].

GOBLIN NPCS

A typical rural goblin may have a point in the *spoken* form of the local human (or dwarf) language, plus skills such as Axe/Mace, Camouflage, Climbing, Stealth, and Survival (Woodlands). Goblins' usual behaviours when other races are around involve running, hiding, and sneak thefts. If they must fight, they prefer quick, opportunistic attacks from behind, but may occasionally switch to berserk desperation.

UNGGUE

Traditional goblin "religion" is a reincarnation-based belief system called "Ungue." (Goblins don't think that any god would

be interested in them.) Notably, goblins believe that some of their own body products – particularly snot, earwax, and nail clippings – are in a sense sacred, and they carefully collect and preserve them in "unggue pots" to be entombed with the goblin after death. Goblins make these containers for themselves, and all seem to possess an uncanny ability to create amazingly beautiful pots from whatever crude materials are to hand. This does them little good, though; no goblin would ever sell an unggue pot, and any found in the hands of other races have likely been stolen, usually after the owner-maker was slaughtered. Still, it's *just* possible that a sympathetic employer could persuade a goblin to apply some of this skill to more mundane work.

Stolen unggue pots may not be safe for humans. In particular, the finest – called "soul of tears," made by female goblins who've been obliged by brutal necessity to eat their own infants – may have genuine supernatural power. There have been cases where humans who handled such pots found themselves possessed by a goblin spirit and unable to let go of the pot. The only way to save a human in this state from wasting away within a few days is to take him to a goblin community, where the spirit can find release.

Golems

438 points

Golems are supernaturally powered "robots." They take the form of large, humanoid clay statues, clearly identifiable as pottery at a casual glance (and in fact partly hollow). They're superhumanly strong and surprisingly fast. Burning red lights glow from a golem's eyes – and from its mouth, if and when it speaks. Golems often end up repairing themselves, and most show signs of centuries of patching. A typical golem is about 8' tall (SM +1) and weighs on the order of 350 lbs.

Golems weren't created by magic as such, though there's evidence that some ancient wizards were able to build something similar. They're actually a product of *religion*. They were originally constructed by priests, holy men, or religious scholars who wanted to prove something about the power of words and to get some heavy work done. A given golem isn't empowered directly by any particular god, but by a holy word, written on parchment (its "chem") and placed inside its hollow skull. Golems are made with hinged tops to their heads to facilitate this.

In any case, the secret of golem creation seems to have been lost to humanity for the last millennium (although some *golems* remember it). Modern priests insist that the creation of things that act like living beings is blasphemous, and ordinary Discworlders tend to agree. It's an open question whether this is a sign of insecurity, based on the fact that golems are much stronger than humans, but even trolls and undead look down on golems. There are *lots* of golems still around, however – more than many people realise. For example, quite a few can be found down drainage shafts, operating pumps continuously, day and night (golems use the rules under *Supernaturally Powered Beings*, p. 92).

Golems are initially bound to obedience by the power that creates them; details vary, but normal golems are absolutely law-abiding, and they were created as servants for their makers and anyone to whom they're lawfully assigned. The only common limitation on a golem's absolute obedience is the requirement that it take time off for some kind of minimal rituals on holy days of the religion which created it. Denied this, it simply stops working. (A golem can't be forced to do anything; neither threats, nor torture, nor actual destruction will make it diverge from its assignment.)

Those golems who *continuously* perform some task – or who, say, act as relentless trackers (p. 105) – don't even have that requirement, though.

Golems aren't indestructible. One can be smashed up with a simple sledgehammer – but so long as its head remains intact enough to retain its chem, it can be repaired. Major repairs require a large, hot oven. Generally, the easiest way to disable a golem is to order it to stand still, and then open up its head and remove its chem.

Their absolute obedience to human law makes most golems incapable of lying or of violence against sapient beings, although they can usually be instructed to defend themselves with minimum force. "Minimum force" for something that can snatch a sledgehammer out of a troll's hands is impressive, mind. A few golems can use violence under the instruction of a legally constituted authority, which tends to unnerve humans who discover the fact – especially if they aren't any sort of legally constituted authority themselves.

Many golems were created without tongues, making them entirely mute; if they need to communicate, they carry slates and chalk with which to write. Others can speak. Some can even imitate any speech which they hear, with the exactitude of a mechanical recording.

A small but increasing number of golems have come to legally own themselves, becoming *free* (they insist on this being done formally and correctly by law). The first golem to be freed saved money from his legal employment and bought and freed another, who did the same . . . Free golems can usually speak (it's possible to install a tongue in a mute golem), and they scrupulously debate the limits and implications of their freedom at length. This template represents such a being.

Attribute Modifiers: ST+15 [135*]; DX+1 [20].
Secondary Characteristic Modifiers: SM +1; Will+4 [20]; Per+1 [5].
Advantages: Damage Resistance 5 [25]; Damage Resistance 15 (Only vs. Heat and Fire) [45]; Doesn't Breathe [20]; Doesn't Eat or Drink [10]; Doesn't Sleep [20]; High Pain Threshold [10]; Immunity to Disease [10]; Immunity to Poison [15]; Indomitable [15]; Injury Tolerance (No Blood, No Vitals, Unliving) [30]; Lifting ST 10 [27*]; Night Vision 4 [4]; Photographic Memory [10]; Pressure-Proof [15]; Protected Eyes 4 [4]; Repairable [50]; Single-Minded [5]; Temperature Tolerance 3 (Cold) [6]; Temperature Tolerance 3 (Heat) [6]; Unfazeable [15].
Perks: Boredom Immunity; Longevity; Striking Surface. [3]
Disadvantages: Hidebound [-5]; Honesty (6) [-20]; Selfless (6) [-10]; Unnaturally Fragile [-50].
Quirks: Broad-Minded; Cannot Float. [-2]

* With 10% cost reduction for SM +1.

COMMON CAPABILITIES

Strictly speaking, there's no such thing as a "standard" golem; each is hand-crafted. However, they *are* mostly similar, and the template and these notes define a typical specimen.

If the golem lacks a tongue, add Mute, reducing character cost by 25 points. On the other hand, if the golem can repeat words which it hears exactly as it hears them, buy this as a perk ("Voice Recorder"). The latter *isn't* Mimicry skill, as the golem can't speak new words in someone else's voice; it's more like a mechanical

record. All golems – even Mute ones – can create a wordless "singing" which is inaudible to humans but which other golems can hear. While this travels for miles through rock, the only specific function it serves is to alert other golems when some of their number are buried deep underground. Hence, it's treated here as a special effect rather than as an advantage or a perk.

An exceptionally robust golem might have a bit more DR, and a poorly fired one might have a bit less. Such variation is rare, however, as are significant differences in size or strength.

Golems which are required to observe specific holy days have a Minor Vow. Common skills for free golems include Law, Philosophy, Professional Skill (Potter), and Theology. Most also know several languages from their long existence. Still, they *are* individuals, with distinct personalities and interests.

FREE AND NON-FREE GOLEMS

Golems which are still subject to their "programming" replace Hidebound and Honesty with Arcane Automaton in the racial template, reducing the cost by 30 points. They also tend to be Dead Broke and to have a large Duty, Status -2, and Truthfulness. They don't make good PCs.

Such a non-free golem can be "reprogrammed" by changing its chem. However, it's usually under general instructions not to allow anyone access to the insides of its head except its current owner and maybe the local watch, who generally won't want it changed. If the golem is sold to a new owner, it is simplest just to show the golem that this legal transaction has taken place, at which point it will start obeying its new owner. Many golems have specific commands and rules written on their chems; represent these with extra disadvantages. *Sensible* owners don't change these, even if they're a little inconvenient – it's too easy to mess up.

A free golem character with mental disadvantages representing the words in its head should have a self-control number of 6, where relevant. It might just be able to *think* its way around such limits, but rarely – they're fundamental to its existence. A non-free golem won't even try. Being Indomitable, golems are only subject to Influence skills from people with Spirit Empathy (p. 42).

Free golems have Status -2 or Social Stigma (Second-Class Citizen, Minority Group, or even Monster) in many places. Ankh-Morpork is a *little* more accepting – but even there, the idea of a golem with positive Status would be laughable. The golems don't care, though.

GETTING CREATIVE

Tinkering-crazed players may be tempted to alter or "enhance" a golem's chem to change its psychology. This is *not* recommended; read *Feet of Clay* to understand why. In brief, the rules that empower most golems produce stable, trustworthy, limited personalities. Anything beyond that may contain subtle contradictions, and an insane golem is a terrible thing.

The GM would be within his rights to rule that creating a *viable* new chem requires rolls against both Theology and Philosophy, at -10. Golems *might* do it with a straight IQ roll, although their one attempt in the chronicles was a disaster.

The processes involved in creating a completely new golem, without any clay from an old specimen, are effectively forgotten. Would-be creators would require the assistance of several existing golems to create a new one – and afterwards, they would have a lot of angry priests to contend with.

TRACKER GOLEMS

A few golems have the ability to track individuals reliably over seemingly unlimited distances by locking onto "psychic signatures." Such a golem can have only one target at a time.

To set up the initial link, the golem needs a name and a description or picture of the target. It must then concentrate for a minute and make an IQ roll. The GM can give bonuses to this roll for good descriptions and pictures, full baptismal names, or being in the target's presence, or penalties for poor or inaccurate data. Failure means the golem cannot try again for 24 hours.

After establishing a link, the golem need only concentrate for one second and make a Per roll to know the direction of and distance to the target. This roll takes *no* penalties for distance!

This is an advantage ("Tracker Golem") with a cost of 15 points.

Sapient Animals

Accidents happen . . . and on the Disc, the result is very occasionally an animal capable of abstract thought. These are one-of-a-kind or at least one-of-a-small-community (though there are also camels, p. 353). The usual cause is runaway magic, as with the Librarian (pp. 333-335) or Gaspode (pp. 316-317). Unseen University's emanations cause a

lot of problems; the rats in its basements have a small tribal culture, and the engineering skills of its ant population are quite worrying. However, magic seems more prone to amplify what's already there than to generate anything entirely new – ants are organised creatures by nature, and rats have a great deal of low cunning. Other known examples of animal sapience include certain parrots and ravens; both are noted for their vocal skills, and if a being can talk, people tend to assume that it's pretty smart.

Most sapient animals appear to be ordinary four-legged beasts, but have human-grade brains and likely the ability to talk (though some are mute). This makes it possible to use them as PCs. They may fit better in some campaigns than others, however, and the GM is free to ban them altogether – although when these accidents happen, the creature *does* often seem to find itself caught up in interesting events.

Still, a player intent on running such a character will need an interesting *explanation*. "Hanging around UU" is valid but unoriginal, while a camel might accidentally have let slip that it's bright, but how easy is it to play a camel PC? It would be possible to create a talking horse, but what's the point if that *only* means the other PCs have an extra horse to ride? Try giving the horse a cynical attitude, or a noble nature combined with equine instincts!

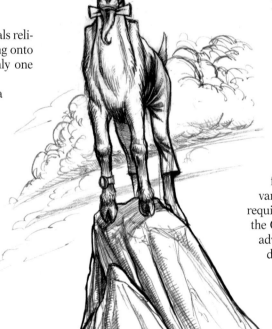

Rather than offer a template for every possible species, it's best to discuss guidelines. First, most animals (apart from apes, birds, fish, etc.) have Quadruped [-35]. Nearly all have a Social Stigma, too – either Logical Impossibility or Valuable Property, both worth -10 points, although a dangerous-looking, seemingly wild animal could have Monster, for -15 points.

It's also necessary to match the traits of the animal's species by adjusting attributes (especially ST and HP) and adding mundane or "racial" advantages and disadvantages. See Chapter 10 for details for several beasts, which can give some idea of appropriate numbers and features. As many of the disadvantages that a sapient animal requires are implicit in its species, the GM should be flexible with disadvantage limits; only "personal" disadvantages ought to count against such limits.

An animal needs an appropriate Size Modifier, which may affect the cost of its ST, as will being a Quadruped. Strength can vary from 3 for a very small dog to 25 for a large horse, or more for even bigger animals. Human-level IQ (around 10) is a sensible baseline, although many sapient animals seem to turn out exceptionally smart – or at least prone to heavy irony – while others aren't *very* sapient. Because such creatures still have "animal senses," many have significantly enhanced Per.

All of DX, HT, Appearance, and Move may also need some thought; for the last, don't forget the option of Enhanced Move (p. 89).

Some sapient animals live entirely outside human society, and hence rate Status 0, which in this case means "no Status either way" rather than "average Status." However, many end up living as "strays" or "wildlife," effectively equivalent to human beggars, with no physical property and receiving no regard in human society, and so should be Dead Broke with Status -2. If you want something better, though, there are plenty of ways to justify it; "Wealth" can represent stuff to which they have informal access, and they can have "jobs" working for humans and probably getting paid entirely in food and maintenance. Still, Struggling and Status -1 are most likely even then – and a lack of *disposable* income is a logical result of those Social Stigmas.

As examples of how to define animals in game terms, here are racial templates for two types that will be useful later in the book: cats and dogs. If a character with either template improves ST or DX, remember the 40% discount for Quadruped. For more on Discworld versions of these beasts, see *Cats* (p. 353) and *Dogs* (p. 354).

DOMESTIC CAT

-82 points

Attribute Modifiers: ST-6 [-60]; DX+4 [48*]; IQ-6 [-120].
Secondary Characteristic Modifiers: SM -3; Will+7 [35]; Per+8 [40]; Basic Move+1 [5].
Advantages: Catfall [10]; Claws (Sharp Claws) [5]; Combat Reflexes [15]; Enhanced Move 1/2 (Ground) [10]; Night Vision 5 [5]; See Invisible (Spirit) [15]; Teeth (Sharp Teeth) [1]; Temperature Tolerance 1 (Cold) [1]; Ultrahearing [5].
Perks: Fur [1].
Disadvantages: Bestial [-10]; Callous [-5]; Cannot Speak [-15]; Dead Broke [-25]; Quadruped [-35]; Short Legs [-2]; Social Stigma (Valuable Property) [-10].
Quirks: Dislikes Water; Distractible; Short Lifespan. [-3]
Racial Skills: Brawling (E) DX+2 [4]-16; Jumping (E) DX [1]-14; Stealth (A) DX [2]-14.

* With 40% cost reduction for Quadruped.

Notes

Even domesticated cats have Bestial, because they don't *really* give a damn about human proprieties. However, they generally understand that annoying the human who gives them food is a bad idea, and they do have a sense of hygiene. Bad Temper, Bloodlust, Bully, Curious, and Uncongenial also fit many cats' personalities. Having up to eight Extra Lives is traditional, but may not be universal.

Some especially aggressive cats have Extra Attack, allowing them to attack twice (or more) per turn – usually a double claw rake, or a bite and a rake.

SMALL SMART DOG

-122 points

This is a smallish, short-legged dog with the sort of exceptional IQ that's possible on the Disc. For something similar but bigger and meaner, see the wolf template (p. 115).

Attribute Modifiers: ST-5 [-50]; IQ-4 [-80]; HT+1 [10].
Secondary Characteristic Modifiers: SM -3; Will+4 [20]; Per+6 [30].
Advantages: Discriminatory Smell [15]; Teeth (Sharp Teeth) [1]; Temperature Tolerance 1 (Cold) [1]; Ultrahearing [5].
Perks: Fur [1].
Disadvantages: Dead Broke [-25]; Illiterate in Native Language (Canine) [-3]; Quadruped [-35]; Short Legs [-2]; Social Stigma (Valuable Property) [-10].
Quirks: Cannot Run Long Distances; Short Lifespan. [-2]
Racial Skills: Brawling (E) DX [1]-10; Tracking (A) Per+3 [1]-15*.

* Includes +4 for Discriminatory Smell.

Notes

"Ordinary" dogs not only have lower IQ, but replace illiteracy (*irrelevant* at IQ 5 or less) with Cannot Speak [-15]. Stray and feral dogs frequently have Bestial [-10], which needn't count against campaign disadvantage limits – although properly domesticated canines are trained to understand at least a bit about human ideas of proper behaviour. Innumerate [-5] is also common among "smart dogs" who haven't had a lot of contact with human thinking, and again it can't be taken by animals who don't have at least IQ 6. Greed and Sense of Duty (to a master or a pack) are common though not universal products of canine instincts. Congenial or even Chummy is the norm for pack animals, but some dogs get used to operating alone.

Trolls

Trolls are discussed at length on pp. 228-230. They come in a wide range of shapes and sizes, size not always closely correlated with strength. A typical, run-of-the-mill troll is about 6'6" tall and weighs 430 lbs., but some are *much* bigger and stronger. As many trolls knuckle-walk some of the time, *apparent* height may be somewhat less.

Trolls have some ideas that are a bit . . . primal, and others that are merely odd. Those with less experience tend to put everything in terms of rocks – to a troll, a rock is currency, possibly food, and always a useful weapon, and the community leader is the troll with the biggest rock. They also think of time as running backwards. This provides many options for customising troll characters with odd little details while staying within the species' normal behavioural range.

When playing a troll, remember that trolls are comically dim but not completely moronic. A troll PC may be the butt of a fair amount of misfortune, but can show off when raw strength is needed. However, Discworld games should *not* be about solving every problem with mindless violence; gamers who want to play trolls because of the gross amount of damage they can do should be gently discouraged.[1] Apart from anything else, they'll probably react badly to laughs at their troll's expense, which are likely to be frequent.

As trolls come in a wide range of sizes, and many racial traits vary with size, three templates appear below. However, *all* trolls are immensely strong, and they are particularly formidable in terms of lifting and dragging strength – powerful in an *unrelenting* way. Thus, all three versions include some Lifting ST and an option to buy more.

---

1. *Point them toward a human barbarian instead.*

MODERATE-SIZED TROLL

83 points

This represents a typical troll, probably sedimentary, about 6'6" or more tall, fittingly broad, and weighing around 430 lbs. It can purchase up to three levels of extra DR; more than +1 DR suggests that it's igneous or metamorphic. It can also buy up to 10 additional levels of Lifting ST (for a total of 14).

Attribute Modifiers: ST+6 [54*]; IQ-2 [-40]; HT+2 [20].
Secondary Characteristic Modifiers: SM +1; Per+1 [5].
Advantages: Damage Resistance 5 [25]; Fearlessness 4 [8]; High Pain Threshold [10]; Lifting ST 4 [11*]; Night Vision 3 [3]; Protected Eyes 3 [3]; Resistant to Disease (+3) [3]; Temperature Tolerance 2 (Cold) [3].
Perks: Longevity; Striking Surface. [2]
Disadvantages: Appearance (Ugly) [-8]; Odious Racial Habit (Hitting People) [-5]; Troll Brain [-10].
Quirks: Brawling Society; Cannot Float; Weak Spot (Neck). [-3]
Racial Skills: Brawling (E) DX+1 [2]-11.

* With 10% cost reduction for SM +1.

Troll Sizes

Trolls come in an extremely wide range of sizes. A troll character *cannot* take Overweight, Fat, Very Fat, or Gigantism (see *Build*, p. 29) – bigger trolls are just assumed to be that way *naturally*. A Skinny troll would be possible but *odd*; it would look weird to other trolls as well as to humans, and it would probably also have Unattractive or Ugly appearance with the Universal modifier (see *Racial and Personal Appearance*, p. 85).

It *is* possible to play a troll with Dwarfism – a stunted specimen who, in the past, may have been sat on a lot by bigger trolls. Take the moderate-sized troll template and add Dwarfism (-15 points). This changes SM to 0, which in turn means that ST+6 now costs 60 points (that is, the standard 10 points/level) and Lifting ST 4 costs 12 points. (Remember also that Dwarfism gives -1 to Basic Move.) Hence, the net cost to play such a troll (template cost plus modifications) is 75 points.

BIG TROLL

115 points

This is a large but not exceptional troll – about 8' tall, quite broad, and around 850 lbs. – such as would be respected in a rural clan or seen as a *big* bruiser in the city. Given its DR, it's probably sedimentary. It can buy one or two levels of additional DR, if it's igneous or metamorphic. It can also purchase up to 15 more levels of Lifting ST (for a total of 20).

Attribute Modifiers: ST+10 [80*]; IQ-2 [-40]; HT+2 [20].
Secondary Characteristic Modifiers: SM +2; Per+1 [5].
Advantages: Damage Resistance 6 [30]; Fearlessness 4 [8]; High Pain Threshold [10]; Lifting ST 5 [12*]; Night Vision 3 [3]; Protected Eyes 3 [3]; Resistant to Disease (+3) [3]; Temperature Tolerance 2 (Cold) [3].
Perks: Longevity; Striking Surface. [2]

Disadvantages: Appearance (Ugly) [-8]; Odious Racial Habit (Hitting People) [-5]; Troll Brain [-10].
Quirks: Brawling Society; Cannot Float; Weak Spot (Neck). [-3]
Racial Skills: Brawling (E) DX+1 [2]-11.

* With 20% cost reduction for SM +2.

HUGE TROLL

190 points

This describes a *really* big, rather lumbering troll, about 12' and 4,000 lbs. (Larger trolls exist, but tend to settle down somewhere quiet and merge with the landscape.) It can purchase one more level of DR, especially if it's igneous or metamorphic, and as much extra Lifting ST as desired. No one makes armour for trolls this size – it would be a seriously hard piece of smith-craft, cost a fortune, and feel superfluous – so they buy their innate DR at a discount.

Attribute Modifiers: ST+23 [161*]; DX-1 [-20]; IQ-1 [-20]; HT+2 [20].
Secondary Characteristic Modifiers: SM +3.
Advantages: Damage Resistance 7 (Can't Wear Armour) [21]; Fearlessness 6 [12]; High Pain Threshold [10]; Lifting ST 7 [15*]; Night Vision 3 [3]; Protected Eyes 4 [4]; Resistant to Disease (+3) [3]; Temperature Tolerance 2 (Cold) [3].
Perks: Longevity; Striking Surface. [2]
Disadvantages: Appearance (Ugly) [-8]; Odious Racial Habit (Hitting People) [-5]; Troll Brain [-10].
Quirks: Brawling Society; Cannot Float; Weak Spot (Neck). [-3]
Racial Skills: Brawling (E) DX+1 [2]-10.

* With 30% cost reduction for SM +3.

TROLL NOTES

- Trolls' Odious Racial Habit might seem low-valued – especially given that some unreconstructed trolls do still sometimes try to eat people. On most worlds, such behaviour would be worth -10, even -15 points. However, as some humans have come to see all this violence as "just trollish ways," while others are terrorised into politeness by it, its practical effect is relatively small.

- While trolls are very robust, some people know that they have weak spots; they're mostly vulnerable to blows to the neck (see *Specific Hit Locations*, p. 183). Treat trolls as having no DR there. Some Assassins are taught this in case they ever take a commission involving a troll (rare, but it could happen). Old-fashioned barbarian heroes tended to discover it by trial and error, or from old tales.

- Although trolls are *rugged*, silicon-based biology has its own diseases, and also its own poisons. Little that poisons a human is likely to worry a troll, but a smart alchemist or researcher could doubtless come up with something that would work. Admittedly, such knowledge is very rare – but that should make the surprise for troll PCs that much greater when they run into sneaky, well-prepared opposition.

- Trolls speak their own language, and there are also older forms of this known by sound to most trolls and understood by a few scholars. However, most trolls in contact with humanity learn a local human language. In all cases, reducing the troll's literacy in its own language doesn't count against campaign disadvantage limits. Old-school trolls rarely went to school – and anyway, it isn't clear that there's any such thing as trollish writing, as opposed to trollish transcribed into human scripts.

● Likewise, while troll culture has its own Cultural Familiarity, most trolls living in human communities learn the local Cultural Familiarity. Some might not comprehend their ancestral culture. However, humans don't always expect much of trolls, and some trolls justify this. Social Stigma (Uneducated) isn't unusual – usually indicating a troll limited to durr-me-got-big-rock sorts of conversation – and Innumerate is downright commonplace.

● *Many* trolls have Intolerance (Dwarfs), but the most prominent trolls in the chronicles have got over this, so the template doesn't include it. However, it shouldn't count against disadvantage limits if a troll character does take it. Quite a few trolls have Callous, Clueless, or Hidebound, but none of these are standard troll features.

● Any troll could suffer from Troll Nocturnalism (pp. 97-98), but if you want a character who can work with non-trolls, it's advisable only to take the version with a mitigator.

● Some trolls walk leaning forward on their knuckles a lot of the time. However, they can operate perfectly well on two legs, and knuckle-walking doesn't seem to make them much faster, just a bit more comfortable, so it isn't treated as having any game effects.

Vampires

107 or 108 points

Discworld vampires are enormously varied. A given vampire's exact nature – both strengths and weaknesses – are shaped partly by beliefs held by nearby humans and partly by the vampire's deep-seated ideas about itself. The latter may be most important, but as the vampire's ideas will be shaped by what it hears from humans, the effects are much the same either way.

Hence, vampires are typically very *traditional* creatures, and the traditions in question tend to be close to the conventions of a certain sort of gothic horror movie – at least among vampires on the Sto Plains and in or near Uberwald. This template defines the commonest general set of vampire traits. It encompasses the sort of vampires who appear as protagonists in the chronicles, such as Otto Chriek, Sally von Humpeding, and Maladict. The extensive notes following the template cover many frequent but not universal features.

By definition, vampires are undead and survive by drinking blood. While they can have many specific weaknesses, almost always including a vulnerability to daylight or comparable bright light, they're *extremely* hard to destroy permanently – although a wooden stake through the heart will usually keep one down. If they're "destroyed," they crumble to dust, but a modest quantity of blood spilled on that dust will restore them to "life." As most humans know this, vampires have to fear being trapped or contained, probably while in dust form, and scattered to the wind, thrown in a fast-flowing river, or in extreme cases dropped in a volcano or over the edge of the Disc. They'll often come back even from those sorts of things, *eventually* – destiny seems to have a weird fondness for vampires in that sense – but it can take a very long time indeed, and culture shock on emerging after millennia aside, a "dead" vampire may have some awareness of the passage of time, making the experience quite unpleasant. Then again, there are those who regard a few years in the tomb as a nice rest.

Vampires are physically strong, fast (sometimes merely *quite* fast, sometimes faster-than-the-eye-can-follow fast), and annoyingly charismatic. Even the hideously ugly corpse-like ones have *style* and a way with words. However, they're also *obsessive*. Most are focussed on their need for blood, but those who swear off human necks typically end up equally intent on some other preoccupation. Many suffer from peculiar hang-ups. They can also display supernatural features such as not showing up in mirrors.

Some vampires are created from humans by a process akin to disease infection, but others are born to vampire parents; this is one of the things that may be influenced by local beliefs. In some cases, vampirism even seems to be inherited through something other than genetics.[1] Vampires certainly don't "turn" others very often; see *Becoming a Vampire* (p. 110). Only humans seem to become vampires; it would be hard to say why dwarfs should be immune, but perhaps a dwarf (never mind gnome) vampire would just be too *unstylish*. Vampirism is about carbon-based blood, and thus has nothing to do with trolls.

Even in a high-powered Discworld campaign, vampires might not make suitable PCs owing to their many foibles – particularly their problems with daylight. However, an "all monsters" game could be amusing (see *Reaper Man* for inspiration), and there are enough vampire protagonists in the chronicles to provide inspiration for mixed-species games at high power levels.

1. *Acquiring a big old gothic castle and a title with a lot of consonants in it has a funny effect on some people.*

Attribute Modifiers: ST+5 [50]; DX+3 [60]; HT+1 [10].
Secondary Characteristic Modifiers: Per+2 [10].
Advantages: Charisma 1 [5]; Doesn't Breathe [20]; High Pain Threshold [10]; Immunity to Disease [10]; Immunity to Poison [15]; Injury Tolerance (No Blood, No Vitals) [10]; Night Vision 7 [7]; Pressure-Proof [15]; Regeneration (Very Fast; Requires Contact with Blood) [60]; Teeth (Sharp Teeth) [1]; Temperature Tolerance 2 (Cold) [3]; Unkillable 2 (Hindrance, Wooden Weapons; Trigger, Contact with Blood) [70].
Perks: Longevity; *males* add Fully Dressed Resurrection. [1 or 2]
Disadvantages: Dread (Holy Symbols; 3-yard radius) [-24]; Dread (Running Water; 1-yard radius) [-10]; Restricted Diet (Blood) [-10]; Supernatural Features (No Body Heat, No Reflection in Mirrors) [-15]; Vulnerability (Cutting Attacks to the Neck* ×2) [-20]; Vulnerability (Wooden Impaling Weapons ×2) [-20]; Weakness 3d (Direct Sunlight) [-120]; Weakness 3d (Holy Water) [-30].
Quirks: Dislikes Garlic [-1].

* For rules for attacking the neck, see *Specific Hit Locations* (p. 183). As cutting attacks there have a wounding modifier of ×2 *anyway*, this gives them an effective multiplier of ×4.

Becoming a Vampire

Yes, sometimes mortals are turned into vampires, thus becoming much more powerful in many ways. No, this does *not* mean that PCs can get themselves bitten and promptly turn into cool creatures of the night. The transformation process is tricky, complex, painful, and varies a bit with the particular vampire type. It isn't 100% reliable, either – and if it fails, you're most likely boringly dead instead of undead. Ethical Black Ribboners (pp. 113-114) don't do stuff like that these days, while old-fashioned vampires have rules against doing it very often for fear of causing food-supply problems. Arranging it should be hard work, and anybody who trusts a vampire who's willing to do the job by appointment is probably an idiot.

Also remember that traditionally (and vampires are all about tradition), the result is a vampire who's in thrall to its "maker" for at least the first few decades. This means "mind-controlled, no resistance possible." Certainly, new vampires have problems controlling their appetites and instincts. The GM is fully entitled to rule that the formerly living PC is now an undead NPC – at least unless the player had enough bonus character points (p. 219) saved beforehand to pay for the upgrade. Vampirism is traditionally viewed as a *curse*, not as a cool power-up, with good reason.

STANDARD VAMPIRE TRAITS

The baseline template above assumes a vampire who – like many in the chronicles – can go around in daylight in long sleeves and a broad-brimmed hat, but who's painfully vulnerable to bright *direct* light. This generally means *clear* sunlight. A vampire can show its face without a hat on a cloudy day, but it will probably act

as if suffering from a bad itch and keep a watch out for threatening breaks in the clouds.

The powerful flash generated by a provoked salamander (p. 358) might overload the vampire's resistance completely; sometimes it just hurts, a lot. If a salamander flashes within five yards, the vampire must make a HT roll at +2. Failure means it goes straight to -10×HP and collapses into a heap of dust. Even success demands a Will roll. If *that* succeeds, the vampire merely has -1 to all rolls on its next turn; on a failure, it falls down and spends the next 1d turns rolling helplessly on the ground in pain.

A vampire is hard to kill and can recover from huge amounts of damage given a bit of blood (by drinking it if still standing, by having it poured on its dusty remains if not), but there *are* ways to put one down and keep it there. Vampire hearts don't beat, so a steel sword through the chest doesn't worry a vampire unduly, and it only bleeds a token amount if cut (a purely visual effect – don't worry about the ramifications for Injury Tolerance), but a wooden stake through the same location or a cutting attack to the neck spells serious trouble (see *Specific Hit Locations*, p. 183). Getting blood poured on the vampire's remains is classed as a common trigger for its Unkillable advantage because, well, it's common for Discworld vampires – narrative causality works that way, as do many faithful Igors.

Vampires can be repelled by holy symbols, making unlife a bit complicated for them on the Disc, where thousands of gods have inspired their followers to adopt all sorts of things as symbolically important. However, vampires don't rear back from random shapes merely because they meant something to a small cult once, millennia ago. The symbol has to be presented as such, by somebody to whom it means something, or placed in a context that the vampire itself recognises as religious (thus, vampires avoid shrines and altars, because something there is bound to be symbolic). Still, a standard symbol of a major local faith will usually keep a vampire off, and someone with True Faith (p. 48) may convince himself that almost anything is a holy symbol, or achieve the same result simply by praying. The GM decides what works, but should bear in mind that True Faith is *supposed* to annoy vampires.

The problem with running water is more of a petty inconvenience. It causes travelling vampires to plot complicated routes, sometimes involving the highest possible bridges.

Finally, vampires dislike garlic. This isn't a big thing for most of them, but they avoid direct contact with the stuff, and may snarl and spit at the smell of it. A Will roll at -3 is required to suppress this response.

OPTIONAL VAMPIRE TRAITS

Individual vampires can vary greatly. Serious vampires – especially NPC horrors who get to threaten whole groups of PCs – are likely to have markedly increased ST or just HP, and several optional abilities (see below). Older ones in particular can acquire a lot of skills over the centuries, some of them oriented to reducing the threat from would-be slayers, along with all manner of social advantages, including Status and Wealth.

Many vampires have Social Stigmas, but this isn't universal and the details vary from place to place: Second-Class Citizen is standard in Ankh-Morpork and similar cities, reflecting less a lack of *formal* rights than a lingering sense of mistrust (although the vampires are trying hard to get rid of that), while Monster is possible in places where people mostly either know vampires only by reputation, or reckon they know them too well and want rid of them. Enemies (vampire-hunters) do also happen.

Most important, vampires can have extra abilities or peculiar weaknesses – often both – of the *supernatural* variety. Below are many possibilities. In most cases, these should be treated as part of the vampire's racial template, meaning that they don't carry over to any Alternate Form the vampire may have, and adjust the primary racial template cost when calculating Alternate Form point costs.

Animal Control: Not many Discworld vampires seem to be able to control animals, but a few manage the trick; certainly, the de Magpyr clan (in *Carpe Jugulum*) were served by a flock of what appeared to be ordinary magpies. This isn't recommended for vampire PCs – it can be a little tiresome to manage in game – but a "Congregation" (p. 38) of low-powered minion animals might be possible. Good with (Animal) or Speak With Animals, for bats, magpies, rats, or wolves, also fit some legends.

Appetite Problems: Vampires need blood to survive (their Restricted Diet disadvantage), but in principle, animal blood – or even very rare steak – is sufficient. However, the sad fact is that human blood, fresh from the vein, tastes best to them, and most have an Uncontrollable Appetite (p. 98) for it. While feeding this desire doesn't *have* to mean killing, accidents happen. For the classic vampire lord with a big gothic castle, this isn't an issue; local peasants and the odd foolish traveller provide adequate supplies. Cunning wanderers can get away with plenty, too. For a careless vampire who can't curb this craving in a hostile society, though, fresh human blood can become a deadly habit. Many modern vampires suffer from this urge (usually with a self-control number of 12) but find a mitigator for it; see *Black Ribboners* (pp. 113-114).

Blinding Speed: For vampires who are scarily fast, buy Combat Reflexes and increase DX, Basic Speed, and/or Basic Move to taste. Extra Attack is appropriate for a "combat monster" who can rip through whole crowds of low-grade vampire-hunters.

Compulsions: Vampires are prone to weird, sometimes crippling, compulsions. Such an issue can *sometimes* be represented by a Compulsive Behaviour (p. 111) or possibly an Obsession (p. 62); vampires seem inclined to extreme meticulousness, and Compulsive Neatness (6) isn't unusual (it might help explain all the full evening dress). A Fixation (p. 95) is often most appropriate, though. For example, in some places, if you throw a handful of poppy seeds at one of the local vampires, it will stop to count them. This is a Fixation on a moderately common item (these stories tend to show up in places where most kitchens have some poppy seeds around) with a three-yard radius, for -12 points.

Different Supernatural Features: The assorted weird touches that mark out a vampire vary greatly from tradition to tradition. Most vampires have at least -15 points in Supernatural Features of *some* sort, but the two in the template are simply the most common. Individuals are welcome to switch them round, or to add or subtract to taste. "Deathly Pallor" is certainly popular among spooky, sinister types.

Flight: Extremely common among vampires who *can't* shapeshift (see *Vampire Shapeshifting*, pp. 112-113). The vampire has either Flight (Winged, Can Hover) [30] (usually swirling a cloak that then transforms melodramatically into temporary wings) or, in flashy cases, Flight (Levitation) [40].

Fresh Blood Requirement: Attempts by vampires to obtain social acceptance depend on the fact that they're able to get by on animal blood, which can be obtained relatively easily from legal sources. If a more restrictive mythology traps a vampire in a need for fresh, human blood, the Restricted Diet disadvantage worsens to -20 points. This is rare, though, and makes it impossible to be

a Black Ribboner and hard to avoid Social Stigma (Monster); thus, it isn't recommended for PCs.

Hunter's Senses: Many vampires have good senses; some are truly superhuman. They may have high Per, Acute Senses (usually Hearing or Taste and Smell), Discriminatory Smell (possibly even with Emotion Sense), Heartbeat Counter, or Ultrahearing.

Hypnotic Gaze: A vampire who can immobilise victims by the power of its stare is really beyond the scope of these rules; see the **GURPS Basic Set** and **GURPS Powers** for options. If you need an NPC with this capability, just say that the vampire can hold its victim stationary each turn that it can win a Quick Contest of Will, but the vampire takes a penalty to his roll equal to the distance in yards from its victim. Alternatively, high Intimidation and Savoir-Faire skills, with the Fearsome Stare and Haughty Sneer perks, might make the point well enough.

Just Comes Back: Vampires are hard to kill – but just to make sure, and to reflect their relationship with narrative assumptions, feel free to buy Extra Life as often as you like.

Mind Control: Some *really* powerful vampires can control mortal minds, making victims obey their commands and even manipulating their memories. However, anything better than Voice of Command (p. 49) is far too much for a PC in most games. If you have an NPC vampire with such an ability, handle it as a Quick Contest between the vampire's IQ (possibly at a bonus if it's especially skilled) and the victim's Will; the margin of success determines how obedient the victim becomes and how long the effect lasts. For more detailed rules and options, consult the **GURPS Basic Set** and **GURPS Powers.**

Must Be Invited In: Stories often mention this problem, but it doesn't seem to slow down most vampires much. It might be an actual Dread of private dwellings into which the vampire isn't invited – a common item – in a one-yard radius, worth -20 points. It could simply be that many old-school, non-Black-Ribbon vampires have a -5-point Code of Honour, "Plays Fair," which says that humans must be allowed some safe havens. Alternatively, a quirk – "Doesn't go where he's not asked" – would explain why, say, the de Magpyr clan seemed to regard a party invitation from the king of Lancre as somewhat significant when they sought to invade the place.

Native Soil Bed: Some vampires need to rest every day on their native soil, leading to much transporting of rattly coffins. This is a special disadvantage, worth -30 points: The vampire must spend at least an hour a day on this "bed" or the vampire starts losing 1 HP per hour, which it can't recover even with Regeneration until it can meet the requirement again.

Phobias: In some cases, vampires' problems seem more like personal psychological foibles than supernatural prohibitions. Major Pyrophobia (p. 62) or Heliophobia (p. 63) would explain a fair amount of vampire behaviour. These would rate as personal rather than racial disadvantages – they carry over when changing shape.

Quirks: Psychological peculiarities and influence from local legends can give vampires any number of quirks. These need not count against normal quirk limits if they're part of vampiric *style.* One favourite is Delusion (Spelling my name backwards disguises it perfectly), and some vampires exhibit Hunter's Habits.

Really Tough: Some real-nightmare vampires swap High Pain Threshold for Supernatural Durability (Killed by beheading, fire, Vulnerabilities, or Weaknesses) [150]. This may replace Unkillable, giving a monster that *just won't stop,* but which can be disposed of eventually given enough firepower.

Reduced Weaknesses: Not all vampires have every disadvantage on the template; a few train themselves out of some of their "flaws," although that demands self-awareness and effort. The snag is that humans find vampires who don't play by the rules *frightening,* and they will put much more effort into killing them *permanently.* The main problems which might be eliminated are the two Dreads, the Weakness to holy water, and the dislike of garlic. Count de Magpyr even dreamed of suppressing the Weakness to sunlight.

Severe Light Susceptibility: Some vampires have far greater problems with sunlight, possibly smoking and collapsing at daylight's merest touch, or recoiling in horror from the slightest glimpse of sunrise. A Weakness which inflicts 4d HP of injury a minute upon exposure to *any daylight at all* is worth -240 points (!). Dread of daylight in a one-yard radius is worth -30 points. Problems of this order can make PCs unplayable, although they fit a certain class of old-school horror-movie monster.

Total Nocturnalism: Vampires who can't even handle the *idea* that the sun is up may have a disadvantage analogous to Troll Nocturnalism (pp. 97-98) – although they don't suffer from Troll Brain, and they collapse back into the tomb rather than turning to stone.

Transform to Mist: Another fairly common vampire trick, this is Insubstantiality [80]. Insubstantiality always requires some way to block or contain the user; here, that's any kind of airtight barrier or container. If someone traps you in, say, a large bottle with a sealed stopper, you can't solidify again until you're set free.

Unkillable Variations: What will or won't kill a vampire varies greatly from case to case. Feel free to tinker with each individual's Unkillable advantage as you see fit; for an example, consider the case of Count von Vonkevve (*Unkillable,* pp. 92-93). Most Achilles' Heels and Hindrances should rate as common or at least occasional – however weird they may look – simply because they can show up in local folklore where the vampire lives, and vampire-hunters come suitably equipped. A low-grade vampire that actually stays dead when killed just has Unkillable 1 (Achilles' Heel, Common, Fire; Hindrance, Common, Wooden Weapons Through the Heart) [13], reducing template cost by 57 points. Such a vampire is still *hard* to kill, mind, but doesn't come back when the job is done competently, for which purpose fire serves admirably (hence the customary peasant mobs with flaming torches). This is appropriate for an NPC vampire intended as a tough one-off adversary.

Weather Control: Yet another powerful advantage that really needs the full **GURPS** rules for proper treatment. For the look of the thing, however, lower-powered vampires can use the Climatic Emphasis perk (p. 50).

VAMPIRE SHAPESHIFTING

The ability of many vampires to change shape is a large topic. In game terms, it's the Alternate Form advantage (pp. 85-87). The secondary form usually has some but not all of the features of the vampire's normal shape. Notably, the shape-changed vampire may not be so hard to kill and keep dead. A vampire that's knocked out or badly wounded might return to its humanoid shape, which *can* regenerate, but if it's actually killed in shape-changed form, that's embarrassingly permanent (see *Witches Abroad*). Hence, sensible vampires only can shift shape for purposes of stealth or escape.

All of the templates below cost fewer points than any serious vampire's basic "racial" template, giving Alternate Form a base cost of 15 points. Male vampires usually have the Absorptive Change (Light Encumbrance) modifier, letting them return to humanoid form fully (and stylishly) dressed; females don't. This is doubtless yet another consequence of the power of human beliefs over the capabilities of vampires, as humans tend to embed a bit too much sexual fantasy in those stories. As Sally von Humpeding says, "It's probably part of the whole underwired nightdress business."

Shapeshift (Bat)

Many shape-changing vampires can become a large but not too unnatural-looking bat. This specific ability is rare among Black Ribboners (pp. 113-114). Apparently, they find the mass change involved in transforming into a *single* bat difficult; it seems to demand a degree of concentration that someone perpetually fighting a taste for human blood can't manage.

. . . the only thing more dangerous than a vampire crazed with blood lust was a vampire crazed with anything else. All the meticulous single-mindedness that went into finding young women who slept with their bedroom window open was channelled into some other interest, with merciless and painstaking efficiency.

– **The Truth**

Vampires with this ability typically change with a couple of seconds of posing and cloak-swirling, possibly giving opponents a chance to get a hit in, though this can vary. The bat has clumsy, blunt claws which can't grip well and which are functionally useless as legs. Not being quite so vulnerable to bright lights as the vampire's normal form, the bat doesn't risk disintegration by a salamander's flash, but it will suffer 1d HP of injury and automatically flee chittering in terror.

This kind of shapeshifting uses the -53-point template below. If changing takes two seconds, a male vampire pays 26 points for the Alternate Form, while a female pays 24 points.

Attribute Modifiers: ST-5 [-50]; DX+2 [40]; HT+1 [10].
Secondary Characteristic Modifiers: SM -4; Per+2 [10].
Advantages: Flight (Winged, Cannot Hover) [24]; High Pain Threshold [10]; Immunity to Disease [10]; Immunity to Poison [15]; Injury Tolerance (No Blood, No Vitals) [10]; Night Vision 5 [5]; Sonar [20]; Teeth (Sharp Teeth) [1]; Temperature Tolerance 1 (Cold) [1]; Ultrahearing [5].
Perks: Fur; Longevity. [2]
Disadvantages: Aerial [0]; Bad Grip 3 [-15]; Bad Sight (Nearsighted) [-25]; Cannot Speak [-15]; Dread (Holy Symbols; 3-yard radius) [-24]; Dread (Running Water; 1-yard radius) [-10]; Restricted Diet (Blood) [-10]; Supernatural Features (No Body Heat, No Reflection in Mirrors) [-15]; Weakness 1d (Direct Sunlight) [-40]; Weakness 1d (Holy Water) [-10].
Quirks: Dislikes Garlic; Hates Any Strong Light. [-2]

Shapeshift (Flock of Bats)

Other vampires transform into entire *flocks* of bats, each individual bat being smaller than the creature defined above. This is simpler and faster to accomplish than becoming a single bat, because it doesn't involve magically changing one's whole body mass. The drawback is that the vampire's mind is divided across the horde, making it hard to remain focussed on a task; the vampire must keep the swarm tightly grouped to avoid becoming highly confused.

Again, the flock isn't as vulnerable to bright lights as the vampire is in human guise. Being creatures of darkness, though, the bats react *very* badly to daylight, usually panicking – which, given those control problems, can leave the vampire confused and incapable of useful action for minutes or hours. And again, a salamander's flash inflicts 1d HP of injury and causes the vampire to flee.

This ability uses the 23-point template below. Changing to a flock takes one second. Alternate Form thus costs 29 points for males, 27 points for females.

Attribute Modifiers: ST-5 [-50]; DX+2 [40]; IQ-1 [-20]; HT+1 [10].
Secondary Characteristic Modifiers: SM +1; HP+3 [6]; Per+3 [15].
Advantages: Immunity to Disease [10]; Immunity to Poison [15]; Injury Tolerance (No Blood, No Vitals) [10]; Night Vision 5 [5]; Sonar [20]; Swarm Body [135]; Teeth (Sharp Teeth) [1]; Temperature Tolerance 1 (Cold) [1]; Ultrahearing [5].
Perks: Fur; Longevity. [2]
Disadvantages: Absent-Mindedness [-15]; Bad Grip 3 [-15]; Bad Sight (Nearsighted) [-25]; Cannot Speak [-15]; Dread (Holy Symbols; 3-yard radius) [-24]; Dread (Running Water; 1-yard radius) [-10]; Restricted Diet (Blood) [-10]; Supernatural Features (No Body Heat, No Reflection in Mirrors) [-15]; Weakness 1d (Direct Sunlight) [-40]; Weakness 1d (Holy Water) [-10].
Quirks: Confused (12) in Daylight; Dislikes Any Strong Light; Dislikes Garlic. [-3]

Shapeshift (Flock of Magpies)

A few vampires – notably the de Magpyrs of Uberwald – become flocks of *magpies*. These lack bats' special senses but handle daylight rather better. Still, being creatures of the night in magpie shape, even vampire-magpies tend to avoid the sun, and a salamander flash inflicts 1d HP of injury on the flock. Vampires that use this trick seem less prone to distraction than those which favour bats, although that may just be because they're often members of the formidable de Magpyr clan.

Use the template for a flock of bats, but reduce Night Vision to one level; change Fur to Feathers, and Sharp Teeth to Sharp Beak; delete Absent-Mindedness, Bad Sight, Sonar, and Ultrahearing; and get rid of the quirk "Confused (12) in Daylight." This gives a template value of 35 points. The actual Alternate Form advantage has the same cost.

BLACK RIBBONERS

Members of the Uberwald League of Temperance are vampires who either retain a sense of ethics, or realise that continuing to act like predators in a well-organised modern society is going to get them permanently killed. Hence, they swear off drinking human blood altogether, wearing small black ribbon badges to advertise the fact and (hopefully) persuade humans of their good intentions. The majority avoid *spilling* any blood if they can possibly help it, because that brings far too much temptation right up to their faces, but few are actually pacifists. Most avoid using the word "blood"; it makes them twitchy.

Because human blood is, when all's said and done, an addiction, "going cold bat" and staying "beetotal" is hard work. Indeed, Black Ribboners tend to be less powerful than other vampires because many vampire abilities demand a level of concentration that they just can't achieve, or require sapient blood as mystical fuel. Much like reformed human alcoholics, they deal with this by forming mutual support groups which meet regularly to provide positive reinforcement and sing heartening songs. (These behaviours are enough to rate as a quirk.) However, the support groups in themselves really aren't enough; the vampires need to sublimate the urge.

The Mitigator

In other words, Black Ribboners still have the Uncontrollable Appetite disadvantage (p. 98), but with a mitigator (p. 53). This mitigator can be almost any form of compulsive or obsessive behaviour intense enough to appear on a character sheet, at least as a quirk. For Otto Chriek (pp. 313-314), it's his Obsession; for Maladict, in *Monstrous Regiment*, it's a quirk-level taste for really, really good coffee; for Sally (p. 328), it seems to involve promoting justice; and for Lady Margolotta (pp. 349-350), it's high-minded but highly manipulative long-term politics. A long-lived being with an obsessive interest will usually pick up relevant skills (Photography, Connoisseur, Politics, etc.), too. However, vampires *never* lose the taste for blood; they *cannot* actually "buy off" Uncontrollable Appetite, although they may reduce the self-control roll to 15.

If a vampire cannot pursue his mitigating obsession – he's kept prisoner away from what he needs, the coffee or photographic supplies go missing, or whatever – the Uncontrollable Appetite kicks in, and being unused to controlling his feeding behaviour, the vampire becomes a potential menace to everyone nearby. However, a dedicated Black Ribboner will attempt to fight the urge. Every *hour* that the vampire is deprived of the mitigator, he must make a Will roll (much like somebody withdrawing from an Addiction, p. 54), initially at -5. Failure means he starts hallucinating, possibly picking up bizarre narrative assumptions from other universes, and may warp reality, causing other beings nearby to share these weirdly scrambled perceptions. Each failure also gives the vampire a cumulative -1 on subsequent Will rolls until he suffers a critical failure (increasingly likely as the penalties mount). At that point, the Uncontrollable Appetite activates, with all penalties for any time spent without feeding, and the vampire goes for someone's throat.

Fortunately, a vampire who hasn't yet drunk human blood will snap out of the hallucinatory state within a few minutes on regaining access to his mitigator. If such a vampire does lose control and drink human blood again, though, he loses the mitigator

on his Uncontrollable Appetite. He can only get this back with a lot of roleplayed soul-searching *and* by spending the appropriate number of bonus character points, all the while living with newly unmanageable impulses.

Werewolves and Wolfmen

Lycanthropes – people who can change into wolves or lupine creatures – come in a huge range of types on the Disc, from the traditional howling, angst-laden monsters, through people who just happen to change into large dogs once a month, to "wolfmen" who retain a bipedal posture even while growing fur. Some are little more than tall, saturnine humans who have to shave a lot. There are even a few "inverted" cases who are born as wolves and transform into rather unhappy humans on nights of the full moon.

Relatively few Disc werewolves are slavering killers, but they *are* part-time wild animals, with carnivore instincts. The more moral of them can control their urges. The worst of them combine these impulses with the less-appealing side of human nature. They kill for food, find it fun, and justify it with intricate arguments.

Discworld lycanthropes are too varied for a single template to handle. What follows, then, are basic templates for two common shapes: the *wolfman*, a humanoid with fur, claws, pointy teeth, and a healthy physique, and the *wolf*, a big, rugged, but essentially ordinary beast. Both have problems with silver – that's practically universal among werewolves. Neither has reduced IQ, the Bestial disadvantage, a Social Stigma, further supernatural advantages, or additional weird disadvantages; you can add such things as required. By varying and juggling these traits when evaluating the Alternate Form advantage, it's possible to generate a character sheet for almost any werewolf on the Disc.

WOLFMAN

131 points

The wolfman form is *monstrous* in a way that few wild animals are, although some people who shift to this shape behave perfectly well. Its hands are more like paws and aren't made for fine work or tool use. Some wolfmen (such as Lupine, p. 116) are *big* – maybe 7' tall – making them SM +1. This reduces the price of ST+3 to 27 points, and template cost to 128 points.

Wolf-shaped lycanthropes cannot speak, but many wolfmen are quite conversational. However, it wouldn't be strange to meet one with Cannot Speak or Disturbing Voice when in "beast" form.

Wolfmen aren't considered "normal" anywhere, so they almost always qualify for some kind of Social Stigma. Second-Class Citizen is a minimum, Minority Group is possible, and in many places, they'll rate Monster. Some are genuinely scary to look at, all teeth and bloodshot eyes, giving Hideous appearance.

Attribute Modifiers: ST+3 [30]; DX+2 [40]; HT+2 [20].
Secondary Characteristic Modifiers: Per+3 [15]; Basic Move+2 [10].
Advantages: Claws (Sharp Claws) [5]; Damage Resistance 1 (Tough Skin) [3]; Discriminatory Smell [15]; High Pain Threshold [10]; Night Vision 2 [2]; Teeth (Sharp Teeth) [1]; Temperature Tolerance 1 (Cold) [1]; Ultrahearing [5].
Perks: Fur [1].
Disadvantages: Appearance (Unattractive) [-4]; Bad Grip 2 [-10]; Vulnerability (Silver Weapons ×2) [-10].
Quirks: Doggy Responses; Hunter's Habits; Silver Aversion. [-3]

Yetis

Humans who know anything at all about yetis generally regard them as high-mountain trolls who are well adapted to life above the snowline, and specifically to jumping out of snowdrifts onto people or goats (light colouration helps). Certainly, some yetis have been known to live that way. If that's what you want in a game, treat yetis as trolls with Camouflage at 15+ and – because of the Troll Brain effect in the cold environment – a scary degree of cunning. However, a few people know that some yetis, at least, are a lot more than that.

These smart yetis – which come across as much more reasonable than the ambush-predator types, at least if addressed politely – have developed a limited ability to control time, in a way comprehensible only to the History Monks (p. 13). They can "save" their lives up to a given point, like characters in a video game, and then start again from that point if anything happens to them. Simulate this by letting a yeti buy any number of instances of Extra Life (p. 43), though it will need a lot of points if it keeps getting killed.

WOLF

63 points

Wolves are wild animals and are usually treated as such by humans, potentially giving them Social Stigma (Monster) – though *not* in parts of Uberwald, where people are all too aware that some are actually members of the aristocracy. However, many Discworld werewolves can pass themselves off as large dogs, which leaves them stuck with Social Stigma (Valuable Property) instead. Angua von Uberwald (pp. 322-324) is particularly fortunate in that regard – her Beautiful appearance carries over to her Alternate Form, and she's forever being "recognised" as a fine specimen of somebody's favourite breed of hunting dog.

Attribute Modifiers: DX+2 [40]; HT+2 [20].
Secondary Characteristic Modifiers: Per+4 [20].
Advantages: Damage Resistance 1 (Tough Skin) [3]; Discriminatory Smell [15]; Enhanced Move 1/2 (Ground) [10]; High Pain Threshold [10]; Night Vision 2 [2]; Teeth (Sharp Teeth) [1]; Temperature Tolerance 1 (Cold) [1]; Ultrahearing [5].
Perks: Fur [1].
Disadvantages: Cannot Speak [-15]; Quadruped [-35]; Short Legs [-2]; Vulnerability (Silver Weapons ×2) [-10].
Quirks: Doggy Responses; Hunter's Habits; Silver Aversion. [-3]

OTHER LYCANTHROPE OPTIONS

The sheer variety of lycanthropes on the Disc suggests several optional traits which can be added to either of these templates:

Bestial: Lycanthropes which fall into an entirely animalistic way of thinking when in nonhuman form have Bestial (p. 95). Lower intelligence (below) usually accompanies this; a creature which has fully human intellect yet thinks like a beast would be very strange. Bestial monsters can also suffer from problems such as Impulsiveness and Pyrophobia. A creature whose natural shape is an animal, but who shifts into a more human guise, might easily be Confused (p. 61).

Killer Instincts: Were-beasts are sometimes markedly more vicious than mere carnivorous animals. Consider adding Bad Temper, Berserk, Bloodlust, Callous, or Sadism.

Lower Intelligence: Many lycanthropes are less intelligent in beast form – brighter than most animals, but not at human levels. Hence, their templates can have reduced IQ. Include penalties that lower IQ to 7 if they're a bit dull, 6 if they're only barely capable of abstract thought and simple tool use, 5 if they're unusually bright animals, or 4 if they function at the same level as a "natural" hunting animal. However, such creatures can have human-level willpower and really impressive senses, so offset every -1 to IQ with +1 to Will and +1 to Per.

Supernatural Resilience: Really serious lycanthropes are *extremely* hard to hurt while in beast form. They can have all sorts of special advantages, from Rapid Healing to Regeneration, and from Unkillable 1 (Achilles' Heel, Fire and Silver Weapons) to – very rarely, fortunately – Supernatural Durability. In most cases, these are added to the template but the Alternate

Form advantage takes the Once On, Stays On modifier; thus, if the werewolf is incapacitated ("killed," if Unkillable) in beast form, it stays that way while it recovers.

Becoming a Werewolf

Lycanthropy, unlike vampirism, appears never to be regularly infectious on the Discworld; rather, it's genetic. If "infection" happens occasionally, it seems to be a fluke. Hence, the issue of human PCs becoming werewolves shouldn't arise – well, unless the GM has a really good plot idea!

PUTTING IT ALL TOGETHER

For any lycanthrope character, the final step is assembling the various forms, linking them using the Alternate Form advantage (pp. 85-87). When doing so, note that some more-than-human abilities might carry over in human form, thanks to a "morphic echo" effect; Discriminatory Smell (sometimes with Emotion Sense) is particularly common. Remove such traits from Alternate Form templates and add them back as personal advantages. In addition, the character may have entirely personal disadvantages such as a Secret – from -5 points for "Finds all the stuff with the hair and the growling deeply embarrassing" to -30 points for "Wiped out a whole village in a moment of excess energy," and with the Secret Identity rule applying (although all that's a lot less common on the Disc these days than it used to be) – or maybe Enemy monster-hunters.

Most Discworld werewolves are obliged to transform during the period of the full moon – usually meaning one week in four – either during the night or full-time. Some can *only* change then and have no conscious control over their transformation. Players who opt to play this type of werewolf may try to manipulate game timescales so that they're never in a dangerous place to change when it happens, and as many fights as possible take place when they happen to be furry death machines. While this isn't wrong of them – good time management is an art that werewolves do try to master – the GM shouldn't let them run the game to fit their calendar. Being a werewolf is definitely supposed to be a curse.

To show how all this works, some characters from the chronicles appear below.

Other Therianthropes?

No were-beasts apart from wolves of various sorts have yet appeared in the chronicles, but given the Discworld's nature, many such beings are presumably possible. Werebears or wereboars would likely originate near the Hub, werecats or weretigers in Klatch, weresharks in the be Trobi Islands, and so on. Essentially, anything big and unloved might be accused of pretending to be insidiously human – like communists in '50s America – and on the Disc, the border between accusation and fact is downright fractal.

Ludmilla Cake

The daughter of Mrs. Cake (p. 267), Ludmilla appears to be some sort of throwback – none of her immediate relatives are werewolves, after all. For three (eight-day) weeks in every (four-week) month, she's human, albeit well-built and perhaps a bit fierce-looking; in the fourth, she becomes a "wolf-woman," hairy and sharp-clawed (and even better built), but perfectly well-behaved. For a long time, Ludmilla's mother was rather ashamed of her, or at least nervous about what would happen if the neighbours *found out,* and insisted that she stay home during her "time." But after Mrs. Cake started running a boarding-house for some of Ankh-Morpork's stranger residents, and Ludmilla met Lupine (below), they both came to feel a little more comfortable about the situation. Currently, Ludmilla helps run the boarding-house.

Ludmilla's base form is standard human, with 10 in all basic attributes. She passes as an ordinary member of human society. Perceptive folk sometimes notice some oddities about her when she's human – a lot of hair, fingernails that seem to grow if she gets annoyed – but nothing that would attract much attention if one had no reason to look.

Being a werewolf, Ludmilla can reasonably be assumed to have picked up the Canine language at Accented level (spoken only), for 2 points. As well, she has Discriminatory Smell [15], even in human form. She seemed a little shy when she first appeared in the chronicles, but she's more assertive these days, especially in defence of other odd nonhumans; either could rate as a quirk (-1 point). She certainly has Broad-Minded [-1], thanks to her upbringing. And she has a modest set of skills: Housekeeping (E) IQ+2 [4]-12, Occultism (A) IQ [2]-10, and Sewing (E) DX+2 [4]-12. These traits come to 25 points.

She also has the Alternate Form advantage. That trait's base 15-point cost takes the modifiers Unconscious Only, -20%, and Uncontrollable (Continuously for eight days in each month), -30%, reducing it to 8 points. Then she selects the wolfman template (p. 114), removes Discriminatory Smell because she has this as a personal advantage, and pays 90% of the remaining 116-point cost. That's another 105 points.

Ludmilla is thus a 138-point character. Most of the time she's just an ordinary human woman with a good sense of smell and the ability to talk to certain dogs – but one week in four, she's more.

Lupine

Lupine is a wereman, an "inverted" werewolf. For three weeks every month, he's a wolf; in the fourth, he becomes a 7'-tall not-quite-human. In the former shape, he's very intelligent for a

wolf – though not on a human level – and self-controlled enough to live in Ankh-Morpork without being hunted down. He's generally taken for a big dog, at least by people who simply *assume* that you don't get wolves in town. He seems to have no control over his changes, but he chose to live in the city, presumably because his human form feels the need for company, and he can hide his nature more easily in a big community. (Even in wolfman form, he can pass as nothing *really* odd by Ankh-Morpork standards.) He used to get help from Reg Shoe (p. 328) in hiding his condition; later, he formed a relationship with Ludmilla Cake (above), despite the fact that they were only fully compatible one week in four.

His normal form uses a version of the wolf template (p. 115) without the Vulnerability to silver or the Silver Aversion, but with -4 to IQ, +4 to Will, and another +4 to Per (total +8), giving it a value of 34 points. He has some "wild animal" skills: Brawling (E) DX+2 [4]-14, Survival (Plains) (A) Per-1 [1]-13, and Tracking (A) Per [2]-14. While an animal has no use for money, he has accumulated a few belongings when in humanoid guise, so he rates as Struggling [-10]. And he has a quirk, "Slightly morose," for -1 point.

He also has the Alternate Form advantage, using the SM +1 variant of the wolfman template (p. 114). Alternate Form's base 15-point cost takes Unconscious Only, -20%, and Uncontrollable (Continuously for eight days in each month), -30%, reducing it to 8 points. The template he uses is worth 94 points more than his base form, costing him 90% of that – another 85 points. (Note that because his Per falls from 14 to 13 when he changes, his Survival and Tracking skills drop by a level apiece.)

Lupine is thus a 123-point character – mostly an exceptionally capable wolf, sometimes a tough not-quite-human with problems.

The von Uberwald Clan

Captain Angua von Uberwald (pp. 322-324), of the Ankh-Morpork City Watch, offers an example of a "high-end" werewolf with a fair amount of control over her changes and some serious supernatural advantages. Her late brother, Wolfgang, had similar abilities but a terrifying attitude: Bloodlust (15), Callous, Intolerance, Sadism (12), and Selfish (12). Unfortunately, he *also* had Status 3 and Very Wealthy, being an aristocrat and leader of a werewolf political movement in Uberwald. He may have had higher ST than Angua, too, although she was fully able to take him on.

Their parents are merely typically arrogant and Callous werewolf aristocrats, lacking Wolfgang's psychotic ambition; they have the same basic abilities as their offspring. Their father, Guye – who is large and physically powerful in human *and* wolf form (+2 to ST) – appears to be slipping into an entirely animalistic, Bestial frame of mind, losing the power of speech. Their mother, Serafine, is merely a vicious snob. Both were scared of Wolfgang. Werewolves are prone to simple pack politics.

Zombies

178 points

A zombie is a dead person who has somehow been reanimated. Generally, the original mind is in control, though without any change to the fact of their being dead. In some cases, however, there's a significant loss of intelligence and personality. While Discworld zombies on average enjoy more free will than their counterparts on other worlds, they have a rather marginal place in the Disc scheme of things.

Zombies are usually the result of a necromancer or voodoo witch spell pp. 206-207), though similar results can be achieved in several ways. Not every dead body can be raised as a zombie. In particular, zombies are almost always deceased humans, as dwarfs appear to possess too strong a sense of propriety, while trolls have their own sort of natural orderliness. It seems that the process requires a little of the former human's soul, which in turn requires that the individual have some urge to stick around – some kind of unfinished business, or at least the basic protectiveness of its own grave-treasures that motivates most mummies.

Some zombies are raised as servants or disposable soldiers; whatever their original reason to refuse to die properly, which may just have been a lack of imagination, they don't hang onto enough personality to pursue it, and end up as automatons with minimal awareness. Others seem to be the result of a very rare act of sheer will: Just occasionally, a human who dies with some deep-seated motivation in his soul can tap into the paranormal nature of the Discworld universe and plain *refuse* to go. This is usually a one-off event, but in a few places it becomes a pattern. For example, many Borogravian military leaders were interred in the crypts of Kneck Keep, and being prone to extreme loyalty, they took to lurching around the place (folk sayings notwithstanding, these old soldiers *did* die – they just didn't let that stop them scowling at younger generations). However, they didn't *do* much with their extended existences; zombies don't tend to adventurous attitudes, and these weren't even great talkers.

Zombies *are* walking corpses, which humans may tolerate but generally find distasteful. They're hard to kill, being dead already; numerous extra HP would be entirely justifiable. Most are very strong – substantially beyond the template level, in some cases – whether because they simply don't worry about hurting themselves when they push hard, or due to necromantic power or sheer will. Because their glands don't do much anymore, they behave in a calm, even lethargic way, although they don't necessarily lose all their emotions. They have an exaggerated reputation for tearing people in half.

Indeed, there are *lots* of legends about zombies, some of which might be true for those which were animated by specific traditional magic. For example, some may have a Dread of ordinary salt. In *most* cases, zombies are vulnerable to fire, thanks to their dried-out bodies.

More self-willed zombies retain the skills they learned in life, which can mean almost anything. On the other hand, while lurching necromantic slaves rarely acquire a little competence with a weapon, or remember a combat skill, most have no skills at all. These throw clumsy punches, rolling against DX to hit and using All-Out Attacks (p. 175) to make this more effective.

While zombies can withstand a lot of damage, and may even be stitched back together again afterward, they don't heal like living creatures, and they cannot use magic or stolen life-energy to repair themselves like vampires. No matter how careful they are, they deteriorate over time. Bits fall off and cannot always be found for reattachment. Zombies with long-term purposes may last for years; unimportant servitors might only get months. Eventually, their bodies go to pieces, at which point Death shows up to complete the deferred job.

Attribute Modifiers: ST+4 [40]; DX-1 [-20]; HT+1 [10].
Advantages: Damage Resistance 1 (Tough Skin) [3]; Doesn't Breathe [20]; Doesn't Eat or Drink [10]; Doesn't Sleep [20]; Fearlessness 3 [6]; High Pain Threshold [10]; Immunity to Disease [10]; Immunity to Poison [15]; Injury Tolerance (No Blood, No Vitals, Unliving) [30]; Night Vision 2 [2]; Pressure-Proof [15]; Repairable [50]; Temperature Tolerance 1 (Cold) [1]; Temperature Tolerance 2 (Heat) [3].
Perks: Longevity [1].
Disadvantages: Appearance (Ugly) [-8]; Social Stigma (Minority Group *or* Valuable Property – choose to fit your situation) [-10]; Vulnerability (Fire ×2) [-30].

Mummies

Mummies, found mainly in Djelibeybi and Tsort, result from subjecting the dead bodies of rulers and other dignitaries to complex funeral rites. This mostly means removing assorted vital organs for separate storage, treating the corpse with enough preservatives and bizarre substances to supply a medium-sized perfume factory for a year, and then wrapping it in cloth bandages. Contrary to vulgar belief, this doesn't in itself leave the deceased able to rise from his sarcophagus and lurch vengefully down pyramid corridors in pursuit of tomb-robbers. Powerful Tsortean rulers prefer to arrange for animated statues and bound demons to handle *that*, rather than do it themselves. The situation in Djelibeybi was more complex (see *Pyramids*), but *deliberately* animating mummies wasn't standard procedure even there.

If such animation does occur, though – thanks to either magic or the same process as produces self-motivated zombies – start with the zombie template (above and add a few points, especially to ST and DR, to represent intrinsic toughness. The main benefit of the mummification process is that it keeps the body intact for a long time. However, all those preservatives are notoriously flammable; increase the Vulnerability to ×3 (worth -45 points) or even ×4 (-60 points).

ZOMBIE VARIANTS

The baseline template represents a zombie intended as a long-term playable character, capable of stitching itself back together after being damaged. A perhaps more typical zombie – if one that's less useful as a PC – would replace Repairable with Unhealing (Total) and Unnaturally Fragile, reducing template cost by 130 points. On the other hand, a *really* motivated zombie might have Unkillable 1, or even swap High Pain Threshold for Supernatural Durability (Killed by fire). A product of serious Mad Doctoring or especially deranged necromancy could add interesting traits such as Patchwork Man.

Becoming a Zombie

A player whose character is careless enough to get killed might notice that this isn't automatically the end for everybody and suggest that his PC should return as a zombie. The GM may respond in several ways.

"No" is certainly a valid answer. On the Disc, destiny and death are matters beyond mortal understanding. The GM can always rule that if the dice say you're dead, the fellow with the scythe has shown up, end of story. Player characters have no *right* to avoid this.

If the party includes a magic-worker with the skill to cast a zombification spell, and the spell is cast and you convince the GM that you'd respond . . . congratulations! Your corpse has become a shuffling, nigh-mindless servitor who'll fall to pieces in a few months. The GM will reduce your IQ and add suitable disadvantages – and what fun *that* is to play. Spells cannot create zombies of the self-willed, blazing-eyed sort with any reliability.

Coming back spontaneously, by effort of will, is *rare:* Roll against Will at *-15* to do so. You get +5 for an unresolved Obsession, or if you have Fanaticism and your cause desperately needs you; +3 for other strong motivations, such as a pressing Sense of Duty; or +1 for a quirk-level drive that might help. Being killed by someone you trusted gives +2, but in that case you'll only come back for as long as you need to take revenge. True Faith means you can only become a zombie if your god officially approves, which most categorically *don't* – but if he's one of the dark and sinister sorts who do, it's worth +5. Even if you succeed, the GM can rule that you don't automatically enjoy full IQ or self-repair capabilities; when you accomplish your goal, you may well keel over with a half-smile on your grey, rotting lips. Long-enduring zombies like Mr. Slant (p. 315) and Reg Shoe (p. 328) are *unusual.*

All of which said, the GM may be somewhat sympathetic if you die with enough unspent bonus character points to pay for zombie template (with maybe a few tweaks), plus some kind of vaguely plausible justification. It's quicker than generating a new character, and he can always give you lots of problems with old-fashioned NPCs who think that walking corpses shouldn't be allowed.

Zombies are subject to the "low-grade undead minion" stereotype. Reduced IQ (as bad as -3), low Wealth, Attentive, Callous, Disturbing Voice (or Mute), Duty (possibly Extremely Hazardous), Hidebound, Incurious, Literal-Minded, Low Empathy, or Selfless – or even Arcane Automaton – need not count against campaign disadvantage limits for them, although these traits make for dull characters. (The Boredom Immunity perk is likewise appropriate.) Bad Smell and Hideous can fit, too; while most zombies stabilise at the leathery yellow skin stage, a few continue rotting. Such decay means that their Social Stigma more-or-less automatically escalates to Monster, a problem that suits *any* zombie in a society less cosmopolitan than Ankh-Morpork or Genua.

Zombies are hard to scare – they're dead already, after all – but the free-willed sort occasionally display sensible levels of caution. For one that really doesn't care, though, perhaps because it's just a lurching servitor, replace Fearlessness with Unfazeable. On the other hand, because of their genuine vulnerability to fire or general monster psychology, many have Pyrophobia. Finally, while they don't have to sleep and aren't bound by the weird rules that afflict so many vampires, some of them do find it restful to return to their grave for a few hours a week.

PLAYING ZOMBIES

A zombie could be at a loose end, or it might still be bound by the magic or supernatural event that created it. In the latter case, it's likely to be an NPC with a rather simple plot function: lurch at intruders until hacked to pieces. If not obliged to attack immediately, it may be willing to talk, which presents ingenious adventurers with opportunities.

"Independent" zombies are one of the Disc's less-happy minorities. For all their physical strength, they aren't best placed to enjoy (un)life. Most need some objective or mission to keep them going; otherwise, it's all too easy for them to lie down and give up. A zombie with a (probably faintly ludicrous) self-appointed role in life can add an interesting twist to many plots.

Zombie PCs have an obvious problem, which is that they're likely to fall apart, slowly but surely. That aside, zombies have wearisome social difficulties. They're probably best limited to tongue-in-cheek "monster club" games or one-off scenarios. Still, they *can* last quite a while in nonviolent professions; Mr. Slant (p. 315) is one example. The template's fairly high point cost might seem troublesome, too, but it's rarely hard to find additional disadvantages for a zombie.

Other Possibilities

The chronicles briefly depict several other sapient races, many of them resembling creatures of Earth myth. The GM can create appropriate templates for these as necessary. However, the majority of such species seem to be rare, are probably getting rarer, and aren't especially bright. Humans, dwarfs, and trolls have out-competed most of them.

The list includes such "traditional" fantasy races as *lizard men* (ugly, scrawny, reptilian creatures, extremely stupid but useful in any fight that doesn't involve tactics) and *centaurs* (half-man and half-horse, but rarely seen outside of remote woodlands, and probably very much half-wild-animal). *Furies,* which originate in Ephebe (p. 235), are bird-like creatures, capable of flight (and apparently quite fast), with claws and beaks; they don't appear terribly intelligent, and their speech sounds like a series of bird squawks, but they're biddable and reliable enough that Lady Margolotta (pp. 349-350) employs a small group of them.

The *kvetch* are found in the deep woods of Borogravia and Mouldavia; they're said to be covered in hair, and it's possible that they complain a lot.

Orcs are probably the most exceptional "minor species" on the Disc. Created as perfect soldiers on the orders of Evil Emperor (p. 241), they gained a name as nearly unstoppable killers – in game terms, a dangerous Reputation. While believed wiped out when the Evil Empire fell, an impoverished community of a few dozen was recently discovered in a remote part of Uberwald. Its members mostly seem unimpressive, but one, Mr. Nutt, has been rescued, given an education, and taken to Ankh-Morpork. He may be exceptional, but it does seem that – along with the strength, speed, claws in the fingers, and rapid regeneration ability that were built into his race – he has exceptional intelligence, probably an extension of what was intended as a keen tactical sense. (In game terms, orcs would be high-point-value characters.) When last heard of, Mr. Nutt was returning to Uberwald to attempt to raise his fellow orcs to civilisation, hopefully without triggering too much of the suspicion which other beings feel toward them.

REALLY BIZARRE BEINGS

In principle, you can play just about any kind of character in a Discworld game; see *Supernatural Personifications as Characters* (p. 104) and *Small God* (pp. 144-145), for instance. On a fantasy world with working magic, set in a large and complex "multiverse," it's difficult to say that anything is completely impossible.

But that doesn't mean that *everything* is a good idea. The Discworld stories concern plausible, more-or-less human characters, who behave in mostly reasonable ways. Playing something gratuitously weird, just because the rules can be twisted to allow it, is missing the point. Certainly, if a player's intention seems to be to gain some kind of extreme benefit purely in game terms, the GM should feel free to impose an Unusual Background (pp. 48-49).

This isn't to say that everyone has to play an ordinary human, although that may be the best way to *start* if you haven't played **GURPS** or a Discworld game before. But a look at the chronicles shows that ordinary humans can be as interesting as anyone else – and if you want something *extra*ordinary, the best thing to do is play your character to achieve that.

> ## Animated Skeletons
>
> Supernaturally animated skeletons (aside from Death) are rare on the Disc but not unknown. They're basically fleshless zombies, sometimes literally: If a zombie's flesh rots off or is lost to bizarre accidents, the zombie might preserve or reinforce its joints enough for the bones to hold together, perhaps through sheer force of will. Other specimens may be deliberate creations.
>
> Animated skeletons are relatively quick but not especially strong or robust. Starting with the zombie template (p. 117), replace the attribute and secondary characteristic modifiers with ST-1 [-10], DX+1 [20], and Basic Move+1 [5]. Add Claws (Blunt Claws) [3] and the quirk Cannot Float [-1]; delete the Vulnerability to fire; change Damage Resistance 1 (Tough Skin) to Damage Resistance 1 [5] plus Damage Resistance 3 (Only vs. Impaling damage) [9]; and upgrade the Temperature Tolerance advantages to Temperature Tolerance 3 (Cold) [6] and Temperature Tolerance 3 (Heat) [6]. This gives a 214-point template.
>
> Most of the optional variant features suggested for zombies suit animated skeletons as well. Many of the disadvantage possibilities noted there – including Arcane Automaton, and Unhealing and Unnaturally Fragile replacing Repairable – show up even more often. Few animated skeletons are really very formidable, although necromancers think that they have their uses.
>
> Like golems, animated skeletons use the rules under *Supernaturally Powered Beings* (p. 92); they have no flesh to get tired.

Occupational Templates

An *occupational* template is a blueprint for a character who can fill a given role or do a particular job. Such templates are intended for new players who want help coming up with PCs, experienced players who need characters in a hurry, and GMs who must create fully rounded NPCs quickly. They're merely suggestions, though; if you want to play a stronger but clumsier watchman, or a wizard who has learned to use a sword, go ahead!

Being designed to accommodate new players, these templates are relatively simple. Each offers a few choices – but *only* a few – to allow for some variation in the end product. Experienced players and GMs will want to swap around points and make more radical tweaks.

Each template generates a complete character with attributes, secondary characteristics, advantages, disadvantages, and skills. The last are broken down into *primary* skills (things which anyone in this role or job really *needs*), *secondary* skills (things at which this sort of character tends to be competent), and *background* skills (things which such a character will likely have picked up incidentally). These templates mostly don't include quirks; you can (and probably *should*) add a few quirks to personalise the character, and spend the points from them on extra or upgraded skills, or on perks. While no particular disadvantage limits (pp. 25-26) are assumed, few of these templates are likely to stretch most campaigns' limits.

Some of these occupational templates are for character types from particular races, in which case they include racial templates in their advantage or disadvantage lists. The others are human by default, but you can always add a nonhuman racial template. See the running example of Hunchbroad Modoscousin for an illustration of this.

As with racial templates, the point value of each trait in an occupational template appears in square brackets; e.g., "DX 11 [20]."

As these templates suggest *specific, absolute* attribute levels, skills are given with difficulty, level relative to the controlling attribute, point cost, and calculated level; e.g., "Naturalist (H) IQ+2 [12]-14" for an IQ 12 character. However, it's often possible to modify attributes a little, in which case any related skill levels will change by the same amount; for example, if that IQ 12 character were boosted to IQ 13, his Naturalist skill would go up to 15. Likewise, if you take a Talent or other advantage that grants a skill bonus – or a disadvantage that gives a skill penalty – remember to check all the relevant skill levels. Similarly, changes to attributes will also affect secondary characteristics.

Low-Powered Characters

These templates cost 25 to 50 points each. They give characters not much different in overall capability to the run of ordinary folks – although they may have minor skills or abilities that are far from ordinary. Such templates can be useful even in campaigns with much higher starting points, as it's always easy to add to them. For instance, to create a muscular, rugged Fourecksian backpacker or a quick-witted, lucky peasant for a 100-point game, simply choose the relevant 25-point template and add, say, +4 to ST, +3 to HT, and 5 points in combat skills, or +3 to IQ and Luck, and then pick one more disadvantage and spend the points from that to round out your skills.

AGATEAN TOURIST

50 points

You're an ordinary citizen of the Agatean Empire who has decided to follow in the footsteps of the legendary Twoflower, visit other parts of the Disc, see exciting things, and find out if the people there are really as strange as everyone thinks. It turns out that your perfectly ordinary gold coins make you quite well-off in foreign parts, and you're pleased to discover that the nice people of Ankh-Morpork publish helpful guidebooks.

Your native language and Cultural Familiarity are of course both Agatean. You'd do well to pick up at least a few words of the local language – and the appropriate Cultural Familiarity – as soon as possible, if not at the start. Someone who enjoys playing a fish out of water is welcome to do things the hard way, though!

Attributes: ST 10 [0]; DX 10 [0]; IQ 10 [0]; HT 10 [0].
Secondary Characteristics: Damage 1d-2/1d; BL 20 lbs.; HP 10 [0]; Will 10 [0]; Per 10 [0]; FP 10 [0]; Basic Speed 5.00 [0]; Basic Move 5 [0].
Advantages and Perks: Status 1* [0] *and* Very Wealthy [30]. ● Luck [15] *or* Unfazeable [15]. ● *One of* Will +2, Per +2, Fearlessness 5, or Language Talent, all [10]. ● Pitiable [5], *or* Resistant to Disease (+3) [3] *and* two of Cultural Familiarity (any), Deep Sleeper, Honest Face, Language (any, Broken/None), or Sea Legs, all [1].
Disadvantages: Social Stigma (Overdressed Foreigner) [-10]. ● *One of* Absent-Mindedness, Charitable (12), Gullibility (9), Honesty (9), or Pacifism (Self-Defence Only), all [-15]. ● *One of*

Chummy, Compulsive Neatness (12), Compulsive Spending (12), Curious (12), Gluttony (12), Ham-Fisted, Klutz, Oblivious, Skinny, Squeamish (15), or Truthfulness (12), all [-5].
Primary Skills: Shouting at Foreigners (E) IQ+2 [4]-12.
Secondary Skills: Photography (A) IQ+1 [4]-11.
Background Skills: *Six of* Riding (Equines) (A) DX [2]-10; First Aid, Games (Aqueduct), Gardening, Gesture, Hobby Skill (Origami), or Savoir-Faire (High Society), all (E) IQ+1 [2]-11; Professional Skill (Filing Clerk) or Writing, both (A) IQ [2]-10; Accounting (H) IQ-1 [2]-9; Fishing (E) Per+1 [2]-11; or Observation (A) Per [2]-10.

* Free from Wealth.

ALCHEMIST

50 points

You're a professional alchemist (p. 290), probably making a shaky income on the fringes of medicine, magic, fireworks manufacture, or white-collar crime. You're supposed to say that your concern is with ancient learning and the secrets of the universe[1], but you dream of wealth.

You may be able to hold down a proper job, or you might resort to the traditional art of persuading kings that you can turn lead into gold, given a research grant.

Attributes: ST 10 [0]; DX 10 [0]; IQ 12 [40]; HT 10 [0].
Secondary Characteristics: Damage 1d-2/1d; BL 20 lbs.; HP 10 [0]; Will 12 [0]; Per 12 [0]; FP 10 [0]; Basic Speed 5.00 [0]; Basic Move 5 [0].
Advantages: *One of* Combat Reflexes, Danger Sense, or Patron (Gullible noble, an extremely powerful individual; 9 or less), all [15]. ● *One of* Per +1, High TL 1, Resistant to Poison (+3), Single-Minded, or Versatile, all [5].
Disadvantages: *Two of* Bad Sight (Mitigator, Glasses), Bad Smell, Clueless, Hard of Hearing, No Sense of Humour, or Struggling, all [-10]. ● *One of* Curious (12), Oblivious, Overconfidence (12), Shyness (Mild), or Stubbornness, all [-5].
Primary Skills: Alchemy (VH) IQ [8]-12.
Secondary Skills: *Two of* Explosives (Demolition *or* Fireworks) (A) IQ [2]-12; or Engineer (Magical) or Metallurgy, both (H) IQ-1 [2]-11.
Background Skills: *Three of* Acrobatics or Sleight of Hand, both (H) DX-2 [1]-8; First Aid (E) IQ [1]-12; Fast-Talk, Research, or Teaching, all (A) IQ-1 [1]-11; Counterfeiting, Herbalism, Natural Philosophy, or Poisons, all (H) IQ-2 [1]-10; Thaumatology (VH) IQ-3 [1]-9; or Scrounging (E) Per [1]-12.

---

1. *Unfortunately, one of the subtler laws of the Discworld universe that alchemists never seem to notice is the Rule of Universal Humour, which is part of the reason that they once got through four guildhalls in two years.*

BANDIT

25 points

You belong to a widespread, hard-working class of rural miscreants. You go to a lot of trouble setting up ambushes and traps, but your handiwork rarely gets you much respect.[1] Still, it's steady work.

As the Discworld attitude to law enforcement is based on a mixture of laziness and uncomplicated morality, a bandit group that merely *robs* travellers on the same remote stretch of road can keep going unhindered for months. However, you have to be careful. If you ever get *too* successful, or get carried away and hurt too many people, some landowner or rich merchant is likely to put together a response – and if you hurt someone popular, even the peasants may turn nasty.

With the addition of some seafaring skills, a pirate character could use this template as well.

Attributes: ST 11 [10]; DX 10 [0]; IQ 10 [0]; HT 10 [0].
Secondary Characteristics: Damage 1d-1/1d+1; BL 24 lbs.; HP 11 [0]; Will 10 [0]; Per 10 [0]; FP 10 [0]; Basic Speed 5.00 [0]; Basic Move 5 [0].
Advantages: One of ST +2, DX +1, HT +2, Born to Hang 2, or Outdoorsman 2, all [20], *or* Combat Reflexes [15] *and* Per +1 [5].
Disadvantages: Status -1 [-5] *and* Struggling [-10]. ● *Two* of Bad Temper (15), Bully (15), Callous, Chummy, Code of Honour (Pirate's), Compulsive Carousing (12), Easy to Read (15), Hidebound, Innumerate, Overconfidence (12), or Sense of Duty (The Gang), all [-5].
Primary Skills: Axe/Mace (A) DX+1 [4]-11 *and* Camouflage (E) IQ+2 [4]-12.
Secondary Skills: Area Knowledge (area of operations) (E) IQ+1 [2]-11; Brawling (E) DX+1 [2]-11; Intimidation (A) Will [2]-10; *and* Survival (usual environment) (A) Per [2]-10.
Background Skills: Four of Crossbow, Fast-Draw (Knife *or* Sword), Knife, Knot-Tying, Shield, or Thrown Weapon (Spear), all (E) DX [1]-10; Bow, Broadsword, Climbing, Riding (Equines), Shortsword, Spear, or Stealth, all (A) DX-1 [1]-9; Carpentry or Current Affairs (local region), both (E) IQ [1]-10; Animal Handling (Equines), Armoury (any), Packing, Smuggling, Streetwise, Teamster (Equines), or Traps, all (A) IQ-1 [1]-9; Naturalist (H) IQ-2 [1]-8; Carousing (E) HT [1]-10; Hiking (A) HT-1 [1]-9; or Observation, Search, or Tracking, all (A) Per-1 [1]-9.

CLACKS FIELD ENGINEER

50 points

You work for a clacks company (pp. 222-225), building towers and keeping them working. This means surveying new areas, surviving whatever you find there, persuading suspicious locals that what you're bringing is good for them, supervising construction work, and fixing whatever goes wrong. Obviously, few people can do all of that singlehandedly, so you're probably part of a team, but you'll get on in the company best if you demonstrate some flexibility.

---

1. *Frankly, you could turn a better living putting that much effort into something more legal – and it isn't that you enjoy all the work. But you live in hope of a big score, and banditry may be an old family tradition with local social standing. Or perhaps you think that girls will be impressed by a rogue who sleeps under a hedge.*

Attributes: ST 10 [0]; DX 10 [0]; IQ 11 [20]; HT 10 [0].
Secondary Characteristics: Damage 1d-2/1d; BL 20 lbs.; HP 10 [0]; Will 11 [0]; Per 11 [0]; FP 10 [0]; Basic Speed 5.00 [0]; Basic Move 5 [0].
Advantages: One of DX +1, IQ +1, or Artificer 2, all [20]. ● *Two* of Per +1, Charisma 1, Eidetic Memory, High Manual Dexterity 1, High TL 1, Single-Minded, or Versatile, all [5].
Disadvantages: One of Bad Sight (Mitigator, Glasses), Clueless, or Truthfulness (6), all [-10]. ● *One* of Curious (12), Duty (To the clacks company; 9 or less), Oblivious, Pacifism (Reluctant Killer), or Post-Combat Shakes (12), all [-5].
Primary Skills: Engineer (Clacks) (H) IQ-1 [2]-10; Mechanic (Clacks) (A) IQ+1 [4]-12; *and* Telegraphy (E) IQ+1 [2]-12.
Secondary Skills: Area Knowledge (one clacks route) (E) IQ [1]-11; Navigation (Land) (A) IQ [2]-11; *and* Survival (one environment) (A) Per-1 [1]-10.
Background Skills: Three of Crossbow or Knot-Tying, both (E) DX [1]-10; Climbing or Riding (Equines), both (A) DX-1 [1]-9; Carpentry, Current Affairs (any), First Aid, or Games (any), all (E) IQ [1]-11; Administration, Fast-Talk, Leadership, Mechanic (Low-Tech Machines), Merchant, Packing, Smith (Blacksmith), Teamster (Equines), or Weather Sense, all (A) IQ-1 [1]-10; Cryptography, Diplomacy, Engineer (Civil *or* Low-Tech Machines), Mathematics (Applied), Natural Philosophy, or Naturalist, all (H) IQ-2 [1]-9; Hiking (A) HT-1 [1]-9; or Fishing or Scrounging, both (E) Per [1]-11.

You'll get on in the company best if you demonstrate some flexibility.

ÉMIGRÉ GNOME

50 points

You're a fairly ordinary gnome who has decided that, now that more of your people have come out from under the toadstool and moved into human society, you're prepared to risk joining them. You have just enough of what it takes to make a living in a job such as pest control or private espionage.

The attributes and secondary characteristics below include modifiers from the racial template. For a tougher being of similar size, see the pictsie occupational template (pp. 141-142).

Attributes: ST 4 [0]; DX 12 [0]; IQ 10 [0]; HT 11 [0].
Secondary Characteristics: Damage 1d-5/1d-4; BL 3.2 lbs.; HP 4 [0]; Will 10 [0]; Per 11 [0]; FP 11 [0]; Basic Speed 6.00 [5]; Basic Move 4 [0].
Advantages: Gnome/Pictsie [18]. ● *Two* of Will +3, Per +3, Combat Reflexes, Danger Sense, High Manual Dexterity 3, Luck, Perfect Balance, or Silence 3, all [15].
Disadvantages and Quirks: Cannot Run Long Distances [-1] *and* Mild Paranoia [-1]. ● *One* of Bad Temper (12), Berserk (12), Low TL 2, Shyness (Severe), or Struggling, all [-10]. ● *Two* of Callous, Code of Honour (Professional), Compulsive Carousing (12), Curious (12), Impulsiveness (15), Status -1, Stubbornness, or Truthfulness (12), all [-5].
Primary Skills: Camouflage (E) IQ+1 [0]-11* *and* Stealth (A) DX+2 [4]-14*.

Secondary Skills: Naturalist (H) IQ [4]-10; Observation (A) Per [2]-11; *and* Scrounging (E) Per [1]-11.

Background Skills: *Five* of Brawling, Knife, or Sewing, all (E) DX [1]-12; Climbing, Filch, or Riding (Birds), all (A) DX-1 [1]-11; Acrobatics (H) DX-2 [1]-10; Area Knowledge (home woods or city of residence) (E) IQ [1]-10; Animal Handling (Birds), Shadowing, Streetwise, or Traps, all (A) IQ-1 [1]-9; Poisons (H) IQ-2 [1]-8; *or* Survival (Woodlands) or Urban Survival, both (A) Per-1 [1]-10. ● Then add +1 to any three of these [3].

* Reflects racial template. The racial Silence advantage (and any added Silence) and the character's small size will often give bonuses to the roll.

ENTERTAINER

25 points

Actors, singers, buskers, and the like abound on the Disc, and often get into trouble. You're one of them. While you're quite competent, if you do say so yourself[1], you're still stuck in the profession's lower ranks. Still, this can be a reasonable, if precarious, existence – especially if you can get the hang of flattering rich people (if you can't, it combines the disadvantages of unemployment with a greater lack of social regard). You have exceptional freedom of movement, anyway.[2] Which said, several art forms enable performers to settle in one place, usually a large city.

You may focus on one form – e.g., music, dance, acting (wandering or settled), or storytelling – but to survive, you probably need a few sidelines. Theatre in Ankh-Morpork is based around the Dysk (see *The Isle of Gods*, p. 252), while opera in that city is similar to opera in our world.[3] Agatean opera audience members definitely require Cultural Familiarity (Agatean) to avoid being completely confused, while dwarf song (which uses only one word, "gold") is more subtle than humans believe. Other forms might be invented, although the precedents of moving pictures and music with rocks in suggest that this might not be a good idea (and the Patrician may have strong opinions there). Fools and clowns are discussed below.

As a wanderer or an urban lowlife, you're at risk of getting involved in all sorts of incidents. After all, given your lack of respectability, you're often the first to be blamed when things get weird.

Attributes: ST 10 [0]; DX 10 [0]; IQ 10 [0]; HT 10 [0].

Secondary Characteristics: Damage 1d-2/1d; BL 20 lbs.; HP 10 [0]; Will 10 [0]; Per 10 [0]; FP 10 [0]; Basic Speed 5.00 [0]; Basic Move 5 [0].

Advantages: *One* of Charisma 3, Daredevil, Empathy, Musical Ability 3, Perfect Balance, or Smooth Operator 1, all [15], *or* Charisma 1 [5] *and* Voice [10]. ● *Two* of Per +1, Ambidexterity, Flexibility, Pitiable, Single-Minded, or Versatile, all [5].

Disadvantages: Status -1 [-5] *and* Struggling [-10]. ● Alcoholism or Lecherousness (12), both [-15], *or three* of Chummy, Code of Honour (Professional), Compulsive Carousing (12), Curious (12), Sense of Duty (The Company), Skinny, Social Stigma (Second-Class Citizen), *or* Wealth reduced further to Poor, all [-5].

---

1. *And oh yes, you do.*

2. *People are always telling you to go somewhere else.*

3. *Possessed of an audience of fanatic followers, incomprehensible to everyone else.*

Primary Skills: *Three* of Hobby Skill (Juggling) (E) DX+2 [4]-12; Dancing (A) DX+1 [4]-11; Acrobatics or Escape, both (H) DX [4]-10; Conducting, Directing, Fortune-Telling (any), Performance, Poetry, Public Speaking, or Writing, all (A) IQ+1 [4]-11; Musical Composition or Musical Instrument (any), both (H) IQ [4]-10; *or* Singing (E) HT+2 [4]-12. ● Then add +2 to any one of these [8].

Secondary Skills: *Three* of Disguise, Fast-Talk, or Fool's Lore, all (A) IQ [2]-10; Carousing (E) HT+1 [2]-11; *or* Sex Appeal (A) HT [2]-10.

Background Skills: *Four* of Brawling, Knife, or Thrown Weapon (Knife), all (E) DX [1]-10; Pickpocket or Sleight of Hand, both (H) DX-2 [1]-8; Carpentry, Current Affairs (Headline News), First Aid, Games (any), Gesture, or Savoir-Faire (Servant), all (E) IQ [1]-10; Acting, Connoisseur (any), Gambling, Packing, or Streetwise, all (A) IQ-1 [1]-9; Artist (any), Diplomacy, or Literature, all (H) IQ-2 [1]-8; *or* Scrounging (E) Per [1]-10.

FOOL/CLOWN

50 points

While many adventurers are *called* fools or clowns, you have the qualifications to prove it. You're a trained member of the Ankh-Morpork Fools' Guild (pp. 262-263), with a vast tradition of japes, foolery, and standard punch lines well drilled into you, and every last vestige of original wit firmly suppressed. You may work in a theatre or a circus, or have a position at a royal court, persuading some paranoid psychotic ruler that he's actually quite tolerant (because he puts up with *you*, even laughs at your jokes). In the latter case, you should do your best to avoid giving people the idea that you're a spy, however many letters you write back to the Guild. Getting involved in adventures or plots may be painful and dangerous, in a Shakespearean sort of way, but you might like the idea more than the prospect of another bucket of custard down your trousers.

Fools and clowns often have quirks like "Regards a clown's make-up as his real face," "Can't see a bucket or a ladder without going into a standard routine," and "Really, really *hates* custard." The GM may let such characters start play with more quirks than are normally permitted – most do leave the Guild school as a bundle of neuroses.

Attributes: ST 10 [0]; DX 11 [20]; IQ 10 [0]; HT 10 [0].

Secondary Characteristics: Damage 1d-2/1d; BL 20 lbs.; HP 10 [0]; Will 10 [0]; Per 10 [0]; FP 10 [0]; Basic Speed 5.25 [0]; Basic Move 5 [0].

Advantages: *One* of HT +1, Per +2, or High Pain Threshold, all [10]. ● *Two* of Basic Move +1, Ambidexterity, Charisma 1, Flexibility, or Pitiable, all [5].

Disadvantages: *Two* of Clueless, Cowardice (12), Disturbing Voice, Hunchback, Odious Personal Habits (Witless witticisms, calling people "nuncle," abuse of custard, etc.), Secret (Spy for the Guild), or Struggling, all [-10]. ● *Two* of Code of Honour (Professional), Duty (To the Guild; 9 or less), Hidebound, Pacifism (Reluctant Killer), Post-Combat Shakes (12), Skinny, or Status -1, all [-5].

Primary Skills: Acrobatics (H) DX+1 [8]-12; Fast-Talk (A) IQ+1 [4]-11; Fool's Lore (A) IQ+4 [16]-14; *and* Hobby Skill (Juggling) (E) DX+1 [2]-12.

Secondary Skills: Gesture (E) IQ [1]-10; Performance (A) IQ [2]-10; Savoir-Faire (Servant) (E) IQ [1]-10; *and* Stealth (A) DX [2]-11.

Background Skills: *Four* of Bicycling (Unicycle) (E) DX [1]-11; Dancing or Climbing, both (A) DX-1 [1]-10; Current Affairs (Politics *or* Regional for home city) (E) IQ [1]-10; Acting (A) IQ-1 [1]-9; Mimicry (any) (H) IQ-2 [1]-8; or Observation (A) Per-1 [1]-9.

FOURECKSIAN BACKPACKER

25 points

With the opening up of EcksEcksEcksEcks, quite a number of its citizens have erupted onto the rest of the Disc to see if it's as interesting as they've heard, and if the beer is as poor. You're one of them. You live off odd jobs, and are happy to explain about the beer. You may have clubbed together with others to buy a battered old cart to get around on, in which case you probably gave it a nice colourful paint job.

Attributes: ST 10 [0]; DX 10 [0]; IQ 10 [0]; HT 11 [10].
Secondary Characteristics: Damage 1d-2/1d; BL 20 lbs.; HP 10 [0]; Will 10 [0]; Per 10 [0]; FP 11 [0]; Basic Speed 5.25 [0]; Basic Move 5 [0].
Advantages and Perks: *One* of ST +2, DX +1, IQ +1, HT +2, or Basic Speed +1, all [20]; or alternatively, *one* of Combat Reflexes, Daredevil, or Serendipity 1, all [15], and *one* of Will +1, Per +1, or Absolute Direction, all [5]. ● *One* of Attractive, Fearlessness 2, Less Sleep 2, or Night Vision 4, all [4]. ● *One* of Alcohol Tolerance, Cold Resistance, Deep Sleeper, Good with Horses, Heat Resistance, Improvised Weapons (Brawling), No Hangover, Sea Legs, or Statuesque, all [1].
Disadvantages: Status -1 [-5] *and* Struggling [-10]. ● *Two* of Chummy, Code of Honour (Pirate's), Compulsive Carousing (12), Curious (12), Impulsiveness (15), Klutz, Oblivious, Overconfidence (12), Sense of Duty (Travelling Companions), Truthfulness (12), or Wealth reduced further to Poor, all [-5].
Primary Skills: Hiking (A) HT+1 [4]-12.
Secondary Skills: Carousing (E) HT+2 [4]-13 *and* Scrounging (E) Per+1 [2]-11.
Background Skills: *Five* of Brawling, Jumping, Knot-Tying, or Thrown Weapon (Axe/Mace), all (E) DX [1]-10; Axe/Mace, Climbing, Dancing, or Sports (any), all (A) DX-1 [1]-9; Sling (H) DX-2 [1]-8; Area Knowledge (any), First Aid, Gesture, Seamanship, or Shouting at Foreigners, all (E) IQ [1]-10; Animal Handling (Equines), Fast-Talk, Mechanic (Animal-Drawn Vehicle), Navigation (Land), Packing, Professional Skill (Bartender), Smuggling, Streetwise, Teamster (Equines), or Writing, all (A) IQ-1 [1]-9; Musical Instrument (any), Naturalist, or Veterinary, all (H) IQ-2 [1]-8; Singing or Swimming, both (E) HT [1]-11; Sex Appeal (A) HT-1 [1]-10; Fishing (E) Per [1]-10; or Survival (any) or Urban Survival, both (A) Per-1 [1]-9.

JOURNALIST

50 points

You're a member of the Disc's newest and most exciting profession. You write for a living and your writing gets fed to one of the fancy new presses, reproduced thousands of times, and read by everyone from kings to beggars. It then gets forgotten the next day, but that's part of what makes the job so exciting. You may work for the first newspaper, Ankh-Morpork's *Times*, or for one of its rivals or imitators, perhaps in another city. The rich and powerful might find you annoying, but the smarter ones normally know better than to harass you *directly* – so when you *do* start getting harassed, you know that you're on to something.

Attributes: ST 10 [0]; DX 10 [0]; IQ 12 [40]; HT 10 [0].
Secondary Characteristics: Damage 1d-2/1d; BL 20 lbs.; HP 10 [0]; Will 12 [0]; Per 12 [0]; FP 10 [0]; Basic Speed 5.00 [0]; Basic Move 5 [0].
Advantages: *One* of Per +3, Danger Sense, Indomitable, Luck, Sense of the City 3, or Serendipity 1, all [15]. ● *One* of Will +1, Charisma 1, Sensitive, or Single-Minded, all [5].
Disadvantages: *One* of Alcoholism (Withdrawn), Curious (6), Laziness, or Struggling, all [-10]. ● *Three* of Callous, Code of Honour (Professional), Overconfidence (12), Pacifism (Reluctant Killer), Reputation -2 (As a nuisance, among local crooks, watchmen, or politicians), Sense of Duty (The Paper), or Stubbornness, all [-5].
Primary Skills: Writing (A) IQ [2]-12.
Secondary Skills: Carousing (E) HT+1 [2]-11 *and* Fast-Talk (A) IQ [2]-12. ● *One* of these packages:

1. *Crime Reporter:* Area Knowledge (city beat) (E) IQ [1]-12; Criminology (A) IQ-1 [1]-11; Current Affairs (Headline News) (E) IQ [1]-12; *and* Streetwise (A) IQ-1 [1]-11.
2. *Critic:* Connoisseur (any) (A) IQ+1 [4]-13.
3. *Foreign Correspondent:* Area Knowledge (assignment area) (E) IQ [1]-12; Current Affairs (Regional for assignment area) (E) IQ+1 [2]-13; *and* Diplomacy (H) IQ-2 [1]-10.
4. *Photojournalist:* Photography (A) IQ+1 [4]-13.
5. *Society Reporter:* Current Affairs (Headline News *or* Regional for home region) (E) IQ+1 [2]-13 *and* Savoir-Faire (High Society) (E) IQ+1 [2]-13.
6. *Sports Reporter:* Current Affairs (Sports) (E) IQ+1 [2]-13; Games (rules for any sport) (E) IQ [1]-12; *and* Games (rules for another sport) (E) IQ [1]-12.

Background Skills: *Five* of Filch, Riding (Equines), or Stealth, all (A) DX-1 [1]-9; Shouting at Foreigners or Telegraphy, both (E) IQ [1]-12; Acting, Interrogation, Research, Shadowing, or Smuggling, all (A) IQ-1 [1]-11; History (something relevant to work) or Psychology (Human), both (H) IQ-2 [1]-10; Body Language or Observation, both (A) Per-1 [1]-11; or Detect Lies (H) Per-2 [1]-10.

MEDIUM

50 points

Mediums are people who have (mostly friendly) dealings with ghosts and other spirits, providing a conduit between the living and the dead. In more traditional areas, the job shades into religion, shamanism, or witchcraft. In urban societies, most mediums are for some reason female, middle-aged, and lower-middle-class.

You're a typical urban medium, the sort who uses genuine spiritual gifts rather than pure trickery. Mind you, a bit of flim-flam doesn't always hurt – people seem to expect it, and a few "people skills" can help with the spirits (or with the *customers* when the spirits aren't cooperating).

There are relatively few mediums in places like Ankh-Morpork, where the dead frequently make haste to get away from their relatives, but there's always work for a few specialists. Talking to spirits can get you involved in all sorts of odd business, too.

Attributes: ST 8 [-20]; DX 10 [0]; IQ 11 [20]; HT 10 [0].
Secondary Characteristics: Damage 1d-3/1d-2; BL 13 lbs.; HP 8 [0]; Will 12 [5]; Per 11 [0]; FP 10 [0]; Basic Speed 5.00 [0]; Basic Move 5 [0].
Advantages: Channelling [10] *and* Medium [10]. • *One* of Indomitable, See Invisible (Spirit), True Faith, or Unfazeable, all [15]. • *Three* of Will +1, Per +1, Charisma 1, five Languages (each Broken/None), Sensitive, or Spirit Empathy (Specialised, Ghosts), all [5].
Disadvantages: *One* of Bad Sight (Mitigator, Glasses), Clueless, Hard of Hearing, Struggling, or Truthfulness (6), all [-10]. • *Two* of Hidebound, Odious Personal Habit (Gossiping about the spirit world), Pacifism (Reluctant Killer), or Stubbornness, all [-5].
Primary Skills: Fortune-Telling (any) (A) IQ [2]-11 *and* Hidden Lore (Spirit Lore) (A) IQ+1 [4]-12.
Secondary Skills: Housekeeping (E) IQ+1 [2]-12 *and* Merchant (A) IQ [2]-11.
Background Skills: *Four* of Sewing (E) DX [1]-10; Area Knowledge (home community), Games (any card game), or Savoir-Faire (Servant), all (E) IQ [1]-11; Fortune-Telling (second type) (A) IQ-1 [1]-10; Intimidation (A) Will-1 [1]-11; or Detect Lies (H) Per-2 [1]-9. • Then add +1 to any one of these [1].

MERCHANT/ENTREPRENEUR

50 points

You're one of the honest (well, *mostly,* for a sensible value of honest) traders who keeps the Disc's economy ticking over. Civilised areas are seeing significant growth in your sort of middle class – and less-civilised parts can expect to see quite a few of the more adventurous sorts of merchant, sooner or later, especially if they produce pearls, furs, or spices. You may be little more than a clever roving pedlar, or you might be a plump and successful urban businessman; choose your advantages and disadvantages appropriately. You'll need some explanation if your Wealth level and Status are too inconsistent.

"Entrepreneurs" are distinct from "merchants" the way that an unbroken wild horse is distinct from a show pony: The former has more energy and is more dangerous to be around, and the greater energy may mean more potential, but after a few years, the two are typically indistinguishable. Effective entrepreneurs are forever looking for the main chance, and they frequently cut corners. In game terms, they may lean on Fast-Talk as much as on Merchant.

Rising merchants and entrepreneurs often go seeking adventure in the company of guides and guards. Richer merchants are more likely to be Patrons than PCs, but their children are sometimes prime PC material – they have access to funds and freedom of movement, and they feel a pressing need to prove themselves.

Attributes: ST 10 [0]; DX 10 [0]; IQ 11 [20]; HT 10 [0].
Secondary Characteristics: Damage 1d-2/1d; BL 20 lbs.; HP 10 [0]; Will 11 [0]; Per 11 [0]; FP 10 [0]; Basic Speed 5.00 [0]; Basic Move 5 [0].
Advantages and Perks: *One* of Charisma 2, Comfortable, or Voice, all [10]. • *Two* of Will +1, Per +1, Absolute Direction, Eidetic Memory, Sensitive, or Status 1, all [5]. • *Two* of HP +1, Languages (any, Broken/Broken), Less Sleep 1, or Lightning Calculator, all [2]. • *One* of Cultural Familiarity (somewhere useful), Haughty Sneer, or Honest Face, all [1].
Disadvantages: *One* of Bad Sight (Mitigator, Glasses), Cowardice (12), Low Pain Threshold, Miserliness (12), Squeamish (12), or Struggling, all [-10]. • *Two* of Callous, Chummy, Code of Honour (Pirate's *or* Professional), Compulsive Spending (12), Curious (12), Gluttony (12), Pacifism (Reluctant Killer), Post-Combat Shakes (12), Selfish (12), Social Stigma (Second-Class Citizen – "Foreign Shyster"), or Very Fat, all [-5].

Primary Skills: Merchant (A) IQ+3 [12]-14.

Secondary Skills: *Three* of Boating (any) or Riding (Camels *or* Equines), both (A) DX [2]-10; Area Knowledge (trade routes) or Current Affairs (Business), both (E) IQ+1 [2]-12; Fast-Talk, Packing, Smuggling, or Teamster (Equines), all (A) IQ [2]-11; or Accounting (H) IQ-1 [2]-10.

Background Skills: *Five* of Brawling, Crossbow, or Shield, all (E) DX [1]-10; Axe/Mace or Shortsword, both (A) DX-1 [1]-9; Current Affairs (Regional for home community), First Aid, Games (Cripple Mr. Onion), Gesture, Savoir-Faire (High Society), Seamanship, or Shouting at Foreigners, all (E) IQ [1]-11; Acting, Administration, Animal Handling (Camels *or* Equines), Connoisseur (any saleable art form), Gambling, Leadership, Navigation (any), Public Speaking, or Streetwise, all (A) IQ-1 [1]-10; Diplomacy, Law (International Trade), or Psychology (Dwarf *or* Human), all (H) IQ-2 [1]-9; Carousing (E) HT [1]-10; Hiking (A) HT-1 [1]-9; Body Language, Observation, or Survival (any), all (A) Per-1 [1]-10; or Detect Lies (H) Per-2 [1]-9.
- Then add +1 to any two of these [2].

Other Small-Time Professionals

For a moderately successful urban craftsman, use this template but reassign some skill points from Merchant or transport-related skills to Professional Skills or repair skills.

William's father, during their last meeting, had gone on at some length about the proud and noble traditions of the de Wordes. These had mostly involved unpleasant deaths, preferably of foreigners, but somehow, William gathered, the de Wordes had always considered that it was a decent second prize to die themselves.

– The Truth

Noble

50 points

You're a scion of one of the Disc's great noble houses, and hence born to rule – the gods wouldn't put somebody in your position without also bestowing all the necessary talent, would they? Oh, you might not *seem* as book-smart as some spinning-eyed wizard, or as cunning as some jumped-up tradesman, but you have *breeding*, and that's what counts. Well, that and the family wealth, but it's vulgar to discuss money. It's also vulgar to discuss how your family achieved this position in the first place.

You could be a total idiot, hell-bent on dying in battle like so many of your ancestors, or a useless fop, only interested in the latest fashions – or you might actually have some of the inherited cunning that has kept your family close to power over the centuries, or an honest sense of *noblesse oblige*. You may even have some modern ideas, which your tenants might dislike. Peasants can be terribly conservative; they like to know where they stand, and they have a habit of showing more respect to spectacularly dissipated nobles than to hard workers. You can try to introduce reforms or try to stop them, but the laws of drama and comedy ensure that you'll have trouble either way.

You might be as wealthy as your manner implies, in which case any adventuring you do is likely for the fun of it. Indeed, if you can find the points for it, even Filthy Rich is perfectly justifiable. Then again, your family may have fallen into financial difficulties, leaving you with Wealth insufficient to support your Status and obliging you to make yourself useful. For game purposes, though, no noble should have *really* low Wealth; even "impoverished" families never seem to have much trouble getting groceries delivered and bespoke tailoring done, thanks to the perceived commercial advantage of being Purveyors to the Elite. It's the leaks in the roof, and the polite letters from the big banks, which give the game away.

In some places, nobles claim the right of "Trial by Peers," meaning that they're bound by most laws but can insist that only fellow nobles *try* them. These nobles might be a bit more relaxed than a commoner court would be, but they may also insist that you not *let the side down*. Certain classes of embarrassing offences (usually involving vulgar money) can lead to the same people insisting that you leave the country for a few years. Nobles in Ankh-Morpork *don't* receive this privilege, although quite a few act as though they do; the Patrician is quite willing to pass judgement on anybody, if asked.

Serious nobles can have significantly higher point values than this, mostly spent on Wealth and Status, plus all manner of advantages (though not without disadvantages). Some have combat skills at low levels, put plenty of points into corresponding Games skills, and add a Delusion: "These skills are fully effective in a real fight." Traditional female aristocrats are more likely to focus on Gardening and Sewing.

Finally, certain nobles and princes disguise themselves as peasants or vagabonds, but they're rarely able to carry it very well. You have to be born to these things.

Attributes: ST 10 [0]; DX 10 [0]; IQ 10 [0]; HT 10 [0].

Secondary Characteristics: Damage 1d-2/1d; BL 20 lbs.; HP 10 [0]; Will 10 [0]; Per 10 [0]; FP 10 [0]; Basic Speed 5.00 [0]; Basic Move 5 [0].

Advantages: Status 2* [5] *and* Wealthy [20]. ● *One* of ST +2, DX +1, IQ +1, HT +2, Military Rank 4, or Patron (Aristocratic house, a very powerful organisation; 9 or less), all [20]. ● *One* of Will +1, Born War-Leader 1, Charisma 1, Legal Immunity (Trial by his Peers), Reputation +2 (As a good chap, among own class), or another level of Status, all [5].

Disadvantages: *One* of Absent-Mindedness, Alcoholism, Code of Honour (Chivalry), Combat Paralysis, Fanaticism (To native land), Lecherousness (12), or Megalomania (9), all [-15]. ● *One* of Bully (12), Clueless, Code of Honour (Gentleman's *or* Soldier's), Compulsive Behaviour (Carousing, Gambling, *or* Spending) (6), Cowardice (12), Delusion ("My superior social class automatically makes me a good warrior"), Dependent (Family member; 50% of own points; Loved One; 9 or less), Easy to Read, Enemy (Similar power; Rival; 12 or less), Gullibility (12), Impulsiveness (12), Incurious (6), Intolerance (Total), Jealousy, Laziness, Odious Personal Habits (Upper-Class Mannerisms), Overconfidence (6), Secret (Deep family shame), Selfish (6), Sense of Duty (Nation), Short Attention Span (12), or Squeamish (12), all [-10].

Primary Skills: Heraldry (A) IQ [2]-10 *and* Savoir-Faire (High Society) (E) IQ+2 [4]-12.

Secondary Skills: *Three* of Broadsword, Rapier, Riding (Equines), Smallsword, or Two-Handed Sword, all (A) DX [2]-10; Flail (H) DX-1 [2]-9; Games (Aqueduct, Chess, or rules for an upper-class sport) (E) IQ+1 [2]-11; Falconry, Gambling, Leadership, or Professional Skill (Farming), all (A) IQ [2]-10; or Carousing (E) HT+1 [2]-11. ● Then add +2 to any one of these [6].

Background Skills: *Four* of Crossbow or Shield, both (E) DX [1]-10; Axe/Mace, Boxing, Dancing, or Spear, all (A) DX-1 [1]-9; Area Knowledge (capital city or family domains), Current Affairs (any), Savoir-Faire (Military), or Shouting at Foreigners, all (E) IQ [1]-10; Administration, Animal Handling (Equines), Connoisseur (any), Poetry, Politics, Public Speaking, or Soldier, all (A) IQ-1 [1]-9; Diplomacy, History (usually related to family), Intelligence Analysis, Law (any civil), Musical Instrument (any), Naturalist, Poisons, Strategy (any), Tactics, or Veterinary, all (H) IQ-2 [1]-8; Sex Appeal (A) HT-1 [1]-9; Intimidation (A) Will-1 [1]-9; or Fishing (E) Per [1]-10. ● Then add +2 to any one of these [3].

* Includes +1 Status from Wealth.

PEASANT

25 points

You're an agricultural labourer – usually an inherited position, if only because few people volunteer for it. This isn't overly exciting in itself, unless you have an overlord with the wrong sort of big ideas, but it's the starting point for many an adventuring career. Such careers are all too often *short,* but the fairy-tales don't talk about those. They do talk about *lucky* peasant youths, although well-developed muscles and basic combat skills are more reliable than luck.

Being a peasant has the advantage of . . . um . . . a lot of company. The more freedom you have from feudal rules, the more you're at the mercy of the free market – and whatever your legal position, any time you aren't engaged in labour, you're prone to being asked annoying questions by men on horseback. Starvation is certainly always an option. However, Discworld peasants mostly seem to manage, venture opinions, and know their rights, which they'll list at length.

Children of better-off peasants and farmers may have enough time and freedom to go off to the Big City. This usually means Ankh-Morpork, but everything is relative; there are those for whom Lancre Town is a metropolis. Most such journeys have a specific purpose – conducting business, getting away before her dad finds out, visiting Great-Aunt Fidity – but anyone who has read a fantasy novel, or indeed who has ever left home on his or her own, will know the rest.

Attributes: ST 11 [10]; DX 10 [0]; IQ 10 [0]; HT 11 [10].

Secondary Characteristics: Damage 1d-1/1d+1; BL 24 lbs.; HP 11 [0]; Will 10 [0]; Per 10 [0]; FP 11 [0]; Basic Speed 5.25 [0]; Basic Move 5 [0].

Advantages and Perks: *One* of ST +1, HT +1, Animal Friend 2, High Pain Threshold, or Outdoorsman 1, all [10]. ● *One* of Will +1, Per +1, Animal Empathy, Rapid Healing, or Resistant to Disease (+8), all [5]. ● HP +1 [2] *or* Acute Senses 1 (any) [2]. ● *One* of Alcohol Tolerance, Cold Resistance, Deep Sleeper, Good with Cattle, Honest Face, or Improvised Weapons (Polearm), all [1].

Disadvantages: Struggling [-10]. ● *One* of Bad Smell, Clueless, Confused (12), Easy to Read, Gullibility (12), Literal-Minded, Paranoia, or Unluckiness, all [-10]. ● *One* of Chummy, Duty

(To feudal lord; 9 or less), Gluttony (12), Ham-Fisted, Hidebound, Incurious (12), Innumerate, Intolerance ("Strange Furriners"), Klutz, Low TL 1, Oblivious, Odious Personal Habits (Downright Picturesque Manners), Sense of Duty (Companions), Shyness (Mild), Skinny, Social Stigma (Uneducated), Status -1, or Wealth reduced further to Poor, all [-5].

Primary Skills: Professional Skill (Farming) (A) IQ+1 [4]-11.

Secondary Skills: Area Knowledge (Home Village) (E) IQ+1 [2]-11.

Background Skills: *Four* of Brawling (E) DX [1]-10; Axe/Mace, Bow, Climbing, Dancing, Polearm, Spear, Sports (something rustic), Staff, or Two-Handed Axe/Mace, all (A) DX-1 [1]-9; Flail or Sling, both (H) DX-2 [1]-8; Carpentry or Gardening, both (E) IQ [1]-10; Animal Handling (Cattle *or* Equines), Teamster (Cattle *or* Equines), Merchant, or Weather Sense, all (A) IQ-1 [1]-9; Law (home region civil) or Naturalist, both (H) IQ-2 [1]-8; Carousing (E) HT [1]-11; Hiking (A) HT-1 [1]-10; Fishing (E) Per [1]-10; or Survival (Woodlands) or Tracking, both (A) Per-1 [1]-9. ● Then add +1 to any two of these [2].

PRIEST

50 points

You're a working representative of an ineffable power. You're probably sincere in your faith – although if you've studied the holy books too closely, it may have crossed your mind in darker moments that you and those to whom you minister seem to take religion a bit more seriously than the big personification whose image is on the altar. However, the god wants worshippers (seems quite *desperate* for them sometimes), and your job is to recruit and keep them. This may mean running a bureaucracy, looking after a temple, or even preaching and performing rites. If you're the better sort – or realise that you can't get much worship (or many donations) from people with serious problems – you might seek to look after your flock, too.

You don't wield much in the way of supernatural power – although if you're truly devout, you may be able to face down some occult problems by raw faith. You do have a measure of *social* power, however, and *sometimes* the god takes care of his own. He might even drop lightning bolts on atheists who argue with you too much, though you personally may regard that as unsporting.

This template makes you a reasonable preacher with some other areas of competence; dark-robed devotees of dubious deities, fat old hypocrites, behind-the-scenes administrators, decrepit timeservers, and learned scholars (of either vanilla theology or Unspeakable Lore) would all look a bit different. As some clerics must look after their god's interests over large "parishes," or are even sent into wild areas as missionaries, "adventuring priests" are perfectly possible. If you're still low in the hierarchy, you may spend a lot of time trekking (if you're lucky, riding) between villages, providing weddings-and-funerals services.

Attributes: ST 10 [0]; DX 10 [0]; IQ 11 [20]; HT 10 [0].

Secondary Characteristics: Damage 1d-2/1d; BL 20 lbs.; HP 10 [0]; Will 11 [0]; Per 11 [0]; FP 10 [0]; Basic Speed 5.00 [0]; Basic Move 5 [0].

Advantages: Clerical Investment [5]. ● *One* of Will +3, Indomitable, or True Faith, all [15]; or alternatively, *one* of Charisma 2, Patron (Actual god or very powerful temple; 6 or less), Patron (Powerful senior priest or fairly powerful cult; 9 or less), or Religious Rank 2, all [10], *and* either Status 1 [5] *or* Tenure [5]. ● *One* of HT +1, Per +2, Comfortable, Congregation (20 people)*, Healer 1, or Voice, all [10].

Channelling, Medium, and See Invisible (Spirit), for shamans. Disadvantages can include an Addiction (to strange fungi) or Low TL, both of which are almost obligatory for shamans. Drop the Administration skill and spend the points this frees up on Naturalist, Poisons, or Survival – or on Computer Programming (Stone Circles), for druids – and add Knife and Shortsword to the background skills options. Combat-oriented druids carry sickle swords (p. 151) and daggers, sometimes coated in interesting natural poisons.

Druids don't often go adventuring, being part of an aggressively staid sort of faith, though they might show up anywhere on the way to a stone-circle maintenance job. Shamans tend to be preoccupied with their dealings with spirits and with their funny little mushroom habits, but may get missions from those same spirits.

RUFFIAN

25 points

The urban counterpart to the bandit (p. 121), you're a small-time professional criminal. While you may be a bit more skilled and versatile than many in your line of work, that isn't saying much. You live a life dominated by low-grade violence – *you* might not use it (perhaps you have just enough class to prefer subtlety), but you certainly have to take care that *others* don't use it on you too often.

If you live in Ankh-Morpork, you don't belong to the Thieves' Guild, and you've managed to avoid their attentions so far (good luck with that). You dream of becoming less small-time; you might even seek Guild membership, although that tends to involve tiresome formalities (they have a *bureaucracy*) as well as explaining why they shouldn't just off you for your past career. On the other hand, if you stick to strong-arm work that doesn't involve theft *as such*, you may be able to avoid their wrath indefinitely. You might be tempted into the adventuring life as a way up and out, or you may just decide that travel is healthy – especially if the Guild is after you.

Attributes: ST 11 [10]; DX 10 [0]; IQ 10 [0]; HT 10 [0].
Secondary Characteristics: Damage 1d-1/1d+1; BL 24 lbs.; HP 11 [0]; Will 10 [0]; Per 10 [0]; FP 10 [0]; Basic Speed 5.00 [0]; Basic Move 5 [0].
Advantages and Perks: Combat Reflexes [15] *or* Luck [15]; alternatively, *one* of ST +1, HT +1, Per +2, or High Pain Threshold, all [10], *and* Basic Move +1 [5]. ● A total of 8 points spent on HP, Acute Senses (any), or Fearlessness, all [2/level]. ● *Two* of Alcohol Tolerance, Check the Exits, Fearsome Stare, or Night Vision 1 [1 each].
Disadvantages: Status -1 [-5] *and* Struggling [-10]. ● *One* of Bad Temper (12), Berserk (12), Bloodlust (12), Bully (12), Impulsiveness (12), Jealousy, Laziness, or Unluckiness, all [-10]. ● *One* of Will -1, Per -1, Callous, Chummy, Code of Honour (Pirate's), Compulsive Behaviour (Carousing *or* Gambling) (12), Hidebound, Incurious (12), Innumerate, Odious Personal Habit (Surly), Skinny, Social Stigma (Uneducated), Status reduced further to -2, or Wealth reduced further to Poor, all [-5].
Primary Skills: Brawling (E) DX+2 [4]-12 *and* Intimidation (A) Will [2]-10.
Secondary Skills: Area Knowledge (home city) (E) IQ+1 [2]-11; Filch (A) DX [2]-10; Knife (E) DX+1 [2]-11; Stealth (A) DX-1 [1]-9; *and* Streetwise (A) IQ [2]-10.

Disadvantages: Duty (To temple/church; 9 or less) [-5] *or* Duty (To temple/church; Nonhazardous; 12 or less) [-5]. ● *Two* of Bad Sight (Mitigator, Glasses), Bully (12), Clueless, Cowardice (12), Delusion ("My god will always protect me"), Disciplines of Faith (Mysticism), Easy to Read, Honesty (12), No Sense of Humour, Intolerance (Religious), Odious Personal Habit (*Never* Stops Preaching), Pacifism (Cannot Harm Innocents), Post-Combat Shakes (6), Selfless (6), Sense of Duty (Entire Faith), Struggling, Truthfulness (6), or Vow (Major), all [-10].
Primary Skills: Religious Ritual (own religion) (H) IQ+1 [8]-12 *and* Theology (same) (H) IQ+1 [8]-12.
Secondary Skills: Administration (A) IQ [2]-11 *and* Public Speaking (A) IQ [2]-11.
Background Skills: *Five* of Riding (Equines) or Staff, both (A) DX-1 [1]-9; Area Knowledge (parish/diocese), First Aid, Savoir-Faire (High Society), or Shouting at Foreigners, all (E) IQ [1]-11; Leadership, Occultism, Politics, Propaganda, Research, Sacred Texts, or Teaching, all (A) IQ-1 [1]-10; Diagnosis, Diplomacy, History (some religious specialisation), Musical Instrument (usually organ), Philosophy, Physician, or Psychology (Human), all (H) IQ-2 [1]-9; Hiking (A) HT-1 [1]-9; or Intimidation (A) Will-1 [1]-10.

* Members of the Congregation of a 50-point priest start out built on a mere 5 points apiece.

Druids and Shamans

For a priest of an archaic nature cult, shift as many advantage points as desired to attributes or the Outdoorsman Talent – or to

Background Skills: *Four* of Fast-Draw (Knife), Forced Entry, or Thrown Weapon (Knife), all (E) DX [1]-10; Axe/Mace or Shortsword, both (A) DX-1 [1]-9; Pickpocket (H) DX-2 [1]-8; Games (Craps) or Panhandling, both (E) IQ [1]-10; Fast-Talk, Gambling, Holdout, Lockpicking, Shadowing, or Traps, all (A) IQ-1 [1]-9; Carousing (E) HT [1]-10; Scrounging (E) Per [1]-10; or Observation or Urban Survival, both (A) Per-1 [1]-9. ● Then add +1 to any one of these or to Stealth [1].

Customisation Notes

For an effective bouncer/splatter, or a superior strong-arm type, raise ST. (A splatter, often a troll, is like a bouncer, only with more force.) Standing around in a doorway, controlling who goes through it, can actually be semi-decently paid as well as technically legal. The problem with a career of rough and tumble, though, is making sure that you provide the rough and the other fellow does the tumbling.

STUDENT WIZARD

50 points

You're an undergraduate at or recent graduate from Unseen University, or maybe a newer institution such as Bugarup or Brazeneck – or perhaps you're in an old-fashioned personal apprenticeship. While you may be a master of cramming for exams, your grasp of *magic* is still patchy. Even a student like you can get involved in some pretty strange matters, though you're probably a geeky sort who doesn't much like the idea of danger.

Attributes: ST 9 [-10]; DX 10 [0]; IQ 12 [40]; HT 9 [-10].
Secondary Characteristics: Damage 1d-2/1d-1; BL 16 lbs.; HP 9 [0]; Will 11 [-5]; Per 10 [-10]; FP 9 [0]; Basic Speed 5.00 [5]; Basic Move 4 [-5].
Advantages: Magery 1 [15]. ● *One* of Magery increased to 2, Mathematical Ability 1, or Patron (Powerful mentor; 9 or less), all [10]. ● *Two* of Basic Move +1, Eidetic Memory, Languages (any, Accented/Native), Resistant to Disease (+8), Single-Minded, or Superior Staff 1, all [5].
Disadvantages: Duty (6 or less) [-2]. ● *Two* of Bad Sight (Mitigator, Glasses), Clueless, Cowardice (12), Disturbing Voice (Stuttering), Easy to Read, Gullibility (12), Laziness, Low Pain Threshold, or Squeamish (12), all [-10]. ● *One* of Will -1, Compulsive Carousing (12), Curious (12), Gluttony (12), Ham-Fisted, Klutz, Oblivious, Octophobia (12), Pacifism (Reluctant Killer), Post-Combat Shakes (12), Pyromania (12), Shyness (Mild), Skinny, or Truthfulness (12), all [-5].
Primary Skills: Magic (Wizardry) (VH) IQ+1 [8]-13*. ● *Two* Magical Forms *and* Thaumatology, all (VH) IQ [4]-12*. ● Then add +1 to any one of these [4].
Secondary Skills: *Three* of Hidden Lore (Demon Lore), Occultism, or Research, all (A) IQ [2]-12; Engineer (Magical) (H) IQ-1 [2]-11; an additional Magical Form (VH) IQ-1 [2]-11*; or Alchemy (VH) IQ-2 [2]-10. ● Then add +1 to any one of these [2].
Background Skills: *Four* of Innate Attack (Projectile) (E) DX [1]-10; Climbing or Sports (Darts), both (A) DX-1 [1]-9; Area Knowledge (university city or mentor's home town) (E) IQ [1]-12; Fast-Talk (A) IQ-1 [1]-11; Astronomy, Astrozoology, Computer Programming (Magical Computers), History (Ancient Magic), Mathematics (Pure), or Natural Philosophy, all (H) IQ-2 [1]-10; or Carousing (E) HT [1]-9. ● Then add +1 to any one of these [1].

* Includes +1 for Magery.

Customisation Notes

The mandatory Duty represents the fact that you can't avoid a certain number of lectures, tutorials, and exams. It isn't classed as Nonhazardous because living in an institution with a large number of powerful, absent-minded, experiment-prone, and sometimes megalomaniac wizards . . . well, that isn't nonhazardous. As student wizards have Status 0 and are effectively supported at that level by the resources they can use at their university or teacher's tower, you're treated as having Average Wealth (with "student" as your Average Wealth-level job). However, you're unlikely to possess much in the way of personal equipment, so you're also considered "settled" (see *Settled vs. Footloose,* p. 147).

Choose Magical Forms to suit your personality – although Elementalism is always good. An incipient megalomaniac will favour Summonation, a premature old fogey might want Divination, while a research nerd will go for Magianism. *Standardised Spells* (p. 203) can be useful for students, who may have got the hang of one or two; to pay for these, reassign points from primary or secondary skills, or use quirks or early bonus character points.

Many student-level wizards have the Non-Improvisational version of Magery (p. 45), saving a few points but making them even less useful as adventurers. Certainly, *most* undergraduates have the No Staff quirk (making them *seriously* ineffective if they're also Non-Improvisational); however, the GM may permit PCs using this template to claim to be recent graduates, or to have acquired a staff somehow as part of a research project or as an heirloom. Alternatively, in games set in or around UU, even undergraduates could have some access to power supplies from the High Energy Magic Building.

TRAINEE WITCH

50 points

You're a country girl – young and uncertain, or possibly young and brash – who's just starting out in the work of witchcraft. You're still being taught by an older witch, but you've picked up a little useful lore. Your first concern is probably to get people in your home area to take you seriously; though you understand that's required for a witch, you haven't quite managed the trick yet. Either that or a sense that witches have *obligations* may get you into a certain amount of trouble. While the basic attitude among witches is that you should then find your own way out again, you *are* still learning.

Attributes: ST 7 [-30]; DX 10 [0]; IQ 12 [40]; HT 10 [0].
Secondary Characteristics: Damage 1d-3/1d-2; BL 9.8 lbs.; HP 7 [0]; Will 11 [-5]; Per 12 [0]; FP 10 [0]; Basic Speed 5.00 [0]; Basic Move 5 [0].
Advantages: Magery 0 [5] *and* Patron (Extremely powerful teacher; 12 or less) [30]. ● *One* of ST +1, HT +1, Will +2, Healer 1, Magery increased to 1, Medium, Outdoorsman 1, or Spirit Empathy, all [10]. ● *Two* of Per +1, Animal Empathy, Animal Friend 1, Charisma 1, Sensitive, or Single-Minded, all [5].
Disadvantages: Duty (To teacher; Nonhazardous; 12 or less) [-5]. ● *One* of ST -1, Bad Temper (12), Clueless, Easy to Read, or Sense of Duty (Everyone you know personally), all [-10]. ● *Two* of Basic Move -1, Code of Honour (Wise-Woman's), Curious (12), Duty increased to 15 or less, Klutz, Low TL 1, Overconfidence (12), Pacifism (Reluctant Killer), Post-Combat Shakes (12), Reputation -2 (As pushy or weird, in and around her home village), Shyness (Mild), Skinny, Social Stigma (Minor), Stubbornness, or Truthfulness (12), all [-5].

Primary Skills: Magic (Witchcraft) (VH) IQ-1 [4]-11 *and* Midwifery (A) IQ-1 [1]-11.

Secondary Skills: Area Knowledge (home village) (E) IQ [1]-12 *and* First Aid (E) IQ [1]-12. ● *One* of Herbalism or Veterinary, both (H) IQ-1 [2]-11; or any Magical Form (VH) IQ-2 [2]-10.

Background Skills: *Four* of Brawling or Sewing, both (E) DX [1]-10; Stealth (A) DX-1 [1]-9; Aerobatics (H) DX-2 [1]-8; Current Affairs (Regional for home area), Gardening, or Housekeeping, all (E) IQ [1]-12; Fortune-Telling (any), Merchant, Navigation (Land), Professional Skill (Cooking *or* Farming), or Weather Sense, all (A) IQ-1 [1]-11; Diagnosis, Naturalist, Physician, or Psychology (Human), all (H) IQ-2 [1]-10; Intimidation (A) Will-1 [1]-10; or Body Language or Survival (home area type), both (A) Per-1 [1]-11. ● Then add +1 to any two of these, Midwifery, or First Aid [2].

Customisation Notes

The Duty here represents the fact that your teacher can and will boss you around. Few older witches will knowingly send a trainee into serious danger, but they *do* expect their charge to learn self-reliance. Buy off the Duty when you become more independent, with your own cottage. Your teacher rates as an extremely powerful Patron *compared to you* – she may be fairly ordinary by witch standards.

As even a trainee witch has Status 0 and is somehow supported at that level – often by her family, occasionally by her teacher – you're treated as having Average Wealth (with "trainee witch" as your Average Wealth-level job). However, because you won't possess much in the way of personal equipment, and witches don't handle cash much, you're also considered "settled" (see *Settled vs. Footloose*, p. 147).

Some trainees have the Non-Improvisational version of Magery (p. 45). They're expected to remedy this (buy it off with bonus character points) before they get their own cottages.

TRIBESMAN

25 points

You're from a part of the Disc that's still at a low level of technological development; the be Trobi islands, perhaps, or maybe Howondaland. You might have fought in very small wars, or simply spent your time hunting and/or gathering. However, the spread of trade and the wanderings of explorers have brought even your homeland into contact with places where getting dressed involves more than one piece of fabric. Now you're out and about, having adventures that entail more than just not getting eaten by the same boring old carnivores.

While you look a bit grubby and underdressed to "civilised" folk, your skills are quite saleable – there are frequently jobs for warriors and those who can work with animals. (And while Ankh-Morpork hasn't caught onto the idea of World Music yet, give it time.) You may be a bit vulnerable to big-city business practises, but your folk have a certain direct way with People-Who-Lie-To-Get-More-Meal-Nuts.

Attributes: ST 10 [0]; DX 10 [0]; IQ 10 [0]; HT 11 [10].

Secondary Characteristics: Damage 1d-2/1d; BL 20 lbs.; HP 10 [0]; Will 10 [0]; Per 12 [10]; FP 11 [0]; Basic Speed 5.25 [0]; Basic Move 5 [0].

Advantages and Perks: Language (any "civilised," Accented/None) [2] *and* Heat Resistance [1]. ● *One* of ST +1, HT +1, Basic Move +2, Acute Hearing 5, Animal Friend 2, High Pain Threshold, Medium, or Outdoorsman 1, all [10]. ● *Two* of Will +1, Per +1, Absolute Direction, Animal Empathy, Flexibility, Rapid Healing, Resistant to Disease (+8), Sensitive, or Silence 1, all [5].

Disadvantages: Literacy in native Language reduced to None [-3]; Low TL 2* [-10]; Status -1 [-5]; *and* Struggling [-10]. ● *One* of Bloodlust (12), Clueless, Confused (12), Gullibility (12), Impulsiveness (12), Literal-Minded, or Social Stigma (Minority Group), all [-10]. ● *One* of Chummy, Code of Honour (Pirate's), Curious (12), Innumerate, Low TL increased to 3*, Oblivious, Odious Personal Habit (Overdoing the Strong Silent Bit), Sense of Duty (Companions), Shyness (Mild), Skinny, Social Stigma (Uneducated), Truthfulness (12), or Wealth reduced further to Poor, all [-5].

Primary Skills: Spear (A) DX [2]-10; Stealth (A) DX [2]-10; Survival (home area environment type) (A) Per [2]-12; *and* Tracking (A) Per [2]-12. ● Then add +2 to any one of these [6].

Secondary Skills: Area Knowledge (homeland) (E) IQ [1]-10; Brawling (E) DX [1]-10; Camouflage (E) IQ [1]-10; Knife (E) DX [1]-10; *and* Naturalist (H) IQ-2 [1]-8. ● Then add +2 to any one of these [3].

Background Skills: *Three* of Jumping, Shield, or Thrown Weapon (Axe/Mace, Spear, *or* Stick), all (E) DX [1]-10; Axe/Mace, Boating, Bow, Climbing, Dancing, Throwing, or Wrestling, all (A) DX-1 [1]-9; Acrobatics or Blowpipe, both (H) DX-2 [1]-8; Carpentry, First Aid, or Gesture, all (E) IQ [1]-10; Animal Handling (Dogs), Armoury (Melee Weapons *or* Missile Weapons), Navigation (Land), Traps, or Weather Sense, all (A) IQ-1 [1]-9; Musical Instrument (any), Poisons, or Tactics, all (H) IQ-2 [1]-8; Swimming (E) HT [1]-11; Hiking, Running, or Sex Appeal, all (A) HT-1 [1]-10; Intimidation (A) Will-1 [1]-9; Fishing (E) Per [1]-12; Body Language or Observation, both (A) Per-1 [1]-11; or Detect Lies (H) Per-2 [1]-10.

* The maximum level of Low TL you can have depends on the campaign TL (pp. 30-31). Usually, you'll be TL0 or TL1, so in a TL4 campaign, you should take at least one more level over the template's starting two. However, you might be from a small community that has reached TL2.

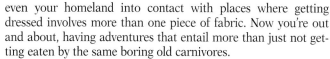

Medium-Powered Characters

This next collection of templates is for 75- to 125-point characters – basically normal people with capabilities that grant them the potential to be serious, if rather specialised, adventurers. Someone like this can handle most problems *within his chosen field*. These templates suit games where the PCs rate the label "heroes," but are heroes of the variety who sneak round the back and use *tactics* rather than burst through the door and bounce axes off their chests.

BARBARIAN HERO WANNABE

125 points

You're a fan of old-style heroic adventuring, with enough talent for the business that you may actually survive for a while. You reckon that stripping down to a leather thong, picking up a big sword, and having pneumatic women drape themselves over your feet sounds pretty cool. Some people say that the age of heroes is over, but you're prepared to prove them wrong. It's a tough life, and you're no Cohen the Barbarian – not yet, anyway – but you're not immediately doomed, either.[1]

Some barbarian heroes are born, some are made, and some have barbarian heroism thrust upon them (up and under the ribcage). You're mostly in the self-made camp, though if you can claim Hubland ancestry and a tribal chief with lousy parenting skills as a father, that's all good. It just isn't required.

In our world's terms, you may look more like a cycle-gang member than a storybook hero – it's the leather and the surliness. You're basically sincere in your ideals, though, and anyone who's prepared to dress like that in pursuit of a destiny is surely *quite* heroic.

Attributes: ST 13 [30]; DX 12 [40]; IQ 10 [0]; HT 12 [20].
Secondary Characteristics: Damage 1d/2d-1; BL 34 lbs.; HP 13 [0]; Will 10 [0]; Per 10 [0]; FP 12 [0]; Basic Speed 6.00 [0]; Basic Move 6 [0].
Advantages and Perks: Combat Reflexes [15]. ● *One* of ST +2, DX +1, HT +2, Basic Speed +1, or Outdoorsman 2, all [20]; or alternatively, *one* of Danger Sense, Daredevil, or Luck, all [15], *and* Per +1 [5]. ● *One* of Will +1, Per +1, Basic Move +1, Absolute Direction, Ambidexterity, Born War-Leader 1, Charisma 1,

---

1. Putting some points into defensive options might not be a bad idea, mind you.

Enhanced Parry (any one weapon), Rapid Healing, Resistant to Disease (+8), or Resistant to Poison (+3), all [5]. ● Attractive [4], or *two* of HP +1, Acute Hearing 1, Acute Vision 1, Fearlessness 1, Less Sleep 1, or Night Vision 2, all [2]. ● *One* of Alcohol Tolerance, Blade-Proof Bare-Chestedness, Cold Resistance, Cultural Familiarity (somewhere interesting), Deep Sleeper, Dual Ready (any two one-handed weapons), Fearsome Stare, Improvised Weapons (any), or Language (any, Broken/None), all [1].

Disadvantages: *One* of Compulsive Barbarian Heroism (9) [-15] or Compulsive Risk-Taking (12) [-15], *or* both Compulsive Barbarian Heroism (12) [-10] *and* Odious Personal Habit (Barbarian Heroism) [-5]. ● *Two* of Bad Temper (12), Berserk (12), Bloodlust (12), Clueless, Delusion ("I am destined for heroic greatness"), Easy to Read, Gullibility (12), Impulsiveness (12), Literal-Minded, Social Stigma (Minority Group), or Struggling, all [-10]. ● *One* of Callous, Code of Honour (Pirate's), Compulsive Carousing (12), Compulsive Vowing (12), Ham-Fisted, Innumerate, Low TL 1, Oblivious, Overconfidence (12), Sense of Duty (Companions), Social Stigma (Second-Class Citizen *or* Uneducated), Status -1, Stubbornness, or Truthfulness (12), all [-5].
Primary Skills: Broadsword (A) DX+1 [4]-13. ● *One* of these packages:

1. Axe/Mace (A) DX+1 [4]-13; Shield (E) DX+2 [4]-14; *and* Spear (A) DX+1 [4]-13.
2. Bow (A) DX+2 [8]-14; Fast-Draw (Arrow/Bolt) (E) DX+2 [2]-14*; *and* Knife (E) DX+1 [2]-13.
3. Brawling (E) DX+2 [4]-14; Fast-Draw (Knife) (E) DX+2 [2]-14*; Knife (E) DX+1 [2]-13; Shield (E) DX+1 [2]-13; *and* Thrown Weapon (Knife) (E) DX+1 [2]-13.
4. Shield (E) DX+2 [4]-14 *and* Sling (H) DX+1 [8]-13.
5. Shield (E) DX+2 [4]-14; Spear (A) DX+1 [4]-13; *and* Thrown Weapon (Spear) (E) DX+2 [4]-14.
6. Two-Handed Axe/Mace (A) DX+3 [12]-15.

Secondary Skills: *Four* of Climbing, Riding (Equines), or Stealth, all (A) DX [2]-12; Camouflage (E) IQ+1 [2]-11; Tactics (H) IQ-1 [2]-9; Carousing (E) HT+1 [2]-13; Hiking (A) HT [2]-12; or Intimidation (A) Will [2]-10.
Background Skills: *Six* of Forced Entry or Jumping, both (E) DX [1]-12; Boating (any) or Wrestling, both (A) DX-1 [1]-11; Acrobatics (H) DX-2 [1]-10; Area Knowledge (almost anywhere), Gesture, Seamanship, or Shouting at Foreigners, all (E) IQ [1]-10; Animal Handling (Dogs *or* Equines), Leadership, Navigation (Land), Performance, Streetwise, or Weather Sense, all (A) IQ-1 [1]-9; Herbalism, Mimicry (Animal Sounds *or* Bird Calls), or Naturalist, all (H) IQ-2 [1]-8; Singing or Swimming, both (E) HT [1]-12; Sex Appeal (A) HT-1 [1]-11; Fishing (E) Per [1]-10; Survival (any) or Tracking, both (A) Per-1 [1]-9; or Detect Lies (H) Per-2 [1]-8.

* Includes +1 for Combat Reflexes.

Customisation Notes

Some barbarians add Gigantism to their disadvantages. In that case, reduce ST and HP costs to reflect the larger SM, spend the points you save on more perks or skills, and don't forget the +1 to Basic Move. If the GM allows the options under *Benefits of the Barbarian Lifestyle* (p. 58), you can often save a few points on advantages, too – which you'll no doubt immediately spend on more weapon skills! Anyone who suggests that Performance is a *primary* skill for this character type is just jealous.

CAREER SOLDIER

125 points

Your job is what pretentious people call "the profession of arms": you fight for a living. Or rather, you *soldier* for a living. That sometimes involves fighting, but fighting is dangerous, and you prefer to do it only when you're at an advantage. Soldiering is for the most part boring, with moments of sheer terror and occasional opportunities for profit – the sort of thing which people reminisce about nostalgically *far* more often than they enjoy at the time. Still, it's a living, and during wartime, plunder is a perk of the job.

Large-scale warfare happens on the Disc, but infrequently; thus, while you might be a loyal trouper in a standing army, you're more likely a mercenary. Between wars, mercenaries mostly find work on a small-scale basis, earning a living wherever a palace needs guards or a city-state wants to look threatening to its neighbours, perhaps training local militias, maybe even bounty-hunting. Some get into law enforcement in places which don't run to a "proper" watch. Resorting to banditry would be an admission of defeat, but it beats starving.

Monster hunters are specialist mercenaries: self-assured, well-armed folk with a keen sense of tradition, unwilling to take on the larger sorts of monster for anything less than half a kingdom and a royal marriage. They favour skills appropriate to the heaviest weapons, and usually wear excellent armour.

Attributes: ST 12 [20]; DX 11 [20]; IQ 11 [20]; HT 12 [20].
Secondary Characteristics: Damage 1d-1/1d+2; BL 29 lbs.; HP 12 [0]; Will 11 [0]; Per 11 [0]; FP 12 [0]; Basic Speed 6.00 [5]; Basic Move 6 [0].
Advantages and Perks: Combat Reflexes [15]. ● *One* of ST +1, HT +1, Per +2, Born War-Leader 2, Enhanced Parry (All), High Pain Threshold, or Military Rank 2, all [10]. ● *Two* of Fearlessness 1, Languages (any, Broken/Broken), Less Sleep 1, or Night Vision 2, all [2]. ● *One* of Alcohol Tolerance, Check the Exits, Crossbow Safety, Deep Sleeper, Fearsome Stare, Good with Soldiers, or No Hangover, all [1].
Disadvantages: *One* of Bad Temper (12), Bloodlust (12), Bully (12), Code of Honour (Soldier's), Duty (12 or less), or Struggling, all [-10]. ● *Three* of Callous, Compulsive Carousing (12), Compulsive Gambling (12), Incurious (12), Intolerance (Civilian Politicians *or* one "old enemy" nationality), Odious Personal Habit (Surliness), Sense of Duty (The Unit), or Stubbornness, all [-5].
Primary Skills: Savoir-Faire (Military) (E) IQ+2 [4]-13 *and* Soldier (A) IQ+2 [8]-13. ● *One* of these packages:

1. Armoury (Heavy Weapons) (A) IQ+1 [4]-12; Artillery (any) (A) IQ+1 [4]-12; Brawling (E) DX [1]-11; Gunner (any) (E) DX+1 [2]-12; *and* Shortsword (A) DX-1 [1]-10.
2. Axe/Mace (A) DX [2]-11; Bow (A) DX+2 [8]-13; Fast-Draw (Arrow/Bolt) (E) DX+1 [1]-12*; *and* Knife (E) DX+1 [1]-11.
3. Bow (A) DX+1 [4]-12; Riding (Equines) (A) DX+1 [4]-12; Shortsword (A) DX [2]-11; *and* Thrown Weapon (Spear) (E) DX+1 [2]-12.
4. Brawling (E) DX [1]-11; Crossbow (E) DX+3 [8]-14; Fast-Draw (Arrow/Bolt) (E) DX+1 [1]-12*; *and* Shortsword (A) DX [2]-11.
5. Broadsword (A) DX+2 [8]-13 *and* Shield (E) DX+2 [4]-13.
6. Broadsword (A) DX [2]-11; Riding (Equines) (A) DX+1 [4]-12; Shield (E) DX+1 [2]-12; *and* Spear (A) DX+1 [4]-12.

7. Fast-Draw (Sword) (E) DX+2 [2]-13*; Shield (E) DX+2 [4]-13; Shortsword (A) DX [2]-11; *and* Spear (A) DX+1 [4]-12.
8. Knife (E) DX+1 [2]-12; Polearm (A) DX+2 [8]-13; *and* Shortsword (A) DX [2]-11.
9. Shield (E) DX+2 [4]-13; Shortsword (A) DX+1 [4]-12; *and* Thrown Weapon (Spear) (E) DX+2 [4]-13.

Secondary Skills: *Three* of Camouflage (E) IQ+1 [2]-12; Animal Handling (Equines), Armoury (any), Leadership, or Teaching, all (A) IQ [2]-11; Tactics (H) IQ-1 [2]-10; Hiking (A) HT [2]-12; Intimidation (A) Will [2]-11; Scrounging (E) Per+1 [2]-12; or Observation (A) Per [2]-11.
Background Skills: *Five* of Forced Entry (E) DX [1]-11; Filch or Stealth, both (A) DX-1 [1]-10; Area Knowledge (past areas of service), Current Affairs (Headline News), First Aid, Games (Craps), or Shouting at Foreigners, all (E) IQ [1]-11; Gambling, Heraldry, Holdout, Interrogation, Merchant, Navigation (Land), Streetwise, or Teamster (Equines), all (A) IQ-1 [1]-10; Strategy (Land) (H) IQ-2 [1]-9; Carousing (E) HT [1]-12; Running (A) HT-1 [1]-11; or Survival (any) (A) Per-1 [1]-10.

* Includes +1 for Combat Reflexes.

There were two men dressed in black standing behind his chair. It wasn't a particularly neat black, more the black worn by people who just don't want little marks to show. They looked like clerks, until you met their eyes.
– Going Postal

DARK CLERK

100 points

You work for the Patrician of Ankh-Morpork – *officially* in an administrative capacity. In reality, you and others like you do all sorts of little tasks that Lord Vetinari needs done but which the Watch would regard as unethical. You also have responsibility for Vetinari's safety, though he can look after himself admirably well and does a good job of making that duty mostly unnecessary. You can get away with many things that ordinary civilians could not, up to and including eliminating people who are a threat to the city, but you're answerable to the Patrician, who expects you to be efficient and tactful. Causing diplomatic incidents, or losing something or someone valuable, could earn you a temporary or permanent loss of privileges.[1] Oh, and you actually do attend to the paperwork as well.

You may have been trained on a scholarship at the Assassins' Guild School, or you might have had a rougher upbringing. Regardless of your past, the thing about you now is that Vetinari picked you for your capacity for loyalty and discretion – and he doesn't make mistakes in matters as important to him as this. You're as meticulous as any clerk, even if your tool is as often a knife as a pen.

1. *Possibly including breathing.*

Dark clerks are natural adventurers in many ways – but they need to be able to keep secrets, which can make dealings with other PCs difficult. They have to obey Vetinari, and they're limited to Ankh-Morpork or places where the city has a political interest or an embassy. Check with the GM before choosing this template!

Attributes: ST 11 [10]; DX 12 [40]; IQ 11 [20]; HT 10 [0].
Secondary Characteristics: Damage 1d-1/1d+1; BL 24 lbs.; HP 11 [0]; Will 11 [0]; Per 11 [0]; FP 10 [0]; Basic Speed 5.50 [0]; Basic Move 5 [0].
Advantages and Perks: Combat Reflexes [15] *and* Legal Immunity (Represents the Patrician) [5]. ● *One of* ST +1, HT +1, Per +2, Basic Speed +0.50, Basic Move +2, Acute Vision 5, Born to Hang 1, High Pain Threshold, Language Talent, or Silence 2, all [10]. ● *One of* Will +1, Ambidexterity, Eidetic Memory, Enhanced Parry (barehanded *or* a single weapon), Resistant to Disease (+8), Sense of the City 1 (Ankh-Morpork), or Sensitive, all [5]. ● *Two of* Fearlessness 1, Languages (any, Broken/Broken), Less Sleep 1, Lightning Calculator, or Night Vision 2, all [2]. ● *One of* Assassin in Good Standing, Check the Exits, Cobblestone Sense (Ankh-Morpork), Crossbow Safety, Cultural Familiarity (somewhere interesting), Dual Ready (any two one-handed weapons), Forgettable Face, Improvised Weapons (any), or Off-Hand Training (any weapon), all [1].
Disadvantages: Duty (To the Patrician; 12 or less) [-10] *and* Secret (More than just a clerk) [-10]. ● *One of* Compulsive Neatness (6), No Sense of Humour, or Sense of Duty (The City), all [-10]. ● *One of* Callous, Duty increased to 15 or less *or* made Extremely Hazardous, Selfless (12), or Skinny, all [-5].
Primary Skills: Acting (A) IQ [2]-11; Area Knowledge (Ankh-Morpork) (E) IQ+1 [2]-12; Crossbow (E) DX [1]-12; Knife (E) DX+1 [2]-13; Shortsword (A) DX [2]-12; *and* Stealth (A) DX [2]-12.
Secondary Skills: *Four of* Brawling or Thrown Weapon (Knife) (E), both DX+1 [2]-13; Climbing (A) DX [2]-12; Acrobatics, Judo, or Karate, all (H) DX-1 [2]-11; Area Knowledge (any), Current Affairs (Ankh-Morpork Regional *or* Politics), or Savoir-Faire (High Society *or* Servant), all (E) IQ+1 [2]-12; Administration, Disguise, Fast-Talk, Holdout, Lockpicking, Professional Skill (Filing Clerk), Research, Shadowing, or Traps, all (A) IQ [2]-11; Accounting, Diplomacy, or Intelligence Analysis, all (H) IQ-1 [2]-10; or Observation (A) Per [2]-11.
Background Skills: *Six of* Fast-Draw (any) (E) DX+1 [1]-13*; Jumping or Knot-Tying, both (E) DX [1]-12; Filch, Riding (Equines), or Smallsword, all (A) DX-1 [1]-11; Blowpipe, Escape, Pickpocket, or Sleight of Hand, all (H) DX-2 [1]-10; Camouflage, First Aid, Housekeeping, or Telegraphy, all (E) IQ [1]-11; Criminology, Heraldry, Hidden Lore (Secrets of Ankh-Morpork), Interrogation, Politics, Smuggling, Streetwise, or Writing, all (A) IQ-1 [1]-10; Cryptography, Forgery, History (Modern Ankh-Morpork), Law (Ankh-Morpork Commercial), Literature, Poisons, or Psychology (Human), all (H) IQ-2 [1]-9; Intimidation (A) Will-1 [1]-10; Body Language or Search, both (A) Per-1 [1]-10; or Detect Lies (H) Per-2 [1]-9.

* Includes +1 for Combat Reflexes.

DARK LORD WANNABE

100 points

Like the barbarian hero (p. 130), you've decided to pursue a dangerous but potentially glorious traditional-fantasy career. However, you've chosen a lonelier and more twisted path than those posing muscle-boys – you want to be *in charge*. That means you have to don blackened armour and find some followers willing to make sacrifices on your behalf, because you're going to be a dark lord! Fortunately, you already have the cunning, resources, and iron nerves you need to start out on this career; getting to the top is surely just a matter of time.

This character type isn't appropriate for every campaign. Leaving aside the tendency to evil, it implies specific goals that might not fit with the GM's plans, and you'll need other PCs who are willing to go along with you. It's also important to remember that dark lording is about *style* at least as much as it's about villainy – using this template as an excuse to be petty or sordid is completely missing the point. It may be best to play a dark lord as a prosperous middle-aged man going through a mid-life crisis; as the Disc doesn't have over-powerful motorcycles, spiky armour and axes will just have to do.

Attributes: ST 10 [0]; DX 11 [20]; IQ 12 [40]; HT 10 [0].
Secondary Characteristics: Damage 1d-2/1d; BL 20 lbs.; HP 10 [0]; Will 12 [0]; Per 12 [0]; FP 10 [0]; Basic Speed 5.25 [0]; Basic Move 5 [0].
Advantages and Perks: Fearlessness 3 [6]; Status 2* [5]; *and* Wealthy [20]. ● *Two of* HT +1, Born War-Leader 2, Charisma 2, Voice, or Wealth raised further to Very Wealthy, all [10]. ● *One of* Per +1, Eidetic Memory, Language (any, Accented/Native), Night Vision 5, or Reputation +2 (As a potential employer, among scum and loser warriors), all [5], *or* Attractive [4] *and* Fearsome Stare [1].
Disadvantages: Code of Honour (Dark Lord's) [-10]. ● *One of* Bad Temper (12), Bully (12), Jealousy, Megalomania (12), Paranoia, or Selfish (6), all [-10]. ● *One of* Bad Smell, Clueless, Cowardice (12), Disturbing Voice, Easy to Read, Enemy (Small group of less-powerful wannabe heroes; Hunter; 9 or less), Hunchback, No Sense of Humour, Odious Personal Habits (Curtness, Ranting, Scowling, etc.), or Unluckiness, all [-10]. ● *One of* Callous, Compulsive Vowing (12), Oblivious, Overconfidence (12), Reputation -2 (As a posing villain; 10 or less), Stubbornness, or Truthfulness (12), all [-5].
Primary Skills: Intimidation (A) Will-1 [1]-11 *and* Leadership (A) IQ [2]-12.
Secondary Skills: Axe Mace *or* Shortsword, both (A) DX [2]-11. ● Riding (Equines) (A) DX-1 [1]-10; Savoir-Faire (High Society) (E) IQ [1]-12; Shield (E) DX+1 [2]-12; *and* Tactics (H) IQ-2 [1]-10.
Background Skills: *Nine of* Knot-Tying (E) DX [1]-11; Stealth (A) DX-1 [1]-10; Area Knowledge (own domains or region *or* the entire Disc), Current Affairs (Headline News, Politics, *or* Regional), Games (Chess), or Shouting at Foreigners, all (E) IQ [1]-12; Acting, Administration, Connoisseur (Fine Art), Hidden Lore (Demon Lore), Interrogation, Occultism, or Traps, all (A) IQ-1 [1]-11; Intelligence Analysis, Poisons, Psychology (Human *or* Troll), Religious Ritual (any dark cult), Strategy, or Theology (any dark cult), all (H) IQ-2 [1]-10; Alchemy (VH) IQ-3 [1]-9; Observation (A) Per-1 [1]-11; or Detect Lies (H) Per-2 [1]-10.

* Includes +1 Status from Wealth.

Customisation Notes

For a traditional evil wizard, add Magery, Magic skill, and two to four Magical Forms. For the glowering high priest of a dark god, take Religious Ritual and Theology, and raise them to higher levels; throw in Clerical Investment, probably Religious Rank, Fanaticism, and the Public Speaking skill; and be sure to acquire a few equally fanatical followers, perhaps as a Congregation. Dark lords of *all* kinds tend to have full sets of quirks.

ENGINEER-INVENTOR

125 points

Discworld folk recognise two basic types of engineer: those who dig stuff out of the ground or make things with it, and those who invent things. You're in the latter category.

Inventors like you are typically either young or quite old (skipping middle age is one of your core accomplishments), and tend to say "Hmm" a lot. You may have found a place in some progressive ruler's court, building fountains in his gardens and new siege engines for his army. Alternatively, you might be an independent consultant-craftsman, selling clever gadgets to people with a taste for novelty or solving problems – from improved plumbing systems in big houses to new stage effects at the opera – while hoping that one of the inventions you produce in your spare time will make you famous.

You're no Leonard of Quirm, sadly, but you respect and admire him and other geniuses such as Goldeneyes Silverhand Dactylos (who combined brilliance with a fatal inability to know when to stop doing brilliant work for ungrateful rulers) and Urn of Ephebe (the first steam engineer). You hope you've learned from all of them. Anyway, you must sometimes venture out of your workshop to make sure that one of your creations is operated and maintained correctly . . .

Attributes: ST 10 [0]; DX 11 [20]; IQ 13 [60]; HT 10 [0].

Secondary Characteristics: Damage 1d-2/1d; BL 20 lbs.; HP 10 [0]; Will 13 [0]; Per 13 [0]; FP 10 [0]; Basic Speed 5.25 [0]; Basic Move 5 [0].

Advantages: Gadgeteer [25]. ● DX +1 [20], IQ +1 [20], or *two* of Per +2, Artificer 1, Comfortable, Photographic Memory, High Manual Dexterity 2, Mathematical Ability 1, Metalwork 1, or Patron (Employer, a powerful individual; 9 or less), all [10]. ● *One* of High TL 1, Single-Minded, Versatile, or Versatile (Inspiration Magnet), all [5].

Disadvantages: *Two* of Bad Sight (Mitigator, Glasses), Clueless, Curious (6), Disturbing Voice (Stuttering), Easy to Read, Hard of Hearing, Hunchback, Low Pain Threshold, No Sense of Humour, or Struggling, all [-10]. ● *Three* of Will -1, Code of Honour (Professional), Compulsive Neatness (12), Duty (To employer or Patron; Nonhazardous; 12 or less), Intolerance (The Ignorant), Oblivious, Obsession (Current project) (12), Odious Personal Habit (Boring), Pacifism (Reluctant Killer), Post-Combat Shakes (12), Shyness (Mild), Skinny, Stubbornness, or Truthfulness (12), all [-5], or Overweight [-1] *and* Unattractive [-4].

Primary Skills: Engineer (any) (H) IQ+1 [8]-14; Engineer (any other) (H) IQ [4]-13; *and* three specialisations of Mechanic, each (A) IQ [2]-13.

Secondary Skills: *Three* of Carpentry (E) IQ+1 [2]-14; Architecture, Artillery (any), Armoury (Heavy Weapons), Cartography, Research, Smith (any), or Teaching, all (A) IQ [2]-13; Artist (Drawing *or* Painting), Cryptography, Mathematics (Applied), or Metallurgy, all (H) IQ-1 [2]-12; or Scrounging (E) Per+1 [2]-14.

Background Skills: *Six* of Crossbow, Forced Entry, or Knot-Tying, all (E) DX [1]-11; Axe/Mace, Driving (any), Piloting (Hang Glider), Submarine (Experimental Submersible), or Two-Handed Axe/Mace, all (A) DX-1 [1]-10; Camouflage, First Aid, Games (Chess), Seamanship, or Telegraphy, all (E) IQ [1]-13; Administration, Armoury (Body Armour, Melee Weapons, *or* Missile Weapons), Explosives (Demolition *or* Fireworks), Lockpicking, Merchant, Navigation (Land *or* Sea), Prospecting, Teamster (any), Traps, Weather Sense, or Writing, all (A) IQ-1 [1]-12; Accounting, Astronomy, Diagnosis, History (Modern Technological), Jeweller, Natural Philosophy, Naturalist, Philosophy (any), or Veterinary, all (H) IQ-2 [1]-11; or Alchemy (VH) IQ-3 [1]-10.

Customisation Notes

Many engineers know Professional Skills such as Glassblowing, Masonry, and Leatherworking, either because they started life in a humble trade or because these help their projects. Feel free to reassign background skill points or use extra points from quirks accordingly.

GRADUATE WIZARD

125 points

You're a fully qualified product of Unseen University, or the equal of such. You may be a junior faculty member, an independent consultant in some provincial town, or something more idiosyncratic. People in the world at large sometimes treat you with respect, based on an exaggerated idea of what you can do – and sometimes they don't.

There are those who say that no *proper* adventuring party is complete without at least one spellcaster. You don't know about that – but adventuring would be a job, maybe, and perhaps a quick route to power, a way to get away from rivals, or even the right thing to do. (In game terms, if you haven't taken Comfortable, the problem of maintaining your Status should make get-rich-quick schemes rather tempting.) Then again, you may just be dangerously curious.

Attributes: ST 9 [-10]; DX 10 [0]; IQ 13 [60]; HT 10 [0].

Secondary Characteristics: Damage 1d-2/1d-1; BL 16 lbs.; HP 9 [0]; Will 13 [0]; Per 13 [0]; FP 10 [0]; Basic Speed 5.00 [0]; Basic Move 5 [0].

Advantages and Perks: Magery 2 [25] *and* Status 1 [5]. ● IQ +1 [20], or *two* of HT +1, Comfortable, Magery increased to 3, or Mathematical Ability 1, all [10]. ● *Two* of Will +1, Per +1, Eidetic Memory, Languages (any, Accented/Native), Single-Minded, another level of Status, Superior Staff 1, or Tenure, all [5]. ● Lightning Calculator [2], or *two* of Good with Wizards, Hyper-Specialisation, Languages (any, None/Basic), Secret Name, or Understands the Librarian, all [1].

Disadvantages and Quirks: Two of Bad Sight (Mitigator, Glasses), Clueless, Cowardice (12), Easy to Read, Laziness, Low Pain Threshold, or Social Stigma (Overdressed Foreigner), all [-10]. ● *Two* of Will -1, Addiction (Chain Smoker), Code of Honour (Academic), Compulsive Carousing (12), Curious (12), Gluttony (12), Ham-Fisted, Oblivious, Obsession (Current research project) (12), Octophobia (12), Overconfidence (12), Pacifism (Reluctant Killer), Post-Combat Shakes (12), Pyromania (12), Reputation -2 (As a menace in a pointy hat, among people who live near him), Shyness (Mild), Skinny, or Truthfulness (12), all [-5]. ● *One* of Autocondimentor, Careful, Imaginative, Minor Addiction (Intermittent Smoker), Overweight, or Proud, all [-1].

Primary Skills: Magic (Wizardry) (VH) IQ+2 [8]-15*; *two* Magical Forms, each (VH) IQ+2 [8]-15*; *and* Thaumatology (VH) IQ+1 [4]-14*.

Secondary Skills: Alchemy (VH) IQ-2 [2]-11 *and* Research (A) IQ [2]-13.

Background Skills: Six of Innate Attack (Beam *or* Projectile) (E) DX [1]-10; Riding (Equines), Sports (Darts), or Staff, all (A) DX-1 [1]-9; Aerobatics (H) DX-2 [1]-8; Area Knowledge (any), Savoir-Faire (High Society), or Shouting at Foreigners, all (E) IQ [1]-13; Administration, Fortune-Telling (any), Hidden Lore (any), Merchant, Occultism, Teaching, or Weather Sense, all (A) IQ-1 [1]-12; Astronomy, Astrozoology, Computer Programming (Magical Computers), Diagnosis, Engineer (Magical), History (Magic in some period), Mathematics (Applied *or* Pure), Naturalist, Natural Philosophy, Philosophy (any), or Physician, all (H) IQ-2 [1]-11; Carousing (E) HT [1]-10; or Intimidation (A) Will-1 [1]-12. ● Then add +2 to any two of these [6].

* Includes +2 for Magery.

Customisation Notes

Choose Magical Forms and optional skills that suit your personality: Divination and Magianism, with Computer Programming and Hidden Lore (L-Space), for a researcher; Necromancy and Summonation, plus Hidden Lore (Demon Lore) and Occultism,

for a demonologist; Necromancy and Magianism, alongside Diagnosis and Hidden Lore (Spirit Lore), for a necromancer; Physiomancy and Sortilege, as well as Fortune-Telling, Merchant, and Occultism, for a practical consultant; Elementalism and Psychomancy, and also Innate Attack and Shouting at Foreigners, for a show-off; and so on. Many wizards feel obliged to be good at throwing fireballs – implying Elementalism and Innate Attack – but that isn't actually mandatory.

GUILD THIEF

100 points

You're part of the Ankh-Morpork underworld or of a similar underworld in another city (a lot of places are imitating Ankh-Morpork in *everything* these days) – but a *respectable* part, a competent professional with a clear social position. You might work directly for the Thieves' Guild (pp. 261-262), at least some of the time, or you could be a freelancer in good standing who drops into the Guild House for the odd dinner. The former may make it more likely that you can get help from the Guild high-ups, but even freelancers can have friends.

Attributes: ST 10 [0]; DX 11 [20]; IQ 11 [20]; HT 10 [0].

Secondary Characteristics: Damage 1d-2/1d; BL 20 lbs.; HP 10 [0]; Will 11 [0]; Per 11 [0]; FP 10 [0]; Basic Speed 5.25 [0]; Basic Move 5 [0].

Advantages: Legal Immunity (Subject to Guild discipline rather than civil law in many matters) [5]. ● *One* of Combat Reflexes, High Manual Dexterity 3, or Perfect Balance, all [15]. ● *One* of ST +1, Born to Hang 1, or Sense of the City 2, all [10]. ● *Two* of Per +1, Basic Move +1, Ambidexterity, Flexibility, Resistant to Disease (+8), or Silence 1, all [5].

Disadvantages: One of Bully (12), Cowardice (12), Laziness, or Unluckiness, all [-10]. ● *One* of Code of Honour (Pirate's *or* Professional), Duty (To Guild; 9 or less), Hidebound, Overconfidence (12), Selfish (12), Shyness (Mild), Skinny, or Stubbornness, all [-5].

Primary Skills: Brawling (E) DX+1 [2]-12; Climbing (A) DX [2]-11; Lockpicking (A) IQ [2]-11; Pickpocket (H) DX-1 [2]-10; *and* Stealth (A) DX [2]-11. ● Then add +2 to any one of these [6] and +1 to another [2].

Secondary Skills: Three of Forced Entry (E) DX+1 [2]-12; Filch (A) DX [2]-11; Sleight of Hand (H) DX-1 [2]-10; Streetwise or Traps, both (A) IQ [2]-11; or Intimidation (A) Will [2]-11. ● Then add +2 to any one of these [6].

Background Skills: Five of Jumping (E) DX [1]-11; Shortsword (A) DX-1 [1]-10; Area Knowledge (the city) or Gesture, both (E) IQ [1]-11; Connoisseur (something portable and valuable), Criminology, Fast-Talk, Holdout, Interrogation, or Merchant, all (A) IQ-1 [1]-10; Carousing (E) HT [1]-10; or Observation or Search, both (A) Per-1 [1]-10.

Customisation Notes

Guild training is broad – encompassing burglary, mugging, misappropriation, and very polite extortion – but most thieves specialise once they're past their apprenticeship, hence the various options here. *Serious* specialists will be very good at one or two skills, but with all the politely prearranged burglaries and muggings these days, many Guild members are losing their edge. Those whose job includes dealing with *unlicenced* thieves will have a significant Duty, more and better combat skills, and quite possibly Bloodlust or Callous.

Senior Guild members may add a level or two of increased Status (and Wealth to match), and probably have some skill in Accounting and Administration, but they're usually too busy with Guild business or running a company to go adventuring. It's theoretically possible to acquire the entire Guild (or at least a faction in the leadership) as a powerful Patron, but that usually implies just as many day-to-day entanglements.

HICK TROLL

75 points

You're fresh down from the mountains – or at least you seem that way – and many people would say that you're not good for much apart from hitting things. Still, even a naïve troll can be remarkably effective at that. You probably employ some large, simple weapon, although your fists often serve just fine. If you're from a *really* remote region, you may be befuddled by art, politeness, crossbows, money, wheels, and other advanced ideas, but you can always find some friends to explain things. If you get involved in adventuring, it's probably by accident; so far as you're concerned, it's just another hitting-things job.

The attributes and secondary characteristics below include modifiers from the racial template.

Attributes: ST 16 [0]; DX 10 [0]; IQ 8 [0]; HT 12 [0].
Secondary Characteristics: Damage 1d+1/2d+2; BL 80 lbs.*; HP 16 [0]; Will 8 [0]; Per 9 [0]; FP 12 [0]; Basic Speed 5.50 [0]; Basic Move 5 [0].
Advantages and Perks: Moderate-Sized Troll [83]. ● Language (local human tongue, Accented/None) [2]. ● *Two* of HT +1, Will +2, Damage Resistance 2, or Fearlessness 5, all [10]. ● *One* of Cultural Familiarity (local human culture), Improvised Weapons (any), or Limited Camouflage (Stone), all [1].

Disadvantages: Innumerate [-5]; Literacy in native Language reduced to None [-3]; Status -1 [-5]; *and* Struggling [-10]. ● *One* of DX -1, IQ -1, Basic Speed -1, or Low Empathy, all [-20]; or alternatively, *two* of Bad Temper (12), Berserk (12), Bully (12), Clueless, Compulsive Carousing (6), Confused (12), Gullibility (12), Literal-Minded, Low TL 2, No Sense of Humour, Short Attention Span (12), or Unluckiness, all [-10].
Primary Skills: Brawling (E) DX+1 [0]-11†. ● *One* of Axe/Mace, Broadsword, Polearm, or Two-Handed Axe/Mace, all (A) DX+1 [4]-11.
Secondary Skills: Intimidation (A) Will [2]-8.
Background Skills: *Three* of Forced Entry (E) DX+1 [2]-11; Area Knowledge (Home Mountains) or Camouflage, both (E) IQ+1 [2]-9; Navigation (Land) or Streetwise, both (A) IQ [2]-8; Musical Instrument (Percussion) (H) IQ-1 [2]-7; Hiking (A) HT [2]-12; or Survival (Mountain) or Urban Survival, both (A) Per [2]-9.

* Includes effects of racial Lifting ST.
† Free from racial template.

HIGHWAYMAN

100 points

You're no vulgar bandit – your variety of highway robbery is *dashing* and *stylish*, and you work alone. You've invested in a horse, good weapons, and expensive clothes with lots of lace at the cuffs. Being robbed by you is more satisfying than an encounter with bandits, because the victim gets a better story to tell, and knows that his money will be spent with style, not spread thinly among a bunch of thugs.

The drawback of having *style* is that you're sometimes pulled into adventures that involve more than "Stand and deliver!" Because one of the Disc's dominant principles is narrative necessity, highway robbery – for individuals of a heroic bent – invariably leads to encounters with vengeful nobles, wizards, supernatural entities, and persons of the opposite sex, romantic inclinations, and a certain age. But that's a risk you're willing to take. Frankly, some of that stuff might make a change from a lot of cold nights on the road, holding up people with barely enough cash to cover your tailor's bill.

Attributes: ST 10 [0]; DX 11 [20]; IQ 11 [20]; HT 11 [10].
Secondary Characteristics: Damage 1d-2/1d; BL 20 lbs.; HP 10 [0]; Will 11 [0]; Per 11 [0]; FP 11 [0]; Basic Speed 5.50 [0]; Basic Move 5 [0].
Advantages and Perks: Charisma 1 [5] *and* Comfortable [10]. ● *One* of DX +1, IQ +1, or Outdoorsman 2, all [20], *or* Per +1 [5] *and* Combat Reflexes [15]. ● *One* of Per +1, Absolute Direction, Ambidexterity, Charisma increased to 2, Reputation +2 (As a dashing rogue, in area of operation), or Status 1, all [5]. ● *One* of Acute Hearing 2, Appearance (Attractive), Less Sleep 2, or Night Vision 4, all [4]. ● *One* of Alcohol Tolerance, Check the Exits, Crossbow Safety, Good with Horses, or Haughty Sneer, all [1].
Disadvantages: *One* of Compulsive Risk-Taking (12), Greed (12), Lecherousness (12), or Trickster (12), all [-15]. ● *Two* of Bully (15), Code of Honour (Pirate's), Compulsive Carousing (12), Compulsive Gambling (12), Compulsive Spending (12), Enemy (Small group of less-powerful local thief-takers; Hunter; 6 or less), Impulsiveness (15), Odious Personal Habit (Smugly Self-Assured), Overconfidence (12), Reputation -2 (As a pretentious bandit, to local high society, *or* as a dashed annoyance, to local law enforcement), or Selfish (12), all [-5].

Primary Skills: Area Knowledge (area of operations) (E) IQ+2 [4]-13; Crossbow (E) DX+2 [4]-13; *and* Riding (Equines) (A) DX+1 [4]-12.

Secondary Skills: Savoir-Faire (E) IQ+1 [2]-12 *and* Survival (Woodlands) (A) Per [2]-11. ● *One of* Broadsword, Rapier, Shortsword, *or* Smallsword, all (A) DX [2]-11. ● *Three of* Stealth (A) DX [2]-11; Camouflage (E) IQ+1 [2]-12; Public Speaking *or* Traps, both (A) IQ [2]-11; Naturalist (H) IQ-1 [2]-10; Carousing (E) HT+1 [2]-12; Sex Appeal (A) HT [2]-11; *or* Intimidation (A) Will [2]-11.

Background Skills: Streetwise (A) IQ-1 [1]-10. ● *Five of* Brawling, Fast-Draw (any), Jumping, Knife, Shield, *or* Thrown Weapon (Knife), all (E) DX [1]-11; Climbing, Dancing, *or* Throwing, all (A) DX-1 [1]-10; Acrobatics (H) DX-2 [1]-9; Current Affairs (Regional) *or* Shouting at Foreigners, both (E) IQ [1]-11; Acting, Animal Handling (Equines), Disguise, Fast-Talk, Gambling, Heraldry, Holdout, *or* Navigation (Land), all (A) IQ-1 [1]-10; Veterinary (H) IQ-2 [1]-9; *or* Observation *or* Tracking, both (A) Per-1 [1]-10.

HUBLANDS MONK

125 points

You're a member of one of the orders which occupy remote monasteries near the Hub (p. 242). You're not so much religious as *mystical*, with years of ascetic living and spiritual study under your belt – which somehow means that you've acquired the ability to leap 70 feet to kick other people in the head (philosophically), although you rarely get to indulge this hobby. You aren't as good at this as some of the legends of monkishness, but you get by.

While you probably ought to be living a life of ritual and meditation, *something* has obliged you to venture out into the world, and it turns out that much of what you learned back in the mountains is useful here. You may be seeking to preserve some kind of cosmic balance (literally, if you're one of the Balancing Monks), or you may have some kind of personal commitment that the monastery is letting you go off to resolve.

Attributes: ST 11 [10]; DX 12 [40]; IQ 11 [20]; HT 11 [10].
Secondary Characteristics: Damage 1d-1/1d+1; BL 24 lbs.; HP 11 [0]; Will 11 [0]; Per 11 [0]; FP 11 [0]; Basic Speed 6.00 [5]; Basic Move 6 [0].
Advantages and Perks: Combat Reflexes [15]. ● *One of these* packages:

1. ST +1 [10]; Will +2 [10]; Cold Resistance [1]; *and* Fearlessness 2 [4]. ● HT +1 [10] *or* High Pain Threshold [10]. ● Rapid Healing [5] *or* Resistant to Disease (+8) [5].

2. DX +1 [20] *and* Perfect Balance [15]. ● *One of* Basic Move +1, Ambidexterity, Flexibility, *or* Silence 1, all [5].

3. IQ +1 [20]; Per +1 [5]; *and* Eidetic Memory [5]. ● Sensitive [5] *or* Social Regard 1 (Venerated) [5]. ● *Five of* Cultural Familiarities (any), Deep Sleeper, Honest Face, Languages (any, Broken/None *or* None/Broken), *or* Longevity, all [1].

4. Per +2 [10]; Danger Sense [15]; *and* Medium [10]. ● Less Sleep 2 [4] *or* Night Vision 4 [4]. ● Deep Sleeper [1] *or* Longevity [1].

5. Basic Move +1 [5]; Enhanced Parry (Barehanded) [5]; Extra Attack 1 [25]; *and* Off-Hand Training (any weapon) [1]. ● HP +2 [4] *or* Acute Hearing 2 [4].

6. Luck [15]. ● Will +3 [15] *or* Indomitable [15]. ● Absolute Direction [5] *or* Single-Minded [5]. ● Less Sleep 2 [4] *or* Mind Shield 1 [4]. ● Deep Sleeper [1] *or* Longevity [1].

Disadvantages: Disciplines of Faith (Asceticism) [-15] *or* Poor [-15]; *or* Disciplines of Faith (Mysticism) [-10] *and* Vow (Vegetarianism) [-5]; *or* Struggling [-10] *and* Disciplines of Faith (Ritualism) [-5]. ● Charitable (12) [-15] *or* Pacifism (Self-Defence Only) [-15]. ● *One of* Clueless, Duty (Mission from the monastery; 12 or less), Gullibility (12), Literal-Minded, No Sense of Humour, *or* Truthfulness (6), all [-10]. ● *One of* Confused (15), Low TL 1, Oblivious, Odious Personal Habit (Enigmatic), Selfless (12), Shyness (Mild), Skinny, *or* Social Stigma (Second-Class Citizen – "Religious Freak"), all [-5].

Primary Skills: Acrobatics (H) DX [4]-12; Judo (H) DX [4]-12; Karate (H) DX [4]-12; *and* Philosophy (Order Doctrines) (H) IQ [4]-11. ● Then add +1 to any one of these [4].

Secondary Skills: Jumping (E) DX+1 [2]-13 *and* Stealth (A) DX [2]-12. ● *Two of* Knife (E) DX+1 [2]-13; Axe/Mace, Polearm, Spear, *or* Staff, all (A) DX [2]-12; *or* Flail (H) DX-1 [2]-11.

Background Skills: *Two of* Thrown Weapon (Spear) (E) DX [1]-12; Climbing *or* Throwing, both (A) DX-1 [1]-11; Escape *or* Sleight of Hand, both (H) DX-2 [1]-10; First Aid, Games (Chess), Gardening, *or* Panhandling, all (E) IQ [1]-11; Navigation (Land) *or* Teaching, both (A) IQ-1 [1]-10; Herbalism *or* Naturalist, both (H) IQ-2 [1]-9; Hiking *or* Running, both (A) HT-1 [1]-10; Intimidation (A) Will-1 [1]-10; *or* Body Language *or* Survival (Mountain), both (A) Per-1 [1]-10.

And up here in the high valleys around the hub of the world, where the snow is never far away, this is enlightenment country.
– Thief of Time

Customisation Notes

Decide exactly what the order to which you belong gets all mystical about, and then choose traits accordingly. Examples include the Balancing Monks (Perfect Balance required, Area Knowledge of the whole Disc a possible addition), the Monks of Cool (for whom Charisma may be considered mandatory), and the Listening Monks (Acute Hearing, Architecture, Natural Philosophy . . .). Full-fledged History Monks (p. 13) are too powerful to be defined by this template (or by the rules in this book!), and severely constrained by their task; even if they stretch a point and intervene in relatively trivial matters, they must be extremely tactful about it.

However, you could be a trainee or an associate of that monastery – and as the "Men in Saffron," History Monks do have a licence to go anywhere in time and space, though novices would only be sent off alone on the most trivial missions.

For *really* fancy fighting, you'll need **GURPS Martial Arts,** which adds more details than you can shake a three-section stick with hidden spikes at.

MAGICIAN/THAUMATURGIST (ALLIED MAGICAL TRADES)

75 points

In strict Discworld usage, a *magician* is a technical assistant in a wizard's laboratory, while a *thaumaturgist* is a lowly minion sent out to obtain the ingredients for magical research – owls' brains, mushrooms harvested by moonlight from the trunk of a 1,000-year-old tree, stuff like that. Magicians are expected to know a bit of theory and perhaps to possess useful magical sensitivity; many are failed Unseen University students who didn't *quite* have what it takes to earn a pointy hat. Thaumaturgists are expected to do what they're told.

Despite every attempt to maintain the distinction, however, it inevitably gets blurred. From time to time, a magician will be sent out to fetch something which the lab needs, while a thaumaturgist may pick up some theory. It's especially useful if a thaumaturgist can tell that the thing he snatched is occult enough to be worth the suicidal risk. Brighter thaumaturgists and venturesome magicians both make plausible adventurers.

This template represents a *competent* wizard's aide. Lots of less-capable people are in the business, although they may not stick around, or even survive, for long.

Attributes: ST 10 [0]; DX 11 [20]; IQ 11 [20]; HT 10 [0].
Secondary Characteristics: Damage 1d-2/1d; BL 20 lbs.; HP 10 [0]; Will 11 [0]; Per 11 [0]; FP 10 [0]; Basic Speed 5.25 [0]; Basic Move 5 [0].
Advantages: One of DX +1, IQ +1, Outdoorsman 2, or Patron (Employer – a powerful lone wizard *or* a fairly powerful research group; 12 or less), all [20], *or* Per +1 [5] *and* Serendipity 1 [15]. ● HT +1 [10], or *two* of Will +1, Per +1, Basic Move +1, Absolute Direction, Languages (any, Native/Accented *or* Accented/Native), Magery 2 (No Spellcasting), Resistant to Disease (+8), or Resistant to Poison (+3), all [5].
Disadvantages: Duty (To employer; 9 or less) [-5]. ● Impulsiveness (12) [-10] *or* Struggling [-10]. ● *One* of Curious (12), Duty increased to 12 or less, Oblivious, Overconfidence (12), Skinny, Status -1, or Truthfulness (12), all [-5].
Primary Skills: Three of Merchant, Occultism, Prospecting, or Research, all (A) IQ+1 [4]-12; Herbalism, Metallurgy, or Naturalist, all (H) IQ [4]-11; or Tracking (A) Per+1 [4]-12.
Secondary Skills: Three of Boating (any), Climbing, or Riding (Equines), all (A) DX [2]-11; Packing or Teamster (Equines), both (A) IQ [2]-11; or Hiking (A) HT [2]-10. ● *Two* of Crossbow, Shield, or Thrown Weapon (Axe/Mace), all (E) DX [1]-11; or Axe/Mace, Broadsword, Shortsword, Spear, Staff, Throwing, or Two-Handed Axe/Mace, all (A) DX-1 [1]-10.
Background Skills: Thaumatology (VH) IQ-3 [1]-8. ● *Four* of Forced Entry, Jumping, or Knot-Tying, all (E) DX [1]-11; Filch (A) DX-1 [1]-10; First Aid or Shouting at Foreigners, both (E) IQ [1]-11; Fast-Talk, Navigation (Land), Photography, Smuggling,

Weather Sense, or Writing, all (A) IQ-1 [1]-10; Computer Programming (Magical Computers), Engineer (Magical), Mathematics (Applied), or Natural Philosophy, all (H) IQ-2 [1]-9; Alchemy (VH) IQ-3 [1]-8; Scrounging (E) Per [1]-11; or Search or Survival (any), both (A) Per-1 [1]-10.

Hunchbroad Modoscousin: The Occupation

Steve looks at the magician/thaumaturgist occupational template (p. 137). This raises Hunchbroad's DX and IQ to 11. These improvements in turn mean that his Will and Per become 11, while his Basic Speed is now 5.50.

For the first, 20-point advantage, Steve decides that Hunchbroad's employers will actually help him (when they remember), making them a Patron – the equivalent of a "fairly powerful" organisation, available on 12 or less. As dwarfs start with decent HT, he passes on that and opts for two 5-point advantages instead. He uses the first to solve a communication problem: Hunchbroad has Dwarfish as his native language but needs to function in human society, so he should know Morporkian. Steve declares that he speaks Morporkian at Native level but writes it at only Accented level (his spelling is a bit eccentric). Also, because this is going to be an Ankh-Morpork-based campaign, Steve reckons that Resistant to Disease is pretty well mandatory, so he takes the +8 version.

The template also offers a choice of disadvantages in addition to a required Duty. Steve selects Impulsiveness over Struggling – he wants Hunchbroad to have dwarf-style armour and adequate gear, and he *is* the sort of dwarf who'll blunder into adventures. Normally, he'd then pick *one* -5-point disadvantage, but because he's in danger of going slightly over-budget, Steve opts to take two of them. The GM agrees that this job can drive a lot of scenarios, so Steve raises the Duty's frequency from 9 to 12. And Truthfulness (12) fits the stolid old-school dwarf image nicely.

Finally, there are skills. As a dwarf, Hunchbroad starts with Axe/Mace at DX (11, in this case). The magician/thaumaturgist template requires Steve to choose three primary skills. Two of these, Prospecting and Metallurgy, get a bonus from the dwarf Metalwork Talent, making them good choices; Naturalist sounds useful for the third. Next, Steve picks secondary skills: Packing, Riding (Equines), and Teamster (Equines) look handy for getting around, while Shield and Throwing offer extra options in combat. For background skills, Thaumatology is mandatory, while Forced Entry, Navigation (Land), Scrounging, and Smuggling provide an array of adventuring possibilities.

Fairy Godmothers

A very few witches have careers as fairy godmothers (good or bad), a role which means a lot of travelling and intervening in people's stories. This function is traditionally passed down from one witch to the next, along with a special wand. How the system got started is unknown. Some people may want to play fairy godmother characters, but there are problems with this.

Godmothers' wands are *extremely* powerful artefacts, capable of transforming almost anything nonmagical to anything else. Consequently, they're likely to dominate game plots. If the GM allows godmother PCs, it's important to bear in mind that while their wands are of unknown origin, they appear to be narrative convention given physical form. This can be as much a curse as a blessing. In particular:

- A wand has an attached Duty disadvantage: godmother work, as depicted in fairy-tales. Tasks just come to the bearer; it's destiny.
- Anybody using a wand without respect for its traditional purpose as a plot device should attract some kind of subtle-but-serious problem; e.g., increasing levels of Unluckiness (p. 65).
- Using a wand calls for Magery. Operation requires an IQ+Magery roll, with further modifiers to the GM's taste. *Targets* who have Magery can resist using Will+Magery.
- Transformations are strictly temporary, lasting at most a few hours. Larger changes are harder (giving more serious penalties) and briefer – and anything bigger than pumpkin-to-coach is simply *impossible*.
- Wands are prone to quirks such as automatically resetting to a single option (e.g., pumpkins or frogs).
- There's no shortage of powerful, *unethical* people who want to get hold of a wand.

VILLAGE WITCH

125 points

You're a respectably competent village figure, probably from the Sto Plains-Ramtops region (witches from other cultural backgrounds may have interestingly different approaches to the craft). Witches have been known to go wandering, and – although you thoroughly disapprove of the idea[1] – to meddle in other people's business. Certainly, given the proper motivation, you'll not only Challenge Evil, but organise the party, make sure that everyone has warm clothes, and keep slackers in line.

Attributes: ST 9 [-10]; DX 10 [0]; IQ 13 [60]; HT 10 [0].
Secondary Characteristics: Damage 1d-2/1d-1; BL 16 lbs.; HP 9 [0]; Will 13 [0]; Per 13 [0]; FP 10 [0]; Basic Speed 5.00 [0]; Basic Move 5 [0].

---

1. Oh yes.

Advantages and Perks: Magery 2 [25]; Social Regard 1 (Feared, Respected, *or* Venerated) [5]; *and* Status 1 [5]. ● *One* of DX +1, IQ +1, HT +2, Basic Speed +1, or Healer 2, all [20]; or alternatively, Will +1 [5] and *one* of Combat Reflexes, Danger Sense, Empathy, Indomitable, or Luck, all [15]. ● *Two* of Will +1, Per +1, Absolute Direction, Animal Empathy, Animal Friend 1, Charisma 1, Reputation +2 (As helpful or Not To Be Messed With, among neighbours), Resistant to Disease (+8), or Social Regard increased to 2, all [5]; or alternatively, Lifting ST 3 [9] and *one* of Cold Resistance, Deep Sleeper, Fearsome Stare, Longevity, or Night Vision 1, all [1].

Disadvantages: Code of Honour (Wise-Woman's) [-5]. ● Ugly [-8] *and* Reputation -1 (As weird, abrasive, etc., among neighbours) [-2]; or alternatively, *one* of ST -1, Pacifism (Cannot Harm Innocents), or Struggling, all [-10]. ● *Two* of Bad Temper (15), Low TL 1, Overconfidence (12), Sense of Duty (Family), Skinny, or Stubbornness, all [-5].

Primary Skills: Herbalism (H) IQ [4]-13 *and* Midwifery (A) IQ+1 [4]-14. ● Magic (Witchcraft) *and* Magical Form (Physiomancy), both (VH) IQ+1 [4]-14*. ● Magical Form (Divination) *and* Magical Form (Psychomancy), both (VH) IQ [2]-13*.

Secondary Skills: Area Knowledge (home region) (E) IQ [1]-13; Brawling (E) DX [1]-10; Current Affairs (Regional for home area) (E) IQ [1]-13; Fortune-Telling (any) (A) IQ-1 [1]-12; Housekeeping (E) IQ [1]-13; Naturalist (H) IQ-2 [1]-11; Physician (H) IQ-2 [1]-11; *and* Psychology (Human) (H) IQ-2 [1]-11.

Background Skills: Five of Knife or Sewing, both (E) DX [1]-10; Stealth (A) DX-1 [1]-9; Aerobatics or Sleight of Hand, both (H) DX-2 [1]-8; Camouflage, First Aid, Gardening, or Shouting at Foreigners, all (E) IQ [1]-13; Acting, Animal Handling (any), Fast-Talk, Hidden Lore (Spirit Lore), Holdout, Leadership, Merchant, Navigation (Land), Occultism, Professional Skill (Cooking *or* Farming), Teaching, or Weather Sense, all (A) IQ-1 [1]-12; Diagnosis, Diplomacy, History (Genealogical for local area), Poisons, or Veterinary, all (H) IQ-2 [1]-11; Carousing (E) HT [1]-10; Hiking (A) HT-1 [1]-9; Intimidation (A) Will-1 [1]-12; Scrounging (E) Per [1]-13; Body Language, Observation, or Survival (home area environment), all (A) Per-1 [1]-12; or Detect Lies (H) Per-2 [1]-11. ● Then add +1 to any two of these [2].

* Includes +2 for Magery.

Voodoo Witches

Voodoo (p. 272) is a branch of witchcraft, but very variant. While voodoo witches can use this template, feel free to tinker with the details – say, shifting points from medical skills to Poisons. Their variety of Social Regard is likely to be Feared. Most favour Cuisinomancy as their Fortune-Telling specialisation, and many have Religious Ritual and Theology (Voodoo Gods). Some, acting as cult leaders, even qualify for Clerical Investment. Most important, they can reapportion their points in Magical Forms, and they frequently have skill at Necromancy or Summonation.

WATCHMAN

75 points

You're an agent of the law – a working copper in some city – and you take your job seriously. Some would say that you're one of a new breed which has emerged with the revitalisation of the Ankh-Morpork Watch, but you may be aware and proud that honest policing is an *old* tradition, although it has been better accomplished at some times than at others.

Attributes: ST 11 [10]; DX 11 [20]; IQ 10 [0]; HT 11 [10].

Secondary Characteristics: Damage 1d-1/1d+1; BL 24 lbs.; HP 11 [0]; Will 10 [0]; Per 10 [0]; FP 11 [0]; Basic Speed 5.50 [0]; Basic Move 5 [0].

Advantages and Perks: Legal Enforcement Powers [5] *and* Watch Rank 0 [0]. ● Combat Reflexes [15] *or* Danger Sense [15]. ● *One* of ST +1, HT +1, Per +2, Basic Speed +0.50, or Sense of the City 2, all [10]. ● *Two* of Will +1, Basic Move +1, Absolute Direction, Enhanced Parry (Barehanded *or* Short-sword), increased Legal Enforcement Powers, Reputation +2 (For corruptibility or fairness, among the local underworld, *or* for effectiveness, among local law-abiding citizens), Resistant to Disease (+8), Sensitive, or Watch Rank 1, all [5]. ● *One* of Acute Hearing 2, Fearlessness 2, or Night Vision 4, all [4]. ● *One* of Alcohol Tolerance, Cobblestone Sense, Cold Resistance, or Fearsome Stare, all [1].

Disadvantages: Duty (To the job, 9 or less) [-5]. ● *Two* of Code of Honour (Watchman's), Duty increased to 12 or less, Selfless (12), or Sense of Duty (Squad Mates), all [-5]. ● *One* of Honesty (12), No Sense of Humour, Pacifism (Cannot Harm Innocents), Social Stigma (Minority Group), or Struggling, all [-10]. ● *One* of Bully (15), Chummy, Ham-Fisted, Hidebound, Reputation -2 (For excess keenness, among the local underworld), or Truthfulness (12), all [-5].

Primary Skills: Area Knowledge (city of operation) (E) IQ+1 [2]-11; Brawling (E) DX+1 [2]-12; Crossbow (E) DX+1 [2]-12; *and* Shortsword (A) DX [2]-11. ● Then add +1 to any one of these [2].

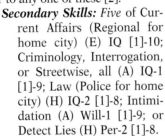

Secondary Skills: *Five* of Current Affairs (Regional for home city) (E) IQ [1]-10; Criminology, Interrogation, or Streetwise, all (A) IQ-1 [1]-9; Law (Police for home city) (H) IQ-2 [1]-8; Intimidation (A) Will-1 [1]-9; or Detect Lies (H) Per-2 [1]-8.

Background Skills: *Five* of Fast-Draw (Arrow/Bolt, Knife, *or* Sword), Forced Entry, or Knot-Tying, all (E) DX [1]-11; Axe/Mace, Boxing, Polearm, Spear, Sports (Darts), Staff, Stealth, or Wrestling, all (A) DX-1 [1]-10; First Aid, Savoir-Faire (Military), or Shouting at Foreigners, all (E) IQ [1]-10; Acting, Administration, Armoury (Melee Weapons), Fast-Talk, Hidden Lore (Secrets of the City), Leadership, Shadowing, or Soldier, all (A) IQ-1 [1]-9; Diplomacy or Psychology (any), both (H) IQ-2 [1]-8; Carousing (E) HT [1]-11; Body Language, Observation, or Search, all (A) Per-1 [1]-9; or +1 to any secondary skill [1].

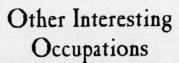

Other Interesting Occupations

All sorts of people become involved in adventures on the Disc, some of them from careers which aren't covered by these templates. Some possibilities:

Beggars mostly have poor attributes; Dead Broke, Status -2, and Unluckiness or physical impairments; and (hopefully) Panhandling, Scrounging, and Urban Survival. Slightly less dysfunctional examples *can* make playable PCs. Consider Area Knowledge, minor advantages representing physical hardiness, a few larcenous skills, and maybe Patron (Beggars' Guild). Beggars see more than almost anyone else, and high-ups such as the Patrician sometimes take advantage of that; they may even remember to pay.

Conjurers are mostly amiable hobbyists, but Animal Handling (Doves and Pigeons *or* Rabbits), Escape, Explosives (Fireworks), Fast-Talk, Holdout, Pickpocket, and of course Sleight of Hand – along with Hobby Skill (Lore of Stage Conjuring) – can be useful anywhere. Dependent (Worried-looking woman in a spangly dress) is traditional, while Odious Personal Habit (Overdoing the Tricks) annoys real wizards far more than it should.

Gamblers primarily require Gambling and several Games skills or Current Affairs (Sports). Body Language, Fast-Talk, Holdout, and Sleight of Hand also help. Eidetic Memory or Lightning Calculator can give a real edge; Luck, too, is useful, but relying on it is *very* dangerous. Compulsive Gambling is *dangerous* in this career, though not unknown. Languages, Cultural Familiarities, and Area Knowledge are possible, along with Danger Sense, Check the Exits, and Streetwise.

Guerrilla Mimes in Ankh-Morpork – where Lord Vetinari bans such street theatre – are hopeless fanatic-romantic rebels who treat mime as symbolic. This isn't a career in itself, but hardened mimes may have Gesture skill and a level or two of Silence, as well as a major Secret, and they pursue all sorts of misguided quests.

Mad Doctors possess wealth, technical brilliance, and advanced knowledge, and they are a significant if disorganised part of Uberwaldian society. They could make interesting PCs. However, they're mad.

Sailors on Discworld ships get to meet a wider variety of cultures and languages than most people, and they try a more interesting variety of booze. Basic requirements are decent HT, adequate DX, and Seamanship; any serious sailor will add Boating and Knot-Tying, and may pick up Languages, Cultural Familiarities, Area Knowledge, and Swimming. Specialists know Navigation; captains need Leadership and Shiphandling. Combat skills can be necessary. Carousing, Survival, and musical skills also fit.

Customisation Notes

To begin play with Rank 2+, shuffle around some advantage points. Nonhuman watchmen may move the points from Short-sword into skill with racially traditional weapons such as dwarf axes or troll clubs.

The extent of your Legal Enforcement Powers depends on how the city is run and on local traditions. For how things work in Ankh-Morpork, see pp. 255-258. In some cities, military-style forces handle law enforcement; the career soldier template (p. 131) with added Legal Enforcement Powers works better in such cases.

High-Powered Characters

These templates are for *powerful* individuals, suitable as PCs in heroic campaigns or as major NPCs.

ASSASSIN

150 points

People throughout the multiverse are prone to hiring each other to impose termi-nally on third parties, but on the Disc, the word "Assassin" means something more. You're a graduate of the school in Ankh-Morpork and a member in good standing of the Guild (pp. 259-261) – an expert in preci-sion killing and in fitting into the milieu wherein Assassins are traditionally employed. You may operate out of the Guild HQ or you might be based elsewhere.

The Assassins' Code (p. 56) has been drilled into you. Even if you don't *actually* live by it, you bear it in mind, as ignoring it can get you into *dangerous* trouble. The template assumes that you either obey it or have some murky secrets in your past. You're certainly no mass murderer – even the most famous Assassins kill perhaps 30 people in an entire career.

Assassins might seem too "un-heroic" for some campaigns. However, remember that many wealthy families send their off-spring to the Guild for a fine all-round edu-cation and some idea of how to defend themselves against jealous relatives, *not* to become working Assassins. Even fully qualified graduates may lose any taste they might have had for killing, going on to pro-vide, say, consultancy in self-protection.

Attributes: ST 11 [10]; DX 12 [40]; IQ 11 [20]; HT 10 [0].

Secondary Characteristics: Damage 1d-1/1d+1; BL 24 lbs.; HP 11 [0]; Will 11 [0]; Per 11 [0]; FP 10 [0]; Basic Speed 5.50 [0]; Basic Move 5 [0].

Advantages and Perks: Assassin in Good Standing [1]; Comfort-able [10]; Legal Immunity (Subject to Guild discipline rather than civil law in many matters) [5]; *and* Status 1 [5]. ● *One of* DX +1, IQ +1, Patron (Guild *or* long-term employer, as a fairly powerful organisation; 12 or less), or Patron (Guild *or* long-term employer, as a very powerful organisation; 9 or less), all

[20]; *or* Combat Reflexes [15] *and* Enhanced Parry (any one weapon) [5]; *or* Flexibility [5] *and* Perfect Balance [15]. ● *Two* of ST +1, HT +1, Per +2, Born to Hang 1, or Wealth increased to Wealthy, all [10]. ● *Two* of Basic Move +1, Ambidexterity, Charisma 1, Resistant to Poison (+3), Silence 1, or Status increased to 2, all [5] – or swap a choice for *one* of Acute Vision 2, Attractive, or Language (any, Accented/Accented), all [4], and *one* of Crossbow Safety, Night Vision 1, or Off-Hand Training (Crossbow *or* Knife), all [1].

Disadvantages and Quirks: Code of Honour (Assassins') [-10] *or* Secret (Bends Guild Rules) [-10]. ● *One* of Callous, Duty (To long-term employer; 9 or less), or Sense of Duty (Brother Assassins *or* Employing Family), all [-5]. ● *Two* of Bully (15), Odious Personal Habit (Radiates Smug Amorality), Overconfi-dence (12), Selfish (12), or Secret (any past indiscretion or fail-ure), all [-5].

Primary Skills: Climbing (A) DX+1 [4]-13; Crossbow (E) DX [1]-12; Savoir-Faire (High Society) (E) IQ+2 [4]-13; Stealth (A) DX+1 [4]-13; *and* Thrown Weapon (Knife) (E) DX+1 [2]-13.

Secondary Skills: Acrobatics (H) DX-2 [1]-10; Dancing (A) DX-1 [1]-11; Knife (E) DX [1]-12; Musical Instru-ment (any) (H) IQ-2 [1]-9; Poisons (H) IQ-2 [1]-9; *and* Traps (A) IQ-1 [1]-10. ● Shortsword *or* Smallsword, both (A) DX-1 [1]-11. ● Then add +2 to any two secondary skills [6].

Background Skills: *Six* of Fast-Draw (any) or Jumping, both (E) DX [1]-12; Bow or Riding (Equines), both (A) DX-1 [1]-11; Blowpipe or Sleight of Hand, both (H) DX-2 [1]-10; Area Knowledge (any), Camouflage, Cur-rent Affairs (Politics *or* Regional), or Games (Chess), all (E) IQ [1]-11; Acting, Architecture, Disguise, Explo-sives (Demolition), Heraldry, Hold-out, Lockpicking, Occultism, or Research, all (A) IQ-1 [1]-10; History (any modern political) (H) IQ-2 [1]-9; Carousing (E) HT [1]-10; *or* Observa-tion (A) Per-1 [1]-10.

IGOR

150 points

You're one of the specialist class of personal servants and laboratory assis-tants who've lately emerged from Uberwald onto the Disc at large. The ulti-mate self-made men, Igors are experts in transplant surgery, which they perform enthusi-astically on themselves. For some idea of Igor capabilities, see *Mad Medicine* (p. 44), *Patchwork Man* (pp. 45-46), and *Uberwaldian Domestic Surgery* (p. 225).

Igors all seem to be blood relatives (insofar as the term means anything – much of the time, they don't so much repro-duce as recycle), forming a sort of extended clan. Igor-recogni-tion is mostly a matter of learning particular patterns of scars.

Igors almost invariably walk with some kind of pronounced limp[1], though they aren't necessarily slowed by it, and they talk with an intrusive lisp. Most have Uberwaldian as their native language but are quite fluent in Morporkian.

Igors come across as amiable individuals to people who've learned to ignore their scars, stitching, and mannerisms. The only annoying behaviours they sometimes display are asking for organ donations ("when the mathter hath finished with you, you won't be needing them") and excessive use of Stealth (materialising right behind the person who's looking for them). They share a common aversion to the idea of burial (all those worms!) and cremation (simply wasteful).

This template illustrates a fairly *basic* Igor. Many Igors display startling abilities with many of the listed skills.

Attributes: ST 10 [0]; DX 10 [0]; IQ 12 [40]; HT 10 [0].

Secondary Characteristics: Damage 1d-2/1d; BL 20 lbs.; HP 10 [0]; Will 12 [0]; Per 11 [-5]; FP 10 [0]; Basic Speed 5.00 [0]; Basic Move 5 [0].

Advantages and Perks: Cutting-Edge Training (Physician/TL5 and Surgery/TL5)* [1]; Gadgeteer [25]; High Pain Threshold [10]; Mad Medicine [15]; Patchwork Man [10]; Resistant to Disease (+8) [5]; *and* Very Rapid Healing [15]. ● *One* of ST +2, DX +1, IQ +1, HT +2, or Healer 2, all [20]. ● *Two* of HP +5, Artificer 1, High Manual Dexterity 2, or Social Regard 2 (Respected)†, all [10]. ● *Two* of Will +1, Ambidexterity, Eidetic Memory, Flexibility, Legal Immunity (Igor Immunity)†, Reputation +2 (As an incredibly useful medic, among neighbours), Resistant to Disease improved to Immunity, Resistant to Poison (+3), Single-Minded, or Versatile, all [5] – or swap a choice for *one* of HP +2, Acute Senses 2 (any), Cutting-Edge Training changed to High TL 1*, Fearlessness 2, Language (any, Accented/Accented), Less Sleep 2, or Night Vision 4, all [4], and *one* of Alcohol Tolerance, Archaic Training (a medical or technical skill), Cold Resistance, Cutting-Edge Training (one Engineer specialisation), Deep Sleeper, Longevity, No Hangover, Off-Hand Training (Sewing *or* Surgery), or There on Call, all [1].

Disadvantages and Quirks: Code of Honour (Igor's) [-5]; Dislikes burial and cremation [-1]; Disturbing Voice (Horrendous Lisp) [-10]; *and* Ugly [-8]. ● Duty (Nonhazardous; 12 or less) [-5] *or* Sense of Duty (Employers) [-5]. ● Low Empathy [-20], or *two* of Clueless, Cowardice (12), Hunchback, Pacifism (Cannot Harm Innocents), or Struggling, all [-10]. ● *Two* of Basic Move -1, Callous, Curious (12), Oblivious, Odious Personal Habit (Asking for Spare Parts), Truthfulness (12), or Unnatural Features 5‡, all [-5].

Primary Skills: Surgery (VH) IQ+3 [20]-15*.

Secondary Skills: Physician (H) IQ+1 [8]-13*; Savoir-Faire (Servant) (E) IQ [1]-12; Sewing (E) DX+1 [2]-11; *and* Stealth (A) DX+1 [4]-11.

Background Skills: *Eight* of Hobby Skill (Juggling), Knife, or Knot-Tying, all (E) DX [1]-10; Area Knowledge (home castle), Carpentry, or Housekeeping, all (E) IQ [1]-12; Architecture, Armoury (Heavy Weapons), Holdout, Mechanic (Clockwork *or* Low-Tech Machines), Research, Shadowing, or Traps, all (A) IQ-1 [1]-11; Diagnosis, Engineer (Clockwork, Low-Tech Machines, *or* really weird stuff), Herbalism, Metallurgy, Poisons, or Veterinary, all (H) IQ-2 [1]-10; Alchemy (VH) IQ-3 [1]-9; Scrounging (E) Per [1]-11; or +1 to any of these skills [1].

1. Pronounced "limp."

* Physician and Surgery *must* be at TL5. In a campaign with a base TL less than 4, buy enough High TL and/or additional levels of Cutting-Edge Training to justify TL5 with these skills.

† Usually, Igors should take Legal Immunity only if based in Uberwald, where it's essentially required; elsewhere, people aren't as understanding. Similarly, in much of Uberwald and adjacent nations, Igors are treated with some deference – nobody wants to alienate them, as their medical services are invaluable – which allows them to buy Social Regard (somewhat compensating for all their reaction penalties). Folk in other places haven't learned this principle yet, though individual Igors may enjoy good Reputations.

‡ On an Igor, Unnatural Features ought to mean something fairly spectacular; scars and stitching are natural to them. However, an Igor living away from Uberwald might take this disadvantage to reflect the effects of his appearance on those unfamiliar with his kind.

PICTSIE (PIXIE)

150 points

You're no mere cowardly gnome, quiverin' an' hidin' under toadstools – you're a *pictsie,* an' proud of it, an' ready to take on anyone who offers you an excuse for a fight. (Och, rilly thoo, who's needin' an *excuse?*) You've somehow become separated from your clan, which is a shame, to be sure, but nae matter – if there's drink to be had an' fightin' to be done, you'll nae be backward in comin' forward. 'Specially not if there's cattle to be moved round, or if anyone looks at you funny.

The attributes and secondary characteristics below include modifiers from the racial template. The ST given here may *seem* high, but given pictsies' cattle-stealing methods and effectiveness in combat, it's entirely justifiable. Pictsies speak their own language (pp. 17 and 102); you've also learned to speak a human language well enough to get by.

Attributes: ST 10 [60]; DX 13 [20]; IQ 10 [0]; HT 12 [10].

Secondary Characteristics: Damage 1d-2/1d; BL 20 lbs.; HP 10 [0]; Will 10 [0]; Per 11 [0]; FP 12 [0]; Basic Speed 6.25 [0]; Basic Move 5 [5].

Advantages and Perks: Gnome/Pictsie [18]. ● Alcohol Tolerance [1]; Combat Reflexes [15]; Fearlessness 5 [10]; Language (any human tongue, Accented/None) [2]; *and* Unfazed by Size [1]. ● DX +1 [20] *or* Basic Speed +1 [20]; or alternatively, Per +1 [5] and *one* of Daredevil, Indomitable, Lifting ST 5, Luck, or Perfect Balance, all [15]. ● *One* of ST +1, HT +1, Will +2, High Pain Threshold, Outdoorsman 1, or Silence 2, all [10]. ● *Two* of Basic Move +1, Rapid Healing, Resistant to Disease (+8), Resistant to Poison (+3), or Silence 1, all [5].

- *One* of HP +2, Fearlessness 2, or Night Vision 4, all [4]. • *Two* of Cold Resistance, Improvised Weapons (Knife), improve literacy in human language to Broken, or No Hangover, all [1].

Disadvantages and Quirks: Brawling Society [-1]; Code of Honour ("Pirate's") [-5]; *and* Respectfully cautious about witches ("hags") [-1]. • IQ -1 [-20], *or* Chummy [-5] and *one* of Absent-Mindedness, Alcoholism, Compulsive Lying (12), Kleptomania (12), or Poor, all [-15]. • *Two* of Bad Temper (12), Berserk (12), Bloodlust (12), Clueless, Impulsiveness (12), or Short Attention Span (12), all [-10].
• *Two* of Compulsive Carousing (12), Odious Personal Habit (Aggressive), Overconfidence (12), or Stubbornness, all [-5]. • *One* of Curious (12), Low TL 1, Oblivious, Reputation -2 (As a brawler or cattle thief, among nearby neighbours), Sense of Duty (Companions), Status -1, Truthfulness (12), or Unattractive (Universal), all [-5].

Primary Skills: Brawling (E) DX+2 [4]-15; Camouflage (E) IQ+3 [6]-13*; Knife (E) DX+1 [2]-14; *and* Stealth (A) DX+1 [0]-14*.

Secondary Skills: Climbing (A) DX [2]-13 *and* Filch (A) DX [2]-13.

Background Skills: *Four* of Jumping or Knot-Tying, both (E) DX+1 [2]-14; Riding (Birds) (A) DX [2]-13; Acrobatics or Pickpocket, both (H) DX-1 [2]-12; Area Knowledge (tribal territory) or Shouting at Foreigners, both (E) IQ+1 [2]-11; Animal Handling (Birds), Armoury (Melee Weapons), Fast-Talk, Navigation (Land), Shadowing, or Traps, all (A) IQ [2]-10; Law (Contract for some region, typically) or Naturalist, both (H) IQ-1 [2]-9; Carousing or Swimming, both (E) HT+1 [2]-13; Hiking or Running, both (A) HT [2]-12; Intimidation (A) Will [2]-10; Scrounging (E) Per+1 [2]-12; or Observation, Survival (Mountain *or* Woodlands), or Tracking, all (A) Per [2]-11.

* Reflects racial template. The racial Silence advantage (and any added Silence) and the character's small size will often give bonuses to the roll.

Customisation Notes

Pictsies may well go over campaign disadvantage limits – many disadvantages are inherent in their nature, after all (though pictsies tend to see these as advantages). It may be best for the GM simply to let them do this. Trying to stop a pictsie taking something he wants is rather hard, after all.

SENIOR WIZARD

200 points

Thanks to your gift for magic, you've risen through the ranks of wizardry to a respectable (and hopefully respected) faculty position at Unseen University or some comparable institution.[1] Alternatively, you might hold a well-paid private post. Or perhaps you do personal research in your own tower (and maybe act like a dangerous throwback).

Having reached this lofty position, you *should* grasp that truly comprehending magic includes knowing when *not* to use it, which is quite a lot of the time. That doesn't make you incapable. With the understanding of when to exercise restraint comes the

1. *Comparable in its own assessment, that is.*

awareness of when to fireball them until they glow and then hex them in the dark.

Attributes: ST 10 [0]; DX 11 [20]; IQ 13 [60]; HT 10 [0].

Secondary Characteristics: Damage 1d-2/1d; BL 20 lbs.; HP 10 [0]; Will 13 [0]; Per 13 [0]; FP 10 [0]; Basic Speed 5.25 [0]; Basic Move 5 [0].

Advantages and Perks: Comfortable [10]; Longevity [1]; Magery 3 [35]; *and* Status 2 [10]. • DX +1 [20] or IQ +1 [20]; *or* Per +1 [5] *and* Basic Speed +0.75 [15]; *or* Combat Reflexes [15] *and* Enhanced Parry (Staff) [5]. • *Three* of ST +1, HT +1, Will +2, Per +2, Magery increased to 4, Mathematical Ability 1, or Wealth increased to Wealthy, all [10]. • *Two* of Eidetic Memory, Legal Immunity (*De facto* government in his tower), Reputation +2 (As leading scholar, among wizards), Resistant to Disease (+8), Single-Minded, Social Regard 1 (Feared – "Power in a Pointy Hat"), Status increased to 3, Superior Staff 1, or Tenure, all [5] – or swap a choice for *two* of HP +1, Fearlessness 1, Languages (any, None/Accented), or Lightning Calculator, all [2], *and one* of Hyper-Specialisation (any), No Hangover, Secret Name, or Understands the Librarian, all [1].

Disadvantages: ST -2 [-20] *or* Low Empathy [-20]; or alternatively, Per -1 [-5] *and* Absent-Mindedness [-15]. • *Two* of Will -2, Per -2, Bad Sight (Mitigator, Glasses), Bad Temper (12), Easy to Read, Hard of Hearing, Megalomania, No Sense of Humour, Paranoia, or Social Stigma (Overdressed Foreigner), all [-10]. • *Two* of Addiction (Chain Smoker), Callous, Code of Honour (Academic), Curious (12), Gluttony (12), Ham-Fisted, Hidebound, Low TL 1, Oblivious, Obsession (Current research project) (12), Octophobia (12), Odious Personal Habits (Shouting, ignoring people, blowing things up, etc.), Overconfidence (12), Pyromania (12), Reputation -2 (As Trouble in a Pointy Hat, among neighbours), Selfish (12), Stubbornness, Unnatural Features 5 (Planets Orbiting Head), or Very Fat, all [-5] – or swap a choice for Fat [-3] *and* Gluttony (15) [-2].

Primary Skills: Magic (Wizardry) (VH) IQ+3 [8]-16*. • *Three* Magical Forms, each (VH) IQ+3 [8]-16*. • *Two* Magical Forms, each (VH) IQ+1 [2]-14*.

Secondary Skills: Alchemy (VH) IQ-3 [1]-10; Innate Attack (Beam *or* Projectile) (E) DX [1]-11; *and* Research (A) IQ-1 [1]-12. • Then add +2 to any one of these [3].

142 NONHUMANS AND OCCUPATIONAL TEMPLATES

Background Skills: Six of Riding (Equines), Staff, or Stealth, all (A) DX-1 [1]-10; Aerobatics (H) DX-2 [1]-9; Area Knowledge (any), Savoir-Faire (High Society), or Shouting at Foreigners, all (E) IQ [1]-13; Administration, Hidden Lore (any), Occultism, Politics, Teaching, or Traps, all (A) IQ-1 [1]-12; Astronomy, Astrozoology, Diagnosis, Engineer (Magical), History (Magic in some period), Mathematics (any), Natural Philosophy, or Philosophy (any), all (H) IQ-2 [1]-11; Thaumatology (VH) IQ [1]-13*; Carousing (E) HT [1]-10; or Intimidation (A) Will-1 [1]-12. ● Then add +2 to any two of these [6].

* Includes +3 for Magery.

Customisation Notes

Choose your Magical Forms to suit your style. Most wizards go for Elementalism, and many use it a *lot* – although there *are* some quiet ones, and those who are creepy enough to prefer Necromancy or Summonation. Smart wizards also pursue Divination; time spent on reconnaissance is never wasted. Magianism is useful for anyone who wants to get *technical*. Psychomancy and Sortilege are less popular, though they have their enthusiasts, and Physiomancy has the charm of allowing one to change opponents into frogs, which can be more satisfying and less legally complicated than fireballing them.

Social Regard applies mostly to freelance tower-dwelling wizards, who are treated with caution due to their power but who aren't granted actual social standing. In Ankh-Morpork, wizards have parlayed that power into Status. If you raise your Wealth to Wealthy, don't forget that this gives you an extra Status level for free.

SERIOUS WITCH

250 points

You're a witch at the top of your profession. (Some would say *near* the top, but part of being a serious witch is not putting up with any mealy mouthed nonsense.) You might be much like the village witch (p. 138), only especially competent. Alternatively, you may be a more idiosyncratic figure, pursuing private interests.

You should remember that, say, building a cottage out of confectionery deep in the woods is a sign that you're losing your grip – it puts you on a narrative path with no good endings – but the temptations of the iron oven and a good cackle can be hard to resist. Power notoriously comes with a price, and for a witch, that price means going along with the story. The trick is to make sure that *your* story is one of the longer, happier ones.

Attributes: ST 10 [0]; DX 11 [20]; IQ 14 [80]; HT 12 [20].
Secondary Characteristics: Damage 1d-2/1d; BL 20 lbs.; HP 10 [0]; Will 14 [0]; Per 14 [0]; FP 12 [0]; Basic Speed 6.00 [5]; Basic Move 6 [0].
Advantages and Perks: Longevity [1]; Magery 3 [35]; Social Regard 3 (Feared, Respected, *or* Venerated) [15]; *and* Status 1 [5]. ● *One* of DX +1, IQ +1, Healer 2, or Outdoorsman 2, all [20]; or alternatively, *one* of Will +1, Per +1 *or* Enhanced Parry (Barehanded), all [5], and *one* of Combat Reflexes, Danger Sense, Indomitable, or Unfazeable, all [15]. ● *One* of ST +1, HT +1, Will +2, Per +2, Animal Friend 2, Comfortable, High Pain Threshold, or Magery increased to 4, all [10], *or* Cold Resistance [1] *and* Lifting ST 3 [9]. ● *One* of Absolute Direction, Animal Empathy, Charisma 1, Reputation +2 (As helpful, not to be messed with, etc., among neighbours), Resistant to Disease (+8), Resistant to Poison (+3), Sensitive, Silence 1, or Single-Minded, all [5]. ● *One* of HP +2, Fearlessness 2, Language (neighbouring region's, Native/Broken), Less Sleep 2, Mind Shield 1, or Night Vision 4, all [4]. ● *One* of Climatic Emphasis, Deep Sleeper, Fearsome Stare, or Oggham Reader, all [1].
Disadvantages: One of Callous, Code of Honour (Wise-Woman's), or Curious (12), all [-5]. ● *Three* of Bad Temper (12), Bloodlust (12), Bully (12), Disturbing Voice (The Cackle), Hard of Hearing, Hunchback, Jealousy, Pacifism (Cannot Harm Innocents), Sense of Duty (Everyone you know personally), or Struggling, all [-10] – or swap a choice for Reputation -1 (As a scary hag, among neighbours) [-2] *and* Ugly [-8]. ● *Two* of Basic Move -1, Compulsive Neatness (12), Hidebound, Low TL 1, Odious Personal Habit (Irascible), Overconfidence (12), Pyrophobia (Minor) (12), Skinny, or Stubbornness, all [-5].
Primary Skills: Herbalism (H) IQ [4]-14; Intimidation (A) Will [2]-14; *and* Psychology (Human) (H) IQ [4]-14. ● Magic (Witchcraft) (VH) IQ+4 [12]-18*. ● *Four* Magical Forms, each (VH) IQ+3 [8]-17*.
Secondary Skills: Area Knowledge (home region) (E) IQ [1]-14; Brawling (E) DX+1 [2]-12; Housekeeping (E) IQ [1]-14; Knife (E) DX+1 [2]-12; Naturalist (H) IQ-2 [1]-12; Occultism (A) IQ-1 [1]-13; Physician (H) IQ-2 [1]-12; *and* Stealth (A) DX+1 [4]-12.
Background Skills: Five of Fast-Draw (Knife), Innate Attack (Beam, Gaze, *or* Projectile), or Sewing, all (E) DX [1]-11; Riding (Equines) (A) DX-1 [1]-10; Aerobatics or Sleight of Hand, both (H) DX-2 [1]-9; Camouflage, Current Affairs (Regional for home area), First Aid, Gardening, or Shouting at Foreigners, all (E) IQ [1]-14; Acting, Animal Handling (any), Fast-Talk, Fortune-Telling (any), Hidden Lore (Demon Lore *or* Spirit Lore), Leadership, Merchant, Midwifery, Navigation (Air *or* Land), Professional Skill (Cooking *or* Farming), Public Speaking, Research, Teaching, or Weather Sense, all (A) IQ-1 [1]-13; Diagnosis, Diplomacy, History (Mystical for local area), Natural Philosophy, Poisons, or Veterinary, all (H) IQ-2 [1]-12; Thaumatology (VH) IQ [1]-14*; Body Language, Survival (any), or Tracking, all (A) Per-1 [1]-13; or Detect Lies (H) Per-2 [1]-12. ● Then add +1 to any two of these [2].

* Includes +3 for Magery.

Customisation Notes

Assign Magical Forms (and background skills) to suit your personal interests. For a healer, concentrate on Physiomancy and Psychomancy, plus medical skills. A research witch should consider Magianism and Sortilege; a regional guardian, Divination and Elementalism. As for a villainess-in-training . . . she might use anything, but *ab*using Necromancy and Summonation is always a "good" start.

To create a voodoo witch at this level, apply the notes under *Voodoo Witches* (p. 138) to this template.

SMALL GOD

275 points

Note: It should go without saying that any campaign in which the GM allows small god PCs may be a trifle unusual. Still, this is what such a character could look like.

You're a genuine god – a thunderbolt-hurling, worshipped, ineffable deity, and don't let anyone forget it. Admittedly, you don't have the biggest temple on the Disc, and your cult still needs careful management (you understand how it works: if you get sloppy and let them drift away, you'll sink down and then fade out). However, you're in this for the long term, and part of being a god is not letting anyone not take you seriously.

Attributes: ST 10 [0]; DX 10 [0]; IQ 10 [0]; HT 10 [0].

Secondary Characteristics: Damage 1d-2/1d; BL 20 lbs.; HP 10 [0]; Will 10 [0]; Per 10 [0]; FP 10 [0]; Basic Speed 5.00 [0]; Basic Move 5 [0].

Advantages and Perks: Burning Attack 2d (Lightning Bolt) [20]; Congregation (50 people)* [12]; Doesn't Breathe [20], Doesn't Eat or Drink [10]; Immunity to Disease [10]; Immunity to Poison [15]; Insubstantiality (Can Carry Objects, Light Encumbrance) [96]; Invisibility (Can Carry Objects, Light Encumbrance; Only While Insubstantial; Substantial Only) [40]; Legal Immunity (Answerable only to other gods) [15]; Longevity [1]; Name Hearing [1]; Pressure-Proof [15]; Recognised Divinity [1];

Temperature Tolerance 3 (Cold) [6]; Temperature Tolerance 3 (Heat) [6]; *and* Tenure [5]. ● *One* of ST +3, FP +10, Flight (Winged, Can Hover), Lifting ST 10, or Very Wealthy†, all [30], *or* Damage Resistance 1 [5] *and* Regeneration (Regular) [25]. ● *One* of DX +1, HT +2, Basic Move +4, Burning Attack increased to 4d, Damage Resistance 4, Enhanced Move 1 (Air or Ground), Social Regard 4 (Feared *or* Respected), Very Handsome/Beautiful (Universal)‡, or Wealthy†, all [20], *or* Medium [10] *and* Spirit Empathy (Full) [10]. ● *Three* of Will +1, Per +1, Absolute Direction, Animal Empathy, Charisma 1, Claws (Sharp Claws), Damage Resistance 5 (Can't Wear Armour; Tough Skin), Eidetic Memory, Rapid Healing, Reputation +2 (As dependable, among a large group of your choice), Silence 1, Speak With Animals (one species), or Ultrahearing, all [5]. ● *One* of Attractive‡, Fearlessness 2, Language (any, Accented/Accented), Mind Shield 1, Night Vision 4, or Protected Eyes 4, all [4]. ● *One* of Climatic Emphasis, Feathers, Fur, Penetrating Voice, Scales, Self-Styling Hair, Statuesque, or Teeth (Sharp Beak *or* Sharp Teeth), all [1].

Disadvantages: Faith Maintenance (21-50 people) [-30]. ● *One* of IQ -1, Bad Temper (6), Hideous (Universal)‡, or Low Empathy, all [-20]. ● *Two* of Bloodlust (12), Bully (12), Clueless, Cowardice (12), Dependent (Chief priest; 25% of own points; Friend; 9 or less), Disturbing Voice, Enemy (Utterly formidable antagonistic religion; Watcher; 9 or less), Impulsiveness (12), Intolerance (Religious), Laziness, Low Pain Threshold, Megalomania, No Sense of Humour, Secret (Running multiple rival cults), Selfish (6), Struggling†, or Supernatural Features (something bizarre), all [-10]. ● *Two* of Callous, Compulsive Carousing (12), Compulsive Neatness (12), Enemy (Deity of equal power; Rival; 9 or less), worsen Faith Maintenance to 51-100 people, Hidebound, Low TL 1, Oblivious, Overconfidence (12), Paranoia, Pyromania (12), Reputation -2 (As a dubious cult figure, among some rival cult), Secret (any past doctrinal inconsistency), or Stubbornness, all [-5].

Primary Skills: *Three* of Area Knowledge (cult's home area) (E) IQ+1 [2]-11; Acting, Disguise, Propaganda, or Public Speaking, all (A) IQ [2]-10; or Mimicry (any), Psychology (Human), Religious Ritual (own cult), or Theology (own cult), all (H) IQ-1 [2]-9.

Secondary Skills: Innate Attack (Beam) (E) DX [1]-10 *and* Intimidation (A) Will-1 [1]-9.

Background Skills: *Four* of Area Knowledge (Cori Celesti), Games (Chess), Savoir-Faire (High Society), or Shouting at Foreigners, all (E) IQ [1]-10; Connoisseur (Music *or* Wine), Fast-Talk, Hidden Lore (Spirit Lore), Leadership, or Occultism, all (A) IQ-1 [1]-9; Naturalist or Tactics, both (H) IQ-2 [1]-8; Carousing (E) HT [1]-10; or Detect Lies (H) Per-2 [1]-8.

* Members of the Congregation of a 275-point small god start out built on 27 points apiece.

† Wealth choices are mutually exclusive.

‡ Appearance choices are mutually exclusive.

Customisation Notes

Small gods come in many varieties, with widely varying powers. This template covers but one common type: an invisible, intangible being who may occasionally manifest in a more-or-less humanoid form defined by its worshippers' beliefs. A god who manifests as an animal might have the Quadruped disadvantage, which in turn means discounting ST and DX costs. Alternate Forms are another possibility, albeit an even more complicated one. Whatever a god's form, it has to materialise before lightning-bolting anyone, and its Invisibility doesn't work against supernatural perceptions.

Choose advantages and disadvantages to reflect the small god's nature and sphere of influence. As for social traits, a god's Wealth level represents material resources that it can call on, with liquid cash taking the form of spare funds at shrines or temples. This template assumes that the god has access to modest sums, with optional lower or higher Wealth implying a poorer or richer cult. It also assumes that the god has Status 0 – or to be precise, *no* particular Status in human society. Social Regard isn't mandatory, but a god with a more substantial Faith Maintenance requirement will need enough to ensure sufficient believers (and *sensible* gods preserve a safety margin).

TOUGH TROLL

200 points

You're something formidable; maybe not a genius, or subtle by human standards, but very good at what trolls do. You might work as muscle in the underworld, or as *heavy* infantry in an army. Your strength is crucial, but surviving in your line of work requires a little bit of cunning – or sense, at least – and you know how to *apply* your strength.

See the hick troll template (p. 135) for more on troll PCs. The attributes and secondary characteristics below include modifiers from the racial template.

Attributes: ST 18 [18*]; DX 11 [20]; IQ 8 [0]; HT 13 [10].
Secondary Characteristics: Damage 1d+2/3d; BL 97 lbs.†; HP 18 [0]; Will 9 [5]; Per 9 [0]; FP 13 [0]; Basic Speed 6.00 [0]; Basic Move 6 [0].
Advantages and Perks: Moderate-Sized Troll [83]. ● Language (local human tongue, Accented/None) [2]. ● DX +1 [20] or Outdoorsman 2 [20]; *or* ST +2 [18*] *and* HP +1 [2*]; *or* Per +1 [5] *and* Combat Reflexes [15]; *or* Damage Resistance 1 [5] *and* Unfazeable [15]. ● *Two* of HT +1, Will +2, or Damage Resistance 2, all [10]. ● *One* of Per +1, Basic Move +1, Rapid Healing, Reputation +2 (As a *solid* troll, among local trolls, *or* as *serious,* in the underworld), or Single-Minded, all [5]. ● *Two* of Acute Hearing 1, Fearlessness 1, Languages (any, Accented/None), or Resistant to Disease increased to (+8), all [2]. ● *One* of Boredom Immunity, Cultural Familiarity (local human culture), Fearsome Stare, Improvised Weapons (any), Limited Camouflage (Stone), or Sulphur Tolerance, all [1].
Disadvantages: *Two* of Bad Temper (12), Bully (12), Clueless, Gullibility (12), Literal-Minded, No Sense of Humour, Struggling, or Unluckiness, all [-10] – or swap a choice for Literacy in native Language reduced to Broken [-2], and *either* Appearance reduced to Hideous [-8] *or* Troll Nocturnalism (Mitigator, Sunscreen) [-8]. ● *Two* of Basic Move -1, Callous, Code of Honour (Pirate's), Ham-Fisted, Hidebound, Incurious, Innumerate, Intolerance (Dwarfs), Klutz, Low TL 1, Oblivious, Overconfidence (12), Reputation -2 (As trouble, in local community),

Social Stigma (Second-Class Citizen *or* Uneducated), Status -1, Stubbornness, or Truthfulness (12), all [-5].
Primary Skills: Axe/Mace (A) DX+1 [4]-12; Brawling (E) DX+2 [2]-13‡; Broadsword (A) DX+1 [4]-12; Polearm (A) DX+1 [4]-12; *and* Two-Handed Axe/Mace (A) DX+1 [4]-12. ● Then add +1 to any one of these [4].
Secondary Skills: *Three* of Camouflage (E) IQ+2 [4]-10; Soldier or Streetwise, both (A) IQ+1 [4]-9; Intimidation (A) Will+1 [4]-10; or Survival (Mountain) (A) Per+1 [4]-10.

> **Background Skills:** *Six* of Crossbow, Forced Entry, Shield, or Thrown Weapon (Axe), all (E) DX [1]-11; Spear, Stealth, or Throwing, all (A) DX-1 [1]-10; Area Knowledge (any), Gesture, Savoir-Faire (Military), or Shouting at Foreigners, all (E) IQ [1]-8; Naturalist (H) IQ-2 [1]-6; Carousing (E) HT [1]-13; or Urban Survival (A) Per-1 [1]-8. ● Then add +1 to any two of these [2].

* With 10% cost reduction for SM +1.
† Includes effects of racial Lifting ST.
‡ Improved from racial level.

Customisation Notes

Alternatively, swap the moderate-sized troll template for the big troll template [115], leave ST at the template base (20), and reduce optional advantages by 14 points (to 36 points' worth). In that case, remember that SM +2 reduces the cost of any extra ST, HP, or Lifting ST by 20%, not merely 10%.

Hunchbroad Modoscousin: Personalisation

Steve has 3 points left with which to personalise Hunchbroad. For a few more, he adds three quirks: "Likes wearing metal to the point of obsession" (Hunchbroad *is* old-school dwarfish), "Thinks that mountain dwarfs are hicks" (Steve feels that Hunchbroad needs a bit of roughness around the edges), and "Works through multiple tasks in alphabetical order" (because this *is* comedy). That gives 6 points to play with.

First, without Cultural Familiarity (Sto Plains/Uberwald), Hunchbroad won't be able to work very well with humans. Steve spends 1 point on this.

Next, Steve recalls Modo the Gardener, who can surely rate as a Contact. Area Knowledge (Unseen University) fits as his "Contact skill," and Steve goes for effective skill 15 (Modo should arguably be better, but he's very focussed on his job), appearing on 12 or less, and somewhat reliable (Modo won't *actually* lie or deliberately inform on Hunchbroad, but may talk in misleading gardening jargon, or let stuff slip). That's another 4 points gone.

That leaves just 1 point. Steve spends it on Mechanic (Animal-Drawn Vehicle), enabling Hunchbroad to fix the carts he drives – especially with the bonus from his Talent.

Hunchbroad is now a 100-point character.

"Are you sure you're in the right place?" the shopkeeper asked, looking at the young woman's expensive clothes and high heels.

"No," sighed Jemzarkiza, "but I need a tent anyway. I'll choose my own, thank you."

Something in her tone made the man retire to the other side of his shop, leaving the two women to their own devices.

"By the way," asked Jemzarkiza, "am I really on expenses?"

"Yes," said Captain Angua. "But."

"'But' isn't a sentence, Captain."

Angua shrugged. "You're working for the city here," she said, "which means that you're working for the Patrician. Who runs things on a budget."

"Oh well." Jemzarkiza turned her attention back to the shelves of equipment. "Whoever's paying, I'm not going out in the perpetual wind-driven hail you people call a climate without a decent tent."

Angua sighed, took off her helmet, unslung her sword, and sank down on a convenient stool with the air of a woman glad to take a load off her feet. "You think the weather here is bad, wait until you get a bit further hubwards," she said.

"I'll look forward to it," muttered Jemzarkiza. "Can we head over to the Thaumatological Park when we're done here?"

"Not on these expenses."

Jemzarkiza shrugged. "No need to account for what I get there, then," she said. "But I've got that advance on the cover mission pay from her ladyship, and I hear that the latest dis-organisers include DPS version 3-and-a-bit. That's worth having."

"DPS?"

"Disc Positioning System," Jemzarkiza explained. Seeing Angua's eyebrow still raised quizzically, she took a deep breath. "With version 1, the imp shrugged and told you that you were positioned on the Disc. These days, it leaps several miles in the air, then tells you **where** on the Disc it **thinks** you are when it comes back down."

There's lots of interesting *stuff* available on the Discworld, ranging from mundane household gear, through the ever-popular swords and axes, to magical devices infested with confused demons, and even *electrical* contraptions built by Uberwaldian mad doctors (don't get too excited – they usually need thunderstorms to power up). For game purposes, the most important slant on the subject is adventuring expenses, although tech level (*Technology Level*, pp. 30-31) plays a large role as well.

Player Characters and Possessions

At the start of play, you get some clothing for free (p. 148); otherwise, you own only what you can afford with your starting money, as determined by the campaign's TL and your personal wealth level (see *Starting Funds*, p. 33). Trying to find something from a higher tech level (TL) than the place you're shopping is often fruitless – but if you *do* find a special import, the price will be at least *doubled* for each TL difference (see *High TL*, p. 31). In addition to a cost and a TL, most purchases have a weight, which becomes important if you carry your gear around with you; see *Encumbrance and Move* (p. 168). Weapons and armour also have specialised statistics which matter if you get into a fight.

SETTLED VS. FOOTLOOSE

An important question at this point is whether your character is *settled*, with a place to live and probably a job, or a footloose *wanderer*. In many games, the GM will require all the PCs to be in the same boat. If you're all watchmen, students at Unseen University, or inhabitants of a big old castle in the Ramtops, you're all effectively settled, while if you're all classic fantasy "adventurers," you won't have such ties. Still, it's *sometimes* possible to mix the two options.

Settled characters have only 20% of their starting money available for "adventuring" gear. The other 80% is tied up in a home, spare clothing, etc. See *What Cost of Living Gets You* (p. 148) for what this 80% buys; don't try to account in detail for every penny. However, that rule assumes Wealth appropriate to Status. If, given a PC's Wealth level, 80% of his starting money is nothing like enough to cover what his Status implies, the GM can decree that his gear is ragged, his servants are mutinous, unreliable, or eccentric, and his home is mortgaged to the hilt – or just lower his *effective* Status to something he *can* afford.

Wanderers, on the other hand, can spend 100% of their starting money on moveable possessions. They must also worry about where they're going to sleep each night. The GM is entitled to ask such questions of footloose characters. If they spend *all* their cash on weapons and other cool gear, they'd better find paying work *fast,* or they're going to be starving on the street tomorrow.

Wanderers rarely have better than Comfortable wealth. Beyond that, you really *have* to settle down, unless you're the sort of old-school hero who rides into town with a pouch full of amazingly negotiable gemstones while wearing enough high-quality armour and weapons to immobilise a carthorse. Conversely, even in a game where every PC is supposed to be settled, Poor characters may be permitted to be footloose – poverty is all about uncertainty as to where the next meal is coming from. For those unfortunate enough to be Dead Broke, the question is academic.

ISSUED EQUIPMENT

Settled characters are also more likely to have jobs in which they're issued the gear they need for their work. In particular, most watchmen and soldiers are issued weapons and armour; likewise, hired craftsmen may use "workshop" tools. However, employees have little say in *what* they're issued, and generally can't take such things home – and if they use them for unauthorised purposes, or lose them, they'll get into trouble. "Issue" gear is often cheap or shabby, too; some workers end up buying better from their own funds.

STUFF YOU NEED AND STUFF YOU WANT

Having determined how much you have to spend, buy the starting possessions you want. Any unspent money is your "bank account" – which might even be held in a bank, if you're a posh city-dweller, but for most adventurers will consist of a collection of coins and negotiable stuff of varying reliability, stowed in a purse, wallet, or old sock. (The GM who wants to get players paranoid can remind them of this and then ask them whether having their home burgled or their pocket picked worries them more, but he should take care not to overdo it, as messing up the PCs' financial situation in trivial-but-annoying ways soon grows tiresome.) Most characters carry at least enough spare cash to buy lunch.

You also start play with a full wardrobe appropriate to your Status, which you need not purchase separately. Cost of living – from the *Status Table* (p. 37) – covers normal wear and tear, but if you suddenly have to replace your clothing, use the prices under *Clothes* (pp. 148-149).

Before you get too excited about the lists of gear later in this chapter, there's one last wrinkle . . .

ARMS CONTROL

A few items, especially weapons, may be legally restricted in some places. Personal armaments are usually tolerated – at least for aristocrats (who claim this as a traditional right), and for hunters and other people who need them for work – but heavy, military-style gear, poisons, and obvious assassination devices may be more-or-less formally banned. Explicitly illegal gear can only be obtained, if at all, with difficulty, personal risk, and much use of Streetwise skill, and at multiples of its list price.

> ## Travel Costs
>
> Travel on the Disc varies enormously in cost, depending on how much comfort and safety you demand, what sorts of vehicles or parties (if any) are going your way, how much of a hurry you're in, and the terrain involved. For basic considerations, see *Travel* (p. 18). Mile for mile, water travel is *much* cheaper – where it's available. Stagecoaches are certainly pricey; the trip from Ankh-Morpork to Lancre or back costs $40 for a single ticket (some of which may still be going to finance road improvements along the route). Air travel would be *very* expensive if money was involved, but usually involves calling in favours rather than paying cash.
>
> Travel doesn't always cost money. If you look tough *and* trustworthy – or, especially, if you're a wizard – people may be prepared to pay *you* to travel with *them,* for the extra security you offer. But if you just look tough, they'll avoid you.
>
> Thus, the GM can set prices, speeds, and options as seems appropriate and amusing at the time. They don't have to be stable, even from day to day.

What Cost of Living Gets You

How and where you live depends on your Status – or more precisely, on the Status which your income lets you support:

Status 8: At least one major palace, and several smaller palaces, fortresses, and hunting preserves. Scary guards, nobles competing to act as your servants, and government departments managing your wardrobe and stables.

Status 7: A large palace or formidable castle, plus other castles or mansions. Professional guards and lots of staff, a larger wardrobe than you could ever use, and plenty of nice horses.

Status 6: A moderate-sized palace, castle, or mansion, and other estates. Competent guards, a modest army of servants, and a large wardrobe and stables.

Status 5: A castle or manor, and some lesser holdings – or the best rooms in Unseen University. Numerous servants (including competent-*looking* guards), a large wardrobe, and adequate mounts or coaches.

Status 4: A castle, manor, or big town house. Enough servants, a nice wardrobe, a good horse or two, and maybe some heavies as guards.

Status 3: A manor, keep, or town house. A few servants (some possibly armed), multiple changes of clothes, and some good horses.

Status 2: A fine house somewhere *or* quarters in some great establishment. Staff to run your home, a good wardrobe (including formal wear), and adequate horses or a carriage.

Status 1: A comfortable house *or* a cottage, or good quarters in a grander establishment. A servant or two (if it fits your style), several changes of clothes, and a horse or mule.

Status 0: A rural cottage, or several rooms in town. Possibly a servant, or at least family members to help you out, and a couple of changes of clothes. In the country, a mule or pony; in town, enough credit to hire or borrow a mount, if necessary.

Status -1: A small cottage belonging to your overlord, a single rented room in town, or minimal quarters in the dingiest corners of some establishment. Clothes for your work, with minimal spares for emergencies.

Status -2: Shared quarters somewhere uncomfortable . . . or whatever space you can find.

Witches and some wizards replace horses or carriages with magic broomsticks. Academic wizards might appear to live a bit below their Status, but they have the resources of a university to call on, and they eat *very* well.

In some cases, weapon laws are "unofficial" but no less serious for that. In particular, the Assassins' Guild regards one or two weapon designs as too much competition in the hands of non-members, and unsporting for members, who can only use them outside of cities (where the Guild assumes that life isn't terribly civilised).

Living Expenses

Rather than account for every last expenditure on meals, room rents, new socks, and broken crockery, the rules assess a monthly *cost of living* payment that covers the basics of daily life. This appears on the *Status Table* (p. 37), as it's intimately linked to Status – it costs more to live like a shopkeeper than like a peasant, more to live like a duke than like a shopkeeper.

This system is something of an abstraction, as plenty of people on the Disc receive payments in kind or live directly off their own products – indeed, some peasants never see coinage in their lives, and many wizards at Unseen University take it for granted that the people of Ankh-Morpork supply them with food (in unspoken exchange for them not blowing things up *too* much). But here as in real life, money is a convenient reference-point. Similarly, the rules measure all transactions in Ankh-Morpork dollars despite the fact that this is far from the only currency in use on the Disc (see *Currencies*, p. 20).

FOOD AND DRINK

Cost of living assumes that you buy groceries and that you, your family, or your staff prepare your meals at home – or that if you always eat out, it's at places one level below your Status. When you eat out or purchase travel rations, use these guidelines:

Restaurant/Tavern: 1% of cost of living for breakfast or lunch, 2% for dinner, based on the Status of the restaurant's typical patron.

Travel Rations: 5% of cost of living for one week. Weighs 14 lbs.

Wine or Liquor: 1% of cost of living per bottle.

In all cases, treat Status greater than 3 as Status 3, except in unusual cases.

Example: Jemzarkiza is on the road. She's Status 1, with an image to maintain, so she frequents taverns of that standard. As her monthly cost of living is $60, lunch costs her $0.60 and dinner sets her back $1.20.

During her travels, she's invited to dinner by a high priest who's Status 5. She's advised that it's the local custom to take an appropriate bottle of wine as a gift for her host. Fortunately, Status tops out at 3 for these purposes. Cost of living for someone at Status 3 is $600, so Jemzarkiza has to spend $6 on one bottle. It's expensive, but she needs to ask a big favour . . .

CLOTHES

Clothing prices, too, are related to Status and given as a percentage of monthly cost of living. There are upper limits to this, though. High-Status individuals own *more* clothes (and the crown jewels of Status 7-8 rulers are worth silly amounts of money), but when buying one outfit, treat Status greater than 3 as Status 3.

Complete Wardrobe: Includes one to four sets of ordinary clothes, nightclothes, one set each of formal wear and winter clothes, and usually at least one outfit appropriate to your job (e.g., a uniform). 100% of cost of living; 20+ lbs.

Ordinary Clothes: One complete outfit, ranging in quality from cast-off rags to designer fashions, depending on Status. At minimum: undergarments, plus a tunic, blouse, or shirt with hose, skirt, or trousers – or a long robe or dress – and footwear. 20% of cost of living; 2 lbs.

Winter Clothes: As above, but heavier – suitable for Chilly temperatures and brief periods in Freezing conditions (p. 191). Includes a hat or hood, boots, and furs. 30% of cost of living; 4 lbs.

Formal Wear: Your best outfit, including accessories (hat, gloves, etc.) or jewellery. 40% of cost of living; 2 lbs.

Example: Jemzarkiza is shipwrecked and loses her luggage. She makes her way to the nearest town, where she decides that she needs a change of clothes. Fortunately, she has some cash in her pouch. With her Status 1, a standard outfit costs her $12 (20% of $60). Then she gets a formal dinner invitation from a friendly local and has to spend another $24 (40% of $60) on a gown for that.

After a week doing magical odd jobs, Jemzarkiza realises that there's an opening here for a consulting expert. However, the GM rules that she must *look* the part to get the business – and "town wizard" means Status 2. Monthly cost of living for Status 2 is $150, and a complete wardrobe will set her back 100% of that. This job had better pay well . . . Though if it works out, Jemzarkiza will have an excellent excuse to buy her Status up to 2 with points – and then to spend more points to raise her Wealth.

Weapons

Adventurers often carry weapons – and not *just* because it makes them look tough. Other people sometimes have a practical or social need to do the same. This might mean a nobleman's elegant fencing blade, without which his outfit would be incomplete; a travelling merchant's crossbow, to deter bandits; or the axe without which any normal dwarf feels naked.

When shopping for weapons, first decide *why* you need them. If your social position requires them, your options are usually predetermined; if they're mostly for intimidation, you want something as big, mean, and spiky as feasible; and if you prefer sneak attacks, look for concealability. In all cases, if there's any chance that you'll actually *use* them (and there is), they should be things you can wield effectively; so review your skills and ST, and *then* look at the weapon statistics. A weapon's damage rating is the basic measure of its effectiveness, but there are also such factors as effectiveness in parrying – and, for missile weapons, range and accuracy.

WEAPON STATISTICS

Weapon tables provide the items of information explained below. A given column will only appear on a table if it's germane to the weapons on that table. In all cases, "–" means the statistic doesn't apply, while "var." means the value varies.

On all such tables, weapons are listed under the skill required to use them. Skill names appear in capital letters, with defaults in parentheses; e.g., "**AXE/MACE (DX-5).**"

TL (Tech Level)

The tech level at which the weapon first becomes widespread. Usually, you may only buy weapons of the campaign's TL *or less.* You may even find yourself in places where the

effective TL is lower – unless the GM rules that special imports are available at accordingly higher cost (see *High TL*, p. 31).

Weapon

The class of weapon in question; e.g., "shortsword" or "longbow."

Damage

For most weapons – swords, axes, javelins, etc. – damage is ST-based, and expressed as a modifier to the wielder's basic thrusting (thr) or swinging (sw) damage, read from the *Damage Table* (p. 28). For example, a rapier does "thr+1"; so if you have ST 11, for a basic thrusting damage of 1d-1, you inflict 1d damage with a rapier. Swung weapons act as levers, and so do more damage. Bows and crossbows are a bit more complicated; see *Missile Weapons and Strength* (pp. 154-155).

However, a few missile weapons give damage as a fixed value. These inflict the same damage whatever the wielder's ST; e.g., an experimental firearm might list "2d+2," meaning that *any* user rolls 2d and adds 2 for damage.

Damage Type: An abbreviation indicates the *type* of injury or effect the attack causes:

Abbreviation	Damage Type	Abbreviation	Damage Type
cr	crushing	pi	piercing
cut	cutting	pi+	large piercing
imp	impaling	pi++	huge piercing
pi-	small piercing	spcl	special

A victim loses HP equal to the damage that penetrates his DR. *Halve* this injury for small piercing attacks; *increase it by 50%* for cutting and large piercing; and *double* it for impaling and huge piercing.

Reach

Melee weapons only.

The distance in yards at which a human-sized wielder can strike with the weapon. For example, reach "2" means that you can only strike at opponents two yards away – not closer *or* more distant. Reach "C" means that you can use the weapon in close combat (defined in *Range, Reach, and Close Combat,* pp. 176-177).

Some weapons have a continuum of reaches; e.g., a spear with reach "1, 2" can strike targets either one *or* two yards away. An asterisk (*) next to reach means the weapon is awkward, requiring a Ready manoeuvre to change reach (e.g., between 1 and 2). Otherwise, you can strike at foes at any distance within the weapon's reach.

Parry

Melee weapons only.

A number, such as "+2" or "-1," indicates a bonus or penalty to your Parry defence when using that weapon (see *Parrying,* pp. 180-181). For most weapons, this is "0," meaning "no modifier."

"F" means the weapon is a *fencing* weapon (see *Fencing Weapons,* p. 77).

"U" means the weapon is *unbalanced:* you cannot use it to parry if you've already used it to attack this turn (or vice versa).

"No" means the weapon *cannot parry at all.*

Acc (Accuracy)

Ranged weapons only.

Add Accuracy to your skill if you took an Aim manoeuvre (p. 175) on the turn prior to your attack.

Range

Ranged weapons only.

Two numbers, separated by a slash; the first is *Half-Damage Range* (1/2D) and the second is *Maximum Range* (Max), both measured in yards. Attacks on targets at or beyond 1/2D inflict half damage. The weapon *cannot attack at all* beyond Max.

Muscle-powered weapons usually list 1/2D and Max as multiples of the wielder's ST (for slings and thrown weapons) or the weapon's rated ST (for bows and crossbows), not as fixed ranges. For example, "×1/×1.5" means that 1/2D is ST×1 and Max is ST×1.5, so someone with ST 10 would have 1/2D 10, Max 15.

Shots

Ranged weapons only.

An indication of how often the weapon can be shot.

"T" means a *thrown* weapon. To "reload," fetch it or ready a new weapon.

"1" followed by a parenthetical number indicates a single-shot weapon that requires preparation between shots; the parenthetical figure is the number of one-second Ready manoeuvres needed to

reload. A bow or sling takes two turns to reload: one to pull the arrow or stone from the quiver or pouch, one to nock the arrow and draw the bowstring or "spin up" the sling. For a crossbow, you must spend a variable amount of time preparing the weapon, depending on your ST and its power (see *Missile Weapons and Strength*, pp. 154-155), and another turn drawing and placing the bolt. You can reduce these times by one turn with a successful use of Fast-Draw (p. 73) to get out the ammunition effectively instantly. Conversely, you may take longer between shots to Aim (p. 175).

"2" or higher is possible for weapons that hold multiple shots: wildly ornate repeating crossbows, overcomplicated siege engines, etc. Use the rules for single-shot devices, but ignore the time needed to draw ammo until after you've taken this many shots.

Cost

The price of a new weapon, in Ankh-Morpork dollars. For swords and knives, this includes a sheath or a scabbard.

Weight

The weapon's weight, in pounds. For missile weapons, the weight of one shot (arrow, bolt, sling bullet, etc.) appears after a slash.

ST (Strength)

The minimum Strength required to use the weapon properly.

For a *melee* or *thrown* weapon, if this is higher than your ST, you suffer -1 to weapon skill per point of ST you lack *and* lose one extra FP at the end of any fight that lasts long enough to fatigue you. With all such weapons, your effective ST for damage purposes cannot exceed *three times* the weapon's minimum ST. For instance, a large knife has minimum ST 6, so its "maximum ST" is 18; if your ST were 19+, you would compute your damage as if you had ST 18.

Missile weapons require some additional special rules; see *Missile Weapons and Strength* (pp. 154-155).

Natural "weapons" (punches, kicks, etc.) have neither minimum nor maximum ST.

"†" means the weapon requires two hands. If you have at least 1.5 times the listed ST (round *up*), you can use such a weapon in one hand, but it becomes *unready* after you attack. If you have at least *twice* the listed ST, you can wield it one-handed with no readiness penalty. But if it requires one hand to hold it and another to operate a moving part, like a bow or a crossbow, it *always* requires two hands, regardless of ST.

"‡" means the weapon requires two hands *and* becomes unready after you attack with it, unless you have at least 1.5 times the listed ST (round *up*). To use it one-handed without it becoming unready, you need at least *three times* the listed ST.

"M" means that the weapon is usually mounted on a heavy tripod or the back of a special cart. *Ignore* the listed ST and Bulk when firing from such a mount.

Bulk

Ranged weapons only.

A measure of weapon size and handiness. Bulk modifies your weapon skill when you Move and Attack (p. 175), and it serves as a penalty to Holdout (p. 76) when you attempt to conceal the weapon.

Notes

Numbers listed here refer to applicable footnotes (if any) at the end of the table.

Improvised Monster-Slaying Weapons

Supernatural creatures are frequently susceptible to things that don't normally rate as very good weapons – consider vampires and their problems with wooden stakes. Also, peasant mobs often show up with the first implements that come to hand. Some common examples:

Flaming Torch: Treat as a small truncheon, but in addition to crushing damage, each attack that hits does 1 point of burning damage (2 points on a critical hit).

Pitchfork: Treat as a spear, but because of poor balance, pitchforks *must* be used two-handed, give -2 to effective skill, and cannot be thrown. The target has -1 to Dodge (twice as many points to avoid), but +1 to Block or Parry (twice as many points to get hung up on things).

Wooden Stake: Treat a small stake as a large knife that can only do thrusting damage, a large one as a spear that suffers -2 to damage (large wooden points aren't very good). Both *can* be thrown.

All of these weapons lack penetrating ability; *double* the target's effective Damage Resistance (if any).

Melee Weapons

If there's more than one way to use a weapon, each method gets its own line on the table.

MELEE WEAPON TABLE

AXE/MACE (DX-5)

TL	Weapon	Damage	Reach	Parry	Cost	Weight	ST	Notes
0	Axe	sw+2 cut	1	0U	$3	4	11	[1]
0	Club	sw+2 cr	1	0U	$1.75	5	12	
0	Hatchet	sw cut	1	0	$2	2	8	[1]
1	Mace	sw+3 cr	1	0U	$2.50	5	12	[1]
1	Small Mace	sw+2 cr	1	0U	$1.75	3	10	[1]
3	Pick	sw+1 imp	1	0U	$3.50	3	10	[2]

BROADSWORD (DX-5)

TL	Weapon	Damage	Reach	Parry	Cost	Weight	ST	Notes
0	Large Truncheon	sw+1 cr	1	0	$0.25	3	10	
or		thr+1 cr	1	0	–	–	10	
2	Broadsword	sw+1 cut	1	0	$30	3	10	
or		thr+2 imp	1	0	–	–	10	

FLAIL (DX-6)

TL	Weapon	Damage	Reach	Parry	Cost	Weight	ST	Notes
3	Agatean Numknuts	sw+1 cr	1	0U	$1	2	7	[3]
3	Morningstar	sw+3 cr	1	0U	$4	6	12	[4]

KNIFE (DX-4)

TL	Weapon	Damage	Reach	Parry	Cost	Weight	ST	Notes
0	Large Knife	sw-2 cut	C, 1	-1	$2	1	6	
or		thr imp	C	-1	–	–	6	[1]
0	Small Knife	sw-3 cut	C, 1	-1	$1.50	0.5	5	
or		thr-1 imp	C	-1	–	–	5	[1]
1	Dagger	thr-1 imp	C	-1	$1	0.25	5	[1]
2	Hatpin	thr-2 imp	C	-2	$0.30	0.1	2	[5]

POLEARM (DX-5)

TL	Weapon	Damage	Reach	Parry	Cost	Weight	ST	Notes
3	Halberd	sw+5 cut	2, 3*	0U	$7.50	12	13‡	
or		sw+4 imp	2, 3*	0U	–	–	13‡	[2]
or		thr+3 imp	1-3*	0U	–	–	12†	
3	Short Glaive	sw+2 cut	1, 2*	0U	$4	6	9†	
or		thr+3 imp	1, 2*	0	–	–	9†	

RAPIER (DX-5)

TL	Weapon	Damage	Reach	Parry	Cost	Weight	ST	Notes
4	Rapier	thr+1 imp	1, 2	0F	$25	2.75	9	

SHIELD (DX-4)

TL	Weapon	Damage	Reach	Parry	Cost	Weight	ST	Notes
0	Shield Bash	thr cr	1	No	var.	var.	–	[6]

SHORTSWORD (DX-5)

TL	Weapon	Damage	Reach	Parry	Cost	Weight	ST	Notes
0	Small Truncheon	sw cr	1	0	$1	1	6	
or		thr cr	1	0	–	–	6	
1	Shortsword	sw cut	1	0	$20	2	8	
or		thr+1 imp	1	0	–	–	8	
2	Sickle Sword	sw+1 cut	1	0	$20	3	10	
or		thr-2 imp	1	0	–	–	10	

MELEE WEAPON TABLE (CONTINUED)

SMALLSWORD (DX-5)

TL	Weapon	Damage	Reach	Parry	Cost	Weight	ST	Notes
4	Smallsword	thr+1 imp	1	0F	$20	1.5	5	

SPEAR (DX-5)

TL	Weapon	Damage	Reach	Parry	Cost	Weight	ST	Notes
0	Spear	thr+2 imp	1*	0	$2	4	9	[1]
	two hands	thr+3 imp	1, 2*	0	–	–	9†	
1	Javelin	thr+1 imp	1	0	$1.50	2	6	[1]

STAFF (DX-5)

TL	Weapon	Damage	Reach	Parry	Cost	Weight	ST	Notes
0	Quarterstaff	sw+2 cr	1, 2	+2	$0.50	4	7†	
	or	thr+2 cr	1, 2	+2	–	–	7†	

TWO-HANDED AXE/MACE (DX-5)

TL	Weapon	Damage	Reach	Parry	Cost	Weight	ST	Notes
0	Big Club	sw+4 cr	1, 2*	0U	$4	12	13‡	[7]
0	Very Big Club	sw+5 cr	1, 2*	0U	$5	15	16‡	
0	Huge Club	sw+7 cr	1, 2*	0U	$7	21	23‡	
0	Monster Club	sw+9 cr	1, 2*	0U	$9	27	29‡	
1	Great Axe	sw+3 cut	1, 2*	0U	$5	8	12‡	
1	Scythe	sw+2 cut	1	0U	$0.75	5	11‡	
	or	sw imp	1	0U	–	–	11‡	[2]

TWO-HANDED SWORD (DX-5)

TL	Weapon	Damage	Reach	Parry	Cost	Weight	ST	Notes
3	Greatsword	sw+3 cut	1, 2	0	$45	7	12†	
	or	thr+3 imp	2	0	–	–	12†	

Notes

[1] Can be thrown; see the *Thrown Weapon Table* (p. 153).

[2] May get *stuck* in victims. If this attack penetrates your opponent's DR and injures him, you must either let go of the weapon or spend your next turn trying to free it, which requires a ST roll. Failure on this ST roll means you must either let go or keep trying on later turns. Success indicates that the weapon comes free and inflicts half the injury it did going in! Until the weapon comes free, your victim has to roll a Quick Contest of ST with you in order to move further away from you. If he wins, he may move, yanking your weapon from your grasp; if you win, he's going nowhere; and on a tie, the weapon pulls free, again inflicting half the original injury.

[3] Attempts to *parry* this weapon are at -2; fencing weapons ("F" parry) cannot parry it at all. Attempts to *block* it are at -1.

[4] Attempts to *parry* this weapon are at -4; fencing weapons ("F" parry) cannot parry it at all. Attempts to *block* it are at -2.

[5] This isn't technically a weapon, but the sort of heavy-duty hatpins favoured by the likes of Granny Weatherwax can do a lot of damage in skilled hands.

[6] For statistics and defensive applications, see *Shields* (p. 155).

[7] Might represent a *huge* blunt instrument for a strong human or dwarf to swing, or a hefty troll club. A warrior with ST 20 can use it two-handed without it becoming unready after an attack – and someone with ST 39 (!) can swing it one-handed (using Axe/Mace skill), and it still won't become unready after an attack. Yes, there are trolls that strong.

MELEE WEAPON QUALITY

You can spend more for especially good *cutting* or *impaling* weapons. Such quality comes in two levels:

Fine: A fine sword-class or fencing weapon costs *four times* as much. Other fine weapons cost *three times* as much if they do only impaling damage (e.g., spears), or *10 times* as much if they're capable of cutting damage. Fine weapons get +1 to damage.

Very Fine: This is limited to sword-class and fencing weapons. Very fine blades cost 20 times as much and get +2 to damage.

High-quality weapons also have less chance of breaking at embarrassing moments if using the optional rules under *Parrying Heavy Weapons* (p. 181).

Weapon quality for combat purposes has little to do with quality of *appearance*. To acquire a "presentation" sword with jewelled pommel and gilded blade, just spend lots of extra money – Discworld craftsmen will happily oblige you! The weapon won't be any more use in a fight, though.

Thrown Weapons

Many weapons can be hurled using specialisations of the Thrown Weapon skill. Most of these double as melee weapons (see the *Melee Weapon Table*, pp. 151-152).

THROWN WEAPON TABLE

THROWN WEAPON (AXE/MACE) (DX-4)

TL	Weapon	Damage	Acc	Range	Weight	Shots	Cost	ST	Bulk	Notes
0	Axe	sw+2 cut	2	×1/×1.5	4	T	$3	11	-3	
0	Hatchet	sw cut	1	×1.5/×2.5	2	T	$2	8	-2	
1	Mace	sw+3 cr	1	×0.5/×1	5	T	$2.50	12	-4	
1	Small Mace	sw+2 cr	1	×1/×1.5	3	T	$1.75	10	-3	

THROWN WEAPON (KNIFE) (DX-4)

TL	Weapon	Damage	Acc	Range	Weight	Shots	Cost	ST	Bulk	Notes
0	Large Knife	thr imp	0	×0.8/×1.5	1	T	$2	6	-2	
0	Small Knife	thr-1 imp	0	×0.5/×1	0.5	T	$1.50	5	-1	
1	Dagger	thr-1 imp	0	×0.5/×1	0.25	T	$1	5	-1	

THROWN WEAPON (SPEAR) (DX-4)

TL	Weapon	Damage	Acc	Range	Weight	Shots	Cost	ST	Bulk	Notes
0	Spear	thr+3 imp	2	×1/×1.5	4	T	$2	9	-6	
1	Javelin	thr+1 imp	3	×1.5/×2.5	2	T	$1.50	6	-4	

THROWN WEAPON (STICK) (DX-4)

TL	Weapon	Damage	Acc	Range	Weight	Shots	Cost	ST	Bulk	Notes
2	Boomerang Croissant	sw cr	2	×6/×10	1	T	$1	6	-2	[1]

THROWN WEAPON (THROWING STAR) (DX-4)

TL	Weapon	Damage	Acc	Range	Weight	Shots	Cost	ST	Bulk	Notes
3	Throwing Star	thr-1 cut	1	×0.5/×1	0.1	T	$0.15	5	0	

Notes

[1] See *Dwarf Bread Weapons* (below). This will return to the thrower if he voluntarily attacks at -5 to skill and *doesn't* hit. He can then catch it if he takes a Ready manoeuvre on his next turn and makes a DX roll. But it's a serious military weapon. Really.

THROWN WEAPON QUALITY

Higher-quality versions of thrown weapons which do *cutting* or *impaling* damage can be purchased using the rules under *Melee Weapon Quality* (p. 152).

Missile Weapons

Discworld societies have an assortment of muscle-powered missile weapons. Perhaps the most common in the chronicles is the crossbow, widely used by both watchmen and assassins, and sometimes handled much as guns are in stories from higher-tech worlds. There are quite a few small "pistol crossbows" around, filling the niche occupied by pistols elsewhere (in some places, high-ST pistol crossbows are known as "horsebows," because they're mostly carried by elite cavalry). However, bows are far from unknown, and slings also exist. Personal firearms (as opposed to cannon; see *Artillery*, p. 155) *are* effectively unknown, although they're within the capabilities of TL4 engineering, even without Leonard of Quirm's absent-minded doodles; the few rulers who know about the theory treat them as highly illegal.

Dwarf Bread Weapons

One ancient dwarf practise that has fallen into decline is the baking of military bread. Dwarf bread (p. 277) is as hard as stone and can hold an edge, allowing a skilled baker to create effective weapons. Treat bread weapons as equivalent to standard-quality metal for cost and durability. These days, though, iron is more convenient and mostly preferred, and battle bread is rarely found outside of the small Dwarf Bread Museum in Ankh-Morpork and traditional sporting events and combat exhibitions in the mountains. (Champion bread-throwers are said to be able to take the tops off a line of six hard-boiled eggs at 50 yards.) Still, even an ordinary dwarfish scone can be deadly in skilled hands.

Known battle-bread weapons include close-combat and guerrilla crumpets, throwing toast, combat muffins, and drop scones (lobbed off walls during sieges). Some of these are equivalent to thrown hatchets or small maces, while daintier confections may be treated as throwing stars. Boomerang croissants – on the *Thrown Weapon Table* (above) – are rare, but stylish. Treat other types as well-chosen rocks weighing 1-6 lbs. (see *Throwing*, p. 78).

Melee loaves are even rarer; they can be made equivalent to any type of one-handed axe, hatchet, or crushing weapon. Defensive bagels are used as shields.

MISSILE WEAPON TABLE

BLOWPIPE (DX-6)

TL	Weapon	Damage	Acc	Range	Weight	Shots	Cost	ST	Bulk	Notes
0	Blowpipe	1d-3 pi-	1	×4	1/0.05	1(2)	$1.50	2	-6	[1]

BOW (DX-5)

TL	Weapon	Damage	Acc	Range	Weight	Shots	Cost	ST	Bulk	Notes
0	Longbow	thr+2 imp	3	×15/×20	3/0.1	1(2)	$10	11†	-8	
0	Short Bow	thr imp	1	×10/×15	2/0.1	1(2)	$2.50	7†	-6	
1	Composite Bow	thr+3 imp	3	×20/×25	4/0.1	1(2)	$45	10†	-7	

CROSSBOW (DX-4)

TL	Weapon	Damage	Acc	Range	Weight	Shots	Cost	ST	Bulk	Notes
2	Crossbow	thr+4 imp	4	×20/×25	6/0.06	1(4)	$7.50	7†	-6	
2	Troll Crossbow	thr+5 imp	4	×22/×28	12/0.1	1(4)	$10	16†	-9	[2]
3	Pistol Crossbow	thr+2 imp	1	×15/×20	4/0.06	1(4)	$7.50	7	-4	[1]
4	Spring Gun	thr+4 imp	3	×20/×25	5/0.06	1(4)	$20	10	-4	[1, 3]

SLING (DX-6)

TL	Weapon	Damage	Acc	Range	Weight	Shots	Cost	ST	Bulk	Notes
0	Sling	sw pi	0	×6/×10	0.5/0.05	1(2)	$1	6	-4	[1, 4]

Notes

[1] Requires *two* hands to ready, but only *one* hand to attack.

[2] Adapted from small siege engines for the use of troll watchmen in Ankh-Morpork – not usually within troll society manufacturing capability.

[3] Basically a metal tube with an extremely powerful internal spring and an ingenious built-in cocking mechanism, equivalent in effect to a "goat's foot" (see *Missile Weapons and Strength*, below). Usually made with a high ST rating (14+) – the user is only expected to get one shot per fight, but that should be by surprise. Effectively highly illegal in Ankh-Morpork, where Commander Vimes will treat any user as a murderer and the Assassins' Guild have it on a banned list. The Guild consider spring guns dishonourable for their people to use and proof of intent to commit unlicenced assassinations for anyone else, but they have a couple in their armoury, and *occasionally* issue them to members on important missions a long way outside of the city.

[4] Can lob stones (TL0) or lead bullets (TL2). Lead bullets give +1 damage and *double* range.

MISSILE WEAPONS AND STRENGTH

The meaning of the ST statistic listed for missile weapons varies by weapon type. For *slings*, ST works as for melee and thrown weapons: Damage and range are based on your ST, and while you can use a sling if your ST is too low, you suffer -1 to skill per point of ST deficit *and* lose one extra FP at the end of any fight that lasts long enough to fatigue you. Your effective ST for damage purposes cannot exceed *three times* the sling's minimum ST.

For *bows*, each individual weapon has its own ST rating, which can vary among bows of that type. The ST listed for each weapon type is the *lowest* for which such a weapon can be made.[1] The bow's damage and range are based on its own ST rating, *not* on its user's ST. Anyone can use a bow if his ST is equal to or greater than the weapon's; you need that much to draw it properly. Thus, if you have ST 15, you can easily use a ST 10 bow – but range and damage are still only based on ST 10.

Crossbows – and the rare, functionally equivalent *spring gun* – are more complicated. As with bows, the ST on the table is the *lowest* possible for the type, and each weapon has its own ST rating used for damage and range. You can draw the string and prepare the crossbow with three one-second Ready manoeuvres if your lifting ST (ST + Lifting ST) is equal to or greater than the crossbow's ST rating. If the crossbow's ST exceeds your lifting ST by no more than 4, you can cock it in 20 seconds with the aid of a lever mechanism such as a "goat's foot" ($2.50, 2 lbs.); something similar is built into the spring gun. Complicated crank mechanisms can let you ready crossbows of almost any ST, but are fiddly and time-consuming. In all cases, add one final Ready manoeuvre to draw and place the bolt. Anyone can *shoot* any crossbow if their personal ST is at least equal to the minimum possible ST rating for the weapon type; if it's too low, they have -1 to skill per point of ST deficit.

Example: Lance-Constable Klump is a burly fellow with ST 13, but he has only just joined the City Watch, which is currently a bit short on weapons, so he's handed a standard-issue crossbow with a ST rating of 10. He can ready it in four seconds (including getting the bolt out of his quiver), and it does damage based on ST 10. As ST 10 means 1d-2 thrust damage, and a crossbow does thrust+4 impaling, that's 1d+2.

While he's on the range, Klump tries a couple of other crossbows out of curiosity. Constable "Tiny Fred" Grudborr's personal crossbow is rated for ST 16; Klump can only draw it with the aid of a goat's foot lever, but if he shot somebody with it, he'd do 1d+5 damage. He also picks up a troll colleague's "troll crossbow," made for a ST 22 user; the only way he could draw it would be with a crank. He shoots it once after its regular user has loaded it for him.

---

1. *In theory, there ought to be maximum possible ST ratings too, but Discworld armourers show great ingenuity about that.*

Minimum ST for a troll crossbow is 16, so he's at -3 to skill, but he can still pull the trigger. It does 2d+5 damage; the target disintegrates, and Klump puts the weapon down and backs away.

Finally, the newly promoted Constable Klump gets a crossbow that really suits him, being rated for ST 13. He can prepare it for use in four seconds – or three if he makes his roll against Fast-Draw (Arrow/Bolt) skill, which he has been learning. When he shoots, he does 1d+4 impaling damage.

AMMUNITION COSTS

An arrow or a crossbow bolt costs $0.10. Lead bullets for slings and darts for blowpipes cost $0.05 for a bag of 10 (but the latter usually carry drugs or poisons that cost a *lot* more). Sling *stones* are free – although the strict GM can insist that users spend time scrounging for them.

MISSILE WEAPON QUALITY

Bows and crossbows can be of *fine* quality for four times list price. This increases 1/2D and Max range by 20%, and grants +1 to reactions from weapons obsessives who see them. (The Disc has a slightly worrying subculture which supports magazines such as *Bows & Ammo*, though few of these people are particularly skilled with weapons themselves.) Arrows and bolts can be *fine* for three times list price, giving +1 to damage.

Shields

Shields are TL1, cost $3, and weigh 15 lbs. They're used with Shield skill (p. 81) to block and to bash. They *also* give +2 to *all* defence rolls – dodges, parries, and blocks – against any attack from a direction where the shield offers protection (a broad arc to the front and to the side where you carry the shield).

A shield usually takes a few seconds to ready for use or to discard, although you may be able to grab one for emergency use in a single second. If it's strapped to an arm, you can use that hand to hold something but not to wield weapons.

Armour

Armour is potentially a remarkably complicated subject, as it can be made of all sorts of materials – e.g., leather, thick cloth, metal plates (bronze, iron, or steel), or interlinked mail segments – and varies widely in style and coverage. Most people who wear it at all go for something solid on the torso (the largest target) and a good helmet on the head (the most important target[1]), with various levels of protection elsewhere. Weight, flexibility, and vision are all concerns, as are style and fashion. However, such complexity is beyond the scope of the combat rules, which don't concern themselves much with precisely where a blow hits, abstracting such questions to a simple system of Hit Points.

Consequently, armour is similarly abstracted here. Each set listed in the *Armour Table* (below) *might* consist of a whole-body suit of a single material, from thick padded cloth to fancy steel plates – but it could just as easily represent a few pieces of rugged protection for important areas, with something lighter but still functional elsewhere. For simplicity, the rules assume that any

---

1. *In most people's opinion, anyway. Some very odd armour has been designed for people with different opinions.*

Artillery

Armies employ an assortment of siege engines and artillery pieces. In the Agatean Empire, these include gunpowder cannon, which are sophisticated in conception but manufactured in a society which regards practical skills as inferior to classical scholarship. The *Missile Weapon Table* includes no weapons used with Heavy Weapon skills (p. 74), because such things are semi-portable plot devices, not personal gear. The general rule is that any ordinary character hit by one is going to be turned into scenery – a *light* bolt-throwing engine might do 5d imp; a typical Agatean "Barking Dog" cannon, 15d pi++ – but such terrors cost hundreds or thousands of dollars, and might take several *minutes* to load.

such variability in armour protection "averages out," and that the results of blows landing on a more or less robust piece are subsumed into the random rolls for damage. Likewise, any suit that provides a given average level of protection is assumed to cost about the same amount of money.

Thus, armour has a single Damage Resistance (DR) value, which subtracts *directly* from the damage inflicted by enemies' attacks: weapons, punches, bites, magical fireballs, and so on. The most effective armour is of course *heavy* – its weight can hinder you (see *Encumbrance and Move*, p. 168), penalising your Dodge score and your attacks and defences with fencing, Judo, and Karate skills.

For example, a human watchman in Ankh-Morpork is issued with a mail shirt, a light breastplate, a metal helmet, and some leather odds and ends. These bits add up to *about* 30 lbs. of weight, so they're classified as "medium armour" with an overall DR of 3. If a drunken dwarf swings an axe at a watchman for 1d+3 cutting damage but rolls only 4 points, getting 1 point through the DR, he maybe hit the watchman's breastplate hard enough to give the copper some unpleasant but survivable bruised ribs. If someone stabs the same watchman with a small knife for 1d-2 damage and rolls the maximum 4 points, again with 1 point penetrating DR, he presumably gashed an unprotected arm, but didn't do as much harm as he would have against an unarmoured victim, because he couldn't aim a solid stab at that well-protected chest.

And before anyone asks – no, you can't layer multiple suits of armour. It gets locked and tangled up, and you fall over, okay?

If you want to go into much more detail on specific locations on the wearer's body, and armour for each area, excellent optional rules appear in the **GURPS Basic Set,** and **GURPS Low-Tech** and **GURPS Martial Arts** add even more sophistication.

ARMOUR TABLE

All suits on this table include any light clothing or padding worn underneath; you don't have to buy that separately. The following information appears for each suit:

Armour: The suit type.
DR: The amount of Damage Resistance the suit gives. Subtract this from the damage done by any blow striking the wearer.

Cost: The suit's price, in Ankh-Morpork dollars.

Weight: The suit's weight, in pounds.

TL: The tech level at which armour of this grade becomes available.

Armour	DR	Cost	Weight	TL	Notes
Very Light	1	$7.50	9 lbs.	1	[1]
Light	2	$17.50	20 lbs.	1	[2]
Medium	3	$26	30 lbs.	2	[3]
Mail	4	$50	75 lbs.	2	[4]
Plate	6	$200	90 lbs.	3	[5]
Jousting Plate	7	$320	110 lbs.	3	[6]

Notes

[1] Typically soft leather and thick fabrics (which can pass as civilian clothes), or maybe studded leathers and unprotected limbs.

[2] Typically heavy boiled leathers, or a mail shirt and some light trimmings.

[3] Mostly light scale and reinforced leather, or a mixture of pieces, such as a watchman's cheap breastplate and nearly bare limbs.

[4] Mail or scale over much of the body – or a chunky breastplate and helmet, and slightly less protected limbs.

[5] Full-body plate, including a helmet that eliminates peripheral vision.

[6] The heaviest available armour, including a helmet that eliminates peripheral vision.

General Equipment

The Disc's shops and markets, especially in big cities full of clever craftsmen, sell all sorts of kit – far more than can be detailed here. If the players want something that isn't listed, the GM who's short on time for detailed research can simply improvise and use common sense. He might make a note in case the PCs want to repeat their purchase (or sale) later, but he shouldn't worry too much about consistency; the Disc is old-fashioned enough that market prices can shift due to random influences. In particular, high demand – or the expressions on the faces of desperate adventurers – can push prices up fast. This gives the GM an excellent excuse to change them if they were too generous the first time round.

The following are a few things that adventurers may want, with the TL at which they become available, and their price and weight.

CAMPING AND TRAVEL GEAR

Backpack, Frame (TL1). Holds 100 lbs. of gear. $5, 10 lbs.

Backpack, Small (TL1). Holds 40 lbs. of gear. $3, 3 lbs.

Blanket (TL1). A warm sleeping blanket. $1, 4 lbs.

Climbing Gear (TL2). Hammer, spikes, etc. $1, 4 lbs.

Compass (TL2). Has an octiron needle, which aligns with the Disc's magical field and points toward the hub. At TL3+, Discworld compasses are good enough to give +1 to Navigation skill. $2.50, 1 lb.

Fishhooks and Line (TL0). Basic gear for Fishing skill; needs a pole. $2.50, 0.1 lb.

Group Basics (TL0). Basic equipment for Professional Skill (Cooking) and Survival for a group. Cook pot, rope, hatchet, etc., for 3-8 campers. $2.50, 20 lbs.

Iron Spike (Piton) (TL2). For climbing, spiking doors, etc. $0.05, 0.5 lb.

Personal Basics (TL0). Minimum gear for camping: -2 to any Survival roll without it. Includes utensils, tinderbox or flint and steel, etc., as TL permits. $0.25, 1 lb.

Pole, 6' (TL0). For pitching tents, fishing, or prodding items. $0.25, 3 lbs.

Pole, 10' (TL0). For things you wouldn't touch with a 6' pole. $0.40, 5 lbs.

Saddlebags (TL1). Hold 40 lbs. $5, 3 lbs.

Sleeping Fur (TL0). Warm unless wet. $2.50, 8 lbs.

Tent, 1-Man (TL0). Includes ropes; no poles needed. $2.50, 5 lbs.

Tent, 2-Man (TL0). Includes ropes; requires one 6-foot pole. $4, 12 lbs.

Tent, 4-Man (TL0). Includes ropes; requires two poles. $7.50, 30 lbs.

Towel, Small/Blanket Patch (TL1). 18" square. The miniature blankets issued to watchmen for inflicting existential paralysis on bogeymen (pp. 361-362) are blue. $0.10, 0.5 lb.

Traveller's Rations (TL0). One meal of dried meat, cheese, etc. $0.10, 0.5 lb.

ASSORTED TOOLS AND EQUIPMENT

Balance and Weights (TL1). For weighing goods. $1.75, 3 lbs.

Bandages (TL0). Bandages for a half-dozen wounds – basic equipment for First Aid skill. $0.50, 2 lbs.

Book (TL2). Book prices vary enormously with size, production quality, popularity, etc., and they are currently falling rapidly with the spread of moveable-type printing. A modest-sized mass-market bestseller such as Nanny Ogg's *The Joye of Snacks* costs $0.50 – but a limited-print-run work, let alone hand-copied volume, could easily go for hundreds. Books concerning magic have always cost more (the safe, trustworthy ones, anyway), and aren't coming down in price, because nobody who understands the subject will let them be printed; the metal of the plates might *remember* the magic.

Bottle, Ceramic (TL1). Holds about 2 pints of liquid. $0.15, 1 lb.

Candle, Tallow (TL1). Smoky! Lasts 12 hrs. $0.25, 1 lb.

Caroc Cards (TL3). See p. 19. A *good* deck, suitable for divination, costs $5. Decks suitable for casual gambling are cheaper; even casinos generally only use $2.50 decks. The cost of a deck that has been marked or otherwise prepared for dishonest use . . . varies with the situation. 0.5 lb.

Cement, Ceramic (TL2). One pot can repair up to 5 HP damage to a golem. Per pot: $1, 2 lbs.

Clockwork Pocket-Watch (TL4). Discworld watches – invented to replace the briefly fashionable imp-infested devices (p. 160) – are often dwarf-made, and they give a degree of reliability not achieved on our world until TL5, at least at these prices. Jewelled, engraved, or otherwise decorated cases can add almost anything to the price. $2.50, 0.25 lb.

Cord, 3/16" (TL0). Supports 90 lbs. Per 10 yards: $0.05, 0.5 lb.

Crowbar, 3' (TL2). Can serve as a small mace in combat, but at -1 to skill. $1, 3 lbs.

First Aid Kit (TL2). A complete kit for treating wounds, with bandages, ointments, etc. Gives +1 to First Aid skill. $2.50, 2 lbs.

Hip Quiver (TL0). Holds 20 arrows or bolts. $0.75, 1 lb.

Hourglass (TL2). $2, 2 lbs.

Lantern (TL2). Burns for 24 hours on 1 pint of oil. $1, 2 lbs.

Lockpicks (TL3). Basic equipment for Lockpicking skill. $2.50, 0.1 lb.

Matches (TL4). Crude by higher-TL standards, and probably quite poisonous, but eminently useful even so. Box of 20: $0.20, negligible weight.

Oil (TL2). For lantern. Per pint: $0.10, 1 lb.

Pouch or Purse, Small (TL1). Holds 3 lbs. $0.50, negligible weight.

Religious Symbol, Silver (TL1). $15, 0.25 lb.

Religious Symbol, Wood (TL0). $0.50, 1 lb.

Rope, 3/8" (TL0). Supports 300 lbs. Per 10 yards: $0.25, 1.5 lbs.

Rope, 3/4" (TL1). Supports 1,100 lbs. Per 10 yards: $1.25, 5 lbs.

Scribe's Kit (TL3). Quills, ink bottles, penknife, paper. $2.50, 2 lbs.

Sewing Kit (TL0). Needles, thimble, and plenty of plain thread, all in some kind of case or pouch. Basic equipment for Sewing skill, enough to fix up to 5 HP to a Repairable zombie, and sometimes required for surgical work on humans. Fancy silks can add almost anything to price. $1, 0.5 lb.

Shoulder Quiver (TL0). Holds 12 arrows or bolts. $0.50, 0.5 lb.

Shovel (TL1). Speeds up digging. $0.60, 6 lbs.

Spyglass (TL4). A simple telescope, mostly used at sea. Gives ×4 magnification, which eliminates -2 in range penalties to observe a particular target *if* you take several seconds to scan with it. $5, 4 lbs.

Surgical Instruments (TL1). Includes scalpels, forceps, etc. Basic equipment for Surgery skill. $15, 15 lbs.

Torch (TL0). Burns for 1 hr. $0.15, 1 lb.

Watchman's Hand-Bell (TL1). $2, 2 lbs.

Wax Tablet (TL1). For writing; erasable. $0.50, 2 lbs.

Whetstone (TL1). For sharpening tools and weapons. $0.25, 1 lb.

Wineskin (TL0). Holds about a gallon of liquid. $0.50, 0.25 lb.

Magical Gear

Some magical or enchanted equipment is common enough on the Disc that it's easily purchased with cash. Most of this stuff is reliable and stable enough to be acceptably safe, although use in a zone of radically unstable magic would be unwise. Some of it is even simple enough for anyone to use, without magical training. Few organisations ever issue any of it to employees, though, and the disclaimers in the small text in the manuals can be extensive.

Shopping (or Not Shopping) as an Adventure

Roleplayers are notoriously diverse in their views of in-character shopping. Some quickly scan the list of available equipment, identify the items that look potentially useful, buy the ones they can afford, write them on their character sheets, and get on with the adventure. Others regard shopping expeditions as *part* of the adventure – more fun than fighting princesses or rescuing monsters – and are happy to spend hours demanding descriptions of the marketplace and haggling over the price of cabbages. Moreover, these types are liable to swap positions when it comes to one specific type of purchase. Players who generally don't care about the details of gear might agonise over choosing the best possible weapons and armour, which can bore the picky clothes-and-groceries shoppers senseless.

None of this needs to matter *too* much, provided that the GM can adapt – well, unless the group turns out to be made up of players with significantly different interests. Then the GM must try to maintain some sort of balance.

One possibility is to include a bit of action and conflict in shopping expeditions. After all, any self-respecting Discworld shopping street is sure to contain its share of pickpockets, con men, muggers, old ladies full of plot-related gossip, and comestibles vendors named Dibbler. It's also possible to persuade action-oriented players that *smart* shopping can be part of the plot; just to start with, stylish or poorly chosen gear can be worth a small reaction modifier when dealing with NPCs of taste.

However, the players who just want to *get on with the game* may have a point. Few stories are about nothing but shopping, after all (though running a Discworld game as a parody of "chick lit" *might* be amusing). Politely reminding people that those princesses won't fight themselves is the first step. If that fails, the GM should track the time taken in the game world by all that haggling, then forcefully convey the importance of *deadlines*. For some tasks, failing to complete the job before the clock stops ticking means failing completely – and then the PCs won't have any money to spend. The GM could even have some shopkeepers hear of the adventurers' mission somehow, and refuse to serve them until they've saved that poor monster who everyone in the town loves so much.

These things are mostly created by tinkering wizards or dwarfs; such work doesn't necessarily require full spellcasting ability, although some of the people involved will then need either Magery (Engineering Only) (p. 44) or high levels of Alchemy (p. 71). Mostly, though, the relevant skill is Engineer (Magical) (p. 73). All this assumes very standardised "industrial magic." Big, high-powered, one-of-a-kind creations – or even devices with slightly variant capabilities – still demand both unrestricted Magery and months or years of design work using Thaumatology (p. 82) and Research (p. 80).

BROOMSTICKS

Flying broomsticks are fairly common on the Disc. Their manufacture represents a profitable line of work for dwarf communities with large workshops and teams of specialist engineer-craftsmen – as do maintenance and repair, because broomsticks are approximately as reliable as the sorts of cars that people always swear are more reliable than their reputation implies. That is, some work fine for decades, while others were clearly run off last thing at night by a trainee. They rarely crash fatally, but may develop quirks (e.g., Granny Weatherwax's requires a running start). Most witches own one, finding them useful when flitting round their rural responsibilities, and a number of wizards have taken to using them in recent years, even incorporating them into larger pieces of *ad hoc* magical engineering. Still, older wizards tend to regard them as a little undignified and, well, *witchy*.

Piloting a broomstick requires the operator to have Magery (to sense the magical energy it uses, which is necessary to activate it) and at least one Magic Point (p. 192) in reserve, although routine flight doesn't consume MP. Routine flight calls for no special skill, either, and isn't overly tiring. However, starting a broomstick in a hurry might need a roll against IQ+Magery, and the GM may apply penalties for unfamiliarity with the specific broomstick – some old broomsticks are terrible starters.

A standard broomstick can fly at up to 36 mph (Move 18) more-or-less indefinitely while carrying as much as 200 lbs. For every 10 lbs. over this weight limit, reduce speed by 2 mph (-1 to Move). It's possible to wring a bit more speed out of a broomstick by tinkering; Granny Weatherwax has induced some local dwarfs to raise the top speed of hers to 40 mph (Move 20). Something similar might be possible for another broomstick by adding 50% to the price. As well, if the broomstick is carrying no more than 200 lbs., it can be pushed to higher speed by raw magical effort. Adding 10 mph (+5 to Move) costs 1 MP per 10 minutes.

Example: In the course of *Wyrd Sisters*, Granny Weatherwax casts a time-stopping spell on the entire pocket kingdom of Lancre. Unfortunately, to get such a spell to work, a witch must start casting it during the "witching hour" (3 a.m.-4 a.m.), and then fly all the way around the chosen area before cock-crow. Cock-crow comes at dawn – which is about 6 a.m. – and Lancre has a border 100 miles long. Flying that distance in two hours is hard enough, but Granny needs to have some magic left to complete the spell at the end of it.

Her plan is to arrange for Magrat Garlick and Nanny Ogg to supply her with extra magic in mid-air. They can supply 5 MP each (after which they'll just have to find their own way down to the ground), and she starts with 7 MP, so she can spend 12 MP, zip around the distance in two hours flat at 50 mph on her souped-up broomstick, and still have 5 MP left at the end to complete the spell.

Of course, it doesn't work out *quite* like that, but the spell does get cast – see the novel!

Flying in a straight line at any speed is easy enough, but complex manoeuvres might demand a roll against Aerobatics (p. 78), at the GM's option. If the flyer ever runs out of MP, one or more Aerobatics rolls (at default, if necessary) are required to make a safe, if bumpy, landing. The GM can be generous at this point; at worst, a witch may suffer 1d or so crash-landing damage. However, landing is *required*.

A typical flying broomstick costs $25 new, though relatively few witches buy their broomsticks, traditionally inheriting solid-but-well-used old models. A settled witch of at least Status 1 can start with one as part of her routine possessions, where *mundane* Status 1 folk would have a horse or a mule (see *What Cost of Living Gets You*, p. 148). With the GM's permission, somebody who has to pay for a broomstick might be able to save 5-20% on the price by purchasing one with persistent maintenance or stability problems. The price reduction should mean real drawbacks, though – the GM can have some fun there! Buying second-hand is generally at the purchaser's own risk; if it's being sold cheap, the seller usually wants rid of it.

Witches actually have some difficulty buying brand-new broomsticks: They rarely do much business in the cash economy, while dwarfs don't accept old clothes and bottles of liniment in trade, being rather attached to gold. The GM can turn the purchasing process into a story in itself.

DEMON-BASED DEVICES

Devices incorporating small, single-minded imps are a fairly recent development on the Disc. These imps aren't evil, despite resembling conventional sulphur-breathing demons in miniature, but they *can* be a little irritable. They exist to do one job (they're created from ambient magical energies, perhaps using a spark of mind from some extradimensional source), and they don't object to this – although they may complain about working conditions. They're sustained by the Disc's background magic. If the device housing them is destroyed, they vanish with a small pop.

Imp-based technology originated in the Agatean Empire, and spread to other lands with the growth of general trade. Unfortunately, the Agateans don't always seem to be exporting their better designs. Ankh-Morpork adopted and then dropped imp-based watches in a few short years, deciding that mundane clockwork was better. Iconographs and dis-organisers, however, still *have* to involve magic. Local wizards have spotted that there's money to be made there, hence the existence of Unseen University's Thaumatological Park (p. 252).

Iconographs ("Picture-Boxes")

An iconograph contains an imp with Artist skill, along with a supply of paints, a tiny easel and stool, and some paper. The imp is a fast worker, able to run off a picture in a second or two after seeing an image for a fraction of a second; the paint then takes a few minutes to dry. The imp also has an excellent memory, and it can repeat any past picture on request. It will stick its head out of the box to say when it has run out of art supplies. A full stock is usually good for 20 or 30 pictures – but if, say, the user requests a lot of pictures of trees, the imp may run out of green after only 10.

Trick iconography is very difficult; the imp paints exactly what it sees, and it may well see through supernatural illusions. It's summoned or created to be reliable, and it doesn't understand requests to "lie." The imp could be considered to have high Artist (Painting) skill, but it's the user's Photography skill that determines the picture's quality.

A functional, basic iconograph costs $3, but prices vary a lot with size, reliability, imp skill level, and so on. Paying just $2 will get you something unreliable and fragile. A professional-grade, large-format model could easily cost $10-$20, while the legendary Akina TR-10 dual-imp model with telescopic seat and

big shiny lever – a specialist studio system – costs $180. The paint and paper for each picture normally costs about $0.10, but this varies as well; fancy boxes may use high-grade canvas and fine oil paints.

Flash photography uses salamanders (p. 358); serious iconographers keep a few cages full of the creatures, which charge up on sunlight and release it in flashes when startled. A salamander needs five minutes in sunlight or proportionately more in lower light levels between uses (strong magical fields generate intense octarine light, which counts as sunlight for this purpose). The iconograph attachment to hold a salamander and startle it when the shutter is activated costs $0.50. Each salamander costs $1. Changing salamanders takes 20 seconds; this time can be halved with a DX roll, but failure means dropping both salamanders, causing the charged one to flash.

Moving images are technically possible, using very fast imps and the magical material known as octo-cellulose. However, since the events of *Moving Pictures*, which showed that moving pictures are inspired by malevolent extradimensional entities, they've been banned in Ankh-Morpork. Bearing in mind that the Patrician, several UU faculty members, and the entire city were all seriously endangered on that occasion, one may be sure that the ban is enforced.

Imp Watches

Imp-based watches are still available for people who don't trust those newfangled mechanical clockwork things (p. 157), and cost and weigh the same. Timepiece-imps have perfect time sense and good voices; when the case is opened, they announce the time, usually in a formal style. This may seem cute at first, but soon becomes irritating.

Personal Organisers ("Dis-Organisers")

Personal organisers are the latest in imp-based practicality and convenience. At least, so the people selling them say.

A personal organiser is a pocket-sized box containing an imp with (at minimum) a photographic memory and a perfect time sense. Its basic job is to remind the user of appointments, take memos, and generally act as a combined timepiece, calendar, diary, and source of moral aphorisms. In other words, it needs to be *organised* – at which point, many users say, the technology's demonic nature becomes evident. Advanced models have precognitive imps, supposedly able to schedule appointments before they're even made. With the market advancing rapidly, some have other functions, including voice recording (the imps have good hearing and can be induced to repeat everything they hear), the Bluenose™ Integrated Messenger Service (the imp runs very quickly to the nearest clacks tower and sends a message), various pointless games, the iHUM function (a trained imp can remember and hum up to 1,500 different tunes), and a kind of spreadsheet/database system (the imp jumps out of its box to add up columns of figures and to sort and collate paperwork).

In fact, it has been said that modern Disc personal organisers have 15 functions, of which 10 consist of apologising for getting the other five wrong. The imps also have irritating habits such as saying "bingledy-bongledy-bing" when activated, offering to change colour on request, and generally being more clever than useful. Some notoriously have handwriting recognition ability[1], but not literacy. See *Jingo* for a case of a personal organiser going *really* off-track.

However, dis-organiser technology is genuinely advancing, to the point that even Commander Vimes has found his latest gadget *useful* on occasion. These devices are completely reliable when instructed to do a job which is within their capacity; it's just a matter of finding uses for them which compensate for the irritation.

A basic dis-organiser – with just diary and memo functions – costs $20. Imp-based technology doubtless has room for further advancement. The GM is welcome to introduce new ideas which will help drive a plot or be sufficiently funny.

FLYING CARPETS

Generations of Klatchian thaumaturgical weavers have produced flying carpets, but the idea doesn't seem to have spread to other lands, and such conveyances aren't exactly common even in Klatch. Magic is magic, and it always takes some effort and skill –

1. *"Yes, that's handwriting."*

while carpets, even when enchanted, are subject to wear and tear, eventually becoming too worn and frayed for use. A carpet that's *almost* disintegrating can present an interesting dilemma for adventurers in a hurry.

For game purposes, carpets are rated by area; each square yard can carry one SM 0 person or 250 lbs. of luggage (less, for old, frail carpets). Normal maximum speed is 40 mph (Move 20). Discworld carpets are started and operated by simple command words like "up" and "down." For steering, "left" and "right" work, but the "pilot" achieves fine control by shifting his weight. Carpets aren't designed for fancy flying, though – Aerobatics rolls are at -3, and any critical failure can involve everyone aboard falling off. The generous GM might give dislodged passengers a DX roll to catch the edge and hang on desperately.

As this suggests, a flying carpet's big advantage over a broomstick is that it doesn't require Magery to operate. It's slightly faster, too. Someone who *does* have Magery and Magic Points to spend can make a carpet he's riding a bit faster, though. Add 6 mph (+3 to Move) for 1 MP, or 10 mph (+5 to Move) for 2 MP, with the boost lasting for 10 minutes.

A *new* flying carpet costs $1,000 for the first square yard of size, plus $500 per additional square yard, if one is lucky enough to find one on sale. Used models may be cheaper – although some are so frayed that flying on them could induce Fright Checks! Klatchian governments reserve the right to requisition carpets in times of war, for scouting and courier work.

SIGNS AND DOOR FURNITURE

A little bit of magic, cleverly applied, can create all sorts of trivial, semi-permanent effects. Small-town commercial wizards often keep a number of extremely minor

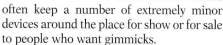

devices around the place for show or for sale to people who want gimmicks.

For example, a brass door plate that speaks the name of a house's occupant when approached is a fairly commonplace piece of engineering, available for $10 in Ankh-Morpork and most other large towns; the vendor will customise it for the specific buyer. A door-knocker in the form of a demonic face that can name the house's inhabitants, or announce visitors to those inside, costs $25. Such a face has a little personality – much like a demon-based device (pp. 159-160) – with effective IQ 8, although it may be rather unimaginative. It's also likely to have a speech impediment owing to the hinged brass ring though its jaws or nose.

Flashier are the magically illuminated signs that optimistic shopkeepers sometimes acquire. These cost about $5 per letter for letters a foot tall. Larger signs cost more in proportion, but smaller ones don't cost much less. They usually last 2d years (larger signs may be shorter-lived), after which they start buzzing and flickering annoyingly.

THAUMOMETERS

A *thaumometer* is a small, green or dark-blue glass device with a dial on the front and a button on the side, intended for measuring ambient magical energy. It's especially useful for determining when one is in an area of high residual magic (p. 270) or another region where supernatural forces are running wild. Most thaumometers are calibrated in thaums (p. 270).

A standard thaumometer is good for up to a million thaums of ambient flux (the level associated with major acts of divine creation), after which it tends to melt.

The standardised thaumometer is a relatively new invention, probably only available at Unseen University and perhaps on the Counterweight Continent. $10, 1 lb.

Special Cases

Some Discworld characters aren't human – or at least aren't *typical* humans – and so face special problems with equipment and living expenses.

UNUSUAL SIZES AND SHAPES

Characters who aren't SM 0 humans often need equipment scaled to suit them. These guidelines cover purchasing such things. For rules on how size affects the way weapons work in combat, see *Size Modifiers, Reach, and Weapons* (p. 176).

Totally nonhumanoid beings (e.g., sapient animals) generally *can't* use weapons or tools, or obtain armour to fit them except on very special order.

Gear for Outsize Humans, Undersize Humans, and Near-Humans

Humans with Gigantism (p. 29) have SM +1. Such individuals require specially made armour and clothing, with *double* the usual cost and weight. However, they use standard human weapons, shields, and tools, having learned to do so out of necessity.

Humans small enough to rate SM -1 (older children, and adults with Dwarfism, p. 29) can get hold of ordinary clothes, which cost 20% less than usual – there's less material, but just as much manufacturing effort. Any armour they wear must be ordered specially, balancing the reduced materials requirement and leaving the cost unchanged. Reduce clothing and armour *weight* by 25%. Such people use standard human weapons. The only smaller humans are children, who don't have to worry much about this stuff.

Races with close-to-human form – and originally human undead – can mostly use human gear (although in some cases, normal humans won't want to use it afterward). Werewolves, vampires, etc. must account for the sartorial effects of changing shape, however; see *Shapeshifter Garments* (p. 162).

Gear for Dwarfs

Typically SM -1 but stocky and well-muscled, dwarfs can share most tools, weapons, and shields with humans. They can also wear helmets designed for humans – there are differences in fit, but then there are differences among humans, too. However, their build means that much armour has to be made for them specifically. Dwarf armour and clothes cost and weigh the same as human versions; they use only slightly less material, and dwarfs tend to be fussy about quality and ruggedness. Dwarf gear, or equipment that's easily adapted for a dwarf to use, is available in most places.

Gear for Trolls and Other Stony Types

At SM +1 or larger, trolls rarely bother with clothing or armour. If they do decide to wear anything, or to acquire shields, increase both cost and weight by a factor based on SM: ×2 for SM +1, ×5 for SM +2, or ×10 for SM +3. (Larger trolls *definitely* don't bother.) For example, medium armour for an SM +2 troll is $130 and 150 lbs. Trolls use standard weapons, albeit usually the heavier types.

Golems and gargoyles don't worry much about tailoring, either. Other gear depends on SM: SM 0 individuals use human-sized items, while larger ones follow the guidelines for trolls.

Gear for Gnomes and Pictsies

These tiny folk can get hold of clothing (doll clothes, if necessary), or have something worked up (usually from rat-skin, by fellow gnome craftsmen), without difficulty; divide prices by 4 and ignore weight. Such garments use a *lot* less material but require especially fine work. Armour small and light enough for gnomes and pictsies would be too flimsy to provide any protection on the scale *GURPS* uses.

Treat almost any weapon usable by a being this size as a dagger for game purposes, whatever its shape. A few fighter-gnomes carry miniature shields, mostly for show. Such shields are $1 and 0.25 lb., but are worthless against anything larger than a dagger.

Gnomes also use human-sized tools when necessary, albeit often in two hands and with much grunting. They won't use the largest tools much, but they can employ the smaller ones quite precisely. A gnome locksmith or jeweller might well be very good, whereas a gnome employed as a carpenter or stonemason will mostly be limited to fine carving, leaving the big stuff to humans and dwarfs.

> # Example of Shopping: Hunchbroad Modoscousin
>
> Hunchbroad is TL4, has a Wealth level of Average, and is "footloose." Thus, he gets $100 to spend. Reading *Gear for Dwarfs* (above), Steve sees that dwarf and human equipment share prices and weights.
>
> Hunchbroad is probably doomed to take the lead when blundering into danger, and is a rather old-school dwarf, so Steve starts by acquiring the heaviest armour he can afford: mail (DR 4, $50, 75 lbs.). Steve suggests that the "clothes appropriate to his Status" that Hunchbroad gets for free consist of a collection of plain, rugged things that he wears under the armour or while getting it cleaned or repaired, plus a winter cloak and a few spare garments which he can stow in his current lodgings. He also needs an axe; actually, he buys two, just in case ($3, 4 lbs. apiece). He purchases a shield ($3, 15 lbs.) and a small knife ($1.50, 0.5 lb.), too, the latter less a weapon than a tool.
>
> To round things off, Steve hangs a wax tablet for notes from Hunchbroad's belt ($0.50, 2 lbs.). Then he puts personal basics ($0.25, 1 lb.), and a whetstone to keep his axes sharp ($0.25, 1 lb.), in a pouch ($0.50). He can add other gear as and when he needs it.
>
> All this adds up to $62, leaving Hunchbroad with $38 – enough to live on for over a month. It also comes to 102.5 lbs., putting him at Medium encumbrance with a modest margin. He won't be quick on his feet (Move 3), but then he isn't supposed to be a sprinter.

LIVING EXPENSES FOR NONHUMANS

Species differences can influence living costs – and not just in size-related ways. If a race with near-human form isn't mentioned here, assume that they pay human expenses.

- *Dwarfs* have the same living costs as humans.
- *Gnomes* and *pictsies* get through a lot less food and drink than humans, bringing their essential living expenses right down. Thus, if they land jobs which pay at human rates – as they often can, at least in Ankh-Morpork – they can live very comfortably indeed (though their expenditure on alcohol may more than balance this). But few of them have got the hang of showing this off so as to raise their perceived Status. Alternatively, they might undercut human workers when bidding for work, but they're often hard bargainers, so they don't get paid much less.

- *Golems* and *zombies* (which don't eat at all), along with *gargoyles* and other creatures with the Cast-Iron Stomach advantage, can live quite cheaply. On the other hand, they tend to end up with low Status. Because they can't show off much in the way of social graces, they get on badly in society, and not many people invite them to parties. They do have occasional peculiar incidental expenses, such as repair costs. Hence, it's simplest to treat them as having normal living expenses for their Status, and then mostly keep Status low. If they do somehow rise in society, they'll have to spend a *lot* on status symbols and fancy housing to convince anyone of the fact.

- *Trolls* live on a mineral diet which costs about the same per troll as human food. They need more mass, but it's cheaper by the pound.

- *Vampires* are treated as humans for *most* purposes. Black Ribboners must make arrangements to get hold of animal blood, but the trouble is balanced by the fact that slaughterhouses will usually sell it cheap. Vampires getting their blood the old-fashioned way have complicated lives balanced by a complete lack of grocery bills.

- *Werewolves* mostly live as humans, with the same costs.

> ## Shapeshifter Garments
>
> Werewolves have a problem with clothes – ideally, they should be able to get them off with paws. They end up spending an extra 10% on clothing and *still* have to make DX rolls at inconvenient moments. A werewolf doesn't magically reacquire clothes when it reverts to human form, either; if it's some distance from "home" at the time, this may lead to much use of old sacks or even barrels. Werewolves who operate in a particular neighbourhood often stash spare clothes in hiding-places.
>
> Shape-changing female vampires have similar problems, although they don't generally have much trouble getting out of a heap of clothing when they assume small bat shape. Males have no such difficulties. This is annoying for the females, who all else aside, often have to purchase new clothes after nights out.

Completed Sample Characters

Here are Hunchbroad Modoscousin and Jemzarkiza of Krull, complete and ready to play. For Hunchbroad, all advantages and disadvantages from the dwarf racial template appear on the character sheet, for ease of reference; this isn't always the norm. Jemzarkiza shows how a completed character sheet (from p. 24) can look; Hunchbroad is given here in a more compact form.

Hunchbroad Modoscousin

100 points

ST 11* [0]; **DX** 11 [20]; **IQ** 11 [20]; **HT** 11* [0].
Damage 1d-1/1d+1; BL 39 lbs.; HP 13* [0]; Will 11 [0]; Per 11 [0]; FP 11 [0].
Basic Speed 5.50 [0]; Basic Move 5 [0]; Dodge 8; Parry 8; Block 8. 3'11"; 125 lbs. (SM -1*).

Social Background

TL: 4 [0].
CF: Dwarfish [0]; Sto Plains/Uberwald [1].
Languages: Dwarfish (Native) [0]; Morporkian (Native/Accented) [5].

Advantages

Contact (Modo the Gardener; Area Knowledge (Unseen University)-15; 12 or less; Somewhat Reliable) [4]; Dwarf [27]; Lifting ST 3* [0]; Metalwork 1* [0]; Patron (Wizard employers; 12 or less) [20]; Resistant to Disease (+8) [5].
Perks: Longevity* [0].

Disadvantages

Duty (To employer; 12 or less) [-10]; Dwarfish Greed (12)* [0]; Impulsiveness (12) [-10]; Truthfulness (12) [-5].
Quirks: Cannot Run Long Distances*; Considers dwarf gender a very private matter*; Likes wearing metal to the point of obsession; Personality Change (gains Bad Temper when drinking)*; Thinks that mountain dwarfs are hicks; Touchy about height and beard*; Works through multiple tasks in alphabetical order. [-3]

Skills

Axe/Mace (A) DX [0]-11*; Forced Entry (E) DX [1]-11; Mechanic/TL4 (Animal-Drawn Vehicle) (A) IQ [1]-11†; Metallurgy/TL4 (H) IQ+1 [4]-12†; Naturalist (H) IQ [4]-11; Navigation/TL4 (Land) (A) IQ-1 [1]-10; Packing (A) IQ [2]-11; Prospecting/TL4 (A) IQ+2 [4]-13†; Riding (Equines) (A) DX [2]-11; Scrounging (E) Per [1]-11; Shield (E) DX [1]-11; Smuggling (A) IQ-1 [1]-10; Teamster (Equines) (A) IQ [2]-11; Thaumatology (VH) IQ-3 [1]-8; Throwing (A) DX-1 [1]-10.

* From dwarf racial template (p. 100).
† Includes +1 for Metalwork.

Equipment

Axes (×2); Mail Armour (DR 4); Pouch (contains Personal Basics, Whetstone); Shield; Small Knife; Wax Tablet; $38.

DISCWORLD
ROLEPLAYING GAME
Character Sheet

Name _Jemzarkiza of Krull_   Player _Anne_   Point Total _250_

Ht _5'7"_ Wt _130 lbs._ Size Modifier _0_ Age _26_ Unspent Pts _0_

Notes _Equipment – Large Knife; Pouch (contains Personal Basics); Quarterstaff; Small Backpack (contains First Aid Kit, Scribe's Kit); Wizard's Wand; $88.75._

							CURRENT		

ST | 9 | [-10]   **HP** | 9 | | [0]

DX | 12 | [40]   **WILL** | 15 | | [0]

IQ | 15 | [100]   **PER** | 15 | | [0]

HT | 12 | [20]   **FP** | 12 | | [0]

CURRENT
MP | 6 | |

Magery: _Magery 3_ [35]
Staff: _____ [ ]

Languages

	Spoken	Written	
Klatchian	Broken	Broken	[2]
Morporkian	Native	Native	[0]
			[ ]
			[ ]

DR 0

PARRY 11 (staff)

BLOCK 7

TL: _4_ [0]
Cultural Familiarities
Klatchian [1]
Sto Plains/Uberwald [0]
[ ]

Reaction Modifiers
+1 (Attractive); -1 (Odious Personal Habit); +2 from Ankh-Morpork xenophiles and wild-eyed romantics (Reputation); -2 from Ankh-Morpork xenophobes and old-school heroes (Reputation); -1 from most Ankh-Morpork citizens (Social Stigma); also has Status 1.

BASIC LIFT (ST × ST)/5 _16 lbs._ DAMAGE Thr _1d-2_ Sw _1d-1_

BASIC SPEED _6.00_ [0] BASIC MOVE _7_ [5]

ENCUMBRANCE / MOVE / DODGE

		MOVE		DODGE	
None (0) = BL	16	BM × 1	7	Dodge	9
Light (1) = 2 × BL	32	BM × 0.8	5	Dodge -1	8
Medium (2) = 3 × BL	48	BM × 0.6	4	Dodge -2	7
Heavy (3) = 6 × BL	96	BM × 0.4	2	Dodge -3	6
X-Heavy (4) = 10 × BL	160	BM × 0.2	1	Dodge -4	5

ADVANTAGES AND PERKS

Animal Friend 1	[5]
Attractive	[4]
Lightning Calculator	[2]
Reputation +2 (As cool, exotic enchantress)	[3]
Resistant to Disease (+8)	[5]
Status 1	[5]
Haughty Sneer	[1]
High-Heeled Heroine.	[1]
	[ ]
	[ ]

Total Points in Advantages and Perks [26]

DISADVANTAGES AND QUIRKS

Acrophobia (12)	[-10]
Curious (12)	[-5]
Odious Personal Habit (Terse, doesn't explain herself much)	[-5]
Reputation -2 (As sinister enchantress)	[-3]
Social Stigma (Overdressed Foreigner)	[-10]
Unnatural Features	[-3]
Annoyed by crass foreign assumptions	[-1]
Loves intellectual argument – gets voluble	[-1]
Small aquatic reptiles fan	[-1]
	[ ]

Total Points in Disadvantages and Quirks [-39]

SKILLS

Name	Level	Relative Level	
Alchemy/TL4	14	IQ-1	[4]
Animal Handling (Reptiles)	15*	IQ+0	[1]
Astrozoology	13	IQ-2	[1]
Fishing	15	Per0	[1]
Innate Attack (Projectile)	14	DX+2	[4]
Knife	14	DX+2	[4]
Magic (Krullian Wizardry)	20†	IQ+5	[16]
Magical Form (Physiomancy)	16†	IQ+1	[2]
Magical Form (Psychomancy)	18†	IQ+3	[8]
Natural Philosophy/TL4	15	IQ+0	[4]
Naturalist	15	IQ+0	[4]
Navigation/TL4 (Sea)	14	IQ-1	[1]
Philosophy (Krullian Scholasticism)	13	IQ-2	[1]
Research/TL4	16	IQ+1	[4]
Savoir-Faire (High Society)	16	IQ+1	[2]
Seamanship/TL4	15	IQ+0	[1]
Shouting at Foreigners	16	IQ+1	[2]
Staff	12	DX+0	[2]
Thaumatology	16†	IQ+1	[2]
Veterinary/TL3	16*	IQ+1	[4]
Weather Sense/TL4	15	IQ+0	[2]
* Includes +1 for Animal Friend			[ ]
† Includes +3 for Magery			[ ]

Total Points in Skills [70]

DOING STUFF

"It's settled," said Klump. "Well, you could send a few people down to Cabbage Street to clear up what's left."

The sergeant nodded thoughtfully. If somebody attacked a watchman with lethal force, and the watchman came home and the somebody didn't, this wasn't anything that the higher ranks in the Watch were inclined to worry about much. On the other hand, if a pair of watchmen could take down a whole gang of violent and insane criminals – well, it suggested competence and enthusiasm that might merit careful watching in future. Just in case. One way or another.

"You . . . got the drop on them?" he asked carefully.

"Some of them," Ingarsson said.

"And the others?"

"They were trying magic," Ingarsson repeated.

"Oh. I get it." The sergeant relaxed a little, then clearly had a second, more worrying thought, and called behind him. "Stolly? Send someone down to the University, ask if we can borrow a couple of their livelier post-grajjit types. Might be worth them running a wand around Cabbage Street, make sure that there's no left-over magic down there. Just to be certain." Then he looked at Constable Ingarsson again, and added, "And while you're at it, send a clacks to Pseudopolis Yard and ask Igor to come down here, pronto. Ingarsson here needs some stitching."

Adventurers will try to *do* all sorts of things, from surviving fights, through climbing mountains, to working magic – and even persuading other people to like them. This demands rules to determine whether they succeed, and what happens as a result.

Constables Ingarsson and Klump, Ankh-Morpork City Watch, were on night duty this week, so nobody in the Chitterling Street Section House was unduly surprised to see them stagger in at approximately the time that the house's cockerel (a recent and unpopular gift from a rustic visitor whom the Watch had saved from unlicenced robbery) sidled out of its temporary quarters and made a token effort at crowing. The improvised bandages around Ingarsson's arm and leg, on the other hand, inspired instant concern.

"Who was it?" demanded Sergeant Vorrgoot, who was on desk duty. "You weren't supposed to be down in the Shades . . ."

"Mimes," grunted Klump, who was never a big talker.

"Oh, Offler," muttered the sergeant. "I thought that they'd got the hint by now."

"New bunch," said Klump.

"It's worse than a hint they've got," said Ingarsson. "They were trying magic."

"Right," said Vorrgoot, reaching under his desk for his crossbow, "let's go find them. We have ways of making them talk . . ."

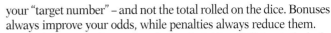

Rolling the Dice

These rules use six-sided dice only (other RPGs use stranger dice), and use "d" as an abbreviation for "dice." The number before the "d" tells you to roll that many dice and add them up; e.g., "3d" means "roll three six-sided dice and add them up." Combat damage (among other things) uses the "dice+adds" system: If a weapon does "4d+2" damage, that's shorthand for "roll four dice and add 2 to the total." Likewise, "3d-3" means "roll three dice and subtract 3 from the total."

Success and Failure

A "success roll" is the commonest type of roll in play, though not the only one. It's made when you need to "test" one of your abilities. Sometimes you roll; sometimes the GM rolls for you. For instance, you might test, or roll against, your Strength to stop a heavy door from closing.

To attempt such a test, roll three dice. The task in question *succeeds* if the total rolled on the dice is *less than or equal to* the number which governs the action – most often a skill or an attribute. Otherwise, it *fails*. For example, if you're rolling against Strength and have ST 12, a roll of 12 or less succeeds. Thus, the higher the stat you're rolling against, the easier it is to make the roll.

Regardless of the score you're rolling against, a roll of 3 or 4 is *always* a success, while a roll of 17 or 18 is *always* a failure.

When to Roll

To avoid bogging down the game in dice, the GM should only require a success roll if . . .

- A PC's health, wealth, friends, reputation, or equipment are at risk. This includes chases, combat (even if the target is stationary and at point-blank range!), espionage, and thievery.
- A PC stands to gain allies, information, new abilities, social standing, or wealth.
- There's a *good* chance that the result might be funny.

The GM *should not* require rolls for . . .

- Utterly trivial tasks: crossing the road, feeding the dog, finding the corner shop, painting a fence, etc.
- Daily work at a mundane, non-adventuring job.

When the GM Rolls

There are two sets of circumstances under which the GM should roll for a PC and not let the player see the results:

1. When the *character* wouldn't know for sure whether he had succeeded.
2. When the *player* shouldn't know what's going on.

It's a good idea for the GM to keep up-to-date copies of everyone's character sheets, for quick reference.

Modifiers

The rules often specify "modifiers" for success rolls. These bonuses and penalties affect the *number you are rolling against* –

your "target number" – and not the total rolled on the dice. Bonuses always improve your odds, while penalties always reduce them.

For instance, when using the Lockpicking skill in pitch darkness, the GM might tell you to roll at -5. If your Lockpicking skill is 9, you roll against 9 minus 5, or 4.

A specific situation might provide modifiers to allow for the relative ease or difficulty of a particular task. For instance, the GM might decide that a lock is +10 to open due to the fact that it's cheap and crude. If your Lockpicking skill were 9, you would roll against 9 + 10, or 19. Since the highest roll possible on 3d is 18, it would seem that success is assured. Not quite; see *Critical Success and Failure* (p. 166).

Modifiers are cumulative unless stated otherwise. For instance, if you tried to open that primitive lock in the dark, *both* modifiers would apply, and you would roll against 9 - 5 + 10, or 14.

BASE SKILL VS. EFFECTIVE SKILL

Your "base skill" is your actual level in a skill, as recorded on your character sheet. Your "effective skill" for a particular task is your base skill plus or minus any modifiers for that task. In the Lockpicking examples above, base skill is 9 in all cases, while effective skill is 4, 19, or 14.

You may not attempt a success roll if your effective skill is less than 3 unless you're attempting a *defence roll* (p. 180).

Degree of Success or Failure

Once you've calculated your effective skill by applying all relevant modifiers to your base skill, roll 3d. If the total rolled on the dice is less than or equal to your effective skill, you succeed, and the difference between your effective skill and your dice roll is your "margin of success."

Example: If you have effective skill 18 and roll a 12, you succeed; your margin of success is 6.

If you roll *higher* than your effective skill, you fail, and the difference between the dice roll and your effective skill is your "margin of failure."

Example: If you have effective skill 9 and roll a 12, you fail; your margin of failure is 3.

Many rules use margin of success or failure to calculate results that matter in play, so be sure to note it when you roll.

CRITICAL SUCCESS AND FAILURE

A "critical success" is an especially *good* result.

- A roll of 3 or 4 is *always* a critical success.
- A roll of 5 is a critical success *if your effective skill is 15+.*
- A roll of 6 is a critical success *if your effective skill is 16+.*

When you roll a critical success, the GM determines what happens. It's always something good! The lower the roll, the better "bonus" he gives you. A roll of 3 can imply a *freakish* and *implausible* success.

A "critical failure" is an especially *bad* result.

- A roll of 18 is *always* a critical failure.
- A roll of 17 is a critical failure *if your effective skill is 15 or less;* otherwise, it's an ordinary failure.
- A margin of failure of 10 or more is *always* a critical failure: roll of 16+ against effective skill 6, roll of 15+ against effective skill 5, and so on.

When you roll a critical failure, the GM decides what happens. It's always bad – the higher the roll, the worse the result – and possibly funny, in a painful or embarrassing way.

Repeated Attempts

Sometimes you get only one chance to do something (disable a deadly trap, jump over a crevasse, please the king with a song). Other times you can try over and over again until you succeed (pick a lock, catch a fish, analyse an alchemical potion). Still other times you won't know whether you succeeded or failed until it's too late to try again (interpret an old treasure map, order in a Genuan restaurant, build a ship). Finally, there are times when you're injured by failure but can afford to fail a few times (climb a wall, impress a suspicious tribesman). The GM must use common sense to distinguish among these cases, according to the exact situation.

Contests

Sometimes a situation arises in which two characters must compare attributes, skills, or other traits to settle a competition. The one with the highest score doesn't *always* win . . . but that's the way to bet. A "Contest" is a way to handle such a competitive situation without playing it out in detail. In a Contest, each competitor attempts a success roll against the ability being tested – with all applicable modifiers – and then compares his

result to his opponent's. There are two different ways to make this comparison.

QUICK CONTEST

A "Quick Contest" is a competition that's over in very little time – often in one second, perhaps even *instantly.* Examples include two enemies lunging for a weapon, or two knife throwers seeing who gets closer to the bull's-eye.

Each competitor attempts his success roll. If one succeeds and the other fails, the winner is obvious. If both succeed, the winner is the one with the largest margin of success; if both fail, the winner is the one with the smallest margin of failure. A tie means nobody won (in the examples above, both fighters grabbed the weapon at once, or the knives hit the same distance from the bull's-eye).

Margin of Victory

The amount by which the winner beat the loser is often important – success by 5 vs. failure by 5 generally means more than success by 2 vs. success by 1! The winner's "margin of victory" is the difference between his margin of success and the loser's margin of success if both succeeded, the sum of his margin of success and the loser's margin of failure if he succeeded and the loser failed, or the difference between the loser's margin of failure and his margin of failure if both failed.

REGULAR CONTEST

A "Regular Contest" is a slow competition with much give and take – for instance, arm wrestling.

Each character attempts his success roll. If one succeeds and the other fails, the winner is obvious. If both succeed or both fail, the competitors' relative positions are unchanged and they roll again. Eventually, one character succeeds when the other fails. At this point, the one who made his roll is the winner.

The length of *game time* each attempt takes depends on the activity and is up to the GM. In a combat situation, each attempt takes one second . . . but in a library-research contest, with the fate of the city hanging on who finds a certain obscure reference first, each attempt could represent hours or even days.

Resistance Rolls

A "resistance roll" is made by someone subjected to an effect that he would consider *bad,* to prevent or limit the consequences. It's usually a success roll against an attribute or a secondary characteristic. Examples include HT rolls to shake off or reduce the effects of disease or poison, and Will rolls to repel mental assaults.

A resistance roll is *sometimes* a Quick Contest between an attacking ability and the defender's resistance, in which case two special rules apply:

The Lady nodded slightly. She picked up the dice-cup and held it as steady as a rock, yet all the Gods could hear the three cubes rattling about inside. And then she sent them bouncing across the table.

– The Colour of Magic

1. The attacker must succeed to win. He cannot win by having the smallest margin of failure. If his roll fails, he loses automatically and his subject doesn't need to attempt a resistance roll.

2. The attacker must win to affect the subject properly. Ties go to the defender (but may sometimes produce momentary or minor effects).

Damage Rolls

A "damage roll" is a roll made in a fight, to see how much harm you did to your foe. Damage rolls use the "dice+adds" system (p. 165). Many things can affect the final injury your attack inflicts: your target's armour (reduces damage), your attack's damage type, poison (causes extra injury if the weapon carrying it penetrates armour), and so on. See *Combat* (pp. 173-184).

Other Dice Rolling

Dice are occasionally used to determine other sorts of random possibilities, too. For example, if there's a 50/50 chance of a gadget working, the notes for it might say, "Roll 1d; on 4-6, it works." Sometimes, these sorts of rolls are made "on a table" – you roll the indicated number of dice, apply any specified modifiers, look up the resulting number on a table, and read off what happens. See *Reaction Rolls* (pp. 171-172) for an important example. Other cases are explained as they arise.

As these *aren't* success rolls, they use the "dice+adds" system, much like damage rolls. Apply modifiers to the dice total, not to anything else.

Settling Rules Questions

In any question of rules, the GM's word is law. The GM decides which optional rules to use, and settles any specific questions that come up. A good GM discusses important questions with the players before deciding – and a good player accepts the GM's decisions.

The GM should know the rules thoroughly. When the rules don't cover a situation – or when a decision about the "real world" is needed – the GM can use several techniques:

Success rolls. A "success roll" is a roll that tests one of a character's attributes, skills, etc.; see *Success and Failure* (p. 165). Use a success roll when a question arises about someone's ability to do some particular thing.

Random rolls. A random roll is often best for a question like "Does the inn have any good white wine?" or "Does one of the warriors have a horse the same colour as mine?" The GM decides what the chances are, then rolls the dice.

Arbitrary fiat. You don't have to use the dice at all. If there is only one "right" answer to fit the plot of the adventure – then that's the answer. "Luckily for you, the flask of alchemical explosive bounced down the stairwell. Nobody was hurt. But now the guards are alerted!"

Physical Feats

Below are rules for common physical tasks of importance to adventurers. For tasks not listed here, make DX rolls for matters of precision and HT rolls for feats of endurance. To determine weight moved or work done, use Basic Lift. Movement speed should generally be proportional to Basic Move.

Climbing

To climb anything more difficult than a ladder, roll against Climbing skill (p. 79). Modify this according to difficulty; e.g., +5 for a tree with lots of branches, -2 for a rope, or -3 for a stone wall. Also, subtract your encumbrance level from your skill.

Make one roll to start a climb and another roll every five minutes. Any failure means you fall (see *Falling*, p. 79). If you secured yourself with a rope, you fall only to the end of the rope unless you critically failed.

Average climbing distance *per second* is 1' on something trivial, like a ladder; 1/2' going down a rope; 1/3' on a tree, or *up* a prepared rope; 1/6' on a typical natural rock face; or 1/15' on a vertical stone wall. For example, climbing a 10' rock face takes 60 seconds and an unmodified skill roll; a 30' tree takes 90 seconds and a Climbing roll at +5.

Triple all climbing speeds if you have Super Climbing (p. 91). You can also triple climbing speed by spending 1 FP per second (see *Fatigue*, pp. 188-189). These multiply together – someone

with Super Climbing who spends 1 FP/second moves at *nine times* normal speed!

Hiking

Sustainable cross-country speed on foot depends on ground Move. To find this, start with Basic Move and reduce it for encumbrance (*Encumbrance and Move*, p. 168), injury (*General Injury*, p. 185), and exhaustion (*Lost Fatigue Points*, pp. 188-189), as applicable. The base distance in miles you can march in one day equals 10×Move.

A successful roll against Hiking skill (p. 79) increases this distance by 20%. Roll daily. A group led by someone with Leadership skill at 12+ may make a single roll against the group's *average* Hiking skill. (Hiking defaults to HT-5 for those who haven't studied it.) Success lets the entire group march 20% more than the slowest member's base distance; failure means the whole group must forgo the bonus.

Further modify distance for circumstances, as follows:

Very Bad: Deep snow, dense forest, jungle, mountains, soft sand, or swamp. ×0.2.

Bad: Broken ground (including streams), muddy roads, forest, or steep hills. ×0.5.

Average: Most roads, light forest, or rolling hills. ×1.

Good: Hard-packed desert, level plains, or the best roads. ×1.25.

Adverse weather conditions – rain, snow, or ice – often reduce these values further.

Jumping

When you want to jump over something much smaller than you, the GM should say, "Okay, you jumped over it," and get on with play. Such jumps succeed automatically. But when the obstacle seems really significant, or if the GM put it there as a deliberate hazard, use the following rules.

Encumbrance and Move

"Encumbrance" is a measure of the total weight you're carrying, *relative to your ST*. Its effects are divided into five "encumbrance levels." All but the lowest level reduce your actual Move to a fraction of your Basic Move, as follows:

Weight Carried	Encumbrance Level	Move*
Up to Basic Lift (p. 28)	No encumbrance (0)	Basic Move
Up to 2×BL	Light encumbrance (1)	Basic Move×0.8
Up to 3×BL	Medium encumbrance (2)	Basic Move×0.6
Up to 6×BL	Heavy encumbrance (3)	Basic Move×0.4
Up to 10×BL	Extra-Heavy encumbrance (4)	Basic Move×0.2

* Drop all fractions.

In addition, note that these levels are numbered from 0 to 4. When a rule tells you to subtract your encumbrance level from (or add it to) a score or a dice roll, this is the number to use. Notably, encumbrance is a penalty to Dodge, Climbing skill, and skill rolls *and* parries with Judo, Karate, Rapier, and Smallsword.

Encumbrance can never reduce Move or Dodge below 1.

Example: Jemzarkiza of Krull has ST 9, giving BL 16. She's out on the town wearing ordinary clothes and carrying gear that comes to 7.75 lbs. in total – No encumbrance. Hence, she can move her full 7 yards/second and use her full Dodge of 9 when a fight breaks out.

During the fracas, she scoops up the huge leather-bound book that everyone seems to be fighting about (it *does* reek of enough arcane power to stun a horse), which weighs 12 lbs., raising her total load to 19.75 lbs. That gives her Light encumbrance, reducing her move to 5 (7×0.8, dropping fractions) and her Dodge to 8 (9 - 1). Fortunately, her opponents are unremarkable humans with ST 10 (BL 20) and Basic Move 5, carrying 30 lbs. of weapons and armour; their Light encumbrance reduces their Move to 4 (5×0.8). Jemzarkiza can get away from them.

Your Basic Move determines jumping distance:

High Jump: (6×Basic Move) - 10 inches. For example, a Basic Move of 6 lets you jump 26" straight up.
Broad Jump: (2×Basic Move) - 3 feet. For example, a Basic Move of 6 lets you jump 9' from a standing start.

For a *running* jump, add the number of yards you run to your Basic Move in these calculations. This cannot more than double your standing jump distances.

In all cases, those with the Jumping skill (p. 79) may replace Basic Move with half their skill level, rounded down, in these formulas.

Lifting and Moving Things

Basic Lift (p. 28) governs the weight you can pick up and move. The GM may let multiple characters add their BL (*not their ST*) whenever it seems reasonable; e.g., to carry a stretcher or pull a wagon.

One-Handed Lift: 2×BL (takes two seconds).
Two-Handed Lift: 8×BL (takes four seconds).
Shove and Knock Over: 12×BL. *Double* this with a running start. The GM can also make allowances for precariously balanced objects, making them easier to upend.
Carry on Back: 15×BL. Thus, you can carry more than you can lift by yourself – but every *second* that your encumbrance is over 10×BL (that is, Extra-Heavy encumbrance), you lose 1 FP.
Shift Slightly: Depending on your footing and how you're braced, you could shift or rock 50×BL.

Example: Hunchbroad Modoscousin has ST 11 but adds Lifting ST 3 from the dwarf racial template, for an effective ST 14 and hence BL 39. He can lift a 70-lb. chest from a table in two seconds and carry it off in one hand while holding his axe in the other, haul a fallen 300-lb. beam off a pinned friend in four seconds, knock a 900-lb. statue off its plinth by running at it, or heave a 1,900-lb. boulder away from a blocked door over a period of several minutes by shifting it an inch or so at a time.

Running

Your running speed, or ground Move, is equal to your Basic Move score modified for encumbrance; see *Encumbrance and Move* (above).

Sprinting is all-out running. It's fast, but also fatiguing. You can sprint if you run *forward* for two or more seconds. Add 20% to your Move *after one second*. For instance, with a Move of 7, you could sprint at 8.4 yards/second after running for one second at 7 yards/second.

If you need to run a long distance, you should pace yourself to avoid exhaustion. Paced running averages exactly *half* of the sprinting speed calculated above.

After every 15 seconds of sprinting or every minute of paced running, roll against HT – or Running skill, if better. Failure costs you 1 FP. Once you're reduced to less than 1/3 of your FP, *halve* your Move for any kind of running; see *Fatigue* (pp. 188-189).

Swimming

Make a roll against Swimming skill (p. 79) any time you enter water over your head, and again every five minutes.

Subtract *twice* your encumbrance level; add +3 if you entered the water intentionally. If you fail, lose 1 FP and roll again in five seconds, and so on until you succeed at a roll, get rescued, or reach 0 FP and drown. If you recover, roll again in one minute; if you succeed, go back to rolling every five minutes.

Humans have water Move equal to Basic Move/5 (round down), minimum one yard per second. After every minute of top-speed swimming, roll against the *higher* of HT or Swimming skill. Failure costs you 1 FP. Once you're reduced to less than 1/3 of your FP, *halve* your water Move; see *Fatigue* (pp. 188-189).

Throwing

You can throw anything you can pick up – that is, anything with a weight of 8×BL or less. If the object isn't already in hand, you must take one or more Ready manoeuvres to grab it. See *Lifting and Moving Things* (p. 168) for details.

Throwing an object in combat – whether as an attack or not – requires an Attack manoeuvre. You can throw objects that weigh up to 2×BL using one hand; heavier objects require a two-handed throw. Roll against Throwing skill or DX-3 to hit a specific target, or against Throwing skill or DX to lob something into a general area. Apply the usual modifiers for target size, speed, and distance.

THROWING DISTANCE
AND DAMAGE TABLE

Use this table to determine how far you can throw an object and how much damage it does if it hits. Read the columns as follows:

Weight: Object's weight in pounds, compared to your Basic Lift (p. 28).

Distance Modifier: Multiply your ST by this value and drop all fractions to find the distance in yards you can throw the object.

Damage: If the object hits something or someone, it inflicts *thrust* damage for your ST (see the *Damage Table*, p. 28), modified as indicated here. Damage is usually crushing. A fragile object or a thrown character also suffers this damage; roll damage twice, once for the target and once for the projectile.

Weight	Distance Modifier	Damage
Up to BL/8	2	Thrust, -2 *per die*
Up to BL/4	1.2	Thrust, -1 *per die*
Up to BL/2	0.8	Thrust
Up to BL	0.6	Thrust, +1 *per die*
Up to 2×BL	0.3	Thrust
Up to 4×BL	0.15	Thrust, -1/2 *per die* (round down)
Up to 8×BL	0.08	Thrust, -1 *per die*

Don't use this table for thrown weapons that were intended as such; instead, consult the *Thrown Weapon Table* (p. 153) for range and damage.

Example: Jemzarkiza (ST 9, BL 16) grabs a 1-lb. pineapple from a market stall and throws it at a passer-by whom she recognises as a disguised demon. (It's a long story.) She can throw it up to 18 yards. If it hits, it does 1d-4 crushing damage; it also *takes* 1d-4.

Her target, who's ST 19 (giving BL 72), retaliates by picking up a 98-lb. bystander and throwing him at Jemzarkiza. He can throw the unfortunate fellow five yards, for 2d-1 crushing damage to whatever he hits and another 2d-1 to his terrified victim. He follows up with a 50-lb. sack of potatoes; range is 11 yards, damage is 2d+1.

Mental Feats

Many adventuring activities involve the mind or the senses.

Sense Rolls

"Sense rolls" include Vision rolls, Hearing rolls, and Taste/Smell rolls. To notice something using a given sense, roll against your Perception modified for any relevant advantages or disadvantages. Sense rolls often take modifiers for range, obviousness, and so on. The GM assigns these as required.

Comprehension Rolls: A successful Sense roll means you noticed something. That's often sufficient, but in some cases, the GM may require a second roll to *understand* what you've sensed; e.g., to realise that the "owl hoot" you heard is really an Howondaland warrior, or that the faint scent you noticed belongs to the flower of a man-eating Howondaland plant (yes, you end up making a lot of rolls when you visit Howondaland). This roll is against IQ for

details that anyone could figure out, or against an appropriate skill if the significance would be lost on anyone but an expert.

Danger Sense: If you have Danger Sense (p. 169) and fail a Sense or comprehension roll for something *dangerous*, the GM will secretly make a Perception roll for you. Success means you sense the danger anyhow!

VISION

Make a Vision roll whenever it's important that you *see* something. Use range and size modifiers as for combat (*Size and Speed/Range Table*, pp. 179-180) – smaller objects at greater distances are harder to see! Penalties for darkness, fog, etc. likewise apply (see *Visibility*, p. 179).

When you try to spot something that's deliberately hidden, the GM may treat this roll as a Quick Contest against a concealment skill (Camouflage, Holdout, etc.), and may allow – or *require* – a skill such as Observation or Search to replace Perception for the roll.

Conversely, when something is *in plain sight*, roll at +10.

Hearing

Make a Hearing roll whenever it's important that you hear a sound. The GM will often require a separate IQ roll to make out speech, especially in a foreign language.

When you try to hear someone who's attempting to move silently, the GM may treat this roll as a Quick Contest against his Stealth skill. If you're *actively* listening for such activity, the GM may allow you to substitute Observation skill for Perception.

Taste/Smell

Taste and smell are two manifestations of the same sense. Make a Taste roll to notice a flavour, a Smell roll to notice a scent.

Will Rolls

When you're faced with a stressful situation or a distraction, the GM may require you to roll against your Will to stay focussed. Success lets you act normally. Failure means you submit to the fear, give in to the pressure, are distracted, etc.

Fright Checks

A "Fright Check" is a Will roll made to resist *fear*. Fright Checks can occur as often or as rarely as fits the campaign "flavour." With only minor adaptation, the GM can use these rules for awe, confusion, etc., as well as fear.

As a general rule, "ordinary" frightening things don't require Fright Checks. Fright Checks are for events so unusual and terrifying that they might stun or even permanently scar someone.

A Fright Check is subject to any number of modifiers, including ones derived from appropriate advantages or disadvantages, and the circumstances surrounding the roll.

When someone fails a Fright Check, the GM rolls another 3d, adds the margin of failure on the Fright Check, and then looks up the result on the *Fright Check Table* and inflicts the associated effects on the unfortunate victim.

Fright Check Table

Many results below give a new mental quirk or disadvantage. The GM assigns this trait, which should be related to the frightening event – and, if possible, to the victim's *existing* mental traits! Rarely, attribute levels may be lost; this also lowers associated secondary characteristics and skills. These quirks, disadvantages, and attribute losses reduce the victim's point value.

4, 5 – Stunned for one second, moaning softly, then recover automatically.

6, 7 – Stunned and silent for one second. Every second after that, roll vs. unmodified Will to snap out of it.

8, 9 – Stunned for one second, and emit a small scream. Every second after that, roll vs. Will, at whatever bonuses or penalties you had on your original roll, to snap out of it.

10 – Stunned for 1d seconds, and emit a loud scream. Every second after that, roll vs. modified Will, as above, to snap out of it.

11 – Stunned and making random gibbering noises for 2d seconds. Every second after that, roll vs. modified Will, as above, to snap out of it.

12 – Lose your lunch. You can do nothing but retch for (25 - HT) seconds; then roll vs. HT each second to recover.

13 – Say "Ah, yes – I *see!*" and acquire a new mental quirk (see *Quirks*, pp. 66-68). This is the only way to acquire more than five personal quirks.

14, 15 – Lose 1d FP, making a horrible gurgling noise, and take 1d seconds of stunning as per **10.**

16 – Stunned for 1d seconds, as per **10** – making semi-coherent gibbering noises throughout – *and* acquire a new quirk, as per **13.**

17 – Gurgle once, faint for 1d minutes, and then roll vs. HT each minute to recover.

18 – Gurgle and faint, as above, and roll vs. HT immediately. Failure means you take 1 HP of injury as you collapse.

19 – Emit a shrill scream and then suffer a severe faint, lasting for 2d minutes. Roll vs. HT each minute to recover. Take 1 HP of injury.

20 – Moan faintly, then go into a faint bordering on shock, lasting for 4d minutes. Also, lose 1d FP.

21 – Panic. Run around screaming, sit down and cry, or do something else equally pointless for 1d minutes. At end of that time, roll vs. unmodified Will once per minute to snap out of it.

22 – Acquire a -10-point Delusion (p. 59). Scream out "Aaargh! Yes! Of course!" and start explaining the Delusion to the nearest being you see.

23 – Acquire a -10-point Phobia (pp. 62-63) or other -10-point mental disadvantage, and shout out "No! Not *that!*"

24 – Major physical effect, set by GM: hair turns white, age five years overnight (more, if you have Longevity), go partially deaf, etc. In game terms, acquire -15 points in physical disadvantages (for this purpose, each year of age counts as -3 points).

25 – If you already have a Phobia or other mental disadvantage that's logically related to the frightening incident, your self-control number becomes one step worse. If not, or if your self-control number is already 6, add a new -10-point Phobia or other -10-point mental disadvantage. Gibber a bit, too.

26 – Faint dead away for 1d minutes, as per **18** but silently, and acquire a new -10-point Delusion, as per **22**.

27 – Faint dead away for 1d minutes, as per **18** but silently, and acquire a new -10-point mental disadvantage, as per **23**.

28 – Make a small noise and fall into a light coma. Roll vs. HT every 30 minutes to recover consciousness. For six hours after you come to, all skill rolls and attribute checks are at -2.

29 – Coma, as above, but with no noise at all. You're unconscious for 1d hours. Then roll vs. HT. If the roll fails, remain in a coma for another 1d hours, and so on.

30 – Catatonia. Sit down on the spot and stare into space for 1d days. Then roll vs. HT. On a failure, remain catatonic for another 1d days, and so on. If you have no medical care, lose 1 HP the first day, 2 the second, and so on. If you survive and awaken, all skill rolls and attribute checks are at -2 for as many days as the catatonia lasted.

31 – Seizure. You lose control of your body and fall to the ground in a fit lasting 1d minutes and costing 1d FP. Also, roll vs. HT. On a failure, take 1d of injury. On a critical failure, you also lose a level of HT *permanently*.

32 – Stricken. You fall to the ground, taking 2d of injury in the form of a mild heart attack or stroke. Clutch at your chest.

33 – Total panic. You're out of control and might do *anything*. The GM rolls 3d: the higher the roll, the more useless your reaction. For instance, you might jump off a cliff to avoid a monster. If you survive your first reaction, roll vs. Will to come out of the panic. On a failure, the GM rolls for another panic reaction, and so on!

34 – Acquire a -15-point Delusion (p. 59), and explain it to someone or something on the spot.

35 – Acquire a -15-point Phobia (pp. 62-63) or other -15-point mental disadvantage. Yell "Hah!" and look smug as well as frightened.

36 – Severe physical effect, as per **24**, but equivalent to -20 points of physical disadvantages.

37 – Severe physical effect, as per **24**, but equivalent to -30 points of physical disadvantages.

38 – Coma, as per **29**, *and* a -15-point Delusion, as per **34**. You mutter about the delusion while you're comatose.

39 – Coma, as per **29**, *and* a -15-point Phobia or other -15-point mental disadvantage, as per **35**. You appear to be having nightmares while you're comatose – lots of twitching!

40+ – As per **39** in every way, but you *also* lose a level of IQ *permanently*.

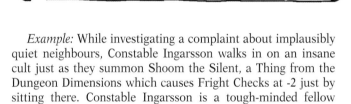

Mental Stunning

As explained in *Knockdown and Stunning* (pp. 185-186), physical injuries can stun you, preventing you from doing much that's useful. Exotic non-injuring attacks, magic, and so on can also cause physical stunning.

It's also possible to be *mentally* stunned, which has much the same effect but comes from confusion in your brain instead of shock to your body. Causes include surprise, terror, and slightly subtler magic. Use the rules for physical stunning, except that the roll to recover is *usually* against IQ rather than HT. (Not always, though; in particular, someone who suffers from Combat Paralysis, p. 57, needs to get his body to override the confusion in his brain.)

Example: While investigating a complaint about implausibly quiet neighbours, Constable Ingarsson walks in on an insane cult just as they summon Shoom the Silent, a Thing from the Dungeon Dimensions which causes Fright Checks at -2 just by sitting there. Constable Ingarsson is a tough-minded fellow (Will 12 and Fearlessness 1), but still . . .

His player rolls, needing 12 + 1 - 2 = 11 or less; unfortunately, he gets 14. The GM rolls 3d, gets 13, adds 3 (the margin of failure), and looks up the result (16) on the *Fright Check Table*. Ingarsson is stunned for 1d seconds (3, as it turns out). After that, he must start rolling against 11 – the same as his initial Fright Check – to resume being useful. He also gibbers while stunned ("*The Not Talking, it's the Not Talking!*"). And he gains a quirk; the GM announces that he has become suspicious of people who don't say much.

Social Concerns

The PCs will often interact with NPCs, and there are rules to cover this. Quite often, the results will be too obvious to bother rolling dice over; e.g., if you go into a grocer's shop and offer the advertised price for some cabbages, the shopkeeper will probably take your money, provided that you don't draw a weapon or do anything equally deranged. In other cases, though, there's an element of uncertainty and maybe skill. It's possible to roleplay many such social interactions – and that's indeed a lot of the fun of roleplaying games – but bringing rules into this serves several purposes:

● It allows the GM to determine what random NPCs think of the PCs without having to decide on full character profiles for all of them.

● It permits players who don't happen to be expert social manipulators to *play* such people by spending character points on appropriate advantages, perks, and skills.

● It enforces the effects of social *disadvantages*, keeping them from being free points. An unattractive, obnoxious, or clueless *character* doesn't get to avoid social difficulties merely because the *player* is a smooth talker!

Reaction Rolls

When the PCs meet an NPC whose reaction to them isn't predetermined, the GM makes a "reaction roll" on 3d. The higher the roll, the better the reaction. The GM then plays the NPC according to the guidelines on the *Reaction Table*.

The GM should keep this roll secret from the players. They don't know, for instance, whether that friendly looking old farmer is giving them straight advice or sending them into a trap.

A reaction roll is *not* a success roll. There are three important differences:

1. There's no "target number" to roll against.
2. A high roll is *good*, not bad.
3. Reaction modifiers apply directly to the dice roll. A reaction *bonus* is any factor that makes NPCs *friendlier*, while a reaction *penalty* is something that biases NPCs *against* the PCs.

Some common reaction modifiers:

Personal appearance and behaviour. This is especially true for the PC who does the talking! Above-average appearance gives a bonus, as do some advantages. Below-average appearance and many disadvantages give a penalty.

Racial or national biases. Dwarfs traditionally don't like trolls, neither of them trust elves an inch, and so on. These are usually penalties, taking the form of an Intolerance disadvantage on the part of the NPC.

Appropriate behaviour by the players! Here's a chance to reward good roleplaying. A good approach should be worth +1 or more. A wholly inappropriate approach that antagonises the NPCs should give the party -1 or -2 on the reaction roll. Don't tell the players, "You blew it!" – just roleplay the offended character, and let them figure it out.

Random reaction rolls are great when they add a note of unpredictability to the game – this is more fun for the GM, too! However, *never substitute random dice rolls for reason and logic.*

REACTION TABLE

Roll 3d and apply any reaction modifiers.

0 or less – *Disastrous.* The NPC hates the PCs and will act in their worst interest. Nothing is out of the question: assault, betrayal, public ridicule, or ignoring life-or-death pleas are all possible.

1-3 – *Very Bad.* The NPC dislikes the PCs, and will act against them if it's *convenient* to do so: attacking, offering grossly unfair terms in a transaction, lying maliciously, and so on.

4-6 – *Bad.* The NPC cares nothing for the PCs, and will act against them (as above) if he can *profit* by doing so.

7-9 – *Poor.* The NPC is unimpressed. He may make threats, demand a huge bribe before offering aid, or something similar.

10-12 – *Neutral.* The NPC ignores the PCs as much as possible. He's *uninterested.* Transactions will go routinely, as long as protocol is observed.

13-15 – *Good.* The NPC likes the PCs and will be helpful within normal, everyday limits. Reasonable requests will be granted.

16-18 – *Very Good.* The NPC thinks highly of the PCs and will be helpful and friendly, freely offering aid and favourable terms in most things.

19 or better – *Excellent.* The NPC is extremely impressed by the PCs and will act in their best interests at all times, within the limits of his own ability – perhaps even risking his life, wealth, or reputation.

Example: Ingarsson's partner, Constable Klump, was off buying some meat pies while Ingarsson dealt with that routine complaint. Hearing sudden screaming in the distance, he guesses that Ingarsson may need help. This sounds like a serious problem, so he calls to a passing street urchin to run to the Section House to tell them to send assistance.

The urchin is a minor NPC, so the GM makes a reaction roll for him. Unfortunately, Klump has a bad Reputation among street urchins, being prone to trying to reform them, which gives him -2 to their reactions. He has no other modifiers that apply here. The GM rolls a 10, which would normally be a "Neutral" reaction – possibly enough to make the urchin helpful in a sluggish sort of way – but with the -2, that becomes 8, "Poor." The urchin sees no reason to help, sneers at Klump behind his back, and doesn't go anywhere.

Influence Rolls

An "Influence roll" is a *deliberate* attempt to ensure a positive reaction from an NPC. A PC with an appropriate "Influence skill" (pp. 74-75) can always elect to substitute an Influence roll for a regular reaction roll in suitable circumstances (GM's decision).

Decide which Influence skill you're using: Diplomacy, Fast-Talk, Intimidation, Savoir-Faire, Sex Appeal, or Streetwise. Choose wisely! The GM may allow other skills to work as Influence skills in certain situations (e.g., Law skill, when dealing with a judge). Then roll a Quick Contest: your skill vs. the subject's Will. In this situation, your skill is subject to all the modifiers that would affect a reaction roll from the same person (pp. 171-172), regardless of whether they would normally apply to that skill.

If you *win*, you get a "Good" reaction from the NPC – "Very Good," if you used Sex Appeal, but the target may have a specific idea of what *you* are going to do in that case. On any other outcome, the NPC resents your clumsy attempt at manipulation. This gives you a "Bad" reaction – "Very Bad," if you attempted Intimidation. *Exception:* If you used Diplomacy, the GM will also make a regular reaction roll and use the *better* of the two reactions. Thus, Diplomacy is relatively safe.

See *Reaction Rolls* (pp. 171-172) for more on what these NPC reactions mean.

Example: Ingarsson and Klump dealt with Shoom before it had completely manifested, by chopping out some timbers and collapsing the building on it. However, the summoners (apart from two whom Shoom ate) escaped through a back door. The constables decide that they need to be caught quickly. Fortunately, they notice a licenced thief lurking nearby.

Klump approaches the man and uses Streetwise to attempt an Influence roll, pointing out that the streets will be far less dangerous for everyone if demon-summoning nutters are stopped, and the Watch will be less inclined to cause trouble for honest working thieves if they're helpful at times like this . . . Klump has Streetwise-10 (he has problems with Shyness), and a +1 Reputation with Thieves' Guild members, as a fair sort of copper, making his effective skill 11. He rolls 7, succeeding by 4, while the thief rolls 9 against his Will of 10, succeeding by just 1; Klump wins the Quick Contest. The thief tells the watchmen about the place two streets away which the Guild had down as a possible unlicenced den of villainy, until they decided it was just a bunch of would-be cultists and so not their problem.

Characters With Jobs

In many campaigns, the PCs will have "day jobs." These pay more-or-less regular incomes, allowing the characters to maintain some level of Status (pp. 37-38). The following rules offer a quick way to handle such things.

Prerequisites

Each job has *prerequisites* – usually one or more skills, but other possibilities include minimum attributes (e.g., ST 11+ for someone hauling heavy loads), advantages (such as Clerical Investment for a priest), and *prohibited* disadvantages (no stuttering town criers!). Prerequisite skills *should* usually be at 12+, or higher if they're a matter of life and death, but the Discworld has plenty of under-qualified people doing jobs badly.

Monthly Pay

Typical monthly pay for an *average* job depends on the campaign TL (pp. 30-31):

TL	0-2	3	4
Monthly Pay	$32	$35	$40

However, each job also has a Wealth level (pp. 33-34), which is the *usual* level of people doing that job. Apply the Wealth Multiplier for the job's Wealth level to the typical monthly rate to determine the job's *actual* monthly pay. Hence, a Poor job at TL1 pays $6.40/month ($32 × 1/5), while a Wealthy job at TL4 pays $200/month ($40 × 5). The GM is welcome to flex these figures a little to reflect good or underpaid employment. For example, a watch constable in Ankh-Morpork is paid $30/month, plus a $5 living-out allowance for those who don't sleep in their watch-house.

Many jobs carry a *lot* of payment in kind. Notably, a wizard at Unseen University gets a comfortable room, some kind of clothing provision, use of *that* library, and all the food he can eat, while many rural witches operate entirely on a barter economy based on old clothes, store-cupboard surpluses, and favours owed. Games can still use this money-based system for such people. Just remember that it's purely an accounting convenience!

It's *possible* to get a job outside of your Wealth level, but hard to get one that pays much higher than your Wealth implies; you must convince a prospective employer that you have the skill and credibility, and they tend to notice that you just don't look the part. If your Wealth level doesn't support your Status (p. 37), you'll be forever chasing unusually well-paid work; the GM should take this as an excuse to keep you continually involved in adventures and plots. And if your income, savings, and lifestyle rise toward a higher Wealth level, the GM can require you to purchase that level with bonus character points (p. 219).

If your Status comes from Rank (see *Special Cases for Status*, p. 38), the salary attached to that Rank will generally be enough to support it, but the job may well have a Duty or other special requirements attached.

Monthly Work and Getting Paid

At the end of every month on the job, roll to determine whether you performed the job competently. This roll is usually against one of the job's prerequisite skills, but possibly against something else; e.g., unskilled labour may require a ST or HT roll. For most jobs, use the *best* prerequisite – possibly at a bonus, for very routine work. A challenging job may use your *worst* prerequisite, though, or require a roll at a penalty. The GM decides.

For ordinary jobs, anything but critical success or critical failure means that you receive the monthly pay for the job, although freelancers may earn 10% extra times their margin of success, or 10% less times their margin of failure. In any case, critical success means something good – maybe a small promotion or bonus, or triple pay for freelancers. Likewise, critical failure means something *bad* – often no pay at all that month, possibly job-related injuries (especially in heavy or combat-related jobs), the sack, arrest (for criminal jobs), or demotion. The GM can use this to start new adventures or just to make trouble for PCs.

Combat

Combat is handled using a fairly detailed set of rules. This is partly because it's capable of rendering characters dead or badly hurt – so it's only fair to resolve this clearly, with opportunities for players to influence events by their choices – and partly because fight scenes are exciting and dramatic. The GM can also use these rules to resolve "action" situations such as chases and tournaments.

The GM decides when to start using the combat rules. This will generally be when fighting seems likely and people begin manoeuvring for tactical advantage.

Turn Sequence

Combat takes place second by second. Each character actively involved in combat gets one opportunity to act per second, referred to as his "turn." A given participant's turn is the one-second period that stretches from when he chooses a manoeuvre (see *Manoeuvres*, pp. 174-176) until his next opportunity to select a manoeuvre. This overlaps other combatants' turns.

The GM shouldn't feel constrained by this one-second timescale. It's merely a way of breaking a battle into manageable chunks!

He should feel free to drop out of combat time whenever dramatically appropriate, and to resume combat time when noncombat action gives way to more fighting.

The "turn sequence" is the order in which active characters take their turns. It's set at the start of the fight and doesn't change during combat. The combatant with the highest Basic Speed goes first and takes his turn, then the one with the next-highest Basic Speed, and so on, in descending order by Basic Speed. Once everyone has taken his turn, the sequence restarts from the top, this cycle continuing until combat time ends.

Tied Speeds: If multiple NPCs on the same side have the same Basic Speed, the GM simply decides who goes first – it isn't really important. If PCs are involved, ties go to the highest DX. If there's still a tie, the GM should roll randomly at the start of combat to determine who acts first, and use that order throughout the fight.

Example: Constable Ingarsson bursts in on a meeting of four renegade street mimes who've taken to summoning monsters from beyond reality in an act of artistic protest, and who aren't in any mood to surrender . . . Constable Ingarsson has Basic Speed 5.75, as does the mimes' leader, Glass Box Graham; the other three mimes all have Basic Speed 5.00. Graham wasn't surprised (he has Danger Sense); the other mimes were. As Graham has better DX than Ingarsson, he gets to act first, then Ingarsson, and finally the other mimes (if they recover from surprise). Then Graham will act again, followed by Ingarsson, and then the other mimes. And so on.

Manoeuvres

A "manoeuvre" is an action you can take on your turn. Each turn, you must choose *one* of the following manoeuvres: Aim, All-Out Attack, All-Out Defence, Attack, Change Posture, Concentrate, Do Nothing, Move, Move and Attack, or Ready. Your choice determines *what you can do* on your turn, and sets your options for movement and active defence (see *Defending*, pp. 180-181).

For the purpose of active defences, your manoeuvre is considered to be in effect until you select another manoeuvre on your next turn. For instance, if you chose All-Out Defence (which gives

a defensive advantage), its benefits would apply if you were attacked after you took your turn, and would persist until it was your turn again and you took a different manoeuvre.

If you're attacked before you've had a chance to choose a manoeuvre – usually at the start of combat – you're considered to be taking a Do Nothing manoeuvre (below).

Manoeuvre Table

Active Defence: Whether the manoeuvre allows active defences (p. 180).

Movement: Movement allowed by this manoeuvre. "Full Move" is Basic Move adjusted as usual for encumbrance, injury, etc.; "Half Move" is half that (rounded down, but at least one yard); "Step" is one yard; and "None" means what it says.

Manoeuvre	Active Defence	Movement
Aim	Any*	Step
All-Out Attack	None	Half Move
All-Out Defence	Any†	Step
Attack	Any	Step
Change Posture	Any	None
Concentrate	Any*	Step
Do Nothing	Any‡	None
Move	Any	Full Move
Move and Attack	No Parry	Full Move
Ready	Any	Step

* Taking an active defence *will* spoil aim and *may* spoil concentration (roll Will-3).

† Gives bonuses under *All-Out Defence* (pp. 175-176).

‡ Defences are at -4 if taking Do Nothing due to stunning or surprise.

DO NOTHING

Anyone who is just standing still is assumed to be *doing nothing.* When combat begins, anyone who hasn't yet taken a turn is treated as if he took this manoeuvre before entering combat.

Someone who's conscious but stunned or surprised *must* take this manoeuvre. On each turn of Do Nothing, he may attempt a HT roll to recover from physical stunning or an IQ roll to recover from mental stunning or surprise. Success means he recovers at the *end* of his turn – that is, he takes Do Nothing this turn but may act normally next turn.

MOVE

Move, but take no other actions except those specified under *Free Actions* (above). You may move any number of yards up to your full Move score. Most other manoeuvres allow at least some movement on your turn; take this manoeuvre if *all* you want to do is move.

Players must tell the GM exactly where their PCs move to so that he can keep track of the combat. The GM decides where NPCs move and will inform any players whose PCs are in a position to witness the movement.

CHANGE POSTURE

This manoeuvre lets you switch between any two "postures." Valid postures are *standing, sitting, kneeling, crawling, lying prone* (face down), and *lying face up.* Any posture other than standing slows your movement and penalises your attack and defence rolls, but also makes you a smaller target for ranged attacks.

You cannot stand up directly from a lying position. If you're lying (prone *or* face up), you must take a Change Posture manoeuvre to rise to a crawling, kneeling, or sitting posture first. A second Change Posture manoeuvre lets you stand from any of these postures. (Going from standing up to lying down, however, only takes one manoeuvre – or none at all, if the change was involuntary!)

You can switch between kneeling and standing (only) as the "step" portion of any manoeuvre that allows a step (see the *Manoeuvre Table*, p. 174) – you don't need Change Posture for that. This is *instead* of using the step to move. Thus, you could go from prone to kneeling with a Change Posture manoeuvre on one turn, and stand up in place on your next turn by taking a manoeuvre that allows a step.

Crouching does *not* require a Change Posture manoeuvre; see *Free Actions* (p. 175).

Posture Table

Attack: Modifier when making a *melee* attack from this posture.
Defence: Modifier to all active defence rolls.
Target: Modifier to hit you with a *ranged* attack.
Movement: Effect on movement.

Posture	Attack	Defence	Target	Movement
Standing	Normal	Normal	Normal	Normal; may sprint
Crouching	-2	Normal	-2	×2/3
Kneeling	-2	-2	-2	×1/3
Crawling	-4	-3	-2	×1/3
Sitting	-2	-2	-2	None
Lying Down	-4	-3	-2	1 yard/second

AIM

This manoeuvre is used to aim a ranged weapon (or a device such as an iconograph or a spyglass). You must choose a specific target. You can't aim at something that you can't see or otherwise detect.

Specify the weapon you're aiming with and your target. If you follow an Aim manoeuvre with an Attack or All-Out Attack with the *same* weapon against the *same* target, you get a bonus to hit. Add the weapon's Accuracy (Acc) to your skill.

If you *brace* a crossbow or similar, you get an extra +1 to Acc. A weapon is braced if you can rest it on a sandbag, low wall, cart, etc. A pistol crossbow or a spring gun is considered braced if used two-handed.

If you Aim for more than one second, you receive an additional bonus: +1 for two seconds of Aim, or +2 for three or more seconds.

You can use an active defence while aiming, but this costs you your aim and all accumulated benefits. If you're *injured*, you must make a Will roll or lose your aim.

ATTACK

Use this manoeuvre to make an armed or unarmed attack in melee or ranged combat. To use a *weapon* to attack, it must be ready.

If you're making a *melee* attack (e.g., with a sword or a fist), your target must be within its reach. Resolve the attack as explained under *Melee Attacks* (pp. 177-178).

If you're making a *ranged* attack (e.g., with a crossbow or a lightning bolt), your target must be within its Max range. Resolve

the attack according to *Ranged Attacks* (p. 178). If you took an Aim manoeuvre last turn, you'll have a bonus to hit.

ALL-OUT ATTACK

Attack a foe, making no effort to defend against enemy attacks. Again, any weapon used must be ready.

If making a *melee* attack, you must specify *one* of these three options before attacking:

- *Determined:* Make a single attack at +4 to hit.
- *Double:* Make two attacks against the same foe, *if* you have two ready weapons or one weapon that doesn't have to be readied after use. Attacks with a second weapon held in the off hand are at the usual -4 (see *Handedness*, p. 29) unless you have Ambidexterity (p. 41).
- *Strong:* Make a single attack, at normal skill. If you hit, you get +2 to damage – or +1 damage *per die*, if that would be better. This only applies to melee attacks doing ST-based thrust or swing damage.

If making a *ranged* attack, your only option is a single attack at +1 to hit.

Untrained Fighters

Amateur combatants (such as most members of peasant mobs) tend not to be especially competent, rolling against DX if unarmed or using weapon skills at default. See also *Improvised Monster-Slaying Weapons* (p. 150). To compensate, they mostly use All-Out Attack (Determined) for +4 to hit while their nerve holds, and then switch to All-Out Defence when they get worried. Mobs are dangerous because of the sheer number of attackers – their victims often resort to All-Out Defence themselves, rather than hit back.

MOVE AND ATTACK

Move as described for the Move manoeuvre (p. 174), but during or after your move, make a single, poorly aimed attack – either unarmed or with a ready weapon.

You attack as described for the Attack manoeuvre (above), but at a penalty. If making a ranged attack, you lose all Aim bonuses, and the penalty is -2 or your weapon's Bulk, whichever is *worse*. If making a melee attack, your penalty is -4, and your adjusted skill cannot exceed 9.

ALL-OUT DEFENCE

The manoeuvre to choose when beset by foes! You must specify *one* of these two options:

- *Increased Defence:* Add +2 to *one* active defence of your choice: Dodge, Parry, or Block. This bonus persists until your next turn.
- *Double Defence:* Apply two *different* active defences against the same attack. If you fail your defence roll against an attack, you may try a second, different defence against it. For instance, if you fail a dodge, you may try to parry or block.

If you try a parry (armed or unarmed) with one hand and fail, a parry using the other hand *does* count as a "different defence."

"You ever done this sort of thing before?"

"What sort of thing?"

"Rushed into a temple, killed the priehsts, shtolen the gold and reshcued the girl."

"No, not in so many words."

"You do it like thish."

– The Light Fantastic

CONCENTRATE

You *concentrate* on one primarily mental task. Examples include making a Vision roll to locate a hidden crossbowman, rolling against Leadership to give orders, working magic to create a fireball to hurl at enemies, and many other IQ-based skill rolls. Some activities require you to Concentrate for multiple seconds. If you use an active defence or are knocked down, injured, or otherwise distracted before you finish, you must make a Will-3 roll. Failure means you lose your concentration and must start over.

READY

Take a Ready manoeuvre to pick up or draw an item and prepare it for use; e.g., to pull a sword from its sheath or to reload a crossbow. Ready is also used to regain control of some unwieldy weapons after a swing, and to adjust the reach of some long weapons.

You may also use Ready to perform physical actions other than fighting: opening or closing a door, picking a lock, lifting, etc.

Example: Glass Box Graham has Fast-Draw (Sword) (p. 73) and he makes his skill roll, so he draws his smallsword as a free action; he *doesn't* have to Ready it. His fellow mimes lack that skill; thus, when they finally get over their surprise, each must take a Ready manoeuvre to draw his knife.

Timing

Knowing when things happen *within* your turn is important.

MARKING TIME

Anything that specifically marks time, expires, or is refreshed on your turn – e.g., spells you've cast, penalties that endure "until your next turn," or active defences – marks its time, expires, or is refreshed at the *start* of your turn, *before you choose your manoeuvre.*

WAITING

When you declare your manoeuvre, you may defer the actual action until if and when something you specify happens; e.g.,

"If the herd stampedes, I'll move out of the way." If the condition isn't met before your *next* turn comes, you stood around waiting the whole time – you never get two turns in a row!

You can make the condition as specific as the GM will accept. If you get too detailed, the GM might require a DX, IQ, or Per roll not to get things wrong – and failures can lead to accidents. "If anyone who isn't on my side comes into view, I'll shoot" is fine, but unless the two sides are clearly different, you'll probably need an IQ roll; at the very least, an opponent will get to attack *you* while you're thinking. Badly chosen conditions make for good comedy!

Range, Reach, and Close Combat

Distance is as critical as timing. At any time, you're a particular distance (in yards) from any given opponent. The GM determines this distance; a rough sketch map can help in complicated situations. If the distance exceeds your melee weapons' reach value, you can only use missiles until someone closes the gap.

Size Modifiers, Reach, and Weapons

Very large and very small fighters – those with a Size Modifier (see *Character Size*, p. 27) other than 0 – function a little differently from the human norm in combat and may find some standard human weapons unwieldy, unmanageable, or flimsy. Much of this is covered by weapons' ST statistic (p. 150), which makes it sensible for stronger or weaker characters to use larger or smaller weapons. Problems of balance can restrict small creatures' weapon choices severely; regardless of ST, a weapon that outweighs the wielder isn't usable, even for a pictsie.

Next, most very small characters have the Short Arms disadvantage (p. 96), which reduces the reach of any weapon they wield by 1. Dwarfism (p. 29) has the same effect. Conversely, large characters enjoy extra reach with their arms. Increase the *upper* end of the reach of any melee attack as follows:

SM	+1	+2	+3	+4	+5	+6
Reach	+0*	+1	+2	+3	+5	+7

* A reach "C" weapon or unarmed attack increases to reach 1, but there are no other effects.

Lastly, you gain +1 to hit when you *grapple* per +1 SM advantage you have over your target.

Example: A huge troll with SM +3 gets +2 to the upper end of his reach – a halberd with listed reach 2, 3 has reach 2-5 in his hands. If he *grapples*, he gets +3 to hit a normal human (SM 0), or +2 against a moderate-sized troll (SM +1).

For further options, see *Relative Sizes in Combat* (p. 179).

Attackers with short-reach attacks can try stepping closer to opponents with longer weapons, who may then have to retreat to preserve their advantage – and *anyone* might retreat for a bonus to defence rolls (see *Retreating*, pp. 181-182), possibly opening a gap large enough that someone must step forward to attack again. Hence, a fight can involve a lot of dancing back and forth.

If you step right up to someone, so that you're touching (more or less), that's "close combat." This requires weapons or unarmed attacks with reach "C." Usually, only two normal-sized humans can be in close combat with each other – whereas a half-dozen people can attack one seriously outnumbered victim from reach 1 by surrounding him, and three of them will count as attacking from behind.

Attacking

An "attack" is an attempt to hit a foe or other target. To do so, you must execute an Attack, All-Out Attack, or Move and Attack manoeuvre. You can attack with a weapon only if it's ready.

The GM always has the option of ruling, for any reason having to do with the situation, that some fighters cannot attack certain opponents. For instance, eight attackers couldn't hit one human-sized foe at the same time. (Even three or four attackers at once would be unlikely, unless their victim had no allies!)

There are two basic types of attack: *melee attacks* (below) and *ranged attacks* (p. 178). Your target must be within reach for the former, within range for the latter. Resolving either type of attack takes three dice rolls:

- First is your *attack roll*. If this is successful, your attack was a good one.
- Now your foe must make a *defence roll* to see if he can defend against your blow. If he succeeds, he evades or stops the attack.
- If your foe misses his defence roll, your blow strikes home and you *roll for damage*.

ATTACK ROLL

Your "attack roll" is a regular success roll. Figure your *effective skill* (base skill plus or minus any appropriate modifiers) with the attack you're using.

If your roll is *less than or equal to* your effective skill, your attack will hit unless your foe successfully defends (see *Defending*, pp. 180-181). If he fails to defend – or if he can't defend – you've hit.

If your roll is *greater than* your effective skill, you missed!

If your roll is a *critical success* (p. 166), you score a "critical hit." This means the blow hits automatically – your foe does *not* get a defence roll. In addition, you get some extra benefit from the attack; the GM decides what, although you can make polite suggestions. You might do the maximum possible damage for the attack, or inflict a *major wound* (p. 185) if any damage at all penetrates the opponent's armour, or your opponent may drop his weapon – whatever fits the situation. In a tavern brawl, you might pull a move so stylish that your opponent feels outclassed and backs down, whereas in battle, you're more likely just to do lots of damage. You can't simply score an automatic kill, although you may do enough damage to make one likely.

If your roll is a *critical failure* (p. 166), you not only miss (a "critical miss"), but you also suffer some kind of embarrassing or dangerous problem. Again, the GM decides the details; this is a wonderful opportunity for comedy, although your PC probably won't find it funny. You may drop your weapon, or have it break (*fine* and *very fine* weapons are largely immune to this, though), be thrown off balance so that you can't do anything until your next turn, lurch past your foe and leave your back exposed, pull a muscle, or do yourself a point or two of damage. Unarmed combatants are prone to falling over or punching brick walls. You won't *kill* yourself, but you might give your opponent a chance to do it for you – and the GM may decide that you knock yourself out, if that fits his plans.

> # Mounted Combat
>
> Occasionally, adventurers will need to fight when mounted on a horse, camel, armoured cart, broomstick, etc. This can get messy.
>
> Mounted combatants who are controlling the thing that's carrying them wield their weapons at the *lower* of the relevant combat skill or the skill used to control their transport: Riding for animals, Aerobatics for broomsticks, a vehicle skill, etc. They can defend by dodging, blocking, or parrying, but if their control skill is less than 12, subtract the shortfall from the defence roll; e.g., someone with Block 11 and Riding (Equines)-10 has an effective Block of 9 on horseback. If they're stunned, they must roll against the control skill at -4 or fall off – or maybe just fall over, if aboard a large vehicle. If they suffer knockback (p. 186), they automatically fall off unless they have saddle *and* stirrups (p. 356), in which case they get a roll at -4 *per yard of knockback* to stay on.
>
> *Passengers* are treated as using a Move and Attack manoeuvre (p. 175) if they attempt an attack, and they may have to make ST or DX rolls to hang on if the mount or vehicle does anything fancy. Seated passengers also suffer all the penalties for the sitting posture (see the *Posture Table*, p. 175). A passenger uses the same rules for being knocked off as the controller, except that he rolls against the *lower* of the controller's skill or his own ST to hang on, at a further -3 in either case.
>
> Nobody can benefit from more than one turn of Aim when making a ranged attack from a moving animal or vehicle. As well, anybody making a melee attack from transport moving at 7 yards/second or faster *relative to the foe* has -1 to hit but +1 to damage.

MELEE ATTACKS

When you take a manoeuvre that lets you make a melee attack, you must specify who you're attacking, and with what. You can make a melee attack using any *ready* melee weapon (including a "natural weapon" such as a kick, bite, or punch).

A one-handed weapon is ready if it's being held in your hand. A two-handed weapon is ready if you're gripping it with both hands. To draw a new weapon from a sheath, scabbard, or belt, you must take a Ready manoeuvre (p. 176) or roll against Fast-Draw (p. 73).

A natural weapon (punch, kick, etc.) is *always* ready unless the body part in question is occupied or restrained; e.g., you can't punch with a hand that's holding a weapon.

You can use some weapons in more than one way; e.g., you can swing or thrust with a shortsword. Such weapons have multiple lines on the weapon tables (pp. 151-154). When you attack with a weapon like this, you must indicate how you're using it *before* you roll.

Example: Glass Box Graham opts to make an Attack. He's two yards from Constable Ingarsson (it's a small room), and he can step one yard closer, while his smallsword has one yard of reach. He has Smallsword-12, but takes -1 to hit because Ingarsson has SM -1 (being a dwarf). Graham must roll 11 or less to hit, and gets 10. He has scored a hit – unless Ingarsson can do something about it.

RANGED ATTACKS

A "ranged attack" is any attack at a distance – from a thrown rock to an experimental gun. You can only make a ranged attack on a target that falls within your weapon's *range*. This appears on the relevant weapon table. Most ranged attacks list Half Damage (1/2D) range and Maximum (Max) range, in yards. Your target must be no farther away than Max range; 1/2D range only affects damage.

All ranged weapons have an Accuracy (Acc) statistic. This is the bonus you get if you take one or more Aim manoeuvres (p. 175) immediately before you attack. When you Aim, you can receive other bonuses for extra seconds of aim or bracing your weapon.

"Thrown weapons" are weapons you must physically hurl at the target: rocks, bubbling flasks, Agatean ninja stars, etc. You can also throw certain melee weapons, such as hatchets, knives, and spears. Treat a thrown weapon just like any other ranged attack.

For information on how long different weapons take between shots, see *Shots* (p. 150).

GENERAL ATTACK MODIFIERS

These apply to most or all attacks.

Attacker's Situation

Bad footing: -2 or more (GM's option)
Major distraction (e.g., all clothes on fire): -3 or more (GM's option)
Minor distraction (e.g., some clothes on fire): -2
Off-hand attack: -4 (*no* penalty with Ambidexterity)
ST below that required for weapon: -1 per point of deficit

Unarmed Combat

Sometimes you have to fight without weapons, or with small, improvised weapons. This is *unarmed combat*. Anyone can engage in unarmed combat, but certain skills make you more effective. The following table gives relevant game details; for explanations, see *Weapon Statistics* (pp. 149-150).

BOXING, BRAWLING, KARATE, or DX

TL	Weapon	Damage	Reach	Parry	Cost	Weight	ST	Notes
–	Punch	thr-1 cr	C	0	–	–	–	[1, 2]
1	Brass Knuckles	thr cr	C	0	$0.50	0.25	–	[1]

BRAWLING-2, KARATE-2, or DX-2

TL	Weapon	Damage	Reach	Parry	Cost	Weight	ST	Notes
–	Kick	thr cr	C, 1	No	–	–	–	[1, 2, 3]
–	Kick w. Boots	thr+1 cr	C, 1	No	–	–	–	[1, 3]

BRAWLING or DX

TL	Weapon	Damage	Reach	Parry	Cost	Weight	ST	Notes
–	Bite	thr-1 cr	C	No	–	–	–	[1, 2]
1	Blackjack or Sap	thr cr	C	0	$1	1	7	[1]

Notes

[1] Boxing improves damage with punches; Karate, with punches and kicks; and Brawling, with *all* attacks on this table. See *Unarmed Combat Skills* (pp. 82-83).

[2] The advantages under *Claws/Hooves* (p. 88) and *Teeth* (p. 92) modify the amount and/or type of damage done by some unarmed attacks – but *not* if you try to combine them with brass knuckles, boots, or Boxing skill.

[3] If you miss with a kick, roll vs. DX to avoid falling.

Judo Throws

On the turn immediately after a successful Judo parry, you may attempt to throw the attacker you parried. This counts as an attack. Roll against Judo to hit. (With an All-Out Attack, you cannot choose Double for two throws, but you can use Determined for one throw at +4.) Your foe may use any active defence – he *can* parry your hand with a weapon. If his defence fails, you throw him and he falls. He must roll against HT; failure means he's stunned!

Target's Size

The target's Size Modifier acts as a modifier to all attack rolls.

Visibility

Blind, target completely invisible, or in total darkness: -10
Cannot see foe: -6, or -4 if you know his location to within a yard
Partial darkness, fog, smoke, etc.: -1 to -9 (GM's option)

MELEE ATTACK MODIFIERS

These affect *melee* attacks, as do posture modifiers (p. 175) for the *attacker's* posture.

Attacker's Manoeuvre

All-Out Attack (Determined): +4
Move and Attack: -4, adjusted skill cannot exceed 9

RANGED ATTACK MODIFIERS

These affect *ranged* attacks, as do posture modifiers (p. 175) for the *target's* posture and modifiers from the *Size and Speed/Range Table* (below).

Attacker's Manoeuvre

All-Out Attack (Determined): +1
Move and Attack: -2 or the weapon's Bulk, whichever is *worse*

Situation

Target in partial cover: -2 (GM's decision)

Other Actions by Attacker

Aim for one turn: +Accuracy of weapon
Braced weapon: +1 if stationary *and* took a turn to Aim
Extra Aim: +1 for 2 seconds, +2 for 3+ seconds

SIZE AND SPEED/RANGE TABLE

The main use for this table is ranged combat. However, size affects melee combat, too – and the GM can also apply these modifiers to Sense rolls and other success rolls that size, speed, and/or range might believably affect.

The table uses the same progression for size as it does for the sum of speed and range, but the modifiers for size have the *opposite sign* from those for speed/range: large size gives a bonus, while large speed and range give a penalty. Thus, if a target is twice as big but also twice as far away and twice as fast, the net modifier to hit stays the same.

Target's Size: The larger the target, the easier it is to hit – in melee or at range. The modifier to hit an object due to its size is its "Size Modifier" (SM). Normal humans have SM 0 (see *Character Size,* p. 27); objects larger than man-sized give a bonus to hit, while smaller objects give a penalty. Look up the creature or object's longest dimension (e.g., height, for a humanoid) in the "Linear Measurement" column of the table, and then read across to the "Size" column to find its SM. If size falls between two values, base SM on the next-highest size. If an object is much smaller in *two* of three dimensions (e.g., a cable 100 yards long but just 2" thick), use the *smallest* dimension instead of the largest.

Target's Speed and Range: Speed and range only affect ranged combat. Add the target's speed in yards/second (which is *half* its speed in mph) to its range in yards, look up the total in the "Linear

Measurement" column, and then read across to the "Speed/Range" column to find the speed/range modifier. If the total falls between two values, use the higher; e.g., treat eight yards as 10 yards. For fighters in melee, assume speed is 0 and use range by itself.

Linear Measurement	Speed/Range	Size
1 foot	0	-5
1 yard	0	-2
2 yards	0	0
3 yards	-1	+1
5 yards	-2	+2
7 yards	-3	+3
10 yards	-4	+4
15 yards	-5	+5
20 yards	-6	+6
30 yards	-7	+7
50 yards	-8	+8
70 yards	-9	+9
100 yards	-10	+10

Example: Constable Klump is making his way around the back of the building with his crossbow out when he runs into the mimes' lookout. Both men failed their Stealth rolls, and the GM rules that this means they come face-to-face at a range of eight yards. The lookout – who recovers from his surprise first – was cleaning his nails with a small knife, which he promptly hurls at Klump. Being eight yards away, he has -4 to hit.

He misses. Realising that he's now dealing with an irritated, armed watchman, he decides to run for it. He's unencumbered and quick on his feet, with Move 7, so he's some way off and rounding a corner before Klump finally gets over his surprise and takes a shot. A target 15 yards away, travelling at 7 yards/second, has a speed/range of 15 + 7 = 22, giving Klump -7 to hit.

Deceptive Attacks

Most people are fairly easy to hit, but a skilled opponent – especially one who parries and retreats – can be tricky. To make combat a bit more interesting, use this optional rule:

You may make a "Deceptive Attack" by taking a voluntary skill penalty on your melee attack roll. You may not reduce your final effective skill below 10 this way. Every -2 you accept gives your opponent -1 on his defences *against that attack only.*

Example: Sasheveralle of Quirm makes a Deceptive Attack on Brother Do-Ko. Sasheveralle has Rapier-15 and attacks at -4, or skill 11 (he couldn't take -6, as that would reduce his skill below 10). If he hits, Do-Ko defends at -2.

Defending

If you make your attack roll, you have not (yet) actually struck your foe, unless you rolled a critical hit (see *Attack Roll*, p. 177). Your attack is *good enough* to hit him – *if he fails to defend.*

There are three "active defences" that a fighter can use: Dodge (see *Dodging*), Parry (see *Parrying*), and Block (see *Blocking*). Calculate these active defence scores in advance and record them on your character sheet.

An active defence is a deliberate attempt to avoid a particular attack. It's only possible if the defender is aware of the possibility of an attack from his assailant *and* is free to react . . . by moving out of the way (a dodge), deflecting the attack with a weapon or a hand (a parry), or interposing a shield (a block). Someone who's unaware of an attack, unconscious, immobilised, or otherwise unable to react gets *no* active defence.

If a foe makes a successful attack roll against you, you may choose *one* active defence and attempt a "defence roll" against it. *Exception:* The manoeuvre you chose last turn will often affect your available defences; see the *Manoeuvre Table* (p. 174). For instance, All-Out Defence (Double Defence) lets you attempt a second defence against a particular attack if your first defence fails, while All-Out Attack leaves you *no* defence.

DEFENCE ROLL

The defender rolls 3d against his active defence score, modified according to *Defence Modifiers* (p. 182). If his roll is *less than or equal to* his effective defence, he dodged, parried, or blocked the attack. Otherwise, his active defence was ineffective, and the attacker rolls for damage.

An active defence roll of 3 or 4 is *always* successful – even if the defender's effective defence score was only 1 or 2! A roll of 17 or 18 always fails.

On the other hand, no defence roll is allowed against a critical hit.

DODGING

A "dodge" is an active attempt to move out of the perceived path of an attack. This is often the best defence when you are not skilled with your weapon, have no shield, or are attacked multiple times. You may dodge *any* attack except one that you didn't know about, and there's no limit to the number of times you may dodge *different* attacks during your turn.

Dodge is the *only* active defence you can take against some "energy" attacks such as magical lightning. This doesn't mean you can actually dodge lightning bolts, but you *can* try not to be where your opponent shoots, by weaving or ducking at the right moment.

Your Dodge active defence is Basic Speed + 3, dropping all fractions. It takes a penalty equal to your encumbrance level (see *Encumbrance and Move*, p. 168).

BLOCKING

A "block" is an attempt to interpose a *ready* shield between yourself and an attack. Your Block active defence is 3 + *half* your Shield skill, dropping all fractions; e.g., Shield-11 would give a Block of 8. You may try to block only *one* attack per turn.

You can block melee attacks, mundane missiles (including thrown weapons), magical fireballs (which move like thrown weapons), and "jets" (like dragon's breath or liquids squirted from alchemical contraptions). You can't block *really* fast-moving attacks: lightning bolts, bullets from anachronistic guns, and so on.

Remember that a ready shield gives +2 to *all* active defences; see *Shields* (p. 155). Thus, if you can block in the first place, you'll *always* enjoy another +2! Also, while you usually have your shield on your "off" arm or hand (e.g., your left hand if you're right-handed), there's no penalty for this (and no bonus if you use your "good" hand) – that's all part of shield training.

PARRYING

A "parry" is an attempt to deflect a blow using a weapon or bare hands. You cannot parry unless your weapon is *ready* – or, if you're unarmed, you have an empty hand.

You can parry with most melee weapons. Your Parry active defence with a weapon is 3 + *half* your skill with that weapon, dropping all fractions; e.g., Broadsword-13 would give a Parry of 9. Check the weapon's Parry stat for modifiers; notably, a quarterstaff gets +2 due to its ability to keep foes at bay, while knives are so short that they give -1.

A parry won't stop anything except melee attacks or thrown weapons. *Exception:* If a foe attacks you with a handheld missile weapon *and* is within reach of your melee weapon or bare hands, you may parry. You're parrying the weapon, not the projectile! For example, if an attacker fired a crossbow at you from only one yard away, you could attempt to parry barehanded.

Success would mean that you slapped his arm or crossbow aside, causing him to fire wide.

You can parry thrown weapons, but at a penalty: -1 for most thrown weapons, or -2 for *small* ones such as knives, throwing stars, and anything else that weighs 1 lb. or less.

Multiple Parries

Once you've tried a parry with a particular weapon or bare hand, further attempts to parry using that weapon or hand have a cumulative -4 per parry after the first – or just -2 per additional parry when using a fencing weapon (one with an "F" on its Parry stat). This penalty only affects multiple parries on the same turn; on your *next* turn, you're back to your full Parry.

Off-Hand Parries

If you parry with your "off" arm or hand (e.g., your left hand if you're right-handed), you take the usual -4 to combat skill. As Parry score is based on half that skill, this gives -2 to Parry. Fighters with Ambidexterity (p. 41) or appropriate Off-Hand Training (p. 52) and a weapon in either hand – and those using Boxing, Brawling, Judo, or Karate – can get two *unpenalised* parries (against different attacks) per turn.

Parrying Unarmed Attacks

If you successfully parry an unarmed attack (bite, punch, etc.) *with a weapon,* you may injure your attacker. Immediately roll against your skill with the weapon you used to parry. This roll is at -4 if your attacker used Judo or Karate. Success means your parry struck the attacker's limb squarely. He gets no defence roll against this! Roll damage normally.

RETREATING

If you're on your feet in melee and can step back one yard from your opponent, you get a bonus to defence rolls: +3 to Dodge, and to Parry with Boxing, Judo, Karate, or fencing skills; +1 to other Parry scores and to Block. If this "retreat" takes you out of your opponent's reach but your defence roll fails, the attack still hits – it arrived faster than you could move.

You can only retreat *once* per turn, from *one* opponent, but you get those bonuses on *all* defence rolls against that foe that turn. If your enemy's attack permits a step and he hasn't yet stepped, he can choose to follow you as you retreat, driving you back. The GM may rule that you eventually run into a wall, are obstructed by other people or things, or must otherwise stop retreating.

You cannot retreat immediately after a Move and Attack manoeuvre.

Dodge and Drop: You can drop to the ground when dodging *ranged* attacks, earning +3 to all Dodge rolls against one opponent that turn (and possibly putting you behind low cover on *subsequent* turns). However, this leaves you lying on the ground!

Example: When Constable Ingarsson is attacked by Glass Box Graham, Ingarsson is considered to be taking a Do Nothing manoeuvre because it's the start of combat. As this manoeuvre isn't due to stunning or surprise, all defence options are open to him. He chooses to parry Graham's smallsword with his axe. Because the axe is an unbalanced weapon, this wouldn't be possible if Ingarsson had attacked with it on his turn – but he didn't. Ingarsson has Axe/Mace-12, giving a Parry of 9. He gets +1 for his

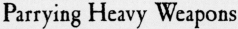

Parrying Heavy Weapons

Surely, interposing a feeble little rapier between oneself and a troll's club is just asking to get the rapier broken? If this worries you, apply these optional rules.

Roll 1d if the attacker's weapon weighed at least three times as much as the parrying weapon. The defender's weapon breaks on a roll of 1 or 2, going up to 1-3 if the attacker's weapon weighed four times as much, 1-4 if it weighed five times as much, and so on. Subtract 1 from this range for *fine* weapons, or 2 for *very fine* ones; see *Melee Weapon Quality* (p. 152). For example, an ordinary rapier (2.75 lbs.) used to parry a halberd (12 lbs.) would break on 1-3, while a *fine* rapier would break on only 1-2. A successful parry still works even if the weapon shatters, unless the chance was 1-6 (that is, automatic breakage).

Regardless of your weapon's weight, you *can't* parry a weapon that weighs more than your Basic Lift if using a one-handed weapon or bare hands, or more than twice your BL if using a two-handed weapon. If you try anyway, and the roll succeeds, all you've done is given your weapon a chance to break – and if it doesn't break, you drop it. If you're unarmed, you're knocked back a yard and must roll vs. DX or fall over.

Example: Thumbik the Gnome (ST 4, BL 3.2) foolishly opts to parry a mace (5 lbs.) using his dagger (0.25 lb.). He makes his roll – but all this means is that his dagger breaks automatically.

Thumbik takes damage but amazingly survives and tries a Brawling parry on his next turn. Again, his roll succeeds, which means that he's sent spinning a yard back and must make a DX roll or fall over.

Unarmed Attacks: Attackers using bare hands, bites, etc., count as weapons with a weight equal to 1/10 of their ST for these purposes.

Example: Henry is fighting a powerful vampire which has ST 22. Its fist counts as a 2.2-lb. weapon. The vampire throws a punch, which Henry parries with a small stake that weighs 0.5 lb.; the stake will break on 1-3 on 1d.

It does, but Henry's colleagues now drop a 100-lb. rock on the vampire. The vampire's BL is 97, so it can't parry the rock . . .

Combat Reflexes and opts to retreat for another +1. Rolling 8 against the 11 he needs, he swipes the sword aside.

Ingarsson's turn comes next, and he goes for broke. He closes the gap and makes an All-Out Attack (Determined), giving him +4. He rolls a 14, which is less than the 16 he needs – a hit! Graham has Smallsword-12, so his Parry is also 9. He retreats, too – and because a smallsword is a fencing weapon, he gets +3, for an effective Parry of 12. Unfortunately for him, he rolls a 13, so Ingarsson hits. We'll come back to this.

Then the other mimes get a chance to act. Two of them succeed at their IQ rolls to recover from surprise; they frown to indicate anger (a free action, like speech). The third fails and stands there with his mouth open. All three Do Nothing *this* turn. *Next* turn, the first two will be able to act while the third continues to Do Nothing and roll against IQ.

Unarmed Defence

When fighting without weapons, or with at least one hand free, you may choose to parry barehanded. You can use an unarmed combat skill for this, in which case your Parry active defence is 3 + *half* your skill, rounded down, but you may incur penalties against some or all weapons, and possibly kicks; see *Unarmed Combat Skills* (pp. 82-83). Alternatively, you can rely on DX, using each hand once per turn; your Parry is then 3 + *half* your DX, rounded down, and has -3 vs. *any* weapon. Beings without hands (like most animals) can't parry unarmed – they can only dodge.

DEFENCE MODIFIERS

Posture modifiers (p. 175) for the *defender's* posture also apply.

Defender's Equipment

Parrying with dagger/knife: -1 to Parry
Parrying with quarterstaff: +2 to Parry
Shield ready in hand: +2*
Unarmed parry vs. weapon: -3 to Parry (0 in some cases; see *Unarmed Combat Skills*, pp. 82-83)

Defender's Manoeuvre

All-Out Attack: no defence possible!
All-Out Defence (Increased Defence): +2 to *one* of Dodge, Block, or Parry
Move and Attack: dodge or block only; no parry (and no retreat)

Defender's Situation

Bad footing: -1 or more (GM's option)
Can't see attacker: -4, and block or parry requires a Hearing-2 roll
Distraction (e.g., clothes on fire): -1 or more (GM's option)
Encumbered: penalty equal to encumbrance level to Dodge, or to fencing, Judo, or Karate Parry
Stunned: -4

Nature of Attack

Attack from behind or critical hit: no defence possible!
Deceptive Attack: -1 per -2 the attacker took to his attack
Flails: -4 to Parry/-2 to Block vs. morningstar, -2/-1 vs. numknuts; fencing weapons *can't* parry
Thrown weapon: -1 to Parry, or -2 to Parry if *small* (1 lb. or less)

Other Actions by Defender

Multiple parries: -4 to Parry per parry after the first, cumulative (halved for fencing weapons)
Off-hand parry: -2 to Parry (no penalty w. Ambidexterity)
Retreat: +3 to Dodge, or to fencing, Judo, or Karate Parry; +1 otherwise

* A ready shield gives +2 against all attacks from the *front* or *shield side* (left, for a right-handed fighter), whether or not the defender is using it to block.

Damage and Injury

If your attack roll succeeds and your target fails his defence roll (if any), you hit him! If your attack is one that can do damage, you must now make a "damage roll." This tells you how much *basic damage* you deal to your target.

Your weapon (and, for muscle-powered weapons, your ST) determines the number of dice you roll for damage. If your target has any Damage Resistance (DR) – from armour, tough skin, etc. – he subtracts this from your damage roll.

If your damage roll is less than or equal to your target's DR, your attack *fails to penetrate* – it bounces off. If your damage roll *exceeds* your target's DR, the excess is the *penetrating damage*. If your foe has no DR, the entire damage roll is penetrating damage.

Once you know your attack's penetrating damage, apply the wounding modifier for damage type (this matters only for cutting, impaling, and certain types of piercing damage; see *Wounding Modifiers and Injury*, below). This gives the *injury* the foe suffers, which is subtracted from his Hit Points.

DAMAGE ROLL

You usually make your own damage rolls, while the GM rolls for NPCs. Damage rolls are expressed as a number of dice, sometimes with a modifier; e.g., "6d-1" or "1d+2." A negative modifier can't reduce damage below 0 if the attack does *crushing* damage, or below 1 if it does *any other type* of damage.

The result of the damage roll (*after* any modifiers, as explained above) is the hit's "basic damage."

If a ranged weapon has two range statistics, the first is its Half Damage (1/2D) range, in yards. If the target is at or beyond 1/2D range, *divide basic damage by 2*, rounding down.

Example: Constable Ingarsson has ST 12, so his axe does 1d+4 damage. He rolls and does 6 points.

DAMAGE RESISTANCE AND PENETRATION

Damage Resistance (DR) rates the degree of protection that tough skin, body armour, etc., afford against damage. Objects have their own DR values that protect against any damage *they* suffer – and if you take cover behind or inside them, their DR also protects *you*. In general, DR from multiple sources is additive; e.g., if your natural DR is 2 and you don medium armour with DR 3, your total DR is 5. Exceptions will always be noted.

Subtract DR from basic damage. The result is the "penetrating damage" that punched through or deformed the armour enough to cause a significant injury.

Example: Glass Box Graham is wearing black leathers – very light armour, with DR 1. Thus, Ingarsson's attack does 5 points of penetrating damage. But there's something else to consider . . .

WOUNDING MODIFIERS AND INJURY

Multiply any penetrating damage by the "wounding modifier" corresponding to the attack's damage type and the target's nature in the table below. This is often lower for *unliving* beings (see *Injury Tolerance*, p. 89) and *homogeneous* objects (furniture, trees, rocks, etc.). Treat complex machines – siege engines, experimental steam chariots, etc. – as unliving here.

Damage Types	Target		
	Living	*Unliving*	*Homogeneous*
Small Piercing (pi-)	×1/2	×1/5	×1/10
Piercing (pi)	×1	×1/3	×1/5
Burning (burn), Crushing (cr)	×1	×1	×1
Large Piercing (pi+)	×1.5	×1/2	×1/3
Cutting (cut)	×1.5	×1.5	×1.5
Huge Piercing (pi++), Impaling (imp)	×2	×1	×1/2

The damage after this multiplier is "injury": HP lost by the target. Round fractions *down*, but minimum injury is 1 HP for any attack which penetrates DR at all. Reduce the victim's current HP total by the injury sustained. The wound's severity and type determine what happens next; see *Injury, Illness, and Fatigue* (pp. 184-191) for rules on injuries and recovery.

Example: Being an axe blow, Constable Ingarsson's attack is cutting. Thus, the 5 points that penetrated Graham's armour are multiplied by 1.5, for 7 HP of injury.

Out back, Constable Klump, too, has scored a hit (he's a keen crossbow marksman). His crossbow bolts do 1d+4 impaling, and the lookout has no armour; so when Klump rolls 9 points of damage, all of it applies. This is *doubled* for impaling vs. a living target: 18 HP of injury!

Flushed with success and under the influence of narrative confusion, Klump later tries to shoot his way through a locked door. The GM points out that a door is homogeneous, and rules that it has DR 1, and that 25 HP will smash it down completely, while half that will break it down enough for Klump to squeeze through. Klump rolls 8 points of damage, so 7 points penetrate – but multiplying by 1/2 makes the injury just 3 HP. The door remains intact; Klump would do better to use a blunt (crushing) instrument.

AFFLICTIONS AND SPECIAL DAMAGE

Some exotic attacks don't do normal damage but are flagged as causing "afflictions" or "special" damage. Affliction attacks inflict unpleasant but usually temporary effects on the victim, and often allow a HT-based resistance roll (pp. 166-167). Such attacks come with notes detailing the specifics; examples include "moderate pain" (-2 to all DX, IQ, skill, and self-control rolls) and "severe pain" (-4 to those rolls). Special attacks have effects described on a case-by-case basis.

GRABBING AND GRAPPLING

Fighters sometimes want to grab opponents instead of bashing them. To attempt this, you must be in close combat (see *Range, Reach, and Close Combat,* pp. 176-177), have at least one hand free, and take an Attack, All-Out Attack, or Move and Attack manoeuvre. Roll against DX, Judo, or Wrestling to hit. Your foe may try to parry, dodge, or block this like any other attack. If he fails to defend, you're grappling him.

Grappling does no damage but gives your victim -4 to DX and all DX-based skills (including combat skills) for as long as you're holding on. He may not move away until he breaks free (see *Actions After Being Grappled,* below) or you let go. *Exception:* If you grapple a foe of twice or more your ST, you don't prevent him from moving away – you're just extra encumbrance.

If you're grappling your foe with all of your hands, the only further attacks you can make are those under *Actions After a Grapple* (below).

Actions After a Grapple

All of these actions require an Attack or All-Out Attack manoeuvre:

● *Takedown:* You may only try this on a standing foe. Roll a Quick Contest, with each contestant using the *highest* of ST, DX, or his best grappling skill (Judo or Wrestling). If you aren't standing, apply the attack penalty from the *Posture Table* (p. 175) to your roll.

Specific Hit Locations

For simplicity's sake, these rules abstract away questions of where an attack lands on a victim. A few useful tricks involve precise targeting, however. They're hard to execute, but All-Out Attack (Determined) can help.

Going for the Throat: Striking the neck with a blow gives -5 to hit, but raises the wounding modifier for *crushing* attacks to ×1.5 and that for *cutting* attacks to ×2. Anyone killed by cutting damage to the neck is beheaded. Decapitation is a great way to ruin a vampire's day or establish your barbarian cred!

Alternatively, you can *grab* the neck (see *Grabbing and Grappling,* above) at -3 to hit. If your grab succeeds, each turn thereafter, you can *squeeze*. Roll a Quick Contest: your ST vs. the higher of your foe's ST or HT. You have -5 if using only one hand. If you win, your victim takes crushing damage equal to your margin of victory. His DR protects normally, but this damage has a wounding modifier of ×1.5 – and if any damage penetrates his DR, he also starts to *suffocate* (p. 190).

Knee to the Groin: Normally, the groin is -3 to hit. However, if you've grappled your opponent from the front, you can roll Brawling-1 or Karate-1 to knee him in the groin; he defends at -2 due to the DX penalties for being grappled, and damage is as for a kick. Male victims suffer *double* normal shock penalties from crushing damage, to a maximum of -8, and have -5 to knockdown rolls.

Knockout Blow: An attacker who has sneaked up behind someone may try to knock out his victim with a *crushing* attack. Roll to hit at -5. If you hit, roll damage normally, subtracting armour DR and another DR 2 for the skull. Instead of suffering injury, the victim must make a HT roll at a penalty equal to penetrating damage (if damage is *exactly* 0 after DR, roll at full HT) or be knocked out for 15 minutes.

On the Chin: A blow to the jaw takes -5 to hit, ignores the victim's armour unless he's wearing a full suit of military plate, and gives -5 to knockdown rolls.

A thrust to the chest takes no attack penalty and produces no special effects. Most attacks hit the centre of mass anyway.

If you *win*, your victim falls down next to you; if he was grappling you, he loses his grip. If you lose, you suffer the same effects! On a tie, nothing happens.

- *Pin:* You may only attempt this if your foe is on the ground. Roll a Regular Contest of Strength. The *larger* fighter gets +3 for every point by which his Size Modifier exceeds his opponent's. The fighter with the most free hands gets +3. If you *win*, your victim is pinned and helpless; you must stay there to hold him down, but you can free one hand for other actions. If you lose or tie, nothing happens.
- *Strike:* You can bite even if all your hands are busy. If you aren't using a hand to grapple your foe, you can use it to Attack or All-Out Attack, either unarmed or with a reach C weapon.

As well, if you aren't using a hand to grapple, you can use it for a Ready manoeuvre. You cannot Aim, Concentrate, or make *ranged* attacks unless you've *pinned* your foe, however.

Finally, you may perform these free actions:

- *Release your grip* with one or both hands, possibly releasing your victim.
- *Drag or carry your victim:* If you've pinned a foe, you can move or step normally, dragging or carrying him. He counts as encumbrance. If you haven't pinned him, moving away from him means you automatically release your grip unless you have at least twice his ST. If you're *that* strong, you can pull or carry him with you.

Actions After Being Grappled

If you're *grappled*, you cannot take a Move manoeuvre unless you have at least twice your foe's ST. You can Attack or All-Out Attack, but you're limited to unarmed attacks (striking or grappling) or attacks using weapons with reach C. You can Ready something if you have a hand free, but you must roll vs. DX; failure means you drop the item. Aim, Concentrate, and *ranged* attacks are completely impossible.

If you're *pinned*, you can't take any manoeuvre that requires physical movement!

Breaking Free: You cannot move away until you break free by *winning* a Quick Contest of ST. Your opponent has +5 if he's grappling you with two hands. If he has you pinned, he rolls at +10 if using two hands or at +5 if using only one, and you may only attempt to break free once every 10 seconds. If your foe is stunned, he rolls at -4. If you successfully break free, you may immediately move one yard in any direction.

Getting Inside Armour

A trick beloved of pictsies and aggressive gnomes is crawling *inside* a foe's clothing (including armour) and getting inventively vicious. In game terms, this is possible only if the larger fighter's SM exceeds that of the smaller by more than six.

The attacker starts by *grappling* his opponent (see *Grabbing and Grappling*, pp. 183-184). If his target fails to break free, he can try a DX roll to infiltrate his quarry's clothes or armour on later turns. The GM may grant up to +4 for loose or voluminous attire, or assess a penalty as harsh as -4 for tight, skimpy, or well-tailored garb. This attempt counts as a step, and it can accompany an Attack or All-Out Attack on the same turn.

Once inside, further attacks are possible; these disregard the larger fighter's armour and shield. Alternatively, the "intruder" may take a Move manoeuvre to climb up inside his rival's clothes. This requires a Climbing roll – at default if necessary – but with +4 because there's so much to hang onto. The GM may inflict a Fright Check (pp. 170-171) on some victims at this point.

All attacks on the intruder are at -3, over and above size penalties, and the DR of any armour he's inside protects *him*. If the victim strikes and misses, he automatically hits himself (the GM may require a Will roll to use a significant weapon attack here). The same is true if someone else tries; the victim may make a defence roll rather than take this risk, but he must opt to do so *before* the dice are rolled to determine whether the blow hits his harasser or him. Where non-protective clothing or very light (DR 1) armour is involved, it's possible – and safer – to grapple the miniature menace.

Discarding clothing or armour to get at the tiny attacker requires one or more Ready manoeuvres per item; the GM rules how many turns are required and how many articles must be discarded. An intruder who wants to keep scurrying from one part of his target's outfit to another must take a Move manoeuvre and *win* a Quick Contest of IQ. A victim who isn't wearing rigid armour can try dropping to the ground and rolling; roll a Quick Contest of DX or Wrestling skill, and if the intruder loses, he takes 1d-3 crushing damage.

Injury, Illness, and Fatigue

Injuries

The life of an adventurer is not all song and glory. You get tired. You get your clothes dirty. You might actually get *hurt* – or even worse, *killed!*

Fortunately, most of these problems can be cured – although death gets kind of tricky. Read on . . .

Wounds and ailments cause "injury": a (usually) temporary loss of Hit Points. Thus, your HP score measures your ability to sustain injury; see *Hit Points* (p. 27).

If injury reduces you to 0 or fewer HP, you'll soon fall unconscious. You can even go to *negative* HP . . . but if you go too far, you risk death. For the average man, the difference between full HP and negative HP is one or two sword blows.

GENERAL INJURY: LOST HIT POINTS

Repeated wounding eventually causes *anyone* or *anything* to weaken and collapse, even if no single injury is very great. The chart below summarises the effects of being at low or negative HP. All effects are cumulative.

Less than 2/3 your HP left – You're *seriously* hurt. There's no specific penalty here, and determined warriors will continue fighting, but if you believed that you had the advantage, or that this was just a minor brawl, consider backing off or giving up.

Less than 1/3 your HP left – You're reeling from your wounds. Halve your Move and Dodge (round *up*). You should think seriously about surrendering or fleeing, as you could get yourself killed if you carry on. The GM should assume that ordinary NPCs will give up at this point, unless they have good reasons to fight to the death.

0 HP or less – You're in immediate danger of collapse. In addition to halving Move and Dodge as above, make an *immediate* HT roll, at -1 per *full* multiple of HP below zero. Failure means you fall unconscious (or simply stop working, if you weren't truly alive or conscious in the first place); see *Recovering from Unconsciousness* (p. 186). Success lets you act normally, but you must roll again *every turn* to continue functioning. *Exception:* If you Do Nothing on your turn, and you don't try any defence rolls, you can remain conscious without rolling. Roll only on turns during which you attempt a defence roll or choose a manoeuvre other than Do Nothing.

-1×HP – In addition to the above effects, make an *immediate* HT roll or die. (If you fail by only 1 or 2, you're dying but not dead; see *Mortal Wounds*, p. 186). If you succeed, you can still talk, fight, etc., as above (until you fail a HT roll and collapse). Roll again at -2×HP, -3×HP, and -4×HP, whether as a result of one wound or many. For instance, if you have 11 HP, you must roll to avoid death at -11 HP. If you survive, you must roll again at -22 HP, -33 HP, and -44 HP.

-5×HP – You die immediately. You've lost a total of *six times your HP!* Nobody can survive that much injury.

-10×HP – Total bodily destruction, if this makes sense given the source of the damage – 200 points of dagger wounds leave a messy but recognisable corpse; 200 points of dragon's breath injury leaves nothing but a lump of charcoal.

Example: Glass Box Graham had 10 HP, of which he has lost 7. He's down to 3 – less than 1/3 of what he started with. He's now at half Move and Dodge. He *should* be thinking about surrendering or running away, but he's a fanatic and his side still has a numerical advantage.

The mimes' lookout had a mere 9 HP, so the 18 he took from Klump's crossbow shot put him at -9, or exactly -1×HP. He must make a HT roll or die on the spot. Fortunately for him, he succeeds. He also has to attempt an immediate HT roll at -1 to avoid unconsciousness.

SHOCK

Whenever you suffer injury, reduce your DX and IQ by the number of HP you lost – to a maximum penalty of -4, regardless of your injuries – *on your next turn only.* This effect, called "shock," is temporary; your attributes return to normal on the turn after that.

Shock affects DX- and IQ-based skills, and also Will and Per rolls, but *not* active defences or other defensive reactions.

MAJOR WOUNDS

A "major wound" is any *single* injury of greater than 1/2 your HP. Any major wound requires a HT roll to avoid knockdown and stunning (see below).

If you thought this was a nonlethal brawl, you now know better. The GM might even require a Fright Check (pp. 170-171), if this level of violence was completely unexpected! For simplicity, the GM may assume that minor NPCs who suffer major wounds are out of the fight, for whatever reason, unless they have good reasons to the contrary.

> ## Biting Animals
>
> Some creatures, especially carnivorous animals, grab and hold on to opponents *with their teeth.* While any combatant can try this, it makes the most sense for beings which have an instinct for sinking their teeth into prey – and maybe claws to rake their victim.
>
> After any successful bite attack, the attacker can declare that he's holding on. Treat this as a *one-handed* grapple, should it matter (e.g., for breaking free); see *Grabbing and Grappling* (pp. 183-184). Until the victim breaks free, a creature hanging on this way can inflict biting damage every turn thereafter, without having to roll to hit, simply by taking an Attack or All-Out Attack manoeuvre. At the same time, it can *also* strike with its limbs – say, raking with claws – or try the same moves as any other grappler.
>
> Some predators – including werewolves – bite for the *neck* (see *Specific Hit Locations*, p. 183) and then hold on. The special wounding modifiers for crushing or cutting damage apply here. As with other grappling attacks to the throat, if any damage penetrates the victim's DR, he starts to *suffocate.*

KNOCKDOWN AND STUNNING

Whenever you suffer a *major wound*, you must make an immediate HT roll. On a success, you suffer no penalty beyond ordinary shock. On a failure, you suffer both "knockdown" and "stunning" (see below). On a failure by 5 or more, or any critical failure, you fall unconscious; see *Recovering from Unconsciousness* (p. 186).

Knockdown: You fall prone (if you weren't already). If you were holding anything, you drop it.

Stunning: You must Do Nothing on your next turn. You may use any active defence, but your defence rolls are at -4 and you cannot retreat. At the *end* of your turn, you may roll against HT. Success lets you recover from this state and act normally on subsequent turns. Failure means you remain stunned; your next manoeuvre must also be Do Nothing, but you get another roll at the end of that turn . . . and so on, until you recover.

Example: Glass Box Graham suffered a major wound (7 being more than half of 10), so he must make an immediate roll against his HT of 11. He rolls 5 and succeeds. He's the next combatant to act and tries another sword thrust – but because attack rolls are DX-based, and he's taking the maximum -4 shock penalty, his Smallsword-12 becomes effectively 8. Fortunately for the watchman, he misses.

Outside, the lookout suffered a major wound (18 is more than half of 9!). He has HT 10, so he must roll 10 or less to avoid knockdown and stunning. If he rolls 15 or more, he'll pass out immediately from the wound. He rolls 12 – he's down but not out. He also has to make that roll to retain consciousness; he rolls 5 and succeeds. He doesn't have to roll again on his turn, as he *must* Do Nothing, so he remains conscious. At the end of that turn, he rolls 9 and recovers from stunning . . . however, he's flat on the ground and empty-handed, and on any turn when he opts to do anything, he'll have to roll to stay conscious.

Knockback

When you hit someone very hard with a *crushing* or *cutting* attack, you may knock him away from you! This is "knockback." A crushing attack can cause knockback regardless of whether it penetrates DR. A cutting attack can cause knockback only if it *fails* to penetrate DR.

Knockback depends on basic damage before subtracting DR. For every *full* multiple of the target's ST-2 rolled, move him one yard away from the attacker; note that some traits modify ST for this purpose (see *Build*, p. 29). If the target's effective ST is 3 or less, knockback is one yard per point of basic damage! If the target has no ST score (like a wall) or isn't resisting, use its HP instead.

Anyone who suffers knockback must attempt a roll against the *highest* of DX, Acrobatics, or Judo. If he's knocked back more than one yard, he rolls at -1 per yard after the first. Perfect Balance (p. 46) gives +4 to this roll. Failure means he falls down.

Example: Stalagmite, a Skinny troll with ST 15, is hit by another troll for 27 HP of crushing damage. Skinny gives -2 to ST for this purpose, so every 11 points of damage knocks him back a yard. He's knocked back two yards and must roll at DX-1 to avoid falling over.

MORTAL WOUNDS

If you fail a HT roll to avoid death by 1 or 2, you don't drop dead, but suffer a "mortal wound." This is a wound so severe that your internal injuries might kill you even after you stop bleeding.

If you're mortally wounded, you're instantly incapacitated. You may or may not be conscious (GM's decision). If you suffer further injury and must make another HT roll to avoid death, *any* failure kills you.

While mortally wounded, you must make a HT roll every half-hour to avoid death. On any failure, you die. On a success, you linger for another half-hour . . . then roll again. On a critical success, you pull through miraculously: you're no longer mortally wounded (but you're still incapacitated). You can also recover from a mortal wound with a successful HT roll whenever medical treatment restores any number of HP – even if you're still in the negatives.

If you recover from a mortal wound, make a HT roll. Failure means you lose a point of HT permanently. On a critical failure, the GM may apply an appropriate disadvantage (pp. 53-66) or some other effect (e.g., reduced Appearance due to scarring).

DEATH

If your character is killed, you may still wish to keep track of further injury – if only out of morbid curiosity. Some supernatural beings can come back from apparent death, often repeatedly. Even ordinary humans may be restored to, if not life, then some kind of *unlife*, by fate or powerful magic (though not usually if they were reduced to -10×HP).

Decapitation, a cut throat, etc., can kill anyone, regardless of HT and HP. If a *helpless* or *unconscious* person is attacked in an obviously lethal way, he's dead. Don't bother to roll damage. Just assume that he drops to -5×HP.

This doesn't apply to a merely *unaware* victim. If you sneak up behind a sentry with a knife, you can't automatically kill him. Game it out. Since it's a surprise attack, he won't be hitting back – make an All-Out Attack! Your attack roll will almost certainly succeed, while your victim will get no active defence. You'll probably inflict enough injury to incapacitate or kill him. But it isn't *automatic*.

When a PC or an important NPC is killed in any but the most sudden and thorough fashion, the GM should allow a "dying action." If this is a final blow at the enemy, it should take no more than a turn. If it's a deathbed speech, the GM should stretch time a little bit for dramatic purposes. This has nothing to do with realism, but whatever – talk about narrativium, if anyone argues.

Then the hooded skeleton shows up and starts talking in hollow capitals.

Example: Klump finally gets into the building and lays into Glass Box Graham, quickly reducing him to -14 HP, which means that Graham has to make an immediate HT roll to avoid death. He fails, but he can and does mime a last passionate show of defiance against the tyranny of language.

Recovery

The *Injuries* rules may seem harsh, but don't despair . . . you can get better!

RECOVERING FROM UNCONSCIOUSNESS

Failure by 5 or more on a knockdown roll, a failed HT roll to stay conscious at 0 HP or less, and many other things can leave you unconscious. It's up to the GM to decide whether you're *truly* unconscious or just totally incapacitated by pain and injury – but either way, you can't *do* anything. You recover as follows:

● If you have 1 or more HP remaining, you awaken automatically in 15 minutes.

● At 0 HP or worse, but above -1×HP, make a HT roll to awaken every hour. Once you succeed, you can act normally. But since you're below 1/3 your HP, you're at half Move and Dodge.

● At -1×HP or below, you're in bad shape. You get a *single* HT roll to awaken after 12 hours. If you succeed, you regain consciousness and can act as described above. But if you fail, you won't regain consciousness without medical treatment – make a HT roll whenever you regain HP that way, with success meaning that you awaken and can act as above. Until you receive help, you must roll vs. HT every 12 hours; if you fail, you *die*.

NATURAL RECOVERY

Rest lets you recover lost HP, unless the damage is of a type that specifically doesn't heal naturally (for an example, see *Disease*, p. 189). At the end of each day of rest and decent food, make a HT roll, at +1 if in the care of someone with the Physician skill (p. 77). Success means you recover 1 HP. The GM may give a penalty if conditions are bad – or a bonus if conditions are very good.

FIRST AID

Immediate assistance for the injured consists of *bandaging* and *treating shock*.

Bandaging

It takes one minute to apply bandages and pressure or a tourniquet to stop bleeding. This restores 1 HP. Anyone can do this – it requires no special skills.

Treating Shock

After bandaging, an aid-giver with First Aid or Physician (see *Medical Skills*, p. 77) may take extra time to apply a more elaborate dressing and treat the victim for shock. Keep the victim warm, comfortable, calm, and still! Stoical witty banter is traditional among those who can manage it; screaming or whimpering, among those who can't. After the time indicated on the *First Aid Table*, roll against skill.

On a success, the medic rolls as indicated on the table to see how many HP the victim recovers – minimum 1 HP. Critical success restores the maximum possible HP! This roll *includes* the 1 HP for bandaging; thus, a roll of 1 HP restores no further HP.

On a critical failure, the victim *loses* 2 HP instead of recovering any HP at all!

Only one person can roll to restore HP to an injured character, and only one attempt is allowed. You can't be restored to full health by a series of first aiders.

First Aid Table

Tech Level	Time per Victim	HP Restored
0-1	30 minutes	1d-4
2-3	30 minutes	1d-3
4	30 minutes	1d-2
5	20 minutes	1d-2

Unfortunately, many doctors on the Discworld operate at TL3 or *below*, whatever their society's TL. See p. 77.

Example: By the end of that fight, Constable Ingarsson has lost 10 of his 14 HP, leaving him with just 4 – which is less than 1/3 of 14, so he's moving slowly. Constable Klump comes to his aid but doesn't have First Aid skill, so all he does is apply basic bandaging, taking one minute and restoring 1 HP, leaving Ingarsson with 5. Thanks to Klump, Ingarsson is now fully mobile, but he's still badly hurt.

Later, Ingarsson is attended by the Igor employed by the Watch, who has Physician/TL5-14. After 20 minutes of muttering and stitching, the job is done; the GM rolls for the skill and succeeds, and then rolls 1d-2 for HP restored. There's a 50/50 chance that he'll only provide 1 HP, and no more benefit than Klump's basic efforts, but fortunately he rolls a 4 and restores 2 HP. That's only 1 HP over what Klump provided, but Ingarsson is up to 6 HP now.

After that, Ingarsson spends a few days in bed, receiving daily visits from Igor with his unnerving green salves and being fed decent-quality rat dishes by fellow dwarf watchmen. He thus gets to roll HT+1 daily, and recovers 1 HP for every success. It takes him a couple of weeks to accumulate eight successes, but after that he's fully fit for duty again.

Drinking

Alcohol, in excess, is bad for your judgement and your health. It's also a staple of comedy. And a huge and sometimes peculiar range of alcoholic refreshments is available on the Disc.

To determine how drunk someone gets, keep track of how many drinks he consumes. A "drink" is a modest mug of beer, shot of spirits, *small* cup of the apple-based rural beverage known as "scumble," teaspoon of Klatchian *orakh*, etc. Weak or strong booze, or variant serving sizes, may well count as less or more than one "drink" per serving.

At the end of any hour in which you consume more than ST/4 drinks, roll against the *higher* of your HT or Carousing skill, at -1 for every full drink over ST/4, +2 if you have Alcohol Tolerance (p. 50) or -2 with Alcohol Intolerance (p. 68), and -2 if drinking on an empty stomach or +1 if this is on top of a good meal. If you continue drinking more than ST/4 drinks per hour, roll again each hour.

Each failure pushes you one step up the drunkenness scale (below). Critical failure moves you *two* steps. If penalties ever reduce your roll to 2 or less, critical failure shifts you *three* steps.

Klatchian Coffee and Knurdness

Everything has an opposite. Well, most things. The opposite of drunk is *knurd*. Knurdness usually results from drinking Klatchian coffee, a beverage so formidable that for safety, it's usually cut with *orakh*: an alcoholic drink made from cacti sap and scorpion venom.

Whenever you drink Klatchian coffee straight, or after more than ST/4 cups with *orakh* added, make a HT roll to avoid knurdness. Failure by 1 or 2 means you become knurd for 2d seconds; if you fail by 3 or more, the state lasts 4d minutes; and on a critical failure, it lasts 3d hours.

On becoming knurd, you must make a Fright Check (pp. 170-171) as you temporarily lose all your illusions. Unfazeable (p. 48) gives +8 to this roll but doesn't entirely protect you. For as long as the condition persists, you're so depressed that you must make a Will roll once per second to attempt any task, even in combat (roll every turn!). You do get +5 to resist magical illusions, but if you fail anyway, you become 100% *convinced* that they're real.

If you've become knurd – however briefly – you must make a Will roll even to *contemplate* drinking any more Klatchian coffee for an hour thereafter. Coffee-drinking in Klatchian taverns is a quiet-but-intense display of competitive machismo; undertaken by philosophers or occultists, it leads to the creation of nihilistic belief systems. The stuff is also pretty harsh on the stomach.

The Drunkenness Scale

There are four increasingly wobbly steps after sobriety:

1. Tipsy: -1 to DX and IQ, and all skills based on them, and -2 to self-control rolls (p. 53) *except* those for Cowardice. Reduce Shyness by one level if you have it (this doesn't eliminate the penalty that Shyness gives to Carousing, however).

2. Drunk: Double the above penalties and reductions. Also make a HT+4 roll; failure means you suffer hallucinations of the GM's devising.

3. Unconscious: You're flat out! You can be partially awakened for a few seconds at a time to take coffee or other remedies.*

4. Comatose: You *can't* be awakened, but get one HT roll after 12 hours to awaken. If you fail, then realistically, you need serious medical attention. In lighter games, the GM can rule that you regain some kind of functional state after a couple of days, looking and feeling disgusting, and suffering whatever negative social consequences strike his fancy.*

* If you reach *unconscious* or *comatose*, make a HT roll. Success means you throw up instead of blacking out, but you still cannot take Concentrate manoeuvres at all and have -5 to any rolls you attempt until you recover. This usually means finding somewhere to pass out.

Instant Cures for Drunks and Knurdness

It's possible to use Klatchian coffee (p. 187) to cure drunkenness instantly, or strong drink to buffer someone's perceptions and cure knurdness, but the balance is delicate. Someone must make a Professional Skill (Bartender) or IQ-based Carousing roll (see *Using a Skill with a Different Attribute*, p. 69) to judge the dosage. You can try yourself, but remember the penalties for being drunk or the problems with being knurd.

Success by 0 or 1 means you become one step less drunk, or stop being knurd; on any better success, you recover instantly from being drunk or knurd. On a failure, you shift from being knurd to being tipsy, or from being any sort of drunk to being knurd. After three failures in succession, you're stuck in the last state you reached; no cure is possible, and you'll find that you really *hate* whoever kept getting the dosage wrong. Especially if it was yourself.

Someone who has been cured of drunkenness this way must still roll for a possible hangover. Klatchian coffee doesn't help with hangovers (few things do); indeed, it probably makes them worse.

Recovering from Drunkenness

Once you stop drinking – and provided that you aren't comatose – you become sober after a full night's sleep, +1d hours if you were unconscious or threw up. If you need to sober up faster, you can roll vs. HT after a number of hours equal to *half* the number of drinks you consumed, at +1 if you're taking effective remedies, being fed ordinary coffee, etc.; on a success, you become one step less drunk. Repeat after the same number of hours until you're fully sober. An experience of sheer terror (credible threat of death, meeting with a monster, etc.) can shift you one or even two steps toward sobriety as the adrenaline hits, at the GM's option, but that only works once a day. Klatchian coffee (p. 187) can sober you up instantly, but a misjudged dose may render you *knurd*.

Also, roll vs. HT, at -2 if you're tipsy or -4 if you became drunk or worse. Failure means you'll suffer a hangover after 1d hours, or when you next wake up if you go to sleep. This puts you at -2 to the rolls penalised for drunkenness *and* gives you Low Pain Threshold (or removes High Pain Threshold, if you have it). It lasts for a number of hours equal to your margin of failure.

Example: Rattled by his partner's brush with Death, Constable Klump goes to the Bucket. He has ST 13, HT 12, and Carousing-10 (not very good, despite an expenditure of points, thanks to his Severe Shyness). Thus, when he consumes five drinks – more than 13/4 – in an hour, he must make a HT roll (as that's better than his Carousing) at -3 for being just over one full drink past his safety margin on an empty stomach.

He succeeds the first time, but repeats the process for another hour, rolls 11, and becomes tipsy. After another hour in which he consumes four drinks, he rolls and fails again, becoming fully drunk. This eliminates his Shyness, and he remembers the young lady to whom he has been failing to express his affection. She's somewhere around . . . it's a shame about the -2 to those social skills which he's about to try using at default.

Stung by rejection, he downs another four drinks in the next hour (more than 13/4, but not by a full drink), rolls against 10 (his HT-2) – and gets 17, a critical failure. This could render him comatose, which is *dangerous*. Fortunately, he succeeds at an unmodified HT roll, and just makes it to the privy, where he throws up.

After that, he lurches home to bed and 8+1d hours of sleep. (As he consumed the equivalent of an extremely unwise 18 drinks, it would be nine hours before he could try to sober up even with help.) But he must make one last HT roll, at -4 for being drunk. Rolling 13 against the required 8 – this just isn't his evening – he's scheduled for a five-hour hangover when he awakes.

Fatigue

Running or swimming long distances, being suffocated, and many other things can cause "fatigue": a temporary loss of Fatigue Points (see *Fatigue Points*, p. 27). Just as injury represents physical trauma and comes off HP, fatigue represents lost energy and reduces FP. Keep track of FP losses on your character sheet.

Lost Fatigue Points

The chart below summarises the effects of being at low or negative FP. All effects are cumulative.

Less than 1/3 your FP left – You're very tired. Halve your Move, Dodge, and ST (round *up*). This does *not* affect ST-based quantities, such as HP and damage.

0 FP or less – You're on the verge of collapse. If you suffer further fatigue, each FP you lose also causes 1 HP of injury. To do anything besides talk or rest, you must make a Will roll; in combat, roll before each manoeuvre other than Do Nothing.

On a success, you can act normally. If you're drowning, you can continue to struggle, but you suffer the usual 1 HP per FP lost. On a failure, you collapse, incapacitated, and can do *nothing* until you recover to positive FP.

-1×FP – You fall unconscious. While unconscious, you recover lost FP at the same rate as for normal rest. You awaken when you reach positive FP. Your FP can *never* fall below this level. After this stage, any FP cost comes off your HP instead!

FATIGUE COSTS

The following activities commonly result in FP loss:

Combat: Any fight that lasts for longer than 10 seconds costs FP. Those who make *no* attack or defence rolls during the conflict are exempt from this fatigue, but other actions still have their usual FP cost. At the *end* of the battle, you lose 1 FP *plus* a number of FP equal to your current encumbrance level (p. 168). This cost is *per fight*, not per 10 seconds of fighting. A very long battle may cost more (GM's decision), but it would have to run for two or three minutes (120 to 180 turns!) before extra FP costs would be realistic.

Dehydration: A human needs two quarts of water a day – three in Hot conditions (see *Temperature Extremes,* p. 191), five in Very Hot! If you get less than you need, you lose 1 FP every eight hours. If you drink less than a quart a day, you lose an *extra* 1 FP and 1 HP per day. You can regain all FP lost to dehydration after a day of rest with ample water supplies. You recover HP at the usual rate.

Hiking: Use the FP costs for fighting, but assess them *per hour* of road travel; e.g., one hour of marching with Light encumbrance costs 2 FP.

Missing Sleep: If you've been awake for more than your normal day (typically 16 hours), you start to get tired. You lose 1 FP if you fail to go to sleep, and 1 FP per four hours you stay awake after *that.* If you've lost half or more of your FP to lack of sleep, you must make a Will roll every two hours you spend inactive (e.g., standing watch). On a failure, you fall asleep, sleeping until you are awakened or get a full night's sleep. On a success – or if awakened – you suffer -2 to DX, IQ, and self-control rolls. If you're down to less than 1/3 your FP due to lack of sleep, roll once per 30 minutes of inaction or two hours of action.

Overexertion: Carrying more than Extra-Heavy encumbrance, or pushing/pulling a very heavy load, costs 1 FP *per second.* See *Lifting and Moving Things* (p. 168).

Running or Swimming: Every 15 seconds of sprinting, or minute of paced running or swimming, requires a HT roll to avoid losing 1 FP.

Starvation: A human needs three meals per day. For each meal you miss, take 1 FP.

RECOVERING FROM FATIGUE

You can recover "ordinary" lost FP by resting quietly. Reading, talking, and thinking are all right; walking around, or anything more strenuous, is *not.* Lost FP return at the rate of 1 FP per 10 minutes of rest. The GM might allow you to regain +1 FP if you eat a decent meal *while resting.* Herbalists and witches may be able to prepare draughts that restore lost FP, but these have bizarre side-effects at the GM's whim.

You can only recover from fatigue caused by *missed sleep* by sleeping for at least eight hours. This restores 1 FP. Further uninterrupted sleep restores 1 FP per hour. You need food or water to recover FP lost to starvation or dehydration.

Other Hazards

Besides swords, spears, troll fists, and swamp-dragon breath, adventurers (and the just plain unlucky) commonly face other hazards.

DISEASE

Maladies and strange diseases may affect adventurers in far-off lands, or even at home (*especially* at home, for some values of "home"). Ordinary infections are a rather sordid and uninteresting topic, but the search for a cure for the Princess' wasting disease or the consequences of what an invader did to your wells are wonderful plot devices.

The important things to know about a given disease are:

Resistance Roll: The HT roll to avoid the disease. Most diseases allow a roll at a modifier from 0 (something trivial) to -6 (a dreadful plague). On a success, the victim doesn't contract the disease. On a failure, he does, but he gets further rolls – once per "cycle" – to throw it off.

Delay: The disease's incubation period – the time between initial exposure and the appearance of the first symptoms in those who fail to resist. This is 24 hours for a "generic" disease, but can vary considerably.

Damage: The disease's effects in game terms. This is typically 1 HP of injury, but it might be higher – up to 1d – for virulent diseases. Damage Resistance doesn't protect against disease! Symptoms (fever, sneezing, coughing, spots, rash, etc.) appear after the subject starts to suffer injury. Injury from disease will *not* heal naturally until the victim makes his HT roll to recover or the disease has run its full course.

Cycles: A disease damages its victim at regular intervals until he makes a HT roll *or* a maximum number of cycles passes. The "default" interval between HT rolls is one day. The number of cycles varies with the disease's deadliness; e.g., a nasty wasting disease might only inflict 1 HP per cycle but endure for 20-30 cycles.

Once a disease's symptoms become apparent, make a Diagnosis roll to identify it. This cannot identify a totally new illness, but a good roll might give enough information to allow treatment. Appropriate remedies – witches' herbal treatments, alchemical drugs, etc. – provide a bonus to the cyclic HT rolls to shake off certain diseases.

Ageing

In campaigns that go on long enough, ordinary people who live past 50 must make four HT rolls a year: one for each of ST, DX, IQ, and HT. Failure means the score drops by one – or by *two* on a roll of 17 or 18. Those with Longevity (p. 52) lose attributes only on a 17 or an 18, and just one level even then. Death shows up when any score reaches 0.

FALLS

People and objects falling significant distances take crushing damage upon hitting the ground, based on how far they fell. A successful Acrobatics roll reduces *effective* falling distance by five yards. Consult the following table.

Falling Damage

Distance	Damage	Distance	Damage
1 yard	1d	30 yards	5d
2 yards	1d+1	35 yards	5d+2
3 yards	1d+2	40 yards	6d-1
4 yards	2d-1	45 yards	6d
5 yards	2d	50 yards	6d+2
10 yards	3d	60 yards	7d
15 yards	3d+2	70 yards	7d+2
20 yards	4d	80 yards	8d+1
25 yards	4d+2	100+ yards	9d+1

Very large or dense individuals suffer more damage. Damage is ×2 for someone (or something) with 20-29 HP; ×3 for 30-39 HP; ×4 for 40-49 HP; and so on.

If you land on something sharp or spiky, this damage becomes cutting or impaling. Landing on something soft *halves* damage; if this is a *person*, you *each* take half the listed damage.

FLAME

If you spend *part* of a turn in a fire (e.g., running through the flames), you take 1d-3 burning damage. If you spend *all* of a turn in a fire of ordinary intensity, you take 1d-1 damage per second. Very intense fires inflict more damage; for instance, molten metal or a furnace would inflict 3d per second.

Burning damage – including burning *attacks* – may also set you ablaze! A *single* damage roll that inflicts at least 3 points of basic burning damage ignites *part* of your clothing. This does 1d-4 burning damage per second and is distracting (-2 to DX, unless the damage simply cannot harm you). To extinguish the fire, you must beat it with your hands. This requires a DX roll; each attempt takes a Ready manoeuvre.

A *single* damage roll that inflicts 10 or more points of basic burning damage ignites *all* of your clothes. This does 1d-1 burning damage per second and is *very* distracting (-3 to DX, except when rolling to extinguish the flames). To put out the fire, you must roll on the ground. This requires a DX roll; each attempt takes *three* Ready manoeuvres. Jumping into water takes only one second and automatically extinguishes the fire.

When extinguishing flames, apply shock penalties to DX if the flame inflicts injury!

Continued exposure to *any* fire may result in intense heat that can rapidly fatigue you even if the flames themselves cannot penetrate your DR. See *Heat* (p. 191).

Lightning

Being struck by lightning can easily cause 6d or more burning damage. The GM who's aiming for comedy can ramp this down some – especially for lightning bolts dropped by irate gods who aren't actually worshipped much.

LACK OF AIR

Sometimes, characters find themselves wanting to breathe when they can't – because they're drowning, being strangled, or trying to avoid the effects of poison gas. Your HT determines the length of time you can hold your breath:

No Exertion (e.g., sitting quietly or meditating): HT×10 seconds.
Mild Exertion (e.g., treading water or walking): HT×4 seconds.
Heavy Exertion (e.g., climbing, combat, or running): HT seconds.

This assumes you have one second – a Concentrate manoeuvre, in combat – to draw a deep breath. If you don't, *halve* these times. Once time runs out, you start to suffocate (see below), or must breathe whatever it was you were trying to avoid.

Suffocation

If you *completely* lack air, you lose 1 FP per second. If you're drowning after a failed Swimming roll, you can get *some* air, but you also inhale water: roll vs. Swimming every five seconds; failure costs 1 FP (see *Swimming*, pp. 168-169).

At 0 FP, make a Will roll every second or fall unconscious. Regardless of FP or HP, you die after four minutes without air.

If you get clean air before you die, you stop losing FP and start to recover FP at the usual rate (see *Recovering from Fatigue*, p. 189). If you're unconscious, you awaken once you have 1 FP. If you were drowning, a rescuer must *also* make a First Aid roll to expel the water from your lungs in order to save you.

MOTION SICKNESS

Some forms of travel – ships on rough seas, camels, etc. – can be miserably nausea-inducing. Seasickness is the most common example, but hardly the only one. Whenever the GM decides that conditions are bad enough, *anyone* can suffer as though they had the Motion Sickness disadvantage (p. 63) – except that people without that problem roll at HT+5, and on a success by 5 or more, or a critical success, they're fine for the rest of the trip.

POISON

Poison can show up on weapons, in food or drink offered by treacherous foes, and anywhere else you didn't expect it. Assassins and druids both make use of it. The important things to know about a given poison are as follows.

Delay: Most poisons require a few seconds to several hours to take effect. This is nearly *always* true for digestive agents.

Resistance: Some poisons allow the victim a HT roll to resist. Roll after the delay, if any, has passed. There's often a modifier; 0 to -4 is typical, but a mild poison might give +2, while one that's almost impossible to resist could give -8! If you're in a poisonous *environment* (like a cloud of gas) and make your initial HT roll, you must roll again once per second until the poison affects you or you leave the area; if the poison has a delay, roll after each delay period instead.

Effects: Poison's most common effect is injury or fatigue. Mild poisons might only inflict 1 HP or FP; more severe poisons can inflict 1d or more. Damage Resistance is of no value here! For a *serious* poison, successful resistance may merely reduce injury or fatigue, not eliminate it completely. These HP and FP losses heal normally.

Like disease (p. 189), poison can cause symptoms or be cyclic, and they may be treatable once identified (roll vs. Diagnosis or Poisons).

TEMPERATURE EXTREMES

As there aren't many reliable thermometers on the Disc, ambient temperatures are rated descriptively, ranging from *Intolerable Cold*, through *Extreme Cold*, *Freezing*, *Chilly*, *Moderate*, *Warm*, *Hot*, *Very Hot*, and *Severe Heat*, to *Intolerable Heat*, in that order. Most people can operate normally in Chilly through Warm conditions without much trouble, if they dress sensibly. Outside this range, they have problems – primarily FP losses. As usual, once you go below 0 FP, you start to lose 1 HP per FP. You can't

recover FP or HP lost to cold or heat until you get into more normal temperatures. For examples of other tolerance ranges, see *Cold or Heat Resistance* (p. 50), *Temperature Tolerance* (p. 92), and the notes on nonhuman racial templates in Chapter 3.

Cold

Humans out in Freezing temperatures must roll vs. HT every 30 minutes – or every 15 minutes in a breeze, or every 10 minutes if there's a strong wind. People in light, thin, or damp clothes have -5 or worse here (thin *and* damp gives -10). Conversely, dry "Arctic" clothing (furs, etc.) grants up to +5. Failure costs 1 FP.

Extreme Cold uses the same rules, but all rolls are at -3, and protective clothing must be very good and quite encumbering to provide a bonus. Intolerable Cold is what it says; at best, HT rolls are at -6, and damage may go straight to HP thanks to frostbite.

Heat

In Hot conditions, humans experience no ill effects (beyond sweat stains) if they stay quietly in the shade. But if you're *active* (fighting, running, or even just walking around without a good hat), roll vs. HT every 30 minutes. Failure costs 1 FP. Critical failure means heatstroke: lose *1d* FP. Heavy clothes give -1 or -2 to the roll – or a penalty equal to twice your encumbrance level, if that would be worse.

The same rule applies in Very Hot conditions, *and* you lose an extra 1 FP whenever you lose FP for other reasons. In Severe Heat, this becomes an extra *2* FP, and almost any activity costs FP. In Intolerable Heat, you can't do much at all – the GM should apply large penalties at whim, including a strong possibility of rapid HP loss, and occasional FP loss even if you sit in the shade.

Messin' With Reality (The Magic Rules)

Discworld magic is complex and mysterious; while academic wizards study it closely and have many *theories* about it (and lots of jargon), even they don't understand it fully. Unfortunately, this complexity – along with the fact that even the most authoritative statements in the chronicles may actually reflect incomplete knowledge or bias – means that no playable set of game rules can cover everything. Thus, the system that follows doesn't attempt to explain how magic "really" works. Rather, it's designed to provide a flexible, playable, *interesting* way of handling Discworld magic – one that lets its users emulate the accomplishments (and failures!) of most magic-wielders in the chronicles and still be worthwhile RPG characters.

Basic Abilities for Magic-Workers

To work magic with any competence and minimal safety, a character needs the Magery advantage (pp. 44-45), Magic skill (p. 76), and some level in one or more Magical Form skills (pp. 76-77) – although the last can come from the Magic skill. It's possible to do *something* with magic without any of these, but that's *not* a good idea.

MAGERY ADVANTAGE

Magery represents sensitivity to magical forces and the associated ability to move them around. It's basically inborn – the kind of thing that wizards and witches refer to as "the gift" or "witchery" – but it can be improved and refined with training and experience. In other words, characters who don't enter play with it can't buy it with bonus character points, but those who *do* start with at least Magery 0 can buy extra levels later, with the GM's permission. Higher levels not only make you more skilled when working magic, but also help you channel more power into some spells.

MAGIC SKILL

Magic skill represents *training* in getting magic to do what you want without your brain exploding or monstrosities appearing through the holes you make in reality. Its specialisations represent alternative approaches – dissimilar bodies of technique based on different ways of thinking. There's rarely any mistaking a witch's way of doing magic for a wizard's, even if they're aiming for the same result. *Wizardry* and *Witchcraft* are the two major specialisations on the Disc, but there are others; see *Types of Magic-Workers* (pp. 271-273).

MAGICAL FORM SKILLS

A Magical Form is a "branch" of magic – skill at getting it to do useful things in one of eight different ways. The Forms are listed under *Magical Forms* (pp. 76-77). For examples of what each can do, see *The Forms* (pp. 202-217).

Which Forms you put points into indicates what sort of magic your character does best. This can reflect his personal interests or prejudices, or the nature of his particular style of magic. And this is where the system gets a bit abstract – while no student of magic on the Disc necessarily thinks in terms of these eight Forms, they can be used to represent a whole lot of loosely related things about magic.

Still, remember that *anyone* trained in magic can potentially use *any* Form – though perhaps not reliably. Some people with Magic skill know so little about certain Forms that they honestly don't believe that they can use them, but that's a personal error.

MAGIC POINTS

Magic Points (MP) represent the raw thaumaturgical *stuff* that you must use to produce all but the smallest effects. They aren't exactly "energy," but they often substitute for it; for example, by pumping more MP into a fireball, you can get it to do more damage. Sometimes, though, MP are less about raw horsepower and more about the degree to which a spell abuses the structure of reality.

It's possible to pull raw magic out of the ether and put it into a spell as part of the casting process; long-winded ritual magic does this, and that's sometimes the only way to get really powerful spells to work. However, individuals with Magery automatically accumulate a little raw magic around themselves – or can see and manipulate the raw magic that settles on anyone, which comes to the same thing – and can use it to power quick spells. Non-mages *can't* do that; they can *only* get magic to work by using long-winded rituals.

To find the maximum number of MP which someone with Magery can carry about with him, add his Will to his Magery level, divide the sum by 3, and round to the nearest whole number. For example, Will 16 and Magery 0 give 5 MP, while Will 9 and Magery 2 give 4 MP.[1]

Spending MP

When a magic-worker successfully casts a spell, he usually has to put a number of MP into it. Deduct this cost from his personal total and/or the total in his staff (if any); *Ritual Casting* (p. 200) and some other methods provide alternative MP sources. If the caster lacks sufficient MP, his spell fizzles and fails automatically.

---

1. *For atmospheric purposes, gamers can refer to Magic Points as "thaums" if they wish. It doesn't really fit the Discworld meaning of the word (p. 270), but never mind. This looks right for wizard characters, less so for witches.*

For further details, keep reading – *General Power Rules* (pp. 195-196) and *Casting the Spell* (pp. 198-200) are especially relevant.

Recovering MP

If you have fewer than your maximum number of MP, thanks to having used them to cast spells, you regain them at a rate of 1 MP per 10 minutes. If you've used up some of your staff's MP, these recover at the same rate, *separately* and *simultaneously*. Neither you nor your staff can recover MP in areas or situations where magic doesn't work, though.

THE WIZARD'S STAFF

Wizards never regard their personal MP reserve as enough, so they've come up with a way to augment it: the magic staff. Every fully qualified wizard has one of these – one is formally presented to each student graduating from Unseen University, and a recognised wizard can take a personal student who has attained graduate level to UU and request that he receive a staff. It acts as a Magic Point "battery." No wizard can have more than one working staff attuned to him at a time.

A standard staff can hold MP equal to the wizard's IQ + Magery level; the Superior Staff advantage (p. 47) adds to that. A wizard can tap his staff for MP so long as it's within two yards of his person and not being held by anybody else. In addition, a spell that requires the wizard to *touch* an opponent or object works just as well if he touches it with his staff. Further, magical telekinesis and similar effects can't affect a wizard's staff so long as it's in physical contact with him. Enemy wizards can fireball the heck out of each other and then loot the body, or even hurl each other around with magical force if they can get a lock-on, but magical disarming doesn't work.

A wizard PC gets his staff for free, without spending cash, and it has the nice bonus that it also works just fine as a support while taking long meditative walks, and as six foot of bashing weapon. A typical staff is made of oak or ash; sapient pearwood (p. 158) is highly desirable but *rare*. A *very* few wizards in the past had metal staffs, which held eminently adequate charges of energy and were certainly durable, but the magic in those tended to become dangerously corrupt – and anyway, that trick has been lost these days.

Losing Your Staff

A wizard would have to be *extremely* careless to lose his staff by accident – although he might deliberately break his staff, as a way of formally giving up magic (sometimes to get married). However, a staff can sometimes be taken away, or hacked apart by opponents. Striking a staff in combat requires an attack at -3 to hit. The wielder can attempt to dodge or parry, the latter representing deflecting the attack in a way that doesn't damage the staff. A staff has DR 5 and can sustain 12 HP of damage before break-

ing; one made of sapient pearwood has DR 7, 15 HP. A staff that's damaged but not destroyed can be mended using magic; each HP repaired requires four hours of work and a roll against the *lowest* of Magical Form (Elementalism), Magical Form (Magianism), or Magical Form (Physiomancy).

A wizard who *does* lose his staff will be greatly inconvenienced (and mocked by other wizards, behind his back or to his face). To replace it, spend 1d days finding a standard quarterstaff ($0.50) that *feels* right to you, then two weeks "attuning" it, during which time you can't do much else. Alternatively, you can acquire another wizard's staff somehow (good luck with that). However you obtain it, it will at first hold only half as many MP as ought to be possible for you; this total increases by 1 MP every two weeks until it reaches your full value. During this process, you may find it necessary to carve the staff with symbols or otherwise embellish it, or it may subtly reshape itself to match your personality. It will always end up with a knob on the end.

A staff formally handed over by a (usually dying) wizard to his successor is immediately, automatically, *fully* prepared and ready to use.

Other Magical Styles and Staffs

Wizards are the only magic-wielders to employ magic staffs, which is one reason why they get so cocky. Witches don't use staffs, and therefore have access to far fewer MP than wizards – though they have subtle ways to get round this (see *Witch Magic Power*, pp. 196-198). Minor magical styles akin to wizardry *might* come up with something similar to the staff, however.

Example: Jemzarkiza of Krull is trained in Krullian Wizardry, which is much like regular wizardry but maybe not quite as good. It has some oddities that sometimes let her surprise people who think in terms of conventional wizardry, though; for instance, her opponents may get the wrong idea about the completely mundane staff she carries, which might give her a useful edge. Her player talked to the GM, and they decided that it would fit the style if she were permitted to carry a *wand* that works a lot like a wizard's staff but holds only 2/3 as many MP. Jemzarkiza has IQ 15 and Magery 3, so her wand stores 12 MP. It's considered a small truncheon (p. 151) for mundane purposes.

Deciding an Effect

To work magic, you must first decide what you want to do. While a large number of standard spells are known to wizardry and a fair number of tricks are widespread among witches, those are mainly teaching shorthand and convenient references – magic can do most things (well, except for the things it can't do), if the user has enough power and skill. Every spell and casting uses a specific Magical Form; a few complex effects draw on more than one Form. Further analysing your objectives determines the skill roll you have to make and how many MP the magic will require. *Complex* spells give lower skill rolls; *powerful* spells cost more MP. Some spells also have special requirements, at the GM's whim: material "ingredients" (see *Props*, p. 274), limited times or places when or where they can be cast, and so on.

The GM has to decide all of this in each case. The player of the magic-worker who wants to try the spell can make suggestions, but the GM's word is final.

Example: Jemzarkiza is trapped in an underground chamber with no exit except a locked trapdoor eight feet above her head. If she can get that open, though, her friends might hear her call for help. A wizard would likely try to smash it with a bolt of force, while a witch might cause the wood of the trapdoor to swell so that it burst from its frame, but Jemzarkiza sees herself as a tidy-minded scholar, so she decides to tell the bolts securing the hinges to undo themselves – an Elementalism effect. This probably wouldn't work if the bolts were iron (to learn why not, keep reading), but Jemzarkiza has noticed that, for whatever reason, all the metal fixtures here are bronze.

ARBITRARY LIMITATIONS

Magic can do a lot, but it's subject to a few limitations. Notably, while it can affect most materials, it can't *directly* damage, control, or deform iron (or steel). This isn't as broad or reliable a way to stymie magic as some people like to think.

Plenty of warriors in steel mail have been taken down with fire-balls (or had their minds comprehensively tinkered with, or their fighting skills cursed to uselessness), and the heat from magical flame can even melt the metal – eventually, although it takes a lot. Also, non-damaging effects can sometimes be routed into iron with a bit of effort, making it useful as a "sink." However, locking a witch or a wizard in iron or steel chains, firmly anchored in the wall, is a rather reliable way of stopping her or him from going anywhere.

Wizard magic has another small limitation: *transformational* spells will only work on another wizard if the caster knows his subject's correct name. This isn't some deeply significant "true name" – it's just the name that would have been on his birth certificate, if he had one. This doesn't stop a sufficiently powerful wizard from fireballing a rival wizard until he glows in the dark, creating a hole in the ground under his feet, or hurling him a mile out to sea; it's only direct transformations of the target's actual body that are banned, *including* attempts to reverse such things. See also *Secret Name* (p. 52).

The GM can declare other, minor limitations or peculiarities in the laws of magic, if he needs them to make a plot work. Be careful with this, though! The players of magic-users are entitled to complain if their expensive abilities are constantly vetoed by arbitrary pronouncements. The GM should make his plot ideas less arbitrary and more robust than that.

GENERAL SKILL MODIFIERS

Every magic-worker has a skill level with each Magical Form. Applying a penalty that depends on spell complexity determines the caster's *Base Spell Skill*. While different sorts of magic encounter different sorts of difficulty, some general guidelines apply:

Simplest, basic applications of a Form (e.g., lighting a pipe using Elementalism, giving someone an itch or making him sneeze with Physiomancy): 0
Slightly more complex/powerful, but straightforward, effects (e.g., using Psychomancy to make someone ignore you for a moment, or Magianism to suppress a simple magical booby-trap for a second): -1 or -2
Displays of raw, but short-term, power (e.g., fireballs for Elementalism, long-distance scrying for Divination, determining the last thing that a fresh corpse saw for Necromancy): -3

Long-Distance Modifiers

If the distance falls between two values, use the *higher*.

Distance	Penalty	Distance	Penalty
200 yards	0	100 miles	-6
1/2 mile	-1	300 miles	-7
1 mile	-2	1,000 miles	-8
3 miles	-3	3,000 miles	-9
10 miles	-4	10,000 miles*	-10
30 miles	-5		

* Will reach anywhere on the Disc. Casting magic beyond that runs into severe technical problems, even if you can find a reason.

Graduate-level stuff (e.g., using Sortilege to curse someone so that he always comes *third* in competitions, or Summonation to summon and simultaneously confine a serious demon): -4 or -5
Intricate or showy spells (e.g., using Magianism to divert, analyse, and take control of any and every spell cast in a given area, or Psychomancy to swap the personalities of everybody in a room between their bodies repeatedly at random while making sure that none of them notice that this is happening): -6 to -10*

* Pulling off a -10 spell in public can get you a free Reputation with other magic-workers – usually positive, unless you were pushing your luck into dangerous territory.

Two other general modifiers may apply in addition:

Blocking spell (p. 199): -2
Spell designed to be invisible in use to anyone lacking Magery: -2

Some spells, especially protective wards, take *no* modifier; however, the amount by which the caster makes the casting roll is crucial. It's fairly easy to cast some sort of protection – but a solid, reliable defence depends on high skill.

Example: Jemzarkiza has an effective skill of 14 with Magical Form (Elementalism). The GM rules that making a dozen bronze bolts undo themselves is *fairly* straightforward, but requires a bit of coordination, so the penalty is -2. Thus, Jemzarkiza's Base Spell Skill is 12.

SITUATIONAL SKILL MODIFIERS

Other modifiers apply for particular circumstances. Adjusting Base Spell Skill for these gives *Modified Spell Skill*, which is what you roll against to cast the spell.

Range is the most important situational modifier. Magic that affects someone or something *directly* generally works best if the subject is close enough to touch. (An *actual* touch isn't usually necessary – the subject just has to be within reach, less than a yard away.) Extending most ordinary magic to work from afar gives -1 to skill per yard. For example, if someone were six yards away, you would have -6 to turn him into a frog.

There are three important details to note here:

1. When casting a spell over an area, only count the range to the nearest edge of your target zone. If you whipped up an area spell with a one-mile radius, and the edge of your chosen circle were immediately in front of you, you would take no penalty.
2. Missile spells (p. 199) provide a way around this. You *cast* the spell into your hand, creating an immaterial missile – so it takes *no* range penalty – and then you throw it later on.
3. Range affects one large category of spells and at least one specific type differently. *Information* spells are designed to scan large areas at long distances. *Teleport* spells transport people or things great distances by stepping outside the normal framework of space. (Summoning spells also more-or-less ignore distance, at least in four dimensions.) Such magic takes the much lower penalties under *Long-Distance Modifiers*.

Example: Reaching up with her wand in hand, Jemzarkiza reduces the effective range to two yards, so her Modified Spell Skill is now 10. If she merely wanted to divine something about the trapdoor, her range penalty would be 0. If she threw a fireball at it, she would suffer no range penalties on the *casting*, but the speed/range penalty for that distance would affect her Innate Attack skill roll to hit.

Trading Power for Skill

You can compensate for low skill through sheer effort, but it's inefficient. Add +1 to Modified Spell Skill for every *extra* 2 MP you assign to the spell, to a maximum of +5 to skill (for +10 MP). This does *not* work for ritual castings (p. 200 It does mean that finding a big source of free magical power gives you a lot of options.

Example: As Jemzarkiza is afraid that her friends are moving out of shouting range, she wants this spell to work. She has a full MP charge at present, so she commits 2 MP to improve her chances, raising her Modified Spell Skill to 11.

Advantageous Situations

Occasionally, spellcasters get a bonus for casting somewhere which is just *right* for them. The most common example is the witch's cottage. Almost every witch has a cottage, if only symbolically – it may actually be an ample-but-cosy booth in a small-town market, or a weird little tenement house in the city. This is, in a way, her fortress. Any magic that she works here is at +1 to Modified Spell Skill – or +5 for spells defending against magic or supernatural effects worked by someone outside.

Also, areas of *aspected magic* (p. 278) may give bonuses to some spells and penalties to others, while *residual magic* (p. 270) might give a small bonus (+1 or +2).

Magical Computer Bonuses

Hex, the magical computer at Unseen University, can provide a large bonus to Modified Spell Skill on ritual castings (p. 200) only, by performing high-speed analysis of all relevant factors as the ritual is performed. At the GM's option, this might mean that Hex rolls against an effective Thaumatology skill of 20 and adds its margin of success as a bonus (critical failures and successes can have whatever interesting consequences the GM wishes), gives a flat +10, or exactly cancels some large penalty from *Long-Distance Modifiers* (p. 194). The point here is that Hex is extremely powerful but not infallible, and sometimes prone to cheerfully excessive optimism. It has also learned how to lie by omission and misdirection.

Pex, the computer recently installed at Brazeneck College (p. 280), probably gives similar but lesser bonuses – say, +5 or the margin of success on a roll against skill 15. It's *supposed* to be more advanced, but Ponder Stibbons has had longer to get Hex working safely.

GENERAL POWER RULES

The MP required to work a spell depend on the raw power, extent, and duration of the effect. As with skill, details vary from case to case, but some general rules apply:

- *Any* magical casting has a basic cost of at least 1 MP, although this can be reduced to zero by high skill (see *Efficiency Benefits*, p. 196). This might create a little energy or a few ounces of matter, channel a single piece of information to the caster, momentarily open a miniature portal, or briefly constrain or manipulate the mind of a living being.
- 2 MP will do something a bit more substantial or persistent; e.g., make materials soften or swell, or confuse someone's mind for several seconds.
- 3 MP will usually do something brief but dramatic, or small and subtle but long-lasting; e.g., summon a petty demon or create a durable illusion.
- For larger effects, the numbers can rise *substantially*. Effectively permanent, large and complex effects have MP costs in double figures.

Although magic can have permanent *consequences* – it can certainly make people dead on a permanent basis – the direct effects usually require a continuing supply of MP to keep going, and hence last only for as long as the caster is awake and willing to provide them. Those that don't are at best structures of stabilised magical energy, obvious to perceptive wizards and witches, and prone to being dissipated by a well-designed counterspell or a metaphysical hiccough.

Sometimes, the GM may rule that spending the minimum MP required for a spell will produce only a minimal effect. The caster has to decide whether that's enough; most will add another MP or two if possible, for certainty. Using too many MP may have dramatic consequences – rarely actually *bad*, but possibly comic.

Areas of significant *residual magic* (p. 270) can reduce a casting's effective MP cost by 20% to 80%, at the GM's option. Some areas of *aspected magic* (p. 278) also modify MP costs.

Damaging Spells

The basic MP cost for a spell (usually using Elementalism) that does damage depends on its scale:

- Damaging a *single target*: 1 MP per die of damage.
- Damaging *everything in an area*: 2 MP per die per yard of radius (see below for more on area effects).

These costs are then multiplied for damage type:

Crushing, burning, piercing, or *small piercing:* ×1
Cutting or *large piercing:* ×1.5 (round halves up)
Impaling or *huge piercing:* ×2

Other Power Sources

A rare few circumstances allow MP to come from other external sources. One significant example in the chronicles is UU's High Energy Magic Building, which can generate as much thaumic energy as the plot requires at any time. Brazeneck (p. 280) may have something similar by now. The main problem there is *controlling* the stuff, as any wizard simply plugging himself into one of its power lines would start moving outwards in all directions at the speed of light[1] soon afterwards. Fortunately, UU has Hex (p. 286) to help with this – there's no point in sneaking into the High Energy Magic Building without also getting time on the computer.

Some witches can tap even more potent, even more dangerous energy sources. The power of narrative (pp. 8-9) is perhaps the *least* of these, merely requiring a bit of arrogance and manipulativeness.

---

1. Not actually all that high on the Disc, but still.

With a *missile spell* (p. 199), you can only put MP equal to your Magery level into the spell during each one-second combat turn (thus, only someone with Magery 1+ can use such a spell), but you can hold the spell in hand while you pump in extra MP on subsequent turns. This is *in theory* only limited by the number of MP you have available; if the GM lets a magic-wielder get hold of huge numbers of MP, he can recover the situation by requiring DX, Will, or Magic skill rolls after a while to keep the magical projectile stable. And would you really want to be standing there with the equivalent of a nuclear hand grenade in your palm, with the pin out?[1]

Area of Effect

Casting a spell over a wider area costs more MP. A *wizard's* spell will have a cost per yard of radius. For instance, if a hail spell costs 2 MP per yard of radius, then raining hail over a five-yard radius requires 10 MP.

Subtle area spells sometimes have *fractional* costs per yard of radius. For example, if a spell costs 1/4 MP per yard of radius, then it could be cast over a four-yard radius for 1 MP, an eight-yard radius for 2 MP, and so on.

All this assumes an approximately circular area of effect. Areas of other shapes are possible, although they usually have to be fairly simple. Use half the longest dimension as the "radius." For a really complex shape – perhaps hitting opponents while avoiding friends (or vice versa) – throw in an extra -1 or -2 to *skill*.

Witch spells sometimes work like this, but witches often cast magic over much larger areas by exploiting the power of story. See *Witch Magic Power* (pp. 196-198).

Duration

Many spells have an instantaneous effect (e.g., setting fire to something or repairing a broken vase), achieve their full effect within a few seconds (e.g., opening a lock or levitating the caster to the top of a tower), or produce a semi-permanent change or consequence (e.g., turning someone into a frog, raising a corpse as a zombie, or summoning a demon). However, other spells generate a continuing effect that requires the input of magical energies to sustain; after a certain amount of time, the *duration*, the caster must pay more MP to keep the effect going (see *Maintaining Spells*, p. 200). Standard durations:

Minor spells: 1 minute.
Subtle, medium-term effects (e.g., adjustments to someone's mood, or attempts to make someone's clothes fireproof): 10 minutes. Also add 1 MP to the base MP cost.
Longer-term spells (e.g., protective wards, or extended explorations of someone's mind or dreams): 1 hour *or* 1 day. Also add 2 or 3 MP, respectively, to the base MP cost.

Efficiency Benefits

If your *Base Spell Skill* (*not* Modified Spell Skill) is 15+, reduce the MP requirement by 1. In effect, you get free power for good technique! If your Base Spell Skill is 20+, reduce the cost by 2. This may mean that you can throw, say, a missile spell that does a die or two of damage without spending any MP – but you only receive the reduction *once per spell*. If you choose to take the option to put more MP into a missile spell on turns after the one on which you cast it, you must pay *all* those points.

Example: Jemzarkiza's spell is simple, but those are hefty, well-tightened bolts. The GM decides that it will cost 2 MP if it works, plus the 2 MP that Jemzarkiza is using to improve her skill roll. Her Base Spell Skill is too low to reduce the cost.

WITCH MAGIC POWER

Whereas wizard magic is all about power and will, witch magic tends to be more subtle. To a large extent, it exploits the innate power of *narrative* (pp. 8-9). Some of it isn't magic at all, exploiting what doctors call the placebo effect. Much of it works – or works *better* – because it's the sort of thing that people expect witches to do in stories. The snag with this is that witches must act the part to reap the benefits.

To start with, witches have to *look* like witches, as much of the time as possible; while occasional disguises and party dresses are okay, they must serve a purpose and not become habitual. A traditionalist like Granny Weatherwax (pp. 339-340) will say that this means dressing in black and wearing a pointy hat, but the truth is that other styles work just as well. Some urban witches go in for colourful costumes with lots of scarves and clattering metal bangles, and Magrat Garlick (pp. 337-339) did okay wearing floaty dresses and weighing herself down with "occult" jewellery and paraphernalia.

Some people – even some witches – say that witchcraft is all about communion with nature, the cycle of the seasons, and ancient rural wisdom. Most competent witches sneer at this, and it's true that there's a lot of sentimental mumbo-jumbo involved, along with confused theories from scholars who've never talked to a real witch. However, there's also a grain of truth, at least insofar as people believe this stuff, and witches certainly can draw on useful traditions and work powerful nature magic. It's all part of the narrative, and it definitely doesn't hurt if a witch chooses to play this up a bit . . . so long as she doesn't start believing it *too* much herself.

---

1. For some wizards, the answer to that will be "yes." Or rather, "Yes, please!"

Finally, witch spells often have a complicating "storybook" component. Where a wizard would stand on a mountaintop and throw wide-scope magic at a whole area at once, a witch might work something similar by flying around the area in question before cock-crow. Subtle witch effects involve herbal preparations or domestic implements, and witch curses involve lots of scowls and muttering. Wizards aren't entirely immune to this sort of thing, but they tend to limit their fancy stuff – all the symbols and chanting and geometry – to their most powerful spells. Low-end wizard magic is snappy and efficient, if not economical. Low-end witch magic has to involve, at the very least, a hard stare.

This slows down witch magic a bit, but confers two huge benefits:

1. If the GM feels that a witch spell has maintained the right style and fits the general tenor of stories about witches, the MP requirement is *half* what the same effect would cost otherwise, rounding halves up.

2. Witch spells can cover larger areas and last for longer, because that makes for a better story.

While wizards arguably have a comparable need to act like "proper" wizards (they certainly seem to feel obliged to wear pointy hats, and then there's the chanting and the symbols), standard narrative assumptions about wizard magic include the idea that it's all about raw power. Thus, their affectations *don't* reduce their MP requirements.

Area

If a witch casts an area spell on a clearly defined location or community (such as a castle or a town) whose inhabitants mostly know or know of her, divide the effective radius by *five*. If the people *don't* know of her, she may be able to fix that immediately before the casting by performing some suitably dramatic action or making a grand entrance; Performance, Public Speaking, or Intimidation skills can help.

Alternatively, if the area is one around which she can travel within some suitably dramatic period, use a multiplier of ×1 to ×8 *instead of* the radius. "While the clock strikes midnight" is worth ×1; "by cock-crow," after starting at some early hour of the morning, is worth ×5; "in a day" is worth ×8. The GM should insist that the witch actually cover the distance and has the right to throw in unexpected obstructions.

Duration

Whereas continuing, non-maintained spells – especially *wizard* spells – tend to have a fixed duration, witch magic is often more poetic, lasting "until sunrise," "until she's kissed by a handsome prince," or "so long as you hold your breath." This makes it a bit less reliable and subject to all sorts of narrative accidents, but handled with care, it allows some very long-duration enchantments. The added MP cost, if any, depends on the details:

A few seconds (e.g., "a dozen heartbeats" or "until your next breath,"): no extra cost
Minutes (e.g., "until a squirrel next enters this perfectly ordinary garden"): +1 MP
Hours (e.g., "until sunrise" or "until you next sleep"): +2 or +3 MP*
Days or weeks (e.g., "until the migrant green geese return" or "until there's a thunderstorm"): +4 to +8 MP*

Longer terms and tricky conditions (e.g., "until she's kissed by a prince"): +10 MP and up*

* The exact premium is up to the GM.

Conditions should always have a touch of the poetic and some degree of plausibility. "Until someone divides an unripe pineapple into five segments, eats two, and puts the others on your head" is just *silly*. This sort of magic taps the power of narrative, which doesn't involve pointless surrealism.

Casters are welcome to work out clever ways to extend such durations – say, driving off squirrels or travelling to remote desert regions to cast until-snow-falls spells. But if a spell is set to last ludicrously long or to be sabotaged too easily thanks to such machinations, narrative forces *will* sabotage things; e.g., a seemingly dead person will draw one last involuntary breath, or the sheikh of the desert kingdom will drop the insulated box of snow he had imported for a party. This cuts both ways, however; a "prince" must be internationally recognised *royalty*, not some nutcase off the street with a tinsel crown.

If the GM feels that the witch has been drifting away from the appropriate style, he should inform the player, and then follow this up by charging the character an extra 1-2 MP per casting or applying an extra -1 or -2 to skill to reflect the problems with working against the power of narrative. These difficulties should increase until the sufferer starts playing the part correctly again, recovering the benefits of witch magic about as quickly as they slipped away.

Mirror Magic

Many witch spells, especially scrying and divinations, use a single mirror; this is routine. However, if a witch ever finds herself standing between *two* parallel mirrors, things can get complicated. The vaguely sensible ones yelp and jump clear. A few get into that position deliberately.

The GM should discourage PCs from experimenting with this sort of thing – double mirror magic is *known* to be stupidly dangerous. If you need a rule, say that a witch can tap the multiple realities of parallel mirrors for several extra MP, but that the reflections also amplify problems: on any critical failure, she rolls multiple consequences. Also, a witch is left attuned to any mirror pair she uses; if the pair is subsequently separated, let alone broken, she may suffer complicatedly dangerous consequences.

Riding the Narrative

As an extension of this, a witch can access even more power by making events follow standard narrative patterns, or by working along with a story that's already under way. A "story" is defined as a series of events with a certain historical momentum, or a bunch of fairy-tale clichés being acted out in real life (as happens moderately frequently on the Disc).

The GM determines whether this is actually happening; not all game scenarios are planned in advance as featuring such a plot, but it isn't impossible for one to develop in play. Fitting plots traditionally have a fairy-tale quality – they involve girls in red cloaks whose grandmothers live in the woods, faintly sad young women of aristocratic ancestry needing to get married, princes going out in the world to seek their fortunes, and so on. However, other sorts of stories might work, if they're archetypical enough. Climactic showdowns at big public events seem almost obligatory.

When a witch needs more power to keep a story on track, or to set up the next part of the plot, she can get it by concentrating for one second and making a roll against Magic (Witchcraft) or Magical Form (Magianism)+2. After each such attempt – successful or not – she must wait 10 minutes before trying again. Success gives her extra MP equal to 1 + her margin of success, multiplied according to their intended use:

Contradicting a standard storyline (e.g., keeping the handsome hero from the princess forever, letting *flagrant* evil go unpunished): ×0 (no MP gained)

Helping one storyline while slowing another (e.g., helping the prince to save the kingdom by keeping him from his true love): ×1/2

Providing a moderate help to the story (e.g., telling the peasant-lad where to look for the sword that will kill the monster): ×1

Generating a standard part of the story (e.g., turning the prince into a frog so that the princess can rescue him and thus make him grateful): ×3

*Doing something **key** to the story* (e.g., putting the castle to sleep for 100 years, or making the volcano erupt just as the explorers flee the decadent city): ×5

The GM is the final judge of whether the intended spell meets narrative requirements. It has to be the *next* spell the witch casts, and she must start the casting within 30 seconds. Any MP not used by that spell are discarded.

After a *successful* attempt, nobody can get more power from the same narrative for 20 minutes.

This technique is *not* inherently "good." Indeed, it's highly abusive to force people to follow stories, denying them free will, just to increase your power or because you think it's tidy. Furthermore, unpleasant spells are at least as important to stories as nice ones, and magic can be used to set up problems as well as to solve them. Nor do stories necessarily guarantee that evil will be punished; someone who has been acting like a fairy-tale villain will generally end badly, but too much quiet low-key nastiness carries on regardless of the grand narratives. Also, some stories – especially modern, "cinematic" ones – seem to guarantee that the villain will get away in order to reappear in a sequel.

Hence, ethical witches often claim to disapprove of narrative magic. However, when a story they didn't start themselves is moving toward an appropriate ending, most witches will go along with it. They just have to remember when to stop, walk away, and leave people to get on with their lives.

Lastly, there's one big danger with this: the temptation to *force* matters to fit stories and to act like a witch (all too often, a *bad* witch) out of those stories. This is a deadly trap; powerful witches too often start as some of the most self-willed people on the Disc, and end up surrendering their free will to habit and tradition. Bad witches tend to end badly. The stories say so.

Casting the Spell

Having defined the spell, worked out its Modified Spell Skill, and determined its MP cost, you can actually attempt the casting.

CASTING TIME

With most spells, casting takes one second (a Concentrate manoeuvre, in combat). If there's a lot of messing about with material ingredients, though, the GM may rule that it takes longer. Once the GM has determined the time, you can opt to take *twice* as long and get +1 to Modified Spell Skill. If you use an active defence or are injured, stunned, grappled, or knocked back or down during the casting process, you must make a Will-3 roll or the spell fails *automatically*. Otherwise, at the end of that time, attempt the roll.

Required Actions

Exactly what you must do to cast a spell depends on your magical style and what the GM thinks is appropriate, although it always counts as a Concentrate manoeuvre (p. 174). Both witches and wizards tend to do more than the magic *really* requires, for show. High skill with a spell makes it a bit less trouble to work, as follows:

Base Spell Skill 9 or less: You must do a lot of chanting, mumbling, hand-waving (with both hands), and possibly fancy footwork. Such a casting will take twice as long as it takes better casters – at least *two* seconds.

Base Spell Skill 10-14: A few audible words and gestures with one hand, while standing still.

Base Spell Skill 15-19: Either a couple of audible words *or* a gesture (e.g., a snap of the fingers); a witch can substitute a hard stare and a successful Intimidation roll at -2. You can step a yard in any direction at the same time. You can often cast with fewer material props (see *Props*, p. 274) than the spell normally demands.

Base Spell Skill 20+: No visible or audible actions whatsoever – just a glance and a thought – while moving up to a yard. You can discard most material props that the spell normally requires.

Example: Jemzarkiza's Base Spell Skill with this magic is 12, so she can cast it by saying a few words in Classical Tsortean while waving her fingers in a complex pattern. The GM tells her player that focussing complex forces on multiple bolts simultaneously is a bit fiddly, so the casting will take two seconds. She opts not to take extra time for +1, as she's seriously worried about her friends moving out of earshot.

Blocking Spells

A "blocking spell" is magic whose sole purpose is to intercept an incoming physical, magical, or mental attack, protecting the caster. It's designed to be cast *quickly,* using just a small gesture; this haste gives -2 to Base Spell Skill. A blocking spell counts as an active defence and thus *doesn't* require Concentrate manoeuvres – and as with any active defence, it isn't permitted against a critical hit. You may try only *one* blocking spell per turn. You can do this while casting another spell, but the attempt causes the other spell to fail *automatically.*

MAGICAL SUCCESS AND FAILURE

Interpret the success roll for a spell as follows:

Critical Success – The spell goes off and you get to keep all *your* MP, but points drawn from narrative to power this specific spell are still lost. For a missile spell (see below), the initial casting is free but you must still pay extra MP added on *subsequent* turns. If the spell could be resisted (see *Resisted Spells,* below), the target can't resist.

Normal Success – If you have the required MP, you spend them and the spell goes off; if there's a chance that the spell could be resisted (see *Resisted Spells,* below), note your margin of success. If you don't have enough MP, you lose all the MP you *do* have but nothing happens.

Normal Failure by 1-5 – Nothing happens, but you don't lose any MP.*

Normal Failure by 6+ – Nothing happens, and you lose MP equal to a roll of 1d or however many the spell would have cost you, whichever is less.*

Critical Failure – You spend the MP that the spell would have cost you (or all the MP you have, if that wasn't actually enough), the spell fails, and you roll on the *Magical Fumble Table* (pp. 201-202).

* In areas of *residual magic* (p. 270), *all* failures count as critical failures!

Example: Jemzarkiza's Modified Spell Skill is 11. If she rolls 3 or 4, she'll get the spell to work without MP expenditure. On 5-11, she'll spend 4 MP and get those bolts out. On 12-16, she'll fail but lose no MP. No failure can be bad enough to cost her MP without being a critical failure.

Unfortunately, she rolls 17. The bolts stay in place, the 4 MP go (she opts to take them from her wand), and the GM demands a roll on the *Magical Fumble Table* . . .

RESISTED SPELLS

Most magic which directly affects another being's mind or body can be *resisted* (see *Resistance Rolls,* pp. 166-167) if the target

wishes – generally using Will or HT, as appropriate. This is a Quick Contest between the magic-user's casting roll and the victim's resistance. *Exception:* No resistance is possible if the caster rolls a critical success!

If the subject has magical training and is conscious, and his effective skill in the Magical Form used by the spell is higher than the score normally used to resist that spell, he may resist with that instead. If the spell uses more than one Magical Form, however, he can only substitute the *worst* of his relevant Magical Form skills. Mind Shield (p. 45) adds to Will or Magical Form when resisting mind-affecting magic.

Unconscious victims can still resist "physical" magic with HT. Mind-affecting spells generally don't do much to unconscious minds, but if such a spell *could* do something, the victim resists with Will at -3.

Example: Earlier in the day, Jemzarkiza tried to use a mental illusion on a hostile dwarf. Her Base Spell Skill with the illusion was 11, and the dwarf was two yards away, so she rolled against 9. She rolled 7, which might have succeeded. However, the dwarf had Will 10 and Mind Shield 1, so his resistance was 11 – and he rolled 8. Jemzarkiza succeeded by 2, while the dwarf succeeded by 3; thus, the spell fizzled.

MISSILE SPELLS

"Missile spells" are mostly damage-producing effects which appear in your hand or on the tip of your index finger or staff – usually in the form of a small glowing sphere. Such a spell can be "thrown" on your next turn or later, using Innate Attack skill (p. 78) to hit. It doesn't cause damage until it's hurled (or dropped). Treat it as a ranged weapon with 1/2D 25, Max 50, and Acc 1. Thus, the magic enjoys greater effective range, at the cost of taking extra time.

The caster can keep a missile spell in hand for as long as he likes, or turn it off and dissipate it harmlessly by taking Concentrate manoeuvre. If he's injured while holding it, though, he must make a Will roll. Failure means the missile spell affects *him.*

Example: After that dwarf resisted Jemzarkiza's illusion, she resorted to a fireball. She took one turn to cast it and spent 2 MP – she reckoned that 2d burning damage was enough. Having cast it, she took another turn to Aim, and then a third turn to hurl it the eight yards to her target (the dwarf was going to raise the alarm). Her Innate Attack (Projectile) skill is 14; with +1 for Acc and -4 for range, she needed 11 or less to hit.

Counterbattery Magic

If a spellcaster has a missile spell successfully cast and ready to throw, and somebody hurls a missile spell at *him,* he can defend himself by expending his spell to intercept the incoming magic. This counts as a defence roll (p. 180) – so the defender doesn't also get a dodge or a block against the attack unless he took an All-Out Defence (Double Defence) manoeuvre (pp. 175-176) – but the defence roll is equal to his appropriate Innate Attack skill at -1. The two spells collide in mid-air with all sorts of colourful special effects.

Example: Jemzarkiza subsequently created another fireball to deal with another dwarf – but before she could hurl it, Krog the Eccentric Wizard popped up and threw a freezing sphere spell at *her.* She hastily countered with the fireball, rolling against Innate Attack at -1, or 13. She succeeded, and fireball met freezing sphere, producing an amazing sound effect and lots of steam.

Maintaining Spells

Spells with a significant *duration* (p. 196) generate a continuing effect which runs for a set period on the MP used in the initial casting. The caster is aware of the spell running, but he can move, fight, talk, etc. while it's active. He can even cast further spells, but his rolls to do so are at -1 per previous spell currently running.

If the caster does nothing about the spell at the end of its duration, it simply "blinks out" at that time. He can always switch it off sooner by concentrating for a second (a Concentrate manoeuvre, in combat).

Alternatively, when the duration expires, the caster can take a second (a Concentrate manoeuvre) to put more MP into the spell to keep it going. This requires *half* the MP he needed to cast the spell (round halves up), ignoring the benefits of any critical success on the casting roll, and buys additional time equal to the original duration. He need not make a further skill roll, but even if the cost is zero, he must make a *conscious decision* to keep the spell going. As witches and wizards have to sleep sometimes, and will remain asleep for longer than most spells' duration, these things will shut down sooner or later.

Ritual Casting

It's also possible to work magic *ritually*. Some spells are *always* cast this way, while others can never be; most can be, if necessary. For examples, see *The Forms* (pp. 202-217).

Ritual casting requires at least three people working together in the same place. They must be free to talk, move around, interact, and wave their arms. One of them – the *leader* – actually casts the spell at the ritual's culmination. The others merely have to be willing to participate.

If everyone involved has the Magery advantage *and* skill in the same specialisation of Magic that the leader is using, the ritual is coordinated automatically. If any participant lacks those qualifications, however, the leader must roll against one of Intimidation, Leadership, or Public Speaking at the start of the ritual. Repeat this roll every 15 minutes thereafter if the ritual goes on for that long. These coordination rolls are at -1 for every full four people who lack Magery or the right sort of Magic skill. A failed roll means that the ritual has to stop, any MP gathered so far are lost, and the leader needs to spend 10 minutes restarting the process.

Qualified or not, *every* participant must make a HT roll every 30 minutes, at -1 per 30 minutes spent so far. Failure means he can't continue. Any such dropouts again stop the ritual. (Moral: Large, extended ritual castings are highly unreliable.)

When working magic ritually, each person participating generates 1 MP for every five minutes taken. For example, four people conducting a 15-minute ritual generate 12 MP. These MP come from the ether, not from anyone's personal supply. Participants cannot contribute additional MP from their personal totals or their staffs – mixing and matching approaches doesn't work.

Once the ritual has generated enough MP, the leader makes the skill roll to cast the spell. He *cannot* spend MP to improve his Modified Spell Skill – in fact, he's at -1 for every full 10 MP that the spell is going to use! If anyone involved in the ritual doesn't

actually want it to work, the leader's roll is at -3 for *each* such person, and they don't have to do anything deliberate or obvious to sabotage the ritual. (Moral: Forcing people to help with rituals is also a bad idea.)

If the casting is successful, the leader decides what to do with the effects if there's any discretion involved; e.g., where to throw a missile spell. If it fails, the MP gathered are dissipated and lost – they were tied up in the failed casting.

Spells cast ritually *cannot* be maintained with further MP input.

Example: Auntie Throgmartin desperately needs to cast a large-scale spell around an entire village to save it from invasion by extradimensional nasties. This will cost at least 18 MP. She decides that it's worth the risk of a rather *ad hoc* ritual casting, and ropes in her apprentice (who has Magery 0 and a point in Magic (Witchcraft)), two stray villagers (who don't), and a visiting trainee wizard (who possesses Magery and Magic (Wizardry), but who hasn't a clue about witchcraft and who's therefore no more useful than the peasants for this). She has to use her Public Speaking skill to get the ritual under way – fortunately at no penalty, because there are only three non-witches involved. She succeeds on the second attempt, so that's 10 minutes wasted.

After 15 minutes, the group of five has gathered 15 MP – not quite enough, so Auntie has to use Public Speaking again to keep the peasants and the trainee wizard in line, fortunately successfully. After another five minutes, the accumulated total is 20 MP, and Auntie can try to cast the spell (using 18 MP – the other 2 MP go to waste). Her Magical Form (Summonation) skill is 15, the penalty for the spell works out as -3, and using 18 MP from ritual casting gives -1, so she needs to roll 11 or less. She succeeds, and the GM says that a shimmering mist rolls over the village, lingering for the next day as it prevents any demonic incursions. The peasants slip away, glad that they still seem to be the same shape; the apprentice asks nervously if that was really a good idea; and the trainee wizard asks a lot of incomprehensible questions about thaumic metastructures.

Untrained Casting

It's *possible*, after a fashion, to work magic without Magery or the Magic skill. It's just *amazingly* unwise. This can only be done ritually – thus, it always involves at least three people being unwise – and it absolutely requires specific, detailed, step-by-step instructions regarding a particular spell.

The necessary instructions typically come from a book or a scroll in the hands of the ritual's leader. Such texts are usually the handiwork of past deranged experimenters (or possibly high-end demons with warped senses of humour). Unfortunately, some general magical textbooks also include detailed discussions of specific methods for one or two spells, and the authors of such works just take for granted that their readers will know about standard safety procedures, protective circles, and so on. This is one reason why wizards work so hard to keep such manuals out of the hands of anybody else.

In game terms, no one can knowingly *buy* a text containing instructions for a spell – getting hold of one should always be an adventure in itself. With the GM's permission, individuals might somehow have the instructions for specific spells memorised; each such spell counts as a 1-point perk (p. 49). A witch or wizard who discovers that a non-expert has such knowledge is liable to lecture that person at great length about why he shouldn't *use* it.

If a foolhardy group nevertheless takes the risk, works through the instructions, and performs the ritual for long enough to collect some MP, the leader gets to roll to perform the casting. His roll is based on IQ-2 or Thaumatology skill instead of Magical Form, modified by the usual penalties for ritual casting and the specific spell.

The group may not know if they've succeeded immediately, as they can't sense the flow of magical energies. They probably also won't know *exactly* what the spell is supposed to do; the classic mistake is performing a summoning without the binding or controlling spell that's supposed to go with it. Oh, and if the ritualists haven't collected enough MP, treat any *success* as a *critical failure* instead!

Example: Readers may wonder how those street mimes on p. 174 managed to summon Shoom. The answer is that Glass Box Graham's lieutenant, White Michael, acquired an old Klatchian scroll which described an appropriate ritual. He was smart enough to understand that this was a bad idea, but crazy enough to do it anyway. Summoning this particular Thing from the Dungeon Dimensions turned out to cost 9 MP and give -3 to skill.

White Michael mustered five other renegade mimes and had Leadership-12. As *nobody* involved had Magery or Magic skill, his roll to coordinate the group was at -1 (for one full multiple of four people). Michael managed that – but he incorrectly deduced from the scroll that he should be able to get the spell to work after five minutes, when the group had in fact only accumulated 6 MP. Michael lacked Thaumatology, so he had to base the casting on IQ-2, with another -3 inherent in the spell (but no further penalties for ritual casting, as it required less than 10 MP). Unfortunately, he had IQ 14 (he was crazy, not stupid), and the GM rolled an 8 for his attempt – an ordinary success, which the MP shortage converted into a critical failure. One roll of 10 on the *Magical Fumble Table* later, everyone involved was involuntarily screaming abuse at each other for several seconds. The neighbours would have complained, but in this part of Ankh-Morpork, they only even noticed because this was more noise than those people had ever made before.

Tragically, White Michael was determined and his friends were fanatics, so they went through the whole business again an hour later, taking 10 minutes this time and thus successfully gathering enough MP. So Michael got the casting to work . . .

Magical Fumble Table

The consequences of critical failures on spellcasting rolls can be embarrassing (if amusing to bystanders who are at a sufficiently safe distance). The botched spell uses up all the MP that the caster intended to spend. As well, roll 3d and look up the number below; the corresponding woes afflict the caster. The Luck advantage *cannot* be used on this roll! For *Ritual Casting* (pp. 200-201), the results of a critical failure affect *each* participant.

3 – Spell fails entirely. Caster suffers a harmless but embarrassing and inconvenient mark of failure lasting for 4d hours; e.g.,
a small rain cloud floating over his head, sneezing *explosively* once per minute, or flowers growing out of his clothing. Treat this as Unnatural Features 5.

4 – Spell is cast on one of the caster's companions (if harmful) or on a random nearby foe (if beneficial).

5 – Spell is cast on one of the caster's companions (roll randomly, but never on one on whom it was meant to be cast).

6 – Spell fails entirely. The caster forgets his own name, and forgets it again instantly if reminded. Make a Will roll after 24 hours, and again every day thereafter, to recover.

7 – Spell fails entirely. There's a momentary dip in local lighting levels, a few seconds of startling (but not harmful) temperature variations, peculiar sound effects, etc. Meanwhile, the caster is drenched in water or custard.

8 – Spell affects someone or something other than its intended target – friend, foe, or random object. Roll randomly, or the GM makes an amusing choice.

9 – Spell fails entirely. Caster suffers 1 HP of injury from a flurry of dramatic octarine sparks, which also singe his clothes.

10 – Spell fails entirely. Caster curses volubly for 1d seconds, and is mentally stunned (p. 171).

11 – Spell produces a strange noise and 1d+1 coloured billiard balls.

12 – Spell produces a weak and useless shadow of its intended effect *and* 1d white doves, coloured frogs, or fluffy mice, which treat the caster with great affection.

13 – Spell produces nothing but a dramatic explosion which leaves the caster with no eyebrows, blackened beard or hairstyle, clothes in rags, and hat 3d yards away, but causes no actual injury.

14 – Spell appears to work, but any roll to resist it is at +5 and all useful numerical results (range, duration, damage, etc.) are halved. Also, the caster suffers surreal nightmares of the Dungeon Dimensions for the next 1d+1 nights, losing 2 FP to missed sleep each night (see *Fatigue Costs*, p. 189); if this reduces him to 0 FP, he's bedridden, gibbering, and basically useless. In a semi-horrific game, the GM should require the victim to make a Fright Check each such night, at +1 per success at a previous Fright Check in the sequence.

15 – Spell fails entirely. Caster's hair (including any beard or moustache) instantly grows 2d yards; his fingernails, 1d inches.

16 – Spell fails entirely, and the caster loses the ability to cast it or anything much like it, forgetting how to work all magic of that sort and suffering the Delusion (p. 59) that it's totally *impossible*. Make a Will roll after a week, and again each week thereafter, until he remembers.

17 – Spell works normally, but the caster is then replaced for the next 3d hours by a version of himself from an alternate timeline, which differs from him in one important fashion – sex, race, profession, sexual orientation, etc. The caster remains unaware that he was ever any different, no matter what anyone says. ("But Magnus, you're a *duck*." "What are you, species-ist?")

18 – Spell fails entirely and something from another dimension manifests somewhere in the area. In a light-hearted game, this can be a dim-witted and mild-mannered demon, although it will *try* to make an evil nuisance of itself. All too easily, though, it can be a Thing from the Dungeon Dimensions – an actual but hopefully short-duration physical manifestation, or more likely partial mental possession of the caster or another vulnerable mind, leading to a temporary split personality (GM's option for details and cure, but there should be plenty of Fright Checks along the way).

The GM is welcome to modify these results at whim, especially if something different would be funny. A "magical fumble" is *meant* to be unpredictable, whimsical, and inconvenient. Big, painful consequences should be fairly rare, else magic-workers wouldn't be as tolerated as they are, and the kind-hearted GM can tone down extreme outcomes if they would derail the entire campaign. Still, magic is *never* supposed to be entirely risk-free – and in areas of residual magic, all bets are off, and failures *must* get weird and dangerous.

Example: Jemzarkiza's player rolls 8 for her magical fumble. The GM interprets the result as meaning that the bolts are too obstinate to shift, causing the twisting force she conjured to feed right back to her. Her wand torques itself from her hands, and a second later, her belt, boot, and backpack straps all start twisting, hard. Jemzarkiza frantically begins wrenching the damned things off before they strangle her – at which point, a passing enemy guard carefully opens the locked door in the nearby wall to discover her swearing and apparently engaged in hand-to-hand combat with her own gear.

The Forms

To give magic-wielders (and their GMs) a better idea of the possibilities, here are descriptions of the eight Magical Forms, each followed by some sample spells.

DIVINATION

This is the magic of information – of scrying and spying, and also of foiling the same. A few manic wizards are a bit sniffy about it, as it can't be used to do damage directly, but most people of any magical persuasion know that knowledge is most definitely power, or at least a lot of fun.

Scry Shield

To protect a person, an object, or a location from being magically spied on, draw a protective circle, scribe some runes on the wall, or make up a warding charm – details vary by magical style, and this is a very widespread sort of spell. Cost is 4 MP to cast on an individual or an item, or 1 MP per yard of radius to shield an area, with a minimum of 4 MP. There's no skill penalty to work this magic, but note the margin of success on the casting roll; any divination magic cast on the subject or into the area must succeed by at least the same amount or it discovers nothing. Duration is one day. The effect *can* be maintained.

Love's Name

For a young woman to find the name of her true love, she should peel an apple so as to have one long piece of peel, and throw that behind her. It will fall in the shape of his name. This "folk charm" allegedly works for any girl, even one without Magery – except that, when tried, it doesn't. That's because it needs a bit more focus. Some hard-eyed old witches might get it to work for themselves or a customer by muttering a few significant-sounding random words, while research witches say that you need the right apple (an unripe Sunset Wonder picked three minutes before noon on the first frosty day in the autumn) and the right peeling technique (left-handed, with a silver knife with a blade less than half an inch wide). Either way, the roll takes no penalty and the cost is 1 MP.

Scrying

Discworld magic allows reasonably accurate and reliable viewing of remote scenes in the present or recent past. The caster must specify an exact location relative to his current position ("307 miles in a direction 11 degrees spinwards of hubward from here") – and, if desired, a time ("three days, four hours, and 19 minutes ago"). The GM should be moderately flexible about this if the intent is clear, especially if the caster has reasonable maps available, and the viewpoint can be moved around a bit when the spell is first cast. Alternatively, the spell can link to another crystal ball or mirror at the target location.

The penalty to Form skill depends on the scrying item used: clear water in a bowl, or a cheap mirror ($0.50), gives -14; a high-quality silvered mirror ($25) gives -8, or -4 for scenes which are visible from another mirror at the target location; and a good crystal ball ($10, 1 lb.) gives -3. Scrying is further subject to *Long-Distance Modifiers* (p. 194) – and, when looking into the past, takes a penalty of -1 per day or part thereof passed since the event. Multiple attempts to observe the same scene in the past generate thaumic interference, giving -1 to Modified Spell Skill for each *unsuccessful* attempt to view that scene, or -3 per successful attempt. All castings cost 3 MP, +1 MP per day or part thereof for events in the past. The spell has a duration of one minute and *can* be maintained.

Only the caster can see the vision, unless the spell uses a rare and insanely expensive enchanted mirror – and even then, things are often shimmery or shadowy. Furthermore, non-magic-users on the Disc have a long tradition of not especially trusting such stuff when it's really important. Hence, the GM can always rule that this spell doesn't *quite* give clear enough information to mess up a mystery plot (and anyway, by widespread custom, the testimony of a scrying wizard won't usually stand up in a court of law).

Unseen University has several scrying mirrors and crystal balls hooked up to the output from the High Energy Magic Building. This allows extended viewing and better two-way communication with wizards elsewhere who can manage an effective casting back to UU. The University also has a few mirrors permanently enchanted with the same sort of magic.

> *What's the good of having mastery over cosmic balance and knowing the secrets of fate if you can't blow something up?*
> *– The Dean, in Reaper Man*

ELEMENTALISM

The magic of energy and *inorganic* matter is the primary concern of most wizards. Witches also know a bit about the subject, but tend to be subtle about it. While wizards love their fireballs, witches will remind solid rocks that they were once molten, causing them to soften and collapse, or quietly deflect damage from "elemental" sources. High-powered witches have even been known to control the weather, although most consider that flashy and too much like hard work. Only the most flamboyant witches will hurl magical bolts of energy, which is so un-witch-like that it never enjoys the MP reductions under *Witch Magic Power* (pp. 196-198).

The big problem with this Form is that mindless materials and forces are *harder* to influence than things with minds, especially in subtle or complex ways. Witches find this especially inconvenient, as living minds and bodies are their prime concern. If something has a mind, that mind can be changed – and such is the nature of things in the Disc's universe that any attached body tends to follow its lead. Even changing someone into a frog is ultimately about *persuading* him that he's a frog. Unthinking matter, on the other hand, has to be controlled directly (or just blasted). Moreover, while magic can overcome many physical "conservation laws" (regarding, for example, momentum or mass), it must still treat them as strong guidelines.

Wizards can accomplish things by pumping raw energy into the problem, but that tends to create semi-random, uncontrolled, disorganised change, such as heat. It's easy for a wizard to blast away a stone wall, given enough MP, but much harder to make the wall move aside smoothly and quietly. This is why wizards (and witches) find it difficult to fly or even levitate using their own magic and favour broomsticks for the purpose; controlling the energy to make every part of themselves move in the same direction simultaneously and at the exact same speed is tricky, and trying to learn how runs the risk of having parts of yourself move in *different* directions at high speeds.

Snap

This magic causes a small quantity of unliving matter – a few ounces at most – to give way *if* it's either inherently fragile (e.g., delicate china) or being pushed toward its limits (e.g., a bowstring under tension). This gives -1 to skill and costs 1 MP. Snapping or shattering something heavier, up to 5 lbs., is possible with -2 to skill and 3 MP.

Visual Illusion

In principle, generating an intangible illusion using Elementalism is easy – you just manipulate a little light to make things look different. The tricky bit is making the effect *convincing*. To fool others, the magic-worker must win a Quick Contest of IQ with each person he wants to deceive; the GM may apply modifiers for the image's complexity and plausibility, limited or extended times to examine it, and so on. Alternatively, the caster can generate a visual illusion to cover his position or movements, either gaining a bonus to Camouflage or Stealth skill rolls equal to his margin of success on the casting roll, or creating effective camouflage without physical materials. Visual illusions can never inflict physical damage, although a really convincing and horrible image might cause a Fright Check.

This spell gives -3 to skill and costs 1/3 MP per yard of radius. Duration is one minute.

Fireball

The classic missile spell (p. 199) gives -3 to skill, costs 1 MP per die of damage, and lets you put up to your Magery level in MP into it each turn.

Magic Lightning

Wizards who want to blast things *quickly,* at a serious cost in range, can hurl electrical damage directly rather than as a missile spell, accepting the usual -1 to Modified Spell Skill per yard to the target. This spell is cast at -3 to skill, and costs 1 MP per die of damage.

Standardised Spells

Some magic-workers may want to master specific spells, casting them more effectively than their skill with the relevant Magical Form implies. Allowing this requires an extra, *optional* rule and may make characters a bit narrow, but it does gives useful effectiveness in those narrow areas.

To raise your effective skill with a "standardised" spell, you must first define the spell very specifically. For example, "inflicts a -15-point mental disadvantage" wouldn't do; you'd have to opt for, say, "inflicts Lecherousness (12)." Likewise, you can't just say, "Stacklady's Morphic Resonator"; you need to specify something like "Change Humans to Pumpkins." You can define it as having variable *power* (a fireball doing a variable number of damage dice is fine, as is an area-effect spell of variable radius), but *not* with any variations that change the Base Spell Skill.

Next, determine your Base Spell Skill with this spell. For example, if you have Magical Form (Magianism)-16, you could choose Dispel Magic (p. 205), with a Base Spell Skill of 11.

Once you've done that, you can spend character points to raise your effective level with *that one spell*. The first +1 costs 2 points; after that, each additional +1 costs 1 point. However, you can't improve any spell past your Magic skill +4.

Example: Walter the Wizard wants to be expert at casting Gindle's Effortless Elevator (p. 204). He has Magic-15 and Magical Form (Elementalism)-14, so he starts at skill 10. He can raise this to 11 for 2 points, 12 for 3 points, 13 for 4 points, and so on, up to skill 19 for 10 points, but no higher. He opts to spend 8 points, and records the spell on his character sheet with a level of 17. If he used it to lift a rock three yards distant, he would roll against 14 (17, -3 for range).

Note: If you use this rule and later want to raise your Magical Form skill, you may have to reassign some points between Magic skill, Form, and spell to keep the character legal.

Balanced Levitation

Wizards say that levitation is harder than people think, because of that annoying conservation-law nonsense to which the universe seems indecently attached. *Smart* wizards know a way around this: They make something else fall to balance the upward impulse they require.

This spell is cast at -3 to skill and costs 1 MP. Within 10 seconds after casting it, the caster must trigger or arrange the balancing fall. A human-sized mass falling from the height he wishes to ascend is most straightforward, but it's just as good to get something twice as heavy to fall half as far, or a third as heavy to fall three times as far. The balance need not be perfect, but should be plausibly close.

For fiddly situations, the GM can require an IQ roll and get whimsical on a failure, having the wizard shoot past his destination or not quite get there, or suddenly overheat or become extremely cold (HT roll to avoid being stunned, or maybe just lose 2d FP) as the energy inequalities find an alternate resolution.

Gindle's Effortless Elevator

This is a fancy wizard name for a simple spell. The caster levitates an object into the air and makes it move around, fairly slowly, by raw magical effort. Some witches know the principles involved, but as it isn't classic witch magic, they can't claim the MP reductions under *Witch Magic Power* (pp. 196-198) when using it. Despite all the problems, this spell is fairly reliable, because the motion it induces is slow and the caster concentrates continuously – but the need for the latter means that a wizard can never cast it on *himself*.

This spell gives -4 to skill, costs 1 MP per 20 lbs. or fraction thereof, has a duration of five seconds, and *can* be maintained. Several wizards working together can combine castings to share the MP cost of moving a heavy object, but each must make an IQ roll to coordinate properly. A living and unwilling target can resist the spell with DX (*not* HT or Will). The magic can move the target at up to two yards per second – not enough to do significant damage, though lifting something over a long drop and then letting go is quite effective.

Rock Soften

Persuading a mass of unliving matter to be less robust than it should be has all sorts of uses – and as noted earlier, this is the sort of magic that witches can pull off by briefly persuading the material that it has a memory. Rendering a volume of rock or similar stuff semi-liquid and highly fragile gives -3 to skill and costs 1 MP per cubic foot influenced. The effect has a duration of 10 seconds and *can* be maintained. The GM determines the quantity that needs to be softened to achieve a given goal; e.g., affecting a couple of cubic feet of stone around a door's hinges and lock will usually allow it to be pushed or pulled away with little effort.

Wind

Basic weather control has many uses, especially for witches and wizards travelling by sailing ship. This area spell takes a skill penalty of -4 and costs 1/25 MP per yard of radius for each change of one "step." A single step can either change wind direction by 45° or shift the wind one notch up or down the following scale: *dead calm, light breeze, moderate breeze, wind, gale, storm,* and finally *hurricane.* For example, a wizard could turn a light breeze into a gale (three steps) and reverse its direction (180°, another four steps) over a 50-yard radius by spending 14 MP. The spell has a duration of 10 minutes and *can* be maintained.

Sumpjumper's Incendiary Surprise

A wizards' favourite, this area spell creates a dense random scattering of burning flares, springing up from often-unexpected places. These fires cover about a third of the area in total. Roll 1d for each individual within the spell's radius; on a 1 or a 2, they take 1d of burning damage. In addition, most large and many small flammable objects in the area will catch fire. Cast in the right place, this magic can quickly generate a real inferno!

This spell has a skill penalty of -4 and costs 1 MP per yard of radius. The caster must have at least Magery 1.

Herpetty's Seismic Reorganiser

Basic earthquake spells are popular with some wizards and a few irascible witches (who of course just call it "Earthquake"). This one is an area spell that takes 30 seconds to cast and gives -6 to skill. Cost is 1 MP per yard of radius if the earthquake is *small*, 3 MP/yard if *moderate*, or 6 MP/yard if *major.* To manipulate such energies, the caster needs at least Magery 1 to create a small earthquake, Magery 2 for a moderate quake, or Magery 3 for a major one. Duration is one minute, and the spell *cannot* be maintained.

A small quake is a slight swaying; it might topple poorly balanced things or people, but mostly it just gives -1 to all DX-based skills used in the area of effect. A moderate quake causes many things to fall over; people must make DX rolls every turn to avoid being shaken off their feet, and everyone in the area suffers -2 to all DX-based skills. A major quake can *collapse* weaker walls and buildings; people in the area have to roll at DX-3 every turn to remain standing and suffer -4 on DX-based skills. Demolishing a reasonably well-built structure requires creating an earthquake under *all* of it – shaking up one corner may crack the stonework a bit, but no more.

MAGIANISM

Direct manipulation of magical energies is useful to anyone who wants to get fancy and complicated with magic. Magianism spells can detect and sometimes dispel almost any other sort of magic and encompass effects that block magical energies. However, they are either complex and rather static, or extremely specific in their "tuning."

Hence, practical witches may see this Form as theoretical and irrelevant to their regular work, while some wizards pay minimal attention to it because it can't be used to blow things up directly. Both are ignoring an important point, though: Magianism can get you more magical oomph for whatever it is you want to do and help you fend off anyone trying to use magic on *you.*

Whatever their style of magic, career magical enchanters *require* skill in Magianism – it's necessary to bind magical energies permanently or semi-permanently into physical objects.

Detect Magic

Although Magery gives magic-workers the ability to sense magical forces, a simple spell can make things far more certain and reliable. This spell can tell whether an object or a phenomenon is magical. If it's successful, a second casting can determine whether the magic is permanent or temporary. Critical success gives full details of the magic, insofar as the caster can understand them. This spell has no skill penalty and costs 1 MP.

Check Thaumic Flux

This spell determines the nature and level of local ambient magical energies. The procedures involved are simple enough that they don't *usually* cause trouble, even in high and/or unstable magical flux levels, except on a critical failure. To get a numerical value, however, the caster must use a certain amount of fiddly instrumentation in the casting – at which point he might as well carry a thaumometer (pp. 160-161). Provided that the local energies aren't doing anything too weird, a margin of success of 2+ also provides a sense of the *orientation* of the magical field, suggesting which direction is hubwards. The spell has a skill penalty of -1 and costs 1 MP.

Analyse Magic

This magic identifies the exact spells on an object or a person. It gives -3 to skill and costs 4 MP. The extended testing process involved means that it takes *30 minutes* to cast – and the caster might need at least a point in Thaumatology or Occultism to have the vocabulary to understand the results! If the subject bears multiple spells, the first casting identifies the one that used the fewest MP and reveals that there are more, the next casting discloses the spell with the next-lowest cost, and so on. For spell-like effects (see below) such as elven mind control, the GM should assign MP-equivalent values to taste.

Octagram

A properly drawn and activated octagram – typically marked on the floor in chalk – generates a magical obstruction which prevents spells and certain magical creatures from passing in either direction. Drawing and empowering such a pattern is treated as an area spell. The resulting barrier projects about 10 to 20 feet up from the symbol traced on the ground and is closed at the top.

Drawing an octagram takes at least a number of seconds equal to five times its radius in yards (minimum five seconds) – longer, if using more robust materials. Activating it – the actual spell-casting process – then requires a *further* five seconds and a skill roll at -3. Cost is 3 MP per yard of radius.

Once successfully created, such a barrier is permanent until broken somehow. If part of the octagram is cut or erased, its power is lost until the caster can remake it. Repairs usually require just a second with a piece of chalk, although worse damage might take longer and/or require another roll. *Magic* can never damage an octagram, but an ordinary person can simply walk up and scuff important chalk lines with his shoe; thus, some wizards have octagram designs inscribed in more durable forms on the floors of their workrooms, ready for activation when needed. Wise spellcasters rarely assume that their octagrams will last forever.

Summoned and *most* extradimensional creatures can neither move, cast magic, nor shift any physical object across an octagram's border. Other beings – including mages and "natural" magical creatures considered "native" to the Disc, such as undead and golems – can cross it without difficulty. Nobody from any dimension can cast spells through an octagram or use magic to traverse it, however. Entities *can* be summoned *within* an octagram (a standard summoner's safety measure), but no being can be called up in an octagram that's too small for any shape it can adopt.

There are exceptions. An octagram will merely inconvenience Things from the Dungeon Dimensions for 1d seconds, as they can absorb its magic and carry on. Such a design will only stop Death (sometimes) if he's summoned into it using the Rite of AshkEnte (pp. 214-215); that particular traditional invitation aside, he can go wherever he has to be. Presumably, the same goes for other beings of similar rank, such as the other three Horsemen (pp. 295-296), and Auditors (pp. 296-297) can simply stop being inside the octagram and be elsewhere instead.

Finally, some trapped entities may be able to *force* their way through an octagram. Roll a Quick Contest between the being's (ST+Will)/2 and the Base Spell Skill with which the octagram was cast. If the creature wins, it destroys the spell. No individual can "test" an octagram more than once per day, and rules-bound types might not even try. The GM decides which creatures make the attempt – but remember that demons in particular are horrendously unimaginative and hardly ever break rules.

Nul Zone

This spell creates an area in which spells simply don't work unless they successfully resist the casting with their own Base Spell Skill. The Nul Zone can be dispelled, but the Dispel Magic spell must resist it first. If the caster – or his staff, in the case of a wizard – is outside the defined area at the time of casting, he's unaffected by it; otherwise, he has to overcome his own magic to cast any further spells within the area. If a spell defeats the Nul Zone, the caster knows immediately and must make a Will roll; failure means his Nul Zone collapses entirely. The Nul Zone only affects spells (and some spell-like effects); magical creatures can walk right through it without noticing, although they can't be magically summoned into it.

Considering its effectiveness, this spell is relatively easy to work. Casting takes five seconds and a skill roll at -3. Cost is 1/10 MP per yard of radius. Duration is one hour.

Spell-Like Effects

Many Magianism spells affect other spells, detecting, controlling, or disrupting them. At the GM's option, these can *also* work against "spell-like effects": powers wielded by innately magical creatures. For example, they could conceivably detect demonic possession (an effect similar to a Psychomancy spell), or dispel a dryad's attempts to spy on someone magically (an effect a lot like Divination). In such cases, if the Magianism working would give a target spell a chance to resist with the Base Spell Skill used to cast that spell, a spell-like effect may resist with the Will of the creature that created the effect.

Dispel Magic

This spell suppresses or disrupts transient magical energies within its area of effect. It does nothing to magical devices, but each spell or spell-like effect *may* be switched off. Each resists separately with the Base Spell Skill used when it was cast. The caster can say that any or all of his own effects caught in the area resist or turn off automatically, as he chooses.

Dispel Magic is cast at -5 to skill and costs 3 MP per yard of radius. It takes a second to cast for every MP put into it.

Emergency Power Drain

This spell works only in an area with above-normal thaumic flux, *or* where there are three or more spells with durations of at least an hour active, *or* where a story is running which the caster has been manipulating (see *Riding the Narrative*, pp. 197-198). It's an area spell, always centred on the caster, with minimum radius five yards, and the area must completely cover the areas of effect of all those active spells. Casting takes one second and a skill roll at -8; the cost is 1 MP per yard of radius.

It functions exactly as Dispel Magic on its area of effect, but the caster's own spells are automatically dispelled. Also, any stories that the caster was manipulating will "break down" in some way as his manipulations fail. Then, the caster recovers half the MP that were used to cast any dispelled spells (round down); if the area has above-normal thaumic flux or a story running which the caster was manipulating, he also gains 2 MP, plus 2 MP for every point of success on this casting.

This can even raise his personal MP reserve above its usual maximum; if so, he immediately starts losing the excess at a rate of 2 MP/second.

NECROMANCY

Death is part of magic, whatever some people mutter about "bad taste" or "disruption of the natural order." Necromancy is all about dealing with death, and the dead, and both material and immaterial *undead*. Necromancers like to talk about confronting ultimate realities and walking the line of shadow, although that's mostly pose.

Nevertheless, animating zombies and skeletons *is* the sort of thing associated more with old-school magical dark lords and scary voodoo witches than with respectable scholars and kindly rural wise-women. Talking to the dead isn't much better; it's widely assumed that they don't want to be bothered by mortals (even if in practise, ghosts who can be contacted at all are often happy to chat). Thus, Unseen University no longer has a Department of Necromancy – although the Department of Post-Mortem Communications (p. 283) still gets its research budget, and what Genua's local witches get up to is strictly their own business.

Detect Haunting

A little careful testing using basic Necromancy can detect the presence of ghosts or similar invisible undead. This has no skill penalty and costs 1 MP. Success by 5+, or a critical success, means that the caster also learns something detailed about the nature of what he has detected.

Exorcise Ghost

Although clearing out ghosts and negative energies is mostly seen as a job for priests – and beneath the dignity of a sophisticated wizard, and none of the business of a hard-working witch – a competent necromancer can handle it. This spell makes its area of effect unpleasant and disconcerting for ghosts, and generally purges it of necromantic energies. Ghosts in the area at the time of casting, or trying to enter it later, can resist it with their Will. By default, they resist at -2, but if they're bound to the site (common among ghosts, who are often doomed to haunt particular places), make that +3 instead.

A ghost who fails to resist simply won't consider going back to the exorcised site unless given an *exceptionally* good reason. In that case, it can try to resist again, but at a further -4 to the previous roll. Ghosts exorcised from places they're supposed to haunt may either go on to whatever afterlife is appropriate for them, or wander more widely with their powers much reduced, trying to fulfil some purpose or task (GM's option).

This spell takes five minutes to cast and gives -3 to skill. Cost is 1/10 MP per yard of radius. Duration is one month. In practise,

most casters rarely bother to maintain it (and suffer the -1 for a running spell) for more than a few minutes – either it drives off the problem or it doesn't.

Speak With the Dead

Necromantic magic can temporarily grant the user the equivalent of the Medium advantage (p. 45), *plus* the ability to understand the languages spoken by any ghosts he contacts (he enters into direct mental communication with them, but he *perceives* this as speech). This spell is also routinely used to communicate with spirits of the dead which have been bound to locations or into physical objects; it's the magical equivalent of a polite knock on the door to them. It's cast at -2 to skill and costs 2 MP. Duration is 10 minutes.

Last Vision

Necromancy is capable of extracting a little information from the physical remains of the dead. This is widely regarded as morbid, and no half-respectable watchman or lawyer would accept information from such a source (for some comments that are relevant here, see *Scrying*, p. 202). Still, it has its uses.

The traditional version of the spell is fairly straightforward: the caster gazes into the eyes of a corpse, works the magic, and sees the last image that the dead person saw. This takes three seconds to cast and gives -3 to skill, plus a further -1 to Modified Spell Skill per full two days since the subject died (it's up to the GM how long a dead body's eyes remain sufficiently intact to work the magic on). Cost is 3 MP. For a similar spell which can reach much further back in time, see *Necromantic Retrocognition* (p. 216).

Chill Finger

While Necromancy isn't primarily combat magic, someone who can juggle "death energies" isn't without options. To cast this spell, the caster points at someone (part of his Concentrate manoeuvre), rolls at -4 to skill, and pays 2 MP. If he succeeds, his victim feels a wave of terror and must make a Fright Check, at -1 per two full points by which the caster made his roll. The target must also resist the spell with HT or lose 1d FP to a supernatural chill.

Steal Zombie

If a necromancer encounters a zombie or similar undead with the Arcane Automaton disadvantage (pp. 94-95), he can "reprogram" it to obey him by casting a spell with skill -4 and a cost of 4 MP. The zombie resists with HT, but at -3.

Animate Zombie

Creating a zombie isn't as easy or common a necromantic procedure as laypeople like to believe. A zombie requires at least a fragment of the life-energy and willpower of the deceased to power it, but the dead usually find themselves *going on* somewhere, leaving nothing of themselves behind. Occasionally, though, the minds of the dead remain quite attached to their bodies – in every sense.

The GM decides whether a particular person had enough unresolved issues or sheer obstinacy to be zombie material; Will 11+ is a fair minimum requirement. If in doubt – e.g., when working with a random corpse – roll 1d. On a 6, the body can be reanimated. The only way to *find out*, though, is to try; thus, most necromancers either put up with a lot of failures or choose their material carefully.

This spell gives -6 to skill, and Modified Spell Skill is at -1 for every three days since death, as the body decays and physically disintegrates. If the dead person's personality was highly motivated to come back for whatever reason (for guidelines, see *Becoming a Zombie*, p. 118), Modified Spell Skill is at +1 to +4, at the GM's option. In all cases, cost is 8 MP. The GM rolls secretly for the casting attempt; thus, if the spell doesn't work, the necromancer won't know whether this was due to an unsuitable choice of body or just a failed casting roll. Multiple attempts *are* permitted with the same body, in the hopes that it's suitable – but even if it is, there's a cumulative -1 per previous attempt by *any* caster.

If the roll succeeds, but by a margin of only 0-4, create the resulting zombie by adding the zombie racial template (see *Zombies*, pp. 116-118) and Dead Broke (p. 33) to a "human" with ST equal to the body's when alive, DX 10, IQ 8, and HT 10. The resulting being also has Arcane Automaton (pp. 94-95) "set" to obey the caster, plus -50 points in other zombie-typical disadvantages (for ideas, see *Zombie Variants*, p. 118). If the margin is 5+, though, the zombie has much more of the deceased's personality – add the racial template and Dead Broke to his *full* character sheet, along with a mere -10 points of zombie-typical disadvantages. In either case, the GM can make a few other tweaks at whim, to keep the spell's results interesting and unpredictable.

The spell is permanent and doesn't need maintenance, in the sense that a zombie will usually keep going until physically destroyed. However, if the resulting zombie has the Arcane Automaton trait, it has three flaws that are likely to limit its useful lifespan:

1. The zombie must make a HT roll *and* a Will+4 roll every month. Both rolls are at -1 for every two other zombies (or animated skeletons) currently serving the same master; zombies need a bit of psychic looking-after. A failed HT roll means that the zombie's ST score drops by one permanently, while a failed Will+4 roll means that its DX drops by one permanently – and in either case, *critical* failure reduces the attribute by 1d instead. The zombie also loses associated secondary characteristics in these cases. A zombie that reaches 0 HP for this reason falls to pieces, while one that drops to 0 DX or Basic Speed simply stops functioning.

2. The magic is vulnerable to Dispel Magic (p. 205). This spell resists being dispelled at +5. If Dispel Magic wins, however, the zombie disintegrates – messily.

3. If the old personality's reasons for not wanting to depart involved hatred of the necromancer, the GM should secretly roll a Quick Contest between the necromancer's Will-3 and the old personality's unmodified Will. If the necromancer loses or ties, the zombie is uncontrollable and seeks to kill him!

PHYSIOMANCY

Physiomantic magic manipulates living things' bodies and life-energies, and tinkers with the form of *organic* matter (such as wood). This can be used for both good and bad ends. It's the mainstay of regular witch medical work, but anyone who knows

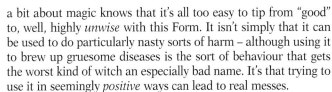

a bit about magic knows that it's all too easy to tip from "good" to, well, highly *unwise* with this Form. It isn't simply that it can be used to do particularly nasty sorts of harm – although using it to brew up gruesome diseases is the sort of behaviour that gets the worst kind of witch an especially bad name. It's that trying to use it in seemingly *positive* ways can lead to real messes.

The problem is that using magic to heal injury or disease directly and quickly (rather than as a subtle aid to mundane medical procedures), or to boost someone's physical capabilities, means binding magic into a living body on a semi-permanent basis. The trouble with *that* is that Discworld magic has, if not exactly a mind of its own, then at least a capacity for independence and a tendency to perversity. Wizards may be megalomaniacs as a breed, but half-sane ones who know much about magic regard the idea of planting magical energies inside a living body as frankly loopy. Witch training makes the point even more directly. Hence, while Physiomancy has many uses, it calls for a degree of subtlety.

Spolt's Forthright Respirator

This is the wizardly name for a spell that witches regard as first aid too basic to be worth naming. It causes someone who isn't currently breathing to start again, taking at least one breath; thus, it's useful for treating respiratory difficulties and can stand in for First Aid skill when dealing with, say, a drowning victim. However, it also has potential offensive uses – for instance, if cast on someone who's trying to hold his breath while underwater. In situations like that, it's resisted with HT. This spell has no skill penalty and costs 1 MP.

Eringyas' Surprising Bouquet

Cast at -3 to skill and a cost of 2 MP, this spell creates a large bunch of roses in the caster's hand. These last for 10 minutes – or longer, if the spell is maintained.

Transfer Pain

This is a standard spell for village witches, anaesthesia being one thing that can make low-tech medicine a lot less *unpleasant* and often more effective simply because it's less traumatic. It's also a kindness for patients whom medicine can no longer help.

The caster must touch the patient with one hand and an inert object (a large rock or an anvil is recommended) with the other, and cast at -3 to skill and a cost of 3 MP. Any pain currently being felt by the patient is transferred to the object, which becomes warm, even hot as a result. The patient remains comfortable for 12 hours, plus six hours per point of success – or one full week, on a critical success. The reduced stress can give from +1 to +4 on medical skill rolls to treat the patient during that period (GM's decision).

Some witches are said to be able to hold pain in an immaterial form, and even use it as an improvised weapon, but that's rare and very tricky.

Catch Wound

This blocking spell (p. 199) *seems* to negate physical harm to the caster's body. In fact, it doesn't – it simply gets around the Discworld problem with healing magic by shifting the injury through time. That makes it easier and more reliable than most defensive magic, but with the snag that the caster must take the damage eventually.

The spell is cast at -4 to skill and costs 3 MP. It can block a single attack that would cause physical damage to the caster alone.

It *doesn't work* against "large-area" damage: explosions, being plunged into acid or molten lava, and so on. The magic-worker must specify some part of his body that can get in the way of the attack – usually a hand or a limb. The attack appears to fail, being stopped dead by the caster's skin.

However, the spell must be maintained, and the caster will take damage when it stops; treat it as having a duration of one day. Calculate the *minimum* damage that the blocked attack could have done, minus any DR that the caster has, plus one. This is the damage that the caster will take to the relevant body part when he stops maintaining the spell (or if it should be dispelled), and *is* modified for damage type. For example, a 2d+3 cutting attack has a minimum damage of 5; if the victim is wearing DR 2 armour, the calculation gives 5 - 2 + 1 = 4 points of damage, which becomes 6 HP of injury with the wounding modifier for cutting. The effect is exactly as if the caster had been hit by the weapon at the moment the spell ends, complete with pain, shock, and any effects from poison or whatever.

Magic-users who can reduce the effective maintenance cost to zero might try to defer the damage indefinitely. Remember that there are penalties to all *other* casting rolls while maintaining spells, though – and there's always the possibility that this magic will be dispelled or otherwise turned off involuntarily at an inconvenient moment. Sensible casters clean and bandage the affected spot carefully, and then "accept" the damage when alone and somewhere safe.

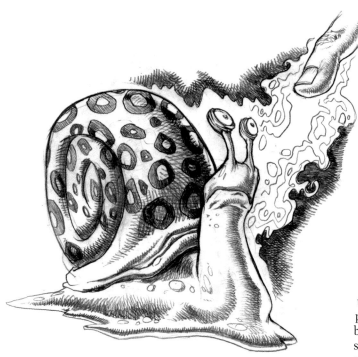

Stacklady's Morphic Resonator

This is a wizard's term for magic to which a witch would give a simpler name (although not as many witches use it as people think). It's plain, old-fashioned turning something living into something *else* living. The technique relies on the fact that most beings' morphic fields (pp. 9-10) are largely controlled by their minds, and so by making a small adjustment to the subject's self-image, his shape can be changed. The effects are temporary, as reality reasserts itself in time.

Perhaps the best-known use of this magic is to transform people into frogs, but it can produce countless other effects.

Pumpkins are popular, and show-off casters have been known to change frogs or cats into *people*. However, the spell cannot create a mind to modify, so ordinary vegetables or rocks cannot be turned *into* anything. The spell also has one fundamental limitation: it can never change the appearance of the target's eyes. Whether the subject's clothes are included in the transformation is up to the GM, who should bear in mind the rule of universal comedy – but armour, valuable jewellery, and magic items are always excluded.

The spell is cast at -6 to skill and is resisted by the subject's Will-4 (it's sneaky and powerful magic) if he doesn't want to change. The results endure for a number of hours equal to the caster's margin of victory – or for hours equal to margin of success plus five, if the target didn't try to resist – and cannot be maintained. If the subject succeeds exactly with his resistance roll, he flickers into the target shape for one second and then returns to normal. Base cost is 5 MP, but for subjects *or* transformed shapes with a Size Modifier greater than 0, multiply this cost by 1 + the SM of the *larger* of the initial or transformed shape. A simple casting of this spell, with no further modifiers than these, can also be used to cancel the effects of a previous working.

However, the spell has a number of peculiarities. *Small* changes are intrinsically harder than large – or rather, it's difficult to specify fine details about the eventual form. This is because kicking a morphic field between shapes is one thing, but sculpting it precisely is quite another. Such transformations give from -2 to -8 to *Base* Spell Skill, at the GM's discretion, while imitating a very specific existing form (such as a particular person) adds a *further* penalty as severe as -4. Further, because morphic fields have levels of similarity, changing a subject's "kingdom" (animal, vegetable, or mineral) gives -2 to Base Spell Skill; turning people into vegetables suffers this penalty, as does turning trolls (walking rocks) into anything but troll animals (also made of rock). Also, *less*-intelligent subjects are harder to transform, because they don't have as much mental power to control their morphic fields; Modified Spell Skill is at -1 for every level by which the subject's IQ is below 8.

The target's ST changes to something appropriate for his new shape, but his DX, IQ, and HT stay the same, and he may retain other features at the GM's whim – again largely depending on what makes a good joke. For example, someone turned into a frog can only go "ribbit," but someone transformed into a pumpkin might well become a *talking* pumpkin. Altering a subject's base HP gives -1 to Base Spell Skill for every 2 HP of difference either way; the caster can say that the transformed shape is exceptionally tough or feeble to avoid this penalty, but the GM can put limits on this (see the example below). Any damage carries over in proportion between forms, so the spell cannot be used to heal wounds; an injured human might become a tough-but-injured frog. Nonsapient creatures changed into sapient beings *might* gain a level or two of IQ from their newly enlarged brains, but no more than that. They also tend to retain their old instincts and habits.

Finally, because the whole business is mental trickery anyway, standard effects and clichés are easier to achieve. Changing a human into a frog grants +2 to Base Spell Skill for a wizard, or +3 for a witch; turning anyone into a pumpkin gives +2, cancelling the "kingdom change" penalty. A transformed shape that's unknown to the subject gives -4 to Modified Spell Skill, as the trickery is much harder. ("He said he'd change me into an okapi, but it didn't work. What is an okapi, anyway?")

All transformations must be approved by the GM, who may demand that specific details and effects be included, or impose extra penalties for less-plausible ideas.

Example: Ferdinand the Long-Bearded, with Magical Form (Physiomancy)-16, decides to change his annoying younger sister into a frog. (He has some childhood issues to work out.) The base skill penalty is -6, with an extra -2 because he specifies that the frog should have purple spots (a family joke). He'd happily leave her with her normal HP score of 9, but the GM refuses to believe in a frog with more than 5 HP, so Ferdinand has to take another -2 for a 4-HP change. He *does* get +2 for the cliché, so his Base Spell Skill is 8. The casting would normally cost 5 MP, but Ferdinand adds another 4 MP to raise his Modified Spell Skill to 10.

Ferdinand casts the spell, taking twice as long as usual (two seconds) because of his low Base Spell Skill (p. 194). His sister, who has been mocking his claims to be a wizard, thinks he's just dancing round the room spouting gibberish. He rolls a 9, succeeding by 1; his sister, with Will 10, rolls against 6 to resist and gets a 12, failing by 6. There's a flash of octarine sparks, and a very angry-looking frog with purple spots, wearing pink lipstick and with characteristic green eyes, crawls out from under the satin party dress now lying on the ground.

She should be stuck like that for seven hours, but after a family argument, Ferdinand grudgingly agrees to change her back; his Base Spell Skill for that is also 10 (his Form skill with only the spell's basic modifier). However, his sister chooses to resist, because she's sulking and wants to make him look bad. Coincidentally, they both make their rolls exactly. She briefly re-inflates to human size, and then collapses back down with an annoying "ribbit."

Note: This spell can become the basis for longer-lasting effects – deliberately or accidentally. For example, Greebo the Cat (pp. 343-344) developed a permanent insta-bility in his morphic field after being transformed once, while in *Witches Abroad*, Lilith worked a semi-permanent transformation on the Duc which also raised his IQ, by tying the transformation into a care-fully constructed narrative. (Lilith was clearly an expert in the "bad witch" variety of Magianism as well as Physiomancy.) Such effects are left for the GM to determine as the plot requires.

PSYCHOMANCY

Magic can produce plenty of flashes and booms, but it's often more efficient to work with thoughts and perceptions. This is the dominion of Psychomancy: mind-magic. The Form can influence any *naturally occurring* mind residing in a *physical* brain, however limited. Hence, it covers the minds of humans, trolls, and animals, down to the smallest insect. Undead are handled by Necro-mancy; spirits, by Summonation.

Most witches dabble in this Form, although some refrain for ethical or other reasons, and some are just better at it than others. The good ones who *do* use it limit themselves to low-powered spells for emergencies only.[1] Witches traditionally believe in free will and prefer tweaking emotions and perceptions to turning humans into puppets.

Wizards tend to be less interested in Psychomancy, although they consider mind and brain perfectly reasonable topics for spe-cialist study. Those who bother with it are rarely terribly consid-erate about *how* they use it. Most wizards reckon that if they have to influence someone's mind, fireballing the scenery will do the trick. After all, a fire spell will light a cigarette, too.

Detect Mind

This may sound trivial, but determining whether there's a mind in residence can save a lot of trouble. The only snag is that, occasionally, a mind can go wandering, leaving its body in a coma but retaining the option to return. Witches can cast this spell with a hard stare and maybe a careful touch of the hand; wizards tend to need a lot more mess-ing about with alchemical preparations or dousing pendulums. This spell gives no penalty and costs 1 MP.

Truth Tell

A basic psychic trick is to look at the surface of someone's mind as he speaks and determine whether he's *consciously* lying. This won't detect honest mistakes, but it can sense uncertainties and ambi-guities (though never *why* the subject is confused or vague). Handling complex cases is left to the GM's judgement. This spell gives -1 to skill, is resisted by Will, and costs 2 MP. If works, it has a duration of one minute, and *can* be maintained.

Mental Adjustment

Psychomancy can be used to change how someone's mind works, at least temporarily and on a shallow level. (Most witches and wizards have enough respect for the con-cept of free will to insist that they couldn't make permanent changes – or at least to say that they *wouldn't* do so.) In game terms, this is a whole collection of spells, each of which implants or suppresses a standard mental quirk or disadvantage, or even a set of closely related traits of this kind. For example, someone could be cursed with Combat Paralysis or have his Shyness temporarily cured. However, com-plex disadvantages generated by conscious decisions, such as Codes of Honour and Vows, aren't possible.

These spells give -3 to skill, and cost 2 MP plus 1 MP per full 10 points of traits added or removed. For example, a spell of self-con-fidence which eliminates someone's Demophobia (12) [-15], Fear-fulness 3 [-6], and Shyness (Severe) [-10], and also gives that same person Overconfidence (12) [-5], makes a total of 36 points' worth of changes, and thus costs 5 MP (2 MP base, +3 MP for 30-39 points of adjustments). The subject resists with his Will, regardless of whether he wants to – minds instinctively resist being changed.

---

1. Honest.

If the magic works, it has a duration of one hour and *can* be maintained.

This is extremely versatile magic. Amoral and manipulative casters simply give victims a Sense of Duty to themselves or to groups to which they belong – although they may also have to eliminate some kind of Intolerance or at least quirk-level dislike, and the favours this gets can be grudging ("I can't say that I like this, but as it's you, I suppose . . ."). An Obsession with seeing the caster happy is a smart addition here. For entertainment value, though, planting Severe Delusions is often the most fun; people who annoy Granny Weatherwax sometimes find themselves trying to sit on lily pads and asking to live in ponds.

Hide from Minds

This spell makes people who might notice the caster not do so. It gives -4 to skill, costs 3 MP, has a duration of one minute, and *can* be maintained. Success grants the margin of success, plus one, as a bonus to the caster's Stealth skill; e.g., success by 4 means +5 to Stealth. Thus, an expert magic-worker can more than compensate for only having Stealth at default.

Naming Spells

Some spells, especially those used by wizards, have interesting and bizarre names; many examples appear in *The Forms* (pp. 202-217). The fact is, the creator of a new technique always wants to be sure of appropriate glory and status, and will usually tag his name to the recipe. (Disc wizards rarely go on grimoire-signing tours, because grimoires don't sell enough copies – wizards are too few, and tend to parsimoniously borrow the books they need from university libraries – but if wizards ever find acceptably safe ways of printing magical tomes, they'll be out there with their quill pens like a shot.) The GM and players of wizards are encouraged to come up with interesting spell names.

Mental Illusion

A skilled magic-user can plant sensory impressions (affecting any or all of the senses) in someone's mind, but this is tricky, because making the results *convincing* requires extremely fine control. The spell is cast at -4 to skill, resisted with Will-3 (the magic is quite subtle), and costs 4 MP. If it works, it has a duration of one minute and *can* be maintained.

On a successful casting, the caster must roll an immediate Quick Contest of IQ with the subject. The illusion's complexity and plausibility modify the caster's roll: from +3 for something trivial and plausible (an ordinary rock in a bit of wilderness that the target has never seen before, or a brief feeling of cold), through no modifier for a fairly straightforward and believable impression affecting a couple of senses (a plate of food with a simple-but-pleasant smell, a glass window suddenly and audibly breaking), down to -5 or worse for the complex and the flagrantly implausible (a group of specific people known to the target, dancing and singing in four-part harmony). If the subject wins, he spots flaws in the illusion – although it can still be distracting, and might cover or drown out other, real impressions – and may

attempt to resist the spell *again* every 10 seconds, as his doubts break down the magic.

The caster can't produce an impression of something that he has never perceived himself, though he might look inside someone's mind with another spell to find images to use. An especially convincing illusion can cause psychosomatic damage – but this always gives the caster at least -2 in the Quick Contest of IQ. If the spell convinces the subject that he has taken damage (been stabbed with a sword, burnt by fire, etc.), he must roll at HT+2, with failure meaning 1d-2 HP of injury (minimum 0). An illusion can only inflict damage once every five seconds.

Borrowing

This spell is a favourite among witches, notably Granny Weatherwax (pp. 339-340); wizards, who call it "psychoproicio," are far less likely to know or use it. On working it, the caster projects her mind into that of another being and can use all of that creature's senses. She can also manipulate the subject, steering it gently toward places she wishes to observe. This isn't absolute control, however – the caster must take care that the creature doesn't realise that it's being steered, or it will probably panic.

This spell works best on beasts with simple, straightforward minds, such as rabbits or small birds. Carnivores are a little harder, being intensely focussed. Intelligent beings – whose minds are a roiling mass of impulses, thoughts, urges, and ideas – are extremely difficult. Ant communities and bee swarms are considered to have a single mind each; these are the hardest of all to Borrow, because even humans don't think about flying in several directions at once while also building a hive and laying eggs. Thus, skill penalty and MP cost depend on the type of creature being Borrowed:

Small herbivore, insectivore, or bird (e.g., mouse, rabbit, sparrow, bat): -4 to skill, 1 MP

Large herbivore (e.g., horse, sheep): -4 to skill, 2 MP

Carnivore or large bird of prey (e.g., cat, wolf, eagle): -7 to skill, 2 MP

Group mind: -10 to skill, 3 MP

Apply these additional modifiers as appropriate when calculating Base Spell Skill:

Creature has IQ 7 or greater: -4

Creature is magical or otherwise "unnatural": -2

Subject is insane or very "strange" (GM's decision): -2

Finally, apply *Long-Distance Modifiers* (p. 194) to Modified Spell Skill.

Success means the caster gains access to the subject's mind. The creature then rolls against IQ as if to resist the spell, at +3 if it has *trained* magical or psychic abilities. If the subject "resists," it doesn't eject the caster but it does become aware that *something* is inside its head. It might become confused or skittish as a result, making it impossible for the caster to steer it or get much that's useful from its senses – although there are situations where confusing a creature for a few seconds can be actively useful, and the caster may choose not to bother hiding, but just throw in some chaos. The subject might also have to make a Fright Check if the GM thinks that it would find the experience disturbing enough. In any event, the caster must wait at least five minutes before trying again with the same creature.

If the casting is fully successful, though, the caster can use the creature's senses and begin trying to steer it. This process consists of placing impulses in its mind, not direct control; all ensuing actions use the subject's own abilities and mental processes.

Each such impulse takes 10 seconds to place and requires a Quick Contest of IQ between caster and creature. Cumulative modifiers apply to the caster's IQ roll:

Impulse is very much in accord with creature's normal behaviour: +2
Impulse is slightly unusual but well within creature's normal behaviour patterns: no modifier
Impulse is slightly unusual but not totally alien to creature: -1
Impulse is significantly unusual for creature, but not actually worrying or unnerving for it: -3
Impulse is radically bizarre for creature: -6
Impulse appears obviously dangerous to creature: -10
Creature is a nonsapient magical creature or carnivore (or both): -2
Creature has IQ 7+: -4
Creature is insane or very "strange" (GM's decision, but includes group minds): -4

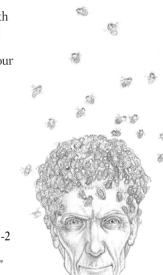

If the caster wins by 5+, the impulse can be specific and complex; otherwise, it must be simple. If the subject wins by no more than 3, the caster can try again after 10 seconds. If the creature wins by 4+, however, it suspects that something odd is happening, and the caster must either leave immediately or spend five minutes lying low.

Two seconds after the spell is cast, the caster's body falls deeply unconscious. It remains thus throughout its period of effect, in a state that's easily mistaken for death by the untrained. (Granny Weatherwax always places a card in her own hands saying "I ATE'NT DEAD" when she goes Borrowing.)

Duration is 10 minutes, and the spell *can* be maintained. When the caster wishes to end the spell, she must make another roll against Base Spell Skill modified for *Long-Distance Modifiers*, the latter being doubled and with a minimum of -3 if the creature is out of sight of the caster's body at the time. Failure means she must maintain the spell for another 10 minutes before trying again. If the caster is reduced to 0 MP before she can return to her body, her body remains comatose and the spell remains active. She can only attempt to return once per *day* thereafter, with an additional -4 to the roll, and each failure costing her a level of HT – and if her HT falls to 0 this way, her body dies and her mind is lost in the wild. During this time, her IQ rolls to influence the animal suffer a cumulative -1 per day passed, and the animal may well wander off if *not* controlled; Borrowing a goose or a swallow, getting lost, and then flying rimwards for the winter can be a tragedy.

Obviously, the risks of Borrowing worry witches who are good at it. What worries them even more is that some of them find Borrowing *addictive* (susceptible individuals might suffer penalties on rolls to return mind to body, at the GM's option). It's thought among witches that some of the greatest of their kind ended up as small birds. Even a witch who successfully recovers from extended Borrowing often half-thinks that she still has wings or paws.

Most witches – especially ethical ones, who tend to be best at Borrowing, being least inclined to force creatures to act in any

particular way – feel a strong sense of obligation to creatures they Borrow, and they usually make sure that they receive food or similar payment.

Follow the Plot, Damn You

Sometimes, a traditional story is well under way (see *Riding the Narrative*, pp. 197-198) but too many people aren't following the script. This area-effect Psychomancy spell gets them acting as they're *supposed* to and hence is often cast with extra MP drawn from the narrative. The results usually count as either "moderate help" to the story or a "standard part."

The spell is cast at -5 to skill and costs 1/5 MP per yard of radius. Everybody within the area can attempt to resist with Will. Individuals who succeed don't prevent others from being controlled – and anyone who has an important part in the story (GM's judgement) resists at -5. However, being influenced to act radically against one's nature, especially in ways contradictory to one's mental disadvantages, grants from +1 to +5 to Will, depending on the details. People can also be made to pause and pay no attention to their surroundings, if that would facilitate the plot; this gives no special Will modifier, but if they're physically injured or attacked, they get another chance to resist, at +5.

SORTILEGE

The magic of chance, fate, and time goes by many names, of which the most feared is probably "Cursing" – but it can be about more than that, so the more academic name of a UU department is used here. The Form covers not just magic that merely allows glimpses of someone's possible future, but also more active manipulations, some of which amount to granting good or bad luck. Discworld witches and wizards generally don't go in for time travel as such (that requires the sort of cosmic enlightenment that's mostly restricted to History Monks, p. 13), but they *can* tweak the flow of time around people or things, and also – a bit more easily, in fact – the way that events will unfold over time.

A Little Luck

This simple spell momentarily improves the caster's luck. It has no skill penalty and costs 1 MP; a caster can only use it *once* per game session. Success grants +3 on the *next* skill or attribute roll that the caster makes, +3 on the *next* reaction roll made when he asks a bystander for aid, or -3 on the *next* attack roll made against him.

Mechanical Failure

Most complicated machines on the Disc are perpetually somewhere near going wrong; canny spellcasters can push them over the brink. This spell is cast at -2 to skill and costs 3 MP. The target device gets to resist; roll against 12 if it's well made, 10 if it has obvious and common failure patterns, or 8 if it involves tightly wound springs or delicately balanced weights. If the spell prevails, the thing fails in some plausible way.

Magical Fortune-Telling

You can foretell something about someone's near future, most often using standard equipment for one specialisation of the Fortune-Telling skill (p. 73): Caroc cards, the Ching Aling, etc. Such paraphernalia helps, if only by making the process more flexible than the alternatives; e.g., reading someone's future in their palm requires the subject to be present, while staring into a fire gives flickering, single-colour visions which are hard to interpret. Witches often use tea leaves; voodoo specialists favour gumbos.

Nonmagical Fortune-Telling

Foretelling the future doesn't *require* spellcasting. Below are two ways to tap into the patterns of destiny that can work for anyone . . . in theory. In practise, these may be better used as props for magical operations, or for applications of the Fortune-Telling skill (p. 73) that have less to do with reading the future than with reading the customer's psychology. To interpret the results of either method correctly, roll against the relevant Fortune-Telling specialisation at -2. Such interpretations should always be vague and conditional; you need a magical gift and training to make this stuff at all reliable.

Caroc

One widespread system uses a *Caroc* deck (the Discworld's tarot; see *Caroc Cards*, p. 19), and gives a fairly complex but subtle set of images relating to a stated question. Readings for anyone but an individual or a couple, in their presence, are at a further -5 to skill. And remember that Death doesn't always mean death. Honest.

The Ching Aling

In certain remote parts of the Disc, fortunes are told using a Hubland method known as the *Ching Aling*, which has also caught on in some circles on the Sto Plains. The subject rolls a set of yarrow stalks (cost at least $2) – preferably so that they all land on the table – and the resulting pattern, or "octagram," is interpreted with the aid of a reference book, which gives terse but immensely *wise* advice. The GM decides exactly what it implies, based on his plans for the current scenario, and then the skill roll serves to interpret it. Unfortunately for would-be seers, most cheap copies of the book are translations and lose something; a *good* version in Morporkian costs $5, and each $1 reduction in price gives -2 to skill. Many small-town wizards don't actually know the skill, but have the requisite stalks and a cheap copy of the book, because the results *sound* impressive ("At evening the mollusc is silent among the almond blossom.").

Advanced practitioners get drunk on alcoholic beverages made from re-annual grapes or other fruit (such as the vul nuts favoured in Krull and the Agatean Empire) which grows before it's planted, thanks to the Disc's intense magical field; this can give very useful memories of the drinker's own future, but the person receiving them is of course drunk. Sufficient re-annual drink for one casting of this spell costs at least $1.50; frequent users may prefer more pleasant, and thus expensive, beverages.[1]

---

1. *Re-annual drunkenness often gives hangovers before the imbiber has started drinking. Resolving what this means for a PC who regularly uses this spell (especially one with mediocre HT) is left as a matter of roleplaying and negotiation between player and GM.*

Whatever the details, props are simply a way of focussing the caster's mind on the future – albeit an important one.

Except for something like palmistry, magical fortune-telling *can* work for people who aren't present, but you need their name and a mental image of their appearance (from a personal meeting or a very good portrait). Some versions require more information. In particular, astrology calls for an accurate date and place of birth.

The spell gives -2 to skill and costs 3 MP. Apply *Long-Distance Modifiers* (p. 194) if the subject isn't present, unless you're using a technique which runs entirely on personal information, such as astrology. Casting always takes some time, which varies by method; reading someone's palm requires just a couple of minutes of examination, whereas preparing a horoscope takes 20-30 minutes.

Whatever the method, success gives clues about probabilities and threats. It doesn't negate causality or free will – this magic is more about warnings than certainties, and the results are *always* a bit hazy and ambiguous in some way. The GM should take the time to come up with something that provides enough wiggle room for the game to veer in whatever direction the players and the dice decide. Indeed, the GM should fine-tune the props, requirements, and revelations of *any* version of the spell to fit the circumstances.

Cursing

While witches have been known to throw around a lot of different bespoke curses, a spell that gives the victim Unluckiness (p. 65) is basic but effective. This is cast at -3 to skill, and the subject resists with Will-2. If the target is unaware that he's being cursed, Modified Spell Skill is at -4 and the caster cannot claim the MP cost reductions under *Witch Magic Power* (pp. 196-198). Witch curses are all about being *known* to have cursed someone!

Cost is 2 MP if the curse is intended to have a duration of one day with the option to maintain it. The effect can instead be set to last a fixed period without further input from the caster, in which case cost is 4 MP for one day, 8 MP for one week, or 15 MP for one month. Alternatively, a witch can work the magic with a conditional duration, as described on p. 197; for instance, cursing someone "until he apologises" might cost 4 MP, while making the condition "until he makes full restitution" for some significant offence may require 8 MP or more. Unluckiness curses aren't cumulative, but a longer-term curse thrown at someone already suffering from a short-term one takes precedence. Even a non-maintained version *might* be broken if the witch dies, at the GM's option – certainly, enough people on the Disc believe this that witches must be careful about using this spell, lest victims get desperate enough to turn murderous.

Suspend Time

This area spell is classic storybook witch magic; a wizard *might* be able to replicate it in a slightly different form, but that would demand a lot of work and MP. The spell takes an hour to cast and gives -7 to skill. Cost per yard of radius is 1/10 MP to stop time for a duration of up to one day, 1/5 MP for up to one week, 1/3 MP for up to one month, 1/2 MP for up to one year, 1 MP for up to 10 years, 2 MP for up to 100 years, and 3 MP for up to 200 years. Longer than that is probably impossible.

Time within the spell's radius is simply *stopped* for the selected period – relative to the outside world, the region's occupants won't move, breathe, age, or think. The caster can place herself inside or outside the area. From the outside, the area appears normal, if a bit hazy, but anyone trying to enter it becomes "lost" and ends up back at their starting point 1d minutes later.

Those who experience this get an IQ roll, with success indicating that they guess that magic was involved and failure meaning that they believe that they simply lost track of the path. Objects thrown into the area seem to move normally, but somehow fall to the ground at the edge. Spells cannot be maintained inside the area by anyone outside, or vice versa, but this spell *is* susceptible to Dispel Magic (p. 205) cast from outside.

This might seem like a spectacularly powerful effect, wide open to abuse. In practise, the uses (and abuses) are relatively limited. For one thing, there's a strong possibility that someone will dispel a long-term working sooner or later, if only out of curiosity – especially if it's located anywhere that enough wizards or witches stumble across it. Moreover, the GM can rule that sufficient random thaumaturgical stress causes the zone to collapse, so that people trying to probe it with scrying spells, enter it while carrying magical swords, fly into it on broomsticks, and/or pursue narratively significant quests involving its contents will end the magic with a brief popping sound.

Narrative Manipulation

A witch can tap into the patterns of story (see *Riding the Narrative*, pp. 197-198) and kick events onto a slightly different track. This spell gives -5 to skill and costs 7 MP. *Long-Distance Modifiers* (p. 194) apply for the distance from the caster to the *furthest* person directly affected; hence, this is magic best worked from in the middle of things. The effects last for 10 minutes and can be maintained – although anyone fighting for that long to keep a story going should consider alternative solutions.

The results are usually subtle but can involve a warping of reality on a par with high-level divine activity. While the spell is in effect, random events that cross paths with the story tend to obey narrative norms and clichés. If it would help the plot, treat individuals who play any part in it as having Luck (p. 44), Serendipity (p. 44), and/or Unluckiness (p. 65), as appropriate. Really crucial dice rolls – attacks made to defeat the villain in the final fight atop the battlements, IQ rolls for someone to recognise a long-lost brother, etc. – take modifiers equal in size to the caster's margin of success.

Any successful casting also permits up to five people entangled with the plot to make immediate Per rolls to notice important facts, Will rolls to break problematic compulsions, and so on. If the caster's margin of success is 5+, information may enter people's heads "from nowhere." They'll regard it as lucky guesses or intuition, but may feel compelled to act on it. For example, in the theatre scene toward the end of *Wyrd Sisters*, Granny Weatherwax uses this spell to cause a Big Denouement In The Theatre, a common narrative event; her casting succeeds by enough to give the actors the "correct" dialogue for the scene, and to make them follow it rather than the script.

Despite all this, *no individual should be able to depend on the spell effect*. Standard plots and stories have a fair amount of flexibility as to who is the hero and who might die heroically or get badly hurt before the ending. Some stories that were heading for happy endings lurch into grand tragedy instead. Moreover, people influenced by the spell in a way that's obviously *disadvantageous* for them can resist it with Will – and nobody will do anything actively suicidal because of this magic, unless he was already inclined to do so and his death would be a significant part of the story.

If two magic-users are trying to manipulate the same sequence of events in different directions, roll a Quick Contest between their spells. Reduce the effective margin of success of the winner's spell by that of the loser's. Narrative Manipulation can be opposed by another casting of the same spell, Dispel Magic (p. 205), Counterspell (p. 216), or various sorts of sabotage, usually using Psychomancy or Sortilege. A caster riding a carefully arranged plot will have a distinct advantage in such a conflict, of course!

Subtle Duelling in Magic

Occasionally, Discworld magic-workers go head-to-head in a *magical duel*. This isn't simply two people trying to blast each other with fireballs or melt each other's brains while desperately throwing up layers of defensive spells.[1] It's a contest of pure ability.

One type of duel – common between witches and perhaps other spellcasters – consists of a formal challenge requiring magical power, and might be as simple as a staring contest. Handle this as a Regular Contest of Will, possibly modified by Magery. The point is to establish who's the most powerful without physical damage to people or the environment. There's no need for such a duel even to involve any specific stakes; knowing who lost and who won, in public, is rather important among witches.

Things like seeing who can out-stare the sun longest (see *Lords and Ladies*) are variants of this. In that specific case, the contestants would have avoided damage to their eyes through some sort of Physiomancy spell – but even with protection, staring at the sun is hard work, requiring an extended effort of willpower focussed through magic. Such a duel might be treated as a Regular Contest of Magic skills based on Will (see *Using a Skill with a Different Attribute*, p. 69).

For more flamboyant contests, see *Flashy Duelling in Magic* (p. 217).

---

1. Okay, in less well-regulated times and places, showdowns between wizards have amounted to artillery duels that reduced the loser to ash. The point is, advanced magical ability permits something more stylish – and hopefully, less lethal.

SUMMONATION

This Form is primarily about summoning and controlling supernatural spirits of many kinds (who aren't as different from each other as they like to claim). Some creatures are not so much summoned as *created* out of raw spiritual energy – but in practise, the distinction turns out to be less important than one might think. Summonation also covers wards and bindings, because summoning certain spirits without protection is suicidal. Since the most basic protective measure, the octagram (p. 205), uses Magianism, career summoners should study that Form as well.

By extension, this Form encompasses dimensional gates and portals, which have other uses. Also, thaumatological engineers employ it to conjure up the small, harmless imps used in mass-produced magical devices. Hence, while high-powered Summonation is largely the preserve of creepy demonologists, most systems of magical instruction encompass the basics. More substantial Summonation spells often fall under the heading of "controlled information," though, taught only to graduate wizards of proven mental stability.[1] The problem being, of course, the number of dimensions adjacent to the Disc's own that are infested with not-very-pleasant entities.

The truth is, however, that many *summoning* spells are dangerously easy because the beings they call desperately *want* to show up. Much harder are all the protective magics that ought to be cast before or integrated with the summoning. Idiotic amateurs disregard that stuff, and even some professionals can get a little sloppy with it – though usually only once.

Gate Scan

Anyone who's competent with Summonation can detect gates, dimensional portals, and weaknesses in reality. This spell reveals all such things within a number of yards of the caster equal to his margin of success, making them glow momentarily. It takes no skill penalty and costs 1 MP.

---

1. Well, stability by wizard standards. They definitely shouldn't be taught to people who are unstable by wizard standards.

The Rite of AshkEnte

This spell summons Death himself (pp. 291-295) and supposedly binds him in the process. It's amazingly easy, partly because Death can and will go anywhere, sooner or later, and partly because it's such a well-tested and standard piece of magic (with a bit too much tradition wrapped around it, if anything). It is cast at -1 to skill and costs 8 MP.

Magic-workers once believed that the Rite required ritual casting by eight wizards standing at the points of a ceremonial octagram (scribed and activated beforehand; see *Octagram*, p. 205), using a lot of swaying, chanting, candles, and incense. Smug junior research wizards have since proved that it can be performed in five minutes by two wizards with three small bits of wood and 4cc of mouse blood. Both casters must have Magery, but they can share the MP cost, and only one needs to make the skill roll. In a pinch, even one person with two bits of wood and a fresh egg can pull it off – although the egg *must* be fresh, there's another -2 to *Base* Spell Skill, and scraping together the MP can be challenging.

Even more annoying junior research wizards say that there are provably nine other, substantially different, ways to perform the Rite, but they all tend to kill you instantly. Senior wizards inevitably suggest that they demonstrate this.

Death will show up whenever the spell is cast correctly. If the caster's margin of success is 5+, he cannot leave the central octagram. Less-successful castings leave him free to wander in and out. While he's usually too polite to do so (he generally just wants to get the thing over with and go about his business), he sometimes forgets.

Death is obliged to answer one question, to the limits of his ability. As he goes (almost) everywhere and is involved in most serious matters, this can be very useful. In theory, he could stick at one question, but as he's polite and dislikes being pestered repeatedly, he usually finds it easier to answer any follow-up queries and expand any details when asked. Wizards who took part in the Rite cannot then do so again for at least 24 hours.

In fact, most wizards try to avoid doing so at all, for the simple reason that they're at least as nervous of dying as anyone else, and attracting Death's attention feels like a bad idea. This is irrational, of course. Death is not capricious or malicious, and merely comes when he's due, and wizards who so choose are entitled to know when that is for themselves – but there you are.

Wizard PCs whose players have read the chronicles may act in a more cold-blooded fashion, casting the Rite daily to answer their smallest questions. This is simply out of character for Discworlders, however, and should be discouraged. Death tolerates use of the Rite, which acts on him as an invitation that cannot be refused, but he *is* known to regard it as an inconvenience, and overuse *will* make him increasingly irritated and evasive. While literal-minded and straightforward, he's capable of a peculiar kind of deviousness, and might omit details or distort his answers.

Then the images began to flicker as shape replaced shape. Stroboscopic shadows danced around the hall. A magical wind sprang up, thick and greasy, striking octarine sparks from beards and fingers. In the middle of it all Esk, peering through streaming eyes, could just make out the two figures of Granny and Cutangle, glossy statues in the midst of the hurtling images.

– Equal Rites

He could even lend indirect assistance to the PCs' enemies, although he would always be subtle about this. Also, a critical failure when attempting the Rite can land users in all sorts of amusing trouble involving involuntary extradimensional travel and lots of amusing Fright Checks.

One last technical detail: The Rite calls up whoever is currently *acting as* Death. In the past, it has almost summoned Mort (Death's apprentice at the time), and brought his "granddaughter" Susan when she was standing in. This sort of thing is unlikely to happen again, but not impossible. Summoning the Death of Rats (p. 295) would presumably require research into a revised version of the Rite.[1]

Summon Thing

This spell – or rather, class of spells – is mentioned here for reference. Such stuff is a really, *really* bad idea in practise, as anyone trained in magic by someone even 10% sane will know. Still, there have been a fair few clammy-palmed scholars over the millennia who couldn't manage that 10%, and who left tattered and flagrantly loopy manuscripts of ideas, half spell and half deranged rant. Somebody had to provide the hideous demonstrations for everybody else, after all, and to cause the occasional annihilation of a city or collapse of a civilisation.

In brief, if someone turns up information that can bring a Thing from the Dungeon Dimensions through to the Disc's universe and provide it with a just-about-stable body in which to operate, that usually rates as a Summonation spell cast at -3 to skill. The MP cost depends on how strong and durable the body is supposed to be. Unfortunately perhaps, Things can't be summoned into really feeble bodies – those would just explode and cover everyone nearby with corrosive green goop, while the Thing got on with subsuming the summoner's brain. Thus, such a spell always needs at least 5 MP, and usually much more.

Once the spell is successfully cast, subsequent events are up to the GM and any heroes and spellcasters in the vicinity. The ensuing scenario is traditionally frantic, with multiple Fright Checks and fatalities.

Exorcise Spirit

Compared to exorcising ghosts (p. 366), casting other kinds of spirits out of places and people where they aren't wanted is seen as slightly more of a job for magic. This spell drives off one chosen immaterial spirit, making it return to wherever it considers home. If it's already there, it won't leave – although it can be expelled from a possessed mortal.

---

1. *But that would seem fairly pointless, unless your question could plausibly be answered by "SQUEAK."*

The spell takes a minute to cast and gives -3 to skill. If the caster lacks a clear idea of what he's dealing with, he has a penalty to Modified Spell Skill. This ranges from -1 (the caster is a bit unsure *exactly* what sort of spirit he's dealing with) to -5 (the caster hasn't a clue what's going on). Cost is 3 MP.

The spirit resists with Will-2. If it fails to resist, it won't even consider going *near* the exorcised area or person for at least a day. Many bothersome spirits have difficulty getting to the physical world anyway, so once they've been driven off, they *must* stay away.

Oracular Demon

Summoning a minor-but-knowledgeable demon to answer three questions, truthfully, is potentially more flexible than other "information spells" – although it suffers from the need to extract *useful* answers from a demon, which will feel obliged by its job description to twist everything and to be annoyingly literal-minded. This spell is one of the few acceptable uses for demons, in the opinions of most witches and wizards. Demons themselves find it irritating, if only because it demotes them from grand powers of evil to speak-your-weight machines.

This spell is cast -3 to skill. The working can take as little as 30 seconds, but it costs 8 MP, so it's often cast ritually (p. 200). In theory, it also requires a cauldron, an octagram, candles, various spices, and so on. In fact, these props amount to a way of focussing the necessary willpower, and the spell has been successfully cast with a washing-bowl, a large spoon, and some cheap soap-flakes. Such cut-price equipment gives an extra -1 to -4 to Base Spell Skill, at the GM's whim.

Strictly speaking, the three questions should all have yes-or-no answers. However, a particularly good reaction from the demon – or a successful use of Intimidation at -3 (resisted by the demon's Will, which is typically 10) – can get more out of it. It will know a fair amount about current supernatural and mundane events in the geographical area around the casting, and may even have a little knowledge of the future, but it cannot be omniscient. When in doubt, the GM should roll vs. Base Spell Skill for each question, treating the results as if these were rolls on a relevant Area Knowledge specialisation or similar skill.

Summon Demon

This is the definitive spell of fully qualified demonologists. As such, it's widely considered a bad idea. However, it's really quite safe if conducted correctly with the basic safety procedures followed. (The same can be said of scientific experiments with highly radioactive materials, of course – and plutonium doesn't actually *want* to pull your liver out through your ears.)

The spell gives -5 to skill and costs 4 MP. The actual casting takes five minutes, but first the caster must inscribe a complicated magic circle on the floor, which takes an hour or so. If

the spell succeeds, a demon appears within the circle and can neither get out nor use abilities of any sort to affect anything outside. This entity can be either a specific, named demon (not one of the rulers of Hell, but something of moderate power by demon standards) or a typical specimen of some well-documented category of medium-powered demons (such as one that will act as a general-purpose servant or – oh dear, they do always ask – a succubus).

What happens after *that* is up to the GM, depending what will work in the campaign and what's funny. Many demons can provide useful services and favours, and can be bound by their sworn word, reinforced by magical invocations, not to harm the caster even after being released from the circle. However, one thing that demons *won't* do for a summoner, by and large, is fight or kill. This may seem odd, but the fact is that there are rules – some written, some not – which are designed to prevent all-out magical warfare in the human world, and which are enforced by much higher powers. Furthermore, most gods promise their human followers protection from demonic power and seem to enjoy delivering on that promise. The priests of such deities are annoyingly good at detecting demonic activities and showing up with enough force to blast a demonic assassin back to a lower circle of Hell and the size and strength of a cockroach for a few millennia.

If the magic-user fails the casting roll, but by only 1-4, *something* may appear in the circle, and probably even be reliably contained there. This may be a totally useless petty demon or some other sort of spirit entirely. The GM should play this for maximum comedy, but with an edge of danger. Discworld demons are unimaginative and often inept, but they're still in the eternal damnation business.

On a critical failure, an unexpectedly powerful demon showing up *outside* the containment circle is certainly a possibility.

However, Discworld demons don't *always* disembowel humans who come within reach, even if they believe that they could get away with it. They often think that there's a chance that they could make some more complicated use of a mortal. The *really* smart ones make sure that humans are actually damned to Hell before causing their deaths, although there aren't many that smart.

MULTIPLE-FORM EFFECTS

Some complex spells draw on more than one Form. Casters working such magic use the *lowest* applicable Form skill and suffer an extra -2 on top of the usual skill modifiers.

Counterspell

Magic-users can cast blocking spells (p. 199) to negate any incoming magic that they know of that's targeted at themselves or an area in which they're located. This calls for a degree of control over the sort of magic involved. The roll is against the *lower* of the caster's skill with the incoming spell's Form *or* Magianism, at -2 for a blocking spell and -1 for every full 2 MP that the rival spell cost (before any reduction for caster skill). For example, someone with Elementalism at 16 and Magianism at 15 could try to Counterspell an incoming 3d bolt of magic lightning (cost 3 MP) by rolling against the lower of those skills with -2 for blocking, -2 for multiple Forms, and -1 for MP cost – in other words, at 10 or less. Each Counterspell costs 1 MP.

As a blocking spell, Counterspell counts as an active defence, preventing the caster from attempting other active defences against the same magic unless he took the All-Out Defence (Double Defence) manoeuvre (pp. 175-176). If it fails, though, he may still attempt any resistance roll the incoming spell allows.

Necromantic Retrocognition

Both Scrying (p. 202) and Last Vision (p. 206) give views of the past but are limited as to how far back. Unseen University's Department of Post-Mortem Communications has recently developed a much more advanced version of the magic, enabling images to be extracted from centuries-old bone fragments. In effect, this is a narrowly focussed version of Scrying that uses human remains as a "sympathetic" link to circumvent problems of distance and time.

Necromantic Retrocognition is a multiple-Form effect using Divination and Necromancy. Treat it as Scrying with *no* penalties or increased MP cost for distance in time or space, but with the extra -2 for multiple Forms. However, all it will show is what the person whose remains are used saw in the last 2d seconds of his life.

Voodoo Doll

This is customarily regarded as a witch's (especially a *voodoo* witch's) spell on the Discworld, but the theoretical principles are well-understood by wizards, who regard them as ancient and rather crude, but interestingly powerful. It's also widely felt to be a rather nasty, sneaky sort of magic, and many people respond badly to anyone believed to have used it. Still, quite a few witches employ it occasionally, when they're sufficiently annoyed.

The witch must make a doll representing someone on whom she wishes to work other magic, and then "activate" it by casting a multiple-Form spell involving Magianism and Physiomancy.

This working has a skill penalty of -3, in addition to the -2 for multiple Forms, and takes 10 minutes. Cost is 5 MP. The doll is traditionally made using personal materials taken from the target – hair, fingernail trimmings, scraps of fabric, and so on. Alternatively, it can be made using an appropriate Artist skill (usually Sculpture or Doll-Making) simply to resemble the subject, which gives an additional -3 to Base Spell Skill but also allows the figure to be used against someone who closely resembles that person.

Once the doll is active, it can be used in two ways. First, if the witch is holding it and is in line of sight of the target, she can cast Physiomancy spells on that individual using *Long-Distance Modifiers* (p. 194) rather than the usual -1 per yard of distance. Second, even if the victim is out of her sight, she can simply stab the doll with a pin to cause him pain. In the latter case, roll a Quick Contest: Base Spell Skill again, this time applying *Long-Distance Modifiers* and a further -3 if the target isn't in the caster's sight, vs. the subject's HT. If the caster wins, the victim is physically stunned (pp. 185-186) for a number of seconds equal to the margin of victory – and if the target loses by 8+, or rolls a critical failure on the HT roll, he falls unconscious for 1d minutes. If the *victim* wins by 8+, however, the arcane link is broken, and that doll can never again be used against him.

Spell Projectile

By taking a standard short-range effect of any Form and bundling it into a nice, semi-stable etheric package using Magianism, the caster can transform it into a missile spell (p. 199) that he can throw with the Innate Attack (Projectile) skill, improving range and flexibility. This is a multiple-Form working involving Magianism and the Form of the converted spell. It adds 1 MP to the effect's usual cost.

Examples: A "shatter bolt" is Snap (p. 203) converted into a projectile. Roll against the worse of Elementalism or Magianism at -3 (-1 for Snap, -2 for multiple Forms), and pay 2 MP (1 MP for Snap, +1 MP for the projectile), to conjure a bolt that will snap small objects. Similarly, one-day Cursing (p. 212) would require a roll against the worse of Magianism or Sortilege at -5, and cost 3 MP, as a projectile.

Spells hurled as projectiles cannot be maintained.

Teleportation

Instantaneous travel over long distances is generally regarded as flashy wizard magic; relatively sensible wizards know that's tricky but sometimes fun. The spell is a multiple-Form working involving Summonation (which is partly about abstract dimensions and portals) and Magianism (needed to balance the complex metaphysics). It gives a *total* of -5 to Base Spell Skill, and Modified Spell Skill is subject to *Long-Distance Modifiers* (p. 194) for the distance travelled. Cost is 5 MP.

Normally, the caster teleports *himself,* along with anything he's wearing, carrying, or touching, up to Medium encumbrance (p. 168); greater encumbrance costs +2 MP for Heavy or +5 MP for Extra-Heavy. Teleporting something else without going oneself gives another -2 to Base Spell Skill, and an additional -1 to Modified Spell Skill per yard from the caster to thing being teleported – and living beings can try to evade the magic by resisting with DX. This costs 5 MP for weights up to 200 lbs., +1 MP per extra 50 lbs. or fraction thereof. *Really* fancy workings can even lock onto something detected and located precisely by

divination spells, and teleport it *to* the caster, but that gives -5 to Base Spell Skill.

If the casting succeeds by 5+, the teleport works perfectly. On success by 1-4, the GM should throw in a nonlethal-but-disruptive side-effect, typically related to the balance of energy or momentum; e.g., the teleport swaps the chosen object with something of similar mass at the destination, travellers become uncomfortably warm or freezing cold, or air explodes outward from the arrival point violently enough to knock bystanders off their feet. If the roll is made exactly, things can get *truly* bizarre.

Teleporting anything very long distances across the Disc runs into relative-velocity problems and is potentially extra-messy; see *Interesting Times.* If a caster attempting a fancy long-distance teleport operation takes the trouble to work in balancing factors – such as deliberately sending an equal mass to replace the thing being teleported – the GM might grant him +1 or +2 to skill.

Playing and Running the Game

The basics of playing a roleplaying game are simple: The GM describes a situation and asks each player what his character is doing. The players answer, and the GM tells them what happens next. At some point, the GM won't be certain that the characters can automatically do what the players say they're doing . . . "You're carrying *what* and jumping the chasm?" . . . and the dice come out.

The Game Session

Games take place in *sessions,* lasting as long as you can manage, or possibly so long as remaining conscious seems wise – three to eight hours is a working approximation. An adventure, story, or "scenario" *might* be completed in one session, but it could stretch over several. Sessions can also include a certain amount of character development, review of what's happened so far, discussion of future plans, suggestions to the GM and other players as to what else should happen, and general chat. However, it's best to try to remain focussed on the active flow of the story told by the campaign and not to get too distracted; "background" stuff can mostly be sorted out through private conversations, e-mail, and the like between sessions.

Ideally, sessions should also involve something for everyone to do – and it's certainly important to make sure that everyone is *entertained.* Those aren't exactly the same thing, though. Many players are happy for their characters to remain in the background for long stretches, as long as they're included in the action at some point, and provided that what's happening to or with the other PCs is fun to watch. Other gamers want to be *doing* something, however, and they're within their rights to ask for some activity for their PCs every session.

The GM's Job

As all of this suggests, the GM has significant responsibilities. These include creating challenges, "managing" the world, and ensuring that everyone has something to do. To cap it all, he needs to make sure that the campaign has some kind of plot or story to it, to stop it from feeling like a bunch of unconnected random incidents . . . despite the near inevitability of players going off on unexpected tangents.

Different GMs handle this in different ways, from painstaking preparation to wildly energetic improvisation. If you're tackling this task, you'll have to work out the method that works best for you – just don't try *too* much improvisation until you've got the hang of the game. Whatever your approach, be sure to keep up-to-date copies of the PCs' character sheets; what will or won't work in a forthcoming session frequently depends on the PCs' capabilities and disadvantages. If you're feeling ambitious, you might even take responsibility for maintaining a campaign log, perhaps using a blog or other online medium – and if you do, the players should try to keep up with reading it, if only to make sure that you haven't been talking at cross-purposes with them about in-game events. Similarly, some players may keep "journals" or "diaries" on behalf of their PCs, which you ought to make an effort to read.

As the GM, it's also important to keep an eye on whether *all* the players are enjoying themselves and to try not to play favourites. This isn't always easy! Almost inevitably, some PCs are more interesting than others, and certain players are more or less assertive. However, every player is entitled to *some* attention, and it's your job to give each some "spotlight time." Don't embarrass quieter players who are happy to play supporting characters and observers – but remember that if they're being entertained by the game, it isn't unreasonable to ask them to put something back in, and to throw a few challenges and problems in their characters' paths.

For much more on the art of setting up a Discworld campaign in particular – including descriptions of various styles of plot, and example settings and adventures – see Chapter 11.

. . . he was nothing more than a comma on the page of History.
– Sourcery

Creating NPCs

Coming up with NPCs is yet another of the GM's many duties. Like PCs, NPCs are characters – and good, *interesting* NPCs can be every bit as complex as PCs. Sadly, not everyone the PCs meet will be that fascinating or important; while we should doubtless respect the dignity of every sapient being, the fact is that shopkeepers who sell routine supplies, and pursuing guards who are doomed to plummet down the unexpected crevasse, really don't need much detail. Even NPCs destined to play major roles in the story, interacting repeatedly with the PCs, don't *necessarily* require full character sheets. Frankly, it's too much work and mostly generates a lot of data that you'll never use.

What matters is having the information that you *will* use – and enough of a vision of the NPC that you can improvise anything you didn't expect to need, in the event that it comes up after all. If the NPC has even minimal plot significance, you should at least note his attributes (although you can assume that these are at the racial average, 10 for a human, if there's no reason for him to be unusual in that respect), any skills that are likely to see use, important advantages or disadvantages, and what equipment he has to hand. You may also need to calculate a few combat-related values from all this if he's likely to be involved in violence.

For example, for some "brawny but otherwise mediocre guards," you might jot down ST 12, DX 10, IQ 9, HT 10, Axe/Mace-12, Shield-10, Bully (15), and Lecherousness (15), with DR 2 armour, axes, shields, and a pound or two of personal gear, giving them Light encumbrance. That in turn means they have Basic Speed 5.00, Move 4, Will 9, Per 9, and 12 HP, and attack with skill 12 for 1d+4 cutting while defending with Block 8 or Dodge 7, at +2 for their shields. They're also likely to behave obnoxiously, in a way that makes them susceptible to some very old distractions. On the other hand, a fastidious and obstructive clerk who the PCs must deal with but can't just beat up could be noted as "IQ 12, Per 11, Will 13, Administration-12, compulsively neat."

All of which said, if you're defining a major NPC who you don't expect to perish too soon, creating a full character sheet can be an interesting exercise. By the time you're done, you should have a good idea of his personality, including some peculiarities and secondary abilities that may surprise or interest the players, allowing you to roleplay him in a more interesting way. This is never required, but feel free if you find that you enjoy it.

Also, if you calculate the NPC's point total and find that it's much higher or lower than the PCs', that *might* be a hint that he's coming out too dominant or weak – unless you *wanted* him to be that way!

The Players' Side

All this might seem to make the GM's job huge and hard – and certainly, it *is* more than is demanded of any one player. For their part, then, the players ought to not only have the basic politeness to thank the GM for all that work, but also try not to increase it gratuitously. They should clearly state what they want their characters to do, let each other and (most important) the GM speak, and accept GM rulings gracefully. If they have a problem with the game, they can say so, but politely; clearing up a problem is better than grumbling incoherently or walking off in an unexplained huff.

Players don't *have* to be as familiar with the rules as the GM, but it doesn't hurt – provided that they don't turn into obnoxious "rules lawyers." Certainly, players should seek to learn enough about basic systems (rolling 3d and hoping the total is less than your skill, monitoring encumbrance levels, tracking Hit Points during fights, etc.) that they don't need things explained to them repeatedly, interrupting session after session. The magic rules in particular benefit from familiarity and the ability to discuss things with the GM in a constructive fashion; if you're new to the game, it's probably best *not* to try playing a witch or a wizard.

All this balancing does call for a bit of give and take. Players traditionally complain a *lot* if they feel that their characters are being "railroaded" – that is, if the GM seems to be following a fixed plot and won't let them jump off. This is certainly a bad habit among some GMs, often caused by excessive planning and falling in love with their own ideas. A strength of tabletop RPGs is that they *aren't* computer games; the GM's brain is more powerful than any computer and should be capable of adaptation and adjustment, even on the fly. However, *the players have an equal and opposite responsibility.*

The GM can't think of everything, has probably made some reasonable assumptions, and is putting in a lot of work. Players who gleefully make things difficult for him are being as selfish as any "railroading" GM. The cry of "My character wouldn't do that!" is *sometimes* an important argument for jumping off the railroad . . . but there are situations where it's just a childish demand for attention. Players who hog the limelight should be reminded that they aren't the only ones present. And if all the players have agreed to play a certain sort of character in a particular type of campaign, trying to play something else, insisting on doing something different, is *very* bad manners. If you really believe that your PC should go off in a wildly different direction, then perhaps it's time to create a new PC.

Character Improvement

At the end of each session, the GM may award *bonus character points.* These are the same kind of points that you used to create your character. They're given as rewards for good play and to represent learning processes and opportunities to get on in society, make useful friends, and so on.

Good play is anything that advances the heroes' mission or shows good roleplaying – preferably both. But roleplaying trumps mission success! If a player did something totally outside his character's personality (for instance, if a total coward performed a brave act), this should not be worth *any* points, even if it saved the day for everyone.

Learning processes encompass deliberate study, training, practising, or working out – mentally or physically – to improve abilities or get rid of weaknesses. (The **GURPS Basic Set** includes rules covering these activities in more detail, if you're interested.) They also include the lessons taught by hard experience during adventures.

The GM is free to award *any* number of points . . . but in general, he should give each player between zero and five points, averaging two or three, *per session.* He might also wish to give an award – perhaps equal to that for a successful play session – upon the conclusion of a lengthy adventure, story arc, or major plot thread, if only to give a sense of completeness. Record awarded points as "unspent" on your character sheet, and then spend them the same way as during character creation. In particular:

Basic Attributes and Secondary Characteristics: To improve one of these, you must spend character points equal to the point-cost *difference* between the old score and the new one. Improving basic attributes will also raise secondary characteristics!

Advantages: Many advantages are inborn and cannot be bought later on. Exceptions include Combat Reflexes and Languages, which can be learned, and social advantages such as Status, which can be earned or granted. To add an advantage, you must pay its cost in points.

Disadvantages: In most cases, a character may get rid of a beginning disadvantage by "buying it off" with points equal to the bonus earned when it was taken, provided that the player and GM can agree on a logical explanation for this.

Skills: Earned points can be spent to improve skills or add new ones. When you raise a skill, the cost is the *difference* between that of your current skill level and that of the new skill level. Adventurers often learn new skills, but the GM is free to prohibit this if it doesn't fit your situation – if you don't have an instructor, opportunities for practise, or the right equipment for a skill, then there's *no way* to acquire it. Even if you think that you're headed for Klatch next week, there's no chance to pick up Riding (Camel) in Lancre!

Buying Success

The GM who wants a more *dramatic* game can allow players to spend bonus character points not just to improve characters, but also to improve the results of success rolls. In that case, 2 points convert critical failure to ordinary failure, 1 point turns ordinary failure into ordinary success, and 2 points improve ordinary success to critical success. Multiple shifts are possible; just add the costs (e.g., 5 points transforms critical failure into critical success). Of course, in situations where success is actually *impossible,* you can't roll – so you can't use this rule.

The GM may also permit players to spend 1 point to reduce the injury from any one attack, however severe, to 1 HP. They ducked or stumbled at the right moment, and it was "just a flesh wound."

The GM might limit these options to moments where they make for a good *or conventional* story, as the PCs exploit the power of narrative. By using that power, though, they forsake the option to become better in themselves.

LIFE and LANDS

*High on a hill sat a lonely clacks tower, and high in that tower sat a lonely clacks operator. Normally, such towers held more than one such individual – they needed at least two at work at all times to forward messages to the next tower, and they needed multiple shifts to keep going day and night. But this tower represented a spur on the great clacks network, so it needed only one man at a time. Also, it had been erected at the suggestion and expense of the local Earl, because he felt that he ought to have this sort of thing these days, rather than because the clacks company saw any hope of profit. The Earl wanted to be up-to-date, but he didn't want to spend **very** much money, or to be bothered with messages at inconvenient times, so he paid the wages for just the one operator, who only worked in daylight, six days in an eight-day week.*

His job was mostly to stare through a telescope at the great tower on the main line, many miles away. When the side-panel on that tower burst into life – as it only did very occasionally – he would respond, sending the signals to confirm that he was doing his job while jotting down the message he received. Then he'd blow on an old hunting-horn which he'd been given, and a lad would scurry up the hill from the village at its foot, collect the message, and run with it to the Earl's house, which was invariably where it was meant to go. Sometimes, especially after he'd received a message, the Earl would want to send one, in which case the operator would be required to remind himself of the codes and systems, and hope that his colleagues in the great tower would see his signals before too long.

*Today, though, a message arrived which puzzled the operator – not so much for its content as for its routing codes. These told him that it wasn't intended for the Earl, which was unusual. The address for which it **was** apparently intended made it downright odd. He almost reached for the horn, but then he noticed other details in the codes, one of which meant that someone had paid an extra dollar for Immediate Delivery By Company Personnel.*

Well, he was the nearest thing to Company Personnel, he supposed. So he set the tower flags to show Temporarily Out of Service, pulled on his jacket, and climbed down the ladder and walked down the hill. At the bottom, instead of turning hubwards for the village or rimwards for the Earl's house, he walked turnwise, for perhaps a mile, until he came to a small hill, and to a cave that he remembered being warned against exploring when he was a boy. So of course, he'd explored it thoroughly, but never found anything.

He looked at the message again. The Special Instructions were quite explicit, and not really unusual. Some recipients were, after all, unable to read, so having Company Personnel read their messages aloud was a sensible use of five pence.

Still . . .

No, the operator knew his duty, and the codes and Special Instructions were unambiguous. Standing straight-backed before the cave, and feeling rather foolish, he read the message aloud, in its entirety.

"Mr. Shine," he read, "Him Diamond."

There was a pause, just long enough to make the operator feel completely foolish. Then, from the depths of the cave, there came a voice.

"WHERE?" it demanded.

The operator blinked, and suddenly found that he wanted to pay attention to nothing but the message. "This message was routed from Ankh-Morpork," he said nervously. "Sir," he added.

There was another pause, and then the voice spoke from the cave again. "I UNDERSTAND," it said. "THANK YOU."

Then the hill began to move.

The Disc is a big world, with a long – if often confused – history. More details are warranted . . .

Disc Society

Current socio-politics of the Disc are best summed up with words like "patchwork." Think of our world in, say, 1850, with democracies, republics, kingdoms, and feudal states. The Discworld has all of these, sometimes in interesting combinations. Ephebe is still based on slavery, but with so many laws about the proper feeding and care of slaves that the slaves themselves have long opposed abolition of the system (a slave must be fed, while a free man is free to starve). Meanwhile, Lancre, in the Ramtops, now seems to operate a sort of reverse feudal system, with a tough and forthright peasantry getting on with their lives while one king works his fingers to the bone governing the place.

Governments and Politics

Ephebe is one of a number of city-states which abound in the lands around the Circle Sea.[1] The greatest and oldest of these is Ankh-Morpork – long ago the hub of a mighty empire held together by military strength, now still immensely powerful because of the strength of the Ankh-Morpork dollar. Think of it as Renaissance Florence and Victorian London rolled together, with some of the outlook of modern New York City. In many respects, its present-day "empire" is the whole of the Sto Plains. If you want a new life, a better job, or just to get away from the farm, you seek your fortune in Ankh-Morpork.

But Ankh-Morpork is a place where you go primarily to make your fortune, rather than *simply* to be free. Strictly speaking, it's a dictatorship – a tyranny, as its tyrant cheerfully reminds people when he needs to get something done immediately. It's just that he works on the principle that people left to themselves as much as possible will make more wealth and less trouble for him, most of the time. This self-balancing oligarchy is relatively sophisticated, as Discworld political philosophy goes. Elsewhere, old-fashioned feudalism is often the norm – but not everywhere. Most systems that people can imagine have been tried, somewhere on the Disc.

For example, other empires have featured in the chronicles. The Agatean Empire is held together by a vast, ancient bureaucracy,

but is nominally ruled by an all-powerful emperor whose position, while supposedly hereditary, is too often taken by whoever can hang onto it. Its politics may currently be a little confused, given that it was conquered a few years ago by a very small barbarian horde who soon abdicated out of boredom. The Omnian Empire, by contrast, is a theocracy, bound together by religion and the fact that the deserts mean that there's nowhere to run to. These days Omnia sees itself as a modern state – it was never that large, as empires go – still dominated by the Church of Om, but subject to the laws and ethics of a genuinely high-minded religion which *tries* to be tolerant.

On the other hand, the "Dark Empire" which once dominated Uberwald and its environs has collapsed entirely, leaving that region without any sort of central authority. It was founded by a megalomaniac who didn't leave any kind of stable political setup behind him. Other lands, high in the Disc's mountains or subject to supernatural instability, have never moved beyond the pocket-dukedom stage, at least in recent millennia.

Thus, adventurers can always *hope* to find a secluded barony or petty kingdom ripe for the taking if their ambitions lie that way. And however hopeless a political system might be, somebody somewhere is trying to make it work. Even democracy has been attempted, with votes for all (at least, for everyone reasonably rich and definitely male); Ephebe uses it, and the Sto Plains city-state of Pseudopolis is said to be trying something similar.

Crime and Law Enforcement

Rural, feudal societies generally get by with informal, local systems of law enforcement, and that's still the way of things on much of the Disc. In most places, "the law" mixes a certain amount of common sense with tradition and whatever some king with a tidy mind once insisted ought to be written down. However, the age of Discworld society ensures that there are a *lot* of traditional laws and old law-books, while a relatively sophisticated system of trade means that formal commercial and banking law has had to develop. At the same time, the growing mercantile cities have come to need a bit more formality and *organised* enforcement. International law remains underdeveloped, though – cooperation is possible ("Yes, he's a mass-murderer all right. Why don't you take him home with you?") but not guaranteed.

---

1. *"City-state" need not mean just a city. Classically, it has usually meant "a city governing a fair-sized area of surrounding countryside."*

As a huge city by Disc (or most other) standards, Ankh-Morpork has usually had *some* kind of Watch or constabulary over the centuries. In recent years, the Night Watch has expanded into a well-organised police force, with many features associated with higher-tech societies in our world's history, such as forensics specialists; see *The Watch* (pp. 255-257). Because Ankh-Morpork is widely envied and respected, other cities across the Sto Plains and perhaps beyond are imitating this idea.

Gender Politics

As mentioned in *Regarding Female Characters* (p. 36), traditional Discworld societies can be quite sexist – similar to our world prior to the last hundred years. However, yet another symptom of some Disc-wide changes is a shift in formal as well as informal rules on this.

Female Education

As the Disc tends to mirror our world, so its male-dominated societies are faced with a disorganised sort of feminist movement. A key concern in this is *education*. Some groups are handling such things better than others.

The Assassins' Guild, for example, has always recognised that women could qualify as worthy members; recently, this acceptance has extended to female students at the Guild school. Other Ankh-Morpork guilds' policies vary with their leaders' personalities, but women are *slowly* finding their way into some. (Meanwhile, the ever-pragmatic Seamstresses' Guild has admitted a few *male* members.) The aristocracy have taken to sending their daughters to boarding schools, albeit mostly ones which concentrate on traditionally feminine accomplishments; the Quirm College for Young Ladies is the best-regarded.

Wizardry, however, remains an all-male pursuit, despite the Eskarina Smith incident (see *Equal Rites*). There are reasons for this, but they aren't much discussed. A GM might consider building a campaign around the foundation and development of independent Colleges of Sorceresses, somewhere on the Disc; their style could be based on that of the female colleges that grew up in association with old-established universities on our world in the late 19th century.

Inheritance and Legitimacy

As a matter less of feminism than of practicality, Discworld inheritance law has long accepted that female children may have a claim to titles and property. Discworld politics has another element that's slightly different to most of our history, too: illegitimate offspring may inherit power. While this isn't quite "legal," it's widely accepted. A legitimate heir will have priority, *if* he wants the title – but in the absence of such a claimant, the old king's mistress' child (for instance) can usually apply for the job. This might be pragmatism or it may be sentimentality, but it is certainly widespread, and it has influenced the recent history of nations including Lancre and Genua.

Incidentally, there are no chronicled "consulting detectives" on the Disc as yet, and few or no people in any sort of "private eye" role. Inevitably, mysteries on the Disc somehow turn out too messy and confused for Sherlock Holmes-style plots (Commander Vimes is especially cynical on this subject). Still, clever-clever PCs who want to enter this business are welcome to try.

BANDITRY AND PIRACY

Travellers away from civilisation are tempting prey for bandits and pirates. Such criminals can be a real threat, although at least some banditry is quite formalised – the risk to one's finances is serious, but many bandits would rather cultivate a raffish reputation than inflict serious harm. Even the fearsome D'regs of Klatch (p. 236) appreciate the advantages of leaving merchants alive to rob again later. Discworld pirates tend to more yo-ho-ho-ing brutality (it's sometimes safer to be caught by slavers, to whom you're at least a valuable commodity), but sensible merchant ships *usually* either avoid the most dangerous routes or carry enough armaments to fight through.

Travellers and people who depend on travelling merchants for supplies and business take a dim view of disruption of communications. Targets worth robbing typically have the wealth or connections to organise armed responses, which are likely if bandits or pirates get too greedy or vicious. Such law enforcement tends to be rather informal, and the punishment applied to the robbers is often quite terminal.

TRIALS AND PUNISHMENT

However, a suspected criminal caught by an organised Watch or a tidier-minded citizen will usually be held for a short time in a rather medieval kind of prison (anything from a damp, rat-infested dungeon to a passably dry holding cell – the Ankh-Morpork Watch tends to the latter end of the scale), and then brought to trial. Most places on the Disc believe in open criminal trials under *some* system of rules, if only for the public entertainment value, but prisoners shouldn't assume too much. By and large, courts are overseen by some local ruler or government officer, who also gets to decide verdicts and penalties. While insane and capricious rulers tend not be well-liked, especially once they start trying and punishing people completely at random, ruler-judges who act in a way that's merely eccentric can be quite popular with the people, who always enjoy a good laugh.

Penalties for lawbreakers also tend to the medieval, with local variations. Disc societies are rarely rich enough to support jails for long-term prisoners – and where such facilities exist, conditions inside are often *really* appalling – so the stocks, whipping, and relatively frequent applications of capital punishment are common. Adventurers should be aware that if a stranger is believed to have committed a minor-to-moderate offence in a smaller community (where outsiders, when available, will be blamed for most things), the locals may not wish to bother a judge. An impromptu beating, financial compensation (all the cash that the accused is carrying), and swift expulsion from the area ("And stay out!") tend to be considered satisfaction enough.

The Semaphore Revolution

Perhaps the most spectacular recent development on the Disc is technological: the creation of a semaphore system, nicknamed "the clacks," whose significance for trade and politics is profound.

Previously, long-distance communications were mostly limited to *ad hoc* letter post. There had been multiple attempts at formal services – the long-disused Post Office building in Ankh-Morpork bore witness to one – but civil war, government corruption, or sheer stupidity always got in the way eventually. Most people simply gave their letters to any passing dwarf, and this worked quite well; dwarfs are continually travelling between their mines and underground cities, and are a stolidly reliable folk. A small payment would usually induce one to pass on a letter or a parcel, perhaps along a chain of several dwarfs, until it reached the addressee.[1] Delivery times were unpredictable to say the least, though. By comparison, the semaphore system is lightning-fast.

The basic mechanism was invented in the Street of Cunning Artificers in Ankh-Morpork. Semaphore – performed with a couple of hand-held flags – had been around for centuries, but this improvement took inspiration.[2] The Patrician either chose not to suppress the idea, or found that it had spread too far, too fast, to stop. Certainly, once a few merchants recognised the profits to be made, it would have been difficult to restrain them. Vetinari quite possibly took the view that, just as Ankh-Morpork had led the world first in the field of arms, and then in the fields of currency and politics, so it should become the nexus of the information revolution. Also, his office enjoys a good view of the central clacks towers on the Tump, and he has people on his staff who are *very* good at breaking codes.

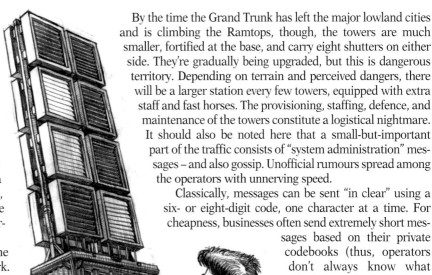

The system involves specially built towers. Mounted on these are arrays of boxes – each about eight feet square – painted black on the inside and with a white-painted "Venetian blind" on the outer face. To an observer, the box appears white when the blind is shut, black when it's open. The shutters are operated by complex lever-and-pulley mechanisms.

At night, a signal is sent down the line indicating that it's time to switch to night operation. Lamps are lit in the boxes, and the codes are "reversed" (because the lamp shows when the shutter is open). Given that the speed of light on the Disc can be as low as 600 mph, "lighting-up time" can vary across the system.

Shutters are arranged in groups of six or eight, and towers are sited 20 miles or so apart, in long chains across the country. Tower crew watch the next tower in each direction through telescopes. The towers of the Grand Trunk, which runs from Ankh-Morpork to Genua, have up to 36 shutters on either side where traffic is heavy, and it can send messages in both directions at once. A junction tower – where a spur of the trunk heads off to another city – has shutters on *three* sides and is extraordinarily busy. The Tump Tower in Ankh-Morpork has 32 shutters on each of its *four* sides, plus six sub-towers to handle local traffic.

By the time the Grand Trunk has left the major lowland cities and is climbing the Ramtops, though, the towers are much smaller, fortified at the base, and carry eight shutters on either side. They're gradually being upgraded, but this is dangerous territory. Depending on terrain and perceived dangers, there will be a larger station every few towers, equipped with extra staff and fast horses. The provisioning, staffing, defence, and maintenance of the towers constitute a logistical nightmare. It should also be noted here that a small-but-important part of the traffic consists of "system administration" messages – and also gossip. Unofficial rumours spread among the operators with unnerving speed.

Classically, messages can be sent "in clear" using a six- or eight-digit code, one character at a time. For cheapness, businesses often send extremely short messages based on their private codebooks (thus, operators don't always know what they're sending). Message cost varies, but is usually about five words per Ankh-Morpork dollar. This may sound exorbitant, but the system is expensive to run, and it's worth every penny to serious users. Clacks companies sometimes work on a first-come, first-sent basis, but are increasingly developing sliding-scale payment systems: customers can pay a lot to get a message off *now*, or less, down to a minimum "night rate" which means their message goes on the rack and is sent overnight, when the system clears its backlog. Yet another streamlining measure is the succinct "c-address"; the first was "We R Igors, Yethmather Uberwald," for an employment agency patronised by those needing cringing toadies in a hurry.

Despite all this, the system is always overburdened. Every part is understaffed, burgeoning local companies use different protocols, and the technology is constantly changing. People keep finding new uses for it, too, adding to the load. For example, some genius has worked out how to transmit pictures in the form of complex numeric codes representing areas of light or dark, enabling newspapers to receive images taken by iconographer-reporters in distant lands, and to publish up-to-date illustrated foreign news. It's a high-speed mess that perpetually has to evolve or die. Still, signals can be passed extremely quickly; when things are working correctly, it's possible to send a message from Ankh-Morpork to Genua within a day.

Originally each chain was run by a separate company, with the whole system being loosely supervised by a new guild. However, much of it soon fell under the control of a single large company, the "Grand Trunk," which in turn fell into the hands of a cabal of unprincipled investors dominated by the unscrupulous Reacher Gilt. After that was sorted out (see *Going Postal*), the Grand Trunk remained, in a reformed and refinanced state. It continues to dominate the system.

Up in the lawless mountains, a company like the Grand Trunk may have its own private army; it's too important for anyone with money to permit local bandits to interfere with it. When a more powerful entity, such as the deranged nation of Borogravia, makes trouble, other nations will step in to slap down the problem.

1. *Provided that it didn't look like money, food, or anything too valuable, anyway. A larger fee would usually persuade the dwarfs not to open letters and read the good parts out to their friends.*

2. *Incidentally, a similar system was developed on our world in the early 19th century.*

Conversely, large organisations in cities have their own clacks towers, generally employing gargoyles as watchers. These are known as personal clacks systems, or "packs."

The creation of the clacks has inspired something of a fashion for semaphore in general. For example, the Ankh-Morpork Watch has taken to using paddles, rather like table-tennis bats, to send signals through a tower on the main watch-house. This *is* faster than the messenger pigeons on which they previously relied. For that matter, some people have taken to hand-semaphoring to each other across crowded rooms, causing a minor public nuisance.

Astronomy and Astrology

Research into the lights in the sky is still mostly at TL3 on the Disc, albeit with plenty of accumulated data. However, the telescope has been invented, so some efforts might approach TL4. Regardless, astronomy is entangled with astrology – although some students may concentrate more on the geometrical, observational bit than on star signs and horoscopes. Of course, on the Disc, astrology *works* (see *Horoscopes*, p. 272). There are 64 constellations in the Discworld zodiac, and the list changes with time as the Turtle moves; current examples include the Celestial Parsnip, Gahoolie the Vase of Tulips, Wezen the Double-Headed Kangaroo, and the Small Boring Group of Faint Stars (Rincewind's sign).

TOWER ARCHITECTURE

Size aside, the main difference between towers is that those in safe, densely populated areas tend to be brick-and-wood structures, whereas those in less-secure areas are heavy stone – at ground level, at least – and fully able to withstand small-scale assaults.[1] But despite the companies' security policies and real-life cautionary tales, towers are never completely invulnerable. Crews are in place for weeks or months at a time, and they cannot help but get bored. In any case, they must sometimes gather firewood and are unlikely to have more than a few days' supply of food and drink in store.

The ground floor (within the stone base of a fortified tower) is a storeroom. Above that are the main living-quarters. In out-of-the-way areas, these consist of a combined mess room and bedroom with two bunks; in safe urban areas, the crew may live away from the tower, and use this space as a place to relax and eat. This level also serves as an office, with a desk for paperwork. The next and highest storey holds the mechanisms that control the shutters.

A trapdoor leads up to the roof and the space behind the shutters, for maintenance purposes. In emergencies, the crew can fire a signal flare, or "mortar," from the roof. A red flare means that the tower is out of action, and a couple of men (armed, in dangerous areas) will be sent from the next tower in the chain, followed by a full maintenance crew from the nearest depot. A green flare means that any problem has been cleared.

---

1. *Some locals just don't like progress.*

TOWER CREW

A *small* tower usually has a crew of three; larger towers can have significantly more. The clacks system is a TL4 development, so these workers' personal TL must be at least that high (see *Technology Level*, pp. 30-31). Crewman use several skills: Telegraphy/TL4 is obvious, Mechanic/TL4 (Clacks) covers routine maintenance, First Aid is recognised as important for emergencies, Housekeeping keeps a tower liveable, and crewmembers with Professional Skill (Cooking) end up being very popular. In the backwoods, a local language may be necessary, and Riding and Survival are often handy. In some regions, combat skills are advisable.

"Tower crewman" is a job with a Wealth level of Average (see *Characters With Jobs*, p. 173); pay may be mediocre by that standard, but crewmembers don't get much chance to spend it. Rates might rise as demand for this expertise increases, or fall as more bright youngsters enter the field. Working in dangerous areas sometimes involves hazard pay, and pushing a new service into raw wilderness is the sort of work that's liable to attract serious adventurers, for corresponding levels of reward (see *Clacks Field Engineer*, p. 121).

The counterweighted mechanisms require no great physical strength to operate, so clacks companies are often equal-opportunity employers, and female operators are sometimes rated highly. Mixed crews may be considered scandalous out in the wilds, though. Gargoyles (pp. 100-101) get a lot of employment in the industry, since they're very good at staring constantly at one thing.

A crewman doesn't have to roll against Telegraphy skill to send or receive messages during routine operation – but poor visibility or other hostile conditions might make things difficult enough to require a roll, at the GM's option. Operators can normally send or receive a number of words per minute equal to their skill level; the operators along a line get to know each other's competences and settle on a rate that everyone can match. They can attempt to send or receive at higher speeds in emergencies or when trying to clear a backlog; this requires a skill roll at -1 for each additional word per minute. Highly skilled operators are valued on the major routes, especially with the spread of encryption (below).

ENCRYPTION

The semaphore system uses a code in the sense that it translates letters and numbers into a series of shutter patterns, but this isn't secret. *Anyone* can learn the Telegraphy skill and read messages passing between towers. Hence, many people have developed encryption systems, and messages often consist of sequences of letters and numbers that are completely meaningless to the crews sending and receiving them – and to casual observers. Sending or receiving encrypted messages in haste or in difficult circumstances gives from -1 to -4 to Telegraphy skill, as the operator won't immediately recognise errors. Most ciphers include checks that let the intended recipient know whether they've been garbled in transmission.

Most encryption is fairly basic and can be defeated by a competent cryptographer using Discworld mathematics, but some systems are quite sophisticated. Wealthy nobles, governments, and trading-houses from Ankh-Morpork to Genua employ experts to devise and crack encryption. The Ankh-Morpork Watch has tolerably secure systems for watchmen operating away from home, and for use in their system of short-range signalling within the city; it shares *some* of this with other city watches.

The Patrician of Ankh-Morpork uses Leonard of Quirm (pp. 308-309) not only to decrypt other governments' messages (Leonard has invented machines to help with this), but also to invent new codes that are carefully designed to be *almost* unbreakable.[1]

Uberwaldian Domestic Surgery

Another, weirder technological oddity has been around on the Disc for much longer than the clacks, but is now spreading rapidly beyond its lands of origin. The startling[2] science of Uberwald has produced some strange accomplishments and even stranger people. In particular, *Igors* are experts in a unique form of all-purpose transplant surgery which enables them to swap body parts seemingly almost at will. They can even perform transplant surgery on *themselves* – though they might need somebody to put a finger on the stitching while they tie off the thread – and no self-respecting Igor has *not* replaced a few of his body parts by the time he has achieved maturity. While usually beneficial, these modifications may be imperfect; Igors can never quite get the eyes level, and their extraordinary skills don't ensure that joins won't show (Igors are notoriously careless about scars and visible stitching). Despite their odd looks, they make popular husbands for young Uberwaldian women.

All this used to be just another one of those odd things about Uberwald. Nowadays, though, Igors are showing up far and wide – often hired through agencies via the clacks. See *Igor* (pp. 140-141) for a character template.

Transplant surgery forms part of the complex belief system that goes into being an Igor. Igors do know that other people have what they regard (but would be too polite to describe) as peculiar hang-ups on this topic, and rarely perform *really* radical surgery on non-Igors, though they often make friendly offers. Still, they tend to regard a badly injured human body as a likely source of useful spare parts (though they'll politely ask relatives for permission first), and another Igor in the same state as an interesting challenge.

WEIRD SURGERY IN PLAY

Igors and some mad doctors have TL5 medical skills (p. 77), allowing them to heal all sorts of problems faster and more reliably than other Discworld medics. Surgery/TL5 lets them perform routine "cut-and-patch" surgery (appendectomies, treatment of internal injuries, etc.) with a reliability otherwise unknown to Discworld medicine. This combined with Mad Medicine (p. 44) represents their extraordinary ability to pull off mix-and-match assembly jobs on human (and other) anatomy, carrying out organ and limb transplants while somehow sidestepping the tissue-rejection problems that bedevil surgeons on more advanced but prosaic worlds.

If the subject has the Patchwork Man advantage (pp. 45-46), almost any surgery can be performed without skill penalties, and routine tasks might even enjoy bonuses. At the GM's option, treating "normal" patients may involve penalties which reflect

the task's complexity, but *never* as extreme as those facing regular Discworld surgeons. Furthermore, when someone with Mad Medicine and appropriate medical equipment (meaning an Igor's bizarre collection of needles, threads, bandages, and ointments) treats someone using the First Aid skill, any roll good enough to be a success on both that skill *and* his Surgery/TL5 skill means that the wounds he treats will heal with impressive speed and efficiency: +3 to subsequent HT rolls for *Natural Recovery* (p. 187).

Generally, Surgery skill grants little special knowledge of anaesthesia, which on the Disc is still mostly at the brandy, poppy juice, and large-padded-mallet stage. However, Igor-style ointments provide fairly effective pain relief.

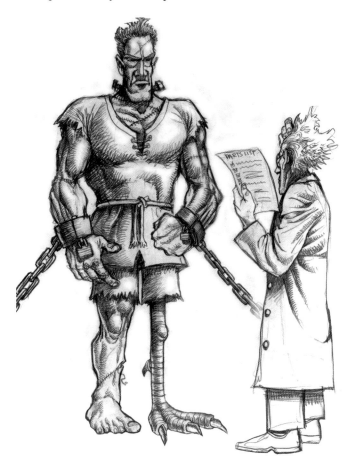

REUSING BRAINS

One final note: Undamaged brains from recently deceased bodies can be used in the creation of completely new individuals – usually Igors. They typically require a jolt of electricity (traditionally from a thunderstorm, through a lightning rod) to get them working again. They start out as "blank slates," essentially, with no guarantee that specific skills or memories will be retained (because on the Disc, a person is more than just his brain). Thus, this isn't a way to get a deceased PC back into play, regardless of whether he's an Igor; it's just a way to create a *new* character.

Brain recipients do tend to be quick learners, however. The GM can rule that they've inherited a random assortment of mental advantages and disadvantages, minor habits, or memory fragments from the donor (with, as the saying goes, hilarious results). Their IQ will usually be within a point or so of the donor's, too. Details are left to the GM's whim, but this could be an excuse for playing a new Igor PC who isn't *too* unlike someone who got himself irreparably mangled.

---

1. *Ensuring that the Patrician always knows what other very intelligent people think they know about what he's thinking.*

2. *And, let's say it, Blasphemous, Strange, and Uncanny.*

Nonhuman Races

As readers have doubtless noticed by now, the Disc is dominated by humans.[1] However, it does also feature other races with whom it's useful to be acquainted.

Dwarfs

Dwarfs are a humanoid race, stockily built, averaging about 4' tall, with a lifespan of around 300 years. For a racial template, see p. 100. Their natural tendency is to live among mountains – especially under them. Almost the entire race displays a constructive obsession with metals and minerals, along with intense attention to detail.

Dwarfs are biologically close to humanity; dwarf-human marriages and offspring, although all but unknown, are possible.[2] In fact, while humans consider dwarfishness to be a genetic matter, dwarfs think of it as much more *cultural*. They might not point it out to humans very often, but there are humans who are shorter than the average dwarf; the question of who was or wasn't brought up in dwarf society, on the other hand, is more sharply determinable, given all the small rules and rituals involved. Hence, Carrot Ironfoundersson (pp. 321-322) is acknowledged as a dwarf even by many dwarf traditionalists. It's actually possible, with some difficulty, for a human to *convert* to dwarfism.

Dwarf culture doesn't seem complex to human eyes, although dwarfs would argue. They have songs that play every possible variation on the word "gold," and they're attached to their culinary tradition, especially their bread (see *Dwarf Bread*, p. 227). They like eating rat, a taste which human entrepreneurs are happy to service.

Dwarfs of both sexes have beards, of which they're very proud. They generally wear multiple layers of clothing – up to a dozen – which, combined with their naturally broad build, makes them look like walking barrels. The layers often include an under-vest of Ramtops wool (p. 237). Other dwarfs wear metal next to the skin; those of delicate sensitivities favour silver underwear if they can afford it. Iron-shod boots (or even solid iron footwear) and helmets are also typical.

In game terms, most dwarfs wear the equivalent of winter clothing at an absolute minimum, will probably be encountered in at least enough layers of fabric and leathers to serve as very light or light armour (pp. 155-156), and consider heavier metal armour acceptable – and in fact stylish – for civilian wear. Those who wear lighter garb than this will be commented on even by humans; other dwarfs will treat them as underdressed, often reacting to them at -1 or worse.

All this makes it impossible for anyone without superhuman senses, even another dwarf, to tell whether a typical dwarf is male or female. Dwarfs don't worry about this; older dwarf dialects don't even include feminine pronouns. Traditional dwarf courtship is a lengthy and delicate process, mainly devoted to determining the other dwarf's sex. Dwarfs really prefer to think about geology or engineering. They reach puberty at about 55, and aren't usually told the facts of life until then. Dwarfs consider other races strange for publicly admitting to gender – but then, they find other races strange in many ways.

Dwarfs often have the Literal-Minded disadvantage (p. 61), although some are able to get rid of this, especially if they've been living among humans for a while. Old-fashioned mine-dwellers, though, find humans at least as annoying as humans find them. To such dwarfs, humans are always offering a meditation on the nature of time and the beauty of fire when you just want to know when the lighted fuse is going to reach the powder keg. Humans would submit that such dwarfs find human speech to be a maze, or a minefield; the dwarfs just say that humans are very confusing.

> ## Dwarf Terms, Sayings, and Battle-Cries
>
> The dwarfish language is generally *spoken* only among dwarfs, but it's often shouted, snarled, or declaimed in mixed company. A few common expressions:
>
> **aaDb'thuk?:** Literally "All correctly beamed and propped?" The dwarf equivalent of "Okay?"
>
> **b'zugda-hiara:** Literally, "lawn ornament." A deadly insult; it can be used as a term of endearment, but the speaker must be *very* certain of the dwarf's affection. (Calling a dwarf a "lawn ornament" in a human language is also a fight-starter, but the dwarfish version works best.)
>
> **g'hruk, t'uk:** "Evening, all." A friendly farewell to a group.
>
> **gr'duzk:** "Good day."
>
> **t'dr'duzk b'hazg t't:** "Today is a good day for someone else to die." The most menacing of battle-cries; once it has been shouted, someone *must* be killed.
>
> **zadkrdga:** Literally, "one who smelts." A temporarily appointed official investigator; one who finds the pure metal of truth in the dross of confusion.

Large dwarf communities always have a "king," though the dwarfish term ("dezka-knik") translates better as "Chief Mining Engineer." Generally, when someone says "I am King of the Dwarfs," he means that he's king of *these particular* dwarfs, not those in the next excavation up the valley. Dwarf society works like a set of efficient industrial companies.

---

1. *At this point, it's traditional to explain at length how, despite the fact that humans are smaller, squidgier, less magical, or poorer at mining than other races, we have some kind of crucial edge – perhaps a willingness to kill, or willpower, or the ability to cooperate, or the favour of the gods, or just the capacity to out-breed everyone else. But the important point is that these stories and games are created by and for human beings. Perhaps there are worlds dominated by yeti, somewhere in the multiverse, where they tell tales of the uncanny humans who live down in those sinister warm valleys. There's certainly a disc, in the same universe as the Discworld, where sea-trolls rule. But reading stories or playing games set there wouldn't be the same.*

2. *If anyone insists on details, treat these offspring as members of one parent race or the other for game purposes – though they may be, say, unusually short, strong humans, or tall dwarfs with embarrassingly skimpy beards.*

The downside is that the "king" usually cares more about the state of the mine than the well-being of his subjects, but other dwarfs understand this perfectly well.[1]

There's one "king" whose title means more, however. The *Low King* rules all those parts of Uberwald (p. 240) which happen to be underground, and he receives great respect from other dwarfs (they don't raise their voices when arguing with him), and so has become the final court of appeal for all matters relating to dwarf law. This makes him the closest thing the race has to an overall leader. Hence, this has become an elected position of sorts; succession is decided by political negotiation among the larger clans. The current Low King is Rhys Rhysson (p. 349).

DWARFS AWAY FROM HOME

For the most part, dwarfs are quiet, obedient, ritualistic, and well-behaved – but only among themselves. When they leave for other areas, such as Ankh-Morpork, they tend to adopt a name that sounds more like a series of threats, wear armour at all times, carry weapons (usually axes, though mattocks, flails, and adjustable wrenches are also popular), drink too much, and erupt into violence at the drop of an iron helmet. Getting away from home gives a dwarf the excuse to get a few decades of frustration off his chest, and this and the commonplace expatriate tendency to play up distinctive cultural features amplify one another. Sensible watchmen regard dwarf bars as extraterritorial, although the Ankh-Morpork Watch now has enough high-mindedness and enough dwarf members to keep some kind of control.

A more radical reaction to seeing the wider world is an urge among a few dwarfs to emulate human-style displays of gender. This may have started with Cheery Littlebottom (pp. 326-327), but it has since become widespread, at least in Ankh-Morpork; female dwarfs are coming out, especially those who find that they don't much enjoy the stereotypically "masculine" aspects of dwarf behaviour. Overt femininity doesn't preclude a bit of clang, though; welding high heels onto boots, and soldering a few sequins onto an axe, combines the two. There's now an actual dwarf fashion industry, which employs beautiful and expensive metals, and which is developing ultra-fine "micromail" fabrics. The latter are amazingly robust but accordingly expensive.

DEEP-DOWNERS

"Deep-downers" is a colloquial term for ultra-conservative dwarfs who revere tradition and don't much approve of other races. The most serious and high-status of them never see sunlight; if they have to come above ground at all, they do so after dark, or carefully travel everywhere in sedan chairs with thick leather curtains, carried by non-dwarfs. At heart, they regard humans – let alone trolls – as *unreal*, a sort of bad dream. Other dwarfs call them "drudak'ak," which translates as "they don't get out in the fresh air enough." In extreme cases, deep-downers might have Disciplines of Faith (Ritualism) (p. 59) and Intolerance (of trolls at least, and probably of all non-dwarfs).

GRAGS

Grags are respected experts in dwarf history and beliefs – the race's honoured lore-masters. There isn't any formal way to gain

1. *Dwarfs are a renewable resource; a good vein of ore is irreplaceable.*

Dwarf Bread

Dwarfs are extremely proud of their bread, which serves many purposes, mostly ceremonial and military (see *Dwarf Bread Weapons*, p. 153) – some even eat it. *Real* dwarf bread is made of grit rather than flour. Sentimental dwarfs insist that it's only worth eating if it has been dropped in a river, dried out, sat on, and contemplated for days on end. It keeps almost indefinitely, making it good marching rations; less purist dwarfs admit that its main use on the march is as encouragement (faced with the prospect of having to eat it, people choose to march another mile in the hope of finding something else). The Low King is crowned while sitting on the (supposedly) ancient Scone of Stone.

"Clang"

Dwarfs love metal and don't mind showing it, but there are degrees to this. An ordinary working dwarf wears a helmet and reinforced boots, and possibly a mail shirt if his budget permits, and carries an axe as a symbol of dwarfishness. Serious dwarf warriors, with nothing to prove, wear armour and carry a *good* axe. Dwarfs with a touch of flamboyance or insecurity, though, wear as much armour as they can afford – with a fancy helmet and metal boots – and lug a couple of axes, along with perhaps a pick, a hammer, and a sword or a morningstar . . . even if they work in a bakery or a toyshop. Such showy swagger is known as "clang."

---

the title; accepted standing among dwarfs is everything. Humans might think of grags as priests, but that would be misleading, as dwarfs don't go in for prayer or religious ritual so much as they see living correctly as the way to honour Tak, their creator. "Living correctly" covers a wide range of things, and grags advise on all of them.

Most grags are deep-downers – but not all. Being fixated on tradition, serious deep-downers can become grags most easily, but it *is* possible for a "surface" dwarf to achieve the status; one famous example is Grag Bashfull Bashfullsson, who was born in Ankh-Morpork and who has acquired a reputation for meditative scholarship, at least among city dwarfs. However, the large dwarf population of Ankh-Morpork feels a need for more grags, so there's now a small community of deep-downers, mostly living in cellars and wearing hooded leather robes that make them indistinguishable.

In game terms, a grag should know an ancient dwarf language or two, have high levels in Philosophy (Dwarfish), Theology (Dwarfish), and several branches of dwarfish History – and probably also Law, Public Speaking, and Teaching. Most of all, however, he should have a +3 Reputation for wisdom among dwarfs. Grags, even the rare liberal sort, don't make good PCs; they have a full-time job advising other dwarfs, and must behave with propriety to retain their standing.

Grags are by definition interested in tradition, and deep-downer grags tend to be socially conservative even by dwarf standards. Grags see their job as keeping dwarfs close to the old ways, and many consider even the cautious, diplomatic Low King Rhys a dangerous radical. They regard dwarfs who live in human society – let alone those who admit what sex they are, or who tolerate trolls – as tragic or despicable. Bashfullsson is an exception to all this, being quietly thoughtful and courteous to everyone, and not wanting dwarfs to be defined by hatred or by living under a mountain. He's on good terms with the Low King.

Dwarfs vs. Trolls

Trolls and dwarfs have a mutual enmity that sometimes seems to have originated about eight or nine minutes after the creation of the universe. Dwarfs call trolls "rocks," trolls call dwarfs "gritsuckers," and neither word could be printed if this book was politically correct and members of either species were reading it.

The source of the problem is fairly simple. Both races are mountain-dwellers, and there's only so much vertical real estate. Even if the dwarfs (for instance) are persuaded to take their operations elsewhere (a situation known in trollish as "We Got Bigger Rocks"), there are probably trolls over there as well. Also, dwarfish mining often leads them into contact with trolls, specifically trolls who have settled down to Think and become one with the countryside. Discovering that his grandfather has been used to resurface a highway is one of the few things that trolls find hard to swallow – and the dwarfish saying "The only good troll is one that's architecturally sound" doesn't help. For their part, trolls are rarely careful of dwarfish constructions that get in their way.

But frankly, all that is explanation, not *reason*. Trolls and dwarfs no longer *need* reasons to fight. There are too many past offences to dredge up, and both races are long-lived, with excellent memories. The conflict goes on because it has always gone on. It *may* be in the process of being partially resolved by a great deal of hard political work and appeals to long-lost historical truths, but that's likely to take decades, and even after the process is complete, there will still be dwarfs and trolls hitting each other *somewhere*.

In game terms, members of either race can easily have Intolerance (p. 60) towards the other. This can subsequently be reduced to a quirk, bought off, or perhaps replaced by a negative Reputation among some members of one's own species ("rock-lover" or "troll who talk to gritsuckers"), but it isn't *surprising*. If a PC group includes trolls *and* dwarfs, though, they should probably all avoid it – nonstop squabbling and surreptitious ankle-kicking is only funny for a while.

There are examples of dwarf-troll friendships. Dwarfs and trolls certainly get along okay in the Ankh-Morpork Watch. Then again, if Completely Mismatched Police Partners Didn't Learn To Respect Each Other Eventually, the narrative universe as we know it would come to an end.

Trolls

Trolls are something between a logical piece of xenobiology (silicon-based life) and a figure of speech run amok (rocks that get up and walk). They're an earthy, stolid species, albeit with some peculiarities. For racial templates, see pp. 107-109. Troll characters typically have their racial template, a few more points in combat skills, and maybe knowledge of something else they need to make a living; rural henhouse-raiders might even have some proficiency with Stealth and Camouflage. Large variations in attributes (*especially* ST) are common, however.

Trolls are *the* Discworld symbol of dumb muscle – if a PC group needs to be shown that an NPC is too rich and busy to fight for himself, then that NPC can hire a troll or six. But they're also an interesting race on their own account; to invert the normal pattern of things, for example, a PC party might be hired by a troll entrepreneur to travel to some hot rimward land and acquire rare minerals, which they must then ship back for sale as food in troll communities. Still, if a Discworld adventure needs an old-fashioned monster with just enough intelligence to be worrying, an NPC troll can meet the need. If the incident takes place in a cold climate, the PCs may be in for a particularly nasty surprise. However, there really is a little more to this race than just hitting people.

Being based on silicon, trolls *are* immensely strong and robust; they sometimes seem slow, but in fact they can move with the speed as well as the force of an avalanche, and little can slow them down. Other races generally regard them as stupid – and not without cause – but the situation is a little more complex. There's a reason why trolls combine this reputation with a name for cunning among those who have to deal with them on freezing winter nights or high in the mountains. The truth is that a troll brain works best at low temperatures (see *Troll Brain*, p. 97), so that in the cold mountains which are their natural environment, they're no more than moderately unintelligent. But when a troll has the bright idea of migrating to the big city, he ends up in a situation where, for practical purposes, he just isn't so bright any more.

Not that being a little dimmer reduces trolls' urban survival ability. They're traditionally employed as doormen, bouncers, enforcers, or in other professions where brute force and ignorance are virtues. Human cities are full of people who are willing to overcome a little species prejudice in the interest of having a walking rock on the payroll. This in turn has generated a market for troll food and entertainment.

A troll can potentially live for an exceedingly long time, but not all trolls fulfil that potential; all that getting hit with rocks takes its toll. Some, however, just keep getting bigger. There are people who think that they also get *dumber*, until they turn into lifeless rocks, but that isn't quite fair. Older trolls don't, strictly speaking, lose intelligence; they just think *slower and deeper*. They start pondering the nature of the world, the meaning of truth, and other imponderables. Eventually, they settle down. What few Discworld inhabitants realise is how many of their most noteworthy hills are actually great philosophers – every now and again, vast and powerful ideas move slowly through the deep rock.

Troll culture is based on rocks in general, and on hitting people with them in particular. "People" definitely includes other trolls; indeed, trolls hit other trolls even more than they hit other races. One troll hitting another with a rock may represent a fight, a business transaction, a casual greeting, or romantic attraction.[1]

---

1. *In the last case, the male troll will try to find a very nice rock, some opal matrix, say, or something with pretty red-quartz inclusions.*

Troll music is percussive. Trolls might seem primitive, except that they grasp the important aspects of new technology[1] quickly enough.

Trolls' reputation for brutality is somewhat unfair. They're capable of loyalty, affection, and even a degree of altruism. They can be reasoned with, using words of one syllable. However, they are *direct,* and do hit things a lot, which leads them too easily into work that counts as illegal if the area has active laws. A truly evil troll is little troubled by conscience.[2]

Trolls usually eat and drink mineral-based substances. It's generally believed that they cannot actually obtain nutrition from carbon-based foodstuffs, implying that they persist in eating people and dwarfs, and raiding henhouses, entirely out of bloody-mindedness. Certainly, they quickly give such habits up in areas where it would be dangerously tactless. On the other hand, even trolls might not have carried on a *completely* pointless tradition at quite such length; certainly, gargoyles, a troll variant of a sort, seem to live on organic matter filtered out of gutters, and the occasional pigeon. Perhaps the trollish digestion and metabolism can do something with organics after all, or can at least benefit from a few trace elements.

Troll teeth, which must deal with solid rock, are diamonds. This is the sort of datum which causes certain old-fashioned role-players (and Disc adventurers) to look thoughtful, and there's no escaping the fact that these diamonds are worth good money – though maybe not quite as much on the Disc as on other worlds. In *Soul Music,* a troll tooth raises $15, although it's probably worth much more. Then again, with so many such stones potentially in circulation, the grade of diamond found in troll mouths probably isn't worth very much.

There are logical reasons beyond stone quality for humans to refrain from dental plunder. To begin with, trolls are tough and hard to render helpless with their mouths open. It's also safe to assume that a troll tooth is easily recognisable, at least until carefully cut. Even if the PCs wish to walk around with this sort of thing in their pockets, odds are that most human jewellers will take one look and refuse the deal. Trolls should likewise exercise caution – a few troll gang bosses wear diamond jewellery, which marks them out very clearly as Not Nice People, even by troll standards. Still, a troll who really wants to extract one of his *own* teeth can do so, usually by punching himself in the jaw; this requires a Will roll, but trolls hit themselves almost as often as they hit other people.

Trolls have a peculiar concept of time. When they're cool enough to be philosophical, they believe that they're moving through time backwards, from the distant demise of the universe toward an end that others think of as birth. Their evidence for this is that they can make out, with some clarity, what the past looks like, but cannot see the future; therefore the past must be in front of them, and the future behind them. This leads to some odd figures of speech. They speak of the "Sunset of Time" when they mean the beginning; they are, after all, naturally nocturnal creatures.

No troll ever seems to have learned magic. Trolls do have a mythology, with gods and heroes, although it isn't exactly complex. A troll priest is basically a storyteller, with a good throwing-rock or two at hand in case of blasphemous hecklers.

---

1. *Whether you can hit things with it.*

2. *Unless required to spell it.*

The Battle of Koom Valley

The Battle of Koom Valley – between trolls and dwarfs – was a genuine historical event, although records and references to it have always been confused and contradictory enough that they can be taken as evidence of the fractured and damaged nature of Disc history (see *Time,* pp. 11-12). Humans who've read about the subject sometimes refer to it as the only battle in history where both sides ambushed each other.

However, a lot of evidence has recently emerged on this subject – perhaps as a result of History Monks (p. 13) patching over the damaged structure of time. It appears that the *original* battle took place about 1,500-2,000 years ago, following a disastrous misunderstanding at what was meant to be a *peace conference.* Partly thanks to some cataclysmic weather and the chaotic geology of Koom Valley itself, it was a messy draw, but it entered the mythology of both races. "Remember Koom Valley!" was what little excuse a dwarf or troll might ever need to start a fight, especially after everyone got organised enough to mark the annual anniversary. On occasion, further clashes would take place between groups visiting Koom Valley itself, some large enough to enter the history books as new Battles of Koom Valley and confuse the issue further.

The recent discovery of the truth about the battle (see *Thud!*) should in theory change the symbolism of the valley, which is now the site of a memorial and meeting-place for peacemaking trolls and dwarfs. How well this will sit with the majority of each species remains to be seen.

The Bad Troll Look

Trolls mostly look like, well, trolls – especially as not many of them wear much clothing. However, a troll who wants to look serious in front of other trolls can always turn to tradition.

Old-fashioned mountain trolls sometimes have lichen growing on them, and with a bit of effort, this can be cultivated, even in the city. Rural troll clans paint traditional graffiti on themselves, and some city trolls imitate this; real hard cases even *carve* designs into their skin. "Wild" trolls also wear belts adorned with human or dwarf skulls, but this really isn't acceptable in human communities, so after a few experiments with monkey skulls (which got the wearers scragged by dwarfs who didn't stop to check fine details), troll would-be gangsters have settled on sheep and goat skulls. They also favour the biggest clubs they can acquire.

Which is all painfully symptomatic. The fact is, *really* tough trolls don't need any of that nonsense. It's all just fashion – if fashion with an aggressive edge.

Trolls mostly dress in a few rags, if at all. If a troll does decide to purchase clothes or armour, see *Gear for Trolls and Other Stony Types* (p. 161) for some important notes.

METAMORPHORICAL NAMING

It's said that trolls are made out of "metamorphorical" rock, which relates to their system of naming. Trolls are usually named after types of rock or geological features; females favour gemstone names. What's odd is that a troll often ends up with an appearance and a physiology suggested by its name, and cause and effect are unclear. A troll named "Granite" is likely to be much more robust than one called "Shale," but no one is sure whether trolls grow into their names, those names change through a troll's life to fit its proven nature, or troll parents are extraordinarily prescient when naming their offspring.

There's definitely an element of social class involved, though. Trolls with low Status are sometimes referred to as "sedimentary" by other trolls, are likely to be named for softer (sedimentary)

rocks, and may be weaker by troll standards. Of course, there may well be a genetic component there.

SOCIETY AND LEADERSHIP

In general, trolls don't organise much. They traditionally live in small, low-tech tribes, where "authority" means "who can be seen to have the biggest club." This can lead to difficulties for trolls in more civilised areas, where politics has advanced to who can establish the reputation of having the biggest rock, or is willing to provide employment to the largest number of subordinate rock-wielders.[1] Trolls in Ankh-Morpork occasionally have to be reassured that the Patrician really does have a rock – sometimes, in the classic manner, by being told that the rock is right there, but only the cleverest and most worthy can see it.

Humans assume that trolls are too stupid to understand anything more complicated, but it's fairer to say that they just prefer things that way. Even trolls in human cities don't borrow human-style rules.

What few humans (or dwarfs) know is that, just sometimes, trolls *do* acquire a higher authority. Occasionally, over the centuries, the peculiarities of metamorphology bring about the birth of a *diamond* troll. This unique troll has a body structure that isn't only diamond-hard, but also enables him to control energy flowing through it. A lesser consequence is that the diamond troll can emit dazzling quantities of light. What's far more important is that he can control the temperature of his own brain, making him highly intelligent. Other trolls don't just respect the diamond troll's wisdom and strength – they seem to defer to him instinctively. A diamond troll is *destined* to be the king of all trolls.

The Disc's trolls currently have a Diamond King, Mr. Shine.

Creatures of the Night

In casual Discworld usage, the term "undead" often encompasses werewolves and all manner of darkness-loving creatures, including bogeymen (pp. 361-362) and similar spirits. There are even a few entirely nonmagical species, such as "natural" banshees (p. 101), which are hard to distinguish from undead when they're bearing down on you with claws out. Not all such beings are particularly evil or vicious; indeed, some are quite likeable when you get to know them. However, most of them do need red meat in their diet, and many have difficulty refraining from staring at people's throats. At the bottom end of the scale are a fair number of more-or-less mindless zombies, who are short of personal motivation – and personal attractiveness.

In some situations, creatures of this sort operate on the fringes of society – or even as a relatively respectable minority group, as in Ankh-Morpork. In other cases, especially in Uberwald (p. 240), they form substantial communities of their own, or rule over humans. However, there are still places where they're hated and hunted; perhaps they're forced to live up to their monstrous reputations to survive, or maybe they simply don't know any better. They do tend to have problems with predator instincts at the best of times.

Vampires are discussed at length on pp. 109-114, as the game treatment of them there has to cover many of their peculiar features.

---

1. *"Landslide victory" is one of the few human political concepts that translates directly to trollish.*

Mr. Shine

Until recently, the current Diamond King of the trolls, Mr. Shine, kept a low profile, living incognito in Ankh-Morpork and going around heavily wrapped up to avoid attention while learning about the world. However, with or without his consent, word of his existence spread in the troll community; numerous walls in the city have been engraved with the graffiti "MR. SHINE, HIM DIAMOND." At the same time, he has become involved in attempts to reduce the conflict between trolls and dwarfs.

In the past, Diamond Kings have organised other trolls to defend and assert themselves, which in practise meant conflict with the dwarfs. Each Diamond King in recent centuries has ended up leading his side in yet another Battle of Koom Valley (p. 229). However, Mr. Shine doesn't want a repeat of that old story and has been working on the problem, even meeting personally with the Low King (p. 349). See *Thud!* for the full story.

Mr. Shine is the equivalent of a formidable troll for his size (ST 22) and hard as only diamond can be (DR 15). He keeps his brain running at IQ 15 *at least*, and may be able to cool it further if necessary. He possesses an array of IQ-based skills (pretty much anything he needs), has deep knowledge of dwarf *and* troll culture, and is a leading teacher of the game of Thud (p. 401); his school takes dwarf, troll, and human students. If Mr. Shine needs to distract or delay people, he can show enough of himself – his face or a hand will suffice – to release a burst of dazzling light. Anyone looking in his direction must make a HT roll once per second, at a basic -5 but with +1 per yard of distance from him, or be blinded for a number of seconds equal to their margin of failure.

As they're varied supernatural beings, shaped by local superstitions, it's unwise to generalise too much. In most cases, though, they're physically strong, don't age or show reflections in mirrors, have a healthy range of vulnerabilities and aversions, are nonetheless ridiculously difficult to dispose of permanently, and can either fly or transform into animals of various kinds, typically bats.[1]

One thing that makes them more acceptable in society is that, although they need blood, it doesn't usually have to be *human* blood, or especially fresh. Many a vampire lives a blameless life on blood puddings and very rare steak. Thus, some find jobs where longevity and a slightly detached view of humanity are positive assets, such as family law. On the other hand, there *is* something about vampirism that can lead to a predatory view of people. It's not that Discworld vampires are particularly angst-prone; it's simply that, after a few centuries of watching humans grow old and never taking summer holidays, they're prone to see themselves as other than human, and probably *better.*

Still, because vampires *can* – for all their strengths – be killed or at least massively inconvenienced, and most humans know how, smart vampires avoid provoking *too much* hostility among their neighbours. Even if they continue to prey on humanity, they rarely kill, and they try to give the humans a sporting chance. A really clever vampire strategy is to make it so easy for people to kill them temporarily that no one ever bothers to kill them permanently. They live in big old castles with easily torn curtains over the windows and furnishings that hunters have no difficulty adapting into wooden stakes or holy symbols – but they also employ servants who can be trusted to arrange something with their dust and a drop of blood after a few years.

This strategy only works in some places, though, and is beginning to look dangerously old-fashioned, which is why the Black Ribboner movement (pp. 113-114) has come into being. Members are mostly *very* peaceable (and nervous), but there are rumours that in some places, including Ankh-Morpork, some members of the League of Temperance work together to *deal with* any vampires who get out of line. It seems that there's no more formidable vampire-hunter than another vampire.[2]

Werewolves are another extremely varied class of being, discussed in connection with game options on pp. 114-116. While they have fewer bizarre peculiarities than vampires, they're almost as varied, ranging from humans with a monthly hair-growth problem and a few anger-management issues to formidable shapeshifting monsters. Werewolf families sometimes even produce *yennorks:* deficient werewolves which cannot change, being stuck in one form. Yennorks are despised by other werewolves and wolves (who can identify them by smell), and by any humans who know what they are.

Their one near-universal trait is an *ambiguous* view of life. In wolf form, they see the world through the eyes of a pack carnivore – not especially vicious or cruel, but short on moral complexity, and full of strong scents and instincts. But they also remember the human viewpoint, even if they shed a little intellect when they grow fur, and when they regain human form, they cannot help but remember the wolf world-view. In some cases, this makes them perpetually a little confused, morally and socially.

---

1. Many also have the quirk "Wears evening dress at all times."

2. Okay, "ethical vampires who hunt unethical vampires" is a blatant roleplaying campaign hook.

Others resolve the problem by becoming *intelligently* predatory and dangerous, seeing themselves as wolves among humanity.

More prosaically, living in human society sometimes gives their wolf form the sorts of opportunities that make foxes in hen-houses so unpopular. Perhaps the worst cases are werewolf families who've acquired the status of aristocracy; they're apt to expound a might-makes-right philosophy, and then demonstrate with their teeth. Because they *do* become dominated by animal instincts from time to time, werewolves have problems living in towns and cities, but some manage. Captain Angua (pp. 322-324) is a shining example, although it has taken her a lot of willpower, if only to overcome the habit of moving on when her monthly changes become too much of an issue.

Minor Races

Being a fantasy world, the Disc is infested with all manner of sapient races. Many of these may actually be close cousins to humanity – after all, in prosaic genetic terms, even dwarfs might just be a branch on the human family tree – but humans can be funny about people with pointy ears or strange-coloured hair, and insist that these things aren't any part of the in-group. In a few cases, such as the furtive gnomes and rare lizard men, a "natural" sapient race may have evolved independently of the primate clan (if evolution as such works on the Disc). In others, sufficient belief among humans might have shaped a whole species out of the ether.

It's sometimes said that some of these races, although known of old, have been rendered more-or-less extinct by competition from men, dwarfs, and trolls. However, the growth of a certain shaky tolerance among humankind for any race that will mind its manners and let itself be overcharged in shops means that several of them have emerged from the mountains and forests in recent years.

When members of a species suffer from the urge to seek their fortunes or get away from their parents, they may decide to head for human towns – usually Ankh-Morpork, because that's the place that everyone has heard of. By now, the sight of an unfamiliar-shaped being wandering up to that city's gates is treated more with casual curiosity and offers of overpriced guidebooks than with overt hostility. It has even become something of a *recognised* cliché that the first such arrivals from each species will end up joining the Watch, where personal shape is treated as less important than mutual loyalty, thus ensuring that

the Watch will have someone on hand to advise on how to deal with later arrivals.

SAPIENT ANIMALS

Discworld humans don't as a rule believe that anything with four legs or wings is likely to be intelligent[1], but that doesn't prove anything. Some remarkably smart animals have appeared in the chronicles; see pp. 106-107 for game ideas. Their chief problem is that people rarely *believe* in them – even when Gaspode the Wonder Dog is telling them to give him a biscuit.

Geography

The Disc is a geographically varied world, although most of the chronicles have focussed on one particular area.

The Sto Plains Region

The people of the Sto Plains consider themselves to be the most sophisticated on the Disc, because they've been civilised longest (except perhaps for the Agateans and the people of Djelibeybi, who are weird foreigners and therefore don't count), are the best-travelled (except for certain Hubland barbarians, who can't count), have the most advanced technology (except sometimes for the Klatchians, who invented the zero and who therefore must cheat when counting), and are the broadest-minded (except when dealing with foreigners, barbarians, and people who quibble).

The Plains are rich, in an agricultural sense, and well-populated. The climate is temperate, mostly ranging from Chilly to Warm (see *Temperature Extremes*, p. 191), although on many nights and some bad days in winter it drops to Freezing, while sometimes in summer it turns Hot or even Very Hot (and nobody does much work). The black soil has been deposited over aeons by the flooding of the River Ankh, and is highly fertile.[2] It grows good cabbages.

The Plains are a patchwork of pocket kingdoms and city-states. Since the land is all good, and there are few major mountains or watercourses, the boundaries of these nations are purely conceptual; they shift every time someone thinks his army is better than someone else's, or signs a royal marriage contract, or slips up at one of the Royal Geographical Societies (which generally consist of one retired cavalry officer who used to know how to read maps). The region is economically dominated by Ankh-Morpork, its largest city (see Chapter 7), but Ankh-Morpork doesn't bother to claim much authority beyond its city limits.

Natives of the Plains have few obvious common attributes in game-mechanical terms, although anyone brought up near the Ankh may have inherited Resistant to Disease. People *susceptible* to disease died out years ago.

AROUND ANKH-MORPORK

Ankh-Morpork sprawls enough that it doesn't have close neighbours so much as suburbs, and it controls the mouth of the River Ankh, making it the primary port for the plains. While it's actually a little way inland, the river is large enough and the relevant vessels are small enough that ships can reach it. A range of what locals like to call mountains – though they would barely rate as hills to most people – runs down to the coast. A few small towns and fishing villages lie along the shores, but mostly, the Circle Sea laps against lonely sandy beaches in these parts.

STO LAT AND STO HELIT

Some people consider the walled city of Sto Lat, 20 miles hubwards of Ankh-Morpork, a dull place. However, its current queen, Kelirehenna (see *Queen Keli*, p. 349), may have a Destiny to start a long-term process of political unification in the region. Fortunately, she's probably the sort to do so by talking.

The adjacent Duchy of Sto Helit is politically subordinate. Its current duchess, Susan (pp. 347-348), lives elsewhere, leaving the running of the place to the city burghers. But she *is* Death's grand-daughter, so what she says goes – eventually.

Sto Lat and Sto Helit are close enough to Ankh-Morpork that they inevitably come under its influence much of the time. In the days when it actually ran an empire, they would have been tributary towns. Today, however, they're proud of their independence, if politely so, and despite the fact that they make much of their income from travellers pausing one last time before reaching the great city.

> *Sto Lat wasn't a big city. Moist had once spent a happy week there, passing a few dud bills . . .*
>
> *– Going Postal*

QUIRM

A town in a wine-growing area overlooking the ocean, with flowers adorning its cobbled streets and a floral clock, Quirm is not merely dull, but is devoted to dullness. Many of the inhabitants *used* to have adventures, and they have consciously given that up. People go there to die, on the basis that after a few years in Quirm, death won't offer many surprises.

Still-active adventurers will on arrival be offered a glass of local wine, a garland of flowers, and a table outdoors. If they don't get the hint, they will be told the equivalent of, "Been there. Done that. Do it somewhere else."

---

1. *Unless it also packs a sheaf of lightning bolts and leers at passing maidens.*

2. *After all, every ounce of it has at some stage been what is politely termed "fertiliser."*

Quirm is mostly famous for making cheese. However, it does feature such notable, if genteel, establishments as the Quirm College for Young Ladies – the principal private school for wealthy females (of all species) in the region, and probably the only good one. (The College works on the principle that if it's going to offer these girls an education, it might as well do so properly.) Hence, many upper-class females spent part of their youth in Quirm, and may be expected to speak at least a little Quirmian (p. 16), which is after all useful when ordering in restaurants.

PSEUDOPOLIS

Pseudopolis, also known as Psephopololis (Discworlders aren't always strong on spelling, or for that matter pronunciation), lies on the turnwise edge of the Sto Plains, where the Carrack Mountains descend to the Rim Ocean. This places it on the route through to the expanses of the Octarine Grass Country. It's considered to be a major city, possibly the nearest thing the region has to a rival to Ankh-Morpork. Quite a few people in the latter city were born or spent time there, including Nobby Nobbs (p. 327), who served – if that's the word – in its army (which suffered a lot of equipment shortages at that time). Pseudopolis remains a place to which a citizen of Ankh-Morpork might think of running were he looking for somewhere nice and distant, but not impossibly foreign.

It's also currently going through something of a dynamic, exciting phase of its own. Its mercantile class has declared it a democracy, and it now has its own newspaper, the *Pseudopolis Herald*, and its own school of magic, Brazeneck College (p. 280). The presence of a new, ambitious magical university may, however, prove to be bad for the city's physical integrity.

FURTHER TO TURNWISE

The lands turnwise of the Sto Plains are similarly temperate and agricultural, but somewhat wilder, with rolling hills rising to actual mountains. This is a more *chancy*, less settled area. The coastal plains are known as the Octarine Grass Country, a sign of their pastoral and magical natures.

The Wyrmberg

The Wyrmberg is at the centre of an area of unstable magic several miles across, and it is therefore a strange and dangerous place. (It may actually be weird and magical enough that, in more prosaic times, it's fading out of reality and into the realm of myth.) Anyone who comes close before they notice the local breakdown of conventional physics will get a large hint: The Wyrmberg is an upside-down mountain, about 20 yards across at the base and widening as it goes up until, a quarter-mile above the green plain, it tops out in a quarter-mile-wide plateau. The plateau has a little forest, some buildings, a lake, and a river that spills over the edge to rain on the plain. Just below this, the mountain is circled by caves, which look suspiciously regular, as if they've been crudely carved.

The problem with getting close is that the Wyrmberg is inhabited, and the inhabitants aren't very polite. The rampant magical field has enabled the development of an exceptionally *heroic fantasy* sort of society – a culture that can get by without obvious forms of economic support and, for that matter, female warriors who manage without normally necessary support, too. This is bulging-muscles-and-minimal-coverage-chain-mail country. It's also *dragon* country.

The magical aura of the area means that a properly trained, or romantically credulous, mind can *create* dragons here, through

The Forest of Skund

The Forest of Skund is a dense woodland between the Sto Plains and the foothills of the Ramtops. Its name means "Your Finger You Fool" in an ancient dialect; an early explorer pointed at it and asked a native what That was called. It's a magic-rich region, with a lot of small-to-medium-sized areas of residual magic or otherwise high thaumic energy (see *Magic*, pp. 270-271).

Casanunda the Dwarf (pp. 344-345) claims to have received the title of Count from the Queen of Skund. However, the wood's only inhabitants seem to be a handful of supernatural beings and evil witches, just enough woodcutters and small villages for them to terrorise, and a community of shamanic priests who appreciate the local magic-mutated fungi. Either Casanunda made the acquaintance of a witch with a heavy power complex, or he's living up to his claim to be an outrageous liar.

"Over Skund way" is an expression often used in the Ramtops around Lancre, especially among witches, to indicate a distant but not completely unknown area where moderately exotic things happen. The words may sometimes be used literally, but mostly it's just a figure of speech.

sheer force of imagination. The dragons thus summoned are of a "noble" sort (see pp. 360-361), but relatively small and manageable by those standards (that is, they're merely irascible, vain, and snappish). The dragon warriors of Wyrmberg ride them to "war" – although because the dragons cannot exist beyond the area's magical field, such "wars" are basically just banditry. Still, it's hard to fight a dragon-rider, though the riders' tendency to wear no armour beyond some leather thongs and a scrap of mail may help, as might the fact that rendering a dragon-rider unconscious or dead causes his dragon to disappear instantly.

It's up to the GM to assess visiting PCs' chances of creating a useful dragon for themselves. In general, the less practical and sensible they are, the better. The actual feat could involve an IQ roll, *reduced* by the difference if the visitor's Will exceeds his IQ, and with a bonus if he suffers from Gullibility. Before dreamers become too pleased with themselves, however, do remind them that the locals have much more experience of the art.

The Wyrmberg rock is shot through with corridors and rooms. In its very centre is a large cavern, the roost of the dragons. Thousands of iron rings have been spiked into the roof. Dragon-riders wearing hook boots use these to walk across the ceiling.[1]

The Wyrmberg is a monarchy. The most recent known ruler was Liessa Wyrmbidder, who murdered her father, the wizard Greicha the First[2], and then had to get around the place's sexist inheritance laws through a scheme that involved forming a liaison with the barbarian hero Hrun. He presumably reigned in collaboration with her for a while, and then wandered off, in the way of barbarian heroes.

---

1. *Yes, upside down. It takes practise.*

2. *Although he refused to actually die for some time.*

Few inhabitants of the Wyrmberg leave for other parts of the Disc, but any who did could be competent warriors or wizards in a posturing sort of way – although the lower general magical field might cause them inconvenience. Overconfidence would be an appropriate disadvantage.

LLAMEDOS

Llamedos is a small country in the mountains hubward of the Octarine Grass Country, inhabited by a dour people with inclinations to Strict Druidism, sombre choral music, and their own stern form of football. It rains constantly[1] – water is the country's principal export, along with stone-circle engineers. Temperatures are often Chilly (see *Temperature Extremes,* p. 191). The only plant that grows reliably is holly; everything else just rots.

In earlier times, the Llamedese were a warlike folk, masters of the human-wave choral assault. Today they're rather more inclined to keep to themselves, having decided that most of the rest of the Disc is too filled with Sinful Temptations.[2] Regardless, Llamedese druid-technicians may be found almost everywhere on the Disc, tuning and maintaining megalithic structures.

There are also a fair number of dwarf clans in mines under the region's mountains. The current Low King of the dwarfs (p. 349) is from a small mine in Llamedos. It wouldn't be unreasonable to expect a few more dwarfs with the lilting Llamedese accent to show up around the Disc, too.

Llamedese PCs might be druids who seek to bring the benefits of religion and decent computing methodologies to the rest of the Disc, mildly rebellious "black sheep" who are prepared to face the risk of Sinful Temptation, or dwarfs of a somewhat political bent. Musical Ability is genuinely common in Llamedos; it's the uses to which it's put that cause problems.

Across the Circle Sea

Rimward of the Circle Sea lies the continent of Klatch. This name is strictly speaking that of an ancient empire, now reduced to a (still substantial) region dominated by the city of Al Khali (below), but the people of Ankh-Morpork never bothered to distinguish

much between empire and region – indeed, they use "Klatchian" as a near-generic term for "foreigner." Klatch is a continent of burning deserts, impenetrable jungles, and all sorts of old-fashioned adventuring opportunities. Temperatures even on the hubward coast are typically Hot or Very Hot (see *Temperature Extremes,* p. 191) by day, but may plunge to Chilly or below in the desert night.

Klatchian humans have dark skin; some are nearly blue-black. Their cuisine involves curries, boiled fish, rice, and sauces containing numerologically significant varieties of ingredients, and it is often ferociously spiced. It's exotic by Sto Plains standards and has become popular in Ankh-Morpork. The coffee is quite remarkable, too.

Klatch is currently going through a certain amount of turmoil as new rulers try to drag it (kicking and screaming, naturally) into the Century of the Anchovy. Outlying tribes whose loyalty was never that strong are threatening to break away. Closer communities are looking at Ankh-Morpork and wondering why it seems to have more fun. All in all, it may well be a land of opportunity for an adventurer with a fast camel and a suitcase full of Ankh-Morpork dollars.

AL KHALI

Al Khali is technically just the capital city of the *nation* of Klatch, but the thing with desert empires is that they consist of a few important cities and a lot of sand, the latter only counting as part of the empire because trade must travel across it and the empire needs an excuse to deal with any desert tribes who try to impose 100% toll rates.

Al Khali is an ancient, sophisticated city[3], ruled by a *Seriph*. Naturally, the real power in the land is sometimes held by a Grand Vizier with a short beard, excellent manners, and a psychopathic temperament.[4] The city is dominated by a great palace, the *Rhoxie*, and a giant garden, or *paradise;* Seriphs traditionally spend their money, not wisely, but very well. The rest of the city is a maze of bazaars and white-walled houses, where the trade of the Circle Sea meets the caravans of the desert. There, everybody spends hours bargaining while hawk-eyed desert nomads work on their reputation for imperturbability.

Jingo described a recent brief, abortive war between Ankh-Morpork and Klatch, occasioned by the (temporary) emergence of the lost city of Leshp from the depths of the Circle Sea. The war's chief consequence was a little more political instability in both countries, especially Klatch.

Player characters from Al Khali could be merchants, desert nomads, wizards of a foreign and melodramatic kind, or bazaar rogues with a lot of luck and nerve. Anyone without a reasonable level in Merchant skill is in danger of being Poor.

AL-YBI

A desert city – some way across a mountain range from Al Khali, and hence usually able to maintain its independence – Al-Ybi has its own Seriph. It's said to be the place where the concept of zero was invented. For complicated reasons, many of its inhabitants are short (a sign of dwarfish blood) and ill-tempered.

---

1. *Except when it drizzles. Or snows.*

2. *That is, people who don't believe in Strict Druidism.*

3. *The temple frescos are X-rated.*

4. *Something must happen at the interview.*

DJELIBEYBI

A country two miles wide and 150 miles long, Djelibeybi basically consists of the fertile floodplain of the river Djel; its name means "Child of the Djel." (During the flood season, the nation is almost entirely under water.) Djelibeybi grows melons and garlic – and, formerly, pyramids. The pyramids nearly squeezed out the edible crops, and since they were the only real industry, the nation was permanently bankrupt. Politically, it could survive only by playing off its more powerful neighbours, Tsort and Ephebe.

It wasn't always so. Djelibeybi is 7,000 years old, and it was once a mighty kingdom, for which it seemed time itself stood still.

In fact, it did. Pyramids slow and even store time rather as capacitors store electrical charge. The necropolis of the Old Kingdom contained thousands of pyramids; it was the second-largest city on the Disc, after Ankh-Morpork. The pyramids charged up with new time every morning, and every night bled it off as a blue flare from their peaks. The Kingdom was using the same day, over and over again. People were born, grew old, and died, but somehow nothing *happened*.

However, since the events of *Pyramids*, change has arrived. Progress has become possible, and the first order of business is to get some decent plumbing installed.

Djelibeybi is ruled by a deified Pharaoh – or rather, these days, by Queen Ptraci I, who is as determined as her subjects to get things moving again. Any PCs who have dealings with her may take her for an airhead. That is, until they discover her amazing ability to brush aside anything that might cause her inconvenience.

It's still mostly underwater in the flood season, though.[1]

Djelibeybi-born PCs could be young peasants or artisans responding to the spirit of the age by looking to travel, or pyramid engineers seeking new employment. On the other hand, a Phobia about pyramids (with a base value of -5 points) would be perfectly understandable.

EPHEBE

A sunlit, relaxed city-state which grows olives and grapes, and makes good use of the local fishing, Ephebe is a small country (population 50,000) with *major* cultural and intellectual traditions.

Ephebians seem addicted to paradox and dispute. The city produces most of the Disc's serious philosophers[2], and the philosophers spend much of their time arguing. Their tendency to turn metaphors into practical experiments leads to much running around and shooting of arrows. The city's defensive strength may seem implausible, but part of the explanation is that a small but significant proportion of the philosophers' ideas turn into something practical, usually in the way of engineering. An assault on Ephebe is prone to run into tower-mounted parabolic mirrors focussing solar rays to burn the attackers, ships with bizarrely shaped hulls that cut through water like marlin, or mathematically designed tactical systems that sound like gibberish but *win*.

Through a (paradoxical) linguistic accident, the ruler of Ephebe is called the Tyrant and is democratically elected for a five-year term. (Admittedly, the electorate excludes anyone who happens to be female, poor, a slave, foreign, mad, or, supposedly, frivolous.) The Tyrant lives in a citadel-palace at the highest point in the city and must want the job enough to put up with the Ephebian contempt for politicians.

Ephebe is one of the few advanced parts of the Disc which officially retains slavery. However, there are many rules surrounding this. Slaves must be given three meals a day, one day off a week, and two weeks being-allowed-to-run-away per year. They cannot be overworked or beaten without permission. After 20 years, they're entitled to their freedom, but most refuse it, knowing that they're better off than their owners. Ephebian slaves fight furiously[3] against political reformers or foreign invaders who threaten to free them.

Ephebian PCs could have almost any abilities. Philosophical or engineering skills are especially easy to justify. An Odious Personal Habit of "Questions Everything" wouldn't be inappropriate.

Brigadoons

Brigadoons are locations – sometimes complete with buildings and populations – which slip in and out of local existence, either randomly or at long fixed intervals. Generally, no time passes in the brigadoon while it is wherever else it is. Most return to the same place, but a few move through space as well as time. Wandering Shops (p. 278) may use similar mechanisms. Signs of a brigadoon include unusual disappearances (of travellers, livestock, or ships), and, less often, appearances of extinct animals or dazed-looking people in funny clothes who aren't up on current affairs.

Whether random or cyclic, brigadoons have a singular tendency to appear when PCs are in the immediate vicinity. Possible Discworld examples include the Lost City of Ee (p. 237) and the village of Turnover in the Ramtops. The land of Chimeria is also sometimes mentioned, although other evidence says that it's consistently real.

OMNIA

A dry country on the Klatchian coast, population about two million, Omnia is ruled by the Church of the Great God Om – or more accurately, Omnia *is* the Church of Om. Its principal city, Kom, is dominated by the Citadel, a temple complex that extends for miles. The Citadel contains dormitories, kitchens, refectories, gardens, barracks, and towers – and these days, printing presses, churning out tracts and sacred texts day and night. There are few staircases, and those that do exist are all shallow, with small steps, suitable for processions of very old men. Other contents include unknown miles of cellars, subterranean corridors, and forgotten rooms, and the chambers of the Quisition.

The Great Temple of the Citadel is a fine example of just how big a building can get when the architects are constrained only by gravity and compressive strength, not money or reason. Its vast dome bears the Golden Horns of Om. Its doors are 100 feet tall, made of 40 tons each of steel-reinforced bronze, and bear the 512 Commandments of Om in golden letters on lead. The Great Temple faces the Place of Lamentations, an open plaza 200 yards across where worshippers gather.

---

1. We haven't seen how Ptraci might deal with six feet of water, but don't bet against her.

2. And probably most of the frivolous ones, too – it's hard to tell.

3. And paradoxically.

Until the events of *Small Gods,* the Church's predominant arm was the Quisition, which dealt with rooting out heresy. It was a suspicious body, which meant that there was clearly a lot of heresy.[1] The army of Omnia was known as the Divine Legion. While sometimes called upon to defend Omnia (often at some distance beyond the border), its principal task was to stamp out heresy within Omnia. Its troops wore "fishmail" (metal scales – medium armour) and, on special occasions, black-and-yellow cloaks.

The Quisition nearly eliminated competent blacksmith-work in the country (smithing being a craft of many small rituals, all of which were naturally considered heretical). Members of the Divine Legion had decent equipment, though, either made long ago or captured from another nation. Since Brutha's rise to power, this situation has changed somewhat, but the best metalwork still has to be imported. Traditions take a long time to restore.

The Church of Om did significantly alter its methods after Brutha became Cenobiarch. However, it remained a theocracy and – in the fashion of governments that have sustained major changes without slaughtering the old hierarchy – preserved many of the forms. Nor did the worship of Om lose much popularity; sheer habit aside, the god had manifested himself in front of whole armies and proved his power, after all.

Also recall that Brutha's tenure as Cenobiarch covered *100 years* of gradual changes. At one time, high-minded adventurers who forgot that the Great God Om, despite some reversals of fortune, is a working god – or worse, who attempted to undermine the Omnian theocracy – were likely to meet an interesting end involving hot metal and pulleys.[2] Today such people will merely find that they're going up against millennia-old habits of thought. In fact, once Omnians lost their reputation for holy wars, they became known and feared over a far wider area; they took to visiting unbelievers with leaflets and lengthy arguments.

Thus, Omnians are always liable to exhibit Fanaticism, possibly with additional Odious Personal Habits or Reputations ranging from "Forever Preaching" to "Spreads Faith by Force," and sometimes still Intolerance. The Divine Legion produced reasonably competent fighters, as they were full-time troops who trained fanatically – albeit with the assumption that Om would guarantee victory, and with more time spent harassing peasants than fighting massed battles. The later missionaries include some who actually preach fairly well (good Public Speaking), many with high levels in Theology (Omnian).

Tsort

Tsort lies along the coast and the Tsort River. While approximately as ancient as Ephebe, it gives the impression of being less self-confident than most nations of the Circle Sea, having a culture that borrows much from its neighbours. The trouble is that the Tsorteans compensate for any inferiority complex in the traditional way: by taking it out on others.

One key moment in Tsort's ancient history was when it was burned to the ground by Ephebian armies following a long war over the legendary Elenor of Tsort. The Tsorteans have yet to forgive and forget – and the Ephebians haven't tried very hard to make up. It's possible that the city is one of those that has been burned down on a periodic basis over the centuries, leading to many different, borrowed, styles of architecture. At one time, the Tsorteans appropriated the idea of pyramids from Djelibeybi and built the single most spectacular (enduring) such structure on the Disc.

The Great Pyramid of Tsort required 60 years and the lives of 10,000 slaves to construct. It contains 1,003,010 limestone blocks, and its height plus its length divided by half its width equals exactly 1.67563. (There are a great many arcane numbers associated with the Great Pyramid, most of them as fascinating and significant as any twelve random digits.) It's honeycombed with secret passages, which are reputed to contain the complete wisdom of the Tsorteans. There are also booby-traps, and probably the standard issue of pyramid guardians, wrapped and unwrapped. In other words, if players insist on a tomb-robbing or mystical-investigation adventure, it can provide them with hours of fun.

Tsortean gods are many, varied, and often borrowed; some seem to be constructed of random parts left over from the creation of other deities. Tsortean PCs could be the varied products of a dynamic imperial power, perhaps tending to minor Odious Personal Habits such as bragging.

D'regs

The deserts of Klatch are home to nomadic tribes of *D'regs,* a robust people with a straightforward view of life. Suffice it to say that, in their language, the words for "foreigner" and "traveller" are effectively interchangeable with the word for "target," and the word for "freedom" is the same as the word for "fighting." D'regs *love* fighting. Their tribal chiefs have only one meaningful task – shouting "Charge!" (preferably at dawn) – and keep their jobs only so long as they do that properly.[1] D'regs rarely take prisoners in serious fights, although they can if the situation demands it.

D'regs are notorious oath-breakers who don't trust their own mothers (their mothers would be ashamed of them if they did), but their *word* is absolutely sacred to them. They hold hospitality to be sacrosanct, too; once accepted into a D'reg's tent, even his worst enemy will be treated with honour for exactly three days. They're also clever enough *not* to kill merchants who cross their territory, or even to take everything the merchants own. Rather, they make sure that merchants can make enough profit to keep coming back – most of the time, at least.

A typical D'reg might have ST 11, DX 11, IQ 10, and HT 11, with Area Knowledge (home lands)-13, Brawling-11, Broadsword-12, Riding-12, Shield-12, Spear-12, Stealth-11, and Survival (Desert)-14.

---

1. However, their tribes also have recognised "wise men" who offer advice on those rare situations not covered by "Charge!"

---

1. Om wouldn't make the faithful suspicious without good cause, after all.

2. Further, there's known to be an alternate history in which Brutha dies without becoming the Prophet, and a century of incessant warfare follows. You wouldn't want to be responsible for that, would you?

THE BURNING RIM

Once one travels into Klatch away from the Circle Sea, one is in pulp adventure territory. Diamond mines, lost cities, Amazonian kingdoms just waiting for Mr. Right, poison-dart-frog breeders, and probably the odd mad scientist with a beautiful unworldly daughter and an urbane robot (well, golem) butler. Oh, and dinosaurs – don't forget the dinosaurs. This is country with the same appeal for adventurers that a cardboard box lined with glue has for household pests. What it is *not* is comfortable.

Howondaland is the quintessentially "dark" and "mysterious" part of Klatch, where mapmakers know better than to tread. *Hersheba* is a small desert kingdom on the edge of this area, said to be ruled by an immortal queen.[1]

People from such areas tend to have Low TL (p. 31), but that isn't the same as stupidity. (After all, Howondaland produced M'Bu, the finest organisational brain on the Disc.) However, some tribes are prone to hobbies such as Bloodlust.

The Great Nef

The Great Nef is a vast desert toward the rimward edge of Klatch. It's so dry that it has *negative* rainfall; temperatures are typically Very Hot (see *Temperature Extremes*, p. 191) at *minimum*. The Lost[2] City of Ee, location of the first pizza ever created on the Disc, is said to lie in the Great Nef. At least, it started there – Ee is a random brigadoon (p. 235) and has been known to appear in more than one location.

In the centre of the Great Nef, under the effects of high temperatures and octarine light, water can enter a state of *dehydration*, becoming like silvery, ultra-fine sand. Well-designed ships can sail through this "dehydrated water," people can sink in it, and it harbours extraordinarily strange fish. It can be rehydrated by adding water. It obviously has interesting magical-alchemical qualities.

> ## On any reasonable map of the area there's barely room for the trees.
> ### – Eric

THE JUNGLE EMPIRES

Widdershins of the Great Nef is a large area of rainforest. In other words, along with the heat (Hot or Very Hot *all the time;* see *Temperature Extremes*, p. 191) and the insects, the inhabitants must tolerate intolerable amounts of precipitation. This is major lost-city territory – at least, it has plenty of cities that would be better lost. Think step pyramids, and tribes who will try any political structure, god, or system of marriage that seems daft enough.

Consider the Tezumen, for example. They're gloomy, irritable, and perverse; they invented the wheel, but use it solely as headgear and jewellery (the axles of their llama-drawn chariots are supported by two people a side). Their music is as painful as their religion. Their pictographic writing is chiselled laboriously onto granite blocks. While their craftsmanship in obsidian, jade, and feathers is impressive, and their garden-style agriculture is efficient, none of this gives them any pleasure.

Partly, this is the fault of the demon Quezovercoatl (see *Demons as Gods*, p. 304), who set himself up as their god and commanded them to bloody conquest and human sacrifice. However, it should be said that his followers were naturals for the role. They also invented hot chocolate, just the thing to settle down with after a long, hard day sacrificing 50,000 people. Following the events of *Eric*, the Tezumen have ceased worshipping Quezovercoatl, and now revere an image of Rincewind's Luggage.[3]

Over the Rim

There are lands beyond the Disc's rim. It was reported by the crew of the *Kite*, Ankh-Morpork's one-off spacecraft, that mountain-sized rocks project through the Rimfall (see *Hub and Rimfall*, p. 16), and that these have evidently caught some things that went over the edge in the past – not just vegetation (there are whole forests there), but also the crews of lost ships. The observers glimpsed houses and villages. Visiting such an outcrop, let alone getting back afterward, would be a truly heroic project.

Toward the Ramtops

The Ramtops are a spectacular mountain chain that runs all the way down from the Hub to near the edge of the Disc's main landmass. However, the term as commonly used refers specifically to the high mountain country hubward of the Sto Plains – an area of duchies and kingdoms that can't grow beyond pocket size because invading the neighbours would require crampons and oxygen. There are also countless dwarf-holds[4], and a lot of goats. The landscape features great expanses of vertical wasteland, mountain lakes, dense forests, and deep valleys. Temperatures are usually Moderate or Chilly, but can plunge to Extreme Cold in winter blizzards; see *Temperature Extremes* (p. 191). Ramtops sheep produce wool that can be knitted into garments of body-armour quality.[5]

A standing wave of pure magical energy lies across the entire Disc. The Ramtops cut through this, acting as a kind of induction coil – raw magic crackles from the peaks and is grounded in the valleys. This has side-effects. Leaves rustle when there's no wind to move them; so do boulders, if they're in the mood. Many of the Disc's greatest witches and wizards are born here. In game terms, there are patches of unstable residual magic (p. 270), some of them intermittent or strangely aspected (p. 278), and plenty of opportunities to acquire components for unusual spells, at proportionate risk.

---

1. *Adventurers who visit places like this tend to get romantically involved with the less-stable locals and cause major volcanic or tectonic incidents, usually within two hours of the opening credits.*

2. *Or possibly just Forbidden.*

3. *If a congregation takes its nature from its god's personality, this may not be much of an improvement.*

4. *Mines.*

5. *At least, they feel that way.*

Krull

This island kingdom is one of the few landmasses to abut the Rim. Krull has some dealings with the rest of the Disc, but is secretive and self-sufficient. Krullians are notorious as slavers (their slaves often used to have their tongues cut out), although these days they mostly just charge exorbitant salvage fees to anyone who shows up on the Circumfence (below). They're scavengers by habit; other people regard them as pirates.

Their capital city (also called Krull) is sited on the highest point of the island, which slopes upward to the very Rim, affording it a magnificent – if disturbing – view. The Krullians combine a plain, pragmatic attitude to many subjects, including magic, with a driving interest in certain areas of pure research, such as astrozoology. Krull's ruler is called the Arch-Astronomer, and he and most of his senior courtiers are wizards. Krull even permits women to study wizardry. Krullian research projects include lowering "chelonauts" over the Rim in experimental vessels, to observe Great A'Tuin. The arrogant Krullians have been known to strike bargains with Fate himself.

Krullian visitors to the rest of the Disc are rare. Those who *do* appear might well be wizards or scholars, or merely sailors. They're likely to suffer from Social Stigma (Overdressed Foreigner) or the Odious Personal Habit of arrogance. On the other hand, they may adhere to Code of Honour (Academic) or harbour an Obsession with scholarship. Some have night-black skin and hair the silver colour of moonlight – exotic, even by Disc standards.

The Circumfence

Krull controls the Circumfence: a structure of posts, ropes, and nets extending thousands of miles to either side of the island, round almost a third of the Rim. It catches the flotsam of the sea, giving Krull a huge – if random – source of treasure. The Circumfence is (or at least used to be) tended by enslaved sailors called *lengthmen*, who man stations every few miles, and is allegedly patrolled by seven navies. It's the source of the wealth which enabled Krull to transform itself into a society dedicated to pure research. This system has had an effect on Krullian architecture – most of the island's buildings were originally the hulls of wrecks or derelicts, caught by the Circumfence, hauled ashore, and mortared together.

LANCRE

A kingdom on the Sto Plains side of the Ramtops, total population (humans, dwarfs, and trolls) about 500, Lancre is

admittedly small even for a fantasy kingdom; however, Lancrastians have a talent for leaving Lancre and becoming famous elsewhere. For instance, the country has produced more than its share of powerful wizards. The local witches are also powerful, though less inclined to leave. It's currently ruled – allegedly – by the hard-working and nervous King Verence (pp. 336-337) and his wife, Queen Magrat (pp. 337-339), a former witch. Actually, the people of Lancre largely get on with doing things as they see fit, and the most *serious* power in the kingdom lies with the local coven, but Verence does get to handle whatever formal diplomacy impinges on the place.

Lancre's geography isn't conducive to urban sprawl. There are a great number of icy mountain peaks that even dwarfs don't find hospitable, and dark forests where you just know that many pairs of beady eyes are always watching you – worse, little beady eyes not in pairs, or really big beady eyes above even bigger teeth. Add in the exceptional quantity of standing stones, barrows, treacherous mountain pathways with rickety little bridges, and gateways to other dimensions, and one gets the feeling that Lancre was intended to be larger, but became badly wrinkled.

Most human Lancrastians live in Lancre Town. "Town" is an extravagant name for it, but it is the biggest habitation, which gives it some of the privileges of a city, such as City Proclamations. One of these states that all pedlars and performance artists must be outside the city gates by sundown. This is universally observed, but since the town has no walls to go with its gates, such folk just come back in again after sundown. It has a tavern, the Goat and Bush, and an inn (well, a house with beds for hire); both are actually fairly comfortable, *most* of the time.

The Lancre River is a tributary of the Ankh, shallow and very swift. It's all winds and rapids around Lancre Town, but there are quiet pools farther into the mountains. Lancre Bridge crosses the river near the town; the road between curves through forested banks, where travellers may be ambushed without undue inconvenience.

On an outcrop of rock above the town stands Lancre Castle. It's much bigger than the country would seem to require, and definitely larger than its current staff (see *Lancre Castle Staff*, p. 336) is capable of maintaining. Their first task each morning is to determine what has fallen off the building during the night.

The castle is certainly atmospheric, if with a sense that the architect was aiming for more atmosphere than the budget

allowed. The caves beneath add to the effect; they're generally, and sensibly, assumed to have a secret connection to the castle. The official dungeons are sadly short on monsters, treasure, or traps (though there may still be some torture instruments, purchased by the late unlamented Duke Felmet), but once one gets into the natural caves, one could meet pretty much anything.

Apart from Lancre Town, Lancre has villages, including Bad Ass, birthplace of Eskarina Smith, the only female ever (yet) admitted to Unseen University.

The roads around Bad Ass have been paved with wooden boards, and the trees have been cut with notches out to a distance of nearly two miles. These precautions have saved the lives of many travellers lost in the snows. This is a good example of the sort of sideways ingenuity that adventurers may encounter in the Ramtops. Then there are Slippery Hollow, Razorback, and Slice.

Oh yes, Slice – a place people are warned about. It's located in a deep, forested cut in the mountains. Other Lancrastians tend to roll their eyes and make woo-woo noises when speaking of Slice's residents. In addition to private lives that would embarrass a mink, Slice is known for containing the original Rock and a Hard Place, and the Place Where the Sun Does Not Shine.[1]

Lancre and Disc-Wide Politics

King Verence is aware that the Disc in general is going through a *complicated* political phase, and feels he that he ought not to ignore this. A somewhat misjudged response was part of what triggered the events of *Carpe Jugulum*. Lancre survived that incident with no serious long-term consequences other than a number of pictsie immigrants, and it's likely that Verence became more cautious as a result, but he's too dutiful to *ignore* the outside world, and he's known to read any reports he can lay hands on about events abroad.

Should a formal banquet be indicated, Verence does his best to put on a show of royal dignity. In fact, he does remarkably well on special occasions – the population of Lancre Town are happy to take up offers of temporary work, confident in the assumption that they'll be invited to any party they help put on. Magrat spends these times trying to introduce Mrs. Scorbic, the cook, to concepts such as freshness and vitamins.

Adventurers and Lancre

Although it's a setting for several Discworld novels, Lancre is *not* a natural spot for old-fashioned adventure scenarios. In purely human terms, it's a sleepy backwater; the occasional problems it suffers are countered by the formidable local coven (see *The Lancre Coven*, p. 339). That said, it's an interesting place for a visit, and an intrepid and broad-minded Unseen University researcher who wanted specific information on witchcraft might be sent there by other wizards, to ask Granny Weatherwax.[2] Proving that one was both serious and trustworthy could be an interesting roleplaying exercise and might lead indirectly to all sorts of adventures. Dealings with King Verence would feel less stressful, but it would be unwise to treat him as a fool, even if that did used to be his job – and remember that his wife is as magically alert as he is hard-working.

Adventurers (and other characters) who *originate* from Lancre are a standard Discworld "bit." Giving them the surname "Ogg" is fine.

---

1. *A dark orifice beneath a huge overhanging rock. The folk of Slice sometimes fasten a rope around one of their number (it isn't something one would ask a stranger to help with) and lower him in, hoping to find something useful. Objects found there include tools, a great number of musical instruments, and unpopular jobs. The Place is another example of the Discworld's refusal to let metaphors remain immaterial. While PCs might well find it interesting, they'd have to deal with the people of Slice (playing the banjo might help; commenting on atypical physiology is less wise).*

2. *While the other wizards struggle to keep a straight face.*

The Standing Stone

A man-sized stele of bluish rock stands in the moors above Lancre. Although there's only one of it, it cannot be counted. If a visitor looks too curious, it will shuffle around behind him; should a team of would-be enumerators show up, it may go off and hide in the bogs. It is one more discharge point for accumulated magic and might be a mobile high magic zone. Or perhaps it's just shy.

Lancre and Elfland

There are at least two ways to reach Elfland (see *Elves*, pp. 362-365) from Lancre, should anyone be feeling stupid.

The Dancers

The *Dancers* are eight great stones standing in a circle, a few miles up an overgrown path from Lancre Town toward the Ramtops. They're thunderbolt (meteoric) iron and detectably very magnetic. (Magnetism is poorly understood on the Disc, although a few theoretician-wizards are taking an interest.) Their arrangement has no astronomical or occult significance; indeed, the circle isn't particularly regular. Three of the stones have names: the Piper, the Drummer, and the Leaper. These names aren't significant.[1]

It's said that rain falls inside the circle a few seconds after it lands outside – and that when clouds dim the sun, the light within fades a moment later than without. In fact, the location is an intermittent portal between the Disc's universe and Elfland. The stones act as a barrier, keeping the portal closed.

Since the events of *Lords and Ladies*, Lancrastians have a fair idea about all this. Visitors who seem intent on tinkering with the Dancers will be run out of town if they're *lucky*.

The Long Man

This is a group of three burial mounds in the forest: two round mounds at the foot of a long one. Long ago, the local men would gather at the Long Man, build sweat lodges, drink scumble (fermented apple cider with some of the character of apples in autumn and some of dimethylhydrazine just before liftoff), put horns on their heads, and dance. Whether this was an ancient mystic rite or the equivalent of a fraternity party is unknown.

At the foot of the long barrow are three large, irregular stones, marking a cave. Within this is a flat rock carved with the image of a horned man and an Oggham (p. 17) inscription. This has been (politely) translated as "Oo, isn't mine big." Underneath the rock is an entrance to the Lancre Caves, including fairly direct access to another gateway to Elfland – one that leads to the King's Court.

---

1. *Sure they aren't.*

COPPERHEAD MOUNTAIN

Copperhead, on the edge of Lancre, is one of the most imposing peaks in the Ramtops. It is home to a substantial independent dwarf community, and the centre of dwarf society in the region. Many dwarfs around the Disc categorise themselves as being "from" Copperhead (as opposed to, say, Uberwald or Llamedos) by ancestry.

UBERWALD

Scrambling over the ridge of the Ramtops, widdershins from Lancre, one eventually arrives in a land of dark pine forests and jagged mountains, many of them topped with glowering castles whose architecture involves a disproportionate number of turrets and spires. Uberwald doesn't have much in the way of central authority, being ruled by an array of barons and margraves. A remarkable number of those aristocrats are . . . unusual. In fact, in the dark reaches of Uberwald, you may well encounter entire societies where not turning into a wolf at full moon is considered strange.

In other words, as the linguistically quick-witted may guess, Uberwald is the Discworld's equivalent of Transylvania, with a Germanic twist to the language. The architecture is Gothic, and so are the stories that happen there.

Loko

Loko is a deep valley in Far Uberwald, circular and about 20 miles across, with mountains all around it. The whole area has exceptional numbers of centaurs, fauns, and other creatures and phenomena considered exotic even by Discworld standards (there's also said to be a tribe of orcs; see p. 119). Current thinking is that the valley was once the site of an extremely successful magical experiment.

Surprisingly, Loko is *not* a zone of low dimensional integrity, although some such smaller areas may be located within the valley. However, there's quite a lot of old magical energy lying around and, more important, magical forces are strangely *distorted* in the region, in a way that can be very dangerous to magically talented visitors. Some people would say that it was cursed, but wizards consider the idea of curses to be mere backward superstition, except when it's them cursing. An expedition from Unseen University once visited Loko; every member contracted some serious magical malady within months of returning home. However, they also recovered a collection of ancient scrolls from a cave somewhere in the valley, which later helped the High Energy Magic team who split the thaum.

Unseen University researchers might want to know more about Loko. If the place is dangerous to wizards, then it follows that it's safe for non-wizards. This might lead to a team of non-wizardly PCs being commissioned to travel there and look for something. They would be perfectly safe – some of the best wizards on the Disc would be happy to reassure them of this.

Most Uberwaldian characters in the chronicles are surprisingly normal – even the werewolves – but the region *does* promote various flavours of stereotyping. The aristocrats tend to disadvantages like Bloodlust (even if they aren't vampires) and Enemies (other aristocrats). Everyone else may be prone to Paranoia, Intolerance (of undead and/or aristocrats), and Scotophobia.

It's believed that when the Disc was still forming and cooling, there was a fifth elephant which slipped from its place under the world, went into some kind of orbital trajectory, and eventually crashed to its doom. Its remains lie under the plateau of Uberwald, and explain the huge fat deposits found there by dwarf miners. In a world where cities such as Ankh-Morpork need tallow and grease for countless purposes, these have become immensely valuable, making those dwarfs quite rich. However, Uberwald might still have remained relatively easy for politicians to ignore if it hadn't been for an accident of technology and geography.

When the builders of the semaphore system (pp. 222-224) decided to run a chain of towers from Ankh-Morpork to Genua, this meant that they cut through Uberwald. At the same time, the great dwarf community at Schmaltzberg, near the Uberwaldian town of Bonk, had to select a new Low King of the dwarfs (p. 349), bringing to light various controversies as to the definition of a dwarf and the proper way for dwarfs to live. This, combined with the activities of various other Uberwaldian rulers, generated the plot of *The Fifth Elephant*, at the end of which international relations were largely stable. But it's clear that the whole region is still going through what historians like to call "interesting times."

Uberwaldian Aristocratic Movements

Some of Uberwald's traditionally all-powerful aristocrats have been shrewd enough to realise that they'll have to adapt if they're to survive and continue to prosper. Unfortunately, Uberwaldian aristocrats are *not,* traditionally, terribly nice people. They may be moving with the times in certain respects, but some of them still believe that they're The Strong, who by that token enjoy the right to rule The Weak.

Carpe Jugulum and *The Fifth Elephant* depict the consequences of two such movements. In each case, although the *leaders* were defeated, there's no proof that all of their *followers* were either wiped out or made to change their ways. This opens obvious possibilities for RPG plots – if any of Count Magpyr's vampire clan or Wolf von Uberwald's werewolf faction survived and decided to leave the scene of their defeats, they could appear in the vicinity of a PC group. And while the vampires might have reverted to full sets of vampiric vulnerabilities (see *Vampires*, pp. 109-114), and the werewolves now lack their leader, either may retain enough big ideas to cause serious local trouble. The generous GM could have these menaces sport fancy waistcoats, or nickel-plated badges showing a wolf's head biting a lightning-bolt, by way of warning.

Indeed, there could be other factions along similar lines. For example, Uberwaldian mad doctors have traditionally been solitary folk, given to keeping their research secret and little interested in terrorising more than one or two villages. One who decided that the point of science was not merely knowledge but its *application* – who, in effect, went into industry – could be a problem for a much larger area. He probably wouldn't have much trouble acquiring students and other followers; indeed, real-world experience suggests that he wouldn't even have to turn a profit in order to receive more backing than he could use.[1]

---

1. *The dedicatedly satirical GM can decide what the Uberwaldian for "IPO" might be.*

Borogravia

Another breakaway component of the old Dark Empire, Borogravia is an agricultural country with a minor sideline in tallow mines. The population is mostly human, with a few trolls and vampires, and wandering clans of Igors. There are also dwarf mines; these closed themselves off for an extended period when the humans took against them for religious reasons, but have since reopened their doors.

Borogravia is noteworthy for only two things: a state religion – now defunct – that tipped from restrictiveness into outright insanity (see *The Story of Nuggan*, pp. 299-300), and a foreign policy that resembled the attitude of an aggressive drunk challenging everyone in the bar. These got Borogravia into increasing trouble over the years, and when the faithful were enjoined to destroy the clacks system, it ended up at war – not only with its neighbours, but also with Ankh-Morpork and Genua. This might well have meant Borogravia falling under the control of the ambitious regional power Zlobenia, except that Ankh-Morpork decided that this would upset the regional balance and gave some quiet support to a few sensible Borogravians who wanted to preserve independence (see *Polly Perks*, pp. 346-347). However, the country is still recovering from its own recent past, and things may remain messy for a while.

Widdershins Regions

Large areas of the Disc widdershins of the Circle Sea and Klatch haven't featured much in the chronicles. Klatchistan, the mountainous borderland on the edge of the continent of Klatch, is doubtless a hotbed of traditional mountain-pass folkways (banditry, feuding, and hawk-eyed sentinels sitting behind rocks). Various lands lie further to rimward, including the substantial coastal land of Muntab. Few details about Muntab have reached the rest of the Disc, other than that its ruler is known as the Pash, but Discworld diplomats are becoming increasingly preoccupied by the Muntab Question.[1]

Further round, there's a temperate area of rolling plains and hills. Much of the country is pleasant, in a fairy-tale sort of way – deciduous woodland, punctuated with farming villages. One of the nations is Brindisi, known in Ankh-Morpork as a land of opera singers and pasta.

At the far widdershins limits of this region, the Trollbone, Rammerock, and Blade mountain ranges are *serious* geology. The Trollbones, especially, are as high, sharp, and generally challenging as such things get, save for the foothills of Cori Celesti itself. They're troll, dwarf, and little-bald-enlightened-monk territory.

The Vieux River

The Vieux River rises in the mountains of Uberwald but leaves as soon as possible, descending into flatter country and slowing down once it's safe. It becomes a broad and useful waterway, navigated by paddleboats (powered by trolls on treadmills), which in turn provide profitable venues for countless professional gamblers. The Vieux enters the Swamp Sea through a broad and marshy delta, dominated by the city of Genua (below).

Genua

As the main port on the Vieux delta, Genua is prosperous, if foetid; the climate is usually Hot (see *Temperature Extremes*,

The Dark Empire

The Dark Empire – sometimes referred to as the Evil Empire or simply The Empire – is defunct, but its *consequences* loom large in the Disc's recent history.

It was founded, some hundreds of years before the chronicles' present, by a sinister figure known simply as the Evil Emperor, who was reputed to be some kind of magical adept – though given the way he operated, that might just have been an inevitable rumour. He was certainly the most successful classical dark lord in Disc history, at least in raw geographical terms. At its height, his Empire dominated what are now Borogravia and Mouldavia, as well as large parts of Uberwald. Igors created armies of orcs (p. 119) as soldiers for him. Quite what stopped him from conquering more of the Disc is unclear.

However, it would seem that the Emperor proved mortal in the end – so far as anyone knows, anyway. Frankly, people like that are just too effective as hero magnets, and he may have grown cocky enough not to bother to make provision for his return in a sequel. His Empire lingered into recent times, but considerably reduced in size; Borogravia and Mouldavia broke away long enough ago to have since developed their own political traditions and rivalries. Uberwaldian towns such as Lipwig were part of the Empire in living memory, though, until it finally, messily disintegrated.

All this helps explain why Uberwald and its neighbours remain so politically disorganised and unstable, despite their long history; they're *still* recovering from this collapse. Fortunately, there are competent and broadly ethical operators – including Lady Margolotta (pp. 349-350) and Low King Rhys (p. 349) – working to patch over the results, with Lord Vetinari assisting from a distance. But dead empires have a nasty way of attracting sentimental admirers. Someone with the nerve and resources to go up against the best politicians on the Disc might regard the Dark Empire's power as something worth salvaging.

p. 191) and also humid. Genua – which has been called the Magical Kingdom and the Diamond City – is an independent city-state, with a population whose ancestors came from all over the Disc, and who have the skin tones to prove it. Centuries ago, it was a colony of Ankh-Morpork, but it broke away.

The dominant local style of magic is voodoo. The place's cooking reflects the same eclectic roots; Genuan cooks are generally brilliant, although a wise gourmet doesn't ask about their ingredients.[2] There are small white buildings around the city's perimeter, large white houses closer in, and at the centre a castle with lots of ice-cream-cone turrets. All this whiteness dazzles against the muted swamp colours.

---

1. *"Where the hell is Muntab?"*

2. *This **is** a swamplands city.*

Genua has had a mixed history recently. A few years ago, it was ruled by the wicked, if charismatic, Baron Saturday. However, this regime wasn't evil enough to ruin the city. That nearly happened once the Baron was overthrown by Lady Lilith de Tempscire (Lily Weatherwax, Granny Weatherwax's older sister) and her protégé, the Duc. Lily was determined to make Genua a happy, well-organised place, using her peculiar expertise in stories. Guardsmen in toy-soldier uniforms of red and blue made sure that everything was very clean, including the cobblestones, and that everybody smiled. There's nothing quite like a life of enforced smiling to break the human spirit.

Following the events of *Witches Abroad*, things are returning to normal under the rule of the young Duchess Ella Saturday, who's probably no worse than most hereditary rulers; if nothing else, she knows what it's like at the bottom of the heap. Adventurers who visited Genua during Lily's reign were bound to get into trouble, at least as soon as their jaws got tired. Those who arrive in a later period might run afoul of the fact that the Genuans know only too well what it's like to live in a fantasy city, and they react very badly to anyone who reminds them of it.

Genuan PCs could be competent voodoo witches, traders, or cooks. Few skills or abilities are unique to the area, although good levels in Boating or Survival (Swampland) are quite plausible. Genuans may suffer from a unique Phobia: a terror of clichés, happy endings, and nice, bright, cheerful communities (worth a base -5 points). Have a nice day.

> ## Oceans
>
> Rimward and turnwise of the Circle Sea is a vast expanse of sea, embellished with archipelagos. Indeed, most of the Disc's landmasses are ultimately edged by the great rim oceans. Some ships sail these waters, but much is under-explored. There are plenty of whales, sea-serpents, ghost ships, and weed-filled seas haunted by undead pirates.
>
> The *Brown Islands* and *be Trobi Islands* lie in these expanses. Most of what trade there is between the Counterweight Continent and the Circle Sea passes this way. These are also the place to go if one wishes to learn the joys of surfing from large gentlemen, or to dive for pearls. The be Trobi Islanders are a cheerful people, but not above fighting tribal wars.

The Hub and Beyond

Toward its centre, the Disc *rises*. Everything here feels high and windswept, if not insanely mountainous.

CORI CELESTI

The Hub about which the Discworld revolves is a spire of grey stone and green ice 10 miles high, and also the site of Dunmanifestin, the home of the gods (p. 301). Cori Celesti acts as a focus or a grounding-spike for the Disc's magical field, which is why energy discharges – the *Aurora Corialis*, or Hublights – crackle around it, sheathing it in blue, green, and octarine. Other mountains cluster nearby, and while they're no

match for it in size and sheer impressiveness, they would be regarded with serious respect anywhere else.

>
> ## The Lost Continent of Ku
>
> The Disc's greatest Lost Land lies beneath the Widdershins Ocean, between EcksEcksEcksEcks, the Counterweight Continent, and the Fjordlands. It sank several thousand years ago, but took 30 years to do so. The inhabitants, having spent a lot of time wading, are unlikely to have left much in the way of arcane technology or pillared temples full of loot. If any of them transformed themselves into amphibious beings and covered their cities with domes of crystal, the fact is not widely known.

BARBARIAN LANDS

The main thing that people elsewhere associate with the Hublands is large, surly gentlemen with more skill in Broadsword than Savoir-Faire. This is *barbarian* country.

The high, cold steppes beyond the Hub are home to nomadic "Horse People" tribes. They eat horse meat, horse cheese, and horse soup, drink thin beer, and complain about the heat on days which are actually Freezing (see *Temperature Extremes*, p. 191). They sleep in yurts (tents) heated by burning dung; as they get quite enough fresh air during the day, their yurts aren't ventilated. Some also herd yok.[1]

These are Mk.1, uncomplicated nomads, with no particular regard for the rights or feelings of people outside the tribe. They usually have good Riding skill, along with bow and sword training, and probably Code of Honour (Pirate's). The tribes also produce competent witches in the shamanic/old-fortune-teller style.

THE FJORDLANDS

This region's coastlands are glacial and heavily indented, and inhabited by people who live in longhouses and sail longships. Yes, they wear furs and horned helmets. Yes, they use axes for many purposes.[2] And yes, they have a rich, lengthy, and boring tradition of sagas. Does anyone really need to know more?

THE VORTEX PLAINS

Also adjacent to the steppes are some slightly more fertile lands, where the people refrain from such baric practises as raiding, having settled down to agriculture and blood sacrifice. The Vortex Plains are the Disc's second centre of Druidism after Llamedos, and they are mainly noted for their large collection of stone circles. The inhabitants are forever being talked into investing in upgrades, but one snag with this sort of computer is that no one has yet found a way to make money from carting away the old ones, and offering them to employees to take home lacks plausibility.

Plains natives have the dour spirituality of a people whose priests are big on holly, mistletoe, and well-sharpened sickles, while lacking even Llamedese cosmopolitanism.

---

1. Like yak, but heavier.

2. Including cleaning their teeth.

The Counterweight Continent

While linked to the Disc's main landmass by a narrow, trackless isthmus, the Counterweight Continent is traditionally classed as a separate body of land, which is how its rulers historically liked it. It has a relatively small area compared to continental regions on the other edge of the hub. Thus, in order for the Disc to be balanced on the four elephants beneath, it must be especially dense.

This is why the Counterweight Continent is reputed elsewhere to be the source of vast quantities of gold; it's sometimes known as the Aurient. Wiser minds in Ankh-Morpork always used to describe it as semi-mythical, because most of the people who sailed off looking for it either came back with nothing but one-that-got-away stories, or didn't come back at all. That's changing fast, though; Ankh-Morpork is becoming downright infested with Agatean tourists.

Actually, although gold *is* abundant there, most of the Counterweight Continent's mass is in large deposits of octiron (p. 275), deep in the crust. And while octiron is even more valuable than gold among the magical professions, it's a dangerously ill-behaved substance. That and the (frankly fortunate) depth of the major deposits mean that it's little traded.

The Agatean Empire

All but a few small parts of the Counterweight Continent are controlled by the Agatean Empire, an ancient, stable, and civilised realm where even making a cup of tea requires a formal ceremony taking up to an hour. Its population is about 50 million and seems to be almost entirely human; if there are any native nonhumans, they keep to themselves. Its capital is Hung-Hung. It's ruled by the Sun Emperor, whose subjects consider him a god.[1]

Long ago, a wall was constructed around the entire Empire to keep out curious strangers – and more to the point, to keep *in* curious Agateans. This wall is patrolled by the Heavenly Guard. Agatean architecture tends toward pyramids, rather squat ones.[2] Gold ornamentation is popular, as gold in the Empire is about as common as copper in other places. This last fact is prone to getting adventurers into trouble.

The Empire traditionally encouraged its people to believe that the rest of the world was a barbaric wasteland inhabited by blood-drinking vampire ghosts. (Nonetheless, a few refugees did get away, often going into the restaurant business in Ankh-Morpork.) It was dominated by five noble families – the Hongs, Sungs, Tangs, McSweeneys, and Fangs – who fought among themselves for power. They tended to regard soldiers and peasants as disposable pawns. Each had a personal army, and between them, they could field 700,000 troops, from samurai warriors, through gunners with sophisticated, unreliable cannon, to quivering conscripts.

Conscript service aside, peasants weren't permitted to possess anything in the way of serious weaponry; the ruling and warrior classes definitely kept such things to themselves. This did lead to the development of a certain amount of fancy martial arts among the non-rulers, but these weren't very widespread. Intruding foreigners with visible weapons would automatically be assumed to be violent barbarians.

---

1. That is, he doesn't have to apologise for anything he does. Or even explain.

2. The better not to see over the wall.

Things have changed recently, though. Following the events of *Interesting Times,* the Empire came under the rule of Cohen the Barbarian (p. 346). However, Emperor Cohen and his friends became bored with that job, and he went off to storm the gates of Cori Celesti instead (see *The Last Hero*). If they left a political mess behind, they won't have worried about it. The five noble families may well have started fighting for dominance once again, but Cohen and the events which brought him to power left their leadership seriously mangled. Cohen certainly installed parts of a more practical governmental apparatus, so the Empire *might* actually have more stable and less vicious leadership at present.

Visits to the old Agatean Empire were tricky and dangerous; visitors would have a very hard time getting in, and if they did manage, would likely be bitterly disappointed in their attempts to bring away gold in public-works-project quantities. It wasn't so much that the Agateans valued the gold itself as the understanding that if you let one bunch get away with it, there would be an unending stream of adventurers following on their heels. Nowadays, things are doubtless a little more open, but the habit of suspicion may endure. With improved communications with the rest of the Disc, fortune-hunters may find that they're too late to make an easy profit in any event; Agatean gold is *already* flowing out in significant quantities.

All suspicion notwithstanding, there's a good chance that the Empire's trade with the rest of the Disc will expand rapidly in the next few years. Given the main things it has to offer – gold, sapient pearwood, magical domestic technology (although since imp-based gadgets became fairly commonplace in Ankh-Morpork, many of them are now being constructed by local commercial enterprises backed by Unseen University), and possibly octiron – the long-term social and economic consequences could be *interesting,* in that "interesting times" sense.

The climate in most of the Empire is Moderate to Warm (see *Temperature Extremes,* p. 191), with enough rainfall to support extensive rice farming. The main seaport – and the only place where contact with foreigners is anything like routine (aside from the embassy quarter of the capital these days) – is Bes Pelargic.

Agatean Gold and Economics

So far, the spread of Agatean gold to other lands has yet to cause total economic anarchy – someone, somewhere may be handling the problem. One suspects that the Patrician of Ankh-Morpork must be riding the wave of potential chaos somehow. A medium-term result may be the disappearance of the traditional gold standard in many economies, in favour of something more *ad hoc* (see *Currencies,* p. 20). But then, for years, the idea that the Ankh-Morpork dollar was backed by precious metal was more of a superstition than anything else; Ankh-Morpork coins certainly haven't been any sort of pure metal for many centuries.

Agateans Abroad

Since the events of *Interesting Times*, the Agatean Empire has also ceased prohibiting its citizens from travelling abroad. Agatean PCs could come from many professions, although the vast majority of its people are peasants of a very stolid kind. Its professional warriors and ninja tend to a formal approach and personal arrogance that makes them ill-suited as wandering adventurers, and its culture regards magic as something to be used almost solely for minor, peaceful purposes.

On the other hand, unusually bold merchants could have a great deal to trade, the Empire's large clerical class might be able to export their efficient managerial methods (once they learn to give up some of their formality), and the local culture is bizarre enough that Agatean entertainers may become fashionable. The first Agatean to appear in the chronicles was also the Disc's first tourist, and thanks to the popularity – and legalisation – of Twoflower's infamous travel book[1], Agatean tourists have become a familiar sight on the streets of Ankh-Morpork (see *Agatean Tourist*, p. 120). Of course, like Twoflower, these tourists all carry what *they* regard as modest quantities of high-purity gold coinage.

BHANGBHANGDUC

This large tropical island lies between the Agatean Empire and EcksEcksEcksEcks. While partly controlled by the Empire, it's mostly inhabited by orang-utans. Not much else is known

about it, which may or may not suggest that it should be of interest to adventurers.

EcksEcksEcksEcks

Not so long ago, "Fourecks" was a semi-mythical continent, usually labelled "XXXX" on maps. EcksEcksEcksEcks (also known as *Terror Incognita*), tales said, was a land of wizards who wore corks around their hats, ate only prawns, surfed on the fresh new light from the Rim, and drank pure golden nectar from bottomless chalices (well, out of tins, anyway). More cynical visitors merely reported dark-skinned people who claimed they lived in a dream, but who could muster a full meal from an apparently empty patch of desert, and good beer.

In fact, Fourecks was a separate creation. While the rest of the Disc was the work of the rather vague figure known as the Creator, EcksEcksEcksEcks was sung and painted into existence by the Old Man Who Carries the Universe in a Sack – a nameless wandering power whose work is always marked by the presence of kangaroos. Unfortunately, following an accident with causality, the continent suffered from peculiar, inconvenient, and persistent weather patterns that meant that, while ships could travel to EcksEcksEcksEcks – usually to be wrecked on its shores – only a remarkably good or extremely lucky crew and vessel could hope to get away without being blown over the Rim. In effect, EcksEcksEcksEcks became a giant prison, mostly inhabited by the descendants of shipwreck survivors.

The newcomers saw a land infested with great leaping rats and giant flightless chickens. Most of the fauna seems to be dangerous to humans (and quite a lot of the flora needs avoiding, too); there are spiders with deadly poison bites (some of which use their webs as trampolines, hurling themselves at incautious humans at head height), and dangerous "drop bears" (p. 355). Even the duck-billed platypus, which looks like a mishmash of random components[2], turns out to include venomous spurs on its hind feet.[3] There are also camels (not strictly native – they allegedly floated in on driftwood), which are just surly and paranoid. In fact, the only creatures guaranteed *not* to be dangerous are some of the sheep. Still . . . no worries, mate.

Those weather patterns not only isolated Fourecks, they also starved it *completely* of rain. The great central Outback was a vast and hostile desert, with temperatures routinely running from Very Hot to Severe Heat (see *Temperature Extremes*, p. 191). The colonists developed a viable nation despite everything, principally on the coastal plains, which are cooled by the sea to mostly just Warm temperatures.

The main coastal city and *de facto* capital is Bugarup, which boasts – not that Fourecksians boast, because it's bloody obvious that anything in EcksEcksEcksEcks is better than anything else in the bloody world – a magical university and an opera house. And a really good jail.

---

1. ***What I Did On My Holidays.***

2. *Because that's approximately what it is; see* **The Last Continent.**

3. *Scientific study suggests that these are used in mating. Which should tell you all you need to know about small, cute animals.*

The Wild Outback

Still, some people moved into the Outback, joining the black-skinned natives there. As settlers attempted to expand, though, they hit practical limits. Naturally, outcasts, criminals, and people with more machismo than IQ[1] insisted on going beyond those limits. They even found ways to prosper a little, either by trading between sheep farms and opal mines, or by robbing the traders. The Outback is now scattered with sheep stations and infested with outlaws of a rather romantic bent. Since the coming of the Wet (see *The Last Continent*), things may have calmed down a little – but it would take a lot to calm down some of *those* people much.

That trade and banditry needed vehicles. Pack camels might have been more cost-effective, but they were too slow to escape from bandits. Hence, a peculiar variety of fast, custom-built carts appeared. These are mostly pulled by horses; a few road-gang vehicles use emus (p. 355), but camels aren't suitable.

Incidentally, the most important trade commodity is *hay*. Long-distance travellers who try to cross the Outback without horses or camels end up, quite simply, dead, and the only way to keep a beast going for a long trip is with proper feed. However, hay and oats have to be brought in from coastal areas. This pushes their value up to get-your-throat-slit levels, and plenty of Outback denizens are willing to slit a few throats.

Backpackers and Opera Stars

Following the events of *The Last Continent*, not only does rain now reach those deserts, but ships can travel to and from EcksEcksEcksEcks, opening the place up to trade – and the rest of the Disc to visits by the dynamic, beer-loving Fourecksians.[2] For a template for these travellers, see *Fourecksian Backpacker* (p. 123). Like Agateans, Fourecksians are becoming well-known in Ankh-Morpork as tourists and émigrés.[3] However, whereas Agateans are clearly *foreigners* from the point of view of the inhabitants of the Sto Plains, Fourecksians make for more low-key, informal encounters.

The culture of the Last Continent draws heavily on that of the Sto Plains. While Fourecksians may strike Ankh-Morporkians as brash and self-regarding (and it takes a lot to look like *that* alongside an Ankh-Morporkian), they speak the same language and share comparable tastes. Likewise, while Fourecksians have much to trade, what they're offering (opals, wool, bananas, and wine) is comparatively familiar to the rest of the Disc. Still, the determination of numerous young, healthy, blond, tanned visitors to see a bit of the old place adds another angle to Ankh-Morpork's burgeoning tourist industry. At the same time, Fourecks' determination to prove how cultured it is could bring some impressive guest stars to the Ankh-Morpork Opera House.

---

1. *Which, many Fourecksians proudly assert, covers most of them.*

2. *Any experienced GM who doesn't recognise that as an opportunity has been spending too long drawing underground menageries on graph paper.*

3. *There's a good chance that, by now, any bartender anywhere will be from Fourecks.*

"Pies! Meat pies! Very reasonable price! Matter of fact, I'm . . ."

"Cutting your own throat?" a voice enquired mildly.

The pie vendor scowled at the speaker. "Evening, Captain Carrot, sir. Can I interest you in some of these fine comestibles?"

"Not just now, Mr. Dibbler." Carrot was looking worried, and C.M.O.T. Dibbler knew enough about how the world worked not to take that personally, but to be concerned nonetheless. "But could you tell me why you're selling in this particular spot this evening? It's not your usual patch."

Dibbler shrugged. "Gotta diversify occasionally, Captain. Can't let the grass grow under me feet. Might be missing an opportunity."

Carrot shook his head. "The waterfront, Mr. Dibbler? Even I can see that there isn't much trade down here. You're a bit close to the Shades, too. Not the safest spot, even for a . . . respected businessman like yourself."

Dibbler looked unhappy. "Don't know fer sure 'til you try," he muttered.

Carrot nodded. "I see that. But the fact is, I notice that you're choosing to sell down here, by the river. At high tide too, when the Smell is at its worst. I think that you only do that when you have a certain sort of supply problem. I'd hate to think that you feel a need to sell to people whose palates are completely paralysed today. You can do better than that, Mr. Dibbler."

"Course I can," Dibbler replied reflexively. "But I can see that you have a sharp eye for the exigencies of business, Captain. I won't deny that the fresh meat trade is going through a bit of a sticky patch just now."

"I thought so," said Carrot. "Thank you, Mr. Dibbler. You've been most helpful." He had dropped his voice to near a whisper as he spoke, for which Dibbler was grateful; they **were** near the Shades, where being thought to be most helpful to the Watch could be very unhealthy.

Carrot turned to leave. "Hey," said Dibbler, startled, "What's all this about, then?"

Carrot turned back to him. "Do you know how many people live in Ankh-Morpork, Mr. Dibbler?" he asked.

"No," said Dibbler. "Lots, I s'pose."

"Yes," said Carrot. "It depends how you count, of course. But however many there are, they all – well, nearly all – need feeding, every day. If something's going wrong with the supply chain, it may require attention. Anyway, take care of yourself, Mr. Dibbler."

Dibbler found himself almost standing at attention as Captain Carrot departed, and with an effort of will, restored his usual slouch.

Then he frowned thoughtfully and turned back to head towards the cellar where he stored his spare stock. He wasn't sure what Carrot had meant by that little speech, but he was pretty sure that there was an opportunity for profit involved, somewhere.

Ankh-Morpork is the oldest surviving city on the Disc (depending somewhat on definitions, of course), and the largest. Its population of about one million, suburbs included, is quite an achievement, given available technologies of transport[1], water supply[2], and waste disposal.[3] It is, technically, *two* cities,
separated by the River Ankh: Ankh, the slightly more prosperous of the two, is on the turnwise side of the river, while Morpork is to the widdershins. Usually, only people trying to sell houses bother distinguishing.

Much of the trade of the Circle Sea and the Sto Plains passes through Ankh-Morpork. It's the centre for mysterious industries such as wizardry, assassination, and banking. It's The City to which young people from the country dream of going, until they become old enough to warn young people against going there.

History

Ankh-Morpork grew up around Unseen University (pp. 279-289) – which, being a magical establishment, makes questions of causality a little uncertain. The University had grown around the Tower of Art (p. 284), and a sort of service village developed nearby. Later, the focus shifted downriver, toward the docks.

This dockside community lay on the site of what's now known as the Shades (pp. 252-253). The growing sprawl eventually absorbed the villages of Dolly Sisters and Nap Hill. Remains of ancient walls still poke up through later buildings, and some foundations in the Shades seem downright timeless.

Then, about 3,300 years before the present, came the Empire of the Kings of Ankh, which lasted about 1,300 years. This is long enough ago to be thought of as a Golden Age of Glorious Deeds. Surviving remnants include a sewer system, which is no longer connected to much in the way of surface plumbing (until recently, only the Assassins' Guild knew of it). As well, a ruin on the hill called the Tump might have been a castle back then. There's also a Throne (actually a throne-shaped heap of dry rot held together by gilt and good intentions), and the legend of a Sword.

The fall of the Kings of Ankh was followed by 17 centuries of the less mythical Ankh-Morporkian Kings. The crown belonged to anybody with soldiers to take it and the poor judgement to keep it. There were wars, betrayals, assassinations, family squabbles about who was going to swim the moat in leg-irons, and prophecies ending in "Beware!" or "Aaaarrggh." The system was actually highly egalitarian; most wealthy families got to be "royal" for at least a generation.

All these monarchs were formally pretenders, since no one knew what had happened to the Kings of Ankh. The population understood that the True King was the one who held The Sword, so a whole series of "true swords" were produced (King Blad carried two bits of wood hastily nailed together, for 51 years). The Sword is now regarded as lost – though like Atlantis and crashed flying saucers, it cannot ever be considered truly gone.

Some of the Kings were a trifle lacking in sanity. Many of these didn't last very long, as sanity is important for self-defence, but others endured for a while, perhaps because none of the plausible replacements were any more acceptable. Anyway, by definition, kings cannot be mad; even "eccentric" is too strong a term to be polite. For example, King Ludwig the Tree gave the city much to remember him by in his four-year rule, not least one of its official

mottoes, "Quanti Canicula Ille In Fenestra?" ("How Much Is That Doggie in the Window?"). His call for the creation of a new kind of frog had less durable results, but amused the population no end. He was harmless, and hence entertaining. Others were more in the Caligula class.

The monarchy ended in 1688 (University dating) with the Civil War. (There had been countless civil wars, of course, but this is the one that gets the capital letters.) This was a genuinely popular uprising against King Lorenzo the Kind, whose private depredations were so unspeakable that people actually *did not* speak of them. Lorenzo wasn't even an effective monster; the city was becoming dominated by Klatch (pp. 234-237), which was going through a dynamic phase.

The end of the monarchy wasn't actually a rebellion against the *idea* of kings, or even their arbitrary, bloody-minded imbecility. Still, from then on, people never *quite* believed that the maniacs in charge of them had been put there by the Will Of The Gods. Not that some of the rulers who replaced the Kings have been much better, mind, but at least they weren't bred for it.

The Smell

A key feature of Ankh-Morpork – perhaps its defining characteristic – is its Smell, a consequence of a million people living around a turgid river with no functioning sewer system. Stories say that at least one invading army was defeated when they sneaked in at night, but their nose plugs gave out.

The citizens are very proud of the Smell. They erected a statue to that victory (though the stone of the monument has somewhat rotted away). People take chairs outdoors on summer evenings to appreciate it. And when they're obliged to travel away from Ankh-Morpork, they talk about their dreams of getting back to the Smell.

The Smell has little effect in game terms, although it makes it effectively impossible to trick an Ankh-Morporkian into thinking he or she is home when that isn't true. At the GM's whim, however, visitors from more refined communities might have to make HT rolls for a few days after arrival to avoid a lot of gagging.

---

1. Poor.

2. Worse.

3. What?

The Patricians

Patricians *aren't* kings. The Patrician of Ankh-Morpork is the ruler, to be sure, and he isn't exactly elected. However, rather than being hereditary, the position goes to the person who, when the post becomes vacant, applies enough cleverness, guile, blackmail,

---

Wellcome to Ankh-Morporke, Citie of One Thousand Surprises – Guild of Merchants publication, mentioned in *Moving Pictures*

---

and other leverage. The process can be thought of as something like musical chairs, in which anyone who has a dagger sticking out of him may not sit down. The office is held for life, which doesn't, of course, prevent anyone with the right resources from changing the office-holder. Officially, the Patrician is merely looking after the place until the longed-for return of the True King – but if you believe *that* . . .

Once in office, Patricians tend to hold it by something like consensus (not necessarily universal consensus, but of the people who count), understanding that they don't have a Divine Right or any other mandate. This hasn't prevented the stresses of leadership from having an effect on Patricians; the names of such past incumbents as Deranged Lord Harmoni, Frenzied Earl Hargarth, and Mad Lord Snapcase (Psychoneurotic Lord Snapcase to his close friends) bear witness to this. Still, the system seems to work to the satisfaction of most Ankh-Morporkians, and lasting long enough in the job to have your name remembered is more than several kings achieved.

Current Government

Ankh-Morpork barely qualifies as having a *system* of government. What it has is an *arrangement*. Ankh-Morporkians say that their government is a democracy, with one man, one vote. The Patrician is The Man, and he has The Vote. For what it's worth, he may sometimes call a meeting of a sort of city council, consisting of assorted guild chiefs, aristocrats, and anyone else whose advice is likely to be useful or whose omission could be fatally tactless. This meeting has purely advisory power; only occasionally is the advice "do this or we'll kill you."

The current Patrician, Lord Havelock Vetinari (pp. 306-308), is exceptional (and very, very sane). He has realised two things. First, that what people want, more than anything else, is stability. Second, that change is currently inevitable, as the Disc is going through one of *those* historical periods.

A lesser ruler might worry about such a contradiction; Vetinari takes it in his stride. If the citizens don't wish to see change, then he won't force them to look. He provides the stability that everyone silently demands. He believes that even a bloody tyranny

would be seen as a Good Thing if it carried on long enough, but he has no wish to test the point. He simply does what must be done, quietly, while taking care not to offend any faction much more than any other.

They all hate him, and the brighter ones even know that they're being played off, while traditionalists cannot help but notice and despise the changes that Vetinari has permitted. To most people, however, keeping Vetinari is categorically preferable to the idea of getting rid of him. Were he to die, the struggle for power would be horrendous – and no one feels certain enough of winning.

That doesn't mean he's never threatened, however. There are always the mad, the desperate, and the supernatural.

THE PATRICIAN'S SPIES

The Patricians have always had impressive spy networks (you didn't get or keep the job without), and Vetinari's intelligence-gathering system is extraordinary. It isn't so much a network, though, as a large number of people who believe – sometimes against all experience – that he pays for information received.

However, his real secret may be less his information sources (such things are often expensive, unreliable, and subject to subversion) than the analysis which the intelligence receives. The routine stuff is first filtered through a small, smart, well-trained team of clerks, while extraordinary material goes straight to Vetinari. Then he *thinks* about it.

Recent Events

If life in Ankh-Morpork is often exciting and has lately come to include quite a bit of technological progress, then the most recent events in the city have sometimes been downright explosive, in a well-contained sort of way.

CHALLENGES TO THE PATRICIAN

Early in his reign, Lord Vetinari convinced most people that it would be very dangerous to challenge him. Persuading everyone with a scintilla of ability not to try took a little longer – and to give them credit, some moves against him have been quite ingenious.

Public Transport

Inventors and entrepreneurs realised some time ago that there are people who want to get around Ankh-Morpork, don't want to walk, have *some* money, but can't afford their own coaches. In the longer term, the Undertaking (p. 250) should help with this. For now, there are a few ground-level services available. These include some uncomfortable horse-drawn omnibuses (which charge a penny or two to carry anyone rather slowly along the major streets) and a number of large trolls who walk around with seats slung in panniers round their necks (which is safe – few people will attack a troll – and surprisingly comfortable, and will get you anywhere within the city walls for $0.05).

Guards! Guards! and *Men at Arms* tell of two such attacks; *Feet of Clay* describes a move that was all the more deadly because it involved keeping Vetinari alive and creating a compromise-candidate replacement; and *The Truth* depicts a ruthless and relatively ingenious variation. In the story of *Going Postal*, Reacher Gilt didn't attack Vetinari directly, but Gilt's high-stakes financial scheming may well have been intended to put him in a position to usurp the Patrician by conventional political means in the longer term. However, none of these plots succeeded, and by the time of the events in *Making Money*, schemes against Vetinari had become the province of the insane and deluded.

Of course, even the insane and deluded can be dangerous, if only because of their unpredictability. Still, it's notable that the Assassins' Guild, whose price for an attempt on Vetinari's life rose to $1,000,000 some time ago, has now declared a refusal even to consider that project. Difficulty aside, the Guild needs a working government to give its own work some kind of reliable meaning; removing Vetinari would be too much of an upset for everyone (which is exactly what Vetinari intended). Meanwhile, the Watch has come under the authority of the worryingly competent and incorruptible Samuel Vimes (pp. 318-321), who heartily dislikes Vetinari, but who openly dislikes and distrusts all his rivals and possible replacements even more.

REFORMING THE CITY

Going back a little, however . . . The process of reform in Ankh-Morpork really got under way after the latest Great Fire of Ankh-Morpork, consequent on the visit of the tourist Twoflower (see *The Colour of Magic*), which enabled a certain amount of rebuilding and revision of the guild system (pp. 258-264). The Merchants' Guild came into being at that time, Vetinari stabilised the Thieves' Guild not long after, and the Assassins' Guild – which had long been ticking over nicely – shed a thuggish underworld element which it had previously incorporated.

The brief reign of Coin the Sourcerer (see *Sourcery*) had no significant long-term effects on the city. Neither did the rise and fall of the Disc's motion picture industry (see *Moving Pictures*). Even the Patrician's brief replacement by a dragon (see *Guards! Guards!*) left him back in charge (although it did create a small area suited to urban redevelopment), and perhaps served to demonstrate that Vetinari isn't the worst thing the city might have to live with. Ankh-Morpork was becoming downright overconfident; a minor international incident, manipulated by a faction in the foreign nation of Klatch, almost turned into a full-scale war, which would have been disastrous for the complacent city's improvised army (see *Jingo*). Vetinari salvaged that situation but was finding that he had whole new classes of problem.

POST AND BANKING

First, the expansion of the telegraph system (see *The Semaphore Revolution*, pp. 222-225) was seized on by an opportunistic group of investors, led by the flamboyant and utterly ruthless criminal businessman Reacher Gilt, who hoped to create a monopoly as a route to financial power and maybe more. The Patrician responded by reactivating the city's moribund Post Office – a slower method of communication, but competition nonetheless. The Patrician's pawn, Moist von Lipwig (pp. 309-311), outplayed Gilt, enabling Vetinari to reform the clacks. Gilt disappeared and subsequently died.

The Post Office is a state monopoly that runs everything from local deliveries to mail-coach services across the Sto Plains. It has its own peculiar traditions, but it needed Moist to develop such "modern" concepts as stamps.[1] It operates out of a grand building on Broadway, recently rebuilt after a fire[2] and once more the centre of mail-coach operations. The blue-uniformed staff now include a number of golems, ensuring that some postmen don't have to worry about bad-tempered dogs.

Then, the Patrician reassigned Moist to another troubled body: the Royal Bank of Ankh-Morpork (and the attached Royal Mint), a formally independent institution responsible for issuing the Ankh-Morpork dollar, which had fallen under the control of the increasingly inept and selfish Lavish family. Moist dealt with the Lavishes and reformed not only the bank but Ankh-Morpork's entire currency, moving it from an old-fashioned system of (highly debased) coinage to paper currency nominally backed by the city's possession of an entire army of ancient golems. Moist also determined that the $5 and $10 notes should be printed with two-dimensional talking imps, making counterfeiting much harder.[3]

---

1. Which done, it rapidly added ideas such as commemorative issues, some of them contentious enough to cause political problems themselves.

2. One of Gilt's ideas.

3. Working through unintended consequences of that could make for an entertaining game or two.

The idea of paper money is still new on the Disc – or at least in Ankh-Morpork (it may have been tried elsewhere) – and people are likely to be suspicious of it for a while yet. However, a master con artist like Moist von Lipwig is well-equipped to persuade the public to accept something this bizarre.

THE UNDERTAKING

One motivation for getting the bank back on its feet was that the city desperately needed a reliable financial system to support the next great project: the Undertaking. This consists of a network of underground tunnels, docks, and warehouses, incorporating a rail-based transport system powered by a peculiar ancient device acquired from the dwarfs but possibly older than the Disc itself. The Undertaking is intended to maintain Ankh-Morpork's dominant commercial position in the Circle Sea region – or, to put it another way, to make a lot of people a great deal of money while keeping as much of that money as possible in Ankh-Morpork.

If Ankh-Morpork is going to get even richer, then the Patrician doubtless intends that some of that wealth should go to maintaining its security and ability to function. Next on his schedule for reform appears to be taxation. For years, the city has been running without much at all in the way of a tax system – just a "Taxmaster," whose method was to hold people upside down over a bucket and give them a good shake. Satisfying as this might be to watch, it notoriously failed to raise much income.

Once again, the Patrician has Moist von Lipwig down as the man for the job. Quite how a semi-reformed criminal pacifist with a flair for improvisation is going to run a tax system is doubtless a question which amuses the Patrician immensely.

Newspapers and Printing

The Disc has long had printing technology of a sort, and moveable type was known in some places. However, the latter was effectively banned in Ankh-Morpork, suppressed by a combination of an Engravers' Guild which maintained a monopoly on old-style woodblock printing, and Unseen University, who were nervous about what might happen if anyone printed *magical* texts.

However, when a group of enterprising dwarfs arrived with an advanced printing press, they discovered that the situation was ready to change. Too many people – including the wizards – had too much use for cheaply produced texts, and the Patrician could see benefits for the city in moving with the times. The Engravers' Guild just had to adapt. Preventing the technology from being used for magical material is going to be a matter of common sense and vigilance.[1]

Moreover, the dwarfs literally collided with William de Worde (pp. 311-312), a young man with good connections, iron nerves, and a talent for writing. This in turn led to the creation of the Disc's first newspaper, the *Times*, and the invention of journalism. The population of Ankh-Morpork rapidly developed a taste for news, not to mention gossip and scandal, and the city's journalists have developed enough of an ethical impulse that most of what they print is true.

Lord Vetinari probably permits this to continue because he doesn't mind being annoyed so long as other people are being even more annoyed. Also, the *Times* did him a genuine service in the course of breaking its first big story (see *The Truth*). While that newspaper continues to annoy a lot of people on a regular basis – including the Watch in general and Samuel Vimes in particular – the smarter ones are learning a bit about news management and public relations.

The *Times* is also making money, and although its first competitor failed in complicated circumstances, other rivals are appearing in both Ankh-Morpork and other cities, none of which can bear to be left behind. Various special-interest magazines existed even before the *Times* (they could afford the time and cost involved in woodblock printing), and the new technology is bringing down the cost of those. There's also at least one dwarf newspaper, *Satblatt*, which few humans see and fewer, of course, can read.

1. *Oh well.*

Geography

Ankh-Morpork is a walled city, but as it hasn't faced siege for many years, the walls are seen as nothing but a nuisance to developers. Most of its million-strong population lives outside, in suburbs and semi-attached villages. However, the great circular heart of the place is what most people think of when they talk about Ankh-Morpork, standing as Manhattan stands to New York.

Because the city has grown with time, there are older plans within the largest circle, some marked out by earlier, fragmentary walls, and all strung out along and around the river.

Thus, from above, Ankh-Morpork has something of the look of a cut onion.[1]

Do note that this is an old-world[2] sort of city plan, not a modern American grid. Right angles are hard to come by. Strangers often have to ask for directions – and are usually confused by the answers. Area Knowledge of the city is valuable for even the simplest errands.

1. *But smells much worse.*

2. *Maybe even Olde Worlde.*

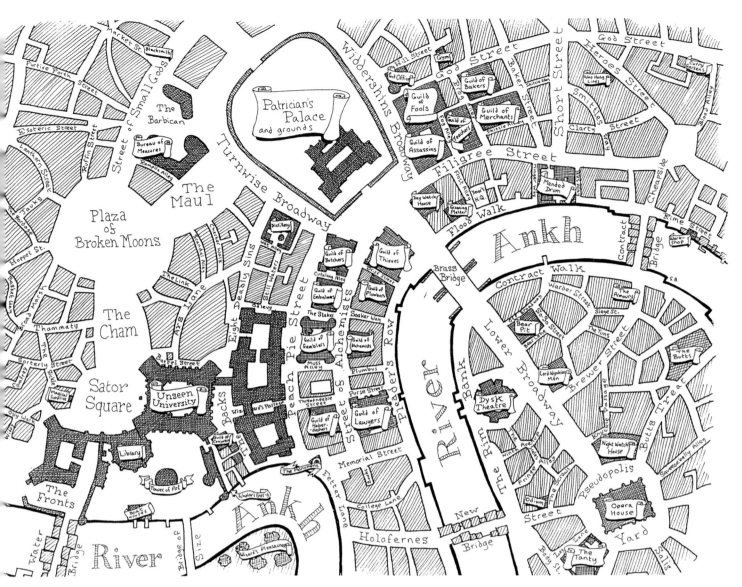

THE RIVER ANKH

The River Ankh rises in the Ramtops and winds in a generally rimward direction down to the Circle Sea. On the way, it collects the silt of the plains, and by the time it reaches the city walls, it's *thick.* In the city, it collects still more silt, along with every form of solid waste created by nature and civilisation; when it leaves, it has the consistency of extremely lumpy oatmeal. The citizens are proud to point out that it's very difficult to drown in the Ankh, but one can suffocate in it. So much material has accreted on the riverbed that it's actually higher than some low-lying parts of the city. When spring snowmelt causes the level to rise, these areas – which, as one might imagine, aren't fashionable – flood, though the actual effect is more like pulling a gravel throw-rug over a dirt floor.

The downriver wall gates, and some bridge gates, can be closed to flood the city deliberately in the event of a fire. This is what city administrators call a "tough choice." Or maybe not. It depends on the administrator, and on where his house is relative to the fire and the river.

The purity of Ankh water is insisted upon by the citizens, who point out that the kidney is one of nature's most efficient filtering devices. The river is known to hold uniquely evolved fish, in a broad sense of the word. These haven't been closely studied, as when removed from their natural habitat, they explode.

The river isn't the city's source of water, however. That's drawn from wells, which need not be deep due to the high water table. The average citizen's resistance to disease is clearly extraordinary. At one time there was an aqueduct on Water Street, but it collapsed centuries ago; a few traces are still visible.

Ankh

The turnwise half of the twin city, known as Ankh, is grander and more expensive than the other half, Morpork; people who spend more money to live there can afford to ensure that it stays that way. Places of note include a park (Hide Park), the apothecary gardens (where medicinal plants are grown) by the river, and a racecourse. Still, Ankh has some of the city's inevitable sordidness, including its original gallows (see *Punishments*, pp. 257-258), and a working docklands area at its rimward side.

At the hubward side of things, the mound of the Tump – with its ancient ruins – is another open space, forcing the city wall outward from its circular plan. Visitors to the city often go there, mostly to spend five minutes looking around and another five wondering why they bothered. There wasn't previously much to see at all. However, the Grand Trunk (see *The Semaphore Revolution*, pp. 222-225 has recently built its largest signal-tower here.

Hubwards Morpork

Unseen University (pp. 279-289) lies on the trailing bank of the river, at the hubwards end of town. The river-facing areas (the gardens and the "Fronts") are adjacent to Water Bridge and the Bridge of Size. Just upstream is the area known as the Unreal Estate (see above).

On the other side of the University from the river is the Plaza of Broken Moons. Beyond that is the Street of Small Gods, which runs down to the temple district. It also cuts across Upper Broadway, which links the Hubwards Gate with the Patrician's Palace (pp. 254-255) and its gardens.

The area between the University, the Plaza, the Palace, and the river contains a number of major guild-houses, including those of the Butchers, Gamblers, Thieves (hard by the river and the Brass Bridge), and Alchemists.[1] Between Broadway and Short Street, which also runs from one of the gates to the river (or rather to the Mended Drum, which is *on* the river) is a bustling area that not only holds most of the temples, but also a lot of mercantile businesses and the Street of Cunning Artificers, traditional home of the city's craftsmen. As well, there's a large area which was opened up a few years ago when a dragon crash-landed on it; this remained undeveloped for some time (unusual in a busy place like Ankh-Morpork, but there were legal complications, and latent superstition about that dragon), but the city's current surge in development may well ensure that this space is soon built over once again. Other major guilds – including the Fools and the Assassins – have headquarters around here, mostly near the river and the palace.

The Isle of Gods

Technically, the Isle of Gods is part of Ankh. But it's actually defined by a looping meander in the river, and some past urban scheme or another drove a canal or an extended dock, the Cut, across the loop, making this into a true island.

Today, it's Ankh-Morpork's theatreland, and also, oddly, the location of its police HQ. At its centre – indeed, at the very centre of the city – is Pseudopolis Yard, at the bottom end of Lower Broadway. This is perhaps the most valuable piece of real estate in the city. Lady Ramkin (see *Lady Sybil Vimes*, p. 320) owns property here, which she gave to the Watch after the dragon demolished their old HQ. Pseudopolis Yard is a large circular plaza, with Ankh-Morpork's huge opera house in the middle. Nearby, on the river, is the Dysk, the city's greatest theatre (somewhat resembling Shakespeare's Globe, in London), home base to Vitoller's Strolling Players, who include the genius playwright Hwel the Dwarf and the uncannily brilliant actor Tomjon.

Rimwards Morpork and the Shades

Much of the city rimwards of Short Street is made up of innocuous residential and shopping areas, ranging from the poor-but-honest to the rich-but-run-down.
And then there's the Shades.

This is an area bounded by Treacle Mine Road, Elm Street, the river, the cattle market, and Cockbill Street.

---

1. The Gamblers' hall is opposite that of the Alchemists. *Think about it.*

To quote from the Merchants' Guild publication, *Wellcome to Ankh-Morpork*:

Thee Shades bee a folklorique network of old alleys and picturesque streets, wherre exitement and romans lurke arounde everry corner and much may be heard the traditional street cries of old time also the laughing visages of the denuizens as they goe about their business private.

What the visitor actually *sees* is a labyrinth of winding little streets – some barely wide enough to expand your chest in – haunted by individuals who always seem to be looking the other way, gods nobody remembers, freelance thieves confident that even the Thieves' Guild won't follow them in here, and people of all descriptions and beyond description selling things that you'll shortly regret owning and have a lot of trouble disposing of.

The typical visitor sees this for approximately 10 minutes before someone puts his lights out with a blackjack. If he's lucky.

Many accounts suggest that visiting the Shades alone is, quite simply, automatically terminal – and there are certainly parts where this is true (these parts expand after dark). However, there are enough locations that folk simply *must* visit, even at dusk, that the Shades simply cannot be as bad as stories suggest. Not quite, anyway.

Obtaining anything unpleasant or illegal that's absolutely necessary to the completion of a game plot probably calls for a trip to the Shades. Area Knowledge (Ankh-Morpork) is a basic survival skill at these times. Turn off your Danger Sense; it'll only give you a headache.

COCKBILL STREET

On the rimwards edge of the Shades, Cockbill Street runs from the city's great cattle market to Pearl Dock, although the term "Cockbill Street" is sometimes used to indicate the whole neighbourhood between here and the city wall. This isn't a completely desolate area – there are many small workshops and such – but it's very, very poor.

The manufacturing round here is sweatshop work. The inhabitants are generally too honest to take the traditional Ankh-Morpork routes out of poverty, so they stay poor.

BEYOND SHAMBLING GATE

The rimwards edge of the wall is pierced by Shambling Gate, so named for its proximity to the livestock market (a "shambles" being a place where animals are slaughtered). This is the closest gate to the point where the Ankh leaves the city. Some way beyond the Gate – though maybe closer to the cattle market than the principles of public health might seem to mandate – in a marshy area by the river, lie the vast city tips and compost heaps. This is part of the domain of Sir Harry King (alias "King of the Golden River" or "Piss Harry"), who has risen from humble origins to great wealth, if not complete social acceptance, by taking control of numerous aspects of waste disposal (and, importantly, recycling) in the city.

The total effect of this geographical layout is best appreciated by trying to think about something else, preferably away from open flames.

The Patrician's Palace

The Patrician rules from the former Winter Palace of the Kings of Ankh, located square across Broadway. (The Summer Palace is some distance outside the city, so that one may enjoy the outside air on a warm summer's day without stiffening and falling to the ground; it isn't much used by any Patrician who realises how long he can afford to turn his back.) Much of the building is presently taken up with clerks' offices, handling both normal city business and the extensive intake of Lord Vetinari's spy network.

When the Patrician wishes to work in private, he occupies the Oblong Office. More-public meetings take place in what was originally the Throne Room, which still contains the Golden Throne of the Kings of Ankh. Lord Vetinari doesn't use the Throne, preferring to sit on a plain wooden chair at the foot of the Throne's dais. This is partly for symbolic reasons and partly because the Throne might collapse under a large weight of sunbeams.

The Palace dungeons are still fully operational, with all the standard equipment. Due to Vetinari's one little foible, any street mimes caught in the city are suspended upside down in a scorpion pit, facing a sign (inverted for easy reading) saying "LEARN THE WORDS." Most of the other cells are quite humane, as such things go.[1]

The Palace also has its share of secret passages and other traditional features, all installed or adjusted to suit the current Patrician. For example, only he knows how the secret passages run. Anyone else would need a lot of skill or luck to find them in a hurry.

One prisoner who is *not* held in the dungeons is Leonard of Quirm (pp. 308-309), who instead resides in a kind of protective custody in a small-but-comfortable attic workshop (with skylight). The corridors leading to his cell are heavily booby-trapped; actually, Leonard invented most of the traps, and he and Vetinari can get past them without even thinking. The Patrician originally treated him *as* a prisoner, albeit very politely, but eventually let him out on occasion to help deal with various peculiar problems. Consequently, Leonard discovered some of the worst things of which humans are capable, and decided that he preferred his prison.

THE GROUNDS

The Palace Grounds are quite splendid, with a small zoo, a bird garden, a racehorse stable . . . and the Gardens. These are a quintessential achievement of Bloody Stupid Johnson. They contain a trout pond (sized to hold one long, thin trout who doesn't mind being unable to turn around), a fountain (which operated once, launching a stone cherub beyond the city boundaries), a chiming sundial (which routinely explodes at noon), a beehive (used to house messenger albatrosses), and a garden maze (which is small enough that people get lost trying to find it).

Guards and Dark Clerks

For most of Ankh-Morpork's history, the kings and Patricians have retained a palace guard for their personal security. These guards also dealt with any little matters that their employer might need attended to (and hence would qualify as having Legal Enforcement Powers, p. 35 . . . in fact, their effective powers exceeded those of the Watch, because people knew that it was a lot less wise to question them). Originally, Lord Vetinari retained this system, and indeed his guards were an exceptionally rough crew – think of the heavies that a Mafia boss in the movies calls in when dealing with people he really doesn't like, and then put them in armour. Furthermore, Vetinari paid them well, and made sure they knew he could outbid anyone who might come along with a bribe.

---

1. Lord Vetinari rarely bothers locking up his enemies, preferring to make use of them in other ways if he can, and to remove them permanently if he must. But if he has to hold on to somebody, he usually wants the option of dealing with them on a civilised basis later, which makes maltreatment counterproductive.

Bloody Stupid Johnson

Bergholt Stuttley Johnson, who lived in the Disc's relatively recent past (the generic "generation ago"), was a landscape gardener and inventor of considerable renown, not all of it positive. He was in many ways a talented man, and many of his creations were elegant and beautiful. His *main* fault lay in the quantitative area. This fault has placed him in the history books as "Bloody Stupid" Johnson.

He seems never to have comprehended the difference between a foot and an inch, or an ounce and a pound – or perhaps he never got ratios right. In any case, the ornamental cruet set he designed for Mad Lord Snapcase may be seen today in Ankh-Morpork's Upper Broadway: four families live in the salt shaker, and the pepper pot is used for grain storage. The triumphal arch commemorating the Battle of Crumhorn is kept in a small cardboard box, and the Colossus of Morpork is not on public view, as it would be too easy for someone to slip it into a pocket. An honest citizen is paid a token fee to take care of such items. Ankh-Morpork contains many of his greatest accomplishments, but he travelled to Quirm to build his famous Collapsed Tower and to mess up the view from the overlord's mansion.

Johnson was never discouraged by what people considered his failures, and he never lacked for work, there generally being people so rich they can spend large amounts on things like a tree-lined promenade four feet long, or a submerged gazebo.

A few of Johnson's errors were downright metaphysical and *dangerous*. For example, when the Post Office (p. 249) commissioned him to build a mail-sorting machine, his design included a driving wheel. However, Johnson was annoyed at the innate irrationality of pi, so he made the wheel a circle with a circumference-to-diameter ratio of exactly 3. This created a flaw in space-time which caused the machine to bring in masses of mail from other times and other dimensions. This device was *probably* completely destroyed in the recent Post Office fire.

Johnson's inventions often work, but for some purpose different than that for which they were built. There may be other "Johnsons" lying in wait around the city for the unwary, ready to induce anything from hilarity to existential terror.

Following the events of *Guards! Guards!*, however, this group was somewhat discredited, while Vetinari grew increasingly confident that anyone who might previously have threatened him was too well boxed-in politically to make trouble. With the restored Watch willing and able to deal with the sorts of problems that had previously required his personal heavies, he has paid them off (doubtless generously – no need to antagonise someone who knows parts of the layout of the Palace). It was increasingly said that Vetinari no longer employed a personal guard force.

Of course, this is an oversimplification. Yes, the Watch now handles law enforcement in the city, which includes protecting the person of the Patrician in the same way that it's their job to protect the persons of anybody else in the city (okay, with a bit more show in *his* case). He's also entitled to ask them to run occasional errands, when someone with armour and a sword is the best choice for the job.

But.

As everyone in Ankh-Morpork knows, the Patrician runs the city by any means necessary, and he can be quite ruthless at times. Certainly, he sometimes needs to have a few dangerous-looking characters on hand at the Palace, just to make a point during informal meetings. Also, there are usually a few guards on the Palace gates, if only to slow down the merely tiresome crazies – while the Patrician has set things up so that only an idiot would attack him (and can defend himself rather well anyway), there are always a few idiots around.

Thus, the Palace staff definitely still includes a few people whose chief qualification is their ability to apply force. Some of these are good at looking ominous. Others are a lot more innocuous and are usually graduates of the Assassins' Guild School (mostly scholarship boys who got there on evident promise, rather

Dark Clerks Campaigns

A group of dark clerks could be PCs in a campaign privileging sneakiness, fine judgement, and ruthlessness. They'd be somewhat amoral types, but they'd also have to be smart and careful – not just brutish thugs. Players who *just* want to play amoral killers should be steered away from this idea, because somebody who acts like a stupid goon while working as a trusted employee of the Patrician will rate as a *problem* to be eliminated as expeditiously as possible. However, playing dark clerks could be a lot of fun for players who enjoy espionage, close protection, the occasional assassination, and a bit of paperwork – and who can be trusted to get them *right*.

See *Dark Clerk* (pp. 131-132) for a template. This is intended purely as a guideline. The main qualification for this job is the ability to be useful to the Patrician and to gain his trust. That's tricky, but it raises all sorts of character possibilities.

than aristocrats). The majority are on the books as "clerks," because that's what the Patrician is *supposed* to employ – and because he likes to get value for money, and needs spies and enforcers with a bit of political awareness, many of them *can* fill in as competent administrative staff, between other missions. Some people refer to them as the "dark clerks."

Law and Order and Defence

Contrary to widespread belief, Ankh-Morpork *does* have law and order. It's just a bit complicated about it.

The Watch

Many years ago, there were four "police" forces in Ankh-Morpork. The *Palace Guard*, or Patrician's Guard, were as described in *Guards and Dark Clerks* (pp. 254-255). The *Cable Street Particulars* were an elite group of investigators and secret police. The *Day Ward* and *Night Watch* were street patrols whose tasks included catching criminals, directing traffic, rousting drunks, and what modern police forces refer to as "animal control."

Over time, however, the Cable Street Particulars became much more secret police than anything else – in the worst sense, acting as viciously underhanded agents of the reigning Patrician. Many were sadists. They were eventually decimated in the course of a political revolution, and disbanded in its aftermath as a popular gesture. Their former headquarters was sold off and became a dwarf delicatessen.

At the same time, the two street patrols found themselves increasingly irrelevant. On one hand, they simply couldn't perform their jobs to anyone's satisfaction. On the other, the guilds and other groups stepped in to handle much practical law enforcement.

When Lord Vetinari became Patrician, he didn't bother trying to reverse this process; instead, he formalised the Thieves' Guild's crime-control function, monitored the other guilds with relaxed efficiency, and deliberately filled the Ward and Watch with dubious characters, drunks, and no-hopers, so as to avoid having armed groups with the wrong attitude on the streets.

However, the brief problem of a dragon pulled the Night Watch together, and Vetinari began to make more subtle use of its Captain Vimes (pp. 318-321). He did fill the expanding Night Watch with racial minorities (trolls, dwarfs, and werewolves), apparently to keep them preoccupied with internal worries, but this had an unexpected effect: instead of falling apart, they began to define themselves as watchmen first, anything else second. When they foiled an attempt on the Patrician's life, he decided to go with the tide. He disbanded the Day Ward (which had faded to little more than a street gang), appointed Vimes to the long-defunct post of Commander and Carrot Ironfoundersson (pp. 321-322) to the rank of captain, and fit them into his political schemes.

The Watch has continued to recruit. It numbers at least 100 and may still be growing, albeit with some turnover as officers are poached by other cities – a process which Vimes doesn't mind *too* much, as it means that the whole Sto Plains region is largely being policed by people who have been trained to salute him. (The widespread slang term for new-style watchmen is "sammies.")

The Watch includes a remarkable number of nonhumans and first-generation immigrants, perhaps because they're more likely to need work than natives who are plugged into the city's network of family connections and favours, and hence are less fussy (the Watch still isn't especially popular), or maybe because Vimes knows that they're less likely to be corrupted by that same network. Vimes has actually resurrected the Cable Street Particulars, despite his disdain for their old nature, presumably because he thinks the name has some resonance; they're now basically a plainclothes division and a place to put people who aren't natural watchmen but who have skills useful for specific purposes. He has also recruited a forensic alchemist, and an Igor as a medic.

Vetinari continues to observe all this with apparent favour; Vimes balances the arrogance of the aristocracy and the growing power of the guilds. On the other hand, Vimes' cynicism could produce a force with little respect for the feelings or nominal rights of the population (he's happy to call the modern Particulars "secret police"), and although Vetinari has no particular regard for "human rights," he knows better than to push people too far. He's assisted in keeping the balance by Carrot's idealism; Carrot *does* believe in human rights, because they're written into the law.

Corruption hasn't been entirely eliminated from the Watch – it still includes Nobby Nobbs (p. 327), after all – but if serious cases show up, the perpetrator is in deep trouble. Furthermore, Vimes and Carrot between them do a good job of instilling a combination of group loyalty and idealism. Among other things, this means that PCs caught breaking laws can't rely on bribery to get them off.

For a character template that represents a competent, fairly experienced watchman, see *Watchman* (pp. 138-140). Some are much better than that (see Chapter 9); a few have more faults and foibles. A "police procedural" campaign could certainly feature a newly formed patrol made up entirely of PCs.

WATCH-HOUSES

The Night Watch was traditionally based in a building on Treacle Mine Road, but that was burned out by a dragon and then replaced by a new HQ in Pseudopolis Yard, a gift from Lady Sybil Ramkin. As the Watch grew, it added several subsidiary watch-houses – in Dolly Sisters, Long Wall, and Chitterling Street – as well as some smaller unmanned stations at the main city gates. Most recently, the Treacle Mine Road building has been reclaimed and is being refurbished to provide more space. Vimes and his older colleagues try not to get too sentimental over this.

There's also another building, across an alley from the Pseudopolis Yard HQ, which acts as a training school and annexe. This is known as the Old Lemonade Factory, because that's what it is.

WATCH RANKS AND POWERS

Rank (p. 35) in the Watch ranges from 0 (Lance-Constable or Constable), through 1 (Lance-Corporal), 2 (Corporal), 3 (Sergeant), and 4 (Captain), to 5 (Commander). Lance-constables are trainees and recent or temporary recruits. Specialists such as forensic alchemists are sometimes ranked as corporals or sergeants – mostly to justify their pay rate – but may be chewed out by a captain if they try to give real orders. There's only one Commander.

Watchmen from lance-constables up to corporals have 5-point Legal Enforcement Powers (p. 35), because Commander Vimes keeps them on a fairly tight leash and Captain Carrot insists on playing by the book. Sergeants and above have 10-point Legal Enforcement Powers, as they're trusted with a fair amount of discretion and the legal system under which they're working is relaxed at best.

Although high Watch Rank grants extra Status (see *Special Cases for Status*, p. 38), sergeants may have only Status 0 in practise – all else aside, because the pay rarely supports more (a *captain's* pay can *just* support Status 1). If a PC reaches this level, the GM may permit the player to keep Status at its former level, thereby recovering 5 points. Thus, moving from Rank 2 to Rank 3 might effectively cost no points – except that the new sergeant also has to spend 5 points on those increased Legal Enforcement Powers. Anyway, achieving that promotion is quite hard; the candidate must demonstrate enough skill and knowledge to win the respect of the rest of the Watch, from the Commander on down. Roleplay it!

WATCH EQUIPMENT

In game terms, standard Watch armour is medium for human and dwarf watchmen (DR 3, 30 lbs.), very light for SM +1 trolls (DR 1, 18 lbs.); gnomes can't carry enough protection to provide any useful DR, while larger trolls don't bother. Dwarf watchmen who want to wear heavier-than-standard-issue armour at their own expense won't be stopped, provided that this doesn't completely immobilise them. It's a genuine cultural tradition with dwarfs, after all, and the Watch is loath to stop its members from having good protection.

A watchman should also carry a shortsword, a small truncheon, a crossbow and ammunition (sometimes left behind when no serious trouble is expected), an hourglass, a hand-bell[1], and various small items of kit, all adding up to at least 15 lbs. Dwarf and troll watchmen usually replace the sword with an axe or some kind of club, respectively, and trolls pack bigger crossbows. Riot duty may call for a "pike" (spear) or a halberd. Bear in mind that this standard load is as much theory as reality. All too often, the Watch is equipped on the principles of Protection, Proper Fit, and Already Paid For – not necessarily in that order.

Assuming a full standard load, and given that the typical human watchman has ST 11 or 12, many watchmen are likely to be carrying at least Light encumbrance – which does slow them down a little (usually to Move 4) and is enough to explain why they take so many surreptitious sit-downs. Roguish PCs may notice this and try the old tactic of Running Away Quickly, laughing as they go.

---

1. *The traditional chief occupation of a night watchman is carrying hourglass and bell, and yelling "Medium-sized pile of sand and all's well!" at approximately correct intervals.*

That's traditional for quick-witted heroes faced with lumbering guards and shouldn't be automatically penalised, but if they make too much of a habit of it, have them run into Captain Angua, or Captain Carrot, or just a watchman who's skilled and swift with his crossbow. And remember: some watchmen know *all* the shortcuts.

City Law

Ankh-Morpork isn't short of laws; in fact, it has 2,000 years' worth. However, they aren't always enforced. Perhaps the only person who actually knows all of the criminal law is Captain Carrot (pp. 321-322), who conscientiously taught himself the book before discovering that there wasn't much point.[1] Mr. Slant (p. 315) probably knows most of it (and wrote a significant fraction of it), but he mostly focuses on commercial law and whatever favours his wealthy clients.

There are a large number of guild rules, mostly of a fairly commonsensical nature, plus what the Patrician defines as "natural justice." The latter means that if someone can get away with something, it's legal – but if the victims object with sharp implements, it's illegal, and the punishment is proportionate to the illegality. Swords and axes are generally tolerated, but the Watch is increasingly inclined and able to treat anyone carrying serious weapons as a troublemaker; someone with a bow or a crossbow had better have a good story ready. Aristocrats and people who look the part are still allowed to wear light swords in public, but if they *draw* them, the Watch will remember that Status isn't supposed to make any difference to them.

THE COURTS

Anyone taken by the Watch has the right to appeal to the Patrician. Serious cases – e.g., rapes, murders, and large-scale robberies and frauds – go before him automatically. Appealing to the Patrician voluntarily may not seem very wise, as he dislikes having his time wasted. However, he is fair, in an ironic sort of way, and finds that unconventional judgements keep everyone on their toes. Strange cases, and those which the Watch feels concern the city as a whole, are likely to be brought to his attention; of course, he'll usually have heard about them already. Other cases go to guild courts, which are as formal as the guild sees fit – but guild-masters do enjoy their pomp and sense of power.

Anyone caught up in the system may hire a member of the Guild of Lawyers if they so wish; this is also recommended for those involved in civil cases, especially given that the Guild now judges such cases. This is an expensive process; the Thieves' Guild regards lawyers with terrified awe, as they make a lot more money than thieves while being a lot less honest, yet manage to enjoy higher social standing. Judges are senior lawyers, appointed by the Patrician; because they're on fixed public salaries, this means a drop in income (unless they get flagrant with their bribe-taking), so Vetinari finds appointment a useful threat to use against lawyers.

PUNISHMENTS

Petty criminals taken by the Watch tend to get off with a fine or some small, appropriate penalty; Captain Carrot has had some bright ideas about community service, which have led to a number of old ladies having their houses redecorated repeatedly. Serious crimes lead to more varied punishments.

Ankh-Morpork has a small prison, known as the Tanty, on the Isle of Gods. This is mainly for holding accused persons and unusual cases temporarily (although minor cases mostly go straight from the watch-house cells to court). The city takes a "medieval" view of the subject – that prisons are a drain on the state and a school for criminals – and prefers floggings and the like.[2] One ancient and rarely used punishment is to tie the miscreant to one of the pillars of the Brass Bridge at low tide, and then untie him one day later. There's also a public gallows, still used occasionally for serious cases. The city's original gallows was located by Hide Park, in Ankh – and there's still a structure there, with a wooden dummy on it for show and to confuse the ravens – but nowadays, public hangings take place outside the front of the prison.

The original theory was that public executions would terrify potential criminals into virtue – but as in our world's history, this completely failed to work, although they provided a lot of entertainment for the masses. They still do. Lord Vetinari regards this sort of thing as part of the necessary pageantry of running the city, and the Ankh-Morpork mob is a bloodthirsty if sentimental beast. The fact that a small proportion of "executed" criminals are merely rendered insensible by a finely calculated drop and then offered some kind of high-risk job by the Patrician remains a deep secret, of course.

---

1. *He's now in a position to make a point of such things, though, if he chooses to.*

2. *Given that the Tanty is quite humanely run, by the standards of the Disc and of low-tech societies generally, it is probably better accommodation than a lot of its inhabitants are used to. It also seemingly offers several options for escape, all of them carefully designed to not quite work, just to keep longer-term inhabitants occupied.*

Public executions are fairly rare, though, which isn't to say that the death penalty is uncommon in the city at large. It's certainly much enforced on, say, non-Guild thieves and individuals the Patrician considers an unalloyed problem – but *informally*. Formally acknowledged capital crimes have been defined as treachery to the city, continuing to commit murder after being told not to, irredeemable stupidity while not being a troll, and persistent street theatre. However, anything bad on a large enough scale may attract the Patrician's attention as deserving discouragement, as Moist von Lipwig (pp. 309-311) discovered to his cost.

Jurisdiction

Ankh-Morpork law applies in the city's suburbs and subordinate villages. *In principle,* it also applies in the holdings of members of the Ankh-Morpork aristocracy. In practise, those aristocrats tend to see themselves as the supreme authority on their own lands and can only be convinced otherwise if the city authorities are prepared to apply serious persuasion and maybe some force. Law enforcement in rural areas is too often left to constables owing allegiance to the local landowner and sometimes just to the landowner's bailiffs.

However, this situation is changing, as the aristocracy are being obliged to recognise that they're no longer feudal warlords. The rural area known as the Shires is currently being brought within the ambit of modern Ankh-Morpork law; see *Snuff*.

The Regiments

Strangely enough, for a long period prior to the very recent past, Ankh-Morpork had no army. The traditional military system was

basically feudal: The city had a lot of aristocrats, each of whom could – given an excuse – raise a few hundred personal troops, known as the Regiments. As usual in a feudal system, this made kingship a tricky business of alliance-juggling and favour-rationing. Like many Ankh-Morpork laws and traditions, though, this arrangement had fallen into disuse. As for the alternatives, the Militia (which could be called up by royal command) was more of an emergency riot-suppression force, the Watch was purely for law enforcement, and the Patrician's Guard just guarded the Patrician.

This didn't look like a problem, however. The usual comment in the city was that any barbarians who wanted to conquer the place were welcome; they were likely to end up being sold a bunch of souvenirs. This was largely true historically, while in recent times, the Sto Plains had grown too densely populated for barbarian hordes to reach the city without tripping over a *lot* of cabbages on the way. The other cities and duchies of the region could be viewed as a greater threat, but in fact serious warfare had become rare in the Plains – the region saw too much trade, and you can't sell things to a corpse, even that of an old trading partner who was also a cousin. Anyway, the essentially libertarian nature of Ankh-Morpork distrusted any large body of men paid to hang around with weapons – they might get bored – while the option of raising the Regiments provided a comforting answer to the theoretical question of what to do if a war *did* happen.

All of which left everybody feeling pleased about all the money they were saving – and then Ankh-Morpork got into a confrontation with Klatch (see *Jingo*). The nobles who were refusing to back down over this took the historically correct path and raised the Regiments. This meant that the army sent to confront Klatch was a hastily mustered horde of untrained amateurs led by even bigger amateurs. Fortunately, its actual effectiveness was never tested against the hardened Klatchian army.

Logically, that should have been the end of the story. However, the Patrician noted that his city was now facing continent-wide problems, and that some of the people who had signed up for the Regiments seemed terribly keen. Thus, he didn't disband them entirely. They became a small standing force, effectively under city authority, and received enough training to survive a real fight, and to act as a cadre – the kernel of a larger army – in the unlikely event of the city being seriously threatened again.

This new force has even been tested in action, as a contingent was sent to Borogravia (p. 241) when that nation's demented aggression was becoming a threat to regional stability (and to the semaphore system on which Ankh-Morpork's trade now relies). It seems to have performed tolerably, despite being under the command of a bunch of aristocrats, including Lord Rust (p. 309). The presence of Commander Vimes (pp. 318-321) helped considerably.

The Guilds

Ankh-Morpork contains over 300 guilds. A guild has an exceedingly broad scope. It controls not only who may practise its trade, but also who may learn the trade in the first place; who the practitioners may hire and fire; where they may set up businesses; how much they charge; what standards apply to the production, quality, and advertisement of their goods or service; and almost anything else that the administrators think of. Ankh-Morpork guilds' activities are limited to the city and its territories, but many of them have subsidiaries or associations with local guilds in other cities.

This is considered a good thing, at least by those who have guild memberships. A guild normally charges a tithe (often 10% of gross income) and provides members with protection from unfair competition, leakage of trade secrets, and ordinary crime. A large guild is effectively a society of its own; many guilds-folk have no social contacts outside their profession.

It's essential for visitors to understand that the guilds protect their territory absolutely. Freelancing in a guild-regulated profession (including theft, begging, and assassination) isn't allowed. Guilds have enforcement powers and act as their own courts.

Almost all schools in Ankh-Morpork are guild-operated, not least because almost all advanced knowledge is considered the private property of one guild or another. Most hospices are also operated by guilds, for the medical care of members and their families.

Standing in the guilds is sometimes determined by an approximate sort of internal democracy in which only some people have a vote, and more often by a lot of politics, back-scratching, and whose turn it is. In a few cases, leadership changes hands on a regular basis, usually yearly. In most, though, someone who gets to the top hangs onto until death – or longer, as in the case of, say, the Guild of Lawyers. Leadership mostly involves bossing people around and eating nice dinners, but it can be a route to something more, at least in theory. For example, when the Patrician was seemingly being pushed out of his place recently, the accepted compromise candidate for his job was Tuttle Scrope, long-time president of the Shoemakers and Leatherworkers.

Ordinary Trade Guilds

The vast majority of the city's guilds deal with unremarkable commercial activities – mostly small-handicrafts manufacture, with a scattering of service industries. Butchers, bakers, haberdashers, and rat-catchers all have guilds. Some guilds have a broader ambit than their name implies; e.g., the Embalmers' Guild also numbers undertakers and gravediggers among its members. Areas of responsibility may owe as much to history as to guild name; for instance, the Engravers' Guild takes responsibility for the new industry of moveable-type printing, because its members handled older forms of printing.

Some guilds run formal schools for junior members (like the Assassins and the Fools, but typically less impressive); others believe in on-the-job training. Those that do run schools can be trusted to produce fairly consistent standards of workmanship[1] and have a care for their image. (The Embalmers teach young gravediggers philosophy, morbid humour, and ventriloquism.) The worst guilds degenerate into protection rackets, as happened with the Musicians (p. 263).

The Merchants' Guild

Oddly enough, the Merchants' Guild is one of the newest in the city. Once upon a time, people professionally involved in buying and selling used to look down on guilds, which they saw as dubious monopoly chasers, unsuited to the naturally dog-eat-dog, freebooting world of commerce. With the invention of tourism and a growth in communications, though, some brighter merchants discovered the benefits of alliance. Part of the inspiration

---

1. Although the Plumbers teach unreliability and procrastination.

was the nuisance caused by the Disc's tradition of heroism, which is largely thievery with a bigger sword; a moderately cooperative guild can afford to have something done about that.

If the PCs wish to conduct *occasional* trade, they'll probably have no problems with the Guild – but generally, anyone who seems set on taking it up full-time will receive a pointed invitation to join. Of course, influential members sometimes seek to warp the system in their favour; that's what it's *for*. Guild members dealing with non-members in the City may receive +1 to Merchant skill, due to their knowledge of obscure Guild regulations. Those who try to rob Guild merchants, save under the terms of the Thieves' Guild charter, are likely to be dealt with severely.

The Merchants' Guild appears to have annual leadership elections, or at least annual taking-of-turns. In one recent year, its Grand Master was Tim Parker, a large, amiable fellow with no volume control who specialises in the grocery trade.

Orphans

By tradition, unwanted newborn babies are sometimes left on the doorsteps of guild-houses. The guild will usually adopt them, give them the surname of a founder or a legendary craft hero, and bring them up within their profession – and if that's impractical, there's always work for servants. While chancy, this system is generally considered a Good Thing compared to the alternative. Guild childcare arrangements are typically adequate and rarely abusive, but not very much more.

Guild-raised PCs will almost always have learned the skills required by full guild members, to professional levels – and perhaps even more usefully, can have Contacts within the guild. If they lack appropriate aptitudes or just weren't needed, then they might have Savoir-Faire (Servant) instead, and probably a resentful attitude. As all guilds have uses for trustworthy muscle (they have rules, and rules need enforcers), those who grew up big and imposing could end up learning Brawling and Intimidation. However, even low-grade servants, will know at least the *basics* of guild business (perhaps meaning a Connoisseur skill). A few, especially those raised by guilds such as the Fools, may end up combining a serviceable set of skills with a *very* bitter view of the profession and a pressing desire to do something – anything – else.

The Assassins' Guild

The Assassins' Guild has been a long time evolving, and its modern form is highly refined, in several senses. It has a beautiful, airy guildhall on Filigree Street, resembling a gentleman's club but incorporating the best school on the Disc. Its weathervane displays a creeping man in a long cloak. The tower clock is set slightly behind every other clock in the city, fashionably late and as a reminder that whoever you are, you may find the Assassins behind you.

Anyone inhumed by an alumnus of the Guild school could go to his rest satisfied that he had been annulled by someone of taste and discretion.

– Pyramids

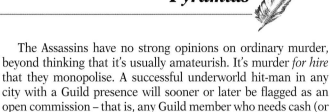

Although the gentlemanly aspect of the Guild goes back centuries, it was previously somewhat underplayed, and the Guild's public face was a bunch of scar-faced throat-cutters. In Ankh-Morpork's old sword-and-sorcery days, there was a place for a large and reliable body of quick, smirking killers, with a few more-gentlemanly types handling the high-end commissions. Today, however, *assassination* has become purely the business of the upper classes (and, more quietly, in some cases the business of their trusted employees – the Guild school's scholarship boys). Cheaper sorts are mere *killers,* who the Assassins would like to ignore but must sometimes remove to maintain their monopoly.

Certainly, someone with a little cash can still find hired killers in the Shades, but these never call themselves Assassins – whether to avoid drawing the Guild's attention or out of inverted snobbery (gentlemanly Assassins are regarded with some contempt by the deep underworld). It's also believed by members of the Thieves' Guild that if they're clumsy enough to turn a mugging into murder, the Assassins will take offence at the demarcation problem and come round to say goodbye. This probably exaggerates the amount the Assassins care, although it's likely that they promote the rumour to keep competition under control.

Banking

As a long-established commercial centre, Ankh-Morpork has a banking system which is probably more stable and sensibly run than most commercial activities in the city – because banks run on trust, and the city needs somewhere people can trust to hold their money. It's hardly perfect or flawless; a smart con artist can often find and profit from a problem somewhere in the system. Still, it has long held together rather well.

The nominal heart of the system is the Royal Bank of Ankh-Morpork (see *Post and Banking,* pp. 249-250), which issues the currency. This was previously run as a private holding of the Lavish family. However, after much of the ownership passed to a small dog in the guardianship of first Moist von Lipwig and then the Patrician, and the Lavishes were exposed as, essentially, embezzlers, it has become much more of an arm of the state.

Ankh-Morpork's banking industry runs on competition, but it's a polite sort of competition, and all of the senior bankers know and essentially trust each other. This ensures that a recognised threat to the system as a whole – such as a too-successful big-time con artist – is living dangerously. The bankers will close ranks and bring their combined personal resources to bear on the problem. This tends to mean a generous bounty offered to the Assassins' Guild, though other solutions are possible.

The Assassins have no strong opinions on ordinary murder, beyond thinking that it's usually amateurish. It's murder *for hire* that they monopolise. A successful underworld hit-man in any city with a Guild presence will sooner or later be flagged as an open commission – that is, any Guild member who needs cash (or likes a challenge) can remove him and claim his price.

THE SCHOOL

Within the Assassins' guildhall is one of the largest libraries in Ankh-Morpork – its collections unsurpassed in its speciality areas[1] – and the Guild school. The Guild actually offers the best general education anywhere on the Disc. An Assassin must be at home in any social environment and able to perform his task with grace and taste as well as technical competence. The school ensures that Guild members meet this standard, with the result that it has become popular among aristocratic families with no interest in their sons becoming paid killers. It doesn't hurt that training in assassination also acts as good training in how to defend oneself against the same.

In fact, only about one in 15 Guild novices actually becomes an Assassin. Most boys are sent there for the education. Sons of dead Assassins receive a free scholarship, as do a few other promising youths. The school has developed as many complex and pointless traditions, and as much peculiar private slang, as any British public school (e.g., "edificeering" for roof-climbing as a hobby and a sport, and "inhumation" for killing); however, slightly more parts of their versions involve ways of killing people.

For most of its history, the Guild took only male students, but it was always *realistic,* acknowledging that many of the finest Assassins were female. Women could attain membership by invitation (how some were chosen for this rather than being eliminated as unauthorised competition is unclear, but doubtless there were procedures), and were even employed as teachers. Today, the school has moved with the times and become co-educational, with the foundation of a couple of all-female houses.

The school's graduation examination is notoriously deadly, designed to ensure that any Guild member will provide reliable services in the Guild's highest traditions – and also that he'll be willing to kill when the moment arrives. Failure in this test is always, and intentionally, lethal. However, given that a large proportion of pupils are members of the aristocracy who aren't intending to become working Assassins, and that a lot of *them* are intellectually mediocre at best, it's safe to assume that many pupils are quietly withdrawn from the school before the end of their final year, with no ill feelings on either side. A decision by an eldest son and heir to go for the test would be a serious matter.

Even full graduates of the school don't necessarily take up careers within the Guild; for examples, see *Pyramids,* in which one goes home as heir to a throne and another returns to his family's not-totally-legal import-export business. It's entirely possible that a qualified Assassin might lose his killing edge, too.

---

1. *Anatomy, poisons, concealable edged weapons, Death and Death Studies, and obscure access routes in major buildings.*

One who has spent years, say, consulting on defensive measures may develop worrying scruples if suddenly offered a commission.

ASSASSIN STYLE

In general, active Assassins have little in the way of morals, but very high standards. The Assassins are by far the most *stylish* of all the guilds. They're nearly always dressed in fine black – and if not, then in dark greys or deep purple. (Junior pupils at the school wear a complex and embarrassing uniform until they advance far enough to "take dark," giving them an incentive to work hard, while teachers wear a purple sash.) Not to be well-dressed when killing someone would be almost as bad as botching the job, though not nearly as bad as not being paid.

This is important. The Guild saying is: "We do not kill merely for a handful of silver. It's a lapful of gold or nothing." The Guild charges exorbitant fees, reflecting the value it places on human life. For an Assassin to work for free would be the gravest breach of the rules.

Guild members salute each other casually by pressing the right thumb against the first two fingers of the right hand, and rubbing gently.

For the code of conduct that the majority of Assassins obey, see *Code of Honour* (pp. 56-57). For a character template, see *Assassin* (p. 140).

GUILD RATES

The Assassins' Guild sets a wide range of charges but is never cheap. The absolute minimum appears to be $10,000. At one point, the stated price for an attempt on Commander Vimes was $400,000, but following injuries to several competent Assassins, and a bloody nose for the head of the Guild himself, this rose. Eventually, the Guild took Vimes off their schedule altogether.

At one time, the price on the Patrician's head was $1,000,000, reflecting both the Guild's sense that his survival may be desirable and their guess as to the task's difficulty. It was further rumoured that they would have charged more to guarantee that he *stayed* dead. The subject is now academic – today, they would simply *refuse* the commission, as they would with Vimes.

These numbers only *seem* impossibly high. There's a huge diversity of personal wealth in Ankh-Morpork.

GUILD LEADERS AND TUTORS

The current Master of Assassins (head of the Guild) is Lord Downey, an amiable-looking, white-haired gentleman whose personal specialisation is poisons – although nobody who has died in his vicinity has ever been found to have been poisoned (he's assumed to be *very good* at his work). He's also a shrewd political operator. In his youth, however, he was an oafish, bullying aristocrat – and one of his victims was the young Havelock Vetinari. Lord Vetinari never refers to this fact, but Lord Downey isn't stupid enough to think that the Patrician ever forgets anything. Presumably, it suits Vetinari to have the Master of Assassins perpetually slightly worried.

Insofar as the Guild has a hierarchy – and it does have a council, which decides major items of policy, including those rare cases when a possible target such as Vetinari or Vimes is put in abeyance – most of its members are senior tutors at the school. Because of the aristocratic bias of Guild selection, a number of them have noble titles (such as the Kompt de Yoyo, house tutor of

Wigblock Prior House, who teaches Modern Languages and Music). Others are termed "Doctor" or "Professor." The Guild quite likely awards academic titles to those who complete its famously rigorous if rather specialised courses of postgraduate studies.

Female instructors at the school include Lady T'malia, who teaches Political Expediency, and whose extensive jewellery carries enough poison to inhume a small town. A more recent recruit is Miss Alice Band, who teaches Traps, Locks and Climbing. A relatively young and notoriously strict woman, Miss Band has been known to send overconfident students on nigh-suicidal tests, such as infiltrating Samuel Vimes' house.

The Breccia

The Thieves' and Assassins' Guilds don't control *all* organised crime in Ankh-Morpork. In particular, they're unable to make much inroad in the nonhuman communities. Dwarfs aren't particularly inclined to this sort of thing, but trolls, with their capacity for direct violence and limited comprehension of human laws, have their own group.

The *Breccia* is a loose syndicate of troll "businessmen," known as the *tons*, who all deny that the Breccia exists (publicly insisting that it *does* can be quite unhealthy). It's led by Chrysoprase, an exceptionally intelligent troll with a taste for human-style suits and diamond jewellery. While Chrysoprase is capable of ruthless brutality and makes sure that his clients and partners know it, he's also capable of long-term planning, and not only when he's sitting in a refrigerated warehouse. Hence, he has withdrawn the Breccia from the troll drug trade, which is increasingly run by rash young trolls who consume their own, ever more dangerous products. He now focuses on finance and property – not actually legitimate, but more respectable. He sometimes acts as a moderate leader figure in the troll community and seems to have some genuine respect for Commander Vimes; peace and stability are better for business, after all.

Chrysoprase's organisation is always willing to lend money to anyone desperate enough to ask. Failure to pay the rather substantial interest rates leads to painful consequences.

The Thieves' Guild

The Guild of Thieves, Burglars, and Allied Trades – like the Assassins' Guild – is a recent organisation of an old practise. It claims descent from various mobs and gangs that existed from time immemorial, but its current form was (again) inspired by Lord Vetinari. The Patrician's idea was based on the belief that, if Ankh-Morpork was going to have crime, then it really ought to be *organised*. He put this to various persons, who were happy to accept an annual quota of tolerated crime – a level of burglary, robbery, and so forth – that lay within acceptable social limits. Of course, they assumed that they could exploit this system for a few years and then drop back into their old ways if it all started getting inconvenient.

By the time they discovered that Vetinari had found out their names and addresses, and those of their families, mistresses, and favourite eating-houses, it was too late. They weren't arrested – they trapped *themselves*, growing fat as pillars of the community. The line between criminal and tradesmen in Ankh-Morpork had often seemed thin; today, it has simply disappeared.

The Guild administration subcontracts Guild crimes to individual members or groups. The quota is spread fairly, so that all members receive an adequate income, unprofitable crime (such as robbing bankrupt businesses) is avoided, and citizens are subject to a strictly limited amount of crime per year. Many citizens arrange to fulfil their quota at a convenient time and place – e.g., one might be robbed at knifepoint in the early evening, in one's side garden, with property damage specified as that awful garden ornament one was given last Hogswatchnight – and spend the rest of the year in perfect safety. People with less foresight sometimes have difficulty accepting muggings as a civic duty, but this is to be expected in a free society.

Naturally, private criminal enterprise represents a danger to this system, and the Guild works swiftly and dramatically against it, generally in a manner that provides a lesson to other would-be freelancers, as well as to students of anatomy.[1]

This has all become rather formalised, even ritualised – but being a guild, the thieves nonetheless ensure that a proper system of training and promotions is in place, and they are quite competent in their field. They have a school which includes renowned experts in lockpicking, pocket-picking, burglary, precise and humane blackjacking, sidling, intimidating repartee, and so on. For a template for a Guild-trained thief, see *Guild Thief* (pp. 134-135).

Disorganised Crime

Not all crime in Ankh-Morpork is sanctioned by the Thieves' Guild. Provided that a villain is discreet, and restricts his actions to people without much social standing – or leaves them unable to complain, ever – it's possible to make a living as a freelance miscreant. As well, there are always a few new arrivals from out of town, idiots, and inadequates whose best chance for survival is that the Watch will catch them before the Guild does. And just occasionally, a genuinely extraordinary rogue shows up and keeps ahead of *everyone* . . . for a while.

For game purposes, this has several implications. For one thing, the Shades contains any number of surly thugs who don't respect possession of a Guild receipt, and who can be used to keep things interesting for visitors. For another, PCs or NPCs with a little nerve and cash, and enough desperate need, can usually acquire the services of such heavies (Streetwise skill and a plausibly dangerous demeanour are both important here, as many thugs, on meeting someone with money in his pocket, may decide to cut out the doing-a-job phase). And if the *PCs* decide to take up freelance crime – well, it's up to the GM to decide which category they belong in.

The Guild's current president is Mr. Boggis, a stout, affable, not-very-subtle fellow who's a pillar of Ankh-Morpork society, even signing up to assist the Watch on a temporary basis during civic emergencies. It doesn't hurt that he brings his bodyguards along on these occasions. At least, it doesn't hurt him, or the Watch.

> *The city **operated**. It was a self-regulating college of Guilds linked by the inexorable laws of mutual self-interest, and it **worked**. On average. By and large. Overall. Normally.*
> **– Men at Arms**

The Beggars' Guild

This is the oldest guild in the city. Allegedly, it's also the wealthiest, since its central principle is not to pay cash for anything that someone can be persuaded to give you. The Guild antedates the other guilds by centuries at least, and indeed it probably originated five minutes after the first hunter-gatherer came back from hunting-gathering with more than he could consume on the spot.

The Guild has a large and, to the uninitiated, bewildering system of types and degrees of beggary: Mumblers, Street-Corner Shouters, People Who Need Tuppence for a Tea, etc. The current leader is Queen Molly, a sharp but essentially good-natured woman who does rather well considering that the Guild's traditional protocol obliges her to ask for nothing less than full banquets, with wine and spirits.

In practical terms, the beggar's living is earned in two ways: begging and not begging. Begging we will assume the reader is familiar with. Not begging as a career involves having, in game terms, Ugly or preferably Hideous appearance, Bad Smell, or Odious Personal Habits – anything that others will gladly pay not to experience close up. Not begging at people's parties is especially profitable.[2]

The Fools' Guild

The Guild of Fools and Joculators and College of Clowns maintains what's probably the grimmest guildhall on the Disc, dank and silent except for the occasional whimper of a student learning that dying is never easier than when you're trying for comedy. It makes a depressing contrast to the modern, cultured guildhall next door, which belongs to the Assassins. It has stern rules about what is or isn't funny, and it regards original humour as nearly blasphemous. Only the greatest clowns may invent jokes.

Visitors to the guildhall should watch out for the small details that members regard as necessary symbols (buckets over the door, trick buttonhole flowers, etc.), although these are invariably rather predictable. Guild ceremonies, even funerals, involve a lot of stock routines and custard.

---

1. *This is considered a matter of internal discipline, and so is of no interest to the Assassins' Guild.*

2. *The citizen pays the Guild a small fee, and no beggars show up.*

The Guild President is known as Dr. Whiteface, though it isn't known whether this is a specific clown or the name used by whoever has risen to the job – probably the latter. Full Guild members spend most of their time in make-up, and they regard their standard design *as their face;* for a clown (or anyone else) to wear someone else's face is an obscenity. Nonetheless, the Guild president may somehow always be a white-face clown. Sinister and utterly unsmiling, white-face clowns are pretty scary individuals . . .

The Dogs' Guild

The Dogs' Guild (which, no, isn't part of the official system) admits only dogs who've been "bad." Members must have at least run away from their owners. The Guild exists because some Discworld dogs are bright enough to comprehend this sort of formal organisation; see *Sapient Animals* (pp. 106-107). It controls scavenging rights, assigns loud-barking and cat-chasing territories, and regulates breeding. Its leader is called the Chief Barker.

While few PCs are likely to join this guild voluntarily, the nature of fate on the Disc means that temporary qualification cannot be ruled out. In such circumstances, one ought to be glad to have a strong professional association.

The Guild once was led by Big Fido, a poodle who dreamed of wolves. Big Fido's burning insanity made him quite capable of dismembering any other dog in the city. Had he been human, the Disc would probably have been in serious trouble, involving jackboots. Since his death, the Guild has gone back to quieter ways, with fewer dreams. But many a flea-bitten stray remembers – it makes gutter life a little bit more tolerable.

The Rats' Guild

The Rats' Guild is only rumoured to exist. If it does, it will certainly have the largest membership in the city.

Some Other Guilds

The following is a selection of some of Ankh-Morpork's more colourful guilds. Do remember that most are more prosaic than this.

The Gamblers' Guild: It's a way of earning a living, and rules are always part of a game . . . This guild permits a certain amount of nonmagical cheating, within strict limits. After all, if everyone does it, the game becomes a contest of skill, whether or not it's "supposed" to be. Non-members may have their own opinions on the matter, mind you.

The Historians' Guild: This small group is basically a club for professional scholars who work as archivists, genealogists, writers, and so on. However, Ankh-Morporkians like to quote precedent at each other, and history can have implications for current events; thus, the Guild is often invited to send a representative to important meetings.

The Musicians' Guild: This small guild lacks the educational and social benefits of the larger organisations, at best running as not much more than a specialist protection racket, charging anyone working as a professional musician in Ankh-Morpork hefty fees not to have their fingers broken by a group of close-harmony enforcers. However, it may not yet have recovered from the bizarre and possibly non-historical Music With Rocks In incident,

which led to the death of its then-president, Mr. Clete – so it might be *relatively* safe to busk in the city at present.

Banned and Irregular Guilds

Most guild business is routine, and most guild members are ordinary craft workers. Still, there's some strangeness at the edges of the system.

Few guilds have ever been banned, although the Patrician reserves the right. Certainly, a guild which seems to have lost control will need to sort itself out – or be sorted out. The *Firefighters' Guild* is one that was prohibited; it worked on the basis that a small monthly payment would guarantee its members' attention in the event of a fire, which turned out to mean that they came round to the houses of people who *didn't* pay, and made Meaningful Casual Remarks. Protection rackets are one thing, as the Thieves' Guild would attest, but fire is altogether too dangerous to the city at large. While there's occasional talk of setting up a municipal fire brigade, that hasn't got anywhere yet.

Creating a Guild

Given that the idea of guilds is widely understood and respected, it's possible that some people in a new or previously disorganised field will decide to call themselves a "guild." This isn't always wise; the existing guilds regard the formal system as important, and they may well decide to Do Something about anyone who seems to be making a mockery of it. However, this *is* how the Merchants' Guild (for example) came into existence, back in less orderly times. A group with a good lawyer, some quick footwork, and no hostility from the Patrician might get a new guild up and running.

One guild that was created thanks to a loophole in the rules was the Guild of C.M.O.T. Dibblers, which has just one member (pp. 315-316). That loophole has been firmly sealed shut.

The Seamstresses' Guild (hem hem): This is a euphemism (and one not unique to the Discworld); the business of the Seamstresses' Guild has nothing to do with needles or thread, and as they say, it believes keenly in on-the-job training. It was granted its charter by Lord Vetinari, after his predecessor broke a promise to do so ("Typical of a man," its members would remark). It's one of the few female-dominated guilds, although it admits a handful of male members; its current leader is the very shrewd Mrs. Rosemary Palm. It runs a more sophisticated medical-benefits scheme than most guilds, and its enforcers – the eccentric, terrifying, and seemingly ageless Agony Aunts, Dotsie and Sadie – are deeply feared by those who've crossed them. They appear to be deadly fighters with handbag and umbrella, but quite what they do is rather unclear; their most *fortunate* victims tend to wake up in the street with hazy memories, completely covered in paint. If the Agony Aunts have to appear in a game, the GM should try to keep them off-stage as much as possible, as a kind of surreal and overwhelming threat.

The Lady Sib

A recent foundation in Morpork, the Lady Sibyl Free Hospital is a charitable institution – sponsored by the Vimes family – which provides free medical care to the city. It's run by Dr. John "Mossy" Lawn, who in game terms has a 5-point Unusual Background, "Klatchian Medical Training," meaning that his medical skills are at TL4 (see *Medical Skills*, p. 77). He enforces the same standards on his staff and may be successfully training some young doctors in exotic ideas such as hygiene.

Ironically, this means that the poor patients who use the "Lady Sib" frequently receive better treatment than wealthy people who employ prestigious traditional doctors. It's quite likely that adventurer PCs will end up there at some point and benefit from this. Unless they genuinely appear to be dying, though, they may well find themselves in a long queue. Also, while the hospital is definitely free, it *is* a charity, and it can always find a use for donations; individuals who look like *successful* adventurers will receive a lot of polite-but-firm hints on this subject before they leave.

Failing to respond appropriately to that is one way to acquire a new negative Reputation in Ankh-Morpork – but making actual trouble at the hospital is *really* stupid. Not only do many of the city's toughest street brawlers receive good treatment there, and want it to remain standing so that they can go back if necessary, but Dr. Lawn is personal physician to the Vimes family. While Lawn has a full set of medical ethics, and he knows the value of discretion after years of work for the Seamstresses' Guild, he isn't required to remain silent about absolutely everything; patients who show up with *interesting* injuries may well be mentioned to the authorities.

The hospital also looks after a few mental illness cases. It has a whole wing dedicated to people who think that they're Lord Vetinari.

The Strippers' Guild: Strictly, the Guild of Ecdysiasts, Nautchers, Cancanières, and Exponents of Exotic Dance, another all-female guild (although it, too, might well be broad-minded enough to accept male applicants; Ankh-Morpork is an unreconstructed sort of society, but if people are willing to pay for something, nobody much argues). This one even has troll members (who specialise in putting clothes *on* – trolls have some odd ways), but no dwarfs, as the idea of removing clothes is largely outside of dwarf experience. The Guild is run singlehandedly by the legendary Miss Dixie "VaVa" Voom, who retired from the stage a few years ago, possibly after causing one riot or heart attack too many.

Food, Drink, and Lodging

Ankh-Morpork derives a lot of income from visitors. There are a great many rooms-to-let available, a variety of food shops and restaurants, and countless places for a drink and a brawl.[1] The following list just skims the surface and leans toward establishments which feature prominently in the chronicles; e.g., the Drum. Because such places *are* so significant, the GM may want to save them for specific encounters or big moments. Then again, *everyone* in the city-based stories seems to end up drinking at the Drum – usually sooner rather than later.

---

1. *The brawl may be included with the cover price.*

The Drum

The Mended Drum, on Filigree Street, is an Ankh-Morpork institution (especially if "institution" is defined to mean "a place with lots of screaming and people with funny ideas about reality"). It's a *well*-established hostelry. It has burned down many times, but somehow, it always gets rebuilt. At times, it has been known as The Broken Drum ("you can't beat it," ho ho), and then renamed after the next fire by a new owner with a quick sense of humour.

The Drum opens directly onto the street; traditionally, the door is guarded by a troll. It backs on the River Ankh. Steps lead down to the main room, which is thick with the smoke of generations, and whose floor is paved with matted rushes and trampled beetles, many of otherwise un-encountered species.

There are also a few rather insalubrious, but just tolerable, rooms for rent upstairs (at Status -1 standards and rates, unless you look like a rich sucker, in which case the prices rise fast).

The tavern serves something identified as beer; food might be available, though the request would be considered odd. The real point of visiting the Drum is its clientèle. It's said that if you spend enough time here, every major hero on the Disc will steal your horse. The Drum is also a favourite haunt of student wizards, who tend to sit in a corner, nursing one drink all night and hoping that their pointy hats will scare off trouble.

It should be understood that the Drum has its own particular sort of indelicate decorum. There will certainly be brawls; that's part of the ambience. People sometimes get killed, but not maliciously. Children are not at great risk (except of expanding their vocabulary), nor are maidens (unless that's the maiden's idea – although their escorts might have to fend off would-be competitors); any ruckus is strictly confined to consenting adults. Still, entering the bar may be considered de facto evidence of consent. There are occasionally quiet nights, usually after some incident (an invasion, a dragon attack) has given everyone enough excitement for a few days, when the owner may even set out bowls of peanuts on the bar – unless the Librarian is expected.

The Drum has changed ownership many times. Any attempt to redecorate usually means a new owner will be along soon; on the Disc, it's difficult to change anything that has been around long enough to develop a personality. The current owner is Hibiscus Dunelm.

Incidentally, one of Dunelm's temporary mistakes was trying to organise musical entertainment. Unfortunately, his customers decided that anyone standing up on stage was a legitimate target, the Librarian took to throwing peanut shells, and the place is now blacklisted by every entertainment guild in the city.

BRAWLING CONTESTS

Lately, brawls in the Drum have become oddly . . . formalised. Thanks to its fame (in Twoflower's memoirs, among other places), the Drum has benefited from the emergence of tourism, but people who come here tend to expect the full traditional range of incidents. And people on the Disc can be simultaneously competitive and traditional.

Hence, many brawls in the Drum are – whisper it – prearranged, even to some extent choreographed. Brawling has become a team sport, with a scoring system based on stylishness and theatricality. Attacks are still delivered with full force, and often with edged weapons, but all teams employ an Igor, so maimed participants can be reassembled afterwards. Professionals are usually tattooed with their own names, in several places, to make sure that they get back their own body parts and not anyone else's. Some PCs might wish to participate in all this; others may just get caught in the chaos.

The sad fact is, though, that with the growth of tourism and would-be social sophistication in Ankh-Morpork, even the Drum may be in danger of becoming an artificial imitation of itself. It'll be a fair few years before it becomes exactly *safe*, however.

Other Bars

Below are a few more bars which have earned mentions in the chronicles. These aren't especially typical of anything, but PCs might find their way to them.

On the far side of the huge room, the evening's fight began with a well-executed Looking-At-Me-In-A-Funny-Way, earning two points and a broken tooth.

– Going Postal

BIERS

This hostelry is in one of the marginally safer parts of the Shades. It used to be called the Crown and Axe, but strictly speaking it no longer has a name; "Biers" is more of a nickname. It doesn't even have a sign outside – there's a sense that people who belong there will somehow find it, while those who don't, won't. Any PCs who actively go looking for it will need an Area Knowledge or Streetwise roll at -4, unless they *belong* (GM's option), in which case IQ+3 will suffice.

Biers' speciality is that it serves beings who don't really fit in at any other bar. Undead, werewolves, and anthropomorphic personifications are regular customers. They make this a rather sinister-seeming place, although it's patronised by Tooth Fairies as well as bogeymen.

Biers never closes, and the lighting is kept low. The barman, Igor (just Igor, not *an* Igor), makes a point of keeping every *thing* his customers might want, within the limits set by Ankh-Morpork's very broad legal system. He's flamboyant enough to decorate some of the drinks – and a few of the decorations are a little startling (Fright Checks optional). Still, you can obtain fruit juices and conventional booze, too; not all the customers want blood. There's no food, apart from bar-top snacks that one wouldn't wish to talk about.

Igor himself appears to be human, apart from a bit too much hair and eyebrows that meet in the middle, and the fact that he seems to mind the bar 24 hours a day. He sets a few *ad hoc* rules, which keep the place viable; these boil down to "no use of excessive supernatural powers, and no brawling." Biers is actually quite a safe bar in that sense. Any "normals" who do somehow wander in usually wander out again rather briskly. If they stay, though, they probably won't suffer worse than cold looks, and the clientèle are unlikely to follow them and rend them limb from limb, unless they make trouble. (There's even one regular local "normal": old, nearly blind Mrs. Gammage, who hasn't realised that the place has changed since her youth, and whom the other regulars have adopted as a mascot.) But the stares in Biers – and some of the drinks that you can get with a misjudged order – are, well, serious.

THE BUCKET

The Bucket, run by a Mr. Cheese, isn't especially highly regarded, although there's nothing actively wrong with it. It serves mediocre beer and a few other drinks, but no food. It almost defines "ordinary," except that customers are certain *not* to get rolled here, which is extraordinary by Ankh-Morpork standards.

The place's crucial feature is simply that it has become the favoured haunt of the City Watch, whose members appreciate a quiet, boring place which gives credit. As they're good customers who don't damage the furniture, this is fine with Mr. Cheese.

Non-Watch drinkers who enter the Bucket won't find any trouble unless they bring it with them, though the atmosphere may seem a little cool. It will get a lot cooler if they look like roistering, brawling adventurers (that is, work for the regular patrons). If they simply drop in for a quiet drink, however, that's their business. Coming here to find Watch members for adventure-related purposes is considered extremely bad manners – the drinkers here are *off duty* – but will lead to silence and scowls rather than a fight. Delivering genuinely urgent messages is fair enough, but don't expect thanks.

THE TROLL'S HEAD
AND THE NAMELESS BARS

Somewhere in the Shades is a tavern whose sign consists of a real troll's head, on a pole. Its customers are not acceptable in the Mended Drum, and can deal with any trolls who feel like complaining about the sign.

There are also some bars in the Shades that are downright nameless. These are places where the murkiest denizens of the underworld go to do business. They're actually quite safe for anyone who's there for what the other customers see as legitimate reasons; after all, the whole point is that people should be able to meet and talk as necessary. Anyone else is highly unlikely to make it out the door breathing.

The Gritz

The Gritz is a hotel with a well-regarded restaurant. Its customers think highly of it. However, those customers are all trolls. Members of other species aren't likely to be impressed by the range of unusual clays in the restaurant and will worry about the floor coverings (they are soft and they are on the floor, but are they carpet?). And, of course, the staff and other guests take a trollish approach to life.

Places to Stay

Ankh-Morpork has countless inns and lodging-houses to which visitors in need of a bed may be directed. Some are even quite tolerable. The trick is to find someone trustworthy to do the directing. Asking a watchman may seem sensible; unfortunately, that isn't always safe. He might try to second-guess your needs, and if he decides that you're an *adventurer* – and therefore trouble – he may send you somewhere that he reckons can handle your sort. Worse, he might be Nobby Nobbs (p. 327).

HOTELS AND LODGINGS

Living costs in Ankh-Morpork follow the general rules under *Status* (pp. 37-38) and *Living Expenses* (pp. 148-149), although short visits can prove expensive. Some inns and hotels charge *much* more (visitors are generally assumed to be gullible rustics by default), but this greed is usually balanced by fierce competition in the local hospitality industry. The hardest sorts of lodging to find may be those corresponding to the highest Status levels; people who are *seriously* well-off often own town houses in the city, or have friends or relations they can visit. Still, there are one or two luxury establishments.

THE Y.M.R-C-I-G-B-S.A.

Relatively impecunious visitors to the city may be directed to the Young Men's Reformed-Cultists-of-the-Ichor-God-Bel-Shamharoth Association. More often referred to as the Young Men's Pagan Association, this charitable establishment provides basic rooms at an affordable price ($0.10 a night). While not quite as respectable as its founders hoped – drink sometimes gets smuggled in, and some underworld types use it when lying low – it's tolerable.

This establishment doesn't serve food or drink. It's a surprisingly secure place to stay; few criminals consider its denizens worth robbing, and criminals currently living there might tell any working thieves they recognise to push off, to avoid having the Watch coming round. However, they may also notice things about other guests for future reference.

MRS. CAKE'S HOUSE

After Ludmilla left home for a while, Mrs. Cake decided that she could acquire some money and company by opening her fairly capacious house to lodgers. With her relaxed view of death, and experience of the practical problems of lycanthropy, she quickly found a gap in the market. She takes in undead, werewolves, and other supernatural beings. She's uniquely tolerant of people who keep strange hours, need a window left open for their return, or require a spare change of clothes kept handy. Particularly strange PCs may find themselves directed to this house – or drawn to it, as like Biers (p. 266), it seems to have developed a kind of psychic resonance.

Mrs. Cake

Mrs. Evadne Cake is a middle-aged woman who runs a *special* boarding-house on Elm Street, on the edge of the Shades (pp. 252-253). She's short, plump (almost circular), and nearsighted. She wears an enormous hat, covered in wax fruit and stuffed birds, all painted black, and carries a huge handbag.

She's also a highly talented medium, well-connected with the Ankh-Morpork spirit world (such as it is), with a spirit assistant named One-Man-Bucket; while she doesn't feel she needs a spirit *guide*, sometimes a direct contact on the other side saves time. Her paranormal perceptions include powerful short-range precognition, which she often has switched on, set about 10 seconds into the future, at which range it's completely reliable; thus, it functions as Danger Sense, which would be handy were she an adventurer. Unfortunately, this leads her to answer people's questions before they ask them (and she gets a headache if they then fail to ask the question she just answered). This can be disconcerting. Moreover, it can be very difficult to play unless the players are prepared to help – the GM may want to have her switch off this gift most of the time when PCs are around.

She *also* has Religion. In Disc society, attending many different temples isn't considered *wrong*, but it's thought a little erratic. Mrs. Cake, however, not only attends many temples, but also tells the priests how they should operate, what to tell their congregations, and generally what to think. Her good works never cease, despite the silent prayers of a thousand clerics. She might rate a -4 Reputation among the city's priests – the whole Disc's priests, it is said – except that they dare not say or do anything.

Mrs. Cake's daughter, Ludmilla (p. 116), is a werewolf.

Mrs. Cake doesn't usually serve food or drink to her lodgers. On the other hand, the chance of being burgled or attacked while staying in her house is negligible.

Eating Houses

The restaurant business in Ankh-Morpork is *really* varied. Prepared food for sale ranges from Mr. Dibbler's sausage inna bun (something of a mandatory experience for newcomers), through "greasy spoon" establishments such as Harga's House of Ribs (noted for its "All you can gobble for a dollar" menu option), and Klatchian and Agatean restaurants (run by the traditional immigrants who work all the hours the gods send, and who have often mutated their national cuisines beyond recognition to meet local tastes, leading to "Klatchian" curries with turnip in them), to Quirmian-style restaurants such as *Le Foie Heureux* (with truly eye-watering prices).

There are also places for the nonhuman trade: dwarf restaurants which sell rat on a stick, and troll establishments which sell all kinds of fine-quality rock. Humans rarely patronise these.

The SUPERNATURAL SIDE

study except after being specifically invited after a very nervous knock on the door. But arguing would merely waste time, which was not in ample supply at this moment, and the student in question was almost certain to recover his hearing within days and his eyebrows within weeks.

"We have a problem, Archchancellor," he began smoothly. "There is some evidence of a diminution of the ontological stability index in . . ."

"Stop right there," said Ridcully. "Is this little speech going to feature the word 'quantum' at any point in the next three sentences?"

Ponder performed a hasty mental adjustment, determining that he could change the second and third sentences of his prepared explanation without excessive loss of precision. Hence, he was able to reply "No, Archchancellor," with complete honesty.

"And was it goin' to before I interrupted?" Ridcully demanded.

Ponder took a deep breath and mentally scrapped five prepared paragraphs. "Sir – stuff is showing up that shouldn't be showing up," he said unhappily.

"Some silly bugger playin' silly buggers with books about demons, is it?"

"Possibly," said Ponder. "Originally. But it's got beyond that now."

"How far beyond?" Ridcully asked, beginning to sound actively concerned.

"We don't know, Archchancellor. But we do know who brought this to our attention. It was your brother, Archchancellor."

"Hughnon? My word . . ."

"This had better be important!" Archchancellor Ridcully roared. "I was conductin' some very important research when that blasted student came bargin' in!"

Ponder Stibbons disregarded both sentences; he heard them every time something arose that was indeed important enough to merit the Archchancellor's personal attention. He might have chosen to quibble, not only about the important research part – Ridcully had his virtues, but any gift for original academic research wasn't very high on the list – but also about the barging in part. He was pretty sure that no student would be foolish enough to enter Ridcully's

But before Ridcully could say any more, there was a sound that might have resembled an elastic band being twanged twice and then breaking, if an elastic band could be made a mile long and 100 yards thick. The windows of the room blew open – despite not having been opened in years, and in some cases never having been designed to open at all – and the sheaf of papers that Ponder was holding were snatched from his hands by a highly localised hurricane and whipped up to the ceiling, where they span in a stately fashion.

"What the blue blazes . . ." Ridcully began.

"The theurgic shielding is failing, Archchancellor!" said Ponder, clutching at his hat. "We have a divine incursion!"

"Gods?" Ridcully roared, "Gods, in here?" Then he paused, and cracked his knuckles. "Right," he said, "we'll see about that . . ."

Being a fantasy world, the Disc features magic, and plenty of gods and demons. (In fact, it has billions of gods, though few of them ever amount to much.) The complication is that things are rarely the way people think but frequently the way people *believe*.

The Basics

The Discworld exists in a universe where magic isn't only real, but is a fundamental part of the structure of reality. It explains the way things work on the invisible level – somewhat like quantum mechanics in our world. But there's more to Discworld reality than that.

The Foundations of Reality

At the top of the Discworld universe's hierarchy of powers – or the base of its structure, choose your metaphor – are the primal forces of creation, which determine not simply how things *are*, but how they *can be*.

This is the stuff which research wizards probe with excessive localised energies and confusing jargon. The fact that it seems to involve a lot of consciousness and intent, so that even *narratives* have power, just adds to the fun. So far as the researchers can tell, they live in a complex polydimensional multiverse in which everything that's possible will have happened *somewhere*. As more senior wizards point out, though, it isn't what happened somewhere else that matters – it's what happens here and now.

In this context, even gods aren't overly important – they're actually just dim-witted metaphysical parasites living off human belief. However, there *are* entities which must be taken more seriously. Some, such as the Old High Ones (p. 291), at least have the manners to keep out of human affairs, mostly. Others, such as the Old High Ones' enforcers, the Auditors (pp. 296-297), are more dangerously interventionist. And a few shouldn't have anything to do with the human world, but sometimes show up anyway.

THE DUNGEON DIMENSIONS

There are wastelands outside of space and time, limitless and all but empty, the ground seemingly consisting of silvery sand. The exception to the emptiness is the sad, angry, unreal beings which dwell there, and which both desire the touch of reality and hate all real beings. This creates *tension*.

These "Things" strictly cannot exist. Not *should* not, not *do* not – cannot. They do not accept this. They're attracted by concentrations of magic, which weaken the boundaries of reality, offering them a chance to break through.

Sometimes the entry point is inside a mind, allowing a Thing to take over the mortal; wizards are particularly attractive targets. Witches are also tempting, but their magic tends to be subtler and less prone to making holes, and their more practical natures offer fewer opportunities for useful insanity. The Things don't exactly seek to *corrupt* humans – they aren't that smart – but they can exploit foibles in a vulnerable intellect. An orderly

mind can be turned into an inhuman tyrant, calmly sacrificing millions in the name of efficiency while *convincing them it is for the best*. A passionate, artistic imagination can be persuaded to think of any number of horrors as beautiful. And the Things do know how to *threaten*.

Alternate Realities, Alternate Creations

The Discworld exists within a universe where magic is not just real, but also powerful enough that a flat world moving through space on top of a turtle is perfectly reasonable. That universe is merely one layer in a *multiverse*, which presumably encompasses our universe, too. Furthermore, some academic wizards have reached conclusions similar to those reached by a number of quantum physicists in our universe: all possible events have some kind of reality, and an infinite number of alternate timelines arise from uncertain events as time passes.

The main use of this stuff is to provide academic wizards with amazingly confusing lines of theoretical waffle, and to create a context for the existence of beings like Azrael (see *The Old High Ones*, p. 291). However, it could also provide an excuse for running Discworld games that don't *quite* fit with the history detailed in the chronicles. If alternate timelines exist, the campaign can be set in one, and the players can't assume that what they read in the stories is always correct – so the GM can surprise them sometimes. They can meet a Rincewind who never returned to Unseen University, visit an Agatean Empire whose old ruling families were never suppressed by the Silver Horde, or deal with a Greater Zlobenia which has subsumed Borogravia. They could even find themselves running the Ankh-Morpork Watch under the authority of a ruling council, because there's no Patrician and no Sam Vimes, or take part in miniature civil wars in an elf-ridden Lancre with no notable witches. The GM should make clear that this is the nature of things before the campaign starts, or the players may get confused and annoyed, but it might save those players from feeling that they can't do much that hasn't been done already.

They can also exploit bizarre *ideas,* even if these aren't explicitly magical. Anything that makes reality less coherent – or minds more confused – represents an opportunity. However, they're then constrained by the shape of the ideas that they're exploiting. They're also attracted to the number eight.

The Things are, in short, the kind of inhuman, Lovecraftian monstrosities that heroes need have no compunction about using extreme force against. The snag is finding a way to do so.

Things in Residence

Some Things have made permanent escapes from the Dungeon Dimensions, trading a little power and potential for a bit of stability. This happened most in the earlier ages of the universe, when nothing was entirely stable. Any ancient, shapeless, tentacled, habitually hostile creature may be an escapee from the Dungeon Dimensions. Or it may be a squid that has been mutated by magical energies, or a god with very poor aesthetic judgement. It's hard to tell, and easier just to get on with killing the thing – though whatever their origins, these sorts of monsters can be annoyingly tough.

One such being is known as Bel-Shamharoth, the Soul-Eater, the Soul-Render, the Sender of Eight. In physical form, Bel-Shamharoth is all tentacles and mandibles, with one enormous eye. Its temples are bigger on the inside than the outside, and they are decorated entirely in black. They have, in short, all the traditional features and were doubtless built by Inhuman Entities Before History. They're also eight-sided, as is every element and decoration inside them. It's suicidally unwise to so much as speak the word "eight" in such a place.

The Necrotelicomnicon

More such creatures are detailed in a volume called the *Necrotelicomnicon,* or *Liber Paginarum Fulvarum,* written by Achmed the Mad (also known as Achmed the I Just Get These Headaches), about whom little is known.[1] It seems likely that he drank far too much Klatchian coffee (p. 187), thus gaining a *real* comprehension of the nature of the universe. The only copy of the first edition is locked away in Unseen University's Library, chained down; most people read heavily bowdlerised 10th-hand copies. The Librarian is unlikely to let anyone gain access to it (it does unspeakable things to careless human beings), but he may look up details in it himself (he isn't human, after all).

---

1. The "About the Author" page of his book spontaneously combusted shortly after his death.

Fighting Invasions

Rule One: If Things erupt into the universe, matters are getting *serious.*

The situation will probably involve magic, but magic is the worst thing to use against Things; they just feed on it. They can

be fought physically – their "natural" forms are in many cases fairly weak, and some wizards carry their staffs into these battles to use as blunt instruments – but Things are often quite large, or possess humans or other vessels. Furthermore, there's no point in dismembering one or two or 10 of them if their means of entry to reality is still open, and a thousand more are coming through.

Thus, the chief concern should be to close the entryway, and then to cut off Things that are already present from any source of magic. Frequently, this will mean dealing with a confused or rogue spellcaster who has given them what they need. Investigations may also discover what rules the Things are twisting but must still obey, which can then be used against them. See *Moving Pictures* for an example of an eccentric but very serious incursion.

Magic

"Magic" has several meanings. *Intrinsic magic,* the basic stuff of the universe, can be manipulated and changed into various forms, including solid matter. However, even individuals who can control it directly – the mercifully rare *sourcerers* – cannot create or destroy it. Local flux levels vary (they can be measured using spells or a *thaumometer,* pp. 160-161), but never fall to absolute zero.

The standard unit of magic used by wizards is the *thaum,* defined as the amount of power necessary to semi-permanently create one small white pigeon or three billiard balls.[1] Academic wizards recognise smaller divisions (millithaums), but these aren't of direct importance to practical spellcasting. It turns out that there's a magical particle which "mediates" this energy; confusingly, this is also known as the thaum. Splitting *that* sort of thaum was one of the great achievements of modern wizardry. The fact that wizardly terminology is hopelessly confusing is fine with wizards.

Magic can also lie around in puddles, because generally, it doesn't decay with time. While sources may be temporarily depleted, they'll usually recharge – often very quickly. This is because magic isn't a substance, like a fossil fuel, but a condition in the nature of reality.

Residual magic is the thaumaturgical equivalent of radioactive waste. Most of it occurs in areas blasted by the long-ago Mage Wars (p. 13); regions such as the Wyrmberg (pp. 233-234) are saturated with it. In such places, even the Discworld's patchy natural laws turn wobbly. Creatures exist that oughtn't, and magical artefacts of the Man Wasn't Meant To level can come into existence. Spellcasting is much chancier in zones of residual magic, but casters can make deliberate use of it, in somewhat the same manner that gasoline can be used to put out small fires (benefits and drawbacks are described in *Messin' With Reality,* pp. 191-217).

Mostly, though, the energy that powers spells either is drawn from across the entire cosmos, or, for those in a hurry, comes from *outside.* The latter is where the danger lies.

---

1. The alternative unit, the Prime (named for its inventor, Augustus Prime), is defined as the amount of magic required to move one pound of lead one foot, with subdivisions into milli-, micro-, and nanoprimes. This was an attempt to put magical measurement on a rational scientific basis. It never caught on.

Because magic tinkers with the nature of things, it weakens the structure of reality, and the Things from the Dungeon Dimensions (pp. 269-270) or lesser menaces may take advantage.

For most practical purposes, however, "magic" is the stuff done by wizards and witches, and it manipulates intrinsic magic to practical ends: weather control, fireballs, making the salt disappear from the dinner table, and so on. It has a huge body of rules and principles, written down in academic texts by wizards, passed down by word of mouth and tradition among witches. What students (and many senior experts) don't realise is that these are less laws of nature than they are laws for witches and wizards. They enable magic-workers to tap and manipulate the raw power of magic without *too* many people's heads exploding.

Really powerful witches and wizards are those who've realised that all rules are merely guidelines. They can do anything because, well, they *know* they can do anything. In game terms, their skills are high enough to enable them to cast many different spells quickly and simply. However, things have evolved so that, by the time someone really understands this, he has also learned the good sense not to overuse the power. Well, usually – in eight cases out of 10, anyway.

Oh yes, eight.

The number eight is crucially significant in the Disc's universe. Wizards inscribe octagrams, the colour of magic is octarine (the eighth colour of the spectrum) which is perceived by octagons in an adept's eye, and so on. Eight is both a crucial number and an unlucky one. Being slightly inherently magical, it tends to attract the attention of Things from the Dungeon Dimensions. Thus, although wizards must often work with it, they tend to be superstitiously (but rationally) careful of actually *mentioning* it. Laymen can *usually* mention it without fear, though.

The Roundworld Project

When it comes to the existence of parallel universes, and the relationship between the Discworld's universe and our own (see *Alternate Realities, Alternate Creations*, p. 269), the simplest point of view is that these two universes lie in parallel dimensions – and this is doubtless true, for numerous values of "true." At least one brief scene early in the chronicles certainly fits this theory. However, the *Science of Discworld* books offer a slightly different frame of reference.

The *Roundworld Project* was originally a thought experiment – a hypothetical idea discussed at Unseen University. Academics theorised that it should be possible to create a zone where *no* magic existed, despite the fact that magic is a basic element of the Discworld universe. However, calculations established that this would require excessive amounts of power. Then, Ponder Stibbons (pp. 332-333) and his colleagues in the High Energy Magic Building (p. 286) succeeded in splitting the thaum, the elementary particle of magic[1], while neglecting to incorporate enough safety factors into the devices they built.[2] Faced with excessive amounts of raw magic, Hex (p. 286) manifested the Roundworld Project on the spot, as an energy sink. The result was an entire universe packed into a convenient globe about a foot across.

This universe proved to lack narrativium (the element that causes events on the Discworld to form sensible stories), deitygen (the elementary substance of gods), and even chelonium and elephantigen (which go to make up world-sized turtles and elephants). However, other elements came into existence, clumped together to form ludicrously large stars and viable round planets, and eventually formed life.

In fact, the Roundworld looks suspiciously like our own universe. However, the wizards eventually got bored with its lack of narrative structure. As it had become self-sustaining, it was handed over to Rincewind (pp. 330-332) for safekeeping. It now sits on a shelf in his office, with a note telling the housekeeper not to dust it. Occasionally, when something untoward happens on Roundworld-Earth, the wizards meddle with it a little to put history right, and then forget about it again.

1. Their justification was that the University's heating system wasn't working well enough, and they could improve it.

2. In the UU squash court, naturally.

Working Spells

Spellcasting is a matter of will and intent. However, it also requires either a vague understanding of what one is doing, in order to gather the requisite energies, or a high-powered, easy-to-use energy source – and it's really nice to have both. The former without the latter is work, but manageable. The latter without the former is a problem that should ideally be solved quickly, before it solves itself (and most other problems in the neighbourhood). *Messin' With Reality* (pp. 191-217) governs how to work magic in game terms; this section is about the look of the thing.

Types of Magic-Workers

The Disc has several different sorts of magic-workers. The two main categories are wizards and witches. Really, though, the various types aren't as different as they like to believe.

The thing that best distinguishes the serious contenders from the dabblers is *Magery* (pp. 44-45) – or rather, the associated sensitivity ("octarine vision"). A spellcaster needs to be able to sense the flows and shapes of magic to work safely. If you've got that, the rest is mostly just training. That said, you may need a *lot* of training, and there *are* people who have the sensitivity but no spells.

(Teatime the Assassin, in *Hogfather*, apparently had some kind of sense for the supernatural thanks to a glass eye made of scrying crystal . . . although any relatively sane wizard told that somebody had implanted magic in his own *eye-socket* would back away, whimpering.)

Horoscopes

Like many other traditional, somewhat occult practises – such as Caroc cards and the Ching Aling (p. 212) – Discworld astrology works, more or less. While it isn't magical, strictly speaking, it requires academic and arcane knowledge. Thus, the working version is generally limited to scholar-wizards and priests.

To cast someone's horoscope, you need to know his star sign. The Disc has 64 signs in its zodiac, which changes periodically (see *Astronomy and Astrology*, p. 224), so you must know his precise birth date. You also have to know his place of birth, to within a few miles. Not all Discworlders know such details about themselves – it's up to the GM to decide what's likely.

Next, you must obtain current astronomical data and have the ability to understand it. Successful use of a stone-circle computer (see *Computer Programming*, p. 72) is one way to get this. Others involve either a working observatory or a small library of almanacs, plus 20 minutes and a successful Astronomy skill roll.

Finally, roll against either Religious Ritual skill for a religion that goes in for this stuff (some kind of Druidism is normal), at -3, or against both Mathematics (Applied) *and* Occultism, with no penalty. This process takes another 30 minutes.

If all the necessary rolls succeed, you get a one-paragraph note saying something about the subject's life for the next day, much like the sort of thing found in "Your Stars" pages in newspapers on our world. It will be quite accurate. The GM should work something out without giving too much away; e.g., "This could be a very good time to think about travel, but be careful of small women and farm implements. Your lucky colour today is green; your lucky number is anything with a fraction."

Making use of a horoscope, without getting too depressed about the glib triviality of the business, is up to you. If players start overusing this stuff, the GM should look thoughtful and then announce that the next horoscope cast reads, say, "You are quite likely to meet a tall skeleton with a scythe today, but don't worry, your friends will meet him too. You don't have a lucky number."

THOSE OTHER TYPES

Individuals who aren't "ordinary" wizards or witches, but who can do something supernatural, are many and varied. A few of the more common sorts are discussed below. The GM, and even players creating unusual PCs (like Jemzarkiza of Krull; see Chapters 2-4), may come up with more. Such inventions should fit either common narrative assumptions or the Discworld's style – preferably both. Campaigns featuring more than one or two new magic-working types are liable to look rather odd regardless.

Demonologists are technically wizards, although other wizards regard them with distaste. It isn't that they don't do real magic or wield real power – but the fact is, they borrow it from beings that have had a lot more practise in politics and contract negotiation. Even wizards can see the snag with *that*. Demonologists tend to be solitary men with warped senses of priorities. However, they deal only with the demons of the Discworld's Hell (p. 304); Things from the Dungeon Dimensions (pp. 269-270) are too icily inhuman to bargain. A demonologist will resemble a regular wizard in game terms, but with a focus on Magical Form (Summonation), and probably also some Magical Form (Necromancy), Occultism, and Hidden Lore (Demon Lore).

Hedge magic is an authentic and respectable branch of wizardry which attracts men who could probably do quite well as druids if they had more interest in blood and slabs of stone. They have extensive knowledge of plant magics via Magical Form (Physiomancy), and of mundane horticulture in the form of the Gardening, Herbalism, Naturalist, and Professional Skill (Farming) skills. They're the sorts of gardeners who *know* that talking to plants helps them grow, because the plants tell them so. This is all a bit rustic and primitive by Unseen University's standards, but the difference is one of emphasis, not deep philosophy.

Voodoo is considered a branch of witchcraft – though with a flavouring of applied religion – and its practitioners are always female (and so would be known as *mambos* in our world). However, voodoo-workers rarely change people into frogs, ride broomsticks, or read tea leaves.[1] Their powers tend to be a little dark in application. They *do* create zombies, and they're very skilled at working with the petty gods of their homelands, who are homely, earthy, temperamental divinities of odd moments and commonplace behaviours, and who are often permitted to "ride" (temporarily take over the bodies of) worshippers. The most powerful practitioners claim that they can actually *make* gods, which would mean identifying an area of religious opportunity, and then generating enough faith and belief in a small congregation – perhaps just the magic-worker herself – that a small god picks up the idea and develops real power. In game terms, voodoo witches tend to concentrate on the Magical Forms of Necromancy and Summonation, backed up by some Divination and maybe Physiomancy or Psychomancy.

While other professional Discworld spellcasters would never admit that *mediums* (for a template, see p. 124) belong in this chapter, they *are* people who employ supernatural abilities for a living. Mediumship requires sensitivity to the unseen and supernatural, which is the first requirement for professional magic, but the medium has a different, limited emphasis.

Priests – including druids and shamans – usually rely on social power and their gods' protection, which enables them to sneer right back at sneering atheist wizards, but a few Discworld religions preserve complex metaphysical doctrines which include a bit of training in some kind of magic, while druids can tap the awesome power of the elements (just ask them), and shamans have regular dealings with the spirit world. Hence, it isn't impossible to encounter a priest with a little Magery and knowledge of a small number of spells, usually appropriate to their deity.

---

1. *For scrying purposes, they prefer gumbos. Everything goes into a good gumbo, so you can see everything in there.*

One example is the classic Evil High Priest who attempts to hold off the Barbarian Hero using Psychomantic fear. Some druids are quite adept at Elementalism, moving impressive quantities of magical energy along ley lines to reconfigure their stone-circle hardware. Access to that sort of energy requires a close connection with the cult hierarchy, though, and should only be *routinely* available to NPCs. For a template that may provide further ideas, see *Priest* (pp. 126-127) – and don't be afraid to increase the point total for a cleric with useful supernatural power.

Disc *fortune-tellers* are generally low-powered witches or wizards with one or two good Divination spells, or mediums who can extract useful information from their allied spirits – or shrewd fairground frauds who carefully avoid contact with real magic-workers while using the Fortune-Telling skill (p. 73).

Sorcerers

And then there are sorcerers.

Sorcerers are *rare*. Exactly one appears in the chronicles, and he leaves after nearly destroying the world. It's hard to imagine a game scenario in which one could appear. However, the basis for their previous existence is important.

On the Disc, the eighth son of an eighth son usually develops magical talents and becomes a wizard. However, if – in defiance of a lot of sensible traditions – such a wizard has eight sons in turn, the eighth will be a sorcerer. It's possible that such individuals had less statistically extreme origins in ancient times, but that's the only way it can happen now. (Once, wizards talked about promising juniors with creative abilities, rather loosely, as "possible sorcerer material." That would be considered rather tasteless today, since some wizards have seen what a *real* sorcerer is like, and some of them survived.)

Conventional wizardry is about nudging the universe your way. Sorcerers grab the thing by the back of the neck and point it where they want it. They're walking sources of power, and – being directly acquainted with the stuff – they can create new spells on the fly.

The trouble is that having the ability to boil the oceans, move mountain ranges around like stage props, and generally treat reality as if it were made of modelling clay, they can't control the desire to do so. And because absolute power isn't really absolute if you have to share it, the cosmos isn't big enough for two of them. They cannot combine their efforts. The Mage Wars (p. 13) – which nearly destroyed the Disc before the Old Ones stepped in, and left pockets of dangerous residual magic (p. 270) which persist to this day – were the sorcerers' equivalent of King of the Hill.

To prevent this from recurring, Unseen University recommends celibacy for wizards. (Contrary to some folklore, one's sexual activity or lack thereof has no effect whatsoever on magical ability or practise, even for wizards and let alone for witches – see Nanny Ogg for proof there.) Some wizards do leave the profession to get married, and although most do so late in life by way of retirement, and marry ladies beyond childbearing age, it's possible that a few become fathers. Still, the symbolism of their renouncing magic – of ceasing to be what they were – is generally enough to ensure that they can't father sorcerers. Symbolism is very important in magic.

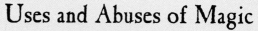

Uses and Abuses of Magic

Faced with something as powerful as magic, many people – including a lot of roleplayers – will want to use it for everything from blowing up their enemies to making the tea. Yet Discworld magic doesn't actually get used that much.

The various reasons for this boil down to enough people understanding how dangerous runaway magic can get. Magic is under the control of clever, often arrogant people who don't take well to being ordered around, and who know the dangers of their art quite well. Meanwhile, politicians and rulers with no magical skill of their own mostly either dislike the idea of power they can't control directly or have the sense to understand those risks; it's common for them to announce that they'll make "No First Use" of magic in warfare, even when they're quite willing to make First (and Last) Use of anything else. There are exceptions to all this: minor, low-powered magical devices are commercially available; some people are willing to cadge a lift on a broomstick, given the opportunity; and persuading a friendly wizard to travel with you, so that *his* acts of self-defence will take down *your* enemies, is considered smart. However, few nonmagical folk actively seek to have their enemies fireballed if there's any alternative.

In game terms, the GM should try to induce the same attitudes among PCs – if necessary, by pointed reference to the rules for magical critical failures. And if the PCs get careless or too enthusiastic about magic, well, the GM can always bring in some powerful witch or wizard NPC to enforce the *unwritten* rules.

Familiars

Discworld spellcasters don't usually have really magical familiars, despite the fact that the *idea* is known. Many wizards in commercial practise keep a raven around their workshop – preferably perched on a skull – but that's a matter of image. Some witches, such as Nanny Ogg, have pet cats (and Nanny's Greebo, pp. 343-344, is no ordinary cat), but that's just old ladies and pets. Others may feel obliged to keep, say, a toad, but there's little to guarantee that it won't wander off or die. Voodoo experts also go for pets, such as huge and malevolent cockerels (roosters), but those don't seem to serve any specific magical function.

All of which said, Disc magic can be a personal thing. It isn't inconceivable that some slightly eccentric magic-workers could have familiars that, say, lend them a few extra Magic Points when required. Players would have to negotiate these sorts of details with the GM, and the full *GURPS Basic Set* rules may prove useful. Such adepts should be ready for a mixture of technical interest and condescension from other magic-users.

Spells

"Spells" are either standardised magical techniques or the results of improvised-but-nonetheless-effective magical operations. Named, documented spells are theoretically optional, but many people find them essential; improvising from first principles all the time is too much work, and boring. For more on this in game terms, see *Standardised Spells* (p. 203).

Wizards sometimes say that they must return to their books to prepare specific spells for use. This usually means that they have only the *Non-Improvisational* form of Magery (p. 45), which is common among inexperienced wizards and those who've allowed their practical skills to get a little rusty. It's also a nervous habit among wizards who are quite *capable* of improvising, but who

want to double-check the safety factors on some high-powered spell before pushing their luck too far. The delay gives such wizards an excuse to ensure that their staffs are fully charged, too.

PROPS

Much Discworld magic involves a lot of candles, bizarre culinary ingredients, and expensive jewellery. While wizards are the worst offenders, witches can be almost as bad, particularly when such paraphernalia is part of how they maintain their image. Most of these props are specific to the spell being cast, but there are a few standard items, of which the wizard's staff (pp. 192-193) is the most obvious example.

However, smart magic workers know that "props" are exactly what these things are. They're mostly used for effect and to save a little effort. The most capable spellcasters are the ones who clank least when they walk.

Exploiting the Laws of Reality

Much Discworld magic is subtle, being based on careful exploitation of the universe's natural laws – not unlike engineering. However, those laws include narrative causality and its corollaries (pp. 8-9). While these *can* be manipulated, the process sometimes gets *complicated*. Any attempt to tweak raw natural forces has its problems. One big difficulty is that a lot of this stuff has a consciousness and may resent being tweaked. Furthermore, little of it is easily quantified, which means that any attempted action may have trivial results . . . or let off the metaphysical equivalent of a nuclear weapon.

Thus, this sort of thing is mostly "encoded" into standard Disc magic, as detailed in *Messin' With Reality* (pp. 191-217). Witches gain much of their power through their understanding of stories and their ability to stand a little aside from them, while certain spells tap raw life forces or even narrative structures in reality. A magic-worker would more likely demolish a wooden door by making it grow and destroy its frame, or move rocks by reminding them of the time when they were molten, than cast a "Disintegrate" spell.

CONSERVATION LAWS

Discworld magic often seems to include the sorts of "conservation" laws that underlie physics in our own universe. For example, levitation is much easier if one causes a heavy object to fall to balance one's own rise, and telekinesis may take the form of leverage, with consequent pressure on the user's brain. All of this is somewhat approximate, from the layman's viewpoint, and often disregarded. However, it *is* a significant part of the flavour of magic in the chronicles. In game terms, GMs can attach a "conservation" effect to any spell that seems to need one.

When It All Goes Wrong

Inevitably, magic sometimes goes wrong. This is rare for standard spells cast by competent, trained experts, but it can happen even then. Castings in zones of residual magic, attempts at new or experimental procedures, and magic in the hands of untrained or unstable users all run far more serious risks. When the players *know* that the PCs are in such a situation yet try magic anyway, the GM is entitled to put the rules aside and get downright malicious. Or at least weird.

Headology

Witches in general – with Granny Weatherwax offering a good example – are experts in practical psychology. Granny, like some others, refers to this discipline as "Headology." In game terms, this is the Psychology skill (p. 80) plus optional helpings of various social skills, including Intimidation (especially from Granny on a bad day). However, it isn't entirely fraud; by making sure that people expect a witch to use magic on their brains, the witch can make it a lot easier to do so for real when the need arises.

It's important to remember that the crucial focus of Headology is *manipulative*, if not always malevolent. A witch should pay constant attention to how others perceive her – because if she handles this correctly, she'll need to cast far less real magic. For one thing, she won't require defensive magic, curses, and so on as often if people respect (or fear) her enough to be polite out of habit. Just as significant, however, is the fact that witches do a lot of practical doctoring, with much use of psychosomatic and placebo effects. Thus, they need patients with plenty of faith in their abilities, who will seriously believe that a bottle of coloured water will make them better.

Important tools for the mistress of Headology include a tall witch's hat and a matching dress. Black isn't mandatory for the complete costume; for that matter, the approach need not be primarily intimidating. Despite Granny Weatherwax's opinions, a witch can earn adequate respect in several ways, provided that she's *clearly* a witch; weirdly colourful and floaty dresses, or (in warmer climes) even the stock-fantasy minimal enchantress outfit, clearly make some kind of relevant point.

The need for what they classify as respect sometimes makes even "good" witches seem rather unlovely, but in fact, Headology doesn't generally call for *active* unpleasantness. If the foundations are properly laid, then whenever someone annoys the witch, any minor, routine misfortune that person suffers in the next five years will be credited to her.

The most likely and immediate threat is that the magic will run amok. It may go in the wrong direction, blow back at the caster, or generate side-effects. Remember, magic is a dynamic and near-conscious force! The *Magical Fumble Table* (pp. 201-202) is designed to bring *low-end* risks of this sort into play. Perhaps the only reason why Unseen University doesn't blow up as often as the Alchemists' Guild HQ – and with stranger colours – is that the wizards have been doing this stuff for longer.

Spells that permanently incorporate magic into the caster's body are troubling even when "successful." No sane magic-worker would do this. The results would be hugely inconvenient at best, hideous at worst. (This also explains the dearth of magical healing on the Disc.)

A deadlier risk comes from the Dungeon Dimensions (pp. 269-270). The Things want to get in, and a trained, magic-using mind gives them an entry that they can prop open. Mostly, magical training is designed to minimise such hazards – a fumbled spell rarely produces much more than a small accident and a sense of a narrow escape – but *powerful* minds and *unusual* magics can mean trouble.

Wizards and witches both keep an eye out for such dangers – especially incursions from the Dungeon Dimensions – and will cooperate with each other or anyone else to deal with them. Unfortunately, the techniques that can be used are often limited; see *Fighting Invasions* (p. 270).

Magic Items

The Disc has a fair number of magical artefacts around, to the point where, nowadays, "technomancy" occupies the niche that the consumer electronics business fills in our world – though "high-end" magic items are rare. Almost anything that a bright graduate wizard or a clever dwarf craftsman can put together will show up sooner or later, because other people will pay enough for it. On the other hand, grand, world-shaping inventions are too much trouble; they take years to make, and then some barbarian thug will, like as not, come along and steal them. If a wizard wants to shape the world, he'll usually do so directly. Besides, poorly designed and over-powered artefacts tend to create annoying etheric emanations. All of which said, a few interesting artefacts do exist.

MAGIC WEAPONS

Among other things, magic is pretty good for injuring people – and not just careless users. For the most part, wizards favour fireballs and witches favour subtlety, but occasionally, someone comes up with dangerous hardware.

Magic weapons are traditional heroic appurtenances, but most of them are rather old. The majority were created by dwarfs with Long-Forgotten Rune Lore, by great wizards, or by blacksmith gods. The first are, well, long forgotten, wizards have long since gone off swords (which always seem to fall into the hands of heroes, who have an unpleasant penchant for using them on wizards), and blacksmith gods these days are usually busy improving the style of the balcony railings and door furniture around Dunmanifestin (p. 301). Wizards also object to the erratic magic of such artefacts – which can scramble the calibration of magical instrumentation for miles around – and tend to arrange for them to be lost at every opportunity.

A wide range of enchanted edged ironmongery certainly *used* to exist, however, some of it even black, sapient, and afflicted with personality disorders. Such things still show up occasionally. This stuff cannot simply be purchased with cash, though – adventurers must track it down to wherever it's being kept, extract it in the face of lethal opposition, and then hang onto it while working out what to do with it.

In game terms, the standard benefits of magic weapons are bonuses to attack and damage rolls, and occasionally to defence rolls. *Really* powerful blades could injure immaterial spirits, slice through armour (reducing the victim's DR by some fraction), glow in the presence of a particular category of enemy (elves, demons, lawyers, etc.), negate magic on touch, or even move under their own power.

Ajandurah's Wand of Utter Negativity

This is an example of *serious* magic weaponry that makes even wizards nervous. Unseen University has prohibitions on such items.[1] A very few are known around the Disc, showing up in the armouries of people with more power than sense.

The wand has the ability to annihilate any matter, living or inert; wizards say that it makes the target somehow *never have existed*, but that may be a slight exaggeration. It requires Magery to use, and costs 1 MP to destroy up to 300 lbs. of mass up to 100 feet away. Larger targets cost +1 MP per extra 150 lbs., while increased range costs +1 MP per 100 feet added. Roll against IQ+Magery+4 to focus it on a chosen target. Control is fine enough to destroy part of a target – such as a single limb – and leave the rest intact, although the GM may reduce the roll to IQ+Magery in such cases.

These wands may go back to the Mage Wars (p. 13). The spells needed to create them aren't currently known on the Disc, and anyone researching the topic would probably be subject to pre-emptive psychological treatment[2] by other wizards. No standard price can be quoted for them. Trading in such things is a bit like dealing in weapons-grade plutonium: You get the best deal you can, and you probably don't want to do business with anyone who wants to do this sort of business.

---

1. Basically, imagine how a loaded assault rifle with grenade launcher and bayonet would go down in a university engineering department. They might be able to tell you how it worked, but they'd rather not have it waved about.

2. A few fireballs.

ENCHANTMENT BY USE

Old and much-used items can gain uncanny attributes through *induced magic*. Long exposure to magical energies can have this effect; for example, a chisel used by a craftsman-wizard in the manufacture of animated puppets for many years might become capable of granting anything it was used on a semblance of life. However, this is an unpredictable process – that chisel might instead become terribly sharp, or develop a voice and critical tendencies, or take to flying round the workshop and hiding in inconvenient places.

The semi-sapient Archchancellor's Hat of Unseen University is an exceptional, very old case of this phenomenon.[1] (Few other wizards' hats are worn on more than one head, as wizards are

---

1. It was believed lost during that unfortunate incident with the sourcerer, but it recently seems to have shown up again. Archchancellor Ridcully rarely wears it, though; he says that it grumbles all the time.

rather possessive of their hats and are often buried in them, usually when they're dead.) *Most* wizardly appurtenances and witches' tools do *not* absorb significant magic over time, though. The whole point of Discworld spells is that they *control* magic, stopping it from seeping. In general, the most that happens is that objects start to shed octarine sparks or mutter to themselves at stressful moments. The GM should use such effects mainly for plot twists and incidental jokes.

A more subtle process involves *belief*, which has power in itself, accessible even to people without magical training. There's plenty of magical energy floating around, so something that begins as a "mere superstition" can eventually gather convincing power. Rituals actually start doing what people wished they could do (and acquire appropriate penalties for improper use), and if enough Discworlders believe that an item has particular properties, it may develop those properties. Objects rarely pick up overtly supernatural powers, though; they tend to become archetypes of themselves.

For example, a famous sword will seem more and more like the ideal of what a sword ought to be. Used by generations of kings, it may become "kingly." If the kings are much given to ceremonies and processions, it might get better at holding a mirror sheen and catching the light with a near-audible *ting* – but because kings who last that long usually know how to *use* a sword, the blade is more likely to improve to *very fine* quality (see *Melee Weapon Quality*, p. 152), even as it becomes increasingly battered and notched. In neither case would it be detectably magical, though. This all works outside the academic mindset of wizards, and it takes a shrewd and sensitive expert in Thaumatology to discern the effect, so wizards often neglect or are contemptuous of it ("Bunch of superstitious peasants, believing in a magic sword!"). That's their mistake.

Items can also absorb *memories* over time without developing overt powers. For example, authentic royal crowns can be a little unnerving for people with psychic sensitivity – they tend to remember the lives and experiences of their past wearers, which inevitably include a fair amount of blood and fire. Wearing a crown, especially if you're not entitled to it, isn't recommended for magical adepts; Fright Checks (pp. 170-171) may be involved.

And just occasionally, *new* nonmagical devices of exceptional quality or power *demand* to be used. This is very unfortunate with weapons.

One fairly common form of induction is for a wizard's staff to absorb power through extended use. The GM might let especially active wizard PCs buy one level of Superior Staff (p. 47) with bonus character points if they use the same staff for many years. Conversely, some staffs may have unfortunate effects on their wielders, thanks to having absorbed personality features in past use. A wizard with Superior Staff might also have some nasty quirks, defined as disadvantages that only cut in when he's employing it (see *Personality Change*, p. 67).

Other Items

The GM who wants to throw *odd* magical items into the game is free to do so – the Disc *does* have a long history of eccentric tinkering. Two examples appear below.

Seven-League Boots

A search round UU's museum will turn up one or two pairs of Seven-League Boots, kept for emergencies and to illustrate to students why high-powered magic isn't always a good idea. The Boots enable the wearer to teleport up to 21 miles with a single step, at a cost of 1 FP. However, this requires careful control; roll against IQ+Magery, at a penalty equal to encumbrance level, for each step (at the GM's option, distractions may give *further* penalties). On a failure, roll vs. DX, again penalised by encumbrance level; success indicates that the wearer restrains the attempt at the last unstable moment, merely losing the FP, while failure means he succeeds in placing one foot 21 miles ahead of the other without properly controlling the dimension shifts. Anyone observing the latter outcome must make a Fright Check. The wearer himself is very, very dead.

Tiny Salad Bar Bowl of Holding

Invented by a student from UU's Faculty of Thaumic Engineering when an Ankh-Morpork restaurant (briefly) instituted an "All you can get in the bowl for 10 pence" offer, the Bowl of Holding can retain up to three tons in a pocket dimension, without becoming any heavier to carry. However, it only works for lettuce and tomato.

Magic Levels

The Discworld is obviously very magical, but exactly *how* magical varies from place to place. While no regions are entirely lacking in magic – that would be impossible – there are certainly areas where there's more of the stuff. Occasionally, this is raw creative energy, generated by some cosmic power; more often, it's *residual magic* (p. 270). Sometimes it indicates a weakness in the structure of reality – the magic is seeping through – and in other cases it causes such a weakness by abrasion. Either way, the effects are much the same.

Signs and Portents

Zones of residual magic vary in area from the county-sized region dominated by the Wyrmberg (pp. 233-234) to small clearings in old-growth forests. There can be no *simple* examples; they all have *personality,* which as anyone who has been sold a crumbling old house by a silver-tongued property dealer can attest, isn't entirely a good thing in a piece of geography. The only sure way to judge their exact extent is by experiment or use of spells or magical instruments, and it's perfectly possible to wander into danger without realising it, but there are often indicators. All such zones should be custom-designed by the GM, with their own quirks, including possible warnings.

The most obvious hints may include a greasy feel to the air and stray sparks of various colours (including octarine) appearing around people's fingernails. These might be obvious to all parties (a *very* strong sign) or only to observers with Magery. Some areas are in perpetual twilight; others are sweltering hot, or freezing cold. Slightly less self-evident, but usually quickly noticeable, are distortions in probability: coins landing on their edges, flying pork (living or cooked), and so on.

Other indicators are the magic's longer-term effects. Natural effects may again be blatant (six-legged rabbits, teleporting ducks, talking trees, and so on), or they might require a successful Naturalist skill roll to spot (such as bushes with the wrong type of fruit, or birds which sing perfect scales). The GM should be imaginative rather than cruel; apples filled with prussic acid are boring, while apples loaded with lysergic acid are *interesting.* Dangerous zones tend to be plastered with large Keep Out notices, signed by famous senior wizards. Sadly, that may be counterproductive. Senior wizards are terrible at explaining their reasons, leaving younger wizards with a natural, often accurate – but more often fatal – suspicion that the old swine are hogging the good stuff.

Lastly, architectural indicators are the result of humans (or other races) being foolish enough to exploit the effect. The traditional witch's gingerbread cottage needs lots of magic to stay intact. Rather less amusing are Twisted Blasphemous Chthonic Temples dedicated to Unspeakable Beings From Beyond Sanity. Such Beings are most likely to show up in these sorts of areas (needing the magic for sustenance, or the associated weak dimensional barriers for ease of manifestation), and somehow acquire a fan club with a taste for heavy, dank pillars and ample cellar space.

In other words, the GM ought to be creative with such regions, and possibly poetic, but more often creatively destructive. With an increased risk of critical failures to worry about, witches and wizards should learn caution. If their casting skills are too high for this to present a serious problem, the GM can always rule that, as they move deeper into an unstable zone, they must roll against IQ at -5 to stop *any* casting from also generating the equivalent of a critical failure.

Incidentally, in a few *highly* magic-saturated zones, such as the immediate vicinity of Cori Celesti (p. 242), any attempt at working magic is akin to lighting a match in a room full of explosive vapours. The GM should always make sure that at least some members of the party realise this – otherwise, you're just going to kill off the lot of them without warning, which is no fun. If a few of them don't, though, you can have the amusing sight of wizards A and B screaming and dog-piling wizard C when he starts muttering and twiddling his fingers.

Wandering Shops

Mysterious shops which appear in little-used alleyways, sell peculiar items with incomplete instructions, and then Are Not There when the victim-shopper goes back are a stock fantasy feature which occasionally shows up on the Disc. Twoflower (pp. 348-349) bought his Luggage from one, he and Rincewind briefly visited another ("Skillet, Wang, Yrxle!yt, Bunglestiff, Cwmlad and Patel, Purveyors"), and the guitar which is central to the plot of *Soul Music* came from a third. Most resemble cluttered junk shops with shelves full of this and that. Traditionally, they carry stock which is far more magical than it looks, in complicated ways, and sell people things they need on a moral or metaphysical level but could *really* do without.

Wandering shops can be moved by the shopkeepers – sometimes using simple mechanical controls, sometimes via arcane hand gestures. However, there are limits to where they can go, primarily the need for a blank wall and a decent number of customers. People who happen to be inside one when it moves will see the door temporarily replaced by yet more shelving.

Various theories seek to explain the existence of these *tabernae vagrantes,* or starshops: a race of supernatural traders from a now-dead universe built them, Fate created them in a distinctly atypical fit of sympathy for humanity, and so on. In fact, at least some of them were once ordinary shops before they were cursed by an extraordinarily powerful wizard who got very annoyed with shopkeepers who looked smug while telling him that they didn't have what he wanted and asking him to come back later (when they would actually be closed). The curse *might* be broken if such a shop ever finds him again and has what he wants in stock.

In games, wandering shops can serve their traditional purpose of distributing overpowered arbitrary plot devices. It's *sometimes* possible to hitch a lift in one, but even if the shopkeeper likes you, the controlling curse-magic may not agree. As most shopkeepers are basically human – if ancient, unageing, and eccentric – adventurers might be able to intimidate or fast-talk them into cooperation. Remember, however, that these traders are *also* most likely protected by great magics and destinies, and they have shops full of incredibly powerful gear which only they can hope to understand. A bit of politeness is safer.

ASPECTED MAGIC

Some Disc background magic is "aspected," favouring particular sorts of spells while making others harder. One way to represent this is with bonuses to some Magical Forms and penalties to others. Such locations should seem strange, even whimsical, and are unlikely to be especially useful to sane spellcasters. The most likely sort of aspect makes summoning spells easier, but with a risk of calling up a particular type of entity instead of the one intended (perhaps if the casting's margin of success is less than 3). Another

example is an area of runaway entropy, making necromantic spells easier (+2 to skill) but doubling *all* spell maintenance costs.

Perhaps the worst, subtlest problems come from zones that let alien *ideas* loose on the Disc. In *Moving Pictures*, these were the clichés of Hollywood, but at least "Holy Wood Magic" proved manipulable for the heroes as well as for the Things. Imagine a region where romantic fiction or soap operas were becoming overwhelmingly true; PCs could find themselves plunged into torrid and complex relationships, and unable to function as a team because of enforced plot complications. Even increases in "life-energy" can make for problems; when Death was temporarily inactive in *Reaper Man*, Ankh-Morpork was assaulted by a bizarre pseudo-living entity.

TEMPORARY MAGIC-LEVEL INCREASES

Some spellcasters may wonder whether ambient magic can be increased, if only temporarily. After all, a moderate increase in the level might make magic easier to work – or at least, easier to work in large amounts.

The first answer is Yes, Probably. It requires some thaumatological (or narrativistic) messing about, but there are ways to accomplish such things. The second is *Don't.*

The reason for the latter is that such an exercise would involve a weakening of local dimensional integrity. A magic-worker might briefly find some benefit in this, but that would soon be irrelevant, because the next thing that would happen would be the arrival of *beings* seeking to exploit the situation. See *Moving Pictures* and *Lords and Ladies* for examples of such temporary windows of opportunity being enthusiastically assailed with metaphysical crowbars – and notice that the witches and wizards present in each case weren't celebrating.

And then, somewhere, somehow, magic would present its bill, which was always more than you could afford.

– Going Postal

LOWER MAGIC

Reduced magic levels are very rare. They represent regions of peculiarly high dimensional integrity – and in general, most processes acting on the Disc seem to make reality thinner, not tougher. Something might suck all the magical energy out of an area, but that's like drawing all the water out of a well: it will flow back before long. An *incredibly* powerful supernatural being could create wards in multiple adjacent dimensions, lowering the region's magic level, but it would need a good reason to do so; this was done to the entire Disc at the end of the Mage Wars (p. 13). As well, there are other dimensions, accessible from the Disc, where magic is "damped"; Death's house (pp. 293-295) is one example (Death doesn't use magic, but wields the much deeper powers implicit in his job).

Low-magic regions might penalise spell skills and increase MP costs, or simply make spellcasting impossible. However, they're of little interest to the individuals who could easily detect them. Wizards and witches don't go looking for things to make their lives *harder,* thank you very much.

Unseen University

Note for American Readers: Much of the humour in the chronicles' description of Unseen University refers to or pokes fun at the British university system – especially the old collegiate universities of Oxford and Cambridge – which differs from the American system in details and terminology. In simplifying things for this book, we've omitted some of these jokes, let others pass without comment, and explained a few (rendering them comprehensible, if no longer funny). Readers interested in the topic are referred to *The New Discworld Companion.* One rule for games, though: Avoid adding too many American university jokes – they just won't fit.

Discworld wizardry is largely an academic endeavour. The principal school is Unseen University, in Ankh-Morpork, but there are other magical colleges around the Disc; see *Rival Universities* (p. 280). As far as Unseen graduates are concerned, though, these other schools are the equivalent of those advertisements in the back of magazines that offer to sell the Wisdom of the Ancients by mail for $29.95.

Officially, Unseen University has established eight formal branches of magic and eight grades of proficiency. In practise, things are far more complicated, with secondary qualifications, associated courses, and so on. Other schools claim to offer up to the 21st grade, and indeed there's nothing in most law-books to prevent a wizard from claiming that he's of any grade he chooses – unless you believe the old saying about wizards with UU diplomas being subtle and quick to anger, and leaving uppity correspondence-school wizards soggy and hard to light. (Unseen University *does* have some remarkably gruesome stuff in its statutes about falsely claiming to be a wizard, but this is only likely to be invoked if the faculty have had a bad night; see also *Magical Law,* p. 257, and *University Law,* p. 282.)

Wizardry isn't *subtle* magic. Senior wizards by and large have a "got-it, flaunt-it" attitude, and they are often given to throwing energy in various forms and turning annoying persons into amphibians. However, junior wizards who are seriously interested in the high-powered stuff are more into research than application (much as in our world, more physicists work with particle accelerators than on nuclear bombs), while most older and less intense wizards have long since discovered the joys of administration (which is power with a lot less responsibility) or really large dinners. The fact is that Unseen University is an ancient system evolved to keep wizards *relatively* harmless, most of the time.

History

The University was founded – or rather, established in its modern form – approximately 2,000 years ago (see *The Disc Year,* pp. 11-12). Before then, the usual first meeting between two wizards was like the first meeting on the main street of Dodge City between two men who were both supposedly the Fastest Gun in the West. Afterward, it was merely like an encounter between two experts on the pipe-rolls of a demolished medieval cathedral who both wondered what the other's position was on certain debated points . . . Except that both of them would be packing the metaphysical equivalent of an anti-tank rocket. Still, there was a net improvement.

The founder was Alberto Malich "the Wise" (see *Death's House,* pp. 293-294). He was the first Archchancellor, and the blueprint for one style of holder of that office: the thin, irritable, explosive

type. Others include the fat, ponderous, decadent type, the very old type (usually elected as a compromise, sometimes without his knowledge), and the seriously insane type.

Throughout ensuing centuries it was generally accepted that the route to promotion in Unseen University might involve stepping into dead men's shoes, but that shouldn't slow down a clever chap. Blatant brawling was considered a little crass, and anything that could seriously endanger the University itself was obviously missing the point, but any number of methods of removing obstacles could be – and were – used. The only limiting factor was the level of power and deviousness this tended to imply at the top of the heap, and the fact that the whole point of getting there, for most contenders, was to settle down to a life of very large dinners.

However, in recent decades, the process accelerated out of hand. Changes in the Disc at large bred restlessness even among wizards. The events of *The Light Fantastic* and *Sourcery* removed a large number of senior figures, giving a lot of middle-rankers inflated ideas of their own chances. Too many Archchancellors were barely making it through their inaugural dinners.

This slammed to a halt with the appointment of Mustrum Ridcully (pp. 329-330) to the Archchancellorship. He was originally intended to be another compromise appointment. He hadn't been seen at the University for over 40 years, having been managing his family's country estates, and was generally assumed to be some kind of hedge wizard. This was incorrect.

In fact, despite his very different personality, Ridcully has had much the same effect on the University faculty that Lord Vetinari has had on the city at large. He's simply too robust, alert, and formidable to assassinate, and he doesn't much approve of such behaviour among his underlings. It isn't that wizards are frightened of danger – they deal with hideous extradimensional horrors as a matter of course – but being shouted at by Ridcully is *stressful*.

Thus, today, the University has become a relatively stable element in Ankh-Morpork society. The occasional horror from beyond time slurping round the city streets is a small price to pay.

Town and Gown: Location and Maintenance

The University doesn't have a clearly defined campus; indeed, some would say that it's very weakly defined indeed, in space and time, as certain rooms appear to contradict the normal rules of architecture and mathematics, and some of the upper floors seem to be older than the sections beneath. For practical purposes, though, it mostly lies between the Ankh and Sator Square (site of a weekly market). It's conveniently located for students looking to waste time on the town, although it has enough walls that they do have to learn one thing: the location of a patch of wall in the alley between the Observatory and the Backs. Here, loose bricks in may be easily removed to create a ladder, which has been used for centuries by students entering after the Main Gate is locked.

Talking of University and City . . . UU is wealthy, but it's a complicated, metaphysical sort of wealth. While it owns much of Ankh-Morpork's real estate, the rents are mostly token and the leases so ancient that even the University's lawyers can't understand them. Most of its actual income comes from donations, usually in kind – that is, gifts of goods and services rather than money. It's generally understood that keeping the wizards fed and content, and on their side of the walls, is worth a few casks of ale and cartloads of starchy vegetables.

However, UU does need some cash flow, and the faculty recently had a nasty moment when they discovered that a large part of their income derived from an ancient bequest with *conditions* attached, one of which ultimately caused them to rewrite the rules of the game of football – the unthinkable alternative being to cut back on their food intake. This should be taken as a hint, for narrative purposes: While Unseen University has huge resources most of the time, it can suffer whatever inconveniences or unexpected shortages a plot may require.

Thanks to the fact that even UU needs cash on occasion, a vague feeling in some quarters that it should move with the times, and a stronger feeling that if there's anything magical being done in the city, wizards ought to be involved in it, the University has recently come up with a new scheme: the Thaumatological Park. This is a collection of commercial enterprises linked to UU and physically grouped together on one (perhaps poorly chosen) site; see *The Unreal Estate and the Thaumatological Park* (p. 252). These businesses mostly manufacture and sell imp-powered devices such as dis-organisers (see *Demon-Based Devices*, pp. 159-160), and are run and staffed by junior wizards who have a bizarre urge to make some cash and perhaps even to talk to ordinary people. Whether this project will turn into a handy money-spinner or an occult disaster remains to be seen. Quite likely it'll be both.

Nonmagical citizens regard UU with cautious amusement. For instance, Ankh-Morpork slang for anything complicated is "dragon magic" (as in, "This isn't dragon magic!"), which relates to academic wizards much as "rocket science" does to scientists in our world.

Rival Universities

Unseen University has never been the *only* source of wizardly training on the Disc. Individual wizards have often trained apprentices, although the more respectable of them would sooner or later transport students of proven competence to Ankh-Morpork for advanced schooling. Unseen was seen as the place where an apprentice would prove himself and "earn his staff." However, there were other supposed colleges of magic scattered round the Disc.

These suffered terribly from credibility problems – Unseen graduates were prone to demonstrating the superiority of their education with magical force – and many of them gave patchy instruction, missing whole areas of important lore, despite their notorious tendency also to give out grandiose titles and fancy costumes. Still, a competent wizard didn't *have* to have spent time in Ankh-Morpork, and isolated nations such as Krull (p. 238) could possess serious arcane resources. In recent years, with the spread of better communications and a *slightly* more relaxed and less lethal attitude at UU toward the whole question of magical superiority, foreign colleges and students have been showing up without immediately getting blown up.

Bugarup University

One such foreign institution is Bugarup University, on Fourecks, which evolved independently while that continent was cut off from the rest of the Disc. Its first contact with Unseen happened to involve a relatively friendly meeting between senior faculty members on both sides. Relations remain polite, if unavoidably distant, with occasional staff exchanges.

Brazeneck College

More recently, the ambitious citizens of Pseudopolis (p. 233) have sought to advance their civic rivalry with Ankh-Morpork by promoting the previously negligible Brazeneck School of Conjuring to full university status, as Brazeneck College. Poaching a few UU faculty members by offering better pay and titles than they could hope for at their previous, rather static institution, Brazeneck has demonstrated steely determination, and it shows off by actually *publishing* the results of research – something considered a bit unwizardly by older, more secretive scholars. This ambition may, however, lead to unfortunate corner-cutting in the area of magical safety, even by the standards set by Unseen. Pseudopolis has already suffered a rather embarrassing attack by a giant chicken; more such incidents may follow, doubtless to the amusement of the UU faculty.

Administration

Unseen University is a complex organisation, divided both vertically and horizontally in a shambolic and casual way. At the top of the heap, the faculty – the tenured professors – try to avoid contact with the lower levels, and mostly succeed. In the past, when promotion at this level was generally achieved by clandestine assassination (the process politely known as *droit de mortis*), the faculty was united primarily by the fact that they spent all of their time watching each other for dirty tricks. Since the advent of Archchancellor Ridcully, they more closely resemble a smug club for crankish old gentlemen with shared tastes in large dinners. Their conviction of their own superiority remains constant.

The University is headed by the Archchancellor, who chairs its Council, the Hebdomadal Board, which traditionally consisted of the heads of the eight Orders (p. 283). Following recent upheavals, however, the Council is now directly appointed by the Archchancellor, mostly from people who didn't move fast enough when they saw him coming; Ridcully has thus acquired considerable power. Then again, most wizards are quite happy to leave the tiresome business of administration to whoever is willing to handle it.

Recently, this mostly meant the Bursar (p. 335), a wizard who long since discovered the small, safe joys of administrative power. (Previous bursars sometimes weren't even wizards, but this one grabbed the post when it came free.) Unfortunately, serving under Ridcully has driven the Bursar to dementia and dried frog pills, but he remains very good at his job. However, the frequent periods when he's just too bursar to be useful have in turn opened an accidental opportunity for Ponder Stibbons (pp. 332-333), who has taken on a series of minor administrative posts and functions. In the process, Stibbons has swept up a majority of votes on the Board, should he choose to risk annoying his colleagues by using them.

Likewise, few senior wizards do much teaching. This is partly due to snobbery, but many of them also find the erratic, sometimes enthusiastic students and graduate researchers faintly intimidating. The University has teaching staff to insulate the higher levels from such horrors – usually mid-ranked graduates, desperate for extra income or still interested in actual scholarship and hence in having bright young minds to bounce ideas off. But there are always exceptions, even among senior wizards, and not just the ones who regard students as useful experimental subjects; those who've advanced rapidly through sheer enthusiasm may still be happy to talk to *interested* students. Established senior wizards regard such zeal with a mixture of disdain, condescension, and nervousness.

Among the undergraduates, recent graduates, and teaching staff, where there are larger numbers of individuals of the same standing, there are more divisions by specialisation, personal interests, and social background. Indeed, some of the most ritualistic and subtle distinctions are drawn among those who aren't officially *members* of the University at all: the University servants (see below).

ADMISSION

Officially, those seeking to become students of the University have a few options for obtaining admission:

1. Perform some recognised service to magic: recover an artefact of power, develop a new spell, whatever.

2. Be sponsored by a practising wizard, after an appropriate apprenticeship (what's "appropriate" being up to the sponsor). A promising youth who has been gifted with a staff by a dying

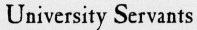

University Servants

Unseen University couldn't function without a lot of underpaid employees behind the scenes. Naïve visitors might wonder why the wizards don't use magic to meet their every want, but no one with a modicum of experience of Disc magic would even consider raising the question.

For one thing, magic takes care and effort, whereas a competent servant manages himself. For another, magic has at least latent consciousness; an enchanted cooking-pot that perpetually had to produce high-quality soup might at best raise objections to its state and at worst start experimenting with *nouvelle cuisine*. And for a third, even the most routine magic carries a tiny but significant risk of Going Wrong – a risk that should only be run for excellent reasons (such as "I felt like it").

Work as servants in such an environment also carries a small but measurable risk, of course. However, it does provide one way in which female characters can get inside the University without attracting attention.

The Bledlows and Their Ceremonies

A special group of servants, the University police force are known as *Bledlows* (the origin of the name is unknown). They tend to be heavyset and elderly, but quick (the term "spry" is sometimes used) and assertive. They're mostly ex-soldiers or watchmen. They have a universal confidence that all students are guilty of something.

Most of the time, their main task is to act as porters. However, they also function as repositories of UU lore – that is, knowledge connected with the University as an historical place of learning, rather than as a magical nexus – which they seem to regard as more important than the concerns of wizards or students. Thus, they spend a lot of their time observing pointless (but possibly once useful) rituals, such as the Ceremony Of The Keys and the Search Of The Laundry.

This sort of thing isn't unusual in a world with a large domestic servant class; Savoir-Faire is ultimately more important to those whose place on the ladder is lower and needs more defending. There are plenty of people behind the scenes at UU who are (wrongly) convinced that their ancient and peculiar job titles make them indispensable. The Bledlows raise ritual to an advanced level, however, frequently annoying the wizards.

wizard is automatically considered to have been sponsored; arrangements may be made for him to obtain apprentice training if necessary.

3. Be an eighth son of an eighth son, and demand admission.

Mostly, though, students get in by demonstrating some talent for magic. It's safer to have such people where other wizards can keep an eye on them. Numerous scholarships and bursaries exist to support poor-but-promising youths through their studentship, but many receive support from their families, or from nobles or factions who like the idea of having a friendly magic-user on tap.

In fact, so long as such support is forthcoming, it's very difficult to get rid of a student; they can keep trying to graduate until they pass.

There's no age restriction on admission. Unseen University wants to have as many wizards as possible within its control.[1] The usual admission age of new students is 16, but the youngest on record was four. This created fewer problems than one might expect, as quite a few of the most senior faculty also need nap time and strained food.

Women are not, and have never been, admitted.[2]

Once accepted, a student studies towards one of a huge array of degrees: Bachelor of Thaumatology, Bachelor of Sortilege,

---

1. Sorry, "fellowship."

2. There was one exception, but that doesn't seem to have set a precedent. Possibly, the administration is making sure that it doesn't happen again – or perhaps the University is still reviewing the consequences of the incident. That can take a while, with wizards.

University Law

The University *theoretically* grants its members immunity to city law – which isn't worth anything in game terms, because there isn't much working city law to be immune to. Still, while the Watch may lock a misbehaving student in the cells for a night, they'll usually hand him over to the University come morning. Hence, UU needs its own legal system. This was never *very* formal, and now consists of the Archchancellor getting annoyed at being interrupted and taking it out on the offender.

The University statutes certainly mention numerous petty offences and specify associated fines, from Acceptable Waggishness ($0.50) and Being a Young Rip ($0.75), to Being found Drunk ($0.80), Being found Rascally Drunk ($0.90), and Being found Objectionably Sober ($1). A wizard committing a really serious civil crime would be a bit of a problem, but that sort of thing tends to be handled on an informal basis in Ankh-Morpork anyway. Such a wizard would quite likely have enemies within the University who would quietly enable his non-wizardly victims[1] to get their own back despite his magical abilities.

Many Discworlders believe that UU has stern laws prohibiting the use of magic against non-wizards. This is in fact only slightly true. Setting fire to large portions of the citizenry is considered a breach of decorum, and wizards don't like psychopaths much more than anybody else does. But they consider magic a perfectly legitimate mode of self-defence, and wizardly dignity as very important. In other words – as Ridcully often says after turning some annoying individual into a frog temporarily – it's more of a guideline. The idea that it's a *law* is mostly promoted by untalented students who are seeking to bluff their way out of sticky situations.

---

1. Even murder victims. Magic is useful that way.

Bachelor of Magianism, Bachelor of Civil Lore, Bachelor of Applied Theurgy, Bachelor of Impractical Necromancy, and so on. There are also master's degrees and doctorates in many of these specialisations.

PROMOTION

Once one is admitted to UU – and certainly once graduated – tenure is practically automatic. A wizard may continue to learn lore, do research, write papers, and potter about in the back stacks of the Library for as long as he desires. There's always a spare study somewhere, and a seat in the Great Hall (though to bring one's own napkin and utensils is a mark of wisdom).

The University recognises eight levels of magical achievement. Level is determined by degrees completed, abilities demonstrated (more-or-less formally – *publication* isn't especially valued, as wizards traditionally tend to be secretive), and the usual academic criteria. At the higher levels, only a certain number of positions are available at any one time. There are, at least officially, only eight wizards of the eighth level: the heads of the Orders. While new positions may be established, generally a level only opens through the promotion or death of a holder. There's only one way to *create* a vacancy at the eighth level, but almost all eighth-level wizards are very old men to begin with, and accidents will happen, perhaps even today.

Some of the faculty also have a sponsored professorship, which, while it carries a decent stipend, requires the holder to actually *teach*. These positions include the Patricius Professor of Magic and the Haudmeritus Professor of Divination.

It must be understood that the system of degrees and honours isn't so much to reward magical achievement as to *control* it. Wizards who are working on the advanced degree they need to reach sixth level, and then (if they're old-fashioned) waiting for one of the existing sixth-levels to walk into an accidentally set deadfall while looking for his scarf, are wizards who aren't out somewhere trying to dominate the multiverse with dark rituals or dodgy shares in a tunnel under the Circle Sea, or to blow big holes in reality to see if it works. They're even slightly less likely to kill other wizards.

In game terms, senior wizards tend to have some combination of skills in actual magic, arcane areas of scholarship where no one else has the knowledge to prove that their accomplishments don't merit promotion, Carousing and Diplomacy (helping them stay in well with other senior wizards), Traps (for the old-fashioned), Administration (if they let themselves be talked into it), and Politics (for those who really know how to work the system).

THE ARCHCHANCELLOR

The Master of the University is its most senior official, with authority over all faculty, staff, and students. He's also the titular leader of all wizards on the Discworld, but this is a title, not a particular fact – not only are there entire countries who don't know who the Archchancellor is, but such is the University's size and complexity that there are wizards across the octangle who don't.

The selection process for Archchancellors is a bit vague, even in the absence of *droit de mortis*. Officially, the Archchancellor is elected, but wizards cannot always be troubled to vote; formally, he's chosen by the gods, but wizards don't believe in gods (or at least, don't believe in troubling them). The selectee – however he gets there – definitely must request entry to the locked Great Hall three times, signifying the consent of wizardry in general to his accession.

THE EIGHT ORDERS

One set of divisions which are as old as the University, and which are ignored half the time and treated as absolutely crucial the other half, is the *Orders*. These are similar to colleges in older British universities. This is *not* the sense of "college" that American universities use to denote separation by discipline (College of Medicine, College of Law, College of Astronomical Athletic Scholarships, etc.). In American terms, the Orders are a *little* like fraternity houses, though much more formal, with a hierarchy extending to the top of the faculty.

Among other things, the shambolic and unpredictable system for assigning undergraduate accommodations mostly places students by Order. Senior wizards largely ignore their Order membership except when cheering on the University's rare and eccentric sporting events[1], or when desperate for an excuse to extend a private squabble. However, they never quite forget these allegiances, and junior wizards may treat them as a source of personal identity.

While there have always been Orders at UU, their names and locations have occasionally changed over the centuries. The exception is Mrs. Widgery's Lodgers, which is an organisation as old as the University itself.[2] The current list is as follows:

> *The Ancient and Truly Original Sages of the Unbroken Circle*
> *The Brotherhood of the Hoodwink* (a.k.a. *The Hoodwinkers*)
> *Mrs. Widgery's Lodgers*
> *The Ancient and Truly Original Brothers of the Silver Star*
> *The Venerable Council of Seers*
> *The Sages of the Unknown Shadow*
> *The Brothers of the Order of Midnight*
> *The Last Order* (a.k.a. *The Other Order*)

DEPARTMENTS

As UU does research and has to organise teaching on some kind of semi-logical basis, it also incorporates a number of *departments,* defined by academic topic. These are considered less *significant* than the Orders, because they're subject to change over time – matching academic theories and systems of nomenclature – and because they inevitably get involved with teaching. Moderately capable faculty members can petition the Council to create a new department or reorganise an old one, whereas the system of Orders is the product of venerable tradition and unlikely ever to change much. Senior wizards are fond of tradition, which encompasses the Orders, but careless about administration, which includes the departments.

Departments cover most branches of magic and many non-magical topics, and correspond approximately to the various job titles and qualifications occasionally mentioned in relation to the University (Applied Astrology, Civil Lore, Recent Runes, Invisible Writings, Eldritch Lacemaking, and so on). Someone dealing with a specific question of magic that can't be solved by a single wizard will have to identify and approach the most relevant active

---

1. Such as its boat races, which, due to the nature of the River Ankh, involve teams of eight students chasing each other on foot while carrying a boat.

2. The Tower of Art was too small to hold all the original students, some of whom therefore boarded with Mrs. Widgery, whose house stood where New Hall does today.

The Department of Post-Mortem Communications

This department *claims* to be a recent addition to the UU system. It occupies an office with gilded letters "NEC..M...." visible underneath the newer sign on the door. But UU has no interest in *necromancy* these days – after all, that's outmoded as well as wrong. Any talking to the dead is done on a modern, rational basis.

The department head is Professor John Hicks, who has changed his name to "Hix" because having an "x" in his name sounds more sinister. This isn't so much because he enjoys being sinister as because he's required to be by University rules. Whatever his department's name, Hix is officially UU's resident evil wizard. After all, he *has* to be evil to run this department . . . and it's sometimes convenient to have someone around to do things like hit the Archchancellor over the head from behind when he's possessed by an evil spirit. The University also needs an expert on death magic and dark forces for defensive purposes, and Hix claims to be kept busy there.

Professor Hix does his best to be and look untrustworthy, being slimmer than most wizards, wearing a black robe and a skull ring, and carrying a staff with a silver skull on it, although it's clear that he finds such traditions a little tiresome. He will, indeed must, ignore University rules and direct instructions from Ridcully, unless Ridcully makes it very clear that he shouldn't this time. He's genuinely skilled, with Magic (Wizardry)-18; the Magical Form skills Divination-15, Elementalism-14, Magianism-14, Necromancy-18, and Summonation-15; and Thaumatology-13. He also has Stealth-12, as he's expected to sneak around and listen at doors, and Performance-12, as he's a leading light in an amateur theatre company.

Apart from Hix, the department's membership varies. It sometimes attracts postgraduates who *may* be interested in its work but who are *certainly* interested in wearing black and looking sinister, because that will (supposedly) turn them into babe magnets. As this is rather unreliable, they don't always stick around for long; if they're lucky, they find out enough about the department's activities that they can blackmail Hix into giving them a qualification before they leave. When last seen, Hix's minions consisted of one free-willed, talking animated skeleton named Charlie, who is at least reliable, if not very magically gifted.

---

department. Some are moribund or forgotten; others are jogging along quietly in remote corners, doing something that makes sense to the people involved. In game terms, the GM is free to make this stuff up, or to declare that some logical, coherent branch of magic is handled by three different departments, all of which will fight viciously dirty political battles to preserve their standing.

Teaching

The education that UU offers is much like the less-formal instruction that old-style wizards provide to their apprentices, although the people who do the teaching are a varied bunch. Anyone seeking formal wizard training at even a half-credible magic school – let alone UU – must, at an absolute minimum, have Magery 0 and full literacy in the local language before they enter the place, so the teachers can assume that as a starting point. Students don't necessarily learn much in the way of useful magic to begin with, though they can pick up a fair amount if they try. The first few years are mostly spent on theory (the Thaumatology skill, p. 82) – on which active wizard PCs should always spend at least one character point – and a variety of background studies. How much of the latter learning sticks depends on the institution, the student, and luck, but wizards can justify knowing any number of medical, philosophical, or scientific skills.

Eventually, of course, the student also picks up some Magic (Wizardry) skill (p. 76). While this grants at least minimal access to all the Magical Forms (pp. 76-77 and 202-217), a half-serious course and a half-attentive student – particularly one planning to *use* magic – will go on from there to focus on at least one and usually two or three Forms. For most wizards, other than those who insist on burrowing off into dubious necromancy, demonology, or hedge wizardry, Elementalism is considered *de rigueur*. All else aside, this Form grants access to blasts and pyrotechnics, ensuring that the wizard can *look* like a wizard to the public at large.

Room 3B

Unseen University's "Room 3B" doesn't exist – but for once, there's nothing darkly metaphysical about this unreality. The fact is that while some lectures and classes are on the timetable, no teacher or student wants anything to do with them. These are always scheduled for Room 3B. Sometimes the entire teaching staff is in there at once. However, an established Discworld fact is that if enough people believe in a thing . . .

The Tower of Art

The University is architecturally dominated by the Tower of Art, a black stone structure 800 feet high. Its age is indeterminate, but it's older than the city, the present University, and possibly most of the Disc. It was, certainly, the original Wizards' College.

The Tower has no windows. Its top sprouts little towers and crenellations, along with small forests, like a Bavarian fantasy castle (with gardens) painted black and stuck on a very tall smokestack. Despite the occasional shedding of stone ornamentation, and clear signs of erosion and wear, it never seems to need repairs. Entire species of bird and beetle have evolved in isolation up there, as if on some jungle plateau, and magic rising from the University has steered that evolution in decidedly *odd* directions.

There's a small door in the base. Inside is a spiral stairway. At one time there were internal floors, but these have long since rotted away, and the Tower is no longer officially used for anything. From its top, one might think one could see the edge of the Disc, once one gets one's breath back. It's a symbol of magic – not just wizardry, but the primal force.

The Library

As a university, UU naturally has a good library. As a *magical* university, it naturally has a slightly unusual one. But UU's Library goes *way* beyond "unusual."

On the Disc, representations of reality tend to double back and modify the reality they illustrate. This is particularly true of books. Large concentrations of books create strong reality fluxes. Add in the fact that many of the University Library's books are actively magical, and one understands that a casual browser risks more than a mould allergy. As with any large library, earnest students disappear in there – but in other libraries they come out again when they run out of junk food.

Magical energy coruscates from the books. Copper rails along the shelves are there to ground this power. There are also corona effects, blue fire dancing over the spines, and a constant rustling. At night, the books talk to one another.

The Library's apparent form is that of a low, circular building, approximately 100 yards across. There are about 90,000 magical texts in there; most are enormous volumes, a couple of feet high and six inches thick, in correspondingly elaborate bindings made from every imaginable substance, a few unimaginable ones, and some you could imagine but wouldn't want to. The more-powerful books are chained to the shelves – not for their protection, but to protect readers. The lower levels hold the Maximum Security Stacks, books that require containment and isolation, books that eat other books, books that eat *anything*. The adult section is especially dangerous to impressionable minds; some volumes there are held under iced water, in plain covers.

There are also thousands of "ordinary" books of magic-related and occult knowledge: astrological ephemerides, herbals, pronunciation guides to nameless horrors, and so on.

By law and tradition, the Library is open to the public, although they aren't allowed as far as the magical shelves. They can usually find what they want to know or see, but rather than consulting a catalogue, there's a good chance that they'll be subjected to an experimental divination procedure by a friendly wizard. This isn't usually too unsafe.

The present Librarian (pp. 333-335) is a 300-pound orang-utan.

THE OCTAVO

The Octavo is the spell book that belonged to the Discworld's Creator. No one knows why it was left behind after he was finished, although Rincewind (pp. 330-332) should have some idea, and some researchers involved with insect culture or marine biology assume a combination of absent-mindedness and a fondness for really odd practical jokes.

The Octavo contains the Eight Great Spells which, presumably, were sufficient to create all time, space, and matter – or at least the Disc. No one really knows what they are. Even the one person who has done anything with them, Rincewind, doesn't understand what he did. However, they did transform a potentially Disc-annihilating situation into an eight-ways happy event (see *The Light Fantastic*).

The book is kept – "imprisoned" might be a better word – in a special room in the Library, warded by signs, pentacles, and the Eight-Fold Seal of Stasis, and fastened to its stand by chains of a very purposeful thickness. No one is allowed to remain in the room for more than 4 minutes, 32 seconds. This figure has been arrived at through many years of trial.[1]

L-SPACE

In one sense, *all* books can be found in the Library.

Students of metabibliology know that knowledge equals power. Power equals energy. Energy equals mass. Mass deforms space. Sufficient concentrations of knowledge can warp and even puncture reality, creating *bookwormholes:* channels of multiply connected space-time linked to other points with similar energy density. According to the theory, it should be possible to travel from point to point through *L-Space,* an in-between universe that connects *all* libraries – everywhere and everywhen – conducting interlibrary loans of books that no longer exist, or that never precisely existed in the first place.

This theory is correct, but at UU, only the Librarian really knows it. Other wizards are aware that venturing too deep into the stacks takes you beyond ordinary spatial dimensions – and also that, approached correctly, the Librarian can seemingly get hold of pretty well *any* book – but they don't quite grasp the

depths of what's going on. The Librarian keeps things that way. The trouble is that L-Space connects all places *and times,* making it a threat to causality. Misuse could lead to a total breakdown in reality; therefore, informed librarians are sworn to secrecy.

L-Space also has its own life forms, some of them dangerous: the kickstool crab, the wild thesaurus, quartohorses (like a leathery *Eohippus*), carnivorous carrel plants, and the unspeakable shushers. There are tales of tribes of lost readers. This is why L-Space calls for its own specialisation of Survival skill (p. 81).

L-Space navigation requires use of a Hidden Lore skill (p. 75), known to only a handful of librarians in the entire multiverse. (Some people stumble into and through L-Space by accident, of course – and sometimes they're found pressed in the pages of old atlases, between Atlantis and Mu.) In our reality, Jorge Luis Borges may have had an inkling. The Librarian has been known to use L-Space travel in pursuit of his own priorities – to rescue some volumes from Didactylos' burning library in Ephebe, and while investigating an especially serious book theft – but even he doesn't do this lightly. Note that both these uses were connected with the *safety of books*.

For the record, the rules of the Librarians of Space and Time are:

1. Silence.
2. Books must be returned no later than the last date shown.
3. Do not interfere with the nature of causality.

Invisible Writings

A recent development of L-Space theory is the study of Invisible Writings. The basic concept is that the L-Space fields of individual books affect all other books, and since L-Space extends in all temporal dimensions, this includes books that haven't yet been written. There are obvious empirical proofs: books written in the past clearly influence later books (plagiarism being the asymptotic case), and books written in the present mention earlier books. Under General L-Space Theory, it's believed that an adequate study of extant books can extrapolate the content of any book yet to be written.

At the last count, UU's Reader in Invisible Writings was Ponder Stibbons (pp. 332-333). As he has other jobs these days, that research may now be pursued more by others. Ponder had an unfortunate experience in the field when early research located (or created) a book seemingly made up of fragments of countless jargon-laden books of management theory from other universes, which fell into the hands of the Archchancellor and gave him *ideas*.

---

1. And error.

High-Energy Magical Research

These days, enthusiastic young research wizards are increasingly intent on taking magical theory off in radical directions. Their *High Energy Magic Building* is the only architecture in the University that's less than a thousand years old, and it generates some tension between the younger wizards who work there and senior faculty, who largely avoid it. The researchers are constantly submitting funding requests for thaumic particle accelerators, superconducting linear athanors, and ever-more-elaborate containment octagons. The seniors have doubts about where all the money is going, and about the actual value of discovering ever-smaller magical particles and finer thaumic-structure constants. Mainly, though, they're worried by the idea that some students are actually enjoying their work.

Emergency Responses

It's entirely possible that a group of PCs might set off a *serious* magical problem in the course of adventures in or near Ankh-Morpork. Fortunately (perhaps), this may allow them to see the UU faculty actually doing something right. Sometimes, this response consists of the Archchancellor with his staff, a crossbow, a pocketful of spells, and as many of the rest of the faculty as he can bully into helping. Perhaps an antiquated broomstick makes a series of low passes with the Bursar on board, dusting the area with rowan-wood sawdust.[1] This has the added virtue of putting Ridcully close to hand when the problem is solved, so that he can shout at the PCs a lot.

However, with all the high-energy magic research that has been going on recently, Ponder Stibbons may have decided to organise a proper Decontamination Team. This could include (but not be limited to) Stibbons and several of his friends, moving slowly in lead-lined robes and with rowan-wood masks[2], carrying crossbows that fire lead-tipped rowan-wood bolts. Or it might be the sort of thing into which a bunch of PCs could be recruited. Whether they like it or not.

1. The effect may be spoiled slightly if the bursar has been sloppy with his dried frog pill dosage and keeps shouting out "Whoops, the laundry is shrinking sideways" or "Hello Uncle Fungus, turned out purple again."

2. Mostly painted with smiley faces or what look suspiciously like portraits of the Archchancellor. Just because you're saving the universe doesn't mean you're immune to student humour.

HEX

A typical High Energy Magic Building project in many ways[1], Hex is the Disc's first thaumaturgical computer. It's a combination of clockwork, ants running round in glass tubes (the builders have got nearly all the bugs in now), and stuff that no one can remember putting in there (including an hourglass that indicates when Hex is thinking). Data entry is through a giant keyboard or experimental voice input; output involves Hex writing with a quill pen. The thing weighs about 10 tons, and nobody understands it any more. Certain components – the mouse's nest, with mouse, and a fluffy teddy bear (FTB) – serve no obvious purpose, but Hex refuses to work without them. Nobody has dared remove the "Anthill Inside" sticker from the side, though no one knows how it got there.

Incidentally, "refuses" is a touchy choice of words. The students deny that Hex is actually intelligent, insisting that it merely talks as though it is.

Despite its oddities, Hex serves its original design function – analysis of magical operations – fairly well. For example, even the UU faculty couldn't teleport people across the full width of the Disc without its advice. Minor side-effects, such as uncertain relative velocities on arrival, are just details.

In game terms, Hex is a plot device supreme. *Magical Computer Bonuses* (p. 195) covers some of its capabilities, but the GM can always allow it to accomplish . . . other things. Its intelligence is eccentric and its capabilities are erratic, but if anyone with a connection to UU needs something done that isn't supposed to be possible, or a question answered that barely makes sense, then Hex *may* be able to help.

Other Features

Unseen University sprawls, sometimes in nonstandard dimensions. A few other details follow.

THE GATES

The first thing that many people see of UU is the Main Gates, which open onto Sator Square. The large doors are plated with octiron, and they are locked each night at sunset by the power of magic.[2]

THE GREAT HALL

Many wizards consider the Great Hall to be the most important part of the University. It is, after all, where they have dinner.

Around the Hall are the portraits and statues of past Archchancellors, bearing objects of wizardly significance and expressions of disapproval at how things have got worse since their terms of office. Some of the portraits are unfinished, the sitter's tenure (of Archchancellorship and existence) having ended before the sitting was complete. A few are represented by pencil sketches or blocks of rough marble with little brass nameplates.

The Hall's floor is covered with a pattern of black and white tiles that shouldn't be looked at too closely or for long. There are long tables and benches. At the turnwise end is a large clock; to widdershins, a great fireplace. The enormous black iron chandelier can hold a thousand candles, creating warm illumination and a partial vacuum in the Hall below.

The wall opposite the doors is mostly taken up by the Mighty Organ, designed and built by Bloody Stupid Johnson (p. 254), who approached his first organ design with his accustomed optimism: "It's only air going through pipes, it can't be that difficult." The Organ has three keyboards, a large number of pedals, uncountable stops, and many unique controls, including one that floods the pipes with poisonous gas to kill the mice.

---

1. "That's a strange idea – let's try it."

2. Actually, by the gardener, a dwarf named Modo, but one must keep up appearances.

Very deep in the cellars is the Other Observatory, a lead-lined room from which the *other* stars may be viewed.

MORE ABOUT THE CELLARS

The cellars also hold the kitchens and their support areas (pantries, butteries, cold rooms, meat lockers, sculleries, bakeries, and taprooms). Unlike most of the University's physical structure – which isn't so much remodelled as built over and allowed to settle together – the kitchens are modern and constantly bustling. Conclusions about the University's sense of priorities may be drawn, but it would probably be pleasanter just to find a seat in the Great Hall and tuck into a pie and a pint.

Other cellar contents include the laundry engines, another Bloody Stupid Johnson design: two floors high, powered by treadmills, and requiring crews of a half-dozen muscular operators.

There's a museum of biological curiosities down here, too. This and the kitchens should probably be visited on different dates.

THE ARCHCHANCELLOR'S ROOMS

Archchancellor Ridcully naturally has very comfortable quarters. Like several other wizards, he has employed dimension-warping magic to adapt his rooms to his personal taste – in his case, installing half a mile of trout stream. He also has access to a bathroom which was designed by Bloody Stupid Johnson on commission from a previous Archchancellor, and then boarded up. Ridcully had this opened up, used it once, suffered an experience of which he will not speak, and ordered it boarded up again.

It can fairly be said to have expanded the possibilities of music itself; a piece has been written for it that seems to the audience not to have commenced until stunned bats tumble into their laps. The use of the Terraemotus pedal has been forbidden; connected to a 128-foot pipe called Earthquake, its last use moved spirits, hearts, and large intestines all over the city, and shifted the building a quarter-inch. The Librarian plays the Organ, by way of a hobby. His arm length and prehensile feet help.

All major University activities are held in the Great Hall, as well as the four main meals daily. Senior faculty once occupied the High Table, so named because it could float several yards above the floor, landing only between courses. The Table is now grounded, following what is known only as the Incident at Dinner.

Also in the same building are the Uncommon Room, which maintains a roaring log fire regardless of season; the small chapel and almost-as-small infirmary (wizards generally being as healthy as they ever get, or dead); and the classrooms, auditoria that slope steeply down to the central teaching areas. The senior wizards' lavatory is here as well. Visitors will note its actual running water.

THE OBSERVATORY AND THE OTHER OBSERVATORY

The Observatory is a glass-domed building with an ornate mosaic floor inlaid with the 64 signs of the Disc zodiac (see *Astronomy and Astrology*, p. 224). Access is controlled by the Librarian.

Non-Wizardly Studies

In addition to magical study, Unseen University maintains departments of medicine, lore (history), minor religions, and other nonmagical topics. However, these are small by comparison with the magical faculty, and all teachers must have trained as wizards. There are also occasional guest lectures from specialists in fields that wizards may or may not respect, but cannot deny are magical, such as witchcraft or shamanism. Thus, many more-or-less scholarly characters with or without borderline magical talent could have contacts at UU.

THE GROUNDS

The neatly maintained grounds, with their rose arbours and gravel paths, lead down to the river's edge, where there are small jetties with moored boats. A footbridge crosses the Ankh to Wizards' Pleasaunce, a small meadow in a horseshoe bend of the river. It's a nice spot for an evening's stroll, when the river wind is blowing away from it. By tradition, wizards are allowed to bathe naked in the river at this spot – but wisely, no one has taken advantage of the privilege for some centuries.

The grounds also include the Archchancellor's gardens and veranda. These are protected by a 20-foot-high wall topped with spikes. A bit further on is a mossy courtyard, crisscrossed by clotheslines hung with damp linens.

The gardens are maintained, it seems singlehandedly, by a dwarf, Modo. He's a calm and amiable character, quite willing to take as long as necessary to restore the lawns to perfection after they've been damaged by rampaging tentacled monstrosities.

OLD TOM

The University clock tower holds a bell, nicknamed Old Tom, which is made of octiron, not bronze. The clapper fell out long ago, but its silences still mark the hours very clearly.

"Numbers" Riktor

"Riktor the Tinkerer" was a former Unseen University lecturer who firmly believed that the universe could be understood in purely numerical terms, and indeed that it *is* numbers, at some very deep level. He was obviously unusually rationalistic for an old-style wizard and built many magical measuring devices. Reproducing them would be a lengthy research project. They included the Mouse Counter[1], the Rev Counter[2], the Star Enumerator[3], and the Swamp Meter.[4]

The Resograph

Perhaps Riktor's most important creation – and typical of his genius – the Resograph ("Reality-Meter") stood for years in a quiet corner of the University. It was housed in an antique vase, with pottery elephants around the side. The partly octiron internal mechanism sensed distortions in the fabric of reality, and it caused the elephants to "spit" small lead pellets in the direction of the event, to a distance proportional to the size of the effect. Riktor calculated that a serious distortion could cause a couple of pellets a month to be projected a few inches. During the invasion of the alien moving-picture imagery, the Resograph became seriously dangerous to be around, firing salvoes of pellets at firearms velocities before it finally exploded. It isn't inconceivable that Riktor might have built a second Resograph, which could show up in the course of a game, if that suits the GM.

---

1. *It counted every mouse in the building.*

2. *Which did much the same for priests.*

3. *Guess.*

4. *Use never explained.*

University-Based Campaigns

Unseen University would be an interesting base for a Discworld campaign. In general, such games can be set at one of three levels.

UNDERGRADUATE CAMPAIGNS

A game could feature low-point-value characters, not terribly competent in magic. Some may have no useful spellcasting abilities at all, while others might be justifiably nervous of using what they do know. For a suitable template, see *Student Wizard* (p. 128).

Plots would probably start with the complications of student life (pretty consistent throughout the multiverse), although they could spin off in countless directions. Trying to recover something lost in the course of a prank before its rightful, high-powered owner notices its absence might lead to adventures across Ankh-Morpork. Doing a favour to ensure a glowing report from a tutor well entail delving through the dark history of Disc magic in a very physical way. Patching Hex's operating system to play games faster could make hacking the Pentagon's missile-control computers look like a really bright idea.[1] Attempts to find a book (desperately needed for an overdue essay) without the Librarian's aid might mean blundering into L-Space and thence almost anywhere. Undergraduates are also likely still to be in contact with their families and old friends, who could involve them in relatively mundane plots.

Do remember, though, that references to Greek-letter fraternities, toga parties, and other stuff from certain all-too-popular movies are completely inappropriate. Likewise, for practical purposes, UU remains all-male.[2]

Alongside actual undergraduates, players could create characters such as University servants, citizens of Ankh-Morpork with whom they strike up acquaintance, relatives of undergraduates who live near enough to visit, demented radicals whose rhetoric might prove dangerously appealing to naïve minds, or people whom undergraduates may choose to consult on specific subjects.

---

1. *The latter, after all, involves only three-dimensional threats.*

2. *Although the happy thought occurs: It **appears** to be all-male, but who knows if all those beards are real?*

How suitable such individuals would actually be as PCs depends on the exact nature of the GM's plans.

GRADUATE CAMPAIGNS

Moving up the scale of age and power, a game could revolve around PCs who are fully qualified wizards but relatively low on the University hierarchy. They might have joined the teaching staff and face the horrors of supervising undergraduates, be deeply engrossed in projects involving Hex or the High Energy Magic Building, or be hanging around the University while trying to establish themselves as freelance consultants. Graduates can be reasonably capable spellcasters, but they also tend to be rather unworldly. For a template, see *Graduate Wizard* (pp. 133-134).

This setup could become the basis of a relatively conventional adventuring game, as researchers and consultants chase after all sorts of problems and solutions, possibly even venturing into underground labyrinths with 10-foot-wide corridors. It might also involve non-wizard and variant PCs, such as thaumaturgists and magicians, brawny warrior bodyguards, senior University servants, and keen undergraduates with nonmagical abilities that balance their lesser academic training. On the other hand, a group consisting of nothing but graduate wizards who never leave the confines of the University could easily have extremely strange adventures, as they're probably the most willing and able of all to take magical research in completely unprecedented directions.

SENIOR WIZARDS CAMPAIGNS

Finally, a game might deal with high-ranking tenured faculty (see the template under *Senior Wizard*, pp. 142-143). Plots would often involve extended jokes about their conservatism and view of magic. Their objectives ought to be coloured by the urge to eat lots of large dinners, avoid undergraduates, and maybe engage in a little academic politics. However, such individuals aren't completely amoral; when serious supernatural forces threaten the Disc, they can show up, fireballs at the ready, and confuse the situation even further. Conversely, by setting the game a few years back – in the era of *droit de mortis* – the campaign could be made as subtle, brutal, and wasteful of PCs as the most exasperated GM could ever imagine.

The problem here is the sheer firepower. Although rigorous application of the game rules for magic can keep this under some control, the main trick is to come up with problems that cannot be solved simply by a big enough spell. Gods, the Things from the Dungeon Dimensions, and anthropomorphic personifications can often simply shrug off magic. Dealings with other wizards may be conducted under rules that say it's impolite to use spells even if they might work. Wizards who become involved in high-level mundane politics may have to contend with the fact that Discworld magic, while powerful, is hard to conceal. And irritated mundane folk – especially those active at that level of politics – can make life tiresome for all wizards, and they may eventually plant an unexpected knife in an arrogant wizard's back.

Witchcraft

Witchcraft on the Disc is practised exclusively by women.[1] Witches are mostly solitary, and they certainly don't form colleges. "Covens" are rare, although a few exist. Discworld witches are driven by tradition and stereotype enough that they usually fit the archetypes of the Maiden, the Mother, or the Crone, as epitomised by the Lancre witches (pp. 337-343). Witches generally don't discuss the theory behind their craft, but this triplet is considered to reflect mental outlook – nice, nurturing, or intimidating – more than it does physical condition.

Most witches can read and write these days, but unlike wizards, they don't derive their power from books. They're taught by other witches, on a one-to-one basis. A witch may have just one tutor or, less often, several in series. While witches' daughters often become witches themselves, it's considered bad practise for mother to teach daughter; the student inevitably absorbs a certain amount of the teacher's style, and magical inbreeding would have the same kind of degenerative effect it has in livestock.

Magic isn't the whole of a witch's training, of course. There are several other village-witch roles to fulfil. These include midwifery, preparing the dead for burial, and folk medicine.

A witch normally has a definite home area, centred on her cottage (see *Advantageous Situations*, p. 195). When she dies, another witch – normally one of her trainees – takes over both locality and

cottage. Some cottages have been in continuous use for centuries. Indeed, the basic unit of witchcraft is essentially the cottage.

Witches are matrilineal – the women are heads of household, and their husbands normally take their surnames, as do their children and grandchildren, male and female. In sparsely populated areas, such as the Ramtops, this is subject to individual variation. Witches aren't really interested in rules, as a rule.

GOOD AND BAD WITCHES

Smarter Discworld witches draw a clear distinction between being *good* and being *nice*. Most are blameless village healers, and some are strong-minded moralists, but all know the importance of *respect*, and soft-heartedness is a liability in their line of work. They aren't all as unsentimental as Granny Weatherwax, but even the kindliest of them exhibit a certain clinical detachment. They have to deal with sickness and death almost daily, after all.

The majority are "good" by most measures, though – they spend their time treating the sick and keeping society ticking over, and witchcraft actually depends on a certain capacity for empathy. Unfortunately, a dangerous minority go another way. Witches operate slightly outside ordinary society, and they can derive power from stories. As a result, they can end up treating everybody else as means to an end. The most famous bad witches become flamboyant fairy-tale characters, living alone in twisted towers or cottages made of confectionery, distorting the lives of everyone in the neighbourhood, until eventually their stories end badly.

Most bad witches are also openly nasty. But a scary minority can actually seem nice, in a sickly sort of way, until you cause them inconvenience.

---

1. The occasional mentions of warlocks apparently refer to male witches, but nobody has ever seen one. The concept seems to be a bit like antimatter: an opposite to normal reality which must logically exist, but of which it's rather hard to imagine the creation.

Witch Training

Girls who become apprentice witches either are selected by their teachers or – in very rare cases – present themselves so persistently that the old witch gives in for the sake of (relative) peace and quiet. Regardless, the teacher will only even *think* of training a girl with Magery. Exact details of training and abilities vary enormously, but there are some basic essentials. Any witch lacking in the following areas requires a good explanation:

1. Witches are trained in folk medicine. Their skill levels at Herbalism[1], Midwifery, and either First Aid or Physician should be at least 12, and many are considerably more competent. Some also know Diagnosis; others don't bother, relying on standard formulae and the placebo effect. Surgery skill is rare – witches work through the mind and herbs, not by gross carving – but witches sometimes learn a little for serious emergencies. There are specialists who know the Veterinary skill, too.

2. Witches learn "Headology" (p. 274), whether or not they call it that, knowing the importance of respect, and how to achieve results without actual magic. This training sticks a lot better in some cases than in others, but even the least assertive or manipulative witch should have *some* talent for getting information out of people she knows. Simulate this with a point or two in an Influence skill (pp. 74-75), and maybe Area Knowledge of her locality. Certainly, Area Knowledge is important to any witch who looks after some region.

3. As part of the process of building up respect and an *image*, a witch usually acquires some kind of Reputation (p. 34) or Social Regard (p. 35) – ideally both. A Reputation may be good or bad, and it is quite often a mixture of the two (and thus may balance out to zero cost); the important thing is *being known*, not what one is known *for*.

As for magic, witches learn Magic (Witchcraft), of course. They're usually competent at Divination, Physiomancy, and Psychomancy. If they study Elementalism, they reserve it for emergencies and less-flashy effects than wizards favour.

Indeed, whatever the game mechanisms, witch magic tends to the *subtle*. Although most witches threaten to turn people into frogs on occasion, they're probably less likely actually to do so than wizards. Their magic treats almost everything as having a mind which can be persuaded to cooperate. They dislike fire, which has no mind at all that they can discern, and they have a *lot* of trouble with iron – even more than wizards do – because it has a cold, rigid intellect at best. (Weather, on the other hand, has distinct personality patterns.) Even witch spells that do direct physical damage tend to take the form of delayed and misdirecting curses, rather than gouts of energy.

Covens

Those witches' covens that do exist are nothing like what rather fevered imaginations envisage; the informal association of Granny Weatherwax, Nanny Ogg, and Magrat Garlick or Agnes Nitt is exceptional.[2] The truth is that a witch is generally a non-joiner by nature, and normally not at home in company. The plural of wizard is "wizards," but the plural of witch is "argument."

Still, many witches enjoy having someone to boss around who can understand what the bossing is all about, or want a structure for their arguments with other witches. A few even grasp the concept of teamwork – or at least the advantage of the weight of numbers. Three is probably the normal number for a coven which lasts for more than a couple of meetings. While the maiden-mother-crone idea has a certain symbolic power, the main reason may simply be that any group of more than three is doomed to disintegrate into sub-factions rather quickly, while two witches isn't a coven, it's just a squabble.

---

1. *Ramtops herbalism is much enhanced by the exceptional, magic-shaped variety of local plant life. Some straightforward "standard formulae" used by local witches produce astonishing results.*

2. *And Granny insists it isn't a coven anyway.*

Alchemists

Discworld alchemy is a borderline-supernatural profession with quite a few members, especially in major cities. Alchemists are seen as experts in a technical field, but not as magic-workers – although a lot of what they do would count as supernatural by our world's standards. For example, some understand the procedures for summoning and binding miniature imps into technomantic devices. Mostly, though, alchemy is a sort of low-tech chemistry, disorganised and weird, but with a huge body of background knowledge that occasionally lets alchemists produce impressive effects.

Unfortunately, alchemists' careless and optimistic approach to experiments, the Disc's levels of background magical energy, and the universal laws of humour combine to ensure that a distressingly large number of alchemical experiments end in explosions. The Alchemists' Guild hall in Ankh-Morpork is notoriously prone to blowing up – sometimes several times in a month. Professional alchemists learn to duck behind reinforced benches at the first sign of bubbling, shimmering, or fizzing.

The core goal of alchemical research is the transformation of lead (or anything else cheap, frankly) into gold. Sadly, this seems to be impossible even under the Disc's sloppy laws of nature, but alchemists are optimists. Also, they can be distracted by other potentially profitable ideas (which is how the Disc's short-lived motion-picture industry got started), and while they aren't especially sociable, they exchange knowledge and have rarely been prone to wizardly levels of backstabbing. Their successes are just enough to ensure a supply of hopeful patrons. Still, some of them get tired of years of failure – or run out of gullible patrons – and end up applying their skills to other purposes. One, Cheery Littlebottom (pp. 326-3270), serves the Ankh-Morpork Watch as a forensic investigator.

In game terms, Alchemy skill can do all sorts of things that may serve the plot, as the GM sees fit. Given basic laboratory facilities, an alchemist can test for poisons and other interesting substances, prepare medicines of a scary and kill-or-cure sort, identify magical energies in physical substances, and create lots of explosions – the last, though, not very reliably. For a template, see *Alchemist* (p. 120).

Also, in most rural areas of the Disc, three witches can each cover a worthwhile area in a region small enough to let them remain in fairly close touch.

If a group of witch PCs of comparable power levels worked together regularly, they would probably be classified as a coven by default. This would require some explanation, especially if there were more than three of them. If they were exceptionally low-powered, they might be hanging together – despite any personal friction – to provide adequate witchcraft services for an area with no more powerful practitioners. Otherwise, it might be better to limit the group to three actual witches and have the remaining PCs be other locals, perhaps blood relatives to the witches. Non-witches associating with a coven could help mediate when the witches themselves start squabbling. It's a dangerous job, but somebody has to do it.

Major Personifications

A few Discworld philosophers and well-informed wizards realise that belief can not only move mountains, it can take the form of a mountain-removal-man. In other words, in the literal-minded magical field of the Disc, mortal belief and imagination – with all their complexity and ludicrous limitations – frequently force powers and even ideas to take a *personal* form.

This seems to be distinct from the process which permits small gods to ascend to divinity (see *The Small Gods*, pp. 297-298), although the distinction is blurred. Personifications are interested less in worship and more in getting a job done. They're created by raw belief rather than prayer. However, a mindless small god may be the piece of grit around which a lesser personification accumulates like a pearl. *Major* personifications, though, represent abstractions that pre-date humanity and belief, and they may survive humanity.

Among other things, the great forces of the universe, as represented by the Old High Ones (below), may manifest on the Disc in "local" forms. These are mostly very abstract entities. There's only one such phenomenon which humans consistently insist on personifying, and which therefore often shows up as a person.

Death

The Death of the Discworld is an emissary or an aspect of Azrael (see *The Old High Ones*, below), but also a personification, imagined by humanity. Any paradox in this isn't resolvable by PCs. His task is to separate life from its end. He isn't a god – he neither requires nor accepts worship, and he happens whether people believe in him or not.

Death appears as a polished skeleton, seven feet tall. There are tiny points of light, usually blue, in his empty eye-sockets. He normally wears a robe of absolute black, and sometimes a black riding cloak with a silver brooch, showing his monogram, the Infinite Omega (an omega superimposed on a lazy-eight infinity symbol). HIS VOICE is felt within rather than heard, and he's understandable in all languages, though his statements may sometimes be less than absolutely clear; it's equal to the Voice of Command advantage (p. 49).

Death's scythe has a normal-looking wooden handle, and his sword has an intricate-but-conventional hilt, but their blades are an ice-blue colour, so thin as to be transparent. Both are, for all purposes, infinitely sharp, and they can cut through anything (should it ever matter, they ignore all DR and deal triple damage). Their purpose is to divide body and soul. Death usually uses the scythe, but royalty and a few other important people are entitled to the sword.

In one sense, Death comes to everyone. In another, the personification only seems to manifest as such for "special cases." He appears to collect magic-workers, royalty, and people dying in vaguely interesting ways, such as from a brand-new disease or after being killed by a supposedly nonexistent monster. However, he does occasionally attend some ordinary, even trivial demises just to keep an eye on things. He determines the *nodes* where he'll be needed using arcane charts which are found in the desk in the study of his house (pp. 293-294).

The Old High Ones

The highest powers recognised by Disc theology are eight entities known as the *Old High Ones*, to whom even the gods are answerable. All discussion of these beings is very indirect. They don't intervene in individual affairs; that would be like a human intervening in the affairs of one microbe. Their sole major direct action on the Disc was to end the Mage Wars (p. 13), which were threatening the structure of reality. They might be considered to oppose the Things from the Dungeon Dimensions, but that's housekeeping, not warfare.

The only one of the Old High Ones who has appeared in the chronicles is *Azrael*, the Great Attractor, the Death of Universes, the Beginning and End of Time. Azrael represents not just death but *finality*. He's as large as a universe, with eyes in which a supernova would vanish. The Deaths of all worlds, including the Disc, report to him, and they may just be aspects of his being. He keeps The Clock, which only goes round once. Gods know at heart that their claims to significance are rendered ludicrous by his existence.

Under normal circumstances, Death is visible only to cats, people with magical senses, and those he has come to collect. Persons in a heightened state of awareness (from some forms of trance or just extreme agitation) can sometimes perceive him, though not clearly. He says that he doesn't make himself invisible; people simply choose not to see him, and they reflexively move out of his way to avoid having to pay him attention. In practise, he has an enhanced version of the Unnoticed advantage (p. 48).

Roleplaying Death

Like other characters from the chronicles, Death shouldn't appear overly often in games. Even if people are dying "on screen" and observers have magical senses, the fact is that he's a hard-working entity with little time to hang around and chat. Most encounters ought to be brief and brisk. While he's never less than polite, there will always be some *reason* why he's taking the time to converse, and mortals should consider it a privilege not to be abused.

However, he's also a major element in the chronicles, and players *will* expect him to crop up sooner or later. When he does, the GM can have some fun, but the event is also something of a challenge.

To start with, there's the Voice, written in hollow capitals throughout the chronicles. Ingenious GMs might plan ahead and lay in a stage-effects box to shift them down an octave and add echo . . . Others will just have to depend on player imagination. Remember, although Death may occasionally be confused by human eccentricities, he doesn't gabble or snap; if you can't think what he would say at a particular point, he may restrict himself to a thoughtful "Hmmm?" He does have what might almost pass for a bone-dry sense of humour.

However, he isn't superhumanly bright or alert. He can know everything, before it happens, if he lets himself, but mostly he projects the character of a hard-working, dutiful type who just happens to be the End Of Everything. He's neither cruel nor reliably compassionate; the first is unnecessary, while the second would make his work impossible.[1] He knows that, if he said too much, people would be forever pestering him for "wisdom," so he's taciturn. He dislikes attempts to trick him into talking, but he doesn't bother blaming anyone for their motives.

---

1. Though he does make the occasional minor exception for a mortal who engages his interest or respect.

Even if Death *does* choose to bring himself to others' attention, most people see him as a fairly normal member of their own species, and they mentally edit the things he says so that they fit that appearance. Humans tend to perceive him as a tall, skinny human who evidently likes to dress in dark clothes – an undertaker, perhaps. If he acts in such a way that they have to respond to him,

they generally only half-attend, thinking of him as unthreatening and "just another person." They may later become puzzled at the vague sense that someone was there, but quite what he looked like is evasive. Small children, whose minds haven't yet got the hang of ignoring inconvenient stuff, may see him for what he is.

In his working role, Death can appear in any form. Once, for a time, he tried to reproduce whatever the client's cultural beliefs called for, but he no longer bothers. All those black celestial dragons and giant scarab beetles were merely confusing, and most people had only vague ideas to begin with. The skeleton is illustrative enough.

DEATH'S NATURE

Death is not cruel. He has an appointment with everyone, and he always keeps it, no matter how inconvenient this may be for the mortal involved. He doesn't put the dagger, or the big rock, or the botulinus organism, or the embolism in the victim's way. He no more kills his clients than the postman writes the letters he collects.

He has no emotions in the usual sense. However, he can *disapprove* of things and actions, particularly among mortals who are trying to "cheat" him, and most of all those who use offensively crude methods, such as human sacrifice – and Death's disapproval is cold enough to freeze helium. He can also become depressed when the service he tirelessly performs goes unappreciated.

When major metaphysical problems arise, Death may even work with mortals. Despite his lack of creativity, he can seem ingenious, or at least good at getting people to do what must be done. He can be politely grateful for assistance received, but he's in no position to grant favours; he certainly cannot be expected to change the date of anyone's demise. He's bound by the largest Duty in the universe. If he feels that it's somehow right, he *may* petition the gods to grant rewards or aid, and they're careful enough of him that they usually oblige.

Death also has an intellectual fascination with humanity. This is apparently because of their incessant efforts to swim against the current of time – not just avoiding him personally, but also building tombs for those who can least appreciate them, exploring distant places for no special reason other than They Are There, writing poetry, worrying about the fundamental structure of a possibly unknowable universe, making war, and making more humans to carry on. His study of these things has led to certain acquired preferences that might be considered human: he likes cats, and curry, though it's unnecessary for him to eat.

Death is fundamentally uncreative. He can only imitate what he has seen. This accounts for his lack of artistic sense. He has tried to learn music (the banjo in particular), but with poor results. He *can* dance, rather well; the "Dance of Death" is mentioned in human myth, and he usually lives up to his image.

Still, Death's job is to manage life's endings, not to obliterate it, and human belief gives him a near-human aspect. This is why he finds himself in opposition to the Auditors of Reality (pp. 296-297). Compared to them, he's a close ally of humanity and life.

Death's powers are not finite, but they are limited; he's obliged to play by the rules, although no one but him really knows what those are. He could be considered to have almost human characteristics in his skeletal guise – say, ST 15, DX 15, and IQ 11 – and 30 HP of damage from some appropriate source can dismantle him, although he'll promptly start reassembling himself, completing the process in 2d seconds. However, when he's obliged to use some ability or aspect of his myth, he's usually infallible.

he's shown making in the chronicles actually happened at different times to the main events of the plot involved. He certainly finds human ideas of reality a little hard to grasp. This is why, for example, his house is bigger inside than out, and fixed distances seem to be strictly optional there.

BINKY, THE STEED OF DEATH

Death's horse is an actual, living horse, not skeletal or winged, although he normally leaves no hoof-prints (except when travelling between dimensions, when he sometimes leaves glowing prints in the air). He wears a silver-and-black harness; his ornate saddle has a sheath for Death's folding scythe and a saddlebag for Death's riding cloak. In his function as the Steed of Death, Binky can not only gallop through the air, but also travel anywhere on the Disc or in adjacent sub-dimensions, sometimes carrying a couple of riders, reaching any destination within seconds.

Binky is extremely intelligent and well-cared-for, and Death clearly regards him with whatever Death's version of affection is. He's a truly exceptional cavalry horse (p. 356); notably, he has ST 24, IQ 5, HT 12, HP 24, FP 12, Speed 5.25, and Mount-17. He is not war-trained and therefore not especially hard to handle, unless he has some reason to be difficult. If he *does* wish to be difficult, it'd be an excellent rider indeed who could stay on. Trying to harm him would be very silly.

DEATH'S HOUSE

Death dwells in a pocket dimension, outside of space and time, containing a house and a garden which include structures that imitate human ones – a furnished bedroom and bathroom, for instance. Death created these, though he has no need of either. It just seems to him that a house ought to have them.

Death doesn't *need* assistance in his work, but he seems to find it convenient – or perhaps just *appropriate* – to maintain not only a house, but also a household. However, he reached the conclusion a little while ago that having anything approaching a family around doesn't really work for him, so that household is now down to one person.

This manservant, *Albert*, was originally Alberto Malich "the Wise," founder of Unseen University, who officially died – and definitely disappeared from the Disc – at the age of 67.

If narrative logic suggests that he should have a tiny chance of error, or degrees of possible success, treat him as having skill 20. When he's playing by some rule that says he should have a meaningful chance of failure (such as playing chess for someone's life if they're allowed that challenge), his effective skill becomes 15, while in his private life, he tends to use DX-based skills at 15 and most other skills at 12. If he ever has to make a Will roll or use a Will-based skill, though, treat him as scoring an automatic critical success, with a margin of success of 20.

Death can go anywhere that something can die, which is to say, pretty well everywhere. The fact that he might choose to walk up a flight of stairs, rather than simply "teleport" to the client, is a dramatic choice rather than a practical requirement. The choice, however, is much more mortals' than Death's; although he rather dislikes drama, he always meets reasonable expectations.

Given the number of times a day he's called on to make collections, it should be apparent that time operates differently for Death than for others. Actually, he operates in a realm *outside* of time, and he can stop it for everyone except himself (and a few other beings of comparable power) when convenient – although he can also work in normal human time when that suits him.

There has been speculation that Death might be killed by his own weapons, or by those of another Death, but whether this is would in fact be "dying" or something wholly *else* is difficult to say. Trying to get hold of Death's scythe to test the concept is the kind of thing heroes often set out to do, three or four chapters before the abrupt denouement, but it cannot be recommended. Death can be summoned and temporarily bound by the Rite of AshkEnte (pp. 214-215), but this is a matter of accepted myth and convention, an invitation he feels obliged to accept. Mostly, magic has no effect on him, and he slightly dislikes it, perhaps because he has seen its worst consequences.

Given that space and even time are largely an irrelevance to Death, it would be possible to assume that some of the "side-visits"

Games Death Plays

By ancient convention, Death can be formally challenged to play some kind of game for any life for which he comes – sometimes, anyway. However, it's difficult in practise for anyone to issue such a challenge unless they can see him before he swings his scythe, which essentially limits the privilege to the magically adept, who have their own reasons for not invoking it very often. Some are too wise to mess with this sort of thing, and others are too selfish to risk issuing a challenge on anyone else's behalf.

Because the problem is, the challenge must be balanced. Only someone with very special privileges can play for more life without offering a balancing stake. At the minimum, a challenge for the life of a human might risk another life, preferably that of a human who *must* willingly volunteer. And even if the mortals win, Death must still take something – though a valuable domestic animal may suffice. Anyway, challenging for a life which has reached some kind of clear, ordained conclusion is rather pointless, as the deceased might just be left in some kind of horrible half-living state. Still, witches will *occasionally* challenge on behalf of, say, a child dying before what they think is its time.

In fact, Death cannot be defeated in these contests, *unless he so chooses.* He isn't above bending a rule for people whose motives he admires, but he doesn't make a habit of it. This could be doubly frustrating for a chess grandmaster who challenged him, because Death keeps forgetting the names of the pieces, and then wins anyway.

Death is as aware of narrative causality as the next anthropomorphic personification, and he may look more favourably on someone who gambles his own life to save the life of another. But don't bet on it. Death will play any game the challenger chooses that has a clear winner and loser: chess, cards, obscure board games . . . RPGs aren't acceptable, although it's a tempting thought.

In game terms, this should be used as a rare, highly dramatic plot device, not as a get-out to avoid the loss of a PC. The point to make is not that PC death can be negated, but that on the Disc, even Death is subject to narrative and tradition.

remaining, but that has since been almost entirely used up. Albert's trips outside Death's house are now effectively limited to journeys where he accompanies Death, and Death remains outside the normal flow of time.

Albert is a thin man who appears hunchbacked; actually, he is tall and wiry, but walks bent over. His nose is red and drips constantly; while this doesn't seem to bother him, it makes other people blow their own noses in sympathy. If it becomes important, treat him as having ST 11, DX 12, IQ 14, and HT 12. Any attempt to cause him, an inhabitant of the realm of Death, serious harm is hopelessly paradoxical.

Albert's training as a wizard, followed by centuries serving Death, give him vast if slightly erratic occult knowledge. For game purposes, the GM can treat him as knowing anything about the supernatural – and especially about Death's work – that suits the plot. In his time on the Disc, he was as powerful a wizard as any at Unseen University. However, much of his reason for wishing to avoid dying quite so desperately is that he knows how many extradimensional entities are waiting to get their claws, paws, tentacles, and pseudopods on him, so he tends to be wary of such topics.

Albert is crabby and self-righteous, quick to pass judgements, and as dedicated to his master's duties as Death himself, with even less capacity for compassion. His cookery shows that he isn't worried by the dangers of cholesterol.

LIFETIMERS AND AUTOBIOGRAPHIES

Death's house holds two resources of special interest. One room contains millions of *lifetimers:* hourglasses, each with a design and decorations as unique as a fingerprint. The trickling sand sounds like an ocean. Empty glasses vanish with a pop, and new ones replace them with a ping. Each of the hourglasses is a life, and when the sand is gone – well, the house owner is a busy man. Death himself has a lifetimer, which is larger than normal and decorated in an ornate skull-and-bones motif, and has no sand; those of other major supernatural entities, tucked away in a semi-secret side room, are another matter. Death can produce anyone's lifetimer from his robe if he wishes to know that much.

Also, Death's library is full of the sound of small scratchings, as of countless quill pens. This is because people's *autobiographies* are being written as they live. Browsing these shelves is discouraged (and rather rude), but not impossible; they're organised alphabetically, and the information they contain isn't likely to end any universes, although it can wreck personal privacy. Death can summon any book to his hand while in the library.

If one looks at one's own autobiography, one finds the last page being filled with a description of oneself reading the book.[2] Recovering some forgotten detail from one's own past would require lengthy leafing back and forth, and probably trawl out some unwanted memories. Perusing someone else's autobiography can be a way of finding out what he has done, or even where he currently is, although if he doesn't know – if, say, he has been blindfolded and kidnapped – the book won't say.

He was trying to perform the Rite of AshkEnte (pp. 214-215) backwards, in order to obtain another 67 years of life; instead, he left a big burnt spot and some charred notebooks.[1] He found himself in Death's Domain, where he has remained for the nearly 2,000 years since. Time does not pass there, but happens over and over again *seriatim*. While some people would find this intolerable, Alberto, a man of ritual and habit, fits right in.

He did previously return to the Disc from time to time, mostly for shopping trips. Time does, however, pass for him during such visits, and an accident on one trip compounded the problem. At the time of his translation, he had 91 days of life

---

1. Performing spells backwards isn't as easy as simply reversing the order of a few words and hand-signs; just try talking like a tape of ordinary speech played backwards. Wizard PCs who attempt such tricks generally shouldn't accomplish anything.

2. Think about this too much and the page will fill up with a description of one's thoughts; the feedback involved could lead to headaches, but probably nothing worse.

The back stacks hold the autobiographies of those dead more than 500 years. Go back far enough and the books become scrolls, then tablets of wax and clay, and then scratchings on stones. The autobiographies of gods and other long-lived beings can fill several volumes, occupying whole shelves and even bookcases.

THE DEATH OF RATS AND QUOTH

For the most part, Death takes responsibility for the end of every life on the Disc. Different beings may have their own ideas of what death is, but they all get the animated skeleton with the scythe.

However, following a metaphysical incident, rats gained their own Death. The Death of Rats is a (mostly) bipedal, rat-sized rat skeleton (with bony whiskers, and a blue glow in its eye-sockets) wearing a hooded robe and bearing a small scythe. He turns up when ships sink unexpectedly, barns burn down, or terriers are set loose. While he mostly deals with rats, he may attend mice, gerbils, and hamsters when the senior partner is busy. He communicates with hollow squeaks. He sometimes rides a talking raven named Quoth – the magically mutated pet of a wizard from Quirm – which provides an interpretation service to humans.

He's just as briskly efficient as Death himself, but a little more pragmatic and straightforward. Not having to associate with human beings much, he hasn't picked up human habits of thought (he finds humans rather exasperating, frankly). On occasion, when Death is distracted or in trouble, he may attempt to help.

If he's obliged to act as a physical being, treat him as having ST 5, DX 14, IQ 12, Move 6, and Dodge 10.

There's also an even smaller Death of Fleas, but that keeps out of sight.

The Other Horsemen

In accordance with multi-universal tradition, Death sometimes rides forth with three other sword-wielding horsemen. Assorted prophecies, many apocryphal (although that may not matter), say that they'll certainly ride out together at some sort of end of the world. Thus, they're known as the Four Horsemen of the Apocralypse.

While Death addresses the others as equals, the fact is that he subtly outranks them, and he can refuse their requests if he chooses. *He* is a universal cosmic absolute. *They* are manifestations of human experiences and will probably only last as long as there are humans – or beings who act like humans – to fear them. Because of that if for nothing else, although the things they represent cause death and suffering for countless billions, the three share Death's cold concern for human existence, and they have been known to fight with him against the Auditors of Reality, who regard them as messy and unnecessary.

It's less widely known that there used to be a fifth Horseman, but he retired to live in the mortal world for reasons of his own, which he does not vouchsafe to humans. He seems to have got bored with all the riding forth.

FAMINE

Famine looks like a starving man, and he rides a horse whose protruding ribs make it resemble a toast rack. He can consume any amount of food in moments. While *hunger* pre-dates humanity, *famine* is a problem of human societies; thus, Famine is essentially a human-derived entity.

PESTILENCE

Pestilence, too, is a product of human society, despite his much more ancient roots in ordinary disease; human carelessness and crowded cities can have appalling consequences. Conversely, Pestilence gets annoyed by advances in medical science. He resembles a dying man clad in bandages, and he rides a horse that gleams like a rotten wound. You really don't want to let him breathe in your face.

Fung Shooey

Fung Shooey (also known as Fong Shoy, possibly from the Agatean for "six inches to the left, please") is a mystical art using the arrangement of buildings, gardens, and furniture to bring good or bad fortune. Unfortunately for its credibility in the Circle Sea region, the first person to seek to bring it to the attention of the wider world was C.M.O.T. Dibbler (pp. 315-316).

Dibbler was all set to start selling consultancy services (along with mirrors and wind chimes) – and had even found a couple of customers – when his bad luck and Discworld metaphysics caught up with him. Among other things, he had advised his customers to keep the lid down in their privies, else the Dragon of Unhappiness would fly up their bottoms. Unfortunately, his second customer, a Mr. Passmore, evidently had the sort of capacity for belief that really isn't safe in the Disc's universe. As a result, the Dragon of Unhappiness came to exist, and it manifested while Mr. Passmore was sitting on the privy.

Mr. Passmore survived, but Fung Shooey suffered a fatal blow to its credibility. Still, there's a chance that this has left Ankh-Morpork sadly ignorant of a genuinely powerful Auriental art. Stories hint, for example, that the greatest Fung Shooey masters can travel through time by rearranging bookshelves to create openings into L-Space (p. 285). Probably due to translation errors, some Ankh-Morporkians also believe that Fung Shooey involves advanced head-kicking techniques.

For a treatment of Fung Shooey in game terms, see *Fung Shooey in Port Duck* (p. 374).

WAR

War appears as a large, jolly, maybe slightly clumsy man, usually clad in red armour. His horse looks like the ultimate warhorse; the severed heads of warriors hang from the saddle. He's the only one of the Horsemen to be married, to a former Valkyrie from some pantheon. They have two sons, Terror and Panic – well-scrubbed youths who are still finding their place in the cosmos – and a daughter, Clancy, who resembles an eight-year-old Pony Club member.

War sometimes seems rather henpecked, spending most of his time at home, observing the conflicts of ants in his garden. His wife doesn't much approve of his old friends. However, he can

still appear every bit as overwhelming as an all-out war when sufficiently provoked.

RONNIE SOAK

Ronnie Soak works as a milkman in Ankh-Morpork. Very few people seem to have noticed that he has been doing this for an indefinite period, or that he's able to deliver fresh milk to all of his customers every morning despite holding a city-wide near-monopoly, or that his cart is drawn by a horse for which any warrior would pay a fortune. People just don't *see* these things.

In fact, Ronnie Soak is really *Kaos*, the Fifth of the Four, that which early peoples feared even more than Death, War, Pestilence, or Famine. But he left before they got famous. While mostly forgotten today, he has recently been shown that, as *Chaos*, he has an important place in the modern world, existing at the heart of every atom.

If and when he resumes his original aspect, he wears a helmet with eyeholes that resemble a butterfly's wings or the eyes of an alien creature. His sword glows with a cold so absolute that it twists right round into heat (making it useful for keeping his storeroom nicely chilled), and he sometimes travels swathed in flames of the same cold. Rather than riding his horse, he uses a chariot, of which his milk cart is a kind of disguised manifestation.

Ronnie has ridden alongside his old friends once in recent years, and then returned to his milk round. It would take a *lot* to make him resume his role as Chaos, but it's possible that his mere presence in the city now serves to deter some entities from threatening it – after all, the Auditors themselves (see below) hate and fear him beyond any other being. They embody the rules; he *destroys* rules. When the Four Horsemen seemed to be losing their battle against an infinite number of Auditors, the arrival of Chaos was enough to reverse everything.

The Auditors

The executive arm of the Old High Ones (p. 291) is represented by a category of much lesser beings, the Auditors of Reality. These appear as small, grey, completely empty cowled robes. Indeed, they give a general impression of *absence*. They do not speak; they do not even plant words in the brains of those to whom they communicate, like Death. Rather, they create the memory of something having been said in a quiet monotone.

The Auditors are responsible for enforcing the basic laws of the universe. If something travelled faster than light, the Auditors would be the ones to give it a speeding ticket. They're absolute order, and their idea of the universe is something that runs smoothly, along predetermined curves, and eventually winds down and stops. They claim proudly to represent oblivion.

Theoretical utterly neutral, they're actually hostile to all randomness and imagination. They find life and individuality immensely annoying, even hateful. They cannot act directly against it, but they've recently started taking measures to render it less annoying, inducing humans to behave disastrously (see *Hogfather* and *Thief of Time*). The limits on their power are fortunate, because their control of matter, energy, and the laws of nature is absolute; they can create a room full of gold or a thunderstorm at will. They can also inveigle their way of thinking into human minds; anyone who ever thinks "That shouldn't be *allowed!*" is open to them. They despise the Death of the Discworld, who is, by his nature, intimately involved with the cycle of life, and who has developed a personality and a degree of cold sympathy for living things. Azrael, however, chooses to accept Death's behaviour.

The Auditors never speak of themselves in the first person. If one of them did, it would indicate individuality, which would cause it to cease to exist. This makes little difference, however – another Auditor would appear immediately as a replacement. Their hatred of life is actually a danger to them, because it makes them think like individuals.

It's also possible to turn the Auditors' bland aversion to *feeling* against them. Exposing them to intense or complex experiences can cause them to dissipate, and replacements are slower to show up in such cases. Something as small but potent as the taste of a high-quality chocolate might be enough. Some humans learned this recently, and the idea has spread – Susan Sto Helit may well have let it slip out deliberately – to the extent that Ponder Stibbons learned of it with a very little research. However, opponents can't rely on any trick just because it has worked against the Auditors in the past; although they're rather stupid, they learn from experience and never forget.

Any PCs who somehow get caught up in the Auditors' plots are in vast danger, though those plots are quite subtle and indirect, generally relating to abstract ideas or cosmic forces. The Auditors are most likely to be opposed by Death or Chaos, although The Lady or even Fate (see *Fate and The Lady*, p. 303) might be amused to frustrate them. At these levels, however, all sides are bound by rules that any human will find hard to understand.

Gods, Religion, and Related Issues

Research theologians say that the Discworld has at least 3,000 gods, with more being discovered every week. They are wrong – by several orders of magnitude.

The Power of Belief

The Disc has *billions* of gods. They fill every corner of space. If a tree falls in the forest, hundreds of gods hear it. But most of these deities are tiny and powerless, intangible, with no consciousness beyond a surging ego and an instinctive hunger for that upon which they feed: belief.

It is only when a god receives the prayers of worshippers that it can begin to grow. Every ounce of faith provides the god with power. The more belief it receives, the more it grows – and as it grows, it can perform more miracles. These tend to take the form that the god's worshippers associate with divinity: lightning bolts smiting the ungodly, food for the hungry, and so on. Obviously, such behaviour makes the being more credible as a god, and so a growing religion enjoys positive feedback; as it gains more worshippers, its god can do more, and the more a god can do, the more worshippers it gains.

However, there is a limit. Human beings can only believe so much. There's a fixed amount of faith to go round. (People do tend to believe more in times of stress or danger, but gods can only promote such experiences so far before their worshippers start looking for a less-demanding deity who will make their lives more comfortable.) Thus, all gods are to some extent in competition.

And if a religion can grow, it can also decline.

Behaviour and Appearance

Gods are also *shaped* by the belief that empowers them. Their growing intellects and powers match what humans expect, which is partly the lightning bolts and partly the sort of behaviour that humans would indulge in given power without responsibility. This helps explain the unattractive divine habits seen in many legends: it's what people would do if they could get away with it. That isn't to say that gods are especially moral if left to their own devices, mind you.

One power that most humans give their gods is the ability to appear in any form they like. On the other hand, most deities are assigned a standard appearance that's expected of them in routine manifestations. Furthermore, gods – even, it seems, higher powers – can never change the appearance of their eyes, which are the windows of the soul.

All this also makes gods painfully vulnerable to artistic errors and confusion on the part of their congregations. For example, Patina, the Ephebian goddess of wisdom, was once thought to have a symbolic owl as her companion and messenger. However, a bungling sculptor who couldn't do birds right was commissioned to create an important image for her temple, the image he created became the accepted standard, and Patina is now accompanied and symbolised by an unhappy-looking penguin.

The Small Gods

Returning to the bottom of the heap: The tiny, powerless gods of game-trails and rocky ledges are known as *small gods*. They can just about generate enough psychic energy to move a small stone or project a passing thought, and the vast proportion of them never gain any more. They need to find followers. There's evidence that nonsapient animals can generate a little belief, but not enough to support more than a very few gods; it's thinking beings who must be convinced. Thus, the instinct of a small god is to cluster round human habitations.

However, because they're in competition, and given that they have the power to push each other around, only stronger deities can hold on to positions near large communities. The wildernesses of the Disc are haunted by the weak and the desperate – spirits who try to tempt travellers, wanderers, and shepherds into believing in them. Sensitive souls with a predisposition to faith are the best catches, but of course such people tend to carry existing beliefs with them, which makes it harder for a small god to get through.

Once in a while, though, a small god helps a goatherd find a lost animal or guides a traveller back to the road. If it's lucky, the human may then build a heap of stones as a tribute to the helpful spirit, and perhaps tell his friends about the experience. At that point, faith *might* begin to spread . . . and then a new religion is on the rise.

All of this is kept secret, although a few Ephebian philosophers and cynical theologians have guessed the truth. Gods don't approve of information that might undermine belief, and Discworld gods have the power to do something about "blasphemy." However, Discworlders are dimly aware that an unknown number of small, weak deities are "out there" somewhere and are prepared to be polite to them. A few large cities (including Ankh-Morpork) have temples to the small gods, giving the whole mass of them a few prayers, which help keep them going.

Forgotten Gods

Gods who've lost all of their worshippers have, for the most part, also lost their chances. They're driven out into wildernesses, haunt ruined temples to themselves, and usually go insane. Unlike unworshipped small gods, who still have hope, they're decrepit and set in ways that will never come again. They fade, but perhaps they never entirely die; all they have left is dreams of glory. Given a human to tempt, small gods in the wilderness manifest as whirling djinn or whispering spirits, but a forgotten god displays a more desperate and hopeless personality.

A really cold-blooded religious philosopher, or an insane scholar, might set out to resurrect the worship of a forgotten god. This could just mean attaching an ancient name to a new god (or to a current god who doesn't mind operating under false colours), but it might actually involve resurrecting the god itself. Given that some religions are abandoned for good reasons, and that any such resurrected god would likely have gone utterly mad, the resulting religion would probably develop a strange and sinister flavour. Preventing the ensuing carnage could be a worthwhile project for a PC group.

Pantheons

Despite their inherent competitiveness, gods *can* work together. The obvious way to build up a pool of worshippers is to specialise in a specific area: the weather, metalwork, farming, whatever. Hence, all human life can be divided up among a group of gods, who acknowledge each other's rights and even become almost-friends. These pantheons may be associated with specific areas, nations, or tribes; thus, there are gods of Ephebe, gods of Djelibeybi, and so on.

Pantheons tend to be led by gods of some major force, such as war or the weather, but such a leader is rarely more than first among equals. After all, in times of peace or once the harvest is in, prayers in that temple drop away, while the god of cooking is still getting a steady turnover of moderate faith, because people always have to eat. The result tends to be a sort of soap-operatic family relationship within the pantheon.

Not all regions have a single standard pantheon, though. Especially in the modern age of reasonably extensive travel, believers and religions move around and mix and match. Broad-minded, cosmopolitan lands such as Ankh-Morpork and Tsort are full of temples to contradictory gods; there, belief is a matter of personal choice.

In fact, most major Disc gods know each other, and a kind of aggregated pantheon has developed, with some deities who share interests sticking to specific nations of worshippers, and others subdividing their fields of interest. This mixed group share living space in Dunmanifestin, the "home of the gods" atop Cori Celesti (p. 301).

SOME WIDESPREAD GODS

These near-fixtures on the divine scene include some recurring names:

Blind Io is Chief of the Gods and a thunder-god. In fact, he's the Disc's single major thunder-god, having mastered the art of obtaining additional worship under false names. He has a collection of disguises, 70 different hammers, and a talent for voices. His chief feature (in his primary aspect) is that he has no eyes on his face – just blank skin. Nonetheless, he has eyes; rather a lot of them, in fact. They fly around independently, enabling Io to observe many parts of the Disc simultaneously (a useful talent in a chief). Blind Io isn't as powerful as he likes to think – praying to the thunder seems a rather crude and primitive idea to sophisticated Discworlders, and he's often taken for granted – but neither is he weak.

Offler the Crocodile God ("Six-Armed Offler of the Bird-Haunted Mouth") started out in Klatch and succeeded in spreading from there. He's the patron of the city of Al Khali; his statue stands in the Square of 967 Delights.[1] He has an obvious role in any hot land with big rivers, especially when people have to pray that a log is just a log, but he has somehow acquired worshippers as far afield as Ankh-Morpork and even the Ramtops. This is partly through his taking responsibility for all sorts of reptiles and other scaly things which most gods ignore, and partly through the creation of a visually impressive but largely undemanding cult. Offler's crocodilian mouth-structure causes him to speak with a strong lisp.

The Sea Queen, the all-encompassing deity of the Disc's seas and oceans, is somewhat believed in and greatly feared by pretty well every sailor. She's as powerful as the sea, uninterested in human concerns and believes in taking her own sacrifices without waiting for them to be offered – frequently in large quantities. She isn't especially bright, and has a short attention span, but this causes her little trouble. Sailors try to appease her through assorted superstitions without doing too much to attract her attention. She seems to have a soft spot for dolphins, or at least to make a point of punishing those who harm them.

---

1. *Klatchians are very precise about the things that interest them.*

National Gods and One Gods

Some gods establish themselves as what folklorists would call the *tutelary figures* of tribes or nations. As a rule, straightforward national gods don't bother to deny that other gods *exist* – they just present themselves as all that their people require, governing every aspect of life within a specific bit of geography. They might permit token worship of a few other deities, and they may themselves receive a little worship from people elsewhere (if only expatriates), but mostly they're location-specific. Hence, such national gods tend to be tolerated by other deities, and they may even be fitted into pantheons somehow, but there's a fair amount of scope for worshipper-poaching, rivalry, and jurisdictional disputes.

Some national gods are low-powered, practical sorts with small-but-serviceable followings. For example, there was the tribe of 51 people (at the last count) on the coast of Klatch who worshipped only a giant newt named P'tang-P'tang. This wasn't considered particularly selfish of P'tang-P'tang, and other deities didn't try poaching on his territory; even by the standards of Disc theology, 51 people aren't enough to start wars over. Others are more ambitious and more annoying to other deities.

But even the cockiest national gods don't necessarily set themselves up as *One Gods*. One Gods are the high-risk, high-return strategists of the game of divinity. They take responsibility for every aspect of human life, and they *do* tell their worshippers that no other gods exist. Generally, they say that anything else that looks like a god is really an evil demon.

The benefits of this are obvious: a One God receives an awful lot of prayers and belief. The first drawback is equally clear: One Gods automatically annoy other deities, who see them as hopelessly selfish and greedy, and who may try to undermine their monolithic systems. Of course, the One God probably has the raw power to oppose this, and simple religions find it easier to inculcate fanaticism in their human worshippers – but such belief can be brittle. Once a few worshippers accept that other deities exist, the whole edifice may collapse in short order.

STRATEGIC PROBLEMS

The second danger is more subtle, but far deadlier in the long run and can also afflict national gods. Having taken responsibility for everything, a god may start to be taken for granted. On one hand, it has to take the blame for bad events as well as credit for good (because even if it blames evil on "demons," it could surely stop them if it wanted); on the other, having built up a monolithic idea of reality, the god can be seen as barely logically necessary. The problem is exacerbated if the god – having built a nice, tight system – becomes lazy and complacent. It may take centuries, but the god's religion can become formalised and hollow, with belief concentrating on the system and not on the god. When it then falls, the god has no supporting faith to fight the collapse.

The primary example of a "One God" system in recent Disc history is Omnia (pp. 235-236), which spent centuries elaborating national worship of the Great God Om. Om almost suffered a classic disaster of hollow faith, having built a religion on telling people what to believe rather than convincing them. However, through good fortune more than anything else, Om survived. The prophet Brutha forged a new covenant that guarantees Om continuing worship in exchange for him behaving in an unusually reasonable way for a god. In fact, Omnianism is now one of the Disc's leading religions; missionaries have fanned out from Omnia to every other known land, offering a comforting general-purpose faith that doesn't make too many promises. They can be a little boring and earnest, but at least they're polite, and they've got some good hymns.

At least one national god has been less lucky than Om, however.

Death and the Gods

Death (pp. 291-295) has formal, straightforward dealings with the gods. They sometimes remind him to deal with an annoying or fated individual; he doesn't need such reminders, but he's too polite to say so. Alternatively, they may discuss some complex destiny with him; that, he classes as legitimate professional business. In return, he occasionally requests their aid in straightening out supernatural confusions or modifying certain aspects of human existence; they're better than he is at things like compassion and vengeance, being more human.

For their part, gods (and demons) see Death as a necessary part of the universe they think they run, although they find him annoyingly inflexible. Death, who knows that gods themselves can die, whatever they may think, is unworried. The gods he gets on with best are the most businesslike.

Any god who claims to be "God of Death" is either a mere curator of a collection of souls, or really a god of sadism or carnage. Death regards such beings with detached disdain.

The Story of Nuggan

The classic demonstration of how to play the divine game *wrong* is the story of the Almighty Nuggan, god of Borogravia. This would be told as a cautionary tale to young demigods arriving on Cori Celesti, if older gods didn't think it was far more fun to watch such entities learn everything the hard way.

Nuggan was originally quite successful, inspiring devout worship from Borogravians and earning a place in Dunmanifestin. He manifested as a small, self-important male figure with an annoying moustache. It was somehow typical of him that he also acted as the god of paperclips, correct things in the right place in small desk stationery sets, and unnecessary paperwork.

However, he got carried away with his laws and commandments, known as the Abominations of Nuggan, on the principle of "spare the thunderbolts and spoil the worshipper." From early on, he prohibited chocolate, ginger, mushrooms, and garlic, ensuring that worshippers who lapsed from his laws would be violently averse to going back. He got into the habit of adding more Abominations at periodic intervals, so that his holy book had to be held in a loose-leaf binder. Nugganites were quite proud of this, referring to it as a "living testament."

Perhaps the first stage of Nuggan's fall came when Cohen and the Silver Horde (p. 346) arrived in Cori Celesti on their quest to return fire to the gods, bringing with them a minstrel to document their efforts. The minstrel was a lapsed Nugganite, who grew violently angry with his former deity, berating him and determining in the process that it was impossible for a god to smite anyone within the confines of Dunmanifestin, thereby embarrassing Nuggan severely. The story of that incident may have leaked out somehow – perhaps thanks to the minstrel himself or some malicious rival god – weakening Nuggan's credibility.

Anyway, the real problem came over the next few years, when Borogravia found itself perpetually at war with its neighbours – and losing. Meanwhile, the additions to the Abominations were becoming increasingly bizarre and blatantly ridiculous; by the end, Nuggan was prohibiting rocks, ears, and accordion players. He was sinking into some kind of divine senility, while the people of Borogravia found it impossible to believe in him when he delivered so little. And yet his only response was more Abominations.

Thus, both Nuggan and Borogravia fell into spirals of decline. Eventually, by the time the war staggered to a truce, a team of research theologians from Ankh-Morpork declared that the god was dead, and other cults moved into the country to pick up the pieces.

The Afterlife

Death merely marks the end of a being's life and sometimes transports souls away a little distance. It's sometimes said that souls go to the House of Death, but that isn't how it seems to the occupants; perhaps a few pass through on their way to their own particular afterlives.

The truth about the Discworld afterlife is that, perversely, people get what they really expect. Hubland warriors are picked up by well-built blonde women on horseback and taken to a life of eternal feasting; those who've pursued a life of what they know is considered evil go to Hell (p. 304); some souls are reincarnated, in forms that range from reward to punishment; and some are fated to hang around the world as ghosts, temporarily or for long periods, until something is resolved or just because that's fate.

One near-constant, however, appears to be a desert that souls cross after death. It's black sand under a starry night sky which, at the same time, is brightly lit. What happens to the soul on this trek appears to reflect the way that person acted while alive. Those who know the old folk classic "The Lyke-Wake Dirge" will get the picture.

Death himself knows the nature of afterlife arrangements, but he won't let on too much to living mortals. All else aside, sensible mortals who knew the truth would lynch hellfire-preaching missionaries on sight.

Nature Gods

There are also a number of divinities with vague, broad areas of responsibility in the natural world, who are worshipped in rural areas across much of the Disc, and who receive at least a little belief from nonsapient animals. These include:

- An unnamed *Moon Goddess*.
- *Hoki the Jokester,* who manifests as an oak tree, or as half-man and half-goat. Hoki was once referred to by Granny Weatherwax, who has deep experience of rural metaphysics, as a "bloody nuisance." Many gods would agree; Hoki occasionally shows up on Cori Celesti, before getting banned again for some gag or another.
- *Herne the Hunted,* the god of small furry animals whose destiny is to end their lives with a crunchy squeak.[1] Herne is three feet high, with floppy rabbit ears, very small horns, and a good turn of speed.

DRUIDISM

The priests of nature are *druids,* who are much concerned with the careful study of natural forces, the construction of ever-larger stone circles, and lots and lots of sacrifices. Druidism is popular in Llamedos (p. 234) and on the Vortex Plains (p. 242). The hardcore form is known as "Strict Druidism." Druids are fond of music, poetry, and exotic herbal poisons; outsiders who have experienced all three tend to prefer the poisons.

Druids aren't as close to their gods as most Disc priests, or as interested in their personal lives. They're deeper into the supernatural-in-general view of religion, and they spend much of their time studying astrological forces, engaging in odd cultural traditions (including dour arts and violent ball games), working a fair amount of magic, or just bossing people around.[2] This suits their gods well enough, as nature deities rarely want to be pestered; they get enough belief from superstitious rustics to keep them going without bothering with *worship,* which always seems to have an undertone of wanting something in exchange.

Druids have made themselves expert in the design and construction of silicon chunk technology – even if their stone-circle computers *do* always need to be upgraded within a year or two, and the whole technology is considered way out of date by wizards who work with modern designs such as Hex (p. 286). They have mastered some relevant magical techniques, such as flying full-size monoliths long distances overnight when an upgrade is needed.

Most druids wear long white robes and copper torques and bracelets, and they carry sickle-swords which they seem all too happy to use.

Life on Cori Celesti

Cori Celesti, the 10-mile-high peak at the Disc's very centre, shows divine psychology at its most typical: The gods *have* to be at the middle of everything, above everybody, and inaccessible in the most literal-minded way.

Being sited at the dead centre of the Disc, with the world revolving around it, Cori Celesti is the focus of a sort of silent, invisible, permanent supernatural tornado. The level of ambient magic there is incredible. One mark of the difference between divine power and mortal witch-and-wizard magic is that nobody could get away with working the latter in a place like this; for instance, someone trying to fly to the home of the gods on a broomstick would find their transport blasted to shreds miles short of the destination.

---

1. *There are a lot of them, and they all have something to pray for, although Herne is rarely able to help them.*

2. *Okay, that's typical of many priests – but Strict Druidism has enough power to make it stick.*

The gods, on the other hand, being creatures of primal supernatural power, find the place rather comfortable.

It has been calculated that serious disruption to the physical structure of Cori Celesti would cause a magical backlash which would obliterate all life on the Disc. Fortunately, that's been threatened only once.

ASCENDING THE MOUNTAIN

It was previously assumed by virtually everybody that Cori Celesti was exactly as sheer a mountain as it looked. In other words, it was thought, extraordinarily determined adventurers *might* climb Cori Celesti to reach the gods' abode, but this could be likened to climbing Everest, twice, in an ice storm. Given the unlikelihood of the gods being very gracious hosts, nobody was inclined to try.

However, when the Silver Horde (p. 346) got annoyed enough with life to want to have a word with the gods, and the gods got stupidly amused enough to encourage them to try, the former were allowed to discover a map that revealed a stranger truth. It turned out that the base of Cori Celesti could only be reached through a series of caverns guarded by an excessive collection of monsters, traps, insane warrior-monks, and suchlike traditional impediments. Once they defeated these obstructions, though, the Horde found that the mountain itself was smoothly vertical – and that gravity bent round to be exactly perpendicular to the surface. Hence, reaching the gods from that point was a simple 10-mile trek.

Given that this incident almost led to the Disc's destruction, it's safe to assume that all the traps and obstructions have since been reset, with plenty of undocumented additions. A band of PCs might feel cocky enough to try to recreate the last accomplishment of the Silver Horde, the greatest barbarian heroes in Disc history, but that isn't recommended. After all, even if they succeed, they'll have gone through all that to reach the metaphysical equivalent of a garish housing estate full of extremely boring bourgeois people with short tempers.

DUNMANIFESTIN

The fact is, Dunmanifestin – home of the gods atop Cori Celesti – looks like a stage set for one of Shakespeare's Roman plays, or a Ray Harryhausen movie, designed by someone with a huge budget and not much imagination: lots of white marble columns and endless shiny inlaid floors. The main problem is that since gods can do almost anything they feel like, they have no particular need for imagination, and there isn't much that they've been forced to put off until retirement.

Not all gods live on Cori Celesti, or even visit. Theoretically, anyone with any worshippers (see *Recognised Divinity*, p. 94) is allowed in, but minor deities tend to be treated with ill-concealed snobbery, and One Gods may be openly criticised. At any time, a number of deities will be engaged in feuds and sulks, and they will refuse to go anywhere that they might meet certain others. A few may even have too much taste, but that's rare.

Divine powers cannot be used within Dunmanifestin's walls, either by convention or a quirk of divine nature, although gods there can observe any part of the Disc with ease and project whatever divine effects they like to any point beyond the mountain. In other words, the gods of Dunmanifestin can watch their worshippers and drop thunderbolts on them, but any interactions between deities must be non-supernatural while they're there – and mortal visitors are actually relatively safe within the walls, as the gods aren't generally especially capable brawlers. A mortal attacking a god with physical weapons in Dunmanifestin might even do him some kind of serious, if temporary, damage. That would be risky in the longer term, though; provoked that far, other gods will likely discover an unusual capacity for divine solidarity. Mortal *magic* is explosively unusable there.

Inter-Faith Relations

Relationships between groups of priests mostly reflect those between their patron deities. The gods expect their representatives to share their personal prejudices, and they make a point of keeping their high priests informed of who is friendly and who is the subject of a feud this week (this is the main reason why they grant the Divine News-Feed perk, p. 51). However, such rivalry is mostly limited to name-calling and perhaps a little mud-throwing. For one thing, priests aren't necessarily immune to secular laws against assault or murder; for another, pacts between the gods include rules against serious damage to each other's power structures. A lot of the time, priests recognise that they have more in common than they have differences.

As the overall leader on Cori Celesti, Blind Io gives his priesthood a great deal of clout. In Ankh-Morpork and other cities, the local High Priest of Blind Io is also the chief spokesman for the religious community when they need one. He may take responsibility for state ceremonies, too.

None of which makes outright religious wars impossible, but they represent an extreme situation for the gods involved and a waste of worshippers all round. If the gods are paying attention, they may actually act as a restraining influence for once. Unless, of course, they have side-bets running on the result; then they're likely to get very excited.

One Gods (p. 299) are traditionally prone to provoking *lots* of religious wars, trying to suppress the believers of rival deities, who naturally get annoyed and retaliate. Om (p. 301) used to be as bad as any; nowadays, his believers are instructed to limit their attacks to strongly worded pamphlets and preaching, and rarely provoke physical violence. They still aren't very popular with other priests, though.

Priests and the Priesthood

To sustain themselves, Discworld gods must acquire and maintain congregations. Priests are their agents in this. They manage and supervise the routine business of religion in exchange for personal satisfaction, access to the system's material benefits (which are of interest to the gods themselves only insofar as they can be used to promote belief), and perhaps the occasional bolt of lightning dropped on people who cause them trouble.

Thus, the vast majority of Disc priests are rather unremarkable – middle management in large organisations that impose a strong corporate image on their employees. Of course, some religions do attract particular personality types. Usually this means the bloodthirsty, but some are authentically well-meaning or even saintly.

It's important to realise that priests do *not* generally know much about the underlying nature of divine power. They of all people must believe in the absolute importance of their gods, and they pay minimal attention to blasphemy or philosophy except to condemn them. Indeed, some better-intentioned priests have ideals and ideas that go far beyond anything the gods are intellectually capable of. Some of the Disc's greatest social figures have worked devoutly in the name of divine airheads

who couldn't find their own backsides with an atlas. For a template, see *Priest* (pp. 126-127).

RELIGIOUS RANK

Many larger religions are well enough organised that they grant the Religious Rank advantage (see *Rank*, p. 35). Ranks in different temples have all sorts of exotic titles, complicated by terms which refer to functions or duties rather than standing. As a broad rule, assume that "novices" are always Rank 0, someone addressed as "brother" or "sister" is probably Rank 0-1, a "father" is typically Rank 1-3, an abbot or an abbess may be Rank 3-4, and a bishop or a high priest is likely to be Rank 4-6.

In the Church of Om, the hierarchy runs from Rank 0 (Novice), through Rank 1 (Priest), 2 (Sub-Deacon), 3 (Deacon), 4 (Bishop), 5 (Lesser Iam), and 6 (Archpriest), to Rank 7 (the Cenobiarch). It's one of the few faiths on the Disc with that much hierarchy. At the height of Omnian imperial power, the Cenobiarch was Rank 8.

Other Legends

The sheer power of human belief has brought a number of other figures into some kind of more-or-less physical existence on the Disc. These mostly don't *appear* to be typical Discworld "gods," although it's hard to say for sure. They aren't generally worshipped in the traditional sense, either, and at least one of them actually consists of a franchise operated by human agents. However, it's possible that they started out as small gods, a very long time ago, before settling deeper into the human psyche than most here-today, gone-next-century deities.

Many of them are shadowy figures, mentioned mostly in folksongs or nursery rhymes and content to slip around the periphery of human vision. They include the Soul Cake Tuesday Duck (basically the Disc equivalent of the Easter Bunny), Jack Frost, Old Man Trouble, and the Sandman (who doesn't bother taking his sand out of the bag before using it to send children to sleep – this *is* the Discworld, after all). A few, though, deserve longer notes.

THE HOGFATHER

The Hogfather is a very ancient god indeed, and one who has done a magnificent job of moving with the times and adapting to human cultural evolution. The legend of the Hogswatch holiday is that a kindly, fat gentleman with a long beard and big boots arrives overnight to the sound of hog bells, bringing toys for all good children, who leave a glass of wine and a pork pie for him. An oak tree is erected in a pot and decorated with paper sausages. On Hogswatch day, the family wears paper hats and eats a pork dinner.

This is the modern, safe version of the story. In older times – and not so much older, in places where pig-killing is something that happens close by and in common view – the Hogfather lives all year in a secret palace of pig bones, to emerge on Hogswatchnight in a sledge drawn by four tusked wild boars (Gouger, Rooter, Tusker, and Snouter). He delivers packets of sausage, black pudding, hams, and scratchings (fried pork rinds) to good children, while bad children get a sack of bloody bones (the kind of detail that proves that this is a children's story).

Deeper than this . . . The Disc has had plenty of winter myths and renewal ceremonies, some of them very bloody indeed. In ancient rural communities, unlucky individuals could find themselves first fêted and then hunted by dogs to make the sun rise, for example. They weren't expected to get away; the sun wouldn't have risen if they did.

Hermits

Hermits are a curious phenomenon that requires a little explanation. Many Disc religions revere these people as wise thinkers who retreat from worldly temptation and get on with serious worship in secluded locations such as the deserts of Klatch. The fact that this also gets a lot of rather dotty and dangerously original religious thinkers out from under the feet of the temple hierarchy – and away from people who might ask them too many questions – may or may not occur to the priesthood.

However, the really dangerous truth is that hermits have a perilously close relationship with too many of the *wrong* gods. The wildernesses into which they withdraw are full of small gods and the odd forgotten god, who latch onto strong religious imaginations like leeches, exploiting hermits and their like as a source of the faith they need to survive, and trying to persuade the human to carry their religion away and spread it in the world at large. The hermits perceive the bribes offered by small or forgotten gods as "temptations," and the would-be deities as "demons" or "spirits," but that in itself is a form of belief, which helps keep their tempters going. For that matter, some hermits find far more to enjoy in these tempting visions than a conventional priest could approve.

Sometimes, a hermit may emerge from the wilderness with radical new ideas or beliefs that give a small god a foothold in the wider community of worshippers. Mostly, though, this is a low-level symbiosis: the hermit gives the small gods a little bit of belief, and the small gods give the hermit something to refuse and deny. Accusing a hermit of being mad because he hears voices and propounds strange religious ideas is missing the point – it's a very *functional* sort of madness.

D'regs (p. 236) and other desert-dwellers usually view madness as a bizarre gift of the gods – partly because of their experience of hermits – and hence tend to treat hermits with a mixture of awe, respect, and fear, quietly avoiding them more often than not. It isn't as if they have anything to steal, and you never know what might be watching.

But Hogswatchnight is safely commercialised and secular these days, in most places. Large shops in Ankh-Morpork are staffed by fat actors (assisted by "pixies") receiving queues of variously bored and overexcited children, and fathers desperately try not to wake sleeping offspring as they deliver presents to waiting stockings (or pillowcases, for wealthier or greedier children). Still, the sheer level of belief involved makes the Hogfather one of the most powerful gods on the Disc, in his way.

He's the god of the shortest night of the year, of the renewal of the sun in the depths of winter. He appears to pre-date humanity, and maybe the Disc. This could mean that he was a god who was recognised by the earliest and simplest life forms in the universe, or it might be that the sheer power of belief has pushed his existence back to the dawn of time. Gods don't worry about temporal paradoxes.

The Hogfather doesn't associate with the gods of Cori Celesti (pp. 300-301); they would be too crass and too high-flown for him. He dwells in his Castle of Bones, or in the human collective imagination. Mostly, he doesn't need to manifest – his representatives in the big shops, and those tiptoeing fathers, handle the miracle-working.

THE TOOTH FAIRY FRANCHISE

Another deep-rooted figure, the Tooth Fairy is an anthropomorphic personification of something complicated involving juvenile dentistry and basic economics. She turns up when small children leave milk teeth under their pillows, replacing them with a silver coin. The amount of childish imagination involved makes her as real as the Hogfather, but the arrangement is different.

Tooth Fairy work has long been a franchise operation which provides jobs for young women. The money is poor – waitressing pays better – but the job does have some small advantages. It actually goes back a very long way, to when an ancient being who wanted to protect children realised that those teeth represented a danger, as sympathetic magic could be worked through them. It therefore started collecting and investing money, to provide a steady income, and employed humans to do the work. Today, the money has grown into an empire of investments.

The young women involved gain the Unnoticed advantage (p. 48) and the ability to extract extra teeth without disturbing the child if they have problems making change (there's a fixed rate per tooth). They carry ladders to give them access to children's rooms, and also dental pliers. The teeth are eventually deposited in the Tooth Fairy's Tower, which lies in a realm outside reality created by childish imaginings. See *Hogfather* for details and for the organisation's current standing.

A PC might be a working or former Tooth Fairy. Aside from the effective invisibility, she could acquire Contacts on the fringes of the Disc's supernatural world, Area Knowledge of her "beat," some sort of Hidden Lore, and useful habits of Stealth. Tooth Fairies tend to be financially Struggling, and the job itself is a Duty.

Fate and The Lady

Two extremely powerful beings spend much of their time on Cori Celesti, but they may be older and more terrible than anyone else there. They might represent higher-level powers, rather than having evolved from small gods. Both are deadly players in the games of the gods, though, and seem to find it amusing to show the others how things should be done.

Fate looks like a friendly middle-aged man with neat greying hair and a kindly face, until one looks closely at his eyes. They aren't, as they first appear, dark, but rather are black, bottomless pits of night. He has a few worshippers, who know that their prayers are pointless, as Fate is inexorable and uncaring toward mortals. He isn't very emotional, but he hates having his plans or strategies disrupted. It's sometimes said that he originated in another universe, which he departed after it suffered some terrible and obscure disaster.

The Lady is Fate's chief opponent when playing games with mortals. She appears beautiful, with iridescent emerald-green eyes. She never answers prayers, but sometimes she aids those who least expect it – and sometimes she doesn't. A group of gamblers once tried creating a temple to her, and they all died shortly afterward; she likes gambling, but no lady likes to be taken for granted. She is, of course, Luck, though one thing that all properly educated Discworlders know is that they *must not* mention her by name. She says that she plays games not to lose, rather than to win, and that she never sacrifices pawns . . . but of course it's never safe to depend on anything about her.

BOGEYMEN

Bogeymen – the manifestation of childhood fears about what's under the bed – appear to be spirits pushed into physical shape by belief, much like gods and demons. However, they have a peculiar but relatively stable form; hence, they're described with Discworld fauna in Chapter 10 (pp. 361-362).

Demons

Discworld demons have nothing in common with the Things from the Dungeon Dimensions (pp. 269-270). Demons represent an entirely human concept of Evil[1], and they often find ways to come and go from the Disc's reality. They *need* humans, because the whole point of their existence is bound up with humanity.

In fact, demons have much in common with gods, and they may well originate as latent psychic entities in exactly the same way. It has been observed that the real difference between a demon and a god is the same as the difference between a terrorist and a freedom-fighter.

1. *Often capitalised.*

Demons as Gods

If one thing demonstrates the close relationship between Discworld demons and gods, it's the fact that some demons *are* gods – or rather, some gods are really demons. This usually happens when a wandering demon in astral form encounters a human community that has somehow failed to find a god to suit it. The demon presents itself as a god and proceeds to instruct its new worshippers in whatever it thinks is a worthwhile campaign of evil. For example, the very minor demon Quezovercoatl made itself into the god of the Tezuman Empire (see *The Jungle Empires*, p. 237), the Feathered Boa, God of Human Sacrifices. The resulting wars and general carnage were unpleasantly impressive. However, as Astfgl (see below) angrily pointed out, most of the dead were lost to Hell; a *really* devious demon would have encouraged a less-bloody empire with a bureaucracy and a taxation system that would have driven millions to damnation through sheer, frustrated hatred.

This kind of thing may be one reason why gods dislike demons: they resent poachers. However, it does provide Discworld campaigns with their share of berserk demon-worshipping cults to suppress, as required.

Quezovercoatl, incidentally, appeared as half-man, half-chicken, half-jaguar, half-serpent, half-scorpion, and half-mad – a typical case of demonic excess, except in his height, which was approximately six inches.

If demons are a kind of mutant small god, however, they've discovered a safe (if cramped) niche in the human imagination: the role of eternal jailer, tormentor, and tempter.

People will believe many different things about their gods, but one detail they're always convinced of is the certain expectation of infinite supernatural punishment for their enemies, their neighbours, and (for the really insecure or honest) themselves. Demons provide that service. The snag is that they're amazingly unimaginative about it. Perhaps the best evidence that demons are products of human fantasy is the fact that they *depend* on human beings to provide them with both the evil they're supposed to thrive upon and the punishments they're supposed to inflict. Which is why demons are so keen to tempt human beings – they need the creative imagination that a human who has been promised a few routine rewards can provide.

Demons do *not* get on with the gods, who treat them with a snobbery that's probably fuelled by moral insecurity, but there isn't usually any physical conflict.

Physically, demons can take many forms. The senior ranks and old-fashioned types favour the red cape, horns, and trident look, while many junior entities go for chaotic mixtures of eyes, claws, jaws, legs, and tentacles. Any teeth, claws, spines, or horns are, incidentally, fully functional. While demons aren't as malevolent as humans assume, they aren't at all nice, either, regarding suffering and chaos as their *thing*, and it's unwise to annoy one unless it's safely contained inside an octagram.

Hell

Demons live in Gehenna, Tartarus, the Place of Eternal Punishment, etc. – you know, *Hell*. This is a pocket dimension of sorts, albeit linked to the Disc by physical pathways (the paving on the main one being carefully inscribed with statements of good intentions). Actually, there's scope for a wide variety of different and particular Hells; indeed, the nature of the multiverse is that, in a sense, there are an infinite number. But the Discworld's Hell is an uncreative place; it makes Death's house look aesthetically sophisticated. As most people have formulated their ideas of Hell from a standard model, that's pretty much what it's like. Only duller.

Although the souls who go here are the ones who, at heart, feel that they deserve it, they soon realise that their punishment is limited by the fact that they no longer actually have physical bodies to suffer. Thus, the place is full of rocks being rolled up hills, boiling lakes of blood, and howling storms, all inflicted on souls who spend a lot of time chatting to the demons, with the occasional howl of torment to keep everyone satisfied that the place is being run properly. It's a bit like prisoners and warders in some eternal jail from which no one will ever be freed or fired; they're all in this together, so they eventually learn to get along.

Astfgl and Vassenego

The current Life President of Hell is the demon Astfgl, who, like all demons, has the creativity of a vending machine: you put your dollar in and you get your eternal punishment out. He dresses in a red silk gown, carries a trident with one wobbly point, and has pointed horns, a tail, and a beard. In fact, he looks like Ming the Merciless played by a skinny kid who has seen too many Vincent Price movies. Demons have no fixed shape, however, and when Astfgl is annoyed, his talons rip through the silk and he develops big black bat wings and very serious ram's horns – like a slightly older kid who has read too many underground comics. It has been suggested that this is indeed where Astfgl got his two favourite shapes, though never in his presence.

Actually, the "Life Presidency" is a strictly honorary position, designed to get Astfgl out of the way. (He tried too hard to be up-to-date, which was more than the other Dukes of Hell could tolerate.) He may not have realised this yet.

The *real* current power in Hell is Duke Vassenego, an ancient, suave demon with the soul of an old provincial lawyer. (In fact, he has the souls of *several thousand* lawyers, but one is the soul he was created with.) He's almost human in his deviousness, and aristocratic in his manner. However, Hell is naturally riddled with politics and backstabbing, and supreme power changes hands periodically. Then again, among immortal demons, "periodically" can mean "once every five or ten thousand years."

"SUICIDALLY GLOOMY WHEN SOBER, HOMICIDALLY INSANE WHEN DRUNK"

The Patrician was gazing out of the window of the Oblong Office when the knock came at the door. He recognised that knock and responded with a simple "Come in." He knew that Commander Vimes wouldn't enter without that instruction. Vimes didn't want anyone to think that he was the sort of person who felt entitled to just walk in on the ruler of the city.

Lord Vetinari turned as Vimes obeyed and took his seat. Vimes noticed who else was present. "You!" Vimes barked.

"Your Grace," Lady Margolotta von Uberwald acknowledged, putting aside her knitting. "It is pleasant to see you again. I hope that your vife is vell?"

Vimes merely grunted in reply to that, but stood staring at Vetinari. The Patrician gazed back calmly. "Please do take a seat, Commander," he said. "You're not here as Commander of the Watch, on this occasion, but as Duke of Ankh. It would be inappropriate for you to stand."

Vimes obeyed, but with every sign of disliking the suggestion. "So it's politics, is it?" he said.

"I'm afraid so," the Patrician replied. "A trivial matter, really, but unfortunately the legal niceties require the involvement of three different nobles of high rank, with no connection of alle-giance or blood to each other."

"Huh," Vimes grunted. "So let's get on with it."

"Ah, no," the Patrician replied. "You forget that I am not of noble rank. I am, after all, simply a servant of the city. We are awaiting one more person."

"Oh, gods," muttered Vimes, "don't tell me that Ronnie Rust . . ."

"I said, no connection," Vetinari interrupted. "Lord Rust is of the nobility of Ankh-Morpork, as are you. And I am not sure if his rank is high enough for this purpose. Fortunately, there is at least one noble in the city who qualifies. I have taken the liberty of asking Captain Angua and Constable Dorfl to request her presence."

Vimes furrowed his brow. "I'm supposed to know if there are any foreign bigwigs in town," he muttered, casting a sideways glance at Lady Margolotta. "And why those two? They've both got enough on their plates."

"It seemed expedient to send that pair because our guest might decide not to be found," Vetinari replied. "They might have some chance of detecting her . . . Ah, yes, we can start now."

The door had opened again – without a knock – and a young woman entered, with an angry expression and none of the nervousness that the Patrician usually induced in new visitors. She wasn't dressed like a noblewoman – just in plain black – but Vimes thought that he might have seen her around the city once or twice; there was no mistaking that white hair with a single black streak, although she didn't normally wear it in that tight plait, did she? Vimes hadn't noticed the birthmark on her cheek before, either: three pale lines.

"What do you mean by interrupting my class . . ." she began.

"Ah, Your Grace," the Patrician smoothly cut across her anger. "So pleasant to make your acquaintance. I am sorry about the circumstances, but we do have an emergency . . ."

The chronicles are populated by colourful characters, a number of whom may well appear in a Discworld game. Thus, some descriptions are in order. Many of these include game details – partly to illustrate how such individuals can be depicted in game terms, and partly to give the GM the mechanics he'll need should the PCs meet these people and interact with them in complex ways. It's even possible to use some of them as PCs, although that isn't especially recommended; much of the point of this book is to allow you to create your *own* Discworld denizens, and anyone playing a character from the novels is likely to suffer from other players itching to point out what he's doing *wrong*. Whether or not they're right, that isn't much fun.

One point here: The Disc is a big place. While players will expect to meet characters from the chronicles – and indeed should, when that's helpful to the story – try to resist the temptation to have Granny Weatherwax, the Patrician, Commander Vimes, Death, and Rincewind (with Luggage) appear in every episode. That's too *busy*.

Citizens of Ankh-Morpork

Ankh-Morpork is a huge city (see Chapter 7) and the setting for many Discworld stories. It doesn't have much of a government system, and its celebrity culture is still developing, but it does have a few people who almost everyone acknowledges are significant, one way or another, and a few equally interesting but less well-known characters in its shadows.

The Patrician (Havelock Vetinari)

431 points

Little is known about Lord Havelock Vetinari's background, but the Vetinaris are apparently the sort of wealthy merchant family who can delegate the less-glamorous work; they were able to send Havelock to the Assassins' Guild School. (He still dresses like an Assassin, in black.) After playing a hidden-but-crucial role in the replacement of one Patrician by another, learning the arts of politics from his aunt, the Genua-born Lady Roberta "Bobbi" Meserole, and touring other parts of the Disc – and encountering Lady Margolotta (pp. 349-350) – Havelock inserted himself into the city's hierarchies and ended up in charge.

He's tall, thin, and austere in his habits; vices are a tool for others to use against one. (His view of street theatre is widely regarded as simply an understandable foible.) At one time, he kept a small terrier named Wuffles, but pets are mortal; he's now the *de facto* guardian of another small dog, Mr. Fusspot, which is technically the chairman of Ankh-Morpork's Royal Bank. He likes music, but he reads it on paper for preference; he finds the idea of fallible human musicians getting involved, with all the sweat and spittle, faintly distasteful.

His weakness is that he's dedicated to Ankh-Morpork. He works tirelessly to keep the place safe, although he's far too intelligent to expect thanks. (Admittedly, retiring now might give some people the idea that it would be safe to take revenge for old wrongs, but that could hardly be an insurmountable problem for him – his active enemies used to be a lot more numerous, but now only the deranged try to plot against him.) He's also fascinated by human nature if not impressed by it. Although he has long since learned enough to manipulate it, he continues to observe it finding new forms of self-destruction. He just wishes that it would stop threatening his city in the process.

It has been observed that, whenever the Patrician has problems, the guild leaders who will support him most reliably always happen to be the female ones: Queen Molly of the Beggars, Mrs. Palm of the Seamstresses, Mrs. Manger of the Launderers, and Miss Voom of the Exotic Dancers. While his behaviour these days is entirely respectable, there are suspicions that he has a complicated romantic past. He certainly has the sort of cool style that appeals to some women.

Vetinari walks with a stick, due to an injury from a past assassination attempt, but his reactions are still fast.

Note: The PCs should NOT be encouraged to cross the Patrician. He's ruthless, *very* smart, and has made sure that numerous factions don't want him dead just yet. The problem for anyone who goes up against him will be staying alive. The kind GM can rig such situations so that Vetinari keeps the PCs around for use as tools in another plot.

ST 11 [10]; **DX** 13 [60]; **IQ** 18 [160]; **HT** 11 [10].
Damage 1d-1/1d+1; BL 24 lbs.; HP 11 [0]; Will 18 [0]; Per 18 [0]; FP 11 [0].
Basic Speed 6.00 [0]; Basic Move 5 [-5]; Dodge 10*; Parry 11* (Smallsword).
6'2"; 140 lbs.

He tended it as one tends a topiary bush, encouraging a growth here, pruning an errant twig there. It was said that he would tolerate absolutely anything apart from anything that threatened the city . . .

– *Guards! Guards!*

SOCIAL BACKGROUND

TL: 4 [0].

CF: Klatchian [1]; Sto Plains/Uberwald [0].

Languages: Klatchian (Native) [6]; Latatian (Native) [6]; Morporkian (Native) [0]; Quirmian (Native) [6]; Uberwaldian (Native) [6].

ADVANTAGES

Charisma 1 [5]; Combat Reflexes [15]; Eidetic Memory [5]; Empathy [15]; Indomitable [15]; Less Sleep 4 [8]; Reputation +1 (Do Not Cross This Man) [5]; Resistant to Disease (+3) [3]; Status 6† [25]; Unfazeable [15]; Wealth (Wealthy) [20].

Perks: Crossbow Safety; Dual Ready (Pistol Crossbow/Pistol Crossbow). [2]

DISADVANTAGES

Duty (Running the City; 15 or less; Nonhazardous) [-10]; Enemy (Occasional Over-Optimistic Plotters; 6 or less) [-10]; Obsession (Maintaining the Security of Ankh-Morpork) (15) [-5].

Quirks: Austere habits; Dislikes street theatre and mime; Highly ironical; Walks with a stick; Will kill for the city, but won't sanction atrocities. [-5]

SKILLS

Administration (A) IQ [2]-18; Area Knowledge (Ankh-Morpork) (E) IQ+2 [4]-20; Area Knowledge (Circle Sea) (E) IQ [1]-18; Area Knowledge (Sto Plains) (E) IQ [1]-18; Area Knowledge (The Disc) (E) IQ [1]-18; Area Knowledge (The Patrician's Palace) (E) IQ [1]-18; Area Knowledge (Uberwald) (E) IQ [1]-18; Camouflage (E) IQ [1]-18; Carousing (E) HT+1 [2]-12; Climbing (A) DX [2]-13; Connoisseur (Music) (A) IQ-1 [1]-17; Crossbow (E) DX+1 [2]-14; Current Affairs/TL4 (Ankh-Morpork) (E) IQ+1 [2]-19; Current Affairs/TL4 (Headline News) (E) IQ [1]-18; Current Affairs/TL4 (People) (E) IQ [1]-18; Current Affairs/TL4 (Politics) (E) IQ+1 [2]-19; Detect Lies (H) Per-3 [0]-15‡; Diplomacy (H) IQ-2 [1]-16; Games (Chess) (E) IQ [1]-18; Games (Thud) (E) IQ [1]-18; Hidden Lore (Secrets of Ankh-Morpork) (A) IQ-1 [1]-17; History (Ankh-Morpork) (H) IQ-2 [1]-16; Holdout (A) IQ-1 [1]-17; Intelligence Analysis/TL4 (H) IQ-1 [2]-17; Intimidation (A) Will-1 [1]-17; Judo (H) DX+1 [8]-14; Knife (E) DX [1]-13; Literature (H) IQ-2 [1]-16; Observation (A) Per-1 [1]-17; Poisons/TL4 (H) IQ-2 [1]-16; Politics (A) IQ+2 [8]-20; Psychology (Human) (H) IQ-1 [2]-17; Rapier (A) DX+1 [4]-14; Riding (Equines) (A) DX-1 [1]-12; Savoir-Faire (High Society) (E) IQ [1]-18; Shadowing (A) IQ-1 [1]-17; Smallsword (A) DX+1 [4]-14; Stealth (A) DX [0]-13§; Traps/TL4 (A) IQ-1 [1]-17.

* Includes +1 for Combat Reflexes.
† Includes +1 Status from Wealth.
‡ Default from Per, with +3 for Empathy.
§ Default from IQ.

NOTES

These stats aside, Vetinari *seems* capable of anything (so to speak). A lot of this can be reflected by his excellent default levels – but the GM who needs him to pull some unexpected aptitude out of thin air for plot purposes shouldn't hesitate to add stuff to his character sheet. For reasons discussed above, it's arguable that Vetinari should have, say, Sex Appeal-14, although he wouldn't use it very often. His skills as an Assassin were probably higher in his youth, too.

His exact Wealth level is hard to pin down. He comes from a high-class background, but lives austerely. He *does* have direct access to city funds, which despite the Ankh-Morporkian aversion to paying taxes are fairly substantial, but he rarely exploits this. If something needs paying for, he's more likely to get someone else to cover the cost.

Rufus Drumknott

The Patrician's chief clerk is a young man of considerable skill but little discernible personality. He clearly suffers from Compulsive Neatness (p. 58) – which in him becomes a kind of virtue. He's calm, studious, and *completely* loyal, and as he can move as quietly as his employer (Stealth-14), he can remain conveniently close by Vetinari's shoulder at all times. More important, he's an expert in the arts of paperwork and always has the correct file to hand (Accounting-13, Administration-14, and Professional Skill (Filing Clerk)-16). While an aide, not a manager, he's capable of intelligent observations, and the Patrician sometimes uses him as a sounding board for ideas.

Drumknott's fanatical loyalty and precision are such that he would never take so much as a paperclip home from the office. Vetinari believes that the nearest thing he has to a hobby is the invention of better filing systems. However, Vetinari and Lady Margolotta (pp. 349-350) have made some attempts to promote a relationship between Drumknott and Lady Margolotta's similarly dependable personal librarian, Miss Healstether.

The PCs are only likely to encounter Drumknott in the Patrician's office or the Patrician's company, and he's far too loyal for any attempt to subvert him to work. It is entirely possible that even magic would slide off the polished shell of his exterior. If he delivers an order or a message, the recipients can be entirely confident that it comes from Vetinari.

Arguably, he should have 15 points of Legal Immunity. He can certainly get away with almost anything! However, Commander Vimes of the Watch has been known to arrest him – and in a peculiar sort of way, Vetinari plays by the rules *more* than most people.

Vetinari is said to have specialised in languages in his training at the Assassins' Guild School. It's entirely possible that he actually has Language Talent, and he knows a few more languages that he happens never to have mentioned – or the GM could just give him Multilingual (Smooth Diplomatic Chat).

Leonard of Quirm

264 points

Leonard of Quirm came from a family who could afford to have him well educated despite his eccentricities, which were obvious from an early age. He quickly mastered every branch of engineering, craftsmanship, and art which he studied. He also spent a while wandering the Disc, during which time he may have encountered (and had some kind of *relationship* with) the young Gytha Ogg (pp. 340-341).

Eventually settling in Ankh-Morpork, he built a reputation for universal genius before the Patrician – realising how much damage he could do – had him secretly locked away. Vetinari has had lesser menaces assassinated without a blink, but he finds Leonard fascinating and occasionally useful. For example, Leonard's creation of a dragon-powered spacecraft capable of circling the Disc and reaching Dunmanifestin prevented the destruction of the world.

Imprisonment doesn't worry Leonard. His cell has large windows, and he's supplied with working materials. In fact, faced with the reality of humanity, he has come to see this as the best place to be. It's protected by booby-traps which only the Patrician, and now Leonard himself, know how to avoid (actually, Leonard designed many of them). Most people in the city are vaguely aware that he works for the Patrician these days, and many have seen his most recent masterpiece: the painting of the entire Disc on the ceiling of the Temple of Small Gods, created at the command of the gods themselves.

Leonard may also demonstrate his genius by creating working firearms, blueprints for flying machines, sticky yellow notepaper, his Going-Under-The-Water-Safely Device[1], or unparalleled works of art. He has no sense of priorities and is utterly naïve, especially about human nature; he even believes that his military inventions could bring about world peace, because they're too terrible to use. The Patrician keeps trying to recover his deadlier sketches.

Inspiration-powered inventiveness explains how Leonard has acquired skills above the local TL, but these ratings are merely approximations in any case. If something is physically possible with his tools, in the Disc's quite tolerant reality, then he may have created it – probably to demonstrate an abstract philosophical principle. Indeed, he wishes the inspirations would leave him alone when he's asleep, and he occasionally tries to invent a helmet that will block them (without success as yet).

Leonard is a quiet man, probably in his 50s by now, although it's hard to say – he appears to be older than he is, and his head looks like it has grown up through its hair.

ST 9 [-10]; **DX** 12 [40]; **IQ** 20 [200]; **HT** 10 [0].
Damage 1d-2/1d-1; BL 16 lbs.; HP 9 [0]; Will 17 [-15]; Per 15 [-25]; FP 10 [0].
Basic Speed 5.50 [0]; Basic Move 5 [0]; Dodge 8; Parry 9 (DX). 5'8"; 130 lbs.

SOCIAL BACKGROUND

TL: 5 [5].
CF: Sto Plains/Uberwald [0].
Languages: Classical Ephebian (Accented) [4]; Klatchian (Accented) [4]; Latatian (Accented) [4]; Morporkian (Native) [6]; Quirmian (Native) [0].

ADVANTAGES

Daredevil [15]; Gadgeteer [25]; High Manual Dexterity 2 [10]; Reputation +1 (As a master of his crafts, among alchemists and artificers) [2]; Reputation +1 (Universal Genius; 10 or less) [2]; Resistant to Disease (+3) [3]; Status 2 [10]; Versatile (Inspiration Magnet) [5].

Perks: Archaic Training 1 (Engineer (Artillery), Engineer (Civil), Engineer (Low-Tech Machines), Mathematics (Applied), Navigation (Sea), and Weather Sense). [6]

DISADVANTAGES

Absent-Mindedness [-15]; Curious (12) [-5]; Duty (Under the Patrician's Hand; 12 or less; Nonhazardous) [-5]; Gullibility (15) [-5]; Pacifism (Self-Defence Only) [-15]; Totally Oblivious [-10]; Truthfulness (15) [-2].

Quirks: Broad-Minded; Delusion ("Better war machines are less likely to be used"); Doodles compulsively, often in mirror writing; Dreamer; Responsive. [-5]

---

1. *It operated submerged in a marine environment. Leonard is hopeless at thinking of snappy names for his inventions.*

SKILLS

Alchemy/TL5 (VH) IQ-3 [1]-17; Architecture/TL4 (A) IQ-1 [1]-19; Artist (Painting) (H) IQ+1 [8]-21; Carpentry (E) IQ [1]-20; Cryptography/TL5 (H) IQ-2 [1]-18; Diagnosis/TL4 (Human) (H) IQ-2 [1]-18; Engineer/TL5 (Aerospace) (H) IQ-2 [1]-18; Engineer/TL4 (Artillery) (H) IQ-2 [1]-18; Engineer/TL4 (Civil) (H) IQ-2 [1]-18; Engineer/TL5 (Clockwork) (H) IQ-2 [1]-18; Engineer/TL4 (Combat) (H) IQ-2 [1]-18; Engineer/TL4 (Low-Tech Machines) (H) IQ-2 [1]-18; Engineer/TL5 (Small Arms) (H) IQ-2 [1]-18; Engineer/TL5 (Submarine) (H) IQ-2 [1]-18; Explosives/TL4 (Demolition) (A) IQ-1 [1]-19; Explosives/TL4 (Fireworks) (A) IQ-1 [1]-19; Mathematics/TL5 (Applied) (H) IQ-2 [1]-18; Metallurgy/TL4 (H) IQ-2 [1]-18; Natural Philosophy/TL4 (H) IQ-2 [1]-18; Naturalist (H) IQ-2 [1]-18; Navigation/TL5 (Sea) (A) IQ-1 [1]-19; Observation (A) Per+1 [4]-16; Piloting/TL5 (Swamp Dragon-Powered Space-craft) (A) DX+2 [0]-14*; Seamanship/TL5 (E) IQ [1]-20; Submarine/TL5 (Large Sub) (A) DX+2 [0]-14*; Traps/TL4 (A) IQ-1 [1]-19; Weather Sense/TL4 (A) IQ-1 [1]-19.

* Default from IQ.

NOTES

Leonard may need Mechanic skills to build and maintain the designs he creates using Engineer, but he has those at default (15) from his IQ, and DX-based rolls will often get a bonus from his High Manual Dexterity, so he has little trouble with this.

Moist von Lipwig

293 points

Moist von Lipwig was born in the town of Lipwig – in Near Uberwald, a region still in political confusion following the collapse of the Evil Empire (p. 241) – and brought up by his grandfather, who bred dogs, after both his parents died. He learned to live by his wits, but so do a lot of people. The difference was that

The Rusts

Lord Ronald "Ronnie" Rust is the *de facto* leader of the aristocratic faction in Ankh-Morpork politics. His ancestor was ennobled after singlehandedly killing 37 Klatchians while armed only with a pin, and Ronald preserves a tradition of rampant military stupidity, sometimes tipping over into mindless bravery; as he's also exceptionally lucky, he has frequently survived when many of his command have been killed. The Patrician seems to have put him in charge of the city's armed forces to keep him away from anything more dangerous, and then put other people, such as Samuel Vimes, in charge of actual policy. (Rust and Vimes have never liked each other.) Rust has blue eyes, a curly moustache, and an aristocratic drawl. However, age is catching up with him these days, and he's often confined to a wheelchair.

Rust's son, Gravid, is a greedy, amoral businessman. After the events of *Snuff*, he's facing a prison term followed by exile to Fourecks. Given how he offended the Patrician, he'll probably die there, very possibly soon. His father has disinherited him, so the heir to the title is now his sister, Regina, whom Vetinari considers hot-headed and dangerously intelligent.

Moist was good at it, and he discovered that he enjoyed it. He became a con man, briefly studying under one or two more-experienced criminals before deciding that he was better than them. That is, better mostly in the technical sense, but also perhaps in what little he had of a moral sense; while they were greedy and sometimes vicious, Moist was charming, efficient, and *preyed* on human greed. Even the large amount of money he accumulated was really just his way of keeping score. He always hated violence, because he reckoned that he would lose if he got into fights.

In a career of white-collar crime and short cons, Moist left a trail of ruined businesses and failed banks across the Sto Plains, eventually arriving in Ankh-Morpork. There, however, he ran into *determined* law enforcers, who tracked him down and assembled a solid case against him – or rather, against Albert Spangler, as Moist was then known. Even they apparently couldn't break through *all* of his disguises and aliases (although Lord Vetinari eventually determined his real identity), and Moist had a vague sense that he shouldn't disgrace his family name, or just an instinctive aversion to admitting anything that happened to be true. The Patrician, noting the sheer quantity of financial and commercial damage which Moist had left in his wake, sentenced him to hang.

However, Vetinari never likes to waste talent, and he had a problem: the city's Post Office needed to be restored as a counterbalance to the dubious management of the new clacks system, and several good agents had already died mysteriously on that project. Hence, Moist's hanging was very precisely faked, and Moist was offered the job. He didn't get much choice, but he did get a golem probation officer.

Despite everything, Moist survived, prospered, and acquired a conscience of sorts along the way, as well as an affection for Adora Belle Dearheart (pp. 314-315). Hence, he didn't flee the city even when he got the chance, but stuck with his new job.

He'd learned to be personable, but something in his genetics made him unmemorable.

– Going Postal

Unfortunately, this left him in a perilously respectable position, and Adora Belle wasn't always around to give his life the necessary spice of danger. This enabled Lord Vetinari to manoeuvre him into taking charge of the City Bank, where Moist engineered the transformation of one great confidence trick (Ankh-Morpork's debased metal coinage) into another (paper money). At the climax of that operation, however, Moist found himself cornered in a court of law and threatened with exposure. So he revealed the truth himself, relying on his ability to charm the public and his proven record of success. Having learned to play the dim-witted, sentimental Ankh-Morpork mob like a musical instrument, Moist got away with that, too. The Patrician has more plans for him; see *The Undertaking* (p. 250).

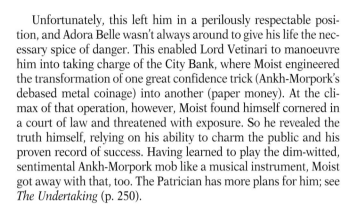

The Aristocracy

Ankh-Morpork was once much more of an aristocratic state than it is now. The fall of the monarchy took away the hub around which the old system revolved, but noble titles still exist and are mostly attached to people with a lot of property and thus power. Most of these titles were created when some ancestor got a few hundred men killed in some glorious military defeat.

Although a lot of aristocrats are strictly average intellects and suffer from a full set of aristocratic delusions (primarily, that being aristocratic makes up for all other deficiencies), they often run to a certain hereditary cunning, or at least survival instinct. Politics in Ankh-Morpork have been down and dirty for long enough that *really* irretrievable stupidity has largely been bred out. Some of them are actually quite sharp; most Patricians have been from this class, after all.

Politically, they tend to be thoroughly conservative, regarding every change as being for the worse, anyone with money or power but no title as fundamentally *wrong*, and nonhumans with disdain. They see the Patrician as an upstart, but they've noticed that he has somehow made himself essential. They have real difficulties with Samuel Vimes; many of them try to ignore his existence, even when he's in the room.

Notable families include the Rusts (p. 309), the Selachiis (Lord Robert Selachii, current head of the house, was previously a working Assassin), the Venturis (who have an ancient feud with the Selachiis, and who have produced many noted soldiers and famous explorers), the Monflathers, the Skaters, and the de Wordes (see pp. 311-312). At least one house, the d'Eaths, has recently become defunct.

If the PCs encounter Moist, they'll most likely find him personable and interesting. However, if they think that they're reading him, they're probably dead wrong – though one or two people *have* managed the trick. While not a bad person these days, he's usually looking for an angle on his latest problem, and he has a certain healthy cynicism about other people's motives.

Moist isn't generally religious, but he has become an occasional devotee of Anoia, Goddess of Things That Stick In Drawers. After he invoked her once while bamboozling the public, because he liked her name, her cult gained a much-increased following. Her one priestess, Miss Extremelia Mume – who looked after several gods from a multi-purpose temple over a bookmaker's office in Cable Street (and worked in a bar in the evenings to make ends meet) – is now a moderately significant figure in Ankh-Morpork. Moist feels that there may be some advantage to having a goddess who owes him. Also, in his days as Head Postmaster, Moist himself may accidentally have become an avatar of some messenger god, but he never felt particularly divine. He feels that he understands how religions work, though, thanks to his background.

Moist has been described, mostly on Watch reports and wanted posters, as appearing to be 20 or maybe 30 years old, 5'9" to 6'2" tall, with hair anything from mid-brown to blond. He instinctively tries to avoid being photographed clearly, although that habit may be superfluous now. He found the Postmaster's uniform – a gold suit and a gold hat with wings attached – embarrassing, but he employed it as a prop, and it distracted people from his actual appearance.

ST 11 [10]; **DX** 13 [60]; **IQ** 13 [60]; **HT** 10 [0].
Damage 1d-1/1d+1; BL 24 lbs.; HP 11 [0]; Will 13 [0]; Per 13 [0]; FP 10 [0].
Basic Speed 6.00 [5]; Basic Move 6 [0]; Dodge 10*; Parry 10* (DX).
5'11"?; 160 lbs.?

Social Background

TL: 4 [0].
CF: Sto Plains/Uberwald [0].
Languages: Morporkian (Native) [6]; Uberwaldian (Native) [0].

Advantages

Born to Hang 4 [40]; Charisma 1 [5]; Combat Reflexes [15]; Luck [15]; Reputation +1 (Entertainingly Clever, in Ankh-Morpork) [2]; Resistant to Disease (+3) [3]; Status 3 [15]; Wealth (Comfortable) [10].

Perks: Check the Exits; Forgettable Face; Haughty Sneer; Honest Face. [4]

Disadvantages

Compulsive Risk-Taking (9) (Mitigator, Company of Adora Belle Dearheart) [-8]; Pacifism (Reluctant Killer) [-5].

Quirks: Gets nervous and twitchy if he has to handle a weapon; Loves beating systems; Occasionally steals small items, just for practise. [-3]

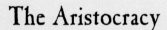

Skills

Accounting (H) IQ-2 [1]-11; Acrobatics (H) DX-1 [2]-12; Acting (A) IQ+2 [8]-15; Administration (A) IQ-1 [1]-12; Animal Handling (Dogs) (A) IQ-1 [1]-12; Area Knowledge (Ankh-Morpork) (E) IQ [1]-13; Area Knowledge (Sto Plains) (E) IQ [1]-13; Artist (Engraving) (H) IQ-1 [2]-12; Carousing (E) HT+1 [2]-11; Climbing (A) DX+1 [4]-14; Counterfeiting/TL4 (H) IQ+2 [1]-15†; Current Affairs/TL4 (Business) (E) IQ [1]-13; Diplomacy (H) IQ-1 [2]-12; Disguise (A) IQ+3 [1]-16†; Fast-Talk (A) IQ+4 [2]-17†; Filch (A) DX+4 [2]-17†; Forgery/TL4 (H) IQ+3 [2]-16†; Gambling (A) IQ+1 [4]-14; Games (Cripple Mister Onion) (E) IQ+1 [2]-14; Holdout (A) IQ+3 [1]-16†; Knot-Tying (E) DX [1]-13; Lockpicking/TL4 (A) IQ+3 [1]-16†; Merchant (A) IQ-1 [1]-12; Observation (A) Per [2]-13; Propaganda/TL4 (A) IQ-1 [1]-12; Psychology (Human) (H) IQ-1 [2]-12; Public Speaking (A) IQ [1]-13‡; Research/TL4 (A) IQ-1 [1]-12; Riding (Equines) (A) DX [2]-13; Savoir-Faire (High Society) (E) IQ [1]-13; Sleight of Hand (H) DX+3 [2]-16†; Smuggling (A) IQ+3 [1]-16†; Stealth (A) DX-1 [1]-12; Streetwise (A) IQ-1 [1]-12.

* Includes +1 for Combat Reflexes.
† Includes +4 for Born to Hang.
‡ Includes +1 for Charisma.

Notes

This is Moist as an unwilling pillar of Ankh-Morpork society, with his new Status supported by income and benefits tied to his jobs. He really hates having acquired Administration skill. In his old career, he functioned mostly at around Status 0 or 1, although he had considerable wealth: $150,000, buried in a box in the woods. (Yes, he could have retired to live in comfort – that wasn't the *point*.) Back then, his past record and current scams would have qualified as a large Secret; later, between his hanging and his declaring himself in court, he had a slightly different but no less tricky Secret. His Compulsive Behaviour has grown as a reaction to his new and discomforting respectability, with his relationship with Adora Belle Dearheart also developing to keep it under control.

Adora Belle Dearheart might rate as a Contact, giving some kind of golem-related skill. Moist has also cultivated sources in Unseen University, although they mostly help on a case-by-case basis, as Moist brings them interesting puzzles. Lord Vetinari might qualify as a Patron, but he tends to assume that Moist can look after himself, and he would set conditions or prices on any favours that he did perform.

William de Worde

133 points

William de Worde was born the second son of Lord de Worde, an aristocrat of the unpleasantly old-fashioned kind. William turned out to have a mind of his own and liberal tendencies, so his relationship with his father was difficult. He was educated at Hugglestones, a not-very-good boarding school where he embraced literacy with enthusiasm, quite enjoyed fencing lessons, and avoided everything else. As a second son, he was expected to go into the priesthood, the military, or land management, but he had no enthusiasm at all for those options, leading to a complete falling-out with his father. William then went off to

do what he found he wanted, which was to become a professional scribe in Ankh-Morpork.

He made an adequate living there, mostly by compiling a newsletter regarding events in the city and having copies run off by woodblock printing, for which he was paid a modest subscription by various rulers in other nations. Later, his older brother Rupert was killed during the brief non-war with Klatch (pp. 234-237), so William technically became the heir to the de Worde titles and estates. Both he and his father do their best to ignore this.

Later again, William had a chance meeting with a group of dwarfs who were looking to introduce moveable-type printing to the city. This in turn led to the accidental invention of newspapers, and William found himself the editor and chief reporter of the *Ankh-Morpork Times*. His first major story involved the exposure of a plot against the Patrician, which may help explain why he was allowed to continue. William discovered a talent for improvisation, getting the paper published despite the attempts of various groups to stop him.

William was supposed to have been brought up to follow the code of his social class, but somehow he turned out differently. He has a clear sense of right and wrong. This means that the *Times* tries very hard to tell the truth and serve the public good, even if William has to decide what those words mean as he goes along.

William is not universally popular in Ankh-Morpork. Aside from all the individuals and factions whom the *Times* has inconvenienced, many people think that he's pompous or arrogant, especially if they judge him by his editorials – and they may have a point. However, he's a good writer and an even better, instinctive editor. Player characters may come to regard him as an ally or a problem, depending on what story they're involved in, but they'll find that he's essentially fair and honest. Do *not* patronise him, though; that sets off the aristocratic pride which he denies having.

William is naturally truthful, although he can be clever about telling the *exact* truth – and anyway, being told the truth conveniently confuses some people. He was brought up to disdain non-humans, but this never took. He has never displayed more than quirk-level discomfort around dwarfs and even vampires, and he has trained himself out of even that.

ST 10 [0]; **DX** 11 [20]; **IQ** 13 [60]; **HT** 10 [0].

Damage 1d-2/1d; BL 20 lbs.; HP 10 [0]; Will 13 [0]; Per 13 [0]; FP 10 [0].

Basic Speed 5.25 [0]; Basic Move 5 [0]; Dodge 8; Parry 9 (Smallsword).

5'9"; 145 lbs.

SOCIAL BACKGROUND

TL: 4 [0].

CF: Sto Plains/Uberwald [0].

Languages: Borogravian (Accented) [4]; Latatian (Broken) [2]; Morporkian (Native) [0]; Quirmian (Broken) [2].

ADVANTAGES

Fearlessness 1 [2]; Reputation +1 ("That clever man who writes down the news," in Ankh-Morpork; 10 or less) [1]; Status 3 [15]; Wealth (Comfortable) [10].

Perks: Cold Resistance. [1]

DISADVANTAGES

Curious (15) [-2]; Pacifism (Self-Defence Only) [-15]; Reputation -2 (For nosiness or impertinence, in Ankh-Morpork; 7 or less) [-1]; Sense of Duty (Sacharissa Cripslock) [-2]; Truthfulness (12) [-5].

Quirks: Deeply dislikes his father, despite basic family loyalty; Habitual news-collector; Hates being patronised; Pedantic about spelling; Strong moral sense. [-5]

SKILLS

Area Knowledge (Ankh-Morpork) (E) IQ+2 [4]-15; Area Knowledge (Sto Plains) (E) IQ [1]-13; Current Affairs/TL4 (Ankh-Morpork) (E) IQ+1 [2]-14; Current Affairs/TL4 (Headline News) (E) IQ+3 [8]-16; Detect Lies (H) Per-2 [1]-11; Diplomacy (H) IQ-2 [1]-11; Fast-Talk (A) IQ+1 [4]-14; Games (Sport Fencing Rules) (E) IQ+1 [2]-14; Literature (H) IQ-1 [2]-12; Merchant (A) IQ-1 [1]-12; Observation (A) Per-1 [1]-12; Printing/TL4 (A) IQ [2]-13;

Propaganda/TL4 (A) IQ-1 [1]-12; Psychology (Human) (H) IQ-1 [2]-12; Research/TL4 (A) IQ-1 [1]-12; Riding (Equines) (A) DX-1 [1]-10; Savoir-Faire (High Society) (E) IQ+1 [2]-14; Scrounging (E) Per [1]-13; Smallsword (A) DX+1 [4] 12; Sports (Hugglestones Football) (A) DX-1 [1]-10; Writing (A) IQ+1 [4]-14.

NOTES

William previously got into danger at least once because he felt a strong, if limited, loyalty to his family, but he has since closed that chapter in his life. He may now actually have a Sense of Duty to the whole *Times* instead.

His Status reflects his aristocratic background and effective standing in Ankh-Morpork; he might be unpopular in some circles, but he runs an important enterprise and has occasional audiences with the Patrician. However, although the *Times* is doing well commercially, his personal income may not cover a Status 3 lifestyle – and anyway, he doesn't have *time* to live at that level. (Before the journalism started up, he was living at a rather bohemian Status 0 and had shed the habits required to look like an aristocrat.) He may *appear* to be about Status 1 or 2. On the other hand, the paper can afford to send him thousands of miles in pursuit of a story.

Sacharissa Cripslock

78 points

Sacharissa Cripslock was the daughter of a struggling professional engraver and helped look after his business. When the arrival of moveable type threatened to take away the work her father was getting from William de Worde, she went round to complain, and promptly found herself recruited into William's new project. She thus discovered a previously completely unsuspected gift for journalism, and particularly the ability to think in headlines. The income from this new job keeps her family quite adequately.

Sacharissa is a woman with a tendency to strong principles. Originally, this took the form of an attachment to respectability – she worried a great deal about whether anything she had to do was *proper* – but a little experience of the realities of news reporting in Ankh-Morpork soon led her to a more realistic attitude. She and William seem to have ended up married, but she persists in using her maiden name for professional purposes. Doubtless, this is a matter of principle, too.

If the PCs do something publicly noteworthy in Ankh-Morpork, they may well be asked for an interview by Miss Cripslock. If they agree, the GM should bear in mind that being interviewed by her is regarded by Moist von Lipwig and the Patrician himself as an *interesting challenge*. She has learned or invented every trick of the (mostly ethical) journalistic interviewer, and she has a genuine desire to discover the truth – but also to sell newspapers. Sloppy interviewees with secrets to keep or images to preserve may feel that they've been hit by a very polite tornado, although they might not realise what they said until the *Times* appears the next morning. The GM should take notes, but remember that Miss Cripslock gets many of her best quotes after she has put her pen away. She has an excellent memory and an annoying habit of printing exactly what people say.

If the PCs refuse an interview, they will inspire a lot of natural journalistic curiosity in Miss Cripslock. Threats would make her *very* curious if also rationally cautious.

Sacharissa is a self-possessed woman, with fine but mismatched features and an excellent figure. She tries to distract people from the latter by dressing plainly; it doesn't work. Still, it seems to make some men want to talk to her. Her manner is always professional, although her instinctive enthusiasm for a good story often slips through.

ST 8 [-20]; **DX** 10 [0]; **IQ** 12 [40]; **HT** 10 [0].
Damage 1d-3/1d-2; BL 13 lbs.; HP 8 [0]; Will 12 [0]; Per 12 [0]; FP 10 [0].
Basic Speed 5.00 [0]; Basic Move 5 [0]; Dodge 8; Parry 8 (DX). 5'8"; 125 lbs.

SOCIAL BACKGROUND

TL: 4 [0].
CF: Sto Plains/Uberwald [0].
Languages: Latatian (Broken) [2]; Morporkian (Native) [0]; Quirmian (Broken) [2].

ADVANTAGES

Fearlessness 2 [4]; Indomitable [15].
Perks: Good Memory for Quotes (Effectively Eidetic Memory for one-line comments); Statuesque. [2]

DISADVANTAGES

Pacifism (Reluctant Killer) [-5]; Sense of Duty (William de Worde) [-2].
Quirks: Code of Honour (Basic Press Ethics); Feminist principles; Somewhat curious. [-3]

SKILLS

Acting (A) IQ-1 [1]-11; Area Knowledge (Ankh-Morpork) (E) IQ+1 [2]-13; Current Affairs/TL4 (Headline News) (E) IQ+3 [8]-15; Detect Lies (H) Per+1 [8]-13; Diplomacy (H) IQ+1 [8]-13; Fast-Talk (A) IQ [2]-12; Housekeeping (E) IQ [1]-12; Interrogation (A) IQ-1 [1]-11; Psychology (Human) (H) IQ-1 [2]-11; Savoir-Faire (High Society) (E) IQ+1 [2]-13; Writing (A) IQ+2 [8]-14.

NOTES

Like William, Sacharissa may actually have a Sense of Duty to the whole *Times*. As they're married, her Wealth and Status will doubtless be rising to match his. An earlier version of Sacharissa might have had only Struggling Wealth, and possibly an Obsession with maintaining respectability or a Delusion that respectability is all that matters.

As a diligent journalist who also happens to be a striking-looking woman, Sacharissa tends to accumulate informants. Most of these are transient or of limited usefulness, but the GM is welcome to give her any Contacts that help a scenario.

Otto Chriek

232 points

Otto Chriek is a vampire, originally from Uberwald. He currently lives in Ankh-Morpork when not off on some assignment for the *Times*, which employs him as an iconographer. As an expert picture-maker, he also gets work taking "society" portraits.

He's a Black Ribboner (pp. 113-114), and like most such, he has had to replace his obsession with human blood with another – in his case, a devotion to the art of iconography and the science of light. Unfortunately, bright light causes him intense pain, and very often he collapses into a heap of dust after taking a salamander-flash photograph, but as he says, "It iss a bit of a bugger, but zere you go." Fortunately, he can be restored to full function after one of these incidents by dropping a small quantity of blood onto the dust. He has taken to carrying a vial of animal blood around his neck; when it falls to the ground, it usually breaks, restoring him instantly. If it doesn't, then hopefully a helpful human will read the little card that he also carries and break the vial for him.

Otto has experimented with the possibility of taking pictures using anti-light, the opposite of light, but most people who know much about that subject think that he's insane. Many dwarfs react to the mere idea at -2. The results can certainly be nightmarish – anti-light, which is emitted by certain invertebrates found in deep Uberwaldian caves, illuminates the darkest depths of the soul.

Otto is thin and pale, and wears small, oval-lensed dark glasses. He dresses in traditional vampire style and has never shed his Uberwaldian accent. All this may simply be a way of amusing people so that they don't get dangerously scared of him. However, he does still have enough vampiric powers to take on whole gangs of human opponents, although he'd much rather be taking pictures. He's a nice person, and loyal to his friends; if that loyalty obliges him to use his speed and strength to save their lives, he'll do so. Still, iconography is his first concern, and his evening dress and cloak have numerous pockets and compartments for photographic equipment.

ST 15* [0]; DX 14* [20]; IQ 12 [40]; HT 11* [0].
Damage 1d+1/2d+1; BL 45 lbs.; HP 15 [0]; Will 12 [0]; Per 14*
    [0]; FP 11 [0].
Basic Speed 6.25 [0]; Basic Move 6 [0]; Dodge 9; Parry 10
    (Brawling).
5'10"; 120 lbs.

SOCIAL BACKGROUND

TL: 4 [0].
CF: Sto Plains/Uberwald [0].
Languages: Morporkian (Accented) [4]; Uberwaldian
(Native) [0].

ADVANTAGES

Flight (Winged, Can Hover) [30]; Patron (The *Times,* a
fairly powerful organisation; 12 or less) [20]; Reputation +2
(As a harmless eccentric and honest working stiff, in Ankh-
Morpork; 10 or less) [2]; Vampire (Male) [108]; Versatile [5].
Perks: Climatic Emphasis. [1]

DISADVANTAGES

Obsession (Perfect the Art of Photography) (12) [-10]; Sense of
Duty (Close Friends) [-5]; Social Stigma (Second-Class Citizen)
[-5]; Uncontrollable Appetite (Zer B-Vord; Mitigator, Photography Obsession) (12) [-6].
Quirks: Black Ribboner (pp. 113-114); Broad-Minded; Hams
up the old-school vampire style. [-3]

SKILLS

Alchemy/TL4 (VH) IQ-3 [1]-9; Animal Handling (Lizards) (A)
IQ-1 [1]-11; Area Knowledge (Ankh-Morpork) (E) IQ+1 [2]-13;
Area Knowledge (Sto Plains) (E) IQ [1]-12; Brawling (E) DX+1
[2]-15; Current Affairs/TL4 (Headline News) (E) IQ [1]-12; Fast-
Talk (A) IQ-1 [1]-11; Intimidation (A) Will-1 [1]-11; Natural Phi-
losophy/TL4 (H) IQ-2 [1]-10; Observation (A) Per-1 [1]-13;
Photography (A) IQ+4 [16]-16; Printing/TL4 (A) IQ-1 [1]-11;
Savoir-Faire (High Society) (E) IQ [1]-12; Stealth (A) DX-1 [1]-13.

* Modified for racial template.

NOTES

Given his proven ingenuity – for example, training his imps to
create etched printing plates by "painting" in acid, and more-or-less
inventing colour printing within a day or two of being introduced
to the printing press – Otto might also qualify for Gadgeteer.

Adora Belle Dearheart

152 points

Adora Belle Dearheart – known as "Killer" to her friends and
as "Spike" to Moist von Lipwig (pp. 309-311) – is the daughter
of Robert Dearheart, one of the founder-creators of the clacks
system (pp. 222-225). She was always strong-willed and self-
confident, seeking to make her own way in life. Unfortunately,
her father lost his position in the clacks company and was financially ruined thanks to the machinations of ruthless businessman Reacher Gilt, and Adora Belle herself lost her job in a
provincial bank when she mistakenly accepted a set of documents forged by Moist von Lipwig. This gave her an embittered,

cynical world-view, which only grew worse when her brother
John was killed – as she guessed, also by Gilt's agents.

She took a job with the Golem Trust, an organisation that finds
work for free golems (pp. 104-106) and helps them buy other
golems out of human ownership. She likes and respects golems for
their absolute and uncompromised integrity, and she became their
champion. Then she met Moist von Lipwig, who fell for her –
largely because she refused to fall for his usual charm – and eventually confessed his past to her, though only after carefully extracting her promise not to kill him. She eventually decided that she
found him interesting enough to forgive, and after he defeated Gilt
with her help, their relationship developed further. They plan to
marry when she can find the time (they say that he's her fiancé, not
vice versa). Since Gilt's frauds were exposed, her family are again
quite well off.

Adora Belle is a stern-looking woman with a taste for plain
grey dresses and high heels. Early ballet lessons and a capacity for
directed aggression give her a formidable kick. She's also a full-
time chain smoker who can be tracked by her accompanying
cloud of cigarette smoke.

ST 9 [-10]; DX 11 [20]; IQ 13 [60]; HT 11 [10].
Damage 1d-2/1d-1; BL 16 lbs.; HP 9 [0]; Will 14 [5]; Per 13 [0]; FP
    11 [0].
Basic Speed 5.50 [0]; Basic Move 5 [0]; Dodge 8; Parry 10
    (Brawling).
5'7"; 130 lbs.

SOCIAL BACKGROUND

TL: 4 [0].
CF: Sto Plains/Uberwald [0].
Languages: Ancient Golem Language (Broken/Accented) [3];
Latatian (Broken) [2]; Morporkian (Native) [0]; Omnian (Bro-
ken) [2].

ADVANTAGES

Appearance (Attractive) [4]; Contact (Father; Engineer
(Clacks)-18; 15 or less; Completely Reliable) [27]; Fearlessness 2
[4]; Indomitable [15]; Resistant to Disease (+3) [3]; Sensitive [5];
Unusual Background (Golem Friend) [10].
Perks: High-Heeled Heroine. [1]

DISADVANTAGES

Addiction (Chain Smoker) [-5]; Bad Temper (9) [-15]; Code of Honour ("Pirate's") [-5]; Odious Personal Habit (Irascible and Sarcastic) [-5]; Sense of Duty (Golems) [-5].

Quirks: Broad-Minded; Likes golems more than people; Not big on small talk. [-3]

SKILLS

Accounting (H) IQ-2 [1]-11; Area Knowledge (Ankh-Morpork) (E) IQ [1]-13; Brawling (E) DX+3 [8]-14; Crossbow (E) DX [1]-11; Dancing (A) DX-1 [1]-10; Detect Lies (H) Per+2 [8]-15*; Hidden Lore (Golem Secrets) (A) IQ [2]-13; History (Golems) (H) IQ [4]-13; Intimidation (A) Will [2]-14; Merchant (A) IQ-1 [1]-12.

* Includes +1 for Sensitive.

NOTES

When she's working on behalf of the Golem Trust, Adora Belle has access to its considerable financial reserves. Also, if they're paying her what she deserves, and given her family background, she may qualify for Comfortable Wealth in her own right.

Aside from her access to her father, Adora Belle is friendly with "the Smoking Gnu," a trio of clever young clacks engineers who might rate as another Contact.

C.M.O.T. Dibbler

87 points

Cut-Me-Own-Throat Dibbler, alias "Throat" or just "Dibbler" (he has never admitted to any other name, though some believe the truth to be "Claude Maximillian Overton Transpire Dibbler"), is one of Ankh-Morpork's best-known figures. His most frequent activity is selling snacks on the street, but he has engaged in all manner of other commercial activities. He isn't technically a merchant; he isn't *technically* anything, not even a criminal, despite the opinions of those who've bought his meat pies. He is, rather, a quintessential entrepreneur. He's the sole member of the Guild of C.M.O.T. Dibblers (see *Creating a Guild,* p. 263).

Dibbler is a skinny, rodent-like figure who's perpetually on the lookout for sales opportunities and who never has the right change. He runs his schemes from a cellar near the Shades. No one knows where he lives, and there's a theory that he never actually sleeps, because then he might miss a chance of profit. He does have a nephew, Solstice ("Soll") Dibbler,

Mr. Slant

The president of Ankh-Morpork's Guild of Lawyers is Mr. Slant, of the firm of Morecombe, Slant and Honeyplace. He's a zombie, which suits him fine; it lets him get on with his job without tiresome metabolic distractions. Other lawyers regard him with quiet fear. He's at the top of a competitive profession, he has been there a *long* time, and he knows where the bodies are buried – and while he may be dead, he shows no interest in joining them.

Whenever the upper reaches of Ankh-Morpork society are up to something dubious, Mr. Slant will be peripherally involved and carefully consulted. He's completely reliable with regard to the Guild's rules of confidentiality and discretion. However, because lawyers aren't supposed to condone or assist with anything illegal, he's generally careful not to become *too* closely involved – so nobody ever pins anything on him later. He usually shows up when the city government needs legal counsel, too.

Mr. Slant has the standard zombie template, an IQ of at least 13, and skill 16+ in all branches of Ankh-Morpork law. He probably rates as having Eidetic Memory, too, at least in regard to legal matters; he doesn't have to consult the books to determine precedent. Very often, he set it himself.

Being a zombie, Mr. Slant is rationally nervous of fire. He's even more nervous of words like *pro bono publico.*

who shares his instincts, but in a slightly more sophisticated – or at least yuppified – form.

Dibbler's schemes have included selling self-help books (on topics such as martial-arts techniques and barbarian heroism) and dragon detectors. He spent brief periods as a moving-picture mogul and (in an uncertain timeline) as a music promoter, both professions ideally suited to his nature. He also briefly found employment when the city's first, short-lived tabloid newspaper needed writers, but left when it was pointed out to him that he was working for someone else. While in fact quite ingenious, he suffers from a fundamental lack of *judgement;* he can never resist the prospect of a bigger return. Thus, his income goes up and down wildly; his effective Wealth level could be almost anywhere at any given time, and he seems to have a knack for raising funds for his projects. It's unclear what he does with his profits, though, or what he would do if one of his grander schemes ever held together to fruition – probably invest the money in some less-wise project.

Dibbler might *occasionally* get peripherally involved in political schemes, mostly in the hopes of profiting from being on the winning side. A measure of his marketing skills (and of the effect of the smell of fried onions on the human palate) is that he not only sells a fair number of meat pies, but actually gets repeat custom.

ST 9 [-10]; **DX** 11 [20]; **IQ** 12 [40]; **HT** 12 [20].
Damage 1d-2/1d-1; BL 16 lbs.; HP 9 [0]; Will 11 [-5]; Per 12 [0]; FP 12 [0].
Basic Speed 6.00 [5]; Basic Move 6 [0]; Dodge 9; Parry 8 (DX). 5'9"; 105 lbs.

SOCIAL BACKGROUND

TL: 4 [0].
CF: Sto Plains/Uberwald [0].
Languages: Morporkian (Native) [0].

ADVANTAGES

Less Sleep 4 [8]; Resistant to Disease (+8) [5]; Versatile [5].
Perks: Honest Face. [1]

Other Dibblers

The chronicles have shown or mentioned numerous people filling the same role as C.M.O.T. Dibbler in different Discworld communities, and the phenomenon extends across time as well as space: Disembowel-Meself-Honourably Dibhala, vendor of strangely fresh thousand-year-old eggs in the Agatean Empire; Cut-Me-Own-Hand-Off Dhblah, who sold disturbingly live yoghurt in Omnia; Al-Jiblah of Al Khali; May-I-Never-Achieve-Enlightenment Dhiblang, presumably a Hublander; Dib Diblossonson, vendor of topless and bottomless smorgasbord in NoThingfjord; May-I-Be-Kicked-In-My-Own-Ice-Hole Dibooki, of some frozen region; and Swallow-Me-Own-Blow-Dart Dlang-Dlang, possibly of Bhangbhangduc or Nafooi. Fair Go Dibbler, of Bugarup, is notable for being more inclined to express political opinions than most Dibblers – probably because the citizens of Fourecks don't need to be convinced to eat bizarre and unnerving foodstuffs.

The Nature of Dibblerdom?

It's possible that some of these Dibblers are related by blood, but mostly, the phenomenon is put down to parallel evolution: Wherever there's a large enough group of people, someone will come along and sell them pork products in a stale bun – and on the Disc, the power of narrative makes that someone fit a pattern. However, it's *possible* that there's something a little more arcane going on.

Conceivably, narrative power might be not merely influencing all these Dibblers, but actually *creating* them. Like bogeymen, Dibblers may be a fundamental human expectation regularly precipitated from the Disc's supersaturated spiritual field. If so, it seems that they don't know their own nature – but then, self-knowledge isn't a Dibbler attribute. And it would certainly explain things like the Dibbler immunity to permanent defeat and seeming lack of need for sleep.

DISADVANTAGES

Delusion ("Everybody can see that past results of my schemes are no guide to future performance!") [-5]; Greed (12) [-15]; Impulsiveness (12) [-10]; Reputation -1 (Among anyone who has ever eaten one of his meat pies) [-2]; Skinny [-5].
Quirks: Always says that a deal is "Cutting me own throat"; Broad-Minded; Dreamer; Tone-deaf. [-4]

SKILLS

Accounting (H) IQ-2 [1]-10; Acting (A) IQ-1 [1]-11; Area Knowledge (Ankh-Morpork) (E) IQ+2 [4]-14; Current Affairs/TL4 (Business) (E) IQ+1 [2]-13; Current Affairs/TL4 (Headline News) (E) IQ [1]-12; Fast-Talk (A) IQ+3 [12]-15; Finance (H) IQ-2 [1]-10; Holdout (A) IQ [2]-12; Law (Ankh-Morpork Commercial) (H) IQ-2 [1]-10; Merchant (A) IQ+1 [4]-13; Packing (A) IQ-1 [1]-11; Propaganda/TL4 (A) IQ [2]-12; Public Speaking (A) IQ-1 [1]-11; Scrounging (E) Per [1]-12; Smuggling (A) IQ [2]-12; Stealth (A) DX-1 [1]-10; Streetwise (A) IQ-1 [1]-11; Writing (A) IQ-1 [1]-11.

Gaspode the Wonder Dog

73 points

Gaspode was born an ordinary mongrel in Ankh-Morpork and promptly thrown in the river in a sack. The river being the Ankh, he was able to walk out (in the sack), but he feels that this set the tone for his life. He soon acquired a truly startling range of diseases – including one normally limited to pregnant sheep – which he claims must be so busy fighting each other that none of them can kill *him*, and indeed he never seems to get any worse. This, and some diligent effort, gives him a serious stray-dog smell. He's also scruffy and generally unprepossessing.

He spent some moderately contented years as an ordinary street dog, until the side-effects of the events of *Moving Pictures* temporarily granted him full sapience. After a brief-but-heroic few weeks, he returned happily enough to his old nature. However, his psyche had been sensitised, and a few days' careless rooting round the rubbish bins at Unseen University accidentally gave him back full colour vision and speech.

Few people ever believe that a dog can talk, but Gaspode has found that this has one advantage: humans respond to what he says without realising that *he* said it. Mostly, what he says is, "Give the nice doggie a biscuit." Speech gives him power over other dogs, too, as he can snap out "Bad dog!" or "Sit!" and drill right into their hindbrains; however, he's nervous of using this power, because the effects rarely last for more than seconds and the victims hate him for humiliating them. He's also a superb tracker; his sense of smell may not be much better than that of most dogs, but he combines it with abstract intelligence. When he's tracking by smell, the GM may allow him to add his Acute Taste and Smell bonus to his Tracking skill.

Gaspode has found himself helping the Watch with a number of problems. Captain Angua – who, being a werewolf, can talk to dogs – has no psychological difficulty with chatting to him, and Captain Carrot has got the hang of doing so, too. He also associates with Foul Ole Ron (pp. 317-318), one of the few beings who smells even worse than him, acting as the world's first thinking-brain dog. There are now stories told in the city of a talking dog, but nobody who doesn't already know Gaspode believes them.

Quirks: Bowlegged; Cynical; Mildly phobic about being domesticated; Proud of his accomplishments (including his tracking ability, his disease collection, and his smell); Wants to be a "good dog," save the day, and have his ears scratched. [-5]

SKILLS

Area Knowledge (Ankh-Morpork) (E) IQ+3 [8]-13; Brawling (E) DX [0]-11*; Fast-Talk (A) IQ-1 [1]-9; Filch (A) DX [2]-11; Merchant (A) IQ+1 [4]-11; Observation (A) Per-1 [1]-13; Scrounging (E) Per [1]-14; Stealth (A) DX+1 [4]-12; Streetwise (A) IQ-1 [1]-9; Tracking (A) Per+3 [0]-17*; Urban Survival (A) Per-1 [1]-13.

* Modified for racial template.
† With 40% cost reduction for Quadruped.

NOTES

From the usual descriptions given of him, Gaspode might qualify for Unattractive or worse Appearance. However, people don't take against him that badly, so his lack of visual appeal is mostly reflected in his low Status, while Pitiable (hopefully) mostly compensates for that and his Bad Smell. If anyone does turn nasty on him, he'll use his Voice of Command. Also, his Resistant to Disease advantage affects new or seriously dangerous infections; the ones already in residence don't trouble him unduly.

Gaspode's quirks may seem contradictory. They are. All dogs are caught between a lust for freedom and a wish to be petted. Gaspode's tragedy is that he *knows* it.

Foul Ole Ron and Friends

In Ankh-Morpork, there's a level below even the Beggars' Guild, and people for whom even Guild beggars feel too much pity to enforce Guild regulations. (Some of these people *might* be Guild members, but they may not remember this fact well enough to follow the rules.) Probably the best-known of these are the group which meets under the Misbegot Bridge, and which is sometimes known as the Canting Crew.

Of these, the most notable member is *Foul Ole Ron,* if only for his Smell, a truly appalling odour which is said to have a life of its own, and indeed to attend the opera without Ron from time to time. Foul Ole Ron is a professional mutterer; he walks around behind people, holding a deranged conversation with himself (favourite phrases include "Millennium hand and shrimp" and "Bugrit") until they give him money to go away. Ron dresses in a huge, filthy overcoat and an ancient felt hat. He's often accompanied by Gaspode (pp. 316-317), who acts as his thinking-brain dog, and indeed sometimes helps the Canting Crew to moderately profitable endeavours, such as acting as newspaper vendors. (They don't *work* as that, or anything else, though – the Canting Crew would never *work.*) Given their generally tenuous grasp on reality, the Crew have no problems with a talking dog.

ST 5* [0]; **DX** 11 [12†]; **IQ** 10* [80]; **HT** 11* [0].
Damage 1d-4/1d-3; BL 5 lbs.; HP 5 [0]; Will 11* [-15]; Per 14* [-10]; FP 11 [0].
Basic Speed 5.50 [0]; Basic Move 5 [0]; Dodge 8.
About 1'; 15 lbs. (SM -3*).

SOCIAL BACKGROUND

TL: 4 [0].
CF: Sto Plains/Uberwald [0].
Languages: Canine (Native/None*) [0]; Morporkian (Native/Broken) [4].

ADVANTAGES

Acute Taste and Smell 3 [6]; Patron (The Watch, through Angua and Carrot, a fairly powerful organisation; 9 or less) [10]; Pitiable [5]; Resistant to Disease (+8) [5]; Voice of Command (Only vs. people who don't believe that he can talk, and all dogs; +10 to IQ roll) [105].

DISADVANTAGES

Bad Smell [-10]; Sense of Duty (Close Friends) [-5]; Small Smart Dog (Social Stigma changed from Valuable Property to Logical Impossibility) [-122]; Status -2 [-10].

"You can talk?"
"Huh. That don't take much intelligence," said the dog.

– Men at Arms

Other regular members of the Crew are *Coffin Henry*, its unofficial leader, who has a positively volcanic cough plus a fine collection of skin diseases, and who again has little difficulty getting people to pay him to go away; *Arnold Sideways*, who has no legs but gets around on a rickety four-wheeled cart; and the *Duck Man*, who's actually completely sane and who knows that he doesn't have a duck permanently sitting on his head, whatever the rest of the world chooses to believe. *Altogether Andrews*, a recent addition, suffers from multiple personalities – eight in total, one of whom, Burke, is regarded with fear by the rest of the Crew, being a dangerous psychotic. Fortunately, the other seven keep Burke out of sight.

Members of the Crew generally have below-average attributes, no discernible advantages apart from Resistant to Disease (they *are* still alive, after all), truly stupendous disadvantages, and no skills to speak of except Panhandling, Urban Survival, and maybe a bit of Current Affairs (Ankh-Morpork) – although Arnold Sideways is said to be a terror in street brawls (his teeth are at groin level), and some of Altogether Andrews' personalities may have unexpected (or, in Burke's case, merely horrible) talents. However, they could represent useful Contacts – they see and hear things while people look straight through them or try to ignore them – if someone were willing to take a stab at interpreting their ramblings. Some of them also convey street-level gossip to the Patrician from time to time, although Vetinari, always careful with his finite funds, may neglect to pay for this.

Should the PCs seek to do the Crew serious harm, they may find this unexpectedly difficult. Aside from the fact that the Beggars' Guild might decide to object, the Crew are part of Ankh-Morpork's narrative structure. *Reality* might decide to object.

The Watch

Ankh-Morpork's City Watch has evolved dramatically in recent years, from a small group of no-hopers led by a drunk to a competent law-enforcement agency. The odd thing is, the no-hopers are still on the strength and the drunk remains in charge, although he has sobered up.

Another peculiar fact is that, when members of a previously rare nonhuman race begin to show up in Ankh-Morpork, it has become more-or-less customary for some of the first of them to be recruited into the Watch. This means that there's somewhere for those initial, strange and widely mistrusted individuals to find work, and it ensures that the Watch has members who understand the race's peculiarities when others of them begin getting into trouble. The problem with this is ensuring that these early recruits become trustworthy and competent watchmen – but so far, the combination of Commander Vimes' training and Captain Carrot's charisma has always been up to the task.

Commander Samuel Vimes (The Duke of Ankh)

460 points

Samuel Vimes' ascent from lowly policeman to, by most measures, second-most-powerful man in Ankh-Morpork has been one of the most spectacular recent phenomena on the Disc. He was born in Cockbill Street (p. 253), which shows how poor his family was – but they had a long tradition of Watch membership and similar, going back to a distinguished ancestor, "Old Stoneface" Vimes, leader of the Ankh-Morpork Revolution of 1688, who executed the unspeakable King Lorenzo the Kind (p. 247) and was subsequently himself executed for regicide. Samuel signed up for the Watch in his teens.

He was always one of nature's honest coppers, never getting the hang of corruption. Some of his contemporaries worked their way up from street gangs to positions of power; he worked more sideways. Vimes' honesty, linked to a policeman's tendency to look closely at his surroundings, eventually drove him to drink (he has been described as being permanently slightly *knurd* when sober). He ended up in the Night Watch, which the Patrician was filling with no-hopers to keep it from causing trouble, and became captain because no other candidates existed. In game terms, he definitely had Alcoholism (pp. 54-55) at this point, and was Status 0, his Watch Rank 4 just compensating for the low general Status of watchmen at the time.

However, events then turned Vimes completely around. He met Lady Sybil Ramkin (p. 320) – the richest woman in the city – when he consulted her about a dragon-related problem, and they fell in love and married. He still considers the money and social position to be hers, but she is an old-fashioned woman and assigned her entire property to him. Thus, his nominal wealth became phenomenal – the character sheet below may seriously underestimate it, given that the Ramkin estates are said to generate $7 million *a year,* though a lot of that goes to maintaining the family homes, the Sunshine Sanctuary for Sick Dragons, and the Lady Sybil Free Hospital, and Vimes has never used it much.

As well, Vimes defeated his Alcoholism by force of will and through his more powerful addiction: to police work. The situations where he might be most likely to drink are precisely those where his obsession with justice drives him to keep a clear head. This made the disadvantage Withdrawn and subsequently converted it to the Former Alcoholic quirk.

With the Watch restored to some kind of respectability, Vimes rose in Status – although his exact level was uncertain for a while, especially as most of high society regarded him with disdain. After he helped foil two serious plots against the city, though, he was given a knighthood (Status 2 or 3). At first it was assumed that entering the upper classes would remove Vimes from the Watch, but instead, he received the newly resurrected position of Watch Commander. While his wealth meant that he could move in the highest level of society, many of the aristocracy can never forget his origins or forgive his blunt code of honour (which amuses the Patrician).

Vimes also renewed the skills which he'd learned through decades of police work, and he added some more. For example, his willingness to arrest even aristocrats led to more than one contract for the Assassins,

but Vimes survived – partly through sheer alertness and partly by booby-trapping his own home. He never found it necessary to terminate any of his uninvited visitors; they left chastened but not seriously damaged, although in some cases they left tied up, on ships heading for distant parts of the Disc, with the captains paid off to keep them aboard for the voyage. This earned Vimes a great deal of respect from the Guild, and their price for attempts on his life rose rapidly.

In due course, the Patrician decided to move Vimes into a position of even greater power, as he served to balance other factions so effectively. He was appointed Duke of Ankh (Status 5) and the old official stain on his family name – its link to a regicide – was wiped away by some deft footwork by the Historians' Guild. Subsequently, the Assassins took him off their register, declaring that they would no longer accept contracts on him, which Vimes finds oddly worrying. Meanwhile, his reputation has spread across the Sto Plains and the Circle Sea, and maybe even beyond; people call him "Vetinari's Bulldog," regarding him as incorruptible and tenacious, even if they don't actually like him. Other cities are fond of recruiting watchmen whom he has trained, and really devious schemers sometimes make sure that he'll be obliged to confirm what they want people to know, because then no one will question it.

He remains a dedicated, if cynical and authoritarian, copper; he believes that everybody is guilty of something. (His cynicism is well enough known that people may play on it.) Within the Watch, Vimes is balanced by the more idealistic Captain Carrot. He has also served on diplomatic and military missions, which has given him a little more knowledge of the wider Disc and a glimmering of political insight. Mostly, though, he's sent to get something done by being blunt and undiplomatic.

Vimes has a straightforward manner, but there's more than one side to him. He subconsciously knows the perpetually alert, ruthless component which makes him deadly in street brawls as "the Beast," and the iron self-control which makes him play by the rules as "the Watchman." These are just metaphors, but given that the Watchman once sent a pre-human vengeance spirit packing, they're *powerful* metaphors.

While obliged to dress to suit his position, Vimes is at his most comfortable in uniform. His wife has given him a fine-quality crossbow; he appreciates its reliability. She has also presented him with a series of personal disorganisers (p. 160), which he at first found deeply annoying. However, the latest model has enough interesting features, and works well enough, that Vimes has grudgingly begun to find it helpful.

Vimes sometimes seems to have general Intolerance, but over time, he has demonstrated a grudging willingness to judge people as individuals, including accepting any and every species into the Watch. He despises anyone who deliberately exploits those weaker than themselves, though. For a long time, his big sticking-point was vampires, whom he distrusts for their manipulative tendencies and inclination to prey on others. He recognises that some vampires are citizens of Ankh-Morpork, so his duty includes protecting them so long as they don't go for anyone's throat, but he doesn't have to like it. He has now been obliged to accept *one* vampire, Sally von Humpeding (p. 328), into the Watch, and he puts up with her. (It doesn't hurt that she once saved his life.)

Lady Sybil Vimes

Lady Sybil Ramkin, heir to the noblest (that is, richest) family in Ankh-Morpork, seemingly went to the Quirm College for Young Ladies (see *Quirm*, pp. 232-233) with half of the female aristocrats of the Sto Plains and Uberwald. Her husband thinks of her correspondence circle as the Ladies Who Organise; she can exert huge amounts of indirect political pressure if she has time to write a few letters. She admits that *some* of her old schoolmates aren't nice people, though.

She never found men of her own class especially interesting, instead directing her considerable energies into her hobby: the breeding and care of swamp dragons (pp. 359-360). An acknowledged expert on the subject (+3 Reputation among dragon-fanciers), she has written several books on dragon diseases. This was what brought Sam Vimes to her door – and that acquaintance soon blossomed into romance. The Watch know and respect her; Ankh-Morpork high society regards her as *odd*, but her Status 5 means that they ignore that.

Some people think of her as fat, but she's just rugged, and passably handsome, although her chestnut hair is a wig (normal among those who keep dragons); her family bred for health, not chinlessness. She's tolerant and broad-minded, and rarely shocked by anything apart from cruelty to dragons. She isn't used to violence (sometimes suffering Post-Combat Shakes), and she worries about her husband's safety, but she doesn't let this show, and she handles crises well.

In games, she is a wonderful device for moving things along, with a combination of Status, high-mindedness, self-confidence, and the Penetrating Voice perk. She's willing and able to face down anybody, up to and including the Patrician, although he has worked out how to plant ideas in her mind. She has skill levels in the 10-13 range in "noble-lady" accomplishments such as Savoir-Faire and Singing (but *not* at knitting or darning socks, at which she's hopeless), and a 15 in anything to do with swamp dragons. She can't lie well (she turns red if she tries), but she's too skilled at refraining from telling the truth for this to be a serious problem.

Technically, she has no wealth of her own, having signed it all over to Sam. (She's old-fashioned that way.) In practise, though, "Filthy Rich" would barely describe the resources she can throw at a problem without even *thinking*.

A little while ago, Vimes was possessed by the Summoning Dark, a primordial vengeance demon known among the dwarfs and goblins. Although Vimes resisted and expelled the demon (a unique achievement, according to experts), it left its mark – literally, in the form of a scar on his wrist – and it may return on rare occasions, usually to push him into avenging some crime of darkness. It could give him all manner of abilities, including perfect dark vision and the ability to understand any language, or it might just offer him berserk fighting ability. However, Vimes wouldn't know how to summon it even if he wanted to, which he doesn't, and the Dark serves only its own inscrutable, vengeful concerns; thus, it's best treated as a very occasional plot device. A Dark-possessed Vimes should cause Fright Checks in many dwarfs.

ST 12 [20]; **DX** 12 [40]; **IQ** 12 [40]; **HT** 12 [20].
Damage 1d-1/1d+2; BL 29 lbs.; HP 12 [0]; Will 18 [30]; Per 14 [10]; FP 12 [0].
Basic Speed 6.00 [0]; Basic Move 6 [0]; Dodge 10*; Parry 12* (Brawling).
5'11"; 150 lbs.

SOCIAL BACKGROUND

TL: 4 [0].
CF: Sto Plains/Uberwald [0].
Languages: Dwarfish (Accented/Broken) [3]; Morporkian (Native) [0]; Trollish (Broken/None) [1].

ADVANTAGES

Combat Reflexes [15]; Danger Sense [15]; Extraordinary Luck [30]; Indomitable [15]; Legal Enforcement Powers [10]; Reputation +1 ("Vetinari's Bulldog") [5]; Resistant to Disease (+3) [3]; Status 5† [5]; Watch Rank 5 [25]; Wealth (Multimillionaire 3) [125].

Perks: Cobblestone Sense (Ankh-Morpork); Improvised Weapons (Brawling). [2]

DISADVANTAGES

Code of Honour (Watchman's) [-5]; Dependent (Infant Son; 0 or fewer points; Loved One; 6 or less) [-15]; Duty (The Watch; 12 or less) [-10]; Intolerance ("Exploiters") [-5]; Odious Personal Habit (Grumpy and Abrasive) [-5]; Reputation -2 (As an old and hated enemy, in the Ankh-Morpork underworld; 7 or less) [-1]; Reputation -3 ("Jumped-up rabble," among old-school Ankh-Morpork aristocrats) [-5].

Quirks: Chauvinistic; Dislikes royalists and social deference; Former Alcoholic; Hates obvious clues and classic detective stories; Throws himself into his duty, but avoids the paperwork. [-5]

SKILLS

Area Knowledge (Ankh-Morpork) (E) IQ+4 [12]-16; Brawling (E) DX+4 [12]-16; Criminology/TL4 (A) IQ+2 [8]-14; Crossbow (E) DX [1]-12; Current Affairs/TL4 (Ankh-Morpork) (E) IQ [1]-12; Fast-Draw (Knuckledusters) (E) DX+2 [2]-14*; Holdout (A) IQ-1 [1]-11; Intimidation (A) Will-1 [1]-17; Knot-Tying (E) DX+2 [4]-14; Law (Ankh-Morpork Police) (H) IQ-2 [1]-10; Leadership (A) IQ+4 [16]-16; Observation (A) Per-1 [1]-13; Savoir-Faire (Watch) (E) IQ+2 [4]-14; Search (A) Per [2]-14; Shortsword (A) DX [2]-12; Stealth (A) DX [2]-12; Streetwise (A) IQ [2]-12; Tactics (H) IQ [4]-12; Teaching (A) IQ+2 [8]-14; Traps/TL4 (A) IQ+1 [4]-13; Urban Survival (A) Per-1 [1]-13; Wrestling (A) DX+2 [8]-14.

* Includes +1 for Combat Reflexes.
† Includes +1 Status from Rank and +3 from Wealth.

NOTES

Vimes' son ("Young Sam") is classified as a Dependent because an enemy did once try to strike at Vimes that way. It was an incredibly stupid thing to do, though, and isn't very likely to happen again unless someone *wants* to tip Vimes over the edge into insane vengefulness. Still, Vimes might sometimes get distracted from his work by the need to look after his family; he used to make a point of *always* getting home to read a bedtime story. His wife isn't treated as a Dependent because people would know that it was just as stupid an idea to go after her, and she can look after herself.

Captain Carrot

430 points

Carrot Ironfoundersson was brought up as the adoptive son of the "king" of a Ramtops dwarf mine, having been discovered as a baby amidst the remains of a human travelling-party that had been wiped out by bandits. Affectionate-but-practical dwarfish family life, lots of mountain air, hard work down the mine, and good plain food produced a young man who was built like a tree; it did not, however, produce a dwarf. Come puberty, this caused problems, so someone suggested that he seek his fortune in human society. Rumour, centuries out of date, suggested that the Ankh-Morpork City Watch offered an admirable career.

When Carrot arrived in the city, he still possessed dwarfish absolute literal-mindedness and had spent the trip from the mountains memorising the city's laws. As the Night Watch was then at its lowest ebb, this led to conceptual dissonance – Carrot persistently tried to arrest criminals and enforce laws. However, a couple of problems appeared for which his talents proved a useful solution, and gradually, he learned to understand people in general and Ankh-Morpork in particular a little better. What emerged through this was a mind of peculiar precision; Carrot tends to solve problems by direct but very effective means, uncluttered by presuppositions. Thus, when the Watch was reorganised, Carrot was made a captain.

Carrot's true ancestry remains generally unknown, but a number of people have observed his apparently congenital charisma, the old but *extremely* effective sword that was found with him by the dwarfs (a *very fine* shortsword, although it doesn't look it), his instinctive love for Ankh-Morpork, the crown-shaped birthmark on his left arm, and the content of some ancient prophecies. They strongly suspect that he's the city's rightful king. This idea used to be known to only a few people, but by now it has become an open secret. There has even been supporting documentary evidence. However, Carrot himself takes the view that kings aren't what the city needs these days, and he has destroyed any such documents that he can get his hands on.

Carrot has short red hair and walks with a slight stoop due to his mine upbringing (his dwarf name, *Kzad-bhat*, means "Head Banger"). His clean-living nature is such that he can actually swear audibly in asterisks ("Oh, *****!"), on the rare occasions when he shows that much annoyance. He mostly seems cool-headed and controlled about his romantic involvement with Captain Angua (pp. 322-324), but he *did* once resign his post and leave the city to follow her. Mind you, Commander Vimes was off in the same direction on city business, Ankh-Morpork was relatively quiet at the time, and Carrot must have known at heart that he'd be able to walk back into his job.

Carrot is a terror in combat, with weapons or fists, although his honourable nature occasionally trips him up. His intelligence is difficult to assess. When he first arrived in Ankh-Morpork, he seemed almost simpleminded, but he soaks up knowledge like a sponge, and his simplicity sometimes shows him the direct route to an answer, uncluttered by complications. Conversely, some of his remarks seem naïve at first, but hint at deep ambiguities and subtleties; even his friends aren't sure what to make of them. Certainly, things seem to just *work* for him, though that might be luck. In fact, he may have a mystical destiny as a Rightful King, with all that entails – charisma, good fortune, the ability to show up whenever the city needs saving – which is continuing to work for him despite his refusal to let it make him any more than a captain of the Watch.

His spelling and writing style remain a little eccentric, although that isn't unusual in a society which hasn't had printing for long enough to flatten out variations.

ST 17 [70]; **DX** 13 [60]; **IQ** 12 [40]; **HT** 14 [40].
Damage 1d+2/3d-1; BL 58 lbs.; HP 17 [0]; Will 14 [10]; Per 13 [5]; FP 14 [0].
Basic Speed 7.00 [5]; Basic Move 6 [-5]; Dodge 11*; Parry 11* (Axe, Boxing, or Shortsword).
6'6"; 250 lbs.

SOCIAL BACKGROUND

TL: 4 [0].
CF: Dwarfish [0]; Sto Plains/Uberwald [1].
Languages: Dwarfish (Native/Accented) [-1]; Klatchian (Accented/Broken) [3]; Morporkian (Native/Accented) [5]; Uberwaldian (Broken) [2].

ADVANTAGES

Charisma 4 [20]; Combat Reflexes [15]; Contact (Gaspode the Wonder Dog; Tracking-18; 12 or less; Completely Reliable) [18]; Eidetic Memory [5]; High Pain Threshold [10]; Indomitable [15]; Legal Enforcement Powers [10]; Less Sleep 2 [4]; Luck [15]; Night Vision 2 [2]; Reputation +1 ("That nice Captain Carrot who may be the Rightful King," among Ankh-Morpork natives) [2]; Resistant to Disease (+3) [3]; Sense of the City 3 (Ankh-Morpork) [15]; Serendipity 1 [15]; Status 1† [0]; Unusual Background (Raised by Dwarfs) [5]; Watch Rank 4 [20]; Wealth (Comfortable) [10].

Perks: Off-Hand Training (Throwing); Understands the Librarian. [2]

DISADVANTAGES

Duty (The Watch; 12 or less) [-10]; Honesty (9) [-15]; Pacifism (Cannot Harm Innocents) [-10]; Sense of Duty (Ankh-Morpork) [-10].

Quirks: Clean-living – usually teetotal, fights as fair as possible, swears in asterisks if at all; Literal-minded and occasionally boringly fact-obsessed; Pays close attention to the Watchman's Code of Honour and is loyal to Angua, but the city comes first; Rarely tells direct lies; Writes home regularly. [-5]

SKILLS

Acrobatics (H) DX-2 [1]-11; Area Knowledge (Ankh-Morpork) (E) IQ+5 [4]-17‡; Axe/Mace (A) DX+1 [4]-14; Bow (A) DX-1 [1]-12; Boxing (A) DX+2 [8]-15; Crossbow (E) DX [1]-13; Current Affairs/TL4 (Ankh-Morpork) (E) IQ+4 [2]-16‡; Engineer/TL3 (Mining) (H) IQ-2 [1]-10; First Aid/TL4 (Human) (E) IQ [1]-12; Games (Old-Fashioned Football Rules) (E) IQ [1]-12; Games (Sport Boxing Rules) (E) IQ+1 [2]-13; Hidden Lore (Secrets of Ankh-Morpork) (A) IQ+2 [1]-14‡; History (Ankh-Morpork) (H) IQ+1 [1]-13‡; Intimidation (A) Will-1 [1]-13; Knot-Tying (E) DX [1]-13; Law (Ankh-Morpork Criminal) (H) IQ+2 [12]-14; Leadership (A) IQ+3 [1]-15§; Observation (A) Per+1 [4]-14; Savoir-Faire (Watch) (E) IQ [1]-12; Search (A) Per-1 [1]-12; Shortsword (A) DX+1 [4]-14; Teaching (A) IQ-1 [1]-11; Teamster (Equines) (A) IQ [2]-12; Throwing (A) DX [2]-13; Thrown Weapon (Axe/Mace) (E) DX [1]-13.

* Includes +1 for Combat Reflexes.
† Free from Rank.
‡ Includes +3 for Sense of the City.
§ Includes +4 for Charisma.

NOTES

When Carrot first arrived in Ankh-Morpork, he suffered from Literal-Mindedness and naivety amounting to full Truthfulness, and some of his skills were lower (along with his Rank). His Honesty is left over from that time; he tries to obey the confused and largely moribund laws of Ankh-Morpork, and he has read and absorbed all of them. He arguably still has Truthfulness, but he chooses his words so effectively when necessary that this doesn't limit him significantly in practise.

Carrot's Unusual Background does more than allow him to have dwarfish as well as human Cultural Familiarities. In the minds of most dwarfs – some ultra-traditionalists aside – he *is* a dwarf, under dwarf law. Thus, he can talk to dwarfs about matters they would simply never discuss with outsiders.

Carrot arguably has an enormous number of Contacts across Ankh-Morpork, but for the most part this is covered by Charisma,

Area Knowledge, and Current Affairs; he knows who to ask, and they tend to answer. Taking Gaspode as a Contact might seem superfluous when he has Angua on his team, but sometimes, a second opinion (and a second nose) with *really* low-level knowledge of the streets is useful. Gaspode protests volubly when Carrot asks him for help, but he would be unlikely to refuse, let alone betray Carrot.

"And you're a wolf and human at the same time, right? Tricky, that. I can see that. Bit of a dichotomy, sort of thing."
– Gaspode to Angua, in Men at Arms

Captain Angua

383 points

The daughter of an Uberwaldian werewolf-baron, Delphine Angua von Uberwald rebelled against the aristocratic werewolf tendency to treat neighbours as lunch on the hoof, left home, and wandered the Disc for a while before joining the Watch. Shortly after doing so, she formed a relationship with Captain Carrot (pp. 321-322). She remains worried by her wolf side, which sometimes takes the odd chicken (for which Angua *always* pays, anonymously), but she seems to have become more confident in her ability to control it.

She may not quite have shed the feeling that she might have to move on eventually, but she's an important figure in Ankh-Morpork and the Watch these days, and not just as a peerless tracker and searcher; she recently made captain. She knows that her feelings for Carrot may resemble a dog's attitude toward its beloved master – what *is* a dog but a domesticated wolf? – but she has come to terms with this.

Angua mostly operates either as a human or a wolf. The third, "wolf-woman" form on her character sheet actually represents her ability to shift shape slightly from moment to moment in a fight in search of a killing advantage from human or wolf features, but about the only time she has employed this was in a deadly brawl with her brother, who also used the trick. Angua doesn't *like* people to see her changing or part-changed; she's presentable enough as human or wolf, but the intermediate stage is blatantly monstrous. She even makes Carrot look away and close his eyes, fearing that he would be disturbed. Probably the only being who gets to watch her change is Gaspode the Wonder Dog (pp. 316-317), with whom she has formed a kind of friendship; he's used to disturbing sights (often as his dinner), and anyway it would be hard to stop him.

It is *not* universally known that Angua is a werewolf – although most of the Watch and a number of other people are aware of it, so it can't count as a Secret. It *is* well known that the Watch *has* such a tracker, and the city's criminal classes have responded by employing "bombs" filled with aniseed, peppermint, or other strong smells to cover their own scent.

Many people think that the werewolf must be Nobby Nobbs (p. 327) if only because they can't see any other reason why Vimes keeps him around. Angua goes along with this accidental deception.

As a human, Angua is a very striking ash-blonde woman. Her athletic figure and long hair add to her attractiveness, although her colleagues (aside from Carrot) have learned not to pay too much attention to this. She still has slight problems with self-confidence; she gets irritated by vampires, especially attractive females like Sally von Humpeding (p. 328), who she thinks of as better-looking than herself because they're so damned *confident.*

She has always been an effective instinctive fighter, and informal Watch training in streetfighting has enhanced this. However, she's no more than competent with weapons; she prefers to rely on quick wits and, frankly, good looks – or *in extremis,* her wolf form – to resolve problems. Socially, she's likeable, if sarcastic, with a stock of off-colour jokes that shock her colleagues, but she sometimes tires of being treated as an honorary male. Her attractiveness carries over to her wolf form, making her a good-looking canine; humans often think she resembles some kind of pedigree wolfhound. Her nonhuman forms aren't as intelligent as she is as a human, but because she's learned to use her brain in any form, they're brighter than an ordinary animal.

ST 11 [10]; **DX** 13 [60]; **IQ** 11 [20]; **HT** 12 [20].
Damage 1d-1/1d+1; BL 24 lbs.; HP 11 [0]; Will 11 [0];
Per 13 [10]; FP 12 [0].
Basic Speed 6.25 [0]; Basic Move 6 [0]; Dodge 9; Parry 11 (Brawling).
5'8"; 145 lbs.

SOCIAL BACKGROUND

TL: 4 [0].
CF: Sto Plains/Uberwald [0].
Languages: Canine (Native/None) [3]; Morporkian (Native) [6]; Uberwaldian (Native) [0].

ADVANTAGES

Alternate Form (Wolf-Woman*; Once On, Stays On; Reduced Change Time, 1 second) [134]; Alternate Form (Wolf†; Once On, Stays On; Reduced Change Time, 2 seconds; Uncontrollable, 8 nights in a month and if touched directly by moonlight) [29]; Appearance (Beautiful) [12]; Contact (Gaspode the Wonder Dog;

Hidden Lore (Dark Corners of Ankh-Morpork)-12; 12 or less; Somewhat Reliable) [2]; Discriminatory Smell [15]; Legal Enforcement Powers [10]; Resistant to Disease (+3) [3]; Status 1‡ [0]; Watch Rank 4 [20]; Wealth (Comfortable) [10].
Perks: Good with Dogs. [1]

DISADVANTAGES

Berserk (15) [-5]; Duty (The Watch; 12 or less) [-10]; Sense of Duty (Captain Carrot) [-2].
Quirks: Doesn't let any human watch her transformation or see her in "wolf-woman" form if she can help it; Respects other people's secrets; Respects the Watchman's Code of Honour; Slightly insecure. [-4]

SKILLS

Acrobatics (H) DX-1 [2]-12; Area Knowledge (Ankh-Morpork) (E) IQ [1]-11; Brawling (E) DX+3 [8]-16; Carousing (E) HT+1 [2]-13; Criminology/TL4 (A) IQ-1 [1]-10; Crossbow (E) DX [1]-13; Intimidation (A) Will-1 [1]-10; Jumping (E) DX+1 [2]-14; Law (Ankh-Morpork Police) (H) IQ-2 [1]-9; Naturalist (H) IQ [4]-11; Observation (A) Per-1 [1]-12; Savoir-Faire (Watch) (E) IQ+1 [2]-12; Search (A) Per-1 [1]-12; Shortsword (A) DX-1 [1]-12; Stealth (A) DX [2]-13; Streetwise (A) IQ-1 [1]-10; Survival (Mountain) (A) Per-1 [1]-12; Survival (Plains) (A) Per-1 [1]-12; Survival (Woodlands) (A) Per+1 [4]-14; Tracking (A) Per+4 [2]-17§.

* Start with *Wolfman* (p. 114); remove Discriminatory Smell; add IQ-2, Will+1, Regeneration (Slow, Not vs. Fire or Silver), Social Stigma (Monster), and Unkillable 1 (Achilles Heel, Fire; Achilles Heel, Silver); improve Per+3 to Per+4. Form cost: 99 points.
† Start with *Wolf* (p. 115); remove Discriminatory Smell; add IQ-2, Will+2, Regeneration (Regular, Not vs. Fire or Silver), Social Stigma (Valuable Property), and Unkillable 1 (Achilles Heel, Fire; Achilles Heel, Silver); enhance personal Discriminatory Smell with Emotion Sense; improve Per+4 to Per+6. Form cost: 66 points.
‡ Free from Rank.
§ Includes +4 for Discriminatory Smell.

"WOLF-WOMAN" FORM

This summary represents Angua in her "transitional" form.

ST 14; **DX** 15; **IQ** 9; **HT** 14.
Damage 1d/2d; BL 39 lbs.; HP 14; Will 10; Per 15; FP 14.
Basic Speed 7.25; Basic Move 9; Dodge 10; Parry 12 (Brawling).
5'10"; 145 lbs.

Social Background

TL: 4.
CF: Sto Plains/Uberwald.
Languages: Canine (Native/None); Morporkian (Native); Uberwaldian (Native).

Advantages

Claws (Sharp Claws); Contact (Gaspode the Wonder Dog; Hidden Lore (Dark Corners of Ankh-Morpork)-12; 12 or less; Somewhat Reliable); Damage Resistance 1 (Tough Skin); Discriminatory Smell; High Pain Threshold; Night Vision 2; Regeneration (Slow, Not vs. Fire or Silver); Resistant to Disease (+3); Teeth (Sharp Teeth); Temperature Tolerance 1 (Cold); Ultrahearing; Unkillable 1 (Achilles Heel, Fire; Achilles Heel, Silver).

Perks: Fur; Good with Dogs.

Disadvantages

Appearance (Unattractive); Bad Grip 2; Berserk (15); Duty (The Watch; 12 or less); Sense of Duty (Captain Carrot); Social Stigma (Monster); Vulnerability (Silver Weapons ×2).

Quirks: Doesn't let any human watch her transformation or see her in "wolf-woman" form if she can help it; Doggy Responses; Hunter's Habits; Respects other people's secrets; Respects the Watchman's Code of Honour; Silver Aversion; Slightly insecure.

Skills

Acrobatics-14; Area Knowledge (Ankh-Morpork)-9; Brawling-18; Criminology/TL4-8; Intimidation-9; Jumping-16; Law (Ankh-Morpork Police)-7; Naturalist-9; Observation-14; Savoir-Faire (Watch)-10; Search-14; Stealth-15; Streetwise-8; Survival (Mountain)-14; Survival (Plains)-14; Survival (Woodlands)-16; Tracking-15.

WOLF FORM

This is Angua when she has shifted to wolf shape.

ST 11; **DX** 15; **IQ** 9; **HT** 14.
Damage 1d-1/1d+1; BL 24 lbs.; HP 11; Will 11; Per 17; FP 14.
Basic Speed 7.25; Basic Move 7; Dodge 10; Parry 12 (Brawling).
2'6" at shoulder; 145 lbs.

Social Background

TL: 4.
CF: Sto Plains/Uberwald.
Languages: Canine (Native/None); Morporkian (Native); Uberwaldian (Native).

Advantages

Appearance (Beautiful); Contact (Gaspode the Wonder Dog; Hidden Lore (Dark Corners of Ankh-Morpork)-12; 12 or less; Somewhat Reliable); Damage Resistance 1 (Tough Skin); Discriminatory Smell (Emotion Sense); Enhanced Move 1/2 (Ground Speed 10); High Pain Threshold; Night Vision 2; Regeneration (Regular, Not vs. Fire or Silver); Resistant to Disease (+3); Teeth (Sharp Teeth); Temperature Tolerance 1 (Cold); Ultrahearing; Unkillable 1 (Achilles Heel, Fire; Achilles Heel, Silver); Watch Rank 4.

Perks: Fur; Good with Dogs.

Disadvantages

Berserk (15); Cannot Speak; Duty (The Watch; 12 or less); Quadruped; Sense of Duty (Captain Carrot); Short Legs; Social Stigma (Valuable Property); Vulnerability (Silver Weapons ×2).

Quirks: Doesn't let any human watch her transformation or see her in "wolf-woman" form if she can help it; Doggy Responses; Hunter's Habits; Respects other people's secrets; Respects the Watchman's Code of Honour; Silver Aversion; Slightly insecure.

Skills

Acrobatics-14; Area Knowledge (Ankh-Morpork)-9; Brawling-18; Criminology/TL4-8; Intimidation-10; Jumping-16; Law (Ankh-Morpork Police)-7; Naturalist-9; Observation-16; Savoir-Faire (Watch)-10; Search-16; Stealth-15; Streetwise-8; Survival (Mountain)-16; Survival (Plains)-16; Survival (Woodlands)-18; Tracking-21.

NOTES

Angua has Discriminatory Smell as a personal advantage, so it's deleted from the templates for her Alternate Forms. However, her wolf form gains the Emotion Sense version, and she hence pays the difference in cost from the basic trait (8 points).

If Angua's Berserk is triggered, she's likely to shift to wolf form. The disadvantage actually represents her bestial side emerging under extreme stress, and she instinctively regards that as her fighting shape. She prefers to suppress this instinct and fight intelligently, but anyone near her during life-or-death moments may notice her jaws and fingernails growing more prominent.

Most important, Angua is the kind of high-powered werewolf who, when in nonhuman form, can only be killed permanently by silver or fire (or perhaps by being hacked and pulverised to bloody fragments if you want to get gruesome). Her injuries from sources other than those also heal supernaturally fast – fastest when she's in wolf form, merely quite quickly when she's in the intermediate form which has more of the human to it. Fortunately, there aren't *too* many silver weapons around. On the other hand, fire, from burning torches to collapsing barns, is an all-too-traditional response to monsters; while it's relatively rare as a weapon in Ankh-Morpork, mostly because it's such a threat to buildings, it's rather common as an accidental phenomenon.

Lastly, Angua is shrewd as well as observant, and she has learned to use her brain on Watch business. Her IQ may rise to 12 – making that of her alternate forms 10 – in later parts of the chronicles.

Sergeant Colon

48 points

In another life, Frederick Colon might have become a pork butcher or a schoolteacher. As it was, he joined an army somewhere on the Sto Plains, and he rose to his natural rank of sergeant (he isn't any sort of warrior, but overweight, steady, pipe-smoking, perspiration-prone individuals fit into the backwaters of NCO duty). He subsequently signed up with the Night Watch, where he has spent more than 30 years. His wife worked days while he worked nights, so they communicated mostly by notes, but somehow they produced a family. With the recent restoration of the Watch's standing in the city, Colon's rank of sergeant has pushed him to borderline Status 1, which his Watch pay just about supports, but he's really a very ordinary member of society.

He's often found guarding the Brass Bridge or the Opera House. They might be hard to steal, but any bold thief who tries will have to deal with Fred Colon. He avoids combat (though he did win prizes for archery in his youth); as he can't run, he mostly spends time thinking about safe choices. After one occasion when Colon and Nobby (p. 327) came in useful, the Patrician created a Watch traffic division, and moved them into that safe, quiet, trivially corrupt duty, where Colon still often serves.

At other times, Vimes employs Colon's knowledge of the streets, and his steadiness helps with new recruits. He's happy in a rut, though, and can't handle serious responsibility.

Recent changes in the Watch have left Colon trailing somewhat, and he *is* pushing 60. Thus, he has talked about retiring, and at one point thought about buying a farm, despite his complete ignorance of agronomy. However, some traumatic experiences in the Ankh-Morpork cattle-yards changed his mind; he's now determined to stay in the Watch for as long as possible.

ST 9 [-10]; **DX** 10 [0]; **IQ** 10 [0]; **HT** 9 [-10].

Damage 1d-2/1d-1; BL 16 lbs.; HP 11 [4]; Will 10 [0]; Per 11 [5]; FP 9 [0].

Basic Speed 5.00 [5]; Basic Move 4 [-5]; Dodge 8; Parry 8 (Brawling). 5'10"; 210 lbs.

SOCIAL BACKGROUND

TL: 4 [0].
CF: Sto Plains/Uberwald [0].
Languages: Morporkian (Native) [0].

ADVANTAGES

Legal Enforcement Powers [10]; Night Vision 1 [1]; Resistant to Disease (+3) [3]; Status 1* [0]; Watch Rank 3 [15].

DISADVANTAGES

Cowardice (15) [-5]; Duty (The Watch; 12 or less; Nonhazardous) [-5]; Fat [-3].

Quirks: Borderline Clueless; Chauvinistic; Dull; Habitual pipe smoker; Pays some attention to the Watch Code of Honour. [-5]

SKILLS

Area Knowledge (Ankh-Morpork) (E) IQ+4 [12]-14; Bow (A) DX+1 [4]-11; Brawling (E) DX [1]-10; Broadsword (A) DX-1 [1]-9; Carousing (E) HT [1]-9; Crossbow (E) DX [1]-10; Current Affairs/TL4 (Ankh-Morpork) (E) IQ+1 [2]-11; First Aid/TL3 (Human) (E) IQ [1]-10; Savoir-Faire (Military) (E) IQ+1 [2]-11; Savoir-Faire (Watch) (E) IQ+3 [8]-13; Soldier/TL4 (A) IQ+1 [4]-11; Spear (A) DX-1 [1]-9; Sports (Darts) (A) DX+1 [4]-11; Streetwise (A) IQ [2]-10; Teaching (A) IQ+1 [4]-11.

* Free from Rank.

NOTES

Colon might be considered to have numerous Contacts around Ankh-Morpork, mostly men of similar age and physique to himself. However, what he gets from them is general background gossip, so this is subsumed into his Area Knowledge, Current Affairs, and Streetwise. His wife and family aren't treated as Dependents because they never become involved in

his work. His Duty to the Watch is considered Nonhazardous because he does mostly avoid risk – the occasions when he's been in danger were isolated accidents.

Sergeant Detritus

285 points

Detritus is, or at least used to be, a troll's troll – a creature with an uncomplicated nature and the ability to punch through walls. He was born in the mountains of Uberwald, but his family migrated to Ankh-Morpork when he was "just a pebble," and he thinks of himself as belonging to the city.

When he grew up, he found work as a splatter (see *Ruffian*, pp. 127-128) at the Mended Drum (pp. 264-265), where he was chained to the wall between the times when he had to hit someone. Later, he was employed in the short-lived Discworld motion picture industry, in which time he met a troll singer named Ruby. Love inspired him to improve himself, and he signed up with the Watch when it began to expand. His biggest problem at that time was a tendency to punch himself out when saluting. He has stuck with the Watch and become one of their best officers, both patrolling the streets and working as a drill sergeant. Holding down a job that needs more than brute force, and dealing with complicated issues of police work, have obliged him to learn to use his brain more; while he's still often *assumed* to be trollishly stupid, even by his colleagues, he sometimes shows flashes of striking shrewdness.

It's also very hard to misdirect Detritus – his physical and mental inertia are too great. He has a trollish resistance to boredom, which makes him good at interrogations; he keeps asking the same questions ("You dunnit, didn't you?") until the suspect cracks and promises to talk if Detritus will just explain what he's supposed to talk *about*. While he was completely illiterate when he joined the Watch, he can now read and write, with a little effort. His marriage to Ruby remains happy but childless, which may explain his tendency to act as a father figure to younger trolls, especially watchmen. His Sense of Duty might be considered to encompass them these days. On the other hand, he shows mild contempt towards trolls who remain unthinkingly violent.

ST 19* [27†]; **DX** 12 [40]; **IQ** 9* [20]; **HT** 13* [10].

Damage 2d-1/3d+1; BL 180 lbs.; HP 19 [0]; Will 11 [10]; Per 10* [0]; FP 13 [0].

Basic Speed 6.25 [0]; Basic Move 6 [0]; Dodge 10‡; Parry 11‡ (Brawling).

6'6"; 480 lbs. (SM +1*).

SOCIAL BACKGROUND

TL: 4 [0].
CF: Sto Plains/Uberwald [1]; Trollish [0].
Languages: Morporkian (Native/Accented) [5]; Trollish (Native/Broken) [-2]; Uberwaldian (Broken/None) [1].

NOTES

When on duty, Detritus wears Watch-issue armour (DR 1) and carries a club in the form of a large truncheon. If the situation demands, he brings along a *special* crossbow (see below). He also has a helmet – made for him by a dwarf friend (now deceased) – which incorporates a complex mechanism that can cool his brain, temporarily giving him a point or two of extra IQ. If he sits down to think, this *sometimes* enables him to achieve remarkable results. He may switch this on if anyone tries to talk their way past him.

Piecemaker

Detritus has adapted a siege engine for use as a personal weapon. *Piecemaker* is effectively an overpowered troll crossbow (p. 154) with an integral winding mechanism, increasing weight to 25 lbs. and minimum ST to fire it accurately to 18. It requires all Detritus' strength to draw, taking 40 seconds between shots. It discharges a whole sheaf of arrows at once, which often splinter and sometimes catch fire as they leave the crossbow. This gives +6 to hit, but reduces Acc to 3.

Targets within five yards are hit as if by a single blast. Treat this as 12d of huge piercing damage – or just assume that anything hit (up to and including reinforced doors and stone walls) *disappears*. At longer ranges, the target is struck by one arrow, *plus* one for every point by which the attack roll is made (e.g., if Detritus needs a 13 to hit and rolls 9, five arrows hit); each does 1d+1 impaling. People or objects near to or behind the target will probably be hit by other arrows, at the GM's whim.

Detritus sometimes carries Piecemaker ready to fire if he expects serious trouble, or just to intimidate annoying people – a practise that causes every other watchman around to stand well behind him. Somehow, his forgetfulness regarding the safety catch has never caused any disasters, although there have been several near-misses. This good luck might be regarded as a perk or simply unusually benevolent narrative at work.

ADVANTAGES

Combat Reflexes [15]; Damage Resistance 6* [5]; Legal Enforcement Powers [10]; Lifting ST 11* [19†]; Moderate-Sized Troll [83]; Reputation +2 (For a *really impressive* punch, among Ankh-Morpork trolls; 10 or less) [2]; Watch Rank 3 [15].

DISADVANTAGES

Code of Honour (Watchman's) [-5]; Duty (The Watch; 12 or less) [-10]; Sense of Duty (Ruby) [-2]; Status 0§ [-5].

Quirks: Dull; Hates troll drug dealers. [-2]

SKILLS

Area Knowledge (Ankh-Morpork) (E) IQ+2 [4]-11; Armoury/TL4 (Missile Weapons) (A) IQ-1 [1]-8; Axe/Mace (A) DX [2]-12; Brawling (E) DX+3 [6]-15*; Broadsword (A) DX [2]-12; Criminology/TL4 (A) IQ-1 [1]-8; Crossbow (E) DX [1]-12; Current Affairs/TL4 (Ankh-Morpork) (E) IQ+1 [2]-10; Forced Entry (E) DX+1 [2]-13; Intimidation (A) Will+1 [4]-12; Law (Ankh-Morpork Police) (H) IQ-1 [2]-8; Leadership (A) IQ [2]-9; Polearm (A) DX-1 [1]-11; Savoir-Faire (Watch) (E) IQ+2 [4]-11; Search (A) Per-1 [1]-9; Streetwise (A) IQ-1 [1]-8; Teaching (A) IQ+3 [12]-12.

* Modified for racial template.
† With 10% cost reduction for SM +1.
‡ Includes +1 for Combat Reflexes.
§ Bought down from free level from Rank.

Sergeant Cheery Littlebottom

Cheery (or Cheri) Littlebottom came to Ankh-Morpork from Uberwald in search of a new life; she didn't enjoy traditional

dwarf occupations such as mining or metalwork. After a brief, embarrassing, but not unusual misunderstanding about the Guild of Seamstresses, she joined the Alchemists' Guild. However, she then blew up the Guild Council, and they hinted that she should go and find a job elsewhere. (She seems to have learned her lesson, though, and rarely causes explosions these days.) By chance, the Watch were looking for a forensic alchemist, and Cheery was recruited.

Cheery then met Angua (pp. 322-324), who recognised her as female by scent. Talking to Angua about her problems led Cheery to decide to be true to herself, and she came out publicly as female – probably the first dwarf in the city to do so. She took to wearing a leather skirt, welding slightly higher heels onto her boots, and sticking glitter on her dress axe.

Since then, she has learned about general police work and earned promotion to sergeant. With an Igor now on the staff, the Watch needs her scientific skills less often, so she frequently acts as an orderly to Commander Vimes (Administration-12). She still isn't supposed to take part in street-level operations, but when she has done so, her solid intelligence (IQ 12) has proved more than sufficient. She's likely to be encountered at the scene of strange or mysterious crimes, with a bag of alchemical equipment and an iconograph in hand, seeking evidence (with Alchemy/TL4-14, Criminology/TL4-11, Metallurgy/TL4-11, Natural Philosophy/TL4-10, Photography-12, Poisons/TL4-12, Research/TL4-11, and Search-13). She rarely gets into fights, but if she loses her temper, her dwarfish nature can overcome her dislike of violence. She still carries that axe, after all (Axe/Mace-10).

Socially, Cheery mostly associates with Angua and other female officers, although she's still getting the hang of human socialising; she finds it weird to watch, but interesting. She doesn't mind drinking, in moderation, but prefers cocktails to beer.

Corporal Nobbs

-7 points

Cecil Wormsborough St John ("Nobby") Nobbs was born and brought up in an especially sordid Ankh-Morpork cellar. He eventually decided to leave home and spent a period in the army of the Duke of Pseudopolis. Unfortunately, they made him their quartermaster.

Normally, Nobby restricts himself to petty theft, but he's *instinctively* dishonest; he allegedly stole the entire inventory. (This may have been when he acquired his interest in the fine details of weapons technology.) Following the ensuing disaster, he returned home and joined the Watch. He somehow became a corporal, which suits him – in a force with more regulations, he would be a barracks-room lawyer.

He has stayed in the Watch despite its recent improvements; it's loyal to its members, and he now shares traffic work with Fred Colon (pp. 324-325). Commander Vimes also uses the pair as a source of news from the streets. Nobby somehow gets on with people, despite everything – they tend to see him as "colourful." Even the rest of the Watch almost like him, although whenever a crime appears to be the work of a warped criminal mind, they do wonder.

Nobby has one principle: Never Volunteer. He has dived headfirst through a plate glass window sooner than accept responsibility. There's some evidence that he's actually the rightful Earl of Ankh, but since he learned that this might imply *duties*, he has ignored it. His Duty to the Watch is considered Nonhazardous, because even if his superiors ordered him to take some kind of risk, he'd find a way to avoid it. The time the Patrician made use of him was a one-off incident.

Nobby is shorter than many dwarfs, pigeon-chested, moves at the sidle, talks out of the corner of his mouth, and stores cigarette ends behind his ears. He carries

an official document attesting his humanity, despite which some people in the city believe that he's actually the Watch's werewolf. His known hobbies include doing tricks with his boils, country dancing, historical re-enactment (an excuse to talk about weapons), and painting (probably because of the nude models). When off duty, he sometimes dresses in astonishingly flamboyant style, and he has discovered a peculiar fondness for dressing in women's clothing, though there honestly doesn't seem to be anything sexual about this. He has had girlfriends: one female acquaintance, who threw fish at him, replaced another, much more attractive lady because the latter couldn't cook, and then dropped him. He's currently growing close to a female goblin.

ST 8 [-20]; **DX** 11 [20]; **IQ** 10 [0]; **HT** 9 [-10].
Damage 1d-3/1d-2; BL 13 lbs.; HP 8 [0]; Will 10 [0]; Per 11 [5]; FP 9 [0].
Basic Speed 5.00 [0]; Basic Move 4* [0]; Dodge 8; Parry 8 (DX).
4'; 60 lbs. (SM -1*).

SOCIAL BACKGROUND

TL: 4 [0].
CF: Sto Plains/Uberwald [0].
Languages: Morporkian (Native) [0].

ADVANTAGES

Born to Hang 1 [10]; Legal Enforcement Powers [5]; Night Vision 1 [1]; Resistant to Disease (+8) [5]; Watch Rank 2 [10].

DISADVANTAGES

Appearance (Ugly) [-8]; Clueless [-10]; Cowardice (12) [-10]; Duty (The Watch; 12 or less; Nonhazardous) [-5]; Dwarfism [-15]; Kleptomania (15) [-7]; Laziness [-10]; Odious Personal Habits (Tricks with boils and general sordidness) [-10].

Quirks: Bowlegged; Dull; Flashy dresser when off duty; Peculiar fondness for women's clothing. [-4]

SKILLS

Acting (A) IQ-1 [1]-9; Area Knowledge (Ankh-Morpork) (E) IQ+3 [8]-13; Armoury/TL4 (Melee Weapons) (A) IQ-1 [1]-9; Armoury/TL4 (Missile Weapons) (A) IQ-1 [1]-9; Connoisseur (Weapons) (A) IQ+3 [12]-13; Crossbow (E) DX [1]-11; Dancing (A) DX-1 [1]-10; Fast-Talk (A) IQ [1]-10†; Filch (A) DX+1 [2]-12†; Forced Entry (E) DX+1 [1]-12†; Holdout (A) IQ [1]-10†; Law (Ankh-Morpork Police) (H) IQ-1 [2]-9; Savoir-Faire (Military) (E) IQ-4 [1]-6‡; Savoir-Faire (Watch) (E) IQ-4 [1]-6‡; Scrounging (E) Per [1]-11; Smuggling (A) IQ [1]-10†; Sports (Darts) (A) DX [2]-11; Stealth (A) DX+2 [8]-13.

* Modified for Dwarfism.
† Includes +1 for Born to Hang.
‡ Includes -4 for Clueless.

Other Notable Watchmen

The Watch's expansion has brought in a startling range of characters of many different species – as a matter of policy, in fact, although this generally means the *Patrician's* policy, over the objections of Commander Vimes (who isn't a racist, but who doesn't trust anyone easily). Some additional members of the organisation are described below. For an idea of typical skills, see the watchman template (pp. 138-140).

CORPORAL SHOE

Some decades ago, Reg Shoe was a young political idealist – always a sad thing to be in Ankh-Morpork, and downright fatal for him when he became involved in a short-lived revolution. However, he came back from the dead as a self-willed, self-motivated zombie (pp. 116-118). Subsequently, he took up the cause of civil rights for the undead, without much success until the Night Watch started expanding, and he went along to complain about their treatment of the metabolically challenged. Somehow, Carrot talked him into signing up, so he could fix the problem from inside. After that, other undead started complaining about Reg.

Reg is still an idealist, but a slightly more jaded one these days; he frequently becomes exasperated with people, especially his fellow zombies, who so often spend their time lurching and groaning when they could be getting out and doing something constructive. He actually has a knack for talking to them, and can help keep them in line; it's possible that Reg is the only being on the Disc who can bore a zombie into submission. Still, he means well and is competent with standard Watch skills.

CORPORAL SWIRES

A gnome, with the unexpected physical strength and attitude sometimes found in the race, Buggy Swires would make a useful officer in any event. However, as the Watch's airborne section, he's *really* valuable. He knows the secrets of training various bird species, favouring a sparrowhawk for its ability to hover but also using a heron to carry more equipment. During difficult pursuit situations, he's likely to take up a position on some high tower with a telescope and a portable semaphore rig.

CONSTABLE WEE MAD ARTHUR

Another recent supposed gnome recruit, Wee Mad Arthur, was subsequently discovered to be a pictsie, explaining his even greater aggression and strength. Arthur has recently displayed a supernatural ability to fly long distances at high speeds on bird-back, learned from his fellow pictsies.

CONSTABLE DORFL

The first known free-willed golem, Dorfl has a voice, and no "chem" to limit him. He has all the features in the golem racial template (p. 105), is notably intelligent (IQ 12), and speaks *firmly*, As Though Every Word Began With A Capital Letter. He has a Sense of Duty to his fellow golems and uses his Watch pay to buy them out of servitude. He is also interested in metaphysics and is happy to discuss religion (very logically) for hours. The city's priests initially objected to his existence, but each of them is now too busy trying to prove that they can convert him. Being effectively lightning-proof, he's the safest agnostic on the Disc.

CONSTABLE VISIT

Visit-The-Infidel-With-Explanatory-Pamphlets is a devout-but-polite Omnian (pp. 235-236), who spends his off-duty hours living up to his name. People tend to avoid him because of his dedication, but he's a reliable policeman. He has the skill Sacred Texts-15, which occasionally even comes in useful.

CONSTABLE DOWNSPOUT

As a gargoyle, Downspout makes a superb surveillance officer. It's unlikely that he or the other gargoyles on the strength have much training in other Watch skills, but they don't need it.

LANCE-CONSTABLE SALACIA (SALLY) VON HUMPEDING

The Watch's first vampire officer was actually a member of the Watch in Bonk, in Uberwald, who was sent on a quiet mission to Ankh-Morpork and who agreed to act as an agent of the dwarfish Low King at the same time. She joined the Ankh-Morpork Watch to facilitate this work, which makes her a spy, but Commander Vimes has chosen to has chosen to keep her on despite knowing this. She's a useful watchman – and anyway, he's going to have spies in the Watch, so he might as well know who they are.

Sally is a Black Ribboner with IQ 12, Acute Hearing (for a Hearing roll of 18), Attractive appearance, Discriminatory Smell (Emotion Sense), Language Talent, a number of languages (including Dwarfish, Morporkian, and her native Uberwaldian), Shapeshift (Flock of Bats), Heartbeat Counter, Delusion (Spelling my name backwards disguises it perfectly), passable Watch skills, and Musical Instrument (Cello) at a professional level. She wears her hair short and looks a bit like a boyish teenager. She also has a slightly overactive sense of humour; she makes somewhat tasteless jokes about her vampirism and will flirt outrageously with *anyone*.

INSPECTOR A.E. PESSIMAL

Originally a government inspector sent to examine the Watch's finances and administration, A.E. Pessimal (who's never named, just initialled) found a vocation there. Commander Vimes took him on for his ability to read and analyse even the most boring paperwork (the Attentive perk, with Administration-15 and Accounting-15), but requires him to go on regular street patrols so that he understands Watch priorities. Inspector Pessimal is happy with this, displaying a fanatical Sense of Duty and insane courage when pressed.

BRICK

Formerly a low-status slab addict, this troll has since been taken in hand by Detritus (pp. 325-326). He may have formally joined the Watch – but if so, his starting rank is actually *below* lance-constable. However, Detritus hopes to make something of him. Brick *seems* spectacularly dim even by troll standards, but that might just be the effects of all the drugs, which are gradually wearing off. Years of abuse have left his brain hardened against the most potent chemicals (some kind of Resistant), and he seems to have an especially high HT, given that his old habits didn't kill him.

Noteworthy Wizards

Most but not all of these wizards are based at Unseen University.

Mustrum Ridcully

390 points

The social significance of "Ridcully the Brown" is described in the account of recent UU history (pp. 279-280). He is not, as his colleagues expected when they gave him the job, a rustic hedge wizard. Rather, he's a huntin', shootin', and fishin' man who also happens to be extremely competent with magic. He achieved seventh level at the extraordinarily young age of 27 – and while 40 years as a gentleman-farmer didn't involve much wizardry, and his staff had been supporting a scarecrow, he never lost his edge.

His favourite spells include divination with a scrying mirror, because as much as he loves hunting, he finds *tracking* rather boring. Although he regards combat magic in the field as unsporting – preferring to employ a crossbow – he's well able to look after himself when things get messy, magically or physically, and he has defended Ankh-Morpork from more than one supernatural threat. He not only throws a serious fireball, but is also a skilled staff-fighter. He survives as Archchancellor, when many others have fallen to ambitious underlings, through a combination of ingenuity, caution, and slamming people's heads into doors; this has made rivals for his job careful to the point of nonexistence these days.

Ridcully has a huge personality, of the sort that demands beer with breakfast and never seems to need sleep. He shouts a lot. He's far from stupid, but his intelligence is based on a thundering ability to *focus*, which makes it very difficult for other people to get ideas through to him. He also suffers from a degree of Discworld-style literal-mindedness. While capable of some charm, he doesn't waste it on the rest of the faculty; the Bursar's fragile mental condition is largely his fault.

When he was young, Ridcully had a friendship – which might have become a romance, but didn't – with the young Esmerelda Weatherwax (pp. 339-340). They've recently come into contact again, and despite a little friction, they remain friendly and can call on each other for aid, given the need. His brother Hughnon is Ankh-Morpork's chief priest of Blind Io, and hence the city's leading religious figure; neither can afford to mention this much, given what priests and wizards traditionally think of each other, but they're actually on good terms.

Ridcully usually wears rugged tweed robes (or, when out for a healthy run, a baggy trouser suit in garish blue and red) and a hat which he designed himself. While the official Archchancellor's

Hat (p. 276) is a badge of office, Ridcully's personal hat is a masterpiece of practical engineering, with fishing flies stuck on it, a miniature pistol crossbow in the hatband, and a bottle of brandy and some iron rations stowed inside; the tip unscrews to become a cup. It's even said that it can expand to become a tent, and that it contains a small spirit stove.

ST 12 [20]; **DX** 12 [40]; **IQ** 16 [120]; **HT** 13 [30].
Damage 1d-1/1d+2; BL 29 lbs.; HP 12 [0]; Will 15 [-5]; Per 16 [0]; FP 13 [0].
Basic Speed 6.50 [5]; Basic Move 5 [-5]; Dodge 9; Parry 11 (Staff).
6'; 270 lbs.

SOCIAL BACKGROUND

TL: 4 [0].
CF: Sto Plains/Uberwald [0].
Languages: Morporkian (Native) [0].

ADVANTAGES

Charisma 1 [5]; Contact (Granny Weatherwax; Magic (Witchcraft)-21; Can obtain information using supernatural talents; 9 or less; Completely Reliable) [15]; Contact (Hughnon Ridcully; Theology (Research)-18; Can obtain information using supernatural talents; 12 or less; Completely Reliable) [24]; Immunity to Disease [10]; Indomitable [15]; Less Sleep 3 [6]; Magery 3 [35]; Status 5* [20]; Tenure [5]; Wealth (Wealthy) [20].

Perks: Alcohol Tolerance; Deep Sleeper; Longevity; No Hangover; Penetrating Voice; Understands the Librarian. [6]

DISADVANTAGES

Delusion ("What everyone needs is lots of exercise and fresh air") [-5]; Fat [-3]; Odious Personal Habit (Poor Listener) [-5]; Sense of Duty (Unseen University) [-5]; Stubbornness [-5].

Quirks: Autocondimentor; Makes loud jokes but never gets other people's; Polite to women (of all classes); Somewhat literal-minded; Trophy-taking hunter and fisherman. [-5]

SKILLS

Animal Handling (Dogs) (A) IQ-1 [1]-15; Brawling (E) DX [1]-12; Camouflage (E) IQ [1]-16; Carousing (E) HT [1]-13; Crossbow (E) DX+2 [4]-14; Fishing (E) Per [1]-16; Innate Attack (Projectile) (E) DX+2 [4]-14; Intimidation (A) Will-1 [1]-14; Leadership (A) IQ [1]-16†; Magic (Wizardry) (VH) IQ+2 [4]-18‡; Magical Form (Divination) (VH) IQ+1 [2]-17‡; Magical Form (Elementalism) (VH) IQ+1 [2]-17‡; Magical Form (Magianism) (VH) IQ [1]-16‡; Magical Form (Physiomancy) (VH) IQ+1 [2]-17‡; Magical Form (Summonation) (VH) IQ [1]-16‡; Naturalist (H) IQ-2 [1]-14; Professional Skill (Farming) (A) IQ-1 [1]-15; Riding (Equines) (A) DX-1 [1]-11; Savoir-Faire (High Society) (E) IQ [1]-16; Sports (Modern Ankh-Morpork Football) (A) DX-1 [1]-11; Staff (A) DX+1 [4]-13; Stealth (A) DX-1 [0]-11§; Survival (Mountain) (A) Per-1 [1]-15; Survival (Woodlands) (A) Per-1 [1]-15; Thaumatology (VH) IQ [1]-16‡; Traps/TL4 (A) IQ-1 [1]-15.

Standardised Spells (p. 203): Stacklady's Morphic Resonator (Human to Frog)-14 [4]; Stacklady's Morphic Resonator (Human to Pumpkin)-14 [4]; Teleportation-14 [4].

* Includes +1 Status from Wealth.
† Includes +1 for Charisma.
‡ Includes +3 for Magery.
§ Default from IQ.

NOTES

Ridcully's effective income as Archchancellor is sufficient to keep him in Status 5 style, although much of it is in kind.

Rincewind

208 points

Little is known about Rincewind's origins; allegedly, his parents ran away before he was born. He started his adulthood as a student at Unseen University, but although he possessed octarine vision, supposedly implying magical ability, he proved singularly incompetent at both the theory and practise of magic. After several years of study in which he learned virtually nothing, Rincewind opened the Octavo (p. 285) on an unwise bet, and one of its incomparably powerful spells impressed itself upon his mind. For this, he was expelled from the University. He then took to exploiting his genuine talent for languages in the shadiest parts of Ankh-Morpork that weren't obviously dangerous.

Since then, he has suffered more adventures than anyone could ever expect – and certainly far more than he wanted. He became guide to the world's first tourist; fell off the edge of the Disc; played a role in the defeat of a sourcerer; travelled to the Dungeon Dimensions, through time, and to Hell; and went cheerfully insane on a desert island. Then he accidentally assisted a revolution in the Agatean Empire, before being magically transported to EcksEcksEcksEcks, where he helped correct an ancient metaphysical and meteorological problem.

None of this was voluntary. Rincewind hates excitement. The closest thing he has to a useful supernatural ability is a sense for danger, coupled with long legs, which he uses to try to leave danger far behind.[1] Unfortunately, Discworld metaphysics guarantee that someone with so little interest in crises will find himself endlessly at the centre of them. Rincewind is possibly the most widely travelled being on the Disc, excepting of course Death, whose country he has also visited (Death knows him by sight, but the sight Death usually sees is the back of his retreating head). He is in fact a favourite pawn of The Lady (p. 303) – but while she never sacrifices a pawn if she can help it, he *is* still a pawn.

Hence, Rincewind was happy to return to UU, where his past services to magic finally received a reward of sorts: He was appointed Egregious Professor of Cruel and Unusual Geography, as well as receiving various other job titles that nobody else wanted (including Health and Safety Officer). All of this was under the condition that he should have no salary, influence, or opinions. However, it gets him accommodation, food, and coal for his fire (whether or not he wants it – thus, his room is horrendously overheated in summer), so he doesn't complain.

---

1. His "Combat Reflexes" are entirely untrained, reflecting his instinctive reactions to danger. He fights, if he must, in a frenzy of fists and knees, with no technique whatsoever.

. . . Clad in a dark red robe on which a few mystic sigils were embroidered in tarnished sequins. Some might have taken him for a mere apprentice enchanter . . . Yet around his neck was a chain bearing the bronze octagon that marked him as an alumnus of Unseen University . . .

– The Colour of Magic

Unfortunately, his incredible breadth of experience, and the fact that anyone else on the faculty can tell him what to do, means that he's still sometimes dragged into interesting events; he even ended up on the crew of the Disc's one and only space mission. Despite his officially lowly status, he's now allowed to sit in on University Council meetings, if only so that he's near to hand when someone needs an unwelcome job done. He tries to insist on being called *Professor* Rincewind, with little success.

Rincewind is tall and scrawny, with an unhappy attempt at a beard. He usually wears a robe with imperfectly embroidered magical symbols; this is badly worn and rarely clean. He also sports a pointy hat with a star on top and the word WIZZARD in crooked letters, and the octagonal bronze pendant of an Unseen graduate. He's emotionally deeply convinced that he's a wizard, despite being fully aware of his own incompetence, and he's a non-smoker, which is quite unusual in a wizard.

Rincewind nominally owns, and is frequently accompanied by, the most lethally malicious sapient pearwood luggage in the history of Agatean carpentry (see below).

Given his history and possible metaphysical status – Death theorises that he might in fact be the Disc's incarnation of the Coward with a Thousand Retreating Backs – Rincewind could turn up any place, anytime. If encountered by PCs, he'll do his level best not to share whatever trouble they're getting into. If there's no option, he'll lend what assistance he can[1], but use any excuse to get away, unless the situation really does seem to be Disc-threatening, in which case he may get confused and behave admirably. In a campaign, he's best used as a source of comic relief, a one-time *magus ex machina,* or a source of down-at-heel common sense when the PCs are making things too complicated.

Although Rincewind lacks both magical skill and proper theoretical understanding, he has spent long enough at UU to recognise common magical phenomena and artefacts. Mostly this means that he knows what to be most frightened of. It's said that he can scream for mercy in 19 languages, and just scream (*correctly*) in another 44. He can get by conversationally in most languages he has encountered, and he made a serviceable assistant in the University Library.

ST 9 [-10]; **DX** 12 [40]; **IQ** 12 [40]; **HT** 11 [10].
Damage 1d-2/1d-1; BL 16 lbs.; HP 9 [0]; Will 12 [0]; Per 12 [0]; FP 11 [0].
Basic Speed 6.00 [5]; Basic Move 7 [5]; Dodge 11*†; Parry 10* (Brawling).
5'11"; 123 lbs.

SOCIAL BACKGROUND

TL: 4 [0].
CF: Sto Plains/Uberwald [0].
Languages: Morporkian (Native) [0].

ADVANTAGES

Combat Reflexes [15]; Danger Sense [15]; Enhanced Dodge [15]; Extraordinary Luck [30]; Magery 1 (No Spellcasting) [3]; Multilingual (Screaming and Begging for Mercy) [20]; Reputation +3 (As "The Great Wizzard," in the Agatean Empire; 10 or less) [3]; Resistant to Disease (+3) [3]; Serendipity 2 [30]; Status 1 [5].
Perks: Understands the Librarian. [1]

DISADVANTAGES

Cowardice (9) [-15]; Delusion ("I AM a wizard, and that's important, whatever people think") [-5]; Laziness [-10]; Reputation -1 (A bit of an idiot, with That Luggage, among UU Faculty) [-1]; Unluckiness [-10].
Quirks: Habitually misspells "wizard"; Likes boredom; Never trusts strangers who are being nice to him; Sentimental about Ankh-Morpork; Sometimes tries to talk sense to people when he can see it's pointless, and may even do the right thing himself out of desperation. [-5]

SKILLS

Area Knowledge (Unseen University) (E) IQ [1]-12; Brawling (E) DX [1]-12; Carousing (E) HT [1]-11; Fast-Talk (A) IQ-1 [1]-11; Hiking (A) HT-1 [1]-10; Jumping (E) DX [1]-12; Occultism (A) IQ-1 [1]-11; Research/TL4 (A) IQ-1 [1]-11; Riding (Equines) (A) DX-1 [1]-11; Running (A) HT+2 [8]-13; Stealth (A) DX-1 [1]-11; Streetwise (A) IQ-1 [1]-11; Survival (Fourecks Outback) (A) Per [2]-12; Survival (Island/Beach) (A) Per [2]-12; Thaumatology (VH) IQ-3 [1]-9.

* Includes +1 for Combat Reflexes.
† Includes +1 for Enhanced Dodge.

---

1. *Not usually much, although the Luggage can complicate matters.*

NOTES

In the past, Rincewind's Wealth – and hence his effective Status – was often lower, and his Reputation with the UU faculty was worse, although they mostly feared his Luggage enough to avoid him rather than do anything worse. He still has only modest Status for a wizard, thanks to his marginal position, but he *is* legally allowed to wear a pointy hat now. His income-in-kind is enough to support this, though it sometimes takes inconvenient forms.

He might almost be given The Lady (p. 303) as a Patron, or have a Duty to her. However, she's remote and subtle in her manipulations; her patronage is largely represented by some of his advantages, and his duty by his Unluckiness and the fact that he just keeps encountering interesting events.

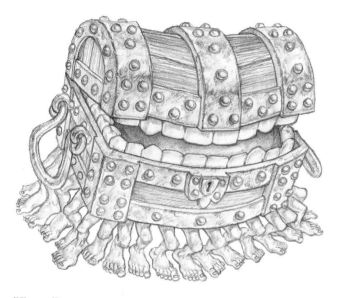

THE LUGGAGE

The trunk-sized Luggage originally owned by Twoflower (pp. 348-349) and later given to Rincewind is often referred to as if it were a typical example of Agatean sapient pearwood joinery, but in fact seems to be far more psychotic and self-willed than most. As a one-off phenomenon with a mind (or at least, a seriously bad attitude) of its own, it's best treated as a unique campaign feature rather than as a character or an item of property with a cash value. Like other such cases (see *Sapient Pearwood*, p. 158), it runs around on lots of small legs (Move 6), is completely immune to magical damage and robust against mundane harm (DR 8, at least, and completely immune to high pressure – although carpentry tools might worry it), and instinctively knows *wherever* its owner is and will faithfully follow him anywhere. If he's on the same world, it will make its way toward him across any terrain, not stopping by day or night until it reaches him. If he's elsewhere, it can apparently shift across universes and dimensions to rejoin him. Indeed, it seems capable of accelerated travel speeds even on the same world, when so inclined; for game purposes, it just turns up when the GM wants it to.

It also appears to have some special features. It has a dimensionally transcendent interior, holding all the personal belongings its owner stows in it, and will return clothes clean and pressed once they've been in there for at least a few minutes. More seriously, it's vicious – if its owner is being threatened, or if it's physically attacked by someone seeking to damage it, it will fight back. Treat it as having ST 15, DX 13, Move 6, Intimidation-12, and

Stealth-14. It can kick at reach C (attack roll of 11) for 1d+1 crushing damage, or possibly more if it gets really angry (it has kicked some very large monsters to death), but its most feared attack is to engulf opponents. No one swallowed by the Luggage has ever been seen again, except for Tethys the water troll, whom it apparently chose to release, and who doesn't need to breathe.

The Luggage seems to be able to swallow someone only if it can sneak up on him. If the would-be victim notices it at the last moment, roll a Quick Contest of his DX or Acrobatics, at +2 if he has Combat Reflexes, against the Luggage's DX. If the target wins, he evades the snapping lid. Most opponents then flee, but Cohen the Barbarian (p. 346) made a good attempt to get the better of it; his approach involved a lot of grappling attempts followed by trying to get the lid open (Contests of ST), on the grounds that a barbarian hero always seeks to get at any treasure in the vicinity.

Despite its reputation and temper, the Luggage won't generally attack anyone who doesn't threaten its owner; it finds Ridcully (pp. 329-330), who approaches it with bluff curiosity, confusing. It can also be moody, is capable of getting drunk when it's unhappy and can get at enough alcohol, and enjoyed a romantic interlude when it met other walking luggage in the Empire. Its experiences on Fourecks included a lot of sparkly decoration, to which it didn't object – it's quite self-confident.

Twoflower said that he bought the Luggage from a Wandering Shop (p. 278), which might help explain its unlimited malice, infinite capacity (and ability to launder clothes), and extreme lethality. It's certainly hard to imagine the Agatean Empire permitting its ordinary citizens to own suitcases that could chew through a regiment of guards like an armoured-vehicle fan's fantasy. It isn't known how much Twoflower originally paid for it; in practical terms, some people might consider it priceless and most would pay a lot of money *not* to have it around. The GM may throw something similar into a game for comic effect (though an identical item would merely be repetitive), but any PC who *wants* to own such a thing should probably be prevented from doing so.

Ponder Stibbons

164 points

As a student at Unseen University, Ponder Stibbons accidentally received a rigged final exam paper which enabled him to graduate with a score of 100%. This suited him, as it enabled him to go on to postgraduate work; his ambition was to find some comfortable corner and enjoy the food for the rest of his life. He soon obtained the position of Reader in Invisible Writings (p. 285), the first in a series of titles he has accumulated over the years.

However, and to his own confusion, Ponder found that he possessed not only real academic talent, but also an inquiring mind. He has become the effective head of the High Energy Magic Lab (p. 286) and a leading figure in the construction of Hex (p. 286). Archchancellor Ridcully gets annoyed at Ponder's use of words such as "quantum" and "continuum," but turns to him when faced with problems that require logic rather than experience. Ponder thinks of himself as the University's token sane person, and he spends much of his time trying to avoid Ridcully's attempts to make him take exercise. His accumulation of academic posts has genuine intellectual justification – since the Dean (pp. 335-336) departed, Ponder has taken charge of much of the University's routine administration. He eventually realised that all the job titles and offices actually give him a singlehanded majority on the University Council.

Ponder is a pale and slightly plump young wizard, with no great love of work until he gets interested. However, his tidy mind means that he can find even University bureaucracy interesting. He's a classic nerd and can seem clueless, but in fact he's pretty good at practical matters when he tries. He has travelled through time, fought elves and Auditors, and run mission control on a space programme – and he *learns*. He has never been seen to cast a useful spell, apart from assisting the Archchancellor with the Rite of AshkEnte and other rituals (although he discovered his talent for magic in childhood by accidentally setting fire to a school bully), but he effectively runs the Hex project and now has direct access to most of the material resources of Unseen University. He's even got the hang of basic politics.[1] These days, he really is the sort of wizard in whose affairs it's a bad idea to meddle.

If the PCs visit UU, they may well encounter Ponder – and he'll probably show up if a serious magical problem arises anywhere in Ankh-Morpork and someone thinks to consult the experts. He can baffle all but the most scholarly or sharp-witted listeners with jargon (he can be thrown off course if anyone actually pays enough attention to work out what he just said), but he'll then proceed to do what needs doing.

ST 9 [-10]; **DX** 10 [0]; **IQ** 14 [80]; **HT** 10 [0].
Damage 1d-2/1d-1; BL 16 lbs.; HP 9 [0]; Will 14 [0]; Per 14 [0]; FP 10 [0].
Basic Speed 5.00 [0]; Basic Move 5 [0]; Dodge 8; Parry 8 (DX).
5'8"; 165 lbs.

SOCIAL BACKGROUND

TL: 4 [0].
CF: Sto Plains/Uberwald [0].
Languages: Morporkian (Native) [0].

ADVANTAGES

Luck [15]; Magery 1 (Non-Improvisational) [11]; Mathematical Ability 1 [10]; Reputation +1 (As the University's Sane Wizard, in Ankh-Morpork; 10 or less) [1]; Resistant to Disease (+3) [3]; Single-Minded [5]; Status 3 [15]; Tenure [5]; Wealth (Comfortable) [10].

1. *While short on general social skills, he has worked out how to keep the University Council in line, and he has had the chance to observe the Patrician at work. He'll never be in Vetinari's league, but he has picked up some tricks.*

Perks: Multiple votes on the University Council; Understands the Librarian. [2]

DISADVANTAGES

Bad Sight (Nearsighted; Mitigator, Glasses) [-10]; Code of Honour (Academic) [-5]; Curious (12) [-5]; Duty (The University; 12 or less; Nonhazardous) [-5]; Pacifism (Reluctant Killer) [-5].
Quirks: Blinds other people with (completely accurate) jargon; Tidy-minded; Tries to avoid physical work. [-3]

SKILLS

Accounting (H) IQ [2]-14*; Administration (A) IQ [2]-14; Area Knowledge (Ankh-Morpork) (E) IQ [1]-14; Computer Programming (Magical Computers) (H) IQ [4]-14; Engineer/TL4 (Magical) (H) IQ [2]-14*; Games (Modern Football Rules) (E) IQ+1 [2]-15; Magic (Wizardry) (VH) IQ-1 [2]-13†; Mathematics/TL4 (Applied) (H) IQ+2 [8]-16*; Natural Philosophy/TL4 (H) IQ [4]-14; Politics (A) IQ-1 [1]-13; Research/TL4 (A) IQ [2]-14; Thaumatology (VH) IQ+4 [20]-18†.

   * Includes +1 for Mathematical Ability.
   † Includes +1 for Magery.

NOTES

Ponder's Status comes from his position at the University, which also gives him sufficient income in kind to support it. However, he's frugal in his habits, and may not appear to be higher than Status 1 to anyone who doesn't know him. He focuses on rational wizardry and practical administration; if he ever learned much about the arts or humanities, he has worked to forget it.

The Librarian

345 points

Unseen University's Librarian used to be human, but he was accidentally magically transformed into an orang-utan. Today, no one – except possibly Rincewind, who has been convinced to remain silent – can remember exactly who the Librarian used to be, and the relevant page in the UU yearbook is missing (a banana peel was found in its place). Coincidentally, this lack of information makes it impossible for any wizard to transform him back. Rumour suggests that he was once the quiet and inoffensive Dr. Horace Worblehat, B.Thau, D.M., but it's best not to mention this.

He now speaks only the language of his new species, which consists of a single word ("Ook"), sometimes heavily inflected ("Ooook-Eeek-Ook!"). Those who know him learn to extract a considerable amount of information from his tone and gestures (p. 53). He can *read* a huge range of languages, seemingly including some from other universes, and comprehend the spoken form of most of them more than well enough, although he can only know as much about pronunciation of dead or obscure languages as happens to be documented – not a great problem, given his inability to speak them. Still, he would be totally ignorant of any undocumented language with no written form.

The Librarian is entirely, vociferously happy with his form. It isn't that he's unaware of the glory and richness of the human condition; it's just that, compared to the practical advantages of his present shape, you can shove all that into an obscure geographical formation in Lancre. In his human days he was a wizard, but he hasn't been known to use any magic whatsoever since his transformation. He is, however, an *ex officio* member of the University Council (no one can find any grounds for keeping him out), and a wizard for all legal and symbolic purposes. He wears a tatty robe for formal occasions as well as after having a bath.

He lives in a cubbyhole in the Library, surrounded by books and an old blanket. He is of course a lover of books, but like many librarians, feels a certain distress at the way people disorder them by taking them off the shelves and putting wear on them. This aside, he mostly gets on well with others, and he has a soft spot for Rincewind (pp. 330-332), who once worked as his assistant and who peeled a competent banana. He does tend to resort to violence when anyone calls him a monkey, though – he is an *ape*. (He can, however, spot a joker when he sees one; anyone setting up someone else to use the wrong word in the Librarian's presence is likely to come off worst.) Despite his preference for keeping books safe, he occasionally goes out of his way to lend *relevant* volumes to people whom he likes and who seem to need particular sorts of knowledge.

Although he enforces rules of silence vigorously when at work, he's far more boisterous in his own time. He spends many of his evenings in the Mended Drum (pp. 264-265). Bar-room brawls are no problem for him; 300 pounds of muscle, with prehensile feet, can give even a troll problems. He also enjoys the theatre, where he insists on slapstick scenes even in tragedies – and given his

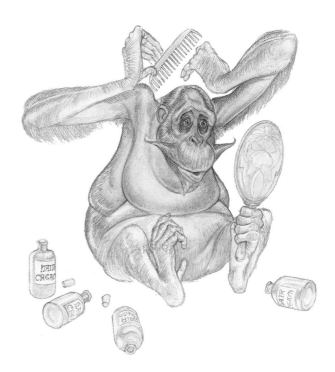

accuracy and force with a thrown peanut shell, companies tend to oblige. His fondness for bananas and peanuts can actually be used against him; a poisoned banana temporarily took him out of his first game as goalkeeper for the UU football team.

He does not, incidentally, have the heavy cheek-pads that indicate the dominant male in an orang-utan troupe. Archchancellor Ridcully becomes very tetchy when this curious fact is discussed.

ST 16 [60]; **DX** 14 [80]; **IQ** 14 [80]; **HT** 14 [40].
Damage 1d+1/2d+2; BL 51 lbs.; HP 16 [0]; Will 14 [0]; Per 14 [0]; FP 14 [0].
Basic Speed 7.00 [0]; Basic Move 6 [-5]; Dodge 10; Parry 11 (Brawling).
5'6"; 300 lbs.

Social Background

TL: 4 [0].
CF: Sto Plains/Uberwald [0].
Languages: Orang-utan (Native) [0].

Advantages

Acute Taste and Smell 4 [8]; Ambidexterity [5]; Brachiator [5]; Damage Resistance 2 (Can't Wear Armour; Tough Skin) [2]; Foot Manipulators [4]; Magery 0 (No Spellcasting) [1]; Multilingual (Bibliographic Work) [20]; Reputation +2 (As amiable enough but a terror in bar-room brawls, among established Ankh-Morpork residents) [5]; Resistant to Disease (+3) [3]; Status 2 [10]; Super Climbing [6]; Temperature Tolerance 1 (Cold) [1]; Tenure [5].
Perks: Alcohol Tolerance; Fur; Secret Name. [3]

Disadvantages

Appearance (Unattractive) [-4]; Bad Temper (15) [-5]; Cannot Speak [-15]; Code of Honour (Personal) [-5]; Semi-Upright [-5].
Quirks: Banana and peanut addict; Bowlegged; Off-duty carouser; Reacts violently to being called a monkey; Twitchy around carnivores. [-5]

The UU Faculty

The staff roster at UU is large – probably not even Ponder Stibbons knows exactly how many people have academic tenure – and includes people who rarely venture out of their rooms. (The fact that some of them have constructed comfortable pocket dimensions *inside* their rooms doesn't help.) However, there are a number of senior wizards who frequently dine with the Archchancellor and who may get called on to assist when trouble starts.

As well as those detailed in this chapter, these include the Senior Wrangler (the least-plump of the old-school senior wizards, who seems to carry a small torch for Mrs. Whitlow, the University housekeeper), the Chair of Indefinite Studies, and the Lecturer in Recent Runes. For game purposes, the University can have a Professor of (or Lecturer in, or Reader in, or Chair of) virtually anything vaguely relevant to the PCs' current concerns. This wizard will usually be quite fat; any such title carries access to the Senior Common Room. It also brings the assumed ability to address the Archchancellor as an equal (unless it's held by Rincewind, which several less useful titles now are), along with the risk of being roped in to assist with supernatural problems.

SKILLS

Acrobatics (H) DX [4]-14; Area Knowledge (Circle Sea Region) (E) IQ [1]-14; Brawling (E) DX+2 [4]-16; Carousing (E) HT [1]-14; Climbing (A) DX+1 [1]-15*; Gesture (E) IQ [1]-14; Hidden Lore (L-Space) (A) IQ+1 [4]-15; History (Publishing) (H) IQ [4]-14; Literature (H) IQ [4]-14; Musical Instrument (Keyboards) (H) IQ-2 [1]-12; Occultism (A) IQ-1 [1]-13; Professional Skill (Book-Binding) (A) DX-1 [1]-13; Research/TL4 (A) IQ+3 [12]-17; Sports (Modern Ankh-Morpork Football) (A) DX-1 [1]-13; Stealth (A) DX [2]-14; Survival (L-Space) (A) Per [2]-14; Thaumatology (VH) IQ-1 [4]-13; Throwing (A) DX-1 [1]-13; Wrestling (A) DX [2]-14.

* Includes +2 for Brachiator.

NOTES

Arguably, the Librarian should have an orang-utan racial template, but as he's probably the Disc's only fully sapient orang-utan and operates entirely in a mostly human society, it's simpler just to give him appropriate racial traits on a one-off basis. For practical game purposes, he *does* qualify for Cannot Speak. He can make only one sound, which ignorant folk will treat as animalistic gibbering – humans need a perk (p. 53) to interpret his vocalisations, which even then might not convey everything he wants.

His Status is that of a full member of the UU faculty, moderated by the facts that (a) he's an ape, and (b) he doesn't worry much about status symbols. Like most faculty members' Status, it's supported by his University income-in-kind. He usually has the cash on him somewhere for a drink, though. His Code of Honour seems to be his idea of a professional code, based partly on the rules of the Librarians of Space and Time (see *L-Space*, p. 285); it obliges him to protect and preserve books to the limits of his ability (sometimes adventuring through L-Space to do so), to help people who he judges deserve well-chosen texts, and not to disrupt the causal structure of reality.

The Bursar

The Bursar (actually Dr. A.A. Dinwiddie, but always addressed by his colleagues as "Bursar") is officially in charge of UU finances. Unlike some previous bursars, he's a genuine, competent wizard – he can be quite gung-ho with incendiary spells. He's also very good with figures. He probably once specialised in mathematically based magic, before discovering the even greater power that lay in a set of investments going back two millennia.

Unfortunately, after the arrival of Mustrum Ridcully as Archchancellor, the Bursar found life increasingly stressful. Ridcully's attempts to make him take some exercise were bad enough, and all the shouting really got him down. Today, his nerves are shot to pieces[1], and he hallucinates more-or-less continuously. (Hex once cured him by conversing more weirdly than he did, but the effect didn't last.) This can often but not always be moderated by dried frog pills, the state of the art in Discworld psychiatric medication, which work by making the user hallucinate that he's completely sane, if someone has got the mix right. Unfortunately, they sometimes have side-effects, such as making him hallucinate that he can fly – and, being a wizard, he tends to react to such hallucinations by making them come true. "Bursar" has become Ankh-Morpork slang for "wibblingly insane."

His usefulness is thus erratic. When he's in the right phase, he's a genius of financial administration, but too often, he's someone who regards decimal points – like gravity – as a trivial inconvenience. Hence, Ponder Stibbons has come to run most of the University's routine financial affairs.

The Bursar dresses much like the rest of the senior faculty, but is skinny, as his nerves burn off a lot of calories. During the random phases when his condition renders him rigidly catatonic, he can be used as a crowbar or a plank.

In game terms, he has IQ 13 with Lightning Calculator, Magery 2, and Mathematical Ability 3. His skills include Accounting-16, Finance-15, Mathematics (Applied)-14, and Magic (Wizardry)-16. He's also competent in various Magical Forms, starting with Elementalism.

Henry the Ex-Dean

The former Dean of Unseen University was always known, even by his old contemporary and sort-of friend Ridcully, simply as "Dean." However, since he accepted a new job (through the undignified route of a newspaper advertisement) as Archchancellor of Brazeneck College (p. 280), everyone has been obliged to remember that his name is actually Henry.

He's a typical senior wizard in that he's elderly but healthy, and enjoys very large meals as often as possible, as his waistline illustrates (Very Fat). Brazeneck's tighter budgets have put a bit of a crimp in his eating, though, which causes even the UU faculty to look at him sympathetically. They don't have to like his college, but a wizard not getting several large meals a day just isn't *right*.

---

1. *Almost literally, thanks to Ridcully's fondness for the crossbow.*

He's also a competent manager (Administration-14); he previously handled much of the running of UU, and today, while Brazeneck had some teething problems, it's working quite well.

Henry's personality has some oddities, though. He isn't especially mentally resilient or stable (IQ 14 but only Will 10), and he's *immensely* susceptible to outside influences. This verges on a psychic talent; he seems to pick up on fads, fashions, and metaphysical distortions of society before they've even started. The one good thing about this is that people who know him can use him as an early warning system – when he starts acting oddly, *something is happening.* His new job may well reflect this susceptibility, too; the creation of a new magical college as a rival to UU was the first sign of a shift in society, so Henry *had* to become involved. Even *Ridcully* used to find his enthusiasms somewhat wearing; they could be classed as Compulsive Behaviour or an Odious Personal Habit, or perhaps a sort of Gullibility.

If pushed into combat – unlikely these days, but not impossible – Henry is likely to charge in with cries of "Hut! Hut!" and let fly with a lot of high-powered magic. He'll probably quickly burn himself out, but the damage he does before that should be substantial.

Henry wears normal magician's robes, or sometimes a leather robe with the words "BORN TO RUNE" across the back in metal studs.[1]

---

1. *Only a wizard could wear a fashion souvenir from a piece of history that didn't even happen.*

Lancre

The tiny nation of Lancre (pp. 238-239) is noted for producing people, many of whom it exports. It is technically a kingdom, complete with a royal palace – actually a castle. Unfortunately, it can't really support much in the way of royalty, let alone a full palace staff. (Previous monarchs did a little better, but they were prepared to get a lot more heavy-handed with tax policies than the present incumbent.) The current court consists of one king, one queen, and four indoor servants.

Lancre Castle Staff

King Verence and Queen Magrat are served by Mrs. Scorbic the cook (a large woman who thinks that cabbage should be cooked until it is yellow and meat until it is grey), Spriggins the butler, Millie Chillum the (small, nervous) maid, and Shawn Ogg, whose titles and responsibilities are too numerous to list. The known outside staff consists of Hodgesaargh the heavily scarred falconer and Mr. Brooks the beekeeper, a master of his trade.

King Verence II

93 points

The current King of Lancre was originally the court fool, before a dubious bit of alleged genealogy gave him the throne.

He didn't like his old job, but an intense sense of duty compelled him to *work* at it, and he graduated from the Fools' Guild School (pp. 262-263) with distinction. However, having left that line of work, he would be happy never to see another bucket of whitewash in his life. He might almost be considered to have No Sense of Humour, although he isn't a cold or unsympathetic person.

Verence is a short, thin man who doesn't look much of a king, but he's neither stupid nor inflexible. He does believe strongly in information obtained from books, and his attempts at improving his kingdom's agriculture have thus run headfirst into his people's bloody-minded conservatism. Similarly, his efforts to introduce democracy have met the response that, as he's king, it's his blasted job to rule the country, and will he please stop bothering other folk about it?

On the other hand, the people of Lancre aren't inclined to complain too much about a king who means well – they've experienced the other sort. His serious efforts and willingness to learn, and the involvement of his wife, will probably achieve a lot of good in the long term. Any PCs who become involved in the state affairs of Lancre shouldn't underestimate him or push their luck.

Verence has a permanently harassed expression, runny eyes, slightly sticking-out ears, and clothes that never seem to fit right, even though he can afford moderately well-made garb. Still, he's presentable and ordinary-enough looking, now that he has shed his old, trained habit of walking bent over and hunched. He does have a weak chest, but his wife keeps an eye on his health.

ST 10 [0]; **DX** 11 [20]; **IQ** 12 [40]; **HT** 10 [0].
Damage 1d-2/1d; BL 20 lbs.; HP 10 [0]; Will 12 [0]; Per 12 [0]; FP 10 [0].
Basic Speed 5.25 [0]; Basic Move 5 [0]; Dodge 8; Parry 8 (DX).
5'7"; 135 lbs.

She gave Verence a withering look. "And I remember you when you were just a man in a funny hat."

Even this didn't work. Verence merely sighed again and turned towards the door.

"I still am, Nanny," he said. "It's just that this one's a lot heavier."

– Carpe Jugulum

SOCIAL BACKGROUND

TL: 4 [0].
CF: Sto Plains/Uberwald [0].
Languages: Morporkian (Native) [0].

ADVANTAGES

Status 6* [25]; Wealth (Wealthy) [20].

DISADVANTAGES

Berserk (15) [-5]; Dependent (Infant Daughter; 0 or fewer points; Loved One; 6 or less) [-15]; Pacifism (Reluctant Killer) [-5]; Sense of Duty (Lancre) [-10].

Quirks: Deeply in love with Magrat; Great believer in book learning and natural ingredients; Responsive; Shuddering aversion to custard and clowning props. [-4]

SKILLS

Acrobatics (H) DX-2 [1]-9; Acting (A) IQ [2]-12; Area Knowledge (Lancre) (E) IQ [1]-12; Current Affairs/TL4 (Headline News) (E) IQ [1]-12; Current Affairs/TL4 (Politics) (E) IQ+1 [2]-13; Diplomacy (H) IQ-2 [1]-10; Fool's Lore (A) IQ+3 [12]-15; Performance (A) IQ+1 [4]-13; Professional Skill (Farming) (A) IQ-1 [1]-11; Savoir-Faire (High Society) (E) IQ+1 [2]-13.

* Includes +1 Status from Wealth.

NOTES

As ruler of a kingdom with no formal law enforcement, Verence might be considered to have 10-point Legal Enforcement Powers; if anyone committed a serious crime, it would theoretically be his job to sort matters out. However, the people of Lancre mostly deal with such things among themselves, and Verence really isn't *inclined* to use his authority like that. If he travels to other lands, he can claim Legal Immunity – he *is* a king, after all.

Verence's daughter is a Dependent he would protect with his life. Her low frequency of appearance reflects the fact that she wouldn't be taken into danger if anyone in Lancre could avoid it – and even if an enemy *could* get to her, the smart ones know just who that would anger. Verence's Wealth might rate considerably higher if one counted the theoretical value of Lancre Castle, but his actual cash reserves are limited. Still, he lives comfortably and can afford to put on an occasional state banquet.

Verence may well have a point in each of Administration and Law (Lancre Criminal) by now – but to begin with, at least, he frequently ended up using these (and Research) at default. In his days as a fool, he had Code of Honour (Professional), fewer skills, and of course lower Status and Wealth.

Queen Magrat

196 points

Magrat Garlick was selected for witch training by Goodie Whemper, a research witch – one of the few members of the profession who really cared about the significance of specific herbs or the structure of spells. (Research witches are regarded as crankish by other witches, but undeniably do some useful work.) It's possible that the choice of Magrat, an impractical character for all her genuine talent, was itself some kind of experiment.

Magrat inherited Goodie's interest in the new and unorthodox, but combined it with a tendency to romanticism and an urge to melodrama. She was forever acquiring books about exotic foreign mystical arts – a few of them genuinely relevant, most totally useless, many published by C.M.O.T. Dibbler.

wooden door demolish itself by outgrowing its frame (a bit of concentrated Physiomancy), but she was less happy with working magic on people, let alone rocks. While she assisted when the coven performed other feats, she would probably only happily try things like that on her own after discussing the details with another witch. However, the GM in need of a plot device could say that she has learned almost *anything* from Goodie Whemper's notes.

In one respect, Magrat even has an edge over the coven's senior members: Because she thinks that details *matter*, she has become at least as good an herbalist as them, and frankly, she makes a better doctor when things get complicated. She actually has Diagnosis skill, where the older two just treat similar symptoms the same way (which usually works because people believe in them). Thus, Magrat is more likely to diagnose correctly in the first place. She might sometimes resort to crankish or experimental treatments, but they have a basis in logic.

Personally, Magrat is short, pointy-nosed, and flat-chested, with uncontrollable hair.

ST 9 [-10]; **DX** 12 [40]; **IQ** 14 [80]; **HT** 12 [20].
Damage 1d-2/1d-1; BL 16 lbs.; HP 9 [0]; Will 14 [0]; Per 14 [0]; FP 12 [0].
Basic Speed 6.00 [0]; Basic Move 5 [-5]; Dodge 9; Parry 9 (Brawling).
5'6"; 115 lbs.

SOCIAL BACKGROUND

TL: 4 [0].
CF: Sto Plains/Uberwald [0].
Languages: Morporkian (Native) [0].

ADVANTAGES

Magery 2 [25]; Serendipity 1 [15]; Status 5* [20]; Wealth (Wealthy) [20].

DISADVANTAGES

Charitable (15) [-7]; Code of Honour (Wise-Woman's) [-5]; Dependent (Esmerelda Margaret Note Spelling; 0 or fewer points; Loved One; 6 or less) [-15]; Pacifism (Cannot Harm Innocents) [-10]; Sense of Duty (Lancre) [-10].

Quirks: Believes in wisdom from distant lands and books that use the word "folk"; Deeply attached to Verence; Generally truthful; Lectures people on healthy eating; Likes "witchy" paraphernalia, and loads up on impressive-looking hardware when she's nervous. [-5]

SKILLS

Brawling (E) DX+1 [2]-13; Diagnosis/TL4 (Human) (H) IQ+1 [8]-15; Fortune-Telling (Caroc Cards) (A) IQ-1 [1]-13; Gardening (E) IQ [1]-14; Herbalism (H) IQ+1 [8]-15; Knife (E) DX [1]-12; Magic (Witchcraft) (VH) IQ [2]-14†; Magical Form (Divination) (VH) IQ-1 [1]-13†; Magical Form (Physiomancy) (VH) IQ [2]-14†; Magical Form (Psychomancy) (VH) IQ-1 [1]-13†; Magical Form (Sortilege) (VH) IQ-1 [1]-13†; Midwifery (A) IQ [2]-14; Musical Instrument (Guitar) (H) IQ-2 [1]-12; Naturalist (H) IQ [4]-14; Occultism (A) IQ-1 [1]-13; Physician/TL4 (Human) (H) IQ-1 [2]-13; Poisons/TL4 (H) IQ-1 [2]-13; Savoir-Faire (High Society) (E) IQ [1]-14; Sewing/TL4 (E) DX [1]-12; Veterinary/TL4 (H) IQ-2 [1]-12.

* Includes +1 Status from Wealth.
† Includes +2 for Magery.

She loved (and still likes) new ideas and interesting "witchy" paraphernalia: candles, cards, ancient disciplines of unarmed combat, and so on. She wore green silk, and so many rings that they could function as brass knuckles, but never felt comfortable in a pointy hat. Her mind was so open that it tended to get cluttered, and it took a while for her hopeless sentimentality to abrade down to a more practical kind-heartedness. But she *was* always an accomplished witch, and, like many cute little creatures, dangerous if cornered.

Originally the third and youngest of the Lancre coven, Magrat became romantically involved with the court fool, and remained close to him when he became king. Although the relationship always involved a great deal of embarrassment on both sides, the pair did eventually marry, making Magrat perhaps the most implausible witch-queen in Disc history. They subsequently started a family, their first daughter being named Esmerelda Margaret Note Spelling (due to a baptismal accident), and she formally retired from witchcraft. However, she still does some medical potion-work and hasn't forgotten much; if Lancre needs defending, she may show up. Having become a little more worldly with time and being fiercely loyal to her family, she could probably surprise opponents with some weirdly effective defensive moves – magical, physical, or even political.

Her magical abilities are patchy but not ineffective, when she chooses to use them. In the past, she was able to make an old, solid

NOTES

Early in her career, Magrat was a lot *more* nervous and shy, with the Delusion that bad things only happen to bad people, and possibly even Clueless. She was always capable of flares of temper and stubbornness when pushed far enough, though, and she has learned from her adventures and settled down to married life. These days, she might not even have as many problems as implied above.

Magrat's Status as a queen – albeit of a tiny kingdom with a not-very-respectful population – has effectively subsumed the Social Regard that she eventually acquired as a witch. Her Status isn't quite as high as her husband's because most people she meets remember her too well as a commoner. The kingdom's resources are just about enough to maintain her family as royalty, and she has effective access to it at need, although there are no guarantees as to the money or equipment she could muster at any given time (still, there's an *amazing* amount of old stuff in the castle attics). If she travelled to other lands, she might claim Legal Immunity as visiting royalty.

Her daughter is rated as a Dependent because Magrat does have to care for her and she could be threatened by a sufficiently ruthless foe, although in practise, that would turn the entire kingdom into a problem for whoever made the threat.

Granny Weatherwax

392 points

Many people consider Granny Weatherwax the greatest witch on the Disc. She certainly does. She was trained by several other witches, and when she had learned all they had to teach, she completed her training on her own.

At first sight, Esmerelda ("Esme") Weatherwax appears so wicked-witch-like that one expects a Kansas farmhouse to drop on her at any moment. (The only farmhouse to try, missed, and hit Nanny Ogg instead.) She is old (although to her annoyance, neither warty nor especially wrinkled), wears black, has a pointy hat, a pointier temper, and a positively scalpel-grade tongue, and is at all times convinced that she's in the right. She hates losing, and her mental and sorcerous abilities, coupled with an absolute willingness to do what has to be done, mean that she doesn't lose often, if ever. She doesn't understand the concept of "coming a good second."

However, Granny's record is definitely that of a good witch. She understands with preternatural clarity that what people want, what they need, and what somebody else thinks they need, are three different things, and that giving them the one on either end usually comes out very badly. She sometimes says that you can't help people using magic, despite the fact that she *does* exactly that at times – frankly, she's a supreme mistress of "Do as I say, not as I do." She is also a mistress of Headology (p. 274), manipulating people into doing what's right or making them think that she accomplished with (or maybe without) magic what they had to do for themselves.

Her older sister Lily ended up proving the wisdom of Esme's philosophy by trying to use magic to fix everything – and everyone – in the kingdom of Genua. This was eventually straightened out. Lily has not been seen since.

Granny's self-confidence is also her weakness in dangerous situations. She's bad at asking for help, and terrible at sharing important information with others. She doesn't really trust anyone else to deal with problems in the way that she sees is right.

Granny is a formidable witch, despite her oft-declared preference for not using magic. She has duelled an Archchancellor of Unseen University to a standstill, held off the Queen of the Elves, expelled the infection of vampirism from her own body (and in the process projected some of her own personality into the vampires involved), and defeated voodoo experts and her own sister. She's particularly fond of Borrowing (pp. 210-211), and she is adept at narrative manipulation (but only uses it with extreme caution).

The Lancre Coven

Lancre *can* support three working witches, but they're often forced into each other's company, forming a coven, whether or not Granny Weatherwax wants to admit that's what it is. (There are several more witches within fairly easy travelling distance, and they occasionally hold larger meetings, but usually it's just the three.) They typically meet on local hillsides – mostly on pleasant nights, as they find the idea of dancing around in thunderstorms as silly as anyone else would – to share a meal and gossip. They'll also collaborate against supernatural threats; while no self-respecting witch would happily admit to needing *help*, they're prepared to compare notes.

The social dynamics here are a little complex. Granny Weatherwax and Nanny Ogg are very old friends, but left alone together, they quickly get on each other's nerves. Having a third, younger person around moderates the interactions. A simple description would be that Granny Weatherwax needs someone to boss around, but it's more that she needs one old friend and one alternative viewpoint, however nervously expressed, to stop her mind wandering into dangerous realms. Nanny Ogg, in turn, gets people she can gossip with on topics that a non-witch wouldn't understand, and the younger witch gets a chance to learn something.

She lives in a cottage outside the village of Bad Ass. Like most witches, she owns a broomstick; it was originally another witch's, but every part in it has been replaced over the years. Despite endless tinkering by the best dwarfish mechanics, it requires a long run-up before takeoff. She flies with an air of especially fierce determination, rarely using Aerobatics skill when Intimidation might serve. Whole species of bird have recently changed their migration patterns to avoid Lancre.

Granny is barely literate by many standards – she can read well enough, but only writes slowly, and her spelling is bizarre – but very numerate, to the point where she can read accounts skilfully (she gets her full default for that purpose, or uses Merchant instead). She's known to trolls as *Aaoograha hoa*, "She Who Must Be Avoided," and to dwarfs as *K'ez'rek d'b'duz*, "Go Around the Other Side of the Mountain."

ST 11 [10]; **DX** 13 [60]; **IQ** 17 [140]; **HT** 13 [30].
Damage 1d-1/1d+1; BL 34 lbs.; HP 11 [0]; Will 17 [0]; Per 17 [0]; FP 13 [0].
Basic Speed 6.50 [0]; Basic Move 6 [0]; Dodge 10*; Parry 11* (Brawling).
5'10"; 140 lbs.

SOCIAL BACKGROUND

TL: 4 [0].
CF: Sto Plains/Uberwald [0].
Languages: Morporkian (Native/Accented) [-1]; Uberwaldian (Broken/None) [1].

ADVANTAGES

Charisma 1 [5]; Combat Reflexes [15]; Contact (Mustrum Ridcully; Thaumatology-18; Can obtain information using supernatural talents; 9 or less; Completely Reliable) [12]; Indomitable [15]; Lifting ST 2 [6]; Luck [15]; Magery 3 [35]; Resistant to Disease (+3) [3]; Sensitive [5]; Social Regard 2 (Feared) [10]; Social Regard 2 (Respected) [10]; Status 1 [5].

Perks: Archaic Training 1 (Physician); Controllable Disadvantage (Callous); Longevity. [3]

DISADVANTAGES

Bad Temper (15) [-5]; Code of Honour (Wise-Woman's) [-5]; Pacifism (Cannot Harm Innocents) [-10]; Selfish (9) [-7]; Sense of Duty (People of Lancre and thereabouts) [-10]; Stubbornness [-5].

Quirks: Absolutely protective of children; Dangerously addicted to Borrowing when bored; Doesn't know when she's beaten and tends to bluff on a weak hand; Prefers to be paid in old clothes; Says that magic is the wrong way to solve problems (but does it anyway). [-5]

SKILLS

Aerobatics (H) DX-2 [1]-11; Area Knowledge (Lancre) (E) IQ [1]-17; Brawling (E) DX+2 [4]-15; Fast-Draw (Knife) (E) DX+1 [1]-14*; Fortune-Telling (Palmistry) (A) IQ+1 [1]-18†; Fortune-Telling (Tea-Leaf Reading) (A) IQ+1 [1]-18†; Games (Cripple Mr. Onion) (E) IQ+1 [2]-18; Herbalism (H) IQ [4]-17; Hiking (A) HT-1 [1]-12; Housekeeping (E) IQ [1]-17; Intimidation (A) Will [2]-17; Knife (E) DX+1 [2]-14; Knot-Tying (E) DX [1]-13; Magic (Witchcraft) (VH) IQ+3 [8]-20‡; Magical Form (Divination) (VH) IQ [1]-17‡; Magical Form (Elementalism) (VH) IQ [1]-17‡; Magical Form (Physiomancy) (VH) IQ+1 [2]-18‡; Magical Form (Psychomancy) (VH) IQ+3 [8]-20‡; Magical Form (Sortilege) (VH) IQ [1]-17‡; Merchant (A) IQ-1 [1]-16; Midwifery (A) IQ-1 [1]-16; Naturalist (H) IQ-1 [2]-16; Occultism (A) IQ-1 [1]-16; Physician/TL4 (Human) (H) IQ-2 [1]-15; Poisons/TL3 (H) IQ-2 [1]-15; Psychology (Human) (H) IQ [4]-17; Sleight of Hand (H) DX [4]-13; Stealth (A) DX-1 [0]-12§; Survival (Woodlands) (A) Per-1 [1]-16; Veterinary/TL4 (H) IQ-2 [1]-15.

* Includes +1 for Combat Reflexes.
† Includes +1 for Charisma and +1 for Sensitive.
‡ Includes +3 for Magery.
§ Default from IQ.

NOTES

Granny has the maximum four levels of Social Regard, in a *mixed* form – she's both Feared and Respected. People don't argue with her, but they don't usually run away from her, either; they go to her for advice, and they tend to pay attention to what she says. And she can go pretty well wherever she likes.

Like many witches, she definitely has positive Status in her community, although she doesn't have very much material Wealth – her cottage and clothing are comfortable, but nothing about her looks new. Still, she has little difficulty getting enough old clothes and provisions to live on. Again like many witches, she works almost entirely in the barter economy, rarely handling cash.

Nanny Ogg

299 points

Thrice-married, outgoing, and with 15 children and a past that would be disreputable if anyone in Lancre cared (or dared comment), Gytha Ogg is very unlike her contemporary and friend, Granny Weatherwax. She's easygoing, understanding, and ridiculously proud and defensive of her family. She does terrorise her daughters-in-law, none of whom she ever considers quite good enough for her sons, and thoroughly enjoys family feuds. Both witches and Oggs tend to be matrilineal; her husbands would never have suggested that she might change her name to theirs, and indeed, *they* took *her* name. Her cottage is in the centre of what passes for a town in Lancre, close to her family, and is capacious, comfortable, and full of cheap, colourful knick-knacks sent home by Oggs who've gone travelling.

Nanny is only an occasional spellcaster, but she has her moments. She has employed curses and divinations, has assisted with more powerful spells, and occasionally invokes oracular demons to answer pressing questions (Granny Weatherwax darkly suspects that Nanny likes those demons because they're evidently male). She certainly seems to *enjoy* her magic more than the others of the coven. There's also good reason to believe that she's the most skilled midwife in the entire history of the Disc.

Under the pseudonym of "A Lancre Witch," Nanny wrote *The Joye of Snacks*, an adults-only cookery book. Any of her readers who identified her as the author would be most impressed.

ST 11 [10]; **DX** 11 [20]; **IQ** 13 [60]; **HT** 13 [30].
Damage 1d-1/1d+1; BL 39 lbs.; HP 11 [0]; Will 13 [0]; Per 13 [0]; FP 13 [0].
Basic Speed 6.00 [0]; Basic Move 5 [-5];
Dodge 9; Parry 9 (Brawling).
5'5"; 195 lbs.

SOCIAL BACKGROUND

TL: 4 [0].
CF: Sto Plains/Uberwald [0].
Languages: Dwarfish (Accented) [4]; Morporkian (Native/Accented) [-1]; Quirmian (Broken) [2]; Trollish (Accented) [4]; Uberwaldian (Broken) [2].

ADVANTAGES

Fearlessness 1 [2]; Lifting ST 3 [9]; Luck [15]; Magery 2 [25]; Resistant to Disease (+3) [3]; Sensitive [5]; Social Regard 3 (Respected) [15]; Status 1 [5]; Wealth (Comfortable) [10].
Perks: Alcohol Tolerance; Archaic Training 1 (First Aid); Longevity; No Hangover; Oggham Reader. [5]

DISADVANTAGES

Code of Honour (Wise-Woman's) [-5]; Fat [-3]; Pacifism (Cannot Harm Innocents) [-10]; Sense of Duty (Lancre in general and family in particular) [-10].
Quirks: Bosses her family and bullies her daughters-in-law; Broad-Minded; Likes a drink and a family party, with an adult-rated sense of humour; Sentimental – dotes on children, treats Greebo as a sweet little kitten; Terrifying Singer. [-5]

SKILLS

Aerobatics (H) DX-1 [2]-10; Area Knowledge (Lancre) (E) IQ+2 [4]-15; Brawling (E) DX+1 [2]-12; Carousing (E) HT [1]-13; Current Affairs/TL3 (Lancre) (E) IQ+2 [4]-15; Fast-Draw (Knife) (E) DX [1]-11; First Aid/TL4 (Human) (E) IQ [1]-13; Fortune-Telling (Palmistry) (A) IQ [1]-13*; Fortune-Telling (Tea-Leaf Reading) (A) IQ+2 [4]-15*; Games (Cripple Mr. Onion) (E) IQ [1]-13; Gardening (E) IQ [1]-13; Herbalism (H) IQ+1 [8]-14; Hold-out (A) IQ [2]-13; Housekeeping (E) IQ+1 [2]-14; Knife (E) DX+1 [2]-12; Knot-Tying (E) DX [1]-11; Leadership (A) IQ-1 [1]-12; Magic (Witchcraft) (VH) IQ+2 [8]-15†; Magical Form (Divination) (VH) IQ+1 [4]-14†; Magical Form (Physiomancy) (VH) IQ+1 [4]-14†; Magical Form (Psychomancy) (VH) IQ-1 [1]-12†; Magical Form (Sortilege) (VH) IQ+1 [4]-14†; Magical Form (Summonation) (VH) IQ [2]-13†; Merchant (A) IQ [2]-13; Midwifery (A) IQ+6 [24]-19; Musical Instrument (Keyboards) (H) IQ-1 [2]-12; Naturalist (H) IQ [4]-13; Observation (A) Per-1 [1]-12; Occultism (A) IQ-1 [1]-12; Poisons/TL3 (H) IQ-2 [1]-11; Professional Skill (Cooking) (A) IQ+1 [4]-14; Psychology (Human) (H) IQ-2 [1]-11; Public Speaking (A) IQ-1 [1]-12; Sewing/TL4 (E) DX+1 [2]-12; Shouting

at Foreigners (E) IQ+1 [2]-14; Stealth (A) DX+1 [4]-12; Veterinary/TL4 (H) IQ-1 [2]-12.

* Includes +1 for Sensitive.
† Includes +2 for Magery.

Agnes "Perdita" Nitt

349 points

After Magrat became Queen of Lancre, a position that makes full-time witch-work impractical, Nanny Ogg realised that the coven needed a new third member. Agnes Nitt was the only young woman in Lancre who looked to have magical talent.

Agnes is the kind of fat person of whom everyone comments that she has good hair and a nice personality. She's definitely very fat, though. (It *is* good hair; it's also extremely *big* hair.) She wasn't entirely comfortable with the life of a farmer's daughter, already had a sneaking suspicion that she might have some kind of unusual ability, and had even played at magic with an unwise group of friends at one stage, but she found the witches too annoyingly self-righteous to wish to join them. However, magic will out; Agnes' magic manifested in the form of a truly extraordinary voice, for singing (she can sing in harmony *with herself*) and, it eventually emerged, with other uses. Her dreams of something better than Lancre also caused her temporarily to adopt the more romantic name of Perdita X. Nitt.

After a short stint in the chorus of the Ankh-Morpork Opera, though, Agnes was convinced that she was fated or doomed to become a witch – she's simply too intelligent and *aware* for any other life. Thus, she took over Magrat's role and began learning from the other two. This unlocked her basic magical sensitivity, and she began picking up magical, medical, and other skills.

However, these developments also helped release Perdita. They say that inside every fat person is a thin person trying to get out, and Perdita is the one inside Agnes. She's a sort of subroutine in Agnes' psyche, or perhaps a childhood invisible friend who never went away.

Perdita *doesn't* have a nice personality. She represents everything that Agnes would like to be but isn't, and thinks all those thoughts that Agnes is too moral, sensible, or scared to think. But she's also the sort to find things "cool," which Agnes sees as silly; both of them can be cynical, but in different ways. Perdita spots things Agnes misses, and in times of stress may try to take over their body and attempt to solve problems her way. This division grants Agnes exceptional mental defences – when something attacks Agnes' mind, it sinks down and Perdita rises up to take charge, and vice versa. This divided personality isn't entirely a disadvantage, but others who learn about it do find it peculiar, and when Perdita gets out, she sometimes says things that shock people who only know Agnes. Thus, these personality changes can give -1 or worse to reactions at times.

Agnes is a practical individual whose first instinct is to help others; while she can be harshly unsentimental, she can't bring herself to walk away. She tries not to *meddle*, but others don't always see the distinction. This combination of practicality and helpfulness may be part of what makes her witch material.

The Oggs

Nanny Ogg (pp. 340-341) comes from a large and *very* long-established Lancre family – she has more-or-less hinted that they invented Oggham script (p. 17), although that was probably spinning a line. Some stay in the area; others go abroad to make their fortune.

Jason Ogg, Nanny's eldest, is Lancre's town smith. He has great talent (Smith (Blacksmith)-17, plus the Good with Horses perk and Animal Handling (Equines)-14), but he also benefits from an ancient, secret, arcane pact: Lancre's smith can shoe anything that is brought before him, *provided that he shoes anything that is brought before him.* Jason once put shoes on an ant, for a bet – and once a year, he dons a blindfold while a very polite gentleman who speaks in HOLLOW CAPITALS brings a superb horse to his forge for attention. Jason carefully keeps the iron from those shoes separate from anything else; his mother has borrowed some of it just once, knowing that it can go anywhere. Jason looks every inch the classic blacksmith (ST 18 and HT 14) and is a formidable brawler (Brawling-14 and Wrestling-15) but a gentle giant; he occasionally gets called in to break up trouble in the town tavern, which he does by picking up overexcited participants and holding them in the air until they calm down.

Shawn Ogg, Nanny's youngest, is employed at Lancre Castle as the guard, handyman, and entire male indoor staff. He also works as the town postman and is commander of the Lancre armed forces (that is, himself). It's mostly a dull job – or rather, a dull set of jobs – even if King Verence occasionally encourages Shawn to attempt potentially profitable projects such as inventing the Lancrastian Army Knife, with its numerous blades, fittings, and capabilities.

"Our Nev," another of Nanny's sons, has migrated to Ankh-Morpork, where he has taken to a life of crime, including stealing the lead from the opera-house roof. Presumably, he's a Thieves' Guild member; that isn't the sort of job which a freelance gang could get away with.

Two of Nanny's grandchildren of note are *Shane*, who went off to become a brave sailor lad (and hence to send Nanny even more exotically useless presents than most of the clan), and Jason's youngest son, *Pewsey*, who's believed to be the stickiest child in the world.

Perdita, on the other hand, is definitely a meddler; she'll generally go along with Agnes' helpful urges because it gives her an excuse for digging into other people's lives, but she'll be even more sarcastic about it.

Agnes has inherited the cottage formerly used by Magrat, and by Magrat's tutor Goodie Whemper before her. This is thus the cottage of a line of literate "research witches," and Agnes has a large library by Ramtops standards (two whole shelves of books) and presumably also Goodie Whemper's extensive, ill-organised notes. At one point, she formed a nervous friendship with the Omnian missionary Pastor Oats (pp. 345-346), which might conceivably blossom into romance one day, but they're both busy people and usually hundreds of miles apart.

ST 10 [0]; **DX** 11 [20]; **IQ** 13 [60]; **HT** 11 [10].
Damage 1d-2/1d; BL 20 lbs.; HP 10 [0]; Will 13 [0]; Per 14 [5]; FP 11 [0].
Basic Speed 5.50 [0]; Basic Move 5 [0]; Dodge 8; Parry 8 (DX).
5'8"; 250 lbs.

Social Background

TL: 4 [0].
CF: Sto Plains/Uberwald [0].
Languages: Brindisian (Broken) [2]; Morporkian (Native) [0].

Advantages

Magery 0 [5]; Mind Shield 5 [20]; Social Regard 1 (Respected) [5]; Stunning Scream* [195]; Voice [10].
Perks: Penetrating Voice. [1]

Disadvantages

Code of Honour (Wise-Woman's) [-5]; Pacifism (Cannot Harm Innocents) [-10]; Sense of Duty (Friends, colleagues, and neighbours) [-10]; Very Fat [-5].
Quirks: Briefly gains Callous, Obsession (Stylishness), and Proud after using Mind Shield or otherwise letting Perdita surface; Can't ignore others' problems – looks for ways to help; Still slightly irritated at becoming a witch. [-3]

SKILLS

Connoisseur (Music) (A) IQ-1 [1]-12; Detect Lies (H) Per-1 [2]-13; First Aid/TL4 (Human) (E) IQ+2 [4]-15; Herbalism (H) IQ-1 [2]-12; Housekeeping (E) IQ [1]-13; Magic (Witchcraft) (VH) IQ-1 [4]-12; Magical Form (Physiomancy) (VH) IQ-1 [4]-12; Midwifery (A) IQ-1 [1]-12; Mimicry (Animal Sounds) (H) IQ+1 [2]-14†; Mimicry (Bird Calls) (H) IQ+1 [2]-14†; Mimicry (Speech) (H) IQ+2 [4]-15†; Musical Instrument (Piano) (H) IQ-1 [2]-12; Sewing/TL4 (E) DX+2 [4]-13; Singing (E) HT+7 [16]-18†.

* This unique ability is the most extreme manifestation of Agnes' extraordinary voice. She must Concentrate for a second and spend 1 FP to use it. When she does, everyone nearby must roll against HT or be physically stunned (pp. 185-186). This roll is at -5 for victims within a yard of Agnes, but improves by +1 for every full yard of distance from her (e.g., someone four yards away rolls against HT-1), out to a maximum of eight yards (HT+3 roll). It has no stunning effect beyond eight yards, although it's still highly audible for a very long distance. Total deafness would render someone immune.

† Includes +2 for Voice.

NOTES

This is Agnes as of the end of *Carpe Jugulum*. She may well have learned more advanced magical and medical skills by now, and so acquired more Status and Social Regard. In fact, given her intelligence and two good teachers, she may have become quite formidable.

Greebo

180 points

Greebo, Nanny's Ogg's cat and the dominant member of his species in Lancre, is a huge, one-eyed tom, theoretically grey but in practise mostly scars with a bit of fur around them. His good left eye is yellow; the other one is pearly white. He smells as if someone saved up essence of tomcat for six months, simmered well, and served it with a decaying cabbage side salad.

His main activities are eating, sleeping, and making kittens – he's the father (and often also the grandfather and great-grandfather) of many of the region's other cats. He's acknowledged by most people who know him to be a psychopath. He has terrified wolves and alligators for fun. Among the few things that have ever seriously scared him were a cockerel with voodoo connections, a vixen defending her cubs, and a pack of elves; he becomes very unnerved on the rare occasion when he meets a creature that he can't face down. When he gets annoyed, he'll take on virtually anything; his tally to date includes two vampires (only one of them in bat form at the time) and an elf. To Nanny, however, he's still a soft, sweet little kitten.

Although Greebo will happily slaughter anything herbivorous or avian, he doesn't necessarily try to kill things that he *fights*. He wants to be the most feared cat in the neighbourhood, and a dead opponent can't fear him.

However, Greebo has a problem these days. In the course of an adventure, the coven, needing assistance, worked a spell which temporarily transformed him into a human. This was supposed to be a strictly temporary measure, but Greebo's morphic field was permanently affected; as a result, he tends to flip back to human

guise whenever his subconscious suggests that this might be a way out of a stressful situation (members of the coven can trigger the change, too, using a simple spell). Unfortunately, his subconscious can't manage the small additional spell that the coven used to give him clothes. In any case, Greebo doesn't really have the hang of being human – he finds the social relationships and subtleties far too confusing. He is, however, terrifying in a fight (or anywhere else), and he radiates a kind of raw animal charisma. He generally changes back when he goes to sleep, and he might also do so if his subconscious decides that being a cat is a better idea.

Greebo-as-a-human retains certain useful features from his cat shape – wiry muscles, feline agility and reflexes, retractable claws, and pointy teeth – along with a voice that sounds like a feline growl.

ST 6* [12†]; **DX** 15* [12†]; **IQ** 5* [20]; **HT** 13 [30].
Damage 1d-4/1d-3; BL 7.2 lbs.; HP 6 [0]; Will 12* [0]; Per 13* [0]; FP 13 [0].
Basic Speed 7.00 [0]; Basic Move 8* [0]; Dodge 11*.
About 1' at the shoulder; 25 lbs. (SM -3*).

SOCIAL BACKGROUND

TL: 4 [0].
CF: N/A.
Languages: N/A.

ADVANTAGES

Absolute Direction [5]; Alternate Form (Felinoid Human‡; Reduced Change Time, 5 seconds; Trigger, Witch Invocation, Easily Obtained; Uncontrollable, When Under Stress) [206]; Charisma 1 [5]; Fearlessness 1 [2]; Resistant to Disease (+3) [3]; Resistant to Poison (+3) [5].

Perks: Fearsome Stare. [1]

DISADVANTAGES

Bad Smell [-10]; Berserk (12) [-10]; Bully (9) [-15]; Domestic Cat [-82]; Gluttony (12) [-5]; Lecherousness (12) [-15]; Odious Personal Habit (Habitually Scruffy) [-5]; One Eye [-15]; Reputation -2 (As damn nuisance, among Lancre housewives and poultry-keepers) [-3]; Sense of Duty (Nanny Ogg) [-2].

Quirks: Nosy; Uncongenial. [-2]

SKILLS

Brawling (E) DX+2 [4]-17*§; Climbing (A) DX+1 [4]-16; Intimidation (A) Will+8 [32]-20; Jumping (E) DX [0]-15*; Stealth (A) DX+1 [2]-16*; Survival (Woodlands) (A) Per-1 [1]-12.

* Modified for racial template.

† With 40% cost reduction for Quadruped.

‡ A "racial template" with ST+1 [10], DX+4 [80], IQ-1 [-20], Will+2 [10], and Per+2 [10]; the cost reductions for Quadruped on his personal +2 ST and +1 DX bought off [16]; the advantages Appearance (Attractive) [4], Catfall [10], Claws (Sharp Claws) [5], Combat Reflexes [15], Night

Vision 2 [2], See Invisible (Spirit) [15], and Teeth (Sharp Teeth) [1]; the disadvantages Callous [-5], Dead Broke [-25], Disturbing Voice [-10], and illiteracy in his native language [-3]; no Bad Smell [10]; the quirks Dislikes Water [-1] and Distractible [-1]; and the racial skills Brawling at DX+2 [4], Jumping at DX [1], and Stealth at DX [2]. Form cost: 130 points. Template cost difference (from Domestic Cat): 212 points.

§ Includes -1 for One Eye.

NOTES

In cat form, Greebo has the usual feline willingness to try to eat anything he can catch. This isn't exactly Cast-Iron Stomach (cats are too fastidious to eat rotten meat), but Greebo *did* catch that vampire in bat form, and it hasn't been seen since.

GREEBO AS A HUMAN

In human form, Greebo appears as a darkly – even demoniacally – handsome man, dressed in leather for preference and with an eye-patch.

ST: 13	**HP:** 13	**Speed:** 7.00
DX: 15	**Will:** 12	**Move:** 7
IQ: 10	**Per:** 12	
HT: 13	**FP:** 13	**SM:** 0
Dodge: 11	**Parry:** 12 (Brawling)	**DR:** 0

Bite (17): 1d cut. Reach C.
Claw (17): 1d cut. Reach C.

Traits: Absolute Direction; Appearance (Attractive); Berserk (12); Bully (9); Callous; Catfall; Charisma 1; Claws (Sharp Claws); Combat Reflexes; Dislikes Water; Distractible; Disturbing Voice; Fearlessness 1; Fearsome Stare; Gluttony (12); Lecherousness (12); Night Vision 2; Nosy; Odious Personal Habit (Habitually Scruffy); One Eye; Resistant to Disease (+3); Resistant to Poison (+3); See Invisible (Spirit); Sense of Duty (Nanny Ogg); Teeth (Sharp Teeth); Uncongenial.

Skills: Brawling-17; Climbing-16; Intimidation-20; Jumping-15; Stealth-16; Survival (Woodlands)-11.

Wanderers and Foreigners

The chronicles have featured a wide range of characters, some of whom had no fixed abode when last seen. Many of these individuals could crop up in games set practically anywhere.

Count Giamo Casanunda

Casanunda is a highly atypical dwarf. Two of his best skills are Sex Appeal-15 and Smallsword-17, while his defining disadvantage is Lecherousness (9). He wears "fop" clothes (periwigs, satins, and lace), understanding that conventional dwarfish attire – especially the iron boots – isn't thought modish by ladies. He even shaves his beard. He makes a living as a mercenary, highwayman, courtier, gambler, and all-purpose rogue, and carries business cards which read:

"And it wasn't as if I didn't play fair," said Evil Harry. "I mean, I always left a secret back entrance to my Mountain of Dread, I employed really stupid people as cell guards –"

– The Last Hero

But then, he means it about the "Outrageous Liar." If anyone asks about the "Second Greatest," his cheerful comment is "We try harder."

Casanunda may be encountered almost anywhere, and he can serve many purposes in a plot. However, he shouldn't be used as a mere adversary – he's sharp-witted, broadly skilled, eternally optimistic, and can come in on any side or none. He's somewhat amoral, and sadly sometimes meets people who won't take him seriously until he has climbed up a stepladder and laid them out, but he's never evil.

Evil Harry Dread

Evil Harry Dread is one of the Disc's last dark lords. He started out in a small way decades ago and never got much bigger, despite trying various forms and styles of evil lordship over the years; he claims that he was repeatedly driven out of business by larger, less-stylish competitors. However, he did well enough to

attract the attention of various old-school heroes – and as he largely played by the rules, they let him live.

Eventually, Harry was reduced to plundering ancient tombs with a handful of minions. In one, he stumbled across a map (actually planted by the gods) that was designed to draw adventurers to Cori Celesti (for amusing effect, as the gods, dim-witted as ever, saw it). Harry ended up allying with the Silver Horde (p. 346) on this quest, and although his retinue was wiped out, he ascended the mountain with the heroes. He waited outside the gates of Cori Celesti, though (a dark lord is supposed to be cowardly), and eventually returned to mortal lands with the minstrel who had also accompanied the party. The two men formed a temporary alliance, as the minstrel set about telling the world the tale of the Horde's last adventure, with Harry mentioned in a key supporting role.

Harry has mediocre attributes (partly due to age) and Unattractive Appearance, though he rates IQ 12 with a level or two of Fearlessness. He also has Clerical Investment – being dedicated to a demon-god or two – and an array of Reputations. His Wealth and effective Status have ranged from adequate to severely depleted over time, and he's evil enough to demonstrate flashes of Bad Temper and Selfish. His skills are broad but shallow, including a little Administration, Intimidation, Leadership, Religious Ritual (Dark Cults), Stealth, and Tactics, along with basic weapons training.

Pastor Oats

Mightily-Praiseworthy-Are-Ye-Who-Exalteth-Om ("Mightily") Oats was born in Omnia and raised in the Church of Om. He was quite devout, mostly by default, which made things complicated for him, as the Church was going through a schismatic period – new doctrines were getting nailed to church doors so often that some doors were more nail than wood. Oats became deeply divided; he could see all sides of every question, and he suffered continuing crises of belief. Still, he joined the priesthood and was assigned to a foreign mission.

Oats' mental divisions turned out to have one unsuspected advantage, however: they made him highly resistant to psychic assaults, much like Agnes Nitt (pp. 341-343). Anyone trying to attack his mind found that they lacked a well-defined target. As a result, when his missionary work took him to Lancre and into the middle of a vampire invasion, he was able to resist the mind-control powers of the formidable de Magpyr clan and provide the locals with valuable assistance.

By the end of that incident, Oats had acquired a much more robust faith, and he decided to carry his mission into Uberwald itself. When last heard of, he was still there, and still carrying a double-headed axe which he transformed into a holy symbol by raw belief, and which he calls "Forgiveness." He was involved in the recent discovery of a surviving community of orcs (p. 119), and in attempts to bring them into contact with other races without bloodshed. His thoughtful letters home may have an important influence on the Church's development, and they include valuable information on the dark corners of Uberwald.

Cohen the Barbarian

Cohen the Barbarian was a heroic legend in his own lifetime – literally. The trouble was, part of the point of barbarian heroism is *irresponsibility*. Cohen never got the hang of saving money, let alone investment (the kind of thing that he associated with fat merchants). But he *kept going*, never losing his combat edge despite the loss of an eye, arthritis, and other geriatric problems. He was incredibly old when he appeared in the chronicles – shrunken and bald, with a long beard and a body covered in varicose veins and scars – but *spry* and very experienced. His sword wasn't blindingly fast, just *always* in the right place (Broadsword-30!), and he fought dirty. He used false teeth made of diamonds from a troll's mouth.[1]

Eventually, Cohen's band of similar heroes, the "Silver Horde," stole the entire Agatean Empire. However, that turned out to be less fun than they'd hoped, and mortality pressed ever harder. So they set out to storm the gates of heaven.

Literally.

The problem was, the gods had secretly encouraged this, for fun, without considering what would happen if, say, somebody detonated a keg of Agatean Thunder Clay on Cori Celesti. Fortunately, the Horde were dissuaded at the last moment, and they were last seen going over the edge of Cori Celesti with a fizzing keg. Seconds later, the explosion obliterated a nearby mountain. However, even that didn't kill the Horde; they entered the realm of myth, on stolen horses. Their current location is probably, metaphysically, unknowable.

The Silver Horde

This group included *Caleb the Ripper* (violent even by the Horde's standards), *Mad Hamish* (wheelchair with scythed wheels, deaf as a post), *Truckle the Uncivil* ("LOVE" and "HATE" written on his walking-sticks), and *Boy Willie* (the youngest, at under 80). *Thog the Butcher* left due to prostate problems before they arrived in the Empire. *Old Vincent* died shortly afterward, choking on a cucumber. The rest of the Horde didn't talk about this, but it helped tip them over the edge.

Ronald "Teach" Saveloy was an honorary member, a former schoolteacher who decided that their job sounded less stressful than his, and he helped them with Agatean customs. Sadly, he died just as they completed their conquest of the Empire.

---

1. *Giving +1 to biting damage – and more to the point, +1 to Intimidation if Cohen grinned.*

If encountered, Oats should come across as a robust, intelligent man and an experienced traveller and preacher (Area Knowledge (Uberwald)-14, Axe/Mace-13, Diplomacy-11, First Aid/TL4 (Human)-14, Hidden Lore (Vampire Secrets)-12, Hiking-12, Leadership-12, Naturalist-11, Navigation/TL4 (Land)-12, Occultism-12 Public Speaking-14, Religious Ritual-14, Riding (Equines)-12, Survival (Woodlands)-12, and Theology-12). He has also developed a good prose style (Writing-13), which has helped build him a +2 Reputation over a surprisingly wide area. His True Faith is overtly in Om, although it's really in the universe as much as anything. It absolutely is *not* blind; Oats reached his current position the long way round, and still sees all sides of every question, but now he can work his way to the best answer.

Polly Perks

Polly was born the daughter of an innkeeper in a small town in Borogravia, and she grew up during Borogravia's wars with all its neighbours. When she was 16, her brother – who had joined the army – went missing in action, so she disguised herself as a boy and enlisted in order to look for him. She promptly became involved in the events that led to the end of the war, and she helped ensure that the conclusion wasn't disastrous for her nation. She also discovered some peculiar facts about her army's leadership (Hidden Lore (Peculiar Secrets of the Borogravian Ruling Classes)-14). Her own secret was exposed, but she returned home with her brother, her status as a soldier formally acknowledged, and a certain amount of glory.

She would have been happy to remain an innkeeper for the rest of her life, but a few months later, the war threatened to start again. Deciding that she might be able to do something about this, Polly donned her uniform once again and returned to the world of international politics.

Player characters involved in diplomacy or military affairs in or near Borogravia might well encounter Polly. She's bright and perceptive (IQ 13 and Per 14), and mostly just wants what's best for her family – but that may involve her becoming a politician. She has first-hand experience of the power of the press, and a better grasp of such things than most of her nation's leaders (Current Affairs/TL4 (Borogravia)-14, Diplomacy-11, and Leadership-13). She dislikes being patronised; Borogravian society is traditionally highly sexist, if only because of the Abominations of Nuggan (see *The Story of Nuggan*, pp. 299-300), but Polly understands just how ridiculous that really is, and her personal history and sheer determination mean that she can avoid the Social Stigma that Borogravian women once suffered (Second-Class Citizen, maybe even Valuable Property). She has a +2 Reputation in Borogravia, knows things that make certain people she has to deal with nervous and very polite, and has some extremely useful Contacts (granting Engineer (Clacks) and Propaganda skills).

Polly is a slim, blonde teenage girl, with an androgynous enough figure that passing as a boy wasn't too difficult for her, although she isn't unattractive. Her adventures have given her visible self-confidence (Charisma 1). Borogravian is her native language, but she can get by in Morporkian. These days, she generally carries a pair of cutlasses (treat as shortswords) and a pistol crossbow with which she habitually practises (Crossbow-13 and Shortsword-11), and she dresses in a "feminised" version of a sergeant's uniform.

Susan Sto Helit

519 points

Susan is the daughter of Mort (Death's former apprentice) and Ysabell (Death's adopted daughter), and she has inherited the Duchy of Sto Helit (p. 232), which was granted to her father. Her parents, nervous of the oddities of the family connection, brought her up to be a very practical, rationalistic person, never telling her about her relationship with Death. They also ensured that she received an unusually good schooling, at the Quirm College for Young Ladies (see *Quirm*, pp. 232-233).

This approach was successful in many ways, but it couldn't suppress the fact that, through the oddities of Disc genetics, Susan had inherited a number of attributes from her "grandfather," including a talent for psychic invisibility, a voice that can drive straight into the human subconscious, and the ability to see what is or isn't actually there.[1] She turned into a rather cold, albeit intelligent young woman – a social outsider – who was exceptionally good at subjects she found interesting but who *disappeared* in classes she found boring. Her parents died while she was still at school, but this didn't seem to affect her much, at least at the time.

The discovery of her heritage, and the need to stand in for her grandfather briefly, was a shock, but she adapted. On leaving school, she became first an extremely capable professional governess in Ankh-Morpork, and later a schoolteacher in the same city; she has a usefully cynical view of young children. She can see the bogeymen and monsters imagined by her charges, and her strong will and honorary position in the supernatural hierarchy enable her to beat the daylights out of them. The only signs of her oddity, to public view, are a self-modifying hairstyle and a tendency to drink in Biers (p. 266) on her evenings off. However, the Assassins' Guild, and probably the Ankh-Morpork College of Heralds, have become aware of her peculiar history (they've been doing their jobs for a long time, and they *know stuff*). Still, she *is* rather lonely, knowing at heart that she isn't entirely human, and she has recently developed a romantic involvement with the anthropomorphic personification of Time, another part-human being who can understand how she feels.

Susan rarely exploits her aristocratic title. Presumably, the Duchy of Sto Helit is being managed for her in her absence by competent staff. She formally owes allegiance to the throne of Sto Lat, and she would get on with its strong-willed Queen Keli (p. 349), who was a close friend of her parents. If Susan became involved in the politics of the Sto Plains, her practical approach and unnerving style would doubtless have interesting effects.

---

1. She also exhibits a talent for any activity involving waving a long-handled implement.

The other way she could become entangled in adventures is through her supernatural connections. Her grandfather has manipulated her into helping him with a couple of problems since she left school, and this may happen again. Past events have acquainted her with the Unseen University faculty, who find her unnerving; she regards them as crazy but usefully qualified to deal with certain questions. She would probably form a similar opinion of many PC groups. She's also on speaking terms with one or two gods, and with Nanny Ogg (pp. 340-341), to whom she occasionally takes pupils on field trips.

If Susan *does* appear in plots, she should be a stabilising force with special connections. She'll usually play her part in events in her own way, intersecting with other factions at odd moments. When she's standing in for Death (and on some other occasions), she gains use of his full range of powers, including the ability to stop time, intangibility, and the capacity to speak and understand any human language. She can operate outside of time when somebody else stops it, too.

Susan is a little thin but not unattractive, with pure white hair with a black streak. She normally dresses in the style of a governess or a schoolteacher, but she may switch to a black lace dress when on supernatural duties. Her face bears a birthmark, three pale parallel lines, that only shows up when she's angry (quite often) or when she blushes (rarely). She also has something about her that unnerves perceptive observers, even if they're superhumanly capable themselves.

The game stats below represent Susan when she's consciously *trying* to be human. She has spent much of her life trying to deny (or rather *avoid*) her heritage. However, like Death, she has the power to step outside reality, and even when working as a schoolteacher, she sometimes takes her class psychically (perhaps even physically) through time and space to see great historical events and important geographical features. When she's obliged to involve herself in Death's business, she allows herself to remember that she has access to a fragment of his nature, possibly making her more powerful than mere gods. However, she still has a mortal body, and she tries to hang onto her humanity; she can be hurt, and she *acts* mostly human.

ST 10 [0]; **DX** 13 [60]; **IQ** 14 [80]; **HT** 12 [20].
Damage 1d-2/1d; BL 20 lbs.; HP 10 [0]; Will 16 [10]; Per 14 [0]; FP 12 [0].
Basic Speed 6.25 [0]; Basic Move 6 [0]; Dodge 10*; Parry 11* (Polearm).
5'9"; 130 lbs.

SOCIAL BACKGROUND

TL: 4 [0].
CF: Sto Plains/Uberwald [0].
Languages: Morporkian (Native) [0].

ADVANTAGES

Combat Reflexes [15]; Contact (Archchancellor Ridcully; Thaumatology-18; 12 or less; Usually Reliable) [12]; Contact (Nanny Ogg; Naturalist-18; 12 or less; Usually Reliable) [12]; Eidetic Memory [5]; Fearlessness 2 [4]; Indomitable [15]; Lightning Calculator [2]; Night Vision 3 [3]; Resistant to Disease (+3) [3]; See Invisible (Spirit) [15]; Spirit Empathy [10]; Status 1 [5]; Universal Translator [30]; Unnoticed [70]; Unusual Background (Death's Granddaughter) [20]; Voice of Command (+6 to IQ roll) [105]; Wealth (Comfortable) [10].

Perks: Fearsome Stare; Improvised Weapons (Broadsword); Improvised Weapons (Polearm); Self-Styling Hair. [4]

DISADVANTAGES

Duty (Occasional favours for Death; 6 or less) [-2]; Pacifism (Cannot Harm Innocents) [-10]; Secret (Supernatural Connections) [-10]; Sense of Duty (Family and employers) [-5]; Unnatural Features 1 (Self-styling hair, occasional skeletal aspect) [-1].

Quirks: Distinctive Features (White hair with a black streak); Gets on best with other "outsiders"; Terse; Treats children like adults; Tries to avoid using supernatural abilities. [-5]

SKILLS

Area Knowledge (Circle Sea Region) (E) IQ [1]-14; Brawling (E) DX+1 [2]-14; Broadsword (A) DX [2]-13; First Aid/TL4 (Human) (E) IQ [1]-14; Hidden Lore (Spirit Lore) (A) IQ-1 [1]-13; Housekeeping (E) IQ [1]-14; Intimidation (A) Will+2 [8]-18; Literature (H) IQ-1 [2]-13; Mathematics/TL4 (Applied) (H) IQ-1 [2]-13; Philosophy (Sto Plains Classical) (H) IQ-1 [2]-13; Polearm (A) DX+1 [4]-14; Psychology (Human) (H) IQ-1 [2]-13; Research/TL4 (A) IQ-1 [1]-13; Riding (Equines) (A) DX [2]-13; Savoir-Faire (High Society) (E) IQ [1]-14; Sewing/TL4 (E) DX [1]-13; Shortsword (A) DX [2]-13; Sports (Hockey) (A) DX-1 [1]-12; Sports (Lacrosse) (A) DX-1 [1]-12; Sports (Rounders) (A) DX-1 [1]-12; Staff (A) DX [2]-13; Teaching (A) IQ [2]-14.

* Includes +1 for Combat Reflexes.

NOTES

Death might be considered a Patron for Susan, but she avoids calling on him for aid, while he prefers to admire the way she solves her own problems. She lives in Ankh-Morpork on a schoolteacher's salary, but if she ever chose to claim her rights in Sto Helit, she could act as Status 4, and the income from her holdings would probably be enough to support this.

Twoflower

The Disc's first tourist was a very ordinary little citizen of the Agatean Empire, a clerk in an insurance office. However, somewhere along the line, he acquired a bizarre urge to see the world and take pictures of it. This should have seen him murdered in short order for his huge stock of gold coins, but perverse good fortune kept him alive – at least until people realised that he was protected by his Luggage (later owned by Rincewind, pp. 330-332), or that he was more profitable alive than dead. It seems that he enjoys the personal attention of The Lady (p. 303) – sometimes, anyway – which could arguably justify giving him multiple levels of Serendipity, if only when she's playing him as a game piece.

Twoflower dragged Rincewind through many of his early adventures, and then decided to go home to tell people about what he'd seen. His story, published in the Empire as *What I Did On My Holidays*, inspired a revolutionary movement with its tales of lands in which people weren't always tortured to death for speaking out of turn. Twoflower wasn't a natural rebel, but he became personally involved with the movement after his wife was killed during a minor manoeuvre in the internal politics of the old regime.

Thus, Twoflower was around when Cohen the Barbarian acquired the throne, and as Cohen knew and liked him, he was promptly appointed Grand Vizier. As a long-time clerk and nice person, Twoflower is probably better suited for this job than most candidates. It isn't known what happened to the Empire's politics after Cohen and friends left, but Twoflower may well have retained some kind of position.

Twoflower is unremarkable in many ways – ST 9, IQ 11, Bad Sight (Nearsighted; Mitigator, Glasses), Curious (15), and Pacifism (Cannot Harm Innocents) – but he has demonstrated a degree of apparent Fearlessness, originally based on the belief that bad things don't happen to well-meaning bystanders. He eventually shed some of his Gullibility, too. His book earned him a +3 Reputation among Agatean radicals and a -4 Reputation among ultra-traditionalists; his unexpected promotion later gave him Administrative Rank 7. He doubtless developed his competent Accounting and Professional Skill (Filing Clerk) into some level of Administration thereafter. He also has experience of Photography and Writing.

Other Rulers

Most Discworld countries are monarchies of various degrees of absolutism, although some leaders get their jobs by manipulating their way through a power structure (as in Ankh-Morpork), and one or two places (notably Ephebe, p. 235, and Pseudopolis, p. 233) purport to be democracies. Hence, the Disc's many rulers claim diverse titles, command varying degrees of real authority, and have armies that differ widely in size and loyalty. A few interesting examples appear below.

RHYS RHYSSON

The Low King of the dwarfs (p. 227) dwells in the royal mine in Uberwald, although he was born into a small coal-mining clan near Llamedos. He's short even for a dwarf, and he wears leather and home-forged mail – although he has expressed an interest in the new wave of dwarf fashions and even hinted that he may purchase some of them (implying that "he" is really a she).

As this suggests, he seems to be quite progressive, though he must be careful to carry dwarf opinion with him – his position isn't hereditary but is attained by an election of sorts and a lot of *politics*. On the other hand, the job is held for life, and Rhys is showing every sign of being willing to act as *he* thinks best, ignoring the traditionalists. He has even negotiated a peace agreement with the Diamond King of the trolls (Mr. Shine, p. 230), although getting dwarfs and trolls to respect that may take work. He possesses dwarfish stubborn determination, plus the support of both Lord Vetinari (pp. 306-308) and Lady Margolotta (below).

Player characters – especially but not only dwarfs – might find themselves involved in Rhys' plans. Those who succeed at some undertaking for him can expect a fair (but not excessive) reward. Those who cross him may face stern dwarf justice, or something less formal.

QUEEN KELI

Princess Keli was a young, inexperienced heir whose destiny was supposed to be to die young, leaving Sto Lat in the hands of an older, deadlier, and much more political ruler whose own destiny was to be part of a process of unification on the Sto Plains. Instead, she ended up as Queen Kelirehenna I, Lord of Sto Lat, Protector of the Eight Protectorates and Empress of the Long Thin Debated Piece Hubwards of Sto Kerrig. This means she's had to take over that bigger destiny; fortunately, she seems able to manage and can be relied on to defend her kingdom with royal determination. (She's more likely to order nuisances exiled than anything more final, but she'll be prompt about the decision.) She may still be advised by Igneous Cutwell, a former consulting wizard who doesn't do much magic these days. Mentioning the rumours about their relationship would technically be *lese-majesty*, but anyway, he's definitely intelligent enough to be a useful aide.

LADY MARGOLOTTA

Uberwald isn't at all united, but much of the real power in most of the region – above ground, at least – is wielded by Lady Margolotta Amaya Katerina Assumpta Crassina von Uberwald, a vampire of some age, considerable intelligence, and surprising moral sense (but don't push your luck). The Patrician of Ankh-Morpork treats her as an equal and plays Thud against her over the clacks; they first met when he was a young man touring the Disc, but she claims to have learned from *him*. Uninformed PCs may not guess any of this when they first meet her, though – she looks like someone's mother (someone with money, mind), often wears pearls, a pink jumper (embroidered with bat designs), and sensible flat shoes, and keeps a lapdog (which admittedly looks like a rat). People sometimes assume that they've met her when they've only yet encountered her librarian, who's tall, thin, dark, and generally looks the part. This confusion suits Lady Margolotta just fine.

. . . New powers are emerging. Old countries are blinking in the sunlight of the dawning millennium. And of course we have to maintain friendships with all blocs.

– Carpe Jugulum

Margolotta is a Black Ribboner (pp. 113-114), and she does her best to reduce bloodshed and keep Uberwald peaceable (although, like the Patrician, she sometimes achieves this by having troublesome people *removed*). Like any vampire who has sworn off human blood, she has had to replace that driving obsession with something of equal strength – in her case, a drive for political control. The GM should assume that her level with any skill relevant to this goal is at least 15, if not higher.

"Lord Vetinari, I know, believes that information is currency. But everyvun knows that currency has alvays been information. Money doesn't need to talk, it merely has to listen."
– Lady Margolotta,
*in **The Fifth Elephant***

PRINCE KHUFURAH

The current Prince of Klatch got the job when his older brother, Prince Cadram, retired in a hurry after an unfortunate misunderstanding (*not* a war) with Ankh-Morpork. Khufurah is a tall, bearded man, previously athletic but a little too fond of the pleasant aspects of his position, including the big dinners, the odd bottle of wine, and attractive company. However, he's also smart, trained in politics, and loyal to his nation. He isn't likely to start anything too dangerous, but PCs should recognise that he's pretty much the standard competent ruler whom it wouldn't be clever to annoy, because he *has* got a bigger army than you.

QUEEN PTRACI OF DJELIBEYBI

Formerly the favourite handmaiden (and, it turned out, daughter) of King Teppicymon XXVII, Ptraci was an attractive young woman during the events of *Pyramids*, usually seen in the heavy make-up and minimal costume of her profession. However, she refused to take poison "voluntarily" and join the old king in his funeral pyramid, which got her into trouble with the priesthood. The new king, Teppicymon XXVIII, secretly rescued her from prison, and after they discovered her parentage, he abdicated and she took the throne. The priests were happy enough with this, thinking that a naïve young handmaiden would be easily manipulated. They instantly discovered that they were wrong.

Assuming that she's still in charge, she may be noticeably older now, and she might have filled out a little, though she's not the sort to let herself go too badly. Her regular asses' milk baths and the installation of modern plumbing in the palace have probably helped. She didn't strike people as especially intelligent in her youth, but as well as a strong will, she displayed a certain whimsical deviousness and practical character judgement. She's likely to be a serious wildcard in the politics of the Circle Sea region, although she'll be well aware that Djelibeybi doesn't have the power to assert itself too much.

Any PCs who have dealings with Ptraci will probably find her confusing but essentially reasonable. If they annoy her, though, she'll work out some way to annoy them right back – and she *is* queen.

BARONESS ELLA OF GENUA

"Ella Saturday" was the (technically illegitimate) daughter of Genua's old ruler, Baron Saturday, and the witch Erzulie Gogol. Her father was killed by Lilith de Tempscire when Lilith took over the city, and her mother was driven into exile in the swamp. Ella grew up into a striking young woman with dark skin and fair hair; Lilith planned to set her up as a character in a Cinderella-style narrative, while Mrs. Gogol had her own ideas about how things should go. However, the Lancre witches intervened, leaving Ella as ruler entirely in her own right.

After a lifetime as a pawn and kitchen worker, Ella's first concern was to enjoy herself (not difficult in Genua, once Lilith was removed), but she showed signs of having a mind of her own. Genuan politics doubtless remain complicated and messy, but Ella is presumably still on top. With five different witches having asserted her right to rule, deposing her would seem like a bad idea.

PRINCE HEINRICH OF ZLOBENIA

Heinrich was born into a complex regional mess of royal families, and he is in fact the nephew of the long-deceased Duchess Annagovia of Borogravia. He's an unpleasant aristocratic-military bully, fond of uniforms; he claims to admire Ankh-Morpork, but this mostly means that he admires its power. Borogravia's incessant warmongering gave him all the excuse he needed to invade the place; if he could prove that Annagovia was dead, he had a good claim to her throne, and so could double the size of his territory. Thanks to the events of *Monstrous Regiment* and the political machinations of Ankh-Morpork, however, the truce that ended the war didn't give him what he wanted. But until Borogravia is properly stabilised and a full peace treaty is signed, he still has a chance.

Heinrich may be a vain braggart, but he's an experienced soldier and not entirely a fool. He also still holds most of the cards in the game of regional politics. If the PCs find themselves working against him, they should watch their backs. He's likely to be nervous around Polly Perks (pp. 346-347), who once kicked him in the crotch.

BEWARE the AMBIGUOUS PUZUMA

High in the Ramtops, an expedition was making an exhibition of itself.

At the top of a long slope with more than enough loose rocks, a pair of young women had fallen into an argument. They'd been teetering on the brink of this for days, and now they were in the middle of the long, emotional plummet that was likely to end with an unpleasant smash. In the years they'd known each other, at school and while volunteering at the Sunshine Sanctuary for Sick Dragons, they had rarely argued, and never seriously. Then again, they had never had much to argue about. Now, weeks from home and halfway up a mountain, their friendship was being truly tested for the first time. And not all tests are passed.

Voices – with impeccable upper-class Morporkian accents – were being raised.

Halfway up the slope, a dwarf and a pair of local guides, left unable to progress by the failure of the women to clear a tangle in their ropes, rested and watched.

And at the bottom of the slope, another young woman was taking a deep breath and counting to 100. Jemzarkiza of Krull could see several ways to resolve this problem. Unfortunately, none of them worked if the person who could see them was at the bottom of the slope. It didn't help that Jemzarkiza hated heights. She'd been avoiding edges and precipices for days now, and getting up even this slope was going to be a trial; she wasn't going to rush anything. Nearby, a small string of pack mules eyed that same slope with the air of animals who were blowed if they were going to attempt the climb at all, even if anyone should ask them.

"You have a problem, ducks?"

Jemzarkiza did her best not to jump, and turned carefully. She discovered that the speaker was a woman of mature years, wearing a black dress and a pointy hat, and holding a broomstick. Jemzarkiza drew the obvious conclusions.

"Just some . . . organisation issues," she said.

The witch nodded. "Forgive me asking," she said, clearly not worrying about forgiveness at all, "but why do you want to come all this way up here anyway?"

"I don't," Jemzarkiza replied, "but someone thinks that there's something up here."

"Well," said the witch, "there's plenty of rock, and quite a bit of moss. And a few trolls, you might want to bear in mind. Even some troll ducks, I believe."

"Troll ducks?"

"They don't float well."

"I suppose not. But that's not what we're after."

"So what . . ."

The witch's question was interrupted by a sudden shout from the top of the slope. The young women suddenly sounded far happier, despite which, they were both now retreating downhill, risking a literal plummet leading to a literal smash. The reason became a little clearer a moment later, when a burst of flame erupted from somewhere beyond them, causing them to retreat faster and more dangerously.

"At last!" said Jemzarkiza.

"At last?" asked the witch, trying to conceal the fact that she was suddenly the person present with the least idea of what was going on.

*"The Greater Mountain Miniature Swamp Dragon!" Jemzarkiza announced. "**Draco vulgaris montanus maximus**! It isn't extinct after all!"*

Most Discworld creatures (and flora) are similar to those of our world. However, the magic-laden environment does throw up some oddities . . .

For a description of the chimera we shall turn to Broomfog's famous bestiary Anima Unnaturale: "It have thee legges of an mermade, the hair of an tortoise, the teeth of an fowel, and the winges of an snake. Of course, I have only my worde for it . . ."

– Sourcery

CREATURE DETAILS

The game details used to describe creatures are similar to those given for people, but simplified, as not all of the information which is important for playable characters is relevant for animals and monsters. In particular, there are no point values, because those would add a lot of arithmetic which wouldn't have any effect on play. Readers who like that sort of thing are welcome to calculate point totals, but they should realise that points measure little of importance here. A monster worth few points because it's stupid, ugly, and intolerant is still a dangerous encounter if it's also strong and tough; it just wouldn't be much fun to *roleplay.*

Details which *do* appear include:

Attributes and Secondary Characteristics: These mean exactly what they do for PCs. ST 0 is usually limited to intangible spirits that can't pick up objects, while anything with IQ 0 is mindless and acts purely reflexively.

Dodge and Parry: These are prefigured from DX, Basic Speed, and combat skills, and *already* include bonuses for Combat Reflexes and Enhanced Defences – don't add those again.

DR: This is *total* DR from both natural and artificial sources. If a creature isn't noted as wearing armour, it doesn't. The GM is free to add more DR if, say, an evil wizard has cast protective spells on his pets, or clad them in metal plates.

Attacks: These are listed by name. The number in parentheses is effective skill with the strike, grapple, fiery breath, or whatever. Damage scores *already* include bonuses for the Brawling skill, the Claws advantage, etc. Possible damage types are burning (burn), crushing (cr), cutting (cut), impaling (imp), piercing (small, normal, large, and huge are noted as pi-, pi, pi+, and pi++, respectively), and "special" (spcl). If a tiny non-crushing attack can never do more than the minimum 1 point of damage (see *Damage Roll,* p. 182), it's listed as "1 point."

Traits: Advantages or disadvantages which are important for game purposes. For brevity's sake, DR and attacks aren't listed here a second time. Also, it can be taken as read that beasts behave in an "animalistic" fashion, cannot talk, and so on; domestic animals behave somewhat better, from a human point of view, but aren't as good at looking after themselves.

Skills: Any skills possessed by all creatures of this type. Exceptional specimens may have different skill lists. Those with IQ 6+ are sapient and capable of learning almost any skill.

Notes: Anything else of importance – including exceptions to these guidelines.

All attributes assume a typical adult member of the species. If the GM wants to get detailed, then young or sickly creatures can be given lower numbers, especially ST (and thus HP), while big, dangerous specimens can go a bit higher. Remember to recalculate secondary characteristics and damage as necessary.

There's a fair degree of variation in animals' *physical* attributes – an incredibly strong elephant, a faster-than-average camel, or a sickly swamp dragon would all be common enough – but few animals vary much from the species-normal IQ given here. However, there are exceptions to every rule. For example, Gavin, the wolf pack leader who appeared in *The Fifth Elephant,* may have qualified for IQ 5 or even 6. He was still an animal, though; he was capable of something *verging* on abstract thought, and he was an excellent judge of character, but he couldn't speak or use tools. Of course, when magic enters the equation, all bets are off!

(Relatively) Ordinary Animals

The Disc does have many animals that the inhabitants of our reality would find quite familiar, although sometimes they're a bit bigger, smarter, or weirder. It also has species that aren't so familiar, but which are, in the end, just animals – either "plausible" in our terms, or recognisable types warped by magic or other local influences.

Such animals tend to behave in *fairly* realistic ways. That is to say, they don't like getting hurt, and they know instinctively that even a moderate injury will most likely kill them, either by infection or by rendering them unable to feed themselves. Hence, most of them will back off from determined-looking humans with pointy weapons. However, some are big, stupid, or crazy – or too heavily influenced by the nature of narrative reality – and pounce first and worry about the odds later, while they're either eating or dying.

.303 BOOKWORM

The .303 bookworm is an example of accelerated Discworld evolution. It's extremely dangerous to hang around magical books for long – even for an invertebrate – so this species eats through whole rows of tomes at projectile-weapon velocities. It doesn't *intend* to be dangerous, but anyone in the way of a .303 bookworm when it comes off the end of a shelf could take, say, 2d pi damage.

AMBIGUOUS PUZUMA

The fastest animal on the Disc, the ambiguous puzuma can approach relativistic velocities. Unfortunately, it's less good at stopping. Adventurers are unlikely to encounter a live specimen.

CAMELS

Discworld camels *appear* very much like those of our own world, right down to the behaviour (surly) and the smell (*distinctive*). They're often domesticated, being useful for load-carrying rather than for speed. Their legs appear to work by a complex system of consensus planning, which makes them slow to get moving from a sitting or lying posture, although real emergencies can persuade them to make haste.

What no one else fully realises is that camels are actually intelligent beings – perhaps the most intelligent on the Disc. Their highly accurate stone-spitting attack isn't instinctive but based on instant mental calculation of trajectories, factoring in local wind speeds and anything else relevant. They are dedicated hobbyist mathematicians.

They don't reveal this because they have a very good idea what humans would do if they found out. They regard a life of contemplation in stables and deserts as perfectly satisfactory, and have no worries about being hit with sticks by sub-numerate herders. They cheerfully adopt human-given names, such as "Evil-Minded Brute" or "Filthy Maniac." However, if mathematical problems or questions of theoretical physics ever become *really* important to a party with a baggage camel, strange hints may begin arriving from obscure directions.

Camels are remarkably tolerant (insofar as a camel is *ever* "tolerant") of being heavily laden. They'll carry loads up to Heavy or even Extra-Heavy encumbrance (582 or 970 lbs., respectively, with ST 22), although Medium encumbrance (up to 291 lbs.) is a safer bet for long distances. They are of course still slowed as per *Encumbrance and Move* (p. 168), and if they get annoyed by their treatment, they won't hide the fact.

A healthy adult camel weighs 900-1,100 lbs. and costs about $75.

ST: 22	**HP:** 22	**Speed:** 5.50
DX: 10	**Will:** 13	**Move:** 7
IQ: 13	**Per:** 13	
HT: 12	**FP:** 12	**SM:** +1
Dodge: 8	**Parry:** N/A	**DR:** 1 (Tough Skin)

Bite (10): 2d-5 cr. Reach C.
Kick (8): 2d cr. Reach C, 1.
Spit (12): Camels are notoriously prone to spitting, usually when eating something reasonably moist. Treat this as a ranged attack with Max 3 and Acc 2. On a hit, the dollop of cud blinds the victim for 1d-2 turns.
Spit Stone (16): A camel that happens to be eating dates can spit the stones. Treat this as a ranged attack with 1/2D 5, Max 10, and Acc 2, doing 1d-3 cr. Camels won't *usually* use this on humans, but they enjoy stunning passing birds.

Traits: Enhanced Move 1 (Ground Speed 14); Hooves; Mathematical Ability 4; Obsession (Pursuit of pure mathematics) (12); Quadruped; Stubbornness; Tacitly Sarcastic (a quirk); Weak Bite.

Skills: Mathematics (all specialisations)-19; Survival (Desert)-15.
Notes: Camels need far less water than their size implies – or rather, they can subsist on little or no water for days, and then make up for it at the next oasis.

CATS

Ordinary Discworld domestic cats are much like those on our world – sneaky, vicious, borderline psychotic, sometime paranoid or neurotic, but *furry* and *cute* – although some of them may be moderately bright. But they're still only called "domesticated" by courtesy; no one can teach a cat tricks it doesn't want to do.

There's nothing especially supernatural about cats in general; if witches often keep cats, it's because old ladies like having pets, not because of anything more mystic. However, cats *can* see invisible spirits, and hence also notice beings using the Unnoticed advantage (p. 48). There doesn't seem to be any deep arcane reason for this – they just can. If you need game statistics for a cat, see *Domestic Cat* (p. 107), adjusting the template details for age, size, and demeanour.

CROCODILES

The statistics below represent an average-sized crocodile, as encountered in rivers throughout Klatch. They could also be used for one of the larger alligators in the swamps around Genua, although those tend to be somewhat smaller and *slightly* less aggressive toward humans. Both species actually vary quite a bit in size. Universal features are a big mouth but short legs (giving these creatures a bit of extra biting damage but a little less power with their claws than their ST implies), and an extremely muscular tail (useful for swimming and if anyone tries to get behind them).

It is interesting to note that, owing to this mathematician's particular species, what he was eating for his supper was his lunch.

– Pyramids

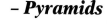

Crocodiles are ambush predators. Their use of Stealth skill is less about sneaking up on things and more about lurking just below the surface of the water, looking like a log, until something unwisely comes close to the banks – or even better, goes for a swim. Being cold-blooded, they don't really get moving until the sun has been up for a few hours, and they spend a lot of time lazing on sandbanks, but they'll always defend themselves if necessary. While they breathe air, they can go without for minutes at a time; they often drag prey underwater in the hope that it will drown before the crocodile has to surface.

Crocodiles have powerful muscles that close their jaws, but much weaker muscles to *open* them. If you can get a grip around a crocodile's jaws, you need only win a Quick Contest of your ST vs. 1/4 of *its* ST to keep them shut. Well, that and worry about 1,500 lbs. of crocodile rolling on top of you, flailing with its tail and claws, and diving under the nearest water.

ST: 23	**HP:** 23	**Speed:** 6.50
DX: 13	**Will:** 10	**Move:** 8 (Water)
IQ: 2	**Per:** 12	
HT: 13	**FP:** 13	**SM:** +2
Dodge: 9	**Parry:** N/A	**DR:** 4

Bite (13): 2d+1 cut. Reach C.
Claw (11): 2d-1 cut. Reach C.
Tail Slam (11): 2d+1 cr. Reach C. Can only be used on opponents to the crocodile's rear. Anyone struck must also roll vs. the better of his DX or Acrobatics or be knocked off his feet.

Traits: Cast-Iron Stomach; Night Vision 4; Quadruped; Sharp Claws; Sharp Teeth; Short Legs; Ugly.
Skills: Stealth-13; Swimming-13.
Notes: A crocodile has Move 4 on land, but only in short bursts – if it has to walk any distance, it's limited to Move 2. It has only DR 2 on its underside.

CURIOUS SQUID

The curious squid is a small species found in the Circle Sea. Curious squid may in fact be highly intelligent – it's possible that they actually constructed the city on the (usually) sunken island of Leshp, or at least adopted it for their own use – but their chief mental attribute is their intense curiosity, which far exceeds their sense of self-preservation. Hence, they can be caught by fishermen simply showing a few lights, or just dropping vaguely interesting-looking nets or hooks into the water. They don't taste very good, but unfortunately for them, they're fashionable in expensive restaurants, whose chefs can hide the taste, or simply leave the squid out of the finished dish altogether.

DOGS

Much as on our world, Discworld dogs are pack hunter-scavengers that could fairly be described as wolves that have been domesticated and then bred into a huge range of often faintly ludicrous forms. Some remain essentially wild, or have strayed and reverted to the feral pattern, even within human cities. Hence, people encountering dogs may regard them as friendly, useful, or dangerous, depending on the circumstances.

ST: 3 to 10	**HP:** 3 to 10	**Speed:** 5.00 to 6.00
DX: 10 to 11	**Will:** 10	**Move:** 5 to 10
IQ: 4	**Per:** 12	
HT: 10 to 12	**FP:** 10 to 12	**SM:** -4 to 0

Dodge: 8 to 10	**Parry:** N/A	**DR:** 0

Bite (10 to 14): 1 point to 1d-2 cut. Reach C.

Traits: Chummy; Discriminatory Smell; Quadruped; Sharp Teeth; Short Legs; Ultrahearing.
Skills: Brawling-10 to 14; Tracking-13 (or better – sometimes *very* high).
Notes: Because dog breeds vary so much, many of these statistics are given as ranges of possible values. In particular, ST and HP can vary enormously, which in turn affects biting damage. A tiny miniature lapdog might have ST/HP 3 and SM -4, and bite for 1 point; a 15-lb. terrier could have ST/HP 5 and SM -3, and also do 1 point; a 70-lb. retriever could have ST/HP 8 and SM -2, and inflict 1d-4; and an impressive hunting beast would have ST/HP 10 and SM 0, and bite for 1d-3. (Fighting dogs may have Brawling at DX+2 or better, for +1 to damage.) Use higher DX and HT scores for fighting or working dogs, lower values for pampered pets. Move tends to be a function of size and breed – long-legged hunting dogs are quicker than short-legged terriers or lumbering bulldogs. *Serious* fighting dogs may have Combat Reflexes, giving +1 to Dodge.

Smart Dogs

Through a combination of narrative causality and background magic, some Discworld dogs – in places including Ankh-Morpork – are significantly smarter than the "realistic" type above, with IQ 6 or even higher, meaning that they've been able to develop their own language. Normal humans *cannot* learn this. The problem is partly one of not having the right sort of throat and partly one of mindset; talking like a dog means truly understanding how a dog thinks. Hence, werewolves *can* learn the Canine language and can use it even when in human shape. There's no written form, and the sounds don't fit any human alphabet. A human who wants to talk to ordinary, even smart dogs will need to find a werewolf or a fully sapient dog such as Gaspode (pp. 316-317) to act as an interpreter – or use magic. Very smart dogs may also learn other skills (Intimidation, for a start).

DROP BEARS

Drop bears are native to the Fourecks Outback (p. 245) and are close relatives of the koala. They have ST 6, DX 10, SM -2, Climbing-14, and Stealth-14. Their carnivore teeth and claws inflict 1 point of cutting damage on a hit. However, the drop bear's most significant feature is a pad of muscle and fat on its rear end, which can absorb impacts with no significant harm to the animal (DR 5, posterior only).

Their hunting method involves sitting around in trees, habitually in family groups of a dozen or so, until an animal passes underneath, at which point one bear . . . drops, aiming with instinctive precision (attack roll 14) for the head. Being good at lurking, they usually achieve surprise; a 25-lb. bear landing on one's head is quite surprising, and typically inflicts 1d-2 crushing damage. If such an attack hits someone who was caught unaware and didn't try to defend, treat it as a knockout blow attempt (see *Specific Hit Locations*, p. 183), giving the bear a fair chance of rendering its target unconscious. Then the rest of the group gather round to finish off the victim and eat.

Drop bears never think to inspect possible prey for pointy or spiked headgear. Also, the members of an overexcited pack will sometimes start dropping as a group.

ELEPHANTS

The elephants found in the jungles of Howondaland are much like those on our world[1]: big grey pachyderms with dexterous trunks, a certain amount of intelligence, and a slightly nervous nature. A large number were transported to Ankh-Morpork during the brief motion-picture craze (see *Moving Pictures*). It isn't clear what happened to them.

Wild elephants behave as wild animals. Captive elephants can be trained to do quite a lot, given time.

ST: 45	**HP:** 45	**Speed:** 4.00
DX: 12	**Will:** 10	**Move:** 4
IQ: 5	**Per:** 10	
HT: 12	**FP:** 12	**SM:** +3
Dodge: 7	**Parry:** N/A	**DR:** 4 (Tough Skin)

Trample (12): 5d cr. An elephant can *trample* SM +1 or smaller opponents – or even SM +2 creatures, if it knocks them down first. The victim's only permitted defence is a dodge. A charging elephant that knocks down its victim and then keeps moving *automatically* tramples (no defence permitted), but for only 2d cr.

Trunk Grapple (12): An elephant can grab with its trunk (see *Grabbing and Grappling*, pp. 183-184), which has ST 11, to throw around smaller foes or because it feels the need to immobilise someone. Reach C-3.

Tusk Strike (12): 5d+5 cr. Reach C.

---

1. Elephants under the Discworld are four in number and not like those in any other universe. See p. 8.

Traits: Enhanced Move 1 (Ground Speed 8); Quadruped (but with one manipulator); Trunk (acts as a ST 11 "hand" with Reach C-3); Tusks (can be used in close combat); Weak Bite.

Hermit Elephants

A variant species, also found in Howondaland, is the *Hermit Elephant*. This shy, thin-skinned (DR 1) sub-species has adapted well to the presence of humans; it adopts deserted human-built huts for camouflage and extra protection. (Mysteriously, it has little difficulty finding such – every hut that an elephant enters seems to be deserted by its inhabitants soon after, if not before.) Growing Hermit Elephants add extensions to their mobile dwellings. A standard lightly built Howondaland hut is worth +5 DR to the elephant, but better buildings may give better protection.

FOURECKSIAN EMUS

This flightless bird is another of the peculiar creatures of Fourecks (pp. 244-245). It's quite a bit bigger and more muscular than our world's emu, or even its ostrich. Indeed, it's pretty intimidating by *any* standards – including those of Outback fauna. Some foolhardy locals use these things to pull single-seat (sometimes single-*wheeled*) personal transports. A trained emu sells for around $25 in the Outback.

ST: 13	**HP:** 11	**Speed:** 5.50
DX: 11	**Will:** 10	**Move:** 7
IQ: 3	**Per:** 11	
HT: 11	**FP:** 11	**SM:** 0
Dodge: 8	**Parry:** N/A	**DR:** 0

Kick (10): 1d+1 cr. Reach C, 1.

Peck (12): 1d-1 pi+. Reach C, 1.

Traits: Bad Temper (15); Blunt Claws; Enhanced Move 1 (Ground Speed 14); Long Neck (Reach 1 with beak); No Arms; Sharp Beak.

Skills: Brawling-12.

Horses and Mules

Horses are a very important means of transport on the Disc, where they're both ridden and used to pull coaches and carts. They aren't *terribly* bright, but the best of them look impressive. They'll carry up to Medium encumbrance (p. 168) fairly happily; light cavalry and messengers aim for Light.

Cavalry Horse

A light warhorse, expensively trained for use by some of the most rash and impetuous professional soldiers, sells for about $200.

ST: 22	**HP:** 22	**Speed:** 5.00
DX: 9	**Will:** 11	**Move:** 8
IQ: 3	**Per:** 12	
HT: 11	**FP:** 11	**SM:** +1
Dodge: 9	**Parry:** N/A	**DR:** 0

Bite (10): 2d-5 cr. Reach C.
Kick (8): 2d cr. Reach C, 1.

Traits: Combat Reflexes; Enhanced Move 1 (Ground Speed 16); Hooves; Quadruped; Weak Bite.
Skills: Brawling-10; Mount-12.

Equestrian Equipment

Working horses appear at TL1, when bridles ($1.75, 3 lbs.) become available; Riding skill rolls are at -2 with such minimal kit. At TL2, full tack ($7.50, 15 lbs.) allows unpenalised skill use; at TL3, such gear includes stirrups, allowing more hands-free riding. Horseshoes ($2.50, 4 lbs. a set) are also TL3; without these, a working horse's feet need a lot of care, and the beast may go lame whenever the GM decides that this would fit the plot.

Draft Horse

A serious working beast, worth $100.

ST: 25	**HP:** 25	**Speed:** 5.25
DX: 9	**Will:** 10	**Move:** 6
IQ: 3	**Per:** 11	
HT: 12	**FP:** 12	**SM:** +1
Dodge: 8	**Parry:** N/A	**DR:** 0

Bite (9): 2d-3 cr. Reach C.
Kick (7): 2d+2 cr. Reach C, 1.

Traits: Enhanced Move 1 (Ground Speed 12); Hooves; Quadruped; Weak Bite.

Pony

Serving sometimes as a hobby for well-off children and sometimes as versatile cross-country transport, a pony is worth $75. A well-trained riding pony has the Mount skill at 11+, increasing cost by $5 or more.

ST: 18	**HP:** 18	**Speed:** 5.25
DX: 10	**Will:** 11	**Move:** 7
IQ: 3	**Per:** 12	
HT: 11	**FP:** 11	**SM:** +1
Dodge: 8	**Parry:** N/A	**DR:** 0

Bite (10): 1d-1 cr. Reach C.
Kick (8): 1d+2 cr. Reach C, 1.

Traits: Enhanced Move 1 (Ground Speed 14); Hooves; Quadruped; Weak Bite.

Saddle Horse

This ordinary long-distance transport costs $60.

ST: 21	**HP:** 21	**Speed:** 5.00
DX: 9	**Will:** 10	**Move:** 6
IQ: 3	**Per:** 12	
HT: 11	**FP:** 11	**SM:** +1
Dodge: 8	**Parry:** N/A	**DR:** 0

Bite (9): 2d-5 cr. Reach C.
Kick (7): 2d cr. Reach C, 1.

Traits: Enhanced Move 1 (Ground Speed 12); Hooves; Quadruped; Weak Bite.
Skills: Mount-11.

Small Mule

A horse/donkey crossbreed – useful as a pack animal in all sorts of terrain, but notoriously *difficult* – a small mule costs $50.

ST: 18	**HP:** 18	**Speed:** 5.50
DX: 10	**Will:** 12	**Move:** 5
IQ: 3	**Per:** 12	
HT: 12	**FP:** 12	**SM:** +1
Dodge: 8	**Parry:** N/A	**DR:** 0

Bite (10): 1d-1 cr. Reach C.
Kick (8): 1d+2 cr. Reach C, 1.

Traits: Bad Temper (12); Enhanced Move 1/2 (Ground Speed 8); Hooves; Quadruped; Stubbornness; Weak Bite.
Notes: A *large* mule has ST/HP 22 (giving bite damage 2d-5 and kick damage 2d), Move 6, and Ground Speed 9, and costs $100.

"Spirited" Horse

This is the sort of animal that gets passed off to people who request something "fast" and forget to specify other details. It uses its Mount skill mostly to throw riders. It probably costs about $60, but a lot depends on how desperate the seller is to be rid of the thing or the buyer looks to procure some sort of horse. Someone who can control it might pay a lot more, if they're careless.

ST: 21	**HP:** 21	**Speed:** 5.50
DX: 10	**Will:** 12	**Move:** 9
IQ: 3	**Per:** 12	
HT: 12	**FP:** 12	**SM:** +1
Dodge: 8	**Parry:** N/A	**DR:** 0

Bite (11): 2d-5 cr. Reach C.
Kick (9): 2d cr. Reach C, 1.

Traits: Bad Temper (6); Enhanced Move 1 (Ground Speed 18); Hooves; Quadruped; Weak Bite.
Skills: Brawling-11; Mount-12.

KANGAROOS

Typical Fourecksian kangaroos are similar to their counterparts on our world, if a bit more cinematic. Energetic herbivores, they can cover nine yards or more in a single leap. If cornered, they lash out with their clawed feet. Being sociable Fourecksian creatures, they travel in mobs. Curiously, although they're no smarter than most grazing herbivores, they have their own gesture-language.[1]

ST: 12	**HP:** 12	**Speed:** 6.50
DX: 14	**Will:** 10	**Move:** 8
IQ: 3	**Per:** 12	
HT: 12	**FP:** 12	**SM:** 0
Dodge: 9	**Parry:** N/A	**DR:** 1

Kick (12): 1d-1 cut. Reach C.

Traits: Bad Grip 3; Enhanced Move 1.5 (Ground Speed 24); Sharp Claws; Short Arms; Weak Bite.
Skills: Gesture-12; Survival (Fourecks Outback)-12.

POINTLESS ALBATROSS

Albatrosses are large seabirds (ST 6, and wingspans of over 11' are possible) capable of flying very long distances (flight Move 12). The most prominent species on the Disc is the *pointless albatross*, which has been known to fly from Hub to Rim without landing, although nobody knows why. Some have been domesticated for message-carrying, and they represent the only swift, reliable form of communication between the Agatean Empire and the Circle Sea. This was previously a minor state secret at both ends, as the Agateans found few reasons to communicate with foreigners, and the Patricians of Ankh-Morpork knew that any messages that did arrive were nothing but trouble. However, in these more open times, the secret may be slipping out.

Annoying an albatross can get you pecked for 1 point of large piercing damage, but mostly they're only dangerous if you're a fish.

QUANTUM WEATHER BUTTERFLY

While rare, this species is known in the Agatean Empire and possibly further afield. It is the butterfly which, when it flaps its wings, so changes air-flow patterns that it can cause a thunderstorm a thousand miles away. It rarely bothers with a thousand miles, though – it mostly generates localised thunderstorms for troublesome creatures in its immediate vicinity, although it can probably also control other weather effects to suit its convenience. It's potentially the deadliest standard-sized butterfly in the multiverse.

A butterfly which feels threatened can use the Lightning Bolt ability (see *Burning Attack,* p. 87) to inflict 1d damage, or 2d if it spends an extra turn preparing. (It will often do less – a minimal zap will deter most animals, after all.) It has Innate Attack (Beam)-12. Alternatively, by taking a turn to control local winds, the butterfly can cause storm-force gusts to buffet every creature within five yards of it. Each victim must roll vs. ST or be knocked down, or hurled into a spin if flying.

Disc Flora

The Disc has a wide variety of plant life, but relatively little that would startle anyone from our world but a botanist. Some plants in zones of unstable magic develop intelligence and speech, but they rarely do much with these gifts. (In fact, *many* Discworld trees are intelligent, but their thoughts take about a season each to process.) In certain areas, residual magic has had *interesting* effects on the local flora. Travellers in such regions should be careful what they eat.

The greatest vegetable oddity is the class of re-annual plants, which have four-dimensional DNA and only grow in magic-rich environments. These often come up a year or more before they're planted. They can be farmed, despite the risks (this is the only branch of agriculture where failure to plant seeds can disrupt the structure of causality); the most popular re-annual crops are those used to make alcoholic drinks. Re-annual drinks give the imbiber hangovers (or rather, *hangunders*) before they're actually drunk. These tend to be severe, so the sufferer usually drinks a lot by way of compensation and to forget, which . . . well, causality is preserved, only backwards.

Re-annual fruits include *vul nuts*, which make a wine that can mature for up to eight years before the seed is sown. In the Agatean Empire, such wine is freeze-distilled to make a drink called Ghlen Livid. There are also more "conventional" re-annual grapes. Re-annual wine can be used for divination; see *Magical Fortune-Telling* (pp. 211-212).

---

1. Scratching the left ear means "Yes," right ear means "No," wrinkling the nose means "Come quick, someone's fallen down a deep hole."

The quantum weather butterfly seems to be more intelligent than most small insects – after all, it can manipulate its environment. It also has very pretty fractal patterns on its wings.

SALAMANDERS

Salamanders are desert-dwelling creatures that resemble small, mouthless lizards. They feed entirely on magical energy, absorbing octarine frequencies from sunlight and becoming comfortably well-fed in any high-magic environment. They excrete waste energy in the form of bright light. Thus, they can be persuaded to act as torches or, by inflicting sharp surprises on them (especially when they've fed well), as flashbulbs; some iconographs (pp. 159-160) come with salamander-based flash systems.

Anyone looking toward a salamander when it flashes must roll vs. HT, at a base -3, +2 per yard of distance, and -2 per salamander after the first if looking at a group that all flashes simultaneously. Failure means the victim is blinded for a number of seconds equal to his margin of failure. Vampires can suffer much worse; see *Standard Vampire Traits* (p. 110). Otherwise, salamanders are harmless.

Salamanders have Move 4 and SM -9, but they rarely try to escape if handled correctly. They cost about $1 each. They are easy to look after, requiring only bright sunlight or a fair amount of ambient magic, but they are a little unreliable as a practical light source, as they may stop excreting at critical moments. Anyone with Photography skill knows how to get them to flash reliably.

Troll Animals

It has been said that, along with humanoid trolls, there are species of "troll animals" – silicon-based life in animal shapes. These haven't been seen in the chronicles yet. Presumably, most of them live in the high mountains where trolls originally dwelt. Rumour mentions troll dogs, a sort of huge and shapeless troll horse, and troll ducks (which sink a lot).

To create a troll animal in game terms, start with the stats for a carbon-based species of the same general shape and size; add 50% to ST (and hence HP) and +2 to HT; and give it DR 1 or 2 if it's smaller than human size, 3 if it's around human scale, or 4 or more if it's larger. Such creatures might also have the Troll Brain disadvantage (p. 97), but temperature-induced IQ variations are likely to be smaller than for humanoid trolls.

TURTLES

Discworld turtles are large, placid creatures whose only problems in life are finding safe breeding-beaches and avoiding people who've discovered turtle soup. Some may grow far bigger than any on our world – after all, turtles large enough to be mistaken for islands are a well-known myth, and the Disc has a thin myth-reality divider. Those would need a heck of a lot of beach.[1] The other danger they face is being studied by wizards and astrozoologists who want reference points when theorising about Great A'Tuin.

---

1. *And would make quite a bit of soup.*

VERMINE

Vermine are small, black-and-white, Hubland-dwelling rodents, related to the lemming. Unlike their cousins, however, vermine are much too level-headed to commit suicide. They only throw themselves over very small stones, abseil down cliffs, and use small boats to cross water. Their evolution – having started out toward good sense and intelligence – may even be accelerating. Currently, typical traits include ST 2, DX 13, IQ 5, HT 11, Will 12, Per 12, Combat Reflexes, Night Vision 2, Sharp Teeth, Temperature Tolerance 2 (Cold), and the skills Climbing-12, Mechanic/TL0 (Simple Vehicles)-8, Observation-12, and Survival (Mountain)-12.

Vermine fur is used to trim formal robes worn by certain wizards and other dignitaries. If vermine *are* becoming smarter, they may eventually have something to say about this.

Contrary to legend – and there are so many legends about wolves, although mostly they are legends about the way men think about wolves – a trapped wolf is more likely to whine and fawn than go wild with rage.

But this one must have felt it had nothing to lose. Foam-flecked jaws snapped at the bars.

– The Fifth Elephant

WOLVES

Wolves are widespread pack predators, commonest in cooler regions. They have animal intelligence but a certain instinctive practicality; humans who can communicate with them regard them with respect. They don't waste time or effort if they can help it – their lives are just too chancy. A few pack leaders can be surprisingly (and worryingly) smart; the GM might add one or even two levels of IQ for a really cunning wolf.

In general, wolves avoid humans, preferring less-risky prey, but a lone human out in the forest when the local pack hasn't fed for a while should be very worried. Contrary to what many people assume, wolves *don't* like werewolves, and they may well attack a lone werewolf on sight. This is for much the same reason that *humans* don't like werewolves: Werewolves aren't human and they aren't wolf, but they *are* trouble – wolves seem to know that werewolves get wolves a bad name. As ever, though, there are exceptions to this rule.

ST: 10	**HP:** 10	**Speed:** 6.00
DX: 12	**Will:** 11	**Move:** 9
IQ: 4	**Per:** 14	
HT: 12	**FP:** 12	**SM:** 0
Dodge: 9	**Parry:** N/A	**DR:** 1 (Tough Skin)

Bite (14): 1d-2 cut. Reach C.

Traits: Discriminatory Smell; Night Vision 2; Quadruped; Sharp Teeth; Short Legs; Temperature Tolerance 1 (Cold); Ultrahearing.
Skills: Brawling-14; Tracking-14.

No wonder dragons were always ill. They relied on permanent stomach trouble for supplies of fuel. Most of their brain power was taken up with controlling the complexities of their digestion, which could distill flame-producing fuels from the most unlikely ingredients. They could even rearrange their internal plumbing overnight to deal with difficult processes. They lived on a chemical knife-edge the whole time. One misplaced hiccup and they were geography.

– Guards! Guards!

Dragons (of All Sizes)

Being a fantasy world, the Disc has dragons. Fortunately, most of them aren't overly fantastic. The fantastic ones are bad news.

Swamp Dragons

Most Discworld dragons are in fact *swamp dragons* – a natural species, but bizarre all the same. They are vaguely reptilian, with four legs as well as wings, and usually grow to about 2' long (SM -3, typically ST 4); however, adult sizes ranging from 6" (SM -6, ST 1) to a yard (SM -2, ST 6) have been reported. They mostly trot around on foot (although one that has to run too much may get dangerously excited), but they can fly for short distances, and indeed they mate in the air. They do not manoeuvre well.

Their most unusual attribute is a truly phenomenal digestive system, which can reconfigure itself to handle almost anything and use that material to generate quantities of flammable gas. Thus, they can quite literally *breathe fire* (combat details appear below); a dragon is likely to have enough gas for 2d-2 flame attacks when first encountered. Swamp dragons recharge by eating bizarre meals (high-grade coal is good). Their senses of taste and smell are highly refined, enabling them to perform instinctive chemical analysis on anything they might consider eating. However, they have to store these gases internally, and they're insanely excitable; consequently, they frequently explode. This seems to constitute a suicidal sort of species defence mechanism.

Swamp dragons will explode because of almost any strong emotion, including boredom. In the breeding season, males fight duels that mainly consist of attempts to provoke each other into screaming, detonating rages; sadly, the excitement of victory can also lead to explosion. (Swamp dragons aren't gentle victors – if the loser rolled over and acknowledged defeat, the winner would disembowel it.) It's very easy to make a male dragon explode by showing it its own reflection in a mirror. Even the sight of any sort of flame can look like a challenge to a swamp dragon.

Indeed, almost anything will make a swamp dragon detonate. In rules terms, any time one gets into a fight or a screaming contest, roll 3d every turn from the third onward, subtracting 3 from the result for males in the breeding season. The dragon explodes if the total is less than or equal to the number of turns fought so far. An exploding swamp dragon usually does 2d crushing damage to everyone nearby, rising to 3d or more for a large, well-fed male with lots of flame-gas. Divide damage by the distance in yards between dragon and victim. In addition, anyone within three yards takes one point of burning damage, and flammable materials in that radius may catch fire.

A dragon killed by a cutting or impaling weapon probably won't detonate (only on a roll of 6 or less on 3d). One that's battered to death might (9 or less) – and one that's killed with fire almost certainly will (15 or less). Hence, fighting swamp dragons tend to finish each other off with fang and claw.

Swamp dragons are prey to a huge range of diseases, some beyond the realm of conventional biology. As well, most of their internal fluids are corrosive – or at best disgusting – and their stomachs sound like antiquated plumbing. Nonetheless, rich and/or silly people occasionally adopt them as pets. They aren't exactly domesticable (the damage they do to carpets by dribbling is too expensive for the word to fit), but they sometimes demonstrate the personality of a particularly dim and messy dog. However, too many owners become bored with them and abandon them on the streets. They may then be rescued by sentimental dragon-lovers, if they're lucky.

Otherwise, they might end up being used as cigarette-lighters or paint-strippers. (One, of a breed with a very hot flame, was once used as a cutting torch in a bank heist.) This is considered heartless by true dragon-lovers, but the biggest danger is that the dragon will get excited by something. They've also been used as *ad hoc* weapons, although that runs even more of the same risk. There's at least one case of a dragon being used as a demolition charge (in a box, with a mirror to provoke it).

The GM may modify all swamp dragon capabilities for large, small, or mutant specimens.

ST: 1 to 6	HP: 1 to 6	Speed: 5.00
DX: 11	Will: 9	Move: 6 (Ground)
IQ: 4	Per: 10	
HT: 9	FP: 9	SM: -6 to -2
Dodge: 9	Parry: N/A	DR: 1

Bite or Claw (11): 1 point cut. Reach C.

Flaming Breath (12): Treat this as Short-Range Flame (see *Burning Attack*, p. 87) doing dice of burning damage equal to half the swamp dragon's ST score (rounded up), but with two changes.

First, this costs no FP; instead, the dragon gets a limited number of uses (see above). Second, at the GM's option, a well-fed dragon may achieve a range of two or three yards if sufficiently provoked.

Traits: Acute Taste and Smell 5; Bad Temper (9); Berserk (9); Burning Attack (Short-Range Flame, with limited uses instead of FP cost; see above); Cast-Iron Stomach; Combat Reflexes; Discriminatory Smell; Flight (Winged, with air Move reduced to 9 and a cost of 1 FP per second); Quadruped; Self-Destruct (see above); Sharp Claws; Sharp Teeth; Short Legs.
Skills: Innate Attack (Breath)-12.

Moon Dragons

When the Ankh-Morpork space programme's one expedition made an unscheduled visit to the Disc's small moon, it discovered a new species of miniature dragon. These "moon dragons" resemble swamp dragons in size, but are slim, sleek, and silver in colour. Leonard of Quirm has theorised that both species share a common ancestor which may have come from another world altogether. Like Errol, they flame from the rear; as they feed on energy-absorbing lunar vegetation, they're fast and agile flyers in the moon's low gravity. It's uncertain whether they could survive in the Disc's higher gravity.

SUPERSONIC SWAMP DRAGONS

The versatile swamp dragon genome has, on just one recent occasion, thrown up a curious variant: Errol, a swamp dragon with a streamlined head and body, and stub wings, who was initially dismissed as a "whittle" (runt). After his genes and metabolism came to grips with things, Errol also acquired the ability to generate a *very* hot flame, out the opposite end of his digestive system to the norm. The result was the fastest flying creature ever seen on the Disc.

Some breeders are hoping to retrace the genetic path that led to this – but given the damage done by Errol's sonic booms, this may not be a good idea.

Draconic Monsters

There is a rumour, at least among barbarian heroes – for whom the miniature swamp dragon is a joke beneath notice – that there once existed "swamp dragons" worthy of a hero's attention. The fact that traditional barbarian heroes attended to these creatures would explain why they're now extinct. According to legend, these beasts did actually live in swamps but didn't breathe fire – although their breath smelled disgusting, and they did collect firewood (and, supposedly, treasure). The last of this species was supposedly killed a couple of centuries ago.

This sounds like a mutant swamp dragon which lost much of its chemical-processing capability in an evolutionary push for body mass. Presumably, such creatures collected firewood instinctively, to build bonfires outside their lairs.

Any "treasure" they accumulated would be a result of ancestral memories motivating them to gather unusual substances in the hopes of finding a digestive use for them. Statistics for such a beast appear below for the GM who wants to set a game in the heroic past or simply have an unexpected survivor come crawling into play, giving heroic types something to fight or more sensible PCs something to run away from.

ST: 18   **HP:** 18   **Speed:** 6.00
DX: 11   **Will:** 11   **Move:** 6
IQ: 3   **Per:** 12
HT: 12   **FP:** 12   **SM:** +2

Dodge: 10   **Parry:** N/A   **DR:** 4

Bite (12): 1d+1 imp. Reach C.
Claw (10): 1d+2 cut. Reach C-2.
Noxious Breath (special): The creature can breathe choking fumes that engulf anyone within three yards of its jaws. Anybody caught in this area must roll vs. HT. Failure means the victim is nauseated, suffering -2 to all attribute and skill rolls, and -1 to active defences, for a number of seconds equal to his margin of failure. If the fumes meet open fire (e.g., a torch), they generate a flare of sickly purple flame, inflicting 1d-3 burning damage on anyone immediately adjacent.

Traits: Bad Temper (9); Berserk (12); Cast-Iron Stomach; Combat Reflexes; Fangs; Quadruped; Sharp Claws.
Skills: Brawling-12.

Noble Dragons

Noble dragons are apparently descended from swamp dragons which learned to feed on magic. This enabled them to grow to huge size and gave them spectacular flight and fire-breathing ability.

Fortunately, noble dragons are effectively extinct – most of the time. When ambient magic on the Disc fell to sensible levels, they migrated into the only reliable ecological niche for a magical species: the human imagination. Unfortunately, they have an occasional chance of escaping back into the real world when a supply of magic comes available and a human offers them a channel.

The results vary with exact circumstances. In the vicinity of the Wyrmberg (pp. 233-234), the local high-energy magical field permits a sufficiently imaginative mind to manifest a dragon with attributes at the lower end of the ranges given below. However, that's strictly a local issue. Much more dangerously, the right sort of ill-advised magic can conjure up something far more powerful.

One grimoire, Tubul de Malachite's *The Summoning of Dragons*, describes a ritual that does this. The author thought that a wizard of sufficient nobility of purpose and mental discipline could summon a truly noble and benevolent dragon. Only one copy of the book is known to exist, and much of that – like its author – was burned to ash in an inexplicable fire. The surviving tome is in the library of Unseen University, and the Librarian doesn't permit borrowing.

The fact, discovered the hard way by everyone who has ever tried it, is that the dragon produced by such a ritual is only marginally controllable and will break free sooner or later – probably sooner. Combining the most spectacular power that human imagination can conceive with the darkest lusts and urges of the human soul, a "noble" dragon is essentially an unstoppable force with a bad attitude. Noble dragons are *not* sociable; a key description of

their mindset is that the nearest thing that they have to a friend is an enemy who isn't dead yet. They're also quite sneaky.

A fully formed noble dragon is capable of almost anything and nearly invulnerable to any harm that humanity can throw at it. Because it effectively feeds on magic, it's also functionally immune to spells; it simply soaks up anything cast at it. The one that briefly ruled Ankh-Morpork weighed around 20 tons (about ST/HP 70), was effectively immune to arrows (*at least* DR 10), and had teeth that would rate as Fangs (inflicting impaling damage). It could breathe fire over a broad area, engulfing whole groups of human victims or annihilating small buildings in one attack – and this flame was hot enough to vaporise a human body (at least 6d×5 burning damage). It was knocked out of the sky by a close-quarters sonic boom, but survived even that.

ST: 20+	**HP:** 20+	**Speed:** 6.00+
DX: 12+	**Will:** 10 to 16	**Move:** 6+
IQ: 7 to 12	**Per:** 14	
HT: 12+	**FP:** 12+	**SM:** +2 or larger
Dodge: 9+	**Parry:** N/A	**DR:** 3+

Bite (DX): thrust-1 cut (2d-2 at ST 20). Reach C.
Claw (DX): thrust-1 imp (2d-2 at ST 20). Reach C-2 or more.
Flaming Breath (DX): Treat this as Flame Jet (see *Burning Attack*, p. 87) doing at least 3d damage.
Tail Buffet (DX-2): thrust cr (2d-1 at ST 20). Reach 1-3 or more. Used to attack opponents to rear.

Traits: Acute Taste and Smell 3; Bad Temper (15); Burning Attack (Flame Jet; see above); Discriminatory Smell; Enhanced Move 1 (Air Speed 24); Flight (Winged); Night Vision 3; Quadruped; Sharp Teeth; Talons.
Skills: Typically Aerobatics at DX, Innate Attack (Breath) at DX, and Stealth at DX+2. Noble dragons can be highly intelligent, and might learn other skills, but would be very unlikely to bother.
Notes: For SM above +2, increase claw and tail reach according to *Size Modifiers, Reach, and Weapons* (p. 176).

> *It wouldn't play with you, or ask you riddles. But it understood all about arrogance and power and cruelty and if it could possibly manage it, it would burn your head off. Because it liked to.*
> *– Guards! Guards!*

Supernatural Beings

The Disc's fantastical nature means that there are a number of types of more-or-less sapient supernatural creature, not all of whom have (yet) moved to Ankh-Morpork and started opening delicatessens.

Bogeymen

The power of belief calls some weird anthropomorphic personifications (pp. 291-297) into being, but usually on a one-of-a-kind basis. Bogeymen, however, are such a universal archetype that they can be treated as a species. They embody the childish fear of scary monsters under the bed or in the cellar.

Bogeymen aren't actually evil. It's simply their nature to hide in dark corners and to jump out and frighten people. They can no more help this than a troll can help being made of rock. Some could even be called shy or retiring; after all, their main attribute is hiding. (A few can bring themselves to venture out in company if they carry a door with them to hide behind.)

But they're no *nicer* than other races, either, and many actively enjoy being a nuisance.

Bogeymen are hideous, shaggy creatures, with fangs, claws, and dinner-plate eyes. Or so most accounts go; those who meet one rarely get a clear view, and it's likely that these beings vary considerably. They certainly have a habit of bending and stretching in strange ways, making it hard to assess their actual size. They can also get into hiding places apparently without crossing any intervening space – although sometimes, when among friends, they ask people not to look while they move, so they may just be fast and stealthy.

On paper, bogeymen should be formidable combatants. However, that isn't the *point* with them – all the claws and teeth and attitude are there to make them effective as the monsters in the closet. They're often rather nervous, especially when faced by someone who shows a steady willingness to use force against them; they're used to being feared, not confronted, and will quickly back down. Still, bogeymen *are* physically powerful, and they can make dangerous opponents if pushed or useful allies if given a good reason to be helpful.

Bogeymen feed on rats, spiders, and whatever else they find under the stairs and in the backs of disused wardrobes. They also collect and hoard old shoes, much like a squirrel collects nuts, though not to eat. This is why wardrobes often have old shoes in them that no one remembers putting there.

ST: 15   **HP:** 15   **Speed:** 5.00
DX: 10   **Will:** 9   **Move:** 7
IQ: 9   **Per:** 11
HT: 10   **FP:** 10   **SM:** +1

Dodge: 8   **Parry:** 8 (bare hands)   **DR:** 2 (Tough Skin)

Claw or Bite (10): 1d imp. Reach C, 1.

Traits: Appearance (Hideous); Cast-Iron Stomach; Dark Vision (see below); Existential Confusion (see below); Fangs; Flexibility; Talons; Teleportation (possibly; see above).

Skills: Scrounging-11; Stealth-15.

Notes: Dark Vision lets the bogeyman see in pitch darkness (disregard *all* darkness penalties). *Existential Confusion* means that, as a figment of childish imagination, a bogeyman has a problem: If all the other beings in the room have their heads under blankets[1], it will temporarily cease to exist. It will fade back into reality – mentally stunned – 1d minutes later, provided that its existence is no longer being denied. If it somehow gets its *own* head under a blanket, then it can no longer believe that it exists and goes into existential shock; it will stand around stupidly for 1d minutes after the blanket is removed, not even defending itself if attacked. Otherwise, bogeymen vary quite a bit, depending on whose bad dreams and fears formed them. The exact size and nature of their claws and teeth differs between individuals, as can their personal skills.

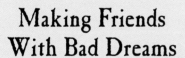

Making Friends With Bad Dreams

Bogeymen aren't always easy to talk to, nor are they actually the monsters they appear. This can make them far more interesting as Contacts than as opponents. Anyone trying to solve the Mystery of the Murder in the Mansion might learn a lot from the creature that was hiding under the stairs when the Duke fell down them.

Dryads

Dryads (*hamadryads*, to give them their full name) are tree spirits as anthropomorphic personifications. Each lives, not inside the trunk of its tree, but in a capacious pocket dimension defined by its tree's psyche. Females are dominant and are green-skinned, with

long, mossy hair. Males are built like bodybuilders, with skins of walnut. Both have luminous green eyes.

Fortunately, very few trees have resident dryads, who are tough, ferociously defensive of their trees, and ruthless, and possess considerable mystic powers. The females are the equal of most witches, with telepathic and scrying abilities. The males are every bit as tough as they look. If PCs encounter a dryad, their main concern should probably be to escape with their skins intact, but it *might* be possible to make some kind of deal with the spirit, gaining brief supernatural aid in return for services rendered. This won't be easy, though – dryads tend to be arrogant and consider the safety of their trees to be a right, not an option.

Elves

Elves aren't a Discworld species, but a race of extradimensional beings. While they appear similar to humans, this is deceptive. Elves are psychic parasites – and, in a very true sense, *monsters*.

They occasionally obtain access to the Disc (or other worlds) and start amusing themselves. They're often later remembered as wonderful. The nature of their amusements is such that beings with *better* communal memories – such as dwarfs and trolls – regard them as one might regard an intelligent plague virus.

Elves used to be widespread on the Disc, millennia ago, but were driven away by the growing use of iron among native races, coupled with the determined opposition of local witches and other magic-workers. The gradual decline of magic may have robbed such defenders of some of their power, but it also reduced the number and reliability of dimensional gateways. The elves left behind a number of elf-human crossbreeds, some of whom retained a distinct social identity. These eventually became known simply as "elves," though they might more correctly be called "elf-kin" (p. 102).

---

1. *Fluffy blue woollen blankets seem to work best. The Ankh-Morpork Watch carry squares of blanket material in case bogeymen cause them trouble.*

ELF NATURE

Elves are psychopaths and sadists. Conscience – the idea that any possible concern should be taken for the lives or feelings of anyone who isn't an elf, or who is an elf but isn't you in particular – doesn't exist for them. If an elf thinks that something might be amusing and believes that it can get away with the deed, then it will act without hesitation. The trouble is that elves usually *can* get away with things, because of their quasi-psychic abilities, known as *glamour*.

Elves make themselves appear beautiful to humans and render them fascinated and obedient. "Getting away with murder" doesn't begin to cover it. In fact, elves aren't especially attractive by human standards – they actually resemble very tall, rather thin, pointy-faced humans, graceful but too obviously predatory. However, they have an enormous sense of *style;* they wear scruffy furs and random bits of armour with unlimited panache. Their illusions *are* beautiful, though not terribly original.

They like to be surrounded by beautiful things, obtaining them by enslaving human artisans, but it's questionable whether this is truly a desire for beauty or merely a hunger to have something that someone else doesn't have. Indeed, elves find all human creativity – even the simplest rustic dancing – fascinating. They seem to use human languages rather than anything of their own (language is creative), although most communication between elves is likely telepathic.

While elves are fairly intelligent, the race doesn't include the sort of extraordinary individuals that any human population produces. They rarely study, but being ageless, they have millennia of experience. They usually know how to ride, handle weapons, and hunt. Many also have Interrogation and medical skills (which aren't exactly used for healing). Most lack much sense of personal identity, with the exception of their monarchs and some of the aristocracy.

Aside from their rulers, elves are sexually indeterminate (genuinely so – not just difficult to distinguish, as with dwarfs). Like almost everything else, in an elf's world-view, sex itself is dull; it's only interesting as a way of messing up other beings. The population of Elfland doesn't grow very quickly, despite elvish immortality, because elves know what other elves are really like.

Elves are creatures of winter and of moonlit nights, and their pale skin burns easily in strong sun. This isn't a serious weakness, but it does affect their behaviour.

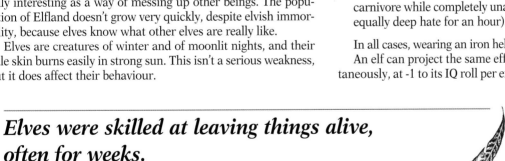

Elves were skilled at leaving things alive, often for weeks.

– Lords and Ladies

ELF POWERS

An elf can detect what's going on inside a human's brain and manipulate it. While this capability appears to be "psionic," it's actually based on a sensitivity to magnetic fields (a highly refined form of the sense believed to enable pigeons to navigate), just like elves' senses of direction and balance. Elf powers can therefore be blocked or disrupted by *iron*. It takes a fair

> ## Elf-Shot
>
> Elves sometimes use small bows to fire stone-tipped arrows bearing exotic psychoactive poisons. These do little or no physical harm (1d maximum), but they may send the victim's mind off wandering in a dreamworld or make humans easy to control (reducing Will).

amount of iron to stop elves cold, but even quite small quantities cause them distress and may persuade them to go elsewhere – and they find strong magnets even more distressing. This is the origin of many rural superstitions, such as nailing up a horseshoe over a doorway "for luck."

When an elf wants to probe or influence a human's thoughts or perceptions, roll a Quick Contest between the elf's IQ+5 and its subject's Will, modifying Will for the effect's complexity:

Extremely subtle (e.g., picking up a human's emotional state, or making a "tweak" like rendering the subject slightly more or less happy, or causing him to fail to notice a single passing thing): -2

Routine (e.g., a trick like seeing through another creature's eyes – or making the subject pause for as long as the elf concentrates, or believe that something is beautiful that isn't, or hear voices, or feel deeply inferior): no modifier

Tricky (e.g., generating a complex illusion with no relation to reality, or rummaging through a human's deep memories at leisure, or setting up a persistent pattern of thoughts that lasts until the victim makes a successful IQ-5 roll, trying once per day): +5

Suicidal or radical (e.g., causing the human to approach a large carnivore while completely unarmed, or changing deep love to equally deep hate for an hour): +10

In all cases, wearing an iron helmet gives the human +5 to Will.

An elf can project the same effect on multiple humans simultaneously, at -1 to its IQ roll per extra target. Each subject resists separately. Range isn't usually a great problem, but the elf must have a line of sight (possibly through another creature's eyes) or know *exactly* where the victim is, and apply *Long-Distance Modifiers* (p. 194) for the range to the most distant person it's trying to influence. Even a bit of iron in the way of such an indirect attack – like that horseshoe over a doorway – can grant the victim up to +3 to resist. Multiple elves within 50 yards of each other can collaborate to strengthen the effect; roll for the elf with the *highest* IQ in the group, at +2 per "assistant."

Elves instinctively use their power to make humans see them as Attractive. This requires no dice roll, but it wears off if the elf is rendered unconscious or trapped within an iron cage.

Elf power is primarily *insidious* – elves cannot generate much raw energy. Notably, they're incapable of moving physical objects around, teleporting, or emulating other "high energy" psychic powers. Moreover, their own nature prevents them from reading emotions especially well or manipulating them except on a gross level, let alone doing anything *helpful*. Although a few of them use a form of extra-sensory perception, being locked in the here-and-now, they could never use any kind of precognition, either (this gives some human magic-workers a real edge). And they find certain nonhuman brains harder to control.

As a special effect more than anything else, elves often sing while using their mind control. This isn't especially musical – they have to kidnap human bards for that – but it is part of their image. However, their victims usually convince themselves that it sounds wonderful.

For those who might wonder, elves could *in theory* learn to sense magnetic fields as such. In practise, they simply don't think in those terms. They would find high technology – with all its steel and magnetism – terrifying.

By working together in a sizeable group to distort the perceptions of a good many humans, elves can exploit the power of belief to warp reality on a large scale, overlaying aspects of their home dimension on parts of another world to make it more hospitable to them. The GM should treat this as a special effect – something that happens at the climax of a large-scale elf incursion, which PC heroes have to stop.

Elves don't use much magic as such, although their powers appear similar. However, some aristocratic elves know a little magical theory and can teach it; they can even seem to grant magical power to humans, when it suits them. What they actually do is use their influence over human brains to unlock the subject's magical gifts, if any. Some of them do know a magical trick that enables them to fly on yarrow stalks at Move 15.

TYPICAL ELF

This represents an ordinary denizen of Elfland. Some variation is possible – elves do amuse themselves in slightly different ways. Elves of this ordinary type usually show up in groups, although these are poorly coordinated unless there's a powerful elf noble along and being assertive.

ST: 11	HP: 11	Speed: 6.25
DX: 14	Will: 10	Move: 7
IQ: 10	Per: 11	
HT: 11	FP: 11	SM: 0

| Dodge: 9 | Parry: 10 (Shortsword) | DR: 0 |

Shortsword (14): 1d+1 cut or 1d imp. Reach 1.

Traits: Absolute Direction; Ambidexterity; Bloodlust (15); Bully (6); Callous; Curious (12) (but only regarding creativity or radical novelty); Dread (Significant quantities of iron; 1-yard radius); Elf Powers (pp. 363-364); Fixation (Mortal creativity, 3-yard radius); Hidebound; High Pain Threshold (which may help explain elves' complete lack of empathy); Illusion Resistance (see below); Immunity to Disease; Night Vision 5; Overconfidence (12); Perfect Balance; Sadism (9); Selfish (9); Vulnerability (Iron and Steel ×2).

Skills: Acrobatics-13; Acting-9; Bow-13; Disguise-11; First Aid-10; Knife-14; Naturalist-8; Riding (Elfland Equines)-13; Savoir-Faire (High Society)-10; Sex Appeal-10; Shortsword-14; Stealth-13; Tracking-12.

Notes: Illusion Resistance means the elf gets +5 on any IQ, Will, or Perception roll to resist or recognise illusions, from magic or other sources – they know all about illusions. Elves use human-style weapons and often wear light (DR 2) or medium (DR 3) armour. Some find it amusing to become good with weapons (skill levels of 18+); others rely more on their powers.

ELF ROYALTY

Elf society is run as a monarchy; elves aren't exactly democratic by nature. It's quite possible that there are multiple elf monarchies, all run in very much the same way by extremely similar kings and queens – elves aren't innovative, either. There's no easy way to tell how many elves there are in the multiverse, or how many similar shifting Elflands, but it's easiest to talk in the singular.

The King of Elves appears as a horned man with goat legs and hooves. He's less interested in scheming than in waiting, certain that sooner or later, the other races will abandon their childish use of metals and agriculture, and the proper elvish dominion will be restored.

The Queen is often seen as the shapely Dark Lady in a flowing dress of a thousand Gothic-novel covers; she knows what humans like. She can easily construct an appearance that rates as Beautiful or Very Beautiful, although she's really no more appealing than any other elf. She's constantly engaged in numerous intrigues, usually complex and inevitably nasty. She has no more use for the King than any elf has for anyone else, but their power is linked in some unknown but definite way, and the King has influence over her.

The average elf would be happy to overthrow the monarchy (in favour of another monarchy – meaningful change is beyond them), for the entertainment value as much as the power, except for the part about getting away with it.

The Queen appears often enough in person in dealings with humans that her personal details merit listing:

ST: 10	HP: 10	Speed: 6.50
DX: 15	Will: 12	Move: 7
IQ: 12	Per: 12	
HT: 11	FP: 11	SM: 0

Dodge: 10   **Parry:** 10 (Knife)   **DR:** 0

Dagger Thrust (15): 1d-3 imp. Reach C.
Punch (15): 1d-3 cr. Reach C.

Traits: As *Typical Elf* (p. 364), plus Combat Reflexes.
Skills: Acrobatics-15; Acting-11; Disguise-11; First Aid-12; Intimidation-12; Knife-15; Naturalist-10; Politics-14; Riding (Elfland Equines)-15; Savoir-Faire (High Society)-12; Sex Appeal-12; Shortsword-14; Stealth-14; Teaching-10.

ELVES IN THE CAMPAIGN

Elves are thought of as creatures of beauty by hopeless romantics and anyone else who buys into their "enchanting" image, but they're remembered with burning hatred by dwarfs, trolls, and humans who know their true nature (most witches, some antiquarian wizards, and these days, the entire population of Lancre). They should primarily serve as opponents in adventures where the PCs are wearing white hats; they have the classic villain combination of sadism, style, and a certain gullibility. However, they're difficult opponents – they're dangerous enough on a purely physical level, and they can get inside other people's heads.

Some players might suggest the idea of elf PCs, but this isn't advisable. Aside from the fact that every dwarf and troll they met would try to kill them, the more correctly an elf is roleplayed, the less fun it is for everyone trapped in their company. Indeed, a perfectly roleplayed elf would be bored all the time anyway. Also, giving them a reasonable representation of standard elf powers would require **GURPS Powers** and a lot of points.

Terminology

It's unwise to use the word "elf," except with plenty of iron around, if any of the species are likely to be in the neighbourhood. They may be surveying the area psychically, and they often notice mention of themselves and *take an interest*. Moreover, if they're discussed at all, the power of belief may actually make it easier for them to manifest. For this reason, witches and others are prone to euphemism. Common words for elves include "Lords and Ladies," "Fair Folk," "Gentry," "Shining Ones," and "Star People."

Elfland Animals

The elves' extradimensional "Elfland" has its own fauna, including unicorns, which are basically horses with large spears on their heads, minor glamour powers of their own (enabling them to scramble and probe minds), and the traditional bizarre unicorn concern with virginity. There are also elf riding-horses, which are psychotic carnivores. Elves keep hunting dogs, too, but they would find cats altogether too much like themselves to tolerate. Elf-animals share the elven resistance to illusion, as there's a lot of it about in their homes.

Genies

Al Khali being a land full of camels, viziers, and meaningful lamps, it naturally has a number of genies, too. These have significant power over space, energy, and matter, and they can sometimes grant wishes, though not always competently.

Genies are probably spirits who've found a niche in the human mythic imagination – less powerful than gods and less sordid than demons, but quite a good career nonetheless. Some may be visitors from other universes where powers on this level are normal. Mostly, they can and should be played as talking plot devices who can do as much as the GM wants, and they always find wonderful excuses for not doing more.

"I am somewhat over-committed on lamps," the genie agreed. *"In fact I am thinking of diversifying into rings. Rings are looking big at the moment. There's a lot of movement in rings. Sorry, people; what can I do you for?"*

– Sourcery

Rarities and Unique Creatures

The nature of the Disc, the universe in which it resides, and the multiverse beyond *that* means that all sorts of beings might show up in games, sometimes as truly unique one-offs. For example, *The Colour of Magic* featured Tethys, a "water troll" – a creature of living water from another disc. The GM can create such beings with appropriate abilities, attributes, and game mechanics, if they're useful for a story. Don't worry too much about details that won't matter in play. The only thing to watch out for is ambitious players trying somehow to take control of the creatures.

It *might* even be possible for determinedly adventurous players to run such unique beings as PCs. However, this can lead to complications. For one thing, they may well need the full **GURPS Basic Set** (and possibly the extended rules in **GURPS Powers**) to assign character point values to unusual abilities. For another, they might confuse or overwhelm an inexperienced GM. Hence, the GM should only permit this option if he's confident of his ability to handle things and prevent the player from hogging the spotlight.

Ghosts

Life after death is a complex subject on the Disc (see *The Afterlife*, p. 300), but sometimes, dead souls stay around. It's far from clear what determines whether this is going to happen, but noble (or even better, *royal*) birth, some kind of unfinished business, violent death, and dying in a high-magic area all seem to be contributory influences. Lancre Castle (see *Lancre*, pp. 238-239) has – or had – a large number of ghosts, most of them kings, many with grudges against the people who replaced them.

Ghosts always have Invisibility (p. 90) – typically always on or at least Usually On, and with Substantial Only. Cats (p. 353) can see them, though, as can some other beings, while someone with Medium (p. 45) can sense and speak with them. They may, with effort (usually requiring both a Will roll and expenditure of FP), generate minor physical effects in the real world. A very few, with exceptional sense of identity, can even produce "poltergeist" effects, moving around small objects. For game purposes, such ghosts should make a Will roll once per second; their margin of success is the ST they can exert in the material world.

Many ghosts are restricted to a "haunting site" (such as Lancre Castle). Most others have only a tenuous link to the material world and must work through a medium if they're to accomplish anything.

Mr. Ixolite

Creatures called "banshees" on the Disc come in two varieties: the rare but "natural" race (p. 101), and an even rarer type of supernatural being. The latter sort is said to appear when someone is about to die, and to indicate doom by its terrifying wailing. However, only one supernatural banshee is known to survive; its name is Mr. Ixolite. What happened to any others is unclear.

Unfortunately, Mr. Ixolite isn't a happy banshee, perhaps partly because he's a male in what is traditionally an exclusively female vocation, but mostly because he suffers from a speech impediment. He is also – probably in consequence – painfully, cripplingly shy. Thus, rather than wailing, he creeps up to doomed people's doors, slips notes under them saying "OooeeeOooeeeOooeee," and then runs away.

If the players are showing too much knowledge of the chronicles and becoming over-confident as a result, the GM might wish to have their characters receive such a note one night. Whether it actually comes from Mr. Ixolite is *their* worry.

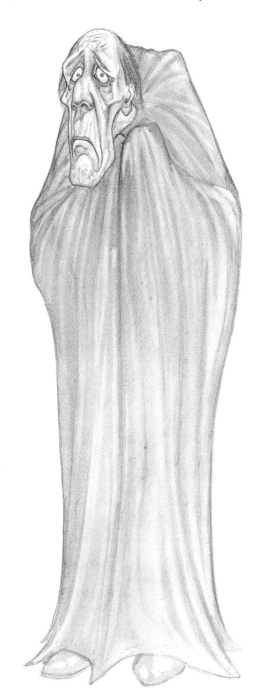

BAD FOOD, NO SLEEP, and STRANGE PEOPLE

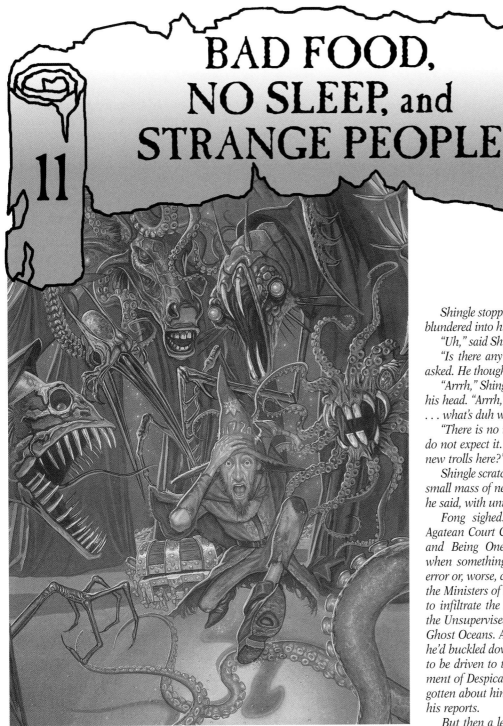

Shingle stopped suddenly, so that Fong nearly blundered into him. "What is it?" Fong asked.

"Uh," said Shingle thoughtfully, "uh . . . stop."

"Is there any trace of the new trolls?" Fong asked. He thought it was worth a try.

"Arrrh," Shingle said, then carefully scratched his head. "Arrrh," he repeated, "there they be. Me . . . what's duh word . . . oh yeah. Me hearties."

"There is no need for all that," said Fong. "I do not expect it. Honestly, I do not. But are the new trolls here?"

Shingle scratched his head again, dislodging a small mass of newly grown lichen. "Sumfin' is," he said, with unusual confidence.

Fong sighed. He'd been halfway through Agatean Court Correct Assassination Protocols and Being One With the Shadows training when something – he suspected either clerical error or, worse, clerical inerrancy – had inspired the Ministers of the New Dynasty to assign him to infiltrate the Accursed Maritime Bandits of the Unsupervised Island Provinces of the Angry Ghost Oceans. As a faithful servant of the state, he'd buckled down and accomplished this, only to be driven to the conclusion that the Department of Despicable Necessities had, in fact, forgotten about him, and that no one was reading his reports.

But then a letter had arrived, requiring him to investigate certain matters. Pleased that he had not been forgotten, he'd talked his new colleagues into assisting. It had seemed like a good idea at the time, but now he was wondering if he couldn't have achieved more alone.

The problem was, his lengthy immersion in the attitudes of his new shipmates had caused him to develop doubts about the practicality of his previous training – despite the fact that his upbringing and grasp of subtlety made him fully aware of the ludicrousness of his shipmates' behaviour. So now, although he could both scream while hurling a throwing star and go "Yah!" while wielding a cutlass, he couldn't quite keep a straight face while doing either. He didn't fit in anywhere.

The jungle was thick and green and damp, and something in the back of Midshipman Fong's mind kept making him want to make the obvious joke about that and his current companion, the troll Shingle. The two of them were making progress, but it was unpleasant and hard work even for a troll – especially for a troll, really, as despite the complicated water cooling system that their allies had rigged up and strapped to his back, Shingle was suffering badly from the heat. The pair had long since given up dreaming of stealth, as the noise of them hacking vegetation aside with their machetes was only exceeded by Midshipman Fong's reflexive swearing at the insects who were treating him as a walking buffet.

A loud crash from ahead of him interrupted that train of thought. His cutlass and numknuts were in his right and left hands before he had time to think.

"Tree fell in duh forest," Shingle observed. "Wonder if anyone saw it?"

The Discworld is a place where stories happen.

All sorts of stories – not just comedies. Tragic and dramatic things happen here, too. If anyone really wanted,

they could use the setting for an old-fashioned game in which heroes and wizards beat up monsters and take their treasure. Or they could create gloomy sagas about angst-ridden vampires on the streets of Ankh-Morpork. There's no obvious reason to do so, but nothing to stop anyone, either.

But stories set on a flat world on the back of a giant turtle do somehow lend themselves to comedy . . .

Running for Your Laugh

Everyone knows the saying: Dying is easy, comedy is hard. (Actually, people are careful about saying that in Ankh-Morpork. The Fools' Guild became nervous that it might be tested on them and took steps to suppress the expression.) Fortunately, in RPGs, PCs might die, but not the players. But RPG rules *are* better at talking about negative Hit Points than they are at raising a smile.

Comedy comes in several forms – there are many ways to get a laugh – but, at the risk of sounding negative, it's worth starting with a couple of things that *don't* fit in too well on the Disc.

First, it isn't a setting that suffers from puns. There are quite a few plays on words in the chronicles, and some silly names, but no grinding, humourless punning (except in Discworld heraldry, which is run by clever people with no sense of humour). Certainly, nothing exists solely to justify a pun.

Second, the Disc is light on slapstick. The chronicles have their share of physical comedy – some of it carefully and intricately choreographed – but the violence is basically as serious as in real life. If people get hurt, it *hurts*. That's one good reason for using a realistic RPG system like **GURPS** for this setting.

A Touch of Horror

The Disc may be a comedy setting, but that doesn't mean that you can't have moments of horror in games. Some of them may even be quite serious. But the chronicles don't feature the horror of blood as often as the horror of *ideas*. The Disc is never more threatened than it is by someone who thinks that everything should be changed for the better. Spellcasters, while rarely actively evil, have to be careful not to open conceptual doors that are better left closed. The conventional "monsters" of the Disc, by contrast – the vampires and werewolves – are often misunderstood and have enough free will to refrain from throat-ripping.

Playing the Game

The GM has a large job, in all sorts of ways, but like most large jobs, it becomes much easier when you break it down into manageable chunks and when you learn not to worry about parts that don't actually matter. An adventure is typically a series of encounters with NPCs (not *all* of them violent), discussions of what to do

next, descriptive bits where the GM sets the scene, and careful applications of skills and other abilities, all driven along by motivations and problems from the PCs' characters sheets (though "earn enough to pay the rent" and "don't get killed" are sometimes implicit rather than explicit). The GM should plan a bit and cultivate the skills of description, improvisation, and roleplaying minor characters – but after a while, a lot of that starts to take care of itself. Indeed, the problem can be preventing the players from spending whole sessions in intra-party interactions and character development. Because most people are happiest if there's some kind of continuing plot going on.

This is why RPGs have campaigns as well as scenarios.

CAMPAIGNS

A one-off adventure or "scenario" can resemble a short story, or a movie, or a novel, depending on its length. It has a beginning, a middle, and an end, after which everyone can go and do something else. But many roleplayers think that this is a waste of the creativity that goes into characters and settings, and want to play in a *campaign*: an extended series of games that form a linked string of stories and adventures with common characters and settings. This might resemble a series of novels (more "the Watch novels" or "the Witches novels" than "the Discworld novels"), but it can often be more useful to think of a campaign as a bit like a *television* series – a police show, maybe, or a soap opera. Each session is a fairly short episode, which should contain a few interesting or exciting events, but there's no need to expect huge revelations or major resolutions every time. An episode may be self-contained, or multiple episodes might be strung together to form a longer story.

Campaigns can also have objectives: maybe somebody wants to found a new college of wizardry, or become a nobleman, or find out who killed his father and get revenge. Different PCs may have different objectives, though hopefully interlocking ones. And eventually, everyone may agree that it's time for everything to come to a grand climax, with big revelations, deaths, fortunes made, and maybe some explosions or weddings (or both). But that's a matter of taste. Some campaigns carry on happily for years. And even if one does come to a climax, there might be a sequel, with the same PCs – or their students or offspring – going on to new goals.

But that's the high-level view. At any given moment, during any game, you'll probably be more worried about short-term concerns.

MOOD AND PACING

Roleplaying is collaboration. The players and GM must work together. And perhaps the single most important thing they should work *on* is *mood*.

Even assuming that everyone is expecting a comedy, a campaign is doomed if the GM is attempting complex satire, half the players are trying for slapstick, and the other half are making incessant puns. The GM must determine what the players want. Is it to revisit locations from the novels or to explore hitherto-ignored areas of the Disc? To come up with original characters or to emulate old favourites? To have adventures or to have as many laughs as possible?

At least this sort of thing can be sorted out with a bit of discussion. Provided that everyone is prepared to put in a little work, constructing a mood isn't too difficult. What can be harder is *pace*.

Games can't be played at the same tempo throughout – that's boring. Equally, key events shouldn't just be neatly, predictably spaced out one-per-hour. It's better to start slow, accelerate until a big comic or dramatic climax, and then perhaps include a calmer "epilogue." On the other hand, there's a lot to be said for dropping people into the middle of some action at the start, to get the adrenaline flowing. Such a scene should *not* usually involve key NPCs, particularly not major villains. Too much can happen if the players show unexpected ingenuity (or stupidity), or the dice run amok.

Be aware, too, that combat is *exciting* but not especially *fast*. Because it involves lots of decisions and details, a fight that lasts mere seconds in the game world can take much of the session to run. The GM should *avoid* combat if the current aim of the game is to get to the next important plot point quickly.

Switches of pace are important to comedy (and to many other forms of storytelling). Trying to play every scene at maximum velocity is exhausting. Rather, the GM should keep moving along at "walking" pace much of the time, throwing in jokes or slapstick action when the players aren't expecting them. Plots can also involve false climaxes, with a series of failed attempts to slow the escalating pace before something really special ends the scene. Then, everyone can draw breath before moving on, preferably in an unexpected direction that emerges from preceding events. In this sense, comedy is strangely akin to horror.

If in doubt, the GM can start with an even-paced, low-key plot, throwing in choice set-pieces at intervals, and let the players develop characterisation. As with most skills, practise is the best way to learn.

THE LIGHT TOUCH

In general, Discworld games should run fast and light. Stopping every five minutes to check a detailed point of rules interpretation is likely to kill any humour. However, GMs who *always* emphasise plot over system too often end up with mild cases of megalomania. A roleplaying game, humorous or not, is a cooperative project, and if the GM takes too much power from the players, they'll ultimately become frustrated. Everyone should be allowed input.

The GM should not be afraid of using the dice, although the results they give can certainly be interpreted freely. The Disc is a place where the random peculiarities of fate are very significant, and risky endeavours genuinely can go right or wrong. Honest use of dice can keep both players and GM on their toes, expecting the unexpected.

Plot/Campaign Categories

So what can Discworld comedy be about? As the chronicles show, quite a lot of things – sometimes several at once.

1,000,000-1

Everyone knows about the *Million-to-One Rule* (see *Further Corollaries*, p. 9). It's generally believed that if heroes can adjust the odds against themselves to 1,000,000-1, they can pull the dumplings out of the cauldron (at the last moment, when else?). Note that the odds must be *exactly* 1,000,000-1; 999,998-1 or 1,000,003-1, and you're toast.

This is one of those ideas that some players seize upon like a piranha on a blood sausage. Given a chance, they'll try to turn every even remotely doubtful encounter into a case of million-to-one odds. Of course, in a "realistic" game, the idea is just silly – how do you evaluate odds that accurately, let alone fine-tune them? – but it *is* something that appears a couple of times in the chronicles. And players who've got their heads around things like narrative manipulation and the rules of barbarian heroism may argue that what they're *actually* doing is setting themselves up as underdog-heroes, who are supposed always to win. To which the answer is that being the underdogs is only half the equation. The other half is to be heroes, which means buckling down and being *heroic*.

Anyway, if this becomes a problem, make the players work for their benefits. Require them to explain just how they're shifting the odds ("Well, Bjorn's going to fight without his left boot, and I'm going to use fresh eggs instead of crossbow bolts . . ."). Limit uses – one million-to-one per adventure should be enough for anyone. Requiring that the party spend *all* of their remaining uses of Luck and Serendipity would also be reasonable. Then, if it looks like the group is getting cocky, strike pre-emptively; after they've spent two or three hours huddled in the inn, working out the odds, somebody in a game of Cripple Mr. Onion on the other side of the room leaps up to display the legendary, unbeatable, Nine-Card Run.

And if all else fails, work it to death. Set up an adventure (preferably short) in which every last encounter involves million-to-one luck. Hopefully, they'll get the hint.

DEATH AND TAXES

It's possible to run a fairly straightforward blood-and-guts adventure, but with an eye to comedy. Such stories can include other non-comedy elements, such as mystery or even horror.

Most Discworld stories work as straight adventures, and many sound serious if summarised in a single sentence. *Guards! Guards!* is about a band of watchmen who defend a city against a monster. *Lords and Ladies* is about an invasion of supernatural aliens. Several plots are partly detective stories (although some of the detectives are cynical about Sherlock Holmes-style deduction); *Men at Arms*, *Maskerade*, and *Feet of Clay* are all murder mysteries. *Small Gods* is a drama about religion and war. Thus, there's a good argument for setting up a Discworld game as a fantasy RPG campaign first and a comedy second.

Campaign Theme: Watchmen

Building a campaign around the adventures of a city watch has many obvious advantages. First, several novels in the chronicles – from *Guards! Guards!* onward – show how it can be done. Second, beyond those works, there's an enormous body of fiction to draw on. The Watch novels are classic police stories with a Discworld-fantasy twist: Commander Vimes is the grizzled, cynical senior cop; Captain Carrot is the idealistic younger officer; the department is a multi-ethnic organisation with its own subculture; and there are forensic analysts, undercover investigations, rookies to train, civic unrest, traffic management, and obstreperous members of the public. There are also wizards and vampires, though – and every once in a while, the impossible crime may be the result of magic or divine intervention. This adds up to an interesting mixture of sitcom, parody, and mystery.

The problems for a GM are the flipside of the advantages. For one thing, a lot of possible stories have already been told in the chronicles; coming up with something original may be hard. For another, all the supernatural powers and general fantasy weirdness may make it hard to put together a decent, soluble mystery. A good GM can get around this, though; consider consulting a guide to creating mystery stories (e.g., **GURPS Mysteries**).

If the campaign is set in Ankh-Morpork, you'll have the advantage of familiarity and also a city which has been – literally – fully mapped out (at least in the centre). However, there's a real danger that the players will feel overshadowed by characters from the chronicles, or that they'll be *too* familiar with the setting. Hence, it might be better to set the campaign elsewhere.

The Ankh-Morpork Watch's recent successes have been widely noticed, and many smaller cities are following that lead. This represents a job opportunity for competent-looking PCs. Of course, not everyone in *any* town will want such projects to succeed. Faced with corruption, incompetence, and their own personal problems, PCs can look forward to a long and varied campaign – maybe with guest appearances by visitors from Ankh-Morpork when a problem crosses national borders. See *New Smarlhanger* (p. 385) for a possible venue, and be careful out there.

Picaresque

If a group wishes to concentrate on the comedy aspect, they may be content to wander through the landscape, meeting strange people. Such stories often involve quirky protagonists as well as quirky encounters. Literary critics call this a *picaresque*.

The problem with this approach from a gaming point of view is that, sooner or later, players get bored with pure tourism. There are two solutions: Either make some of the individual encounters into short adventures of a more focussed kind, as in *The Colour of Magic*, or give the journey a little more point.

The Confused Quest

This more focussed version of the picaresque can turn into a *quest*, on a classic heroic-fantasy model. See *The Light Fantastic* for an example of such a plot emerging out of unplanned journeying, *Sourcery* for a circular expedition, *Eric* for a magical quest through space and time, and *Witches Abroad* for a quest leading to an urban adventure.

The problems with quests in games are, firstly, keeping the PCs on track – players have an astounding capacity for becoming sidetracked, worrying red herrings to death, and finding subplots more interesting than the main event – and secondly, deciding what to do next, without anticlimax, when the plot is complete. Thus, quest plots often work best for groups who don't mind taking a hint and ending the campaign at a fixed point. Alternatively, limited quests may be worked into larger games.

Comic quests are mainly distinguished by the degree of confusion and unwillingness on the part of the protagonists (meaning that they need the right PCs), and the oddness of the people encountered, in a picaresque sort of way. Thus, they probably work best with players who are prepared to throw themselves into things and enjoy the comic atmosphere.

Social Comedy

Classic intelligent comedy is usually comedy of manners, or comedy about realistic personalities interacting in complicated ways.[1] This is a recurring theme in Discworld stories, despite the fantastical setting; most have at least a bit of it, and certainly every story set in Ankh-Morpork plays off the city's social complexity. *Men at Arms* and *Maskerade* are among the stronger examples.

This sort of thing can be difficult in RPGs, because PCs must be played on the fly, which makes complex relationships and motivations hard to depict. However, a good, determined group of players may manage. One stock theme of this kind of comedy is social climbing. As PCs are often determined to rise in the world, making this ambition social rather than defining it in terms of combat ability could make for a lot of comedy.

Sitcoms

Sitcoms are more As Seen On TV than novel-ish. A sitcom is usually a kind of low-level social comedy.

---

1. *Farce, somebody said, is tragedy played at 120 revolutions per minute – and tragedy is all about people who can't get on with each other or the world.*

It starts with a simple situation like "Family with three kids living in the suburbs," "Single yuppies sharing an apartment," or "Dimwitted mother in the media, clever schoolgirl daughter, decadent parasite friend." From this, the creators spin off a new plot every episode. Because the audience soon becomes familiar with the main characters, it's easy to get a new story moving each time.

This could be a very good model for a Discworld campaign. The GM should agree to a theme with the players, who then create characters to fit. To give the players the chance to feel that they're achieving and building something, the situation probably ought to include a clear starting point and an opportunity for long-term growth. For some possible themes, see *Sitcom Campaign Ideas* (see below).

PARODY

Parody is an easy, effective, but rather unsubtle style of comedy, wonderful in small doses but tiresome in large lumps. Of course, the Discworld and everything about it is a parody of the fantasy genre, but there's a lot more to it than that. Individual elements and some plots are parodies; Discworld dwarfs and magicians are jokes about their counterparts in other worlds, and *Wyrd Sisters* is a sort of parody of Shakespeare's tragedies (with a very Shakespearean theatre troupe in starring roles). *Maskerade* builds on a parody of *The Phantom of the Opera*, while *Moving Pictures* and *Soul Music* parody the habits of the real-world movie and music industries, respectively.

It's hard to parody complete plots in RPGs, because the players are entitled to some control over the game's plot. Struggling to keep them on a track that they can predict in advance, or that they don't understand at all, is a futile exercise. However, one can spoof individual elements and "bits," as *Wyrd Sisters* and *Lords and Ladies* do with Shakespeare. It would also seem logical to parody some old RPG traditions in a game (and *The Colour of Magic* contains several RPG references). One could send a totally inappropriate party on a dungeon raid, say, or have a merchant ship crew who forever accept bizarre jobs from noble patrons in dockside bars.

SATIRE

Satire isn't the same as parody – it's more subtle and complex. Parody is comic imitation; satire is a (more-or-less) comic way of commenting on other matters.

A lot of satire is political or otherwise concerned with the sort of thing that gets into the newspapers, but this isn't common in Discworld stories. All else aside, that sort of satire quickly becomes outdated, and is incomprehensible to people who don't recognise the targets. However, some Discworld stories do satirise social topics: *Equal Rites* is about gender roles and sexism, *Pyramids* concerns itself with a tradition-driven society, and *Small Gods* looks at religious faith. *Maskerade* mostly parodies opera, but it also says some satirical things about the art and its audience.

A game plot can contain as much satire as the GM is able to squeeze in. For example, a setting could be designed as a satire on contemporary society; a game doesn't have to travel and endure the way a novel should, so the GM is welcome to try some political satire if their players will put up with it. (The only catch is that a GM who tries to impose political ideas on players could be in for a lot of arguments, possibly unpleasant.) Players should also note that player-character concepts can be satirical – if only at the level of a six-foot human who insists that he's a dwarf, or a wizard

Adventures vs. Stories

Traditionally, roleplaying games are about having "adventures." Player characters are expert at getting into and out of trouble, and do so for a living. In other words, they're useless hangers-on in a world full of people trying to do an honest day's work.

The Discworld is a good setting for this sort of thing. However, it's also a good venue for a different kind of story: tales of people building communities, trying to avoid trouble, dealing with weird stuff because *it* comes to *them*, and generally doing their best. The chronicles are full of "adventures," but few of the characters are actively seeking that sort of thing, and some are desperate to avoid any sort of excitement whatsoever. There *are* "adventurers," but they are a minority, and generally regarded with that distrust always shown by people in trousers toward those who persist in wearing tiny leather pouches whatever the weather.

This book is intended to assist both sorts of game and to impose neither. Feel free to play either way – but most important, remember that you have a choice.

Sitcom Campaign Ideas

● The PCs are a group of trainee rural wisewomen whose NPC mentor has an appointment with Death in the first episode. They have to divide up herb-gathering rights and cackling responsibilities, establish credibility with the locals, and clean out the old lady's cellar (which turns out to be bigger than the cottage above – *much* bigger). Non-witch PCs could include peasant allies and local priests.

● High in the Ramtops sits a great castle which has just emerged from a century-long sleeping curse. The PCs are nobles, guards, servants, and perhaps a confused traveller or a helpful wizard who somehow broke the curse. They need to re-establish contact with the outside world, and repopulate the forgotten nearby village or otherwise develop an economic basis for survival.

● Not all wizards live at Unseen University. Even those who do may have fallings-out with department heads. Perhaps a group of such academics, too proud to go off to the Brazeneck College about which they themselves have recently been so rude, could found a new college of their own, in a remote rural spot or some smaller city?

who's incapable of casting magic. Certainly, anyone familiar with academia will almost certainly end up treating any game set in Unseen University as more-or-less satirical, and the relationship between the press (meaning primarily the *Times*) and the government and the Watch in Ankh-Morpork is bound to end up reflecting some real-world concerns.

To Bear in Mind . . .

There are a couple of important things that the GM running Discworld stories should remember.

NOT EVERYTHING IS COMPLETELY KNOWN

Even after dozens of books, maps, and porcelain figures, there are an infinite number of details of Discworld place, life, and reality that remain questionable, even blank. It's possible, for instance, that Death is actually a subordinate aspect of Azrael the Great Attractor. Or maybe all the Deaths are independent beings who work as Azrael's branch managers. It really isn't given to mortals to know this kind of thing, but they still worry about it. Mostly, though, such uncertainties shouldn't have much effect on what mortals do.

Campaign Theme: The Press

With the invention not only of the moveable-type printing press, but also of newspapers (p. 250), a whole new sort of adventurous career has opened up: *reporting*.

In a "Fearless Reporters" campaign, the PCs would work for the press and seek to feed it with the stories it lives on – though how fearless they really are is up to them. They might be new hires at the Ankh-Morpork *Times*, employees of a rival paper in the same city (hopefully competing on accuracy and timeliness of reporting, and not just making stuff up), or inhabitants of some other town where somebody has decided to play a round of the ever-popular game of "Imitate what's fashionable in Ankh-Morpork." They could even be freelancers, based in an area where no newspaper has yet sent staff and trying to place stories with whatever publication might find them interesting.

Most will be reporters or iconographers; for a template, see *Journalist* (p. 123). However, roguish street-level contacts, muscular "minders," and Watch officers assigned to keep an eye on these idiots would all work as well.

Plots could involve any number of mysteries surrounding crimes, diplomatic incidents, espionage, or something like archaeology. Reporters will want to discover and publish as much as possible, despite all the people inconvenienced by this – and if they can solve any mysteries before the people who are supposed to do so, that makes them look good in print. Longer-term plots may involve either politics, with the reporters perhaps supporting one faction against their enemies (although there's also press neutrality to consider), or large-scale criminal conspiracies. The reporters might not even realise that there's a connection between some incidents until they're up to their necks in sinister plotting.

On a more mundane level, one can't say for certain what sort of weapons and armour any given Ankh-Morpork City Watchman will have when encountered. Not only is the issue less than perfectly uniform, but when a Guardsman lays aside his breastplate and helmet at the end of his shift, he can't be sure that they won't have turned to flakes of rust and scraps of mouldy leather by next duty call. The best one can say is that a watchman will be wearing something somewhat protective and carrying an object capable of causing personal injury. Maybe the adventurers' weapons will get through the armour, maybe not – do you feel lucky today?

And then there are the ale-barrel philosophers who really want to know about the intimate lives of dwarfs and the refractive index of octogen. Curiosity about the world one is vicariously living in is healthy, but on the Disc, as in the real world, wanting to know an answer – even *needing* very badly to know it – doesn't mean that an answer is forthcoming. If the players make an issue of the price of a double-order of chicken vindaloo at the Klatchian Curry House, or the airspeed velocity of an unladen albatross, think upon the published material and invent a plausible response. You might even make a note of it for future reference.

IT ISN'T ALL A JOKE

To be sure, humour is an essential part of the Discworld, and some of this humour can be a bit silly. But the things that happen in Discworld stories – wizardly plots, palace intrigue, battles and sieges and wars – are the same things that happen in terribly serious fantasy yarns, just warped by the sheer cussedness of the environment. The frantic defenders trying to stop a really big, bad dragon from crisping first them and then Ankh-Morpork are *really* scared of the dragon, even though their plan for stopping it consists of adjusting the odds against them to exactly a million to one.

While Death (the individual) is the kind of person one can only wish our world's Death was, death (the event) is just as scary and final (sparing a few undead) as it is for us. On the Discworld, Palace Guards have an *opinion* about being disembowelled in passing by Heroes on their way to something Heroic.

And now and then something happens that's quiet and even moving, like Death's last dance in *Reaper Man*. Earning moments like that takes a lot of work.

Certainly, laughter is the big reason for roleplaying on the Disc. But a lot of that laughter comes from the fact that Discworlders respond to their incredible surroundings in a more, well, *realistic* way than most fantasy characters.

Sample Campaign Setting: The Brown Islands

The following is one possible setting for a Discworld campaign – a location which appears on maps of the Disc, but which isn't detailed or depicted directly in the chronicles, leaving it wide open for the GM to develop. It's also a place where all sorts of interesting characters might collide.

There's much more trade and communication these days between the Counterweight Continent and the Circle Sea than there was only a few years ago, and the traffic is growing. A lot of this seaborne commerce must pass through the Brown Islands, an archipelago in the Turnwise Ocean previously noted only for surfing and beaches. (Ships might instead hug the coastline of the Disc's main landmass, passing Gonim, Hergen, and Chimeria. However, those coasts are prone to storms, whirlpools, tricky currents, and regions of thaumic instability, so sailors with enough confidence to head out of sight of land prefer the open-ocean route, with the Brown Islands as a stop along the way.) This has *consequences*.

On one hand, when a lot of ships find the same bay convenient for anchoring overnight, and their crews and passengers all start looking for supplies, entertainment, and beds that don't go up and down all the time, other people soon see the profit in supplying those wants. Before you know where you are, you have young, bustling communities.

On the other hand, there are people who decide to skip the tedious business of buying and selling. They have to get hold of armed ships, shabbily fancy costumes, and sinister flags, and cultivate a taste for rum, loud conversation, and even more nautical slang than honest sailors, but there are always volunteers.

CAMPAIGN CATEGORIES

The Brown Islands can serve as a setting for death-and-taxes adventures of a nautical sort, and they are great for picaresque wanderers or questers to visit. Port Duck offers opportunities for social comedy, from its brawling inns to its diplomatic quarter, while sitcoms could be set in native villages or on pirate ships. The setting is built around a double parody, of the "swashbuckling pirate" and "Hong Kong action movie" genres. And as for satire – the Brown Islands are all about international relationships, trade, and collisions between money, power, crime, and tradition.

History

Before the recent trade boom, the Brown Islands had the good fortune to be short on recorded history. They were also short on many other amenities, and the natives weren't above a little interpersonal violence even without someone else writing about it, but at least the weather was nice.[1] There were a few trading-posts and small villages on some of the better natural harbours, supporting the thin trade that did pass through, but these were definitely the sorts of places where a person could go to get away from it all for decades at a stretch, getting by on the friendship of the locals and one frayed change of clothes.

THE NATIVES

It would be a mistake to assume from the lack of major-looking events that the original Brown Islanders were unambitious or unimpressive. Indeed, no one who met them ever called them the latter. They're large, robust folk with bronzed skin and dark hair, built of slabs of muscle that look misleadingly like fat until one of the locals gets annoyed with you. The men don't develop beards or much else in the way of facial hair, giving them a bodybuilder look. The women are similarly imposing, and the slimmer ones have the kind of athletic figure that causes much throat-clearing and awareness of the heat among male visitors.[2]

Nor are these people "mere" tribal fishers and floral garland manufacturers. In fact, their tribes are quite large, and their kings are usually on the lookout for ways to extend their influence. Brown Islands warfare typically involves a mixture of jungle skirmishes, ambushes and hit-and-run raids, and brutal head-on canoe battles.

---

1. *Outside of hurricane season, anyway.*

2. *Especially as said heat has always discouraged much in the way of tailoring.*

Canon Concerns

The sample settings and adventure outlines in this chapter fit what's known about the Disc, but they aren't "canon." Their purpose is to illustrate how to set up various styles of game using the Discworld as a frame. Because the details of these locations aren't drawn from the chronicles, they give GMs and players alike the freedom to develop ideas from scratch, changing or extending what's written without the sense of sacrilege that's sometimes felt when game material tinkers with its primary sources.

Which said, though everything in this chapter – and indeed, this entire book – strives not to contradict the Discworld novels, a campaign set on the Disc will almost inevitably drift in directions that don't coincide exactly with the chronicles. This is true even when its starting point is canon rather than one of the situations described here. It's also a good sign – a *fun* roleplaying game is an exercise in imagination, after all.

The GM whose adventure or campaign runs into an apparent contradiction with a Discworld story can – with a little fast-talking, improvisation, and low cunning – use *the contradiction itself* as inspiration for further gaming. Has one source or the other always been false? Was somebody very powerful running an elaborate charade, and if so, why? Is this due to the other gods leaning on Fate to change something after a lost bet, or is the problem due to flaws in the Disc's fractured and unreliable history? And if the latter is true, do the History Monks (p. 13) need someone to patch things over? Or – perhaps toughest but most brilliant of all – were *both* sources correct, in some complicated but perfectly logical way?

Impossible problems require unlikely solutions – and often, the more unlikely the solution the better, especially on the Discworld.

Given that the canoes may carry 20-30 warriors and achieve a fair turn of speed with all that muscle rowing, things can get fairly messy. Even full-sized merchant ships tend to turn and head the other way rather than get into fights with a couple of war canoes.

Brown Islanders are skilled sailors, and their idea of peacetime fun includes canoe racing. However, they're even fonder of *surfing*. Their tribal heroes tend to be the best surfers[1] and many spend all their free time at the beach. They adopt a studiedly casual manner when discussing the subject, which masks the fact that surfing is virtually a religion. The GM can have them employ as much surfer slang as he can remember, but use it the way some people use biblical quotation. In game terms, surfing is a Sports skill (p. 74); feats that attract Brown Islander admiration, and the

sorts of waves they consider interesting, impose large penalties on skill rolls.

The Gnarly Waves aside, Brown Islanders worship an assortment of minor deities concerned with fish or vulcanology. They deny that they're in the habit of throwing sacrifices – especially human sacrifices – into the handful of volcanoes that dot the Islands, but have a worrying way of adding "we stopped doing that years ago" in a tone that seems to imply that they can't quite remember *why* they stopped.

Old-style Brown Islanders would be TL0, with TL1 boat-building. However, many of them are now in regular contact with newcomers, so characters with this background may easily achieve higher TLs. They have their own language (actually a family of related dialects), but a few members of most tribes have picked up some of the Morporkian that's now the area's trade language.

The natives mostly have only intermittent contact with the newcomers, though, and there's a fair amount of mutual suspicion, as the tribes have a slightly relaxed view of personal property, while the newcomers often have a large dose of colonial arrogance. Still, friendly dealings are possible, with effort. In most games, natives should be an odd feature on the margins of the story, with full-scale visits to non-urban areas coming as a change of pace. Culture clashes can make for entertaining problems, regardless of whether they involve volcano gods.

Brown Islanders are skilled sailors who love canoe racing and surfing.

Trade and Piracy

These days, capitalism has come to the Brown Islands with a vengeance. Agatean junks laden with tourists coming one way meet speculative expeditions from the Circle Sea heading the other, and everyone stops for supplies. At the same time, some of the more secluded coves have become bases for pirate ships.

However, the pirate business sometimes seems a touch lopsided. The trouble is that the richest potential prey is those Agatean junks, but they're also big, rugged, and well-equipped. More to the point, traditional Agatean thinking with regard to assaults on the citizenry by Foreign Dogs favours massive retaliation, and this was one part of traditional Agatean thinking that Emperor Cohen could understand. These days, Agateans leave their homeland with the consent of the rulers, and while many Agatean tourists find the idea of being robbed by authentic, picturesque foreign pirates fascinating, they tend to protest to their government if the pirates are impolite about it. Thus, after a few bad experiences with Agatean navy junks, the most sensible pirates have instituted a hands-off policy, though some enterprising souls have taken to sailing alongside tourist ships, waving their cutlasses and shouting "Arrrh" a lot, and charging very reasonable rates to have their pictures taken.[2]

---

1. *Given that these tend to be big, healthy lads with catlike reflexes, they're usually quite good at more general heroic stuff, too.*

2. *Older pirates consider this demeaning, but their younger colleagues observe that it pays the bar tab.*

Still, this does leave scope for some good old-fashioned mayhem in relation to other vessels. Although Discworld maritime technology is advanced (see below), ships' weapons typically don't include much in the way of artillery. Catapults aren't unknown, but most sailors regard them as more trouble than they're worth. Sea-spray invariably gets to strings, cords, and springs, so they don't work when they're needed. Thus, pirates mostly employ cutlasses, spears ("boarding pikes"), one-handed axes, and whatever else comes to hand, with maybe a few bows and crossbows for use in the early stages of an action.

What most pirates really rely on, though, is *intimidation* – weapons make their calls for surrender more convincing. Faced with this, some cautious merchantmen carry plenty of weapons and make sure that their crews are willing and able to fight. This pushes costs up, so other captains sail light, relying on speed if they sight pirates.

SHIP TYPES

Discworld shipbuilding has a long history, and despite a great deal of conservatism, ships are quite well-built. In game terms, while ships from major nations are still sometimes built to late-TL3 standards, they're generally heading into TL4. Apart from the smallest canoes, all vessels met around the Brown Islands have sails, if only as a backup for oars, and often as their only means of propulsion – oars and oarsmen take up space that could be used for cargo, and the seas around the Brown Islands are rough enough that open oar-ports are risky.

Most merchant ships are designed for capacity and robustness, making them relatively slow and easily outpaced by anything built as a raider or a courier. The more advanced nations of the Circle Sea mostly favour squat, clinker-built vessels with one to three square-rigged masts. Conversely, Brown Islands canoes and designs inspired by Klatchian warships have the sort of long, slim, elegant lines that give a real speed advantage. Single-masted ships (*sloops*) are rarely considered large enough for ocean travel, so any seen in the Brown Islands are likely to be locally built. These include small craft used for support and reconnaissance by large pirate forces. Rams indicate purpose-built warships, but are rare, as pirates prefer to capture ships rather than sink them. However, what pirates sail is very much down to what they can get hold of rather than what they might want.

Klatchian ships and Klatchians themselves are still rare enough in the Brown Islands to be treated as curiosities. However, Klatch has a venerable tradition of piracy, and their home ports have sometimes become a little too warm for upholders of this tradition in recent years, so a handful of Klatchian corsairs have relocated to the Brown Islands and built a reputation for scimitar-waving vigour. Back home, corsairs often use small, oar-powered galleys (giving them an advantage over sailing ships on calm days), but these are too small to reach the Brown Islands, so the few in use here had to be built locally. Klatchian vessels generally are longer, slimmer, and faster than those from Sto Plains ports and have a fairly distinctive style of rigging, with more use of triangular sails – though it takes an expert to identify a Circle Sea ship's nation with much certainty at any distance.

The standard Agatean design is the *junk*. This name often induces predictable hilarity among Ankh-Morporkians, but not among sailors who've had a close look at one. They're well-built, with simple-but-functional compartmentalisation that makes them very hard to sink, and intricate-but-efficient rigging. They may carry a few cannon on deck – *crude* and *unreliable* cannon, admittedly, but when they work, they can hole a hostile ship at some distance, and they have a serious deterrent effect.

Swashbuckling (of Several Sorts)

The Brown Islands are depicted here as a venue for swashbuckling adventure, both sincere and in parody. Swashbuckling is close to self-parody at the best of times, and on the Discworld, the perpetual collision between the irresistible force of narrative tradition and the immovable object of common sense creates many opportunities. Anyone swinging from chandeliers will succeed impressively, crash painfully to the floor, or find himself dangling above a smiling enemy with an upward-pointing sword. *Unimpressive* success is rarely an option.

In this setting, swashbuckling comes in two contrasting flavours. On one hand, there are pirates, sailing ships, slender swords, and some deliberate references to the traditions of 1930s Hollywood. On the other, Port Duck is not *only* based on Port Royal in 1660. It owes as much to Hong Kong in the present day – or rather, to the image of it created by its film industry. The bustling, Aurient-meets-Turnwise atmosphere, the fast food, and most especially the melodramatic unarmed combat all evoke a specific cinematic atmosphere. Some flying-jump-kick and weird-looking-blade-weapon action can enhance the ambience. And while the comedy of silly accents gets tiresome *very* quickly, there's no denying that the numerous Agatean denizens of this location talk in such a way as to make it clear that Morporkian isn't their first language.[1]

When the two styles collide, serious devotees of combat rules can test fencing against kung fu, high-points heroes can compare swinging from the chandeliers with running up the walls, and everyone else can see whether "Arrh, there, ye lubbers!" is more or less deadly than "Hah so!" Players who can't get enough detail when it comes to fighting will appreciate **GURPS Martial Arts,** which offers comprehensive treatments of both fancy fencing and several sorts of kung fu.

1. Having their lips move out of synch with their words would be cheap, though.

PIRATE ORGANISATION

The odd thing about some Brown Islands pirates is that they're remarkably democratic, in a rough-and-ready, high-mortality, alcoholic sort of way. Pirate crews are in effect collectives, who share out the spoils of their raids according to carefully worded articles of agreement. They elect captains, but the captain's job is to decide strategy (or at least chair crew meetings).

However, things invariably get a little messy. When a crew first gets together, haggling over the articles of agreement is often resolved by a crossbow being pointed up someone's nose, and illiterate pirates have to rely on their literate colleagues to tell them what an agreement says.[1] As for the elected captains, they're a bedraggled bunch, worn out by the effort of chairing extended policy meetings, often involving much quaffing of rum, sometimes called in the middle of a fight. Captains are also obliged to lead from the front in battle (ahead of a bunch of people who may still be arguing over their interpretation of some point of order). In fact, the highest rate of nautical desertion on the Disc occurs among Brown Islands pirate captains.

On the other hand, there are the non-democratic ships. Sometimes, the big, mean-looking so-and-so is unambiguously in charge and has a carefully selected band of especially non-sociable thugs at his side to emphasise the point. Adventurers facing pirates should not assume anything either way until they have a chance to talk – if they're given one.

Still, a meeting with a Brown Islands pirate ship may leave you with your life and a tale to tell your grandchildren. It's never likely to be good news for your insurance company, though.

Port Duck

Although several Brown Islands bays have recently been developed as transit ports and trading-posts, one especially has been triumphantly successful.

Port Duck was founded a few years ago by Trossig the Defensive, a Pseudopolitan engineer-turned-maritime entrepreneur, who discovered a well-sheltered natural harbour with a defensible rocky bluff dominating its entrance. He immediately named the site, claimed it as his own property, and ordered the construction of a fort on the bluff. "So far, so good," thought the people he had persuaded to finance his scheme.

However, when Trossig showed them his plans for reinforcing the fortress walls, then adding more walls for safety, then reinforcing those, and then clearing the surrounding forest to a distance of a mile or so, they began asking when the trading-post and its profit-making shops would be built. Trossig accused them

of wanting to leave his fortress vulnerable, probably so that they could break in and take his money. They stopped funding him and set to work building more-profitable operations. Trossig declared himself King of the Brown Islands, and spent a few days trying singlehandedly to sabotage the building work, before disappearing. Rumours variously claim that he drowned himself in a fit of pique, or is wandering the island's forests talking to parrots (some of whom *do* seem to possess a remarkably wide vocabulary of engineering terms), or is locked in a comfortable room somewhere eating through a straw, or is off building the world's biggest fortress for a mad duke somewhere else on the Disc.

Trossig was a good engineer, though. He was right about the harbour's qualities, and his unfinished fortress still stands above the town, whereas the shops and houses built by less-visionary folk keep burning down or falling over. Indeed, some of their builders claim that this is due to Trossig (or perhaps his ghost), who they say still lurks around the place, sabotaging their efforts. This is certainly a more interesting explanation than the one about them building four-storey buildings in three days flat, from whatever materials come to hand, with unskilled labour.

THE POPULATION

Port Duck's inhabitants are a mixed bunch. Essentially, the permanent residents are people who reckon that they can make their fortunes off the temporary residents before their luck runs out. This can be a challenge, since the transient population consists of ships' crews (most of whom would deny that they're pirates, though not always with a straight face), travelling merchants who can't make the living they want elsewhere, wanderers who've left cities such as Ankh-Morpork because things are getting too quiet (or too hot) for them, Agatean tourists, and the odd outcast tribesman.

At first, the only thing that kept the whole place from burning down in the middle of a bloodbath was an unspoken agreement between some of the tougher, smarter pirate crews, who realised that they needed somewhere to resupply, get drunk without the risk of falling overboard, and pick up rumours about merchant activities. Subsequently, other factions appeared with their own forms of order, if not law. Several merchants and keepers of larger shops recruited groups of mercenaries to look after their parts of town.

---

1. *Some pirates not only press-gang carpenters, coopers, surgeons, and musicians, but also lawyers. The life of a buccaneer-lawyer is a complicated one.*

The Agatean Repeating Crossbow

Where the repeating crossbow invented in our world's history was a weak and ineffective weapon which never caught on, the one that appears in the hands of some Agateans in Port Duck is somewhat more impressive (if expensive). It incorporates a magazine which holds six bolts, and it can be fired once per second by pulling a lever which operates a complicated internal feed-draw-release mechanism. The user should have ST at least equal to the crossbow's rating; someone who falls short, but by no more than 3, can shoot it once every three seconds, at -2 to skill; someone with lower ST than that can't use it at all.

Most important, it makes a sinister "kerr-chunk" noise when operated.

CROSSBOW (DX-4)

TL	Weapon	Damage	Acc	Range	Weight	Shots	Cost	ST	Bulk
4	Repeating Crossbow	thr+2 imp	1	×10/×20	8/0.06	6(4*)	$50	7†	-7

* Time to reload *per bolt.* Reloading a magazine of six bolts takes 24 seconds.

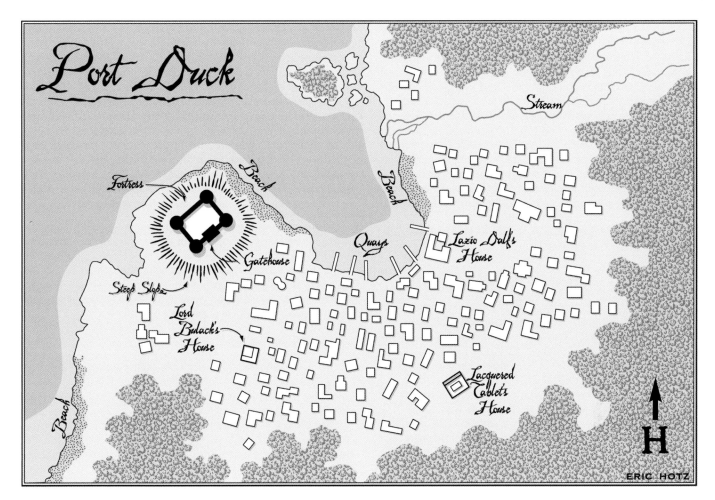

And then several people decided to follow the Ankh-Morpork example and make sure that any crime in this town was properly *organised* crime. After a week or so of chaos, the would-be Thieves' Guilds were whittled down to three, who are currently in a very uneasy armed truce.

Then, someone important somewhere else heard about Port Duck.

GOVERNMENT

Actually, as a number of important people in several places heard about it at much the same time, Port Duck very nearly became the subject of a war. The only thing that saved it – as had saved the Brown Islands throughout history – was its sheer remoteness. Although various nations had set up colonies among the Islands, and some had tried to claim sovereignty on that basis, there had never before been enough economic cause for anybody to sail all this way just to take charge. Now, despite some excessive rhetoric, no one could summon *enough* interest in a few new towns. Shrewd chancellors observed that sending tax-collecting expeditions would cost far more than could be raised in taxes. Somehow, tempers were kept, quiet agreements were signed (or remained unwritten), and a joint authority was set up.

Essentially, Port Duck is now overseen by emissaries of several nations.[1] These professional diplomats, many of whom regard the

---

1. *That's "overseen" as in "not paid attention to by people who are looking too high."*

place as a punishment posting, spend most of their time going to parties at each other's well-fortified mansions and getting drunk. There are three leading figures:

Lord Bulack represents Ankh-Morpork. The Patrician heard about the Brown Islands situation and settled the politics before the city's aristocracy picked up so much as a whisper. He made the point about taxes clearly enough for the council to understand and sent Bulack – an enthusiastic, callow individual in his early twenties who had just inherited his title from a relative who hadn't left the family mansion in 20 years. The new lord was very keen to serve the city, which Vetinari found worrying, and this posting seemed to resolve the matter quite nicely. Vetinari thinks that the lad will either lose his excessive zeal, suffer a decisive misfortune, or (just possibly) learn sense; so far, Bulack has retained his energy, but he's burning some of it off in learning to surf. When he does take an interest in government, it tends to involve him in serious attempts to assist visiting Ankh-Morpork citizens . . . which can be good *or* bad for the visitors.

Rear-Admiral Lazlo Dalf represents Quirm's interests. Quirm is almost entirely non-expansionist these days, but at one stage in history, it produced some impressive naval adventurers, some of whom tried to lay claim to this archipelago. The Rear-Admiral more-or-less embodies the term "old sea-dog" and has never quite burned off his sense of adventure: he volunteered for this post because retirement was boring him. He can seem tiresomely bluff and jovial, but he's probably the single greatest expert in naval matters in town (any relevant skills at 16 – but all at TL3).

He's also acquainted with several of the local pirates, from his sailing days (which doesn't *necessarily* mean that he was ever a pirate himself), and his bodyguards are a tough, informal-looking bunch. Invitations to his wine-and-cheese parties are much sought after; he believes in maintaining the best traditions of Quirm while abroad, so both the wine and the cheese are excellent.

Lacquered Tablet, a member of a long-established bureaucratic family, is the Agatean representative. The Agatean Empire has only weak claims in the Islands, having always avoided any more contact with the outside world than it could help, but its recent governments have displayed more interest in the world, no one thinks it tactful to argue with the Agatean Empire when it expresses a polite interest in something, and there's no denying that there are

a lot of Agateans passing through these days. Lacquered Tablet is a stout, intelligent, middle-aged man who got this job because several of his superiors were finding him too inflexible to fit into the new regime at home. He's habitually conservative, but having been (as he, at heart, sees it) exiled into a realm of angry cannibal ghosts, he has methodically built up his defences. Someone once told him that the rest of the world saw Agateans as inscrutable, and he decided that this was a good idea. He's very inscrutable and goes everywhere with a gang of rather large guards selected for inscrutability. He thinks that the Agatean tourists he has to assist are disloyal dolts for leaving home, however temporarily, but he'll be damned to a hell full of even worse cannibal ghosts before he lets anyone take advantage of one.

This doesn't add up to actual government, and Port Duck is currently basking in serious claims to the status of Wickedest City on the Disc. Even some tough customers from Ankh-Morpork have shown up and muttered that it reminds them of the Old Days. However, official representation from several major powers represents the *threat* of government, and wise heads suspect that the place will settle down eventually.

THE COP

In fact, Lacquered Tablet decided some time ago that Port Duck needed better law enforcement and requested assistance from home. His superiors responded by sending one man. Fortunately (perhaps), that man was Prop Lee (p. 379).

Lee set to work cleaning up the streets, or at least making a more *stylish* mess, and quickly became noted in Port Duck for his tinted eyeglasses, and for hurling himself across rooms full of wrongdoers, pumping bolts from a repeating crossbow (p. 376) into all of them before they could even react. If he runs out of bolts before he runs out of targets, he'll Fast-Draw a pair of pistol crossbows, and then eventually resort to unarmed combat or to melee weapons (used at default). He's dedicated to his job, but he also *loves* to look good. He's *extremely good* at what he does – he wouldn't last long otherwise – and insanely lucky. He seems to be riding his own personal heroic narrative. But his dedication to being the coolest thing in any room is hardly destined to win him friends.

Not that he cares. Actually, he not-*very*-secretly despises anyone whom he thinks might believe that they're better than him, leading him to clash with his superiors, rich civilians, and adventurers.

No one knows *why* he's like this. It's entirely possible that he's venting some suppressed rage or seeking vengeance on the criminal classes for something. On the other hand, it's possible that he just enjoys it. He works out of Lacquered Tablet's modest-but-elegant Agatean-style house on the edge of town, on the rare occasions that he needs an HQ.[1]

TRADE AND HOSPITALITY

Ultimately, though, Port Duck remains a pirate town, where the distinction between "ship's chandler," "pawnbroker," and "fence" is hazy. Many of the local inns see plenty of roistering.[2] On the other hand, an increasing number of respectable traders, and not least the Agatean tourist ships, are encouraging a more legitimate sort of business.

---

1. But, of course, as a Maverick Cop, Prop Lee Does Not Get On With His Superiors. It's in the job description.

2. Not to mention quaffing.

Llapffargoch-Wokkaiiooii

Despite being the wettest (and least pronounceable) of the Brown Islands, Llapffargoch-Wokkaiiooii is becoming a popular tourist spot. Its culture – a curious blend of Druidic religion and traditional native practises – offers the strongest evidence that the legendary missionary-explorer Llamedos Jones really existed and reached these parts.[1] The most obvious difference from other islands is that the locals don't surf. Instead, they engage in terrifying choral singing and in religious ceremonies involving two teams of 15 men, who ritually maim each other in pursuit of a small ball which isn't even properly round.

There are only two traditional roles for the men of Llapffargoch-Wokkaiiooii: shepherd or miner. The nearest thing to ore on the island is a powdery black rock of no known value, which is piled up in untidy heaps all over the place. Since the birth of the tourist industry, this has been marketed as "Brown Islands rock" and sold to visitors.

Piracy

The men of the island are heavily built, and more obviously aggressive than their neighbours. Piracy comes naturally to them. They blacken their faces with rock powder. They grimace at their victims before combat, sticking out their tongues and shouting. They sing. In short, they're terrifying. Many trading ships surrender immediately.

These pirates resolve disputes using a technique called "the Scrumm." Each side bends down in a huddle with the heads of the men behind between the buttocks of those in front[2], and the two groups face off, trying to push their opponents over the side.[3]

---

*1. The accents **are** a bit of a giveaway, too.*

2. It isn't a good idea to make jokes about this.

3. This is the origin of the old local saying, "Everything can be solved if we just put our heads together."

The tourists are also, unknowingly, encouraging some legitimate businesses that *look* otherwise. The new profession of travel agent, which has emerged on the Counterweight Continent, has taken to offering all-inclusive holiday voyages to the Circle Sea which incorporate visits to "The Wicked Pirate City." While Port Duck has no trouble living up to most of its reputation, these visitors don't really want to see anything *too* disturbing, and the tour organisers certainly don't want to provide much genuine risk. Consequently, various entrepreneurs have got together and set up a cluster of taverns near the tourist lodging-houses, where one can witness a brawl or two, overhear discussion of which ships to rob, be scowled at by some fearsome bruisers, and still go home with your drink unspilled and your gizzard unslit. Old-fashioned pirates tend to weep at the very mention of these places if only because they have such stupid names.[1]

Other businesses include small boatyards, brokers, and so on. The place is still totally dependent on maritime commerce.

If Moist was any judge, any judge at all, the man in front of him was the biggest fraud he'd ever met. And he advertised it. That was . . . style. The pirate curls, the eyepatch, even the damn parrot. Twelve and a half per cent, for heavens' sake, didn't anyone spot that?

– Going Postal

Culture and Society

Port Duck is a new town with an exceptionally diverse population. It doesn't have a culture so much as a collection of borrowed cultures, none of them working quite right, and all of them regularly crashing into each other. People are still learning how to live together without more than a couple of serious riots a week. Eventually, things may settle into something almost civilised, but don't expect that to happen soon.

Religion

The town doesn't yet have a "temple quarter" as such, although one is visibly developing. While Discworld temples are simply places where the priests can gather large groups of worshippers and really get some belief going, most religions have very standardised architectural styles, to give the faithful a comfortable sense of familiarity wherever they go. Thus, in large cities, one may find Strict Druids worshipping in open-air stone circles, alongside Ephebian shrines with columns and marble sculptures. Currently in Port Duck, a new sect seems to show up every week and insist on changing the skyline.

---

1. *There's quite a competition in the naming. "Ye Well-Hanged Scurvy Knave, Arrrh" is currently considered to lead the field.*

Prop Lee

368 points

In game terms, the only serious full-time law-enforcer in Port Duck looks like this:

ST 12 [20]; **DX** 16 [120]; **IQ** 11 [20]; **HT** 12 [20].
Damage 1d-1/1d+2; BL 29 lbs.; HP 12 [0]; Will 11 [0]; Per 13 [10]; FP 12 [0].
Basic Speed 7.00 [0]; Basic Move 7 [0]; Dodge 12*†; Parry 13* (Judo).
5'7"; 140 lbs.

Social Background

TL: 4 [0].
CF: Agatean [0].
Languages: Agatean (Native) [0]; Brown Islander (Accented) [4]; Morporkian (Accented) [4].

Advantages

Ambidexterity [5]; Appearance (Attractive) [4]; Charisma 1 [5]; Combat Reflexes [15]; Daredevil [15]; Enhanced Dodge [15]; Fearlessness 5 [10]; High Pain Threshold [10]; Intuition [15]; Legal Enforcement Powers [10]; Patron (Agatean Consulate; 6 or less) [5]; Rapid Healing [5]; Reputation +2 (As dutiful cop and not a man to cross, in Port Duck) [5]; Ridiculous Luck [60].
Perks: Crossbow Safety; Fearsome Stare. [2]

Disadvantages

Duty (As cop; 15 or less) [-15]; Impulsiveness (12) [-10]; Jealousy [-10]; Odious Personal Habit (Full-Time Cool) [-5]; Stubbornness [-5].
Quirks: Taciturn; Uncongenial; Vengeful; Wears tinted glasses everywhere. [-4]

Skills

Acrobatics (H) DX-1 [2]-15; Area Knowledge (Port Duck) (E) IQ [1]-11; Armoury/TL4 (Missile Weapons) (A) IQ-1 [1]-10; Criminology/TL4 (A) IQ [2]-11; Crossbow (E) DX+2 [4]-18; Current Affairs/TL4 (Port Duck) (E) IQ [1]-11; Fast-Draw/TL (Arrow/Bolt) (E) DX+1 [1]-17*; Fast-Draw (Pistol Crossbow) (E) DX+1 [1]-17*; Hidden Lore (Port Duck City Secrets) (A) IQ-1 [1]-10; Holdout (A) IQ+1 [4]-12; Interrogation (A) IQ-1 [1]-10; Intimidation (A) Will-1 [1]-10; Judo (H) DX+2 [12]-18; Karate (H) DX-1 [2]-15; Law (Agatean Police) (H) IQ-2 [1]-9; Shadowing (A) IQ-1 [1]-10; Stealth (A) DX-1 [1]-15; Thrown Weapon (Throwing Star) (E) DX [1]-16.

* Includes +1 for Combat Reflexes.
† Includes +1 for Enhanced Dodge.

To add to the confusion, in a town as diverse as this one, certain religions aren't as different as they like to think. For one thing, some gods go looking for worshippers in different lands, under different names (Blind Io, p. 298, is the greatest expert at this). This makes life complicated for priests in a theologically diverse place like Port Duck. Just as two temples are getting a really good holy feud going, a pair of embarrassed and oddly worded revelations may suddenly arrive from Cori Celesti, telling them to make peace.

Scenario: A Little Job

This story starts in Ankh-Morpork, where the PCs are recruited to perform a job for the Patrician. While they might actually be hired, it would be more in character for him if they were manipulated or tricked into it. Perhaps Vetinari wants them out of town for a while and won't be too upset if they don't make it back. Anyway, he explains the mission very straightforwardly.

One of his continuing concerns is recovering the scattered notebooks that a younger Leonard of Quirm (pp. 308-309) filled with designs for devices that might have unfortunate effects if actually built. Recently, his agents located one of these, only to be beaten to their goal by someone else, who had been hired to acquire the notebook and send it to an address in the Brown Islands. The PCs must follow, locate, and recover the notebook, or see that it is destroyed; Vetinari hates to see the products of genius lost entirely, so he'd prefer the former.

After the requisite voyage and some investigation in Port Duck (not a place where questions are always welcome), the trail leads to a building in the jungle belonging to *Soso Sung*, an Agatean nobleman of impeccable manners, technical genius, and no great sanity. Unfortunately, the PCs arrive too late: Sung has used designs in the notebook to build a giant humanoid machine, controlled from the head and powered by five hired trolls (one in the body, one in each limb).

The GM should manipulate things mercilessly to ensure that Sung gets to try out his contraption, which is assembled by the trolls with much chanting of "Put It Together!" Naturally, Sung wants revenge on everyone who has ever annoyed him – starting with some overcharging local tradesmen – and only the PCs can stop him. Fortunately for them, the trolls keep overheating and slowing down, so the machine has to stop stomping opponents and go lie down in a river until the trolls can think again.

If the PCs need more assistance, they can discover that Sung has a sideline in collecting interesting fauna, and there's a giant reptilian monstrosity in a holding pen behind his tower. If released, it will get into a fight with the machine. Hopefully, the winner will then be damaged and weakened enough for the PCs to have a chance of stopping it.

Scenario Seeds

When setting games on the Brown Islands, much depends on the PCs – natives, wanderers from Ankh-Morpork, and agents of the Agatean government have different problems to deal with.

The Islands are filled with buried treasure, pirates, navy vessels, and assorted other adventures.

SEAFARING ADVENTURES

The Islands are a suitable venue for any number of standard pirate plots, including quests for buried treasure while being shadowed by shiploads of ruffians (who *do* have as much right to it as anyone else), mutinies against power-crazed captains, and cat-and-mouse struggles between pirates and navy vessels. Equally, tropical islands can have problems involving archaic tentacled deities, or attempts by the natives to fend off colonialism. Below are some further possibilities.

He Ain't Very Heavy

Somewhere among the Islands is a pirate crew that includes a self-exiled Ankhian nobleman. Now, others of his family want him to come home. Has he been as successful a swashbuckler as he naturally expected? (The nobility always assume that breeding will tell.) And will his crewmates let him be taken away, or will they start talking ransoms?

Picture **This**, Me Hearties

A couple of years ago, an Agatean trading ship was wrecked on the coast of a small, uninhabited island during a storm. The PCs have come to the same island – perhaps by chance, perhaps seeking salvage. What they don't know is that (a) the ship was carrying a cargo of imp-based iconographs, personal organisers, and watches (pp. 159-160), and (b) through some quirk of the local magical field, the imps escaped, survived, and *bred*. The resulting tribes of tiny supernatural creatures have bizarre mental powers and are very determined that they should *not* go back in the boxes.

What Is This Thing Called "Spandex"?

Like any self-respecting archipelago, the Brown Islands include less-often-visited islands inhabited by amazon tribes genetically blessed with perfect skin and hair. An exile from one such tribe recently reached Ankh-Morpork, where she sensibly traded her (minimal, two-piece) tribal costume for more practical garb before getting a job as a companion/bodyguard to an upper-class lady. However, her old clothes fell into the hands of a Morporkian entrepreneur, who has now arrived in the Brown Islands seeking their source. The robust, elastic, comfortable plant fibres used to make them could revolutionise the textile industry.

PORT DUCK ADVENTURES

A *bustling, brawling* town like Port Duck is such natural adventure territory that adventurers will quite likely get through a handful of bar-room brawls, a dozen rumours of treasure, and a week in the cells before they can even think about a plot. However, when the need arises, there are numerous possibilities.

You Spilled My Drink (By Arrangement)

Being a professional Evil-Looking Customer in one of the Port Duck bars which exist to keep tourists *safely* entertained is a Struggling-level job; Performance, Intimidation, and perhaps Brawling skills would be useful. The supervisor gets Average-level wages and would add Directing and Leadership skills. As well as keeping bystanders enjoyably unnerved but not actually harmed, employees have to deal with real-but-naïve ruffians who've wandered into the wrong bar, looking for real trouble.

Something There Is That Doesn't Love This Wall

Few people believe the legend of Trossig's Revenge, but *something* is disrupting the latest attempt to build a fortified trading-post for an Ankh-Morpork merchant company. Every night, whatever work was done during the day falls down. Is it the crazed but still-living Trossig (with a flock of weirdly intelligent parrot allies), his ghost, the company's competitors, or poor-quality foundations? To find out, the PCs are hired as night watchmen, consulting priests or wizards, or engineers.

. . . She Had To Stalk Into Mine

Brick's Café Ankh-Morporkian is one of the more authentic establishments in Port Duck, despite its "theme." It's a replica of Ankh-Morpork's Mended Drum, complete with a troll doorman, "Brick." (After dark, Brick almost cools down enough to be useful, though he has never become smart enough to notice that he isn't getting paid.) It's also the town's centre for trade in small and intangible valuables, such as documents and information. Now, however, its proprietor and chief broker seems distracted – an old girlfriend of his has shown up, and what's more, she seems to be a were-leopardess. His business partners think that she's up to something and hire the PCs to investigate.

More Settings

These are some other possible settings, which can be used as written or taken as examples of how to develop typical Discworld themes and ideas for games. There are plenty more possibilities, though. *Vast* areas of the Disc remain unexplored. Less than a third of the land area has been covered by the chronicles – and who knows what lies under the sea? Outside of Ankh-Morpork and Lancre, even "known" lands have largely been traversed rather than examined. There could be *anything* out there.

possibility of smaller states being converted to rubble if they weren't very careful. However, Wadi El-Rukl was remote and minute enough that only small missions were sent, and the sultan kept them happy with vague responses. Then, just as things were getting worrying, political turmoil in Al Khali following the abortive war with Ankh-Morpork put the entire question on hold. Still, Al Khali never quite forgets such things, and ambitious frontier generals might choose to prove themselves at any moment.

Wadi El-Rukl

Wadi El-Rukl is a caravan town in the deserts of Klatch, lucky enough to have escaped direct rule from Al Khali so far. There has been some kind of community here for a *long* time (hieroglyphs and ruins survive from the days when Djelibeybi ruled the continent and this was an unpopular army posting), but the place's emergence as a town goes back two or three centuries. A local petty chieftain gained enough tax income and credibility to erect a palace and call himself a sultan, and his heirs have built on that. In particular, one previous sultan managed some improvements in the water supplies to farms around the town, giving the economy a firm basis.

Success can lead to trouble, though. The recent aggressive expansion of Al Khali included some careful assessment of every neighbouring statelet. This was followed by polite diplomatic missions discussing treaties, tax harmonisation, joint anti-banditry operations, and the

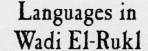

Languages in Wadi El-Rukl

The native language in Wadi El-Rukl is the Klatchian of Al Khali. The town has its own recognisable accent and a few quirks of vocabulary, so a visitor from Al Khali will usually be identified as such by a native, and vice versa; roll vs. IQ for this. The difference in accents can be hidden with a roll against Acting at +1 or Mimicry (Speech) at +3. Roll once per hour during long conversations. As a widespread "trade language," Morporkian is spoken by many merchants, and anyone who habitually ventures across the desert is also likely to know something of the D'reg dialect. Other languages are limited to a few travellers, wide-ranging merchants, and scholars.

THE PALACE

The current ruler is Sultan Khodrian ibn Alg al-Ieee, Warden of the Wells and Guardian of the Seven Tax-Paying Temples, known to his friends as Alg-Ieee, and to citizens of the town as Him In The Palace.

Khodrian is a quiet, middle-aged man of moderate appetites, average intellect, and reasonable sense. He's aware that tradition requires him to appoint as his vizier a sinister figure with a short beard and a polite way of being very dangerous, but this is tempered by the knowledge that anyone too well qualified for the job would sooner or later start thinking about promotion – and the only rank above vizier is sultan. So he appointed a perfectly competent tax accountant named Dabil al-Intri (inventor of a new accountancy system that he's too modest to name after himself), and then insisted that Dabil grow a short beard and dye it black, and practise his polite manners and sinister smiles. Dabil does his best to oblige, but secretly finds all this tiresome and uncomfortable. He's also missing something important.

THE HAREM

Like any self-respecting sultan, the lord of Wadi El-Rukl maintains a harem. And like any sensible harem, the inhabitants have found extra ways to make themselves useful. Traditionally, they engage in spinning, weaving, embroidery, and similar domestic industry, and sell their surplus production through contacts in the local bazaar, enhancing the palace's funds.

The complication is that most members of *this* harem have time on their hands. The sultan long ago formed a very affectionate relationship with his first wife, Ameeth, who has given him a couple of heirs, who are still quite young. Khodrian only added a bunch of concubines to his household for the sake of appearances, and largely forgets that they're there. Ameeth – who, as tradition dictates, has charge of the harem – has allied with them.

Working with the shrewd lower-class women who sell the harem's products in the bazaar, Ameeth and her colleagues took up speculative trade, aided by titbits of palace gossip. They built their funds steadily over time and are now rich on their own account. Through a combination of contacts and palace influence, they effectively control the town. They have to be subtle, but they've become good at that.

Their agents drop hints, trade favours, and engage in extremely polite bribery. Meanwhile, Ameeth chats to the sultan when he needs to relax, and occasionally makes suggestions. These tend to be blatantly very stupid, but to contain some core of an idea that Khodrian can be expected to pick up and develop, thinking all the while that it's his own. Dabil does realise that the harem is making a healthy profit, but sees this merely as giving him a buffer of funds for emergencies. He doesn't realise that about half the harem's income never even crosses his books, but is salted away in the form of gold, gems, and "frivolous luxuries" such as high-value silk cloth and gold jewellery.

Fortunately for the town, the harem has its best interests at heart – just on their own terms. They want prosperity, security, and stability, they can be appallingly ruthless in pursuit of these ends, and they aren't above commissioning the odd assassination when

someone seems to be a threat. A couple of the shrewder and less-moral denizens of Wadi El-Rukl's small underworld know that they've received some well-paid commissions "from the palace," but assume that these have come from the sultan or his vizier.

THE BAZAAR

The key to the feel of Wadi El-Rukl is that someone will always be buying or selling. Hang around the town gates and sooner rather than later, a caravan will pass through, a camel will step on your foot, and its driver will insult you. If you're seeking somebody important, the bazaar is always the best place to start. Try to find some*thing* important, and – well, bargaining is a basic survival skill in these parts.

The bazaar is open through the daylight hours, seven days out of eight. It takes place in the town's central square – which is largely covered in temporary stalls and surrounded by permanent booths with awnings and lockable shutters – and in a maze of surrounding streets. These lanes are only slightly wider than a camel with a full pack on it, as is continually demonstrated by camels with packs.

One consequence of all this is that fight or chase scenes will be chaotic. The bazaar is cramped and full of people, many of whom will get loudly annoyed, panic, or become extremely curious the moment things start happening. Furthermore, they share the space with flimsy awnings, precarious stacks of stuff, camels, chickens, and rather rickety buildings. The GM shouldn't bother even trying to put everything on a map – just assume that something will end up broken, get in the way, or fall down at some crucial moment. Highly accurate camel expectoration, pedlars trying to sell stuff, and broken oil jars creating traction-free slicks are specially recommended.

LAW, ORDER, AND MILITARY POWER

The sultan of Wadi El-Rukl maintains a body of robust mercenary guards who double as law enforcers. However, being soldiers first, they may not be the Disc's most efficient police force. A squad of them will usually show up when a crime is reported loudly enough, and arrest anyone obvious. This force also occasionally gets involved in fighting D'regs (p. 236), although they try not to, valuing breathing as they do. Fortunately, the local tribes are relatively small and restrained in their robberies, for now.

The sultan has heard that the rulers of Al Khali appoint *walis* (officials) to deal with serious crimes across their large territories. However, Wadi El-Rukl has neither the need nor the resources to follow suit – yet. Adventurers wanting that job would have to be exceptionally convincing. Still, it's a possibility.

MAGIC

Wadi El-Rukl has a handful of small-time wizards, trained by apprenticeship. They tend to dress flamboyantly and hang around the bazaar, casting showy spells by way of public entertainment or taking small-time commissions, usually to work their unreliable divinations. However, it's dangerous to underestimate them.

They're quick and clever with the spells they do know; if it comes to a showdown, some will get off a distracting illusion and a couple of painful fire spells in the time it takes an over-educated UU snob to decide which language to incant. Their greatest weakness is that the offer of a lamp or a ring of unknown origin, however blatantly mundane, attracts them like a scuttle of anthracite attracts swamp dragons.

There's one flying carpet (p. 160) in the sultan's treasury, and at least one more (unknown to the sultan) in the harem.

WADI EL-RUKL CAMPAIGNS

Wadi El-Rukl has enough violence, intrigue, and espionage for death-and-taxes adventures, and it is remote enough to feature interestingly in picaresque campaigns. It's certainly full of opportunities for social comedy, while a sitcom might be set in a caravanserai or a trading-house. Arabian Nights fantasy is ripe for parody, and the situation with the harem is designed as satire of traditional views of the place of women. Some specific game ideas follow.

Profit and Loss

Particularly ambitious newcomer merchants may have to deal not only with the usual shrewd bazaar-dwellers, but also with the sense that they're being watched and out-thought. Potential customers are distracted, everything they want to buy rises in price thanks to a dozen seemingly unconnected rival purchasers, and *someone* tips off potential competitors in the next town along. Eventually, the newcomers may be smart enough to identify who's making trouble for them and to reach some kind of compromise with the harem.

Intelligence Tests

There aren't *many* spies in town at the moment, but some visiting merchants and diplomats have a tendency to take notes. The harem keeps an eye on such people, as do some smarter members of the palace guard. Not all foreign observers will be from Al Khali; nations from Hersheba, Tsort, and Ephebe to Ankh-Morpork are watching Klatch these days. Given a few provocative rumours, the place could turn into the venue for a multi-sided secret war.

Be Careful What You Wish For

Supernatural events in this part of the Disc often involve powers greater than mortal wizards can control. Wizard PCs may be convinced that *they* are the exceptions. Mind you, not all lamps, rings, and carpets are worth the asking price.

Prophet and Less

The desert sun helps religions germinate. Perhaps the next faith fated to sweep the nations of Klatch is currently forming in the solar-heated brain of a hermit (p. 302) outside Wadi El-Rukl. Magical diviners, priests of rival deities, and History Monks may all be drawn to the scene, along with potential acolytes.

Cart Wars

Much of the continent of EcksEcksEcksEcks (pp. 244-245) is taken up with desert, and despite recent improvements in the climate, it's still *serious* desert, some of it too hot and remote even for Fourecksian sheep-farmers. Parts, however, are crossed

---

Scenario: Rug Addiction

The oasis village of Abrl Mrekk, about three days' ride from Wadi El-Rukl, is noted for one thing: the wonderful (nonmagical) carpets which its inhabitants weave. Lately, however, nothing has been heard from that direction, and the last trade caravan is overdue. Contacts say that the D'regs deny having anything to do with this (and they rarely bother to conceal their raiding). The PCs are hired to investigate.

On the way, they're harassed in the night by a couple of bogeymen (pp. 361-362). If captured or cornered, the monsters seem confused as to why they've manifested here, but they clearly felt obliged to cause fear in sleepers, as is their nature. When the party reaches Abrl Mrekk, they find all the villagers and the lost caravan lying around fast asleep, in broad daylight.

The cause is an ancient, nearly defunct small god, whose last shrine was buried in the desert on the edge of the oasis. This deity is concerned with dreams and creativity. So long as it was weak, it survived by giving the carpet-weavers vivid dreams, which inspired their artistry and induced just enough belief. Recently, however, a villager digging a new well exposed the shrine, and this generated a brief surge of superstitious awe that fully awoke the god. Driven mad by centuries of enfeeblement, it sent all the villagers to sleep, and is now sustained by the belief that they feel in their dreams. It can work just enough miracles to keep them alive, although they're growing emaciated, dehydrated, and sunburnt.

The PCs must keep most of the villagers awake for long enough that the god's power fades below a critical level. Force-feeding them lots of Klatchian coffee should do the trick. However, the god itself can manifest through countless rugs and carpets that have its ancient symbols woven into them. It might produce anything from minor poltergeist effects to a giant animated figure constructed entirely of carpets, according to the GM's taste and what will challenge the PCs. The trick is to stay ahead of the angry carpet-god for long enough to get most of his unwitting worshippers onto a serious caffeine high.

---

occasionally by fast, armed carts. They're armed, fast, and only occasional because these roads are also prowled by "road gangs": bandits with speedy carts of their own, attitude problems, and a distinctly punk fashion sense.

Yes, it's a tough land with tough people and lots of conflict. Some roleplayers find that strangely appealing.

ARENA COMBAT

The Outback's culture of road-based violence has evolved in peculiar ways. Even in EcksEcksEcksEcks, not everyone feels that banditry is the way to spend their time. It's easier to organise proper betting on the results if you have a set venue and maybe a few rules.

Thus, someone had the bright idea of building arenas, complete with civilised facilities.[1] Anyone who wants can come along and prove himself in front of a large and cynical audience. These arenas are rough affairs – rickety stands arranged around oval dirt tracks, dotted with betting kiosks and fast-food stands, and semi-sapient security staff prowling everywhere – but no worries.

Predictably, though, some older cart aces think that rules and confined spaces are for wimps. With "real road warrior" types saying that arena fighters can't cut it in a fight without tying their opponents' hands behind their backs, and arena fighters saying that road warriors are a bunch of crooks who can't go down to the shops without cheating on the way, there's plenty of scope for bar-room brawls. And the fact that many drivers cheerfully switch between the two modes means that you can't be sure who'll be on your side in the next brawl.

The XCDA

Even among Fourecks' cart duellists, *someone* ended up suggesting that things ought to be more organised. The EcksEcksEcksEcksian Cart Duel Association ("XCDA") is the result. The popular local opinion of it is "buncha wowsers," but it does serve a purpose in laying down rules for arena combats, and more relaxed guidelines for open-road combat.

The XCDA is an assortment of enthusiastic organisers, racers who want to prevent the organisers from making excessive changes, and bookies fighting to ensure that any changes don't involve them paying out too much. It meets annually in some large Outback bar, mostly to elect a committee of five to 15 people (depending on how the annual meeting went), who in turn meet roughly every month. Both annual and committee meetings invariably degenerate into alcoholic disputes, and committee members are advised to wear armour. Indeed, there's talk of setting up an association to regulate combat at XCDA meetings.

The XCDA's other self-appointed function is publishing league tables and ratings. The job of assessing these is now anonymous, following several disputed calls leading to violence.

CAMPAIGN CATEGORIES

The Outback is (still) a big location for death-and-taxes adventure – with emphasis on the death part. It first appeared in the chronicles as somewhere that archetypical picaresque wanderer, Rincewind, passed through on a quest he wasn't even aware he was pursuing. It's a bit less appropriate for social comedy, but even hay-smugglers and cart duellists have their relationships. A sitcom could certainly be set here. It's also all about parody, specifically of the "post-catastrophe road warriors" genre, and of board games and movies about duels between armed cars. Satire might focus on

---

1. Betting kiosks.

the pseudo-Australian style of the setting: the frontier-colonial economy, the brash egalitarianism, and the accents.

OPEN ROAD ADVENTURES

Fourecks' Outback is one of the few remaining areas of the Disc where old-fashioned, run-around-screaming heroism is still a viable, indeed admired, option. Experienced gamers who don't wish to give up all their old habits should feel at home, with the unique cart-based lifestyle adding novelty. How morally or otherwise they choose to play their characters is up to them – but remember, even the most psychotic road-gang member needs a sense of *style*. Admittedly, it's style without taste, involving a lot of studded leather and filed teeth, but the self-aware nature of Fourecksian myth-making has infected these people.

In games set after the end of *The Last Continent*, things may have calmed down a bit; with the coming of the Wet, hay and oats will be worth a little less, reducing the incentive for banditry. But the Outback is still mostly desert – and then there's all those sheep farms, which seem to attract rustlers and other larrikins like, well, flies to a dead sheep. On the other side of the law, there are bush police and freelance carters. And there are also the aboriginal people, with their unique magic and traditions.

Needed – Another Hero, ONO

On top of all the above, innocents may get caught up in Outback adventures. Perhaps a town full of people has been flooded out by the Wet, or a bunch of refugees have sailed in from elsewhere on the Disc, somehow having got the idea that this is a land of opportunity. Unfortunately, the villains of the piece have this group tagged as an exploitable resource – as, in a nicer way, have the heroes.

This is when real heroes get to stand tall, or at least to fight a lot of running battles with road gangs while, they hope, attracting the attention of farmers' daughters (or, to be fair, farmers' sons). Of course, the innocents *will* be Discworlders, and therefore stubborn, opinionated, and difficult.

But I Don't Like Waltzing

Then there's the fine tradition of Outback Ballads, mostly written by city-dwellers who've never been more than five miles from the Opera House. Suppose that one such balladeer decided that he ought to do some actual research? Keeping him alive amongst road gangs and spiders could be a challenge for professional bodyguards.

Arena Adventures

Gamers who just want to play out a bit of cathartic vehicular violence can always switch off their roleplaying instincts and run some straight cart combat on a map. Other PCs can bet on their friends[1], or become involved in plots to sabotage favoured vehicles, spy on new designs, or dope horses or drivers. This being the Outback, though, there's little formal law, and gamblers who suspect that they've been swindled are likely to demonstrate their unhappiness with extreme prejudice.

Nor need such games entirely lack opportunities for roleplaying. Even arena duellists have personalities, and there's always the old gladiator-movie cliché of the fighter who gets coerced into this business against his better nature. A couple of other plot ideas appear below.

But Prove Yourself WHAT?

The newest driver in the arena is being watched at a discreet distance by some very large gentlemen. It turns out that he's the would-be black-sheep son of a wealthy family, who don't want him to come to harm before he comes to his senses. Adventurers could be hired to look out for him, find themselves as his opponents in a high-risk destruction derby, or just see this as an interesting betting opportunity.

A Dish Best Served Cold (With Pea Soup)

The attractive young woman hanging around the arena isn't actually the sort that your mother warned you about (though perhaps she should have). It turns out that the lady's boyfriend went missing a couple of years ago, presumed killed by a notorious road-gang member who's now the regional duelling champion. She's keen to see justice served. Or so she says.

Will the adventurers help, for cash or honour? If so, will they survive? And what's the *real* story? Maybe the boyfriend just wanted out of a relationship with the sort of girl who goes around commissioning assassinations, and he rigged a cover story . . .

---

1. Or bet against them. Friendship and money don't mix.

Sample Scenario: Lost and Found

This scenario starts in Ankh-Morpork but soon departs. It can stand alone or be used as the starting point of a longer campaign – a disparate group pulled together for this mission might decide to stick together afterward.

Background

Unseen University has a problem: The supply of bananas in Ankh-Morpork has dried up, and the Librarian (pp. 333-335) isn't a happy ape. The library continues to run passably well, but he's becoming morose, unhelpful, and testy.

The undergraduates are getting by, as most of the books *they* need are in well-catalogued open stacks, and they take any small

disruption as a welcome break. Likewise, the senior faculty, while admitting that there may be a problem, are not losing sleep[1] – the Librarian is still keeping the more dangerous grimoires in line, and they're sure that something will turn up eventually.[2]

For more-dedicated junior graduates such as the pale, obsessive denizens of the High Energy Magic Building, however, things are becoming impossible. Every time they want to find some moderately obscure tome, they're confronted with the fact that the only being who really understands the place is sitting disconsolately on top of a very tall bookshelf, flicking peanuts at people.[3]

---

1. And certainly not missing any meals.

2. They might add that the last time they got involved in this sort of thing – and it was a **serious** problem that time, mark you – they got dragged across the Disc and several thousand years back in time, and they don't want any more of that, thank you.

3. And not even hard enough to sting.

The cause of the trouble is a mystery. Stall-holders in the city market report that no ships have put in from the tropical lands of further Klatch for weeks now, and no one can say what the problem is. Bananas are sometimes shipped in from further afield – even from EcksEcksEcksEcks – but it's the wrong season for those. There's nothing for it. Someone will have to investigate.[1]

GETTING PCs INVOLVED

At this point, PCs who are wizards at the University can simply draw a short straw, metaphorically or literally. Undergraduates may be bribed, bullied, or blackmailed by their supervisors, while more senior wizards could be subject to subtler persuasion. Some might even volunteer. Graduate wizards may be persuaded by

---

1. If you like guest appearances, bring in Rincewind (pp. 330-332) during this scene – as a known expert on banana-peeling – and then have him flee screaming at the first mention of the word "adventure."

Background Research

Intellectual PCs involved in this scenario – especially wizards – may try more sophisticated information-gathering. Divination magic is patchy and unreliable at these ranges, but it might get something. Exact results are up to the GM and the dice, but remember that the problem lies hundreds of miles distant, and is somewhat peculiar, with a certain amount of unconventional magic involved. Answers are likely to be, at best, hard to comprehend until the mystery is solved. If anyone consults Hex (p. 286), it will spend some time attempting to resolve the problem of getting divinations to work, and then suggest that the best approach is to go and look.

It's unlikely that any wizard will want to cast the Rite of AshkEnte (pp. 214-215) for this purpose, and even if one does, it's even less likely that he'll find enough others willing to assist. If it *is* cast, Death will answer as politely as ever, but will be a little aggrieved at being summoned over *fruit*, and may be a bit terse. He'll confirm that several people have died recently *en route* between Howondaland and Ankh-Morpork, which is probably why the ones transporting fruit haven't got through lately, but he isn't required to go into detail and chooses not to.

University-based PCs may also try more prosaic sorts of research before setting out, perhaps looking for guides to Klatch or information on bananas. The trouble is that even such routine nonmagical references are stored *in the library*. Still, the adventurers can be allowed a Research roll. They'll probably survive, but on a critical failure, the lack of aid from the Librarian might mean that they get into trouble. At worst, they could be gone for some time. They may even get lost in L-Space (p. 285) – in which case the GM can add complications like having them emerge before they went in. More likely, though, they'll end up with an indifferent travel guide to Howondaland.

---

offers based on their known tastes; e.g. the chance of a few hours of completely free time on Hex might prove irresistible. For University employees, this could be when they discover the small print in their contracts, saying that they have to go *wherever* they are told.

As this is a University project of sorts, the University will fund it, so far as possible. The High Energy Magic crew may even be prepared to divert some of their research funds. Perhaps special emergency grants were set up in the University's distant past. The level of funding available is left to the GM, depending on what expenses the GM expects the adventurers to meet; the idea is to persuade them to get involved and to give them a fair reward at the end, not to annoy them or unbalance the game.

Other PCs need not have University backgrounds; in fact, the entire party might be recruited by NPC wizards – a group of nerdy, verbose, and nervous academics trying to hire some muscle. Anyone who *is* recruited from the University may be encouraged, by other UU members, to ". . . hire some more help. Hey, there are always plenty of those heroic swordsmen hanging around the Drum." (If the GM doesn't mind a digression, this can be an opportunity for a bar-room brawl.) A little manipulation might also be required to get incompatible individuals – such as dwarfs and trolls, or wizards and barbarian swordsmen – to sign up for the same mission. As always, money may help.

The Quest for Fruit

With the scene set, the next step will probably consist of the adventurers discussing their exact plans. In some cases, it might be necessary to explain what bananas *are*. Optimists may insist on scouring the city markets, but apart from C.M.O.T. Dibbler (pp. 315-316) trying to sell them substitutes ("No, Mr. Dibbler, these are potatoes."), they'll be out of luck. It seems that a trip to Howondaland is unavoidable, which means starting at the city docks. An indirect route is usually advisable for any visit to the docks, incidentally – natives can explain to visitors that a shortcut through the Shades is Not A Good Idea.

Enquiries about bananas will garner the same answers at the docks as they did in the market, along with occasional remarks about *nothing* having come in from Howondaland lately. The adventurers are highly unlikely to have enough funds to charter a ship (the graduate wizards certainly don't provide that much, and if anyone has really excessive Wealth, well, tell them that there are no ships for sale this week), so they should end up asking about vessels that are already planning to go that way. The GM can run through as much roleplaying, dockside banter, and use of *Reaction Rolls* (pp. 171-172) as he likes – but eventually, the PCs will be pointed toward a ship moored at the end of Pier Three.

By Sea to Re'Durat

The ship at Pier Three is the *In Nomine*, commanded by a Captain Chadwick, a dapper fellow with Charisma 1 and pleasant manners. If the PCs try asking around, Psychology or Body Language will determine that many sailors and dockhands are a bit cautious talking about this vessel, while Streetwise may turn up that it has some underworld associations. However, Chadwick and his men seem fairly straightforward, and the *In Nomine* is definitely the only ship heading toward Howondaland in the near future.

In fact, the *In Nomine* is the latest name of the *Nameless*, a vessel used in smuggling and speculative anti-piracy work. This may be familiar to players who've read *Pyramids*, but the GM should let smart-aleck fans work this out for themselves.

Anyway, when they accept that they have little choice but to visit this craft, the adventurers will be directed to speak with Chadwick – who is in fact Chidder, from *Pyramids*, a graduate of the Assassins' Guild School. No game details are given for him here; the GM should simply assume that he's pretty good (skill 14+) at anything he turns his mind to, and really quite *serious* in a fight, but laid-back when off duty.

Chadwick will acknowledge that he's departing tomorrow for far Klatch. He'll also be open about the reason: When imports from an area fall below demand, there's an opportunity for profit. Although he has no idea what may be causing the problem – he'll listen politely to any suggestions, but not jump to conclusions – he seems confident that he can deal with any obstacles. (Actually, his ship can outrun almost anything on the water and outfight just about anything that it may end up fighting.)

He'll be happy to take on passengers, especially those who look like they might be able to assist in the event of trouble. In truth, he thinks that a bunch of adventurers could help, but he's a merchant first and foremost, so he'll charge them for passage. How much is up to the GM; this is a good opportunity to try a Quick Contest of Merchant skill. Chadwick will neither bankrupt the PCs nor take it badly if he's out-haggled. If pushed skilfully, he'll bring them along for nominal rates – maybe even for free – but they would have to agree to handle any fighting on the way.

Accommodation details will be one subject to settle. Any trolls will have to sleep in the ballast – nothing personal, it's just that the ship's furniture isn't built to bear that much weight, and on deck, they might roll over and fall into the sea in their sleep. (And trolls sink like, well, stones.) Male travellers can have an adequate cabin or two between them. If there are any females in the group, especially attractive ones, Chadwick nods politely: "The ladies can sleep in my cabin."[1]

The *In Nomine* sails at dawn. Once it has made its way into the Circle Sea, there's time for roleplaying and minor clue-dropping. This should go by easy stages. The voyagers have a long journey ahead of them, with little to do at first, and the GM can skip over most of it, use minor incidents as punctuation, or invoke *Motion Sickness* (p. 190).

Those who know ships, or who are lucky with IQ or Per rolls, may notice some oddities. Anyone specifically looking over the bow *might* glimpse a solid-looking metal spike cutting through the water (below the waterline, so it isn't automatically visible). Also, although the hold is empty, there are a couple of nailed-up crates on deck. If asked about any of this, Chadwick shrugs, smiles charmingly, and says something vague.

As the weather gets warmer to rimwards, the crew – burly fellows, with a tendency to wear one gold earring each – take their shirts off. This will reveal some quite amazing adults-only tattoos. Wizards, and other humans who aren't used to such things, may have to make Will rolls or go and lie down for a while. Increasing warmth will also make thinking somewhat harder for any trolls in the group.

Chadwick's attempts to apply his (entirely genuine) charm to any female passengers, to while away the voyage, can be roleplayed out or not, as the GM chooses.

MONSTERS! MONSTERS!

The *In Nomine* makes its way into the great ocean and heads along the coast of Klatch. The coast remains in sight, but the ship doesn't put in anywhere – it doesn't have to, being well-supplied and provided with excellent navigation equipment, and the point of the trip doesn't involve digressions. It *does* involve finding out what happened to other vessels, which – in part, anyway – happens fairly soon.

The trick with this next scene is to make sure that the adventurers are the stars of the show without giving the impression that the crew are completely useless.[2] Assuming that at least some of the party spend time on deck, the GM can require Vision rolls. Whoever succeeds by the greatest margin spots a pair of reptilian heads, on the ends of long, sinuous necks and sporting impressively large teeth.

The monsters attack 15-20 seconds after being sighted. A bit of missile fire may be possible before they reach the ship, but much of each creature is underwater and hence not really a feasible target. In current weather conditions, the ship isn't able to evade them – and anyway, its captain doesn't especially wish to try. He believes that he can win the fight. Chadwick and his crew get busy, doing a lot of nautical things, donning good armour, and prying the lids off those unexplained crates. Meanwhile, since the adventurers were brought along as spare hero types, it's time for them to show off.

---

1. *At no stage does he say that he'll move out of his cabin. But he's smooth.*

2. *Not that this should be hard if the adventurers act like typical PCs.*

The sea-monsters are basically what an Earth palaeontologist would identify as medium-to-large plesiosaurs. They have ST 15, DX 13, IQ 3, HT 14, and water Move 7; Dodge 9; and DR 1 with 15 HP. They can bite for 1d impaling damage at reach C-3 – they have long, flexible necks. While they're technically about SM +4, the adventurers are likely to spend most of their time striking at the approximately human-sized (SM 0) head/neck area, with the rest of the creature out of reach or underwater.

This isn't intended as a *terribly* hard fight, although a plesiosaur bite can be nasty. The creatures do attack from different sides of the ship, though, obliging the PCs to divide their attentions. If things become difficult, the crew can lend a hand, but not so quickly as to rob the heroes of their glory. Chadwick may Fast-Draw a pistol crossbow, more for style than lethality in this scene, though a dart in the eye could distract a monster at a crucial moment.

By the time the monsters are dead, the mysterious crates are open, revealing a couple of bolt-throwing artillery pieces. Passengers with appropriate skills may get a chance to man these, if the fight lasts long enough; they take 30 seconds to prepare for each shot, but do enough damage to kill a monster with one hit.

AFTERWARDS

Once the fight is over, Chadwick will congratulate the party on their efforts, with as much or as little irony as seems appropriate. If anyone asks, he'll explain that there aren't *supposed* to be sea-monsters in these parts – certainly nothing this aggressive. He'll also agree that such creatures could explain the lack of trade on this route lately, at least in part.

The fate of any monster bodies is up to the slayers. Their meat tastes horrible, and any trophies will soon rot and start to smell in the tropical heat. On the other hand, a severed monster head mounted on a pole at the ship's bow would be a good way to deter other monsters during the remaining days of travel.

The GM decides whether there are further encounters with the creatures. However, the crew will now be keeping a sharp lookout, the ballistas will be ready for action, and everyone will know what to expect. More full-scale fight scenes are unnecessary unless the GM feels the need to pad things out, or the players are total combat junkies. Any more monsters can be put off by a sufficient show of pre-emptive force, such as a ballista bolt in the face.

Inland

Eventually, the *In Nomine* reaches the Howondalandish banana-port of Re'Durat. (Fannish players may point out that Re'Durat is in Ymitury, not Howondaland proper. The GM should have a suitably durable blunt object on hand against this eventuality.) Re'Durat is the embodiment of the colonial-era tropical cliché: a sun-baked town of grass huts with the occasional whitewashed building, jetties made of bamboo, and laid-back, dark-skinned inhabitants lounging around being aggravatingly cool.[1] The ship arrives in the hottest part of the day, when the locals quite sensibly indulge in a siesta. Any trolls in the group will also be very sluggish. The GM should embellish this scene to taste, throwing in booze-sodden expatriates[2], a run-down temple to Offler (p. 298), and so on.

1. *Metaphorically, that is. Not literally cool. Not in this heat.*

2. *Who can never go home to Ankh-Morpork because of some past shame, but who ask forlornly if the Smell is still the same.*

There are a couple of other light freighters in port, with identifiable monster-bite-sized chunks taken out of their rigging. A few members of their crews will point and stare if the *In Nomine* docks with a trophy on the prow. When the ship comes up to the jetty, local harbour employees will help tie up – in a casual, laid-back fashion.

ENQUIRIES

There are plenty of people around to question about the local situation – other crews, dock workers, random locals, and eventually the harbourmaster – but someone *will* have to ask. It's time for a little bit of roleplaying and some reaction rolls. The known facts are as follows:

1. The monster problem started a few weeks ago. Essentially, at intervals just frequent enough to be a nuisance, assorted reptilian monsters come swimming down the river into the harbour, and either head out to sea or lurch ashore with malicious intent. The latter was a big problem at first, but the locals have rigged ditches, palisades, heavy bows, and warning gongs, so the place itself is no longer seriously threatened.

2. However, the situation is seriously disrupting trade. No one wants to be carting a bale of bananas through the jungle when something big and toothy jumps out, and the creatures that went out to sea have been playing havoc with shipping. The craft visible in port are those that survived monster attacks, but even they were sufficiently damaged to make them limp back for repairs. The *In Nomine*, being armed and ready for trouble, was better able to deal with the situation than most. Others will doubtless get through once they've added some deck artillery, but the crews are already talking big danger money.

3. No one has tried going upriver to see where the monsters are coming from. "Do we look like daft 'eroes? No 'fence, o' course." And nobody knows much about what's up that way – mostly, it's just crocodiles, mud, and jungle. Besides, this whole business is an excuse for taking a holiday and being more laid-back than ever.

THE HARBOURMASTER AND BANANA STOCKS

At this point, Chadwick turns businesslike. The harbourmaster's office is the obvious place to go. It's one of the moderately substantial buildings close to the docks.

The harbourmaster is taking his siesta with his feet up on his desk. He's extremely casual but open with visitors. The situation is a nuisance, and he'll be happy to ensure that anyone who does anything about it gets an excellent price for a worthwhile banana cargo.

Talking of which, there's a *large* stock of bananas available in the warehouses. The quantity worth taking back to Ankh-Morpork is rather smaller. Bananas must be picked while they're green, as they ripen *en route*. They ripen quicker in the heat. Anyone who asks is welcome to inspect the warehouses. The GM may require a HT roll to resist the impulse to leap back several yards from the aroma of *very* ripe fruit when the doors are opened.

Chadwick concludes that, with a little haggling, he can put together a just-worthwhile cargo from the banana stocks, but he knows that this isn't a permanent solution. He and his crew will need a few days to buy and load that cargo. Perhaps the PCs could use the time to identify and deal with the root cause?

Adventure! People talked about the idea as if it was something worthwhile, rather than a mess of bad food, no sleep, and strange people inexplicably trying to stick pointed objects in bits of you.
– Interesting Times

Heading Upstream

Assembling an expedition *should* be fairly straightforward, although the players will doubtless complicate it, seeking to borrow everything from siege engines to elephants. The GM ought to accommodate this so long as the players are reasonable, but should feel free to amuse himself if they do anything daft.[1] Chadwick may rescue them from *some* local difficulties, barely disguising his amusement, in order to get things back on track.

Advice and directions are easily obtained, as are supplies and camping equipment (within reason). A fairly good path – used by banana porters and the occasional hunting party – runs alongside the river, sufficiently close to be useful but distant enough to avoid crocodile problems. It isn't clear how far this goes; the town-dwellers regard "inland" as profitless country full of nothing but trees. Chadwick will wait a week or so, and recommends that the adventurers head upstream for three days and then turn around. If they worry that they might not discover what's going on in that time, he'll suggest that they might want to go back to Ankh-Morpork and raise a larger expedition, but that a preliminary survey would be a good start.

If the PCs voice apprehension about tropical diseases (a realistic concern), the locals will cheerfully offer them a favourite preventative, made from the bark of a local tree. It tastes utterly disgusting. Strangely, it works – anyone who takes it is effectively immune to tropical fevers for the trip's duration.

The PCs may try to find a local guide, and perhaps even bearers. This is best avoided, as it would clog things up with NPCs. It's more fun to make it clear that the visitors are doing something that the locals think is crazy ("Do we *look* like 'eroes?").

It's also possible to travel by water rather than land, if anyone has Boating skill. Of course, the river is where the monsters have been coming from. The adventurers can borrow a ship's boat from the *In Nomine* or hire something local. Rowing upstream all day is hard work, but a healthy group should be able to manage. Having them meet a constant stream of monsters is likely to become tedious, but the odd small crocodile or juvenile plesiosaur can keep combat-loving players entertained. The GM can use the stats under *Crocodiles* (pp. 353-354) for this, perhaps scaling down the size and ST (and thus HP and damage) for a smaller version that makes for an amusing fight scene without wiping out any idiots who insist on going for a swim.

If they *do* walk, though, they'll find that trekking through the jungle isn't too arduous, just muddy and hot.[2] The trail is one person wide, so the players can amuse themselves worrying about marching order.

However the PCs travel, they find a nice, comfortable, convenient clearing where they can pitch camp near the end of the first day. It's visible from the river if they're travelling by boat, but far enough from the water to feel safe from crocodiles. A Survival skill roll will confirm that it's a good choice. The GM should discourage silly ideas like night travel, enjoy watching the players decide who stands watch, and start rolling dice meaningfully if no one does.

Local Wildlife

Shortly after the party settles down, so does another group of wanderers. Anyone keeping watch should roll appropriate Per checks; however good their senses, it's dark and there are trees in the way. If everyone is asleep, they get Hearing rolls at penalties. If no one succeeds, they'll wake at dawn and discover things then.

There's something out there. Something large that wasn't there before. Something that doesn't seem to be moving much. Closer inspection shows the something to be, apparently, a small native village. A herd of Hermit Elephants (p. 355) has settled down here for the night.

Investigating the huts can be mildly surreal: "I look through the window." "You see something large and grey." "What's through the other window?" "A large eye, looking back at you." The huts occasionally shift – just enough that those exploring the "village" must make occasional DX rolls to avoid being knocked off their feet by a wall that wasn't there before. Those who rashly open doors have a good chance of being confronted by the back end of an elephant – which, according to the law of comic inevitability, has an equally good chance of concluding the digestion of a meal at that moment. No one should be seriously gored or trampled, though some adventurers may find themselves pursued through the forest by enraged huts.

In the midst of the herd is a modest but unmistakable two-storey, whitewashed, wood-and-plaster tower. Wizards may find it strangely appealing (being naturally drawn to towers). Other adventurers might investigate it on principle.

The tower contains the herd's dominant bull. He occupies almost all of the ground floor, but the remains of a staircase still lead to the intact-seeming upper storey, and the outside walls are climbable. It previously belonged to a mad wizard, who was conducting experiments out in the jungle, but he isn't in residence. The upper floor holds some furniture, including a chest containing spare wizardly robes. No pointed hat, though; that's still with the wizard (what's left of it . . . and him). His journal (p. 390) might also be here, although since PCs might decide to sit down and read it from cover to cover, playing havoc with the flow of the scenario, it may be better to delay that discovery.

Assuming that no one does anything seriously unwise, the Hermit Elephants will awake around dawn and move off majestically with the bull in the lead.

---

1. *Such as trying to steal the solitary local domesticated elephant. Yes, this scenario **has** been playtested.*

2. *The local insects **are** annoying. Bzzzz-slap! Bzzzz-slap! Bzzzz-slap!*

IMPORTED WILDLIFE

The next day, after an hour or so of travel, the party will have another encounter. Sitting in the middle of the path – or on the riverbank, if they're travelling by boat – is a swamp dragon (pp. 359-360). This is a male (moderately large, with ST/HP 5) with a group of nesting females to guard, and it's feeling irritable. Even if it isn't attacked, it will bounce up and down screaming for a second or two, and then take to the air and attack the nearest intruder.

This fight is likely to be short, but messy. Intelligent parties may scatter, leaving the problem to missile-users. A successful roll against Naturalist skill will recall that swamp dragons are warm-temperate-zone animals, so what this one is doing here is a mystery. Then the adventurers can regroup and carry on around the next bend . . .

. . . straight into a small clearing which has become a nesting colony for swamp dragons. Lots of them.

The PCs will probably jump at the sight, but these dragons are quieter, being incubating females. The smart response is to skirt carefully around the clearing.

Campaign Theme: Travelling Professionals

In rural areas of the Disc, many skills and services are needed occasionally, but not regularly enough to support a specialist in every village. As in our history, this problem is solved by a class of travellers who wander from place to place, hopefully showing up sufficiently often that people's needs are more-or-less met. On the Disc, though, rather more different types of work are handled by such folk than has usually been the case on our world. Along with entertainers, pedlars, and craftsmen, the Disc has itinerant priests, accountants (who travel in very tidy carts and help small businesses keep their books), and librarians (though mobile libraries aren't unknown in rural areas of our world). Almost anything else along these lines is possible – just take a professional skill that isn't represented in any normal village and determine whether demand for it could support a roaming expert.

A band of travelling specialists would make a good basis for a Discworld game – probably one tending to the picaresque. They would have skills and knowledge enough to handle all sorts of problems that can't be dealt with by some sturdy peasants with agricultural implements, and the shrewdness to spot patterns of problems and piece together signs of larger trouble that parochial settled folk may miss. Most of the PCs should have their specific professional skills at competent levels, Merchant skill to handle the business side of things, and some "traveller" skills such as Hiking, Packing, Survival, or Teamster. They may be accompanied by apprentices, assistants, and waifs and strays, who might have other skills and advantages.

Resolution

After a bit more walking, the river meanders around a bluff, where the higher ground has been cleared of vegetation. In fact, there was clearly some kind of building here – perhaps even a small community. All that's left is some debris and fragments of shattered plaster. Yes, the wreckage is consistent with a herd of elephants having passed through.

STUFF TO FIND

A brief search will turn up two things: a wooden chest among the rubble, and – beneath a collapsed beam – a flight of stairs leading down.

The chest contains an assortment of clothes, mostly more robes. There's also a book (unless the GM decided that it already showed up in the herd-bull's tower). This small, leather-bound volume has no title on the outside, but inspection reveals it to be a journal, written in a distinctive style. It's very abbreviated and cryptic – only educated readers with some idea about magic are likely to be able to get anything out of it – but every few lines, there's something like "The fools! They dared to laugh at me!", "Mad? I, mad? Consider my accomplishments!", "My theories are vindicated! This will show them!", or just "Ha! Ha! Ha! Ha!"

A wizard, living alone, who *wrote* maniacal laughter. Not a good sign.

Actually working out what the wizard was up to will take a while and some IQ rolls. Much of it is quite cryptic – it's clear that this journal was written for personal reference only. There are a number of references to "SDs," and also much discussion of carefully numbered experiments (1, 2, 3, 7, 7a, 9, 37b, 42c, 49x, 147-blue . . .). Deeper reading will discover much use of words like "morphology," "biological reversion," and "regressive inheritance." The general thrust of the author's work was clearly biological magic.

With any luck, a wizardly or scholarly member of the party will settle down with the book, leaving everyone else to get bored and start looking for trouble. Oh yes – stairs leading down.

THE BASEMENT

The short staircase leads to a landing which is just big enough to enable a large door to open outward. The door has a latch-and-bar arrangement – easy to shift, two-handed, from either side, but proof against anything without hands. Beyond is a corridor that runs for a few yards and then opens out into a larger space. Sufficient sunlight reaches the passage to illuminate it, but not the cellar beyond. Someone will have to venture in with a torch or a lantern.

When someone does so, have them make a Per roll to see if they notice what's coming at them from one side, jaws gaping.

If somebody is back up on the surface with the book, this is a good time for the reader to discover a passage, evidently written fairly late:

Latest experiment v. successful. Fascinating regression. Combined modern and archaic anatomy! (Note: Specimen somewhat excitable. May be a little dangerous.)

The results of that experiment are waiting in the dark for something to jump on. The *High-Velocity Rapacious Monstrosities* have long, powerful back legs, vestigial front legs, big teeth, and an attitude problem. They also retain some capabilities from the swamp dragons (pp. 359-360) from which they were derived.

ST: 8	HP: 8	Speed: 6.50
DX: 14	Will: 10	Move: 6
IQ: 3	Per: 11	
HT: 12	FP: 12	SM: 0
Dodge: 10	Parry: N/A	DR: 1

Bite (14): 1d-4 cut. Reach C.

Flaming Breath (14): Treat this as Short-Range Flame (see *Burning Attack*, p. 87) doing 1d+2 damage, but it doesn't cost FP; instead, each monstrosity gets four uses per day.

Kick (12): 1d-3 cut. Reach C, 1.

Traits: Bad Temper (9); Berserk (12); Burning Attack (see above); Combat Reflexes; Enhanced Move 1.5 (Ground Speed 18); No Arms (effectively); Self-Destruct (see below); Sharp Claws; Sharp Teeth.

Skills: Innate Attack (Breath)-14; Stealth-13.

Like swamp dragons, these beasts are prone to exploding in moments of excitement, or if killed the wrong way. Fortunately, although larger than swamp dragons, they have slightly better-contained stomachs, so they only do 2d+1 crushing damage to adjacent targets, with reductions and side-effects as for standard swamp dragons. The cruel GM may fudge things so that this always happens. The kind GM – or one who doesn't want to wipe out an already-injured party of PCs – can ignore it, or just have the creature stagger off and *burst,* messily.

There are two of them, and they're hungry. The bolder specimen quickly jumps the first person into the room. It might not be too hard to kill, but it may do some damage. Then the second beast leaps up onto one of the benches scattered around the cellar and hisses, showing lots of teeth (pure pose, of course).

With any luck, the PCs should be feeling battered enough at this point to use *tactics.* There are numerous possibilities. Tossing something unexpected and provocative of explosions into its open jaws (and then diving for cover) is always good.

THE LAST PIECES OF THE PUZZLE

With the monsters finished off, people can have a look around the basement, where they'll find a few not-very-surprising bits and pieces. To start with, there are a number of well-gnawed bones of all-too-obviously human origin, and a battered and bloody pointy hat. (The mad wizard paid the ultimate price for knowledge.) The party may choose to take the hat home to attempt identification.

Then there's a second, smaller laboratory, closed off by a bolted door. This has a ramp leading down to water; evidently, there's a concealed entrance from the river (the means by which the wizard brought in some larger apparatus back when he was starting work). This room holds some lab equipment, along with a big, low, open-topped box/crate/pen over to one side. This contains many leathery, reptilian eggs of varying sizes. Even as the PCs watch, one of these hatches, and out pops something small and toothy. Left to itself, it will flop across the floor toward the river, and then swim for the sea.

If they didn't come upriver by water, the party may discover a small boat here – there's no harm in making departure easier for them than arrival.

GOING HOME

Thus, everyone can head downstream, announce that the monster problem is solved, and take the *In Nomine* home. The GM can skim over this part; the expedition's objectives have been accomplished. When the ship reaches Ankh-Morpork, the GM can remind the players that wizards *can* use divination spells, and hence the graduates already know about their success. The dock is lined with thaumaturgical nerds, throwing their hats in the air and cheering. Really smug adventurers will want to be the first to deliver a bunch of nice bananas to the library; for that, they'll earn a passionate kiss from the Librarian.

More Scenario Ideas

Here are yet more scenarios, set on other parts of the Disc. The GM can use them "as is" or mine them for inspiration.

Full Court Press

The succession to the Duchy of Applegrove on the Sto Plains is contested between two candidates: Anastasia "Annie" Dapplegrove (age 19), granddaughter of the last formally crowned Duke, and Wynvoe Cadwallader (age 53), whose claim is based on traditional law.

Anastasia is convinced that she's supposed to be Duchess of Applegrove. She's also convinced that a handsome prince will marry her and add his vast lands to hers, that babies are brought by a large bird (possibly an owl), and that she looks ravishing in yellow. She's supported by Captain Vaughan of the Applegrove Lancers, the Duchy's standing army (two corporals and a dozen sergeants). Vaughan is in love with her, but torture wouldn't get it from him. Despite the difference in their ages, he would probably make a good consort and co-ruler.

Wynvoe has a lot of friends among the farmers, who agree that he's the best-qualified person to be Duke. Research actually shows that the title has always belonged more to the candidate most accepted by the rich local farmers than to any heir-by-birth.[1] The Cadwalladers have been cider-masters of Applegrove for almost as long as the Crabtree-Dapplegrove dynasty has been ruling it – longer, if you believe Wynvoe.

---

1. *That's a polite way of saying there've been a lot of small civil wars. But precedent is precedent.*

A one-man third faction consists of Doctor Aufidius Roskilde, D.M. (Unseen), D.Plant.Sci. (U.Minn.), wizard, horticulturist, and chancellor. Dr. Roskilde came to Applegrove during the reign of Anastasia's great-great-grandmother, Tisane. Some say that he was a very young man then, others that he has always looked like he does now. He was brought in to modernise the orchards that make up almost the entire national economy. While there was little he could do to improve fructiculture in the Duchy, his organisational skills proved of great practical value, and the fact that Applegrove is now comfortably wealthy is to his credit. He's a competent wizard if out of practise; his staff resembles a walking-stick made of live applewood. Taciturn and cryptic, he could be up to anything – or even nothing.

A Death and a Quest

The death of Duke Danton, some months ago, involved a crossbow bolt of uncertain origin while he was out hunting (creating suspicions that aren't helping Wynvoe). Since then, various legal complications have prevented Annie's coronation – courtesy of Wynvoe. Mumblings at the court about Anastasia's "unsuitability" were coming to a head. But then the castle cook's son came back from a trip to the big city and said in passing that he'd seen a piece of metalwork with the Ducal symbol on it in the market there. This was immediately identified as part of the ceremonial Ducal Cider Press, ancient and revered symbol of the Duchy.

(Why was it rediscovered now? Narrative causality? Wynvoe fixing to get his problem out of the way temporarily while he plotted?)

Anastasia promptly announced that *she* would recover the Press, and she even refused more than a token bodyguard.[1] Vaughan insisted on being the token. Somewhere along the line, the PCs should get involved, but Annie will insist on the fiction that they aren't *with* her, however much they tag along and help her.

When she arrived in Ankh-Morpork, the unworldly and under-funded Annie found a room in the cellar of a run-down boarding house. Looking around, she saw what she thought was a piece of ornamental stonework, which she said was "nice." The sentiment, and the sound of what he thought was his name ("How did lady know, unless was supposed be?"), went straight to the brain of Gneiss, a rustic troll who was hiding out there after a misunderstanding with a group of dwarfs. Since then, he has been her utterly devoted follower. He'll take orders from Captain Vaughan, but only if he agrees with them. For the Duchess, he would happily jump into a volcano.

Involving the PCs

If the PCs are mercenary swords, they could be recruited into the Applegrove Palace Guard, while wizards might be asked by a patron to look up an old friend of his who, in a recent letter, mentioned having problems. ("Name's Roskilde. Clever chap. Bit obsessed with plants, though. Seems to be lookin' after the books for some tinpot duchy.") Anyone employed by the Patrician – directly or indirectly – may be told that his sources have determined that a foreign aristocrat is coming to town *incognito* on some kind of idiot quest, and

that their job is to prevent diplomatic incidents while protecting the city's interests.

Alternatively, if the PCs are street-level operators in Ankh-Morpork, they can be staying in a flophouse on Elm Street when they become aware of some odd neighbours. They might decide to do something traditional about this, such as burglary, but Anastasia and Vaughan have little worth stealing. The GM should set up as many coincidences as are necessary for the adventurers to fall into conversation with the visitors, who reveal their quest. The possibility of getting on the good side of a full-powered Duchess, who may have wealth back home, ought to be tempting.

Even if it isn't, an agent of Wynvoe Cadwallader will approach them within a day or two. Through this messenger, Wynvoe presents himself as the rightful and plausible ruler of Applegrove. ("Can you imagine an airhead like that doing any good for a modern nation?") Ideally, he would like to get hold of the Press himself, but merely preventing Anastasia from recovering it would be enough. Wynvoe does *not* want Anastasia harmed, though. He'll say that this is because he isn't a murderer – he just wants justice. The PCs *might* also suspect that Anastasia's death would throw a lot of suspicion onto Wynvoe's head, given Danton's accident, and make her into a martyr.

It's up to the PCs whether they take Wynvoe's part (and his cash), tell him where to go, or try playing off both sides.

But the thing about saving the world, gentlemen and ladies, is that it inevitably includes whatever you happen to be standing on.

*– Lord Vetinari,
in The Last Hero*

Parts One and Two

The Press consists of three components: an open-topped oak barrel; the frame that clamps around the barrel, holding a large-diameter screw and a wooden-faced piston; and the handle, a bar of metal about two feet long, with a wooden handgrip at each end. The metal parts are cast iron, sporting the Ducal crest (a coronet around an apple) in several places.[2] The Press disappeared at some uncertain time very close to Dr. Roskilde's arrival in the Duchy.

The mechanism is on sale at a stall in the weekly market in Sator Square. (A good excuse for a few encounters: Thieves' Guild operatives, C.M.O.T. Dibbler[3], wizards, PCs' Enemies, whatever.)

---

1. *Far too many romantic stories, that one.*

2. *Realist nitpicker's note: No part of a cider press that comes into contact with the apples or juice can be made of iron or steel, as this will damage the flavour.*

3. *Try to stop Anastasia buying a sausage in a bun just because she thinks he looks "sweet."*

If the PCs are acting against Anastasia and Vaughan at this stage, the GM should rig events so that Anastasia reaches the stall first. The stallholder will be secretly glad to be rid of the thing, but he's an Ankh-Morpork merchant, so he'll bargain anyway. The visitors' funds are limited, and they aren't good bargainers . . .

Once the deal is done, the stallholder will throw in a free answer to the next question. "Oh yes, I got this as scrap off old Cheese at the Bucket." So it's time to get some more directions and then visit that hostelry (p. 266).

There, Anastasia will go into raptures at her good fortune, for the barrel is plain to see: it has become the Bucket's sign. The only snag is that Mr. Cheese thinks that it makes a good sign, and his regulars[1] tend to get slightly unhappy if anything changes around the place. So it's time for more bargaining, punctuated by interruptions from various watchmen, who want to know why their favourite quiet drinking spot has suddenly become so noisy. Anyone suggesting stealing the sign is welcome to try. The place opens long hours and has watchmen inside for all of them.

Eventually, some arrangement should be possible, and Mr. Cheese will also throw in a clue. "Mmm. Sold the contraption to that fellow down the market as a curio, but he wasn't interested in that big handle thing. Too bulky, he reckoned, and after all, any old handle would do. So I chucked it on one of the junk carts. It'll be down City Tip Four[2] by now."

If anyone asks for more details, Cheese might add that the Press originally came to him on a cart with a load of cider from the country. "I kept it because I was always thinking of making my own stuff. Can't be hard, can it, it's just apples?" (Anastasia winces prettily.) "But it never came to nothing. And then the other day, some fellow came with another cartload and saw it sitting back of my cellar, and said that them markings were some kind of bad luck charm or curse or something. Sends cider bad, he said. Well, I wasn't worried, but – ah, it was just junk."

If the PCs get to the Bucket first with the intent of foiling Anastasia, and succeed, they can stay ahead of her – but she'll look tragic enough that Mr. Cheese will tell her about the handle for free.

THE TIP

City Tip Four is part of Harry King's empire of waste. Stuff transported there is sorted for reuse, recycling, or composting. However, the big point is that it *smells* like a rubbish heap. When she gets close, Anastasia will pale visibly – but she'll insist on going on, despite the fact that logically, the chance of recovering the handle is zero. And she'll be vindicated. But first . . .

Depending on which side the PCs appear to be assisting, the other side will have a few friends back at Applegrove who are less subtle or romantic than their leader, and who decide to intervene. This is the moment when these stout country lads catch up with all and sundry.

Use as many heavies as will make for interesting chaos, with Vaughan attempting to shield Anastasia, and Gneiss leaping out of the shadows at the wrong moment and hitting all the wrong people. Any PCs who cut loose with magic during this fight should see it produce some interesting effects, as the tip produces all sorts of reactive outgassing, and some of the solid matter may interact with spells. Those who prefer simple violence should be reminded that escalating a blunt-instruments brawl to use of edged weapons is frowned upon, even in Ankh-Morpork, and that Anastasia will be deeply shocked and unhappy.

In the midst of all this, *Ivan Shallowpans*, the tip manager, will wander in, trying to determine who's making a mess of his nice, tidy rubbish. When it's all over, he'll cock his head, look at people, and ask what all this was about. Ivan is a Solid Wastes Handling Specialist – one of Harry King's trusted lieutenants. He likes cleaning things up, and he's a hands-on sort of person. He'll be slightly charmed by Anastasia, but not as much as some people; all human beings are remarkably similar from his point of view. His natural instinct is to help anyone who asks, although he doesn't approve of anyone who makes his job harder.

This is fortunate, as he's the only way that anyone is going to find the handle. He knows his tip as well as the Librarian knows his library. What look like mounds of rubbish to anyone else are, in his orderly mind, accurately categorised by date and origin: "Oh yes, the Bucket. That's area four. Last week, y'say? Three feet down, seven over."

Of course, this still means that someone will be spending several minutes digging through rubbish.

COMFORT WITH APPLES

With all the parts located – and perhaps even in the same hands – it's time for a quick bath, then Applegrove. There, the population will respond to the return of their ancient symbol by assuming that a party is indicated, with lots of cider. The Press will be formally reassembled, and everyone will settle down to some serious politics. Anyone who has been on the cider beforehand may not be at their best during these debates.[3]

---

1. Yes, all those polite gentlemen in armour.

2. For our American readers, a "tip" is a dump site.

3. "Cider" has the same meaning on the Disc as it does in Britain – it isn't the sweet, unfermented children's drink served in certain other countries. Apple juice ferments quite nicely, with results rather stronger than beer. Also, given the presence in apples of various trace chemicals, the rougher versions can be very insidious indeed. The best Applegrove cider isn't rough, but the stuff served in the market square varies. And the locals like playing little jokes on visitors.

Inne Juste 7 Dayes I wille make You a Barbearian Hero!
– Publication credited to
Cohen the Barbarian, in **Sourcery**

Wynvoe's support turns out to be strong. Many of the farmers are unhappy with the idea of their newly prosperous land being run by "some slip of a girl." If Wynvoe cannot actually snatch the title, he may still be able to reduce the Duchess to a ceremonial figurehead, with himself as prime minister. Even if he is in fact honest and not a murderer, his instincts will be to engineer a lot of power for himself. If he isn't restrained, he's likely to end up as a dictator, with all the ducal powers and none of the *noblesse oblige*. On the other hand, he's competent, and the PCs may by now have become aware of just how bubble-headed Anastasia can be.

Meanwhile, Dr. Roskilde is looking enigmatic. He's *respected* – the locals recognise how much good he has done, and if there are any bodies, he knows where they're buried.[1] And Gneiss is looking confused and having to be dissuaded from hitting anyone he thinks has been nasty to Anastasia.

How things develop depends on what the GM has decided about the true history and motivation of the NPCs, as well as on the PCs' actions. A little detective work concerning the murder of Danton may be in order, as might some verbal fencing with Roskilde over the family's recent history (and maybe his relationship with Tisane). If things get out of hand, Roskilde could also turn out to be rather more of a serious wizard than he appears. ("My, my – hadn't cast Gherricauld's Flinty Barrier for donkey's years. Nice to know one can still manage.")

Matters should culminate in the revelation of some truth, at least to the PCs. Other people might better be left in ignorance, depending what the truth *is*. This can be followed by a coronation and more partying (and more cider) – a suitable setting for any last-minute revelations and reversals of fortune.

Rewards for the PCs are more likely to involve useful social contacts, and a place where they're always welcome, than sacks of jewels – but a small-but-well-filled purse apiece from the new ruler wouldn't be inappropriate. Either Wynvoe or Vaughan can become a new enemy for the group. Gneiss will probably end up with a lease on one of the Duchy's bridges.

Sektoberfest in NoThingfjord

As has been noted elsewhere, with the opening up of EcksEcksEcksEcks, many young citizens of that land went forth to see the world. The first landfall they made on the Disc's main continent was in the Fjordlands (p. 242) – usually meaning NoThingfjord, the region's largest community. Having said g'day to the locals and bought a few souvenir horned helmets, most set out for the big cities, but a few hung around to sample the local beer, which was at least cold (having typically been left outside for some time).

Then one of the locals happened to mention that once a year, in Sektober, they often held a major festival, to celebrate the big batch of beer that they brewed around that time. The visitors declared that this sounded like a bloody good idea, and they

resolved to come back for the event. Some of them remembered or wrote to friends who remembered, or other Fourecksians happened to be passing through, or . . . Anyway, NoThingfjord had plenty of Fourecksian visitors around Sektober.

Thus are traditions born.

THE SETUP

This scenario takes place at one such festival. It's ideal for backpacker, tourist, or Fjordlander PCs, but almost anyone could *happen* to be present: wizards on their way between UU and Bugarup University, merchants hoping to make some money from the festival crowds, and so on.

NoThingfjord consists of a collection of wooden longhouses, currently surrounded by tents. Most backpackers bring simple, sturdy two-person things, but a few wealthier visitors show up with miniature pavilions. There are also several large marquees. Some backpackers are sleeping in the carts they use for travel. Sanitation arrangements are, well, basic.

The weather is cool but survivable – and anyway, most people spend the majority of their time in the marquees, investigating the local brew and (being hardy and broad-minded types) listening to the folk music. This consists of a mixture of Fjordlander sea-shanties and Fourecksian ballads of bold sheep-rustlers.[2] Festival policy, enforced by a crew of burly Fjordlanders, is for weapons to be left at home, which means that usually, the occasional brawl that breaks out is mostly harmless. (It helps that the participants are typically too stewed to aim a punch reliably.) Mutton and rough bread are available to soak up the beer.[3]

Incidentally, Fjordlander beer was traditionally made from herrings. The local brewers have become more cosmopolitan in recent years, and most of the modern brews are more conventional, but there's a small contingent of full-figured men who campaign vociferously for what they term "Reäl Äle." Some Fourecksians have been persuaded to sample this, and one or two thoroughly recommend it.[4]

THE COMPETITION

One smaller marquee is dedicated to the saga recitation competition, in which middle-aged male Fjordlanders sit around, look thoughtful, and then launch into lengthy recitations. *Very* lengthy, as it turns out – the GM may require any PCs present to make rolls against the lower of HT or Will to stay awake. The speakers are competing for the Lars Larsnephew memorial drinking-horn.

---

1. *Under apple trees, mainly.*

2. *The chief topic of conversation among the audiences is people asking each other what various words, in Fjordlander or Morporkian, mean.*

3. *From the stomach or the floor. In whatever order.*

4. *Fjordlanders are proud of their Reäl Äle. Fourecksians are proud of their straight-faced practical jokes.*

The judges (slightly greyer men with even more thoughtful expressions) award points based on accuracy of recollection of the ancient sagas, flatness of tone, and consistency of unrelenting rhythm. Originality and excitement are not mentioned on the scorecards.

This marquee has been erected around a well (complete with a circular stone wall and a winch to lower the bucket). If anyone asks, the only reason given for this is that it is tradition, but the practical considerations should soon become clear. Because of all the ale-quaffing that goes on, even serious saga fans – and there are some – are prone to dozing off. Anyone observed to slump or heard to snore is promptly awakened with a traditional bucket of very cold water over the head. Fjordlanders profess to find this exhilarating. Serious competitors also drink water rather than beer, at least some of the time, to help maintain their concentration on the all-important flat tone and lengthy recounting of characters' ancestry.

Fjordlanders have mixed feelings about their extensive native tradition of epic narrative. On one hand, they're intensely proud of it, and they will become upset if it's criticised or insulted in any way; on the other, they find it as mind-numbing as everyone else. They'll recommend – perhaps even insist – that any visitor who enquires about the competition should go and admire it, but they have a lot of skill at avoiding it themselves. Needless to say, slipping away in mid-saga must be done with some care, else word will get around that a skald was *insulted,* and the outlanders may find themselves involved in a brawl.

PLOTS

Once people have settled down and had their fill of jokes involving accents and horned helmets, you can get on with the plot. This isn't actually mandatory, though – Sektoberfest *can* be run as a string of loosely connected gags, or used as the starting point for picaresque quests. However, there *is* somebody ready to cause more dramatic trouble.

A day or two into the festival, in the small hours of the morning, when everyone has drunk their fill and retired, a commotion erupts. A hulking figure comes striding into the festival grounds, generating a lot of screaming and shouting, starting with some random fellow who'd got up to relieve himself (and who does so immediately). It strides up to the saga competition marquee, tears off the roof, reaches inside, picks up an old skald who has perfected the traditional skill of slumping unconscious over a bench, turns around, and walks back to the nearest fjord. There, it sinks from view, prey in hand.

It should be hard for anyone to do much to stop this. The creature is a huge, ancient troll with ST/HP 50, HT 14, and DR 8. Even a fireball wouldn't slow it significantly. It also has Move 10, thanks to its sheer size, so it will get away quite quickly. (The GM doesn't *have* to use the word "troll," by the way – the players will probably guess, but talking vaguely about a "monster" or a "creature" can help maintain an air of mystery.)

People will doubtless *try* to intervene, though, so there's plenty of scope for chaos in the darkness. One or two backpackers may assume that this is some kind of practical joke, dash up to the monster, and try to pull its mask off. They, and anyone else trying to grapple, will probably be flung through the air. In accordance with narrative tradition, they'll land on something soft but discomfiting, such as a vat of beer, a tent full of lightly clad sleeping backpackers of the opposite sex (if the GM is feeling kind), or a privy (if the GM has had a bad day).

Anyway, once the creature has departed, silence will fall, broken after a moment by the traditional NPC filling in the basic facts: "It got Hengist!"

REACTIONS

Then the shouting begins. It isn't entirely clear who's responsible for recovering or avenging the skald when this sort of thing happens, but consensus among the locals is that *somebody* should. The trick here is persuading the players that they ought to mount this mission, or at least handle the reconnaissance. This is going to depend a great deal on the nature of the party. Some heroic sorts will volunteer immediately; others will respond well to vague offers of fame, as much beer as they can drink, and the gratitude of blond persons of their gender of choice; and yet others might take a little coercion. There seems to be a vague idea among the skalds present that it's traditional for some foreign hero to demonstrate his worth in these circumstances, and this may be mentioned pointedly within earshot of non-Fjordlanders. It isn't that the locals aren't brave enough to tackle the job themselves; it's just that Fjordlanders are very respectful of tradition (and that thing was *big*).

It's also possible that some of the PCs will be natural peacemakers. In that case, the GM should make it clear that after the locals have finished arguing and getting drunk in memory of Hengist, they're likely to mount a mob-handed rescue mission involving a lot of axes. In addition, once the word "troll" is used, a great deal of rather nasty anti-troll-ish sentiment will develop, with the locals remembering ancient Fjordlands traditions of unending warfare with local trolls. It would probably be a good thing for race relations if the troll in this case was proved to be a solitary rogue, and perhaps induced to apologise. Troll PCs may have a particular interest in this.

The first problem is to work out what to do and where to go to do it. All but the most impetuous adventurers ought to be thinking about *preparation* at this point. Someone should eventually remember that trolls can't breathe water. This may hint at where the thing was going, and increase the hope that Hengist could still be alive.

There's also the fact that monsters (especially trolls) live in caves. It's traditional. The locals can confirm that there are quite a few caves in this area, and it's entirely possible that the creature has access to an underwater entrance. This may encourage some heroes to think about following the thing. With the right magic, clever improvisation, or just high HT scores, the idea of diving into cold darkness and finding a cave mouth might seem acceptable. Or maybe not.

There are also cave entrances in the hills above NoThingfjord, and locals will agree that they may well all join up. That implies miles of twisty passages, all alike, so there's still an issue of navigation. Again, magic might help, or the GM may introduce Hengist's faithful hound, Holgar. This works best if at least one PC has Animal Empathy or skill in Animal Handling (Dogs), in order to notice that Holgar is looking tense and eager, and grows more so if taken near a certain cave entrance. Holgar's animal senses are, naturally, leading him to his master.

Finally, with the talk of caves, someone might remember the well. Anyone venturing down will find it extremely cramped (unless they're a gnome), with no human-sized way through from the bottom. It has been excavated a little way into bedrock, and it is fed by a small underground stream – a fair clue as to the extent of the cave systems hereabout. On a Per roll, investigators may discover substantial cracks in the rock walls just above the water-line, and testing with smoke will reveal a draught flowing *into* these. Really determined use of magic or engineering skills could give the party a way through to the cave system by this route, and a shortcut to the next big scene, but it would take some doing.

THE USEFUL NPC

Alternatively, the GM can introduce a local wise-woman, *Bjerka the Crone*. She's a witch whose appearance happens to fit some kind of Viking-style gerontophobic nightmare – all wrinkles, hooked nose, and world-class random cackling, with a proclivity for stirring a cauldron full of unspeakable substances with a long, two-handed ladle – and she can serve as a useful tool for involving the PCs. As she herself puts it, she knows what Fjordlanders are like in this sort of situation: they spend hours getting drunk, and then try to resolve things with axes while hung over. If she can persuade, cajole, bribe, bully, or trick someone into solving this problem quickly and cleanly, she will do so. She can also provide magical aid, specifically cuisinomantic divination.[1] This generates a set of slightly garbled but functional instructions that will lead to Hengist ("Go up to the medium-sized rock that looks like a big rock, and into the cave underneath. Take the third left, then the first passage past the broken boulder . . ." and so on).

> *"Well, it's not like . . . a real saga," said Evil Harry hoarsely. "It's got a tune. You could whistle it, even. Well, hum it. I mean, it even **sounds** like them."*
> – *The Last Hero*

INTO THE CAVES

One way or another, *someone* will venture into the cave system. This scene can run slow or fast, creepy or unremarkable. Penalising the explorers for not taking equipment such as lanterns is reasonable, though of course Discworld caves have several species of luminous fungi. The PCs may well be jumpy, although the only wandering creatures that they're likely to meet are bats.[2] Likewise, any spells or directions they use for guidance should be adequate, if a little vague in places; there's only a limited amount of fun to be had by getting them lost, and having them completely lost and starving to death is dull. But the players might pay more attention if they sense that the GM is thinking about that possibility.

Explorers with knowledge of geology will note that the local rock appears to be limestone, and that these caves were probably carved out by underground streams.[3] This in turn can be used to induce additional nervousness, if the GM *is* feeling mildly sadistic. Mention a cloudbank on the horizon when they're entering the cave, and then emphasise that the walls are noticeably damp in the lower levels, and get them wondering if they're about to be flushed away by a sudden flood.

Before they break down and run gibbering for the surface, though, the adventurers should find what they're looking for. Rounding a bend in the tunnel, they see firelight flickering on one wall. If they pause and listen, they'll hear a *basso profundo* voice and a quieter, rapid clicking sound. If they eavesdrop for long enough, they may make out that the voice appears to be talking, very slowly, about property rights pertaining to a flock of sheep, some time in the past.

Bold warriors might insist on charging in. Hopefully, though, they'll remember that their task is a rescue mission of sorts – and in any case, that creature was *big*. It may be wise to spy out the scene, or even attempt negotiation.

In the cave, Hengist is indeed alive and well, but damp and very cold. He has an old, rough, grubby blanket thrown round his shoulders, and he is sitting close to the small fire in the centre of the cavern. The clicking sound is his teeth chattering.

---

1. *Using a pungent casserole of herring in herring beer.*

2. *And large cockroaches with a taste for luminous fungi.*

3. *Or by eccentric chthonic deities, if you prefer. This is the Discworld, and the gods get the blame for a lot of things.*

Sitting opposite him, further back from the fire, is the troll. It *is* big, and also as ugly as tradition demands (less-bright observers might conceivably mistake it for a rock formation at first glance). Its name is *Lode*.

Lode is an *old* troll, and as slow and persistent as that implies. Even in this nice cool cave, he effectively has IQ 6 – but when he starts thinking about something, he's almost impossible to stop until he reaches a conclusion. He isn't terribly interested in violence, or even in sociable trollish hitting people with rocks, but if adventurers should charge in screaming with swords drawn, he'll defend himself, punching with Brawling-12 for 5d+6 crushing damage.

For the record, there's a dark pool of water around a bend at the far end of the cave. Close inspection would reveal it to be *salt* water, suggesting that it may well be connected to the outside. This is how Lode got in and out.

"MOTHER CAN BE A LITTLE STRANGE"

The *rational* alternatives boil down to sneaking Hengist out somehow, or going in and talking. After all, Lode is already doing the latter, and he doesn't seem to be harming Hengist just now. The problem with the first option is that, however long the party waits in the shadows, Lode simply doesn't *stop* talking, apart from the occasional confused-sounding (and increasingly hypothermic) noise of agreement from Hengist. Some kind of trickery might be feasible – against an IQ 6 troll, it isn't difficult – but getting away may be harder, as Hengist is in no condition to run. In any case, as Hengist will explain, Lode is certain to cause more trouble eventually.

Thus, the PCs will have to find out what's going on. Even if they avoid conversing with Lode, they should get the basics from Hengist, to whom Lode has been explaining matters.

The first thing for the GM to know is that there are cracks high on the walls of this cavern, leading upward. Lode's lair is almost directly beneath the Sektoberfest grounds, and some of those fissures connect to the well. Crucially, the whole system acts as a conduit for sound, in an acoustically unlikely but highly plot-convenient way. Someone who sits in the cave and keeps quiet can hear almost every word that's spoken in the saga competition tent.

To drive this point home, anyone who spends time in the cavern can overhear some conversations. It's up to the GM exactly what's being said, but the PCs will certainly be the subject of much of the discussion. The details will depend on what sort of impression they've made at the Sektoberfest. Among other possibilities, they might hear their quirks and visible oddities dissected at great length, their heroic credentials questioned, and bets made on their survival chances. The unusual acoustics only work in one direction: nothing they say will be carried up to the surface.

This is the cause of the trouble. Lode, an old troll who's close to entering a state of inert geology, has been down here for decades. Recently, once a year, he has had to listen to the saga recitations. That in itself is no problem – if there's one sort of being that can appreciate a Fjordlander saga, it's an old troll. Rather predictably, though, many of these sagas deal with the battles between Fjordlander heroes and trolls. Furthermore, they include lengthy and somewhat prejudiced explanations of the root causes of these conflicts.

In short, Lode feels that his family is being slandered, and he has decided to complain. As he'll explain, he himself isn't too

worried, "But, you see, Mother may hear some of this. And she's a rather proud sort."

"Mother"?

Lode will gesture about himself vaguely. At this point, visitors should make Per rolls to notice the general shape of the walls on the far side of the cave. The hint of a distorted feminine curve, the shape of a huge nose, the suggestion of something like muscle definition . . .

Old trolls can grow *very* big.

CORRECTING THE RECORD

The fact is, people aren't going to be able to fight their way through this one. You can't kill a mountain. Lode's mother is completely inert for now, but Lode believes that she's still capable of awakening. Hengist, while not currently at his best, has already grasped this; he'll be reasonably cooperative with attempts to resolve the problem, which will have to be quick, as sooner or later, a larger and drunker rescue party will show up. However, he's fanatical about the traditions of skaldship, and he will obstruct anything that threatens to debase the traditional text of the sagas. As annoying as this might be, it shows what would-be peacemakers may have to deal with among other saga devotees.

One possibility would be to persuade the people of NoThingfjord to move the saga recitation competition away from the well. This would only be a temporary fix, however. On one hand, Hengist will explain how holding the competition there is *traditional*, so moving it would be a bad thing, and people would probably sneak back to recite sagas there on principle. On the other, Lode will make it clear that not changing the insult to his family will annoy *him*. Thus, the PCs will need to address the underlying problem.

This will mean enduring several minutes of explanations from Lode and Hengist, and making IQ rolls to grasp the subtleties of the issue. Essentially, long ago, the people of NoThingfjord and the trolls in the adjacent hills reached some kind of semiformal agreement by which sheep near the human community would be left alone, while wild sheep further away were fair game for trolls who wanted a varied diet. It wasn't much of a treaty, but it served. The two communities still fought, but at least human shepherds could go out in groups of less than 30, and trolls knew where to grab a snack without being pelted with missiles.

However, as the human community expanded, squabbles over what was "near" to it increased, the agreement had to be renegotiated several times, and some small wars were fought. One of these is the subject of one of the sagas, which includes many remarks on the perfidy and greed of the trollish enemy. *This* is the problem.

Fixing it can be accomplished several ways, depending on what the PCs can do and the players suggest. The ingenuity will have to come from them; while Hengist has effective skill 14 in anything related to skaldic lore, he's also Hidebound. He's just about willing to tolerate suggested changes to the sagas, but he has difficulty coming up with ideas. And Lode – well, he has IQ 6. The best bet is to revise the saga to include references to the trolls' side of things, perhaps including some trollish-language quotes that translate as "we are being perfectly reasonable," or depicting the human heroes as proclaiming that they're going to hit the trolls whatever happens (a sentiment that any troll will find perfectly inoffensive), and deleting references to the humans having the right of the dispute. Working this into the changed saga may involve Poetry skill rolls, but at +2; so long as the saga has a strong rhythm and always rhymes, no one cares if it's any good as poetry. Ingenious characters with Law skill in any version which relates to contracts can suggest clever modifications to the narrative, anyone with Fast-Talk can come up with clever forms of words, and so on.

Hopefully, someone will eventually hammer out an acceptable compromise, and get it past Lode and committed to Hengist's memory. Any PCs with little to contribute may wish to return to the surface. Here, they can placate locals who are about to charge into the caves with heavy weaponry, or fetch supplies and warm blankets, or just have another beer.

CONCLUSIONS

In the end, Hengist and the PCs should return to a moderately heroic welcome on the surface and be bought some drinks to celebrate their victory. Clever heroes will work out versions of the tale that reflect well on themselves while not causing offence if repeated in the vicinity of the well. Other rewards are up to the GM. A small positive Reputation could be good for the party's job prospects, while Bjerka can always provide something in the way of magical aid, training, or good advice. Or the adventurers can just get back to the Sektoberfest.

And More!

Some further brief adventure ideas follow. The GM will have to expand these before use, jotting down notes on the NPCs, adding more details, and working out how to get PCs involved.

LANDSCAPE WITH QUAINT FEATURES

The Marquis of Prostayne-Glumrigg – an intellectual by the standards of the aristocracy[1] – has recently decided that he wants to improve his estates on the Sto Plains, meaning not only that he's telling his peasants how to be better peasants[2], but also that he wants to improve the gardens. The main thing he's doing is changing everything that one of his ancestors did. Among other efforts, this means draining the lake.

The Marquis' great-great-grandfather landscaped the gardens at a time when the fashion was for "naturalism": informal arrangements, twisting paths, and a lake. (He was lucky enough not to attract the attentions of Bloody Stupid Johnson, p. 254.) The fashion this year is for formal gardens, however, and the Marquis wants to be able to go for a stroll without getting lost every five minutes.[3] Anyway, the estate could do with more income, and turning a larger fraction of the land over to farming seems indicated. Draining the lake is the biggest part of the scheme.

This is a big job – nontrivial but relatively straightforward – requiring a lot of hands and some specialised brains. Thus, this scenario can involve all sorts of PCs: gardeners, engineers, down-on-their-luck folk with enough ST to take labouring jobs, upper-class acquaintances of the Marquis, or scholars with an interest in his family's history. Comic inevitability ensures that *something* will go wrong, but any disasters should be fixable.

But *dark hints* soon start accumulating. When a PC is away from the estate, a crazy old gaffer wanders up to him, says "It's rising from the waters! Ye're all doomed!", and wanders off. Later, a group of mysterious travellers takes up residence nearby, casting dour glances and watching the work with strange, unreadable expressions. Eventually, the water starts to drain away – but there's a lot of it, and the process will have to be left running overnight. People toast their success and go to bed.

---

1. He can tie his own bootlaces.

2. No, they aren't listening.

3. There are a lot of overgrown patches. The natural look costs more to maintain than the family can afford.

"That wasn't cheating!" Cohen growled. "Leavin' scrolls around to lure heroes to their death, that's cheatin'!"

"But where would heroes be without magic maps?" said Blind Io.

"Many of 'em'd still be alive!" snapped Cohen. "Not pieces in some damn game!"

– The Last Hero

Come morning, the first thing anybody wandering down to the lake-as-was will see is a lot of mud. The second is the remains of a small village. Prolonged immersion isn't good for walls, but these have survived pretty well, and the shapes of several buildings can be seen. Anyone who wants to investigate more closely may encounter problems with all that sticky mud. It might be wise to wait for things to dry out and then test for sinkholes and boggy patches. If and when the PCs do get out there, they'll find the remains of several cottages and one larger structure (some kind of hall).

Eventually, someone will suggest digging through the old estate records. It turns out that there *was* some kind of hamlet there when the lake was constructed, but no name is given (just "the people in the valley"), and no one seemed bothered that it was going to be flooded out. A careful reading of the old Marquis' private diary in the library (Research roll at -2) may turn up an entry saying "The valley is flooded, and they are gone. Good riddance!"

Now things start to get *weird*. The mysterious travellers *may* be responsible for the lights that are visible among the ruins in the night, when strange chants are heard, though investigators will find it hard to obtain proof. (Wandering onto the mud is still messy at best, dangerous at worst.) Also, there suddenly seem to be a lot of frogs around, some of them getting into the house. If the GM doesn't want too many NPC servants getting in the way, they start suffering horrible fates and/or fleeing (taking the household's horses with them).

In short, this is a pocket-sized version of the old "lost/damned city from the depths" plot, and things should rapidly get horror-movie-ish. The former inhabitants of the sunken village worshipped a minor-but-sleazy god, and now is the Time Of *His* Prophesied Return. The deity himself has been subsisting on the worship of assorted amphibians, many of which are being twisted by resurgent divine power into dangerous (but only slightly larger) forms, or being given strange powers (as appropriate to move the plot along). The travellers may be cultists, or they might be an *opposed* group that wants to *prevent* the return, and who suspect the Marquis and his visitors of deliberately seeking to bring it about.

For that matter, the Marquis might indeed be up to something. He *was* brought up near the lake! In that case, his agricultural reforms were aimed at increasing the local worm supply, to feed the frogs, and he'll eventually sneak off to the ruins. His departure may be concealed for a while, as a frog with supernatural powers

of speech takes his place in his room and tells anyone who knocks on the door to go away.

This can all be played as a straight suspense plot, culminating in a siege of the house by killer frogs (with the odd newt for variety), or for pure comedy. After all, a cult consisting mostly of frogs can't wield *very* much power, can it?

Campaign Theme: Working for a Monastery

Many monasteries are scattered around the Disc's mountains, and the monks in such places are sometimes trained in martial arts. See *Hublands Monk* (p. 136) for a template, discussion of some orders and their members, and notes on tasks which monks might be assigned. Not all members of a monastery-affiliated party have to be monks, though; some missions employ guides or other local help. Few humans or other beings (apart from the Auditors, pp. 296-297) would *deliberately* oppose most of the monasteries' work, but ignorance, confusion, prejudice, or local politics can cause all sorts of *interesting* problems.

LLICENCED RESELLER

A master stone-circle engineer from Llamedos has decided that his craft is only marginally related to Strict Druidism, and that in fact he'd like to establish a start-up organisation and become his own boss. However, as the fundamental tenets of Strict Druidism involve a certain amount of bloody sacrifice, he has decided to leave his homeland to do it. Anyway, he feels that an organisation HQ somewhere warmer and drier might have advantages.

In boring materialist terms, what he's trying to establish is a rationalist astronomically related religion which spends more time on agricultural planning than it does on sacrifices. He also wants to set it up as a sort of franchise operation, with local priests running their own circles and paying him commission. Whether it will *work* is an open question, but the founder isn't totally stupid. He realises that he'll need assistants, technical staff, sales representatives, and – when the Strict Druids find out about him – plenty of guards. Would the PCs mind taking share options in place of salary?

FESTIVAL OF THE DIMMED

The Ephebian philosopher Gastraphetes has recently come up with a theory of drama which says that comedy and tragedy provide the most powerful tool by which human beings can understand the universe. (It says a lot more, too, but that's the important bit.) However, as Ephebian theatre consists entirely of men in masks standing around telling each other about the dreadful things that are happening off-stage, Gastraphetes suspects that he and his fellow countrymen don't understand the universe as well as they ought to.

As a minor sideline, Gastraphetes is also an expert in political economics, whose advice has repeatedly saved Ephebe from financial disaster. The Tyrant will therefore do a lot to humour him.

Thus, Gastraphetes' suggestion that the city-state should host an international festival of theatre was taken seriously.

This has provoked surprising interest – dramatists and performers are flocking to Ephebe from across the Disc. If the PCs aren't themselves involved in the theatre, they may end up here as porters, bodyguards, guides, or tourists. Performers include parties from both Vitoller's Strolling Players and the Ankh-Morpork Opera (see p. 252); the National Theatre of Omnia performing a Mystery Play[1]; an experimental troupe called "That's The Way To Do It," which consists entirely of gnomes and one very small crocodile (widely considered to work quite well on smaller stages); an Agatean opera company; a contingent from Ankh-Morpork's Fools' Guild, out to demonstrate that the Disc has only *one* valid tradition of comedy, and it's theirs; and Lithic's Honey Lane Irregulars, a group of political subversives led by a fanatical troll revolutionary[2], who are determined that their performance will *literally* bring down the house.

There's infinite scope for clashes of artistic temperament, even discounting the 1,000-derechmi prize for best production. If no one dies on stage during the festival, it may not be for want of anyone else trying.

PLUMBING THE DEPTHS

A secret is buried beneath the streets of Ankh-Morpork: the sewer system built millennia ago by the Kings of Ankh. For centuries, these tunnels were known only to the Assassins' Guild. But now that they have been rediscovered and are due to be incorporated into the Undertaking (p. 250), they need to be mapped.

The PCs are probably hired for this job, although it's also possible that the Patrician is discretely blackmailing them, so that he can have an agent or two reporting directly to him. While their expedition is adequately financed, everyone involved has been made keenly aware that budgets aren't unlimited. As well, the Undertaking is big and complicated enough that there may be rival surveying teams, all doing much the same job but working

---

Campaign Theme: League Football

Following the events of *Unseen Academicals*, the traditional Ankh-Morpork sport of football is undergoing a transformation. From a glorified street brawl with few goals and multiple casualties, it's becoming an almost-respectable sport.

The PCs might be employed to represent the interests of some faction or organisation. Several guilds are certainly putting teams together, and these will require healthy, well-coordinated individuals – preferably with some vague connection to the guild – to play for them. Meanwhile, the old neighbourhood teams are reorganising, and they may or may not be prepared to shed some of their animosities.

The teams will also require trainers, scouts, and business managers; there are whole new bodies of rules to get the hang of, on and off the pitch. And the business will need people to arrange matches and competitions, settle disputes, steward crowds, and sell the spectators meat pies and souvenirs.

---

for employers with slightly different interests, or looking at a bonus if they *happen* to report first.

Another wrinkle is that the surveyors are working against the clock. The tunnels are only safely accessible at the end of long, hot summers, when the water table has sunk (and the reek is *appalling*). The rest of the time, they're frequently flooded – the Undertaking pumped drainage system isn't working yet. Don't be down there during a heavy storm!

Complications will certainly emerge. To start with, the Assassins are annoyed that their old secret has been invalidated. They can't stop the Undertaking, but they can slow things down while they recover some old caches and perform a few last-minute assignments. Fortunately for the PCs, no one is paying for any assassinations here and the Guild doesn't believe in blanket commissions; thus, by the Assassins' Code, the Guild can only kill in self-defence (or if someone offers the Guild minimum for someone else down here, but who ventures into a sewer carrying that much cash?). *Scaring*, confusing, or otherwise harassing people, however, is allowed.

Then there are Lithic's Honey Lane Irregulars (see *Festival of the Dimmed*, pp. 399-400), underground (literally) deconstructivist artists who have plans for a major artistic act.[3] Some of Lithic's followers have learned a bit about civil engineering, as appropriate to her artistic conception.

Oh, and there *must* also be albino alligators, which have wandered into the sewers from another set of narrative assumptions. When the intrepid explorers are up to their thighs in these creatures, will they remember that their original purpose was to draw maps?

---

1. The Mystery is why anyone would watch it.

2. The group consists of a mixture of trolls who feel downtrodden in human society and assorted disaffected humans.

3. Involving buildings sinking into the ground.

A BRIEF GLOSSARY

Apocralypse, the: The end of the world, as predicted by debatable Discworld myth.

Archchancellor, the: The head of **Unseen University,** and nominal head of all wizards on the Disc.

autocondimentor: A person who seasons his food before tasting it.

bogeymen: Anthropomorphic personifications of childish fears. Large and unattractive humanoid creatures given to lurking in cellars and wardrobes.

Borrowing: A witches' magical technique; "riding" in the mind of another being, usually an animal.

Breccia, the: Rumoured to be a secret troll criminal society. Such rumours are rarely good for the health of those repeating them.

Caroc cards: The Disc's counterpart to the Tarot, used for both cartomancy and games.

Cenobiarch, the: The supreme head of the Omnian religion.

chelonauts: Krullians appointed to take part in research expeditions over the Rim in experimental vessels.

Circumfence, the: Barrier built round almost a third of the edge of the Disc by the nation of Krull, to catch salvage.

dragon magic: An expression for anything difficult and highly technical – usually encountered in the phrase "It isn't dragon magic!"

dwarf bread: Nearly indestructible baked products created by dwarfs for consumption on the march and use as throwing weapons.

edificeering: Assassins' Guild slang for roof-climbing as a hobby and sport.

Ghlen Livid: Strong alcoholic drink made from **vul nuts** through a process of freeze-distillation.

grags: Renowned masters of traditional dwarfish cultural lore – usually though not always highly socially conservative.

Headology: Psychology, as applied by witches. The placebo effect as a martial art.

Hex: **Unseen University**'s magical computer.

Hnaflbaflsniflwhifltafl: An ancient dwarf board game and direct predecessor of **Thud.** Also known as Hnaflbaflwhiflsnifltafl.

Hogfather, the: The Disc's version of Father Christmas, but with more of a focus on pork and ham.

Hogswatchnight: The primary Discworld midwinter festival.

iam: A rank above bishop in the Omnian religion. *Archpriests* are senior iams; the **Cenobiarch** is the supreme iam.

Igor: One of a class of fawning lackeys/transplant surgeons, noted for their habit of self-modification. Igors originated in Uberwald, but are now found further afield.

inhumation: Assassins' Guild euphemism for killing.

kelda: The matriarch, wise woman, and biological mother to a clan of pictsies.

L-Space: A transdimensional, seemingly infinite realm of bookshelves, accessible from any library of adequate size.

narrativium: The material or principle that holds the Disc together while enforcing the power of stories.

Necrotelicomnicon, the: The Disc's most fearsome work of dark magic (also known as the *Liber Paginarum Fulvarum*). Written by Achmed the Mad (also known as Achmed the I Just Get These Headaches).

octarine: The eighth colour of the Disc spectrum, visible only to the magically adept. Said to resemble a sort of fluorescent greenish-yellow-purple.

octarines: Gemstones that resemble inferior diamonds, but which glow in strong magical fields.

Octavo, the: The Creator's own grimoire, which holds the eight spells that are apparently terribly important to the Disc's position in reality. Held in a secure room in **Unseen University**'s library.

Octeday: The eighth day of the Discworld week.

octiron: A very rare metal, appearing slightly iridescent, with exceptional and complex magical properties, mostly of a rather dark kind.

octogen: A dangerously magical gas.

Oggham: An ancient runic alphabet, still used by some dwarfs in the Ramtops.

Patrician, the: The supreme government executive authority in Ankh-Morpork. Also the supreme legislative authority in Ankh-Morpork. Also the supreme head of government administration in Ankh-Morpork.

Quisition, the: The sharp end of Omnian religious absolutism. Now disbanded.

Ramtops, the: The Discworld's premiere mountain range, stretching from the Hub to near the Rim. Impressive, angular, heavy on magic, and a real problem to get over.

re-annual plants: Magical plants which grow the year before they are planted.

sapient pearwood: A type of tree, extremely rare outside the Agatean Empire, which produces wood with a mind of its own – totally immune to magical damage, but very useful for purposes such a wizards' staffs, and supernaturally loyal to its owner.

Thud: A boardgame, played by both dwarfs and trolls (and a few humans).

turnwise: Clockwise. The way the Disc turns.

Unggue: The goblin religion/philosophy, based on the sanctity of bodily secretions.

Unseen University: The Disc's premier centre of magical learning.

UU: See **Unseen University.**

vermine: A small, cautious mammal occupying colder parts of the Disc. Its fur is much in demand for trimming ceremonial garb.

vul nuts: A type of **re-annual plant** found in the Agatean Empire. Used in the production of vul nut wine and **Ghlen Livid.**

widdershins: Counter-clockwise. The way the Disc doesn't turn.

yennork: A werewolf (biologically and mystically speaking) who is unable to change, and who is therefore stuck in human or wolf form for life. May be the subject of lethal prejudice from "true" werewolves.

BIBLIOGRAPHY

This game represents a merger of two things: the Discworld chronicles and **GURPS.** Hence, its bibliography comes in two halves.

Discworld Books

The following novels, all by Terry Pratchett, make up the Discworld series at the time of writing. They're listed in publication order, which mostly also corresponds to the series' internal chronology.

The Colour of Magic (1983) introduces Rincewind, Twoflower, and the games of the gods, and visits Ankh-Morpork (at its most archaic), the Wyrmberg, and Krull.

The Light Fantastic (1986) continues the saga of Rincewind and Twoflower, and their tour of the Disc, taking in new lands and characters, including Cohen the Barbarian.

Equal Rites (1987) is the story of the only female student yet admitted to Unseen University, partly thanks to Granny Weatherwax, and includes much about both witchcraft and wizardry.

Mort (1987) is the tale of Death's apprentice, showing something of Disc metaphysics.

Sourcery (1988) sees the return of Rincewind, who gets to visit Klatch, and shows why sourcerers are a bad thing.

Wyrd Sisters (1988) reintroduces Granny Weatherwax, as she and the coven deal with a tyrant in Lancre.

Pyramids (1989) concerns Djelibeybi, Assassins, Ephebian philosophy, and excessive pyramid-building.

Guards! Guards! (1989) introduces Carrot Ironfoundersson to the Watch under Captain Vimes, and shows how Ankh-Morpork really works. It also features the only true noble dragon to appear on the Disc in recent times.

Eric (1990) is a shorter tale (also available in illustrated form) in which Rincewind returns from the Dungeon Dimensions and promptly takes his longest journey yet, involving both the Tezuman Empire and Hell.

Moving Pictures (1990) sees Ankh-Morpork under attack from the Dungeon Dimensions through the peculiar magic of motion pictures.

Reaper Man (1991) introduces Azrael and the Auditors of Reality, who force Death to retire. The plot also features an assortment of Discworld undead and the strangest alien invasion of all.

Witches Abroad (1991) sends the Lancre coven to Genua, and to a confrontation with a renegade fairy godmother and the power of voodoo.

Small Gods (1992) illustrates the secret truth about religion by telling the story of the reformation of the Omnian church.

Lords and Ladies (1992) brings the coven back to Lancre just in time to face an invasion of elves.

Men at Arms (1993) shows the Watch growing, changing, and dealing with an attack on the Patrician.

Soul Music (1994) features another invading alien idea, and introduces Susan Sto Helit as Death's occasional understudy.

Interesting Times (1994) brings Rincewind back so that he can be sent to the Agatean Empire and suffer reunions with Cohen and Twoflower.

Maskerade (1995) has Granny Weatherwax and Nanny Ogg seeking a new member for the coven – backstage at the Ankh-Morpork Opera House.

Feet of Clay (1996) presents the much-improved Watch with a complex problem involving golems and heraldry.

Hogfather (1996) explains what Hogswatchnight is really all about, as various established characters deal with a very peculiar assassination.

Jingo (1997) sees Ankh-Morpork (briefly) going to war with Klatch, due to the emergence of the lost city of Leshp from the depths of the Circle Sea.

The Last Continent (1998) sends Rincewind to EcksEcksEcksEcks, where he once again, most unwillingly, stands in for a hero.

Carpe Jugulum (1998) has Lancre infiltrated by *modern* vampires, who present the coven with a very dangerous threat.

The Fifth Elephant (1999) sends Sam Vimes on a diplomatic mission to Uberwald, where he has to deal with werewolf and dwarf politics.

The Truth (2000) concerns the arrival of modern printing in Ankh-Morpork, the accidental invention of newspapers, and another plot against Lord Vetinari.

Thief of Time (2001) pits Death, Susan, and the History Monks against an attempt by the Auditors to put a stop to time itself.

The Last Hero (2001) is another illustrated story, in which the need to stop the Silver Horde from storming Dunmanifestin leads Leonard of Quirm to build the Disc's first spacecraft.

Night Watch (2002) sees Sam Vimes accidentally sent back in time 30 years, to a year when one Patrician is being replaced by another, and his younger self has just joined the Watch.

Monstrous Regiment (2003) is set in Borogravia, as its interminable wars with everybody else draw to their conclusion, and Polly Perks and others do what they can to save the situation.

Going Postal (2004) introduces Moist von Lipwig. After his execution, Moist is given the job of reviving the Ankh-Morpork Post Office, and hence of dealing with threats from and to the clacks system.

Thud! (2005) involves another case for the Watch, concerning dwarf culture and the dwarf-troll wars.

Making Money (2007) sees Moist von Lipwig take charge of the Bank of Ankh-Morpork, despite the objections of various people who have lots of money.

Unseen Academicals (2009) is about the transformation of football in Ankh-Morpork from a chaotic street brawl to a modern game, and features the first orc seen among other races in modern times.

Snuff (2011) sends Commander Vimes to the country, where he promptly discovers a crime involving the previously obscure goblin race.

OTHER DISCWORLD FICTIONS

Some of Pratchett's stories about the Disc are in non-novel form.

A handful of short stories are available in various places. Three to note are "Troll Bridge" (1992), which isn't *quite* a Discworld tale, but can be squeezed in; "Theatre of Cruelty" (1993); and "The Sea and Little Fishes" (1998).

Nanny Ogg's Cookbook (1999), written with Stephen Briggs and Tina Hannan, is a cookbook and etiquette guide as penned by Nanny Ogg.

The Science of Discworld (1999), *The Science of Discworld II: The Globe* (2002), and *The Science of Discworld III: Darwin's Watch* (2005) – all written with Ian Stewart and Jack Cohen – include chapters of fiction, in which the wizards of Unseen University create and monitor what appears to be our universe, combined with nonfiction commentary.

ABOUT THE DISC

The Disc has also been the subject of other publications. The following may be especially useful for games.

The Discworld Mapp (1995), by Terry Pratchett and Stephen Briggs, provides a view of the whole Disc.

The Compleat Ankh-Morpork (2012), by Terry Pratchett and the Discworld Emporium, is a trade directory, gazetteer, and comprehensive map of that city.

Turtle Recall (2012), by Terry Pratchett and Stephen Briggs, is "The Discworld Companion . . . so far": a guide to people, places, and phenomena mentioned in the chronicles.

EVEN MORE

The Discworld has further inspired computer games, board games, diaries, music, figurines, posters, art books, academic studies, a Christmas ("Hogswatch") card, T-shirts, jewellery, the Unseen University college scarf, a microbrewery beer, and tattoos on more devoted fans. A few stories have been adapted into graphic novels,

and several have become animated or live-action films for TV and video release; there have also been radio dramatisations and stage adaptations, the scripts of which have been published. Many of these things might offer additional ideas for games.

GURPS Publications

Steve Jackson Games supports *GURPS* with numerous books and electronic releases, many of them potentially useful in Discworld games. Using these is *optional* and should only be done with the GM's explicit permission, but many people like the idea. (*Note:* To convert prices, incomes, etc. from the "dollars" used in other *GURPS* books to Ankh-Morpork dollars, divide by 20.) The following may be of particular interest.

Dell'Orto, Peter and Punch, Sean. *GURPS Martial Arts.* Covers advanced combat training of all sorts, including fencing and boxing as well as kung fu and karate.

Hite, Kenneth. *GURPS Horror.* Relevant to some Discworld games; see *A Touch of Horror* (p. 368).

Jackson, Steve. *GURPS Basic Set.* The current (fourth) edition, developed by David Pulver and Sean Punch, comes in two volumes: *Characters* and *Campaigns.* It's the "long version" of the *GURPS* rules, with more character traits, more equipment, and more things to do with them.

Masters, Phil and Punch, Sean. *GURPS Powers.* Extended rules for exotic abilities, which might be useful for games involving characters with unique talents.

Pulver, David. *GURPS Mass Combat.* Rules for large-scale combat, for occasions when the Patrician's manipulations don't achieve enough.

Punch, Sean, et al. *GURPS Dungeon Fantasy.* A lengthy *series* of works that should appeal to fans of Cohen the Barbarian.

Riggsby, Matt. *GURPS Fantasy-Tech 1.* Gear that might have been created by Leonard of Quirm.

Stoddard, William H. *GURPS Fantasy.* A guide to creating fantasy settings in general.

Stoddard, William H. *GURPS Social Engineering.* Extensive guidelines and optional rules for social interactions of all sorts.

Stoddard, William H., with Peter Dell'Orto, Dan Howard, and Matt Riggsby. *GURPS Low-Tech.* A *lot* more detail about equipment available at TL0 to TL4: swords, armour, clothing, coaches, ships, survival gear, etc. The three *GURPS Low-Tech Companion* volumes by the same authors offer even deeper treatments of early technologies.

As well, a large number of books published in support of earlier editions of *GURPS* are available as PDFs from **warehouse23.com.** A lot of these dealt with historical eras or places that are reflected in parts of the Disc (*GURPS China* for the Agatean Empire, *GURPS Arabian* Nights for Klatch, and so on). The old-edition rules are similar enough to those in this game that conversions are rarely a problem; a free guide to the subject, *GURPS Update,* is available from Warehouse 23.

SOFTWARE

GURPS Character Assistant, a program for Microsoft Windows computers, can be purchased as a download from **warehouse23.com.** It facilitates *GURPS* character creation and recordkeeping. Specific support for Discworld games will be available from the program's active online community.

INDEX

Traits Index

This index includes select characteristics. If you cannot find a game term here, please turn to the text. For attributes, see pp. 26-27 For secondary characteristics, see pp. 27-28. For advantages, see pp. 28-49 or 85-93. For perks, see pp. 49-53 or 93-94. For disadvantages, see pp. 28-49, 53-68, or 94-98. For quirks, see pp. 66-68 or 98-99. For skills, see pp. 70-82.